The Sage Handbook of
Political Marketing

Editorial Advisory Board

The Sage Handbook of
Political Marketing

Edited by
Paul Baines
Phil Harris
Denisa Hejlová and
Costas Panagopoulos

Sage

Sage

1 Oliver's Yard
55 City Road
London EC1Y 1SP

2455 Teller Road
Thousand Oaks, California 91320

Unit No 323-333, Third Floor, F-Block
International Trade Tower Nehru Place
New Delhi 110 019

8 Marina View Suite 43-053
Asia Square Tower 1
Singapore 018960

Editor: Rhoda Toweh
Editorial Assistant: Benedict Hegarty
Production Editor: Gourav Kumar
Copyeditor: Niketha
Proofreader: Girish Kumar Sharma
Indexer: TNQ Tech Pvt. Ltd.
Marketing Manager: Danielle Nemeth
Cover Design: Ginkhan Siam
Typeset by: TNQ Tech Pvt. Ltd.
Printed in the UK

Library of Congress Control Number: 2025941015

British Library Cataloguing in Publication data

A catalogue record for this book is available from the British Library

ISBN 978-1-5296-0970-7

Contents

List of Tables and Figures

TABLES

FIGURES

Notes on Editors and Contributors

EDITORS

Paul Baines is Professor of Political Marketing and Head of Executive Education at the University of Leicester School of Business, and a Visiting Professor at Cranfield and Aston Universities. He is (co) author/(co)editor of 150+ published journal articles, book chapters and books, and frequent media commentator, on political marketing and propaganda issues. He co-edited the *SAGE Handbook of Propaganda* (SAGE Publications, 2020, with Nicholas O'Shaughnessy & Nancy Snow) and has published in, inter alia, the *European Journal of Marketing*, *Marketing Theory*, *Journal of the American Statistical Association*, *International Journal of Management Reviews* and *Journal of Business Research*. He is a Fellow of the Market Research Society, and a member of the Academy of Marketing and (US) Market Research Council. He was an Impact Advisor on Research England's 2021 Research Excellence Framework (REF) university research evaluation exercise. Paul has worked on strategic communication research projects for the UK Foreign and Commonwealth Office, Home Office, Ministry of Defence, UK Law Enforcement and overseas government departments. He is Councillor, Deputy Leader of the Conservative Group and Past Mayor (2021/2) at Charnwood Borough Council in England. He is also Director, Baines Associates Limited.

Phil Harris is Professor Emeritus of Marketing and Public Affairs at the University of Chester and Woxsen University, Hyderabad, India, Professor Extraordinarius at the University of South Africa (UNISA), Pretoria, Adjunct Professor at the University of Otago, New Zealand, and Director of the Nigerian British University. He is one of the founders of research and theory development in strategic public affairs management, political marketing and economic and governmental communication. Phil is the joint founding editor of *the Journal of Public Affairs*, a member of numerous international editorial and advisory boards and trusts, and has authored over 200 articles and 20 books. He has worked in the chemical, food and media industries and has taught and advised businesses and governments in Africa, Asia, Europe and North America. He has held visiting professorships in Australia, China, Germany, New Zealand, Nigeria, South Africa and the United States, as well as senior academic positions at Otago and Manchester Metropolitan Universities. Phil was made a Knight of the Order of St. Agatha of the Republic of San Marino in London in 2024 in recognition of his work supporting them during COVID-19 and his services to fostering International Education, Public Affairs and Charity. He is a Freeman of the City of London and a Liveryman of the Worshipful Company of Marketors and Chairs the Medical Mission Sisters (MMS) UK 2025 Centenary in London.

Denisa Hejlová is a prominent Czech scholar and communication consultant. She conducts research, teaches and consults in the areas of strategic communication, public relations, public affairs and political communication. From 2011 to 2023, she led the Department of Marketing Communication and PR at Charles University, which hosts one of the Czech Republic's most sought-after programmes. She previously held the roles of vice-dean for PR and PR manager at the Czech Ministry of Foreign Affairs. Hejlová was a Fulbright Visiting Scholar at Columbia University in 2014 and studied intercultural communication at Tokyo University of Foreign Studies from 2005 to 2006. She is the author of comprehensive books on public relations and strategic communication tailored for the Czech audience, published in 2015 and 2025, respectively. A prolific contributor to academic journals, she has also been a guest lecturer at several universities in Germany, Spain, the Netherlands, and Japan. In 2020, she launched the first Czech MA programme in Strategic Communication at Charles University. As of 2023, Hejlová is the director of the Research Centre for Strategic Communication at the Faculty of Social Sciences within Charles University.

Costas Panagopoulos is Distinguished Professor of Political Science at Northeastern University. In Fall 2024, he was Visiting Scholar in the Department of Government and an affiliate of the Center for American Political Studies at Harvard. He was previously Professor of Political Science at Fordham University and Visiting Professor of Political Science at Yale University. He has also taught at Columbia University and New York University. Between 2006–2020, Professor Panagopoulos was part of the Decision Desk team at NBC News. Since the 2022 cycle, he has been on the Decision Desk at Edison Research, which conducts exit polls and analysis for the National Election Pool that includes NBC, ABC, CBS and CNN. He is a leading expert in campaigns and elections. He has authored, coauthored or edited 11 books and over 100 peer-reviewed articles, including *Battleground: Electoral College Strategies, Execution and Impact in the Modern Era* (co-authored with Daron Shaw and Scott Althaus) published by Oxford University Press.

CONTRIBUTORS

Gözde Akdeniz is a Research Assistant at the Department of Production Management and Marketing in the Faculty of Business at Manisa Celal Bayar University. She has a BS degree in both Business Administration and International Business and Trade and an MSc degree in Business Administration from Dokuz Eylul University. Since 2022 she is PhD student at the Department of Business Administration in the Graduate School of Social Sciences at Dokuz Eylul University. Her research focuses on Consumer Behaviour, International Marketing and Sustainable Development.

Maria Cristina Antonucci is a senior researcher at Italian National Research Council, and adjunct professor in Political Communication at Rome Sapienza University. Her research field focuses on the intersection of political communication, public policy and social innovation. With a PhD in Political Sociology and post-doc in Political Science, her work explores the dynamics of public engagement, the role of digital transformation in governance and the evolution of participatory democracy, especially in a gender perspective. She has authored several publications that bridge theory and practice, offering critical insights into how advocacy and communication strategies influence policy outcomes and societal change. Her interdisciplinary approach integrates political science, sociology and communication studies, focusing on research themes such as public advocacy, democratic innovations and gender studies. In addition to her research, she actively participates in civil society collaborations, contributing to debates on open governance and civic engagement.

Guja Armannsdottir is a Senior Lecturer at Nottingham Business School, Nottingham Trent University. Her expertise includes political marketing and political branding, focusing on brand identity and image. She has published her work in various journals such as *Journal of Vocational Behaviour*, *International Journal of Market Research*, *Qualitative Market Research: an International Journal*, *Journal of Political Marketing* and *Politics and Policy.*

Suniti S. Bal is a Vice President at GMMB, one of the most respected full-service communications agencies in the nation. Suniti brings nearly 20 years of nonprofit and political communications experience to GMMB. Currently her portfolio includes reproductive rights, health equity and climate change. She has had the opportunity to support reproductive health organizations navigating media crises like the overturn of *Roe v. Wade* and supported advocacy efforts to elect pro-choice candidates in key states. Working closely with nonprofits of all sizes, she provides strategic communications counsel to support day-to-day communications needs, expert crisis communications support and overall partnership to help organizations reach their goals. Early in her career she served on Senator Mazie Hirono's (then Congresswoman Hirono) staff. Currently she serves on the board of directors for the Praxis Project, a nonprofit dedicated to health equity and social justice. She is also on the board of directors for The Arc Foundation, the nation's oldest and largest disability rights organization.

Anjali S. Bal is an Associate Professor of Marketing and Presidential Research Scholar at Babson College. Bal's research centres on Arts & Entertainment, Sports and Political Marketing with expanded focus on the intersectionality of Diversity, Equity, Inclusion and Accessibility (DEIA) in these markets. She has published in numerous journals including the: *European Journal of Marketing*, *Journal of Advertising Research* and *Journal of Product and Brand Management*. An award-winning educator and advocate for DEIA in higher education, she was named to Poets & Quants' '50 Best Undergraduate Business Professors' in 2023. Dr Bal holds a BA in Theatre from the University of California, San Diego; an MBA from the Rotterdam School of Management, Netherlands; and a PhD in Marketing from The Beedie School of Business at Simon Fraser University, Canada. She frequently comments on marketing-related topics for: *The Wall Street Journal, Forbes, KCBS San Francisco* and more.

George M. Bob-Milliar is an Associate Professor in the Department of History and Political Studies, Kwame Nkrumah University of Science and Technology (KNUST), Kumasi, Ghana. In 2024–2025, he was a Senior Researcher at the Nordic Africa Institute (NAI) based in Uppsala, Sweden. He earned his PhD in African Studies and therefore his research is strongly interdisciplinary and lies at the intersection of political science, history and development studies. His research focuses broadly on democratization in Africa with a focus on electoral politics in Ghana, informal institutions and social/political history, among others. He published in the top-ranked journals in his field of specialization. He has also been supported by numerous grants and fellowships. He edits *African Affairs*, *African Economic History* and *Contemporary Journal of African Studies* and sits on the editorial boards of several other reputable journals.

Bridget Barrett, PhD, is an Assistant Professor of Advertising at the University of Colorado Boulder. Her research is at the intersection of digital marketing and electoral politics with a focus on branding and social identity. Her work has appeared in academic journals including *Political Communication* as well as in the popular press. She received her PhD from the University of North Carolina-Chapel Hill.

Fabio Bordignon teaches Political Science at the University of Urbino Carlo Bo (Italy), where he is director of the LaPolis Electoral Observatory. He is a member of the ITANES (Italian National Election Studies) research group and a researcher at the polling institute Demos&Pi. He is Associate Editor for Communications of the international journal *South European Society and Politics* and member of the Scientific Committee of SISE (Italian Society of Electoral Studies). He is a political columnist for NEM newspapers and contributor and survey analyst for the newspaper *La Repubblica*. He is the author (with Luigi Ceccarini and Ilvo Diamanti) of *Le Divergenze Parallele. L'Italia dal voto Devoto al voto Liquido* (Laterza 2018). With Luigi Ceccarini and James L. Newell, he edited the book *The Italian General Election of 2022. The Right Strikes Back* (Palgrave, 2023). His main areas of research are transformations of democracy, electoral behaviour and the personalization of politics.

Alexander Braun is an international political strategist who has worked on close to a hundred election campaigns around the world. Called a 'campaign magician' by *Forbes*, Alex has founded and leads the research and international political practices at SKDK, a premier political consultancy in Washington DC. In addition to US campaigns, including Biden 2020, Alex has advised prime ministers in the United Kingdom, India and Croatia and presidents in Ukraine, Mexico and the Philippines, among others. The American Association of Political Consultants named him International Campaign Consultant of the Year and inducted him among its '40 under 40', in addition to winning the Reed and Polaris Awards for his campaign work. Alex is also an adjunct professor of political campaign management at George Washington University and frequently lectures on campaign strategy on both sides of the Atlantic.

Patrick Butler is Professor of Marketing and Director MBA Programs at Monash Business School, Australia. He has had academic appointments at Melbourne Business School, Trinity College Dublin, Ireland and Ulster University, Northern Ireland. He has taught in business schools in USA, Japan and has worked with EU and UN organizations in Russia and Africa. Patrick's research on marketing strategy, politics and public sector management has been published in international books and journals. He is actively involved in strategy projects in several industry sectors and jurisdictions.

Furkan Cakmak is a Postdoctoral Researcher in Quantitative Analysis at Wesleyan University. He works with the Wesleyan Media Project, which tracks political advertising, and collaborates with the

Quantitative Analysis Center. Cakmak received his PhD in Political Science from the School of Politics, Philosophy and Public Affairs at Washington State University. His research interests are American Politics, Political Communication and Political Psychology. Cakmak's work focuses on the role of emotions in politics and media choice, utilizing both qualitative and quantitative methods. He also studies affective polarization, including its causes and consequences.

Luigi Ceccarini teaches Public Opinion, Media and Democracy at the University of Urbino Carlo Bo (Italy) where he serves as Head of the School of Political and Social Studies and scientific coordinator of the research centre LaPolis. He is President of the Italian Society of Electoral Studies, and senior researcher for the polling organization, Demos&Pi. His recent books include: *The Italian General Election of 2018, Italy in Uncharted Territory* (with J.L. Newell, eds., Palgrave, 2019), *The Digital Citizen(ship)* (Edward Elgar, 2021), *Postpolitica* (il Mulino 2022), *Constituency Communication in Changing Times* (with R. De Rosa, J.L. Newell, eds., Palgrave 2022), *The Italian General Election of 2022. The Right Strikes Back* (with F. Bordignon, J.L. Newell, eds., Palgrave, 2023). He is particularly interested in studying how citizens participate in politics through diverse forms of engagement in the frame of democratic change.

Sára Cigánková is a PhD candidate in the department of Political Science at Masaryk University. Her main interest lies in political communication, emotions and their possible impact on political behaviour. In her research, she deals mainly with the issue of populism in Central Europe.

Neil Collins is a Professor of Political Science at Nazarbayev University and Professor Emeritus of Political Science at University College Cork. He has previously held academic positions at Ulster University and the Universities of Liverpool and Birmingham. His recent research has focussed on political marketing and neo-mercantilism.

Kenneth M. Cosgrove is Professor of Political Science and Legal Studies at Suffolk University in Boston, Massachusetts, USA. Ken has written extensively about the uses of political branding in the USA and Canada. He holds a PhD in Political Science from the University of Oklahoma.

Wojciech Cwalina is Professor and Head of the Department of Social Psychology at the Maria Curie-Sklodowska University in Lublin, Poland. His research interests include social psychology and political marketing. He is senior editor of the *Journal of Political Marketing*. He is the author or co-author of five books, including *Political Marketing: Theoretical and Strategic Foundations* (Taylor and Francis, 2011/2015), and numerous articles (e.g. in *Media Psychology*; *Journal of Political Marketing*; *European Journal of Marketing*; *International Journal of Market Research*; *Journal of Environmental Psychology*) and book chapters.

Birce Dobrucali Yelkenci is an Assistant Professor at Department of International Trade and Finance in the Faculty of Business at the Izmir University of Economics. Dobrucali Yelkenci received her BS degree in International Trade and MSc degree in Logistics Management from Izmir University of Economics, and her PhD degree in Business Administration from Dokuz Eylul University. Her research focuses on Social Media Analytics, International Marketing and Machine Learning Applications in Marketing. Her research has been published in pre-eminent journals and books at both national and international levels, and her studies have been presented at leading conferences including the American Marketing Association (AMA) Summer Academic Conference and the SERVSIG Conference.

Otto Eibl is the Head of the Department of Political Science at Masaryk University's Faculty of Social Studies. His research focuses on political marketing and communication, emphasizing branding and long-term voter-party relations. Recently, he has explored the role of artificial intelligence in political persuasion and analysis, examining both its potential and limitations. Key challenges include ethical concerns about data privacy, the spread of disinformation and the transparency of AI-driven decision-making processes. He has (co-)authored several papers and book chapters on campaigning, particularly in the Czech Republic, and co-edited notable volumes, including *Thirty Years of Political Campaigning in Central and Eastern Europe* (Palgrave Macmillan, 2019, with Miloš Gregor) and *Issues of Political Marketing – East*

European Perspective (Routledge, 2025, with Miloš Gregor and Bruce Newman). His work examines the evolving landscape of political marketing and campaign strategies in Central and Eastern Europe.

Craig S. Fleisher is a pracademic educator, global researcher and capacity builder in analytics, corporate affairs, health trends, intelligence sciences and strategy. Craig has served in numerous leadership roles in academia, government and industry. He has co-authored/edited 17 books and over 230 scholarly articles on applied intelligence, business analytics, and corporate and public affairs and teaches graduate subjects in these fields at the Medical College of Wisconsin (Milwaukee, WI) and Mercyhurst University (Erie, PA). His most recent co-authored or edited books are the *Palgrave Encyclopedia of Interest Groups, Lobbying and Public Affairs* (Palgrave MacMillan, 2022); *The SAGE Handbook of International Corporate and Public Affairs* (SAGE, 2017); and *Business and Competitive Analysis 2ed.* (Pearson, 2015).

Miloš Gregor is Assistant Professor at Masaryk University, the Czech Republic. He teaches courses on political communication and marketing, propaganda, disinformation and fake news. Among other publications, he has co-edited several volumes: *Thirty Years of Political Campaigning in Central and Eastern Europe* (Palgrave Macmillan, 2019), *Challenging Online Propaganda and Disinformation in the 21st Century* (Palgrave Macmillan, 2021), *Political Communication and COVID-19* (Routledge, 2021) and *Risk Communication and COVID-19* (Routledge, 2025). Together with Petra Mlejnková, he is mentor of projects Choose Your Info (Zvol si info) and Fakescape, both dedicated to media literacy awareness. Both projects were awarded in the international Peer to Peer: Global Digital Challenge competition.

Jennifer J. Griffin is the Raymond C. Baumhart, S.J. Endowed Chair of Business Ethics at Loyola University Chicago Quinlan School of Business. She examines how organizations craft ethical strategies to innovatively address critical social impacts – in short, how firms can treat people with dignity, decency, and do well. Griffin is the award-winning author of the Academy of Management SIM Division Best Book Award, *Managing Corporate Impacts: Co-Creating Value.* Recipient of numerous research awards including the 'Best Paper in 20-years Award', her research on CSR and corporate public affairs are published across multiple disciplines: *Public Administration Review, Journal of Business Ethics, Business & Society, Group & Organization Management, Journal of Management Studies, Corporate Reputation Review,* and *Journal of Public Affairs,* among others. A member of Chicago's Corporation Coalition and a Board Member of Keep America Beautiful, Jenn and her husband are certified (currently, inactive) Commonwealth of Virginia firefighters and enjoy good conversations and making great food with their two adult sons and their partners.

Katherine Haenschen, PhD, is an Assistant Professor at Northeastern University, where she is jointly appointed in the Communication Studies and Political Science departments. Her research focuses on the intersection of digital media and political behaviours and attitudes. She primarily conducts field and survey experiments and analyzes digital trace data. Her work has appeared in the *Journal of Communication, Political Communication, Political Behavior* and other outlets. Haenschen received her PhD from the University of Texas at Austin.

Nada Hashmi is an Assistant Professor of Information Systems in the Technology Operations and Management Information Department at Babson College. Her research focuses on how the intersectionality of gender, race and age play a role in advancement in the workplace. In addition, she studies women's leadership and whether technology, such as generative AI, plays a role in gender equality. In the past, she has also studied group dynamics and group size – specifically, how to measure and predict group performance using metrics such as the Collective Intelligence Scores. She has over ten notable publications and a patent. She is also a social entrepreneur with three startups focusing on women and healthcare and is on the board of two technology startups. She received her PhD from the Sloan School of Management at Massachusetts Institute of Technology (MIT) in the Technology, Innovation, Entrepreneurship and Strategy as well as the Organizational Studies Group. Her Master's degrees are in System Design and Management Department from MIT and Computer Science from the University of Maryland, College Park.

Andrew Hughes is a Lecturer in Marketing in the Research School of Management, College of Business and Economics, at Australian National University. His research explores the role of emotions and emotional responses in communications and marketing, the role of place and space in slow tourism, and political and non-profit marketing. Recent examples include his exploration of the role of stakeholders in political marketing, personal brands in political marketing and the role of negative advertising in different contexts. Andrew has published in *Marketing Theory*, and written a book on the role of digital and social media in political communications, *Market Driven Political Advertising* (Springer, 2018). He has also given numerous interviews on politics and political marketing to national and international television, radio, print and internet outlets.

Burcu İlter is a Professor of Marketing at the Faculty of Business Administration, Department of Business Administration, Dokuz Eylul University. She has been working there since 1995 in the Department of Production and Marketing. She completed her master's degree in international business at Dokuz Eylul University, Institute of Social Sciences in 1996 and received her PhD in 2002 from the same institution. Her research focuses on International Marketing, Retail Marketing, Branding and Corporate Social Responsibility.

Varsha Jain is the AGK chair professor of marketing and co-chairperson of research and dissertation at the MICA, India. She is the deputy editor of *the Journal of Consumer Behaviour* and an associate editor (AE) at: *Psychology and Marketing*, *Journal of Consumer Marketing*, and *the Australasian Marketing Journal.* She has authored over 150+ publications (primarily qualitative research in the digital age), including *the European Journal of Marketing*, *the International Journal of Information Management*, *the Journal of Advertising Research*, *the Journal of Consumer Behavior*, *the Journal of Consumer Marketing* and *the Journal of Business Research.* She is a visiting guest at Emory Business School, Atlanta, Michigan State University, University of Washington, USA, a visiting scholar at Greenwich University, London, and The Medill School, Northwestern University, USA. Her interests are advertising, branding, consumer behaviour and digital marketing, primarily immersive technologies, including Artificial Intelligence (AI), Augmented Reality, Virtual Reality and Metaverse. She co-authored *Consumer Behavior: A Digital Native* (Pearson India, 2019) with Jagdish Sheth and Don Schultz), Artificial Intelligence in Customer Service (Palgrave MacMillan, 2023) and *The Future of Purpose-driven Branding* (Wiley India, 2023) with David Aaker and Varsha Jain. With Sheth, Mogaji and Ambika, she co-edited *Artificial Intelligence in Customer Service: The Next Frontier for Personalized Engagement* (Springer, 2023).

Nigel A. Jones is a visiting fellow in the Defence Studies Department at King's College London, supporting the UK Joint Services Command and Staff College on cyber and information operations. Nigel is particularly interested in the interplay of social and technological factors in real-world communications, security and risk challenges. His work on the human and informational dimensions of security, behaviours and decision-making has taken him to several conflict areas. He advises both public and private sector organizations in critical national infrastructure on security and information risk as strategic issues for Boards and leadership. He continues to advise, research and write on cyber, information, communication and propaganda in security and conflict. He contributed to the *SAGE Handbook on Propaganda* (SAGE, 2020). Nigel is a Fellow of the BCS, the Chartered Institute for IT and a Fellow of the Royal Geographical Society.

Dawood Khan is a PhD scholar and Associate Lecturer at Nottingham Business School, Nottingham Trent University. Dawood's research focuses on exploring the (mis)alignment between the corporate political brand identity and image of *Pakistan Tehreek-i-Insaf* from a multi-stakeholder perspective.

Paweł Koniak is an Assistant Professor at the Department of Social Psychology, Maria Curie-Sklodowska University, Lublin, Poland. His research interests include persuasion, reducing biased processing, framing, attitudes towards restrictions and the role of emotions in attitude formation and change. He is the co-author of one book and the author of numerous articles (e.g. in *Social Psychology, Journal of Communication Management, Social Psychological Bulletin, Polish Psychological Bulletin*) and book chapters.

Marcela Konrádová holds a PhD in political science and works as an Assistant Professor at Charles University in Prague, Department of Marketing Communication and PR. Her research fields combine political and government communication, political marketing, personalization of politics and its consequences and electoral campaigns. Marcela has participated in several internships and trainee programmes for organizations such as KohoVolit.eu or Demagog.cz; she was also an external collaborator of the Institute of Political Marketing and Campaigns. She contributed to preparing the ANO 2011 movement or the Slovak movement Sloboda, a Solidarity election campaign. In analytical positions, Marcela has worked on international projects in Germany, Serbia, Bulgaria and other countries. She also worked as a spokesperson at the Prague 8 City District Office.

Raoul V. Kübler is a Professor of Marketing at ESSEC Business School, France. He obtained his Ph.D. from Kiel University, Germany, in 2012. Following his doctoral studies, he served as an Assistant Professor at Özyegin University in Istanbul from 2012 to 2018. From 2018 to 2022, he held the position of Junior Professor of Marketing and Marketing Analytics at Münster University, Germany. His research interests revolve around gaining and leveraging insights from large amounts of user-generated content obtained from online sources. Kübler is an expert in machine learning, artificial intelligence, digital transformation, political marketing, and digital marketing. His work has been published in premier journals of his discipline, including the *Journal of Marketing, the Journal of the Academy of Marketing Science, the International Journal of Research in Marketing, and the Journal of Retailing*. Additionally, he is a co-author of two influential textbooks on Marketing Analytics, both published by Sage. Kübler serves on the Editorial Review Board of JAMS and is currently an Area Editor for the *International Journal of Research in Marketing* and the *Journal of Business Research*. His contributions to the field have been recognized with awards from esteemed institutions such as the Academy of Marketing Science, the European Marketing Academy, and the Marketing Science Institute.

Darren Lilleker is Professor of Political Communication and Director of the Centre for Comparative Politics and Media Research at Bournemouth University. His expertise is in the intersecting areas of political campaigning and public engagement in politics, and in particular how public engagement can be facilitated, channelled or reduced through the strategies employed by political organizations. He has published over 200 works covering various aspects of campaigning as well as communication psychology including *Political Communication and Cognition* (Palgrave, 2014) and *The Psychology of Democracy* (Taylor and Francis, 2021).

Lauren M. MacLean is the Dean's Professor of Political Economy and Civic Engagement in the Department of Political Science at Northeastern University. Her research focuses on democratic citizenship and the comparative political economy of public service provision in Africa. MacLean has published award-winning books and articles and been supported by grants from NSF, SSRC, the Robert Wood Johnson Foundation, Fulbright-Hays and the Carnegie Corporation. She was the recipient of the APSA QMMR 2016 David Collier Mid-Career Achievement Award.

Kai Manke is a research assistant at the Chair of Marketing & Media at the University of Münster where he received his PhD in 2024. His research focuses on the intersection between media and politics. In 2013, he received a Master's degree in Media Economics at the Technical University of Ilmenau. He then worked as a project manager at hr werbung GmbH, a subsidiary of the Hessian Broadcasting Corporation in Frankfurt am Main. Here, he was responsible for the operation and development of the central database for the processing and accounting of advertising and sponsorship revenues. From 2014 to 2016, he held several teaching assignments in the Media Management programme at the Faculty of Business & Media at Fresenius University of Applied Sciences in Idstein.

Claudia Mariotti teaches 'The Italian Political System' in the Department of Political Science at the University of Roma Tre (Italy) and 'Political Communication' at the University of Arkansas in Rome. She authored refereed articles, chapters in edited international volumes and encyclopaedia entries. She is also the author of a monography on Berlusconi's party, Forza Italia. Her fields of research are about political parties, charismatic leadership, elite theory, and, more recently, her work revolves around political communication, political polarization and lobbying. She was a Visiting Fellow in 2015, 2016 and 2024 at the University Carlos III (Madrid), in 2022 at the University of Cluj (Romania) and in 2023 at the University of Passau (Germany).

Roger Mortimore is Professor of Public Opinion and Political Analysis at King's College London. He co-edits the *Political Communications* series on British elections with Dominic Wring and Simon Atkinson (most recently *Political Communication in Britain: Campaigning, Media and Polling in the 2019 General Election*, Palgrave, 2022), and was co-editor of *Butler's British Political Facts* with Andrew Blick (Palgrave, 2018). He is a member of the Editorial Board of the *Journal of Political Marketing* and was formerly Journals Review Editor of the *International Journal of Public Opinion Research* and on the Editorial Board of the *Journal of Elections, Public Opinion and Parties*. He is also Director of Political Analysis in the UK arm of Ipsos (formerly Ipsos MORI), specializing in political and electoral research in particular, as well as in survey methodology, and has been a member of the Ipsos MORI exit poll team at each general election since 1997, contributing to the highly successful election night forecasts for the broadcasters.

Mona Moufahim is Professor in Marketing at Stirling Management School, University of Stirling. Her research interests include: marketing, consumption and extreme right politics. She is also interested in the mechanisms of power and resistance at the interface of market institutions and consumer-citizens (with a particular focus on marginalized communities). She edited *Political Branding in Turbulent Times* (Palgrave MacMillan, 2022), and her research has been published in *Organization Studies, Tourism Management,* the *Journal of Business Ethics and Marketing Theory.*

Srabanti Mukherjee is Associate Professor of Marketing at Vinod Gupta School of Management, Indian Institute of Technology Kharagpur. Her research interests are in the base of the pyramid market, consumer behaviour and services marketing. Srabanti's research has been published in *the Journal of Business Research, Journal of Political Marketing, Journal of Retailing and Consumer Services, Journal of Strategic Marketing, Journal of Service Theory and Practice, Marketing Intelligence & Planning, Journal of Hospitality Marketing and Management, Tourism Recreation Research, and Journal of Consumer Marketing* among others.

Alessandro Nai is Associate Professor of Political Communication at the Amsterdam School of Communication Research (ASCoR), University of Amsterdam. His work focuses on the dark sides of politics – the use of negativity and incivility in election campaigns in a comparative perspective, the (dark) personality traits of political figures and radical partisanship in voters. His recent work has been published in journals such as the *Journal of Politics, Political Communication, Political Psychology, European Journal of Political Research, Public Opinion Quarterly, West European Politics, International Journal of Press/Politics, Leadership Quarterly* and more. His most recent book (*Dark Politics. The Personality of Politicians and the Future of Democracy,* Oxford University Press, 2024, with J. Maier) won the 2024 ISPP Juliette and Alexander L. George Outstanding Political Psychology Book Award. From 2025, he is Editor of the *European Journal of Political Research.*

David W. Nickerson is Professor of Political Science at Temple University. His research focuses on the tactics employed by political campaigns and how voters react to the tactics. In addition to his academic work, he has collaborated with dozens of civic organizations and political campaigns, including the 2012 Obama and 2016 Clinton campaigns.

Darlington Nyambiya earned a PhD in Political Marketing and Communication from Bournemouth University, where his research provided critical insights into the impact of digital technologies on political processes, with a particular focus on autocratic environments. His expertise is in political marketing with research exploring the evolving nature of elections, political parties, and civil society engagement aligned with the strategic use of digital platforms by political entities, analysing how social media, artificial intelligence, and data analytics are deployed in political campaigns, voter engagement, and civic activism. His research is particularly concerned with how these technologies are used both as tools of political control and as instruments of resistance in non-democratic regimes.

Georgios Patsiaouras is an Associate Professor in Marketing and Consumption at the University of Leicester School of Business, UK. His research interests focus around marketing theory, political branding and sustainability marketing. His work has been published in *Marketing Theory, Journal of Marketing Management, Journal of Macromarketing* and *Journal of Historical Research in Marketing*, among others.

Koen Pauwels is the Associate Dean of Research and Distinguished Professor of Marketing at Northeastern University. Koen's European positions include Adjunct Professor at BI Norwegian Business

School, and Visiting Professor at Vrije Universiteit Amsterdam. For 4.5 years, he was Principal Research Scientist at Amazon Ads, with brand building and budget allocation recommendations reaching hundreds of thousands of advertisers. Koen received his PhD from UCLA, where he was chosen Top 100 Inspirational Alumnus. After getting tenure at the Tuck School of Business at Dartmouth, he helped build the startup Ozyegin University in Istanbul. Named a worldwide top 2% scientist, and 'The Best Marketing Academic on the Planet', Koen published over 100 articles on marketing effectiveness. This research was awarded by managers (Rethink Retail, Google, WPP and Syntec), academics (O'Dell, Davidson, and Varadarajan) and both (Gary Lilien ISMS-MSI-EMAC Practice Prize). Koen is the editor-in-chief of the *International Journal of Research in Marketing*, and Associate Editor for the *Journal of Marketing*, the *Journal of Consumer Research* and the *Journal of Interactive Marketing*. His books include '*Modeling Markets*' and '*Advanced Methods for Modeling Markets*' for analysts and '*Break the Wall: Why and How to Democratize Digital in Your Business*', and '*It's Not the Size of the Data – It's How You Use It: Smarter Marketing with Analytics and Dashboards*' for managers.

Christopher Pich is an Associate Professor in marketing and branding at Nottingham University Business School, The University of Nottingham, United Kingdom. He is an active researcher currently focusing on the application of branding concepts and frameworks to the political environment ranging from brand identity, brand image, brand reputation, co-branding and consumer-based brand equity. Further, Christopher specializes in the use of qualitative projective techniques in interviews and focus group discussions. He has published work in a range of academic journals such as the *Journal of Business Research, European Journal of Marketing, Journal of Vocational Behaviour, Journal of Strategic Marketing, Journal of Marketing Management, International Journal of Market Research, Qualitative Market Research: An International Journal* and the *Journal of Political Marketing*. Christopher is the Managing Editor for Europe for the *Journal of Political Marketing* (2016-present), and Associate Editor for the *International Journal of Market Research* (2023-Present).

Igor Prusa is a Czech scholar in Japanese studies and media studies. He worked at the Czech Academy of Sciences and is currently affiliated with Ambis University Prague where he teaches media theory. Prusa received his first PhD in Media studies at Charles University in 2010 ("Media and Society in Japan"), and in 2017 he defended his second doctoral thesis ("Scandal, Ritual and Media in Postwar Japan") at the University of Tokyo. Prusa's research interests include Japanese media culture, media scandals and cultural representations of anti-heroism. He is the author of *Scandal in Japan: Transgression, Performance and Ritual* (Routledge 2024). His research has appeared in a wide range of publications, including *Media, Culture & Society* and *Contemporary Japan*. Apart from his academic activities, Igor Prusa is a music composer in a band Nantokanaru. He may be contacted at igorprusa@gmail.com.

Marta Rebolledo De La Calle is Associate Professor in Communication and Media Studies and Associate Dean of the Mohammed Bin Rashid School for Communication at the American University in Dubai. Rebolledo holds a double doctoral degree from the University of Navarra (Spain) and l'Université Paris-Est (France). Prior to joining AUD, she was as Associate Professor of Political Communication at the School of Communication of the University of Navarra where she taught in different bilingual undergraduate programmes – Global Journalism and Politics, Philosophy and Economics degrees. She has been visiting scholar at The George Washington University (United States), Loughborough University (United Kingdom) and Université de Montréal (Canada). Rebolledo also has an active research profile with a variety of publications and contributions to international conferences, and is actively involved in several academic associations such as the International Political Science Association (IPSA), being a member of the board of the Political Communication Research Committee (RC22). Her research interests include media coverage, marketing, campaigns, digital communication and public communication from institutions and corporations.

Travis N. Ridout is Thomas S. Foley Distinguished Professor of Government and Public Policy in the School of Politics, Philosophy and Public Affairs at Washington State University. He also serves as co-director of the Wesleyan Media Project, which has tracked political advertising since 2010. Ridout's research on political campaigns and political advertising has appeared in the *American Political Science Review, American Journal of Political Science, British Journal of Political Science, Journal of Politics, Political Communication, Political*

Behavior, Political Psychology, Annual Review of Political Science and in several book chapters. Ridout's most recent book, *Political Advertising in the United States, 2nd edition,* was published in 2021.

Christopher Robertson is Lecturer in Social Science and International Relations at Leeds International Study Centre. Christopher has published widely on political communication, democracy and journalism, in journals such as *The International Journal of Media and Cultural Politics* and *The Journal of Public Affairs*, and in books such as *The Palgrave Encyclopedia of Interest Groups, Lobbying, and Public Affairs and Futures of Journalism: Technology-Stimulated Evolution in the Audience-News Media Relationship.* Current research interests include the marketing and reception of austerity and anti-austerity messages, the contemporary significance of political philosophy to marketing, framing and communications and the role of non-traditional political communications.

Sergei A. Samoilenko is an Assistant Professor in the Department of Communication at George Mason University. His research focuses on issues in the fields of subversive strategic communication, crisis communication, and reputation management. He is a co-founder of the Research Lab for Character Assassination and Reputation Politics (CARP), an interdisciplinary research community, studying strategies and tactics of character assassination and ways to counter them. He is an author and editor of several books, including *Handbook of Social and Political Conflict, Character Assassination and Reputation Management: Theory and Applications, and Handbook of Research on Deception, Fake News,* and *Misinformation Online.*

Filip Scherf is a researcher, published author and policy analyst with the focus on Russia and European security with extensive international experience from the United States, the United Kingdom, Brussels, Russia, and the Czech Republic. He is currently a Researcher at the University of St Andrews and the University of Oxford's Europaeum Scholar. Filip is affiliated as a Research Associate with the Cambridge Margaret Beaufort Institute, lectures on political risk at Charles University, and serves as a Research Director at Princeps Risk Intelligence Institute. Formerly, Filip was a regional Correspondent to the Economist Intelligence Unit and a political risk consultant in Russia. Filip's other academic and professional experience include Columbia University's Harriman Institute for Eurasian Studies in New York, RAND Corporation in Cambridge (UK), Eurasia Group in London and NATO PA in Brussels. Filip holds master's degree in International Affairs from Columbia University's School of International and Public Affairs (SIPA), and a master of letters degree from St. Andrews University in Scotland where he was placed on the Dean's list for academic excellence. For his research, Columbia University awarded Filip the Dasturdaza Dr Jal Pavry Memorial Award for International Peace and Understanding. Filip was also a Harriman Junior Fellow, a member of the International Fellows Program and a recipient of the Robert Legvold Fellowship. Filip's book *The Lost Land: A Story of Modern Russia* was published in Czech in 2024. He has also published articles and essays in print and online media in the United States, the United Kingdom, the Czech Republic and Slovakia. He serves on Columbia University's Global Engagement Committee.

Subhojit Sengupta is an Assistant Professor (Marketing) at the Institute of Management Technology (IMT), Ghaziabad. He has a PhD in Marketing from Vinod Gupta School of Management, Indian Institute of Technology Kharagpur. His research interests are in the bottom of the pyramid market, political marketing, public policy and has been published in the *Journal of Political Marketing, Journal of Financial Crime, Journal of Marketing Communications and Marketing Intelligence & Planning.*

Pooja Sharma is a Fellow Programme in Management (FPM) scholar at MICA, Ahmedabad, specializing in Integrated Marketing Communications and Digital Management. She is currently a visiting scholar at the College of Communication, Arts and Sciences, Michigan State University, where she is affiliated with the Department of Advertising and Public Relations. Her interdisciplinary research integrates political communication, digital media studies, and consumer behavior, with a focus on how strategic narratives, platform infrastructures, and mediated discourses shape public perception, participation, and decision-making in contemporary democracies. She holds a Master's degree in Political Science from Jawaharlal Nehru University and a Bachelor's (Hons.) in Political Science from the University of Delhi. She is also UGC-NET qualified and holds a Bachelor's in Education. Drawing on a mixed-methods research orientation, her work combines thematic analysis, discourse analysis, and statistical modeling to understand communication practices across digital and political ecosystems.

Anna Shavit holds a PhD in Political Science and is an assistant professor at the Faculty of Social Science at Charles University. Her research areas are political marketing (focusing on relations to political parties, citizen participation and democratic process), government communication (covering mainly the Czech environment) and election campaigns (professionalization of campaigns, role of political consultants, etc.). She also works as a campaign strategist and has extensive experience with many campaigns in the Czech Republic and Slovakia. She is a Charles University research team member in ReMeD Horizon Europe. Anna is a former Fulbright scholar.

Nathan R. Shrader is Associate Professor of Politics and Co-Director of the Center for Civic Engagement at New England College in Henniker, New Hampshire, USA. A self-described "professor, pundit, and ward heeler," Shrader is a veteran of over two dozen political campaigns, served as Legislative Aide and Deputy Director of Communications for the Lieutenant Governor of Pennsylvania, Legislative Aide in the Virginia House of Delegates, and Legislative Intern in Washington for U.S. Senator Arlen Specter. Shrader is a regular contributor to news broadcasts covering state, local, and national politics He holds a PhD in Political Science from Temple University.

Aurken Sierra is Assistant Professor in the Department of Public Communication at the University of Navarra's School of Communication. He teaches courses on the History of Communication, Contemporary Political Systems and Comparative Political Systems. His research work includes contributions to the Journalism, Political Communication and Democracy group, as well as the Narrative, Violence and Memory group. Additionally, he is actively involved in the REMED research project, funded by the European Commission. He is also a member of the Spanish team for the Digital News Report, a leading global study that analyzes trends in digital media consumption and the state of journalism across various countries.

Nancy Snow (PhD, School of International Service) is a Professor of Communications Emeritus at California State University, Fullerton, a contributing writer to *Nikkei* and *Nikkei Asia,* and a senior advisor at Kreab Tokyo. Snow was a principal founding faculty member of the USC Annenberg School and Syracuse University Newhouse School master's degree programme in public diplomacy. She was Japan's first distinguished professor of public diplomacy and held an Abe Fellowship at Keio University and a Fulbright professorship at Sophia University. Snow is a senior fellow with the Sympodium Institute for Strategic Communications, an editorial board member of *Defence Strategic Communications* and an Adjunct Fellow with the Institute for Contemporary Asian Studies, Temple University Japan. In addition to her Fulbright in Japan, she was a Fulbright scholar at the University of Freiburg in Germany and a Fulbright professor at Panteion University in Athens, Greece, where she is a non-resident senior fellow at the Institute of International Relations. Snow was a Presidential Management Fellow (PMF) at the Department of State and U.S. Information Agency during the Clinton administration. She is the author, editor and co-editor of sixteen books, including the eighth edition of *Propaganda and Persuasion* (SAGE, 2025) and both editions of the *Routledge Handbook of Public Diplomacy.* She has held strategic communications and public diplomacy teaching and consulting appointments across the globe, including the Schwarzman Scholars Programme at Tsinghua University, and has lectured in more than 30 countries.

Louise Spry is Senior Lecturer at Nottingham Business School. Her research specialism is corporate branding in different contexts. She has published in journals such as *Journal of Brand Management, International Journal of Market Research, Journal of Strategic Marketing* and *European Journal of Marketing.*

Wayne Steger is professor of Political Science and Distinguished Honors Faculty at DePaul University. His research focuses on campaigns and electoral competition, presidential nominations and elections and the American presidency. His books include *A Citizen's Guide to Presidential Nominations: The Competition for Leadership* and *Campaigns and Political Marketing.* His most recent book is *Presidential Nominations: Political Parties as Conditional Arbiters of Democracy.* His current work focuses on the resurgence of left- and right-wing populism, in the forthcoming book, *Resurgence of American Populism: Economic and Social Transformation and Political Discontent.*

Henry Sun is the Chairman of Sun Inter-Technology Corp. He has consulted for various academic institutes, multinational corporations and government, such as The Wharton School, General Electric, General Signal,

Consulting and Audit Canada, and Training and Development Canada. He is the Director of International Affairs at the Institute of Urban Governance, Shenzhen University, and a Member of the Academic Committee of the Institute for Global Cooperation and Understanding, Peking University. His current and past academic affiliations include fellowships at Rothermere American Institute, Oxford University, ASH Center, Harvard Kennedy School, Asian Studies Center, Sciences Po., Paris, American Studies Center, Peking University; Member of Editorial Boards of *Journal of Political Marketing* and *Journal of Public Affairs*; Visiting Professor University of Chester, UK, China University of Politics and Law, Jiangxi University of Economics and Finance and New York Institute of Technology. He has co-authored books on Political Marketing and International Political Marketing. He has a PhD degree in International Politics from Peking University, an MSc degree in Marketing from Pennsylvania State and a BA degree in Trade Economics from Jiangxi University of Finance & Economics.

Jonáš Syrovátka is a Doctor in Political Science who graduated from Masaryk University in Brno, Czech Republic. As a researcher in Czech and international think-tanks, he has been involved in the research of disinformation, conspiracy theories and propaganda since 2016. He led the team of analysts conducting the research series 'Czech elections in the era of disinformation', mapping the role of disinformation in five elections between 2017 and 2021.

Martin Vértеši is a PhD candidate in the department of Political Science at Masaryk University in Brno, Czech Republic. His research interests include political communication, political campaigns and issues in political competition with a focus on political parties and Czech presidents.

Michael Vintr is a Senior Director at Prescient, a Chicago-based global risk management and intelligence services firm. In his role as the Practice Lead of Prescient's Intelligence practice, Michael focuses on the firm's most complex bespoke engagements in business intelligence and manages corporate security solutions with a focus on travel risk intelligence. Michael joined Prescient in 2017 and helped to develop many of Prescient's current best practices around management and research process, including Prescient´s current standards for international due diligence engagements. Outside of Prescient, Michael has held external consultant positions with a focus on identifying early indicators of radicalization on social media, as well as general political risk analysis and forecasting. In 2023, Michael co-founded the Princeps Risk Intelligence Institute ("PRII"), a Prague-based non-profit organization dedicated to developing the risk intelligence industry standards in Central & Eastern Europe. In his role as the Director of the PRII, Michael is responsible for setting the long-term strategy of the Institute. Michael is also an Associate Lecturer at Charles University in Prague, where he teaches courses on risk intelligence. Michael holds a Master's degree in International Affairs from Columbia University's School of International and Public Affairs, where he focused on international security and was a member of the International Fellows Program.

Tom Wraight is a lecturer in Political Economy at Queen Mary University of London. His research specialism is economic nationalism and Anglo-American conservatism.

Jason Voiovich is an independent researcher and practicing marketing professional focusing on innovation, marketing, persuasion and consumer culture. He is the author of multiple academic papers and two books: *Marketer in Chief: How Each President Sold the American Idea* and *Booze, Babe, and the Little Black Dress: How Innovators of the Roaring 20s Created the Consumer Revolution.* His newest book, *Bullfrogs, Bingo, and the Little House on the Prairie: How Innovators of the Great Depression Made the Best of the Worst of* Times, was out in May 2025. Voiovich earned his BS from the University of Wisconsin – Eau Claire, his MA from the University of Minnesota and post-graduate education from the Massachusetts Institute of Technology Sloan School of Management.

Foreword I

After 50 years of running or advising campaigns from Australia to Afghanistan, the United Kingdom to the United States and from Zambia to Zimbabwe, my perspective on political marketing is a practitioner's. Practitioners and academics don't always see eye to eye. Each has some contempt for the other. The practitioner viewing the academic as overly theoretical and the academic viewing the practitioner as opportunistic and cynical. In developing this handbook, the Editors have produced much that can be instructive for practitioners, especially with regard to digital and social media. That this handbook devotes attention to new ways of delivering messages is a useful thing. It draws from across geographies, specialisms and experts to create a breadth and depth of views, although perhaps insufficiently from the centre and centre-right.

Political marketing is an academic's term. Practitioners speak simply of campaigns, as an exercise in influencing or reinforcing the behaviour of a target audience (generally voters). As a campaigner, I seek to ensure our target audience behaves in a particular way. So, an election is like a retail sale but, uniquely, you want people to 'buy' from you on just on one day. Ascertaining what gets them to 'spend' their vote with you is key. What they think before or after the act of voting is interesting but irrelevant. In any campaign, there are three targets – base, swing and 'anti'. These terms are wide, and one of the worthwhile features of this handbook is its discussion of the techniques enabling targeting to be more specific. In any campaign, one seeks to activate the voter base. Because they are your supporters, you do not have to persuade them. You do have to motivate them to action in support of your campaign. Your antis must be contained and neutralized (not in a CIA sense!). Any engagement with them, if at all warranted, must be on your terms and to their detriment. Finally, there are 'swing' targets. These undecided or 'soft' voters have to be persuaded and activated.

When discussing the campaign task, you 'persuade through reason but motivate through emotion'. I believe that observation is the single biggest lesson in political marketing. An effective campaign requires reason *and* emotion. Consideration of these warrants more attention than it currently receives. An election is a choice. As a campaigner, you must help frame that choice in a voter's mind. There is much discussion in this handbook about negative campaigning and candidate attacks and whether they are right or wrong. If you leave a vacuum in a campaign, your opponents will fill it. In presenting the choice voters face, you must define yourself and your opponent. With the latter, that means holding them to account for their views and actions. Such accountability is legitimate and fair, not negative.

I have observed, across five decades, many changes in how campaigns are run. The editors summarize the reality of political marketing well when they say 'The long-term goals of political actors, firms and voters are largely unchanging. It's only the tools that change'. However, a voter receives a message – whether it is from canvassing (a narrowcast message), a television advertisement during prime-time TV (a broadcast message) or a personal message delivered direct to one specific individual using social media, I firmly believe that message matters most. If a voter does not hear or receive a campaign message, then the best message in the world stands for naught. The mechanics of a campaign are therefore vital in ensuring the message is received. You can spend too long thinking about the latest technique and not long enough on the message. Readers can judge for themselves if this handbook gets that balance right.

On occasion, the message and mechanics can be integrated. Barack Obama's message as the first African-American Presidential candidate was one of empowerment: his slogan being 'yes we can'. Social media was emblematic to and enshrined within that campaign. Voters demonstrated 'yes we can' by deploying their own social media in support of Obama. Individuals were empowered by both the candidate and the campaign tools available to them via social media. Today's tools create global connections. They enable low-cost and effective global activism, adding a new, powerful dimension to political marketing. An idea advanced in one country can be picked up and advocated in another, in seconds. Where once money was a powerful proxy for campaign support, now it is the number and volume of voices mustered which are the proxy – all for a fraction of the cost of a more traditional campaign. Digital and social media can however create an echo-chamber easily and effectively as several contributors underscore.

Understanding the crafting of campaign messages is critical. To be influential, there are four elements to an effective political issue or message. These elements are found within the 38 chapters of this handbook even though they may not be brought together in one concise expression. The first is that a campaign issue or message must be salient. As several authors say, context is important. If you talk about issues outside of the context of current debates, voters will ignore you – or worse believe you to be out of touch and undeserving of being heard. So what you talk about must make sense. Secondly an issue, if it is to influence a voter, must be personally relevant. One reason for much apparent disconnect between 'elites' and the 'typical voter' is that the issues that elites focus on or talk about are not seen by many voters as relevant to their lives. You must connect to people in a personally relevant way. This need not be an issue or policy. It could be a value or a belief that matters to the target voter. Whatever it is, it must be relevant or else it will not influence the voter in the right way. The third element is differentiation. You differentiate on your strengths and minimize differentiation on your weaknesses. The final element is giving the voter a role. The voter should be empowered to achieve the outcome they want, for example, to endorse a candidate or policy or send a message to a political party. That role is to consciously vote to achieve their desired outcome. Elections are not about giving observations. They are about giving voters a role and stake in their own futures.

One of the biggest campaign changes I have witnessed – and in some ways this handbook is a reflection of it (although understandably so) – is the focus on campaign process. Today's media focus on *why* a candidate or campaign is doing something. For example, they talk of a Presidential candidate going to a district because it is *swing* district or speaking about *medicare* because it is an important issue for voters in a key state. So, voters are now wise to the political strategies and tactics in a way they were not before. This heightens cynicism and suspicion. The same goes for polls which various contributors discuss at length. There are so many polls published now that they have become *part of the campaign process* itself and are not impartial exercises. Public polls are part of the campaign dialogue and increasingly gamed by political candidates for their own benefit.

The greatest change is happening now. AI and deepfakes pose a real threat to political discourse, campaigns and decision-making. As several contributors tell us: without a moral compass to guide them, they can be turned into potent and democracy destroying tools. That understanding alone makes this handbook well worth reading and referencing.

SIR LYNTON CROSBY AO
Co-Founder and Executive Chairman
CT Group

Foreword II

The *SAGE Handbook of Political Marketing* presents a comprehensive investigation of the constantly evolving relationship between marketing practices and political communications. The scope of this collection is vast, encompassing a large variety of geographical perspectives and political contexts. Both scholars and practitioners will encounter a wide array of content related to political organizing, propaganda, persuasion and the digital revolution. In fact, one can worry that the very breadth of material may be too wide-ranging, as concepts tend to lose precise meaning when used too broadly. Over 60 authors bring diverse backgrounds to this work. This breadth of expertise allows the reader to comprehend a multifaceted view of political marketing that spans different political cultures and contexts. The diversity of perspectives highlights both commonalities and distinctions in political strategies employed in different political systems. Both academics and activists will find great value in this extensive array of content. The Handbook addresses key trends in campaign strategies such as continued reliance upon broadcast media coupled with the increasing influence of social media which, in turn, has facilitated the intensification of populism, as well as the role of digital tools in contemporary political marketing. The Handbook's exploration of trends in political marketing is particularly timely as the political arena becomes increasingly influenced by digital technologies. In that its focus remains largely on democratic systems and the influence of Western marketing techniques; however, the volume may overlook the channels of political communication in authoritarian contexts.

As most of the authors explicitly argue, the significant transformations in political marketing over the 20th century were heavily influenced by technological advances that enabled candidates to reach ever broader audiences. This development also advanced the professionalization of campaigning, heavily shaped by the American model of political marketing that emphasizes branding and message consistency. In recent decades, however, the rise of the internet and social media has expanded the landscape of political marketing. Political campaigns now utilize data analytics, targeted advertising and real-time engagement strategies, allowing for more personalized communication with voters. The use of AI and digital tools has enhanced the sophistication of political messaging, enabling politicians to craft narratives that resonate on an individual level. This evolution reflects a shift from mass communication to a more nuanced, micro-targeted approach, while underscoring the importance of political marketing as an essential component of contemporary electoral strategies. In other words, the Handbook incorporates the simultaneous broadening of the audience for political persuasion and the narrowing of message content towards individual recipients.

Looking ahead, the Handbook posits that political marketing is poised for further evolution, particularly as technological innovations continue to reshape the way political communication occurs. The increasing integration of AI and machine learning into campaign strategies will likely lead to even more refined targeting techniques and voter engagement methods. In this context, one desirable advance could be a growing importance of ethical considerations in political marketing. As concerns about misinformation, disinformation, 'deepfakes', scams, outright prevarication and data privacy rise, political marketers will need to navigate a complex landscape where transparency and ethical practices will carry equal weight as messaging. Additionally, the resurgence of grassroots movements and populism may ultimately shift the focus of political marketing to more community-oriented approaches, emphasizing local engagement, collective activation and community building over traditional top-down strategies.

F. CHRISTOPHER ARTERON
Founding Dean and Emeritus Professor of Political Management
Graduate School of Political Management (GSPM), George Washington University

Introduction

Paul Baines, Phil Harris, Denisa Hejlová and Costas Panagopoulos

The aim of this book is to introduce the theory and practice of political marketing in a global, yet localized, world. The practice of political marketing has changed immeasurably during the 20th and 21st centuries with the rise of the mass media, as political communication has adapted to the logic and processes of marketing communication, advertising and the internet. Culturally, the field has been dominated mainly by US, European and Australasian scholars with a great emphasis on the Americanization and professionalization of campaigning styles (Elebash, 1984; Field, 1994; Scammell, 1998).

Since the start of the new millennium, political marketing has experienced yet another shift with the digitalization of communication and personal data collection and analysis. It has since transformed into a data-driven, specialized profession, with rhetoric crafted by AI, into personally targeted, evidence-based messaging with real-time measurement of engagement and sentiment analysis. This use of political marketing is not restricted to democratic regimes and has been widely adopted internationally by centrally controlled states and systems. Even dictators need to listen to their citizens or they face deposition as events in Iran in 2009, and the Belarussian protests in 2020-21, showed (though without regime change in either case). It seems then like a very good time to update what we know about political marketing and bring what has been written about it firmly into the 21st century.

With the collapse of the Soviet Union in 1991, we might have expected the world to have transformed into one where most nations strive for greater democracy. Sadly, it has not. Democratic-minded uprisings, such as the Arab spring, or developments in other countries with weak democracies, such as Afghanistan, have turned and many of these countries have lapsed back into dictatorships, or civil war. Highly developed and democratic countries in the West like the USA, France, the UK, Hungary and others have experienced a surge in populism (see Chapter 15 for more on this topic).

The new millennium brought us terrorist groups with a global focus like Al Qaeda and ISIS, who both made extensive use of political marketing/propaganda to recruit foreign fighters and to sow mayhem in democratic societies (Jones et al., 2015; O'Shaughnessy & Baines, 2009). While Islamist terrorist groups copied Al Qaeda as a globally marketed terrorist brand archetype (see Baines & O'Shaughnessy, 2014), right-wing examples also abound including Atomwaffen (allegedly disbanded in 2024) and Combat 18 to take two international examples. Chapter 25 covers the rise and increasing allure of the Far-Right and the techniques they use to politically market themselves.

Marketing can be, and has been, applied to popular movements. Revolutions in Egypt, Tunisia, Iran and Moldova, were all facilitated by the marketing of revolution on social media in the late 2000s and early 2010s. Political marketing therefore exists as a phenomenon in almost all countries in the world, from Albania to Zimbabwe to Brazil. The aim of this new SAGE Handbook is to represent the global perspective on political marketing in a variety of contexts, cultures and regimes. We are very proud to note that the Handbook covers perspectives on political marketing from Australasia, Europe, Africa, Asia and the US. We are particularly pleased to be able to provide insights into political marketing in Zimbabwe, Japan, India, Hong Kong and Ukraine; places seldom previously discussed in the political marketing literature. These chapters enrich the debate on what political marketing is and the impact that it can have on democracies and, importantly, also when used pseudonymously in authoritarian societies.

A *SAGE Handbook of Political Marketing* including chapters from well-known contributors in the field is required now more than ever as political marketing morphs, from a method to get people elected, to a multi-faceted phenomenon based on the marketing of ideology, including marketing by terrorist groups, corporates, pressure groups, political parties, popular movements (see Chapter 20) and state governments. Most governments have an army of communication advisors working in various departments. To get some idea of how this approach has been adopted outside of the West, consider that one of our editors was informed that 8 million people now work in government communications in China, which is probably true given the size of the population (1.4 billion in 2024; CIA, 2024) and the ruling Communist Party's strict controls over the dissemination of information to their populace. The growth of advocacy, lobbying and public affairs internationally are all covered in depth, reflecting all of political marketing whether it be direct or indirect.

The Handbook covers 38 chapters in the following four parts, each of which covers a specialist area of study and is carefully curated by each one of the editors with the support of various members of our excellent editorial board in improving each of the chapters submitted over two successive rounds of reviewing.

- *Part 1:* Strategy in Political Marketing: Orthodox and Occidental Perspectives (Paul Baines)
- *Part 2:* Political Marketing, Propaganda, and Digital Evolution: Global South and Eastern European Perspectives (Denisa Hejlová)
- *Part 3:* Ideology in Political Marketing: Advocacy, Movements, Lobbying, and Public Diplomacy (Phil Harris)
- *Part 4:* Contemporary Political Marketing: Cybercampaigning, Fake News and Social Media (Costas Panagopoulos).

Our treatment of political marketing herein privileges topics not always well-treated in similar books on the topic, including the marketing of ideology as political marketing (see Chapter 20), focusing on the marketing of movements and company use of political marketing techniques to affect legislative agendas (i.e. lobbying) and advance governments' own positions internationally. We also tackle the nature of change in political marketing that has arisen from the advent of the internet, including digital marketing and the use of AI in political marketing (see Chapters 29–31) and analytics in campaigns (see Chapter 17). Much early consideration of political marketing has been focused on campaigning in an era of mass TV and radio. Yet the birth of the internet and, particularly social media (see Chapters 9 and 29), has had significant impacts on campaigning and fund-raising practices, though TV advertising still remains important and relevant (see Chapter 8). In the modern world, we also see the use of fake news and disinformation in political campaigning (see Chapter 16). This takes standard practices like negative campaigning, which we cover extensively in a series of chapters (see Chapters 4, 5 and 32), to another level and these effects deserve much greater academic consideration, especially since election interference is now ubiquitous (see Henschke et al., 2020). We are also pleased to cover the use of political marketing techniques in a crisis management context (see Chapters 10 and 24). In addition, to match the increasing discussion of political branding in the political marketing literature, we have a number of contributions on that topic (see Chapters 7, 33 and 35) but also on the older and related discussion of positioning in political marketing (see Chapters 3 and 22). As with the marketing profession, and with the advent of digital communications, there is increasing scope and desire to measure the effects of political marketing practice. This is a topic little written about but covered in this Handbook in Chapters 6, 17 and 37). There is also extensive coverage of narrative and discourse in political marketing, a topic of considerable importance to practitioners (see Chapters 1, 9 and 18). There are numerous other sub-topics covered including propaganda and disinformation (see Chapters 11, 12, 16 and 32), the vetting of political candidates (see Chapter 14), the use of stakeholder influence techniques (see Chapter 21), the role of women in public affairs and lobbying (see Chapter 27) and policy considerations and their link to political marketing (see Chapters 4, 26, 28, 34 and 35).

In the next sections, we provide an overview of the content of the chapters in each part and what each part hopes to contribute to our wider understanding of political marketing as a social and cultural phenomenon and as a set of powerful managerial techniques to influence political outcomes in contested spaces like referendums, protests, elections, political debates and more.

PART 1: STRATEGY IN POLITICAL MARKETING: ORTHODOX AND OCCIDENTAL PERSPECTIVES

Introduction to Part 1

In this opening first section of the Handbook, we consider political marketing strategy in both orthodox and occidental perspectives in political marketing, by which we mean that we focus on the central concepts in political marketing. Much of the writing in the discipline of political marketing derives from Global North perspectives (certainly until around 2010), meaning that it has originated in particular from North American, British, European and Australasian (occidental) perspectives. However, there has been an increasingly important discussion of political marketing from oriental perspectives (see Jain & BE, 2020; Mukherjee et al., 2022). We are delighted to be able to bring occidental perspectives even more to the fore in this Part. Similarly, the political marketing literature incorporates a wide range of subject matter, including political (marketing) communications, political branding, negative campaigning, political strategy development, campaign management and message development, voter research, digital political marketing, political image/reputation management (including crisis management), propaganda and disinformation and much more. In Part 1, we focus particularly on strategies, campaigns and communications.

THE CONTENT: CHAPTERS IN PART 1

Political Marketing Strategy in an Election Context

The first three chapters in Part 1 consider political marketing strategy in the context of election campaigning. Strategy is particularly important because it sets the blueprint for what activity should be undertaken, in what order, why, how and with what resources. Getting strategy wrong means losing an election for candidates and parties and the examples are legion. Consider Barry Goldwater in the 1964 US Presidential, when he failed to offset and anticipate the negative attacks he received from the Johnson campaign. These cleverly articulated that he was a war-monger, through Doyle Dane Bernbach's (DDB) famous 'daisy spot' ad campaign, where a narrator intones in a campaign TV spot to a nuclear countdown that 'these are the stakes, to make a world in which all of God's children can live, or to go into the dark. We must either love each other or we must die'. Such graphic language and visualization of nuclear war invoked the fear of God in viewers, thinking that Goldwater was dead set on pressing the nuclear button and so they duly elected Lyndon B. Johnson. Another example was the failed Brexit campaign of the Conservative government in the UK in 2016, when the Remain ('Britain Stronger in Europe') campaign failed absolutely to make a compelling case for staying in Europe. They allowed the negative attacks of the UK Independence Party (UKIP) and the officially designated Leave party ('Vote Leave') to gain traction with an admittedly already Eurosceptical electorate.

Wider examples of failed political marketing strategy in other countries include the shock drop in votes for Narendra Modi in India that forced him to seek a coalition to stay in office in his third term in 2024, and in Japan's 2024 lower house elections, when the Liberal Democratic Party and its partner, Komeito, lost their majority and were forced into running government with all the chaos accompanying ruling as a minority party (Oxford Economics, 2024). These examples illustrate that parties cannot trust their past success and indeed cannot trust that the strategy they pursued previously will work for them in future campaigns. Voters become tired of seeing the same old thing and hearing promises that are made in manifestos but are not kept. Witness the defenestration of Emmanuel Macron in June 2022 legislative elections in France, when the voters edged him in for a second term in the Presidential elections, but ensured he was a lame duck after he lost his majority in the parliamentary elections that followed (Anon., 2022).

In Chapter 1, 'Strategies and Tactics in Global Political Marketing: Cases and Challenges from the Practitioner's Perspective', Alexander Braun explores what knowledge is essential to running a modern election campaign from years of personal experience. He boils it down to really understanding the electorate and developing a segmented approach to campaigning, developing impactful branding in order to cut through voters' selective perception barriers, and the importance of communicating the brand to the right people using authentic, compelling narratives. Braun provides a series of examples of political leaders who have employed these strategies around the world in the last 10 years.

In Chapter 2, 'Australia – Political Marketing in a Down Under Democracy', Andrew Hughes discusses the unique nature of political marketing in the Australian context, explaining its duopolistic party system and how it has evolved towards a more pluralistic system incorporating new minor parties, compulsory voting and the forced choices it creates in voters, and the 'Washminster' system which characterizes Australian government (mixing elements of the US and British political systems) and how each of these elements impacts upon political marketing practice as a result. Hughes concludes that Australian political marketing practice is market-oriented and, accordingly, has become characterized by person-branded leaders, simple promotions focusing on three core issues, and by positioning using election strategies predominantly targeting women in urban locations aged 28–55 years, and working in medium to high paying occupations, if parties want to win in Australian elections.

In Chapter 3, 'Positioning Presidents: Non-Political Branding in US Elections', Neil Collins and Patrick Butler develop a typology of how previous US presidents have been positioned in presidential elections. They explain how presidents have been positioned on either a predominantly social or professional dimension and on either a Washington insider (i.e. part of the political establishment) or an outsider basis. This they argue leads onto four types of campaign including the Champion (the social-insider), the Challenger (the social-outsider), the Counsel (the professional-insider) and the Combatant (the professional-outsider). They use this typology to characterize presidential campaigns since 1901 in the hopes that it provides a heuristically useful system to both characterize future presidents in elections and to provide candidates themselves with some understanding of where they stand and how they might position themselves accordingly.

POLITICAL CAMPAIGNS: NEGATIVITY AND MEASUREMENT OF EFFECTS

In Chapters 4–6, we also consider negative issue campaigning, electoral attacking strategies in TV debates and the measurement of campaign effects in political marketing. There has been extensive debate on negative political advertising (see Lau et al., 1999; Lau et al., 2007 for meta-analyses) and some discussion of the measurement of effects in political marketing, but this is a more contested area and often but, not always, based on analysis of the effectiveness of a single medium (see Dommett et al., 2024; Goldstein & Ridout, 2004; Iyengar & Simon, 2000; Pareek et al., 2018; for selected useful studies on the topic).

In **Chapter 4, 'Negative (Issue) Campaigning: Towards a Decision-Making Process and Framework'**, Paul Baines and Roger Mortimore seek to outline how political marketers ought to think about how to design negative campaigns and what factors impinge upon those design decisions. This chapter illustrates an attempt to provide a useful framework for political marketers to design how to run future negative campaigns. Such decisions about how to design negative campaigns ought to be taken in the light of polling, social media analyses and qualitative research evidence, but the authors indicate that while there is plenty written on negative campaigning in political marketing, there is not much written on how political marketers should actually do negative campaigning.

In **Chapter 5, 'Electoral Attacking Strategies: Lessons From the Electoral Debates in Spain and France'**, Marta Rebolledo **De La Calle** and Aurken Sierra continue the discussion of the theme of negative (attack) campaigning, but from comparative case and contextual perspectives, taking in the debates between opposition parties in Spain and France. The authors conclude that electoral debates are primary events in political campaigns but that their formats and contexts morph over time affecting their impacts. They conclude that incumbents often receive the most attacks but that in the case of their study, the ideological nature of the parties and the degree of hostility shown towards the other party were different in different contexts.

In **Chapter 6, 'Polarized and Connected: Measuring Campaign Effects in the 2016 and 2020 US Presidential Elections'**, Koen Pauwels, Kai Manke, Raoul Kübler and Costas Panagopoulos discuss how social media interactions and candidate campaigns were linked to election outcomes in two presidential elections in the United States. They use a novel combination of content analysis and time series analysis, finding that quality market research matters as polls in themselves drive some voters' electoral choices, that events can impact voters' choices but most do not, that disinformation can affect election outcomes (as it did with Hillary Clinton in 2016) and that social media channels can boost campaigns (as Hillary

Clinton did using Instagram and Donald Trump on what was Twitter, now X, in 2016). They recommend political marketers optimize their messages for the channels they are using and monitor the campaign discourse carefully to ascertain whether or not it is resonating with the electorate.

POLITICAL MARKETING COMMUNICATIONS: IN ELECTIONS, CRISES AND WAR

In the final section in Part 1 (Chapters 7–11), we consider the very important concept of (political marketing) communications. This is an aspect of political marketing that has long been written about, from both marketing and political communication perspectives. Early pioneering books in the development of the political marketing discipline emphasized the communications angle and how it could be optimized to appeal to the electorate including O'Shaughnessy (1990), Maarek (1995) and Newman (1993). What is different however about this topic in contemporary times, particularly since Bruce Newman's excellent and comprehensive previous handbook on political marketing (see Newman, 1999), is that this publication covers the advances in political marketing practices given the advent of the internet and social media over the last 20 years. Chapters 7–11 encompass branding, TV advertising, social media campaigning and discourse, the important job of managing political communications during crises and strategic (government) communication in the unique context of a war, specifically the Russian-Ukraine war.

In **Chapter 7, 'Political Brand Engagement and Positioning: An Integrated Framework'**, Chris Pich, Guja Armannsdottir, Dawood Khan and Louise Spry analyze branding in elections in the (British) Crown Dependency of Jersey and in Pakistan to support the development of a political brand engagement and positioning framework to identify the difference between actual and intended positioning and the drivers and barriers in achieving (non)alignment between the two. The authors undertake depth interviews with all four main and relatively new parties in Jersey (the 'oldest' being founded in 2014), concluding that it is too early to tell whether these fledgling political party brands will endure and increase engagement with the electorate or whether independents will endure as they have previously. The authors also used focus groups based on stakeholder groups to consider political branding by Pakistan's main opposition party, Pakistan Tehreek-e-Insaf (PTI), the leader of which is former Pakistani team cricket captain and the 19th Prime Minister (2018–2022), Imran Khan. They conclude that of the party, policy, leader trinity of a political brand, in Pakistan, the leader element predominates in the brand's positioning.

In **Chapter 8, 'The Continued Relevance of Political Advertising on Television: A Review of Its Effects and Content'**, Travis Ridout and Furkan Cakmak discuss the central question of whether TV advertising remains relevant in an era where online and digital campaigning has risen to the fore. They discuss the effects and effectiveness of TV advertising. They argue that TV advertising does indeed remain relevant, because it continues to increase knowledge of, and participation in, politics and sets the news agenda but also because the medium is itself evolving into digital formats, for instance, via connected television (CTV) including via YouTube. Contemporary TV advertising allows messages to be tailored to specific types of voters and even individuals. Though their focus is principally the US, they do consider TV advertising elsewhere, though they note these other countries tend to more highly regulate TV advertising in elections, when compared with the US.

In **Chapter 9, 'Social Media Content in the Turkish Presidential Elections: A Functional Theory of Political Campaign Discourse Perspective'**, Gözde Akdeniz, Birce Dobrucalı Yelkenci and Burcu İlter examine discourse during the 2023 Turkish Presidential and Parliamentary elections between incumbent Turkish President, Recep Tayyip Erdoğan, and the leader of the main opposition party (Republican People's Party), Kemal Kılıçdaroğlu. Analysing posts on X, using Benoit's Theory of Political Campaign Discourse, they analyze each leader's messages based on their function (acclaim, attack and defence) and topic (character and policy). Their findings indicate that politicians can and should use platforms like X to achieve real-time voter engagement, track public reactions to their posts and statements and adjust their strategies accordingly. They explain how analysing discourse on X reveals the unique dynamics of a campaign, particularly in the cultural context of that country, which in the case of Türkiye, means contending with the fact that it is a secular, nationalist and predominantly Muslim country.

In **Chapter 10, 'Political Communication and Digital Media in Japan: Trends and Challenges'**, Igor Prusa argues that digital media has had a limited impact on Japanese political engagement despite the fact that it has a strong digital infrastructure. He argues that Japanese society favours government-centric as opposed to citizen-centric services. An important part of the lack of uptake in citizens' digital engagement is that Japan's politics are less polarized, conventional media remain strong, and a single party (the Liberal Democratic Party) has dominated for most of the last six decades since it was set up in 1955. He argues that Japan's relatively immature digital e-democracy hampers civic society as a consequence.

In **Chapter 11, 'Ukrainian Political Communication in the Russo-Ukrainian War: A Case of Strategic Communication and Political Marketing?'**, Nigel Jones and Paul Baines seek to illustrate how strategic communications (as a discipline in defence and strategic/communications studies) and political marketing theory might explain the impressive, rapid (initial) success of President Zelensky in mobilizing the Ukrainian people to 'fight to the finish' and repel the Russian invasion and in gaining the financial, intelligence and logistical support of Western partners, without whom he simply could not hope to defeat the Russian invasion. They highlight that in the same way that political marketing has developed the concept of the 'permanent campaign' (i.e. campaigning not purely during a formal election campaign) so strategic communications are increasingly being used by governments during peace *and* wartime (especially by Western adversaries such as Russia, China and Iran).

Overall, Part 1 highlights how political marketing concepts and practices are becoming increasingly used in both Western and Eastern contexts. This maturation of political marketing practice has brought about an increasingly sophisticated use of political branding, negative campaigning, political advertising and social media in election campaigns and other political contexts, but these same techniques can also be used in war and other conflict scenarios as the chapter on the Russia-Ukraine war highlights. Political marketing has been described as a marketing-propaganda hybrid (O'Shaughnessy, 1990), and nowhere is this more apparent than in the Russia-Ukrainian war. The use of political marketing techniques in future war and conflict scenarios is likely to become increasingly ubiquitous.

PART 2: POLITICAL MARKETING, PROPAGANDA AND DIGITAL EVOLUTION: GLOBAL SOUTH AND EASTERN EUROPEAN PERSPECTIVES

Introduction to Part 2

The rapid rise of digital communication tools has profoundly reshaped societies on a global scale. This transformation extends beyond our everyday interactions, fundamentally influencing political decision-making and civic engagement. Smartphones and social media have become gateways to people's minds, emotions and political opinions and actions, impacting citizens in both economically developed and under-developed regions. The influence of platforms like TikTok on elections has become increasingly evident (Duncombe, 2018). 'Twitter diplomacy' has emerged both as a recognized academic term and a new foreign policy tool. Social media's capacity to amplify political messages has fuelled a surge in populism, a phenomenon linked to the decline of interest in 'hard news' and the rise of 'news fatigue'. This fatigue, particularly pronounced among women and young people, often leads to disengagement from political news because they do not want to be stressed by politics (Reuters Institute/University of Oxford, 2024).

In Part 2, we focus particularly on digital communications, not just in their use in enhancing political marketing effectiveness but also in their use as a tool for more insidious forms of political combat. These include foreign interference (Dowling, 2021), manipulation (Kõváry Sólymos, 2023) cyber espionage (Segal, 2013) and cybercrime (NCSC, 2024) though these contexts are not all explored in this Handbook. The gap between democratic, semi- and even non-democratic states has widened significantly. Democracies are typically bound by ethical norms prioritizing transparency, accountability and openness (often with freedom of information rules in place). In contrast, authoritarian regimes face no such constraints and frequently deploy manipulative tactics and propaganda aimed at both domestic and international audiences without regard for ethical considerations. This disparity highlights the need to explore how digital tools, including the use of analytics, are employed for propaganda, political vetting and voter targeting in political campaigns. This part also considers political marketing in the Indian context, including an explanation of how Bottom of the Pyramid voters are coerced into voting for particular candidates through treating and information manipulation and a discussion of the focus of Indian political leadership messaging.

POLITICAL COMMUNICATION AND HUMAN NATURE

The transformative power of digital tools reflects a fundamental shift in political communication. Yet, as futurologist Alvin Toffler predicted, while digital communication would alter how people communicate, it did not change human nature (Toffler, 1970). The desire for influence, control and dominance persists, manifesting through both ethical engagement and manipulative tactics. This duality underscores the complex ethical questions surrounding digital political communication, as these tools amplify both the constructive and destructive tendencies inherent in human political behaviour.

Francis Fukuyama's prediction of an 'end of history', in which liberal democracy would become the universal model of governance, has proven overly optimistic (Fukuyama, 1992). Today, only about half of the world's nations are democracies. Even within democratic regions like the European Union, populist movements continue to gain traction, challenging established norms. This populist wave, particularly prominent in Central and Eastern Europe, complicates the trajectory towards democratic consolidation. In India, the world's largest democracy, political engagement is further shaped by deeply rooted cultural and religious dimensions. Digitalization has transformed political marketing in India, but local cultural practices – such as storytelling and religious traditions – remain influential. Outsiders often find it challenging to fully comprehend these intercultural dynamics. Nonetheless, India demonstrates that democracy is adaptable and manifests differently in different cultural contexts.

NAVIGATING POLYCRISES AND SOCIETAL DISTRUST

Today's global society faces what scholars refer to as a 'poly-crisis' – an overlapping convergence of economic instability, environmental degradation, geopolitical conflicts and social fragmentation (see Henig & Knight, 2023). This climate of uncertainty has given rise to a pervasive sense of nihilism, particularly among younger generations who view political institutions with scepticism. The resulting mistrust creates fertile ground for populist and authoritarian movements, which exploit public discontent to gain influence. Digital platforms provide an ideal medium for these groups to disseminate their narratives. Political marketing strategies have thus evolved to address, and sometimes exploit, this environment of scepticism and polarization.

ETHICAL CHALLENGES AND DIGITAL OPPORTUNITIES

The rise of digitalization brings not only new possibilities but also significant ethical challenges. Social media analytics, AI and big data have revolutionized political communication by enabling highly personalized messaging. While these tools allow political campaigns to target specific demographics with precision, they also raise concerns about privacy, consent and potential manipulation. The ability to micro-target and tailor messages to individual voters can create echo chambers, where people are exposed only to information that reinforces their existing beliefs. This technical feature limits open debate and critical thinking, deepening societal divisions and polarization. Political marketers must navigate the fine line between effective engagement and ethical responsibility, ensuring that digital tools serve to inform rather than manipulate.

THE COMPLEX INTERPLAY OF SOFT AND HARD POWER

Joseph Nye's concept of 'soft power' (Nye, 1990a) – influencing others through attraction rather than coercion – takes on new dimensions in the digital age. Digital soft power often operates alongside elements of hard power, such as economic sanctions or cyber operations, making influence campaigns more complex and multifaceted. States and non-state actors leverage digital platforms to covertly shape public opinion, sometimes promoting understanding and dialogue, but often sowing discord and division. Influence campaigns targeting Western democracies have used soft power tactics to erode public trust in democratic institutions, spreading misinformation and divisive narratives. The integration of soft and hard power in the digital era highlights the blurred lines between attraction, persuasion and manipulation, emphasizing the need for vigilance and robust countermeasures in democratic societies.

THE CONTENT: CHAPTERS IN PART 2

The Digital Evolution – Rise of Propaganda and Manipulative Digital Tools

The first set of chapters in Part 2 (Chapters 12–14) open with a focused examination of how digital technologies have reshaped political communication, emphasizing both the opportunities and ethical challenges presented by these tools. In **Chapter 12, 'Political Marketing and Propaganda: Definitions, Evolutionary Changes, and Their Implications for a Taxonomy of Regime Types'**, Denisa Hejlová explores the historically contested distinction between political marketing and propaganda. Hejlová frames both as powerful tools of persuasion aimed at mobilizing citizens to act according to specific political aims but emphasizes that their ethical boundaries differ significantly across different political and socio-cultural contexts. Hejlová traces the evolution of propaganda, discussing how modern digital technologies such as computational propaganda and cyber propaganda blur the line between reality and manipulation. The chapter illustrates how digital communication enables new forms of control over public opinion and integrates surveillance technologies that introduce new layers of censorship and self-censorship. By positioning political marketing and propaganda within historical and digital contexts, Hejlová's work deepens our understanding of their impact on contemporary political persuasion.

In **Chapter 13, 'Strategic Market Segmentation and Targeting in the 21st Century: Ethical Challenges, Trends and Innovations'**, Otto Eibl and Miloš Gregor examine the sophisticated targeting methods that have become central to modern political campaigns. Eibl and Gregor discuss how technological advancements, including AI, machine learning and data-driven analytics, allow for personalized voter profiling and micro-targeting. They address the ethical dilemmas inherent in these practices, questioning whether such methods should be used to influence voters and the impact they have on a democracy's quality. The chapter balances practical insights into segmentation and targeting with a critical reflection on the risks posed by AI and data-driven manipulation, particularly when used by both legitimate democratic actors and hostile non-democratic forces (including hostile states). This work highlights the need for ongoing ethical debate regarding the use of advanced technologies in political marketing.

In **Chapter 14, 'Vetting Political Candidates in the Digital World'**, Filip Scherf and Michael Vintr explore how digital technologies have revolutionized candidate vetting. Traditionally confined to internal party processes (often through 'interrogations' as a means of determining whether one's candidate had 'skeletons in their closet'), vetting now extends to broader public scrutiny through digital tools and open-source intelligence (OSINT). Scherf and Vintr introduce a theoretical framework that redefines surveillance and control in political contexts, showing how digital tools shift power from traditional institutions to the public, enabling 'sousveillance' or 'watching from below'. This chapter critically examines both the opportunities and risks of digital vetting, cautioning against the potential for exclusionary practices, misinformation and reputational damage. By emphasizing the need for balance, transparency and ethical use of such vetting tools, the authors contribute an essential perspective on both democratic accountability and reputational damage minimization for political parties or other candidate sponsors in the digital age.

Together, these chapters offer a comprehensive overview of the digital evolution in political marketing and the manipulative potential of modern tools. They raise crucial ethical questions about the integrity of democratic processes, highlighting the dual potential of digital innovation to either enhance transparency or deepen manipulation.

THE HEATED CEE REGION: POLITICAL MARKETING AMID GEOPOLITICAL SHIFTS AND THE RISE OF POPULISM

The second set of chapters in Part 2 (Chapters 15–17) delves into the dynamic and often contentious landscape of political marketing within Central and Eastern Europe. These chapters examine how populism, disinformation and data analytics shape political strategies and voter behaviour, emphasizing their implications for democracy and electoral integrity in this geopolitically significant region.

In **Chapter 15, 'Political Marketing and the Strategic Populism in Poland'**, Wojciech Cwalina and Paweł Koniak offer a detailed analysis of how populism has become a central feature of Polish politics. While populism was traditionally used by outsider or challenger parties, it has increasingly been adopted by mainstream politicians seeking to counter populist challengers and mobilize their voter base. Cwalina and Koniak provide a marketing-centric view of populism, treating it as both a 'thin' ideology and a strategic approach to voter segmentation and party positioning. The chapter contextualizes the rise of populism within Poland's post-communist history, highlighting socio-political factors such as the challenges of economic transition, public dissatisfaction with state institutions and cultural tensions. By identifying key populist narratives – ranging from historical grievances to economic and cultural dissatisfaction – the authors shed light on the multifaceted appeal of populism and its implications for political marketing strategies.

In **Chapter 16, 'Disinformation and Elections: Old Challenge in the New Context',** Sára Cigánková, Jonáš Syrovátka and Martin Vérteši focus on the pervasive impact of disinformation on elections and democratic politics in the region. The authors trace the historical roots and evolution of disinformation, emphasizing its heightened relevance in the aftermath of the 2016 US presidential election. By examining case studies of electoral campaigns influenced by disinformation, the chapter illustrates how fake news, conspiracy theories and other manipulative tactics shape voter behaviour and can undermine democratic processes. Cigánková, Syrovátka and Vérteši also explore strategies to combat disinformation, emphasizing the importance of media literacy, transparency and cross-border cooperation to safeguard electoral integrity. This chapter provides valuable insights into the complex and evolving threat of disinformation, offering both a theoretical framework and practical recommendations for political actors and researchers.

In **Chapter 17, 'Use of Analytics in Political Marketing: Data-Driven Campaigns, Theory and Examples',** Anna Shavit and Marcela Konrádová explore the increasing role of data-driven campaigns in contemporary political marketing. Building on the concept of 'permanent campaigning' (see Blumenthal, 1982), the authors discuss how data analytics has become a cornerstone of modern electoral strategies, allowing political actors to gather and analyze voter data to inform campaign decisions. Shavit and Konrádová provide a detailed overview of the phases of analytics in political marketing, using examples from the Czech Republic to illustrate how data-driven approaches differ across various types of elections. While the chapter focuses primarily on practical applications, it also addresses ethical considerations related to data privacy and voter manipulation, calling for a balanced approach to the use of analytics in democratic processes.

Together, these chapters illuminate the complex interplay of populism, disinformation and data analytics in political marketing within Central and Eastern Europe. The rise of populist rhetoric, the prevalence of disinformation and the use of sophisticated data-driven strategies present both challenges and opportunities for political actors, underscoring the need for ethical guidelines and regulatory measures to preserve democratic integrity in the region.

POLITICAL MARKETING IN THE WORLD'S LARGEST DEMOCRACY: INDIA

The next set of chapters (Chapters 18 and 19) offer a focused exploration of the unique dynamics shaping political communication and marketing in India, an important democracy, and indeed the world's largest. As India increasingly modernizes, and grows more economically important, its elections and government decision-making are also likely to become increasingly important. This section highlights how traditional cultural elements and modern digital tools intersect, creating a multifaceted and evolving political landscape. In **Chapter 18, 'Role of Content and Narrative in Indian Political Leadership Communication: A Narrative Paradigm Theory Approach',** Pooja Sharma and Varsha Jain investigate the role of content and narrative in the political communication strategies of Indian leaders. The chapter explores how social media has become a key platform for Indian politicians to connect with voters, using thematic and narrative-driven content to engage and influence public opinion. Sharma and Jain provide a thematic analysis of social media engagement, illustrating how political leaders employ storytelling and strategic narratives to foster relationships with their target audiences. By examining the interplay between digital platforms and political messaging, the authors offer insights into the evolving nature of political communication in India, highlighting its impact on voter engagement and democratic discourse.

In **Chapter 19, 'Political Marketing at the Bottom of the Pyramid: Shreds of Evidence From India',** Subhojit Sengupta and Srabanti Mukherjee explore the unique challenges faced by Bottom of the Pyramid (BOP) voters in India. The chapter explores how political branding and communication strategies influence the decision-making of BOP voters, who are often characterized by poverty, limited education and restricted access to information (see also Mukherjee et al., 2024). Through a qualitative phenomenological approach, Sengupta and Mukherjee analyze the factors driving BOP voting behaviour, including short-term incentives, coercive tactics and a sense of belonging. Their findings offer a nuanced understanding of political marketing at the grassroots level, emphasizing the need for policy interventions to protect and empower vulnerable voter groups. This chapter contributes to the broader discourse on political communication by proposing a conceptual framework for understanding the BOP segment and offering policy recommendations to enhance democratic engagement and voter protection.

Together, these two chapters illustrate the complex and diverse nature of Indian political marketing, emphasizing the interplay between digital tools, traditional cultural elements, and socio-economic factors. By examining both high-level digital narratives and grassroots political engagement, this section provides a comprehensive overview of how political marketing shapes democracy in India, offering critical insights for scholars, practitioners and policymakers alike.

Overall, Part 2 highlights a critical divide between democratic and non-democratic states, with far-reaching implications for international political cooperation and conflict. The rapid evolution of digital communication tools has not only reshaped how political campaigns are conducted but has also opened new arenas for foreign interference, particularly in cyberspace. This digital battleground frequently translates into real-world consequences, impacting political stability, trust in institutions and the effectiveness of democratic governance.

Democracies operate under ethical norms emphasizing transparency, accountability and openness; these are principles essential to maintaining public trust. However, these same values often make democracies more vulnerable to covert influence campaigns, disinformation and manipulation orchestrated by hostile non-democratic states. Authoritarian regimes, of which there has been a global expansion, are unrestrained by such ethical considerations, employ sophisticated propaganda, cyberespionage and manipulative political marketing strategies to destabilize rivals, undermine democratic norms and assert their influence on the global stage. This asymmetry creates a significant challenge, as democracies must find ways to defend themselves without compromising the very values that define them.

The chapters in this part have explored how populism, disinformation, data-driven political marketing and cultural narratives intersect with these broader geopolitical realities. They reveal the dual nature of digital tools as both instruments for engagement and levers for manipulation. In the future, international collaboration, ethical frameworks and regulatory measures will become increasingly crucial to mitigating the risks posed by digital influence campaigns. Democratic societies must not only enhance their resilience against foreign interference but also strive to foster informed citizen engagement, promote media literacy and ensure that digital tools are wielded in ways that strengthen, rather than erode, the democratic process. This nuanced understanding is vital to navigating the evolving digital landscape and preserving democratic integrity in a world increasingly shaped by the complex interplay of soft and hard power in cyberspace.

PART 3: IDEOLOGY IN POLITICAL MARKETING: ADVOCACY, MOVEMENTS, LOBBYING, AND PUBLIC DIPLOMACY

Introduction to Part 3

How do we market policy and share power, ideas and ideals with the people and in international and multi-cultural societies in an increasingly digital world? This question is in essence, at the heart of political marketing and, consequently, its policy equivalent public affairs management. Public affairs has always been complex, and the actual craft of leadership and good fortune or 'fortuna', as Niccoló Machiavelli (the Italian renaissance diplomat and author) would have said, is to succeed for the most significant number and the public good (Harris, 2022). This is as complex as ever, and today, we have a global market of consumers, communications and polluters. Things have changed, and communications are more diverse and, in some ways, controlled. We now have 5 billion internet users out of 8 billion citizens worldwide allowing a diverse and divergent group of communications and views to be expressed often with no accountability or consistency. Many means of communication, many forms of government and governance and a range of tools and methods to achieve ends now exist. Part 3 of the handbook explores how we communicate digitally and through traditional campaign methods in political marketing. It also looks at how women are playing more significant roles in causes and professionally in political marketing, providing greater balance. It assesses international government and trade, right-wing parties and pressure group campaigning. Such foci hopefully inform and educate those interested in political marketing and its methods in the 21st century.

THE CONTENT: CHAPTERS IN PART 3

Social Movements in America, Asia and Europe

Part 3 in particular addresses gaps in knowledge in our understanding of how political marketing is used to advance new social movements (NSMs) in America, Asia and Europe. For example, in **Chapter 20, 'The Marketing of an Ideal: The Hong Kong Pro-Democracy Movement',** George Patsiaouras assesses modern political advocacy, campaigning and lobbying. His chapter brings together political marketing and the phenomenon of the NSMs by outlining the evolution and development of the Hong Kong Umbrella movement as a case study and example. NSMs emerged after the 1960s and are characterized by their focus on identity, lifestyle and ethics rather than economics. They are distinct from the 'old' working-class movement-based organizations, which was the primary challenger to capitalist-based systems in Marxist theory. NSMs focus on issues related to human rights rather than economic concerns such as economic development or trade. One example is Black Lives Matter (a movement challenging inequality and mobilizing for justice and democracy). The Shahbag Movement in Bangladesh (a mass movement that demanded a trial for crimes against humanity) and the Disability Rights Movement. NSMs often focus on lifestyle, ethical or identity concerns rather than economic goals. They also often work outside of formal institutional channels. Well-known NSMs include *Occupy, MeToo, Black Lives Matter, Extinction Rebellion and the Gilets Jaunes, which differ from older movements.* The Chapter outlines the realities of advocacy in the modern global world, protecting values, civil liberties and international good governance.

In **Chapter 21, 'Pick-Six: How Grassroots Organizations in the United States Can Use Core Stakeholder Influence Techniques in Political Marketing',** Craig Fleisher and Jason Voiovich, primarily focus on North American advocacy and how influence and dialogue can be developed and targeted within one of the world's most sophisticated media communications systems. They argue that targeting and focusing on issues and points of influence is critical for success in this diverse, multi-complex society and state. Grassroots political marketing organizations often need help to plan, execute, evaluate and measure the impact of their advocacy, influence and lobbying tactics. Did they work? Why did they work? Did they work well enough to 'win'? Are such tactics the most effective way of influencing within a complex and sophisticated society? These are the sort of questions considered. By the time organizations get around to measuring their campaign effectiveness, the urgency has often passed and, along with it, the opportunity to impact policymakers and other relevant stakeholders. In short, grassroots political marketers must use proven influence strategies that can be deployed quickly, as they are needed, and without time-intensive pretesting. That was especially relevant during the COVID-19/Flu/respiratory syncytial virus (RSV) 'Tripledemic' season of 2022/2023, the context in which Chapter 21 is written.

Digital lobbying has emerged as a crucial tool for grassroots influence success and is a growing industry in modern public affairs. The most advanced models allow us to see digital lobbying as a six-step process based on: (1) monitoring, (2) analysis, (3) strategic evaluations, (4) positioning, (5) acting and (6) evaluating outcomes. By vigilantly tracking issues and stakeholders in social and traditional media, grassroots leaders can better analyze and prioritize their communication outreach strategy to lawmakers and related external stakeholders' contexts.

In **Chapter 22, 'It's all About Position, Position, Position: The Case of the Five Star Movement in Italy'**, Fabio Bordignon, Luigi Ceccarini and Claudia Mariotti discuss the place of a populist, digital party and its impact on political marketing. They discuss this in the context of the Italian protest party Movimento 5 Stelle (Five Star Movement, FSM), explaining how it has evolved along the path of change from protest stage towards institutionalization. The authors particularly focus on 'place' and 'political positioning', referring to FSM's revolutionary extended use of the internet as an alternative space for engagement and political action.

In **Chapter 23, 'Soft Power, Art of the Media and International Political Marketing: A Cross-Cultural Perspective',** Henry Sun and Phil Harris assert that the monitoring and knowledge of the soft power of nation-states is a critical component of modern political marketing. They assert that since Joseph Nye first developed the concept (Nye, 1990b), it has evolved and become the cornerstone of much political thinking and policy-making. They outline how conflict can harm a nation's soft power but that it can be bolstered with military and economic strength. This might sound contradictory but in fact the point is to project military and economic strength not necessarily wield it; the latter of course is the remit of war and sanctions. International political marketing, they assert, is the public face of a government's efforts to bolster a particular country's image through persuasive communications aimed at international organizations and foreign subjects. Their notion of international political marketing therefore has parallels with the notion of public diplomacy, defined as 'government-sponsored efforts aimed at communicating directly with foreign publics' (typically to build support for that government's strategic objectives) (The Editors of the *Encyclopaedia Britannica,* 2024). Sun and Harris explain how international political marketing concerns how states maintain and enhance long-term relations between governments.

In **Chapter 24, 'The Pandemic Olympics: Japan's COVID-19 Crisis Communications',** Nancy Snow explores how Japan (mis)managed the communications associated with the Olympic Games of 2021 against the backdrop of the COVID-19 pandemic. It gives a historical perspective and compares and contrasts Japan's response with South Korea's response to COVID-19. Like other countries, Japan suffered swift and devastating consequences from COVID-19 on its economy and society, but Snow concludes that the initial euphoria of hosting the games turned to fear, and the event needed to be managed to avoid contagion. All attending used masks and adopted strict quarantine methods and, as a result, financial costs and public opposition grew. The games were eventually seen as successful, but significant political marketing activity needed to be undertaken to help Japan achieve this during a traumatic global health crisis and the Japanese government boxed themselves into this situation by treating the hosting of the games during the COVID crisis as an inevitability. The chapter provides an excellent and timely reminder of the need to have built-in contingency planning and effective management of pandemics and international sporting events to be maintain public confidence and stability and reminds us the impact such soft power initiatives can have on a government's international reputation.

In **Chapter 25, 'Marketing the Far-Right: How Do They Get it Right?',** Mona Moufahim examines Belgium's far-right and secessionist party, Vlaams Blok/Vlaams Belang (V.B.), and how the party uses political marketing from an etic (outsider's) perspective. Her chapter reviews the literature associated with the far-right and then outlines the key concepts in political marketing and (re)branding, particularly positioning, image and identity. When tackling the study of parties like the Flemish V.B., the Austrian Freedom Party (FPÖ), or the French Rassemblement (formerly known as the Front National), the catch-all labels of far-right, extreme-right or (extreme) right-wing populism are commonly used. There are several designations, many of which are used interchangeably, complicating and confusing their study. To further complicate matters, some organizations are formal political parties operating within parliamentary democratic systems; others are more akin to social movements. The steady rise of rights and nationalism in Europe and even worldwide is attracting attention and putting strain on parliamentary and democratic systems. How far-right parties win adherents is an area of significant study. These parties are not reflective of media stereotypes and are invariably very digitally and mathematically aware of their geo-demographic targeting in elections. Moufahim concludes that V.B. has been successful because it has managed to rebrand itself into a new right-wing conservative party brand while retaining the brand heritage of its parent, the Vlaams Blok party. Importantly, the new entity remains attached to its anti-immigration stance (winning it votes) but retains its Flemish nationalism at heart and promotes this with often controversial media outbursts to ensure it courts public visibility.

In **Chapter 26, 'The Political Marketing of Austerity and Anti-Austerity Policies in the UK',** Chris Robertson focuses on how austerity – a government policy to reduce government debt by reducing government spending – is so unpopular to voters (Hübscher et al., 2020), but was marketed and sold to electorates, particularly after the 2008 Global Financial Crisis. The chapter also explores how anti-austerity communities have emerged and responded in attempts to challenge what have become perceived by some sections of society as regressive austerity policies. In so doing, this chapter considers how austerity has been marketed across two different timelines in the UK and, consequently, how the meaning of austerity has changed and become contested. While it was previously associated, consensually, with post-war frugality (necessary during and after rationing), austerity is now frequently perceived as linked more with neoliberal conservatism and consequently its use is highly contested by those on the left-wing of politics. Robertson questions why this is, considering how the term's usage has evolved from government and society prudence into what he argues is an ideological, regressive policy in less than 75 years? Robertson's work focuses on interrogating critical debates in the manufacturing and marketing of austerity and anti-austerity policies, indeed policy in general, determining current issues of concern in the discipline, including how policy debates shift from the fringes of society to the mainstream.

In **Chapter 27, 'Women in Public Affairs and Lobbying',** Maria Cristina Antonucci considers the gendered nature of the public affairs/lobbying profession and how it has changed. She explains how the sector is becoming increasingly feminized, particularly in areas like event management, network building, monitoring/reporting and issues management. Antonucci's discussion considers present challenges such as women's access to the lobbying and public affairs profession, and the 'sticky ground' they must overcome to advance their careers to gain new heights, while simultaneously overcoming the 'glass ceiling'. Antonucci argues that this is necessary because greater gender diversity within the lobbying and public affairs sector enhances organizational dynamics, improves collaboration and creates innovation. The chapter explores the shift from a male-dominated profession to a more inclusive and equal one, where women assume leadership roles in consultancy firms and corporate public affairs departments. A two-step approach, comprising data analysis and a review of the literature on the topic, aims to elucidate two key aspects: firstly, the ongoing issue of the persistent underrepresentation of women in lobbying and public affairs careers, and secondly, the potential solutions to this issue. The proposed solutions include adopting the gender mainstreaming approach endorsed by the 1995 Beijing Conference on Women and the European Commission and integrating gender considerations into Diversity, Equity, and Inclusion (DEI) systems. These practices are increasingly implemented by organizations that adhere to the Environmental, Social, and Governance (ESG) model, thereby offering, in addition to a gender mainstreaming approach, a pathway to achieving gender balance in lobbying and public affairs careers.

In **Chapter 28, 'Going Blue in the Deep Red: How Kansas Voters Shocked the Nation and Protected Choice',** Nada Hashmi, Suniti S. Bal and Anjali S. Bal examine how pro-choice political advertisements played on the intersectionality of Kansas voters during the 2022 Kansas abortion referendum. Their chapter considers a unique context: specifically, the aftermath of the United States Supreme Court judgement *Dobbs v. Jackson Women's Health Organization* which overturned *Roe v. Wade*. *Roe v. Wade* had been a landmark decision ensuring the right to abortion was legal across the whole of the United States. With the *Dobbs* decision, the right to access abortion was no longer federally mandated but in the hands of individual states (Coen-Sanchez et al., 2022). One such state was Kansas, where Republicans controlled the state legislature and held many nationally elected positions. Three months after *Roe* was overturned, Kansas politicians moved to ban nearly all abortions within the state. Many believed that with the Republican stronghold in the state, this ballot initiative would quickly pass. Kansas defied the odds and protected reproductive health care access. Hashmi, Bal and Bal propose that this sentiment was driven by younger, more diverse audiences – groups not well-represented in traditional polling. This meant that the poll results released did not give a comprehensive view of sentiment towards the initiative. Subsequently, related media coverage was not wholly accurate. Their findings highlight the need for public polling to be approached from an intersectional perspective. Kansas provides an important example of how traditional polling might have overlooked a significant portion of public sentiment. They highlight how abortion bans/restrictions are linked to systemic racism because they disproportionately impact ethnic minority groups. These very groups played a crucial role in voting down the Kansas ballot initiative, and Twitter-based sentiment underscored their strong opposition to the initiative. This research shows that if traditional polling had tapped younger and more diverse audiences, polls would have predicted a negative outcome for the Kansas abortion referendum.

Overall, Part 3 makes a contribution to the Handbook by highlighting and discussing an area of political marketing less well-served in the literature: the marketing of social and political movements, fringe political groups, countries' efforts to influence other countries, political crisis communications, women's increasing emancipation in public affairs and the surprising effects of political advertising during an abortion referendum. These perspectives enrich our understanding of political marketing and its application in different contexts, cases and countries.

PART 4: CONTEMPORARY POLITICAL MARKETING: CYBERCAMPAIGNING, FAKE NEWS AND SOCIAL MEDIA

Introduction to Part 4

The rise of digital political marketing, both in the Global North and the Global South, is explored in depth in Part 4 of the Handbook. Drawing from numerous national examples, including the United States, China, South Korea, Zimbabwe, Ghana, Austria and others, the authors conceptualize and explicate a range of concepts that help explain the ever-evolving world of political marketing. The authors bring new theories and empirical insights to bear on digital political marketing across the political sphere, not only from the perspective of political parties and candidates but also from governments, nations, and firms.

The first section (Chapters 29–31) provides insight into the role of AI and AI-generated content in political marketing, for example, in microtargeting, character assassination, grassroots organizing, democratization and state censorship. The following section (Chapters 32–34) integrates political marketing with perspectives from political candidates, national governments and firms. The last section (Chapters 35–38) contributes a focus on historical and experimental analyses with cases from Zimbabwe to the United States. Altogether, the chapters review large bodies of research on the effects of political marketing and illuminate areas ripe for new research.

THE CONTENT: CHAPTERS IN PART 4

Digital Political Marketing

Although the goals of political campaigns remain largely unchanged, the technologies and strategies used in political marketing have changed dramatically over the last two decades due to the ascendance of social media and digital technologies. In **Chapter 29, 'Digital Political Campaigning and Social Media',** Katherine Haenschen and Bridget Barrett review the research on the growth and usage of social media in political campaigns through the lenses of candidates and their campaigns, users and the platforms themselves. The authors illuminate how the loss of the press's power to gatekeep information related to political campaigns opened up numerous avenues for campaigners and voters to interact. They enumerate these unique capacities and affordances of social media, touching on, for instance, how campaigns can raise funds, candidates can exhibit their personal qualities, users can mobilize their peers, and platforms can tailor their algorithms. They highlight many of the methodological challenges and shortcomings in our understanding of the causal effects of these new methods, helping set the stage for further research. They also call attention to the need for empirical descriptive work on the content of digital political advertising on social media sites in countries around the globe for comparative research. We do not know much about what campaign professionals do, they point out, and even less on what the effects of their strategies may be.

In **Chapter 30, 'The Role of Artificial Intelligence in Political Marketing',** Chris Robertson and Phil Harris discuss how new challenges for trust in political marketing and advertising have emerged with the advent of AI. Robertson and Harris provide an interdisciplinary approach to the development and maintenance of trust in democracies and apply it to AI. The issue the authors focus on is the ability of political actors to use AI to produce content that voters fail to perceive as synthetic and potentially false or misleading. They apply a theory of the 'social becoming' of trust in which trust is given as a sort of bet about another actor's future behaviour that may or not may pay off. If it fails to pay off, then trust is damaged. With failed bets about the veracity of AI-generated political advertising comes a growing awareness of its use and a weakening of the culture of trust in the political system, and political marketing specifically. Rampant distrust or mistrust – scepticism – could leave citizens with little confidence in the pronouncements of politicians and the technology itself. A society weak in trust, the authors warn, is averse to taking risks that are necessary for cooperation. Their prescription is to recognize that tech platforms that produce and disseminate AI-generated content are Machiavellian in that they seek to portray themselves as representing the public interest while preventing harm to their brands. To foster a culture of trust, then, requires trust in both the technology and the actors behind it, especially the politicians using it. They argue that advertisements should disclose when they were created using AI, which would increase accountability for tech firms and political actors, and raise familiarity and trust in the technology.

In **Chapter 31, 'Digital Political Marketing: Informing, Mobilising and Interacting During the 2023 Zimbabwean Election',** Darren Lilleker and Darlington Nyambiya call attention to the impact of digital technologies in Zimbabwe. As a developing country under the rule of a single dominant party that has almost complete control over state media, it is an instructive case of the role digital marketing technologies can play to foster democratic competition. First the authors review a large body of literature on how social media platforms inform, mobilize and foster engagement among citizens. Then they demonstrate their effect on Zimbabwean civil society and politics. Their rich exposition of the Zimbabwean case follows the path of the Citizens Coalition for Change (CCC), a political newcomer, as it challenged the dominant Zanu PF party in the 2023 election. The CCC leveraged social media and other digital technologies like WhatsApp to build trust with voters and counter political apathy, in part by speaking to everyday problems and eliciting participation from citizens in the urban centres and rural areas. However, while digital platforms fostered political pluralism and citizen engagement, the authors also demonstrate how they can lead to political mudslinging, misinformation and resulting polarization.

POLITICAL MARKETING FOR POLITICAL CAMPAIGNS, COUNTRIES AND FIRMS

As candidate-centred elections have spread around the globe, so has the focus on the leaders standing in those elections and the desire to bring those leaders down by their respective oppositions. In **Chapter 32, 'Character Assassination in Electoral Negative Campaigns',** Sergei A. Samoilenko and Alessandro Nai's comprehensive analysis helps us understand an increasingly important form of strategic political communication: character assassination. They explicate its various forms, such as name-calling and questioning moral character, through the use of numerous examples taken from contemporary politics in both the United States and Europe. Leveraging these examples, they enumerate five elements – attacker, target, audience, context and the media – that clarify the roles of different actors and how each contributes to the impact of character assassination. With these elements, they describe three strategies character assassination campaigns often take: provocation, contamination and obliteration. Exposing the media to a scandal involving a political actor is one form: provocation. A specific tactic is misquoting, which involves purposefully taking the target's words out of context to portray them in an unfavorable light. Push polling is perhaps an even more nefarious tactic given its increased feasibility using AI and microtargeting. It involves contacting voters in the guise of a survey house and asking them questions designed to spread rumours or raise other doubts about the target. Contamination and obliteration strategies are described in turn, providing a thorough understanding of modern character assassination strategies. This chapter provides a unique overview of how a particular and pernicious form of negative campaigning has developed in recent times.

In **Chapter 33, 'What Can Nation Branding Research Learn From Political Marketing?',** Tom Wraight argues for recognizing the inherently political nature of nation-branding and incorporating insights from political science into nation-branding research. In particular, he emphasizes the benefits of drawing from literature on the state's relations to society and business, ultimately proposing that the field evolve towards a model of International Political Marketing (see also Chapter 23). Nations' brands are intricately connected with the brands of their most prominent businesses, and depend on states' administrative capacity, centralization and involvement in these businesses. They are also influenced by states' strategic goals and ambitions domestically and internationally. Wraight draws from a range of case studies to illustrate that the nation-branding strategies of great powers, such as the US and China, middle powers, and smaller states, are part of their geopolitical positioning in international affairs. These strategies are part of what some have called 'soft power' and others 'cultural diplomacy' or 'corporate public diplomacy'. In China, for instance, the state has set out to reposition itself from a manufacturer of consumer goods to an innovator of high-tech products. Looking to the US, Wraight focuses on the industrial and foreign policy of Trump and Biden in explaining how America's national brand is perceived abroad. He showcases the strategies of middle powers by discussing the UK, Brexit and the subsequent Global Britain campaign. Smaller nations, such as South Korea, he shows, instead rely on specialized branding around key industries or regional collaboration.

In **Chapter 34, 'Challenges to Political Marketing: Overcoming Risks When Engaging in Socio-Political Issues',** Jennifer J. Griffin addresses how firms can adapt to the ongoing, complex world of politics and policy-making. She addresses the ways companies can fall behind if they stick to old strategies, and charts new paths for firms to navigate socio-political issues. She underscores that businesses may be rewarded for pursuing collective goals, ones that benefit all of society, instead of their short-term, firm-specific goals, which may backfire in the long term. Companies should develop an enterprise-wide perspective, rather than one driven by a single department. Though the tendency is for various departments to operate in isolation, an enterprise-wide approach draws expertise and generates buy-in from across the firm. Towards this end, CEOs should collaborate early-on with corporate affairs colleagues, prior to fielding political marketing campaigns. Corporate affairs colleagues help mitigate the errors of one-way communications intended to manage influencers, employees and others; instead, they can foster two-way communication aimed at engagement with those stakeholders. Firms should widen their perspective even further at times, forming coalitions with other firms and stakeholders. Because public policy is a slow, complex process, firms will benefit from taking wider and longer-term perspectives.

Griffin is cognizant of the hurdles that often prevent firms from taking those perspectives, and lays them out in detail with numerous examples. To become successful in the political sphere, ultimately firms should not expect quick victories, but rather anticipate the need to integrate a variety of interests.

EMPIRICAL CASES OF POLITICAL MARKETING

If the electorate is a marketplace, then political parties are firms trying to sell their product. Like a fast-food chain, political parties can benefit from a national brand that can be replicated in constituencies across the country. A national brand provides consistency across the marketplace. In **Chapter 35, 'Entrepreneurs or Franchisees? The Use of Individual Versus Party Branding in Contemporary American Politics'**, Kenneth Cosgrove and Nathan R. Shrader take this allusion further explaining that, unlike economic firms, political parties are based on coalitions of actors. Competition among intraparty factions and influence from party leaders, along with candidates' need to tailor their platforms to local constituencies, all mitigate against strong national brands in American political parties. The authors trace decades of brand-building within both the Republican and Democratic parties. Beginning with the 'Make America Great Again' slogan of Ronald Reagan's 1980 campaign and leading into its reuse by Donald Trump in his 2016 presidential campaign, the authors show how candidates mix both entrepreneurship and franchising in their branding. The adoption of Trump-like branding by other Republican candidates, to varying success, also demonstrates the effectiveness of the franchise model. The authors also detail the successes and pitfalls of branding in the Democratic Party, starting with FDR's heritage brand into Obama and through to Biden and Harris. Looking towards the impact of technological change on franchise-like branding, they integrate the rise of social media and microtargeting technologies into their analysis.

In **Chapter 36, 'Political Marketing Amid the Rise and Fall of Democratic Regimes in Africa'**, George M. Bob-Milliar and Lauren M. MacLean broaden our understanding of the variables that shape political marketing strategies and outcomes, through the lens of African nations' experiences. The continent's young demographics, post-colonial status, large diaspora and variety of political regimes offer novel insights into political marketing. Following the histories of countries across the continent beginning in the 1960s and into the 2020s, the authors further describe how urbanization, democratization and the consolidation of party systems in post-colonial contexts have affected the behaviour of repressive governments, the marketing strategies of upstart political parties and the political participation of the citizenry. Numerous case studies demonstrate the ebb and flow of increased access of digital communication technologies and media freedoms, along with the influence of diasporas and transnational marketing agencies. The authors argue forcefully for a broadening of the study of political marketing to include the range of cases in Africa; an important point since its study in the wider literature is indeed sparse.

In **Chapter 37, 'Persuasion and Persistence: A Large-Scale Field Experiment in a Presidential Campaign',** David W. Nickerson explores the impact of political marketing efforts in the context of a high-information political race in the United States. He reports the results of a field experiment conducted during Obama's 2012 re-election campaign. Over the course of four weeks, campaign volunteers attempted 350,000 calls to registered voters in 19 states to persuade them to vote for Obama over his Republican opponent. The experiment targeted voters who were undecided, and therefore were likely open to a persuasive message. Much in the way that digital political marketing attempts to foster organic engagement among users, the volunteers in the experiment crafted their persuasive message, in this case by choosing from a list of talking points provided by the campaign. Compared to the control group, voters who received a persuasive message were more favourable towards Obama and were more likely to vote for him. In a two-way race question between Obama and Romney, the Republican candidate, people who received a phone call were 5.3 percentage points more likely to vote for Obama than they otherwise would have been. One key effect of the phone call was to help 'bring back' many voters who had been dissatisfied with Obama, and who may have otherwise defected or abstained. The phone call's effect lasted for some time as well, persisting 81% up to 6 weeks afterwards. By 12 weeks, however, the effect had dissipated. Nevertheless, this randomized trial shows the significant impact of volunteer-based persuasion in the context of a highly competitive race in an established democracy.

In **Chapter 38, 'The Challenge of Responding to Populism',** Wayne Steger first tackles the tricky question of what populism actually is, as to define it is an important stage in countering it. He argues that a narrow focus on populism, such as defining it as anti-elitist or as nationalist, fails to take account of the differences between right-wing and left-wing variants and that social and economic circumstances impact on the relative success of different types of populist. He also discusses how populists take advantage of, and exploit, the media, including social media, in order to reinforce certain values and cultural beliefs in the people, essentially by telling them what they want to hear, sometimes in the form of disinformation and conspiracy theories that suit their political agendas, and the difficulty opponents have in countering these types of political message given supporters' natural confirmatory bias when receiving these statements.

Overall, the future of politics, as with so many other areas of human life, will be impacted by the evolution of digital technologies. Part 4 has sought to help us better understand their diverse applications in political marketing, so that we can study the growth and effects of digital technologies on the political outcomes scientists and practitioners care about. It's important, however, as these chapters reiterate, not to lose sight of the things that stay the same. The long-term goals of political actors, firms and voters are largely unchanging. It's only the tools that change. Further research on how technologies will change and impact on political consumption behaviour is necessary, both to protect democracy and to protect citizens and political consumers more generally.

ACKNOWLEDGEMENTS

The editors would like to thank each and every one of the reviewers for their guidance and support in evaluating the chapters (often on more than one occasion) and whose constructive comments helped make a significant improvement to the final (accepted) versions of the chapters. Their support, analysis and ability to respond to tight deadlines and last-minute requests have been admirable. The reviewers have included, among others, the following:

Duygu Akdevelioglu, Rochester Institute of Technology, USA
Alberto Bitonti, American University, USA
Patrick Butler, Monash University, Australia
Ken Cosgrove, Suffolk University, USA
Wojciech Cwalina, Maria Curie-Sklodowska University, Poland
Barbara DeSanto, Maryville University, USA
Gary Davies, Manchester Business School, UK
Dianne Dean, Sheffield Hallam University, UK
Otto Eibl, Masaryk University, Czechia
Katherine Haenschen, Northeastern University, USA
Andrew Hughes, Australia National University, Australia
Varsha Jain, MICA, India
Nigel Jones, Right Objective, UK
Wing Lam, University of Bangor, Wales, UK,
Darren Lilleker, Bournemouth University, UK
Philippe J. Maarek, University Paris-Est Créteil, France
Roger Mortimore, King's College London, UK
Mona Moufahim, University of Stirling, Scotland, UK
Srabanti Mukherjee, IIT Kharagpur, India
David Nickerson, Temple University, USA
Aron O'Cass, LaTrobe University, Australia
Nicholas O'Shaughnessy, Queen Mary, University of London, UK
Ozlem Ozdemir, University of East London, UK
Patricia Nicholls, Manchester Metropolitan University, UK
Chris Pich, University of Nottingham, UK
Maria Irene Prete, University of Salento, Italy

Marta Rebolledo De La Calle, American University in Dubai, UAE
Travis Ridout, Washington State University, USA
Chris Robertson, Leeds International Centre, Leeds, UK
Toshiasu Sakata, University of Tokyo, Japan
Christian Scheucher, Christian Scheucher Consulting, Austria
Anna Shavit, Charles University, Czechia
Nancy Snow, California State University Fullerton, USA
Wayne Steger, DePaul University, USA
Arco Timmermans, Leiden University, Hague, The Netherlands
Christine Williams, Bentley College, USA.

We first began discussing the idea of the need for a *SAGE Handbook of Political Marketing* in 2019 with Matt Waters, our Publisher at SAGE. Then COVID occurred and derailed the project for two years. Matt helped us get it back on track and take it forward to the contract stage. SAGE formally accepted our proposal in April 2022, and we were delighted to release the book in August 2025. We also want to thank Delia Alfonso-Martinez, Director at SAGE, who inputted on the contract. Matt's guidance and support helped us ensure we got an editorial team with a more global remit and consequently a better product. We also want to thank Colette Wilson, SAGE's Reference Manager at that time, who helped us scope out what the book should look like, who might write for us, and how we would ensure the quality of the work was as good as it could be. Her early work supporting the book's design and the review process set the tone for the whole project, which broadly ran as she had expected it to. The editors would particularly like to thank Ben Hegarty, who started with us as an Editorial Assistant (but by the end of the project had been made an Associate Editor), for his excellent support in the second half of the administration of the project. He helped us set up the editorial board, the editorial review panel, organize the reviews of the chapters during two separate rounds and generally ensured the trains ran on time. It is to his credit that we delivered, and with the quality that we did, on the contract. Without his excellent assistance, we would not have been able to produce this Handbook on time.

As an editorial team, we must also thank our editorial advisory board, for their support during the review process (see insert at the start of the Handbook). We are delighted that they come from far and wide, taking in India, Europe, the US and Australia. They helped provide strong guidance to our authors, significantly improving their work, particularly but not solely in the second review round, and on occasion recommending potential authors to us. There were a number of chapters that sadly did not make it through the review process, often for a variety of reasons. We would like to thank those authors (anonymously, of course) for the time they invested in developing and submitting a chapter to us. We hope that the time they spent, and the guidance they received on improving their work, has been useful in getting that work published elsewhere.

Finally, we'd like to thank the 65 authors who shed blood, sweat and tears writing the chapters that make up this Handbook. They come from all corners of the globe and their chapters represent unique perspectives on political marketing in Australia, Spain and France, the US, Türkiye, Italy, Japan, Ukraine, Poland, the Czech Republic, India, Zimbabwe (and Africa more generally) and Hong Kong (and China more generally). Without their sustained efforts, over two rounds of reviews, and around 21 months in time, we would have no Handbook and the political marketing discipline would not have the insights that their chapters provide.

FINAL WORD

While we have made every effort to ensure that this editorial and the chapters herein are as accurate as they can be, and that any permissions have been suitably sourced, any remaining errors contained herein are the result of the editors and authors only. If you require us to obtain outstanding permission, please contact the publisher and we will be happy to consider your request.

It is of course a cliché to say that our work here has been a labour of love, but in truth, that is what it has been. The editors and authors all share a resounding and deep interest in political marketing and its continuing evolution and we hope that is apparent in the individual chapters contained within the Handbook.

It is now time, finally, to say that we hope, dear reader, that you enjoy this Handbook as much as we and the authors have enjoyed editing, writing and producing it for you. If you are an academic, may it inspire you to further productive research; if you are a practitioner, may it help you run more effective political or government campaigns, or better counter your opponents' disinformation campaigns; and if you are a member of the public, may it inspire you to more critically question the political messages you receive.

REFERENCES

Anon. (2022, June 19). Macron loses absolute majority as far right makes historic breakthrough and left surges. *Le Monde*. https://www.lemonde.fr/en/politics/article/2022/06/19/french-legislative-elections-macron-loses-absolute-majority-as-far-right-makes-historic-breakthrough-and-left-surges_5987355_5.html. Accessed on 21 December 2024.

Baines, P., & O'Shaughnessy, N. J. (2014). Al Qaeda messaging evolution and positioning, 1998–2008: Propaganda analysis revisited. *Public Relations Inquiry*, *3*(2), 163–191.

Blumenthal, S. (1982). *The permanent campaign: Inside the world of elite political operations*. Simon & Schuster.

CIA. (2024). *World Factbook – China*. Central Intelligence Agency. https://www.cia.gov/the-world-factbook/countries/china/#people-and-society. Accessed on 13 December 2024.

Coen-Sanchez, K., Ebenso, B., El-Mowafi, I. M., Berghs, M., Idriss-Wheeler, D., & Yaya, S. (2022). Repercussions of overturning Roe v. Wade for women across systems and beyond borders. *Reproductive Health*, *19*(1), 184.

Dommett, K., Mensah, S. A., Zhu, J., & Stafford, T. (2024). Understanding the communicative strategies used in online political advertising and how the public views them. *The British Journal of Politics & International Relations*. https://doi.org/10.1177/13691481241287

Dowling, M. E. (2021). Democracy under siege: Foreign interference in a digital era. *Australian Journal of International Affairs*, *75*(4), 383–387.

Duncombe, C. (2018). Twitter and the challenges of digital diplomacy. *SAIS Review of International Affairs*, *38*(2), 91–100.

Elebash, C. (1984). The Americanization of British political communications. *Journal of Advertising*, *13*(3), 50–58.

Field, W. (1994). On the Americanization of electioneering. *Electoral Studies*, *13*(1), 58–63.

Fukuyama, F. (1992). *The end of history and the last man*. Penguin.

Goldstein, K., & Ridout, T. N. (2004). Measuring the effects of televised political advertising in the United States. *Annual Review of Political Science*, *7*(1), 205–226.

Harris, P. (2022). Machiavelli, Nicollo (1469–1527): Machiavellianism, moralism, and his contribution to the development of international public affairs management. In P. Harris, A. Bitonti, C. Fleisher, & A. Skorkjaer Binderkrantz (Eds.), *The Palgrave encyclopedia of interest groups, lobbying and public affairs* (pp. 861–874). Springer Nature.

Henig, D., & Knight, D. M. (2023). Polycrisis: Prompts for an emerging worldview. *Anthropology Today*, *39*(2), 3–6.

Henschke, A., Sussex, M., & O'Connor, C. (2020). Countering foreign interference: Election integrity lessons for liberal democracies. *Journal of Cyber Policy*, *5*(2), 180–198.

Hübscher, E., Sattler, T., & Wagner, M. (2020). Voter Responses to fiscal austerity. *British Journal of Political Science*, *51*(4), 1751–1760. https://doi.org/10.1017/S0007123420000320

Iyengar, S., & Simon, A. F. (2000). New perspectives and evidence on political communication and campaign effects. *Annual Review of Psychology*, *51*(1), 149–169.

Jain, V., & BE, G. (2020). Understanding the magic of credibility for political leaders: A case of India and Narendra Modi. *Journal of Political Marketing*, *19*(1–2), 15–33.

Jones, N., Baines, P., Craig, R., Tunnicliffe, I., & O'Shaughnessy, N. J. (2015). The Islamist cyberpropaganda threat and its counter-terrorism policy implications. In J. L. Richet (Ed.), Cybersecurity policies and strategies for cyberwarfare prevention. IGI Global.

Kõváry Sólymos, K. (2023, October 31). *Slovakia: Deepfake audio of Denník N journalist offers worrying example of AI abuse*. International Press Institute. https://ipi.media/slovakia-deepfake-audio-of-dennik-n-journalist-offers-worrying-example-of-ai-abuse/. Accessed on 19 December, 2024.

Lau, R. R., Sigelman, L., Heldman, C., & Babbitt, P. (1999). The effects of negative political advertisements: A meta-analytic assessment. *American Political Science Review*, *93*(4), 851–875.

Lau, R. R., Sigelman, L., & Rovner, I. B. (2007). The effects of negative political campaigns: A meta-analytic reassessment. *The Journal of Politics*, *69*(4), 1176–1209.

Maarek, P. J. (1995). *Political marketing and communication*. John Libbey.
Mukherjee, S., Datta, B., & Baines, P. (2024). Safety in numbers? Why Indians at the base of the pyramid herd their votes and the policy implications. *Journal of Political Marketing*. https://doi.org/10.1080/15377857.2024.2440005
Mukherjee, S., Srivastava, A., Datta, B., & Sengupta, S. (2022). Impact of political marketing strategies on the BOP voters in India. *Marketing Intelligence & Planning*, *40*(8), 994–1009.
NCSC. (2024, September 5). *UK and allies uncover Russian military unit carrying out cyber attacks and digital sabotage for first time*. National Cyber Security Centre. https://www.ncsc.gov.uk/news/uk-allies-uncover-russian-military-carrying-out-cyber-attacks-digital-sabotage. Accessed on 19 December, 2024.
Newman, B. I. (1993). *The marketing of the president: Political marketing as campaign strategy*. SAGE.
Newman, B. I. (Ed.). (1999). *Handbook of political marketing*. SAGE.
Nye, J. S. (1990a). Soft power. *Foreign Policy*, *80*, 153–171.
Nye, J. S. (1990b). *Bound to lead: The changing nature of American power*. Basic.
O'Shaughnessy, N. J., & Baines, P. R. (2009). Selling terror: The symbolization and positioning of Jihad. *Marketing Theory*, *9*(2), 227–241.
Oxford Economics. (2024, October 28). Japan's shock election defeat for the LDP, but policy shift unlikely. *Research Briefing*, https://www.oxfordeconomics.com/resource/japans-shock-election-defeat-for-the-ldp-but-policy-shift-unlikely/. Accessed on 19 December 2024.
O'Shaughnessy, N. J. (1990). *The phenomenon of political marketing*. The Macmillan Press Ltd.
Pareek, B., Ghosh, P., Wilson, H. N., Macdonald, E. K., & Baines, P. (2018). Tracking the impact of media on voter choice in real time: A Bayesian dynamic joint model. *Journal of the American Statistical Association*, *113*(524), 1457–1475.
Reuters Institute/University of Oxford. (2024). *Digital news report*. https://reutersinstitute.politics.ox.ac.uk/digital-news-report/2024. Accessed on 11 November 2024.
Segal, A. (2013). The code not taken: China, the United States, and the future of cyberespionage. *Bulletin of the Atomic Scientists*, *69*(5), 38–45.
The Editors of the Encyclopaedia Britannica. (2024, November 3). Public diplomacy. https://www.britannica.com/topic/public-diplomacy. Accessed on 29 December 2024.
Toffler, A. (1970). *Future shock*. Random House.

PART 1

Strategy in Political Marketing: Orthodox and Occidental Perspectives

Strategies and Tactics in Global Political Marketing: Cases and Challenges from the Practitioner's Perspective

Alexander Braun

INTRODUCTION

Running a campaign seems like juggling a hundred balls. There are so many things to take care of: What is our message? Are we staying on message? What creative ways are we using to bring our communications to life? Through what means are we sending the message? Who do we want to send the message to? Those are just a few questions a campaign strategist needs to ask and answer all the time.

What complicates this further is that these questions are asked in the background of a time crunch. During campaigns, there is never enough time to think through these sufficiently and every day consists of numerous quick, imperfect decisions and trade-offs. Campaign strategists therefore need to ask another larger question – which area of the campaign needs more focus and resources than others? Unlike with juggling, where the juggler needs to pay equal attention to all the balls all the time, a campaign strategist must determine which areas require more attention than others. A wrong focus can easily lead to misplaced priorities, too much motion (busy work) and too little movement (in making progress in convincing voters).

How does a campaign know what that the right focus is? I make the case that there are three key campaign strategy pillars that are central to a successful campaign. Having worked on presidential campaigns in the United States, Mexico, Indonesia or Ukraine, parliamentary elections in Great Britain, Czechia, Japan or Ecuador and constantly using and experimenting with new campaign techniques, I argue that campaigns need to primarily keep focused on these fundamentals before venturing further. Despite all the advances in big data modelling, generative Artificial Intelligence (AI) or digital outreach methods, winning campaigns still first need to primarily focus on the following:

1 a good understanding of voters;
2 good branding;
3 telling a good story.

Campaigns that do not properly develop these areas and lose focus on them tend to lose elections. The Hilary Clinton 2016 campaign is an illustration of this. Arguably, she was a substantially better qualified candidate than her opponent Donald Trump, with decades of political experience and a superior campaign infrastructure. Notwithstanding the polling errors that year (such as underrepresenting less-educated white male voters), her campaign did a great job in its focus on the first pillar of understanding the voters through extensive polling, big data analysis and modelling. However, it never quite got the other pillars right. The campaign failed to sufficiently articulate Clinton's brand and voters didn't have enough reasons or emotional connection with her to turn out for her on election day. Her campaign narrative was not well-defined and kept wavering, resulting in an uninspired Democratic electorate that voted significantly more *against* her opponent than *for* her. It wasn't enough and Clinton lost.

In contrast, Barack Obama's 2008 campaign is now a textbook example of excellent branding (see Baines & Fill, 2014), great storytelling and very good voter research. His brand of an embodiment of change was evident, his narrative combining change and hope ("Yes, we can!") inspired large swaths of voters and his voter research and big data analyses started many new trends still in use today.

Of course, there are myriads of other factors, but practical experience has led me time and time again to ensure that these three pillars at the forefront of any campaign strategies and decisions. This chapter explores each of the three building blocks, explains their utility and provides a practical guide on how to use them as learned on the campaign trail. It contains a little bit of theoretical background but is really meant to provide a view from a campaign practitioner's perspective.

Voters

The level of an election campaign's accomplishment is gauged simply – by maximising votes on election day. Since the number of voters is *the* success metric of a candidate in an election, it is critical for campaigns to understand the electorate as much as possible. Figuring out who the voters are, how they think and what makes them tick is crucial from the inception of the campaign all the way to the election day.

Voters are not a homogenous group. They are diverse. They have different priorities. They think differently. They change how they think. Understanding voters early on and throughout the campaign is simply paramount. The way to do that is not through assumptions but through solid voter research and analytics.

This is still not something that all campaigns realise or admit. While in most countries with decades of competitive elections some kind of voter research is ubiquitous, many candidates and campaign operatives still believe they already "know" what their voters want or use basic research in a perfunctory way. Such an approach is a bad idea and leads to missed opportunities or oftentimes worse.

No matter how long one has been immersed in local or national politics, staking a strategy on a gut feeling is risky at best. Voters' minds are not stationary – opinions change, situations change and voting dynamics are faster than ever before. Social media has made this even more perilous – while one can access many more opinions than ever before, it is often illusory as many algorithms are built to accentuate opinions that are similar to each other and de-emphasise those that are from a different camp (Kreiss, 2016). This can easily result in a false echo chamber effect, validating wrong assumptions and leading campaigns astray.

This is not to say that experience is useless. On the contrary, a historical analysis is most often used as the basis for initial strategy contours and hypotheses formation. It is useful to look at past election results and estimate future behaviour, just as it is to learn about past voting dynamics from past actors and observers of the process. It is also important to keep the perspective that these insights need to be updated and validated, and then checked on and calibrated all the way until the election day.

The best way to figure out who voters are, how they think, and what currently makes them tick is through voter research. Simply put, voter research is the collection and analysis of data about voters. It involves understanding voters' preferences, opinions, emotions and behaviours, as well as the demographic, economic and cultural factors that influence them. It can be done through a variety of methodologies including quantitative research (like polls), qualitative research (like focus groups), digital performance measurements, social media listening (getting insights from social media can be very useful if it is not the only source) and combining various data streams into deeper analytics.

Voter research has two main utility levels. First, it *describes the situation*, the composition of the electorate and their attitudes at the time. This is eminently useful as it removes the guessing game and provides data that help gauge and answer speculations. Second, it can be *prescriptive*, providing evidence-based guidance for what the campaign should do or say to sway voters' opinions. While the first element is something that the public can often see in the media, albeit not in such detail as campaigns, the second element is something that is unique to strategic campaigns.

What are some of the key areas of inquiry that are useful in campaign research?

1 *Likelihood of voting:* If a voter doesn't show up on election day, they are of no interest to the campaign. Polling can estimate the likelihood of individuals turning out to vote based on various factors such as past voting behaviour and interest in the election.
2 *Political preferences:* An obvious key element of any voter research is understanding which candidates or political parties people favour. This can be measured mainly in terms of overall support, likelihood to switch, second choice voting or consideration to vote.
3 *Favourability and job approval ratings:* Liking a candidate or a party is the first step towards converting a voter to get their vote but doesn't guarantee it. Voters might not particularly like a candidate, but they might think she has been doing, or would do, an effective job. Polling measures both and helps set the overall strategy through these key questions.
4 *Candidate attributes:* What is behind the attitudes? Research uncovers perceptions of candidate's characteristics, like trustworthiness, leadership abilities and empathy. This knowledge is especially important for the formation of the brand of the candidate.
5 *Voter sentiment:* Polling captures voters' sentiments towards the present political climate, such as whether they feel the country is heading in the right direction or is off on the wrong track, or whether they feel better off today than they did a few years ago.
6 *Opinions on issues:* Polling gauges voters' awareness of and positions on different policy matters, such as healthcare, education or immigration. This helps campaigns align their priorities with what voters care about.
7 *Demographics:* This might include age, gender, ethnicity, religion, educational background or geographic location. Polls can reveal patterns among different demographic groups and is critical for targeting.

Good strategic voter research goes beyond these elements and looks further. Other research categories that are often used in drafting blueprints for campaigns:

8 *Story testing:* Campaigns need to figure out the best elements of the candidate's or leader's biography–including specific stories and anecdotes that highlight the candidate's brand – and positions they should accentuate, and what the biggest strengths of their opponents are to try to deposition them.
9 *Message testing:* What is the best way to talk about positions and policy proposals? Besides the content itself, this includes the words used to describe them, tone and the overall semantic frame. Research should not only measure what is the best way to frame the message but crucially also if the message moves voters' attitudes.
10 *Psychographics:* Unlike demographics, which categorise people based on firm and quantifiable variables like age or gender, psychographics focus on qualitative properties that relate to the mind and emotions. Psychographics can help strategists understand what drives voters at deeper values-based and emotional levels. Mark Penn's polling famously identified "soccer moms," a key swing voter group in Bill Clinton's 1996 election, through a combination of psychographic factors and demographic information.
11 *Media consumption habits:* Campaigns need to know how and where their target groups get their information to efficiently reach them. Polling allows you to cross refence voter groups with information sources.

More broadly, understanding the voters means the campaign will segment the electorate into smaller groups it can then work with. The most basic but eminently useful division is breaking the likely electorate down into the following three groups:

1 *Base voters:* These are loyal supporters of the candidate or party who are unlikely to switch. The campaign should ensure these voters turnout on election day and inspire some of them into activists.
2 *Swing voters:* This is usually the most important group and campaigns target most of their persuasion (and attention and budget) towards this group. Swing voters are undecided or deciding between two or more choices, without being firmly committed.
   - Swing voters are often a large group, and strategists can divide them into the easier to convince group and those who can be conceivably but less likely persuaded.
   - An increasingly large group of voters that require attention are disconnected voters. These are people who are at least somewhat likely to turnout (if they were so disconnected they wouldn't vote on election day they would be of little interest to campaigns) but have been mostly uninterested in politics and decide much more intuitively and usually just days before election day.
3 *Unreachable voters:* No matter what the candidate or campaign do, these people will never vote for the candidate. The campaign should not waste time and money on them, with the exception of strategies aimed at discouraging their turnout or encouraging ticket splitting.

Campaigns need to divide the electorate into these categories early on so that they can prepare actionable strategy plans. This is typically done through benchmark polls, which are extensive, large sample size polls conducted in the beginning of the campaign. Often, either before or after the benchmark poll, campaigns also explore specific voter groups through in-depth through focus groups to better understand their mindsets, their emotions and the language they use.

Campaigns need to continue measuring the public sentiment and calibrating their strategy throughout the campaign period. Typically, the frequency of polling increases in the last couple of months because that is when many swing voters start to tune in and begin making their decision, the race becomes more dynamic and the campaign needs to have more real-time guidance.

Besides polling and qualitative research, campaigns increasingly rely on additional, digital means to understand the electorate. Big data analysis was pioneered especially by Barack Obama's 2008 election, which used multiple data sources, not just polling, for voter modelling to increase the accuracy of its targeting and advertising. Since then, most large campaigns in the West, but also in India and elsewhere, try to include advanced analytics and digital measurements, although its real impact is still questionable.

Augmenting surveys is not only an attempt to improve the accuracy of polling, which – although still the best existing method of measuring the electorate and its sentiments – suffers from inaccuracies related to sampling difficulties or low response rates. The inherent deficiency of campaign polling is that it estimates results and attitudes onto *groups* of voters, not on individual voters. Since everyone is different, campaigns know that they are forced to generalise and deploy communications strategies that do not accurately reflect the mindset of each specific voter. Being able to effectively target each voter *individually* is the holy grail of campaign strategists – but at present, we are still far from it.

Time will tell if generative artificial intelligence or other tools can truly help with translating the findings from multiple data sources into truly individual-level strategies. But even if we had that level of specificity and were able to understand and target voters on the individual level, the question remains how this would be used in practice. In reality, campaigns are almost always short on time and finances, and ways to physically or digitally reach voters are always limited, especially on the individual level. For now, the question of successfully scaling the campaign delivery to the individual voter level remains elusive.

Brand

Besides understanding the voters, campaigns need to also understand the candidate and the opponents, meaning that they need to figure out the brands of the main actors in an election. Not dissimilar to general marketing, a political brand comprises the unique identity and image of a candidate or a party that differentiates them from their competitors. A strong political brand can help a candidate build recognition, establish an emotional connection and build credibility with voters and communicate their values and programme effectively (Scammell, 2015). There are many branding theories that describe the utility of branding, including those from corporate branding, such as Aaker's brand equity model with its emphasis on brand awareness, brand associations, brand loyalty and brand's perceived quality (Aaker, 2014). However, in real life, many candidates and even strategist do not focus enough of their attention on properly developed branding. Unlike in the corporate world, the realm of political campaigns guarantees some level of people's and media's attention which may make some candidates think that proper branding is secondary. That is a mistake – branding is foundational.

How to begin developing a successful political brand? There are several important elements for crafting a successful political brand. Political branding needs to combine candidates' image with their core values and their party or campaign's identity and needs to be able to convey the brand consistently (Newman, 1999). This is where voter research is eminently useful, as it helps flesh out how to describe the identity of the candidates – self and of the opponents – with all their strengths and weaknesses. A candidate will not have a successful brand if their communication fails to lean into who they authentically are and what has led them to this point in their life journey. Michael Duakakis's 1988 tank riding blunder is a famous example of inauthentic branding.

The brand needs to be not only clear and credible but must also be distinct from others. Elections are about a choice and voters need to decide not only which candidate is great but which candidate is better than the alternative (Smith & French, 2009). This is harder when many candidates have a similar brand. In commercial marketing, this is called the unique selling proposition, or USP, and this concept is sometimes undervalued in political campaigns. While, for example, all candidates might want to improve the economy, if all candidates are presented as reformist economists, voters are left with a tough choice and decide on other factors.

The third consideration for forming a political brand is how compelling it is to voters in that specific election. It is great to have a brand of, for example, being a compassionate listener, but if voters demand a strong decisive leader, it will not work. This does not mean candidates should try to mould themselves into whatever the prevailing desires are at that moment, but rather the brand needs to address the overall context of the election – while remaining true to the candidate.

Let's look at a couple of examples. When Barack Obama ran in 2008, his brand was that of "Change" and "Hope." This was not only congruent with who he was and what his political life reflected but also what the electorate wanted after what many saw as two fumbling terms of George W. Bush. Many anti-immigration candidates run on the brand of protectors, such as LePen in France, AfD in Germany or Jobbik in Hungary. Salvadorian Nayib Bukele or the Philippines' Rodrigo Duterte have the brand of crime fighting politician. The branding in these cases addresses one of the main prevailing sentiments in the country, contrasts with the opponents' and is authentic to the candidates behind it.

A good brand can also handle less-flattering characteristics of the candidate and turn them into an advantage. Such was the case of the Slovak-born, Andrej Babis, when he ran in the 2013 Czech parliamentary elections and came 2nd in the polls and entered the government. His brand was that of a common-sense businessman entering politics, and when his opponents mocked his far-from-perfect command of the Czech language, the campaign turned it into an advantage. Babis drew a sharp contrast between the well-spoken but ineffectual traditional politicians and himself, for his no-frills, no-nonsense approach to getting things done. It worked well and Babis's party joined government, and he became deputy prime minister.

SO, HOW TO DETERMINE WHAT THE RIGHT BRAND SHOULD BE?

Political marketing literature is replete with theories on branding. From the use of Jungian archetypes (Mark & Pearson, 2001) to contemporary brand theory (such as Keller, 2013), there is a common thread – need for clarity and consistency. In practice, it is useful to focus on singularity, which means that campaign strategists should keep working on narrowing down positioning concepts and selecting only a few, or ideally one, to build out a fuller strategy.

The positioning concepts are essentially elevator pitches for why voters should vote for a candidate or party. Successful political marketing needs to be disciplined in sticking with one positioning concept or meta-narrative and consistently presenting the candidate that way. This is not easy. In practice, most candidates believe their competencies span at least two or three concepts and are reluctant to "box" themselves into one. They find it restricting and argue that different voters want different things. They are technically right, but they need to keep in mind that getting through to voters with one narrative is far more valuable than expressing multiple narratives that fail to penetrate voters' consciousness at all.

The main problem with using multiple positioning frames is communication noise. Voters need to hear one thing at least 7–10 times to internalise it. Presenting a candidate as a strong leader and also a wise innovator can leave people confused or unengaged. Rather than convincing people that the candidate is great in both aspects, the campaign is more likely to completely fail in capturing voter attention with their message. Voters might not only fail to internalise both of these avenues of communication, but they might not even notice. Like chatter in a restaurant, one might not make out any specific conversation from patrons sitting at the bar despite them being loud.

This is often evidenced when we conduct strategic campaign polling – we ask voters what they have heard, read or seen about Candidate X. If Candidate X tends to speak about multiple topics or their branding highlights multiple character traits, voters not only cannot name anything specific about them, but often say they did not hear or see *anything* about them at all. In contrast, Candidate Y who sticks to one theme in their communications, just about every time, receives higher ratings on the awareness questions. Less is more in this case.

There are other reasons for selecting and sticking to a clear singular brand. Brands become more effective if they manage to align themselves with an existing concept in the minds of the voters. Much of modern psychology harks back to Jung's theory of archetypes and the subsequent work applied to branding. Whether one subscribes to Jungean archetypes or not, in practice, it seems that certain types of "brands" have been with humans most of our existence and are inherent to our thinking and even subconsciousness, and thus are universal and people respond to them regardless of time and place (Mark & Pearson, 2001). Examples of such archetypes in politics include The Ruler embodied in Vladimir Putin or Donald Trump; The Hero, such as Vaclav Havel or Volodymyr Zelensky; or The Sage, such as the Dalai Lama.

The idea here is that a good political brand requires a low cognitive load from voters if it can tap into existing thought circuits. Since we are social creatures, this often means 'personalising' the brands, as voters find it easier to form an emotional connection to concepts that involve personalities. This is true even for races that involve political parties rather than individual candidates, and political branding should not underestimate this. The importance of personal branding as a useful mental shortcut in political campaigns is explained in Samuel Popkin's The Reasoning Voter. He argues that "it is easier to take personal data and fill in the political facts and policies than to start with the political facts and fill in the personal data," and "personal information can drive more relevant political information out of consideration" (Popkin, 1991, p. 79). Kamala Harris, abruptly entering the US presidential race in the summer of 2024, is a good example of this – with low public familiarity of her political stances and proposals, she quickly and significantly changed the dynamics of the presidential race mainly on personal characteristics and general atmospherics rather than priorities (her subsequent downfall is a different story).

Branding works both ways, assertively and defensively. Understanding brand weaknesses allows you to know when an attack is likely to land versus one that will leave little to no mark. The key here is to determine whether the attack undermines the core brand attributes of the candidate. If so, the attack should work. This is best shown through an example. Criticising Vladimir Putin for not being jovial is useless, as his core branding rests on strong leadership. People expect their archetypal Ruler to lead well; they do not expect him to be relatable. On the flip side, showing that Putin has lost control of a situation would go directly against his core attributes and undermine his position in the eyes of voters.

Donald Trump understands this well and has been often effective in exploiting his opponents' perceived weaknesses. In his case, he literally creates nicknames for them. Consistently calling Hillary Clinton 'Crooked Hillary' (i.e. somebody who cheats and cannot be trusted by people) in 2016, Trump went after one of her key brand weaknesses (her perceived trustworthiness) and arguably solidified it in the eyes of undecided voters. On the positive side, Trump's brand was that of a hard-charging businessman, so attacks on his character as being 'insensitive' or 'politically incorrect' did not land.

NARRATIVE

Having a good brand and understanding the voters are two crucial building blocks of a good campaign, but these are really brought to life for the voter in the narrative the campaign tells. Simplified, a narrative is a pattern of stories set in a context that produces cognitive and emotional responses. Campaign narratives can be viewed as crafted stories used to provide a comprehensible structure for understanding and interpreting political situations. Ideally, they capture voters' imagination and create a sense of identity.

Many candidates tend to enumerate policy proposals, list facts and logic and assume voters will perform a rational analysis to determine who to vote for. Clearly, that is not the case. Countless studies and experiments show that people have a much harder time recalling facts than stories. A narrative can therefore serve as a potent shortcut for voters to learn facts, place them in a meaningful and compelling context and persuade. "Narratives are more easily compiled and are retained longer than facts," Samuel Popkin writes in The Reasoning Voter. "Narratives, further, require more negative information before they change" (Popkin, 1991, p. 78).

It is important to establish that a story is only a subset of a narrative. While "story" and "narrative" are often used interchangeably, it would be more appropriate to talk about "storytelling" as something closer to what campaign narratives do. Campaign narratives are usually built on multiple stories and are contextualised into a specific period (campaign season) and for specific voters (different target groups can perceive different narratives). As such, narratives have a stronger persuasive power than individual stories. "Narratives are far more powerful than stories because they actively call for participation – they are open-ended... The outcome depends on us. What will we choose to do?" (Hagel, 2014).

In sum, narratives can distil complex issues into understandable and relatable constructs, elicit powerful emotional responses and can cultivate a sense of identity among voters. By fostering empathy and an emotional connection between the voters and the candidate, narratives make political concepts more comprehensible and personal (Westen, 2007). In other words, good storytelling moves people.

HOW TO WEAVE A GOOD NARRATIVE?

This has been the subject of a millennia of thinking and writing by writers, philosophers and politicians. Even today, it is useful to look at some of the classics, such as Aristotle who identified that a good story follows a simple but powerful structure. Aristotle argued that a great story line must have a beginning that sets the scene and introduces the protagonist and the challenge they will face. Then comes the middle, which explores the conflict and how the protagonist deals with the challenge. The end brings a resolution to the conflict and concludes the story or ties it to the present and the future, and as such gives it meaning (see Aristotle, 1961).

To use an example that Aristotle would have known, the battle of Thermopylae introduces Spartans led by their king Leonidas (the protagonist/s) posed with the threat of a giant army of invading Persians. Then comes the heroic stance of a small and vastly outnumbered army of well-trained Spartans defending the Persians' advance in a pass at Thermopylae and concludes with the Spartans' demise in one of the most famous last stand battles. The Spartan's epic resistance buys Greece more time and aids in the Greeks' eventual victory.

More than 2,000 years later, we still tell the story and Hollywood blockbusters are made about it (e.g. *The 300* Spartans (1962),[1] *300* (2006)[2]). Good political narratives follow similar narrative patterns and present a protagonist (the candidate or the political party), a (political or societal) conflict or challenge to overcome and a resolution (proposal or vision). The political narratives serve to summarise and illustrate the candidate's core values, overarching objectives and policy prescriptions, and most importantly appeal to voters' cognition and their emotional state.

An example of such narrative is Bill Clinton's 1992 election campaign, encapsulated in his one-minute introductory ad, *Hope*.[3] It introduces Bill Clinton as a scrappy boy from the backwaters of Arkansas, working hard to earn a good education, foregoing a well-paid career for public service and, after improving his state as governor, making a case why he should be the right person to lead the whole of America. The ad follows an Aristotelian story arch of introducing the protagonist, describing the challenges and conflicts he has faced and ending with a denouement that brings it all together.

Besides the Aristotelian story arch, there are key principles underlying good political narratives, which include the following:

The Narrative Should Elicit an Emotional Response

We have already established that our brains are significantly more likely to internalise story lines over facts. This has been exacerbated by the constant and enormous deluge of information we are exposed to in the digital age, making it even more difficult for rational arguments to break through. What cuts through and gains attention and prominence in good communications is an emotional response by the receiver (Heath & Heath, 2007).

Good narratives vibrate a responsive chord inside voters, a term coined by the legendary political ad maker, Tony Schwartz (see Schwartz, 1973). The responsive chord evokes a dominant feeling that has a power to change the perspective of the receiver and sets facts into a meaningful and memorable setting. It employs the voter's imagination, it is suggestive and lets the voters form a picture in their heads, rather than telling them what is what. Schwartz was the creator of arguably the most famous political ad in history, the 1964 Daisy Ad,[4] which artfully shows the power of the responsive chord. In the ad, a little girl is counting leaves on a daisy flower. As she reaches ten, the frame freezes and a countdown begins until it reaches zero and a nuclear explosion is reflected in her eye. Without mentioning Barry Goldwater's name or any proposals but hinting that he was the ultimate warmonger, it solidified President Johnson's election victory – because it responded to a deep-seated primal emotion in the people and helped them place it into the election context. As Maya Angelou, the American memoirist and poet, is commonly quoted as saying: "people will forget what you said, people will forget what you did, but people will never forget how you made them feel."

The Narrative Should Transcend Everyday Issues and Provide a Broader Meaning

Most elections have a central, underlying question. Do we want a change or a continuation? Do we vote for a leader or a party? Do we feel our children will have a good future? A good political narrative captures that dominant question, clarifies it for the voter and leads them to answer it. It transcends short-term wants of voters, offers a lens through which to view the situation and gives the situation significance.

Joe Biden's 2020 election campaign demonstrated this concept with its focus on painting the danger of Donald Trump's re-election. In Biden's words, "Donald Trump and the MAGA Republicans represent an extremism that threatens the very foundations of our republic" (Biden, 2021). Clearly, in Biden's narrative, there was more at stake than a regular election – he felt the need to battle for the soul of the whole nation. Other examples can include a rags-to-riches narrative that inspires people and taps into hope and optimism, underdog stories that can feel relatable to voters who otherwise feel powerless, or voyage and return stories that are meaningful in parts of the world experiencing brain drain and high emigration.

The Narrative Should Draw Voters in and Build a Personal Connection With Them

Political narratives need to form a personal bond with voters even more strongly than commercial campaigns. They should make voters understand they are not alone and can be part of a larger collective, with a shared journey, sense of belonging and mutual support in the campaign. This ideally leads to a feeling of a social movement and increases voters' desires to shape its direction.

The Arab Spring in Tunisia in early 2010s was a good example of this. What started as a local protest decrying the economic stagnation in the North African region turned into a national movement calling for, and succeeding in, the removal of Tunisian long-time dictator, Zine El Abidine Ben Ali. It mobilized people across the country, unified individuals from various walks of life and convinced them to risk their well-being and their lives. Its narrative was so powerful that it spread into other Arab countries, including Egypt, Libya, Yemen, Syria, and Bahrain.

The Narrative Should Be Clear and Simple to Understand

Good political narratives need to be clear and easy to understand (McNair, 2011). If voters need to spend too much time thinking about what a narrative is about, they are likely not to respond and move on. As mentioned earlier, this can be well illuminated on Hillary Clinton's 2016 election campaign. Her deep experience, superior campaign operation, advanced data modelling and an army of activists were not enough to defeat Trump who mostly flew on his instincts and did not have a comparable campaign infrastructure. The main reason for Trump's success was that his narrative was clear and concise, epitomised in four words, *Make America Great Again*. Through them, Trump clearly conveyed who he was and what his vision for America was. His voters knew what he meant by it, and it vibrated the responsive chord among them, as it played on a powerful campaign concept of "taking power back." In contrast, what was Clinton's narrative? It remains unclear and even at the time it seemed like she could not decide what her narrative was, as it oscillated between being well-qualified, being the first female president, togetherness, fairness and other concepts. Voters were confused and unmoved. The end of Kamala Harris's campaign was similarly unfocused and inconsistent – leading to the same result of losing to Donald Trump.

The Narrative Often Uses Symbols

Although not required, using a symbol is often a hallmark of successful campaign narratives. Symbols cut through the informational noise, help voters understand the meaning faster and aid with recall. Human brains are primed to respond to symbols, and this has become even more salient in the age of social media where our attention has been drastically reduced. We notice symbols easier than most other information pieces.

Many parties use their colours as the most basic symbolic identifier, such as the use of red by European socialist and social democratic parties, other use logos. Donald Trump's red hat, with the *Make America Great Again* words, is another example of using a symbol to deliver a narrative. But the symbol does not need to be a physical object. Ronald Reagan's 1984 re-election campaign framed their narrative in the concept of a morning. In its famous "It's Morning Again in America" ad[5] in 1984, Reagan's campaign begins and ends with describing that the dawn of better times has begun and argues that people should not want to go back to dark times. The concept of a national 'morning' was used as a symbol.

The Narrative Needs to Be Told Consistently

A key point about a campaign narrative is that it is imbued in all the communications through different channels and all messages. Campaign consultants know that a voter needs to hear each message at least seven times to really notice it, process it and connect it to the narrative. Being disciplined enough to repeat the narrative many times is important – but it does not mean using the same words. Trump's consistent use of phrases such as 'Drain the Swamp', 'Crooked Hillary', 'Build the Wall' or 'War on Radical Islamic Extremism' in 2016 all fit into the macro narrative of *Make America Great Again* and reinforced it.

Organizing the Narrative

How should this all be tied together to start articulating a good campaign narrative? This is the secret sauce of campaign strategists and communications experts, but there are methodological structures that should help any campaign bring narrative ideas into practice. The Message House is a well-known scheme that categorises a campaign's communications and organises it to ladder up to a central idea. The roof is the central positioning (or, roughly, the narrative), resting on several pillars of key messages, which are in turn grounded in facts and figures. It is a useful tool to keep the communications operation disciplined.

Another useful approach is a message triangle, the centre of which conveys the overall value proposition (similar to the roof of the message house) in between three corners that each contain a supporting point. This triangle has been updated by Stephen Krupin, Barack Obama's senior speechwriter, who developed the Message Story, a structure that ensures each of the sub-points have a relationship to one another and overall tell an intuitive, chronological story (see Figure 1.1). It begins by invoking a central value that explains the motivation for the campaign, then defines the conflict – a problem that violates the core value. This is followed by the campaign's solution and closes by painting what success or failure looks like, an ending that would ideally bring the core value into reality. Any and all of the three categories can be supported with facts and examples to make often abstract themes as concrete, vivid and relatable as possible.

Additionally, campaign teams always debate about the right proportion of rational and emotional elements in their communication. Some argue that candidates should not appeal to voters' emotions because it is "cheap" or somehow morally wrong. Such reasoning is misplaced and misses how the human mind works. When it comes to cognition and approaching new concepts, "intuition comes first, strategic reasoning second" (Haidt, 2012, p. 106). Jonathan Haidt talks of an apt metaphor of a rider (reasoning) sitting on an elephant (intuition) and not controlling but rather serving the large animal wherever the elephant decides to go. If the elephant decides to go to one side (e.g. the voter *feels* negative about something), the rider will look for which way to go on that side (i.e. explain and ex-post rationalise why the voter feels negative) and will stop looking in the other direction. Humans routinely ignore rational reasons that conflict with our intuitive feeling, otherwise also called confirmation bias. "Reasoning matters, particularly because reasons do sometimes influence other people, but most of the action in moral psychology is in the intuition" (Haidt, 2012, p. 108).

The fact that voters are driven mainly by their inner intuitive leanings and, often subconsciously, follow their inner compasses or group allegiances is a profound insight for campaign communications writ large. Successful narratives work on the intuitive level. A candidate whose communications do not respond to the makeup of voters' inner psyche risks not only failing to convince voters they are the right person for the job, but the candidate can fail to be understood or even heard.

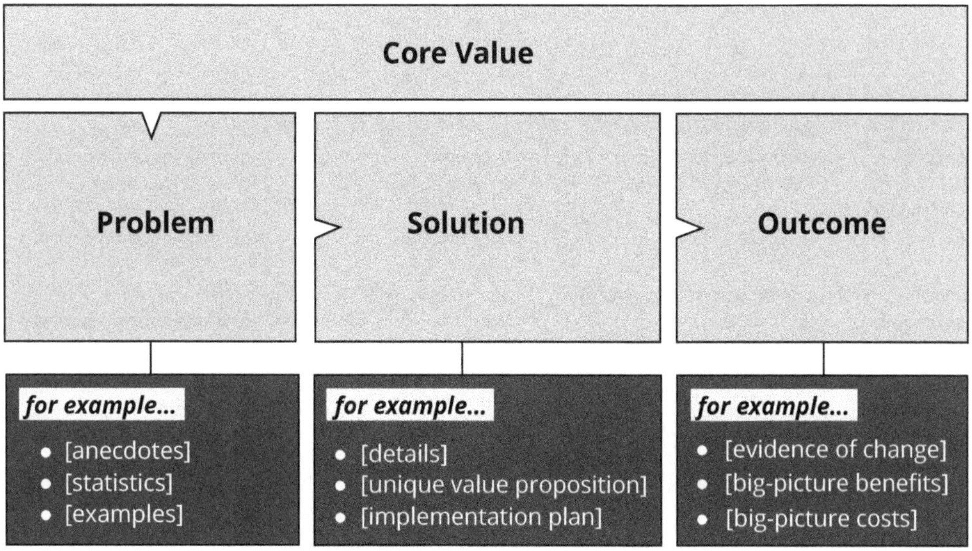

Figure 1.1 The Message Story Concept for Narrative Design

Finally, campaign narratives need to fit into a cadence of the election timeframe. If the candidate is a newcomer, they would typically want to have a strong introduction and capture voters' attention, while a well-known candidate might have more leeway in the initial intensity. The narrative also needs to consider the fact that many voters, often a third or more of the electorate, pay only scant attention to politics until the last weeks or days before the election. This usually means that the storytelling of the campaign has a strong closing argument that solidifies the base voters, convinces the swing voters and also convincingly summarises the narrative of the campaign to the voters who might just be starting to tune in. While brands should be more or less constant and consistent, narratives need to be flexible and evolve with external circumstances and with the campaign calendar.

BRINGING IT TOGETHER

Successful campaigns manage to bring all three elements together in a seamless fashion – a well-established and forceful brand telling a compelling narrative to the right sets of voter groups. While no campaign can be adequately summarised in a few words, it is in fact a useful exercise to do during the campaign. What is the elevator pitch of the campaign and who are we talking to? If the candidate or strategists cannot answer this succinctly, they would be well-advised to go back to the drawing board and try to figure it out before focusing on other activities.

There are numerous recent examples of parties and candidates from around the world that have managed to weave the three elements together successfully and win elections. Table 1.1 outlines a few examples. It is important to acknowledge that other factors do play a role in campaigns, from a well-organised field operation, get-out-the-vote programme, social or traditional media communications, or exogenous factors outside the campaign's control. However, in a tightly run campaign, there is always clarity on the three elements: brand, narrative and (connection to) voters.

Table 1.1 Examples of Successful Political Branding Campaigns

Campaign	*Brand*	*Narrative*	*Voters*
Narendra Modi (2014 General Election, India)	Strong, decisive leader with a pro-business stance, emphasising development and good governance and also playing on nationalism.	"Achhe Din" (Good Days) – positioned as the candidate who would bring development, economic growth, and good governance, breaking from ineffective Congress rule.	Targeted middle-class, business owners, rural poor and youth. Modi's message resonated particularly with voters frustrated with corruption and lack of development under previous governments, and also patriotic Hindus.
Leave Campaign (2016 Brexit Referendum, UK)	Anti-establishment, nationalistic, focused on sovereignty and control.	"Take Back Control" – Framed as a movement to reclaim sovereignty from Brussels, promising more control over immigration, laws, and national destiny.	Appealed to older voters, working-class citizens, and those in economically struggling areas who felt left behind by globalisation and the EU.
Emmanuel Macron (2017 Presidential Election, France)	A fresh, centrist alternative to the traditional political establishment, positioned as pro-European and reformist.	"Neither left nor right" – promoted himself as the candidate for a new France, transcending traditional parties, with a focus on reform, renewal, and European unity.	Targeted dissatisfied voters, including moderates from both left and right, and youth who were disillusioned with the existing political system.
Jacinda Ardern (2020 Re-election	Compassionate and energetic crisis manager. Especially recognised for her handling of the COVID-19 pandemic, the	"Strong, Kind Leadership" – Ardern's campaign focused on her ability to lead with empathy and strength during	Broad appeal across New Zealand, particularly among women, urban dwellers and younger voters who appreciated

Table 1.1 (Continued)

Campaign	*Brand*	*Narrative*	*Voters*
Campaign, New Zealand)	Christchurch mosque attack and other major crises.	crises, and promised a recovery based on kindness, inclusivity and well-being.	her empathetic leadership. Her strong COVID-19 response attracted a large coalition of supporters.
Gabriel Boric (2021 Presidential Election, Chile)	Young, leftist candidate advocating for social justice, human rights and deep structural reforms. Positioned as a symbol of a new political generation pushing for equality and systemic change.	"Chile for All" – Boric framed his campaign around inclusivity, a fight against inequality and the need to address the systemic injustices that sparked widespread social unrest in Chile.	Mobilised younger voters, progressives and those disillusioned with traditional politics. His appeal extended to those advocating for the social movements that emerged after the 2019 protests.
Claudia Sheinbaum (Mexico, 2024 Presidential Campaign)	Progressive, technocratic leader who was a guarantor of the continuation of her predecessor Andrés Manuel López Obrador (AMLO) from the same party.	"Continuing the Transformation" – A focus on building on AMLO's legacy with promises to extend social programs and focus on climate change and equity. She emphasises her scientific background and pragmatic approach to solving issues.	Appeals to urban, progressive, and younger voters who support AMLO's policies and seek continuity in social welfare and environmental reforms. Also appeals to women and those advocating for gender equality.

CONCLUDING REMARKS

Campaigns are complex, exhausting endeavours with a lot of moving pieces. It is not uncommon to get lost in the process, lose efficiency, and eventually lose the election. While there are constant improvements to the process of running campaigns, certain elements remain crucial in all campaigns, big or small. I draw on practical personal experiences from dozens of campaigns around the globe and argue that there are three key areas that the campaign needs to get right to succeed.

First, campaigns need to have a solid understanding of the electorate. Since the measure of success is the number of votes on election day, understanding the people casting the votes is critical. I make a case for rigorous voter research and explore the role it plays in segmenting the electorate into (i) base voters, (ii) swing voters and (iii) unreachable voters, and how to study each of these cohorts more in depth. I also provide practical information on what dimensions are useful to explore and how to tie the various information streams together.

Second, campaigns need to figure out the appropriate branding needed for the candidates. Voters pay limited attention to politics and tend to form snap and hard-to-change judgements of candidates based on their perceived strengths and weaknesses, or just anecdotal insights. Brands are the frames through which voters see the candidates and campaigns need to strive to control the brand frames as much as possible. I discuss various approaches and tools for crafting the right brands in political marketing and making them impactful.

Third, I describe the process of combining the previous two concepts and activating them for the purposes of a campaign through storytelling. Successful campaigns communicate clear, authentic and compelling narratives that appeal not only to voters' reason, but more importantly to their intuition. This chapter deciphers key building blocks for the development of good narratives and provides practical guidance on how to weave them together.

Notes

1 See: https://www.imdb.com/title/tt0055719/.
2 See: https://www.imdb.com/title/tt0416449/.
3 See: https://www.youtube.com/watch?v=Xq_x3JUwrU0.
4 See: https://www.youtube.com/watch?v=riDypP1KfOU.
5 See: https://www.youtube.com/watch?v=pUMqic2IcWA.

REFERENCES

Aaker, D. A. (2014). *Aaker on branding: 20 Principles that drive success*. Morgan James Publishing.

Aristotle. (1961). *Aristotle's poetics*. Hill and Wang.

Baines, P., & Fill, C. (2014). *Marketing 3e* (p. 589). Oxford University Press.

Biden, J. (2021, September 1). *The battle for the soul of the nation*. Speech.

Hagel, J. (2014, January). What is to be done? *Edge Perspectives*. https://edgeperspectives.typepad.com/edge_perspectives/2014/01/what-is-to-be-done-part-3.html

Haidt, J. (2012). *The righteous mind: Why good people are divided by politics and religion*. Pantheon Books.

Heath, C., & Heath, D. (2007). *Made to stick: Why some ideas survive and others die*. Random House.

Keller, K. L. (2013). *Strategic brand management: Building, measuring, and managing brand equity* (4th ed.). Pearson Education.

Kreiss, D. (2016). *Prototype politics: Technology-intensive campaigning and the data of democracy*. Oxford University Press.

Mark, M., & Pearson, C. S. (2001). *The Hero and the outlaw: Building extraordinary brands through the power of archetypes*. McGraw-Hill.

Newman, B. I. (1999). *The mass marketing of politics: Democracy in an age of manufactured images*. SAGE.

Popkin, S. L. (1991). *The reasoning voter: Communication and persuasion in presidential campaigns*. University of Chicago Press.

Scammell, M. (2015). Political brands. *European Journal of Marketing*, *49*(5/6), 615–628. https://doi.org/10.1108/EJM-02-2014-0082

Schwartz, T. (1973). *The responsive chord*. Doubleday.

Smith, G., & French, A. (2009). The political brand: A consumer perspective. *Marketing Theory*, *9*(2), 209–226. https://doi.org/10.1177/1470593109103068

Westen, D. (2007). *The political brain: The role of emotion in deciding the fate of the nation*. PublicAffairs.

Australia – Political Marketing in a Down Under Democracy

Andrew Hughes

INTRODUCTION

While there have been singular level works that have examined aspects of political marketing in Australia, there has not been one that has sought to outline how the context, process and systems influence how political marketing is practiced in Australia. This work seeks to address that gap.

Firstly, the chapter will consider the context facing political marketing in Australia. This is of the nation itself currently, but also its history as a former British colony. Next, the work will briefly examine the Australian political system. There will be a brief description of the Australian political system from a historical perspective, which will then be followed by how voting works in Australia and the role this has in framing approaches to political marketing in Australia. Keeping with the historical background, there will be a discussion of elections and party leaders over time in Australia. How political parties are funded at elections will be examined next.

The chapter will then look at the nature of political exchange in Australia. After this, there will be a brief overview of earlier works that have examined political marketing in an Australian context. The role of stakeholders in Australian political marketing will conclude this section.

The chapter will then move into a more marketing focus, examining each of the four different elements that make up the marketing mix, and how each influences the market orientation in the Australian system. The chapter will finish with some concluding thoughts about Australian political marketing.

CONTEXT

Australia, one of the newest and most advanced Western democracies in the world, provides insights into how political marketing is adapting and evolving in the digital age in a market with compulsory voting. Driven by one of the richest first-world economies on the planet, the state of the discipline in Australia has reached industry level, with thousands now employed to assist with the marketing and branding of governments, organisations, leaders, candidates and campaigns daily, and parties offering formal courses to political staff in marketing, branding, public affairs and communications (Grattan Institute, 2022).

With a diverse population and culture, Australia is undergoing an era of social and technological change. It is establishing its own unique culture, and breaking away from the English Colonial connections that helped lay the foundations for the political system that now operates in Australia. As a first-world nation, it has also enthusiastically adopted digital and social media and technologies. This unique mix makes

Australia an important testing ground for innovative ideas, methods and approaches in political marketing. Some global political campaigners of note, including Sir Lynton Crosby, Mark Textor and Isaac Levido, are Australians who developed their skills in campaigns in Australia (Saunders, 2019).

Australian political parties have heartily embraced a relationship marketing orientation (O'Cass, 2001), with active and passive stakeholders playing an important role in the development of policies. Similar to other Western systems, recently wealthy oligarchs, most notably Clive Palmer (a former politician and businessman with mining interests), are becoming directly involved in election campaigns. They either run their candidates through their own created political parties, or support those which best represent their views. With the rapid change in Australian society and culture, especially due to a high migration intake, party identification is shifting rapidly. Once generational, party identification is becoming more fluid and allowing for the rise of minor parties and independents who have (largely) effectively implemented marketing and branding methods into their campaigns and relationships. These parties are created rapidly and often have few policies other than those directly targeting segments they see as being key to winning electoral influence.

As a highly developed nation, Australians have always embraced centrist policies and parties. The two major political parties in Australia, the Labor Party (centre left), and the Liberal Party (centre right) once dominated the vote in Australian elections at all levels. But correlating with the drift in identification, there has been a steady flow to parties on the fringes of the centre since the 2000s (see Table 2.1), where one in three Australians now vote for one of these parties.

These changes, and the unique political system that Australia has, are seeing the most dynamic era for Australian politics for decades. This chapter will discuss how a young democracy is evolving within a dynamic market dominated by a relationship marketing approach. It should be noted that Australia, as a federation, is examined from a national political perspective, with states considered only in the context of the national perspective.

UNDERSTANDING THE AUSTRALIAN POLITICAL SYSTEM – HISTORY AND VOTING

Australia is a constitutional monarchy with a representative democracy for a population of 27 million in 2024 (Australian Bureau of Statistics, 2024). Colonised by the British in 1788, and only federated as a nation in 1901, the English monarch remains officially the head of state, represented in Australia by the Governor-General. The Governor-General is appointed by the Monarch of the United Kingdom, but only following advice from the Prime Minister of the day. The constitution of 1901, which is also a British Act of Parliament, provides the overarching powers for how the country is governed.

As Australia is a nation, the Governor-General's role is seen as analogous to that of a figurehead and acting in the same way as the Monarch in Great Britain. However, from time to time, such as during the constitutional crisis of 1975, and when the former Prime Minister, Scott Morrison, was secretly sworn into additional ministries in 2020/2021, the existing constitutional power of this role has raised questions on scrutiny and governance. Australian Republicans, who lost a close vote in 1988 to cede altogether from the United Kingdom, have long cited the constitutional powers of the Governor-General as a significant reason for this position to be replaced with an Australian head of state.

Australia, as a Westminster-based system, has three arms of government: (i) the legislative,

Table 2.1 Primary Votes at Australian Elections Since 2007

Election Year	*ALP*	*Coalition*	*Total 2 Party*	*Greens*	*Ind/Other*	*Result*
2007	43.4	43.3	86.7	7.8	5.5	Labor Win
2010	38	43.2	81.2	11.8	7	Labor Minority
2013	33.4	45.2	78.6	8.6	12.8	Coalition
2016	34.7	41.7	76.4	10.2	13.4	Coalition
2019	33.3	41.1	74.4	10.4	15.2	Coalition
2022	32.5	35.7	68.2	12.2	19.6	Labor Win

Source: Australian Electoral Commission, 2023.

(ii) the executive and (iii) the judiciary. The Executive is led by the Prime Minister and Cabinet, and other ministry roles, who are in charge of the public service. The Judiciary in Australia is led by the 7-member High Court, appointed directly by the Federal Government, and then the state and local judicial systems.

Legislative power is held by Parliament. Federally, this comprises a lower house (House of Representatives) and an upper house (Senate), loosely based on the United Kingdom's Westminster system (of Houses of Commons and Lords). The party or parties with the largest number of seats in the lower house, which comprises roughly 150 members (dependent on population changes), is invited by the Governor-General to form government. The Senate, or Upper House, has 76 members, 12 for each of Australia's six states, and two each from its two Territories. It is often called the House of Review as convention means legislation is passed first by the House before being reviewed and then passed by the Senate. The Senate also being where Senators represent entire states is also partly due to the influence of the US system on the drafting of the Constitution where Senators in Congress represent states. Hence the term 'Washminster', a portmanteau of Washington and Westminster, is used by some to describe Australia's system.

However, if the Senate blocks legislation, it is sent back to the House for amendment, and the process is started again. The Lower House has three-year maximum terms, the Senate six years, with half the Senate elected at each Federal election unless there is a double dissolution election. A double dissolution election can only be called by the Prime Minister under the conditions outlined in the Constitution, which is having a piece of legislation twice rejected by Parliament, which usually happens in the Senate.

Australia's states follow similar models, except in Queensland which abolished its Upper House in 1922. Each state has a Governor who acts in much the same way as the Governor-General. Federal law overrides State law other than in certain areas defined in the Constitution, and State governors follow a similar precedence with the Governor-General, although it is incredibly rare for a state Governor to have a dispute with the Governor-General.

Forced Choice and the Australian System

Australia is one of only 22 democracies in the world that have compulsory voting of any type, and one of only 11 to enforce it legally (Australian Parliament House, 2004). This applies to nearly all levels of government in Australia. Many Australians feel they are in a forced or compulsory choice scenario. Some argue, when combined with the consumer culture and widespread negative perception of the methods used by Australian parties and candidates, that this aspect of the Australian system is leading to voter fatigue (Crabb, 2022; Sinnerbrink, 2019). This is supported by early voting and postal voting in Australian elections being at all-time highs, roughly 35% now of all votes cast at federal elections, with many citing the switch-off factor as being a key reason why they do so. Despite this, political engagement around key issues in Australia remains strong. The challenge then for parties in the Australian system is to reconnect and re-engage with voters, and to use methods that enable this to occur. The Teals showed how this could be done federally, and independents such as Justine Davis in the Northern Territory also provide good examples (Garrick, 2024).

While many Australians dislike the forced choice of voting, there is no doubt that it has had the desired effect of keeping most engaged in issues and politics in Australia (Winchester et al., 2016). Compulsory voting is seen as a key reason for the identification of parties and candidates in Australia being a significant factor in outcomes on election day as people know that come the day they will have to vote for someone. This identification was heavily influenced by close peer and family groups initially (Gauja & Grömping, 2020), but over time cultural factors have also started to permeate relationships between political brands and political consumers. Identification and the role it has in election outcomes though remain an important factor in why many parties and candidates do not support any move away from compulsory voting in Australia.

Voting in Australia

A final and important note on the Australian system is on voting itself. Voting is compulsory at all levels for people aged over 18, with fines varying depending on the level, for example, $A20 federally, but in Queensland, this is $A161.30 (Electoral Commission of Queensland, 2024). In practical terms, in the 2022 Australian Federal Election, over 92% of people voted (Parliamentary Education Office, 2024).

The Preferential System

Nearly all voting in Australia is based on preferential voting, which is as per the *Commonwealth Electoral Act 1918*. Only Tasmania (state level), the Australian Capital Territory (territory level) and the Senate (Federal level) use a proportional system. As the Parliament of Australia (2024) states about the preferential system:

> The preferential voting system used is an absolute majority system where for election a candidate must obtain more than 50 per cent of the votes in the count. The voter is required to mark his or her vote on the ballot paper by placing the number one (1) against the name of the candidate of first choice, and to give contingent votes for all the remaining candidates in order of preference by the consecutive numbers 2, 3, 4 and so on; all squares on the ballot paper must be numbered, although one square may be left unnumbered, in which case the blank square will be deemed to be the voter's last preference, provided a first preference has been indicated.

Proportional Voting

Tasmania (state level), Australian Capital Territory (territory level) and the Senate (Federal level) use a proportional system. The following description of proportional voting in Australia relates to the Federal level.

> Under proportional voting, a candidate must obtain a certain percentage of the votes in the count, usually referred to as the 'quota', to be elected. This system is only appropriate to multi-member constituencies, such as those for the Senate, where each State votes as one electorate. For Senate elections, the voter has the option of marking the ballot paper preferentially by party/group or, alternatively, by individual candidate. The special feature of proportional representation is contained in the method of counting the votes which ensures that the proportion of seats won by each party in a State or Territory closely reflects the proportion of the votes gained by that party. There is thus greater opportunity for the election of minority parties and independents than in the House. (Parliament of Australia, 2024)

The proportional system allows minor parties a greater chance of being elected compared to the preferential system due to the use of the quota, therefore requiring a lower primary vote to be elected.

Another notable feature of using these systems is that minor party votes can be important in determining election outcomes in Australia. The Greens, for example, often have a strong preference flow (80%) to Labor, so if one of their candidates obtains a 10% primary vote, but is then eliminated from the count due to where they place, then their 8% would be highly likely go to Labor. So even if Labor obtains an initial primary vote of 30%, they could still win the seat with preference flows from minor parties who prefer it over other candidates.

A HISTORY OF POLITICAL PARTY SUCCESS AND LEADERS

Australia has a reputation for being a politically stable nation dominated by centrist economic policies but with progressive social, cultural and technological policies. Federal and state governments have been held either by the Labor Party or the Coalition for several decades now (AustralianPolitics.com, 2024).

In recent times, there has been a change in political culture as parties have become more focused on polls and retention of power once in government. The reliance on leaders as the centrepiece of the party and then the government has meant that once a leader sees their ratings starting to dip in the polls, then they are likely to be seen as a liability and not an asset by those within their party (see Table 2.2 for an indication of the volatility of, and change in, party leaders since 2007). Consequently, Australia has had 10 Prime Ministers serving two terms or less, the majority of whom have been in the last decade. In fact, since 2013, there have been four elections and six Prime Ministers, with one, Kevin Rudd, serving twice in a three-year timeframe. It has had two minority Federal governments. This is not a pattern usually associated with a stable democracy, yet the Australian system has survived this upheaval by parties within it and is still seen as one of the most open democracies in the world (Transparency International, 2024).

Table 2.1 showing lower house primary voting figures at elections indicates that the majority of the population vote for either Labor or a Coalition. As mentioned earlier, since the advent of social and digital media and increased overseas migration, especially from 2010 onwards, the primary vote share of the major parties has been slowly falling, and that of independents and minor parties growing.

This fall in the two-party vote was seen as a sign by the major parties of them not being sufficiently market-oriented, especially when it came to how voters perceived their leaders. Yet, it could be equally argued that the major parties had not worked on relationships with key emerging segments in Australia, especially middle-class women aged 25–55 in inner urban areas where many Australians now live.

Table 2.2 Number of Federal Leaders by Party Since 2007

Party	*Number of Leaders Since 2007*
Australian Labor Party (ALP)	6 (Kevin Rudd twice)
Liberal Party (Lib)	6 (Malcolm Turnbull twice)
National Party (Nats)	6 (Barnaby Joyce twice)
Greens	4

In search of a renewed relationship with such key segments, parties have changed their leaders to ensure they could re-establish a connection with the electorate. Even minor parties, such as the Nationals and the Greens, who adopted the same strategy, changed leaders consistently over the last 15 years. Parties still had not recognised that markets were splintering, however, and that identification by younger voters, and those who had only moved to Australia recently, was not present to the level that gave them the support required to achieve majority government.

As marketing knowledge advanced within political parties, there was a realisation of the importance of understanding that opinion polls were not necessarily effective at predicting election outcomes as Australia itself became more diverse and splintered, reflecting global trends in Western nations (Firat & Shultz, 1997).

The development in Australian political marketing has helped provide clarity to parties on what has been affecting their performance. Slowly over time, it has moved from a top-down, managerial approach, similar to marketing as a whole in society, to a more holistic approach (Keller & Kotler, 2015) which considers a wider range of factors, such as culture and society, when evaluating the effectiveness of methods, strategies and brands.

This was an important but significant development because, in this same timeframe, Australian society has undergone societal, cultural and technological transformations. As an example, the fastest-growing household type has now become single parents, especially males. House prices have nearly doubled (Australian Bureau of Statistics, 2024), with many Australians now more likely to rent for their entire lives than own a house in the suburbs, or the 'Great Australian Dream' (Turnbull, 2024). The cost of living and other economic issues dominate other issues in Australia. While Australia is one of the richest nations on earth, with the 9th highest GDP per capita (Australian Department of Foreign Affairs, 2024), it is also seeing the development of increased inequality in society with all government welfare payments below the recognised poverty line (Melbourne Institute, 2024).

The uptake of technology in Australia, which helps overcome the tyranny of long distances between urban centres which is so common in Australia, means that in 2024, the average adult Australian has on average eight social media accounts, and spends more time on their device than with traditional media such as television or radio (Meltwater, 2024). These transformations have made the Australian political market awash with knowledge from diverse content providers, something which was not present in 2007. The deeply ingrained Australian cultural value of being given a 'fair go' and 'standing up for the underdog' means many still favour progressive policies, but only with a foundation of economic stability.

One of the key lessons Australia can teach about political marketing from its development is that opinion polls are a basic form of market research. Relying upon them as primary evidence of the perception of political brands in the community is fraught with danger. They are reliable as indicators of electoral-level trends, and may not necessarily correlate with what leaders and parties perceive to be so in the national electorate. Instead using modern and open marketing research which considers wider environmental factors and is correlated with the parties' analyses is more likely to provide an accurate picture of how the electorate is evolving and changing in the modern Australian political era.

The old saying in Australian politics that governments are usually voted out and not in seems to remain the case in the modern era, although it is far less likely as a premise when contextualised with the development and implementation of policies by parties and candidates who use marketing research effectively. As shown in Table 2.3, the change in prime minister in the last 15 years or so of Australian politics has been largely due to a market orientation by parties.

FUNDING AUSTRALIAN PARTIES

By far one of the most contentious issues in Australia is the funding of political parties. In Australia, this is achieved publicly via electoral commissions (such as the Federal figures in Table 2.4) and privately by the parties themselves.

Table 2.3 List of Australian Prime Ministers Since 2007

Prime Minister	*Party*	*Date and Reason for Election as PM?*	*Date and Reason for Leaving as PM?*	*Term Length*	*Elections Contested as PM*
Kevin Rudd	ALP	3 Dec 2007, election win	24 June 2010, party room spill	2 years, 203 days	0
Julia Gillard	ALP	24 June 2010, party room spill.	27 June 2013, party room spill.	3 years, 3 days	1
Kevin Rudd	ALP	27 June 2013, party room spill	18 September 2013, election loss	83 days	1
Tony Abbott	Lib	18 September 2013, election win	15 September 2015, Party room spill	1 year, 362 days	0
Malcolm Turnbull	Lib	15 September 2015, party room spill	24 August 2018. party room spill	2 years, 343 days	1
Scott Morrison	Lib	24 August 2018, party room spill	23 May 2022, election loss	3 years, 272 days	1
Anthony Albanese	ALP	23 May 2022, election win	In power presently		

Source: Museum of Australian Democracy, 2023.

Table 2.4 2022 Federal Election AEC Funding, Top 10 Parties

Political Party	*Total Election Funding Paid*
Australian Labor Party – Federal	$27,104,944.03
Liberal Party of Australia	$26,550,112.02
The Australian Greens – Victoria	$3,023,677.14
Pauline Hanson's One Nation	$3,003,118.86
The Greens NSW	$2,961,026.14
National Party of Australia-NSW	$2,401,012.16
Queensland Greens	$2,204,033.40
United Australia Party	$1,925,262.31
Australian Greens	$1,401,351.35
The Greens WA Inc	$1,170,451.81

Source: Australian Electoral Commission (AEC), Election Funding, 2023.

Both Federal and State laws regulate fundraising by political parties and how it ought to be undertaken. At the Federal level, funding is provided to parties that receive 4% of the primary vote of the total first preference votes in a seat at an election. This amount was set at $A3.22 per vote in 2024.

However, according to returns lodged with the Australian Electoral Commission (AEC), the major parties and the United Australia Party spent roughly over $A120 (US$82) million on their Federal election campaigns in 2022. This means that there is a significant funding shortfall between what the taxpayer pays and what is spent. This gap is usually filled by donations to the major parties from external entities. These donations are somewhat scrutinised through legislation, but most of it can be excluded from being declared through loopholes in the legislation that no significant party in the federal Parliament seems keen to close, perhaps for obvious reasons.

Yet this reluctance to close the door on one funding avenue has also kept it open for a newer set of stakeholders to have increasing influence on election campaigns in Australia. Along with most of the developed world, campaign costs have escalated in the era of digital and social media, the 2022 Federal Election being the most expensive to date in Australia with an estimated spend by parties and candidates of close to $A500 million (AEC, 2023b), parties and candidates have had to turn to major donors to fund campaigns.

These donors then want a return on their investment, which can range from friendly legislation to Public Private Partnerships (PPPs) which have become the norm for funding large-scale projects in Australia such as roads and airports.

Yet it is through fundraising that Australia also reveals a dichotomy of the use of political marketing in a still-evolving Western democracy. That is, how, if the market and democratic structures allow, minor parties and independent candidates can successfully challenge a long-established duopoly such as that enjoyed by Labor and the Liberal-National Party Coalition? Does the lack of donation laws help and assist minor parties and independents to mount more effective campaigns against duopolies? Do donation laws prevent challenges to the major parties and make it more likely that Australians will only ever have one of two parties in government? These are some of the questions Australia faces when it comes to grappling with the cost of marketing in politics.

Australia also provides an example of how purpose-built well-financed movements can re-engage disaffected voters in seats presumed to be safely held by major parties in a duopoly system. It could be argued that only because there are funding loopholes in the Australian system that minor parties and independents can now spend money on marketing methods to help them compete with the majors. In 2022, this was demonstrated when some inner-city seats went from Labor to the Greens and some from the Liberals to the Teals. Of particular note here was the 'Indi' campaign, a Federal Lower House Seat, in 2013 where digital marketing research methods were used, most notably NationBuilder which Obama used effectively in the US (McKelvey & Piebiak, 2018).

This integration of research, with the data and access from Australians' use of social and digital media, helped minor parties and independents to more effectively plan and strategise. They could finally be competitive against larger competitors as they could move more dynamically in fluid segments, such as young voters, who were attracted by more progressive policies and brands, but also candidates who better reflected this segment.

AUSTRALIAN POLITICAL MARKETING: FOUNDATIONAL PREMISES OF EXCHANGE

Australian political marketing derives its foundational premises from existing political marketing constructs (O'Cass, 1996, 2001). As a market-based economy, exchange is the foundation stone of Australian political marketing. Firstly, as with any exchange in marketing, there is the central or primary exchange between two actors where value is co-created, each actor exchanging a thing of value for another thing of value from the other actor (Lusch & Vargo, 2012). However, this primary exchange then usually creates a secondary exchange between other stakeholders in the political market.

As exchange underpins all marketing, this helps shape and form how political marketing can be defined (Kotler & Zaltman, 1971; Lock & Harris, 1996). When a political candidate or party applies this concept to the political process, they must be in a position to adapt to and satisfy voters' needs (Mauser, 1983; Newman & Sheth, 1987; O'Cass, 1996; Reid, 1988). Prior research (Houston, 1986; Newman & Sheth, 1987) identified the need to apply the marketing concept to the political process to understand the values that voters will place on selective criteria that will generate an effective exchange between a consumer and a voter.

While the instability may have disappeared in the 2020s as parties that pursued an opinion poll-driven approach suffered swings against them in elections, one of the other noted enduring effects was trust in government and government communications. It could be argued that this effect may be partly due to some government communications undertaken during COVID-19, such as the negativity towards the infamous *Sydney Woman* TV ad[1], trust in government in Australia has plunged to new lows in the 2020s as the flow-on effect from market-driven approaches such as changing leaders to increase poll fortunes become discernible to the electorate.

POLITICAL MARKETING IN AUSTRALIA: A RESEARCH OVERVIEW

Prior research in political marketing in Australia has focused on two main areas: a broad marketing managerial perspective (O'Cass, 2001) or a more communications and campaigns perspective (Van Onselen & Errington, 2007). The latter area also touches on aspects of the brand, but while written in a marketing context does not usually delve deep into aspects of it. Most prior work has focused on the 4 parties with the most significant representation in Australian parliament: Labor, Liberals, Nationals and the Greens. Some work has also studied political marketing in Australia from a stakeholder perspective (Hughes & Dann, 2009).

O'Cass's work (1996, 2001) provides the most-highly cited papers in the Australian context. These articles established how Australian political parties were operating with a market orientation, but were slowly moving towards a marketing orientation (Ormrod, 2006; O'Shaughnessy et al., 2012; Shama, 1976), a difference that is now less noticeable in the mid-2020s. Lees-Marshment (2003) offers some critique of these works, primarily on research method, but alternatively, she suggests that parties in Australia use and apply a more comprehensive political marketing managerial approach. As the relationship marketing orientation became dominant in Australia, parties and candidates were seeking out more knowledge and understanding of marketing methods and strategies, and less so from political science.

Parties started to work more closely with similar parties internationally to share ideas and knowledge. A consequence of which parties started to integrate more marketing theories and methods to become more market oriented. Professional campaign organisations, such as Crosby Textor, now CT Group, which worked closely with conservatives, or Labor's via Lawrence Creative, also infused new ideas and concepts into Australian politics from a commercial brand and campaign perspective.

The 2013 Independent e-campaign of Cath McGowan was the pioneering campaign in Australia for making use of social media with a database platform, in that case NationBuilder, to mount a grass roots campaign against a major party. This took many by surprise for its use of technology, despite the precedent set by Obama in 2008 (in a campaign in a safe rural conservative seat many saw as unwinnable by a non-major party candidate). Many minor parties and independents, such as the Teal[2] candidates, have adopted and modified this strategy with significant success in recent times.

This raised the importance of understanding the role of brand and relationship marketing principles in Australian political marketing. Some researchers' work has focused on this aspect in political marketing, with researchers such as Hughes and Dann (2009) looking at aspects of political branding in Australia, focusing on aspects of relationship marketing.

However, political marketing research in Australia is limited due to a lack of support for the discipline at an academic level. This is primarily due to the points raised above – many in Australia see it as being more of an application of separate theories by parties in a system driven by relationships with stakeholders, rather than a whole-of-managerial, or top-down, approach applied by parties, candidates and stakeholders in the Australian political system.

Even in the discipline of political communication, there is a reluctance to support the political marketing field, with many practitioners afraid to go on record about methods and strategies as, for many, some of their biggest clients are government departments. In this way, while Australia may like to think of itself as a first-world democracy, there are aspects where executive control is stifling debate, discussion and development of knowledge of how commercial ideas and concepts, such as marketing and branding, are influencing and affecting the system of government and democracy.

STAKEHOLDERS: THE GOLDEN RULE – THOSE WITH GOLD MAKE THE RULES AND GET INFLUENCE

Like any Western democracy, stakeholders who use networks, power and wealth to obtain influence exist in Australian politics. Figure 2.1 provides a conceptual view of how stakeholders operate in Australia.

But what makes how they operate in Australia perhaps unique compared to other nations is how some, such as the Palmer United Party, backed and founded by billionaire coal miner Clive Palmer, seek influence over seats in Parliament. This is because of how powerful preferences are in the political system in Australia. With the last few governments being elected with only slim majorities of 3 seats or less this makes these preferences incredibly influential on election outcomes for major parties.

More recently, in 2022 the pro-environmental Climate 200 group, backed by several wealthy individuals, most anonymous, supported candidates who had a mix of centre-right economic and green policies but were running as independents in conservative-held electorates. This policy mix led to these candidates being called Teal, and 6 were elected into both Houses of Parliament. This did not come cheap with an estimated campaign cost of around $A20 million (Hornsey et al., 2022). Without the existing funding loopholes, such as those detailed by Griffiths and Einslie (2022), it is debatable if these candidates would have been successful in 2022 on a far lower budget.

In addition, Australian election campaigns have always attracted high spends from those who support the major parties. Trade unions will often spend over $A20 million to support Labor, and a

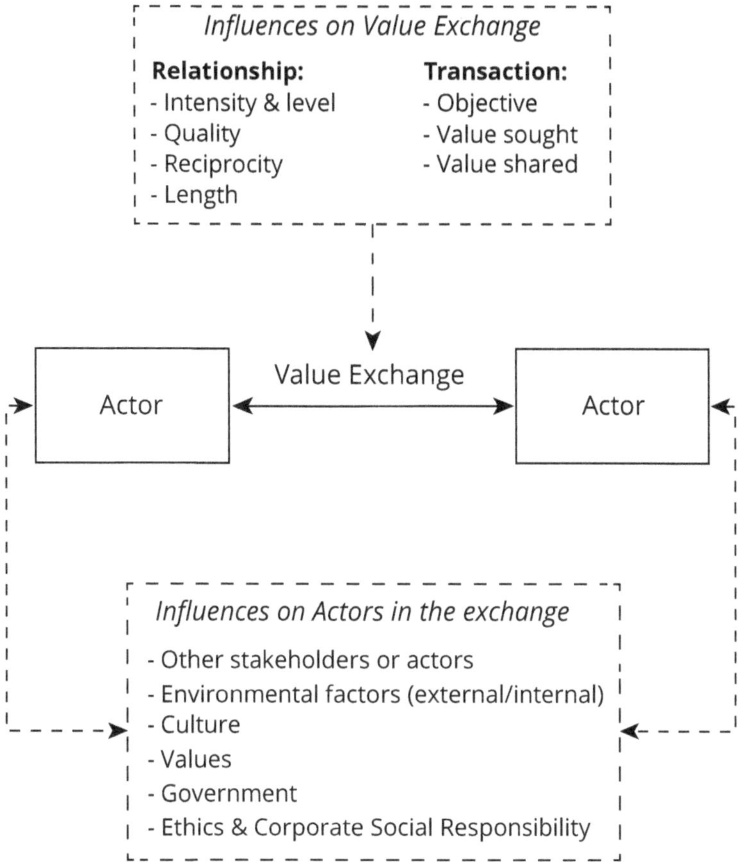

Figure 2.1 Actor-to-Actor Stakeholder-Based Model of Value Exchange in Political Marketing (Hughes, 2018)

similar figure is spent by business groups backing the conservative Liberal and National parties. Then there can be independent campaigns run around certain issues by special interest groups, such as pro-mining organisations who advocate for the role of resources in Australia. With cut-through harder to achieve due to the splintering of the media market, the scale of advertising spend in the 2022 Federal election was at levels never before seen in Australia. This raised concerns over campaign financing and influence by stakeholders.

The high advertising and campaign spend also fed into the notion of a political arms race in Australia. Some felt that in the Australian context this undermined the cultural importance of equity and fairness, and that it was changing the perception of democracy and democratic institutions in Australia as being transparent and above influence. Along with existing beliefs that the concentration of power in the executive was becoming greater, and harder to influence, this has allowed for those on the fringes of the left and right to start narratives about elites. Suddenly comparisons were being made with Trumpian notions of power being shifted away from all to just a few wealthy elites, a finding common in other Western systems where duopoly power exists.

Yet stakeholder influence in Australia is also creating a more diverse party and candidate offering (see Figure 2.1). With compulsory voting deterring switch-off factors which affect voluntary voting systems, minor parties and candidates stand a chance of being considered worthy of votes. The use of preferential and proportional voting is a further significant reason why these parties can consider running with some degree of optimism.

An example of this was in the 2022 Federal elections where there were an increasing number of electorates where two candidates preferred (2CP) polling provided little accuracy in predicting the outcome as they had become three candidate contests. The tyranny of distance in Australian politics (Gibson et al., 2008) also played a role here as, outside the large urban centres, traditional campaign methods based on a generational relationship=centric approach meant that, in rural areas, many of these issues had minimal influence.

Stakeholders in Australian politics also highlight that most parties perhaps are still operating to a relationship marketing context as opposed to a more transactional model. They may be becoming more managerial when it comes to how they operate, but Australian political marketing strategy is built around the relationships voters have with brands, even if that has not progressed to formal identification with that brand.

THE AUSTRALIAN WAY: METHODS AND STRATEGIES IN AUSTRALIAN POLITICAL MARKETING

Political marketing in Australia is unique through how methods and strategies are applied in a preferential and proportional voting system with compulsory voting. There are few other systems in the world similar to Australia. While the Western Democracy franchise has dozens of nations, Australia is unique for the very reason it is Australia. It is also one of the newest democracies on earth, formed as a nation only in 1901.

So, while there is much similarity in the methods discussed in this chapter with other nations, it is not possible to simply just generalise and apply findings in other nations to Australia. In fact, to say that the methods which may be effective overseas can be undertaken in the same way here to the same level is contradicted by many commercial brands, like Dr Pepper, or running a majority positive campaign as Obama did in 2008. This section will therefore focus on the methods and concepts which make political marketing different but also consider points of parity with other systems.

The embrace of branding, for example, has become noticeable in Australian political marketing. It has even extended to brand leveraging through the use of government advertising for policy communications, often linked implicitly to party platforms. With a more pronounced relationship marketing orientation though parties, candidates and other stakeholders also became reliant upon nearly all aspects of modern marketing, such as database driven analysis, research, product development, market and environmental analysis, as the foundation for campaigns and government. Political marketing is less about the permanent campaign, and more about being part of a larger ongoing brand management of parties and leaders.

PARTY AND PARTY STATUS AS BRAND

The perceived power and role of a leader and party has been combined and is represented by status. Status referring to the role in Parliament a party has. For example, using the leader as part of a co-brand with the government, such as the Albanese Government, the Dutton Opposition, the Greens led by Adam Bandt.

Increasingly governments are branded less on patriotic grounds in Australia, for example, the Australian Government, and more on who leads it. But the same can be said of other parties. Having a status brands the party and the leader, and in a way allows it more flexibility in the eyes of the market if it acts in a way consistent with that brand status. For example, voters expect a far-right brand to be more outspoken on right wing issues such as immigration, national identity or religion. A left-wing party and leader would expect or allow for views which differ from the mainstream on issues such as climate change, social welfare, housing and health.

The key is that as long as those issues match up to the perceived brands of the party, leader and status, then voters will allow for flexibility in that area. In a way, this is political service delivery (Lees-Marshment, 2019). A far-left minor party would be expected, but also encouraged by those engaged with it from its community, to be outspoken and prepared to even risk arrest at protests on issues cognisant with the leader and party brand. The same could be said for a far-right party.

Status therefore considers the role of ideology, and there is overlap with the other two elements but this overlap is consistent with how a voter may see all three elements working together in a political system such as Australia's.

PRODUCT: PERSON BRANDS: LEADERS, MPS AND CANDIDATES

The term personal brand was first used in 1997 in an article in management magazine, *Fast Company,* by Tom Peters, although no definition was given (Lair et al., 2005). Lair et al. (2005) argue that personal branding perhaps started earlier, in 1936 with Dale Carnegie's *How to Win Friends and Influence People*. The first definition given to personal branding was by Lair et al. (2005, p. 309) who described it as involving '. . .the concepts of product development and promotion are used to market persons for entry into or transition within the labour market'.

There is no reason why the other aspects of branding could not be extended to personal brands. A personal brand would also easily identify a product or service and is a sellers promise to deliver consistently a specific set of features, benefits and services to buyers (Kotler & Keller, 2006) and it has four important characteristics: attributes, benefits, values and personality (Kapferer, 1992; Keller, 1993). A personal brand's meaning to a consumer is based around each of these four characteristics, and it is up to the marketer to decide what emphasis to place on each so that a brand can be established (Kapferer, 1992).

A personal brand can be defined as being a person, name, term, sign, symbol or design, or a combination of these, intended to identify the goods or services of one seller, or group of sellers, and to differentiate them from those of competitors (Hughes, 2007).

In Australian political marketing, personal branding has become one of the most dominant marketing methods in use today, extending from candidates to leaders. Successful examples are found at all levels of politics in Australia. Personal branding is nearly always used as part of a co-branding strategy.

PROMOTION – THE RULE OF THREE: KEEPING IT SIMPLE

In the heavy cognitive environment which is the modern era, having three simple policies is becoming important in Australia in winning elections. Gone are the days of six-point plans, such as those put forward by then Liberal leader, Tony Abbott, which some candidates failed to remember. There are simple connections to the brand built around three key points. Perhaps this is a nod to the famous rule of the three-word slogan in advertising and communications, which has been shown to assist with recall (Kohli et al., 2013), but in Australia, it is effective. For example, Pauline Hanson's One Nation campaigns was built around three key issues, specifically identity, immigration and Islam.

The Greens have been successful as they usually have a rotating list of three key issues which match up with their brand identity although as they start to move more and more into the centre this has now meant one environmental policy, one social welfare policy and one policy built around integrity or health.

Having the rule of three helps support the use of a more focused, and narrow messaging strategy, which has become perhaps the dominant one now in Australia and ensures consistency across a nation as large as Australia with multiple time zones where it can be incredibly difficult to manage a large campaign. Keeping in mind the rule of three also helps in the high cognitive load environment which is the Western world in the post lockdown 2020s.

PRICE – POLITICAL SOCIAL ACCOUNTABILITY: GENDER, DIVERSITY AND CHANGE

Australian political marketing has struggled with gender issues for a long time. Perceived as being misogynistic, highlighted by the famous 2012 speech in Parliament by then Prime Minister, Julia Gillard. The major centre-left parties, Labor and the Greens, both have quotas in place when it comes to representation by gender. The major conservative parties, the Liberal and the National Party, do not. Although the leading far right party in Australia, One Nation, is built around Pauline Hanson, its long-term leader. Yet the electorate itself, like so many counterparts in Western democracies, has undergone significant changes in relation to gender representation in society, culture and the economy. These changes have meant that in Australia, one of the most critical segments of the market to win at any election is that of women, especially those aged 28–55 who live in urban areas and work in medium to high paying occupations, usually services.

Once seen as the bedrock of the Liberal vote in the cities, this segment moving from the Liberal Party to the Teals at the 2022 election (primarily as many Teal candidates themselves fitted this profile), was a key reason why so many Teals were elected and yet why so many Liberal Party sitting members were defeated as the vast majority were perceived as conservative men. With more formal funding and support being given to groups such as the Women's Electoral Forum, whose aim is to see more women elected to Parliament, regardless of political persuasion, gender in political marketing in Australia is only rising in prominence. Having more diversity in candidates in general in Australian politics has always been welcomed by the electorate, especially considering the very nature of Australia itself as a nation comprised nearly entirely of people who are perhaps only a small number of generations Australian as the nation was only formed formally in 1901.

Diversity in candidates is like that of gender: it should reflect the community a party is seeking to represent. Yet in this area, some parties are still struggling. While both major parties in Australia have solid track records in being diverse, with Labor perhaps better than the Liberal Party in more recent times, they remain far from being reflective of modern Australia.

CONCLUSION

Australian political marketing is dynamic, fluid and modern. Loose electoral laws relating to all aspects of marketing have allowed for a unique environment in which to study how methods are used, and the role of stakeholders.

Yet Australia as an example of political marketing practice also highlights the concerns we ought to have on how a market-oriented approach impacts upon the nature of democracy itself. These primarily relate to how a market orientation comes into conflict with some democratic principles due to how stakeholders exercise power. Future researchers may want to examine how marketing orientation and stakeholder influences are helping creating multiple meanings of what democracy represents to the electorate. The role of social and digital media in allowing for the emergence of new brands in a duopoly, and how this may be changing the market itself into a more competitive and effective market, may also interest researchers in an Australian context.

Australia is recognised as a highly developed nation in many ways. However, those in politics and institutions which maintain, regulate and develop its democracy must do so with the modern era in mind to ensure the electorate knows it is the right system for the unique culture and society that is Australia.

Notes

1 The *Sydney Woman* television advertisement was an Australian Government advertisement which depicted a woman in her thirties suffering from COVID-19, especially difficulty breathing, in a hospital bed as she had not got vaccinated. In Australia, at the time only those aged over 55 were eligible for a vaccination.

2 Teals are a group of candidates who stood as notionally independents but were supported financially by a Climate Change group. While many of their policies were similar to the Liberal party, especially on economics, their strong support for environmental policies gave rise to the nickname Teal in reference to the colour.

REFERENCES

Australian Bureau of Statistics. (2024). https://www.abs.gov.au/. Accessed on September 23, 2024.

Australian Bureau of Statistics. (2024). *Total value of Dwellings*. https://www.abs.gov.au/statistics/economy/price-indexes-and-inflation/total-value-dwellings/latest-release. Accessed on September 23, 2024.

Australian Department of Foreign Affairs and Trade. *Australia is a Top 20 Country*. https://www.dfat.gov.au/sites/default/files/australia-is-a-top-20-country-all-topics.pdf. Accessed on September 24, 2024.

Australian Electoral Commission. (2023a). *Election results*, https://results.aec.gov.au/. Accessed on June 20, 2023.

Australian Electoral Commission. (2023b). *Financial disclosure – Transparency register*. https://www.aec.gov.au/Parties_and_Representatives/financial_disclosure/transparency-register/. Accessed on June 20, 2023.

Australian Parliament House. (2004). *Joint standing committee on electoral matters*. https://www.aph.gov.au/Parliamentary_Business/Committees/Joint/Completed_Inquiries/em/elect04/appendixg. Accessed on July 2, 2023.

AustralianPolitics.com. (2024). *Federal election dates and outcomes*. https://australianpolitics.com/elections/dates/federal-election-dates-and-outcomes/. Accessed on September 23, 2024.

Crabb, A. (2022). *Australian voters took their rage and despair to the ballot box, and major parties can no longer take them for granted*. Australian Broadcasting Corporation. https://www.abc.net.au/news/2022-05-26/australian-election-voters-rage-despair-major-parties-on-notice/101095010. Accessed September 22, 2024.

Electoral Commission of Queensland. (2024). Do I have to vote? https://www.ecq.qld.gov.au/how-to-vote/do-i-have-to-vote. Accessed on September 26, 2024.

Firat, A. F., & Shultz, II, C. J. (1997). From segmentation to fragmentation. *European Journal of Marketing*, *31*(3/4), 183–207.

Garrick, M. (2024). *Independent politicians join forces to hold new CLP government to account in NT*

Parliament. Australian Broadcasting Corporation, https://www.abc.net.au/news/2024-09-02/nt-independents-yingiya-guyula-justine-davis-join-forces/104294666. Accessed on September 24, 2024.
Gauja, A., & Grömping, M. (2020). The expanding party universe: Patterns of partisan engagement in Australia and the United Kingdom. *Party Politics*, *26*(6), 822–833.
Gibson, R. K., Lusoli, W., & Ward, S. (2008). Nationalizing and normalizing the local? A comparative analysis of online candidate campaigning in Australia and Britain. *Journal of Information Technology & Politics*, *4*(4), 15–30.
Grattan Institute. (2022). Your money, their ads. https://grattan.edu.au/news/your-money-their-ads/. Accessed on October 23, 2022.
Griffiths, K., & Einslie, O. (2022). $177 million flowed to Australian political parties last year, but major donors can easily hide. *The Conversation*. https://theconversation.com/177-million-flowed-to-australian-political-parties-last-year-but-major-donors-can-easily-hide-176129. Accessed on September 26, 2024.
Hornsey, M. J., Chapman, C. M., Fielding, K. S., Louis, W. R., & Pearson, S. (2022). A political experiment may have extracted Australia from the climate wars. *Nature Climate Change*, *12*(8), 695–696.
Houston, F. S. (1986). The marketing concept: What it is and what it is not. *Journal of Marketing*, *50*(2), 81–87.
Hughes, A. (2007). Personal brands: An exploratory analysis of personal brands in Australian political marketing. In *Australia and New Zealand Marketing Academy Conference*. 3–5 December. University of Otago.
Hughes, A. (2018). *Market driven political advertising: Social, digital, and mobile marketing*. Springer.
Hughes, A., & Dann, S. (2009). Political marketing and stakeholder engagement. *Marketing Theory*, *9*(2), 243–256.
Kapferer, J. (1992). *Strategic brand management: New approaches to creating and evaluating brand equity*. Kogan Page.
Keller, K. L. (1993). Conceptualizing, measuring, and managing customer-based brand equity. *Journal of Marketing*, 1–22.
Keller, K. L., & Kotler, P. (2015). Holistic marketing: A broad, integrated perspective to marketing management. In *Does marketing need reform?: Fresh perspectives on the future* (pp. 308–313). Routledge.
Kohli, C., Thomas, S., & Suri, R. (2013). Are you in good hands? Slogan recall: What really matters. *Journal of Advertising Research*, *53*(1), 31–42.
Kotler, P. (2000). *Marketing management* (10th ed.). Prentice Hall.
Kotler, P., & Keller, K. L. (2006). *Marketing management* (12th ed.). Pearson.
Kotler, P., & Zaltman, G. (1971). Social marketing: An approach to planned social change. *Journal of Marketing*, 3–12.
Lair, D. J., Sullivan, K., & Cheney, G. (2005). Marketization and the recasting of the professional self: The rhetoric and ethics of personal branding. *Management Communication Quarterly*, *18*(3), 307–343.
Lees-Marshment, J. (2003). Political marketing: How to reach that pot of gold. *Journal of Political Marketing*, *2*(1), 1–32.
Lees-Marshment, J. (2019). Political delivery marketing. In *Political marketing* (pp. 211–239). Routledge.
Lock, A., & Harris, P. (1996). Political marketing. *European Journal of Marketing*, *30*(10/11), 14–24.
Lusch, R. F., & Vargo, S. L. (2012). The Forum on Markets and Marketing (FMM) advancing service-dominant logic. *Marketing Theory*, *12*(2), 193–199.
Mauser, G. A. (1983). *Political marketing: An Approach to campaign strategy*. Praeger.
McKelvey, F., & Piebiak, J. (2018). Porting the political campaign: The NationBuilder platform and the global flows of political technology. *New Media & Society*, *20*(3), 901–918.
Melbourne Institute. (2024). Henderson poverty line 2024. https://melbourneinstitute.unimelb.edu.au/research/labour/henderson-poverty-line
Meltwater. (2024). 2024 social media statistics for Australia. https://www.meltwater.com/en/blog/social-media-statistics-australia. Accessed on September 24, 2024.
Museum of Australian Democracy. (2023). *Australian Prime Ministers*. https://apm-origin.moadoph.gov.au/prime-ministers. Accessed on July 1 2023.
Newman, B. I., & Sheth, J. N. (1987). *A Theory of political choice behavior*. Praeger Publishers.
O'Cass, A. (1996). Political marketing and the marketing concept. *European Journal of Marketing*, *30*(10/11), 37–53.
O'Cass, A. (2001). Political marketing – An investigation of the political marketing concept and political market orientation in Australian politics. *European Journal of Marketing*, *35*(9/10), 1003–1025.
Ormrod, R. P. (2006). A conceptual model of political market orientation. In *Current issues in political marketing* (pp. 53–70). Routledge.
O'Shaughnessy, N. J., Baines, P. R., O'Cass, A., & Ormrod, R. P. (2012). Political marketing orientation: Confusions, complications, and criticisms. *Journal of Political Marketing*, *11*(4), 353–366.
Parliament of Australia. (2024). Method of voting. https://www.aph.gov.au/About%20Parliament/House%20of%20Representatives/Powers%20practice%20and%20procedure/Practice7/HTML/Chapter3/7chap03_2_9.html#_ftnref102. Accessed on September 26, 2024.

Parliamentary Education Office. (2024). How many people voted in the last election? https://peo.gov.au/understand-our-parliament/your-questions-on-notice/questions/how-many-people-voted-in-the-last-election. Accessed on September 26, 2024.

Reid, D. M. (1988). Marketing the political product. *European Journal of Marketing*, *22*(9), 34–47.

Saunders, J. (2019). Lynton Crosby and the dark arts of democracy. In *Media ethics, free speech, and the requirements of democracy* (pp. 53–68). Routledge.

Shama, A. (1976). The marketing of political Candidates 1. *Journal of the Academy of Marketing Science*, *4*(3), 764–777.

Sinnerbrink, R. (2019). Election fatigue and what to do about it. *The Lighthouse*. https://lighthouse.mq.edu.au/article/may-2019/Election-fatigue-and-what-to-do-about-it. Accessed on September 24, 2024.

Transparency International. (2024). Australia. https://www.transparency.org/en/countries/australia. Accessed on September 23, 2024.

Turnbull, T. (2024). *The year the Australian dream died*. British Broadcasting Corporation. https://www.bbc.com/news/world-australia-67723760. Accessed on September 24, 2024.

Van Onselen, P., & Errington, W. (2007). The democratic state as a marketing tool: The permanent campaign in Australia. *Commonwealth & Comparative Politics*, *45*(1), 78–94.

Winchester, T., Hall, J., & Binney, W. (2016). Conceptualizing usage in voting behavior for political marketing: An application of consumer behavior. *Journal of Political Marketing*, *15*(2–3), 259–284.

Positioning Presidents: Non-Political Branding in US Elections[1]

Neil Collins and Patrick Butler

INTRODUCTION

The 2016 presidential election in the United States presented exceptional issues for parties, pundits and public alike. The most extraordinary topic was the rise of Donald J. Trump as the nominee of the Republican Party despite the opposition of the power brokers in that organisation. His election platform included many appeals to populist opinion that appalled most analysts but found favour with large sections of the electorate. Indeed, his election and his behaviour in office continued to enthral and appal. Shortly thereafter, in the Democratic primaries in 2019/20, young American voters responded enthusiastically to the elderly Bernie Sanders, notwithstanding his being perceived as a radically left-of-centre contestant.

This is not a new phenomenon; distinctive personalities and their positioning in the minds of the electorate have historically been important in American politics:

> [George] Washington's actual presence was almost guaranteed to trigger genuine public displays of expressive silence… a real person riding a great white horse – people reported not only that they were speechless, but also that they were able to read profound meaning in the man's face… they could see – even feel – for themselves the most inspiring aspects of the president's character. (Breen, 2016, p. 127)

As Breen (2016, p. 73) notes, the 'iconic image… was the product of carefully crafted political theatre'. It was designed to create the Washington brand that was fashioned for a largely illiterate electorate. As well as employing posters and cartoons, Washington's campaign staff doled out hand-painted portraits and engraved buttons that supporters sewed onto their clothing (Glassman, 2015).

For political scientists, presidential primaries and elections offer analytically-interesting issues of policy, representation, power-broking and societal dynamics. The clash of political ideas is seldom more dramatically rehearsed than during the race to presidency. However, when observed through a marketing analytical lens, a fresh perspective on political campaigning exists that may help clarify often confusing or seemingly inconsistent situations. In political campaigns, the competition between the parties and the candidates may usefully be explained not by the politics of the contest but by the non-political positions candidates take up, and how they are communicated to the electorate. Thus, the marketing analysis here concentrates not on particular policy positions but rather focuses on the place of the candidates in the public's mind on dimensions other than policy relative to their political rivals. Here, politicians are seen as creating a brand by their perceived association with the personal and social features that have meaning and symbolic value to sections of the electorate.

Despite the long-established practice of branding, Winchester et al. (2016, p. 259) assert that an understanding of 'branding philosophies and practices is still a gap in political marketing'. The theory of human branding is applied here to construct a typology using the brand identities of US presidents. A *post hoc* segmentation approach and a longitudinal study sets out the relative market positions of the candidates in presidential elections from the beginning of the 20th century to the present. In doing so, it does not seek to address the significance of the holders of this office as democratic leaders but rather to refocus on some of the explanations for their electoral success. Reviews of earlier presidential election campaigns show that, despite not always consciously marketing, all presidents have leveraged their brand image.

BRANDING POLITICS

In marketing, branding is an essential topic for research because brand is a core concept underpinning an understanding of customer value, market positioning, consumer experience and management performance (Speed et al., 2015).[2] An increasingly significant aspect of political marketing research is the 'human brand', described by Thomson (2006, p. 104) as 'any well-known persona who is the subject of marketing communications efforts'. As Needham and Smith (2015, p. 1) say, '[p]olitical branding has gained increased attention within marketing and political science journals, highlighting the growing consensus that parties and politicians can usefully be conceptualised as brands'.

> Branding is ultimately about forging a differentiating identity, for which people... or person-like qualities... are often used to manufacture. Periodically, individuals themselves become brands... and serve as the primary source of identity. Candidate brands are similar to the latter, where political leaders and their associations define the brand. (Parker, 2012, p. 209)

This review will examine the role played in the brand creation of American presidents in their election campaigns by their character or personality,[3] social background, professional career and political profile.[4] It will attempt to gauge the relationship between human brands and an evolving party system (Speed & Butler, 2011). The typology developed is generalisable and aims to facilitate marketing analysis in other non-American political contests. The power of a typology arises from the ease with which cases can be accurately classified and the degree of insight that is generated by the differences between the ideal types. Accordingly, the paper seeks the simplest possible conceptual framework that yields useful results. It suggests that the brand association of politicians will be affected by two factors – one summarising their social or professional background and the other their relationship to the political system itself. It also seeks to distinguish between those whose political capital derives primarily from a close association with central government and the related establishment and those whose associations are with other political structures.

Brand image is restricted to the presidential candidates' first election to office so that presidential performance is not relevant for the voter. Almost all presidents see their popularity decline in office. As Mueller (1985, p. 233) concluded, if a president aimed to buck this trend, 'he should either (1) be Dwight David Eisenhower or (2) resign the day after inauguration.

CHARACTERISTICS OF THE POLITICAL MARKETING CONTEXT

A well-established literature presents political campaigns as analogous to the product development and launch process in the world of enterprise. In his early contribution to the field of political marketing, Mauser (1983) highlighted some important distinguishing features: commercial markets typically support a large number of business firms, whereas most political systems tolerate only a small number of political parties; markets usually run virtually continuously, whereas elections are periodic; and political organisations are not motivated by the imperatives of profit.

The American political system or marketplace then has its own distinctive characteristics that inform the application of marketing logic and models and that influence the application of positioning and branding strategy. In presidential elections, these include the predominant duopoly structure and related first-past-the-post winner, the exceptional scale of candidate campaign budgets and the interest in, and impact of, the contest internationally. The duopolistic features of party competition in America add to the complications of branding by association because they present

> ... limited channels for the expression of multiple social identities, the Democratic Party became a big tent for constituencies that might remain separate in multiparty systems while the Republican Party incorporated nationalist elements, which become far-right parties elsewhere, under a banner of conservative ideology. (Grossmann & Hopkins, 2016, p. 135)

Also distinctive, given the declaratory absolutes experienced in campaigning, in the American system, the candidate is relatively free to change policy positions; they are not compelled to agree with their Congressional party (Marland & Wagner, 2020). Post-election, the candidate may present policy change as responding to new circumstances or, Volle (2015, p. 1) suggests, for electoral reasons. As Butler and Collins (1994, p. 22) put it, '[a] notable property of political marketing is that the "purchase" is alterable even in the post-purchase setting'.

Critically for the case argued here, this kind of mutability makes it more likely that American voters will rely on unchanging aspects of the candidate before them; brand position takes on the central responsibility of dependability and reliability and trust where volatility characterises the environment and the political domain.

The American presidency offers a particularly useful focus for research on the human brand because of the distinctive role of the person in the party organisation and the constitutional character of the office as the only nationally contested position. As Wattenberg (2016, p. 125) states, 'American presidential elections are inherently personal contests, as unlike in parliamentary systems, voters are able to cast a vote directly for the nation's chief executive'.

Given the complexity of a fully rational voting choice, it is not surprising that brand image offers an attractive heuristic path chosen by a broad range of voters: 'The myth that the better educated are less concerned with personal attributes of presidential candidates than the less educated is simply that – a myth' (Glass, 1985, p. 523).

From the pioneering 1950s work of Campbell et al. onwards, it has been clear that '[p]erceptions of the personal qualities of candidates proved to be of critical importance for partisan turnover in the White House, overcoming evaluations of issues and social groups' (Norpoth, 2009, p. 523). To draw on Holian and Prysby's (2014, pp. 5–6) research on candidate character traits in presidential elections, 'perceptions of the personal traits of the candidates play an important role in presidential elections'. Reviewing the literature, Holian and Prysby (p. 23) offer leadership, competence, integrity and empathy as the traits most often identified as relevant to voters' judgements. These are not policy positions; rather, they are personal, social, perceptual and impressionistic.

At several points in American history, the functions of the presidency have changed. The tenures of Andrew Jackson, Abraham Lincoln, Theodore Roosevelt and Franklin D. Roosevelt are often seen as turning points. For example, from the beginning of the New Deal and the end of the Second World War, the president's responsibilities for the economy became more prominent, though as Lynch (2002, p. 29) argues: 'Government economic policy in the late 19th and early 20th centuries did affect important blocs of voters – specifically farmers and industrial workers – albeit in different ways that government policy affects voters today'.

The elements of the presidential brand may have altered in their salience over time as the functions of the presidency have changed (Lynch, 2002), but, it is argued here, there are significant continuities. And though brand is the focus here, there is no doubt that partisanship and ethnicity influence the individual elector to either cast their vote, even for candidates to whom they are not attracted, or to abstain. Voters' judgements will also be framed by economic and political circumstances such as unemployment, international tension and the moral climate of the time. Similarly, the cleavages formed by the Civil War weighed more heavily than any brand association based, for example, on class or personality traits, for most presidential elections. Party allegiance is generally long term, but 'it can change under some circumstances. In particular, national crises have had large effects on the distribution of partisanship' (Lewis-Beck, 2014, p. 401).

Such fundamental shifts are rare. Yet, even if brand considerations were overridden by the power of the dominant political cleavages, each successful presidential candidate seeks to project an image that will resonate with some or all sections of the electorate. Further, though their likely behaviour may be predictable, voters do make choices and their ultimate decision is influenced, in part, by the characteristics of the offer before them. As Michael Deaver, Ronald Reagan's campaign manager, said before the 2000 presidential election: 'People are going to make their decision based on the impression a candidate makes more than anything else' (as cited in Boller, 1999, p. 419).

Simply by being elected, the individuals who held the position of President of the United States were successful to some degree in establishing a brand image. Of course historical circumstances, the quality of their opponents and other factors influenced their success.

Nevertheless, the politics in each of the periods favoured different brands by association. So, for instance, if the parties are more polarised at elite level in the current party system, it may favour the outsider. In the United States, as Kuo and McCarty (2015, p. 54) point out, 'since the 1970s, ideological divisions have increased polarization between the Republican and Democratic parties... Congress has become increasingly unproductive... Public trust in democratic institutions has declined considerably, and partisanship in the electorate [has] exacerbated polarization in national politics'.

AMERICAN PRESIDENTIAL BRANDING THROUGH HISTORY

While this article covers the elected presidents since 1901,[5] the 1840 'Log Cabin Campaign' between William Henry Harrison and John Tyler represented a turning point in campaign tactics (Gunderson, 1977) and highlighted the critical influence of personalities and what we now refer to as the human brand. A rhetorical attack on Harrison by *The Baltimore Republican* greatly misjudged the public mood and seemed to denigrate the hardworking frontier community: 'Give him a barrel of hard cider and a pension of two thousand a year, and... he will sit the remainder of his days in his log cabin' (as cited in Davies, 2002, p. 14). Symbols and mock-ups of log cabins appeared everywhere and the Whig candidate defeated Tyler handsomely:

> During the 1844 campaign, techniques used in the 1840's Log Cabin extravaganza were more widely applied and further refined – although 'refined' is perhaps not the most appropriate word for the frenzied rallies, parades, "poll-raisings", "musters", picnics and barbecues used to arouse mass enthusiasm. (Benson, 2015, p. 124)

The campaign became the touchstone for successful branding by association. As Brookes (2012) explains the trope: 'to live up to a "log cabin" ideal... candidates need to "connect with majority values," showing that they experience "common emotion with uncommon intensity"'. There is a great wealth of research on American elections to demonstrate that 'voters use information shortcuts to electoral decisions by making inferences about candidates based on the candidate's social, political and demographic characteristics' (McDermott, 2009, p. 606).

Much has been made of the changing technologies available to presidential candidates such as radio, television, the internet and social media. While changes to the media landscape may not have changed the fundamentals of the brand, the near saturation news cover gave rise to what Tulis (1987, p. 18) called the 'rhetorical presidency', a process of 'active and continuous presidential leadership of popular opinion'. Here, the assumption is made that, whatever the technological or communication means available, the brand projected is unaltered. As Schlozman et al. (2010, p. 489) speculate, the effect of online communications may be not to raise political activity but instead to repackage it.

Nevertheless, it does make sense to suggest that the use of the media reflected the sensibilities of the period:

> Candidates began to campaign for themselves in the middle decades of the [19th] century, with little of the damage that self-promotion had caused earlier. In the 1820s and 1830s, self-promotion was deemed about a badge of dishonor for any candidate. One Jacksonian stalwart expressed the common wisdom of the age when he noted that those with the 'lust for office' deserved no respect. (Baldasty, 1992, p. 38)

After the 1850s, explicit campaigning became the norm, though candidates had brand images before then as well as prototype campaign managers. Even the best-known non-campaigning presidential candidate of the 19th century, William McKinley, who ran in 1896, had previously been a vigorous congressional candidate. In the presidential election itself, his strategist Mark Hanna sought to portray him as 'the advance agent of prosperity' (Deskins et al., 2010, p. 258) and the candidate gave speeches to all who turned up to his Ohio home. By the time of the McKinley 'non-campaign', the political parties were themselves established and expensive organisations.[6]

AMERICAN PRESIDENTIAL BRANDING THROUGH ASSOCIATION

Brand association is taken here to be both positive and negative information related to a brand in a consumer's memory (Keller, 1993). As French and Smith (2013, p. 1357) state, 'brand information is recalled from memory by an "activation" process when one association stimulates the recall of another, linked association'.

For a sceptical political 'customer', a candidate's association with positive images or ideals can be more important than overt promotional tactics. As Lilleker (2014, p. 199) suggests in a review of communications theory:

> ... many citizens across democracies will have low interest, or low involvement, in politics and so be likely to rely on the peripheral processing of political communications....it means that simple images, phrases and slogans come stored in the schema of the receiver, so forming associations.

This chapter proposes a branding typology to examine the electoral success of recent American presidents with particular reference to their background, their professional career and political experience. For example, cowboy imagery, military background, public service record and family values are assessed as signifiers relevant to holding presidential office. In relation to the childhood home especially, associations with rural, small town or farming images, which play an important role in the American cultural imagination, are examined. As with charismatic leaders as understood in the psychological literature, references to their social background help candidates associate themselves with 'a collective's history and tradition, their own identification with followers, shared values and moral justifications, and so forth' (Emrich et al., 2001, p. 527).

Morreale (1996, p. 9) suggests one phenomenon central to this model and analysis: that all presidential candidates fall into one of two categories depending on where they line up on the dual promise contained in America's core myth – the American Dream of rugged individualism and a caring and united nation:

> ... presidential candidates' images... typically emphasize one or other of the myths... They are wise and virtuous leaders whose unique talents enable them to rise above the people: or they are populist men of the people who are mere instruments of the popular will.

The contrasting associations were neatly displayed in one of the closest races in recent time during which Al Gore was presented on his web site as 'a candidate who appeared active by interacting with ordinary American citizens, dressing casually, and appearing in places like schools, restaurants, and kitchens... By contrast, Bush's images seemed to convey a dignified leader' (Verser & Wicks, 2006, p. 194).

Following Speed et al. (2015), the analysis here will examine brand authenticity and brand authority in the context of American presidential electoral competition. As in marketing more generally:

> ... authenticity is used to refer to the genuineness, reality or truth of something... Consumers experience authenticity differently and use a range of cues to evaluate the authenticity of an object, which may be based on their interest in, and knowledge of, a subject. (Napoli et al., 2014, p. 1091)

Brand authenticity addresses the level of social association of the candidate; brand authority relates to the level of competence of the individual (Cecciobelli & Di Gregorio, 2022)

The analysis here presents a wider set of associations by which candidates seek their brand identity. It also assumes that 'effective campaigns coordinate images, commercials, news releases, and speeches in ways that will reinforce reoccurring themes of the candidates' (Verser & Wicks, 2006, p. 182).

For purposes of this typology, the broad range of significant and positive brand associations are sorted into two groups which are treated as binary variables to form discrete categories:

1. The source of primary band association derived from either social factors or professional factors (Social–Professional).
2. The source of brand association derived from either a close relationship with the Washington DC political system or an outsider position separate from that establishment (Insider–Outsider).

The four ensuing categories are:

Social–Insider described here as Champion.
Social–Outsider described as Challenger.
Professional–Insider described as Counsel.
Professional–Outsider described as Combatant.

The strength of these categories is dependent on their ability to offer insights into the use of branding by association as applied to politicians. Importantly, the complexity of human identity as well as the multifaceted nature of brand means the categories are not entirely independent of each other. The categories *insider* and *outsider* need to reflect the dominant brand association rather than the formal titles (see King, 2002). Similarly, the brand association with business as a profession does not imply eschewing public service; rather, it is about being viewed as not primarily a politician. While Carter served as governor of Georgia, for example, his brand position here is primarily based on his social/personal identity as a champion of human rights and his work on peace accords. Similarly, as Wilson (1992, p. 118) writes of Hoover:

> He projected an image of service, efficiency, morality, and prosperity... It was an image that will serve Hoover well in the presidential election of 1928... Hoover... a self-effacing ideologue... perfected the systematic administrative use of publicity and then used it to popularise the progressive ideal of the nonpartisan manager of government.

In seeking to identify the President of the United States according to their brand, this article does not suggest that each president can only be associated with one brand. Indeed, it is likely that individual segments of the market associated each individual with differing images. As Newman (1994, p. 71) puts it:

> ... political images do not exist apart from the political objects (or their symbolic surrogates) that stimulate political thoughts, feelings, and inclinations... [A] candidate's image consists of how voters perceive him, sections based upon both the subjective appraisals made by the voters and the messages utterances, attributes, qualities, etc. transmitted by the candidates.

It is also not suggested that the brand of each politician was their most obvious characteristic. So, for example, Kennedy was the first Catholic president, but this was not an essential part of his brand image.[7] Referring to that brand image, O'Brien (2014, p. 82) suggests that 'Kennedy retained an aura of youthfulness, now enhanced by the quality of maturity and its associated experience, wisdom and judgement. Pictures of Kennedy with his wife Jacqueline and two children promote the devoted husband, father and all-round family man'.

Similarly, we are not suggesting that each president consciously cultivated brand but by habitually using references to his background, profession, personal traits, etc. they may become associated with a particular brand image.

Figure 3.1 shows the US presidents since 1901 in these brand categories:

In this schema, the 'Champion' is an insider whose social associations engender trust and whose record lends credibility. So, for example, as his vice president, Charles G. Dawes, wrote: 'The popularity of Coolidge, notwithstanding the opposition he has encountered from a Congress nominally Republican, is due to the fact that he, not it, best understood the people and they him' (as cited in Fleser, 1990, p. 51). Similarly, Truman emphasised continuity with the New Deal, strong leadership in foreign affairs, a commitment to social welfare and civil rights, integrity and honesty and the defence of democratic values. Nevertheless, he was also known for his humble rural background and was the last president not to have a university degree.

The 'Challenger' may be similarly admired as reflecting the values of an important constituency, but their credibility based on having worked the political system of Washington may be questionable. Often their political experience is outside the mainstream and difficult for most voters to assess. As Winter (1998, p. 370) suggests, based on his analysis of his speeches, Clinton's appeal was based on his 'high goals and aspirations, tinged with warmth and compassion. But [despite] all his experience as governor of Arkansas, he might not be comfortable or effective in the quicksands of Washington federal politics'. Similarly, FDR, when first elected in 1932, despite being from a prominent political family and having been Assistant Secretary of the Navy under Wilson, pitched himself as a challenger to the status quo and traditional power structures.

The 'Counsel' draws strength from the presumption of credibility and being associated with achievement in their profession, even if that profession is essentially long-standing political office and Washington establishment insider status. They may not enjoy as much social empathy but they are expected to achieve policy goals: 'Nixon sought to close the growing gap between the elites and ordinary people. Typically, he tailored his policies to left-leaning opinion leaders while crafting his rhetoric to propitiate the right-leaning "silent majority"' (Barone, 1999, p. 24).

To be a 'Combatant', the successful candidate appeals on the basis of assumed professional standing but being untainted by strong association

Relation to core Washington DC political system

Source of primary brand association

	Insider	**Outsider**
Derived from social factors	**Champion** Harding 1921–23 Coolidge 1923–29 Truman 1945–53 Kennedy 1961–63	**Challenger** Roosevelt F.D.1933–45 Carter 1977–81 Reagan 1981–89 Clinton 1993–2001 Obama 2009–17
Derived from professional factors	**Counsel** Roosevelt T. 1901–09 Taft 1909–13 Johnson 1963–69 Nixon 1969–74 Bush GHW 1989–93 Biden 2021–2025	**Combatant** Wilson 1913–21 Hoover 1929–33 Eisenhower 1953–61 Bush GW 2001–09 Trump 2017–2021

Figure 3.1 US Presidents Positioned Relative to Social-Professional and Insider-Outsider Factors

with the central government. So, for example, Norpoth (2009, p. 527) suggests that:

> A detailed breakdown of favorable references [in opinion surveys] to Eisenhower... points to some explanations... war hero, above all, with experience, a reputation for both leadership and honesty... This was a rare mix of qualities, and all of it acquired before the candidate's first day in the White House.

DISCUSSION

As a 'champion' in this framework because of his 'social' brand, Warren G Harding was owner/publisher of a small-town newspaper in his native Ohio. Given the low reputation he now enjoys, it is worth noting that Harding was seen on election as 'a "regular guy" – culturally distinct from such elitists, bluebloods, and academics as Franklin Roosevelt and Woodrow Wilson – a representative of American small-town masculinity' (Fine, 1996, p. 1171). The 'regular guy' image can be enhanced even by an apparent lack of rhetorical skill, but he was regarded as the consummate 'insider' party man.

Coolidge also presented the image of an insider best suited to running Washington efficiently. Voters were urged to 'keep cool with Coolidge' (Boller, 1999, p. 216). It is difficult for a vice president-cum-candidate to avoid association with the previous regime be that an advantage or burden. William Taft, who seems to have found electioneering a real chore, also presented himself as the competent administrator 'perfecting the machinery' (Lurie, 2011, p. 83).

Richard Nixon is positioned as professional insider: his time in the national limelight was surpassed only by John Quincy Adams and he was nominated for national office by his party on five occasions. He nevertheless defeated the incumbent vice president in 1968 at a time of great national turmoil in part by spanning the divide. Nevertheless:

> During the 20th century, the stature of vice presidential candidates improved. This could be attributed to changes in campaigning style, as well as changes in the role of the media in elections. As vice presidents began to actively campaign during the general election, they became known to the electorate and were better able to build their own constituency. (Marchant-Shapiro, 2015, p. 49)

Another set of insiders are vice presidents who finished out their predecessors' terms. Since 1901, only Theodore Roosevelt, Calvin Coolidge, Harry Truman and Lyndon Johnson were successful presidential candidates at the subsequent election. Of these, Johnson was the most clearly associated with the effective management of Washington and a classic insider 'counsel' here. As Goodwin (2015, n.p.) suggests, he 'played a dominant role... in transforming opportunity into achievement... the perception of Johnson – one that was accurate and that he encouraged – [was] as the gargantuan manipulator, the tireless practitioner of political skills'.

The 'challenger' is typified by former governors Reagan and Clinton. In terms of an electoral competitive advantage, the more turmoil, the better the chances for Washington establishment outsiders. On the outsider criterion, executive experience can derive from political roles apart from federal or Washington positions such as state governor, in particular. According to Marchant-Shapiro (2015, p. 91), due to their proactive role in the Populist Era:

> ... governors became increasingly more influential politically and increasingly more likely to become powerful contenders for the presidency. Today, it is commonplace to assume that service as the chief executive of a state is a good preparation for service as a national chief executive.

As Ambar (2014, p. 92) suggests, Reagan, Clinton and GW Bush were 'equipped – unlike senators or vice presidents – to take office with the mandate of outsiders'. So the prefix Governor, as opposed to Senator or Vice President, can have an impact by association, though not inevitably[8]. Similarly, in 1979, 'Jimmy Carter, a relatively unknown outsider who had served one term as governor of Georgia and before that as a state senator in Georgia, won the Democratic nomination [and] went on to defeat incumbent president, Gerald Ford' (Jackson, 2014, p. 94). Barack Obama was also an outsider in Washington terms:

> ... in the 2008 American presidential election... Hillary Clinton [had] been in the public eye on the national level for a period of 16 years... Unlike Hillary, Barack Obama, the former senator from Illinois, with seven years in the Illinois state Senate and one term in the U.S. Senate, was a Washington outsider, starting from scratch. (Ilie, 2009, p. 548)

As Critchlow (2015) observes: 'Successful presidential candidates from the earliest days in American politics ran as outsiders and against the status quo'. Indeed, 'the [George W.] Bush Web site presented the candidate as a professional public servant ready for leadership' (Verser & Wicks, 2006, p. 189).

Although as outlined above, the analysis here does not cover incumbent presidents seeking another term, the insider's Washington experience is leveraged as an advantageous primary brand association. In all, 27 presidents have had experience in Congress – six in the Senate only, twelve in the House only and nine in both (Marchant-Shapiro, 2015, p. 69). Joe Biden's campaign platform relied almost entirely on his professional insider status as the foil to opponent Trump's period in office. Washington experience can, of course, also be framed as disadvantage. Trump, Eisenhower and Arthur were the last presidents not to hold federal or state-wide office but, even among other politicians, whether the key association is as a Washington insider or outside is significant.[9] As Ambar (2014, p. 76) observes, 'Washington insiders proved more electable to the presidency during periods of relative consensus, as was the case between 1945 and 1976'.

The category *social* is taken to incorporate the brand appeal of a 'humble background'. This may be set within various narratives, but triumphing over social disadvantage to achieve success is a common form of brand by association in America. For example, candidates Reagan and Obama appealed to different demographics, but their brand referenced a common theme of overcoming challenging family circumstances. The social category is also taken to encompass the 'og cabin',[10] working class, small town and rural associations of successful presidential candidates. Of the Trumans, Donovan (1996, p. 146) suggests that on arrival, '[i]n contrast to the aristocratic Roosevelts, they imparted the flavour of small-town life to the White House'.

Infrequently, the big city social background is seen as an asset with which to have your brand associated, but:

> Michael Dukakis [unsuccessful candidate, 1988] is one of the only candidates who makes a virtue out of coming from East Coast suburb, and who fails to pay tribute to America's heartland. In his [campaign] film, his cousin Olympia Dukakis takes viewers on a tour of Brookline, one of Boston's wealthy areas. The image lacks mythic resonance. (Morreale, 1996, p. 9)

Much more common in the campaign films, the genre of which candidates have complete control, are references to evoke 'the agrarian myth that equates virtue with the land' (Morreale, 1996, p. 9). In relation to the common touch, Democratic candidates have, at least since FDR, enjoyed the advantage as their party 'still enjoys a groundswell of good feeling for favoring the "common man," "little people," "working people," the "poor," and the "needy," whereas the Republican Party is chastised for being in bed with "big business," the "rich," the "upper class," etc'. (Norpoth, 2009, p. 525). This advantage has been reduced somewhat by Trump's championing of the 'brand of aggressive anti-elite and ethno-nationalist politics' (Pierson, 2017, p. S109).

Another dimension of branding by association categorised here as social is that of *family values*. In the American context, family values are often assumed to be more firmly rooted in small town or rural contexts, but they are also appealed to more directly. Thus, for example: 'Pictures of the young and attractive John F. Kennedy family contributed to the presumption on the part of the audience that the former president represented family values' (Verser & Wicks, 2006, p. 182).

The family values theme was given something of a twist by Bill Clinton in that his 'man of the people stature was strengthened by his standing up for his mother and younger brother against his alcoholic father. Herbert Hoover, on the other hand, always hid his 'emotionally and materially insecure childhood' while exaggerating his business and technical success' (Wilson, 1992, p. 15).

As Norpoth (2009, p. 529) states: 'Without the test of the office, the challenger finds it nearly impossible to impress the public [on the issue of leadership] unless he has proven his leadership ability in a non-political career'. The *professional* category can also cover those whose brand is associated with success in a non-political arena. Calvin Coolidge (1925) famously said to have remarked that 'the chief business of the American people is business'. Success in business suggests to some voters that similar talents would be usefully applied to politics. As a *New York Times* commentary on a 2016 primary candidate with significant business success summarises the association, 'the American dream still holds sway... In general, Americans, even those with few means, end up aligning themselves with the wealthy in the hope that they, too, will eventually get rich' (Covert, 2016 n.p.).

Twenty-five presidents have had legal qualifications, including 10 of the last 20, but few have leveraged this profession as a brand association (Gross, 2009). John Adams, Rutherford B. Hayes and Benjamin Harrison are among the most notable lawyer-presidents in terms of brand image but none are in the group analysed here. In contrast, although 'military voters have rarely had much impact in swaying elections' (Inbody, 2016, p. 156), a professional background in the military can be a major branding clue for a candidate. Clearly, George Washington's brand image is as a successful military leader but others, such as Andrew Jackson, Zachary Taylor and Ulysses S. Grant, also became president being associated with professional military success. In the post-1901 group, Theodore Roosevelt and Dwight D. Eisenhower also used their military fame to establish their brands. It is not entirely clear, however, whether the favourable association is with rank or perceived leadership qualities: 'as Eisenhower's case indicates, military service all by itself conveys little advantage with the American electorate' (Norpoth, 2009, p. 528). For John F. Kennedy and George H. W. Bush their military decorations supplemented other branding by association.

Successful businesspeople have increasingly entered politics in recent years. They point to their private sector success as evidence of their ability and argue that their professional skills and experience are transferable to high office. Hoover, George H.W. Bush and, most recently, Trump used their professional achievements in business to strengthen their brand.

The promise to tackle the problems 'inside the Belt Way' could be a winner with the non-Washington candidate: 'This critique partisanship is one thing that Barack Obama and his challenger, John McCain, agreed on in the 2008 campaign. Each promised to defang the poisonous partisanship in Washington and seek bipartisan solutions to the nation's problems' (Jackson, 2014, p. 94).

In 2016, one of the two candidates was distinctly outside the Washington milieu:

> One, a former senator, former secretary of state, a former candidate for president, the spouse of a former president, and the heir apparent to the outgoing two-term president, was the embodiment of the very political establishment that populist uprisings rail against. The other candidate... wasn't. (Schier, 2017, p. 3)

CONCLUSIONS

The brand positioning typology offered here is based on a longitudinal study. It reflects the notion that voters, like customers, make choices based not on detailed knowledge but broad understandings of the offers being made. The brand is a coping mechanism to facilitate complex decisions. In the cases examined, brand characteristics allow judgements to be made based on which social cleavages are most pressing to the particular voter. The analysis focuses not on specific policies but rather how the electorate imagine a particular candidate relative to his opponents. The brand matters in elections and it is conditioned by associations among the electorate.

Electioneering has evolved. The sophisticated, research-driven, data-based intelligence now driving campaign direction and decision-making is, in one sense, a long way from earlier campaign strategies. But, in another way, the fundamentals are the same. A value judgement informed by personal circumstance and social position is translated into a decision to vote for a candidate or to abstain. The intellectual capacities and constraints of voters are unchanged. The mechanics of the electoral system will condition the process of voting and the ability to express a range of preference. Nevertheless, on the day of an election, the voter is sovereign.

Motivating the study is the realisation that the assigning of presidents to the non-political categories results in some highly unlikely bedfellows that solicit explanation. The analysis looks at the individual's brand on the day of taking office for the first time. Thus, for example, Trump and Obama are both seen as outsiders though their degree of distance from the 'swamp' varied. At his inauguration, Trump (2017, n.p.) declared: 'a small group in our Nation's Capital has reaped the rewards of Government while the people have borne the cost'. Righting the imbalance of power was also promised by Obama (2009, n.p.): 'our time of standing pat, of protecting narrow interests and putting off unpleasant decisions – that time has surely passed'. One promised to 'remake America', the other to 'make America great again'.

Though this analysis primarily addresses a marketing and political science audience, its starting point is confirmed by other research. In their anthropological study, Lempert and Silverstein (2012) also suggest that presidential campaigns are essentially more about a candidate's brand than the issues debated. For them, the quantity of material in the public arena during presidential campaigns militates against rational discourse. The psychology of voting has similarly informed the dominant model used by political science since the 1960s (McDermott, 2009; Steenbergen, 2010).

The human branding literature relied upon here does not radically question the analysis offered by other disciplines though, like them, it sits incongruously with democratic rhetoric. It also offers similarities between candidates in terms of brand that may seem counter-intuitive in the popular narrative suggesting, as it does, the same category for Reagan and Obama or Nixon and Johnson. Though some analysts may disagree with the position assigned to individual presidents, the article hopes to offer a heuristically useful typology of a kind that may be developed to allow comparisons between not only American but also other presidential systems.

Context and evolving political systems and priorities are important: the current rise in the influence of populism has focused increasing attention on the head of government as the nation's leader in many countries even with very different institutional characters. The COVID-19 pandemic also emphasised the role of the political leader in the presentation and coordination of the response to a definite emergency. The personal brand of individual politicians is likely to become even more critical at the next round of elections as people reward their champions or flock to the challenger.

Notes

1 An earlier version of this paper is published as Collins (2020).
2 Despite this, '[t]here is no consensus about how to define "brand"', according to Jones and Bonevac (2013, p. 112).
3 Character is assumed to be developed early in life but to be mutable, and personality is taken to be the superstructure of character. See Renshon (2013).
4 For a psychological typology, see Rubenzer et al. (2000).

5 Excluding vice-presidents who assumed office on the death or resignation of the incumbent.
6 The 1896 McKinley 'non-campaign' cost $3,350,000. See Davies (2002).
7 Kennedy did benefit from the voters of Catholics who normally supported Republicans but this was outweighed by anti-Catholic support for Nixon. See Polsby et al. (2008, p. 25).
8 Though in the early decades having been Secretary of State seemed to confer an advantage on Buchanan, who was the last holder to become President.
9 Chester A. Arthur assumed the presidency on the death of Garfield in 1881. Not included in the analysis.
10 James Garfield was the last president to live in a log cabin. See Feldman (2005).

REFERENCES

Ambar, S. M. (2014). The rise of sunbelt governors: Conservative outsiders in the white house. *Presidential Studies Quarterly*, *44*(1), 72–94.

Baldasty, G. J. (1992). *The commercialization of news in the nineteenth century*. University of Wisconsin Press.

Barone, M. (1999, September 20). *Nixon's America* (pp. 20–27). US News and World Report.

Benson, L. (2015). *The concept of Jacksonian democracy: New York as a test case*. Princeton University Press.

Boller, P. F. (1999). *Presidential campaigns: From George Washington to George W. Bush*. Oxford University Press.

Breen, T. H. (2016). *George Washington's journey: The president forges a new nation*. Simon and Schuster.

Brookes, S. (2012, October 15). The art of the campaign Gaffe: What we learn when candidates stuff up. *The Conversation*. https://theconversation.com/the-art-of-the-campaign-gaffe-what-we-learn-when-candidates-stuff-up-9982

Butler, P., & Collins, N. (1994). Political marketing: Structure and process. *European Journal of Marketing*, *28*(1), 19–34.

Cecciobelli, D., & Di Gregorio, L. (2022). The triangle of leadership: Authenticity, competence and ordinariness in political marketing. *Journal of Political Marketing*, *21*(2), 113–125.

Collins, N. (2020). Campaigning by human branding: Associating with American presidents. *Fudan Journal of the Humanities and Social Sciences*, *13*, 495–515.

Coolidge, C. (1925, January 17). *Address to the American society of newspaper editors*. The American Presidency Project. UC Santa Barbara. http://www.presidency.ucsb.edu/ws/?pid=24180.

Covert, B. (2016, March 3). Whose American dream flies? *New York Times*.

Critchlow, D. (2015, August 21). Hillary Clinton's problem: She can't run against Washington. *The Conversation*. https://theconversation.com/hillary-clintons-problem-she-cant-run-against-washington-45128

Davies, P. J. (2002). The material culture of US elections. *Journal of Political Marketing*, *1*(2–3), 9–24.

Deskins, D. R., Walton, H., & Puckett, S. C. (2010). *Presidential elections, 1789–2008: County, state, and national mapping of election data*. University of Michigan Press.

Donovan, R. J. (1996). *Conflict and crisis: The presidency of Harry S. Truman, 1945–1948*. University of Missouri Press.

Emrich, C. G., Brower, H. H., Feldman, J. M., & Garland, H. (2001). Images in words: Presidential rhetoric, charisma, and greatness. *Administrative Science Quarterly*, *46*(3), 527–555.

Feldman, R. T. (2005). *James Garfield*. Twenty-First Century Books.

Fine, G. A. (1996). Reputational entrepreneurs and the memory of incompetence: Melting supporters, partisan warriors, and images of president Harding. *American Journal of Sociology*, *101*(5), 1159–1193.

Fleser, A. F. (1990). *A rhetorical study of the speaking of Calvin Coolidge*. Edwin Mellen Press.

French, A., & Smith, G. (2013). Measuring brand association strength: A consumer based brand equity approach. *European Journal of Marketing*, *47*(8), 1356–1367.

Glass, D. (1985). Presidential candidates: Who focuses on their personal attributes? *Public Opinion Quarterly*, *49*(4), 517–534.

Glassman, E. T. (2015, May 18). The branding of an American president. *The Conversation*. http://theconversation.com/the-branding-of-an-american-president-40451

Goodwin, D. K. (2015). *Lyndon Johnson and the American dream*. Open Road Media.

Gross, N. (2009). *America's lawyer-presidents: From law office to oval office*. ABA Museum of Law.

Grossmann, M., & Hopkins, D. A. (2016). *Ideological republicans and group interest democrats: The asymmetry of American party politics*. Oxford University Press.

Gunderson, R. G. (1977). *The log-cabin campaign*. Greenwood Press.

Holian, D. B., & Prysby, C. L. (2014). *Candidate character traits in presidential elections*. Routledge.

Ilie, C. (2009). Talking the talk, walking the walk: Candidate profiles in election campaign interviews. In G. Gobber, S. Cantarini, S. Cigada, M. C. Gatti, & S. Gilardoni (Eds.), *Proceedings of the IADA workshop word meaning in argumentative dialogue* (Vol. II). Università Cattolica.

Inbody, D. S. (2016). *The soldier votes: Wall, politics, and the Ballot in America*. Palgrave Macmillan.

Jackson, J. S. (2014). *The American political party system: Continuity and change over ten presidential elections*. Brookings Institution Press.

Jones, C., & Bonevac, D. (2013). An evolved definition of the term 'brand': Why branding has a branding problem. *Journal of Brand Strategy*, *2*(2), 112–120.

Keller, K. L. (1993). Conceptualizing, measuring, and managing customer-based brand equity. *Journal of Marketing*, *57*(1), 1–22.

King, A. (2002). The outsider as political leader: The case of Margaret thatcher. *British Journal of Political Science*, *32*(3), 435–454.

Kuo, D., & McCarty, N. (2015). Democracy in America, 2015. *Global Policy*, *6*(S1), 49–55.

Lempert, M., & Silverstein, M. (2012). *Creatures of politics: Media, message and the American presidency*. Indiana University Press.

Lewis-Beck, M. S. (2014). *The American voter revisited*. University of Michigan Press.

Lilleker, D. G. (2014). *Political communication and cognition*. Palgrave Macmillan.

Lurie, J. (2011). *William Howard Taft: The Travails of a progressive conservative*. Cambridge University Press.

Lynch, G. P. (2002). US presidential elections in the 19th century: Why culture and the economy both mattered. *Polity*, *35*(1), 29–50.

Marchant-Shapiro, T. (2015). *Professional pathways to the presidency*. Palgrave Macmillan.

Marland, A., & Wagner, A. (2020). Scripted messengers: How party discipline and branding turn election candidates and legislators into brand ambassadors. *Journal of Political Marketing*, *19*(1–2), 54–73.

Mauser, G. A. (1983). *Political marketing: An approach to campaign strategy*. Praeger.

McDermott, M. L. (2009). Voting for myself: Candidate and voter group associations over time. *Electoral Studies*, *28*(4), 606–614.

Morreale, J. (1996). Playing politics: Mythical portraiture in presidential campaign film. *Visual Communication Quarterly*, *3*(1), 8–12.

Mueller, J. E. (1985). *War, presidents, and public opinion*. University Press of America.

Napoli, J., Dickinson, S. J., Beverland, M. B., & Farrelly, F. (2014). Measuring consumer-based brand authenticity. *Journal of Business Research*, *67*(6), 1090–1098.

Needham, C., & Smith, G. (2015). Introduction: Political branding. *Journal of Political Marketing*, *14*(1–2).

Newman, B. (1994). *The Marketing of the president: Political marketing as campaign strategy*. SAGE.

Norpoth, H. (2009). From Eisenhower to Bush: Perceptions of candidates and parties. *Electoral Studies*, *28*(4), 523–532.

Obama, B. (2009, January 20). Obama's inaugural address: The full text. *Time*. http://content.time.com/time/politics/article/0,8599,1872715-2,00.html

O'Brien, D. (2014). *Classical Masculinity and the spectacular body on film: The mighty sons of Hercules*. Palgrave Macmillan.

Parker, B. T. (2012). Candidate brand equity valuation: A comparison of U.S. presidential candidates during the 2008 primary election campaign. *Journal of Political Marketing*, *11*(3), 208–230.

Pierson, P. (2017). American hybrid: Donald Trump and the strange merger of populism and plutocracy. *British Journal of Sociology*, *68*(S1), 105–S119. https://onlinelibrary.wiley.com/doi/full/10.1111/1468-4446.12323

Polsby, N. W., Wildavsky, A. B., & Hopkins, D. A. (2008). *Presidential elections: Strategies and structures of American politics*. Rowman & Littlefield.

Renshon, S. A. (2013). *The psychological assessment of presidential candidates*. Routledge.

Rubenzer, S. J., Faschingbauer, T. R., & Ones, D. S. (2000). Assessing the US presidents using the revised NEO personality inventory. *Assessment*, *7*(4), 403–420.

Schier, S. E. (2017). *The Trump presidency: Outsider in the oval office*. Rowman & Littlefield.

Schlozman, K. L., Verba, S., & Brady, H. E. (2010). Weapon of the strong? Participatory inequality and the internet. *Perspectives on Politics*, *8*(2), 487–509.

Speed, R., & Butler, P. (2011). Towards a typology of human brand – Organisation relationships. In *Proceedings of Academy of Marketing Annual Conference*. University of Liverpool.

Speed, R., Butler, P., & Collins, N. (2015). Human branding in political marketing: Applying contemporary branding thought to political parties and their leaders. *Journal of Political Marketing*, *14*(1–2), 129–151.

Steenbergen, M. R. (2010). The new political psychology of voting. In T. Faas, K. Arzheimer, & S. Roßteutscher (Eds.), *Information – Wahrnehmung – Emotion: Politische Psychologie in der Wahl-und Einstellungsforschung* (pp. 13–31). VS Verlag.

Thomson, M. (2006). Human brands: Investigating antecedents to consumers' strong attachments to celebrities. *Journal of Marketing*, *70*(3), 104–119.

Trump, D. (2017, January 20). Donald Trump inauguration speech full transcript. *Belfast Telegraph*. https://www.belfasttelegraph.co.uk/news/world-news/donald-trump-inauguration-speech-full-transcript-35386639.html

Tulis, J. (1987). *The rhetorical presidency*. Princeton University Press.

Verser, R., & Wicks, R. H. (2006). Managing those impressions: The use of images on presidential candidate web sites during the 2000 campaign. *Journal of Communication*, *56*(1), 178–197.

Volle, J. J. (2015). *Twenty-five years of GOP presidential nominations: Threading the needle*. Palgrave Macmillan.

Wattenberg, M. P. (2016). The declining relevance of candidate personal attributes in presidential elections. *Presidential Studies Quarterly*, *46*(1), 125–139.

Wilson, J. H. (1992). *Herbert hoover: Forgotten progressive*. Waveland Press.

Winchester, T., Hall, J., & Binney, W. (2016). Conceptualising usage in voter behaviour for political marketing: An application of consumer behaviour. *Journal of Political Marketing*, *15*(2–3), 259–284.

Winter, D. G. (1998). A motivational analysis of the Clinton first term and the 1996 presidential campaign. *The Leadership Quarterly*, *9*(3), 367–376.

Negative (Issue) Campaigning: Towards a Decision-Making Process and Framework

Roger Mortimore and Paul Baines

INTRODUCTION

Political marketing campaigns around the world make frequent use of negative campaigning, to gain an advantage by informing voters of their opponents' failings. This is nothing new: there have probably been negative campaigns for as long as there have been election campaigns (Haselmayer, 2019); nevertheless, it is a controversial practice. Moreover, its use may be increasing: for example, in an analysis of the 2016 US Presidential campaign ads, negative ads were far more ubiquitous than in previous campaigns, by both the Donald Trump and Hillary Clinton campaigns (Parry-Giles et al., 2017).

It is the more extreme examples that are most prominent and longest-remembered, often depending primarily upon character assassination, and such campaigns are often treated as synonymous with the entire notion of 'negative campaigning'[1]; they are also frequently designed with the intention of persuading more through their emotional impact than through rational argument. The practice has been refined to a fine art (Mark, 2009) and is typically implemented using malicious, targeted 15-second and 30-second advertising spots assassinating the characters of political opponents. Consider, for example, three of perhaps the most famous examples in US election history: the daisy spot campaign (1964) where Lyndon B. Johnson, the Democratic Presidential candidate, implied that Barry Goldwater, the Republican Presidential nominee, would make use of nuclear weapons to end the Vietnam War in 1964[2]; the 'Willie Horton' ad used to discredit Michael Dukakis (Democrat) by the Republican campaign for George H.W. Bush in 1988[3]; and the successful Republican 'swift boat veterans for truth' untruthful campaign to discredit John Kerry's run for President despite him being a decorated war hero[4] (McIntyre, 2018). All these negative campaigns were devastating for the opponent targeted in the ad.

Because these advertisements are often hard-hitting, and sometimes economical with the truth, they can be highly controversial as well as being risky for the campaigner. An example was the 'New Labour New Danger' campaign used by the British Conservatives to try to discredit Tony Blair by portraying him with 'demon eyes' in the 1997 British General Election. The ad even won an advertising industry award for having generated £5m of free publicity from a campaign spend of £125,000, despite having been described by the United Kingdom's Advertising Standards Authority as 'unacceptable' (Culf, 1997), and yet the expert consensus was that it failed in its political objectives (Butler & Kavanagh, 1997, pp. 36–8). Similarly, a 1993 advertisement by the Progressive Conservative Party in Canada, appearing to attack Liberal leader Jean Chrétien by focusing on a facial deformity caused by a harmless medical condition, seems to have been directly counter-productive (Haddock & Zanna, 1997) and may have contributed to the Progressive Conservatives' overwhelming defeat.

Nevertheless, not all negative campaigning is nearly as extreme as this and is arguably often much less morally objectionable and serves a useful function (Mattes & Redlawsk, 2015; Mayer, 1996); indeed, much campaigning is sufficiently ambivalent that measures of its negativity are subject to substantial partisan bias (Walter & van der Eijk, 2019). The term as normally used by scholars is much wider and encompasses all elements of a campaign that involve challenging an opponent's credentials or policies rather than proclaiming one's own. Some studies, indeed, classify even comparative claims as a form of negative advertising. Viewed in this light, it is hard to see how any candidate or party could hope to make their case without resorting to negativity on some level (see Lau & Pomper, 2002, pp. 48–49): to argue rationally that they better deserve to be elected than their opponents, they can hardly avoid commenting upon their opponents' capacities and policies as well as their own. Every campaign manager must therefore almost inevitably propose some degree of negative campaigning; the choice they face is more over the balance between positive and negative, and how this mix should be varied across the different issues which the campaign will debate.

Historically, the vast majority of academic papers published about negative campaigning have been concerned with its use in the United States, reflecting not only the size of the political science community in the United States but the number of elections that are held in that country and perhaps also the prevalence of negative campaigning there. Nevertheless, there have been many other studies of the practice in other countries around the world, especially in recent years, some of which have highlighted that conclusions drawn from the American experience are not necessarily universal ones (e.g. Elmelund-Præstekær, 2010; Nai, 2020; Ridout & Walter, 2015; Sigelman & Shiraev, 2002; Walter, 2014). On the other hand, some of the more important of those conclusions, such as that negative campaigning tends to be more widely used by challengers than by incumbents, seem to have much wider validity (Valli & Nai, 2022).

Negative campaigning seems a potentially powerful tool, and much scholarly study of it has concentrated upon assessing its effects. While its most obvious intent is to worsen public perceptions of the targeted opponent, other possible consequences are also frequently posited; these include the possibility that it could be counter-productive for the advertiser and even that it might pose a long-term threat to the democratic health of the nation. It is argued that negative campaigning can distort political discourse, polarize and demobilize the electorate and be used to (mis) dis-inform the electorate (Haselmayer, 2019) and may even result in a net loss of votes rather than a net gain to the campaigner (Lau & Pomper, 2002; Shapiro & Rieger, 1992), presumably especially if poorly designed or poorly executed. Nevertheless, despite considerable academic investigation, there is no consensus on the effectiveness of negative campaigning in securing election victories or on its other impacts (Chou & Lien, 2010; Lau et al., 1999, 2007; Merritt, 1984), nor is there any specific guidance or decision-making framework for practitioners on how to undertake negative campaigning.

Of course, it would be simplistic to suppose either that negative campaigns always work to the advantage of the campaigner or that they never do so. Naturally, therefore, much of the more recent research on the topic seeks to identify the circumstances in which it is most effective and characteristics that may modify its effectiveness, or dissects the techniques used and explores the mechanisms by which it has an impact, whether sociopolitical or psychological. In the former category comes the recognition that in a modern election, the most powerful impact of negative campaigning is often its perceived ability to generate free publicity, given the controversial nature of the claims made: Major and Andersen's (2016) work analyzing the news coverage associated with negative ads bears testament to this, concluding that the free publicity advantages the attacking campaign, allowing it to control the news narrative by ensuring more quoted sources and more favourable headlines compared to the campaign being attacked; similarly, Poljak (2024) finds that using negativity significantly increases politicians' chances of gaining media access. Meanwhile, a growing body of research explores the psychology of the voters faced with such campaigns, and this too often points to more conditional conclusions about their effectiveness, such as the suggestion that advertisements evoking some emotions are more powerful than others (e.g. Petković, 2022; Roseman et al., 2020).

Scholars have also discussed whether it may be more effective for certain classes of candidates: their suggestions include its being more effective on issues where the campaigner is strongest (Damore, 2002) and most effective for challengers running against incumbents (Lau & Pomper, 2002).

A smaller number of papers have also explored the situations in which negative campaigning is used in practice. They have found that: it is most used by candidates who are perceived as weak on personal attributes (Harrington & Hess, 1996), tends to be used by parties or groups rather than by candidates (Dowling & Wicholwsky, 2015) and is more likely to be used by candidates further from the ideological centre (Nai, 2020) and by right-wingers (Valli & Nai, 2022), and more by trailing candidates than by those with a polling lead (Skaperdas & Grofman, 1995). Damore (2002) has also noted that candidates become more likely to turn to negative tactics as election day draws closer, and that candidates who are attacked by their opponents' negative campaigns become more likely to retaliate with negative campaigning of their own. There is also some evidence that negative political advertising on Facebook is more likely to be used by underdog candidates in less competitive races while personal attacks are more likely in competitive races (Auter & Fine, 2016). Meanwhile, Nai et al. (2022) have explored the personality traits of candidates that choose to go negative.

Unfortunately, from a more practical perspective, these studies have all been primarily empirical: they study the decisions that have been made in real elections, but by concentrating on seeking common factors across elections to explain those decisions can only touch upon the contextual features of a specific election in a very broad-brush way. In particular, they offer some insight into whether negative campaigns are adopted in particular circumstances but not into *how* they will be conducted or what their content will be. They tend to implicitly assume that all negative campaigning is one-and-the-same phenomenon, and there has been little attempt to explore why negative campaigning of a particular type or around a particular issue might or might not make strategic sense in a specific situation. Because negative campaigning poses a risk of backfiring, the decision to undertake it is a difficult one – it might conceivably swing the result of an election in either direction – and even if one negative message might be successful in a given case, a different negative message in the same situation might be disastrous. Consequently, a formal framework for analyzing the strategic situation in an election, and how negative campaigning might change that, could help practitioners who have to make such decisions. That is what this chapter attempts to do.

The research study outlined in this chapter provides a structural framework for viewing the issues in an election and how they relate to each candidate and the public's voting behaviour, in order to understand whether positive or negative campaigning on each issue is worthwhile. We postulate that how the public sees issues in the political debate is not symmetrical in its effects on candidates, so that in practice, this framework presents different imperatives to different candidates, and also that, under certain circumstances, this creates a scenario where a negative campaign on a particular issue is the rational choice for at least one of the candidates. Using polling data from the 2019 British General Election campaign, we outline on which issues a given candidate has most to gain from a positive campaign and which from a negative campaign.

THE CONCEPT OF NEGATIVE CAMPAIGNING

To demonstrate the principles, we will consider the possibilities in the last few weeks of an election campaign. In these final few weeks, there are some things that it is too late to change including: the candidates (they are chosen) and their policy programme (that will have been published). Campaigning at this stage depends not upon changing the substance of the 'product' but on improving the impression it makes.

We discuss the simplest situation: an election with a choice between only two viable options for the voters, as is normally the case in a US Presidential election (where there are only two candidates with a chance of winning) or a UK parliamentary general election (where only the two largest parties can realistically hope to see their leader become Prime Minister [PM] and form a government). The same considerations apply in a multi-party or multi-candidate election but with a much more complicated interaction between the options since a strategy that benefits one candidate may not be equally to the detriment of all the other candidates, and vice-versa (see Galasso et al., 2023).

It must be remembered that even in a 'two-option election', the voters actually have three options: they also might choose not to vote at all.[5] (In practice, if directing the campaign of one of the two major candidates, we can treat voting for minor candidates or parties as functionally equivalent from our point of view to not voting.) In the last few weeks of the election campaign, some voters will still be wavering between the two candidates, although the proportion of voters in this situation might be expected to vary considerably depending on the political context and the previous course of the campaign. Others may be sure which of the two candidates they prefer yet still be susceptible to campaign influence on whether or not they will turn out at all. Therefore, campaign planners have three possible routes to impact:

i. they can sway the waverers in their direction;
ii. they can get out their own vote;
iii. they can depress the turnout of their opponent's supporters.

Each of these three aims targets a different group of voters and may need a different strategy. There is no guarantee that making the same arguments or instilling the same impressions will have similar impacts on each group.

We take as a practical example the UK general election of 2019, from which we have the evidence of a commercial opinion poll taken at precisely this stage of the campaign. This poll allows us to judge the relationship between voting intentions, the image of the two candidate parties and the willingness of voters to consider changing their minds before election day. (The practical campaign manager in this situation would conduct their own private polling, but we suggest that it might profitably proceed along the same lines as our poll, although taking the opportunity to explore opinions in much greater detail.)

DATA AND CONTEXT

In a British general election, the formal campaign is generally considered to last around five weeks, from the dissolution of the previous Parliament until polling day, although the date of the election is typically announced before the dissolution and practical campaigning will frequently begin at that point, if not before. In 2019, it was uncertain that there would be an election until 29 October, when Parliament voted for a bill to circumvent the provisions of the Fixed Term Parliaments Act (which had automatically set a date in 2022 for the next election) and hold an early general election. Parliament was dissolved on 6 November and voting took place on 12 December 2019.

The UK uses a plurality voting system ('First-past the-post') in which voters elect a single Member of Parliament (MP) to represent their electoral district ('constituency'). Almost all candidates with a reasonable chance of success will be standing as members of one of the national political parties, and campaigning is conducted largely on a party basis and through the national media. A party wins by securing a majority of elected MPs, in which case its leader will become (or remain) PM. The image of the party leaders is often an important factor in the voting as well as the image of the parties more generally and their promised policies. Although numerous parties participate in the election, only two – the Conservative Party and the Labour Party – have had a realistic chance of winning a British general election in recent decades.

Our data are taken from an opinion poll conducted by Ipsos MORI on 15–19 November 2019, the results from which were published in the *London Evening Standard*. This was towards the start of the formal campaign but at a stage when most voters would have already been aware of the election issues and of the party leaders. With more than three weeks to go before polling day, it would still have been early enough for the parties to have modified their campaigning tactics had the survey been conducted for political marketing purposes rather than for a newspaper. The poll interviewed a quota sample of 1,228 adults by telephone and included both landline and mobile numbers.[6] The questionnaire included questions on: voting intention, with a follow-up asking whether the respondent had 'definitely decided' to vote for that party or might still change their mind; whether the Conservative leader, Boris Johnson, or the Labour leader, Jeremy Corbyn, would make the most capable PM; whether the respondent liked or did not like each of the major parties and their leaders; and a list of 11 possible descriptions of a political party, some positive and some negative, from which respondents were asked to select any that they felt applied to each of the two major parties. Data were weighted to match the known demographic profile of the population.

The full sample was designed to be representative of all adults of voting age across Great Britain[7], but to be better illustrative of the possibilities available to the campaign manager aiming to sway votes, we confine our analysis only to 'waverers' – those respondents within the sample who said they intended to vote either Conservative or Labour and yet were not 'definitely decided' on how they would vote. It is symptomatic of the uncertainties and feverish atmosphere surrounding the 2019 election that as many as 40% of those who gave a voting intention said they might still change their minds, a considerably higher proportion than is normally the case at that stage of a British election campaign. Our sample for analysis comprises 233 cases; this relatively small sample size ensures that any effects need to be substantial to register as statistically significant. Conservatives were significantly more likely than Labour supporters to have definitely decided how to vote, but the Conservatives had a substantial overall lead in voting intentions at this stage of the campaign, with the result that the sample is roughly equally split between Conservative and Labour supporters. It also means that Labour would have needed to win over the vast majority of waverers to have a chance of victory, whereas the Conservatives could win by maintaining the status quo[8].

We excluded from our sample those intending to vote for smaller parties or not giving any voting intention; including them led to unsatisfactory or perverse models, perhaps because these other groups react so differently to the image factors we were measuring that the normal statistical assumptions may not hold in building a combined model. Our analysis therefore relates solely to campaigning tactics to sway voters between the two major parties, and separate analyses would be required to design tactics to use with these other target groups.

ANALYTIC METHOD

To assess the tactical situation in the election, we considered both the relative importance of the party and leader image attributes as determinants of voting intention and which issues are strong/weak for each party. A party is most incentivized to raise issues where its position is strong, although it may also need to rebut issues its opponent(s) or the media raises where it is weaker; but issues that are not closely related to voting intentions are much less important than those that are.

To assess the relative importance of the issues to voting intention, we used a binary logistic regression analysis to identify the opinions that most effectively distinguish those who intend to vote Conservative from those who intend to vote Labour: for each of the image attributes, a respondent could apply it only to the Conservatives, only to Labour, to both or to neither. Each of these variables was treated as categorical (rather than assigning some numerical score to each response), with 'neither' as the reference category – this meant that we could directly compare the impact on voting intention of applying each description to each party. For the questions which asked whether respondents liked the two party leaders, we recoded their responses into a single variable with corresponding categories (like Boris Johnson, like Jeremy Corbyn, like both, like neither) so that it could be included in the same analysis.

Our original intention was to build a multivariate model in which each of the 13 available factors (choice of best PM, liking or not liking the leaders and the 11 party image attributes) would be simultaneously included if statistically significant. However, it turned out that choice of best PM was so closely correlated with voting intention that including it with the other 12 variables in a single model to predict voting intention produced perverse results, with many of the other variables apparently associated with voting in the 'wrong' direction – controlling for leader preference is not a useful way of analyzing the impact of the other image factors. Therefore, we show one model for the relationship between voting intention and choice of best PM, and a separate multivariate model including the other 12 factors (although, as demonstrated, only 5 of the 12 prove to be statistically significant).

For the other half of the analysis, party strength on each issue is indicated by which party has an advantage on the topline score among the same sub-sample of respondents, and by how much. (We rely on the natural interpretation of whether a description should be considered positive or negative, i.e. if more voters say they think the Conservatives 'will promise anything to win votes' than think that Labour will, that is taken as being a Labour lead on the issue since the characteristic would be an undesirable one.)

Then, drawing all three elements together, the differential impact of each issue points towards what a party's optimal tactics on the issue might be (although it then still needs to identify effective messages to put these into practice).

RESULTS

Table 4.1 shows the 'topline' results of the relevant questions (the weighted percentages of 'waverers' giving each answer). For clarity, the image statements are arranged in order of party advantage, from biggest Conservative lead to biggest Labour lead. (Those marked with an asterisk are negative statements, so a party is judged to be leading on those where fewer apply that description to that party than their opponents. The description 'different to other parties' might

Table 4.1 Party and Leader Image – Topline (Marginal) Percentage Data

Image Statement	*Only Conservatives* %	*Only Labour* %	*Both* %	*Neither* %	*Party lead*
Leader is most capable PM	43	30	n/a	27	Con 13
I like the party leader	35	32	4	29	Con 3
Fit to govern	32	19	17	32	Con 13
Divided	10	23	48	19	Con 13*
Extreme	15	27	16	43	Con 12*
Has a good team of leaders	22	17	14	46	Con 5
Out of date	23	20	24	33	Lab 3*
Keeps its promises	13	17	12	57	Lab 4
Different to other parties	10	18	38	34	Lab 8
Will promise anything to win votes	24	12	48	16	Lab 12*
Understands problems facing Britain	14	27	33	25	Lab 13
Looks after the interests of people like me	19	40	16	25	Lab 21
Concerned about people in real need	9	43	23	24	Lab 34

Base: n = 233 'waverers', November 2019

in theory be either a positive or a negative attribute, but in this case, it was clearly considered positive, as many more respondents applied it to the party for which they intended to vote than to the other party.)

It will be seen that Labour had the advantage on a higher number of the image statements than the Conservatives. Their strongest issue positions would seem to be that they were seen as being 'concerned about people in real need' and as looking after 'the interests of people like me', on which Labour's lead was much higher than the Conservatives' lead where they had the greatest advantage, on their leader being the most capable PM, on being 'fit to govern' and on being less divided or extreme than their opponents. However, the real implications of these numbers cannot be judged until the relationship of each with voting intention is considered.

The relationship between voting intention and the choice of 'most capable Prime Minister' is shown in Table 4.2. As expected, there is a strong correlation between the two, with those judging Boris Johnson to be most capable being significantly more likely to vote Conservative, and those preferring Jeremy Corbyn significantly less likely to do so, than those who say neither is better than the other. (A negative coefficient indicates tendency towards Labour, a positive one towards the Conservatives.)

The impact of preferring Corbyn is marginally stronger than that of preferring Johnson (indicated by the absolute size of the coefficient), but both are substantial. Each party could expect to gain votes if they could persuade wavering voters either of the capability of their own man or the incapability of their opponent.

The impact of the image attributes on voting intentions is shown in Table 4.3: five of the twelve show a significant independent effect and are included in the final model, while the remaining seven are omitted. In each case, the reference category is 'none', with the impact of the description being applied to either or both of the parties measured separately.

We need concern ourselves only with the terms in the model that are statistically significant. The most powerful factor explaining a Conservative vote (i.e. the biggest positive coefficient) is the belief that the Labour Party is extreme; operating in the same direction, but slightly less powerfully, is a belief that the Conservative Party keeps its promises. On the other side, Labour gains most strongly from being seen to be described by 'looks after the interests of people like me', and a little less (but still substantially) from being thought of as 'different to other parties' and from the perception that the Conservatives are out of date. Note that even the weakest of these five associations is still a close one: the odds ratio for Labour being different to other parties is 0.037 (roughly 1/27), indicating that the odds of somebody who believes this being a Labour rather than Conservative supporter is 27 to 1.

Note also that none of these descriptors has a symmetrical effect: believing that Labour 'looks

Table 4.2 Predictors of Voting Intentions (Binomial Logistic Regression) – Best Leader

	Coefficient	*S.E.*	*Odds Ratio*	
Constant	−0.664	0.247	0.515	**
Leader is most capable PM				
Labour (Corbyn)	−2.774	0.680	0.062	***
Conservative (Johnson)	2.600	0.372	13.467	***
−2 Log likelihood	205.820			
Nagelkerke R Square	0.624			

Note: Base: n = 233 'waverers', November 2019
***= significant at 99.9% significance level
**= significant at 99%
*= significant at 95%

Table 4.3 Predictors of Voting Intentions (Binomial Logistic Regression) – Image Attributes

	Coefficient	*S.E.*	*Odds Ratio*	*Significance*
Constant	1.471	0.672	4.352	*
Keeps its promises				
Labour	−0.746	1.017	0.474	
Both parties	0.321	1.198	1.379	
Conservative	3.721	1.485	41.324	*
Extreme				
Labour	4.100	1.104	60.312	***
Both parties	0.038	0.970	1.039	
Conservative	−18.099	5062.896	0	
Looks after the interests of people like me				
Labour	−4.852	1.047	0.008	***
Both parties	−0.458	0.927	0.633	
Conservative	1.361	0.905	3.901	
Different to other parties				
Labour	−3.289	1.106	0.037	**
Both parties	0.723	0.923	2.060	
Conservative	0.422	1.140	1.525	
Out of date				
Labour	−1.477	1.150	0.228	
Both parties	−0.702	0.776	0.496	
Conservative	−3.882	1.138	0.021	***
−2 Log likelihood	90.237			
Nagelkerke R Square	0.866			

Note: Base: n = 233 'waverers', November 2019
***= significant at 99.9% significance level
**= significant at 99%
*= significant at 95%

after the interests of people like me' is a strong driver of voting intentions but believing the same thing about the Conservative Party has no statistically significant effect at all; parties therefore need to select their messages on each issue with care if they are to be effective.

Finally, in Table 4.4, we can draw these various elements together to demonstrate both how

Table 4.4 Summary of Tactical Situation on 13 Attributes

	Link With Vote if Applied to Conservatives	*Link with Vote if Applied to Labour*	*Party and Lead*
Leader is most capable PM	**Yes**	**Yes**	**Con 13**
Fit to govern	No	No	Con 13
Divided	No	No	Con 13*
Extreme	**No**	**Yes**	**Con 12***
Has a good team of leaders	No	No	Con 5
I like the party leader	No	No	Con 3
Out of date	Yes	No	Lab 3*
Keeps its promises	Yes	No	Lab 4
Different to other parties	No	Yes	Lab 8
Will promise anything to win votes	No	No	Lab 12*
Understands problems facing Britain	No	No	Lab 13
Looks after the interests of people like me	No	**Yes**	**Lab 21**
Concerned about people in real need	No	No	Lab 34

relevant they are to voting for each main party as well as what advantage a particular party has on that issue.

In the latter stages of the campaign, both parties will probably prefer to concentrate on those issues where they already have a lead in public perceptions. While they could in theory aim to turn around perceptions and reduce or reverse their opponents' lead on the issues where they are weaker, this is likely to be more difficult – voters tend more to align their opinions with a prevailing majority than against it, especially where that view is held by elites (Levendusky, 2010), and the existing state of opinions is likely to exist because it is inherently more plausible in the current context and is probably reflected in the media narrative. Although Labour dared not entirely abandon its efforts to establish Jeremy Corbyn as the more capable of the two candidates to be PM, it will surely be the Conservatives who can be more confident of winning converts on that basis at this stage. The Conservatives are therefore best advised to concentrate on the comparison between the leaders and on Labour being the more extreme party, while Labour's best hope is to drive home the opinion that they are the party that 'looks after the interests of people like me', and perhaps also that they are different to other parties, although this may not be so easy a task. Where the lead is much narrower (on whether the Conservatives keep their promises, and whether they are out of date), there is probably less to be gained by campaigning effort.

Table 4.4 illustrates that the campaigning situation creates some very clear incentives for negative campaigning, although this is not appropriate for every issue. On which leader would be the better PM, opinions about both leaders can sway votes and either party might reasonably choose to promote their own man or denigrate their opponent, depending on which message they expect to be most credible. And Labour should clearly campaign positively on 'Looks after the interests of people like me', since believing this about Labour is strongly linked to voting whereas it seems to make no difference whether people think this description fits the Conservatives or not. However, it seems that the Conservatives have much to gain by negative campaigning to portray Labour as 'extreme' – this perception is closely associated with voting intention and the Conservatives have a strong lead on the issue which they cannot exploit by positive campaigning (since believing that the Conservatives are not extreme has no statistically significant effect). Labour might also consider negative campaigns to argue that the Conservatives are out of date and do not keep their promises, although their lead here is lower so the voters might be less receptive. Again, though, a positive campaign on the same issue by Labour would be ineffective since opinions about Labour on these issues are not strongly tied to voting. (The Conservatives, on the other hand, might defend themselves against Labour's accusations by positive campaigning on these two counts.)

DISCUSSION AND CONCLUDING REMARKS

Our presentation sets out a more comprehensive structural framework for understanding the tactical possibilities in a given electoral situation than has hitherto been proposed. By tabulating image dimensions against favorability towards candidates and determining each image dimension's impact on voting intention, and the candidate's relative standing vis-à-vis one another, campaign teams can identify issues on which they are likely to be able to more effectively campaign negatively. This framework shows how some issues are better suited than others to negative campaigning for a particular candidate. Our polling example applies this in a real situation, offering a simplified view of the Johnson-Corbyn campaign.

We must emphasize that our analysis is aimed only at establishing possibilities, not at providing a fully comprehensive understanding of voter behaviour in the election which we studied, hence the title of this chapter. We had at our disposal only a single opinion poll, including a relatively small sample of the kind of voters of interest to us, and designed to inform a journalist reporting on the election rather than a campaign manager fighting it. It covers only a selection of newsworthy issues and does not explore them in depth. A real campaign manager would almost certainly want to use a more sophisticated segmentation of target voters and would need to be satisfied that not only would a proposed tactic be successful with one target group but also that it would not backfire by alienating other voters outside the target group. Moreover, we have assumed that perceptions of the parties and their leaders drive voting intention, rather than the opposite being the case. Almost certainly this is a simplification, and it is possible that some positive evaluations follow so strongly from party support rather than being a cause of it that it is futile to attempt to promote them in themselves. Again, this is a point that wise campaign managers would research for themselves, and the precise dynamics of image and voting intention are probably context-dependent and different in every election. Nevertheless, the analysis demonstrates that certain situations can create an incentive for negative campaigning and not purely around those issues where this can only mean character assassination. Further, these issues are not the same for every candidate in a given election; a corollary to this is that direct retaliation to an opponent's negative campaigning is not necessarily the best defence to it. If, in our example, the Conservatives were to campaign negatively on the basis that Labour was an extreme party, it would be wasted effort for Labour to try to show that the Conservatives were also extreme; they should instead try to disprove the Conservatives' claim or launch an attack on an entirely different front.

This framework does not amount to a comprehensive campaigning recipe; that requires considerable further research. At most, it rules out certain possibilities. Having chosen a particular issue on which to campaign and a particular tactic, the candidates and their teams still need to identify appropriate messages to implement that decision. It is at this stage that they will have to weigh up the advantageous impact of each chosen message against any possible deleterious effects of a backlash against being seen to campaign negatively. Nevertheless, our data establish the possibility that political marketers ought to approach and position their candidates differently on different issues. It provides a framework they can use in determining how to do so and that observers can use in analyzing how they made their decisions. Candidates and campaign managers already, frequently, make the decision to go negative without resorting to any formal framework, relying instead on instinct and experience to interpret the implications of what they know about voter opinion. Moreover, our study takes a step towards advancing our understanding of real-world decisions to adopt negative campaigning tactics. By recognizing that the key decision may be to campaign negatively on a particular issue in a particular way, rather than merely a general go-ahead to 'go negative', we allow for the detailed study of an election and its voters that campaign managers may undertake before making reasoned decisions, going beyond the broad features of the strategic situation on which previous researchers have relied as independent variables in their explanatory models. The next step for researchers is to explore how closely empirical campaigning practice fits this theoretical structure of optimal choices and to incorporate personal as well as issue attacks.

Notes

1 Collins dictionary defines negative campaigning simply as 'Political campaigning in which a

politician or party focuses on criticizing another politician or party rather than emphasizing their own positive qualities'. (Collins, n.d.); and similarly, Geer (2006, p. 23), 'negativity is any criticism levelled by one candidate against another during a campaign'.

2 To watch this campaign video, see: https://www.youtube.com/watch?v=riDypP1KfOU.

3 To see this political advertisement, see: https://www.youtube.com/watch?v=sdJ97qWHOxo.

4 To see this political advertisement from the 'Swift Boat Veterans for Truth' campaign, see: https://www.youtube.com/watch?v=phqOuEhg9yE.

5 A few democracies, such as Australia, practise compulsory voting, but even there, in practice, some citizens will fail to get to the polls despite making themselves liable to a fine by doing so, and others will spoil their ballot paper or leave it blank; the third option always exists.

6 The published summary findings of the poll and technical details including full question wordings can be found at https://www.ipsos.com/en-uk/labour-party-image-falls-2017-seen-more-divided-more-extreme-and-less-fit-govern, accessed on 21 February 2022.

7 The main national political parties in UK elections do not run candidates in Northern Ireland, and our poll – like most British political polls – therefore covers only Great Britain (England, Scotland and Wales) and excludes Northern Ireland.

8 In the event, Labour narrowed the gap slightly during the remaining weeks of the campaign but were still beaten by a very substantial 12 percentage points of the vote.

REFERENCES

Auter, Z. J., & Fine, J. A. (2016). Negative campaigning in the social media age: Attack advertising on Facebook. *Political Behavior*, *38*, 999–1020.

Butler, D., & Kavanagh, D. (1997). *The British general election of 1997*. Macmillan.

Chou, H.-Y., & Lien, N.-H. (2010). How do candidate poll ranking and election status affect the effects of negative political advertising? *International Journal of Advertising*, *29*, 815–834.

Collins. (n. d.). *Negative campaigning*. https://www.collinsdictionary.com/dictionary/english/negative-campaigning. Accessed on 26 April 2024.

Culf, A. (1997, 10 January). Demon eyes ad wins top award. *The Guardian*. https://www.theguardian.com/politics/1997/jan/10/past.andrewculf. Accessed on 26 April 2024.

Damore, D. F. (2002). Candidate strategy and the decision to go negative. *Political Research Quarterly*, *55*, 669–686.

Dowling, C. M., & Wichowsky, A. (2015). Attacks without consequence? Candidates, parties, groups, and the changing face of negative advertising. *American Journal of Political Science*, *59*(1), 19–36.

Elmelund-Præstekær, C. (2010). Beyond American negativity: Toward a general understanding of the determinants of negative campaigning. *European Political Science Review*, *2*, 137–156.

Galasso, V., Nannicini, T., & Nunnari, S. (2023). Positive spillovers from negative campaigning. *American Journal of Political Science*, *67*, 5–21.

Geer, J. G. (2006). *In defence of negativity. Attack ads in presidential campaigns*. University of Chicago Press.

Haddock, G., & Zanna, M. P. (1997). Impact of negative advertising on evaluations of political candidates: The 1993 Canadian Federal Election. *Basic and Applied Social Psychology*, *19*, 205–223.

Harrington, J. E., & Hess, G. D. (1996). A spatial theory of positive and negative campaigning. *Games and Economic Behavior*, *17*, 209–229.

Haselmayer, M. (2019). Negative campaigning and its consequences: A review and a look ahead. *French Politics*, *17*, 355–372.

Lau, R. R., & Pomper, G. M. (2002). Effectiveness of negative campaigning in U.S. Senate elections. *American Journal of Political Science*, *46*, 47–66.

Lau, R. R., Sigelman, L., Heldman, C., & Babbitt, P. (1999). The effects of negative political advertisements: A meta-analytic assessment. *American Political Science Review*, *93*, 851–875.

Lau, R. R., Sigelman, L., & Rovner, I. B. (2007). The effects of negative political campaigns: A meta-analytic reassessment. *The Journal of Politics*, *69*, 1176–1209.

Levendusky, M. S. (2010). Clearer cues, more consistent voters: A benefit of elite polarization. *Political Behavior*, *32*, 111–131.

Major, M., & Andersen, D. J. (2016). Polls and elections: Swift boating reconsidered: News coverage of negative Presidential ads. *Presidential Studies Quarterly*, *46*(4), 891–910.

Mark, D. (2009). *Going dirty: The art of negative campaigning*. Rowman & Littlefield.

Mattes, K., & Redlawsk, D. P. (2015). *The positive case for negative campaigning*. University of Chicago Press.

Mayer, W. G. (1996). In defense of negative campaigning. *Political Science Quarterly*, *111*, 437–455.

McIntyre, L. (2018). Fighting post-truth. *The Humanist*, *78*(2), 20–22.

Merritt, S. (1984). Negative political advertising: Some empirical findings. *Journal of Advertising*, *13*, 27–38.

Nai, A. (2020). Going negative, worldwide: Towards a general understanding of determinants and targets

of negative campaigning. *Government and Opposition*, *55*, 430–455.
Nai, A., Tresch, A., & Maier, J. (2022). Hardwired to attack: Candidates' personality traits and negative campaigning in three European countries. *Acta Politica*, *57*, 772–797.
Parry-Giles, S., Hunter, L., Hess, M., & Bhat, P. (2017, November 21). 2016 presidential advertising focused on character attacks, not policy. *Huffington Post*. https://www.huffpost.com/entry/2016-presidential-adverti_b_13090306. Accessed on 26 April 2024.
Petković, V. (2022). Emotions as the impetus of negative campaigning effects. *SocArXiv Papers*. https://doi.org/10.31235/osf.io/72mcn. Accessed on 26 April 2024.
Poljak, Ž. (2024). Give the media what they need: Negativity as a media access tool for politicians. *The International Journal of Press/Politics*. https://doi.org/10.1177/19401612241234861. Accessed on 26 March 2024.
Ridout, T. N., & Walter, A. S. (2015). Party system change and negative campaigning in New Zealand. *Party Politics*, *21*, 982–992.
Roseman, I. J., Mattes, K., Redlawsk, D. P., & Katz, S. (2020). Reprehensible, laughable: The role of contempt in negative campaigning. *American Politics Research*, *48*, 44–77.
Shapiro, M. A., & Rieger, R. H. (1992). Comparing positive and negative political advertising on radio. *Journalism Quarterly*, *69*, 135–145.
Sigelman, L., & Shiraev, E. (2002). The rational attacker in Russia? Negative campaigning in Russian presidential elections. *The Journal of Politics*, *64*, 45–62.
Skaperdas, S., & Grofman, B. (1995). Modeling negative campaigning. *American Political Science Review*, *89*, 49–61.
Valli, C., & Nai, A. (2022). Attack politics from Albania to Zimbabwe: A large-scale comparative study on the drivers of negative campaigning. *International Political Science Review*, *43*(5), 680–696.
Walter, A. S. (2014). Negative campaigning in Western Europe: Similar or different? *Political Studies*, *62*(1), 42–60.
Walter, A. S., & van der Eijk, C. (2019). Measures of campaign negativity: Comparing approaches and eliminating partisan bias. *The International Journal of Press/Politics*, *24*(3), 363–382.

Electoral Attacking Strategies: Lessons From the Electoral Debates in Spain and France

Marta Rebolledo and Aurken Sierra

INTRODUCTION

Election campaigns are the most extensively researched area of political communication. The focus of election studies is often on the evolution of campaigning and changes over time. As research on elections has expanded beyond the United States, the term "Americanization" has become a core concept in electoral studies. This term refers to the transposition of American campaign practices to other countries. Specifically, the term refers to the "elements of electoral campaigns and related professional activities that were first developed in the United States and subsequently applied and adapted in different ways in other countries" (Swanson & Mancini, 1996, pp. 5–6). The term highlights that certain features of American campaigns have been transported to other contexts outside the United States, including negative campaigning (Walter, 2014).

A negative campaign is based on attacking the opponent constantly. Negative campaigns are mainly based on criticism rather than proposing solutions. Research on this topic has focused on analyzing the effects of negative messages (Gerstlé & Nai, 2019). Additionally, there is a significant body of research devoted to analyzing the messages themselves, with political advertisements being a recurrent topic.[1]

Research suggests that negative campaigning can have various effects. In their book "Going Negative" Ansolabehere and Iyengar (2010) analyze the effects of political advertising in six presidential campaigns. Their conclusions point in two directions: firstly, negativity can cause non-partisans to become disillusioned and refrain from participating in the electoral process; secondly, negative messages can reinforce partisans' loyalties. In summary, negative campaigning can have a detrimental effect on the electoral process by reducing elector participation and polarizing the electorate. While there is no consensus on the impact of negative campaigning, research suggests that it can distort political discourse, demobilize voters, and be used to spread disinformation (Haselmayer, 2019). According to Shapiro and Rieger (1992) and Lau and Pomper (2002), the use of biased language can result in a candidate losing votes rather than gaining them. Another main approach regarding negative campaigns beyond effects has to do with which kind of candidates are prone to go more negative. Research points out that challengers or trailing candidates are more likely to use negative appeals while incumbents are less likely to use negative campaigning (Ridout & Searles, 2011). In this line, candidates from extreme and populist political parties rely more on attacks, aggressive rhetoric, and use of fear appeals (Gerstlé & Nai, 2019; Oliver & Rahn, 2016; Scheller, 2019).

Debates are an important setting for analyzing messages and strategies in political campaigns. Electoral debates are considered the main events of campaigns and are often seen as the climax of the election season. There is a consensus that debates play a crucial role in democracy, as they attract the attention of the audience, identify essential issues, invite deliberation, and provide an opportunity to listen directly to the candidates. Unlike typical media coverage, a televised debate provides voters with the opportunity to hear directly from the candidates and learn about their positions on campaign issues, as well as their qualities as politicians, without mediation or filtering. Therefore, a televised debate can be recognized as the most visible and public test of political candidates (Norton & Goethals, 2004) or even a sort of dramatic conflict consisting of answering the audience (Benoit & Harthcock, 1999). The debate ultimately represents political strategies and tactics (Pérez-Ruiz & Melgosa, 2015) pursued primarily by candidates who, for various reasons, are at a disadvantage in terms of electoral preference.

During electoral campaigns, televised debates serve as the focal point of the campaign. Among other reasons, electoral campaigns today tend to personalize political discourse (Campus et al., 2010; Langer, 2007; Rebolledo, 2017). This trend is accompanied by a growing negativity in political discourse and an increase in interpretive coverage based on a horse race game scheme (Reinemann & Wilke, 2007).

Research on electoral debates traditionally focuses on their impact on voting decisions. While debates can foster interest in the campaign and motivate participation, their influence on the final vote remains a topic of debate among researchers. However, electoral debates have a limited conversion effect, only being impactful during specific moments of elections such as technical ties or high volumes of undecided voters (Díez Nicolás & Semetko, 1995). Debates can influence this segment of the population, as well as abstainers, to vote for a candidate and political party consistent with their initial predispositions. Luengo (2011) conducted an analysis of the immediate micro-level effects of electoral debates in Spain. Using the electoral debate between José Luis Rodríguez Zapatero and Mariano Rajoy on 3 March 2008, and aided by a computer system designed for this purpose – Continuous Response Measurement (CRM) – Luengo was able to verify citizens' impressions in real-time about the performance of the two candidates.

Electoral debates generally crystallize voting tendencies and reinforce voters' positions (Crespo et al., 2011; Luengo, 2011). During this period, selective perception occurs (Marín, 2003), as citizens are exposed to the debate with their own political biases, falling into motivated reasoning (Leeper & Slothuus, 2014). They tend to ignore negative information about their preferred candidate and perceive positive information. It is important to note that this phenomenon can lead to a lack of objectivity in the evaluation of candidates. Consequently, viewers interpret the information based on their political beliefs and perceive their candidate as the winner. Electoral debates also play a crucial role in setting and controlling the campaign agenda, as well as persuading the electorate. Their influence is established from the moment they are announced, creating a scenario in which parties compete to shape the public and media agenda. During debates, the audience gains knowledge of the political issues discussed, which can have cognitive effects. López et al. (2015) found that electoral debates are important tools for influencing the political agenda and the electorate during European Parliament elections. However, only a few years ago, some studies began to focus on the processes that occur during the debates. This approach identifies other important aspects beyond the debates' influence on the vote, such as determining the immediate reactions to specific topics, approaches to them, and the tone of the interventions, and so on. This proposal aims to contribute to the discussion on the importance of electoral debates with a comparative approach. The primary source of analysis are two multiparty debates in France and Spain in 2017 and 2019. The proposal explores the development of candidates' performances.

THE EVOLUTION AND CONTEXT OF DEBATES

The debate model used is the result of the country's reality, and is influenced by political history and culture, the party system, and the media system. In the literature, sometimes we tend to use the category European electoral debate format in contrast to the American format (Morales & García Gordillo, 2023). In this case, Spain has never been considered a perfect two-party system, but rather an imperfect one, with the Spanish Socialist Workers' Party (PSOE) on the center-left and the *Partido Popular* (PP) on the center-right as the main political parties. Since the first televised electoral debate in 1993 and until 2015, political broadcasts had portrayed only the candidates from the two main political parties. Since the inaugural presidential election in 1974, France has traditionally engaged in a distinctive post-first-round debate between the two candidates advancing to the second round. However, this established pattern underwent a notable shift in 2017.

Historically, the format in both cases was quite similar. First, there is a direct exchange of ideas between candidates, that is, they have a real conversation where they exchange ideas, intervene and interrupt each other. Second, journalists who participate in the debate adopt the role of moderators. Third, regarding the scenography, the candidates stood behind the tables and there was no public on the set. In both cases, prior negotiations take place between politicians and journalists. These discussions usually concern the choice between armchairs and lecterns, or the possibility of including questions from the public, but can also include topics. In both Spain and France, journalists are usually praised for not accepting political restrictions and for presenting themselves as the ones who control the context in which the presidential debates take place (Brandariz Portela, 2021). However, some political influence did find its way into the organization of the Spanish debate that was analyzed. Specifically, and given the intense political competition of the 2019 elections, the five topics discussed in the debate were agreed upon by the five political parties that participated in the debate.

THE SPANISH CASE

Electoral debating has not been a long tradition in Spain. In the democratic context, most electoral processes have been developed without having an electoral debate. In fact, until the 2015 elections, in 11 general elections in Spain, only five debates between candidates were held on television. The scarcity of televised debates is explained by the absence of specific legal regulation, which leaves it in the hands of politicians acting according to their interests to decide whether or not to hold electoral debates. Despite this fact, the Spanish electorate is very accustomed to the presence of politics and politicians on television and they have naturalized with extraordinary rapidity the existence of televised debates between the main candidates running for prime minister (López et al., 2015).

The debate between Felipe González (PSOE) and José María Aznar (PP), during the 1993 general elections, marked a turning point in the democratic history of Spain. There was a technical tie in voting intention according to the polls, so it was necessary to encourage participation through million-dollar hearings (the last abstention rate was 29.9%) and capture the undecided vote (estimated at six million). The certainty that president González would clearly prevail led the PSOE to accept the face to face. The results of the 1993 debates set the tone for the following elections: 1996, 2000, and 2004. On all three occasions, the PP refused to debate with the socialists.

In 2008, there was a new element imported from the American model: a debate also among the vice-presidential candidates was introduced. Three years later, in the 2011 general elections, the debate between PSOE and PP represented through the candidates Rubalcaba and Rajoy, served to consolidate a model in Spain. Electoral debates were limited to the two main candidates.

In 2015, this dynamic underwent a significant change as the electoral debate diverged from past norms. The electoral outcomes marked a definitive departure from the existing two-party system, exerting a direct influence on the subsequent debates, including those in the 2019 elections. On the one hand, the participation of two new parties – *Podemos*, on the left side, and *Ciudadanos*, on the center-right – made the vote dispute greater. On the other hand, this debate introduced important formal changes (Zamora-Medina & Rebolledo, 2017).

The emergence of these two new political parties forced the layout of the stage to be modified, the moderators had an active role and acted as journalists, and there were 300 people invited as public. Another novelty was that the event was broadcasted on social media and the audience was able to follow and interact (Zamora-Medina & Rebolledo, 2019). In this new political landscape, the strategies portrayed by candidates grew in complexity. The incumbent president, the conservative Rajoy, opted for acclaiming significantly more and attacking less than the rest of the contenders, a strategy which can be seen with incumbents in other countries (Benoit & Sheafer, 2006).

With regard to the electoral debate on 5 November 2019, this chapter highlights the political instability of the time. Throughout the year, the stage was set for a compelling general election, which would be the second time citizens would vote in 2019. The first attempt, on April 28, failed because the PSOE, despite winning, couldn't secure support for a government, necessitating a second round later in the year. The PSOE's slogan for the second election was "Ahora sí" ("Now's the time"). Notably, 2019 saw increased support for the radical-right wing party, *VOX*, leading to a polarized political landscape (Rodríguez-Virgili et al., 2022). After performing well in the first election of 2019, *VOX* became the primary focus of the televised debate on November 5th (Zamora-Medina & Rebolledo, 2019).

THE FRENCH CASE

In France, since the first 1974 debate between François Mitterrand and Valery Giscard d'Estaing, televised debates between the two candidates for the final round of the election became the peaks of presidential campaigns.[2] An observation made in France for some time was the fact that frequently, the politician leading the polls managed the best performance in the debate, and then won the election. This strong correlation would mean that the debates might not have been so decisive (Maarek, 2016). The steady pattern of a single televised presidential debate changed in 2017. So far, the presidential debate remained with the same format and with no major changes (Maarek, 2014). The aspect that used to make each of these electoral appointments different was particular soundbites used by the candidates.

The 2017 presidential campaign was a turnover in French electoral politics for several reasons (Durovic, 2019; Gougou & Persico, 2017; Maarek & Mercier, 2018). In political terms, the President François Hollande decided not to stand for a second term. This was the first time in the history of the 5th Republic that a president didn't go for a second term. There was a change of the leadership of the main traditional parties after a process of primaries in both cases: Benoît-Hamon was elected as new leader of the Socialist Party (PS), and François Fillon, of *Les Républicains* (LR). Another relevant novelty was the creation of a new political party by Emmanuel Macron, Hollande's former minister of economy, challenging the bipolar format of the French party system (Grunberg & Haegel, 2007). His new party, *La République En Marche*, (LREM) was created one year in advance of the elections and assembled politicians from the left and the right, activists from civil society as well as from the private sector. On the far left, Jean-Luc Mélenchon's movement, *La France Insoumise* (FI), also set up only one year before the elections, equally benefited to some extent from the turmoil among the governing left.

There was a pluralization of the political scenario and the fact that there were four candidates in the presidential elections who seemed to have an equal good chance of qualifying for the second round showed how fragmented the political context was. This paradigmatic shift was labeled as an "electoral earthquake" (Martin, 2017) considering the consequences for the French party system.

Another major surprise in this election was that for the first time in the history of the 5th French Republic, the candidates of the two traditional governing parties were disqualified during the first round of the presidential elections (Kuhn, 2017). The duel between the centrist Macron and the radical-right Le Pen in the second round of the elections constitutes an unprecedented configuration.[3] The two parties, which had been alternating in power for decades, were the Socialist Party, and the Gaullist Party and its successors. They lost the presidency for the first time to relative newcomer Macron, who had never previously been elected to any political position.

In terms of campaigning, for the first time in the history of French presidential campaigns, two debates were held before the first round of the election (Maarek, 2020). The first one, on the main French private channel, TF1, on 20th March, gathered only five candidates out of 11. The second debate before the first round of the election played simultaneously on most of the News Channels on 4th April. All 11 candidates were present.[4]

METHODOLOGY AND SAMPLE

Our research sample consists of two electoral debates held in France and Spain before the presidential elections in each country.[5] The selection of these debates was based on their relevance and comparative nature.

First, in both cases, these debates marked a milestone in the history of televised debate. In the French case, this was the first time a televised debate was held before the first round of presidential elections. The changing political environment made it possible to hold two electoral debates before the first round of elections.[6] The first one, the one selected in this work, was organized by the main French private channel, TF1, along with LCI and France 24, and was held on the 20th March, gathering five candidates out of 11. TF1 decided to include only the politicians polling at above 10%, namely Macron from *La République En Marche* (LREM), Hamon from the Socialist Party (PS), Fillon representing *Les Républicains* (LR), Mélenchon from *La France Insoumise* (FI), and Le Pen from *Rassemblement National* (RN).

The unusual scenario following Hollande's decision not to run for re-election was compounded by Emmanuel Macron's candidacy, embodying novelty. The singular political context of 2017 required the structure of the debate to be modified: the discussion was organized between five candidates. Other changes were made regarding the stage: as in the 2019 Spanish electoral debate, lecterns were used on the stage instead of a traditional table. Also, there was a live audience in the studio and social media was also part of the debate dynamic. An aspect criticized of "*Le Grand Débat*" was the lack of control exercised by the moderators. In the traditional French debate format, they don't have a really active role because the discussion is carried out by the candidates. Even if the 2017 French debate was different since there were more politicians participating, the hosts didn't modify their participation.

The Spanish debate was organized by the Academy of Television and Audiovisual Sciences. Like in the French case, this debate marked a historic moment in the renewal of the Spanish political landscape, which began after the elections in December 2015 (Hutter et al., 2018; Simón, 2016). The emergence of multipartisanship in the Spanish political system, historically dominated by two parties, made parties more inclined to participate in debates to prevent their absence from being used by their opponents (Hutter et al., 2018; Rodríguez Teruel et al., 2018). This fact became evident during the 2015 elections, when the repeated absence of the *Partido Popular* in the electoral debates organized by various entities was used against the Spanish Prime Minister Mariano Rajoy.

In particular, the debate held on 4 November 2019 marked the inclusion of an extreme right-wing candidate for the first time in the history of Spanish television (Rodríguez Teruel et al., 2018); until April 2019, the Spanish Central Electoral Board, the highest body of the electoral administration, had continuously refused the participation of the Spanish extreme right in electoral debates, since *VOX* had not managed to obtain representation in the national parliament. This situation was surpassed in April of this year, when the extreme right secured its first seats in a general election. This debate represented the highest level of sophistication in Spanish debates, with the participation of five candidates in a dynamic environment compared to the rigidity of previous debates until 2011. The participants in the debate were Pedro Sánchez (PSOE), Pablo Casado (PP), Albert Rivera (*Ciudadanos*), Pablo Iglesias (*Unidas Podemos*), and Santiago Abascal (*VOX*). The situation was worrying for some parties, including the establishment parties. On the one hand, the November national elections resulted from the failure of the elected members of parliament to elect a president. This was the second time that Spaniards had voted in a national election that year, which gave the November election a second-round feel. On the other hand, the strategies of the parties in second and third place in the April elections had to change dramatically. The *Partido Popular*, the natural alternative to the Socialist Party, had reached its all-time low in April and needed an electoral boost if it was to survive. *Ciudadanos*, for its part, had almost overtaken the *Partido Popular*, but a terrible postelection performance had made the November elections its last attempt at survival. The results of the November elections brought relief to the *Partido Popular* and political annihilation to *Ciudadanos*.

Second, the selection of the two debates was based on comparative criteria. Despite taking place in different years (2017 for the French debate and 2019 for the Spanish debate), both debates share similar characteristics that facilitate comparisons. In addition to the number of candidates, five in both cases, both debates show a clear division between candidates representing establishment parties and those whose parties claim to be outsiders. In the French debate, Fillon and Hamon stood out on one side and Macron, Mélenchon, and Le Pen stood out on the other. In the Spanish debate, Sánchez and Casado faced Rivera, Iglesias, and Abascal.

Similarities can also be identified in the level of experience of participants in the debates in both countries. In both France and Spain, some candidates had extensive experience with this format. Despite the novelty of a multicandidate debate in France, Jean Luc Mélenchon and Marine Le Pen, due to their long political careers and leadership in their respective movements, had already been exposed to public scrutiny in the past. This contrasted with the situation of Fillon (LR), Hamon (PS), and Macron (LREM), who, despite years of political experience, had not held leadership positions until shortly before the electoral campaign.

In Spain, a clear distinction can be made between left- and right-wing candidates. Both Sánchez (*PSOE*), Rivera (*Ciudadanos*), and Iglesias (*Unidas Podemos*) had not only led their parties for more than four years but had also participated in multiparty electoral debates in 2015 and 2016. In contrast, the situation of right-wing leaders was different. Casado (PP) had participated in the electoral debates of April 2019 but had been at the helm of his party for less than two years. Santiago Abascal (*VOX*), on the other hand, had not participated in such a debate until November 2019. It is worth mentioning that he came close to participating in April 2019, but the Central Electoral Board suspended a debate organized by Atresmedia[7] because VOX had yet not secured parliamentary representation.

Beyond these similarities, there is a clear difference when it comes to their political systems that requires a clarification. Spanish debates are held between the representatives of competing parties in a parliamentary election, whereas those in France are between candidates for the presidency. Even if the President of the Government in Spain is equivalent to a Prime Minister or Chancellor in other European countries, and not to a President, there are some characteristics from Spain that soften this apparently major difference. The presidential elements in the Spanish Government are visible from its very configuration (Bar & Blondel, 1997). "In constitutional terms, the president occupies the center of the Spanish political system," according to Heywood (1991, p. 111). The 1978 Constitution underlines the preeminence of the head of Government by explaining his powers: he "directs the action of the government and coordinates the functions of its other members" (art. 98.2, Spanish Constitution). Likewise, it is the President of the Government who decides the dissolution of the chambers, "under his exclusive responsibility" (art. 115.1 SC), as it is the case for the French President (art. 12, French Constitution). In this line, Presidential practices extend to the other parties that compete for the Government, since "the same processes that strengthen the heads of the executive also favor the leaders of the opposition parties with government potential" (Poguntke & Webb, 2005, p. 351). Thus, although the candidates in the Spanish debate are running in a parliamentary rather than a presidential election, the configuration of the Spanish party system makes both debates similar in terms of the public projection of the political leaders who participate in them.

In addition to all this, in analyzing the debates, we pay attention to the legitimization strategies used by the candidates. For this, we follow the classification created by Raupp (2022). Following van Leeuwen (2007), Raupp (2022) distinguishes four types of legitimization in constructing discourse: firstly, authorization, which includes personal authority, role authority, rules and laws authority, and tradition authority. Secondly, moral evaluation, which legitimizes through appeals to shared ethical values. Thirdly, rationalization, which is based on logical arguments and the practical utility of actions. And lastly, mythopoesis, which uses narratives and symbolic stories to justify practices and decisions. These strategies allow candidates to effectively justify their positions and actions to the public.

PROPOSITIONS AND CODING

Taking into account the differences in the French and Spanish party systems and the results of previous electoral cycles, we propose the propositions below.

Since the political context in Spain is more polarized than in France (Müller & Schnabl, 2021), and traditionally the tone in Spanish debates tends to be hostile and based on confrontation comparing to France (Zamora-Medina & Rebolledo, 2017), we propose:

P1: The French debate will be less hostile than the Spanish one.

In relation to the typology of the interventions distinguished by Raupp (2022), and based on the competitive dynamics of the preceding elections:

P2: Most of the attacks that will be directed at the Spanish candidates will fall into the category of "direct attacks."

Based on the assertions of Haselmayer (2019) and Ansolabehere and Iyengar (2010) regarding negative campaigns and their effects on electoral dynamics and following research pointing out that extreme and populist political parties rely more on attacks (Gerstlé & Nai, 2019; Oliver & Rahn, 2016; Scheller, 2019), we propose the following propositions:

P3: Incumbents will be the focus of negative campaigning by other opponents and will receive more attacks.

P4: Candidates representing extreme ideological spectrum parties will be using more attacks than the center ideological candidates.

In our analysis, we used candidates' interventions as our unit of analysis (UA), assigning them numbers for identification. Each time a candidate takes the floor and starts speaking, we consider it as a single intervention or UA, which continues until the candidate concludes their speech or voluntarily decides to interrupt it. Even if a candidate is interrupted by someone else during their speech, we continue to regard that intervention as a single UA, unless the candidate chooses to stop speaking because of the interruption. In summary, an intervention can conclude in two ways: when the candidate finishes their speech or when the candidate is interrupted and chooses not to continue.

We conducted a discourse analysis of each UA, considering five different categories. These categories included the speaker, the mentioned candidate, the type of intervention, the type of attack, and the type of legitimization used by the speaker. We identified three types of interventions: attacks, defenses, or statements, depending on the speaker's objective. Given the adversarial nature of electoral debates (Blas Arroyo, 2003), we decided to add an additional level to our analysis to distinguish the type of attack made by the speakers based on intensity or resources used. The attacks can be:

a Irony/sarcasm: the speaker uses an ironic tone to convey their message, allowing them to question other candidates in a soft manner.
b Veiled criticism: the tone employed by the speaker becomes more serious when questioning other candidates, but they do not directly mention them by name or organization.
c Direct critique: the tone becomes harsher, and the speaker directly mentions other candidates in their intervention, but a degree of restraint in discourse is observed.
d Personal attacks: the questioning goes beyond the ideas presented in the debate, and the speaker uses a personal characteristic to criticize another candidate.
e Incivility: the speaker expresses disdain for another candidate and accompanies their message with clear gestures of disgust, such as hand or facial expressions.

Finally, in the case of legitimization, we follow a similar framework to the one proposed by Raupp (2022). Thus, the code used to analyze the speeches of speakers during both electoral debates is as follows:

a Speaker: a category aimed at distinguishing who was delivering the message.
b Type of intervention: attack, mixed attack, defense, defensive attack, defensive statement or statement.[8]
c Type of attack: irony/sarcasm, veiled criticism, direct critique, personal attack, or incivility.
d Candidate addressed: the candidate to whom the speech is directed.
e Type of legitimization used: authority, morality, rationalization, or mythopoesis.

RESULTS

The analysis of two electoral debates revealed significant differences in message typology, candidate interventions, and interpellation dynamics among participants, shedding light on the nature and development of political debates in both Spain and France. Notably, the distribution of interventions exhibited distinct dissimilarities between the debates in the two countries.

In Spain, candidates' interventions were distributed more evenly; this fact is linked to the debate's stricter format. Since the 2019 Spanish elections took place in a context of great polarization, great care was taken with the candidates' interventions, so that no candidate was favored by the format, and all had similar opportunities to discuss and defend their positions. A special "time room" was created, where the intervention time was controlled to ensure equal participation of all members of the debate. In this way, the difference between the candidate who intervened the most, President Sánchez (24), and the one who intervened the least, Rivera (21), was minimal. In contrast, even if it is not a major difference, the flexibility of the debate format in France led to more candidate intervention variability. Macron had the highest number of interventions with 23, while Fillon had the lowest number with 18. These discrepancies point to the potential role of debate structure and organization in impacting the allocation of speaking time among the contenders (Figure 5.1).

Regarding the typology of the messages (see Figure 5.2), there are notable differences between the debates in Spain and France. In general, the Spanish debate was characterized by a more adversarial character compared to the French, where the messages were more neutral or mixed. In the Spanish debate, more than 56% of the interpellations can be classified as "attacks." In contrast, only 7% of the messages could be classified as defensive. Throughout the debate, there were numerous instances where candidates started their interventions defensively but ended up adopting an offensive tone in their speeches. Thus, the 7% of purely defensive messages is supplemented by another 4.5% that we have labeled "defensive attack." Together, both categories make the total of defensive speeches grow to represent 11.5% of the messages during the Spanish debate, a number that contrasts with the 56% of attacks mentioned. Only 17% of the interventions were neutral in nature, focusing exclusively on the candidates' proposals. All candidates made some statements at some point in their participation, but the adversarial nature of the Spanish debate also influenced this typology. Thus, a significant number of interventions that started out neutral ended up taking on an offensive character, a behavior we reflect with our label "mixed attack" (15%). The

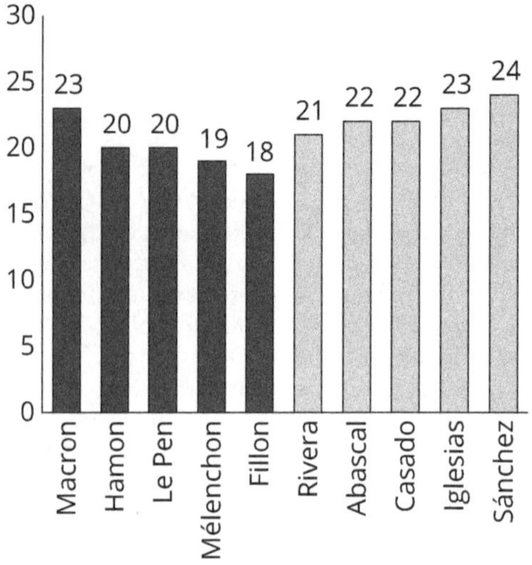

Figure 5.1 Interventions per Candidate

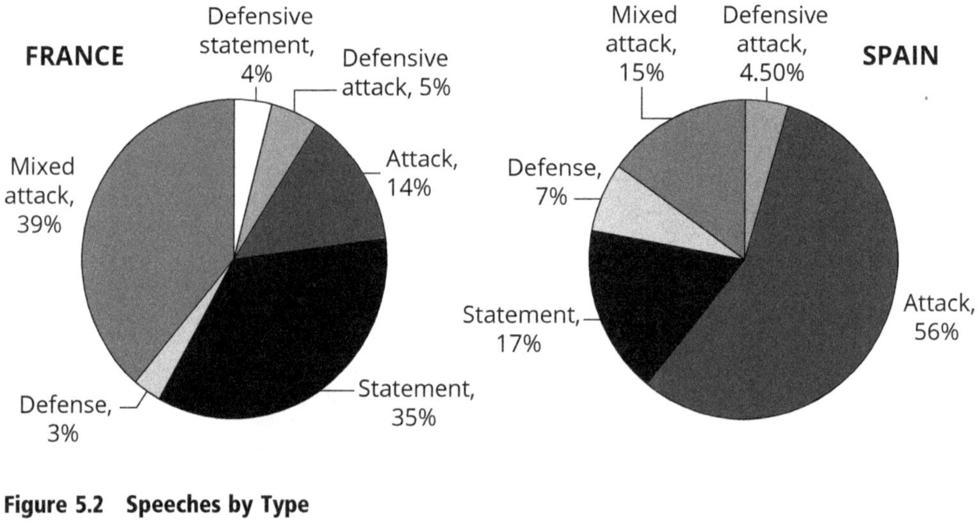

Figure 5.2 Speeches by Type

adversarial nature of the Spanish debate is evident, with 75.5% of messages containing some adversarial element when combining pure attacks, defensive attacks, and mixed attacks. This contrasts sharply with the more neutral tone observed in the French debate.

With regard to the French debate, it was characterized by a more neutral approach, which contributed to a calmer image. Although nearly 55% of the interventions had some adversarial tone, only 14% of them can be considered purely attacks, while the majority of the adversarial messages had a mixed nature (39%), mixing statements with some attacks against other candidates. Similar to the Spanish case, defensive messages represented a minimal percentage of the total number of interventions. Only 5% of the messages were purely defensive and 4% had a mixed defensive character. A point of contrast with the Spanish debate is the number of neutral messages: 35%, twice as many as in the Spanish debate. Thus, while the Spanish debate showed an influence of adversarial messages toward neutral ones, contributing to an increase in hostility, the opposite occurred in the French case. By opting for a more neutral approach, the candidates did not contribute to the emotional charge of the debate, projecting an image of greater calm. These results confirm that the French debate was less hostile than the Spanish one (P1) and in the latest case, most of the attacks fall into the category of "direct attacks" (P2) (Figure 5.3).

The Spanish candidates who launched the most attacks during the debate were Abascal (25 attacks) and Sánchez (23), representing the far right and the socialists, respectively. The combined interventions of these two candidates account for almost 50% of the attacks made during the speeches of all the candidates. However, it is with the far-right candidate that these attacks constitute the majority of his interventions, amounting to 59% (see Figure 5.4). On the other hand, the other two representatives of the new political landscape, Iglesias and Rivera, opted for a strategy that tended towards messages of a mixed nature: 14% of the messages of the far left representative, Iglesias, began as statements and later turned into attacks. This value is balanced by the neutral messages he delivered, representing 27% of his interventions and contributing to balance the nature of his speeches (see Figure 5.4). As for the liberal candidate, he took a more adversarial stance, with 48% of his messages being attacks and more than 33% being mixed attacks. In addition, he is the only leader who did not deliver any defensive messages.

A more nuanced analysis by candidate shows that French participants were less aggressive than their Spanish counterparts. Among the Spanish candidates, the conservative candidate Casado (PP) emerged as the most confrontational. Of all his interventions, 73% were classified as attacks, indicating a deliberate effort to attract attention. This strategy was likely employed in response to the conservative PP's significant losses in the previous national elections, prompting Casado to seek ways to regain traction. In the French debate, the two most aggressive candidates came from radical or reactionary parties. Both the far-left candidate, Mélenchon, and the far-right candidate, Le Pen, exceeded a 20% attack rate, although not all of their verbal assaults were explicitly categorized as "direct attacks" (see Figure 5.6).

The approaches of the winning candidates are also noteworthy, with both showing a more restrained demeanor in their speeches. In particular, the future president Macron refrained from making purely offensive remarks. Instead, the liberal candidate opted for mixed attacks, using this strategy in 30% of his interventions during the debate. In contrast, the more adversarial tone of the Spanish debate favored Sánchez, who adopted a more aggressive stance than his French counterpart, although less than the other Spanish candidates. After winning the general election in April, Sánchez assumed the presidency, which was evident in his frequent use of interventions to defend his positions and his government. The comparatively less aggressive tone of the French debate led most candidates to adopt an approach similar to Macron's. More than half of the messages from the conservative candidate Fillon, the

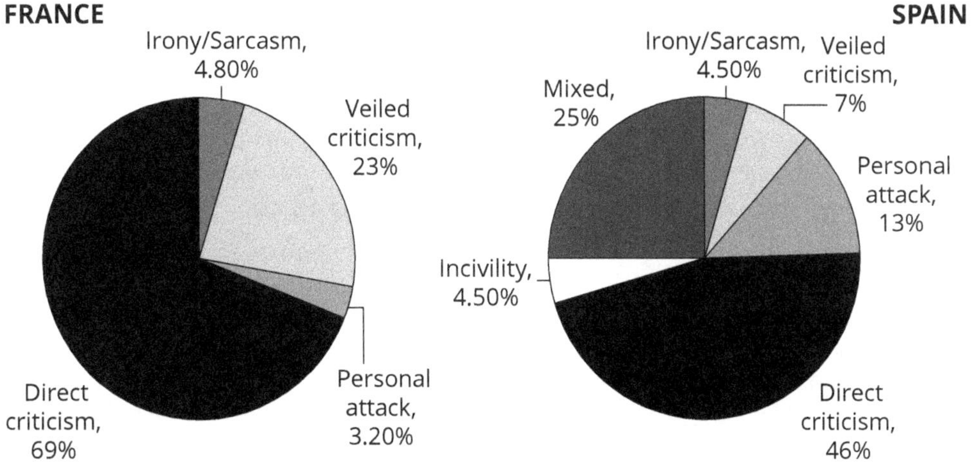

Figure 5.3 Speeches by Attack Type

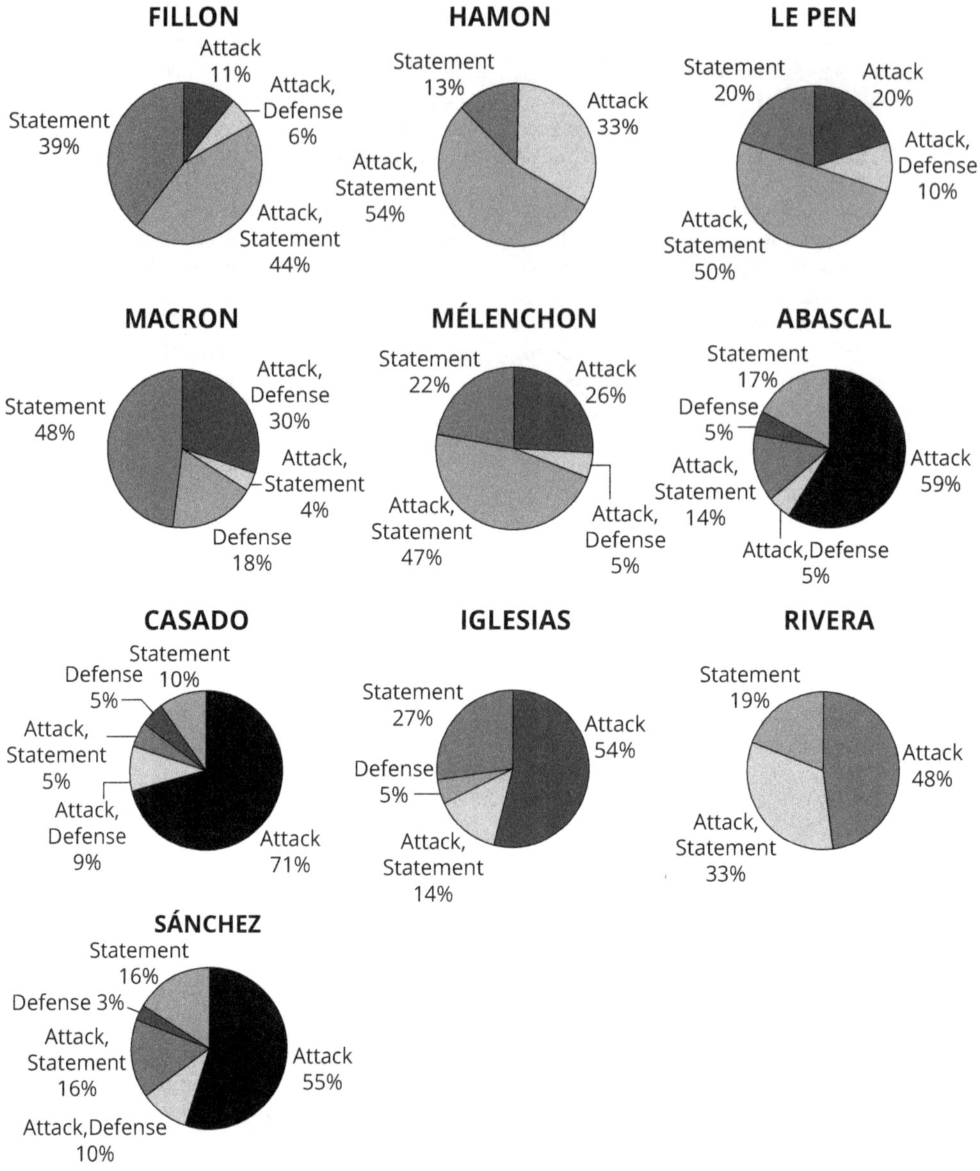

Figure 5.4 Intervention Typologies by Candidate in France and Spain

far-right candidate Le Pen, and the far-left candidate Mélenchon were mixed attacks. The Socialist candidate Hamon was the only exception, with neutral messages making up 60% of his total interventions. These results suggest that the two countries do not follow the same pattern in terms of candidates' use of attacks. In the French context, candidates representing parties at the extremes of the ideological spectrum (Mélenchon and Le Pen) relied primarily on attacks, while in Spain, this strategy was not as conclusive, as it was used by Abascal from the extreme right but also by Casado from the center-right.

A more detailed analysis of the candidates' attacks shows that they also adapted their speeches in order to project a specific image. Comparing the

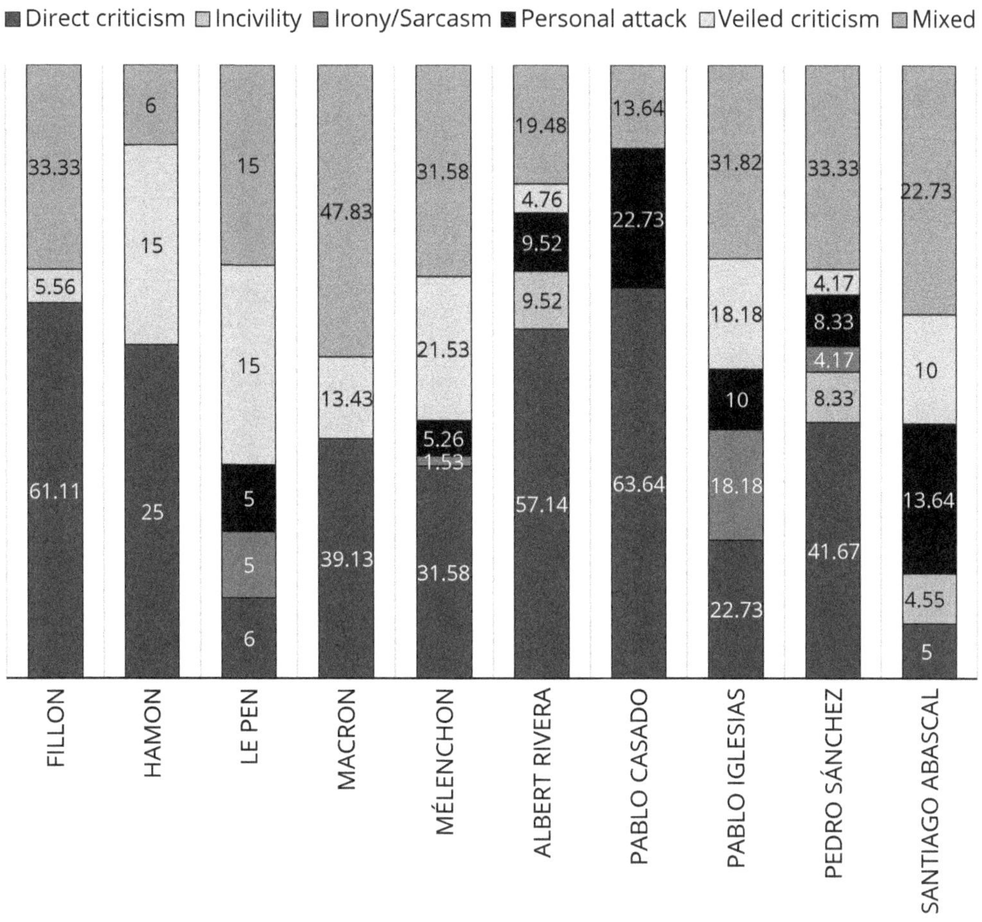

Figure 5.5 Type of Attacks by Candidate in Both Debates

interventions of all candidates, both French and Spanish, it can be observed that the more radical candidates followed a less confrontational strategy than their counterparts belonging to the mainstream parties. Looking at the weight of direct criticism in the overall messages of far-right candidates, such as Abascal and Le Pen, or far-left candidates, such as Iglesias and Mélenchon, we see that the radicals resorted to direct criticism less often. In none of these cases did they account for more than 35% of the total messages, reaching figures as low as 9% for the *VOX* candidate. Instead, the more extreme candidates articulated their criticisms in a more subtle or balanced way. This behavior corresponds to the strategy of candidates who, aware of their radical position, try to project a more moderate image of themselves. On the other hand, representatives of traditional parties, such as Sánchez, Hamon, Fillon, and Casado, who take advantage of their positions closer to the center, opted for a more direct style of criticism.

As for lack of civility, only three of the ten candidates resorted to inappropriate language during the debates. This was the case of Abascal, Sánchez, and Rivera, all Spanish politicians who used it as a resource to discredit their opponents. Although these comments were out of place, especially compared to the French debate, it is important to consider that this type of accusation is part of the tradition of some candidates in electoral debates in Spain (Blas Arroyo, 2003).

Content also played a key role in shaping the level of confrontation (see Figure 5.6). As the debates between the candidates progressed, the

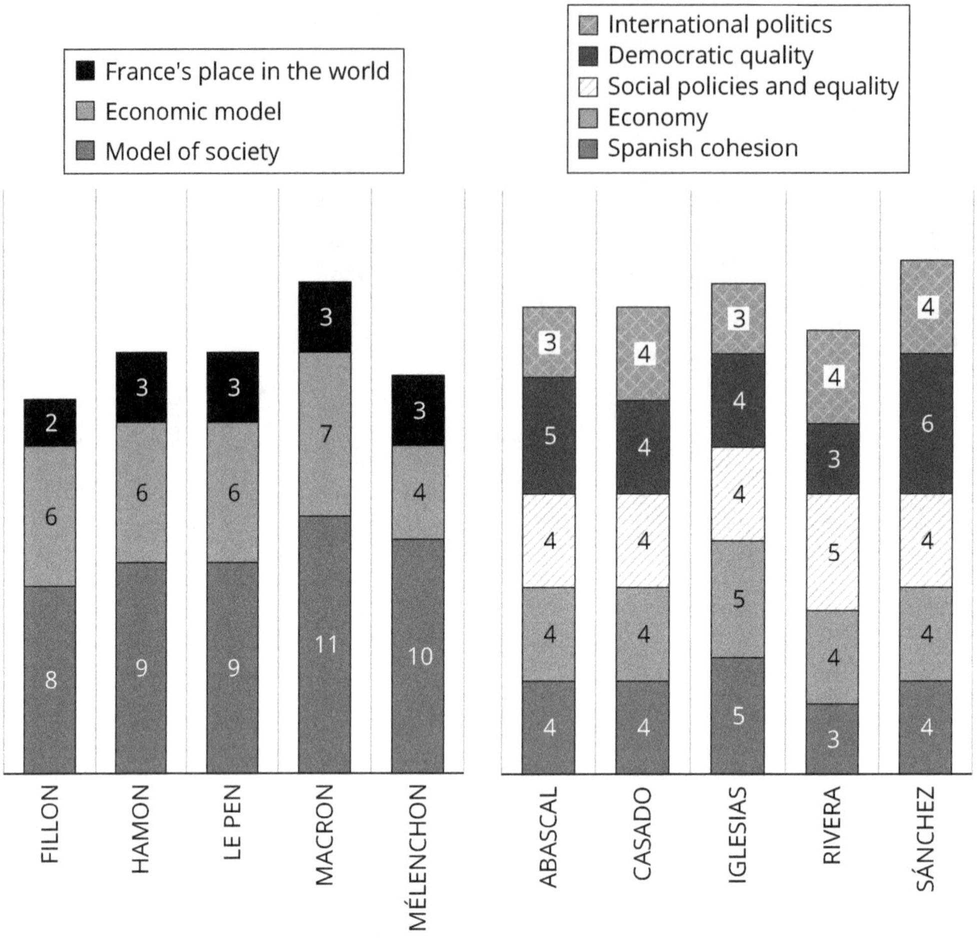

Figure 5.6 Number of Speeches per Topic in Both Debates

atmosphere became increasingly charged with confrontation. Each country approached the debate differently, with the French dividing it into three main sections and the Spanish structuring it into as many as five. Despite these differences, however, the themes of the debate remained largely similar. Certain sections, particularly those on national unity or social policy, saw a notable escalation in disagreement. Candidates used these topics to illustrate their different approaches, while others, such as international policy, were discussed in a more explanatory manner. This variance could be attributed to the different salience of these issues for the candidates of certain participating parties. For example, the issues of national cohesion and social policy emerged as significant factors in the parties' arguments, leading to heated debates during these segments (Figures 5.4–5.6).

Throughout both debates, a trend was noted in which certain candidates were targeted by their opponents for questioning. In both cases, the candidate who faced the most questions ended up winning the election. In the Spanish debate, Sánchez was the most frequently questioned candidate (see Table 5.1), receiving an impressive 38% of all questions, putting him well ahead of Casado, who received only 18% of the questions. Despite all the candidates addressing the incumbent candidate, those who focused on him the most were the candidates from the right, Casado, and the far-right, Abascal. The candidate from the far-left, with whom a few months later Sánchez formed the first coalition government, only questioned him on nine occasions. In the French context, questions were distributed fairly among the candidates. However, it is

Table 5.1 Interactions Among Candidates in Spain

Candidate	*Sánchez*	*Casado*	*Rivera*	*Iglesias*	*Abascal*
Sánchez		9	7	7	5
Casado	15		3	2	1
Rivera	11	5		4	6
Iglesias	9	4	3		6
Abascal	13	6	6	8	
TOTAL	48	24	19	21	18

noteworthy that the questions directed at Macron (26%) and Fillon (25%) together accounted for over 50% of all questions during the debate. These results point out that incumbents tend to be the focus of negative campaigning by other opponents and receive more attacks (P3). In France, there are some nuances though. Since there was not a proper incumbent from the socialists, the attacks were directed to the candidates representing the other main traditional section of the ideological spectrum, the center-right, here represented by Fillon and Macron (Table 5.2).

Some candidates stood out by focusing their interventions significantly on one of their opponents. In Spain, this behavior was observed between the leading candidate in the polls and the candidate in second place (see Table 5.1). For example, the sum of Casado's interventions against Sánchez was more than double the sum of his interventions against the other candidates. A different behavior can be observed among the candidates of the newer parties. The candidates of *VOX*, *Unidas Podemos*, and *Ciudadanos* questioned Sánchez more often than the others. However, when we analyze the rest of the interventions, we find a dual pattern. On the one hand, the far-left and the liberals, who had already participated in the 2015–2016 electoral cycle, directed more attacks at Sánchez, but also questioned Casado several times, practically ignoring each other during the debate. On the other hand, the behavior of the far-right candidate clearly stands out as an atypical case with respect to the rest of the candidates. With 33 interventions directed at the other candidates, he was the participant who questioned the others the most, followed by President Sánchez with 27.

The calmer nature of the French debate was also reflected in the number of questions. Compared to the 138 questions asked by the Spanish candidates in their debate, the French questioned each other only 98 times, a number that was mostly taken up by the representatives of the extreme left and the extreme right. The interpellations that Mélenchon (22) and Le Pen (30) addressed to the rest of their opponents exceeded 50, a fact that illustrates how both candidates behaved during the debate. Thus, and despite the fact that the general tone of the debate was characterized by the aforementioned "mixed attack," the most extreme candidates directed their criticism at the rest of the opponents, with one exception: both Mélenchon and Le Pen practically ignored each other. Of the 22 interpellations made by the leader of the far-left, only twice did he address Le Pen. In turn, the latest, mentioned him only once (Figure 5.7).

In terms of the legitimacy strategies used by the candidates to build their arguments, rationality as a strategy predominates. Macron was the candidate who used it most (52%), while Mélenchon used it least (5%). The latter's case is particularly striking because, instead of relying on rationality, he used morality to structure his arguments in almost 90% of his speeches. French candidates used morality to legitimize their arguments more often than their Spanish counterparts. Thus, the average of moral arguments in the former case is 52.2%, while in the Spanish case, it is 8.2%. The scarce use of authority to legitimize the arguments used is also noteworthy, especially in the French case. In France, only Macron (22%) and, to a lesser extent, Fillon (12%) used authority to argue. The situation was similar in Spain, where only the far-right candidate Abascal used this strategy frequently (18%).

DISCUSSION

This research aims to contribute to the discussion on the importance of electoral debates with a comparative approach exploring the development

Table 5.2 Interactions Among Candidates in France

Candidate	*Fillon*	*Macron*	*Hamon*	*Mélenchon*	*Le Pen*
Fillon		3	4	7	5
Macron	4		3	5	7
Hamon	2	3		1	2
Mélenchon	6	9	5		2
Le Pen	13	11	5	1	
TOTAL	25	26	17	14	16

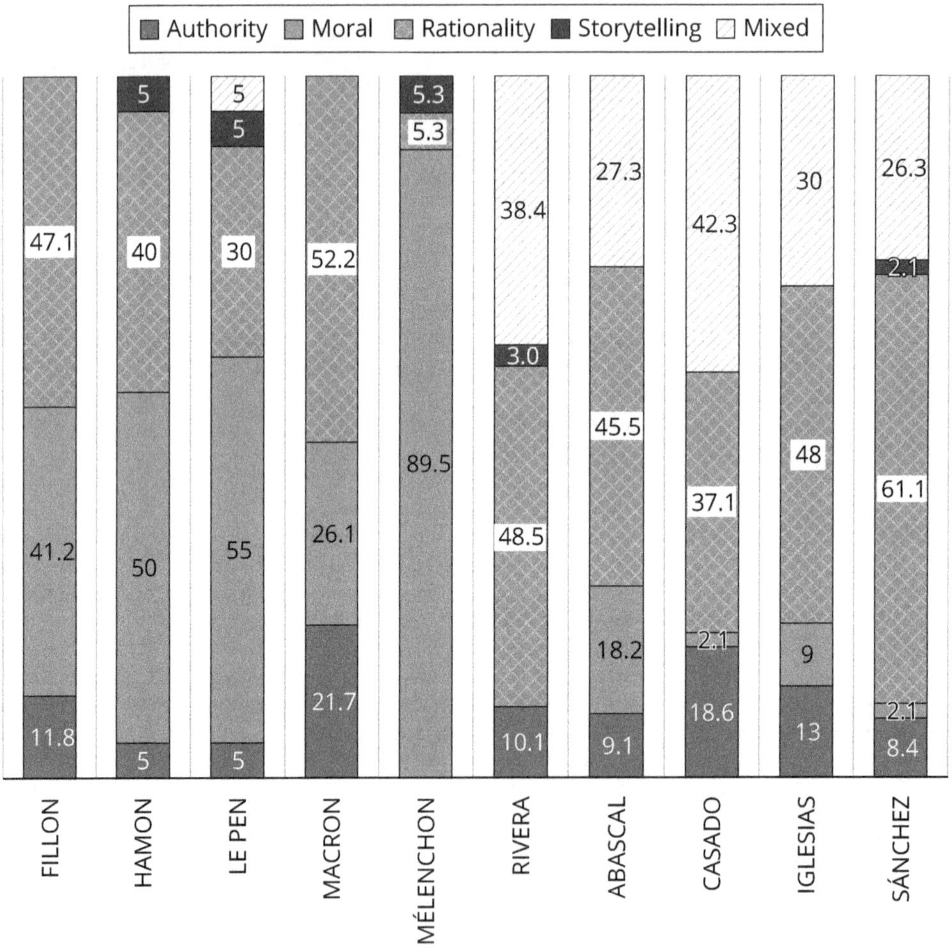

Figure 5.7 Legitimization Types

of candidates' performances. By comparing France and Spain, the study draws conclusions that could assist political consultants and marketers in developing debate strategies. As explained earlier, both countries are interesting case studies for comparing since both share some aspects. On the one hand, both have been holding debates in a steady traditional pattern until recently (2015 and 2019 for Spain and 2017 for France). On the other hand, the political scenario changed radically in both countries, with the appearance of new parties and new leaderships.

The situation of political instability that the Spanish party system has experienced since the 2015–2016 electoral cycle translated into greater hostility in the debate, confirming our first proposition. As we will see in the following paragraphs, the changes in the right-wing bloc, which experienced enormous electoral volatility in the 2019 national elections, combined with the institutionalism that the left-wing parties, especially the PSOE, tried to convey, made the Spanish debate very aggressive.

This hostility can be seen at a glance by comparing the weight of aggressive messages in the two debates. While in France the sum of attacks and mixed attacks reached 53% of the total, in Spain this percentage rises to 71% of all messages. This percentage increases when analyzing the behavior of certain candidates, such as the centrist Rivera, whose attacks accounted for 81% of his interventions, with most of them qualifying as "direct attacks," which increased the overall hostility of his speeches.

In the Spanish case, there is a clear predominance of pure attacks as opposed to mixed attacks, both in general and in particular, which also confirms our second proposition. While in France the sum of all types of attacks reaches 53%, in Spain this percentage is surpassed by counting only purely aggressive messages (56%). The same happens with the classification of the messages of the candidates. Iglesias, the leader of *Unidas Podemos*, was the candidate who used statements the most, but even in his case, the attack messages represent 55% of his interventions. This figure contrasts sharply with the situation in France, where no candidate exceeds 30% in this category, with one of them, the future president Macron, not using them at any time.

With regard to our third proposition, our analysis confirms that candidates who were ahead in the pre-election polls received a greater number of questions. This is the case of Sánchez in the Spanish debate, who with 48 interpellations was the candidate most addressed by the other participants, and also of Macron, although with a very small difference compared to the Spanish Prime Minister. Thus, while Sánchez received twice as many questions as the second candidate (48 as opposed to Casado's 24), in the French case, Macron was only one question ahead of Fillon. After analyzing the political context in each country, we argue that this is due to two reasons: the adversarial tone and the novelty of Macron.

On the one hand, as has been shown throughout this chapter, the Spanish debate was much more adversarial than the French debate, which was more programmatic. By moving away from a proactive vision and focusing on attacking the other participants, Spanish candidates turned the debate into a confrontation. Instead of considering the debate as an opportunity to present their ideas, the leaders of the five main Spanish parties behaved as if they were in a duel, trying to convince the viewers that their party was the best by attacking the other candidates. In other words, they relied not only on the merits of their proposals, but rather on the shortcomings of their opponents. In this adversarial context, it is normal that the number of questions was higher in the Spanish debate, and therefore that the leader who had the best chances of winning the elections was questioned more often.

Second, it is worth distinguishing between who was leading the polls in Spain and who was leading the polls in France at the time of the two debates. Unlike in the Iberian Peninsula, Macron was not an incumbent candidate. Although the leader of *La République En Marche* was leading the polls at the time of the French debate (March 20), the future French president was still a distorting agent of the French party system. Until May of that year, when Macron reached the Elysée, conservatives and socialists had shared the French presidency. By defeating Le Pen and succeeding François Hollande (PS), Macron became the first president since the beginning of the Fifth Republic (1958) to not belong to any traditional establishment parties. For this reason, during the debate analyzed in this chapter, Macron shared the limelight of the interpellations with the person who would traditionally have been the natural alternative to the Socialist Party in government: the leader of the conservative party, Fillon. Therefore, the number of interpellations Macron received was not as remarkable as that of Sánchez.

Similarly, the behavior of the incumbent candidate in Spain differs somewhat from proposition1 and from what the literature suggests. It is true that he received more attacks than the rest, but he is also the second candidate who made more interpellations to the rest of the participants, 27, only five less than *VOX*. This is explained by the strategy of the *Socialist Party* in the 2019 elections. Since these were the second national elections in which *VOX* could obtain parliamentary representation in the Congress of Deputies, the PSOE gave a very adversarial approach to its campaign and approached it from a two-block perspective. Thus, it conveyed the idea that voters had to choose between socialism and the extreme right, including its main opponent, the conservative PP, in the second bloc. It is not surprising, therefore, that Sánchez, the incumbent candidate in Spain, took a more adversarial stance in the debates than is usual for this type of candidate.

Our fourth proposition is clearly confirmed in the French case, but not in the Spanish one. The candidates at the ideological extremes, Le Pen and Mélenchon, were by far the most aggressive. 86.7% of the messages of the candidate of the French extreme right had an aggressive tone, a figure that decreases, although slightly, in the case of the leader of the extreme left, who was aggressive in 82.2% of his interventions. However, these data are influenced by the general tone of the debate, which is based more on proposals than on attacks. For example, both extreme candidates made clearly offensive statements on 30% of the occasions and mixed proposals with attacks in just over 50% of their interventions. It is precisely in the analysis of the clearly offensive messages that the difference between the extreme candidates and the rest of the participants in the French debate can be observed. While these messages represent 30% of the total for Le Pen and Mélenchon, they fall to around 15% for the representatives of the traditional parties, Fillon and Hamon. A striking case is that of Macron, who did not make any messages in this category during the first debate, concentrating on mixed attack messages.

In Spain, our fourth proposition does not hold. Despite the fact that all the candidates are very evenly matched in terms of aggressiveness, the most belligerent one was the candidate from the center party. 86.6% of Rivera's messages during the debate can be classified as some kind of attack. He is accompanied on the podium by the conservative Casado (76%) and the leader of the extreme right, Abascal (75.1%). Thus, what explains the aggressiveness of the messages of the candidates is not only their ideological position but rather the situation of the political party the candidates belong to. The arrival of *VOX* in the Congress of Deputies in April 2019 meant a crisis of the ideological space of the right in Spain. Until that time, *Ciudadanos* and the *Partido Popular* had been the dominant forces on the right of the ideological spectrum. However, the emergence of *VOX* forced both parties to redefine their positions, particularly in relation to the far-right party. The competition on the right and the volatility of the vote for the right-wing bloc reached unprecedented levels in the history of Spanish democracy. This explains the hyper-aggressiveness of right-wing candidates during the debate, with bittersweet outcomes. The performance of *Partido Popular* and *VOX* was regarded as satisfactory, whereas the hyperactivity of Albert Rivera (*Ciudadanos*) was perceived as indicative of despair. In this context, the electoral prospects of *Partido Popular* and *VOX* as predicted by pre-election polls played a pivotal role. The electoral prospects of *PP* and *VOX* were optimistic, with the expectation that both formations would secure a greater number of seats in the rerun election. Conversely, the hyperactivity of *Ciudadanos* was perceived as a consequence of the party's desperation, particularly in light of the frequent position shifts it had undergone in the preceding months.

The two left-wing candidates, aware of this situation, opted for a more institutional image. Particularly, this strategic approach is clearly visible in the behavior of the far-left candidate in the debate and implied a major strategic change for the party. Until the 2019 electoral cycle, *Unidas Podemos*, as well as its leader, Pablo Iglesias, had been characterized by a brassy style of doing politics. Its arrival to the institutions in 2015 occurred in a climate of great political tension, a situation that the far-left formation was adept at exploiting. The leaders of *Unidas Podemos* were not reluctant to engage in direct confrontation with the traditional parties, PP and PSOE. However, this changed in 2019. In contrast to Rivera, Iglesias presented himself as a more central figure in the political landscape. His messages remained assertive and advocated for a radical transformation of the system. However, he employed a more measured approach to expressing these ideas, opting for neutral statements and avoiding direct attacks as a strategy.

The *Socialist Party* was not the only one that understood the arrival of the far-right formation as an outlier in relation to the rest of the previous elections. The two formations that were in the right-wing bloc in the 2019 elections, the *PP* and *Ciudadanos*, had difficulty defining their position on *VOX*. As a result, both the conservatives and the liberals did not question Abascal as assiduously as they did the rest of the candidates. For his part, the representative of the far-right referred to all the candidates on the stage. The fact that the leader of *VOX* had not yet achieved significant power allowed him greater freedom to criticize the other candidates, whose parties were experiencing a certain degree of wear and tear due to their roles in territorial governments. On the French side, interestingly, Le Pen was also the candidate less questioned by the rest. This fact could be interpreted under different angles. On the one hand, the other candidates did not want to give Le Pen more space and attention. On the other hand, they wanted to present themselves as far away from what Le Pen represented politically. Also in France, the extreme parties from different sides, Mélenchon and Le Pen, followed the same practice of going negative like *VOX*. In this sense, it was a success for them because they improved compared to the 2012 elections: Le Pen got 21.3% and Mélenchon, 19.6% in 2017 compared to 17.9% and 11.1% in 2012, respectively. In addition, Le Pen was finally able to advance to the second round as she was the candidate with the most votes along with Macron.

As our results show, there are many options when it comes to competing. Candidates and campaign managers often make the decision to go negative, especially when they seem to be in a disadvantaged position or threatened by new political options. Sánchez in Spain is an example that even as an incumbent, when his position seemed to be under threat from various sides of the political scene, he clearly based his strategy on going negative. Going negative also has to do with trying to occupy extreme positions, as shown by Mélenchon and Le Pen. However, this was not the case in Spain, where *Unidas Podemos* preferred to have a lower profile compared to previous elections, while *VOX* based its strategy on attacks. Real practice in politics shows that there are different options and not one unique solution. An interesting comparison is the approach adopted by Macron and Rivera, both of whom represent moderate and centrist positions in the political spectrum. The French candidate chose to present himself as a calm, firm candidate while Rivera opted for a more aggressive strategy.

CONCLUDING REMARKS

The intriguing matrices showing which candidates attacked which in the debates studied seem under-exploited at the moment, and might offer a jumping-off point for some tentative suggestions of new theories and/or avenues to research. From the consultants' side, they will have to consider their responsibility in advising candidates to go negative. Among the positive aspects of this negative strategy, one notable point is the clarification of candidates' positions. The aggressiveness displayed by Spanish candidates helped shed light on their stances, which can be highly beneficial in fiercely competitive electoral environments, such as the 2019 period for the Spanish right-wing. However, this strategy was not always successful. There were cases, like that of *Ciudadanos*, where instead of projecting strength and clarifying their positions, it had the opposite effect. When advising candidates to adopt a negative approach, it's important for advisors to consider that attitude in debates is crucial, but not everything. The actions of parties and candidates in the months leading up to debates play a crucial role in how citizens perceive them during those debates.

Rivera's main flaw during the debate was precisely that his demeanor lacked the stability his party projected. While Rivera had more debate experience than others, his actions did not align with the party's situation. After numerous position changes in preceding months, *Ciudadanos* was no longer seen as a stable and reliable party. Additionally, it's important to be aware that opting for aggressiveness can lead to unintended consequences such as escalating the debate into a vicious cycle of attacks.

Furthermore, adopting an assertive stance may result in unforeseen consequences, such as intensifying the debate into a cycle of attacks, which could potentially alienate voters. The Spanish debate, with its excessive emphasis on attacks, demonstrated that this approach could complicate discussions and drive voters away from candidates. In contrast, the French debate permitted more distinct delineations in positions and facilitated idea exchange, exemplifying a more balanced approach.

The political context also plays a pivotal role. The political instability that has prevailed in Spain since the 2015–2016 electoral cycle has led to a greater degree of hostility in debates. The changes that have occurred within the right-wing bloc, combined with the institutionalism that has been projected by the left-wing parties, especially the PSOE, have resulted in a highly aggressive Spanish debate. This adversarial tone has transformed the debate into a confrontation, where candidates have been inclined to rely more on attacking their opponents' shortcomings rather than presenting the merits of their own proposals.

Moreover, candidates who are leading in pre-election polls tend to receive more questions, as evidenced by Sánchez in Spain and Macron in France. However, the number of questions received also depends on the debate's tone and the candidates' novelty. Macron, as a nonincumbent and a distorting agent in the French party system, shared the limelight with Fillon, the traditional alternative to the Socialist Party. In contrast, Sánchez, as the incumbent candidate in Spain, received more attacks but also made significant interpellations, reflecting the PSOE's strategy in the 2019 elections.

While negative strategies can clarify candidates' positions and offer competitive advantages, they require careful management to avoid unintended consequences. Political consultants and campaign managers must consider the broader context, including the candidates' actions leading up to the debate and the overall tone of the electoral environment, in order to effectively advise on and implement these strategies.

Notes

1 As far as research is concerned, there is a long tradition in the study of television political advertisements in the United States. It is remarkable the existence of longitudinal studies on this topic. This is because political advertising in the United States is the central axis of every political campaign and has been a pioneer in its use, as well as political marketing. Furthermore, the fairly permissive regulation favors the conditions for the use of spots and these are not comparable in any other country (i.e.: ; Johnston & Kaid, 2002; Kaid & Johnston, 1991; Ridout & Searles, 2011).

2 In France, for the presidential election, a first-round vote is followed two weeks later by a second vote opposing the two politicians heading the score, unless someone obtains more than 50% of the ballots in the first round.

3 Actually, in the 2002 campaign, for the first time, there was an unusual situation in French politics. Lionel Jospin, the socialist candidate, did not pass to the second round, Jean Marie Le Pen, from the Front National, did instead. This extreme right candidate and Jacques Chirac, representing the center-right party, ended up being the protagonists of the debate.

4 A third debate was initially planned for the 20th of April, three days before the vote. It was finally cancelled because it was too close to election day.

5 In Spain, the President is elected through legislative elections. The name used for this position is President even if it doesn't correspond to the head of the state, but to the head of the government instead.

6 In France, for the presidential election, a first-round vote is followed two weeks later by a second vote opposing the two politicians heading the score, unless someone obtains more than 50% of the ballots in the first round.

7 A Spanish communication group that operates in various sectors of activity, especially audiovisual, and which is made up of several media outlets.

8 This typology includes three mixed types-mixed attack, defensive attack, and defensive statement – that result from combining the pure types – attack, defense, and statement. During the debates, participating candidates may choose to begin their remarks from a defensive position in order to move to an attack or to elaborate on a particular point. In these cases, we believe that a mixed type may capture the nature of the speech more accurately than using a pure type alone. The label "mixed attack" was given to all those speeches that contained a mixture of attack and explanation.

REFERENCES

Ansolabehere, S., & Iyengar, S. (2010). *Going negative: How political advertisements Shrink and Polarize the electorate*. Simon & Schuster.

Bar, A. (1997). Spain: A prime ministerial government. In J. Blondel & F. Müller-Rommel (Eds.), *Cabinets in Western Europe*. Macmillan.

Benoit, W. L., & Harthcock, A. (1999). Functions of the great debates: Acclaims, attacks, and defenses in the 1960 presidential debates. *Communication Monographs*, *66*(4), 341–357.

Benoit, W. L., & Sheafer, T. (2006). Functional theory and political discourse: Televised debates in Israel and the United States. *Journalism & Mass Communication Quarterly*, *83*(2), 281–297.

Blas Arroyo, J. L. (2003). 'No diga chorradasi…' la descortesía en el debate político cara a cara. Una aproximación pragma-variacionista. *Oralia: Análisis del Discurso Oral*, *4*, 9–45.

Brandariz Portela, T. (2021). El debate electoral del 10-N de 2019 en España: Los candidatos políticos y RTVE. *Revista de Ciencias de La Comunicación e Información*, 1–25.

Campus, D. (2010). Mediatization and personalization of politics in Italy and France: The cases of Berlusconi and Sarkozy. *International Journal of Press Politics*, *15*(2), 219. https://doi.org/10.1177/1940161209358762

Crespo, I., Garrido, A., Carletta, I., & Riorda, M. (2011). *Manual de Comunicación Política y estrategias de campaña. Candidatos, Medios y Electores en una nueva era*. Biblos.

Díez Nicolás, J., & Semetko, H. A. (1995). La televisión y las elecciones de 1993. In A. Múñoz Alonso & J. I. Rospir (Eds.), *Comunicación Política* (pp. 243–304). Editorial Universitas.

Durovic, A. (2019). The French elections of 2017: Shaking the disease? *West European Politics*, *42*(7), 1487–1503.

Gerstlé, J., & Nai, A. (2019). Negativity, emotionality and populist rhetoric in election campaigns worldwide, and their effects on media attention and electoral success. *European Journal of Communication*, *34*(4), 410–444.

Grunberg, G., & Haegel, F. (2007). La France Vers le Bipartisme?: La Présidentialisation du Ps et de

L'ump. *Presses de Sciences Po*. https://doi.org/10.3917/scpo.grunb.2007.01
Gougou, F., & Persico, S. (2017). A new party system in the making? The 2017 French presidential election. *French Politics*, *15*(3), 303–321.
Haselmayer, M. (2019). Negative campaigning and its consequences: A review and a look ahead. *French Politics*, *17*, 355–372.
Heywood, P. (1991). Governing a new democracy: The power of the Prime Minister in Spain. *West European Politics*, *14*(2), 97–115.
Hutter, S., Kriesi, H., & Vidal, G. (2018). Old versus new politics: The political spaces in Southern Europe in times of crises. *Party Politics*, *24*(1), 10–22.
Johnston, A., & Kaid, L. L. (2002). Image ads and issue ads in US presidential advertising: Using videostyle to explore stylistic differences in televised political ads from 1952 to 2000. *Journal of Communication*, *52*(2), 281–300.
Kaid, L. L., & Johnston, A. (1991). Negative versus positive television advertising in US presidential campaigns, 1960–1988. *Journal of Communication*, *41*(3), 53–64.
Kuhn, R. (2017). The 2017 French presidential and parliamentary elections. *Modern & Contemporary France*, *25*(4), 335–358.
Langer, A. I. (2007). A historical exploration of the personalisation of politics in the print media: The British Prime Ministers (1945–1999). *Parliamentary Affairs*, *60*(3), 371–387.
Lau, R. R., & Pomper, G. M. (2002). Effectiveness of negative campaigning in US Senate elections. *American Journal of Political Science*, 47–66.
Leeper, T. J., & Slothuus, R. (2014). Parties and motivated reasoning. *Political Psychology*, *35*, 129–156.
López, G., Gámir, J., Garcí, F., Llorca, G., Lorena, C., & González, J. L. (2015). El debate sobre Europa en Twitter. Discursos y estrategias de los candidatos de las elecciones al Parlamento Europeo de 2014 en España. *Revista de Estudios Políticos*, *170*, 213–246.
Luengo, Ó. G. (2011). Debates electorales en televisión: una aproximación preliminar a sus efectos inmediatos. *Revista Española de Ciencia Política*, 25, 81–96.
Maarek, P. J. (2014). *Communication et marketing de l'homme politique*. LexisNexis.
Maarek, P. J. (2016). Televised presidential debates: Parallel lessons from the 2012 American and French elections. *French Politics*, *14*, 178–205.
Maarek, P. J. (2020). French television debates. Just audience or true influence? In J. Juárez-Gámiz, C. Holtz-Bacha, & A. Schroeder (Eds.), *Routledge international handbook of electoral debates* (pp. 197–209). Routledge.
Maarek, P. J., & Mercier, A. (2018). *2017, La présidentielle Chamboule-tout. La Communication Politique au Prisme du "Dégagisme*. L'Harmattan.
Marín, B. (2003). Debates electorales por televisión. In S. Berrocal (Ed.), *Comunicación Política en Televisión y Nuevos Medios* (pp. 207–243). Ariel.
Martin, P. (2017). Un séisme politique. L'élection présidentielle de 2017. *Commentaire*, *158*, 249–264.
Morales, R., & García Gordillo, M. (2023). Entre el "cara a cara" y la multiplicidad de candidatos: el debate electoral televisado en Europa (2019-2022). *Ámbitos. Revista Internacional De Comunicación*, *59*, 127–146.
Müller, S., & Schnabl, G. (2021). A database and index for political polarization in the eu. *Economics Bulletin*, *41*(4), 2232–2248.
Norton, M. I., & Goethals, G. R. (2004). Spin (and pitch) doctors: Campaign strategies in televised political debates. *Political Behavior*, *26*, 227–248.
Oliver, J. E., & Rahn, W. N. (2016). Rise of Trumpenvolk: Populism in 2016 election. *The ANNALS of the American Academy of Political Science*, *667*(1), 189–206.
Pérez-Ruiz, M., & Melgosa, F. (2015). Los debates electorales realizados en España en 2008: cuando la política se convierte en espectáculo televisado. *Contratexto*, 024, 113–132.
Poguntke, T., & Webb, P. (Eds.). (2005). *The Presidentialization of politics: A comparative study of modern democracies*. Oxford University Press.
Raupp, J. (2022). "The situation is serious": Angela Merkel's crisis communication in the COVID-19 pandemic. In P. J. Maarek (Ed.), *Manufacturing government communication on COVID-19 – a comparative perspective* (pp. 231–252). Springer.
Rebolledo, M. (2017). La personalización de la política: una propuesta de definición para su estudio sistemático. *Revista de Comunicación*, *16*(2), 147–176.
Reinemann, C., & Wilke, J. (2007). It's the debates, stupid! How the introduction of televised debates changed the portrayal of Chancellor candidates in the German press, 1949—2005. *Harvard International Journal of Press/Politics*, *12*(4), 92–111.
Ridout, T., & Searles, K. (2011). It's my campaign I'll cry if I want: How and when campaigns use emotional appeals. *Political Psychology*, *32*(3), 439–458.
Rodríguez Teruel, J., Barberà, O., Barrio, A., & Casal Bértoa, F. (2018). From stability to change? The evolution of the party system in Spain. In M. Lisi (Ed.), *Party system change, the European crisis and the state of democracy* (pp. 248–270). Routledge.
Rodríguez-Virgili, J., Portilla-Manjón, I., & Sierra-Iso, A. (2022). Cuarenta años de polarización ideológica en España. *Revista Empresa y Humanismo*, *25*(2), 75–103.
Scheller, S. (2019). The strategic use of fear appeals in political communication. *Political Communication*, *36*(4), 1–23.
Shapiro, M. A., & Rieger, R. H. (1992). Comparing positive and negative political advertising on radio. *Journalism Quarterly*, *69*(1), 135–145.
Simón, P. (2016). The challenges of the new Spanish multipartism: Government formation failure and

the 2016 General Election. *South European Society & Politics*, *21*(4), 493–517.

Swanson, D. L., & Mancini, P. (Eds.). (1996). *Politics, media, and modern democracy: An international study of innovations in electoral campaigning and their consequences*. Praeger.

van Leeuwen, T. (2007). Legitimation in discourse and communication. *Discourse & Communication*, *1*(1), 91–112.

Walter, A. S. (2014). Negative campaigning in Western Europe: Similar or different? *Political Studies*, *62*, 42–60.

Zamora-Medina, R., & Rebolledo, M. (2017). La personalización como recurso estratégico en los debates electorales. El caso del 7-D: El Debate Decisivo en las elecciones generales de 2015. In P. Vázquez-Sinde(Dir.) (Ed.), *Personalización en Comunicación Política: de la Técnica a la Estrategia* (pp. 11–36). Egregius Ediciones.

Zamora-Medina, R., & Rebolledo, M. (2019). La estrategia de la personalización: los debates de las elecciones 2015 y 2016 en España. *Estudios sobre el Mensaje Periodístico*, *15*(3), 1649–1662.

Polarized and Connected: Measuring Campaign Effects in the 2016 and 2020 US Presidential Elections

Koen Pauwels, Kai Manke, Raoul Kübler and Costas Panagopoulos

INTRODUCTION

The last decades have witnessed a substantial change in the political landscape and how politicians and political parties engage with citizens (Diamond, 2010). The advent of social media has offered new channels, allowing more interactive engagement between voters and political candidates, as well as across voters and between voters, and other stakeholders. However, the rise of populism, ideological and partisan polarization and the unexpected outcomes of elections and referenda across the globe has led many to question whether democracy and the American political system are able to cope with the challenges of the internet era (Persily, 2017). Growing levels of misinformation and disinformation in the electoral arena only complicate the picture for candidates and political marketers. How can candidates best market themselves in an age of polarization and disinformation?

While disinformation has been around since ancient times, social media has greatly expanded its reach and potential importance (Aral, 2020). An increase of disinformation has been shown in the 2016 Brexit referendum (Bastos & Mercea, 2019) and has been associated with the rise of populist parties within the European Union (Monti, 2018; Shao et al., 2018) and Latin America (Ferrara et al., 2016). Despite considerable attention to disinformation also in the United States, the focus has been on its origin, prominence, and dissemination mechanisms, and less on the empirical quantification of its actual impact on election outcomes (Aral, 2020; Jamieson, 2020; Silver, 2017a). Disinformation research has shown that factually false messages travel faster and farther than real news on social media (Vosoughi et al., 2018), but not whether it influences polls or votes. On this score, the evidence is decidedly mixed to date. Allcott and Gentzkow (2017) find that factually incorrect claims had no impact in the 2016 election, for example, while others find links between disinformation and the 2016 polls (e.g., Guess et al., 2020; Gunther et al., 2019), but without controlling for other potential drivers or distinguishing different disinformation topics and their effects on different polls. This leaves central questions about how social media and disinformation shape political preferences unanswered, and especially how such developments interact with other strategies and tactics deployed by political operatives to advance their clients' interests in campaigns.

Contemporary political marketers are blessed with seemingly endless amounts of data to track political preferences over the course of an election campaign but simultaneously cursed with the possibility that preference polls and election surveys may be biased, inaccurate, potentially misleading or send mixed or inconsistent signals (Jennings & Wlezien, 2018; Kennedy et al., 2018). Importantly, such polling may also distort the decision-making of campaigns if they base shifts in strategy on these polls, such as adapting the content and tone, as well as the allocation of their marketing communication (Gordon et al., 2012). As political marketers have access to multiple streams of information, including prediction markets, traditional polls, and probabilistic polls, a better understanding of these predictive metrics would help assess their value in political marketing in the polarized era.

We aim to answer at least some of these questions by combining rich, daily data from the last two US presidential elections. Our data set includes several predictive metrics, including the candidates' owned media (statements and social media posts), TV advertising, campaign contributions, news coverage, and social media posts with interactions on Twitter, Facebook, and Instagram. We carry out natural-language processing of the candidates' owned media to identify both linguistic and moral foundations and organize advertising by topics obtained from structural topic models (STMs). Relying on state-of-the-art time series econometrics, we show whether and to what extent each variable affected various types of polling metrics, enabling us to quantify their relative importance in shaping pre-election preferences in the 2016 and 2020 US presidential elections.

Our research contributes to the political science, marketing and social media, and disinformation sharing literature streams. First, whereas political science has focused on the foundational context (e.g., state of the economy, incumbent party) and the identity of the candidates (e.g., gender, race) and their followers (Sides & Vavreck, 2013), we contend that candidates' *actions* in statements and topic/media combinations matter most for different predictive metrics. Moreover, our findings yield specific recommendations on *which topics* candidates and political marketers should focus on in *which media*.

Second, marketing literature has moved beyond a focus on for-profit companies to demonstrate the societal impact of marketing strategies (Moorman et al., 2018). While past marketing models in a political context have focused on media market-level differences in candidates' marketing spending (Gordon & Hartmann, 2013; Shachar, 2009; Spenkuch & Toniatti, 2018), we are the first to analyze different predictive metrics, campaign content, and channels. To do so, we select leading drivers of the predictive metrics with Granger (1969) causality tests among hundreds of variables, estimate their dynamic interactions in a flexible model, and uncover which ones mattered most.

In both elections, fear appeal ads benefitted the Republican candidate, while ads on the economy and unity benefitted the Democratic candidate. In contrast, the incumbent's ads on COVID-19 backfired. Moreover, different topics played well on some channels, such as Twitter, but poorly on others, such as Facebook. Likewise, social media disinformation about a candidate's emails or support for "Defund the Police" harmed their chances a great deal, but disinformation on connections with Muslims or fraud allegations did not. Finally, our empirical results suggest that candidate's statements and external events differently affected traditional and probabilistic polls. While, for example, traditional polls show a positive reaction to Clinton's own social media posts on women rights, we also find that the probabilistic (and likely more accurate) polls decreased once Clinton posted on this topic. Similarly, the spread of disinformation on Clinton's emails did not significantly alter the traditional polls, but we observe that when the volume of email disinformation posts on social increases, the probabilistic polls decrease for Clinton, helping Trump. These differences in impact across the two different types of polls and the fact that campaign managers commonly only focused on the traditional polls (Kübler & Pauwels, 2021), strongly suggest that this divergence may have mislead candidate campaigns on citizen reactions to topics, platforms, moral language, and disinformation, a key lesson for upcoming elections.

THEORETICAL BACKGROUND

We base our conceptual development on four research streams. The first involves the predictive value of metrics, such as polls and prediction markets, the second focuses on the intersection between politics and marketing, the third on disinformation and fake news, and the fourth on other factors that drove the outcome of the 2016 US presidential election.

Tracking Candidate Preferences

Political science has a rich history of analyzing survey data to understand what matters to voters and whom they plan to vote for (Converse & Traugott, 1986; Hillygus, 2011). Traditional polls typically probe respondents about their likelihood of voting in the election as well as about their candidate preferences. Both of these dimensions are potentially problematic since preferences and vote intentions may be fluid or uncertain, sometimes systematically so. A newer alternative, probabilistic polling, aims to address some of these drawbacks and has been shown to predict election outcomes more reliably. Probabilistic polling estimates the vote outcomes as respondents' probability of appearing at the polling station multiplied by the likelihood of prospective voting for the candidates. Respondents are asked about all candidates running, and scales ranging from 0% to 100% capture the respective likelihoods (Delavande & Manski, 2010; Gutsche et al., 2014). However, probabilistic polling still relies on asking citizens whom they are likely to vote for.

Still another election prediction mechanism leverages the "wisdom of crowds": prediction markets (Surowiecki, 2004, p. XIV). Prediction markets offer contracts whose payoffs are linked to the (as yet unknown) occurrence of future events. Because prices react immediately to new information (following the efficient market hypothesis), traders have an incentive to disclose all news available to them (Mann, 2016; Wolfers & Zitzewitz, 2004). Some prior research has found prediction markets to be superior to polls in terms of accuracy in predicting both the vote share and the victor of elections (Rothschild, 2009; Williams & Reade, 2016), even as other studies dissent (see Erikson & Wlezien, 2008).

Political Marketing and Candidate Preferences

Since Lazarsfeld et al.'s (1944) work, political marketing has investigated the role of mass media and interpersonal interactions in elections. The economy typically comes out as the most important issue for voters. For example, in May 2012, 52% of voters said that the economy and jobs were the single most important issue in their choice for president. Not discussing those issues makes a candidate appear inattentive or uncaring. By contrast, the extent of news coverage was only important in driving candidates' success during the primaries; in the 2012 election, for instance, news coverage followed rather than drove pre-election preferences in polls. Likewise, perceived "blunders" by candidates have less impact than pundits may believe, as most Americans are unaware of these or, if they are, unlikely to change their opinions (Campbell, 2005; Sides & Vavreck, 2013).

A wealth of political science literature focuses on fundamentals (e.g., state of the economy, which party is currently in power) and the candidates' identities (e.g., race, past record). Only a handful of studies specifically discusses how marketing activities shape political outcomes, focusing on either *marketing spending* or the *framing* of political messages. On the impact of marketing spending, empirical studies rely on county-level advertising and voting data to show the impact of TV advertising and grassroots campaigning. While political advertising can increase voter turnout, it only explains 1% of the variance of political preferences (Shachar, 2009). Applying different endogeneity controls to county-level ad allocation strategies, Gordon and Hartmann (2013) find that TV ads have a party preference elasticity of 0.033 (Republican) and 0.036 (Democratic), both below the typical TV ad elasticities for consumer goods (0.05). Likewise, Zhang and Chung (2020) show that field operations and political advertising by PACs were more effective in counties with stronger levels of support for a candidate, while a candidate's advertising was more effective in counties with lower levels of support for a candidate in the 2004 to 2012 elections. They report elasticities of 0.034 for candidate ads, 0.026 for political action committee ads, and 0.078 for field operations. Finally, Wang et al. (2018) find that negative advertising sponsored by political action committees is significantly less effective than that sponsored by candidates, with a 0.015 elasticity on the candidates' unconditional vote shares in the 2010 and 2012 US senate races. These authors specifically call for research to go beyond the tone and analyze the issues discussed in the ads using content analysis. Recent political science studies find similar results on marketing spending effectiveness (Coppock et al., 2020; Haenschen & Jennings, 2019; Spenkuch & Toniatti, 2018).

Early work with a focus on manipulation (Herman & Chomsky, 1988; Lippmann, 1922) versus information (Bernays, 1928; Downs, 1957) mainly discussed the framing of political messages conceptually. Insights into content are rather limited, with Stewart and Schubert (2006) failing to find a significant impact of hidden cues in advertisements on behavioral intentions. By contrast, several studies find that the moral foundations of candidate statements have important political consequences. According to Haidt (2008, p. 70), moral systems are "*interlocking sets of values, practices, institutions, and evolved psychological mechanisms that work together to suppress or regulate selfishness and make social life possible.*" Moral foundations theory advances the five moral foundations of care/harm, fairness/cheating, loyalty/betrayal, authority/subversion, and sanctity/degradation (Graham et al., 2013), which in turn can be categorized into individualizing and binding foundations. Individualizing foundations, including care/harm and fairness/cheating, are based on considerations of individual rights. Binding foundations, including loyalty/betrayal, authority/subversion, and sanctity/degradation, are based on efforts made to support group cohesion (Hadarics & Kende, 2017; Weber & Federico, 2013).

Finally, studies at the intersection of politics and (social) media find a strong positive relationship between (social) media usage and political participation (Boulianne, 2015; Dimitrova & Bystrom, 2013; Knoll et al., 2018). None of these studies, however, take specific content or actions of politicians into account to explain political will-formation and preferences.

Research on Fake News and Disinformation in the Wake of the 2016 Election

Fake news refers to "*information fabricated to mimic news media content with the intention to undermine public opinion, and the credibility of the political system as well as traditional media*" (Lazer et al., 2018, p. 1094). However, opinions differ on the exact criteria. Economists such as Allcott and Gentzkow (2017) consider only factually incorrect information, while others include highly partisan or "slanted" news (e.g., Tandoc et al., 2018; Zimdars & McLeod, 2020). In their comprehensive review, Tucker et al. (2018, p. 3) define online *disinformation* as "*a broad category describing the types of information that one could encounter online that could possibly lead to misperceptions about the actual state of the world.*" We uphold this definition, consistent with several recent studies on the exposure to and spread of such disinformation during the election (Guess et al., 2020; Gunther et al., 2019; Vosoughi et al., 2018). Contributing to that literature, we focus on the *topic* of disinformation (e.g., sharia law, email scandals) as an underresearched area.

The spread of and exposure to disinformation has received the lion share of research attention. Bovet and Makse (2019) find disinformation in a quarter of tweets with links to political news websites, and Grinberg et al. (2019) show that an average user was exposed to 204 potential fake news items on Twitter. Vosoughi et al. (2018, p. 1150) find that such disinformation triggers fear, disgust, and surprise and hence diffuses "*farther, faster, deeper, and more broadly than the truth.*" Disinformation exposure is higher for right-wing than left-wing supporters, and senior white voters are most exposed to and share most disinformation (Grinberg et al., 2019; Guess et al., 2019). However, evaluations of the medium-to-long-term impact on political behavior of exposure to disinformation "*are essentially nonexistent in the literature*" (Lazer et al., 2018, p. 1095).

In sum, while a great deal is known about the spread of disinformation, its impact on candidate preferences, as compared with other factors, is unclear. Closing this research gap is important to give better recommendations to political operatives and marketers as well as to policy makers (Lazer et al., 2018; Persily, 2017). Our study is the first of which we are aware to combine disinformation volume and topics directly with political preference data, such as polls, donations, and user-generated content on social media.

Research on the 2016 US Presidential Election

The 2016 US presidential election generated interest from a wide spectrum of research disciplines (Abramowitz & McCoy, 2019; Francia, 2018; Persily, 2017). A key focus was the *positioning* of the two candidates and which specific *topics* appealed to which types of *voter subgroups*. From their surveys, Abramowitz and McCoy (2019) conclude that Trump's victory was largely due to his ability to mobilize white working-class voters in the swing states of the Northeast and Midwest. Kahane's (2020) county-level analysis of election results shows that Trump won in nonmetro, metro-adjacent, and mainline Protestant counties. Within this demographic, Trump benefited from factors such as the strong identification with the Republican party, racial resentment, economic conservatism, antigay rights, and anti-free trade (Abramowitz & McCoy, 2019). From 2012 to 2016, foreign trade, race, and unemployment issues shifted to classic Republican positions (Green, 2020). While some voters had changed political sides since 2012, black voters were not mobilized as strongly as racial or ethnic groups that favored Trump. Gunther et al. (2019) find disenchantment in some Obama 2012 voters who abstained from voting for Clinton in the 2016 election, and believe the disinformation against the candidate may have amplified this behavior.

Another stream of research on the 2016 election focuses on *paid and earned media*. Franz et al. (2020) find that neither campaign took advantage of the opportunities of online microtargeting and adapting positioning strategies to the different preference structures of voters. Compared with online advertising, TV ads covered mostly the same topics, with a slightly stronger focus on the economy and terrorism. Attack ads were common for both campaigns, especially targeting Clinton's competence (Tedesco & Dunn, 2019), and 2016 had the highest number of negative words used by a Republican candidate (Rhodes & Vayo, 2019). Trump received more media coverage and benefited from the increased public interest (Reuning & Dietrich, 2018). Francia (2018) credits Trump's provocative social media use for gaining $5 billion in free media coverage compared with $3.2 billion for Clinton. Building on these insights, our study combines the two campaigns' social media and advertising with news coverage and the reaction of social media users to quantify their longitudinal impact on polls, prediction markets and the final election outcome.

CONCEPTUAL DEVELOPMENT

Communication research and political science show that candidates have different political persuasion pathways, such as in-group building and stirring emotions (Clifford et al., 2015; Gordon et al., 2012; Simas et al., 2020). Different media and topics are better suited to persuade voters on their action intentions (as measured by polls) and their actions (as measured by votes). Moreover, polls and prediction markets provide feedback mechanisms to the candidates' campaigns, influencing their actions over time. Our conceptual and empirical framework follows the suggestions of Kübler and Manke (2023) and accounts for the various dynamics in political decision-making, as visualized in Figure 6.1.

First, in-group building is demonstrated in a variety of ways, including the candidates' *social*

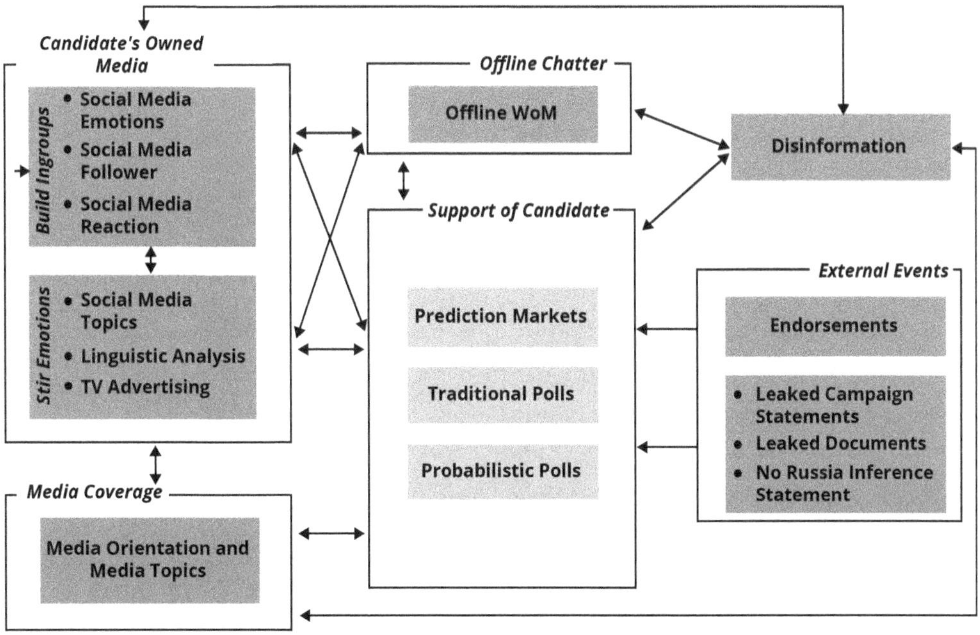

Figure 6.1 Conceptual Model

media following and *sentiment*, just as it does for commercial brands (e.g., Colicev et al., 2018). *Sharing* of stories among the in-group indicates a level of engagement and help further strengthen group cohesion (Ilhan et al., 2018).

Second, the stirring of emotions is driven by (social media) *topics and disinformation*. Economic topics have enduring appeal for decades (and are hence called "fundamental" in political science) but may not be as stirring as cultural topics, such as minorities and women, or law and order issues (e.g., linking the opponent to the "Defund the Police" movement), and threats such as health and terrorism. Moreover, these *topics likely interact with the media*; as marketing literature shows that the social media platform matters (Schweidel & Moe, 2014). In their general classification of social media platforms, Zhu and Chen (2015) distinguish *relationship* platforms, which are profile based and consist mostly of customized messages (e.g., Facebook) from (1) *self-media* platforms, which allow users to manage their own communication channels (e.g., Twitter); and (2) *creative outlet* platforms, which are content based and allow users to share their interests and creativity (e.g., Instagram). Specifically, relevant for information exchange, Instagram is typically used to share visual content and its user base skews young and female (Schmidbauer et al., 2018). Thus, positive cultural topics relevant to young female voters should play well on that platform. In contrast, Twitter is suitable for broadcasting short texts to many (lesser known) followers, and shows more experience of negative content-related emotions such as threats. As a key social media platform in politics, Facebook is suitable for social interaction and sharing longer texts and story links with fans and friends, about whom much information is known, making it effective for in-group building. In contrast, TV ads should help more for highlighting a candidate's stance on enduring issues such as the economy (Voorveld et al., 2018).

For each specific candidate, which topics (what?) and (social) media (where?) would be most useful for these persuasion pathways? Regarding *topics*, people choose among alternatives that share "points of parity" (held by all considered alternatives) but are distinguished by their "points of difference" (Keller et al., 2002). In political branding, this means a focus on topics that are relevant to voters and for which the candidate has or can develop positive associations (Keller, 1993). To some extent, this topic choice depends on the candidates' own records and that of their party; for example, conservatives are motivated to avoid negative outcomes through constraints, while liberals are motivated to advance positive outcomes through interventions (Janoff-Bulman, 2009). However, voter response to such topics also depends on the fundamentals of which party has been in power and voter perceptions of the state of the country (Sides & Vavreck, 2013). In 2016, a Democrat had been in the White House for eight years, and Clinton was considered part of the establishment responsible for the economy as well as foreign policy and faced strong criticism for both. Thus, the Trump campaign could focus on the economy and terrorism, as both issues had been important to US voters for decades, and made it possible to establish points of difference with Clinton. Better and cheaper health care could be touched on to establish a point of parity. By contrast, the Clinton campaign could focus on women, civil rights, and gun control issues to establish points of difference not easily imitated, and thus negated, by her opponent. The economy could be her point of parity. In contrast, the 2020 election occurred in the midst of (1) a pandemic, for which the incumbent's response was criticized, (2) a down economy, for which he was not, and (3) disunity/polarization, which he was criticized for having furthered during his presidency. Marketing theory suggests that every branding message should strengthen either a point of parity or a point of difference (Keller et al., 2002).

The topics, sentiment, and (moral) language used by the candidates should help them build in-groups and drive people's emotions enough to take action (e.g., by inducing them to donate to their campaigns and vote for them) (Clifford et al., 2015; Gordon et al., 2012; Simas et al., 2020). We measure in-group building by social media reaction: (1) *volume* of followers on Facebook, the dominant source of online news for Americans (Lazer et al., 2018; Shearer & Gottfried, 2017), and (2) follower *engagement* on the three main social media platforms, (3) the *sentiment* expressed by these followers, and (4) the *topics* they discuss (O'Connor et al., 2010; Tumasjan et al., 2011; You et al., 2015). In turn, these are influenced (see bottom of Figure 6.1) by both news and disinformation topics shared by followers (Allen et al., 2020; Vargo et al., 2017). Regarding the bidirectional arrows, journalists may report on social media, and social media may pick up on news articles (Francia, 2018; Hennig-Thurau et al., 2010; Kreiss et al., 2018), and all these potential poll drivers can also be driven by the polls (Gordon et al., 2012; Hillygus, 2011). The only exogenous variables (bottom right of Figure 6.1) are external events (Gordon et al., 2012), which include leaked candidate statements (e.g., Clinton's "basket of deplorables" statement, Trump's "grab them" tape), leaked documents (e.g., Wikileaks), and third-party actions, such as FBI announcements (Gambino & Pankhania, 2016; Stracqualursi, 2016). Finally, all these effects could materialize with some time delay, requiring a longitudinal data set and analysis (Anderl et al., 2016; Srinivasan, 2022; Srinivasan et al., 2016).

Given the many mixed findings and divergent opinions discussed in the extant research, we do not formulate explicit hypotheses on the importance of these factors. Instead, this importance emerges from the flexible long-term modeling approach to our comprehensive data set.

DATA DESCRIPTION

For each major-party campaign, we combine prediction markets and polling data, donation data, traditional TV advertising data, and a set of event-specific control variables. In addition, we enrich our data set with a unique set of social media interactions, including all posts of the two candidates on the leading social media platforms Twitter, Facebook, and Instagram. Our data set also includes user reactions on social media for each candidate that we extracted through web crawling following the approach described by Yildirim and Kübler (2023). For Twitter, we collected more than 80 million tweets, with 10 million mentioning only Clinton, 17 million mentioning only Trump, and the remainder mentioning both candidates. For Facebook, we collected 4.5 million and 2.5 million user comments from Trump's and Clinton's official pages, respectively. For Instagram, we extracted 2.7 million and 2.2 million user comments from Trump's and Clinton's official accounts, respectively. Variable operationalizations follow the approach shown in Kübler et al. (2020) (further details are available from the authors upon request).

Voter Preferences

To track the trajectory of candidate preferences over the course of the 2016 campaign, we leverage available prediction markets, traditional polling, and probabilistic polling for the two candidates (Converse & Traugott, 1986; Gordon et al., 2012; Hillygus, 2011). Using daily measures since both presidential candidates were known (July 11, 2016, when Bernie Sanders endorsed Hillary Clinton), we have 119 data points until November 7, 2016, the day before the election. Specifically, we use PredictIt for prediction markets and Poll Tracker (2016), which summarizes all available daily polls, for traditional polling. For probabilistic polls, we use the USC Dornsife/*Los Angeles Times* Presidential Election Poll (https://cesrusc.org/election), which surveys one-seventh of the representative sample of 3,000 members of its online panel on a daily basis (Gutsche et al., 2014). Figure 6.2 depicts these three predictive metrics from July to November 2016. While traditional polls and prediction markets move together (correlation of 0.66), they each have a lower correlation with probabilistic polls (correlation of 0.48 and 0.49 respectively). Face validity comes not only from showing a tight race, with Trump in the lead from mid-September until Election Day, but also from likely influential events, such as the "basket of deplorables" leak (September 12) and Comey's letter about Clinton's emails to Congress (October 28).

Following political science research (Kennedy et al., 2018), we calculate the national *gap* as the difference between Clinton's and Trump's numbers for each predictive metric. A decrease in the poll gap indicates that Trump gains in public support, while an increase in the poll gap indicates that Clinton gains in public support.

Voter Engagement on Social Media: Volume, Emotion, Moral Language, and Topics

For brands (Colicev et al., 2018), three major components include (1) the size of a candidate's following, (2) the volume of user-generated content (UGC), and (3) the sentiment of UGC (valence and arousal level). We adapt this approach for presidential campaigns by adding (4) the moral foundations of the UGC text, which may be especially relevant in political discourse (Smith et al., 2017; Weber & Federico, 2013), and (5) the topics discussed, which matter for brand-related actions (Pauwels & Joshi, 2016) as follows.

First, we collected the daily number of followers of Facebook, via its API, from the candidates' official pages. Trump maintained a substantial lead over Clinton, growing from 6.2 million followers in July 2016 to 8.4 million followers by election day (2.2 million and

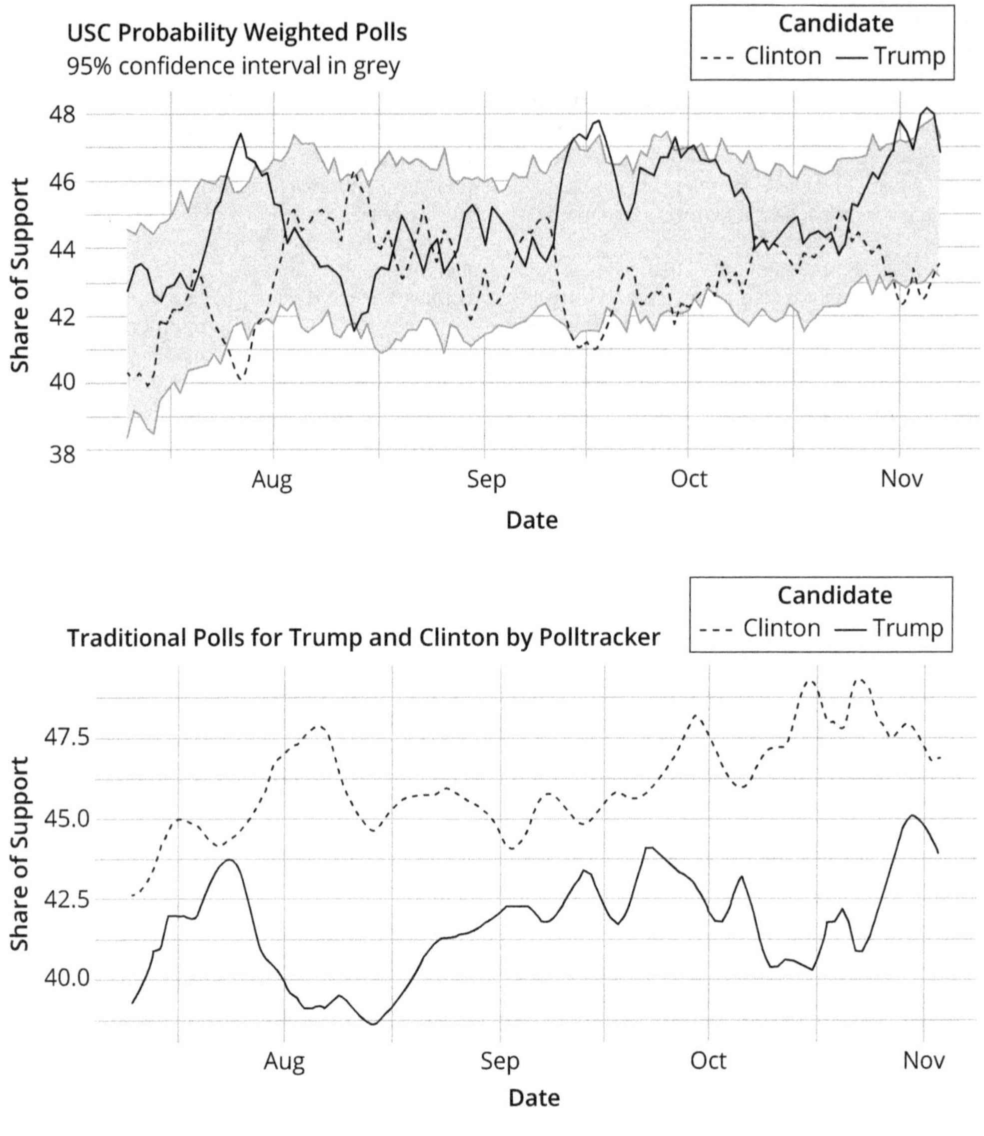

Figure 6.2 Probabilistic Polls and Traditional Polls for Trump and Clinton

3.8 million for Clinton, respectively). Trump also had more Instagram (Graham, 2016) and Twitter followers in September 2016 (Day, 2016; Statista, 2016). We concede that following a candidate does not necessarily mean endorsing him or her.

Second, to collect all related UGC, we extracted all posts, tweets, and comments mentioning one of the two candidates from Twitter, Facebook, and Instagram. Our data crawling respected the specific privacy requirements of each platform (e.g., Facebook's API allows tracking of all comments on candidates' public pages but not conversations in closed groups, in private messages, and on private walls). Similar to the size difference in followers, the 4.5 million user comments on Trump's Facebook page showed higher UGC volume (often used as a measure of "engagement"; see Kupfer et al., 2018) than the user comments (more than 2.5 million) on Clinton's page.

Third, we analyze the sentiment in all user posts and user comments (for a political science application, see O'Connor et al., 2010). Specifically, we conducted a "top-down" dictionary sentiment analysis (Humphreys & Wang, 2018). As Kübler et al. (2020), we combine two customized dictionaries: VADER (Hutto & Gilbert, 2014) and Senti Strength (Thelwall et al., 2010), which have been developed for short texts originating from social media sources, and handle typos, slang, internet specific abbreviations, emojis and other symbols, as well as negations. Each dictionary provides a relative sentiment score that accounts for the share of positive and negative words in a document. We further validate this approach by calculating the correlation of the dictionaries for each document (Berger et al., 2020), which yields an average of 0.89. In the next step, we rely on the NRC emotion dictionary (Mohammad & Turney, 2013) that provides us with relative scores for fear, anger, disgust, sadness, surprise, joy, trust, and anticipation.

Fourth, we measure morality with the moral foundation theory dictionary developed by Graham et al. (2009). For example, "authority virtue" moral language is expressed by this user statement on Clinton's Facebook page: "*You can not take America Back and Make America Great again if you do not recognize the Law which has been stolen from you. The very law which says Hillary Clinton is Ineligible to hold ANY public office of trust or profit.*"

Fifth, we combine *disinformation* lists from Pennycook and Rand (2019), Vosoughi et al. (2018) and Zimdars (2016) to count all user comments or posts that link to URLs for websites known to publish fake news (Zimdars & McLeod, 2020). In total, we identified 29,359 links referring to disinformation stories: 18,119 were shared on Clinton's Facebook page and 11,240 on Trump's page. To understand which topic a disinformation link addresses, we apply an STM[1] to the title information within each identified link because the vast majority (99% of the disinformation links captured) use the story's title as part of the URL (see also Giomelakis & Veglis, 2016). In total, we identify four disinformation topics shared on Hillary Clinton's social media domain, while we find five disinformation topics shared on Donald Trump's. Interestingly, all nine topics intended to harm Hillary Clinton's election chances (a detailed description of the identification of disinformation topics is available from the authors upon request).

Candidates' Marketing: TV Ad Topics, Social Media Topics, and Sentiment

We account for a candidate's marketing activities in two ways. First, we create a daily time series for the air time devoted to each TV ad topic based on the airing times for both candidates' TV advertisements and a list of their topics provided by a political marketing research company. Second, we track the content of the candidates' statements on Twitter, Facebook, and Instagram using text-mining techniques. To match the topic information of the TV ads, we also apply an STM to all these candidate posts. Moreover, we apply the same sentiment analyses as for UGC, to reveal a candidate's posting style following the approach of Kupfer et al. (2018).

Offline Social Media Sentiment

Word-of-mouth data were provided by the social data and analytics firm Engagement Labs, who ask a representative sample of 700 US consumers to conduct a 24-hour diary in which they document WOM incidents including every face-to-face or phone conversation (Fay et al., 2019; Lovett et al., 2013). Just as for commercial brands, they measure volume and sentiment of offline conversations about the presidential candidates at the weekly level. We bring these weekly measures to the daily level by applying linear interpolation.

News Media Coverage

The news media agency AllSides classifies the political orientation of 56 major US news media. We approximate news coverage by tracking all tweets sent out by any of the 56 news sources, mentioning a candidate. While this approach may miss coverage that has not been forwarded to Twitter, it is the best available measure that provides volume together with content information. To test the reliability of the measure, we conducted a correlation analysis of tweet volume and Google News volume. The correlation coefficient of 0.81 supports our proxy selection. For each account, we track all tweets mentioning one of the two candidates. We apply again a structural topic analysis to the Twitter texts featuring each article. For each candidate, the STMs' coherence scores identify an optimum of five latent topics.

The variable operationalization table in Appendix 6.1 provides a summary overview of all variables in our analysis.

Longitudinal Analysis

Our longitudinal data allow us to analyze the *dynamic* relationships among the conceptually motivated metrics. This requires a methodology that is flexible in terms of the temporal hierarchy and complicated relationships among metrics, including dual causality (Ansolabehere et al., 2003; Gordon et al., 2012; Hillygus, 2011). Moreover, as effects may take several days to materialize, a flexible treatment of lags is important (Pauwels, 2014); to our knowledge, no theory in marketing or politics prescribes effect timing. Thus, our methodology needs to allow for recursive effects among polls, prediction markets, candidate actions (statements, advertising, and social media posts), media coverage, and the public's social media reaction, with multiple paths and alternative hierarchies.

To satisfy these requirements, we apply the persistence modeling approach (Chanley et al., 2000; Dekimpe & Hanssens, 1999; Freeman et al., 1989), which selects variables that are leading performance indicators (Granger causality tests), quantifies dynamic relationships in a vector autoregressive (VAR) model, and derives the relative importance of each variable in driving the outcome with forecast error variance decomposition (FEVD). Given the possibility of simultaneity between several of our endogenous variables, using vector autoregression is particularly appropriate for two reasons (Freeman et al., 1989). First, VAR "*does not impose a priori structural relations between potentially endogenous variables, reducing the risk of omitted variables bias,*" and second, it is "*flexible enough to ... specify variables that are distinctly exogenous*" (Chanley et al., 2000, p. 248). Table 6.1 summarizes the steps in this approach.

In the first step, we verify that each variable has a finite variance with augmented Dickey–Fuller unit-root tests, the most popular test in economics and business applications (Colicev et al., 2018; Dekimpe & Hanssens, 1999; Enders, 2004). In the second step, we conduct Granger causality tests on each variable pair. We validate our selection of variables by applying LASSO. In the third step, we capture the dynamic interactions from Figure 6.1 in the VAR models, in which a vector of variables is regressed on its past (Dekimpe & Hanssens, 1999). By treating all variables with "incoming arrows" in Figure 6.1 as endogenous (explained by the model), we capture the dynamic relationships among them without imposing a priori restrictions (Sims, 1980). At the same time, we add strictly exogenous events to each equation to quantify their impact on each endogenous variable (Chanley et al., 2000). Equation (1) displays the structure of the VAR model in matrix form:

Table 6.1 Analytical Procedure

Methodological Step	*Relevant Literature*	*Research Questions*
1. Unit-root test Cointegration test	Enders (2004); Johansen et al. (2000)	Are variables stationary? Are evolving variables in long-term equilibrium?
2. Variable Selection:		Do the variables:
a Multivariate regression	Leeflang et al. (2015)	a add incremental explanation;
b Granger causality	Granger (1969); Freeman (1983); MacKuen et al. (1992); Sides and Vavreck (2013)	b change in time before outcome variables do, so that outcome is better predicted with the variable;
c LASSO	Hastie et al. (2001), Zou and Hastie (2005)	c have effect strong enough to survive shrinkage for complexity?
3. Vector Autoregressive (VAR) model	Sims (1980); Freeman et al. (1989)	How do all endogenous variables interact over time?
4. Out-of-sample forecast accuracy of VAR model	Theil (1966)	How large is the forecasting error compared with a naive model?
5. Generalized Impulse Response Functions (GIRF)	Dekimpe and Hanssens (1999)	What is the net outcome effect of a change in each variable?
6. Forecast Error Variance Decomposition (FEVD)	Lütkepohl (1990); Nijs et al. (2007)	What is the relative importance of each variable in driving outcomes?

$$Y_t = A + \sum_{i=1}^{p} \Phi_i Y_{t-i} + \Psi X_t + \sum_t \quad t = 1, 2, \ldots, T, \qquad (1)$$

where $\boldsymbol{Y_t}$ is the vector of the endogenous variables, $\boldsymbol{A}$ is the vector of intercepts, p is the number of autoregressive lags, and $\boldsymbol{X_t}$ is a vector of exogenous variables. The full residual variance–covariance matrix Σ contains the same-day effect of each endogenous variable on the others (Colicev & Pauwels, 2022).

We evaluate the models' in-sample fit by (1) the information criteria for the full model (which also determine the optimal lag length, balancing forecasting accuracy with model parsimony), (2) the (adjusted) R-square of each equation, for which we expect a higher explained variance for our performance variables (the poll and prediction market gaps) than for the candidate actions, as observed in branding literature (e.g., Srinivasan et al., 2010), and (3) out-of-sample forecasting performance at different times before the election.

In the final step, we show the VAR model's *substantive results* in three ways. First, for the exogenous variables (the events in Figure 6.1), we directly show the estimated coefficients on the performance variable of interest. Second, for the endogenous variables (depicted using an arrow in Figure 6.1), we calculate the impulse response function (IRF), or the net daily effect combining all estimated dynamic coefficients in Eq. (1) relevant to the impulse variable (e.g., the TV ads on the economy) and the response variable (e.g., the poll gap). We obtain the same-day (immediate) effect by calculating the expected contemporaneous shock in the residual variance–covariance matrix (Evans & Wells, 1983; Pesaran & Shin, 1998). This allows us to compute the generalized impulse response functions (GIRFs), which do not depend on a prespecified causal ordering. Following best practices, we apply a one-standard-error band to each GIRF in each period (Sims & Zha, 1999) and sum the significant effects to obtain the total effect under the curve, often called the "cumulative effect" of a one standard deviation *change* in the impulse variable on the response variable (Slotegraaf & Pauwels, 2008; Trusov et al., 2009). Third, the FEVD reveals the *relative importance* of each variable in having contributed to the variation in the outcome variable, analogous to a "dynamic R-square." For example, while each news coverage may have had less of an impact than each candidate statement, the much higher occurrence of news coverage can still result in a higher overall importance than candidate statements in driving the poll gap. FEVDs always sum up to 100%, and the standard errors allow us to evaluate statistical significance (Srinivasan et al., 2010).

VAR Model Variable Selection

We use three methods to narrow down the list of 210 variables. First, multivariate regression requires a variable to add significant explanatory power in the context of the other variables (e.g., Leeflang et al., 2015). Second, the variable should significantly Granger-cause at least one predictive metric (Pauwels & Joshi, 2016). We run the Granger causality test for up to 14 daily lags and classify a variable as driving the outcome variable if it Granger-causes it at the 5% significance level for any of these lags (Trusov et al., 2009). Third, the variable's coefficient estimate should not be shrunk to zero in a LASSO regression, which penalizes model complexity (e.g., Hastie et al., 2001). We retain a variable in the VAR model if it is chosen by any of these three methods for any of the predictive metrics.

RESULTS

2016 Candidate Marketing Strategies and Voter Reaction

A qualitative interpretation of the various topic model outputs (TV ads, news coverage, and social media) suggests that candidates developed and changed the content of their campaigns throughout the race. First, Clinton TV ads show a shift from the economy in the summer to civil rights, family, and terrorism in the fall. While Trump TV ads discuss the economy, immigration, and the military in the summer, terrorism becomes more important as a topic in the fall. Second, disinformation on Clinton and Muslims peaked in early August, when Trump criticized the parents of a slain Muslim US soldier and saw his poll numbers decline (Figure 6.2). By contrast, disinformation about Clinton's emails on her own Facebook page peaked after Comey's Congress letter of October 28.

Unit Root and Cointegration Tests

While the traditional and probabilistic polls for a candidate have a unit root, they are not cointegrated, underscoring the different information they provide throughout the race. Subtracting Trump's poll numbers from Clinton's yield our "poll gap" variable, which is stationary for both the traditional and the probabilistic poll. Likewise, our remaining explanatory variables are stationary and can thus be included in the model.

2016 Variable Selection

Among the predictive metrics, prediction markets are driven by the traditional polls and fail to drive either the traditional or the probabilistic polls. Moreover, they failed to predict the 2016 election outcome, pointing to over 75% probability of a Clinton win at closing time.[2] As a result, we do not incorporate them in our model. Table 6.2 juxtaposes the variable selection with three methods: (1) multivariate regression, (2) Granger Causality, and (3) LASSO.

Several variables are selected by all three methods, some by two out of three, and a few by a single method. Interestingly, more variables are selected for the probabilistic poll gap than for the traditional poll gap. We keep all 17 selected variables in both models to ease comparison.

Each VAR model therefore includes 17 explanatory variables and 1 outcome variable for 18 endogenous variables, and three exogenous events, for 21 variables in total, which is similar to the reduction from 99 to 17 variables in a marketing application (Pauwels & Joshi, 2016). Table 6.3 shows the descriptive statistics and correlations of each variable in the model.

The first observation from Table 6.3 is the modest (0.48) correlation between the traditional and probabilistic poll gaps. Among candidate actions, Clinton's TV ads on the economy have the strongest correlation with the probabilistic poll gap, but Trump's TV ads on terrorism have the strongest correlation with the traditional poll gap (−0.31). Overall, the strongest correlation with

Table 6.2 Variable Selection by Granger Causality Tests Versus LASSO Regression

	Variable Selection for the Probability Poll Gap in 2016 Election		
	Regression	*Granger Causality*	*LASSO*
All three selections	TV economy Clinton	TV economy Clinton	TV economy Clinton
	TV terrorism Trump	TV terrorism Trump	TV terrorism Trump
	FB Authority Virtue	FB Authority Virtue	FB Authority Virtue
	Disinformation Emails	Disinformation Emails	Disinformation Emails
	Disinformation Muslims	Disinformation Muslims	Disinformation Muslims
In two selections	TV gun control CL	TV gun control CL	
	Twitter Vader pos Trump	Twitter Vader pos Trump	
	Media Clinton Sanders	Media Clinton Sanders	
	Trump Media Sex scandal	Trump Media Sex scandal	
	Clinton Insta Supreme		Clinton Insta Supreme
	Trump Twitter Putin		Trump Twitter Putin
In one selection	Trump Media Sex scandal	Clinton FB Women	WOM positive Trump
	Clinton Twitter Supreme	Clinton Twitter Women	
		Clinton Twitter No Trump	

	Variable Selection for the Traditional Pol Gap in 2016 Election		
	Regression	*Granger Causality*	*LASSO*
All three selections	Trump Media Sex scandal	Trump Media Sex scandal	Trump Media Sex scandal
	WOM pos trump	WOM pos Trump	WOM pos trump
In two selections	News Clinton Sanders	News Clinton Sanders	
	TV economy Clinton		TV Economy Clinton
	TV Terrorism Trump		TV Terrorism Trump
	Disinformation Emails		Disinformation Emails
		Authority Virtue Clinton	Authority Virtue Clinton
In one selection		FB Fairness Vice	Clinton Twitter Women
		Twitter Joy Trump	
		Clinton FB Women	

Table 6.3 Descriptive Statistics and Correlations of All Continuous Variables in the Traditional and Probabilistic Poll Gap Models

	Probabilistic Poll	*Traditional Polls*	*PredictIt*	*TV ad Clinton Economy*	*TV ad Clinton Gun Control*	*TV ad Trump Terrorism*	*Authority-Virtue*	*Fairness-Vice*	*Disinformation Clinton Emails*
Mean	−1.76	4.48	0.71	1,105.43	112.26	886.49	3,456.66	0.26	15.76
Median	−1.71	4.00	0.71	66.57	0.00	420.50	2,989.00	0.00	2.00
Maximum	4.78	8.90	0.83	6,029.00	660.00	5,500.00	12,733.00	3.00	204.00
Minimum	−7.29	0.60	0.62	0.00	0.00	0.00	310.00	0.00	0.00
Std. Dev.	2.51	2.14	0.06	1,617.31	186.26	1,209.03	2,134.68	0.59	33.04
Probabilistic poll	1.00	0.48	0.50	0.41	0.28	−0.26	−0.50	0.08	−0.33
Traditional poll	0.48	1.00	0.66	0.05	0.09	−0.31	−0.38	−0.17	−0.13
PredictIt	0.50	0.66	1.00	0.25	0.04	−0.31	−0.37	−0.14	−0.02
TV ad Clinton Economy	0.41	0.05	0.25	1.00	0.37	−0.07	−0.11	0.00	−0.11
TV ad Clinton Gun Control	0.28	0.09	0.04	0.37	1.00	0.03	0.00	0.03	−0.06
TV ad Trump Terrorism	−0.26	−0.31	−0.31	−0.07	0.03	1.00	0.12	−0.04	0.13
Authority-Virtue	−0.50	−0.38	−0.37	−0.11	0.00	0.12	1.00	0.04	0.68
Fairness-Vice	0.08	−0.17	−0.14	0.00	0.03	−0.04	0.04	1.00	−0.05
Disinformation Clinton Emails	−0.33	−0.13	−0.02	−0.11	−0.06	0.13	0.68	−0.05	1.00
Disinformation Clinton Muslims	0.29	−0.12	−0.08	0.46	0.23	0.12	−0.07	0.03	−0.15
Twitter VADER Positive Trump	−0.22	−0.47	−0.29	−0.24	−0.24	0.17	0.21	0.15	0.07
Clinton Facebook Women	−0.38	−0.09	−0.02	−0.22	−0.31	0.00	0.48	−0.13	0.42
Clinton in media about Sanders	−0.32	−0.19	−0.28	0.02	−0.08	0.05	0.25	−0.15	−0.06
Clinton Instagram Supreme Court	−0.32	−0.20	−0.20	−0.11	−0.12	0.02	0.10	−0.14	−0.05
Clinton Twitter Supreme Court	−0.28	−0.01	0.09	−0.16	−0.21	0.16	0.11	−0.16	0.04
Clinton Twitter Women	−0.27	−0.06	0.17	−0.13	−0.24	0.11	0.42	−0.13	0.52
Clinton Twitter No Trump	−0.10	−0.20	−0.25	−0.01	−0.09	0.03	0.13	−0.04	−0.07
Trump Twitter Putin	0.10	0.39	0.63	−0.11	−0.28	0.00	−0.07	−0.17	0.12

Trump in Media about Sex	0.09	0.34	0.20	0.15	0.20		0.14	−0.03	−0.25	0.11
Positive word-of-mouth on Trump	−0.41	−0.75	−0.79	−0.31	−0.18		0.11	0.35	0.17	0.03

Disinformation Clinton Muslims	*Twitter VADER Positive Trump*	*Clinton Facebook Women*	*Clinton in Media About Sanders*	*Clinton Instagram Supreme Court*	*Clinton Twitter Supreme Court*	*Clinton Twitter Women*	*Clinton Twitter No Trump*	*Trump Twitter Putin*	*Trump in Media About Sex*	*Positive Word-of-Mouth on Trump*
11.90	0.10	2.58	91.01	0.12	5.51	3.54	3.28	27.47	216.32	0.26
4.00	0.10	2.00	74.00	0.00	4.00	3.00	2.00	7.00	212.00	0.25
88.00	0.11	14.00	445.00	2.00	24.00	21.00	13.00	237.00	400.00	0.32
0.00	0.09	0.00	31.00	0.00	0.00	0.00	0.00	0.00	51.00	0.21
18.43	0.01	2.45	65.57	0.38	4.99	3.73	2.89	46.39	66.51	0.03
0.29	−0.22	−0.38	−0.32	−0.32	−0.28	−0.27	−0.10	0.10	0.09	−0.41
−0.12	−0.47	−0.09	−0.19	−0.20	−0.01	−0.06	−0.20	0.39	0.34	−0.75
−0.08	−0.29	−0.02	−0.28	−0.20	0.09	0.17	−0.25	0.63	0.20	−0.79
0.46	−0.24	−0.22	0.02	−0.11	−0.16	−0.13	−0.01	−0.11	0.15	−0.31
0.23	−0.24	−0.31	−0.08	−0.12	−0.21	−0.24	−0.09	−0.28	0.20	−0.18
0.12	0.17	0.00	0.05	0.02	0.16	0.11	0.03	0.00	0.14	0.11
−0.07	0.21	0.48	0.25	0.10	0.11	0.42	0.13	−0.07	−0.03	0.35
0.03	0.15	−0.13	−0.15	−0.14	−0.16	−0.13	−0.04	−0.17	−0.25	0.17
−0.15	0.07	0.42	−0.06	−0.05	0.04	0.52	−0.07	0.12	0.11	0.03
1.00	−0.09	−0.32	0.07	−0.10	−0.21	−0.26	−0.04	−0.25	−0.08	−0.10
−0.09	1.00	0.27	0.25	0.23	0.28	0.23	0.14	−0.03	−0.25	0.51
−0.32	0.27	1.00	0.34	0.19	0.34	0.63	0.14	0.32	0.15	0.19
0.07	0.25	0.34	1.00	0.33	0.28	0.23	0.47	−0.13	0.12	0.23
−0.10	0.23	0.19	0.33	1.00	0.12	0.15	0.10	−0.09	−0.01	0.25
−0.21	0.28	0.34	0.28	0.12	1.00	0.28	0.18	0.29	0.17	0.01
−0.26	0.23	0.63	0.23	0.15	0.28	1.00	0.27	0.41	0.29	−0.01
−0.04	0.14	0.14	0.47	0.10	0.18	0.27	1.00	−0.16	0.12	0.25
−0.25	−0.03	0.32	−0.13	−0.09	0.29	0.41	−0.16	1.00	0.19	−0.42
−0.08	−0.25	0.15	0.12	−0.01	0.17	0.29	0.12	0.19	1.00	−0.26
−0.10	0.51	0.19	0.23	0.25	0.01	−0.01	0.25	−0.42	−0.26	1.00

the traditional poll gap was positive WOM about Trump (−0.75), while for the probabilistic poll gap, it was Clinton's Facebook page user comments on Authority Virtue. This moral language variable is also 0.68 correlated with Disinformation about Clinton's emails. This "model-free" evidence suggests a complex web of relationships among the 2016 election drivers and different effects on the different polls.

2016 VAR Model Order and Fit Statistics

We selected the VAR order (lag number) of 1, based on modified likelihood ratio tests and all four information criteria (Bayesian, Akaike, Akaike's final prediction error, and Hannan–Quin). Thus, we need to estimate 21 parameters (17 lagged endogenous variables, three exogenous events, and one intercept) from 177 observations. This 8.43 observation-to-parameter ratio is above 5 that Leeflang et al. (2015) recommend, and estimation converged immediately for each model. Analysis of the residuals detected neither serial correlation nor autoregressive conditional heteroskedasticity in any of the equations.

Our predictive metrics are significantly explained by the model, with an R^2 of 0.87 (adjusted R^2 = 0.82) for the probabilistic poll gap and 0.95 (adjusted R^2 = 0.92) for the traditional poll gap. Consistent with the in-sample fit, our model is able to forecast the traditional poll better than the probabilistic poll. Even when forecasting 12 weeks before the election, the traditional poll's Theil Inequality Coefficient stays below 0.25 and the probabilistic poll's below Lindberg's (1982) 0.55 benchmark for a "very good" forecast. In summary, our models show satisfactory in-sample fit and out-of-sample forecasting accuracy for both the traditional and probabilistic polls.

Impact of External Events

Our first main result pertains to the effect of external events on each of the endogenous variables, as directly represented by the estimated coefficients. First, Comey's Congress letter[3] significantly increased Clinton's Twitter posts on women (8.51, t = 3.23) and decreased the Clinton–Trump probabilistic poll gap (–2.69, t = –2.36) benefiting Trump. Our analysis is consistent with Silver's (2017a) result of 2.5 points and confirms that "*the Comey Letter probably cost Clinton the Election.*" Second, Clinton's "basket of deplorables"[4]-statement increased Trump ads on terrorism (2.81, t = 4.36) and decreased the Clinton–Trump probabilistic poll gap (–3.25, t = –2.50) by 3.25 points – the strongest effect in favor of Trump for any event. Notably, these effects are substantially smaller and not significant for the traditional poll gap (for Comey: –0.92, t = –1.56; for deplorables: –0.63, t = –1.07). By contrast, Trump's "grab them"[5] tape increased the traditional poll gap (2.30, t = 2.89) helping Clinton but did not significantly affect the probabilistic poll gap (–2.51, t = –1.40) or any other endogenous variable at the 95% significance level. This finding is consistent with survey literature arguments that traditional polling induces social desirability bias ("*I should be offended and reflect this in my voting preferences*") and may produce misleading results when voters do not act on such survey responses (Coppock, 2017).

Dynamic Effects of Each Poll Gap Driver (GIRFs)

Figure 6.3 shows the GIRFs for the probabilistic poll gap response to a 1 standard deviation impulse in respectively Clinton's TV ads on the Economy, her Facebook posts on women issues and disinformation about her emails.

While TV ads on the Economy did benefit her election chances, Clinton's Facebook posts on women did not, but the impact of both returns to 0 within 10 days. In contrast, disinformation about Clinton's emails continues to lower her probabilistic poll gap. All these GIRFs come with standard errors, and our main interest lies in the cumulative impact of all significant effects. Table 6.4 and Figure 6.4 show this cumulative poll gap impact from increasing every driver by one standard deviation.

We observe the highest probabilistic poll gap effect of *disinformation* on Clinton's emails, followed by pro authority comments on her Facebook page and her tweets on women's issues, together with the deplorables statement. All harmed Clinton's probabilistic poll standing, while her TV ads on the economy benefited her the most. By contrast, the traditional poll gap shows the highest effect of Trump's TV ads on terrorism, pro-Trump sentiment on Twitter, and user statements on fairness and vice on Clinton's Facebook page. While both polls agree that disinformation on Clinton and Muslims benefited Clinton, they dramatically differ on Trump's "grab them" event (only benefiting Clinton in the traditional poll), news coverage on Clinton versus Sanders, and disinformation

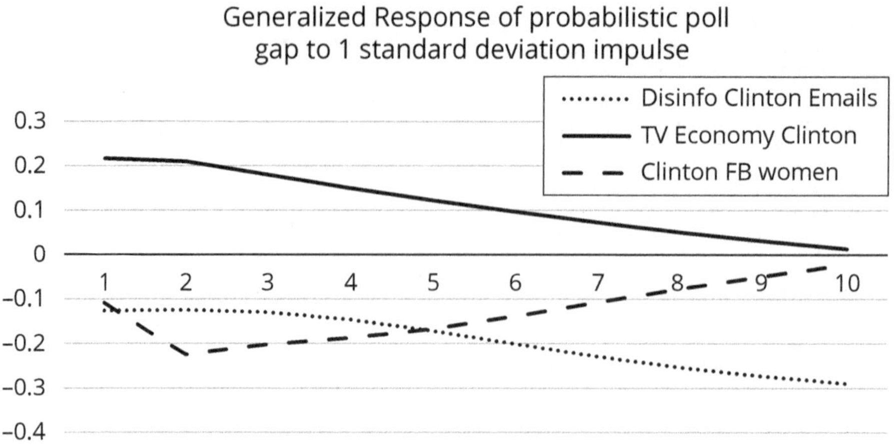

Figure 6.3 Impulse Response of Probabilistic Poll Gap to Clinton TV Ads on Economy, Facebook Posts on Women Topics, and Disinformation About Her Emails

Table 6.4 2016 Election Poll Gap Response to a 1 Standard Deviation Generalized Impulse*

Poll Gap Effect of	*Traditional*	*Probabilistic*
Clinton TV ads on the economy	0	0.425
Clinton TV ads on gun control	0	0.134
Trump TV ads on terrorism threats	−0.206	0
Authority virtue language about Clinton on her FB page	0.194	−0.102
Fairness vice language about Clinton on her FB page	0	0
Disinformation related to Clinton and emails	0	−1.262
Disinformation related to Clinton and Muslims	0	0.131
VADER positivity score related to Trump on Twitter	−0.371	0
Clinton statements on Facebook on Women Issues	0.284	−0.224
News coverage related to Clinton and Bernie Sanders	0.164	−0.125
Clinton statements on Instagram on the Supreme Court	0.040	−0.120
Clinton statements on Twitter on the Supreme Court	0.171	0
Clinton statements on Twitter on Women Issues	−0.067	−0.134
Clinton statements on Twitter against Trump	−0.112	0
Twitter coverage of Trump and Putin	0	0
News coverage related to Trump and sexual misconduct	−0.084	0.117
Positive word-of-mouth about Trump	−2.749	−3.256
Clinton's "basket of deplorables" statement	0	−3.25
Comey's letter to Congress on Clinton's email	0	−2.69
Trump's "grab them" tape	2.30	0

*The last three variables are exogenous, so their effect is the coefficient estimate, when significant, in the model.

on Clinton's emails (benefiting her in the traditional poll, but harming her chances in the probabilistic poll).

In summary, our analysis shows that, against common wisdom, *disinformation had diverse effects* on the probabilistic poll gap in the 2016

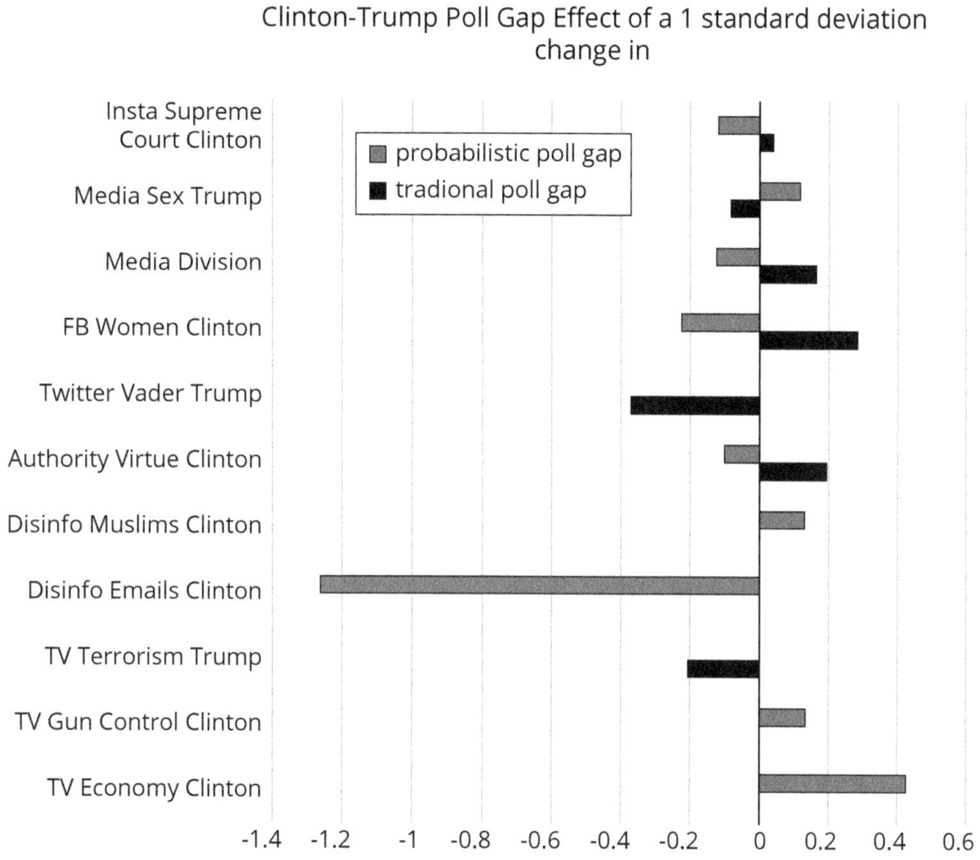

Figure 6.4 Clinton–Trump Poll Gap Effect for Each Endogenous Variable

US presidential election. An increase in disinformation targeting Clinton's connection with Muslims benefited instead of harmed her election chances. Examination of the response of disinformation to an impulse in the poll gap (the reverse arrow in Figure 6.1) shows that such posts surged when Clinton was further ahead in the traditional polls, in an apparent, but unsuccessful, attempt to halt her poll rise. The one topic of disinformation that did hurt Clinton's election chances was her emails. Based on the estimates, the Clinton campaign would have needed 2.97 more standard deviations in TV economy ads, or 9.40 more in TV Gun Control ads to compensate for one standard deviation more disinformation about her emails. How important, however, is each of these drivers in explaining the poll gap?

Relative Importance of Each Driver in Explaining the Poll Gap

Figure 6.5 shows the FEVD of the probabilistic poll gap; for ease of exposition, we omitted the poll gap's own past (whose FEVD drops from 81% on day 1–39% on day 21) and any driver explaining less than 3% for the full 30-day period. Initially, the probabilistic poll gap is increased most by Clinton's TV ads on the economy (see the IRF results), and decreased most by positive sentiment about Trump on Twitter on the negative side. Over time, the importance of the economy ads declines to end up explaining only 2% of the probabilistic poll gap. By contrast, other drivers become more important over time, including Clinton Facebook page users' moral language supporting

Authority, Trump TV ads on terrorism, and especially disinformation about Clinton's emails becomes the dominant driver after six days, accounting for 12% of the probabilistic poll gap variance after 21 days (the related FEVD plots can be received from the authors upon request).

Predicting the 2020 US Presidential Election

Based on the framework developed above, we analyzed the 2020 US presidential election and publicly predicted the outcome two weeks before the vote. That prediction was correct, and we collected all the information we had in 2016 to analyze the 2020 with the same procedure. Key differences in this election, besides being held in a global pandemic, included a broad agreement between probabilistic polls, traditional polls, and prediction markets. However, similar themes emerged as for the 2016 election about disinformation and the importance of topics and channels with different effects of the different types of polls (see Table 6.5).

First, our model again has a higher explanatory power for the traditional poll gap ($R^2 = 0.97$) than for the probabilistic poll gap ($R^2 = 0.87$). Moreover, we again find a different effect of variables on the polls. The size of the effects, however, is typically larger on the probabilistic than on the traditional poll gap.

Second, disinformation was substantially more widespread than during the 2016 election, with us counting 531,345 occurrences in 2020 versus 36,149 in 2016. Moreover, only certain topics of disinformation harmed candidates' support in the pre-election polls. Biden saw his probabilistic poll gap decline with disinformation about his alleged support for "Defund the Police" and belief "America is not Great" as well as his alleged fraud. In contrast, disinformation about his son Hunter helped Biden's election chances in both types of polls.

Third, the impact of TV topics reiterated the importance of the economy benefitting the Democratic candidate and division benefiting the Republican candidate. Trump's TV topics about division within the Democratic party had the largest immediate impact, but they were quickly overshadowed by Biden's TV ads about the economy.

As to channels, we collected additional information on ad spending on Facebook and Google,

Table 6.5 2020 Election Poll Gap Response to a 1 Standard Deviation Generalized Impulse

Poll Gap Effect of	*Traditional*	*Probabilistic*
Biden TV ads on the economy	0	0.44
Trump TV ads on the military	0	−0.54
Trump TV ads on COVID-19	0.074	0.00
Trump TV Ads on Division in the Democratic Party	0	−0.87
Biden Facebook Ad spending	0	0.08
Trump Facebook Ad Spending	0	0.09
Trump Google Ad Spending	0	−0.06
Disinformation on Biden "Defund the Police"	−0.06	−0.21
Disinformation on Biden "Fraud"	0	−0.26
Disinformation on Biden "Hunter Biden"	0	0.27
Disinformation on Biden "No America Great Again"	0	−0.95
Biden's Facebook page comments on Fairness Vice	−0.07	0.33
Biden's Facebook page comments on Authority Virtue	−0.06	0.00
Biden's Instagram Anticipation comments	0.00	0.06
Media Topic 1 on Biden	0.00	0.10
Media Topic 3 on Biden	0.00	−0.24
Media Topic 3 on Trump	0.06	0.00
Media Topic 4 on Biden	0.20	0.00
Media Topic 5 on Biden	0.08	0.00
Positive Word of Mouth about Biden	0.09	0.37
Positive Word of Mouth about Trump	0.00	−0.25

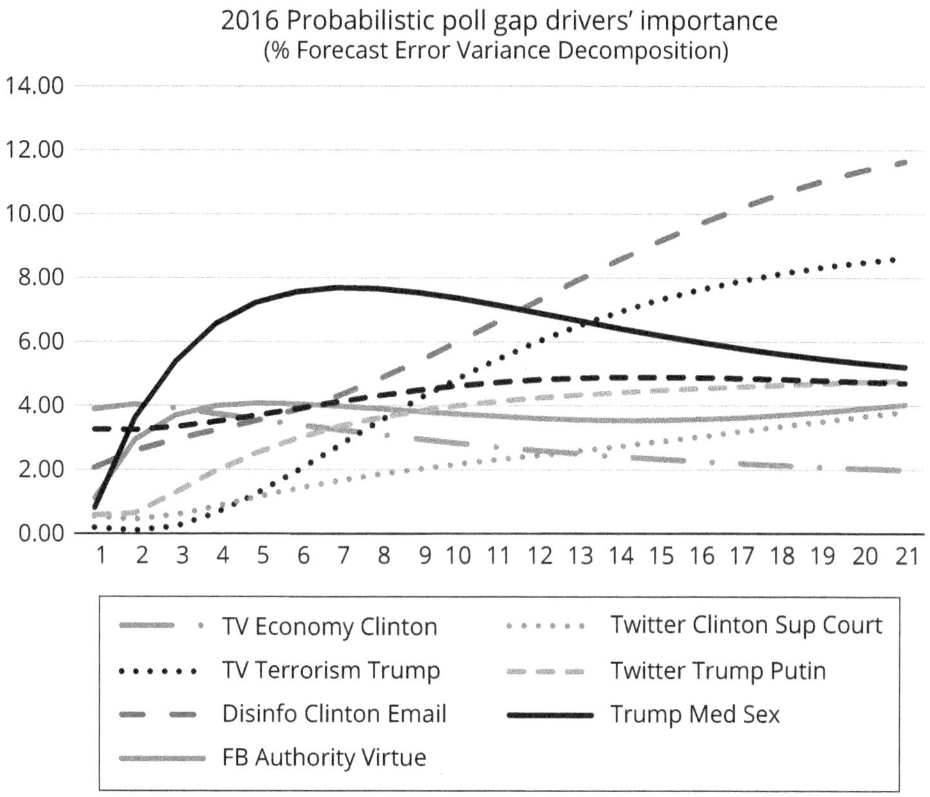

Figure 6.5 Forecast Error Variance Decomposition (FEVD) of Probabilistic Poll Gaps

which showed interesting differences. Biden's probabilistic poll standing is helped by his Facebook ads, while Trump benefits from his Google ads. Finally, offline word-of-mouth showed strong benefits for either candidate.

The probabilistic poll shows more significant effects benefitting Trump, including his military and Democratic division ads, and disinformation about Biden's alleged fraud and objection to America being great. It also shows a Biden benefit of referring to moral unfairness via Fairness Vice language, such as this May 30 tweet: "*You can't defeat bigotry, it only hides. And when leaders give it oxygen as Donald Trump has done, it comes roaring back. We all have the moral obligations to stand up, speak out and hold people accountable.*"

In contrast, the traditional poll gap shows Biden benefiting from Trump's COVID-19 ads and from several news coverage topics. It also picks up Biden hurting his standing with his use of moral pro authority language attacking Trump with statements such as "*I am not running for office to be King of America*" (Twitter, June 2nd).

Among the studied variables, Trump's TV ads about Democratic division have the highest short-term effect (explaining 12% of the poll gap in the first days) but are superseded by false news about Biden's alleged support for Defund the Police. Biden's TV ads about the economy take several days of wear-in to reach their peak impact of about 6%, while other drivers show exponential wear-out after their immediate peak impact for Biden: fake news about "America is not Great," Fairness Vice moral language, and offline word-of-mouth (Figure 6.6).

In sum, we find empirical evidence that our modeling framework and major findings generalize from the 2016 to the 2020 US presidential election: channels (TV vs. social media) and topics matter substantially, and they show

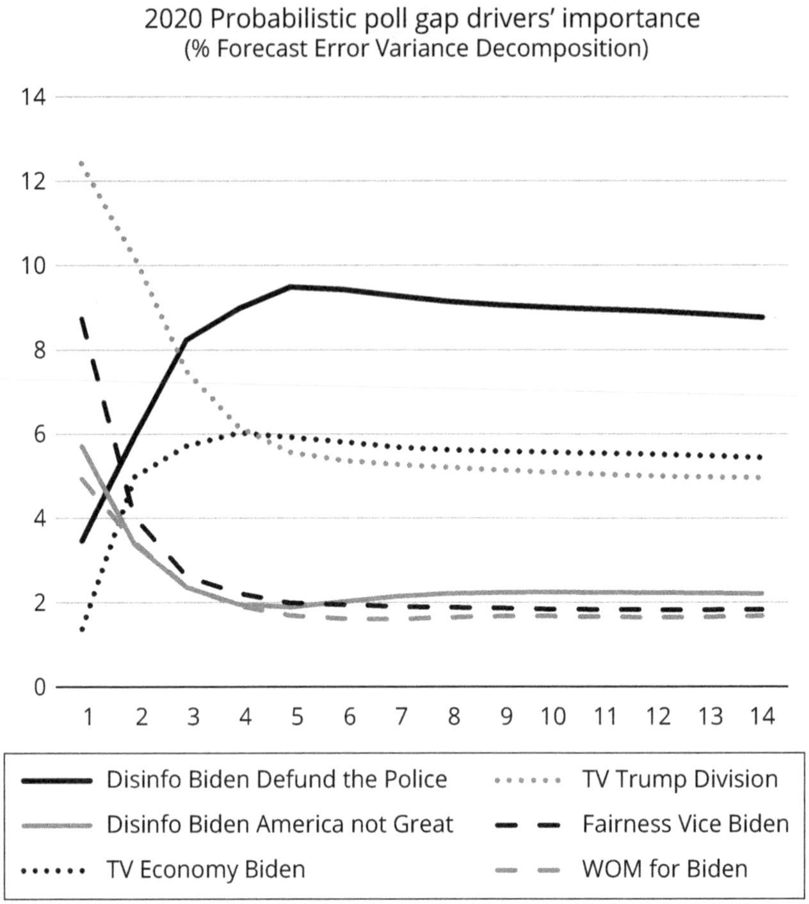

Figure 6.6 2020 Probabilistic Poll Gap Drivers' Importance

different effects on various predictive metrics. Moreover, the importance of disinformation grows over time, the Republican candidate gets the most benefits from using fear appeals and from disinformation about the opponent, while the Democratic candidate gets most benefit from talking about the economy.

To what extent would our findings generalize to other elections? We don't believe they generalize to 20th century elections, with the exception of the importance of fundamentals (economy and party in power). Both of our studies analyzed public use of social media, disinformation, and a populist candidate. These features are likely to stay in coming decades and matter worldwide, as experiences and research from the Philippines to France, from Germany to Brazil show (Gerstlé & Nai, 2019; Machado et al., 2019; Ong & Cabañes, 2018).

KEY FINDINGS AND MARKETING LESSONS FOR FUTURE ELECTIONS

Key research questions motivating this study included: (1) To what extent did disinformation versus candidate actions drive the polls for the 2016 US presidential election? and (2) Did the election predictive metric matter? Figure 6.4 visualizes our answers.

Earned social media (the sentiment and moral language in social media user comments) are important drivers for both poll types, explaining the Clinton–Trump gap by 13% for the traditional and 23% for the probabilistic polls. This social media influence outshines the effect of news coverage (approximately 9% in each poll). However, insights into the effects of candidate actions starkly differ between the polls. Judging from the traditional poll gap, the campaign managers may have concluded that the Trump campaign's TV ads were most influential and *six times more powerful* than Clinton's TV ads. Clinton's coverage in news and disinformation come next and are about equally important. By contrast, the probabilistic poll gap is more than one-third explained by *disinformation about Clinton* and shows a 9% (vs. 5% for Trump) impact of Clinton's own moral language. Clinton's TV ads explain more than Trump's TV ads, demonstrating the power of Clinton's ad themes on the economy and gun control to improve her election chances.

Two key contributions of our research are the importance of topic and platform. We find that topics matter a great deal, even reversing the sign of voter impact of false news about a candidate (Clinton's email vs. Muslim associations). Moreover, we find starkly different effectiveness for topics pushed by the campaigns. We recommend that campaigns focus most on topics that are of high importance to voters (e.g., point of parity, the economy) and that represent the candidate's point of difference (e.g., terrorism for Trump, women's issues and gun control for Clinton). However, platforms matter as well, and they interact with topics in new ways. "Creative outlet" platform Instagram works for showing support for women's issues, but "self-media" platform Twitter does not and is better suited to stir sentiment. At the same time, offline marketing (in our study, TV ads) remains a powerful vehicle to get the candidate's message across, especially on topics voters care most about, such as the economy, terrorism, and gun control. Finally, mainstream news mostly matters for its coverage of scandals and the general understanding it provides for interpreting fake news on the same topics.

What lessons can we draw from these findings for future elections? The first key lesson is that *quality market research matters in politics*. Commenting on the apparent overconfidence of at least some media and campaigners concerning the traditional poll gap, Silver (2017b) asks: "*Could this misreading of the polls – and polling-based forecasts – actually have affected the election's outcome?*" Whereas political science has focused on the prediction accuracy of different polls (Gutsche et al., 2014; Jennings & Wlezien, 2018; Kennedy et al., 2018), we show that the choice of poll matters for the size and even the sign of campaign actions on voter preferences. Further research could dive deeper into the conditions of and explanations for these differences and use these insights to better design and/or combine polls. Moreover, we advise candidates against relying on a single predictive metric, and to leverage probabilistic polls and their breakdowns to monitor voter reactions and adapt tactics based on this information. Clinton campaign's TV ads initially focused on the economy and gun control, points of parity and difference, respectively, in our conceptualization and the two topics that increased her probabilistic polls most in our analysis. However, this focus shifted to family, crime, and justice as well as terrorism threats, none of which is effective to move probabilistic polls in our analysis. According to Silver (2017a), Clinton's campaign "*went off script in the final 10 days.*" Clinton (2017) acknowledges the campaign pivot (considered necessary after the Comey letter) but also shows a chart of how many times she mentioned "jobs" to support the claim she continued to pay attention to the economy. Our data show that the Clinton campaign indeed continued to run economy ads, but this message likely did not come across because of heavy spending on other issues. Marketing has repeatedly demonstrated the importance of consistent brand messaging over time to build and maintain the clarity and strength of the brand's position (Braun-LaTour & LaTour, 2004; Erdem & Swait, 2004). In summary, fundamental marketing concepts appear important to political strategies as well.

Second, *events matter less* than how they resonate in the candidates' strategies and people's social media interactions and disinformation sharing. Of the 18 events we analyzed, only 3 had a significant impact on 2016 daily poll numbers: Comey's letter to Congress, Clinton's "basket of deplorables" statement, and Trump's "grab them" tape (only for the traditional poll gap). Likewise, in the 2012 election, 68 moments were described as "gamechangers" by pundits, but most were not (Sides & Vavreck, 2013, p. 1). Thus, we agree with Silver (2017a) that,

> *'if I were advising a future candidate on what to learn from 2016, I'd tell him or her to mostly forget about the Comey letter and focus on the factors that were within the control of Clinton and Trump'*

Indeed, how candidates and their supporters or opponents react to events can be significant. While Trump succeeded in diverting attention from poor debate performance with a tweet about a "big announcement" (Newman, 2016, p. 789), Clinton's lesser relative emphasis on the economy in

TV ads hurt her in the polls. Marketing theory recommends that, though a brand can ride an opportunistic wave (e.g., denouncing an opponent's ethical lapses) or defend against attacks by denouncing them, it should return to its core (Erdem & Swait, 2004; Keller, 1993). In this respect, Trump showed a long-term adherence to authentic branding, being perceived relatively similar in the 2016 primaries to his persona on *The Apprentice* (Dholakia, 2016). Moreover, Trump matched his message to himself in public and in advertising, "*ranting and raving if he chooses, thereby creating the image of a macho politician who is stronger and bolder than any of his opponents*" (Newman, 2016, p. 790). When Trump did publicly experiment with messages and taglines (e.g., crowdsourcing how to call his opponent at a rally), he consistently used the result #CrookedHillary in later messaging, making it easy for his fans to repeat it. By contrast, none of the negative hashtags for Trump became dominant, and the "grab them" leak did not hurt his chances.

Third, a main long-term driver of Clinton's polls in our analysis was *disinformation* posts/comments related to her emails on her Facebook page. Mainstream news coverage also mattered but was much less important in our analysis. Again, this is consistent with Sides and Vavreck's (2013) finding of a limited impact of news coverage on polls. A completely new finding is that the impact of disinformation depends on the topic, with the continued discussion of division in her party hurting her, but hints of her connections with Muslims actually helping her in the polls. It could be that such connections were seen as positive. However, assimilation-contrast theory (Sherif et al., 1958) offers an alternative explanation: While exaggerated claims about Clinton's email scandal hurt her chances, as voters perceived them as having some grounds in truth (assimilation), exaggerated claims about Clinton's Muslim connections were too outlandish to be believed (contrast). Likewise, allegations of Biden's fraud and support for Defund the Police hurt him in the polls, while Trump's TV ads about COVID-19 did not hurt, but even helped Biden. Further research could explicitly investigate this theory-derived explanation, as it has important implications for which fake news topics might matter for future elections. We recommend that candidates carefully monitor not only polls but also social media interactions, as well as disinformation sharing and its impact on polls. Appropriate action on disinformation depends on whether it helps or hurts the brand (Ilhan et al., 2018). Unfortunately, platform and regulatory interventions to disinformation, whether to empower people to evaluate the disinformation they encounter or to prevent their disinformation exposure in the first place, have been met with little success (Kozyreva et al., 2023; Lazer et al., 2018). Disinformation is here to stay, and counteracting its negative impact will remain the responsibility mostly of the targets themselves.

Fourth, *place matters*. For example, Clinton got a boost from discussing women's issues on Instagram but not on Twitter. Moreover, her own Facebook page was full of negative comments using authority virtue language, which substantially hurt her in the polls. These examples confirm that different social media platforms attract different people and trigger different dynamic interactions (Kreiss et al., 2018; Schmidbauer et al., 2018). While Instagram focuses on sharing beautiful images and supportive words among the like-minded, Twitter and Facebook interactions are often angry discussions among followers, who can be lovers or haters (Ilhan et al., 2018). Conversely, Trump benefited from Twitter as a direct broadcasting to likely voters, bypassing the typical gatekeepers of media and party apparatus. In the Obama campaigns, for example, urging followers to post, share, and become involved in any way they could enabled them to effectively create their own campaign (Francia, 2018; Newman, 2016). However, such open sharing also allows "haters" to directly address the candidate's fans. In contrast with findings that allowing such negative comments is good for commercial brands because it "*rallies the troops*" (Ilhan et al., 2018), the substantial harm (from authority virtue comments on Clinton's own Facebook page) indicates different considerations for political brands. The widely acknowledged *differences* between commercial and political branding battles are a likely explanation for this discrepancy. Political battles are winner-takes-all and, without freedom to vote in many countries and a de facto two-party system in the United States, can be won on the margin by simply discouraging citizens from voting for a candidate they mildly prefer over the other candidate (e.g., Bump, 2018). Such Clinton-negative comments on her own Facebook page (as captured by our example in the data section) often referred to her alleged lack of authority and virtue, which are typical Republican talking points in moral foundations research (Graham et al., 2009). Thus, our findings reveal an important caveat to the advice to use "*virtually all possible social media platforms*" (Newman, 2016, p. 786).

We recommend that campaign managers carefully match their messages to the optimal platform and monitor the moral language in negative comments posted on their owned media. In contrast with recent findings in marketing science for commercial brands (Ilhan et al., 2018), political brands should take action to mitigate the harm of such social media discourse. If such negative comments only receive a weak push-back from the candidate's fans, this may indicate a deeper issue that should be addressed. Our cross-platform analysis also contributes to political science, as Tucker et al. (2018) specifically call for research on Facebook to move beyond the typical Twitter focus of political and disinformation studies.

LIMITATIONS AND FUTURE RESEARCH

We acknowledge several limitations of our research. First, our data are on the aggregate (national) level and do not address either the candidates' successes or their actions in specific states. Therefore, we highly recommend additional research for different states, given both their importance of the US political system and the potential to assess geographic differences in the observed effects. However, we note that some of the most influential drivers (e.g., disinformation and moral language on social media) occur across counties and states and that explaining national polls is of key importance, given that a national advantage exceeding two points yields electoral victory in the United States (Silver, 2017a). Second, our findings for the studied variables may partly be due to the omitted variables with which they correlate. Though we include both offline and public online conversations, private messages (including direct messages and WhatsApp conversations) are unavailable for ethical reasons. Even if our social media data represent only the proverbial "tip of the iceberg," our main findings hold up insofar as these other sources show a similar relative importance of topics, sentiment, and so on (Awad et al., 2004). Third, several variables included in previous research are missing from our data, such as field operations (Wang et al., 2018). Although Silver (2017c) finds that these did not explain the 2016 election outcome, further research should include field operations, to the extent that they do not correlate highly with the many other candidate variables in our analysis. Fourth, our methodology provides flexible treatment of time lags and allows complex interactions among the endogenous variables. This is appropriate when the literature's body of knowledge is unclear on the lag structure and/or unidirectional causality, but it makes precisely testing specific hypotheses more difficult (Freeman et al., 1989). Drawing on our insights, research could build causal models and isolate incremental effects through counterfactuals (Gordon et al., 2012). Fifth, our model does not account for changes in economic situation and consumer sentiment, as they were rather stable in 2016. By contrast, 2020 witnessed large shifts in health and economic threats, and one of the candidates for US president was up for reelection.

Overall, we show the relative importance of several factors believed to have driven election results, from external events and social media interactions to the topics, channels, and moral language chosen by the candidates. The results reveal a blend between old-school insights and newer developments due to both new market research tools and new ways for candidates and citizens to express themselves through social media. While people were previously limited to influencing a few others they knew personally, now they can influence "*hundreds, maybe thousands, and maybe even millions of people who follow a person's thinking*" (Newman, 2016, p. 794). Capturing this rich information and analyzing it for actionable insights are key opportunities. We hope that our longitudinal analysis of the 2016 and 2020 US presidential elections will inspire researchers, politicians, political marketers, operatives, and citizens to act, refine, and improve on what we learned.

Notes

1 STMs belong to the latest developments in topic modeling and allow contrary to classic latent Dirichlet allocation models the inclusion of co-variates which account for factors such as time or platform, which lead to a better topic identification (Roberts et al., 2019). This makes STMs especially suitable for latent topic identification in a political context (see Roberts et al., 2014) as underlined by recent applications in the context of US human rights politics (Bagozzi & Berliner, 2018), the analysis of disinformation during the Ukrainian crisis (Mishler et al., 2015), and political speeches in the US primaries (Lucas et al., 2015).

2 The likely reason for this prediction failure was neither market manipulation nor incorrect knowledge about the functioning of prediction markets, but the Clinton preference of the prediction market participants, whose education profile matched hers rather than Trump's base (Graefe, 2017;

Wolfers & Zitzewitz, 2018). Granger causality test results can be provided by the authors upon request.

3 FBI Director James Comey sent out a letter on 28 October 2016 (just 11 days before the US presidential election) in which he informed Congress that the FBI had discovered additional emails related to its investigation into Hillary Clinton's use of a private email server while she was Secretary of State.

4 The phrase "basket of deplorables" was used by Hillary Clinton on 9 September 2016, at a fundraiser in New York City, where she said: "*You know, just to be grossly generalistic, you could put half of Trump's supporters into what I call the basket of deplorables. Right? The racist, sexist, homophobic, xenophobic, Islamophobic – you name it.*" The "basket of deplorables" comment was widely publicized.

5 The "grab them" tape refers to a 2005 recording of a conversation between Donald Trump and Billy Bush, then a host of the entertainment news program "Access Hollywood." In the tape, Trump and Bush were heard having a lewd conversation about women. The most infamous part of the conversation involved Trump bragging about how his celebrity status allowed him to make unwanted sexual advances toward women. He said: "*I just start kissing them. It's like a magnet. Just kiss. I don't even wait. And when you're a star, they let you do it. You can do anything. Grab them by the p****. You can do anything.*" The recording was made public by The Washington Post on 7 October 2016 and caused a significant public outcry and led to widespread condemnation from both Democrats and Republicans.

REFERENCES

Abramowitz, A., & McCoy, J. (2019). United States: Racial resentment, negative partisanship, and polarization in Trump's America. *The Annals of the American Academy of Political and Social Science, 681*(1), 137–156.

Allcott, H., & Gentzkow, M. (2017). Social media and fake news in the 2016 election. *The Journal of Economic Perspectives, 31*(2), 211–236.

Allen, J., Howland, B., Mobius, M., Rothschild, D., & Watts, D. J. (2020). Evaluating the fake news problem at the scale of the information ecosystem. *Science Advances, 6*(14), 1–6.

Anderl, E., Becker, I., Von Wangenheim, F., & Schumann, J. H. (2016). Mapping the customer journey: Lessons learned from graph-based online attribution modeling. *International Journal of Research in Marketing, 33*, 457–474.

Ansolabehere, S., De Figueiredo, J. M., & Snyder, J. M. (2003). Why is there so little money in US politics? *The Journal of Economic Perspectives, 17*(1), 105–130.

Aral, S. (2020). *The hype machine: How social media disrupts our elections, our economy, and our health – And how we must adapt*. HarperCollinsPublishers.

Awad, N. F., Dellarocas, C., & Zhang, X. (2004). Is online word-of-mouth a complement or substitute to traditional means of consumer conversion? In Paper presented at the *Sixteenth Annual workshop on Information Systems Economics (WISE)*, Washington, DC.

Bagozzi, B. E., & Berliner, D. (2018). The politics of scrutiny in human rights monitoring: Evidence from structural topic models of US state department human rights reports. *Political Science Research and Methods, 6*(4), 661–677.

Bastos, M. T., & Mercea, D. (2019). The Brexit Botnet and user-generated hyperpartisan news. *Social Science Computer Review, 37*(1), 38–54.

Berger, J., Humphreys, A., Ludwig, S., Moe, W. W., Netzer, O., & Schweidel, D. A. (2020). Uniting the tribes: Using text for marketing insight. *Journal of Marketing, 84*(1), 1–25.

Bernays, E. L. (1928). *Propaganda*. Horace Liveright.

Boulianne, S. (2015). Social media use and participation: A meta-analysis of current research. *Information, Communication & Society, 18*(5), 524–538.

Bovet, A., & Makse, H. A. (2019). Influence of fake news in Twitter during the 2016 US presidential election. *Nature Communications, 10*(7), 1–14.

Braun-LaTour, K. A., & LaTour, M. S. (2004). Assessing the long-term impact of a consistent advertising campaign on consumer memory. *Journal of Advertising, 33*(2), 49–61.

Bump, P. (2018) *4.4 million 2012 Obama voters stayed home in 2016—More than a third of them black*. www.washingtonpost.com/news/politics/wp/2018/03/12/4-4-million-2012-obama-voters-stayed-home-in-2016-more-than-a-third-of-them-black. Accessed on June 1, 2020.

Campbell, J. E. (2005). The fundamentals in US presidential elections: Public opinion, the economy and incumbency in the 2004 presidential election. *Journal of Elections, Public Opinion, and Parties, 15*(1), 73–83.

Chanley, V. A., Rudolph, T. J., & Rahn, W. M. (2000). The origins and consequences of public trust in government: A time series analysis. *Public Opinion Quarterly, 64*(3), 239–256.

Clifford, S., Jerit, J., Rainey, C., & Motyl, M. (2015). Moral concerns and policy attitudes: Investigating the influence of elite rhetoric. *Political Communication, 32*(2), 229–248.

Clinton, H. R. (2017). *What happened*. Simon & Schuster.

Colicev, A., Malshe, A., & Pauwels, K. (2018). Social media and customer-based brand equity: An

empirical investigation in retail industry. *Administrative Sciences*, *8*(3), 1–16.
Colicev, A., & Pauwels, K. (2022). Multiple time series analysis for organizational research. *Long Range Planning*, *55*(2), 1–14.
Converse, P. E., & Traugott, M. W. (1986). Assessing the accuracy of polls and surveys. *Science*, *234*(4780), 1094–1098.
Coppock, A. (2017). Did shy trump supporters bias the 2016 polls? Evidence from a nationally-representative list experiment. *Statistics, Politics, and Policy*, *8*(1), 29–40.
Coppock, A., Hill, S. J., & Vavreck, L. (2020). The small effects of political advertising are small regardless of context, message, sender, or receiver: Evidence from 59 real-time randomized experiments. *Science Advances*, *6*(36), 1–6.
Day, C. (2016) *Can twitter analytics predict a trump v. Clinton winner?* www.agorapulse.com/blog/clinton-trump-twitter. Accessed on June 1, 2020.
Dekimpe, M. G., & Hanssens, D. M. (1999). Sustained spending and persistent response: A new look at long-term marketing profitability. *Journal of Marketing Research*, *36*(4), 397–412.
Delavande, A., & Manski, C. F. (2010). Probabilistic polling and voting in the 2008 presidential election: Evidence from the American life panel. *Public Opinion Quarterly*, *74*(3), 433–459.
Dholakia, U. (2016). *What Mr Trump's success teaches us about authentic branding*. www.psychologytoday.com/us/blog/the-science-behind-behavior/201605/what-mr-trump-s-success-teaches-us-about-authentic-branding. Accessed on June 1, 2024.
Diamond, L. (2010). Liberation technology. *Journal of Democracy*, *21*(3), 69–83.
Dimitrova, D. V., & Bystrom, D. (2013). The effects of social media on political participation and candidate image evaluations in the 2012 Iowa caucuses. *American Behavioral Scientist*, *57*(11), 1568–1583.
Downs, A. (1957). *An economic theory of democracy*. Harper & Brothers.
Enders, W. (2004). *Applied econometric time series*. John Wiley & Sons.
Erdem, T., & Swait, J. (2004). Brand credibility, brand consideration, and choice. *Journal of Consumer Research*, *31*(1), 191–198.
Erikson, R. S., & Wlezien, C. (2008). Are political markets really superior to polls as election predictors? *Public Opinion Quarterly*, *72*(2), 190–215.
Evans, L., & Wells, G. (1983). An alternative approach to simulating VAR models. *Economics Letters*, *12*(1), 23–29.
Fay, B., Keller, E., Larkin, R., & Pauwels, K. (2019). Deriving value from conversations about your brand. *MIT Sloan Management Review*, *60*, 72–77.
Ferrara, E., Varol, O., Davis, C., Menczer, F., & Flammini, A. (2016). The rise of social bots. *Communications of the ACM*, *59*(7), 96–104.
Francia, P. L. (2018). Free media and twitter in the 2016 presidential election: The unconventional campaign of Donald Trump. *Social Science Computer Review*, *36*(4), 440–455.
Franz, M. M., Fowler, E. F., Ridout, T., & Wang, M. Y. (2020). The issue focus of online and television advertising in the 2016 presidential campaign. *American Politics Research*, *48*(1), 175–196.
Freeman, J. R. (1983). Granger causality and the times series analysis of political relationships. *American Journal of Political Science*, *27*(2), 327–358.
Freeman, J. R., Williams, J. T., & Lin, T. (1989). Vector autoregression and the study of politics. *American Journal of Political Science*, *33*(4), 842–877.
Gambino, L. and Pankhania, M. (2016). *How we got here: A complete timeline of 2016's historic US election*. www.theguardian.com/us-news/2016/nov/07/us-election-2016-complete-timeline-clinton-trump-president. Accessed on June 1, 2020.
Gerstlé, J., & Nai, A. (2019). Negativity, emotionality and populist rhetoric in election campaigns worldwide, and their effects on media attention and electoral success. *European Journal of Communication*, *34*(4), 410–444.
Giomelakis, D., & Veglis, A. (2016). Investigating search engine optimization factors in media websites. *Digital Journalism*, *4*(3), 379–400.
Gordon, B. R., & Hartmann, W. R. (2013). Advertising effects in presidential elections. *Marketing Science*, *32*(1), 19–35.
Gordon, B. R., Lovett, M. J., Shachar, R., Arceneaux, K., Moorthy, S., Peress, M., et al. (2012). Marketing and politics: Models, behavior, and policy implications. *Marketing Letters*, *23*, 391–403.
Graefe, A. (2017). Prediction market performance in the 2016 US presidential election. *Foresight*, *45*, 38–42.
Graham, J. (2016, August 12). Trump vs Clinton: how the rivals rank on Twitter, Facebook, more. *USA Today*. https://www.usatoday.com/story/tech/news/2016/08/04/trump-clinton-social-media-twitter-facobook-youtube-snapchat/87974630/
Graham, J., Haidt, J., Koleva, S., Motyl, M., Iyer, R., Wojcik, S. P., & Ditto, P. H. (2013). Moral foundations theory: The pragmatic validity of moral pluralism. *Advances in Experimental Social Psychology*, *47*, 55–130.
Graham, J., Haidt, J., & Nosek, B. A. (2009). Liberals and conservatives rely on different sets of moral foundations. *The Journal of Social Psychology*, *96*(5), 1029–1049.
Granger, C. W. J. (1969). Investigating causal relations by econometric models and cross-spectral methods. *Econometrica*, *37*(3), 424–438.

Green, A. D. (2020). *From the Iowa caucuses to the white house - understanding Donald Trump's 2016 electoral victory in Iowa*. Springer Nature.

Grinberg, N., Joseph, K., Friedland, L., Swire-Thompson, B., & Lazer, D. (2019). Fake news on twitter during the 2016 US presidential election. *Science, 363*(6425), 374–378.

Guess, A. M., Nagler, J., & Tucker, J. (2019). Less than you think: Prevalence and predictors of fake news dissemination on Facebook. *Science Advances, 5*(1), 1–8.

Guess, A. M., Nyhan, B., & Reifler, J. (2020). Exposure to untrustworthy websites in the 2016 US election. *Nature Human Behaviour, 4*, 472–480.

Gunther, R., Beck, P. A. and Nisbet, E. C. (2019). 'Fake news' and the defection of 2012 Obama voters in the 2016 presidential election. *Electoral Studies*. https://doi.org/10.1016/j.electstud.2019.03.006

Gutsche, T. L., Kapteyn, A., Meijer, E., & Weerman, B. (2014). The RAND continuous 2012 presidential election poll. *Public Opinion Quarterly, 78*(S1), 233–254.

Hadarics, M., & Kende, A. (2017). The dimensions of generalized prejudice within the dual-process model: The mediating role of moral foundations. *Current Psychology, 37*, 731–739.

Haenschen, K., & Jennings, J. (2019). Mobilizing millennial voters with targeted internet advertisements: A field experiment. *Political Communication, 36*(3), 357–375.

Haidt, J. (2008). Morality. *Perspectives on Psychological Science, 3*(1), 65–72.

Hastie, T., Tibshirani, R., & Friedman, J. (2001). *The elements of statistical learning*. Springer.

Hennig-Thurau, T., Malthouse, E. C., Friege, C., Gensler, S., Lobschat, L., Rangaswamy, A., & Skiera, B. (2010). The impact of new media on customer relationships. *Journal of Service Research, 13*(3), 311–330.

Herman, E. S., & Chomsky, N. (1988). *Manufacturing consent*. Pantheon Books.

Hillygus, D. S. (2011). The evolution of election polling in the United States. *Public Opinion Quarterly, 75*(5), 962–981.

Humphreys, A., & Wang, R. J. H. (2018). Automated text analysis for consumer research. *Journal of Consumer Research, 44*(6), 1274–1306.

Hutto, C. J., & Gilbert, E. (2014). VADER: A parsimonious rule-based model for sentiment analysis of social media text. In Paper presented at *The Eighth International AAAI conference on Weblogs and Social Media*, Ann Arbor, MI (June 1–4).

Ilhan, B. E., Kübler, R. V., & Pauwels, K. H. (2018). Battle of the brand fans: Impact of brand attack and defense on social media. *Journal of Interactive Marketing, 43*, 33–51.

Jamieson, K. H. (2020). *Cyberwar: How Russian hackers and trolls helped elect a president*. Oxford University Press.

Janoff-Bulman, R. (2009). To provide or protect: Motivational bases of political liberalism and conservatism. *Psychological Inquiry, 20*(2/3), 120–128.

Jennings, W., & Wlezien, C. (2018). Election polling errors across time and space. *Nature Human Behaviour, 2*(4), 276–283.

Johansen, S., Mosconi, R., & Nielsen, B. (2000). Cointegration analysis in the presence of structural breaks in the deterministic trend. *The Econometrics Journal, 3*(2), 216–249.

Kahane, L. H. (2020). Determinants of county-level voting patterns in the 2012 and 2016 presidential elections. *Applied Economics, 52*(33), 3574–3587.

Keller, K. L. (1993). Conceptualizing, measuring, and managing customer-based brand equity. *Journal of Marketing, 57*(1), 1–22.

Keller, K. L., Sternthal, B., & Tybout, A. (2002). Three questions you need to ask about your brand. *Harvard Business Review, 80*(9), 80–86.

Kennedy, C., Blumenthal, M., Clement, S., Clinton, J. D., Durand, C., Franklin, C., et al. (2018). An evaluation of the 2016 election polls in the United States. *Public Opinion Quarterly, 82*(1), 1–33.

Knoll, J., Matthes, J., & Heiss, R. (2018). The social media political participation model: A goal systems theory perspective. *Convergence: The International Journal of Research into New Media Technologies, 26*(1), 135–156.

Kozyreva, A., Herzog, S. M., Lewandowsky, S., Hertwig, R., Lorenz-Spreen, P., Leiser, M., & Reifler, J. (2023). Resolving content moderation dilemmas between free speech and harmful misinformation. *Proceedings of the National Academy of Sciences, 120*(7), 1–12.

Kreiss, D., Lawrence, R. G., & McGregor, S. C. (2018). In their own words: Political practitioner accounts of candidates, audiences, affordances, genres, and timing in strategic social media use. *Political Communication, 35*(1), 8–31.

Kübler, R. V., Langmaack, M., Albers, S., & Hoyer, W. (2020). The impact of value-related crises on price and product-performance elasticities. *Journal of the Academy of Marketing Science, 48*(3), 776–794.

Kübler, R. V., & Manke, K. (2023). Data Driven Campaigning: Wie Einfluss messbar gemacht werden kann und wie wir damit effizientere Kampagnen gestalten können. In M. Fuchs, & M. Motzkau (Eds.), *Digitale Wahlkämpfe – Politische Kommunikation im Bundestagswahlkampf 2021* (pp. 121–144). Springer.

Kübler, R., Pauwels, K., & Manke, K. (2020). *How social media drove the 2016 US presidential election: A longitudinal topic and platform analysis.*

papers.ssrn.com/sol3/papers.cfm?abstract_id=3661846. Accessed March 22, 2024.

Kübler, R., & Pauwels, K. (2021). Metrics gone wrong: What managers can learn from the 2016 US presidential election. *NIM Marketing Intelligence Review*, *13*(1), 30–35.

Kupfer, A. K., Pähler vor der Holte, N., Kübler, R. V., & Hennig-Thurau, T. (2018). The role of the partner brand's social media power in brand alliances. *Journal of Marketing*, *82*(3), 25–44.

Lazarsfeld, P. F., Berelson, B., & Gaudet, H. (1944). The people's choice. In *How the voter makes up his Mind in a presidential campaign*. Columbia University Press.

Lazer, D. M. J., Baum, M. A., Benkler, Y., Berinsky, A. J., Greenhill, K. M., Menczer, F., et al. (2018). The science of fake news. *Science*, *359*(6380), 1094–1096.

Leeflang, P. S., Wieringa, J. E., Bijmolt, T. H., & Pauwels, K. H. (2015). *Modeling markets*. Springer-Verlag.

Lindberg, B. C. (1982). International comparison of growth in demand for a new durable consumer product. *Journal of Marketing Research*, *19*(3), 364–371.

Lippmann, W. (1922). *Public opinion*. Harcourt, Brace and Company.

Lovett, M. J., Peres, R., & Shachar, R. (2013). On brands and word of mouth. *Journal of Marketing Research*, *50*(4), 427–444.

Lucas, C., Nielsen, R. A., Roberts, M. E., Stewart, B. M., Storer, A., & Tingley, D. (2015). Computer-assisted text analysis for comparative politics. *Political Analysis*, *23*(2), 254–277.

Lütkepohl, H. (1990). Asymptotic distributions of impulse response functions and forecast error variance decompositions of vector autoregressive models. *The Review of Economics and Statistics*, *72*(1), 116–125.

Machado, C., Kira, B., Narayanan, V., Kollanyi, B., & Howard, P. (2019). A study of misinformation in WhatsApp groups with a focus on the Brazilian presidential elections. In *WWW '19: Companion proceedings of the 2019 world wide web conference, San Francisco, USA, May 13–17, 2019* (pp. 1013–1019). Association for Computing Machinery.

MacKuen, M. B., Erikson, R. S., & Stimson, J. A. (1992). Peasants or bankers? The American electorate and the US economy. *American Political Science Review*, *86*(3), 597–611.

Mann, A. (2016). Market forecasts. *Nature*, *538*(7625), 308–310.

Mishler, A., Crabb, E. S., Paletz, S., Hefright, B., & Golonka, E. (2015). Using structural topic modeling to detect events and cluster twitter users in the Ukrainian crisis. In *HCI international 2015 - Posters' extended abstracts* (ed C Stephanidis), Los Angeles, USA, August 2–7, 2015 (pp. 639–644). Springer.

Mohammad, S., & Turney, P. (2013). Crowdsourcing a word-emotion association lexicon. *Computational Intelligence*, *29*(3), 436–465.

Monti, M. (2018). *The new populism and fake news on the internet: How populism along with internet new media is transforming the fourth estate*. papers.ssrn.com/sol3/papers.cfm?abstract_id=3175280. Accessed March 22, 2024.

Moorman, C., Chandy, R., Johar, G., & Roberts, J. (2018). *Call for papers | Journal of marketing special issue: Better marketing for a better world*. www.ama.org/2018/11/20/call-for-papers-journal-of-marketing-special-issue-better-marketing-for-a-better-world. Accessed June 1, 2020.

Newman, B. I. (2016). Reinforcing lessons for business from the marketing revolution in us presidential politics: A strategic triad. *Psychology and Marketing*, *33*(10), 781–795.

Nijs, V. R., Srinivasan, S., & Pauwels, K. (2007). Retail-price drivers and retailer profits. *Marketing Science*, *26*(4), 473–487.

O'Connor, B., Balasubramanyan, R., Routledge, B. R. and Smith, N. A. (2010). *From tweets to polls: Linking text sentiment to public opinion time series*. www.cs.cmu.edu/~nasmith/papers/oconnor+balasubramanyan+routledge+smith.icwsm10.pdf. Accessed June 1, 2020.

Ong, J. C., & Cabañes, J. V. A. (2018). *Architects of networked disinformation: Behind the scenes of troll accounts and fake news production in the Philippines*. scholarworks.umass.edu/communication_faculty_pubs/74. Accessed March 22, 2024.

Pauwels, K. (2014). *It's Not the Size of the data - It's how you use it: Smarter Marketing with Analytics and dashboards*. Amacom.

Pauwels, K., & Joshi, A. (2016). Selecting predictive metrics for marketing dashboards: An analytical approach. *Journal of Marketing Behavior*, *2*(2/3), 195–224.

Pennycook, G., & Rand, D. G. (2019). Fighting misinformation on social media using crowd-sourced judgments of news source quality. *Proceedings of the National Academy of Sciences*, *116*(7), 2521–2526.

Persily, N. (2017). The 2016 US election – Can democracy survive the internet? *Journal of Democracy*, *28*(2), 63–76.

Pesaran, H. H., & Shin, Y. (1998). Generalized impulse response analysis in linear multivariate models. *Economics Letters*, *58*(1), 17–29.

Poll Tracker. (2016). *US presidential election 2016: Poll tracker*. www.telegraph.co.uk/news/2016/05/26/us-presidential-elections-2016-poll-tracker. Accessed June 1, 2020.

Reuning, K., & Dietrich, N. (2018). Media coverage, public interest, and support in the 2016 republican invisible primary. *Perspectives on Politics*, *17*(2), 326–339.

Rhodes, J. H., & Vayo, A. B. (2019). The historical presidency: Fear and loathing in presidential candidate rhetoric, 1952–2016. *Presidential Studies Quarterly*, *49*(4), 909–931.

Roberts, M. E., Stewart, B. M., & Tingley, D. (2019). stm: An R package for structural topic models. *Journal of Statistical Software*, *91*(2), 1–40.

Roberts, M. E., Stewart, B. M., Tingley, D., Lucas, C., Leder-Luis, J., Gadarian, S. K., Albertson, B., & Rand, D. G. (2014). Structural topic models for open-ended survey responses. *American Journal of Political Science*, *58*(4), 1064–1082.

Rothschild, D. (2009). Forecasting elections. *Public Opinion Quarterly*, *73*(5), 895–916.

Schmidbauer, H., Rösch, A., & Stieler, F. (2018). The 2016 US presidential election and media on Instagram: Who was in the lead? *Computers in Human Behavior*, *81*, 148–160.

Schweidel, D., & Moe, W. W. (2014). Listening in on social media: A joint model of sentiment and venue format choice. *Journal of Marketing Research*, *51*(4), 387–402.

Shachar, R. (2009). The political participation puzzle and marketing. *Journal of Marketing Research*, *46*(6), 798–815.

Shao, C., Ciampaglia, G. L., Varol, O., Yang, K. C., Flammini, A., & Menczer, F. (2018). The spread of low-credibility content by social bots. *Nature Communications*, *9*, 1–9.

Shearer, E. and Gottfried, J. (2017). *News use across social media platforms 2017*. www.journalism.org/2017/09/07/news-use-across-social-media-platforms-2017. Accessed June 1, 2020.

Sherif, M., Taub, D., & Hovland, C. I. (1958). Assimilation and contrast effects of anchoring stimuli on judgments. *Journal of Experimental Psychology*, *55*(2), 150–155.

Sides, J., & Vavreck, L. (2013). *The gamble - Choice and Chance in the 2012 presidential election*. Princeton University Press.

Silver, N. (2017a). *The Comey letter probably cost clinton the election*. fivethirtyeight.com/features/the-comey-letter-probably-cost-clinton-the-election. Accessed June 1, 2020.

Silver, N. (2017b). *Clinton's ground game didn't cost her the election*. fivethirtyeight.com/features/clintons-ground-game-didnt-cost-her-the-election. Accessed June 1, 2020.

Silver, N. (2017c). *The media has a probability problem*. fivethirtyeight.com/features/the-media-has-a-probability-problem. Accessed June 1, 2020.

Simas, E. N., Clifford, S., & Kirkland, J. H. (2020). How empathic concern fuels political polarization. *American Political Science Review*, *114*(1), 258–269.

Sims, C. A. (1980). Macroeconomics and reality. *Econometrica*, *48*(1), 1–48.

Sims, C. A., & Zha, T. (1999). Error bands for impulse responses. *Econometrica*, *67*(5), 1113–1155.

Slotegraaf, R. J., & Pauwels, K. (2008). The impact of brand equity and innovation on the long-term effectiveness of promotions. *Journal of Marketing Research*, *45*(3), 293–306.

Smith, K. B., Alford, J. R., Hibbing, J. R., Martin, N. G., & Hatemi, P. K. (2017). Intuitive ethics and political orientations: Testing moral foundations as a theory of political ideology. *American Journal of Political Science*, *61*(2), 424–437.

Spenkuch, J. L., & Toniatti, D. (2018). Political advertising and election results. *Quarterly Journal of Economics*, *133*(4), 1981–2036.

Srinivasan, S. (2022). Modeling marketing dynamics using vector autoregressive (VAR) models. In C. Homburg, M. Klarmann, & A. Vomberg (Eds.), *Handbook of market research* (pp. 515–547). Springer Nature.

Srinivasan, S., Rutz, O. J., & Pauwels, K. (2016). Paths to and off purchase: Quantifying the impact of traditional marketing and online consumer activity. *Journal of the Academy of Marketing Science*, *44*, 440–453.

Srinivasan, S., Vanhuele, M., & Pauwels, K. (2010). Mind-set metrics in market response models: An integrative approach. *Journal of Marketing Research*, *47*(4), 672–684.

Statista (2016). *Number of twitter followers of 2016 US presidential candidates as of September, 2016*. www.statista.com/statistics/509579/twitter-followers-of-2016-us-presidential-candidates. Accessed June 1, 2020.

Stewart, P. A., & Schubert, J. N. (2006). Taking the 'low road' with subliminal advertisements. *Harvard International Journal of Press/Politics*, *11*(4), 103–114.

Stracqualursi, V. (2016). *Key moments of the 2016 election*. abcnews.go.com/Politics/key-moments-2016-election/story?id=43289663. Accessed June 1, 2020.

Surowiecki, J. (2004). *The Wisdom of crowds*. Anchor Books.

Tandoc, E. C., Lim, Z. W., & Ling, R. (2018). Defining 'fake news'. *Digital Journalism*, *6*(2), 137–153.

Tedesco, J. C., & Dunn, S. W. (2019). Political advertising in the 2016 US presidential election: Ad Hominem Ad Nauseam. *American Behavioral Scientist*, *63*(7), 935–947.

Theil, H. (1966). *Applied economic forecasting*. Rand-McNally & Co.

Thelwall, M., Buckley, K., Paltoglou, G., Cai, D., & Kappas, A. (2010). Sentiment strength detection in short informal text. *Journal of the American Society for Information Science and Technology*, *61*(12), 2544–2558.

Trusov, M., Bucklin, R. E., & Pauwels, K. (2009). Effects of word-of-mouth versus traditional marketing: Findings from an internet social networking site. *Journal of Marketing*, *73*(5), 90–102.

Tucker, J. A., Guess, A., Barberá, P., Vaccari, C., Siegel, A., Sanovich, S. et al. (2018). *Social media, political polarization, and political disinformation: A review of the scientific literature*. hewlett.org/wp-content/uploads/2018/03/Social-Media-Political-Polarization-and-Political-Disinformation-Literature-Review.pdf. Accessed June 1, 2020.

Tumasjan, A., Sprenger, T. O., Sandner, P. G., & Welpe, I. M. (2011). Election forecasts with twitter: How 140 characters reflect the political landscape. *Social Science Computer Review*, *29*(4), 402–418.

Vargo, C. J., Guo, L., & Amazeen, M. A. (2017). The agenda-setting power of fake news: A big data analysis of the online media landscape from 2014 to 2016. *New Media & Society*, *20*(5), 2028–2049.

Voorveld, H. A. M., Van Noort, G., Muntinga, D. G., & Bronner, F. (2018). Engagement with social media and social media advertising: The differentiating role of platform type. *Journal of Advertising*, *47*(1), 38–54.

Vosoughi, S., Roy, D., & Aral, S. (2018). The spread of true and false news online. *Science*, *359*(6380), 1146–1151.

Wang, Y., Lewis, M., & Schweidel, D. A. (2018). A border strategy analysis of Ad source and message tone in senatorial campaigns. *Marketing Science*, *37*(3), 333–355.

Weber, C. R., & Federico, C. M. (2013). Moral foundations and heterogeneity in ideological preferences. *Political Psychology*, *34*(1), 107–126.

Williams, L. V., & Reade, J. J. (2016). Forecasting elections. *Journal of Forecasting*, *35*, 308–328.

Wolfers, J., & Zitzewitz, E. (2004). Prediction markets. *The Journal of Economic Perspectives*, *18*(2), 107–126.

Wolfers, J., & Zitzewitz, E. (2018). The 'standard error' of event studies: Lessons from the 2016 election. *AEA Papers and Proceedings*, *108*, 584–589.

Yildirim, G., & Kübler, R. (2023). *Applied marketing analytics using R*. Sage Publications.

You, Y., Vadakkepatt, G. G., & Joshi, A. M. (2015). A meta-analysis of electronic word-of-mouth elasticity. *Journal of Marketing*, *79*(2), 19–39.

Zhang, L., & Chung, D. J. (2020). The air war vs. the ground game: An analysis of multichannel marketing in US presidential elections. *Marketing Science*, *39*(5), 872–892.

Zhu, Y. Q., & Chen, H. G. (2015). Social media and human need satisfaction: Implications for social media marketing. *Business Horizons*, *58*(3), 335–345.

Zimdars, M. (2016). *False, misleading, clickbait-y, and/or satirical 'news' sources*. docs.google.com/document/d/10eA5-mCZLSS4MQY5QGb5ewC3-VAL6pLkT53V_81ZyitM/preview. Accessed June 1, 2020.

Zimdars, M., & McLeod, K. (2020). *Fake news: Understanding media and misinformation in the digital age*. MIT Press.

Zou, H., & Hastie, T. (2005). Regularization and variable selection via the elastic net. *Journal of the Royal Statistical Society Series B: Statistical Methodology*, *67*(2), 301–320.

APPENDIX 6.1 VARIABLE OPERATIONALIZATION

Category	*Variable*	*Description*	*Source*
Performance Variables	Probabilistic Polls Clinton	Daily Poll Clinton, weighted by intention to vote	USC Dornsife polls
	Probabilistic Polls Trump	Daily Poll Trump, weighted by intention to vote	USC Dornsife polls
	Prediction Market Clinton	Daily Average Share Prices of Bet Clinton Winning 2016 US Presidential	PredictIt.com
	Prediction Market Trump	Daily Average Share Prices of Bet Trump Winning 2016 US Presidential	PredictIt.com
	Donations Clinton	Daily sum of donations (in USD) to Clinton made by private US citizens	Federal Election Commission
	Donations Trump	Daily sum of donations (in USD) to Trump made by private US citizens	Federal Election Commission
	Followers Clinton	Daily number of US based followers of Clinton's official Facebook, Twitter and Instagram page, as well as YouTube Channel	Facebook, Twitter, Instagram, and YouTube APIs
	Followers Trump	Daily number of US based followers of Trump's official Facebook, Twitter and Instagram page, as well as YouTube Channel	Facebook, Twitter, Instagram, and YouTube APIs
	Aggregated Daily Traditional Polls Clinton	Daily Poll Clinton (averaged over all major US polls)	Polltracker
	Aggregated Daily Traditional Polls Trump	Daily Poll Trump (averaged over all major US polls)	Polltracker
TV Advertising	TV Advertising Time Trump	14 variables indicating daily sum of seconds of ad time related to candidate's biography, civil rights, crime and justice, economy, education, environment, family, foreign policy, gun control, health care, immigration, military, terrorism, and women	AdSpend database
	TV Advertising Time Clinton	12 variables indicating daily sum of seconds of ad time related to candidate's biography, civil rights, crime and justice, economy, education, environment, family, gun control, health care, immigration, terrorism, and women	AdSpend database
Content Marketing by		STM analysis of all social media channels with 6 topics	

(Continued)

Category	Variable	Description	Source
Candidates on Social Media	Topics of Social Media Posts from Clinton on Twitter, Facebook, and Instagram	per channel: Spanish Posts, Rallies and Support, Democratic Party, Building New USA, Attacking Trump, and Women and Family (18 variables in total)	STM analyses of Clinton's posts in all social media channels
	Topics of Social Media Posts from Trump on Twitter, Facebook, and Instagram	STM analysis of all social media channels with 6 topics per channel: Political Agenda, Trump Campaign News, MAGA, Attack Clinton, Clinton Emails, and Direct Interaction with Trump (18 variables in total)	STM analyses of Trump's posts in all social media channels
Social Media Post Valence per Candidate	Valence for Clinton's and Trump's posts on Twitter, Facebook, and Instagram	VADER and Senti Strength Compound Scores (daily number of positive words – number of negative words) divided by total daily number of words of a candidate in a social media channel	Python 3.63 Vader Sentiment module SentiStrength JAVA tool
	Emotions for Clinton's and Trump's posts on Twitter, Facebook, and Instagram	NRC-based count of daily words associated to the 8 emotions: Anger, Disgust, Fear, Sadness, Anticipation, Joy, Surprise, and Trust. For each dimension, candidate, and social media channel one daily count variable is calculated (48 variables in total)	NRC emotion dictionary provided by R package syuzhet
	Morality for Clinton's and Trump's posts on Twitter, Facebook, and Instagram	Moral foundation theory dictionary–based daily sum of all words associated with moral emotions. For each candidate and social media channel one variable is generated (6 variables in total)	MFT dictionary as provided by Graham et al. (2009)
Sentiment and Emotions of User Reactions in Social Media	Valence for user-generated comments on Clinton's and Trump's own Facebook and Instagram pages and from all tweets mentioning Trump or Clinton	VADER and Senti Strength compound score (daily number of positive words – number of negative words) divided by total daily number of words in comments on the official Facebook page of a candidate (2 variables in total)	Python 3.63 Vader Sentiment module SentiStrength JAVA tool
	Emotions for user-generated comments on Clinton's and Trump's own Facebook and Instagram pages and from all tweets mentioning Trump or Clinton	NRC-based count of daily words associated to the 8 emotions: Anger, Disgust, Fear, Sadness, Anticipation, Joy, Surprise, and Trust. For each dimension and candidate, one daily count	NRC emotion dictionary provided by R package syuzhet

(Continued)

(Continued)

Category	*Variable*	*Description*	*Source*
		variable is calculated (16 variables in total)	
	Morality for user-generated comments on Clinton's and Trump's own Facebook and Instagram pages and from all tweets mentioning Trump or Clinton	Moral foundation theory dictionary–based daily sum of all words associated with moral emotions. For each candidate one variable is generated (2 variables in total)	MFT dictionary as provided by Graham et al. (2009)
Disinformation	Disinformation Topics Clinton	4 variables with daily number of links associated to 4 disinformation topics resulting from STM analysis: Emails, Muslims, FBI Investigation, and Clinton Foundation	STM analysis of all disinformation links posted by users on Clinton's Facebook page referring to any website listed in Pennycook and Rand (2019), Vosoughi et al. (2018) and Zimdars (2016).
	Disinformation Topics Trump	6 variables with daily number of links associated with 6 disinformation topics resulting from STM analysis: Clinton Foundation, Muslims, Election Fraud, Wikileaks, Clinton Emails, and Main Stream Media	STM analysis of all disinformation links posted by users on Trump's Facebook page referring to any website listed in Pennycook and Rand (2019), Vosoughi et al. (2018) and Zimdars (2016).
Media Coverage	Media Coverage Clinton	25 topic variables with daily number of links for each of the 5 topics and each of the 5 media categories Topics: • FBI Investigation • Comparison with Trump • Democratic Party and Bernie Sanders • Email Investigations • Polling Results	STM analysis of all tweets from center, lean-left, left, lean-right, and right media outlets referring to a news article on their own website.
	Media Coverage Trump	25 topic variables with daily number of links for each of the 5 topics and each of the 5 media categories Topics: • Trump Endorsements • Trump vs. DNC • Polling Results • Trump Sex Life • Mike Pence and Rally Coverage	STM analysis of all tweets from center, lean-left, left, lean-right, and right media outlets referring to a news article on their own website.

Political Brand Engagement and Positioning: An Integrated Framework

Christopher Pich, Guja Armannsdottir, Dawood Khan and Louise Spry

INTRODUCTION

The exploration of branding and politics continues to be an inescapable phenomenon and developed into a specialised topic of political marketing (Lilleker & Moufahim, 2022). Further, the application of branding concepts and frameworks to the political setting remains a contemporary field of study for practitioners, researchers and academics due to the abundant theoretical implications and managerial opportunities derived from research in this area (Lloyd, 2022; Pich et al., 2020; Scammell, 2015). Indeed, the diversity and abundance of research on different types of political brands in international settings has expanded and continues to capture the imagination and curiosity of multiple stakeholders including academics, researchers-strategists, politicians, political parties and most importantly voters to name but a few (Baines et al., 2014; Marland et al., 2017; Newman & Newman, 2022). Nevertheless, two related priority issues continue to represent under-explored areas of study supported by explicit calls for further understanding. Firstly, investigating how voters engage with brands continues to be a key issue for marketers and brand managers within and beyond the realms of political marketing (Boleat, 2023; Poorrezaei et al., 2023). Secondly, examining how a political brand manages and communicates an intended position representing 'what it stands for', versus the realised position brought to life in the mind of voters (Baines et al., 2014; O'Shaughnessy & Baines, 2009; Pich et al., 2020; Smith & French, 2009). In order to frame the exploration, the engagement and positioning associated with political brands, this chapter of adopts intrinsically linked concepts such as consumer brand engagement (CBE), brand identity and brand image, which serve as appropriate theoretical lenses (Bolton & Saxena-Iyer, 2009; Brodie et al., 2011; Carvalho & Fernandes, 2018; Gambetti et al., 2015; Hollebeek, 2011b; Hollebeek et al., 2014; Leckie et al., 2016). This in turn will satisfy demands for a deeper understanding into engagement and positioning yet also explore the 'inter-relationships' between the concepts of CBE, brand identity and brand image (Hollebeek, 2011a). Investigating how voters engage and interpret political brands equips marketers and brand managers with the knowledge to devise strategies and tactics to strengthen existing behaviours, enhance long-term relationships and maintain desired positioning.

This chapter adheres to four objectives. First, the chapter presents the different typologies of political brands. Second, the chapter discusses the interactions and relationships between stakeholders and political brands through the theoretical construct of CBE. Third, the chapter presents the antecedents-drivers of consumer (political) brand engagement namely the concepts of political brand identity and political brand image. The chapter concludes with two short empirical case studies to illustrate application of the key constructs. Case one focuses on political brand positioning and identity in the British Crown Dependencies of Jersey. Case two focuses on presenting an integrated political brand engagement and positioning framework in the context of Pakistan with a specific focus on the PTI (Pakistan Tehreek-e-Insaf) party brand. The British Crown Dependencies of Jersey and Pakistan were chosen as they represent two under-explored yet dynamic contexts. Further, the two cases were in no way selected as comparisons but served to illustrate two unique international settings and home to different types of political brands. Finally, the two cases demonstrate the transfer potential of branding concepts to politics however acknowledges that core branding theory may need to be tailored to address the unique settings and contexts. The chapter concludes by presenting the political brand engagement and positioning framework (Figure 7.8), underpinned by the related yet distinct concepts of political brand identity, political brand image and CBE. Strategists and researchers should adopt the Political Brand Engagement and Positioning Framework as a mechanism to capture the engagement and/or positioning associated with political brands particularly from a multi-stakeholder perspective. Further, the chapter argues that it is important to routinely audit and track the positioning and engagement of political brands as this may reveal coherency or misalignment of desired and actual positioning, which strategists can respond and develop strategies to maintain alignment or devise repositioning-engagement strategies (Baines et al., 1999; Collins & Butler, 2002; Pich, 2022; Smith, 2005).

POLITICAL BRANDING

The exploration of brands and branding continues to be an inescapable phenomenon and research topic (Bastos & Levy, 2012; Richelieu, 2018). Further, research demonstrates that there is no limit to the application of branding concepts and frameworks to different contexts and settings. For example, branding principles can be transferred to products, services, people, institutions, religions, monarchies, campaigns, nations, cities, destinations, philosophies and politics (Bendisch et al., 2013; Mirza, 2016; Needham & Smith, 2015; Richelieu, 2014; Salzman, 2013; Speed et al., 2015; Zenker, 2014). Thus 'branding is everywhere and everything is a brand' (Richelieu, 2018, p. 354). However, it should be recognised that the transfer of branding concepts and frameworks to diverse settings is not a simple straightforward process and the branding principles may require adaptation and refinement to reflect the unique environment (Speed et al., 2015). Nevertheless, brands are more than names, images and logos (Shepherd, 2005). Brands are amalgamations of multiple tangible and intangible dimensions strategically designed to stand out from competitors, communicate a consistent message and build long-term relationships with their target markets (Marland et al., 2017).

One area of research that has witnessed advancement is the development of political branding. Further, the study of branding and politics has expanded in sophistication and scope over the last 30 years and has become a specialised area of political marketing (Pich et al., 2020; Scammell, 2015; Speed et al., 2015). Brand-related principles applied to the political environment enable parties, politicians and campaign groups to identify desired positioning, create, manage and communicate an envisaged identity, tailor campaigns-messages to distinct groups and stakeholders, which in turn provides a means of differentiation from political competitors (Baines et al., 2014; Lin & Himelboim, 2019; Marder et al., 2018; Nielsen, 2016). Indeed, political brands need to ensure they are perceived as authentic, united, engaging, trustworthy and understood in the desired manner by multiple stakeholders for success (Marland, 2016; Marwick & Boyd, 2010; Speed et al., 2015). Nevertheless, there are many related yet distinct typologies of political brands (examples outlined in Table 7.1) and this represents the complexity and multifaceted nature of political brands (Pich & Newman, 2020).

Indeed, some progress has been made in political branding in terms of conceptualising different typologies in diverse contexts such as Canada, USA, Australia, India, Iceland, Indonesia and British Crown Dependency of Guernsey (Armannsdottir et al., 2019; Falkowski & Jabłonska, 2019; Jain & Ganesh, 2019; Marland & Wagner, 2020). Existing research has tended to focus on 'established' rather than with new/recent political brands often with an emphasis on traditional electoral 'party systems' opposed to independent 'non-party' settings. Further,

Table 7.1 Different Typologies of Political Brands

Political Brand Typologies	*Example*
Corporate	National and international level such as the Democratic Party (US), The Labour Party (UK), Bharatiya Janata Party (India).
Local-Sub	Regional level yet affiliated with the corporate political brands such as Nottingham Labour (UK), New York Republican State Committee (USA), Pakistan Tehreek-e-Insaf Women Wing (Pakistan).
Politician-Personal	Politicians-personal brands of individual politicians/candidates at national level, for example, President Macron (France), Prime Minister Jacinda Ardern (New Zealand), Chief Minister Gavin St Pier (Guernsey), or regional-local level such as Members of Parliament, Assembly Ministers, Councillors or local representatives.
Coalitions-Groups	Multi-party governments at national level such as the Republic of Iceland, Grand Coalition in Germany and international level such as the Alliance of Liberals and Democrats For Europe in the European Parliament.
Political Movements	Political campaign groups at local, national and international level that are independent yet endorse political parties, politicians or campaigns to achieve a common goal such as *Momentum* (UK), *Greta Thunberg's fight against climate change* or *Greenpeace*.
Pop-up Brands	Created around campaigns and political events such as 'Yes Scotland' referendum group in the 2014 Scottish Independence Referendum, 'Vote Leave' campaign group that supported a leave vote in the 2016 UK EU membership referendum.
Political Events	Campaign activities during elections as local, national and international level such as 2021 London Mayoral Election (UK), 2020 Presidential Elections (USA) and 2019 European Parliamentary Elections (EU).

existing studies have investigated the typologies of political brands through a distinct theoretical lens. These include brand identity, brand image, brand reputation, co-branding, brand equity, self-branding, brand communities, positioning, orientation often from an internal strategist perspective and/or from an external voter perspective (Pich & Newman, 2020; Lin & Himelboim, 2019; Marder et al., 2018; Nielsen, 2016; Van Steenburg & Guzmán, 2019). Irrespective of the theoretical construct, what seems to be clear and the common factor across studies is that they all aim to investigate how political brands are positioned by political stakeholders and how citizens interpret and perceive the communicated political brands (Baines et al., 2014; Nielsen, 2016; O'Shaughnessy & Baines, 2009). Therefore, political branding 'is an evolution of image management' (Marland & Flanagan, 2014, p. 952) and a strategic process of communicating a clear vision brought to life through physical and intangible dimensions and touchpoints (Marland et al., 2017).

Despite advancements in political branding research, there continues to be explicit calls for the additional understanding of different types of political brands from different perspectives and in diverse settings and contexts. More specifically, future research should examine two important characteristics such as how citizens *perceive* and *engage* with political brands particularly from a 'voter centric perspective' (Ahmed et al., 2015; Nielsen, 2016; O'Shaughnessy & Baines, 2009). This will build a convincing account into the relationship between political brands and citizens (Needham & Smith, 2015). This in turn will address calls for more insight into diverse cases of political brands and consider distinct theoretical lenses as this will continue the develop of the subject area (O'Cass & Voola, 2011; Pich et al., 2020; Rutter et al., 2015; Scammell, 2015; Simons, 2016). However, the next step is *to* conceptualise how consumers-citizens *engage* with brands followed by conceptualising how to investigate the *perceptions* of brands.

POLITICAL (CONSUMER) BRAND ENGAGEMENT

The exploration of how consumers (or citizens) engage with their brands continues to be a priority issue for marketers and brand managers (Gambetti et al., 2015). Consumers interact with thousands of brands on a daily basis; however, they only develop an 'intense connection' and relationship with a small number of these tangible-intangible entities (Carvalho & Fernandes, 2018). Consumers are fluid in terms of their relationships with brands due to increased competition, fading loyalty and identification and dynamic markets (Hollebeek et al., 2014; Van Doorn et al., 2010). Further, the notion of 'engagement' and how consumers 'engage' with brands continues to attract interest and promise (Halaszovich & Jaques, 2017; Raed et al., 2018). Indeed, understanding how consumers engage with brands equips marketers and brand managers with the knowledge to devise strategies and tactics to strengthen existing behaviours, enhance long-term relationships and maintain desired positioning (Raed et al., 2018).

According to Hollebeek et al. (2014), the engagement process can be uncovered by investigating a two-way interactive relationship between the subject and object. More specifically, the consumer is seen as the 'engagement subject' and the brand is defined as the 'engagement objective' (Carvalho & Fernandes, 2018; Halaszovich & Jaques, 2017; Verhoef et al., 2010). In addition, the majority of studies frame their research around 'engagement contexts', for example, technology, services, politics and psychology, which in turn provides a focus for the subject, object and investigator (Carvalho & Fernandes, 2018). Therefore, understanding the relationship between the consumer and brand grounded in a specific context will reveal insight into the engagement process and highlight how these interactions between the object, subject and context develop over time (Carvalho & Fernandes, 2018; Halaszovich & Jaques, 2017; Hollebeek, 2011; Hollebeek et al., 2014; Verhoef et al., 2010). However, engagement is a complex and multifaceted concept (Hollebeek, 2011). Further, engagement is not a new construct within the marketing literature with origins yet interest in this area continues to capture the imagination of researchers across diverse disciplines including psychology, sociology, organisational behaviour, brand management and political science (Brodie et al., 2011; Carvalho & Fernandes, 2018; Hollebeek, 2011; Powell, 2016; Raed et al., 2018). Indeed, engagement is often conceptualised differently in studies and contexts (Dessart et al., 2015; Halaszovich & Jaques, 2017) and often approached from different perspectives (Brodie et al., 2011; Raed et al., 2018). This has resulted is continued confusion and a lack of consensus with defining the concept of engagement (Brodie et al., 2011; Dessart et al., 2015; Machado et al., 2019).

DIMENSIONALITY VARIATION

Indeed, there remains 'variation in the dimensionality of the concept' of engagement (France et al., 2016, p. 121). In its simplest form, engagement is often constructed via three dimensions including cognition, emotion and/or behaviour (Hollebeek et al., 2014). Further, existing research has defined engagement as unidimensional (focusing on cognition, emotion or behaviour) alternatively multidimensional (cognition, emotion and behaviour) (Brodie et al., 2011). Therefore, irrespective of whether a single or multiple dimensional approach is adopted, the majority of studies concur that engagement is underpinned by cognition, emotion and/or behaviour (Ahn & Back, 2018; France et al., 2016; Gambetti et al., 2015; Gong, 2018; Halaszovich & Jaques, 2017). What seems to be distinct is the variation of different theoretical lenses blended with the engagement literature, which has resulted in the development of numerous similar yet distinct concepts (Hollebeek et al., 2014). For example, we have seen the development of customer engagement, customer brand engagement, CBE, online engagement, brand community engagement and advertising engagement (Bowden, 2009; Brodie et al., 2011; Calder et al., 2009; Carvalho & Fernandes, 2018; France et al., 2016; Hollebeek et al., 2014; Leckie et al., 2016; Raed et al., 2018; Vale & Fernandes, 2018). However, existing studies acknowledge that there is 'semantic confusion' (Hollebeek, 2011) with engagement research and 'similar conceptual scope despite employing differing concept designations' (Hollebeek et al., 2014, p. 152) particularly with the concepts of customer brand engagement and CBE.

Customer brand engagement emphasises the relationship between the customer and brand (France et al., 2016; Halaszovich & Jaques, 2017) and focuses on a 'customer's motivational, brand related and context-dependent state characterised by specific levels of cognitive, affective and behavioural activities' (Ahn & Back, 2018, p. 145). Further, customer brand engagement acknowledges a psychological, motivational state concerning the individual and brand/organisation, which is manifested through a customer's actions, sentimental attachment and informed reasoning (Carvalho & Fernandes, 2018; Gambetti et al., 2015). Similarly, CBE is recognised as a dynamic relational process (Gambetti et al., 2015) and focuses on a 'consumer's positively valenced (feeling of quality) cognitive, emotional and behavioural brand-related activity during, or related to, specific consumer/brand interactions' (Hollebeek et al., 2014, p. 151). However, what about negative experiences and behaviours and how does this relate to engagement (Gong, 2018)? In addition, CBE is considered a 'multidimensional concept...which plays a central role in the process of relational exchange where other relational concepts are engagement antecedents and/or consequences in iterative engagement processes within the brand community' (Brodie et al., 2011; Hollebeek et al., 2014, p. 151). Nevertheless, both customer and consumer brand engagement appear to comprise rationalised interest related to the brand under study, emotional subjective feelings associated with the brand and behavioural exchanges between the individual and brand (Ahn & Back, 2018; Brodie et al., 2011; Halaszovich & Jaques, 2017; Machado et al., 2019). Further, it is important to note that the customer-consumer engagement process 'does not follow an orderly sequential progression of phases over time' (Carvalho & Fernandes, 2018, p. 25) and this suggests that all three dimensions have equal importance and relevance. However, CBE is considered more comprehensive and multidimensional than customer brand engagement (Hollebeek et al., 2014; Leckie et al., 2016; Machado et al., 2019).

DRIVERS AND CONSEQUENCES

Irrespective of definition and dimensionality, existing research has focused on 'drivers-antecedents' and 'consequences' of CBE. For example, examining an individual's involvement (Leckie et al., 2016; Raed et al., 2018), participation, self-expression (Leckie et al., 2016), experiences, activities (Gambetti et al., 2015) interactivity, rapport, perceived quality, satisfaction, trust, commitment, customer value and loyalty (Carvalho & Fernandes, 2018; Hollebeek, 2011) with brands will explain current engagement. Equally, existing research has also investigated 'consequences' of engagement that relate to the potential or improved relationship between the individual and brand. More specifically, consequences of understanding engagement can influence loyalty, retention, positive word-of-mouth, (Leckie et al., 2016), satisfaction, commitment and trust (Carvalho & Fernandes, 2018; Raed et al., 2018), identification (Carvalho & Fernandes, 2018), familiarity, ownership, identification, (Gong, 2018; van Doorn et al., 2010) and empowerment (Vale & Fernandes, 2018). Therefore, there appears to be some overlap between 'drivers-antecedents' and 'consequences' of CBE. The 'drivers-antecedents' of CBE have the potential of managing 'consequences' of CBE and this has implications for marketers and brand managers. Thus, generating deep insight into the cognitive-emotive perceptions, associations and attitudes, combined with knowledge on the behaviours and experiences of individuals and brands could lead to a greater understanding of CBE by providing additional drivers-antecedents and consequences. Further, this may also reveal whether the consequences are intended or unintended by the brand's creator.

Despite the advancements and topical nature with CBE, there continues to be calls for further research in this area (Gong, 2018; Powell, 2016; Verhoef et al., 2010). Recent work has inductively captured 'the essence of the CBE process' from the brand decision makers such as marketers, brand managers and advertising executives (Gambetti et al., 2015). However, there continues to be limited research on the CBE process from the first-hand accounts of consumers (Bowden, 2009) and from a multi-stakeholder perspective (Gambetti et al., 2015). Therefore, CBE remains a 'prominent construct' and can impact on the development of future relationships between individuals and brands (Carvalho & Fernandes, 2018).

As the CBE process can be dissimilar across different settings and contexts (Halaszovich & Jaques, 2017), future studies must focus on specific brands (Leckie et al., 2016) and other contexts and settings (Ahn & Back, 2018; France et al., 2016). Indeed, CBE represents an under-explored and promising area of study (Hollebeek et al., 2014). Conceptual scope within existing CBE studies have been aided by adopting an interdisciplinary approach and employing different theoretical constructs to frame the investigations and debates. Theoretical constructs include consumer culture theory, service dominant logic, relationship marketing (Brodie et al., 2011; Hollebeek et al., 2014), social identity and brand loyalty (Leckie et al., 2016), psychological ownership theory and regulatory focus theory (Gong, 2018), systems theory (Bolton & Saxena-Iyer, 2009) and social exchange theory (Raed et al., 2018). However, existing studies on CBE argue further research is required and future studies should consider an interdisciplinary approach and framed through appropriate and relevant marketing-based theoretical lenses (Bolton & Saxena-Iyer, 2009; Brodie et al., 2011; Carvalho & Fernandes, 2018; Gambetti et al., 2015; Hollebeek, 2011b; Hollebeek et al., 2014; Leckie et al., 2016). More specifically, Hollebeek (2011a, p. 569) explicitly called for future research to address 'the nature of CBE interrelationships with other concepts' including how brands are positioned and how they are interpreted by consumers. Therefore, construct of positioning, brand identity and brand image could be considered drivers-antecedents of CBE and may provide deep insight into CBE, which in turn would address demands for more empirical research in this area (Bolton & Saxena-Iyer, 2009; France et al., 2016; Hollebeek, 2011a; Hollebeek, 2011b; Hollebeek et al., 2014; Leckie et al., 2016).

POLITICAL BRAND POSITIONING

Political strategists aim to project a clear, relatable and comprehensible position which signifies how the political brand intends 'to be seen' in the mind of the voter (Baines et al. 1999, 2014; O'Shaughnessy & Baines, 2009; Pich, 2022; Smith & French, 2009). Further, successful positioning allows political brands to communicate clear points of differentiation compared to competitors and serves to illustrate relevance by addressing the wants and needs of stakeholders (Newman & Newman, 2022; Smith, 2005; Wring, 2022). In addition, positioning is strategic in orientation and represents a process that candidates, political parties and/or campaign groups follow to efficiently and effectively portray the political brand's product offering (Baines, 1999; Gurău & Ayadi, 2011). However, political brand positioning is a complex procedure that can be interpreted as a 'two-way communication process' involving the producer (insider the organisation) and consumer (outside the organisation) (O'Shaughnessy & Baines, 2009, p. 239). Nevertheless, intended *and* actual positioning can differ, and it is the role of strategists to work towards aligning the two related yet distinct perspectives (Newman, 1999; O'Shaughnessy & Baines, 2009). Aligned political brands have the potential to be perceived as credible, trustworthy, authentic and united, which can lead to greater success at the ballot box (Smith & French, 2009). Therefore, positioning has a 'central place within political branding theory as it provides insight into the political brand's product offering; responds to the wants and needs of voters; and enables strategists to create a competitive differentiation in the political marketplace' (Pich, 2022, p. 121). However, it is important to routinely audit and track the positioning of political brands. For instance, voters might have unintended perceptions (O'Shaughnessy & Baines, 2009). Therefore, routinely investigating political brand positioning will may reveal coherency or misalignment of desired and actual positioning, which strategists can respond and develop strategies to maintain alignment or devise repositioning strategies (Baines et al., 1999; Collins & Butler, 2002; Pich, 2022; Smith, 2005).

Research on the positioning of political brands has received some attention. However, existing research has tended to focus on the measurement of how political brands are positioned (positioning scales) or appraisal of strategies and communication tactics implemented by political brands during election campaigns (Baines et al., 1999; Collins & Butler, 2002; Gurău & Ayadi, 2011; Johnson, 1971; Newman & Newman, 2022; Norris et al., 1999; O'Shaughnessy & Baines, 2009; Smith, 2005; Smith & French, 2009). For instance, Smith (2005) examined the positioning strategies of the three main political parties (Labour, Conservatives and the Liberal Democrats) during the 2005 UK General Election. It was found from the beginning of the campaign that all three political brands faced political positioning 'dilemmas' and this included the UK Conservative Party brand. The Conservative Party brand faced the internal problem of appeasing not only the previously silenced pro-European wing of the party but also the core anti-European constituency (Smith, 2005). In addition, the UK Conservative brand was still positioned by the party's past, they failed to develop a clear point of differentiation from political competitors, especially Labour. They were perceived as an opposition party, not credible, and a 'nasty' uncaring party for the 'rich and privileged' (Smith, 2005). Furthermore, Smith (2005) concluded they had failed to produce an integrated long-term strategy and needed to develop new approaches to address the political brand's dilemmas.

Subsequently, there continues to be a paucity of research dedicated to investigating the intended and actual positioning of political brands (Baines et al., 1999; Gurău & Ayadi, 2011; O'Shaughnessy & Baines, 2009; Pich, 2022; Smith, 2005). Further, the positioning of political brands 'is often difficult to capture' (Baines et al., 2014; Pich, 2022, p. 121) and may be due to the complex and nebulous nature of political brand positioning. This may be a key factor for the limited studies on political brand positioning. To address this, perhaps appropriate theoretical lenses are needed to help structure the investigatory process of political brand positioning. To reiterate positioning is a 'two-way communication process' which focuses on a political brand's intended vision created-communicated by a producer and brought to life in the mind of the consumer (O'Shaughnessy & Baines, 2009). Therefore, the related yet distinct constructs of brand identity and brand image could be seen as important dimensions of positioning and serve as unproblematic theoretical constructs to frame the investigatory process of political brand positioning.

Political Brand Identity

In order to conceptualise how a political brand creates a desired position in the minds of stakeholders, the construct of brand identity is a suitable theoretical lens to help structure the envisioned characterisation (He et al., 2016; Su & Kunkel, 2019). More specifically, brand identity represents an internally created strategy designed to communicate what brands intend to 'stand for' and constructed to appeal to multiple stakeholders inside and outside the organisation (Nandan, 2005; O'Shaughnessy and Baines 2009; Savitri et al., 2022; Silveira et al., 2013). Further, brand identity enables organisations to map out a distinctive intended narrative from competitors and express their relevance, which in turn provides rationale for stakeholders to identify with their offering and establish a long-term relationship between organisations and their target markets (Foroudi et al., 2018; O'Shaughnessy & Baines, 2009; Pich & Armannsdottir, 2022). Brand identity can be created and managed around physical and intangible touchpoints (Baines et al., 2014; Plumeyer et al., 2017; Propheto et al., 2020; Schneider, 2004). For example, physical touchpoints include components such as symbols, logos, signage, messages, policies and communication platforms-methods-tools devised to raise awareness, communicate differentiation and resonate with specific target markets. Intangible touchpoints can include components such as brand values, vision, goals, ideology, heritage-culture, feelings, attitudes and associations often brought to life by the physical touchpoints. A visualisation to illustrate the key components of desired brand identity and envisaged positioning is outlined in Figure 7.1.

Successful identities irrespective of their manifestation depend on brands adhering to three simple rules (Pich & Armannsdottir, 2022). First, all stakeholders inside the political brand have a responsibility to ensure coherency between the physical and intangible elements. Further, internal stakeholders should be united and remain 'on message' (Marland et al., 2017; Marland & Flanagan, 2014). This increases the likelihood of projecting a clear, unambiguous identity and maintaining an authentic, credible political brand. Second, relevant, clearly differentiated and appealing identities can lead to the establishment

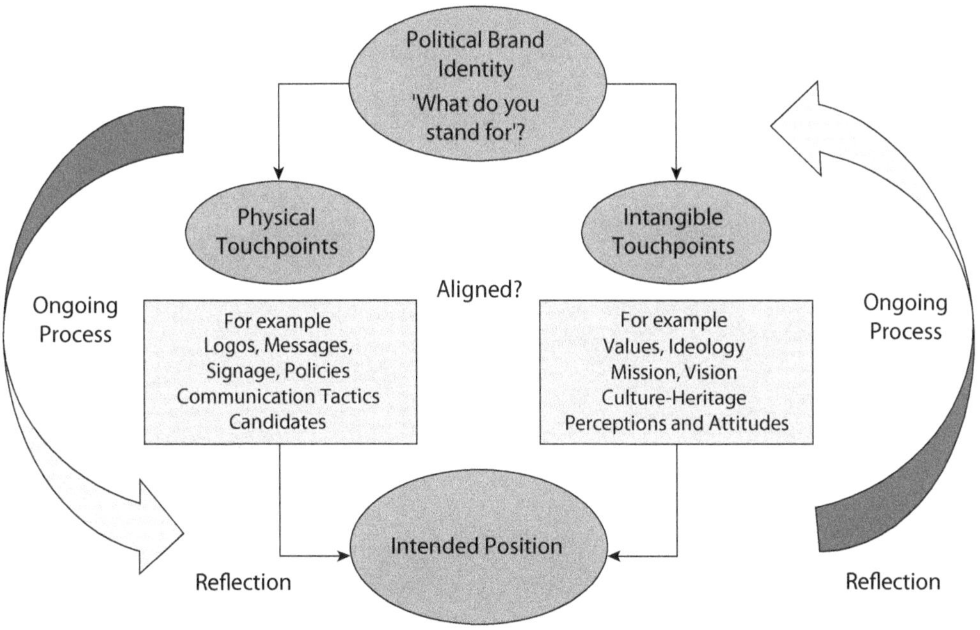

Figure 7.1 Visualisation of Brand Identity and Brand Positioning

of a close relationship and a sense of loyalty between the political brand and citizen (Armannsdottir et al., 2019; Foroudi et al., 2018; Savitri et al., 2022). Therefore, political brands need to ensure their intended identities are believable, grounded on style and substance, live up to expectations, coherent across all touchpoints and be prepared to amend their offering in relation to an ever-changing dynamic political environment (O'Shaughnessy & Baines 2009). Third, strategists, politicians and communication directors need to routinely reflect on the physical and intangible touchpoints and audit the identities of their political brands and recognise the benefits and implications of strong political brand identities (Marland et al., 2017). Further, by routinely reflecting and carrying out a holistic audit on the current identities of political brands, internal stakeholders can develop strategies to maintain positive, strong, aligned identities or design tactics to correct any misalignment, ambiguity and weaknesses associated with the desired position (Pich & Armannsdottir, 2022). Therefore, adhering to the three simple rules provides a series of motivations, which in turn will raise the prospect of long-term success. Key motivations for strong political brand identities can be seen in Figure 7.2.

Subsequently, designing and managing political brand identity is not just about raising awareness. Indeed, political brand identities should demonstrate positive unique characteristics that allow political brands to project a clearly differentiated position compared with political rivals (Armannsdottir et al., 2019; Baines et al., 2014; Silveira et al., 2013). Further, it is important that citizens recognise the uniqueness and distinct identities, and this can lead to alignment between the communicated identity and understood image in the mind of the public, which in turn can lead to success at the ballot box (Nandan, 2005; Pich et al., 2020). Therefore, periodically assessing political brand identity is not the only construct that needs to be monitored and individuals need to consider the concept of political brand image.

POLITICAL BRAND IMAGE

Brand image has been defined 'as the current/immediate associations perceived and formulated in the mind of the consumer' (Pich, 2022: 193). Further, brand image has also been recognised as a set of actual 'beliefs, attitudes, stereotypes, ideas, relevant behaviours or impressions that a person holds regarding an object, person or organisation' (Panda et al., 2019, p. 237). Brand creators develop and communicate the brand identity; however, they have little control over how the brand is actually perceived by consumers (Marland et al., 2017). For

Figure 7.2 Motivations for Successful Political Brand Identities Developed From Pich and Armannsdottir (2022)

example, brands can become associated with undesired and unintended imagery, perceptions and attitudes (O'Shaughnessy & Baines, 2009). Therefore, it is important to understand what benefits brands offers consumers and what experiences consumers have or want to have with a brand. Alignment between intended brand identity and actual brand image is critical for organisations if brand is to be considered as 'authentic' (Pich et al., 2020).

Political brand image has been defined as the manifestation of the communicated identity combined with perceptions associations and attitudes in the mind of the citizen or voter (Pich et al., 2018). Political brand image should reveal distinct factors of differentiation which can represent unique selling points for brands. However, political strategists can often have little control over how voters understand or engage with their brand. Further, misalignment between political brand identity and image can damage the clarity of the message or positioning while strong alignment will help with voters' engagement and trust.

Similarly, to brand image, political brand image is seen as the voters' understanding of the political brands, their perception of what they stand for and their experiences with brands (Pich & Armannsdottir, 2022). It should also be perceived as authentic and should differentiate the brand from other competitors. Furthermore, political brand image should encourage involvement with multiple stakeholders, live up to voter expectations and help create a feeling of trust in the minds of voters. Figure 7.3 summarises a series of motivations for political brand image associated with successful political brands.

For politicians and political strategists, a strong political brand image should help with creating and managing their branding strategy. It is important that politicians manage and monitor their brand image to be able to establish a positive relationship with their voters (Plumeyer et al. 2017). Figure 7.3 summarises implications of political brand image. Political brands can be seen as a trinity of three elements, including the party leader, political party and party policy (Butler et al., 2011; Davies & Mian, 2010; Smith & French, 2011). Previous research on brand image has focused on one or two elements of the trinity but few have investigated all three elements of political brand as will be done here.

CASE STUDIES: APPLICATION

So far, we have discussed the different typologies of political brands and the interactions and

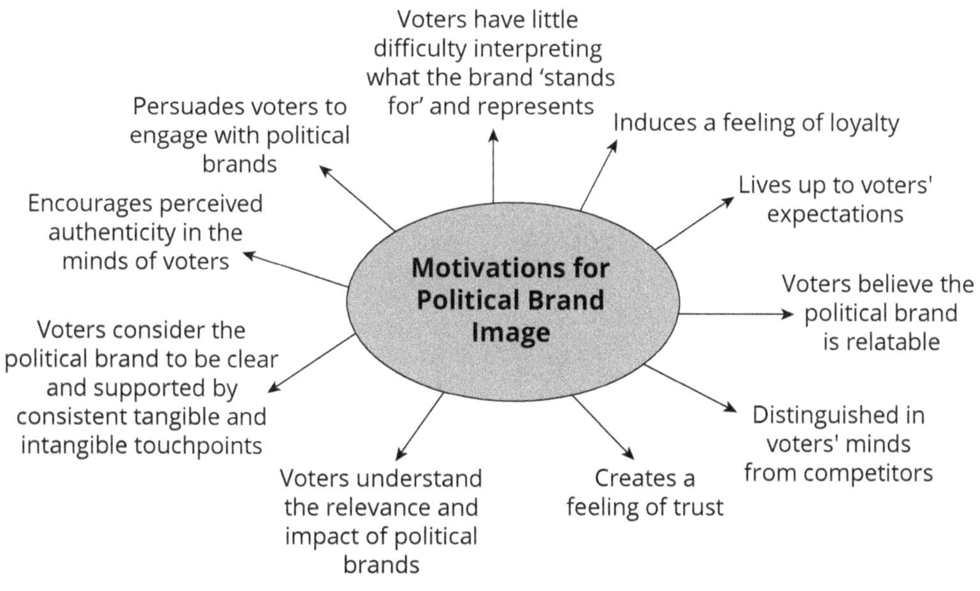

Figure 7.3 Motivations for Successful Political Brand Image Developed From Pich and Armannsdottir (2022)

relationships between stakeholders and political brands through the theoretical lens of CBE. We have also presented the antecedents-drivers of consumer (political) brand engagement namely the concepts of political brand identity and political brand image. Political brand identity and political brand image remain two related yet distinct constructs and allow political stakeholders (politicians, political parties, supporters and activists) to create and manage a desired position in the mind of voters. This section will focus on two specific case studies to demonstrate the applicability of political brand engagement, identity and image to international contexts and settings. The British Crown Dependencies of Jersey and Pakistan contextualise the two cases. The two cases were in no way selected as comparisons and represent two unique international settings. Jersey and Pakistan are home to different types of political brands and represent two under-explored yet dynamic contexts. Further, existing studies on political branding call for further research in under-researched electoral systems (Armannsdottir et al., 2019; Falkowski & Jabłonska, 2019; Jain & Ganesh, 2019; Marland & Wagner, 2020). Firstly, we discuss the political brand position through the concept of political brand identity in the context of the Channel Island of Jersey. Finally, we will discuss the political brand position with the aid of the theoretical concept of political brand image in the context of the PTI (Pakistan Tehreek-e-Insaf) party brand in Pakistan. The two cases demonstrate the transfer potential of branding concepts to politics however acknowledges that core branding theory may need to be tailored to address the unique settings and contexts.

CASE 1: POLITICAL BRAND POSITIONING AND IDENTITY IN JERSEY

Introduction

Case one focuses on investigating the political positioning and identity of the four political party brands in the context of the British Crown Dependency of Jersey. To reiterate, brand identity can be interpreted as the desired position developed by internal stakeholders (strategists, politicians and communication directors) and communicated to external stakeholders including voters (Baines et al., 2014; Nandan, 2005; Su & Kunkel, 2019). Thus, brand identity represents the political brand's aspirations and vision structured around physical touchpoints such as logos, symbols, communication platforms-tools, messages and policies and also developed from intangible elements such as values, heritage-culture, mission, vision and ideology often designed to appeal to different groups or target markets (Pich & Armannsdottir, 2022). Further, successful identities are coherent, unambiguous and perceived as authentic, which in turn can encourage multiple internal and external stakeholders to engage and form a connection with political brands (Armannsdottir et al., 2019; Foroudi et al., 2018; Savitri et al., 2022). Existing research on political brand identity has tended to focus well-established political party brands in party systems such as the United Kingdom, Canada, the United States and India (Jain & Ganesh, 2019; Marland & Flanagan, 2014; Marland & Wagner, 2020; Pich & Dean, 2015). In addition, there is limited research on new or emerging political party brands especially from an insider-internal perspective. This is supported by explicit calls for further research on different typologies of political brands in dynamic contexts and settings (Needham & Smith, 2015; Newman & Newman, 2022; Pich & Newman, 2020). In order to contextualise this case study, the British Crown Dependency of Jersey serves as an appropriate setting. Jersey is an independent small island state situated off the north-coast of France and has a population of just over 103,000 citizens (Boleat, 2023). Until recently, Jersey has been dominated by independent politics with a paucity of political parties. However, ahead of the 2022 Jersey General Election, three new political parties (Progress, Jersey Alliance and Jersey Liberal Conservatives [JLC]) were created to join the only established political party (Reform Jersey) and fight for representation in the 49-seat Parliament. Further, 40% of the 93 candidates contested the 2022 General Election under the banner of the four political parties, which was a huge change from previous elections where 'independent politics was the norm' (Boleat, 2023). Therefore, this case focuses political brand identity as its theoretical concept to assess the political brand positioning of the four party brands in Jersey. In addition, this case demonstrates the applicability and useful nature of using the construct of brand identity to deconstruct the desired positioning which can impact on consumer-voter brand engagement.

Research Design

As this case aimed to explore the creation and management of political brand identity and positioning from the perspective of key internal stakeholders within Jersey's four political parties, a qualitative interpretivist approach was adopted. A qualitative interpretivist approach is ideal for exploratory research and under-explored settings as it can delve beneath the surface to capture deep insight and detailed understanding of the phenomenon under study (Warren & Karner, 2010). Further, qualitative interpretivist studies allow researchers to build an in-depth understanding and uncover rich explanations based on the testimonies and perspectives of participants (Bell et al., 2019; Zikmund, 2003). This case utilised online semi-structured interviews with key stakeholders from all four political parties in Jersey including Reform Jersey, the Progress Party, Jersey Alliance and the JLC. Key stakeholders included candidates-politicians, activists and party members. Participants were invited via email to take part in this study. Interviews were carried out online via MS Teams and Zoom due to the travel restrictions which were in place during this time. Eleven participants came forward to take part in this study. Interviews were conducted from November 2021 to February 2022. Table 7.2 outlines the profile of our sample.

As outlined in Table 2, participants were given a unique code to ensure anonymity, for example, 'participant 1' was coded as 'P1' and the coding process was repeated for all participants. Websites, campaign materials (manifestoes, leaflets, posters) and social media posts associated with all four parties were also examined as part of our analysis. To analyse the interview transcripts and additional content, Braun and Clarke's (2006) six stages of thematic analysis were adopted as our analytical strategy, which in turn provided a systematic process and transparency to our analysis.

Aspired Identity and Positioning

The four political party brands in Jersey created desired identities and aspired positioning based on three inter-related themes including *party or alliance*, *values and ideology*, and *personality and leadership* as illustrated in Figure 7.4 below.

Party or Alliance?: Party

The first key theme uncovered relates to structure and construct of the four political party brands. It is worth remembering that up until recent years, Jersey's Parliament was dominated by independent politicians (politicians not part of political parties but stood as individuals in elections). Thus, the introduction of political party brands was novel to the political landscape. An overview of the lifecycle and structure of the four political party brands is set out in Table 7.3.

Reform Jersey founded in 2014 remains the oldest and most established political party brand in the Bailiwick and contested several elections prior to Jersey's General Election in 2022. Nevertheless, Reform Jersey can trace its origins back to 2012 having evolved from a grassroots 'political movement' before registering as an official party ahead of the 2014 Jersey General Election. Further, Reform is 'mature, professional, strategic and continues to evolve' (P3) and each election serves as an opportunity to reflect and improve their electioneering and messaging, sharpen their policies and demonstrate their existence and relevance as an authentic party brand. However, it could be argued that Reform's three competitors (Progress, Alliance and JLC) were 'late for the party' (i.e. 2022 General Election). The Progress political brand was founded in January 2021,

Table 7.2 Sample Profile of Our Sample

Participant Code	*Party Membership*
P1 = (Participant 1)	Jersey Alliance
P2 = (Participant 2)	Progress
P3 = (Participant 3)	Jersey Liberal Conservatives
P4 = (Participant 4)	Reform Jersey
P5 = (Participant 5)	Jersey Liberal Conservatives
P6 = (Participant 6)	Reform Jersey
P7 = (Participant 7)	Progress
P8 = (Participant 8)	Jersey Alliance
P9 = (Participant 9)	Progress
P10 = (Participant 10)	Jersey Liberal Conservatives
P11 = (Participant 11)	Jersey Alliance

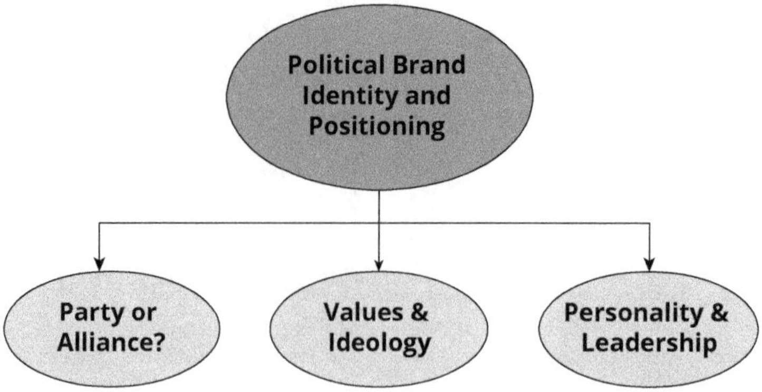

Figure 7.4 Core Themes Identified Related to Political Brand Identity and Positioning

Table 7.3 Lifecycle and Structure of the Four Political Party Brands in Jersey

	Reform Jersey	*The Progress Party*	*Jersey Alliance*	*Jersey Liberal Conservatives (JLC)*
Founded	2014	January 2021	July 2021	January 2022
Political Brand Slogan	'Social and economic justice' 'New deal for Jersey'	'Balanced policy for Jersey's future prosperity and wellbeing, policies that will be delivered for good for every islander'.	'Pride in our Past. Purpose in our Future'.	'Socially liberal, fiscally conservative'.
Party	'Tradition Party'	'Tradition Party'	'An Alliance not a Party'	'Tradition Party'
Structure	-Constitution and Whip System -Regular meetings – Chair -150+ members -Membership fee £2 -Youth branch -Free membership	-Constitution and Whip System -Limited resources -100 members -Bottom-up, members driven	-Current Ministers in Government 2018–2022 -No whip -3-tiered membership -Selective recruitment	-Inclusive -Trying to persuade people to join -Committee-led – 9 individuals
Outcome General Election 22nd June 2022	*Out of 49 Seats* **2022 = 10 Seats** **2018 = 5 Seats**	*Out of 49 Seats* **2022 = 1 Seat**	*Out of 49 Seats* **2022 = 1 Seat**	*Out of 49 Seats* **2022 = 2 Seats**

Alliance July 2021 and JLC in January 2022; therefore, the three new political brands were established 17 months – 6 months before Jersey's 2022 General Election.

In terms of structure, three of the four political brands (Reform, Progress and JLC) positioned themselves as 'traditional political parties' with 'constitutions', adhering to the 'whipping system', an official leader and internally governed by a 'committee' or 'working group' with members with distinct roles such as 'chair', 'treasurer' and 'co-founders'. Further, Reform, Progress and JLC promoted a culture of inclusion in terms of practicing a bottom-up, member-led approach in terms of developing polices and feedback on values and positioning. However, Alliance did not practice the 'whipping-system' and promoted a selective top-down approach in terms of recruiting candidates-members and approaching individuals 'with a track record', 'like-minded individuals' and belief 'they could work with [them]'. Nevertheless, all parties revealed that they had members-supporters and had developed membership schemes (paid and unpaid membership); however, the membership base for each party brand remains unknown.

Values and Ideology: Policy

Firstly, the envisaged identities of all four party brands were created around values and ideological positioning designed by a small number of founders and party leaders. For example, Reform Jersey were positioned as a 'social democratic party' and a very much 'centre-left' political brand with a strong belief and 'track record' for 'inclusivity, diversity with progressive policies and opportunities for all'. In contrast, the Progress Party, positioned as a 'big tent' political brand favouring 'practical solutions' rather than a focus on ideology campaigned on broad values such as 'transparency and accountability'...and the pledge to deliver on housing, immigration and change for all islanders. The centre-right Jersey Alliance, positioned as a 'political group' rather than a 'party', pledged to 'continue' with the current Government's plan and acted as a champion for an 'open economy' with a focus on 'opportunities for all' and 'investment across the island'. Finally, the JLC, like the Progress Party in terms of 'not keen on ideology' put forward several broad values including 'opportunity and enterprise', belief in personal freedom and responsibility, 'fiscal prudence' and 'competent leadership'.

Despite two of the four political brands arguing that *ideology* was not a core dimension of their desired identities (Progress and JLC), following the analysis of the transcripts and other content such as the party websites, social media platforms and manifestoes, it was deduced that both entities were positioned as 'centre-right' political brands. Therefore, the centre-right position of Jersey's political landscape was 'quite crowed' (P7) with three political brands fighting for a similar position. Whereas Reform Jersey was clearly positioned as a centre-left political brand, which in turn provided differentiation from key competitors.

Personality and Leadership: Leader

It was argued that 'Jersey is so personality based' (P7) and each of the four political party brands were led by 'big personalities...seasoned politicians' (P6) with strong recognition, familiarity and awareness in the mind of islanders. It was revealed that each of the four leaders were part of the founding team or driving force in terms of establishing the four political brands and created their political brands based on their own belief systems or envisaged positions. Further, three of the four party leaders (Progress, Alliance and JLC) were experienced politicians having contested several elections and served as independent parliamentarians for many years before forming their respective parties. However, creating and developing the political party brands was a 'big political experiment' (P4), 'a political poker game' (P2) and a 'treacherous journey of launching a political party' from scratch and the leadership teams had 'no experience...we had to make it up as we went along' (P6). A 'artisan approach' (P1) seemed to be adopted by most political party brands as there was little support or resources from Jersey's Parliament or existing political system to support the development of political party brands. Further, Reform were trendsetters in Jersey politics as they had spent several elections making the argument 'for party politics in Jersey' and had 'won the argument' for the introduction of political party brands (P3). Therefore, Reform had carried out the groundwork for the three new political party brands and moved the debate forward allowing the new political parties to opportunity to explain their identities and positioning rather than spend time justifying their existence.

Case One Summary

This case addresses one of two related priority issues for further research in political branding. More specifically, this case provides first-hand accounts and insight on how four political party brands in Jersey created and managed their intended positioning and attempted to communicate their envisaged identifies designed to encourage engagement (Baines et al., 2014; O'Shaughnessy & Baines, 2009; Pich et al., 2020; Smith & French, 2009). Further, this case addresses explicit calls for additional understanding on different types of political brands including new/emerging political brands and political brands in diverse settings and contexts (O'Cass & Voola, 2011;

Pich, 2022; Pich et al., 2020; Rutter et al., 2015; Scammell, 2015; Simons, 2016). Up until now, existing research has tended to focus on traditional electoral 'party systems' and well-established political 'party' brands (Armannsdottir et al., 2019; Falkowski & Jabłonska, 2019; Jain & Ganesh, 2019; Marland & Wagner, 2020). This case demonstrates that the political party brands in Jersey were positioned by values and ideology often created by the belief system of the party leader, governed by a distinct leader, and supported by a hierarchy of key stakeholders. Figure 7.5 illustrates key elements of the four political brand identities in Jersey.

This case revealed all four political 'party' brands possessed all elements of the political brand trinity including party, leader and policy (Butler et al., 2011; Davies & Mian, 2010; Smith & French, 2011). However, Reform Jersey appears to have developed a clearer position and distinct identity compared with its three rivals. Further, Reform has developed its position and identity over a considerable period having contested several elections and had the opportunity to road-test its policies, vision and relevance, messaging and tactics compared with competitors. Therefore, Reform's political brand position appears to have resulted in stronger engagement with the electorate compared with its political rivals. Despite the dominance of independent politics in Jersey, many believe 'parties are inevitable'; however, 'it will take a few election cycles' (P7) for other political party brands to catch up with Reform. For example, it will take time for the other three parties to develop and establish clear intended identities and professionalise their electioneering strategies and tactics. Further, this case provides insight into the dynamic electoral system of Jersey, one traditionally structured around the personal brands of politicians (independent politicians unaffiliated to political parties) with the limited existence of corporate political party brands (Pich, 2022). Therefore, the jurisdiction of Jersey is witnessing fundamental changes to its electoral system and the metamorphosis of its political brands. It is unknown whether political 'party' brands will become the norm in Jersey. However, this represents an area for further research. Further research on political branding should consider carrying out longitudinal and comparative research, which up until now remains limited. Future research could also investigate whether the small gains made by the three new parties were a result of a crowded political landscape and whether each political party brand projected-communicated a coherent identity, which was clearly differentiated from competitors. In addition, future research could be conducted to examine why independent politicians continue to experience stronger engagement (success at the ballot box) compared with party brands. Finally, future studies could assess whether the success with Reform Jersey was due to a well-established authentic, engaging identity and/or the professionalism and disciplined nature of their political brand. Nevertheless, this case demonstrates the versatility and unproblematic nature of applying the theoretical lens of political brand identity to under-explored contexts to uncover the intended position of an emerging political 'party' brands.

CASE 2: POLITICAL BRAND IMAGE AND ENGAGEMENT IN PAKISTAN

Introduction

A corporate brand image, consisting of the trinity of leader, party and policies (Robertson & Meintjes, 2021; Smith & French, 2011), is the mental picture or total impressions of an organisation held by external stakeholders (Conz, 2019; Greyser & Urde, 2019; Iglesias & Ind, 2020; Koporcic & Halinen, 2018). Several corporate brand images exist for an organisation at any given time (Garas et al., 2018) since it is the sum of comprehensive associations held by a multitude of stakeholders (Markovic et al., 2018; Spry & Pich, 2021). Hatch and Schultz (2001; 2003; 2008) advise organisations to streamline their corporate identity and image to create a coherent corporate brand and use it as a competitive advantage. PTI party is Pakistan's main opposition party, founded and led by former world-class cricketer Imran Khan. Imran Khan founded the party in 1996 and led it to electoral victory in 2018 serving as Prime Minister of Pakistan until 2022. Since its inception, PTI has gained a significant following across various segments of society, advocating for reform, anti-corruption measures and social justice. PTI's policies and initiatives have been of particular interest to journalists, university students, small business owners, public servants and the Pakistani diaspora, making them key stakeholders in assessing the party's corporate brand image. Corporate political brands face challenges in maintaining a coherent image due to their complex and multifaceted nature, resulting in a multiplicity of images (Coker et al., 2021; Rutter et al., 2018). However, current research on brand image has primarily focused on voters, overlooking the involvement of

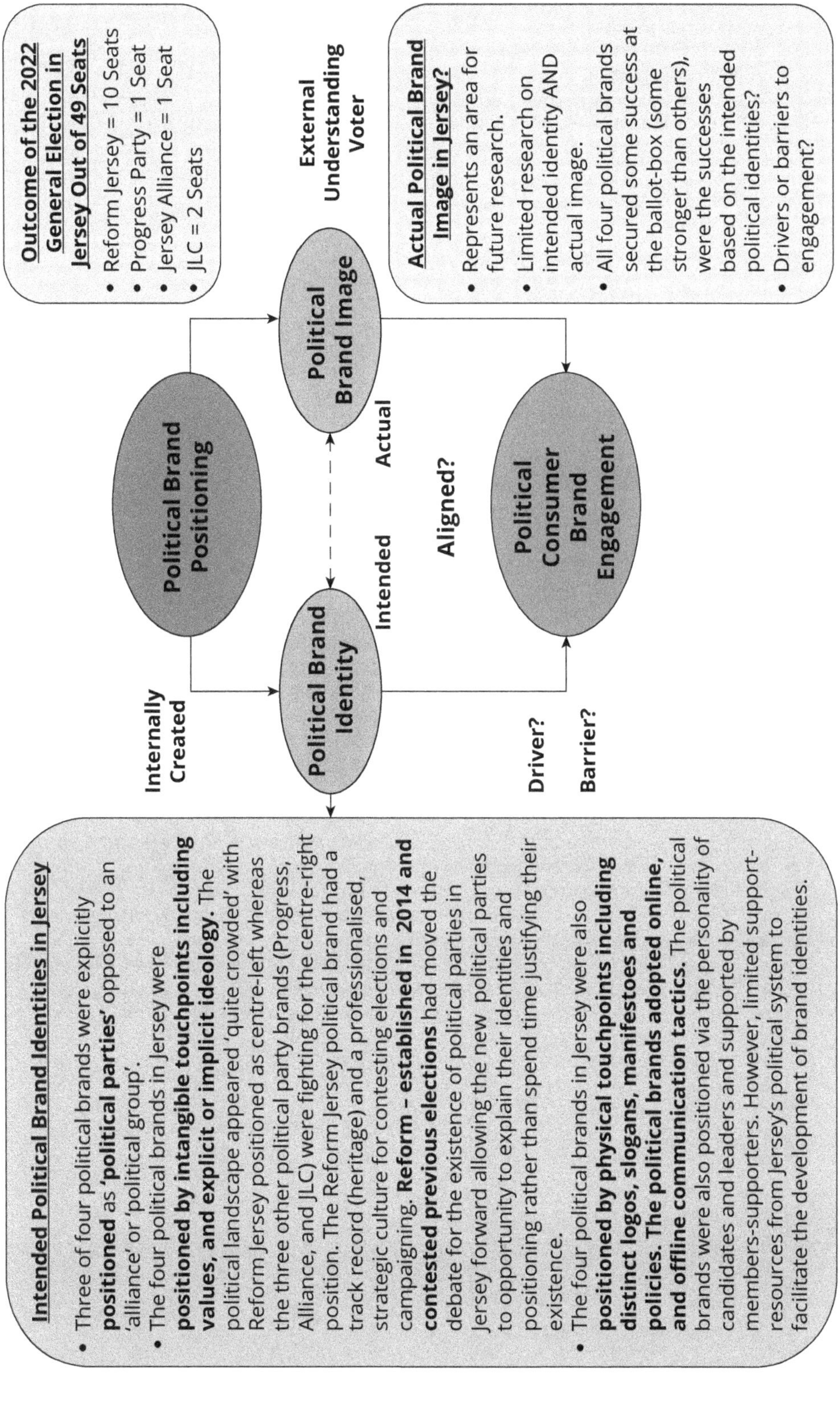
Intended Political Brand Identities in Jersey
Three of four political brands were explicitly positioned as 'political parties' opposed to an 'alliance' or 'political group'.
The four political brands in Jersey were positioned by intangible touchpoints including values, and explicit or implicit ideology. The political landscape appeared 'quite crowded' with Reform Jersey positioned as centre-left whereas the three other political party brands (Progress, Alliance, and JLC) were fighting for the centre-right position. The Reform Jersey political brand had a track record (heritage) and a professionalised, strategic culture for contesting elections and campaigning. Reform – established in 2014 and contested previous elections had moved the debate for the existence of political parties in Jersey forward allowing the new political parties to opportunity to explain their identities and positioning rather than spend time justifying their existence.
The four political brands in Jersey were also positioned by physical touchpoints including distinct logos, slogans, manifestoes and policies. The political brands adopted online, and offline communication tactics. The political brands were also positioned via the personality of candidates and leaders and supported by members-supporters. However, limited support-resources from Jersey's political system to facilitate the development of brand identities.
Internally Created
Political Brand Positioning
Political Brand Identity
Intended
Political Brand Image
Actual
Aligned?
Driver?
Barrier?
Political Consumer Brand Engagement
External Understanding Voter
Outcome of the 2022 General Election in Jersey Out of 49 Seats
Reform Jersey = 10 Seats
Progress Party = 1 Seat
Jersey Alliance = 1 Seat
JLC = 2 Seats
Actual Political Brand Image in Jersey?
Represents an area for future research.
Limited research on intended identity AND actual image.
All four political brands secured some success at the ballot-box (some stronger than others), were the successes based on the intended political identities?
Drivers or barriers to engagement?

Figure 7.5 Key Elements of Political Brand Identities in Jersey and Areas for Further Research

numerous stakeholders in the political branding process (Pich & Dean, 2015; Pich et al., 2018). This oversight calls for an exploration of the brand image from the perspective of multiple stakeholders, which can provide a more comprehensive and nuanced understanding of the brand's perception.

Research Design

The overall philosophy of this study was to focus on exploring the corporate brand image of PTI from the perspective of multiple stakeholders. A qualitative research approach was adopted as it is renowned for providing an in-depth exploration of participants' perspectives (Aspers & Corte, 2019; Azungah, 2018; Erlingsson & Brysiewicz, 2013; Gelo et al., 2008; Gephart, 2004; Mohajan, 2018). Further, focus groups were chosen due to their ability to uncover unexpected aspects of social phenomena from the participants' perspectives, rather than the researcher's (Acocella, 2012; Guest et al. 2017; Kruger et al., 2019). The focus group discussions were held with journalists, university students, Pakistani diaspora, business owners and government officials between May 2020 and November 2020 in Lahore and Karachi. A six-step 'contextualist thematic analysis' (Braun & Clarke, 2006) was then utilised to analyse the transcripts and reveal rich insights into the corporate brand image from the perspective of multiple stakeholders.

Key Findings

From the perspective of these five external stakeholder groups, the PTI corporate brand can be divided into a trinity of leader, party and policy. The main themes that emerge about this trinity are charismatic and competent leader, inclusive yet contentious party, and progressive policies (Figure 7.6). The leader element of the corporate political brand is the strongest and most coherent dimension for the brand image. The other two elements, that is, the party and policies were next in order respectively. The leader was always associated with positive attributes even by those who were otherwise critical of the party brand. The party element was consistent across all stakeholder groups with positive and negative associations. Whereas there was greater diversity in opinion among stakeholders when it came to policies.

Leader: Leader as the Ace of the Pack

All five stakeholder groups saw the leader element of the brand trinity in a positive light. The leader, Imran Khan, the former World Cup-winning cricket captain (Mehmood et al., 2021), was widely praised for his integrity and stakeholders from all groups highlighted this trait as a key strength. Additionally, it was seen that the leader exuded charisma, and stakeholders across all groups acknowledged this characteristic. Journalists and university students emphasised the leader's visionary and progressive approach and his success in handling the COVID-19 pandemic. For example, a journalist from Karachi was of the view 'He (Imran Khan) opposed the (COVID-19) lockdown which is why we are in a much better position than other countries in the region. You can imagine how bad it would have been if we had locked down'. Another respondent, a university student in Lahore commented on the leader's vision by saying, 'All of his (Imran Khan) policies have resulted in more women empowerment… torch bearer of women's rights' in reference to PTI's health card, education, and law and order. The health card has benefitted women by providing more prenatal and postnatal care. Education policies have seen more female enrolment in public schools, and law and order measures have

Figure 7.6 Corporate Political Brand Image of PTI

made women safer by tackling crimes against them.

Public servants also identified the leader's strength and unifying leadership style. Small business owners praised the leader for his unifying approach and COVID-19 success. Finally, Pakistani diaspora members highlighted the leader's unifying and charismatic qualities and his honest leadership. Overall, the PTI party's leader was widely praised for his integrity, charisma, unifying leadership style and success in handling the COVID-19 pandemic. It can be concluded that the leader is the strongest element of the PTI corporate brand.

Party: Inclusive yet Contentious Party

The party which is the second element of the corporate political brand was associated with both positive and negative perspectives. All stakeholder groups agreed that the PTI party was inclusive as it represented all segments of Pakistani society. Public servants praised the party for introducing new faces into politics and bringing professionals into the fold, while university students appreciated the party's inclusivity on an ethnic basis. For example, a business owner from Lahore said 'They (PTI) are the only national party today and promote the youth...-under 35 are the majority in Pakistan and PTI champions them'. However, stakeholders also expressed concerns about infighting, poor communication and values dissonance/contradictions within the party. Journalists and university students called out the party for its self-destructive conflicts and disorganised structure. For example, a journalist from Lahore said 'There are many rival groups within the party that are trying to take each other down'. Small business owners were also critical of the selfish/self-interest of some party members and the party's disconnect from the corporate brand. Pakistani diaspora members also cited communication struggles with the party and identified new members who are off-brand as concerns for the brand. In summary, external stakeholders view the party as inclusive yet divided.

Policies: Progressive Policies

Fighting corruption was seen as PTI's central policy by all stakeholder groups, and it was identified by university students, journalists, small business owners, public servants and the Pakistani diaspora. PTI's focus on social issues was also a key finding, with both university students and small business owners highlighting them as a policy priority. For example, a student from Karachi said 'I personally know people who have used the health card to avail private health care'. Small business owners and public servants said that PTI represented institutional reforms and youth empowerment. Journalists and university students also highlighted PTI as the party of change and reform but emphasised the importance of addressing the communication disconnect and social media overreliance. Concerns over the bad shape of the economy were also voiced by university students, journalists, small business owners and public servants. Inflation was identified as a significant issue by small business owners one of whom said 'They have destroyed the economy... everything is so expensive and continues to be'. While public servants called for social policies to be a central area of focus. Finally, Pakistani diaspora members echoed similar opinions about anti-corruption measures, social policies, inflation and the need for institutional restructuring. Overall, it can be said that PTI's policies are seen as progressive.

Case Two Summary

This case study addresses two priority issues in existing research on political branding. First, it explores the under-researched area of corporate political branding within Pakistan, addressing calls for research in diverse contexts (Jain & Ganesh, 2019; Pich & Newman, 2020). While scholars have conceptualised political brands as corporate brands (Jain & Ganesh, 2019; Pich et al., 2018), Pakistan's political landscape offers a unique opportunity to examine this concept in a fresh light. Secondly, this study goes beyond existing research by exploring brand image from the perspective of multiple stakeholders (Pich & Newman, 2020). Although political brands are often conceptualised as corporate entities with various stakeholders (Conz, 2019; Coker et al., 2021; Jain & Ganesh, 2019; Pich et al., 2018), there is a paucity of studies that analyse brand image from multiple perspectives at the same time. By incorporating the perspectives of journalists, students, public servants, business owners and the Pakistani diaspora, this case study provides a more comprehensive and nuanced understanding of a political party's corporate brand image. For example, Figure 7.7 illustrates key elements of the PTI's corporate brand image.

The leader element of the PTI corporate brand trinity appears to be a consistent theme across focus groups. The leader is the strongest and most engaging dimension of PTI. However, opposing opinions emerged among stakeholder groups for the party and policies dimensions which are present but not as coherent. This case demonstrates the complexities of managing a political brand image, particularly when relying heavily on a single leader. While Khan's leadership enjoys strong support, internal inconsistencies within the party and concerns about policy implementation create a disconnect. To strengthen brand image and stakeholder engagement, PTI may need to address these inconsistencies and communicate a more unified message across all elements of the brand trinity (leader, party, policies). Subsequently, political brand creators need to align all parts of their brand (party, leader, policy) to increase engagement, trust and loyalty with all their stakeholders. In this case, barriers to engagement are the internal issues within the party and conflicting views regarding policies. To increase engagement, PTI needs to communicate a clear and 'authentic brand' which is only possible if all elements of the trinity are aligned. Journalists, in particular, were found to be less favourable of the PTI party and policies while students, public servants, small business owners and Pakistani diaspora had a mixed view of the same. This creates a conundrum for brand owners while they aim to align the corporate brand identity and image (Hatch & Schultz, 2001, 2003, 2008; Pich & Newman, 2020). External stakeholders can often have competing interests (Coker et al., 2021; Garas et al., 2018) and treading this delicate path of managing the brand image further reveals its complexity and multi-faceted nature. It is equally important that further research into brand image is undertaken to monitor the perceptions, associations and attitudes as they are subject to change. Equally important is to understand the internal identity of the PTI brand and future research should consider this.

DISCUSSION

This chapter discussed two important characteristics associated with different types of political brands including engagement and positioning. Adopting an interdisciplinary approach, this chapter introduced and applied the concept of CBE to political branding. CBE represents a dynamic, comprehensive and multidimensional construct (Gambetti et al., 2015; Hollebeek et al., 2014; Leckie et al., 2016; Machado et al., 2019), and focuses on a 'consumer's positively valenced (feeling of quality) cognitive, emotional and behavioural brand-related activity during, or related to, specific consumer/brand interactions' (Hollebeek et al., 2014, p. 151). Therefore, this chapter demonstrates the applicability and unproblematic nature of transferring CBE as a construct to investigate the rational, emotional and behavioural exchanges between the individual and political brands (Ahn & Back, 2018; Brodie et al., 2011; Halaszovich & Jaques, 2017; Machado et al., 2019). This in turn answers calls for further research in this area (Gong, 2018; Powell, 2016; Verhoef et al., 2010). Secondly, this chapter presented the related yet distinct drivers of CBE including political brand identity and political brand image and developed the *political brand engagement and positioning framework* as outlined in Figure 7.8.

Political brand identity was conceptualised as the internally created and intended position of the political brand structured around tangible and intelligible touchpoints (Baines et al., 2014; O'Shaughnessy & Baines, 2009; Plumeyer et al., 2017; Propheto et al., 2020; Schneider, 2004). In contrast, political brand image was defined as the actual perceptions, attitudes and imagery positioned in the mind of the voter (O'Shaughnessy & Baines, 2009; Pich, 2022). This chapter demonstrates that political brand identity and political brand image are appropriate theoretical constructs to help structure the investigatory process of political brand positioning, which up until now was difficult to capture (Baines et al., 2014; Pich, 2022). Therefore, political brand positioning can be seen as a 'two-way communication process' (O'Shaughnessy & Baines, 2009, p. 23), which focuses on a political brand's intended vision created-communicated by a producer and brought to life in the mind of the consumer (Baines, 1999; Gurău & Ayadi, 2011; O'Shaughnessy & Baines, 2009). Alignment is an important process of strategically managing political brands. Further, further research should focus on whether intended and actual positioning are drivers and barriers of political CBE.

This chapter goes some way in addressing the paucity of research dedicated to investigating the *intended* and *actual* positioning of political brands (Baines et al., 1999; Gurău & Ayadi, 2011; O'Shaughnessy & Baines, 2009; Pich, 2022; Smith, 2005). In addition, investigating the positioning of political brands will provide insight into how stakeholders engage with political brands and reveal whether the desired identity and understood image are barriers or drivers of

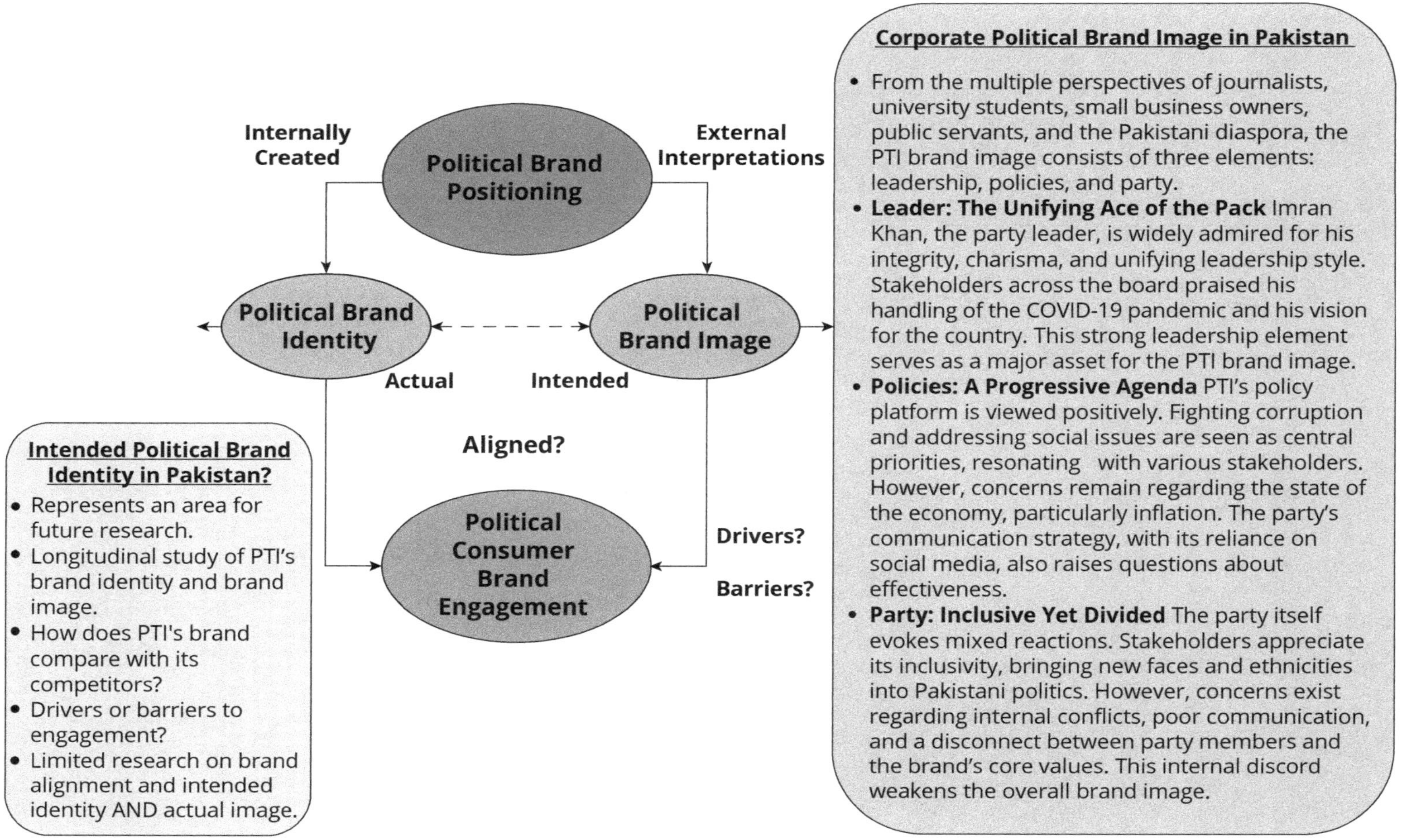
Internally
Created
Political Brand
Positioning
External
Interpretations
Political Brand
Identity
Political
Brand Image
Actual
Intended
Aligned?
Political
Consumer
Brand
Engagement
Drivers?
Barriers?
Intended Political Brand
Identity in Pakistan?
• Represents an area for future research.
• Longitudinal study of PTI's brand identity and brand image.
• How does PTI's brand compare with its competitors?
• Drivers or barriers to engagement?
• Limited research on brand alignment and intended identity AND actual image.
Corporate Political Brand Image in Pakistan
• From the multiple perspectives of journalists, university students, small business owners, public servants, and the Pakistani diaspora, the PTI brand image consists of three elements: leadership, policies, and party.
• Leader: The Unifying Ace of the Pack Imran Khan, the party leader, is widely admired for his integrity, charisma, and unifying leadership style. Stakeholders across the board praised his handling of the COVID-19 pandemic and his vision for the country. This strong leadership element serves as a major asset for the PTI brand image.
• Policies: A Progressive Agenda PTI's policy platform is viewed positively. Fighting corruption and addressing social issues are seen as central priorities, resonating with various stakeholders. However, concerns remain regarding the state of the economy, particularly inflation. The party's communication strategy, with its reliance on social media, also raises questions about effectiveness.
• Party: Inclusive Yet Divided The party itself evokes mixed reactions. Stakeholders appreciate its inclusivity, bringing new faces and ethnicities into Pakistani politics. However, concerns exist regarding internal conflicts, poor communication, and a disconnect between party members and the brand's core values. This internal discord weakens the overall brand image.

Figure 7.7 Key Elements of the External View of the PTI Political Brand Image and Areas for Further Research

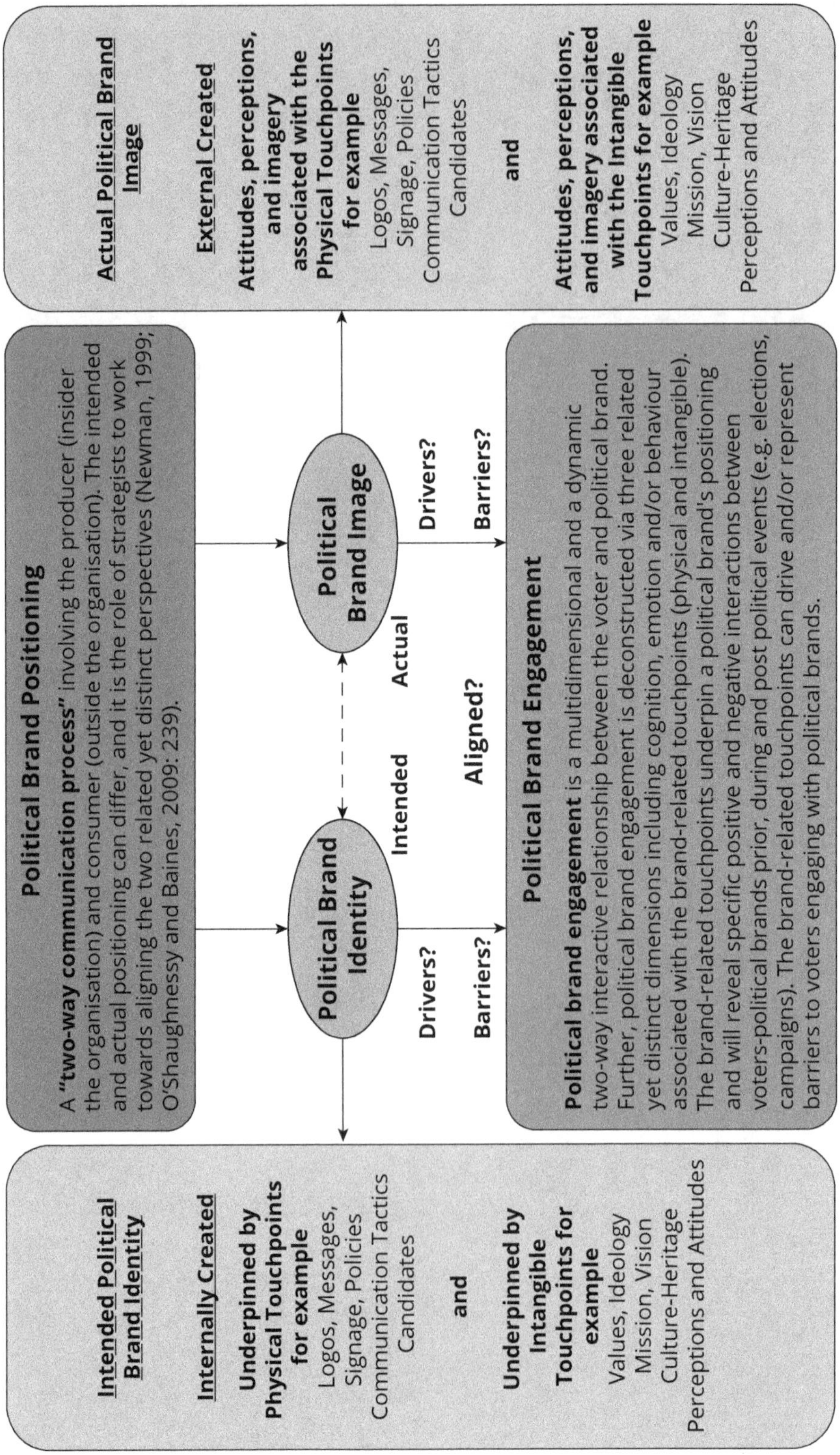
Intended Political Brand Identity
Internally Created
Underpinned by Physical Touchpoints for example
Logos, Messages, Signage, Policies
Communication Tactics
Candidates
and
Underpinned by Intangible Touchpoints for example
Values, Ideology
Mission, Vision
Culture-Heritage
Perceptions and Attitudes
Political Brand Positioning
A "two-way communication process" involving the producer (insider the organisation) and consumer (outside the organisation). The intended and actual positioning can differ, and it is the role of strategists to work towards aligning the two related yet distinct perspectives (Newman, 1999; O'Shaughnessy and Baines, 2009: 239).
Political Brand Identity
Political Brand Image
Intended
Actual
Aligned?
Drivers?
Barriers?
Drivers?
Barriers?
Political Brand Engagement
Political brand engagement is a multidimensional and a dynamic two-way interactive relationship between the voter and political brand. Further, political brand engagement is deconstructed via three related yet distinct dimensions including cognition, emotion and/or behaviour associated with the brand-related touchpoints (physical and intangible). The brand-related touchpoints underpin a political brand's positioning and will reveal specific positive and negative interactions between voters-political brands prior, during and post political events (e.g. elections, campaigns). The brand-related touchpoints can drive and/or represent barriers to voters engaging with political brands.
Actual Political Brand Image
External Created
Attitudes, perceptions, and imagery associated with the Physical Touchpoints for example
Logos, Messages, Signage, Policies
Communication Tactics
Candidates
and
Attitudes, perceptions, and imagery associated with the Intangible Touchpoints for example
Values, Ideology
Mission, Vision
Culture-Heritage
Perceptions and Attitudes

Figure 7.8 Political Brand Engagement and Positioning Framework

engagement. This in turn addresses explicit calls for further research on 'the nature of CBE interrelationships with other concepts' including how brands are positioned and how they are interpreted by consumers and responds to demands for more empirical research in this area (Bolton & Saxena-Iyer, 2009; France et al., 2016; Hollebeek, 2011a; Hollebeek, 2011b; Hollebeek et al., 2014; Leckie et al., 2016). Strategists and researchers should adopt the Political Brand Engagement and Positioning Framework (Figure 7.8) as a mechanism to understand the engagement and/or positioning associated with political brands particularly from a multi-stakeholder perspective. It is important to routinely audit and track the positioning and engagement of political brands as this may reveal coherency or misalignment of desired and actual positioning, which strategists can respond and develop strategies to maintain alignment or devise repositioning-engagement strategies (Baines et al., 1999; Collins & Butler, 2002; Pich, 2022; Smith, 2005).

CONCLUSION

This chapter discussed two related priority issues linked to political brand positioning, which represented under-explored areas of study within political branding. More specifically, this chapter examined how a political brand creates, manages and communicates an intended identity, and discussed how researchers and strategists can capture the actual position associated with a political brand developed in the minds of voters (Baines et al., 2014; O'Shaughnessy & Baines, 2009; Pich et al., 2020; Poorrezaei et al., 2023; Smith & French, 2009). Further, this chapter considered several intrinsically linked concepts including CBE, brand identity and brand image, which served as appropriate theoretical lenses to frame the discussion (Bolton & Saxena-Iyer, 2009; Brodie et al., 2011; Carvalho & Fernandes, 2018; Gambetti et al., 2015; Hollebeek, 2011b; Hollebeek et al., 2014; Leckie et al., 2016). This chapter satisfies demands for a deeper understanding into engagement and positioning yet also explores the 'interrelationships' between the concepts of CBE, brand identity and brand image (Hollebeek, 2011). Investigating how voters engaged and interpreted political brands equips marketers and brand managers with the knowledge to devise strategies and tactics to strengthen existing behaviours, enhance long-term relationships and maintain desired positioning.

Two short empirical case studies were presented to illustrate the unproblematic applicability of the key constructs. Case one focused on political brand positioning and identity in the British Crown Dependencies of Jersey. Case two focused on political brand image and engagement in the context of Pakistan with a specific focus on the PTI party brand. The British Crown Dependencies of Jersey and Pakistan were in no way selected as comparisons but served to illustrate two unique international settings and home to different types of political brands. Therefore, this chapter addresses explicit calls for further research on different types of political brands in under-explored contexts (Ahmed et al., 2015; Armannsdottir et al., 2019; Falkowski & Jabłonska, 2019; Jain & Ganesh, 2019; Marland & Wagner, 2020; Nielsen, 2016; O'Shaughnessy & Baines, 2009) and investigated with the aid of related yet distinct theoretical lenses (O'Cass & Voola, 2011; Pich et al., 2020; Rutter et al., 2015; Scammell, 2015; Simons, 2016). Finally, the two cases demonstrate the transfer potential of branding concepts to politics however acknowledges that core branding theory may need to be tailored to address the unique settings and contexts.

The chapter concludes by presenting the 'political brand engagement and positioning framework' (Figure 8), underpinned by interlinked concepts including political brand identity, political brand image and CBE. Strategists and researchers should adopt the political brand engagement and positioning framework as a mechanism to capture and compare the intended position and actual position. This is turn will reveal coherency or misalignment of intended brand identity and actual brand image, which strategists can respond and develop strategies to maintain alignment or devise repositioning-engagement strategies to help manage and safeguard political brands (Baines et al., 1999; Collins & Butler, 2002; Pich, 2022; Smith, 2005). Therefore, political brand positioning remains a 'two-way communication process' (O'Shaughnessy & Baines, 2009, p. 239), which focuses on a political brand's intended vision created-communicated by a producer and brought to life in the mind of the voter (Baines, 1999; Gurău & Ayadi, 2011; O'Shaughnessy & Baines, 2009).

REFERENCES

Acocella, I. (2012). The focus groups in social research: Advantages and disadvantages. *Quality and Quantity*, *46*, 1125–1136. https://doi.org/10.1007/s11135-011-9600-4

Ahmed, M. A., Lodhi, A. S., & Ahmad, Z. (2015). Political brand equity model: The integration of political brands in voter choice. *Journal of Political Marketing*, *16*(2), 149–179. https://doi.org/10.1080/15377857.2015.1022629

Ahn, J., & Back, K. (2018). Antecedents and consequences of customer brand engagement in integrated resorts. *International Journal of Hospitality Management*, *75*, 144–152. https://doi.org/10.1016/j.ijhm.2018.05.020

Armannsdottir, G., Carnell, S., & Pich, C. (2019). Exploring personal political brands of Iceland's parliamentarians. *Journal of Political Marketing*, *19*(1, 2), 74–106. https://doi.org/10.1080/15377857.2019.1680931

Aspers, P., & Corte, U. (2019). What is qualitative in qualitative research. *Qualitative Sociology*, *42*, 139–160. https://doi.org/10.1007/s11133-019-9413-7

Azungah, T. (2018). Qualitative research: Deductive and inductive approaches to data analysis. *Qualitative Research Journal*, *18*(4), 383–400. https://doi.org/10.1108/QRJ-D-18-00035

Baines, P. R. (1999). Voter segmentation and candidate positioning. In B. L. Newman (Ed.), *Handbook of political marketing*. SAGE.

Baines, P., Crawford, I., O'Shaughnessy, N., Worcester, R., & Mortimore, R. (2014). Positioning in political marketing: How semiotic analysis adds value to traditional survey approaches. *Journal of Marketing Management*, *30*(1–2), 172–200. https://doi.org/10.1080/0267257X.2013.810166

Baines, P. R., Lewis, B. R., & Ingham, B. (1999). Exploring the positioning process in political campaigning. *Journal of Communication Management*, *3*(4), 325–336. https://doi.org/10.1108/eb023496

Bastos, W., & Levy, S. J. (2012). A history of the concept of branding: Practice and theory. *Journal of Historical Research in Marketing*, *4*(3), 347–368. https://doi.org/10.1108/17557501211252934

Bell, E., Bryman, A., & Harley, B. (2019). *Business research methods*. Oxford University Press.

Bendisch, F., Larsen, G., & Trueman, M. (2013). Fame and fortune: A conceptual model of CEO brands. *European Journal of Marketing*, *47*(3–4), 596–614. https://doi.org/10.1108/03090561311297472

Boleat, M. (2023). Election turnout in Jersey, *Policy Centre Jersey Research*, 1-34. https://www.policy.je/papers/election-turnout-in-jersey. Assessed on 8 May 2023).

Bolton, R. N., & Saxena-Iyer, S. (2009). Interactive services: A framework, synthesis and research directions. *Journal of Interactive Marketing*, *23*(1), 91–104. htttps://doi.org/10.1016/j.intmar.2008.11.002

Bowden, J. (2009). Customer engagement: A framework for assessing customer-brand relationships: The case of the restaurant industry. *Journal of Hospitality Marketing & Management*, *18*(6), 574–596. https://doi.org/10.1080/19368620903024983

Braun, V., & Clarke, V. (2006). Using thematic analysis in psychology. *Qualitative Research in Psychology*, *3*(2), 77–101. https://doi.org/10.1191/1478088706qp063oa

Brodie, R. J., Hollebeek, L. D., Juric, B., & Ilic, A. (2011). Customer engagement: Conceptual domain, fundamental propositions & implications for research in service marketing. *Journal of Service Research*, *14*(3), 252–271. https://doi.org/10.1177/1094670511411703

Butler, P., Collins, N., & Speed, R. (2011). The Europeanisation of the British political marketplace. *Journal of Marketing Management*, *27*(7–8), 675–690. https://doi.org/10.1080/0267257X.2011.593540

Calder, B. J., Malthouse, E. M., & Schaedel, U. (2009). An experimental study of the relationship between online engagement and advertising effectiveness. *Journal of Interactive Marketing*, *23*(4), 321–331. https://doi.org/10.1016/j.intmar.2009.07.002

Carvalho, A., & Fernandes, T. (2018). Understanding customer brand engagement with virtual social communities: A comprehensive model of drivers, outcomes and moderators. *Journal of Marketing Theory and Practice*, *26*(1–2), 23–37. https://doi.org/10.1080/10696679.2017.1389241

Coker, K. K., Flight, R. L., & Baima, D. M. (2021). Video storytelling ads vs argumentative ads: How hooking viewers enhances consumer engagement. *The Journal of Research in Indian Medicine*, *15*(4), 607–622. https://doi.org/10.1108/JRIM-05-2020-0115

Collins, N., & Butler, P. (2002). The Marketplace, eGovernment and eDemocracy. *Joint Issue of Irish Marketing Review/Journal of Korean Academy of Marketing Science*, *15*(2), 86–93. https://doi.org/10.1080/10696679.2017.1389241

Conz, E. (2019). A marketing perspective on reshoring: Online corporate brand image and communication of reshored Italian companies. *Economia Aziendale Online*, *10*(1), 75–91.

Davies, G., & Mian, T. (2010). The reputation of the party leader and the party being led. *European Journal of Marketing*, *44*(3–4), 331–350. https://doi.org/10.1108/03090561011020453

Dessart, L., Veloutsou, C., & Morgan-Thomas, A. (2015). Consumer engagement in online brand communities: A social media perspective. *The Journal of Product and Brand Management*, *24*(1), 28–42. https://doi.org/10.1108/JPBM-06-2014-0635

Erlingsson, C., & Brysiewicz, P. (2013). Orientation among multiple truths: An introduction to qualitative research. *African Journal of Emergency Medicine*, *3*(2), 92–99. https://doi.org/10.1016/j.afjem.2012.04.005

Falkowski, A., & Jabłonska, M. (2019). Moderators and mediators of framing effects in political marketing. Implications for political brand management. *Journal of Political Marketing*, *19*(1- 2). https://doi.org/10.1080/15377857.2019.1652221

Foroudi, P., Zhongqi, J., Gupta, S., Foroudi, M. M., & Kitchen, P. J. (2018). Perceptional components of brand equity: Configuring the Symmetrical and Asymmetrical Paths to brand loyalty and brand purchase intention. *Journal of Business Research*, *89* (2018), 462-474, https://doi.org/10.1016/j.jbusres.2018.01.031

France, C., Merrilees, B., & Miller, D. (2016). An integrated model of customer brand engagement: Drivers and consequences. *Journal of Brand Management*, *23*(2), 119–136. https://doi.org/10.1057/bm.2016.4

Gambetti, R., Biraghi, S., Schultz, D. E., & Graffigna, G. (2015). Brand wars: Consumer–brand engagement beyond client–agency fights. *Journal of Strategic Marketing*, 1–14. https://doi.org/10.1002/9781118785317.weom090054

Garas, S. R. R., Mahran, A. F. A., & Mohamed, H. M. H. (2018). Internal corporate branding impact on employees' brand supporting behaviour. *The Journal of Product and Brand Management*, *27*(1), 79–95. https://doi.org/10.1108/JPBM-03-2016-1112

Gelo, O., Braakmann, D., & Benetka, G. (2008). Quantitative and qualitative research: Beyond the debate. *Integrative Psychological and Behavioral Science*, *42*, 266–290. https://doi.org/10.1007/s12124-008-9078-3

Gephart, R. P., Jr. (2004). Qualitative research and the Academy of Management Journal. *Academy of Management Journal*, *47*(4), 454–462. https://doi.org/10.5465/amj.2004.14438580

Gong, T. (2018). Customer brand engagement behavior in online brand communities. *Journal of Services Marketing*, *32*(3), 286–299. https://doi.org/10.1108/JSM-08-2016-0293

Greyser, S. A., & Urde, M. (2019). What does your corporate brand stand for. *Harvard Business Review*, *1*(2), 82–89.

Guest, G., Namey, E., Taylor, J., Eley, N., & McKenna, K. (2017). Comparing focus groups and individual interviews: Findings from a randomized study. *International Journal of Social Research Methodology*, *20*(6), 693–708. https://doi.org/10.1080/13645579.2017.1281601

Gurău, C., & Ayadi, N. (2011). Political communication management: The strategy of the two main candidates during the 2007 French presidential elections. *Journal of Communication Management*, *15*(1), 5–22. https://doi.org/10.1108/13632541111105222

Halaszovich, T., & Jaques, N. (2017). Customer–brand engagement and Facebook fan-page "Like"-intention. *The Journal of Product and Brand Management*, *26*(2), 120–134. https://doi.org/10.1108/JPBM-02-2016-1102

Hatch, M. J., & Schultz, M. (2001). Are the strategic stars aligned for your corporate brand. *Harvard Business Review*, *79*(2), 128–134.

Hatch, M. J., & Schultz, M. (2003). Bringing the corporation into corporate branding. *European Journal of Marketing*, *37*(7/8), 1041–1064. https://doi.org/10.1108/03090560310477654

Hatch, M. J., & Schultz, M. (2008). *Taking brand initiative: How companies can align strategy, culture, and identity through corporate branding*. John Wiley & Sons.

He, H., Harris, L. C., Wang, W., & Haider, K. (2016). Brand identity and online self-customisation usefulness perception. *Journal of Marketing Management*, *32*(13–14), 1308–1332. https://doi.org/10.1080/0267257X.2016.1170720

Hollebeek, L. D. (2011a). Exploring customer brand engagement: Definition and themes. *Journal of Strategic Marketing*, *19*(7), 555–573. https://doi.org/10.1080/0965254X.2011.599493

Hollebeek, L. D. (2011b). Demystifying customer brand engagement: Exploring the loyalty nexus. *Journal of Marketing Management*, *27*(7–8), 785–807. https://doi.org/10.1080/0267257X.2010.500132

Hollebeek, L. D., Glynn, M. S., & Brodie, R. J. (2014). Consumer brand engagement in social media: Conceptualization, scale development and validation. *Journal of Interactive Marketing*, *28*(2), 149–165. https://doi.org/10.1016/j.intmar.2013.12.002

Iglesias, O., & Ind, N. (2020). Towards a theory of conscientious corporate brand co-creation: The next key challenge in brand management. *Journal of Brand Management*, *27*, 710–720. https://doi.org/10.1057/s41262-020-00205-7

Jain, V., & Ganesh, B. E. (2019). Understanding the magic of credibility for political leaders: A case of India and Narendra Modi. *Journal of Political Marketing*, *19*(1–2), 15–33. https://doi.org/10.1080/15377857.2019.1652222

Johnson, R. M. (1971). Market segmentation: A strategic management tool. *Journal of Marketing Research*, *8* (February 1971), 13–18. https://doi.org/10.1177/002224377100800101

Koporcic, N., & Halinen, A. (2018). Interactive network branding: Creating corporate identity and reputation through interpersonal interaction. *IMP Journal*, *12*(2), 392–408. https://doi.org/10.1108/IMP-05-2017-0026

Kruger, L. J., Rodgers, R. F., Long, S. J., & Lowy, A. S. (2019). Individual interviews or focus groups? Interview format and women's self-disclosure. *International Journal of Social Research Methodology*, *22*(3), 245–255. https://doi.org/10.1080/13645579.2018.1518857

Leckie, C., Munyaradzi, W. N., & Johnson, L. W. (2016). Antecedents of consumer brand engagement and brand loyalty. *Journal of Marketing Management*, *32*(5–6), 558–578. https://doi.org/10.1080/0267257X.2015.1131735

Lilleker, D., & Moufahim, M. (2022). The ethical challenges at eh heart of political branding. In M. Moufahim (Ed.), *Political branding in turbulent times. Palgrave studies in political marketing and management* (pp. 141–152). Palgrave Macmillan. https://doi.org/10.1007/978-3-030-83229-2_2

Lin, J. S., & Himelboim, I. (2019). Political brand communities as social network clusters: Winning and trailing candidates in the GOP 2016 primary elections. *Journal of Political Marketing*, *18*(1–2), 119–147. https://doi.org/10.1080/15377857.2018.1478661

Lloyd, J. (2022). Toxic shock: Brexit and the lessons to be learned by UK's political brands. In M. Moufahim (Ed.), *Political branding in turbulent times. Palgrave Studies in Political Marketing and Management* (pp. 87–102). Palgrave Macmillan. https://doi.org/10.1007/978-3-030-83229-2_2

Machado, J. C., Vacas-de-Carvalho, L., Azar, S. L., André, A. R., & Pires dos Santos, B. (2019). Brand gender and consumer-based brand equity on Facebook: The mediating role of consumer-brand engagement and brand love. *Journal of Business Research*, *96*, 376–385. https://doi.org/10.1016/j.jbusres.2018.07.016

Marder, B., Marchant, C., Archer-Brown, C., Yau, A., & Colliander, J. (2018). Conspicuous political brand interactions on social network sites. *European Journal of Marketing*, *52*(3–4), 702–724. https://doi.org/10.1108/EJM-01-2017-0059

Markovic, S., Iglesias, O., Singh, J. J., & Sierra, V. (2018). How does the perceived ethicality of corporate services brands influence loyalty and positive word-of-mouth? Analyzing the roles of empathy, affective commitment, and perceived quality. *Journal of Business Ethics*, *148*, 721–740. https://doi.org/10.1007/s10551-015-2985-6

Marland, A. (2016). *Brand command: Canadian politics and democracy in the age of message control*. UBC Press.

Marland, A., & Flanagan, T. (2014). Brand new party: Political branding and the conservative party of Canada. *Canadian Journal of Political Science*, *46*(4), 951–972. https://doi.org/10.1017/S0008423913001108

Marland, A., Lewis, J. P., & Flanagan, T. (2017). Governance in the age of digital media and branding. *Governance: An International Journal of Policy, Administration and Institutions*, *30*(1), 125–141. https://doi.org/10.1111/gove.12194

Marland, A., & Wagner, A. (2020). Scripted messengers: How party discipline and branding turn election candidates and legislators into brand ambassadors. *Journal of Political Marketing*, *19*(1–2), 54–73. https://doi.org/10.1080/15377857.2019.1658022

Marwick, E. A., & Boyd, D. (2010). I tweet honestly, I tweet passionately: Twitter users, context collapse, and the imagined audience. *New Media & Society*, *13*(1), 114–133. https://doi.org/10.1177/1461444810365313

Mehmood, F., Haroon, O., & Riaz, Z. (2021). It's just not cricket. *Asian Journal of Management Cases*, *18*(1), 80–97. https://doi.org/10.1177/0972820120978708

Mirza, F. (2016, May 25). Changing perception: 3 branding lessons you can learn from pope Francis. www.business.com/entrepreneurship/3-brandinglessons-you-can-learn-from-pope-francis/. Accessed on May 2020.

Mohajan, H. K. (2018). Qualitative research methodology in social sciences and related subjects. *Journal of Economic Development, Environment and People*, *7*(1), 23–48. https://doi.org/10.26458/jedep.v7i1.571

Nandan, S. (2005). An exploration of the brand identity-brand image linkage: A communications perspective. *Journal of Brand Management*, *12*(4), 264–278. https://doi.org/10.1057/palgrave.bm.2540222

Needham, C., & Smith, G. (2015). Introduction: Political branding. *Journal of Political Marketing*, *14*(1–2), 1–6. https://doi.org/10.1080/15377857.2014.990828

Newman, B. I. (1999). A predictive model of voting behaviour. The repositioning of Bill Clinton. In B. L. Newman (Ed.), *Handbook of political marketing* (p. xvii). SAGE.

Newman, B. I., & Newman, T. P. (2022). Introduction: Political marketing – Analysis, synthesis and future considerations. In B. L. Newman & T. P. Newman (Eds.), *A research agenda for political marketing* (pp. 1–15). Edward Elgar Publishing Limited. https://doi.org/10.4337/9781800377202.00007

Nielsen, S. W. (2016). Measuring political brands: An art and a science of mapping the mind. *Journal of Political Marketing*, *15*(1), 70–95. https://doi.org/10.1080/15377857.2014.959682

Norris, P., Curtice, J., Sanders, D., Scammell, M., & Semetko, H. A. (1999). *On message: Communicating the campaign*. SAGE.

O'Cass, A., & Voola, R. (2011). Explications of political market orientation and political brand orientation using the resource-based view of the political party. *Journal of Marketing Management*, *27*(5–6), 627–645. https://doi.org/10.1080/0267257X.2010.489831

O'Shaughnessy, N. J., & Baines, P. R. (2009). Selling terror: The symbolization and positioning of Jihad. *Journal of Marketing Theory*, *9*(2), 227–241. https://doi.org/10.1177/1470593109103069

Panda, S., Pandey, S. C., Bennett, A., & Tian, X. (2019). University brand image as competitive advantage: A two-country study. *International Journal of Educational Management*, *33*(2), 234–251. https://doi.org/10.1108/IJEM-12-2017-0374

Pich, C. (2022). Political branding – A research agenda for political marketing. In B. I. Newman & T. P. Newman (Eds.), *A research agenda for political marketing* (pp. 121–143). Edward Elgar Publishing Limited. https://doi.org/10.4337/9781800377202.00014

Pich, C., & Armannsdottir, G. (2022). Political brand identity and image: Manifestations, challenges and tensions. In M. Moufahim (Ed.), *Political branding in turbulent times. Palgrave Studies in Political Marketing and Management* (pp. 9–32). Palgrave Macmillan. https://doi.org/10.1007/978-3-030-83229-2_2

Pich, C., Armannsdottir, G., Dean, D., Spry, L., & Jain, V. (2020). Problematizing the presentation and reception of political brands: The strategic and operational nature of the political brand alignment model. *European Journal of Marketing*, *54*(1), 190–211. https://doi.org/10.1108/EJM-03-2018-0187

Pich, C., Armannsdottir, G., & Spry, L. (2018). Investigating political brand reputation with qualitative projective techniques from the perspective of young adults. *International Journal of Market Research*, *60*(2), 198–213. https://doi.org/10.1177/1470785317750817

Pich, C., & Dean, D. (2015). Qualitative projective techniques in political brand image research from the perspective of young adults. *Qualitative Market Research: An International Journal*, *18*(1), 1–36. https://doi.org/10.1108/QMR-12-2012-0058

Pich, C., & Newman, B. I. (2020). *Political branding: More than parties, leaders and policies*. Routledge, Taylor and Francis Publications. https://doi.org/10.4324/9781003045199

Plumeyer, A., Kottemann, P., Böger, D., & Decker, R. (2017). Measuring brand image: A systematic review, practical guidance, and future research directions. *Review of Managerial Science*, *13*, 227–265. https://doi.org/10.1007/s11846-017-0251-2

Poorrezaei, M., Pich, C., Armannsdottir, G., Branco-Illodo, I., & Harvey, J. (2023). Young voters' engagement: A customer journeys perspective. *International Journal of Market Research*, *65*(5), 532–565. ISSN 1470-7853.

Powell, S. M. (2016). Year end review 2016. *Journal of Brand Management*, *23*, 601–611. https://doi.org/10.1057/s41262-016-0021-5

Propheto, A., Kartini, D., Sucherly, S., & Oesman, Y. (2020). Marketing performance as implication of brand image mediated by trust. *Management Science Letters*, *10*(4), 741–746. https://doi.org/10.5267/j.msl.2019.10.023

Raed, A., Rana, N. P., Dwivedi, Y. K., Alalwan, A. A., & Qasem, Z. (2018). The effect of telepresence, social presence and involvement on consumer brand engagement: An empirical study of non-profit organizations. *Journal of Retailing and Consumer Services*, *40*(C), 139–149. https://doi.org/10.1016/j.jretconser.2017.09.011

Richelieu, A. (2018). A sport-oriented place branding strategy for cities, regions and countries. *Sport, Business and Management*, *8*(4), 354–374. https://doi.org/10.1108/SBM-02-2018-0010

Richelieu, A. (2014). The strategic management of the brand in the world of sport. *Journal of Brand Strategy*, *2*(4), 403–415.

Robertson, R., & Meintjes, C. (2021). Towards an online risk mitigation framework for political brands subject to computational propaganda. *Communicatio*, *47*(1), 95–121.

Rutter, R., Chalvatzis, K. J., Roper, S., & Lettice, F. (2018). Branding instead of product innovation: A study on the brand personalities of the UK's electricity market. *European Management Review*, *15*(2), 255–272. https://doi.org/10.1111/emre.12155

Rutter, R., Hanretty, C., & Lettice, F. (2015). Political brands. Can parties be distinguished by their online brand personality. *Journal of Political Marketing*, *17*(3), 193–212. https://doi.org/10.1080/15377857.2015.1022631

Salzman, M. (2013, March 18). Branding the pope. www.forbes.com/sites/mariansalzman/2013/03/18/branding-the-pope/#513c3aaa5f7b. Accessed on May 2020.

Savitri, C., Hurriyati, R., Wibowo, L., & Hendrayati, H. (2022). The role of social media marketing and brand image on smartphone purchase intention. *International Journal of Data and Network Science*, *6*(1), 185–192. https://doi.org/10.5267/j.ijdns.2021.9.009

Scammell, M. (2015). Politics and image: The conceptual value of branding. *Journal of Political Marketing*, *14*(1–2), 7–18. https://doi.org/10.1080/15377857.2014.990829

Schneider, H. (2004). Branding in politics – Manifestations, relevance and identity-oriented management. *Journal of Political Marketing*, *3*(3), 41–67. https://doi.org/10.1300/J199v03n03_03

Shepherd, D. H. I. (2005). From Cattle and Coke to Charlie: Meeting the challenge of self-marketing and personal branding. *Journal of Marketing Management*, *21*(5–6), 589–606. https://doi.org/10.1362/0267257054307381

Silveira, C. D. Lages, C.,& Simoes, C. (2013). Reconceptualising brand identity in a dynamic environment, *Journal of Business Research*, *66*, 28–36. https://doi.org/10.1016/j.jbusres.2011.07.020

Simons, G. (2016). Stability and change in Putin's political image during the 2000 and 2012 presidential elections: Putin 1.0 and Putin 2.0? *Journal of Political Marketing*, *15*(2–3), 149–170. https://doi.org/10.1080/15377857.2016.1151114

Smith, G. (2005). Positioning political parties: The 2005 UK general election. *Journal of Marketing Management*, *21*(4), 1135–1149. https://doi.org/10.1362/026725705775194184

Smith, G., & French, A. (2011). Measuring the changes to leader brand associations during the 2010 election campaign. *Journal of Marketing Management*, *27*(7–8), 718–735. https://doi.org/10.1080/0267257X.2011.587825

Smith, G., & French, A. (2009). The political brand: A consumer perspective. *Marketing Theory*, *9*(2), 209–226. https://doi.org/10.1177/1470593109103068

Speed, R., Butler, P., & Collins, N. (2015). Human branding in political marketing: Applying contemporary branding thoughts to political parties and their leaders. *Journal of Political Marketing*, *14*(2–3), 129–151. https://doi.org/10.1080/15377857.2014.990833

Spry, L., & Pich, C. (2021). Enhancing data collection methods with qualitative projective techniques in the exploration of a university's brand identity and brand image. *International Journal of Market Research*, *63*(2), 177–200. https://doi.org/10.1177/1470785320943045

Su, Y., & Kunkel, T. (2019). Beyond brand fit: The influence of brand contribution on the relationship between service brand alliances and their parent brands. *Journal of Service Management*, *30*(2), 252–275. https://doi.org/10.1108/JOSM-02-2018-0052

Vale, L. V., & Fernandes, T. (2018). Social media and sports: Driving fan engagement with football clubs on Facebook. *Journal of Strategic Marketing*, *26*(1), 37–55. https://doi.org/10.1080/0965254X.2017.1359655

Van Doorn, J., Lemon, K. N., Mittal, V., Nass, S., Pick, D., Pirner, P., & Verhoef, P. C. (2010). Customer engagement behavior: Theoretical foundations and research directions. *Journal of Service Research*, *13*(3), 253–266. https://doi.org/10.1177/1094670510375599

Van Steenburg, E., & Guzmán, F. (2019). The influence of political candidate brands during the 2012 and 2016 US presidential elections. *European Journal of Marketing*, *53*(12), 2629–2656. https://doi.org/10.1108/EJM-06-2018-0399

Verhoef, P. C., Reinartz, W., & Krafft, M. (2010). Customer engagement as a new perspective in customer management. *Journal of Service Research*, *13*(3), 247–252. https://doi.org/10.1177/1094670510375461

Warren, C. A. B., & Karner, T. X. (2010). *Discovering qualitative methods: Field research, interviews and analysis*. Roxbury Publishing Company.

Wring, D. (2022). *Stratified electioneering: The political marketing century*. https://doi.org/10.4337/9781800377202.00010

Zenker, S. (2014). Measuring place brand equity with the advanced Brand Concept Map (aBCM) method. *Place Branding and Public Diplomacy*, *10*(2), 158–166. https://doi.org/10.1057/pb.2014.2

Zikmund, W. G. (2003). *Business research methods*. Thomson Learning.

The Continued Relevance of Political Advertising on Television: A Review of Its Effects and Content

Travis N. Ridout and Furkan Cakmak

CAMPAIGN ADVERTISING ON TELEVISION

Election-related advertising on television has been a staple in many democracies for at least 60 years, but the recent growth of advertising on digital and social media requires a reassessment of television's relevance in political campaigns. We argue that television advertising is not dead, nor even close to dying. While television's market share may be declining in many countries, spending on television advertising remains high, especially in the United States (Fowler, Franz, & Ridout, 2021). At the same time, television ads can have an impact on voters, influencing both voter choice (Sides et al., 2022) and other participatory attitudes and behaviors (Jackson et al., 2009). Finally, television advertising itself is changing in ways that make it more attractive to campaigns. Television ads can be increasingly targeted, and the opening of inventory on streaming – often viewed on televisions – has created a new type of television advertising that allows campaigns to reach more voters in different ways (Effectv, 2023).

We conceive of campaign advertising rather broadly, encompassing both advertisements that are paid for and airtime for messaging that is given (typically to parties) for free (sometimes called party election broadcasts or party political broadcasts). Whether free airtime is granted depends on the country. Countries such as Mexico, South Korea, Switzerland, and the United States do not provide for air time for advertisements, while others such as Australia, France, and Spain do (Holtz-Bacha & Kaid, 2006). Campaign advertisements may be sponsored by parties, individual candidates or groups that are independent of parties. Some countries restrict sponsorship of campaign advertisements to political parties, while some allow all three types of sponsorship. Campaign advertisements may air on commercial or public broadcasting channels. Again, this varies depending on the country, with some, such as Germany and Japan, restricting advertisements to commercial television (Holtz-Bacha & Kaid, 2006).

Much of the research we cite in this review is based on advertising from the United States. There are several reasons for this. First and foremost, spending on campaign advertising on television in the United States towers above spending in all other countries. One company that tracks political advertising estimated that $3.5 billion (USD) was spent on television advertising during the country's 2020 elections (Adgate, 2020). Another source estimated $3.2 billion in spending on television advertising in federal and gubernatorial races in the 2021–22 election cycle in the United States (Franz et al., 2023).

The wealth of spending in the United States can be attributed, at least in part, to the lack of regulation. Candidates and political parties may spend unlimited amounts on television advertising provided that the money is raised in ways specified by the law, and groups are able to spend unlimited amounts on television advertising subject to limited reporting requirements (Fowler, Franz, & Ridout, 2021). By contrast, many European nations have either limited spending on televised political ads or banned them entirely. France, for instance, forbids campaigns from purchasing airtime, allowing only free time on public television (Kaid & Gagnère, 2006). In the United Kingdom, a prohibition on the purchase of political advertising on commercial television and radio has existed for decades, though parties are given some amount of free airtime prior to elections in order to air party political broadcasts (Conway, 2019). In Germany, each political party is allowed to run a certain number of ads for free, which is determined by their share of vote in the last election (Holtz-Bacha, 2006). Although German parties can buy additional ads, their budgets are more limited compared to campaigns in the United States. India banned political ads on television in 1995 (Sabha, 1995), but this ban was relaxed in 2004 (Secretary, Ministry of Information and Broadcasting V. Gemini TV (P) Ltd. and Others, 2004). Some countries also place limits on when political ads can be broadcast. In Japan, campaign ads can be broadcast only during the two-week period before the day of the election (Tak, 2006), while in Turkey, there is a moratorium on any campaign material on election day (Can, 2006). Australia has instituted a blackout on television advertising during the day of the election and the two days prior (ACMA, 2022). The upshot is that, due to varied restrictions on spending or the timing of advertising, televised political advertising is a much more important component of political campaigns in some countries than in others.

In what follows, we review the history of political television advertising, starting with the first television ads in the 1950s and exploring the many ways by which television advertising is disseminated nowadays. We argue that television advertising remains relevant for political campaigns today despite the rise of online advertising, and we review the many ways in which exposure to television advertising might influence voters.

A Brief History of Political Advertising on Television

Campaign advertising on television goes back more than 70 years. The first US presidential campaign ad on television aired in 1952, coinciding with the rapid growth in television ownership. The percentage of American households owning a television increased from 1% in 1948 to 75% in 1955 (Putnam, 2000). During the 1952 campaign, Republican candidate Dwight D. Eisenhower released a series of ads titled "Eisenhower Answers America." His short and folksy answers to questions asked by citizens helped burnish his image (Kaid & Johnston, 2001).

In contrast to the mostly upbeat message of the first television ads, campaigns in the 1960s started using ads to attack opponents. Perhaps the most discussed attack ad of the time was the "Daisy Girl" ad, released by US president Lyndon B. Johnson during the 1964 presidential campaign (Mann, 2011). In the ad, a young girl is picking flowers and counting down, and the ad ends with a mushroom cloud as the countdown finishes. The message of the ad was that Johnson's opponent, Barry Goldwater, was unfit to have his finger on the nuclear button. Although the campaign removed the ad after one paid airing, it was controversial enough to be replayed many times during the major networks' news programs (Mann, 2011).

With the proliferation of color TVs in the 1970s, television as a medium had become the dominant source of information. Campaigns doubled-down on candidate-centered advertising, and attack ads increased. Richard Nixon's 1968 campaign was perhaps the best representation of this decade. He released many documentary-style ads to try to humanize himself. At the same time, Nixon ran a series of negative ads that included harsh personal attacks against his opponent, Hubert Humphrey, and used stark images of the military and protesters (Museum of Moving Image, 2023).

In the United States, the 1970s also saw the increased regulation of campaign finance. Following the Watergate scandal, which resulted in Nixon resigning from office, the Federal Election Campaign Act of 1971 was amended to create the Federal Election Commission to regulate spending. The original act heavily regulated the amount of money that could be spent on campaigns and thus television advertising. Although some of the reforms were struck down by courts, this era of change laid the groundwork for later reforms. However, while the United States was early in regulating campaign spending on television, its reforms fell behind those of other countries in the following decades.

The reforms of 1970s in the United States led to two important changes to political advertising on television. First, with the rise of political action committees (PACs), there was more involvement of outside groups in television ad campaigns. Second, the rise of outside group advertising led to more negativity in campaign advertising. An example of this change is the "Willie Horton" ad produced by the National Security PAC that supported George Bush's 1988 presidential campaign. The ad features William Horton, a convicted criminal who committed several crimes while on furlough in Massachusetts when Michael Dukakis, Bush's opponent, was governor. Research in political science has analyzed the "Willie Horton" ad to understand how campaigns use negativity to prime racial attitudes (Mendelberg, 1997; Valentino et al., 2002).

Television habits changed around the globe in 1980s and 1990s with an increased number of channel offerings on cable systems. In the United Kingdom, cable television was liberalized in 1984 with the Cable Broadcasting and the Telecommunications Acts, which allowed cable systems to carry multiple channels. In the beginning of the 1990s, cable infrastructure quickly improved, and cable television became common. In Argentina, cable television became so popular that by 1996, 53% of households had access to it (Arancibia, 1996). Taiwan officially allowed cable television in 1993 with the Cable Television Act, following a huge growth in audience size in 1980s (Liu, 1994). Finally, cable television subscriptions in the United States rose steadily to 68.5 million by 2000 (Federal Communications Commission, 2002). The rise of cable television and inclusion of local coverage enabled more precise targeting of messages to more distinct audiences watching specific cable channels. Consequently, campaigns were free to focus on smaller issues, in addition to the general message.

Today, connected television (CTV), which allows viewers to stream programs via the internet and watch them on their television screens, has become widespread with outlets such as YouTube TV, Sling TV, Direct TV Stream, and Hulu + Live TV, among others. These services attract millions of subscribers. For instance, Hulu + Live TV had 4.1 million subscribers as of 2022, while YouTube TV had over 5 million (Perez, 2022). Thus, CTV has provided an additional venue for viewers to see ads both on and off their televisions.

Contemporary Relevance of Television Advertising

Digital advertising has grown over the past decade – and so quickly that it may threaten the dominance of television. An estimated $743 million was spent on digital ads during the 2020 US presidential campaigns on the Google and Facebook (now Meta) platforms (Ridout et al., 2021). About 39% of Trump's ad spending in that campaign was on digital, compared to 25% for Biden (Passwaiter, 2020). In the US midterm elections in 2022, about $150 million was spent on digital ads by candidates in House and Senate races (Franz et al., 2023).

In countries outside the United States, the amounts spent on digital advertising were less but tended to constitute a greater percentage of ad spending, in part, because television advertising tends to be more heavily regulated. For example, in the 2017 general election in the United Kingdom, about £3.16 million was spent on Facebook advertising, and it is estimated that 43% of reported advertising spending was on digital advertising (Dommett & Power, 2019). In the 2019 federal elections in Canada, the major parties spent over $16 million (CAD) on television advertising, compared to $9.7 million (CAD) on digital advertising (Rabson, 2020). Finally, in Australia's 2019 federal election, it was estimated that more was spent on digital advertising than on ads on traditional media, such as television, radio, and newspapers (Hughes, 2019).

Given all this spending on online advertising, it is worth asking whether television advertising remains relevant. That television advertising is still purchased in large amounts – even after digital advertising has reached maturity – points to the continued relevance of television in contemporary campaigns, especially when it comes to the goal of persuading voters to cast ballots for certain parties or candidates. One reason for this is both the actual and perceived importance of video for persuasion. Video might create an immersive environment that can heighten one's emotions more than text or images alone. Indeed, as Holtz-Bacha and Kaid (2006) note, some countries have banned television advertising on the grounds that it is "a powerful form of persuasive communication and therefore not to be placed in the hands of those striving for power" (p. 5). A recent experimental study argued that people found political ads presented as videos to be more believable than those same ads presented as transcripts, and the video ads, on average, yielded significantly more attitude change than the transcripts, though the effect sizes were not all that large (Wittenberg et al., 2021).

Admittedly, some online political ads are in video format – think of those on YouTube, for instance – but there is an additional concern with digital advertising: that it won't be viewed. Digital ads sometimes do not play automatically and are often quickly scrolled past, clicked away from, closed or swiped off the screen. And even if they are seen, they may not be heard, as often the volume on a device is turned off. While concerns that television viewers are changing the channel or muting the audio when advertisements appear have existed for a very long time, we believe that avoiding a television advertisement is more difficult than avoiding one online.

There are other reasons for the continued relevance of televised political advertising that may be more specific to the United States. Unlike many other countries where campaign spending is limited – and the ability to raise money may be constrained – campaigns in the United States often have large amounts of cash on hand that they must spend quickly before the day of the election. Television advertising offers these campaigns a platform through which they can spend large sums of money quickly, disseminating their message to a large number of voters in quick fashion.

The demographics of television viewers are also attractive in some ways. Those who watch traditional television skew older. Americans in the 18–24 age range spend, on average, just 53 minutes each day watching broadcast television, while those older than 65 spend almost six hours each day watching broadcast television (Fatemi, 2022). People in that oldest age group are the most likely to turn out to vote – 76% of them did in the US 2020 presidential election – making them an attractive audience for campaigns.

Television's continued importance may also stem from the perceived weaknesses of other forms of advertising. First, although a campaign can know the types of people exposed to online political ads, it remains difficult to measure their persuasive impact in the real world (Ridout, 2020). Others worry that no one is opening their mail anymore. Thus, given these real or perceived deficiencies with other avenues for disseminating campaign messages, the use of television remains viable.

Political Advertising Content

Given the importance of television advertising for political persuasion, it is important to consider what contemporary television ads look like. One feature of television advertising that has received considerable attention is its tone. While the tone of an advertisement can be measured in multiple ways, one standard approach is to look at whether an ad includes a mention of an opponent (Geer, 2008). Ads that contain such mentions are considered "negative" or "attack" ads. For example, in 2022, the Australian Liberals ran an ad that attacked Labor leader Anthony Albanese, noting that "he supported higher taxes on retirees, housing, super and inheritances, and unwinding Australia's strong border protection." The ad ends by saying, "Don't risk our recovery with Labor." Ads that contain no such mentions of opponents are considered "positive" or "promotional." One such ad was aired by the Australian Labor Party in 2022, in which leader Albanese states, "I'll work with business to invest in manufacturing. . .I'll help families get ahead by making childcare cheaper. . .and I'll make it easier to see the doctor. It's my plan for a better future."

While this definition (and measure) is easy to understand – and thus likely to be highly reliable across coders – some have criticized it for being too broad. Jamieson et al. (2000), for instance, propose a three-fold categorization in which some negative ads are redefined as "contrast" or "comparative." These ads not only mention an opponent but also mention the favored candidate or party. For example, one Biden ad in 2020 spoke about how Biden went into public service to "make a difference for working families," while Donald Trump "ran for president for himself and for his friends on Wall Street."

Still, both the two-fold and three-fold definitions miss nuance in describing political advertisements. These measures do not take into account whether the ad contains legitimate policy-based criticisms versus mudslinging (Kahn & Kenney, 1999), and they do not take into account production features of the advertisement, such as whether the lighting is bright or dark and whether the music is slow or fast-paced. Nor do they account for the specific emotions that are elicited by the ad (Brader, 2006). All of these factors are likely to influence citizens' perceptions of an advertisement, which matters for the ad's impact. Indeed, Lipsitz and Geer (2017) show that citizens' perceptions of the negativity of advertisements is a better predictor of intention to turn out to vote than are scholars' ratings of the tone of these ads.

What do we know about trends in negativity in political advertising on television? At least in the United States, it appears that negativity on television has increased over time. Geer's (2008) coding of television ads aired during US presidential campaigns between 1960 and 1996 reveals increasing negativity over time. A separate analysis of advertising in all federal races between 1998 and 2020, however, suggests that while there was rising negativity earlier during the period, negativity plateaued (at a fairly high level) in about 2010 (Fowler, Franz, & Ridout, 2021). Yet, this increase in negativity over time is not present in Walter's (2014) cross-level analysis of the Netherlands, Germany, and the United Kingdom. She finds no rise in negativity in party election broadcasts in these countries between 1980 and 2006.

There is evidence from the United States that television is the most negative venue for campaign messaging. One study analyzed television and Facebook ads from the same candidates and found significantly more attack and contrast (comparative) advertising on television than in candidates' online advertising (Fowler et al., 2021). A study of US campaigns in 2010 found that television ads were more negative than messages disseminated on Twitter (Bode et al., 2016). But this finding that television advertising is the most negative medium does not extend to the Netherlands. Walter and Vliegenthart (2010) compares party election broadcasts on television with televised election debates and newspaper articles in the Netherlands. They do not find huge differences in levels of negativity across media but note that it is highest in the debates, not in television advertisements.

Negativity in campaign ads on television may also depend on institutional and structural factors.

Kaid and Holtz-Bacha (2006) perform a content analysis of advertising in twelve countries, finding substantial variation in the degree to which television advertising is negative. The highest levels of negativity were in the United States and Israel, followed by the United Kingdom, while Spain, Poland, and France had the lowest levels of negativity. Walter's (2014) study echoes these results, finding consistently higher levels of negativity in advertisements in the United Kingdom and the United States than in the Netherlands and Germany. Although the number of cases is small, this finding hints that a two-party system, such as found in the United States and (arguably) the United Kingdom, might be more conducive to negativity than a multi-party system.

Indeed, Ridout and Walter (2015) test the idea that negativity is higher when a country has a two-party as opposed to a multi-party system, which are associated with first-past-the-post and proportional or mixed electoral systems, respectively. The authors take advantage of a "natural experiment," coding the tone of television ads and party election broadcasts in New Zealand before and after the country's change from first-past-the-post to a mixed-member proportional electoral system in 1994. They find a reduction in negativity after the change. The logic behind this is that in multi-party systems, parties may need to work with each other after the election to form a government, and thus there is an incentive not to burn one's bridges. But in a two-party system, it is winner-take-all, and thus the risk of going negative may be worthwhile (Walter & Van der Brug, 2013).

In addition to the common complaint that political advertising is "too negative," another complaint is that it lacks issue content. The story goes that ads are more focused on slinging mud against opposing candidates or parties than talking about important policy issues. But the data do not entirely support that story. Sixty-three percent of television ads that aired in US House and US Senate races in 2018 were mostly focused on policy, with another 21% discussing both policy and candidates' characteristics (Fowler, Franz, & Ridout, 2021). Only 16% were focused mostly on the personal characteristics of candidates. Kaid and Holtz-Bacha's (2006) cross-national analysis of the extent to which political advertising focuses on issues versus images finds substantial discussion of issues in long-standing democracies such as the United States, France, Italy, Germany, and the UK, but the focus on issues was less in what they term "evolving democracies," such as Russia, Poland, Israel, Greece, and Turkey. Geer (2008) finds that issue content is common in US presidential ads – and even more common in negative ads.

Other research tries to explain variation in issue content. Early research found evidence of gender-of-candidate differences in the issues discussed, with women candidates more likely to discuss so-called "women's issues" (e.g., Kahn, 1993). But a more recent study that looked at candidate issue emphasis in television ads by US congressional candidates found that for only one of ten issues was there a significant difference in the emphasis that men and women candidates placed on the specific issue (Sapiro et al., 2011).

Moreover, the specific issues mentioned in political ads on television do not appear to be markedly different from the specific issues mentioned online. This is true for comparisons with online ads in the United States (Franz et al., 2020) and with tweets in Argentine campaigns (Pallister & Fitzpatrick, 2023).

One reason political advertisements may be effective is that they are laden with emotional appeals. Brader (2006) found that 72% of the US political ads that he studied contained an appeal to emotion as opposed to an appeal to logic. In a study of US Senate ads, Ridout and Searles (2011) found an even higher level of emotionality. Eighty-four percent of ads in their sample contained an enthusiasm appeal, 85% contained an appeal to pride, 48% contained an appeal to anger, and 23% contained a fear appeal (some ads contained more than one appeal). Kaid and Holtz-Bacha's (2006) cross-national study found that appeals to emotion in political advertising were common in most countries, though again there was variation. At the high end were Spain and France, with at least 70% of ads making an appeal to emotion, while at the low end were Britain, Germany, and Korea, with no more than a third of ads containing an appeal to emotion.

Effects of Televised Political Advertising

Political advertising on television is used to win political battles, whether policy or electoral. Thus, these ads are aimed at controlling the narrative. Political ads can do that by setting the agenda, telling voters, in a sense, what to think about. They can also use a certain perspective to influence how people think about a given issue (i.e., framing). Thus, there are many ways in which exposure to political advertising might affect voters. In this chapter, we focus on four in particular: persuasion, reinforcement, political participation, and learning. We also discuss how political ads can influence coverage by the news media.

Persuasion and Reinforcement

One of the most widely studied media effects in political ads on television is persuasion, that is, changing voters' opinions of parties and candidates and changing their vote preferences. When it comes to persuasion, scholars have discussed whether ads are persuasive, to what extent, and the conditions under which they are most persuasive. Recent scholarship suggests that political ads on television can persuade viewers, but persuasive effects tend not to persist (Gerber et al., 2011; Hill et al., 2013). The persuasive effects of political ads may last for an even shorter period in subnational races (Hill et al., 2013). Spenkuch and Toniatti (2018) agree that exposure to political ads could change a voter's intended vote but suggest that the overall effects of advertising are small given that both sides in an election tend to campaign in a similar fashion, and thus the ad effects cancel out. That said, a balanced ad environment does not characterize all campaigns. In fact, many US federal races in 2022 saw large imbalances in the number of ads aired by competing candidates (Franz, Fowler & Ridout, 2023).

When it comes to when political ads will be more persuasive, studies focus on three characteristics of ads that could condition their persuasiveness. These include the context in which the ad is aired, the sponsor of the ad, and the recipient of the ad.

Sides and colleagues (2022), for instance, found that in the context of down-ballot races (which typically experience less intense campaigning), television advertising is more persuasive on average. This study confirmed the findings of Ridout and Franz (2011), which showed more advertising impact in US Senate and US House races than in presidential races.

Scholars have also found that ad sponsorship matters. For instance, ads sponsored by outside groups tend to be more persuasive than ads sponsored by candidates. One experiment showed that an ad sponsored by an unknown interest group was more persuasive than an ad sponsored by a known interest group or a candidate because viewers deemed it more credible (Weber et al., 2012). Similarly, attacks on candidates contained within ads are more successful when voters know less about the group that is doing the attack (Dowling & Wichowsky, 2013).

In addition, the gender of the candidate sponsoring the ad may condition its effectiveness. Holman et al. (2015) concluded that although both male and female candidates will benefit from gender-based appeals aimed at women, such as references to policies concerning violence against women, the underlying mechanisms will differ. Female candidates will gain support of women voters because their messages will prime women's gender identity. This priming will motivate women voters to be more interested in descriptive representation, causing higher support for women candidates. Male candidates, on the other hand, will benefit from identity-based targeted messages because these messages will change the perception of the candidate in a positive way among women voters.

Other research suggests that the characteristics of the message recipient, including political knowledge and partisanship, conditions the persuasive effects of advertising. When it comes to audience knowledge, Franz and Ridout (2007) found that ads were less powerful in affecting the vote choices of those with more political knowledge. Rather, it was those low in knowledge who were the most persuaded. These findings are in line with Zaller's (1992) "Receive-Accept-Sample" model of public opinion, which suggests that voters who are less aware of politics will accept more of the messages they receive given their inability to identify messages inconsistent with their predispositions.

Zaller's theory also points to the importance of partisanship. Strong partisans are theorized to be more likely to reject messages inconsistent with their partisanship. Huber and Arceneaux (2007) investigate this possibility using a natural experiment in which they compare the effects of advertising among those who live in battleground states in the United States to those who live in non-battleground states but still receive ad messages because media market boundaries cross state lines. They found that viewers are persuaded by political advertising, but the persuasive effects of ads were lowest among strong partisans – who are presumably quite selective in their acceptance of counter-partisan messages. The effects of advertisements, however, are not necessarily confined to those whose partisanship matches the ad's sponsor or political independents. Ridout and Franz (2011), in fact, find fairly widespread effects of advertising – even among those whose partisanship is different from the ad's sponsor.

While most research tends to confirm the persuasive – though often conditional – nature of political ads on television, some research using a different design does not. After conducting a large-scale study with 59 real-time randomized experiments, Coppock and colleagues (2020) found small effects of exposure to political ads, but these effects did not significantly vary by the recipient's partisanship, the ad's sponsor, the race context (battleground v. non-battleground state), or the tone of the ad. Overall, the consensus is that political ads on television can be persuasive, but these effects will be small and short-lived (Motta & Fowler, 2016).

Some scholars suggest that rather than persuading, political ads on television are more likely to reinforce people's existing beliefs (Ansolabehere & Iyengar, 1995). Because of motivated reasoning (Lodge & Taber, 2013), ads are more likely to have an impact on those who are motivated to accept the ad's message. The fragmentation of television media also makes reinforcement more likely to occur than persuasion. For instance, in the United States, with the rise of cable news media, many outlets now appeal to niche audiences. Because there are cable news outlets serving the left, right, and the center of the political spectrum, all people – regardless of their political viewpoints – can find a media outlet that aligns with their views. Thus, media choice can be thought of as a motivated action by viewers to avoid cognitive dissonance (Arceneaux & Johnson, 2013; Stroud & Muddiman, 2019). As a result, political ads on television have a better chance at reinforcing existing opinions.

Another reason reinforcement is more likely to occur with television ads is that the cable television audience is higher in political knowledge than the audience for social media (Pew Research Center, 2020). Thus, cable television audiences have existing opinions on issues and candidates that are difficult to change. Overall, then, reinforcement may be as common as persuasion on television.

Participation

Another potential effect of political ads on television is on political participation. Participation is not only good for democracy but also good for candidates who mobilize their supporters and bring them to the voting booth. Some scholars have suggested that political ads can have a positive effect on turnout because they can make viewers more attentive to what they lose or gain from elections (Freedman et al., 2004). Others suggest that ads can increase participation because they can help viewers learn about the candidates. This new knowledge, in turn, allows them to make quicker decisions about whom to vote for, reducing the costs of voting (Ridout & Holland, 2017).

Whether television advertising, taken as a whole, affects citizen participation is a related, but separate, question from whether negative ads, in particular, have a distinct impact on electoral participation. There is a long-standing debate about whether exposure to negativity demobilizes the electorate, as famously argued by Ansolabehere and Iyengar (1995). Certainly, the idea that exposure to politicians' attacking each other could turn off voters is intuitive, and it also might expose people to reasons not to like specific politicians, reducing the benefits of voting for them. But not all subsequent research has supported the demobilization hypothesis, and some research has concluded that negative advertising stimulates turnout (Goldstein & Freedman, 2002). The idea that exposure to negativity might give people a participatory boost also makes sense given Martin's (2004) findings that negativity – which exposes people to potential problems facing the country – can boost one's sense of duty, increase perceptions of threat (and thus anxiety), and lead one to perceive that a race is close.

Weighing into this debate, Lau et al. (2007) conducted a metanalysis that incorporated 57 studies (some of which examined political advertising other than television). They conclude that negativity does not demobilize and even allow that "if anything, negative campaigning more frequently appears to have a slight mobilizing effect" (p. 1184).

Perhaps, then, the effect of negativity in campaign advertising is conditional. For instance, Krupnikov (2011, 2014) shows that negativity in campaign ads can demobilize, but that only occurs after the voter has decided for whom to vote and only after exposure to negativity about the selected candidate. In his study on the effect of negativity on turnout in Switzerland, Nai (2013) found that the impact of negativity depends on who is sponsoring the ad and whether the ad is supportive of the status quo or a policy change. Negative ads that come from parties that support the status quo result in boredom among viewers and thus aversion to politics. Thus, one should expect decreased turnout. But negative ads coming from challengers induce surprise and enthusiasm, increasing interest in politics and, in consequence, voter turnout.

Learning

Political ads also have the potential to contribute to viewers' knowledge of politics. First, although ads on television are usually around 30 seconds in length, most of them contain policy information (Fowler et al., 2016). Ads, then, have the potential to increase political knowledge. Some studies support this idea that greater exposure to political ads can lead to more interest in politics (Freedman et al., 2004) and, as a result, more knowledge about the candidates and their policies (Ridout et al., 2004). When it comes to the tone of advertising, Lau et al. (2007) conclude that negative ads are no better (or worse) than positive ads in affecting voters' knowledge.

Although scholars generally agree that political ads can increase knowledge regardless of their nature, this effect will not be equal for all viewers. Indeed, learning from ads can depend on the characteristics of viewers. Based on Zaller's (1992) theory of opinion building, one might expect that those who are less politically sophisticated will learn more from ads. However, Valentino et al. (2004) provide experimental evidence that, although viewers learn from ads regardless of prior knowledge, those with higher knowledge learn more because they can easily interpret the meaning of the ad. This could be due to the limitations of television ads, which are too short to provide much political context. Yet Freedman et al. (2004) argue the opposite, suggesting that political ads – because they are short, emotion-laden, and designed to be easy to understand – are more likely to improve interest, knowledge, and participation among those who are the least politically sophisticated.

Overall, research on the effects of political advertising is fairly positive about the role of television advertising in democratic politics and governance. At the very least, exposure to political advertising appears to have few, if any, ill effects on voter participation, appears to foster the acquisition of political knowledge, and the persuasive effects of advertising are small enough – and sufficiently conditional – so as to mitigate concerns about massive manipulation of the electorate. But there remains at least one concerning possibility: that political advertising on television has eroded the sorts of attitudes that are necessary for democracy to thrive. What, then, does research say about this possibility?

By and large, there is little evidence of the deleterious effects of political advertising. For instance, there is no relationship between long-term exposure to advertising (or negative advertising) and party polarization (Ridout et al., 2018). There are no negative effects of exposure to negative advertising on attitudes such as approval of Congress, feelings towards congressional leaders and both internal and external efficacy (Jackson et al., 2009). One study even finds a positive effect of exposure to advertising on political interest, with people watching more news programming after being exposed to political ads (Canen & Martin, 2023). While the research in this area is largely positive, there are some potentially concerning findings from the field of public health. For instance, exposure to greater numbers of television advertisements in the 2016 presidential campaign is associated with more diagnoses of anxiety (Niederdeppe et al., 2021) and increased worry about crime, at least among Republicans (Liu et al., 2023).

News Media

While we have explored the many ways in which exposure to political advertising on television might affect citizens' beliefs, attitudes, and behaviors, there is another way by which political advertising might have an impact: by influencing coverage by the news media. Roberts and McCombs (1994) find evidence of this "intermedia agenda setting" in the 1990 gubernatorial race in Texas, showing that the issue agenda of advertising is positively correlated with the issue agenda of subsequent news coverage.

Further evidence of this relationship is found in the 1996 US presidential race (Boyle, 2001), though research from Spain finds more evidence that the advertising agenda follows the news media's agenda, with the issue agenda on television news leading the issue agenda in television advertising (Lopez-Escobar et al., 1998).

Not only can the issues discussed in political advertising potentially influence the issues discussed by the news media, but specific political ads can drive coverage as well, at least in the US context. Political advertisements on television often serve as fodder for news coverage (Ridout & Smith, 2008), both on television and in newspapers (Fowler & Ridout, 2009). Negative ads, in particular, attract the attention of the news media (Fowler & Ridout, 2009; Geer, 2012). There is also some evidence that negative ads are privileged by the media in New Zealand as well, though not in the U.K. (Ridout & Walter, 2015b).

To summarize, the effects of exposure to televised political advertising on the voter are many, including persuasion and reinforcement; mobilization (and sometimes demobilization); and learning about the candidates, parties, and their issue position. Television advertising can also affect the way in which the news media cover campaigns, multiplying the impacts of that advertising.

Future of Television Advertising

At one point, almost all political advertising on television was distributed through broadcast (free-to-air) television, either nationally or to specific regions of a country served by certain broadcast television stations. But how television advertising is disseminated has evolved as well. In the United States, for instance, the options expanded to include placing ads on national cable networks and on local cable television. Placing an ad on national cable outlets allowed campaigns to target their ads at very specific audiences, such as conservatives watching Fox News. Local cable allowed campaigns to place their ads during commercial breaks on specific cable television programs and in fairly small geographic areas. These new venues for placing television ads allowed campaigns to use their advertising dollars more efficiently, aiming messages at particular audiences who were likely to be receptive and avoiding audiences who were not. The Bush campaign and Republican National Committee trialed this strategy in 2004, aiming television ads at programs that were watched by Republican base voters (Ridout et al., 2012).

While television advertising can still be used to reach a general audience, it can also be used to reach fairly specific audiences, defined by the specific channels and programs that they watch. For instance, in 2008, Barack Obama's campaign aimed relatively more of their ad dollars at programs watched by Black and Latino/a voters, including situation comedies with predominantly Black casts and Spanish-language programs, than did John McCain's campaign (Ridout et al., 2012).

More recently, campaigns have become interested in advertising through CTV (connected TV), which straddles the line between television and online advertising. Essentially, CTV refers to internet-connected televisions, whether a smart TV or a television connected through another device, such as a Roku device or an Xbox (Viant, 2020). Thus, a campaign can now deliver an advertisement to a television viewer through a streaming service, such as Hulu or Roku. The commercial firm, AdImpact, estimates that $1.08 billion was spent on CTV in the 2021–2022 election cycle in the United States, which represents 12% of total political ad spending (AdImpact, 2022). The importance of CTV is that it not only allows targeting of groups of voters, but it allows for targeting of messages to individual voters based on their demographic and other characteristics (Singer, 2022). The upshot, then, is that one of the biggest advantages that online advertising has over television advertising – the ability to precisely target – is reduced, if not eliminated, with CTV. Television as a platform for political advertising, it seems to us, is still very much relevant and will continue to be so.

What sorts of things, then, should future research consider? One possibility is more research on the effects of particular content elements in political advertisements. While the effect of an ad's tone is well-trod ground, there are other elements of content that could make a difference for the effectiveness of an ad, including visual elements (e.g., lighting, color and the presence of symbols) and aural elements (e.g., background music and the voiceover announcer). Scholars must expand the range of ad content features they examine.

At the same time, given the consensus that the effects of television advertising are conditional on the message, the recipient, and the context, we believe it will be important to examine the interaction of ad content features and characteristics of the recipients in multiple contexts. One example of this type of research is the study by Searles et al. (2020), which examines how the gender of the voiceover announcer, the gender stereotypes of the issue, and gender of the recipient work in tandem to influence the effectiveness of political ads.

Moreover, given the importance of online advertising today, campaigns surely want to know whether online ad campaigns can strengthen television ad campaigns – and vice versa. How should campaigns integrate their online and television ad branding and messaging for maximum impact?

Finally, as this review has made clear, the vast majority of studies in this area study advertisements created for US campaigns, and when they examine effects, they do so using US audiences. Clearly, there is room for research on political advertising in countries outside the United States – and room for studies of ad effectiveness that use audiences not based in the United States. Even more fruitful would be cross-national studies of political advertising on television, which would allow us to better understand how context matters for the content and effects of political advertising.

CONCLUSION

Election-related advertising on television has been around for at least 70 years, though the prominence of television advertising in campaigns – and the degree to which it is regulated – varies by country. Yet despite the growth of digital advertising, television remains important. Those who study television advertising distinguish it in many ways, including its tone, issue content, and emotional appeals. Exposure to television advertising can influence voters' choices at the ballot box, their decision to participate in politics, and how much they know about candidates, parties, and their policies. Television ads can also drive media coverage of political campaigns. Although television advertising may seem old fashioned, it is evolving in ways that allow it to be more targeted at specific types of voters and even individuals. The merging of television with digital continues.

This trend will have an impact both on those who study televised political advertising and campaign practitioners who rely on it to disseminate their messages. At one point, one could count on television being the dominant form of advertising in many places, with parties and candidates sending a broad message to a large audience. These were the conditions under which many of the effects of television advertising, such as persuasion and learning, were discovered. But as television advertising has become increasingly targeted to smaller segments of the population – and even to individual voters through connected TV – scholars are less likely to discover these broad impacts. But the possibility of more intense impacts of advertising, but only among carefully targeted segments of the population, may be more likely to occur. Thus, calculating the true impact of television advertising may require far more sophisticated research designs, and ones that incorporate measures of all the different forms of advertising to which audiences are exposed.

REFERENCES

Adgate, B. (2020, August 11). Kantar estimates 2020 election ads will cost $7 Billion. *Forbes*. https://www.forbes.com/sites/bradadgate/2020/08/11/2020-an-election-year-like-no-other/?sh=76179ab838d1. Accessed on March 18, 2023.

AdImpact. (2022, December 16). 2022 cycle in review. *AdImpact*. https://adimpact.com/2022-cycle-in-review/. Accessed on March 18, 2023.

Ansolabehere, S., & Iyengar, S. (1995). *Going negative: How attack ads shrink and polarize the electrote*. Free Press.

Arancibia, P. (1996, September 27). El cable sigue creciendo en la Argentina: La otra televisión. In *Clarín Digital: La otra televisión*. https://web.archive.org/web/20141223011446/http://edant.clarin.com/diario/96/09/27/cables.htm. Accessed on March 14, 2023.

Arceneaux, K., & Johnson, M. (2013). *Changing minds or changing channels? Partisan news in an age of choice*. University of Chicago Press.

Australian Communications and Media Authority. (2022, March). *Political and election matter guidelines*. ACMA. https://www.acma.gov.au/publications/2022-03/guide/political-and-election-matter-guidelines. Accessed on March 18, 2023.

Bode, L., Lassen, D. S., Kim, Y. M., Shah, D. V., Fowler, E. F., Ridout, T., & Franz, M. (2016). Coherent campaigns? Campaign broadcast and social messaging. *Online Information Review, 40*(5), 580–594. https://doi.org/10.1108/oir-11-2015-0348

Boyle, T. P. (2001). Intermedia agenda setting in the 1996 presidential election. *Journalism & Mass Communication Quarterly, 78*(1), 26–44. https://doi.org/10.1177/107769900107800103

Brader, T. (2006). *Campaigning for hearts and minds: How emotional appeals in political ads work*. University of Chicago Press.

Can, B. (2006). Persuading voters and political advertising in Turkey. In L. L. Kaid & C. Holtz-Bacha (Eds.), *The SAGE handbook of political advertising* (pp. 387–397). SAGE.

Canen, N., & Martin, G. J. (2023). How campaign ads stimulate political interest. *The Review of*

Economics and Statistics, *105*(2), 292–310. https://doi.org/10.1162/rest_a_01062

Conway, L. (2019). *Political advertising*. House of Commons Library Briefing. Paper 8673. https://researchbriefings.files.parliament.uk/documents/CBP-8673/CBP-8673.pdf

Coppock, A., Hill, S. J., & Vavreck, L. (2020). The small effects of political advertising are small regardless of context, message, sender, or receiver: Evidence from 59 real-time randomized experiments. *Science Advances*, *6*(36), eabc4046.

Dommett, K., & Power, S. (2019). The political economy of Facebook advertising: Election spending, regulation and targeting online. *The Political Quarterly*, *90*(2), 257–265. https://doi.org/10.1111/1467-923x.12687

Dowling, C. M., & Wichowsky, A. (2013). Does it matter who's behind the curtain? Anonymity in political advertising and the effects of campaign finance disclosure. *American Politics Research*, *41*(6), 965–996. https://doi.org/10.1177/1532673x13480828

Effectv. (2023). *The ultimate guide to reaching voters*. https://www.effectv.com/wp-content/uploads/2023/06/the-ultimate-guide-to-reaching-voters.pdf

Fatemi, F. (2022, November 15). How TV viewing habits have changed. *Forbes*. https://www.forbes.com/sites/falonfatemi/2022/11/14/how-tv-viewing-habits-have-changed/?sh=5e68de284888. Accessed on March 18, 2023.

Federal Communications Commission. (2002). *8th annual video competition report*. Retrieved June, 24, 2002.

Fowler, E. F., Franz, M. M., Martin, G. J., Peskowitz, Z., & Ridout, T. N. (2021). Political advertising online and offline. *American Political Science Review*, *115*(1), 130–149. https://doi.org/10.1017/s0003055420000696

Fowler, E. F., Franz, M. M., & Ridout, T. N. (2021). *Political advertising in the United States*. Routledge.

Fowler, E. F., & Ridout, T. N. (2009). Local television and newspaper coverage of political advertising. *Political Communication*, *26*(2), 119–136. https://doi.org/10.1080/10584600902850635

Fowler, E. F., Ridout, T., & Franz, M. (2016). Political advertising in 2016: The presidential election as outlier? *The Forum*, *14*(4), 445–469. https://doi.org/10.1515/for-2016-0040

Franz, M. M., Fowler, E. F., Ridout, T., & Wang, M. Y. (2020). The issue focus of online and television advertising in the 2016 Presidential Campaign. *American Politics Research*, *48*(1), 175–196. https://doi.org/10.1177/1532673x19875722

Franz, M. M., & Ridout, T. N. (2007). Does political advertising persuade? *Political Behavior*, *29*, 465–491. https://doi.org/10.1007/s11109-007-9032-y

Franz, M. M., Ridout, T. N., & Fowler, E. F. (2023). Television advertising in the 2022 midterms. *The Forum*. https://doi.org/10.1515/for-2023-2005

Freedman, P., Franz, M., & Goldstein, K. (2004). Campaign advertising and democratic citizenship. *American Journal of Political Science*, *48*(4), 723–741.

Geer, J. G. (2008). *In defense of negativity: Attack ads in presidential campaigns*. University of Chicago Press.

Geer, J. G. (2012). The news media and the rise of negativity in presidential campaigns. *PS: Political Science & Politics*, *45*(3), 422–427. https://doi.org/10.1017/s1049096512000492

Gerber, A. S., Gimpel, J. G., Green, D. P., & Shaw, D. R. (2011). How large and long-lasting are the persuasive effects of televised campaign ads? Results from a randomized field experiment. *American Political Science Review*, *105*(1), 135–150. http://www.jstor.org/stable/41480831

Goldstein, K., & Freedman, P. (2002). Campaign advertising and voter turnout: New evidence for a stimulation effect. *The Journal of Politics*, *64*(3), 721–740. https://doi.org/10.1111/0022-3816.00143

Hill, S. J., Lo, J., Vavreck, L., & Zaller, J. (2013). How quickly we forget: The duration of persuasion effects from mass communication. *Political Communication*, *30*(4), 521–547.

Holman, M. R., Schneider, M. C., & Pondel, K. (2015). Gender targeting in political advertisements. *Political Research Quarterly*, *68*(4), 816–829. http://www.jstor.org/stable/24637818

Holtz-Bacha, C. (2006). Political advertising in Germany. In L. L. Kaid, & C. Holtz-Bacha (Eds.), *The SAGE handbook of political advertising* (pp. 163–180). SAGE.

Holtz-Bacha, C., & Kaid, L. L. (2006). Political advertising in international comparison. In L. L. Kaid, & C. Holtz-Bacha (Eds.), *The SAGE handbook of political advertising* (pp. 3–13). SAGE.

Huber, G. A., & Arceneaux, K. (2007). Identifying the persuasive effects of presidential advertising. *American Journal of Political Science*, *51*(4), 957–977. https://doi.org/10.1111/j.1540-5907.2007.00291.x

Hughes, A. (2019, May 1). Facebook videos, targeted texts and Clive Palmer memes: How digital advertising is shaping this election campaign. *The Conversation*. https://theconversation.com/facebook-videos-targeted-texts-and-clive-palmer-memes-how-digital-advertising-is-shaping-this-election-campaign-115629. Accessed on March 18, 2023.

Jackson, R. A., Mondak, J. J., & Huckfeldt, R. (2009). Examining the possible corrosive impact of negative advertising on citizens' attitudes toward politics. *Political Research Quarterly*, *62*(1), 55–69. https://doi.org/10.1177/1065912908317031

Jamieson, K. H., Waldman, P., & Sherr, S. (2000). Eliminate the negative? Categories of analysis for political advertisements. In J. A. Thurber, C. J. Nelson, & D. A. Dulio (Eds.), *Crowded airwaves*

campaign advertising in elections (pp. 44–64). Brookings Institution Press.
Kahn, K. F. (1993). Gender differences in campaign messages: The political advertisements of men and women candidates for US senate. *Political Research Quarterly*, *46*(3), 481–502. https://doi.org/10.1177/106591299304600303
Kahn, K. F., & Kenney, P. J. (1999). Do negative campaigns mobilize or suppress turnout? Clarifying the relationship between negativity and participation. *American Political Science Review*, *93*(4), 877–889. https://doi.org/10.2307/2586118
Kaid, L. L., & Gagnère, N. (2006). Election broadcast in France. In L. L. Kaid & C. Holtz-Bacha (Eds.), *The SAGE handbook of political advertising* (pp. 83–96). SAGE.
Kaid, L. L., & Holtz-Bacha, C. (2006). Television advertising and democratic systems around the world: A comparison of videostyle content and effects. In *The SAGE handbook of political advertising* (pp. 445–458). SAGE.
Kaid, L. L., & Johnston, A. (2001). *Videostyle in presidential campaigns: Style and content of televised political advertising*. Greenwood Publishing Group.
Krupnikov, Y. (2011). When does negativity demobilize? Tracing the conditional effect of negative campaigning on voter turnout. *American Journal of Political Science*, *55*(4), 797–813. https://doi.org/10.1111/j.1540-5907.2011.00522.x
Krupnikov, Y. (2014). How negativity can increase and decrease voter turnout: The effect of timing. *Political Communication*, *31*(3), 446–466. https://doi.org/10.1080/10584609.2013.828141
Lau, R. R., Sigelman, L., & Rovner, I. B. (2007). The effects of negative political campaigns: A meta-analytic reassessment. *The Journal of Politics*, *69*(4), 1176–1209. https://doi.org/10.1111/j.1468-2508.2007.00618.x
Lipsitz, K., & Geer, J. G. (2017). Rethinking the concept of negativity: An empirical approach. *Political Research Quarterly*, *70*(3), 577–589. https://doi.org/10.1177/1065912917706547
Liu, Y. (1994). The development of cable television in China and Taiwan. *Jurnal Komunikasi*, *10*, 137–156.
Liu, J., Avery, R. J., Fowler, E. F., Baum, L., Gollust, S. E., Barry, C. L., Welch, B., Tabor, E., Lee, N. W., & Niederdeppe, J. (2023). Campaign advertising and the cultivation of crime worry: Testing relationships with two large datasets from the 2016 US election cycle. *The International Journal of Press/Politics*, *28*(1), 70–91. https://doi.org/10.1177/19401612211020929
Lodge, M., & Taber, C. S. (2013). *The rationalizing voter*. Cambridge University Press.
Lopez-Escobar, E., Llamas, J. P., McCombs, M., & Lennon, F. R. (1998). Two levels of agenda setting among advertising and news in the 1995 Spanish elections. *Political Communication*, *15*(2), 225–238. https://doi.org/10.1080/10584609809342367
Mann, R. (2011). *Daisy Petals and mushroom clouds: LBJ, Barry Goldwater, and the ad that changed American politics*. Louisiana State University Press.
Martin, P. S. (2004). Inside the black box of negative campaign effects: Three reasons why negative campaigns mobilize. *Political Psychology*. *25*(4), 545–562. https://doi.org/10.1111/j.1467-9221.2004.00386.x
Mendelberg, T. (1997). Executing Hortons: Racial crime in the 1988 presidential campaign. *The Public Opinion Quarterly*, *61*(1), 134–157. http://www.jstor.org/stable/2749515
Motta, M. P., & Fowler, E. F. (2016). *The content and effect of political advertising in US campaigns*. Oxford Research Encyclopedia of Politics. https://doi.org/10.1093/acrefore/9780190228637.013.217
Museum of the Moving Image. (2023). *1972 Nixon Vs. McGovern*. http://www.livingroomcandidate.org/commercials/1972. Accessed on March 15, 2023.
Nai, A. (2013). What really matters is which camp goes dirty: Differential effects of negative campaigning on turnout during Swiss Federal Ballots. *European Journal of Political Research*, *52*(1), 44–70. https://doi.org/10.1111/j.1475-6765.2012.02060.x
Niederdeppe, J., Avery, R. J., Liu, J., Gollust, S. E., Baum, L., Barry, C. L., Welch, B., Tabor, E., Lee, N. W., & Fowler, E. F. (2021). Exposure to televised political campaign advertisements aired in the United States 2015–2016 election cycle and psychological distress. *Social Science & Medicine*, *277*, 113898. https://doi.org/10.1016/j.socscimed.2021.113898
Pallister, K., & Fitzpatrick, E. (2023). The medium and the message in Argentina's presidential campaigns. *The International Journal of Press/Politics*. https://doi.org/10.1177/19401612221149272
Passwaiter, S. (2020, November 23). Political ad spending this year reached a whopping $8.5 billion. *Ad Age*. https://adage.com/article/campaign-trail/political-ad-spending-year-reached-whopping-85-billion/2295646. Accessed on March 18, 2023.
Perez, S. (2022, July 12). YouTube TV now has topped 5 million subscribers and 'trialers', says google. *TechCrunch*. https://techcrunch.com/2022/07/12/youtube-tv-now-has-topped-5-million-subscribers-and-trialers-says-google/. Accessed on March 14, 2023.
Pew Research Center. (2020, July 30). Americans who mainly get their news on social media are less engaged, less knowledgeable. https://www.pewresearch.org/journalism/2020/07/30/americans-who-mainly-get-their-news-on-social-media-are-less-engaged-less-/. Accessed on March 14, 2023.
Putnam, R. (2000). *Bowling alone: The collapse and revival of American community*. Simon & Schuster.
Rabson, M. (2020, June 23). TV, online ads, take Lion's share of party election spending, new reports show.

CTV News. https://www.ctvnews.ca/politics/tv-online-ads-take-lion-s-share-of-party-election-spending-new-reports-show-1.4996155. Accessed on March 18, 2023.

Ridout, T. N. (2020). *Negotiating goals and return: Political campaigns' ad spending on digital and social media platforms*. Working paper. https://labs.wsu.edu/ridout/sample-page/research/

Ridout, T. N., Fowler, E. F., & Franz, M. M. (2021). Spending fast and furious: Political advertising in 2020. *The Forum*, *18*(4), 465–492. https://doi.org/10.1515/for-2020-2109

Ridout, T. N., Franklin Fowler, E., Franz, M. M., & Goldstein, K. (2018). The long-term and geographically constrained effects of campaign advertising on political polarization and sorting. *American Politics Research*, *46*(1), 3–25. https://doi.org/10.1177/1532673x17721479

Ridout, T. N., & Franz, M. M. (2011). *The persuasive power of campaign advertising*. Temple University Press.

Ridout, T. N., Franz, M., Goldstein, K. M., & Feltus, W. J. (2012). Separation by television program: Understanding the targeting of political advertising in presidential elections. *Political Communication*, *29*(1), 1–23. https://doi.org/10.1080/10584609.2011.619509

Ridout, T. N., & Holland, J. L. (2017). The effects of political advertising. In C. Holtz-Bacha & M. R. Just (Eds.), *Routledge handbook of political advertising* (1st ed., pp. 61–72). Routledge.

Ridout, T. N., & Searles, K. (2011). It's my campaign I'll cry if I want to: How and when campaigns use emotional appeals. *Political Psychology*, *32*(3), 439–458. https://doi.org/10.1111/j.1467-9221.2010.00819.x

Ridout, T. N., Shah, D. V., Goldstein, K. M., & Franz, M. M. (2004). Evaluating measures of campaign advertising exposure on political learning. *Political Behavior*, *26*(3), 201–225. https://doi.org/10.1023/b:pobe.0000043453.96025.a8

Ridout, T. N., & Smith, G. R. (2008). Free advertising: How the media amplify campaign messages. *Political Research Quarterly*, *61*(4), 598–608. https://doi.org/10.1177/1065912908314202

Ridout, T. N., & Walter, A. S. (2015). Party system change and negative campaigning in New Zealand. *Party Politics*, *21*(6), 982–992. https://doi.org/10.1177/1354068813509522

Ridout, T. N., & Walter, A. S. (2015a). How the news media amplify negative messages. In A. Nai & A. S. Walter (Eds.), *New perspectives on negative campaigning: Why attack politics matters* (pp. 267–286). ECPR Press.

Roberts, M., & Mccombs, M. (1994). Agenda setting and political advertising: Origins of the news agenda. *Political Communication*, *11*(3), 249–262. https://doi.org/10.1080/10584609.1994.9963030

Sabha, L. (1995). *The cable television networks (regulation) Act, 1995 (7 of 1995)*. https://www.casemine.com/act/in/5a979d9b4a93263ca60b7115#5a979d9b4a93263-ca60b7115. Accessed on March 14, 2023.

Sapiro, V., Cramer Walsh, K., Strach, P., & Hennings, V. (2011). Gender, context, and television advertising: A comprehensive analysis of 2000 and 2002 House races. *Political Research Quarterly*, *64*(1), 107–119. https://doi.org/10.1177/1065912909343583

Searles, K., Fowler, E. F., Ridout, T. N., Strach, P., & Zuber, K. (2020). The effects of men's and women's voices in political advertising. *Journal of Political Marketing*, *19*(3), 301–329. https://doi.org/10.1080/15377857.2017.1330723

Secretary, Ministry of Information and Broadcasting V. Gemini TV (P) Ltd. and Others, Laws(SC)-2004-4-172 Casemine (No. 6679 April 13, 2004). https://www.casemine.com/judgement/in/581181042713e179479eba3d. Accessed on March 14, 2023.

Sides, J., Vavreck, L., & Warshaw, C. (2022). The effect of television advertising in United States elections. *American Political Science Review*, *116*(2), 702–718. https://doi.org/10.1017/S000305542100112X

Singer, N. (2022, September 15). This ad's for you (not your neighbor). *The New York Times*. https://www.nytimes.com/2022/09/15/business/custom-political-ads.html. Accessed on March 18, 2023.

Spenkuch, J. L., & Toniatti, D. (2018). Political Advertising and election results. *The Quarterly Journal of Economics*, *133*(4), 1981–2036. https://doi.org/10.1093/qje/qjy010

Stroud, N. J., & Muddiman, A. (2019). The American media system today: Is the public fragmenting? In T. N. Ridout (Ed.), *New directions in media and politics* (2nd ed., pp. 7–28). Routledge.

Tak, J. (2006). Political advertising in Japan, South Korea, and Taiwan. In L. L. Kaid & C. Holtz-Bacha (Eds.), *The SAGE handbook of political advertising* (pp. 285–305). SAGE.

Valentino, N. A., Hutchings, V. L., & White, I. K. (2002). Cues that matter: How political ads prime racial attitudes during campaigns. *American Political Science Review*, *96*(1), 75–90. http://www.jstor.org/stable/3117811

Valentino, N. A., Hutchings, V. L., & Williams, D. (2004). The impact of political advertising on knowledge, internet information seeking, and candidate preference. *Journal of Communication*, *54*(2), 337–354. https://doi.org/10.1111/j.1460-2466.2004.tb02632.x

Viant. (2020, August 11). OTT vs. CTV Advertising: What's the difference? *Viant Technology LLC*. https://www.viantinc.com/insights/blog/ott-vs-ctv-advertising-whats-the-difference/. Accessed on March 18, 2023.

Walter, A. S. (2014). Negative campaigning in Western Europe: Similar or different? *Political Studies*, *62*(1_suppl), 42–60. https://doi.org/10.1111/1467-9248.12084

Walter, A. S., & Van der Brug, W. (2013). When the gloves come off: Inter-party variation in negative campaigning in Dutch elections, 1981–2010. *Acta Politica*, *48*(4), 367–388. https://doi.org/10.1057/ap.2013.5

Walter, A. S., & Vliegenthart, R. (2010). Negative campaigning across different communication channels: Different ball games? *The International Journal of Press/Politics*, *15*(4), 441–461. https://doi.org/10.1177/1940161210374122

Weber, C., Dunaway, J., & Johnson, T. (2012). It's all in the name: Source cue ambiguity and the persuasive appeal of campaign ads. *Political Behavior*, *34*(3), 561–584. https://doi.org/10.1007/s11109-011-9172-y

Wittenberg, C., Tappin, B. M., Berinsky, A., & Rand, D. G. (2021). The (minimal) persuasive advantage of political video over text. *Proceedings of the National Academy of Sciences*, *118*(47), e2114388118. https://doi.org/10.31234/osf.io/r5yun

Zaller, J. R. (1992). *The nature and origins of mass opinion*. Cambridge University Press.

Social Media Content in the Turkish Presidential Elections: A Functional Theory of Political Campaign Discourse Perspective

Gözde Akdeniz, Birce Dobrucalı Yelkenci and Burcu İlter

INTRODUCTION

Political communication is a persuasive process involving the exchange of political messages (Lock & Harris, 1996, p. 25). Political parties and candidates endeavor to persuade voters by presenting their ideologies and promises through political campaign messages. The ruling party, through political communication efforts, seeks to convince voters that choosing them is a wise decision, while opposition parties strive to persuade voters that electing them in future elections would be a prudent choice (Popkin, 1994). Political campaign communication generally encompasses elements similar to communication processes. During the election process, a political party or candidate conveys a persuasive political campaign message to their target audience, that is, the electorate, through a specific channel. Voters, in turn, receive and process these messages, expressing their feedback through voting or abstaining from voting behavior (Dudek & Partacz, 2009).

According to McNair (2017, p. 6), the components of political communication consist of political actors, the media, and citizens. Political actors convey their political messages to the media and the public through discourse, party programs, advertising campaigns, and public relations. Political actors disseminate messages via diverse campaign tools like advertisements, speeches, and social media, with the latter gaining prominence due to accessibility and real-time engagement (Broersma & Graham, 2013; Papacharissi & de Fatima Oliveira, 2012). Voters engage through televised debates, rallies, and social media aligned with their ideologies.

As a result, voters can engage with political discourse by watching televised debates, following statements given to the press, or attending rallies. Additionally, by tracking the social media accounts of political parties and candidates, voters can gather information and support a party or candidate whose ideological views align with their own. Furthermore, social media allows for the observation of comments and reactions from other voters and experts regarding political campaign messages. In its entirety, social media serves as a strategic communication tool that brings together voters and political campaign messages (Kreiss & McGregor, 2018; Barlas, 2018).

The effectiveness of political campaigns relies not only on message frequency and medium but also on content. Literature scrutinizes message content regarding nature, tone, type, and language structure (Benoit et al., 2011; Bischof & Senninger, 2018; Painter & Rizzo, 2017; Zhang et al., 2017). Critical discourse analysis has been employed to explore the unhighlighted social and political messages beyond the given political campaign message and their impact on voters (Mirzaei et al., 2017; Sriwimon & Zilli, 2017). Additionally, studies in the examination of political campaign messages have been based on Aristotle's Rhetoric Theory and Benoit's Image Repair Theory, along with the Functional Theory of Political Campaign Discourse (Banavand, 2020; Boukala & Dimitrakopoulou, 2017; Dudek & Partacz, 2009; Sheldon & Sallot, 2008; Waymer & Hill, 2023).

The Functional Theory of Political Campaign Discourse examines the political campaign messages according to their functions (acclaim, attack, and defense) and topics (character and policy) (Benoit, 1997). In that way, political campaign discourse strategies can be developed and analyzed, and it shows how candidates differentiate themselves (Benoit, 2003). Within the scope of this study, posts shared by the ruling party leader, President Recep Tayyip Erdoğan, and the opposition party leader, Kemal Kılıçdaroğlu, during the 2023 Presidential elections via their official X accounts were analyzed using the content analysis method in light of the Functional Theory of Political Campaign Discourse. This study represents a novel endeavor aimed at scrutinizing the political campaign dialogues of Turkish politicians on the X platform. The main contributions of this paper can be summarized as follows: Firstly, the utilization of a systematic content analysis methodology that objectively organizes and categorizes the content enables subsequent qualitative interpretation. Secondly, an exploration of the overarching discourse propagated by the two primary candidates via the X platform during the electoral campaign in Türkiye's 2023 presidential election was conducted, delving into the underlying themes and tonalities. Thirdly, a comparative analysis of the political discourses disseminated by these candidates was undertaken. By applying Benoit's Functional Theory, this study not only contextualizes Turkish political discourse within a broader theoretical framework but also provides a detailed empirical analysis that enhances our understanding of the strategic use of social media in contemporary political campaigns. The findings underscore the significance of understanding the functions of acclaim, attack, and defense in shaping voter perceptions and engagement, illustrating how strategic communication via social media platforms can influence electoral outcomes.

FUNCTIONAL THEORY OF POLITICAL CAMPAIGN DISCOURSE

This study will employ Benoit's Functional Theory of Political Campaign Discourse, which provides a framework for analyzing election campaign messages (Benoit, 2017). According to this theory, candidates differentiate themselves from their competitors through political campaign messages. In doing so, they attempt to persuade voters by employing messages that acclaim or defend themselves; or attack their opponents' policies or characters. Voters, in turn, compare and evaluate the political campaign messages of candidates to decide which is more preferable (Benoit, 2003, 2007). In summary, the Functional Theory of Political Campaign Discourse examines politicians' messages during the election period based on their functions (acclaim, attack, defense) or topics (policy, character) (Benoit, 1997, 1999).

In messages containing acclaim, the strong aspects of the party, the candidate, and party policies are lauded. This type of message content is generally the most commonly used (Benoit, 2007). The purpose of messages with acclaim content is to highlight the candidate's strengths and qualities, emphasizing the positive actions they have taken or will undertake (Benoit, 2017; Benoit et al., 1997; Henson & Benoit, 2010).

In messages containing attacks, a political candidate endeavors to expose the weaknesses of their opponent(s) using aggressive language, holding them responsible for undesirable, unlawful, or harmful actions to the electorate. Thus, the goal is to create a perception that the opposing candidate is an undesirable political leader, leading voters to view the candidate as less trustworthy and refrain from voting for them (Benoit et al., 1997; Benoit & Goode, 2006). In these messages, it is common to criticize the policies of the opposing candidate more than their character. However, the use of attack content in political campaign messages is highly risky. This is because messages with attack content can be interpreted by voters as "mudslinging" and may bring them closer to the opposing candidate (Benoit, 1999; Merritt, 1984).

In messages containing defense, accusations against the party or candidate are refuted (Benoit, 2007). The use of defensive content in political discourse is infrequent (Benoit et al., 1997). This is because the deployment of defensive political campaign messages can create a reactive image in front of voters and is not a desired situation where the potential weaknesses of the candidate are detailed and exposed to the electorate. Therefore, candidates often prefer attacking each other's vulnerabilities rather than engaging in a defensive discourse. Additionally, constructing a political discourse based on self-defense by the candidate may divert attention from the messages they need to convey to convince voters. However, it is known that responding to an opponent's attack message with an immediate defensive message does not create a perception of weakness in the eyes of the voters (Benoit, 2010, 2017). A candidate exposed to attack messages from the opposing candidate aims to improve their tarnished image and defend themselves by demonstrating that the accusations are unfounded (Benoit, 2017). The candidate defends themselves by contradicting, apologizing, or being accountable (Benoit, 2001; Benoit & Goode, 2006; Henson & Benoit, 2010).

In conclusion, if messages containing acclaim are perceived and accepted by voters, it is likely that the candidate will be perceived more positively. If messages with attack content are convincing enough, they can lead to a more negative perception of the opposing candidate. Messages containing defense are expected to reduce the perceived cost for the defending candidate and restore or even enhance the candidate's former appeal (Benoit, 2017; Benoit & Goode, 2006; Choi & Benoit, 2009). In most studies, various researchers have found that currently serving political leaders tend to share more messages with acclaim content (54% acclaim, 46% attack) regarding actions taken during their tenure, while opposition leaders tend to share more messages with attack content (55% attack, 44% acclaim, 1% defense) (Benoit et al., 1997).

According to the Functional Theory of Political Campaign Discourse, the content of a political message can also be considered in terms of its subject matter. The topics of political campaign messages are primarily divided into two groups: the character of the candidate and their policies (Benoit et al., 1997). Messages related to the character of the candidate can be conveyed through personal qualities, leadership skills, and ideals. Messages concerning the candidate's policies, on the other hand, are shaped around the candidate's past deeds, future goals, and general goals.

The character of the candidate is explained within the framework of their personal qualities, leadership ability, and ideals (Brazeal & Benoit, 2001). When evaluating the candidate's personal qualities, four key attributes are considered: sincerity, morality, empathy, and drive, in addition to private work experience. Sincerity includes traits such as trust, honesty, consistency, and openness; morality encompasses decency, integrity, responsibility, and fairness; empathy involves understanding, similarity to the voter, advocating for the voter, and compassion; while drive entails courage, diligence, strength, and determination (Benoit, 2017, p. 22).

Leadership ability is assessed by considering the candidate's skills and qualifications, especially taking into account any previous experience in a government position (Benoit, 2017; Benoit & Goode, 2006). At this point, private work experience is more closely associated with personal qualities, while leadership abilities are predominantly explained by governmental experience (Banavand, 2020). The ideals of the candidate consist of principles and values such as democracy, peace, and freedom (Benoit, 2017; Benoit & Goode, 2006).

Political campaign messages reflecting the candidate's policies can be about past deeds, future goals, or general goals. When it comes to past deeds and policies, candidates emphasize their own achievements while highlighting the failures of the opposing candidate (Brazeal & Benoit, 2001). In messages concerning future goals, candidates make promises about the future, articulating projects they are working on and improvements they plan to implement (Benoit, 2017; Benoit & Goode, 2006). Although political messages conveying general goals share similarities with political messages containing future goals, the latter are more specific due to the nature of the improvements planned (Benoit, 2017; Benoit & Goode, 2006). Leaders tend to use messages related to political themes more frequently than messages related to character themes in their political discourse (Benoit et al., 1997). Additionally, with some exceptions, it is generally known that the political messages of an incumbent political leader often revolve around their own policies, while an opposing political leader tends to focus more on personality traits (Benoit et al., 1997).

Finally, the candidate's policy influences the perceived personal characteristics of the candidate, and the perceived personal characteristics of the candidate also affect their policies. Therefore, the concepts of the candidate's character and policies expressed in political discourse are not completely separate from each other and are not mutually exclusive; they influence each other (Benoit, 1999).

Benoit et al. (1997) have reached significant findings from the combination of functions and topics of political campaign discourse messages. Messages containing acclaim and attack are frequently used to highlight or criticize both policies and personality traits. Incumbent political authorities often attempt to weaken the image of their opponents by criticizing their policies more than their character using messages with attack content. In doing so, they also emphasize their own character traits such as presidential qualities and leadership. Political candidates, on the other hand, tend to engage more in political discourse with attack content, focusing on each other's past deeds. This is because it is easier to criticize the past deeds of the opposing candidate than to criticize their current general goals.

In addition to the findings of Benoit, existing literature also provides support and, in some cases, a new perspective to this theory. The political campaign messages in the 2007 parliamentary elections in Poland were compared with data from the United States and Israel and, results suggested that political messages with negative content may take precedence contrary to prevailing assumptions. (Dudek & Partacz, 2009). Additionally, the analysis of political messages during the televised debate program in the 2006 presidential election campaign in Finland also highlighted the prevalence of defense-oriented messages (Isotalus, 2011). It was found that the majority of messages delivered by political candidates during the televised debate program consisted of defense (35%), followed by attack (28%) and acclaim (16%). Political candidates tended to disseminate more campaign messages on policy topics compared to character-related topics. Regarding policy topics, they predominantly discussed general goals (43%), followed by past deeds (26%) and future goals (18%). Candidates aimed to convey campaign messages primarily about their personal qualities (45%), followed by their leadership abilities (22%) to the electorate.

BACKGROUND OF 2023 PRESIDENTIAL ELECTIONS IN TÜRKİYE

In this section, the political atmosphere in Türkiye is examined, providing information on the form of governance, party groupings in the Grand National Assembly of Türkiye (TBMM), types of elections, and recent election results. In Türkiye, citizens periodically go to the polls for local elections, general elections, by-elections, and referendums. In local elections, officials of local and municipal administrations are elected, including mayors, metropolitan mayors, municipal council members, provincial council members, headman of the neighborhood and villages, and council of elders who support the headman in the neighborhood and villages. In general elections, citizens vote for members of parliament. A member of parliament is a representative elected by the public to the legislative council (Türk, 2006).

The Grand National Assembly of Türkiye (TBMM) has legislative, oversight, and representational functions. Until 2017, it was also responsible for government formation and ministerial appointments. However, the Constitutional Referendum on 16 April 2017, caused the downfall of the parliamentary system in favor of a presidential one. This landscape change abolished the prime ministerial position and consolidated executive power under the President. Furthermore, barriers hindering political party members from assuming the presidency were dismantled. Consequently, the prerogatives of appointing ministers and establishing the government transitioned from the TBMM to the President (Öztürk, 2018). Ratified by 51.41% of the populace, this constitutional amendment took effect on 9 July 2018, cementing Türkiye's current presidential governance model. President Recep Tayyip Erdoğan occupies the dual role of head of state and government, alongside his leadership of the Justice and Development Party (AK Party) (BBC News Türkçe, 2017).

In the Parliamentary General Elections of 2002, 2007, and 2011, the AK Party ascended to power unilaterally, clinching a decisive majority in parliament (Supreme Election Council of the Republic of Türkiye, 2024b, 2024c, 2024d). Notably, on 28 August 2007, Abdullah Gül assumed the presidency for a seven-year term following endorsement by the TBMM (Deutsche Welle, 2007). In the Constitutional Referendum held on 21 October 2007, it was decided that the President would be elected by the citizens. Thus, the presidential office, which was previously elected by the parliament for a single term of seven years, began to be elected by the public, with the term reduced to five years and a limit of two terms for any individual to become president (Official Gazette of the Republic of Türkiye, 2007). Alongside the general elections, the AK Party continued its success in local elections as well. The AK Party achieved success as the leading party in the 2009 and 2014 local elections (Supreme Election Council of the Republic of Türkiye, 2024e, 2024f).

By the year 2014, the term of office of Abdullah Gül, who was appointed in 2007, had expired. Following his appointment, the referendum of 2007 decided, with a majority of 68.95%, that the next president would be elected by the public (Supreme Election Council of the Republic of Türkiye, 2024g). Therefore, in 2014, citizens went to the polls for the Presidential election. The candidates were Recep Tayyip Erdoğan, Ekmeleddin İhsanoğlu, and Selahattin Demirtaş. The ruling party at the time, the AK Party, supported Recep Tayyip Erdoğan, while opposition parties such as the Republican People's Party (CHP), Nationalist Movement Party (MHP), Grand Unity Party (BBP), Democratic Party (DP), Democratic Left Party (DSP), among others, supported Ekmeleddin İhsanoğlu. Political parties like the Labor Party, and People's Democratic Party (HDP), among others, declared their support for Selahattin Demirtaş (Euronews, 2014). The election results showed the following vote percentages for the candidates: Recep Tayyip Erdoğan 51.79%, Ekmeleddin İhsanoğlu 38.44%, and Selahattin Demirtaş 9.79% (Supreme Election Council of the Republic of Türkiye, 2024h). In the general elections of 7 June 2015, the AK Party won 258 seats, the CHP won 132 seats, while the MHP and HDP won a combined total of 80 seats in the parliament. However, during that period, in order for a political party to be able to govern independently and form a government, it was required to have at least 276 seats. Therefore, the AK Party engaged in coalition negotiations with opposition parties, but consensus could not be reached. As a result, snap elections were held on 1 November 2015 (Supreme Election Council of the Republic of Türkiye, 2024i).

On 24 June 2018, both the Presidential Election and the 27th Term Parliamentary General Election were held in Türkiye. Prior to these elections, changes were made to the election law to allow political parties to form alliances. Consequently, voters encountered the People's Alliance and the Nation Alliance for the first time in the 2018 general and presidential elections. The People's Alliance was formed between the AK Party and the MHP in February 2018 (Sözcü, 2018). Later, the BBP and the Yeniden Refah Party (YRP) also joined the alliance (Diken, 2022). The Free Cause Party (HÜDA PAR) and DSP also announced their support for the AK Party. The Nation Alliance, on the other hand, was formed in May 2018 and consisted of the CHP, İYİ Party, Felicity Party (SAADET), and the Democracy and Progress Party (DEVA) later joined by the Future Party (GP) (BBC News, 2018a).

On 24 June 2018, the People's Alliance announced only a single candidate for the presidential election – Recep Tayyip Erdoğan – while the Nation Alliance preferred having multiple candidates as Muharrem İnce (CHP), Meral Akşener (İYİ Party), and Temel Karamollaoğlu (Felicity Party). Thus, while the Nation Alliance cooperated in parliamentary elections, they presented separate candidates for the presidential race. Additionally, Doğu Perinçek (Homeland Party-VP) and Selahattin Demirtaş (HDP) were other presidential candidates outside of the alliances. As a result, Recep Tayyip Erdoğan was re-elected as President for the second time, receiving 52.59% of the votes. The vote percentages for the other candidates were as follows: Muharrem İnce (30.64%), Selahattin Demirtaş (8.40%), Meral Akşener (7.29%), Temel Karamollaoğlu (0.89%), and Doğu Perinçek (0.20%) (Supreme Election Council of the Republic of Türkiye, 2024j).

In the general elections held on 24 June 2018, the AK Party obtained 295 seats in the parliament with a vote share of 42.56%. The CHP secured 146 seats with a vote share of 22.65%, while the HDP won 67 seats with a vote share of 11.70%. The MHP gained 49 seats with a vote share of 11%, and the İYİ Party obtained 43 seats with a vote share of 9.96%. However, since the AK Party did not secure a majority in the Grand National Assembly of Türkiye (TBMM), consisting of a total of 600 seats, it formed an alliance with the MHP and the BBP (BBC News, 2018b).

In the local elections held on 31 March 2019, the AK Party emerged as the first party with the highest vote share, obtaining 44.33% of the votes, while the CHP became the second party with the highest vote share, securing 30.12% of the votes. The alliances formed in 2018, namely, the People's Alliance and the Nation Alliance, were continued in this election (Congar, 2019). However, parties that were part of the Nation Alliance in the general elections separated from the alliance, leaving only the CHP and the İYİ Party in the alliance. In terms of alliances, the People's Alliance received a total of 51.64% of the votes, while the Nation Alliance received 37.57% of the votes (Supreme Election Council of the Republic of Türkiye, 2024k). In Istanbul specifically, due to appeals, the elections were rerun on 23 June 2019, and the candidate of the CHP once again won the election (CNN Türk, 2019).

On 28 May 2023, the Presidential Election and the 28th Term Parliamentary General Election took place. Members of parliament were elected in the first round held on 14 May 2023. However, as no candidate received over 50% + 1 of the votes, the Presidential Election proceeded to a second round scheduled for 28 May 2023. In the first round of presidential elections, four candidates competed, and their vote percentages are as follows: Recep Tayyip Erdoğan 49.52%, Kemal Kılıçdaroğlu 44.88%, Sinan Oğan 5.17%, and Muharrem İnce 0.43%. In the second round of the Presidential Election, the number of candidates decreased to two, leading to a competition between Recep Tayyip Erdoğan and Kemal Kılıçdaroğlu. As a result, Recep Tayyip Erdoğan won with a vote share of 52.18%, while Kemal Kılıçdaroğlu lost with a vote share of 47.82% (Supreme Election Council of the Republic of Türkiye, 2024l). The detailed timeline of this presidential election is given in Appendix 9.1.

In this election, the People's Alliance, composed of the AK Party, MHP, and BBP, continued its collaboration. The YRP, HÜDA PAR, DSP, etc., along with Sinan Oğan, the presidential candidate in the first round and leader of the Homeland Party, supported Recep Tayyip Erdoğan without being part of the alliance. The Nation Alliance, on the other hand, saw the reactivation of the alliance formed by the CHP, İYİ Party, SAADET, DP, DEVA, and GP. The primary goal uniting these six opposition parties was to move away from the presidential system and transition to a strengthened parliamentary system. During the election period, they called the "Table of Six" (Sayın, 2023). However, amid internal crises, the İYİ Party initially withdrew from the alliance but later rejoined. While the People's Alliance continued into the 2024 local elections, the Nation Alliance disbanded after the 2023 elections (El, 2023). Following the electoral defeat, the CHP held its 38th Ordinary Congress and elected Özgür Özel as the new party leader, replacing Kemal Kılıçdaroğlu (Euronews, 2023). In the 2024 local elections, CHP participated independently and emerged as the first party with 46.57% of the votes, while the AK Party secured the second position with 37.43% of the votes (TRT World, 2024).

One of the main differences between the United States and Türkiye is that there is no place for the state system and the Senate and the Congress in legislative mechanisms. However, the presidential system which was applied since 2018 is one of the main similarities. The presidential selections vary because in the United States it is enough to get the majority of the votes, but in Türkiye, there is a (50 + 1) % requirement. When it is considered the House of Representatives is the equivalent of the TBMM, the election frequency is also varied: it is two years in the United States and five years in Türkiye (Özdemir et al., 2020). Comparing the political atmosphere in Western Europe with that of Türkiye in depth constitutes a focal point of studies within the field of political science. Western European countries exhibit a variety of mechanisms, such as federal systems (e.g., Belgium, Germany), semi-presidential systems (e.g., France), and constitutional monarchies (e.g., Denmark, United Kingdom). Generally, alongside these mechanisms, there exist institutions similar to those in Türkiye, including a parliament and a Council of Ministers. Numerous parties positioned on the left and right spectrum participate in elections, and in cases where sufficient votes to form a government are not obtained, coalition governments can be formed (e.g., Finland) (TBMM Araştırma Hizmetleri Başkanlığı, 2017; Ministry of Foreign Affairs of Türkiye (n.d.).

METHODOLOGY

The primary objective of this research is to analyze the social media posts made by the Presidential candidates of the People's Alliance, and the Nation Alliance on their respective official X accounts during the 2023 Presidential elections within the framework of William Benoit's Functional Theory of Political Campaign Discourse.

The methodology employed for this analysis is content analysis, a qualitative research method commonly used for examining textual data (Andaç & Akbıyık, 2016; Silsüpür, 2016). To carry out content analysis, various forms of content, including posts, posts threads, reposts, and quoted posts, shared by the candidates on their official X accounts, were collected on a daily basis. The selection of X as the primary platform for data collection in this study is justified by its pivotal role in modern political communication. The electorate's interest in understanding candidates' character and personality to assess their trustworthiness as political leaders is well-documented (Kendall & Paine, 1995; Westen, 2009; Vavreck, 2016), with social media platforms like X, formerly known as Twitter, offering new avenues for constructing and negotiating these images. This study, focusing on the 2023 Presidential elections in Türkiye and analyzing the social media posts of President Erdoğan and Kılıçdaroğlu, recognizes X's significance as a micro-blogging service (Vergeer, 2015) and its popularity among politicians and citizens alike. Within the broader context of the mediatization of politics (Hjarvard, 2008; Strömbäck, 2008) where political communication increasingly emphasizes personalities and personal traits, X provides a direct channel for politicians to share their public image and personal sides. Politicians benefit from X's direct communication channels, circumventing traditional media mediation, and gaining a powerful form of endorsement when their messages resonate widely (Boyd et al., 2010). Therefore, X's unique position as a platform for campaign strategies and public persona representation makes it an ideal choice for this study, offering direct insights into the political communication tactics of President Erdoğan and Kılıçdaroğlu in the context of the 2023 elections.

The data collection process commenced three months prior to the elections, specifically on 14 February 2023. Since the elections on 14 May 2023, did not result in either candidate obtaining more than 50% of the votes, the elections proceeded to a second round, scheduled for 28 May 2023. Consequently, posts shared by the candidates on their official X accounts from 14 February 2023, to 27 May 2023, were recorded for analysis. Although some studies have covered longer periods (Bayraktutan et al., 2014), the rationale behind selecting this timeframe is the observed heightened intensity of political messages on Twitter in the approximately three months leading up to elections, also a timeframe consistent with previous studies (Andaç & Akbıyık, 2016; Silsüpür, 2016). It is important to note that content in the form of videos and live broadcasts was excluded from this study.

Despite the presence of three Presidential candidates in the first round of elections, this study focused solely on two candidates, Recep Tayyip Erdoğan, and Kemal Kılıçdaroğlu, and their political campaign messages disseminated on the X platform. This selective approach was guided by Benoit's Functional Theory of Political Campaign Discourse, which suggests that the theory yields meaningful results when applied to candidates with reasonably high chances of winning the election (Banavand, 2020; Benoit, 2007, 2017).

Content analysis facilitates a thorough understanding of data through an inductive perspective, enabling the analysis of textual data through processes such as collecting, coding, conceptualizing, and thematizing (Yıldırım & Simşek, 1999). For qualitative data analysis using content analysis, a codebook is essential. Researchers may opt for a code list developed with the assistance of a specific theory or one utilized in prior studies (Yıldırım & Simşek, 1999). In this study, a codebook was constructed based on Benoit's Functional Theory of Political Campaign Discourse (Appendix 9.2). Before commencing the coding process based on themes, researchers deliberated on coding rules to ensure a shared understanding among the team regarding the coding protocol.

The coding process involved identifying the most dominant theme in each post. Overall, 1091 posts were subjected to content analysis based on the Functional Theory of Political Campaign Discourse, considering political message topics and functions, and were analyzed as "1 = exists," and "0 = does not exist." It was acknowledged that a single post could encompass multiple topics (such as policy and character) and multiple functions (acclaim, attack, defense).

1091 posts in total shared by two candidates from 14 February 2023, to 27 May 2023, were selected as the sample of this study because it is known that in Türkiye political campaign efforts have gained momentum and intensity within the last two months (TRT World Research Centre, 2024). Additionally, the Supreme Election Council of the Republic of Türkiye announced the election calendar as starting on 18 March 2023 (Supreme Election Council of the Republic of Türkiye, 2024a). However, on 6 February 2023, the south of Türkiye experienced a devastating earthquake. The posts shared by the candidates in the days following the earthquake had purposes such as organizing rescue operations, directing aid, and making official statements to citizens. However, in order to see the impact of this earthquake on the political campaign discourse of the candidates, the researchers determined the exact date 3 months before the election date (14 February 2023) and started collecting data as of 14 February 2023. For all posts, the functions of them were considered and the political campaign discourse topics they contained and sub-themes related to each post were established. For instance, the sub-theme of the post which emphasizes every possible contribution that will be made to ensure the rapid recovery of the earthquake-stricken region was identified as "earthquake-stricken region development." This approach aimed to provide a concise summary of all content, including posts that sometimes exceeded 300 characters, and to group together those with similar political campaign messages. Through this process, the 1091 posts were not only transformed into understandable and interpretable components, but an attempt was made to elucidate the predominant political discourse topics where politicians employed functions of acclaim, attack, and defense.

In qualitative research, the commitment to objective data collection and analysis is tantamount to validity, while providing a clear and detailed account of the research process enhances reliability (Yıldırım & Simşek, 1999). To ensure validity, consistency across the processes of data collection, analysis, and interpretation is crucial. Any inconsistencies within a study can lead to contradictions, thereby diminishing its credibility. Moreover, qualitative studies that lack transferability to other samples, times, or research contexts compromise validity. Therefore, this study presents a detailed account of all steps to enhance validity. To bolster reliability, triangulation and inter-coder reliability were ensured by having three different researchers conduct content analysis (Neuendorf, 2002; Yıldırım & Simşek, 1999). As suggested by Yıldırım and Simşek (1999), the collected data were analyzed by three different researchers, adhering to the theoretical framework.

FINDINGS

Descriptive Findings

In this section, the posts are analyzed in view of their descriptive characteristics, and before the content analysis of the posts, the authors provide an overview of the analyzed posts. In images and findings, the shortened forms of the names of candidates will be used as "RTE" for the ruling party leader President Recep Tayyip Erdoğan, and "KK" for the opposition party leader Kemal Kılıçdaroğlu.

The candidates collectively made a total of 1091 posts. Out of the total posts, the majority (65%) are posted by President Erdoğan, while the rest (35%) are posted by Kılıçdaroğlu as depicted in Figure 9.1. One noteworthy fact is that none of the 1091 posts were appropriate for the application of the Functional Theory of Political Discourse. Some posts were categorized as election promotion campaign efforts and they aimed at raising awareness of their rallies to attend, their TV appearances to watch, voting, safety, their slogans, meetings they have attended, and their messages of congratulations, commemorations, condolences, and celebrations.

When all the posts are divided based on the identified acclaim, attack, and defend themes, it is evident that the leader of the ruling party used the acclaim function frequently. In this case, messages containing attack themes come from the leader of the opposition party more than the leader of the ruling party. Also, there is a balance between the acclaim and attack messages of the opposition party. Whereas the defense function remains the least preferred by both parties. Another significant aspect is that the majority of the candidates employed acclaim, attack, and defense functions combining political and character topics with only two exceptions. Therefore, in Figure 9.2, these two posts as they are only about character or policy topics are illustrated individually.

Some of the candidates' posts utilized only one function, while others contained sentences combining multiple functions. Consequently, single and mixed functions were computed for the candidates. President Erdoğan opted to blend 18% of its posts containing the acclaim function with those containing the attack function as seen in Figure 9.3, while Kılıçdaroğlu chose to merge 41% of its posts containing the acclaim function with the attack function as given in Figure 9.4.

In addition to the functions of political campaign discourse, the topics are also the focal point of analysis in this theory. Thus, the posts of the candidates were divided into two categories: character and policy issues. As earlier noted, the candidates employed messages on character and policy issues in combination with acclaim, attack, and defense roles in their posts on Platform X, except for two. Therefore, the researchers did not categorize the posts into character and policy groups but grouped them under acclaim, attack, and defense. This approach pointed out which topics and functions the candidates favored and stressed in the political debates.

However, in order to see the density of character and policy and their sub-categories in the

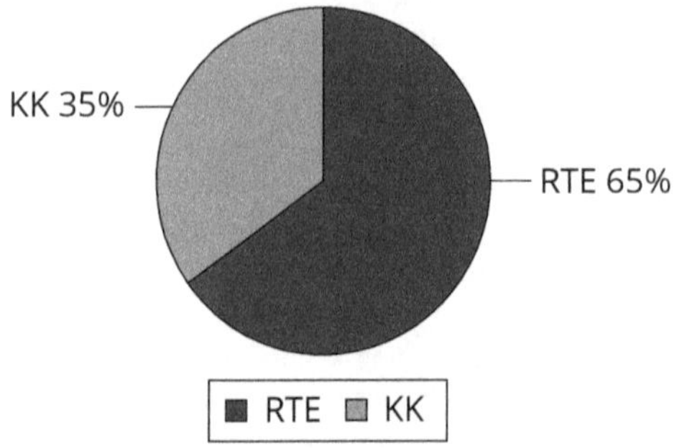

Figure 9.1 Number of Posts for the Candidates

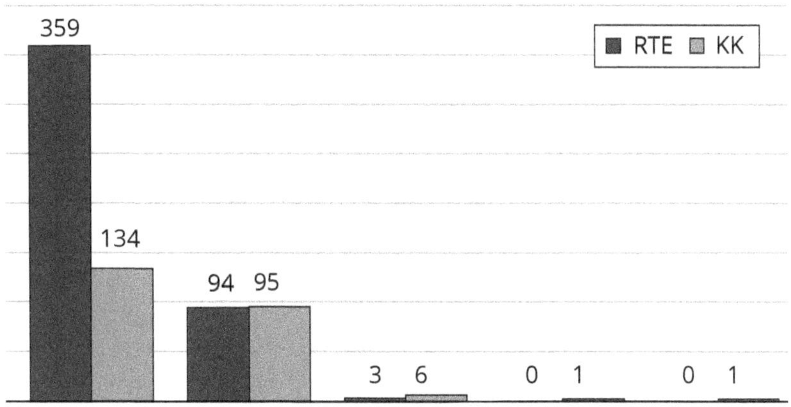

	Number of Acclaim Mentioned Posts	Number of Attack Mentioned Posts	Number of Defense Mentioned Posts	Number of Policy Mentioned Posts	Number of Character Mentioned Posts
RTE	359	94	3	0	0
KK	134	95	6	1	1

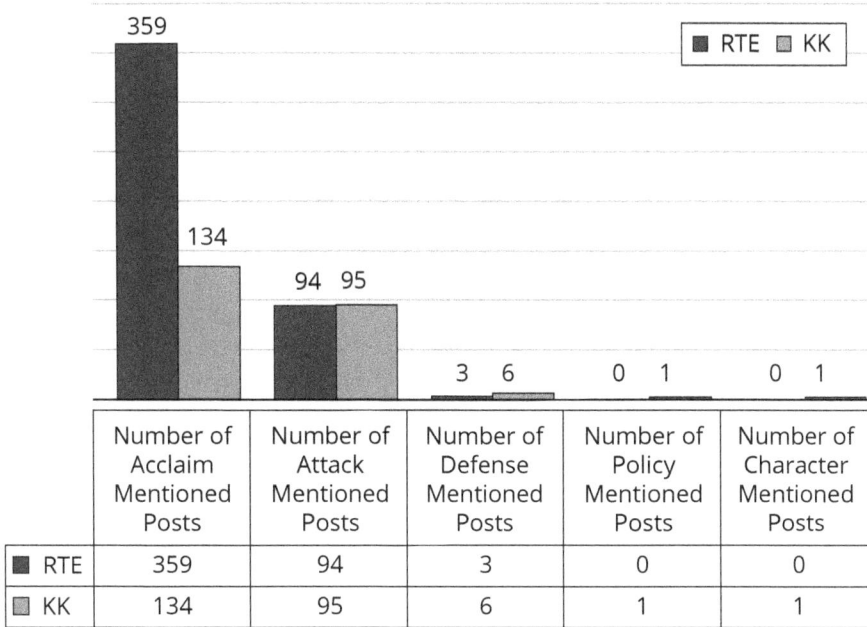

Figure 9.2 The Number of Posts by Candidates according to Topics and Functions

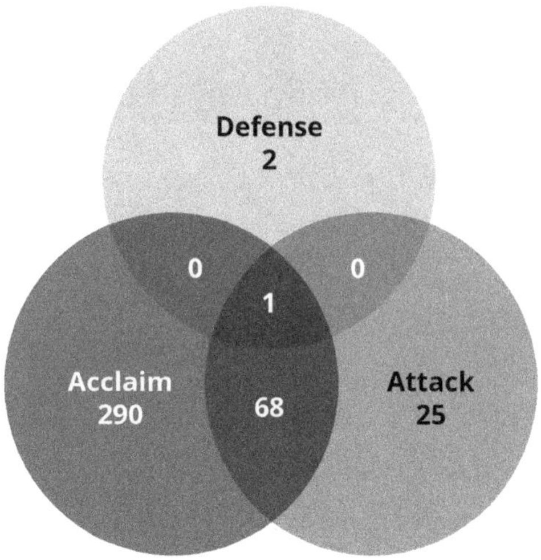

Figure 9.3 Recep Tayyip Erdoğan's Posts Using the Single and Mixed Functions

candidates' posts, see Figures 9.5–9.7. Character topics can be divided into three subgroups as personal qualities, leadership abilities, and ideals. Among these, personal qualities are further divided into five categories: sincerity, morality, empathy, drive, and private work experience. Character topics expressed by candidates in terms of acclaim, attack, and defense functions will be examined ranging from narrow to broad as seen in Figure 9.5. It has been seen that posts utilizing the

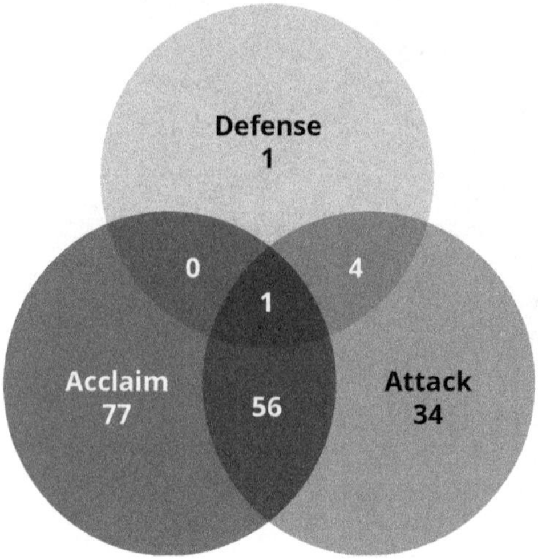

Figure 9.4 Kemal Kılıçdaroğlu's Posts Using the Single and Mixed Functions

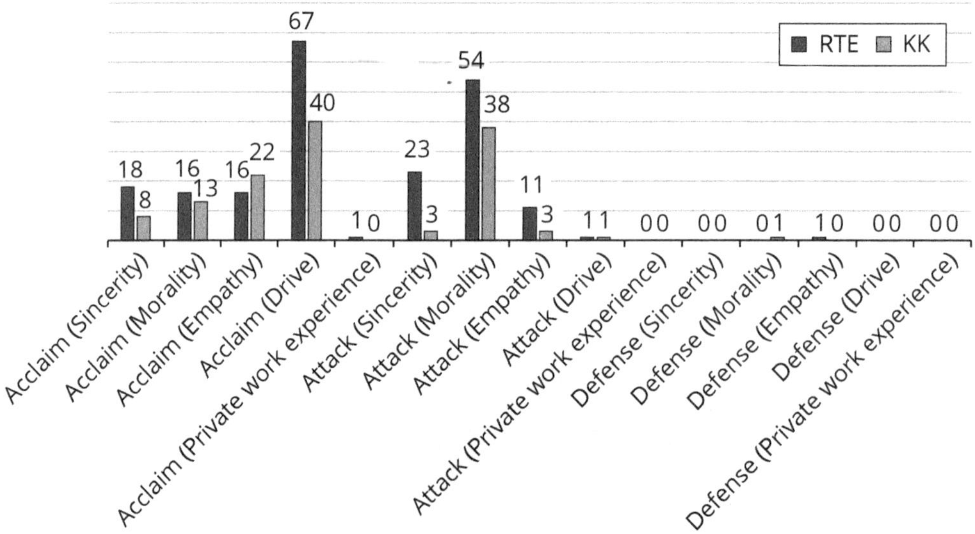

Figure 9.5 The Posts by Candidates About Personal Qualities Using the Acclaim, Attack, and Defense Functions

acclaim function on sincerity, morality, drive, and personal work experience have been more frequently employed by President Erdoğan compared to Kılıçdaroğlu. At the same time, Kılıçdaroğlu has shared more posts acclaiming himself and his party on the topic of empathy. In posts containing the attack function, candidates have predominantly chosen to disseminate messages regarding the morality topic. As for the defense function, since there were only nine posts in total, candidates have only one post each in the morality and empathy topics.

In examining the broader scope of the general characteristics within the subject matter, the presence of personal qualities, leadership ability, and ideals becomes evident. Accordingly, candidates have utilized their acclaim and attack functions in their posts for personal qualities, ideals, and leadership ability topics, respectively, in descending order as seen in Figure 9.6.

Finally, candidates tend to utilize the character theme more for acclaim compared to attack and defense functions as seen in Figure 9.7.

When examining the posts candidates have published about their policies, it is suggested to categorize them into past deeds, future goals, and general goals. Through this categorization as seen in Figure 9.8, it is evident that the leader of the ruling party has shared a significant number of posts focusing on past deeds for acclaim. However, there is almost no post where the leader of the opposition party has utilized the acclaim function regarding past deeds which appears reasonable because the party has been in the opposition for over two decades. Both candidates have shared posts acclaiming future and general goals, but the majority of such posts are from President Erdoğan. Specifically, President Erdoğan has employed the acclaim function in 74% of the posts in the future goals topic and in 61% of the posts in the general goals topic. The posts employing the attack function by candidates have predominantly focused on past deeds.

By comparing the posts that contain policy topics, it can be seen that the ruling party acclaims its own policy, and the opposition party attacks the

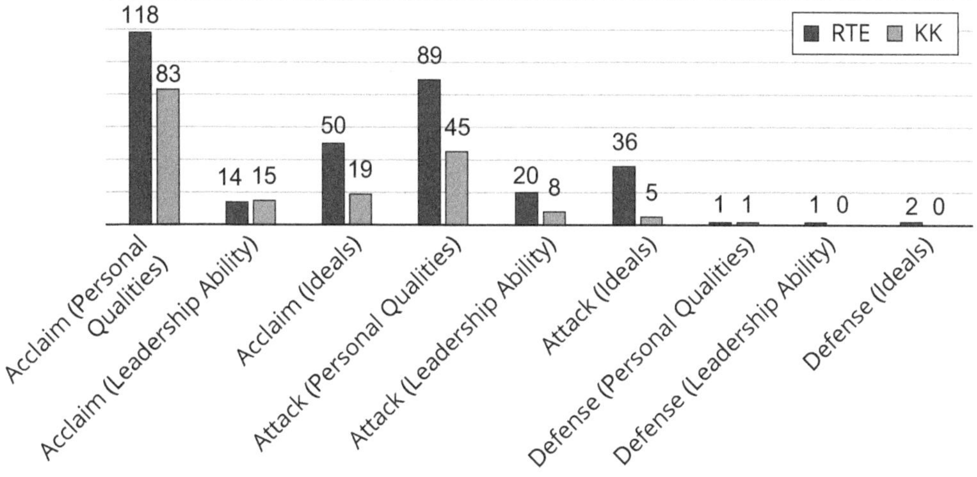

Figure 9.6 The Posts by Candidates About Subgroups of Character Topic Using the Acclaim, Attack, and Defense Functions

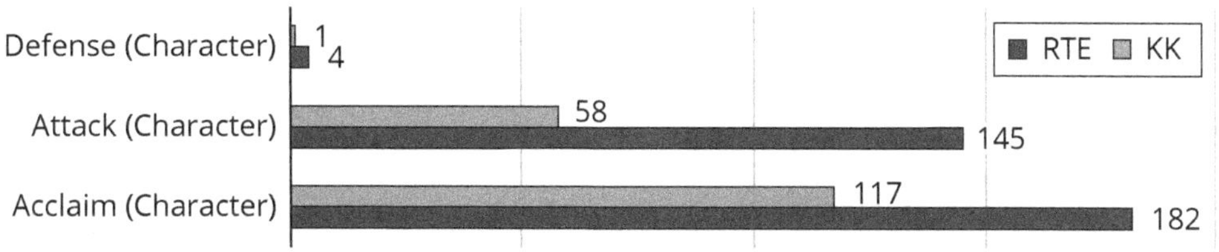

	Acclaim (Character)	Attack (Character)	Defense (Character)
KK	117	58	1
RTE	182	145	4

Figure 9.7 The Posts by Candidates About Character Topic Using the Acclaim, Attack, and Defense Functions

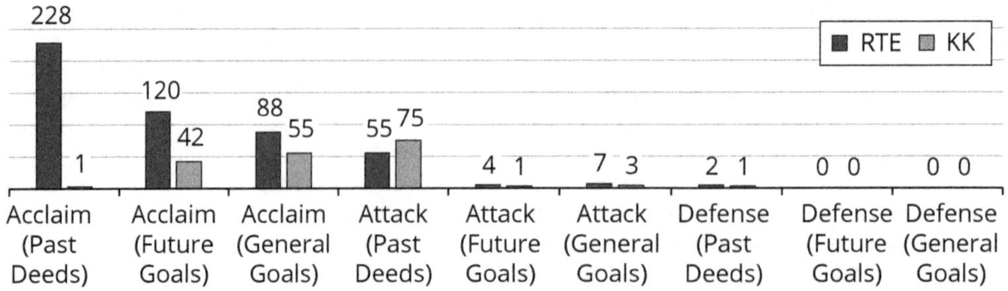

Figure 9.8 The Posts by Candidates Regarding the Subgroup of Policies Using the Acclaim, Attack, and Defense Functions

policies of the ruling party. Few posts contained the defense function (see Figure 9.9). However, if certain topics of the posts are pointed out, then they are mainly related to counterterrorism, freedom of speech, and media freedom.

In addition, posts should also be examined from a temporal perspective. Hence, Figures 9.10 and 9.11 will try to account for the analyzed posts in the context of time. The distribution of post numbers was analyzed from February when the researchers started sampling the posts to May when the elections were held. Consequently, it is seen that the number of posts shared by both candidates also increased with the coming closer to the election date (see Figure 9.10).

Besides, the marked increase of post numbers, the variation of functions according to months is also reflected in Figure 9.11. Hence, while in May, the month of the election, there was a reduction in the number of acclaim messages as opposed to the number of attack messages. Also, the initial defense messages were noted in posts in the month of the election.

Furthermore, it was found that some of the posts only had visuals, videos, or reposts that did not include any textual information (see Figure 9.12). Nevertheless, if these visual and video posts have textual descriptions, they are considered included into the analysis. Reposts, although they evidence the candidate's party identification or support ideas, were not coded because it does not involve the candidate's voice.

The last but not the least concern is that the aspect of inclusiveness, which was not directly discussed in the theory, was quite often highlighted by the candidates in their posts. Posts with an inclusivity theme primarily consisted of content aimed at embracing every segment of society. The candidate embraces all segments of society and appeals to everyone. The candidate includes all the segments of the society and often reminds the audience that every individual is equal to the state, irrespective of his or her religion, language, race, sect, or political preference. They declare equal rights and freedom for every citizen in the country. For example, one of the posts emphasizes that in these elections, everyone will win: the 85 million people of all ages and genders, all 81 provinces, and every segment of society, including Turks, Kurds, Arabs, Sunnis, Alevis, Christians, Jews, Assyrians, and people of different faiths. The supporters of the AK Party, the People's Alliance, the CHP, the İYİ Party, the Felicity Party, and other parties will all benefit. Among 1091 posts, the leader of the ruling party mentioned the given theme in 29 posts, as it was mentioned in 18 posts by the leader of the opposition party. Despite its insignificance in terms of its proportion, compared to the current state of society and the polarization of the elections, the inclusion of the candidates was considered important by the authors and taken into account.

As a result, the descriptive findings of this study are in parallel with the existing literature: Both leaders posted more acclaim messages than attack and/or defense. The current literature indicates that policy topics are heavily preferred in political campaign discourses, especially by the ruling party to attack the opposition party. Both leaders as expected focused on more policy policy-related messages rather than character topics (Benoit et al., 1997). However, and different from the expected, the ruling party leader attacked more on character than the policy of the opposition party's leader. Additionally, it was expected that the ruling party's leader would use acclaim approaches and character features more including their leadership credentials (Benoit et al., 1997); however, in this political campaign, using an acclaim approach for their policies

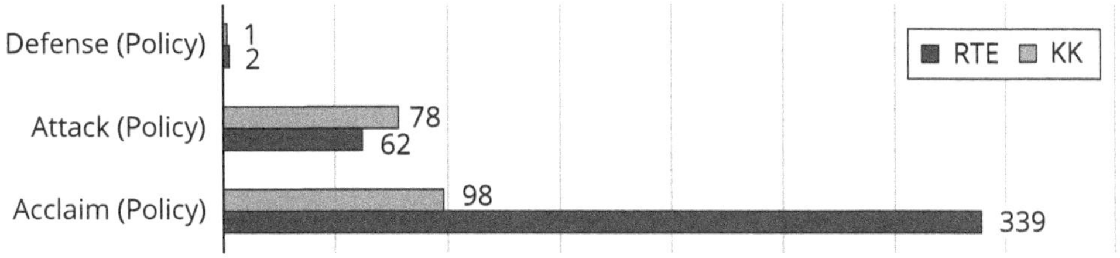

	Acclaim (Policy)	Attack (Policy)	Defense (Policy)
KK	98	78	1
RTE	339	62	2

Figure 9.9 The Posts by Candidates About Their Policies Using the Acclaim, Attack, and Defense Functions

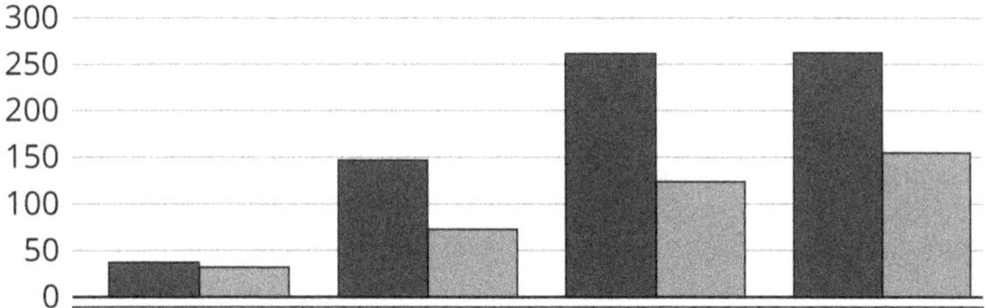

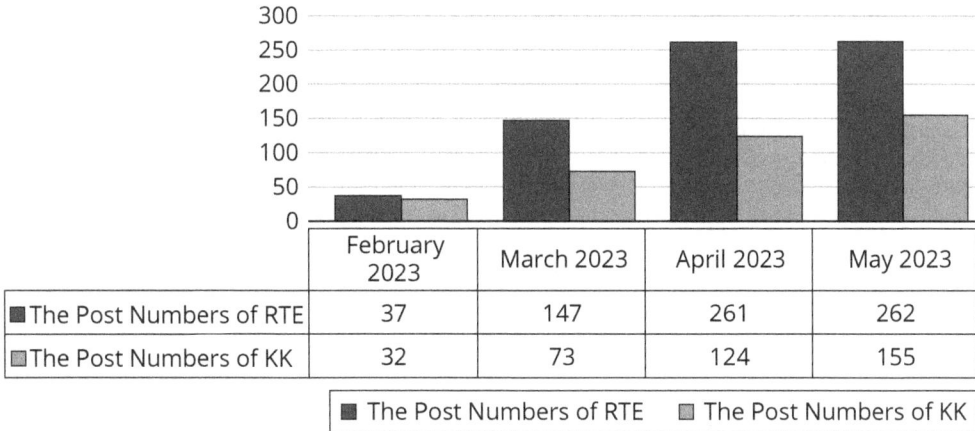

	February 2023	March 2023	April 2023	May 2023
The Post Numbers of RTE	37	147	261	262
The Post Numbers of KK	32	73	124	155

Figure 9.10 The Monthly Post Counts of the Candidates

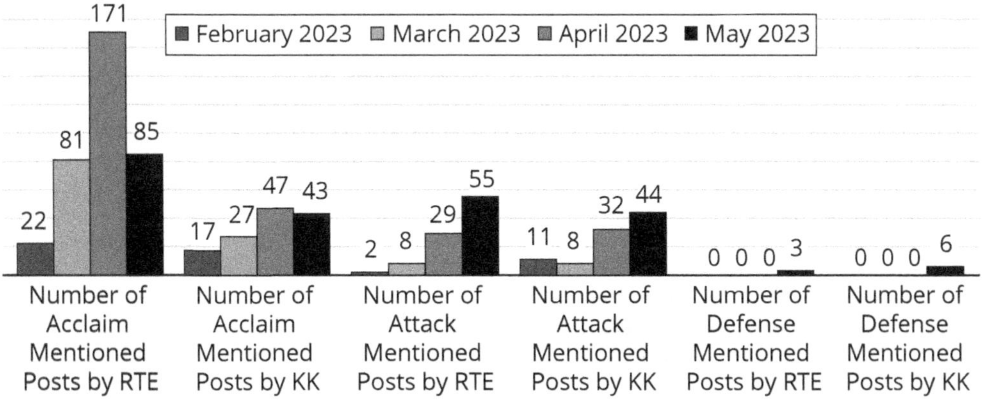

Figure 9.11 Frequency of Posts Mentioning Acclaim, Attack, and Defense by Month

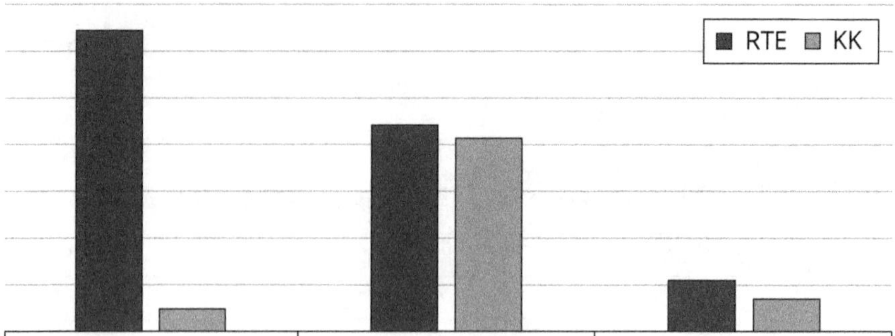

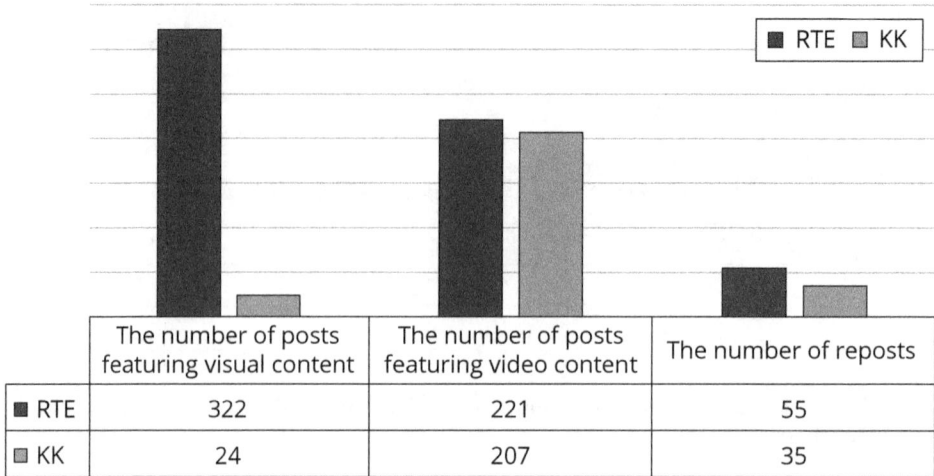

	The number of posts featuring visual content	The number of posts featuring video content	The number of reposts
RTE	322	221	55
KK	24	207	35

Figure 9.12 The Number of Posts Featuring Visuals, Video Contents, and Reposts

(most of them were about past deeds) was more prominent. The opposition party's leaders tended to acclaim their character features also; however, it was almost at the same level as with acclaiming policy-related topics. However, the expectation from the literature from the opposition party's perspective is to have more acclaim-focused messages regarding the character topic. Lastly, as predicted, using a defense approach was a less favorable option chosen.

EXPLORING FUNCTIONS AND TOPICS IN POST CONTENT ANALYSIS

Posts of Recep Tayyip Erdoğan

A total of 707 posts of President Erdoğan were analyzed. As indicated previously, content in the form of videos and live broadcasts was excluded from this study. 707 posts were first divided into categories according to their functions, namely acclaim, attack, and defense. All these functions were further analyzed according to the topics mentioned. In the latter analysis, it was evident that some posts contained more than one topic. For instance, on 7 May 2023, President Erdoğan posted a message which emphasized that since taking over governance in 2002, significant efforts have been made to develop a "great and powerful Türkiye." Major projects in various sectors and a strong economy have been achieved through the contributions of all 85 million citizens across 81 provinces. This success is attributed to the dedication and support of the population over the past 21 years. Beginning May 14th, further progress will be made, continuing to build the Türkiye Century together with the people. This message highlights both the public investments made to date and emphasizes election strategies. Therefore, it should be highlighted that some posts fall under multiple topics.

TOPICS OF POSTS WITH ACCLAIM FUNCTION

Natural Disaster Management: It was found that 531 topics were used to serve an acclaim function, with many of them (24.11%) as seen in Figure 9.13 focusing on natural disaster management. The frequent mention of natural disaster management in election rhetoric is no coincidence; it is a direct consequence of a recent earthquake disaster that unfolded in the near past. The 2023 Kahramanmaraş earthquakes were a devastating series of seismic events that occurred on 6 February 2023. The earthquakes, with magnitudes of 7.8 Mw and 7.5 Mw, were among the most powerful in recent history. The impact was catastrophic, with official figures reporting a staggering loss of at least 53,537 lives in Türkiye, with over 107,000 people sustaining injuries (Anadolu Agency, 2024). Accordingly, in President Erdoğan's posts using the acclaim function, natural disaster management holds a significant

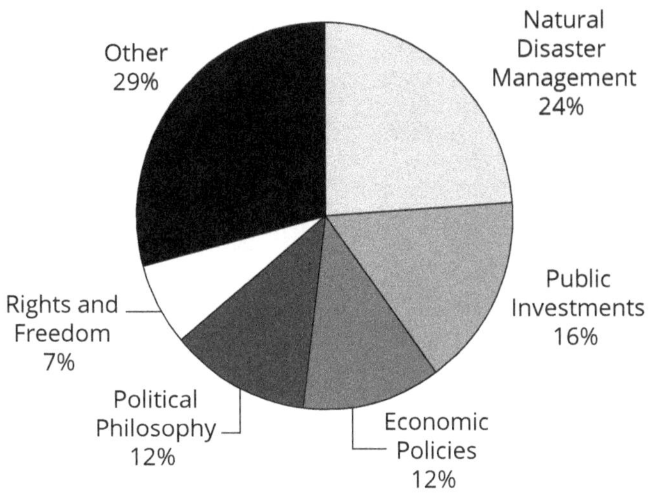

Figure 9.13 Top 5 Topics of Recep Tayyip Erdoğan's Posts Using the Acclaim Function

space. He emphasized their resilience as the ruling party in providing assistance and help to the affected regions and people by also highlighting their future plans regarding the development of the region as well as the need for making the country more resilient to disasters. President Erdoğan also underscored the vitality of empathy and understanding toward earthquake victims, emphasizing that they should not be forgotten. Finally, President Erdoğan announced the establishment of the Disaster Management Policy Board and the importance of international aid in the aftermath of earthquakes.

Public Investments: The second dominant topic in President Erdoğan's acclaim rhetoric was public investments at 16.20% (see Figure 9.13). President Erdoğan emphasized a diverse range of projects and initiatives highlighting their commitment to development and progress. The construction of the 15 July Martyrs Bridge, high-speed train line projects, ferry route openings, the Rare Element Facility opening, investments in internet infrastructure, and hospitality constructions are some of the acclaimed public investments. He also emphasized energy projects including natural gas discoveries in the Black Sea and the Zero Waste Movement. President Erdoğan also underscored AK Party's achievements in urban planning and the government's commitment to national development.

Economic Policies: President Erdoğan's acclaim posts also shed light on a range of economic policies and initiatives at 12.05% (see Figure 9.13). He emphasized the importance of projects targeting families' and youth's economic welfare by mentioning their initiatives like the Family and Youth Bank, Family Shield, the First Land and My First Home, and Protection Programs. Moreover, President Erdoğan announced discounts on electricity and natural gas, assistance for renters, steps to improve retirement pensions for security guards, and reductions in social security premiums. Most importantly, he discussed the enhancement of public worker wages and civil servant salaries, aiming to provide protection against inflation.

Political Philosophy: Another acclaim topic is found to be political philosophy at 12.05% (see Figure 9.13). President Erdoğan frequently emphasized the vitality of unity, solidarity, and diligent governance to advocate for a strong belief in the supremacy of law and the responsibilities of leadership. His messages underscored his dedication to serving the citizens by referring to topics such as nationalism, the politics of affection, and fulfilling promises. He emphasized their contributions to Turkish politics and shared his vision for a united and prosperous Türkiye.

Rights and Freedom: The final major acclaim topic is found to be rights and freedoms at 6.78% (see Figure 9.13). In his campaign discourse, President Erdoğan put an emphasis on Turkish people living abroad by promising recognition of their military service, discussing work opportunities for retirees in foreign countries, mentioning housing projects for those living abroad, and promising mobile consulates. By doing so, President Erdoğan showcased his dedication to improving the lives of Turkish citizens globally. President Erdoğan also emphasized women's rights and freedoms, including positive discrimination, retirement initiatives for housewives, and providing a fair society. He also highlighted their commitment to education and workers' rights, along with minority rights.

Other Acclaimed Topics: The remaining acclaimed topics in President Erdoğan's rhetoric include defense industry investments at 3.95%, "Türkiye Century" as a management philosophy at 3.58%, election campaign strategy at 3.58%, national security and counterterrorism at 3.01%, international relations, and EU membership at 2.64%, urban transformation at 2.64%, technological developments, and space investments at 2.26%, energy investments at 1.88%, TOGG (an EV brand based in Türkiye) investment at 1.69%, agriculture, and animal husbandry at 0.94%, and others.

TOPICS OF POSTS WITH ATTACK FUNCTION

Political Philosophy: It is found that the vast majority of the posts using the attack function (26.67%) focus on attacking the political philosophy of the opponent group as seen in Figure 9.14. President Erdoğan emphasized the discrepancy between promises made to citizens and their fulfillment, condemning the manipulative tactics of political engineering and polarization. Criticizing a lack of satisfaction with multiparty political dynamics and attempts to disregard the will of the people, he underscored actions undermining fundamental values like freedom and democracy. President Erdoğan also accused the opposition of showing arrogance and presenting a democratic appearance despite their incompetence. In addition, President Erdoğan accused the opposition of neglecting self-criticism, vision and ties with the public, and of overlooking the wishes of young people and using historical events for political gain.

Election Strategy: The second dominant topic in posts using the attack function is found to be the election strategy of opponents at 17.22% (see Figure 9.14). President Erdoğan criticized the opposition's election strategy by pointing to controversial issues such as internal alliance negotiations, coalition negotiations, and seat-sharing arrangements. In addition to evaluating the reconciliation policies to be insincere and opportunistic, President Erdoğan also accused the opposition's election discourse of being full of lies and black propaganda. President Erdoğan stated that the opposition practices populism against the will of the people and exemplified the situation with contradictory gestures such as using the heart sign while resorting to confrontational discourses. In these posts, President Erdoğan underlined the issues he perceived as opportunistic and manipulative in the opposition.

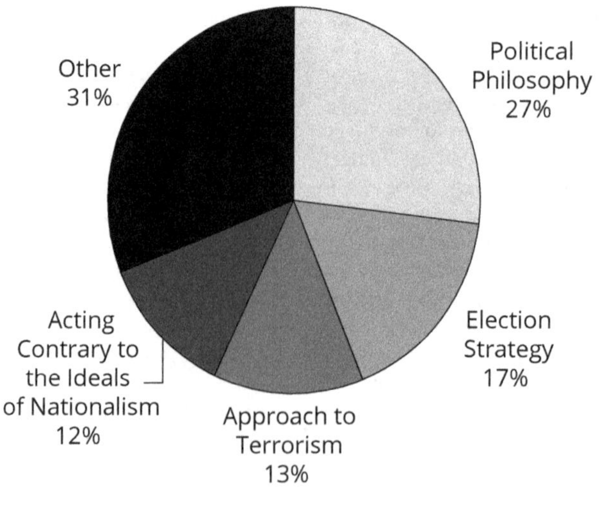

Figure 9.14 Top 5 Topics of Recep Tayyip Erdoğan's Posts Using the Attack Function

Approach to Terrorism: The third major attack topic is found to be the approach of opponents to terrorism at 13.33% (see Figure 9.14). In his pre-election posts, President Erdoğan strongly criticized the opposition's stance against terrorism, especially against terrorist groups such as FETO (also known as the Gülenist Terrorist Organization, which is accused by the Turkish government of planning the failed coup attempt in 2016) and Daesh, also known as ISIS. He drew attention to the allegations of cooperation with these organizations. In addition, President Erdoğan accused the opposition of being involved in the Gezi events,[1] citing the protests in Türkiye in 2013 as evidence. It describes and condemns what it sees as tolerance or cooperation with these groups as a threat to national security and stability. Thus, President Erdoğan, emphasizing the importance of taking a determined stance against terrorism, accused the opposition of undermining efforts to effectively fight against terrorism.

Acting Contrary to the Ideals of Nationalism: The third major attack topic is found to be the approach of opponents to the ideals of nationalism at 11.67% (see Figure 9.14). President Erdoğan criticized the opposition group's approach to the ideals of nationalism, accusing them of belittling and sabotaging national projects vital for development. Moreover, President Erdoğan has condemned what he perceives as their failure to align with the fundamental principles of nationalism, portraying it as a betrayal of the country's interests. These attacks underscore President Erdoğan's commitment to advancing nationalist ideals and his portrayal of the opposition as detrimental to the nation's prosperity and unity.

Other Attack Topics: The remaining attack topics in President Erdoğan's rhetoric have a share of 31% (see Figure 9.14) and include attitude toward earthquake victims and using earthquakes as pretexts for hostility toward Türkiye at 5%, relations with external powers (referring to other countries) at 5%, leadership skills at 5%, discrimination at 4.44%, economic policies at 2.79%, and others.

TOPICS OF POSTS WITH DEFENSE FUNCTION

It was found that President Erdoğan's election discourses generally focused on the acclaim and attack functions, and there were only three posts that provided the defense function. In his posts, President Erdoğan has defended his stance against accusations from opposing parties, addressing allegations regarding 2 in 3 freedom and 1 in 3 supporting terrorisms. He has addressed these allegations directly, using the ongoing election process as an opportunity to highlight the robustness of Turkish democracy, refuting claims of dictatorship and fear-mongering tactics.

POSTS OF KEMAL KILIÇDAROĞLU

A total of 384 posts by Kılıçdaroğlu were analyzed. Content in the form of videos and live broadcasts was excluded from this study. These 384 posts were categorized based on their functions, including attack, defense, and acclaim. Each of these functions was then examined in detail based on the topics mentioned. During this analysis, it became clear that some posts addressed more than one topic at the same time.

TOPICS OF POSTS WITH ACCLAIM FUNCTION

Political Philosophy: The findings reveal the major acclaim topic in Kılıçdaroğlu's discourse to be his political philosophy with 20.48% (see Figure 9.15). Kılıçdaroğlu frequently emphasized peace, inclusiveness, empathy, listening to voters, and serving citizens in his posts. He also highlighted the significance of being accountable, ready for change, and determined to win elections and not forgetting about keeping promises made to voters. In addition to addressing social issues, Kılıçdaroğlu also centered his messages around increasing the global reputation of Türkiye and ensuring social welfare. Through his posts, he demonstrated a comprehensive vision of governance that prioritizes the welfare and interests of all citizens and aims to create a more egalitarian and prosperous society.

Commitment to the Founding Principles of the Party: Kılıçdaroğlu frequently emphasized the issues related to the founding principles of the CHP (see Figure 9.15) like republicanism, folkism, nationalism, laicism,[2] statism, and reformism by clarifying his values and future targets about justice, democracy, freedom, and equality. Accordingly, the second major acclaim theme is found to be a commitment to the founding principles of the CHP with 12.86%. Kılıçdaroğlu emphasized the necessity of change and the importance of democracy in shaping the future of the country, expressing that the country should re-establish state discipline and integrity, and

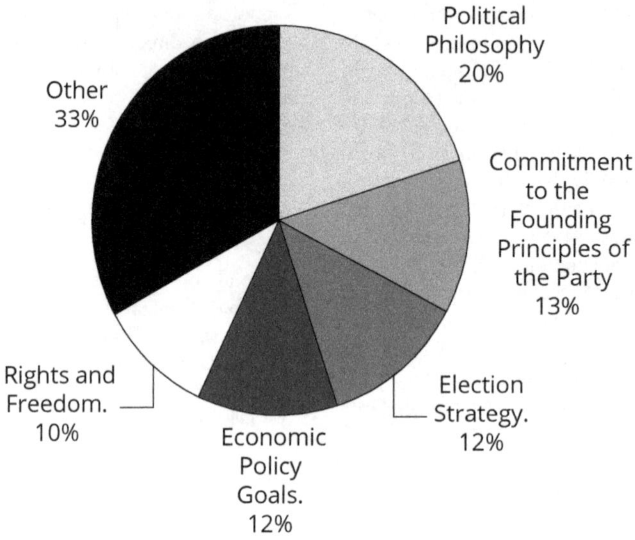

Figure 9.15 Top 5 Topics of Kemal Kılıçdaroğlu's Posts Using the Acclaim Function

promising to bring freedom. Kılıçdaroğlu also underlined his support for the ideal of equal citizenship for everyone and thus offered the vision of a new beginning by creating a more fair, inclusive, and democratic society.

Election Strategy: Kılıçdaroğlu frequently acclaimed their election strategies that focused on unity and solidarity (12.38%) (see Figure 9.15) and invited citizens to vote and build Türkiye with an inclusive and constructive approach. He encouraged the spirit of cooperation and dialogue in his posts, especially avoiding destructive language. He also gave voters hope for change by frequently applauding his team and called on candidates to participate in open televised debates.

Economic Policy Goals: The fourth most popular acclaim topic in Kılıçdaroğlu's posts was found to be economic policy targets with a frequency of 11.90% (see Figure 9.15). He emphasized his economic vision to attract investment to Türkiye, develop the economy, and bring prosperity to the country through various projects such as supporting entrepreneurs, Organized Industrial Zones, and producers. He was also aware of the hardship that housewives and students experienced, thus, he underscored the importance of providing financial aid to them. His determination was seen on his posts to foster economic growth, investment, and wealth for all citizens.

Rights and Freedom: The fifth most frequently mentioned topic was about rights and freedom of society with 9.52% (see Figure 9.15). Kılıçdaroğlu demonstrated his dedication to equality and justice by frequently touching on social and human rights issues in his posts. He promised to preserve and protect fundamental rights and achievements, including women's rights and gender equality. He also promised to protect and promote freedom, democracy, and social justice for all groups such as journalists, miners, academics, police officers, civil servants, artists, and especially for widows and orphans.

Other Acclaimed Topics: The remaining acclaim topics in Kılıçdaroğlu's political discourse have a share of 33% (see Figure 9.15) and included natural disaster management with 9.05%, refugee and immigrant problems with 5.24%, determination in the fight against corruption with 3.81%, determination in the fight against illegal entities and organizations (such as mafias and profit seekers) with 3.33%, improvement plans for agriculture and animal husbandry with 1.43% and others.

TOPICS OF POSTS WITH ATTACK FUNCTION

Political Philosophy: It is found that the vast majority of the posts using the attack function focused on attacking the political philosophy of the opponent group with 22.54% (see Figure 9.16).

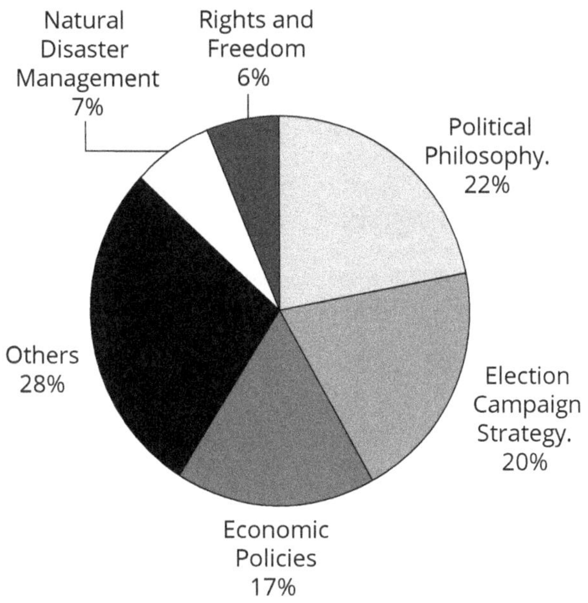

Figure 9.16 Top 5 Topics of Kemal Kılıçdaroğlu's Posts Using the Attack Function

Kılıçdaroğlu frequently addressed a myriad of issues related to the current government's governance approach in his posts, critiquing various aspects such as the repressive regime, lack of openness to criticism, and their political discourse. He highlighted his concerns regarding incompetence, President Erdoğan's oppressive measures, and the propagation of religious ideology for political gain. Additionally, he accused the government of deceiving citizens and neglecting their issues, while also condemning pan-Islamism and the development of a party-state system. Criticisms extended to the leadership approach of those in power, the mentality rewarding social media trolls, and the erosion of common values.

Election Campaign Strategy: It was found that the second most-mentioned topic in Kılıçdaroğlu's posts containing an attack function was the election campaign strategy of the rival party with 19.65% (see Figure 9.16). In this context, Kılıçdaroğlu frequently criticized the other party's black propaganda practices, which include the spread of false or misleading information aimed at discrediting and creating a negative perception in the public. Additionally, he accused the rival party of using insults and poisonous language, as well as montages, tapes, and conspiracies aimed at discrediting opposition figures, and he stated that tactics such as slander and lying create a toxic atmosphere in politics.

Economic Policies: The results revealed that the third most-mentioned issue in Kılıçdaroğlu's posts attacking the other party was the economic policies of the ruling party, with 16.76% (see Figure 9.16). In addition to drawing attention to the harmful effects of practices such as weak economic investment, nepotism, and squandering national assets through disposal on the economic welfare of the country, Kılıçdaroğlu also accused the Central Bank of not having a consistent economic vision. In addition, while accusing the government of neglecting the needs of the people and causing hunger, he stated that tax privileges for foreigners caused housing prices to increase and the welfare level of citizens to decrease.

Natural Disaster Management: In Kılıçdaroğlu's posts, the fourth biggest attack topic against the other party was found to be natural disaster management capability with 6.94% (see Figure 9.16). Kılıçdaroğlu emphasized the need for more effective disaster response measures, drawing attention to the situations where earthquake aid did not reach the earthquake victims. In addition, Kılıçdaroğlu touched upon the deficiencies in interventions during forest fires and drew attention to the lack of preparation and sufficient resources.

Rights and Freedom: Another major attack issue was found to be the other party's approach to issues related to human rights and freedoms, with 6.36% (see Figure 9.16). Kılıçdaroğlu blamed the government for not paying enough attention to women's rights, the rights of widows and orphans, and inadequate working conditions for police officers. In addition, he condemned violence against women and called for greater freedom for art and artists. Kılıçdaroğlu also condemned situations such as the closure of universities and emphasized the need to improve the educational opportunities of young people.

Other Attack Topics: The remaining attack topics in Kılıçdaroğlu's pre-election discourse have a share of 28% (see Figure 9.16) and include the ruling party's inappropriate relationships of interest at 5.2%, lack of transparency and accountability at 4.05%, election security at 2.89%, accusations that Erdoğan and his party collaborated with terrorist groups at 2.31% – although details such as the names of the groups and clear justification for these accusations were not provided in the analyzed posts, they may have been mentioned in other sources – refugee and migrant issues at 1.73%, and others.

TOPICS OF POSTS WITH A DEFENSE FUNCTION

It was found that Kılıçdaroğlu's election discourses generally focused on the acclaim and attack functions, and there were only two posts that provided the defense function. In his posts, Kılıçdaroğlu has defended his stance against accusations from opposing parties, addressing allegations regarding his dishonesty.

COMPARING THE POLITICAL CAMPAIGN DISCOURSE OF RECEP TAYYİP ERDOĞAN AND KEMAL KILIÇDAROĞLU

The pre-election political campaign discourse of both leaders exhibits notable similarities and differences. When the posts were categorized according to their functions, it was revealed that President Erdoğan employed the acclaim function way more frequently when compared to Kılıçdaroğlu who posted more attack-themed messages. Furthermore, while both candidates employed posts blending multiple functions, Kılıçdaroğlu merged a higher percentage of posts containing both acclaim and attack functions compared to President Erdoğan. Regarding character and policy topics, it can be noted that President Erdoğan predominantly focused on the past deeds for acclaim, future, and general goals, whereas it was revealed that Kılıçdaroğlu preferred to share more attack-themed messages on past deeds of the opponents and focused less on past accomplishments of their party. The discourse tendency of President Erdoğan in leaning more toward acclaiming his own policies, and the tendency of Kılıçdaroğlu in preferring to attack the policies of the AK Party are understandable issues when we consider the fact that AK Party has been the ruling party in Türkiye for more than 20 years. However, results reveal that the both leaders emphasized inclusivity in their posts, albeit to varying degrees, reflecting their efforts to appeal to a diverse range of societal segments.

The findings pointed out the fact that differences in leaders' political approaches and goals resulted in differences in the ways they communicated their governance visions and interacted with voters, even though they used similar rhetorical strategies. For example, President Erdoğan's campaign rhetoric was mainly shaped around themes such as natural disaster management, public investments, economic policies, political philosophy, with an emphasis on unity, nationalism, and strong leadership. On the other hand, it was found that Kılıçdaroğlu's discourse covered a wider range and was shaped around the themes of social justice, inclusiveness, and democratic principles. These distinctions shed a light on how leaders reflect their priorities and visions of governance by offering different options to voters.

It was also revealed that while using attack strategies, both leaders criticized each other's political philosophies and campaign strategies, and accused each other of manipulation tactics and ignoring basic values. While President Erdoğan targeted perceived inconsistencies between the opposition's promises and actions, Kılıçdaroğlu criticized the ruling party for repression and spreading religious ideology for political gain. Although the themes they emphasized in their posts were different, it was found that each leader used the attack function to criticize their opponents' governance approaches, election strategies, and approach to issues related to rights and freedoms.

Although both leaders used the defense function in their pre-election campaign discourses to eliminate accusations from the other side, it was found that this function was the least-used function by both leaders. While President Erdoğan used this function to deny accusations of being oppressive and fear monger, Kılıçdaroğlu was using the defense function to deny accusations of dishonesty.

CONCLUSION

This study examines the political campaign discourse of President Erdoğan and Kılıçdaroğlu during the 2023 Turkish Presidential Election and 28th Term Parliamentary General Election using Benoit's Functional Theory of Political Campaign Discourse. By examining a significant but under-explored area of political campaign discourse in Türkiye, findings reveal the nuances in both the topic-based emphasis and the employed discourse functions between two leaders. Accordingly, this study contributes to the political marketing literature by revealing the dynamics of political discourse in Türkiye, which is a secular, nationalist, and predominantly Muslim country. In other words, this research extends the theoretical understanding of political communication, particularly in diverse socio-political contexts. Moreover, the findings of this research provide fruitful insights for researchers, practitioners, and politicians interested in political messaging, and the broader implications of campaign discourse in Türkiye.

The comparative analysis of the political campaign discourses of Mr Recep Tayyip Erdoğan and Mr Kemal Kılıçdaroğlu offers several practical and theoretical implications. Politicians can leverage these findings to refine their communication strategies, recognizing the importance of balancing acclaim and attack functions based on their political status and campaign objectives. For instance, as the findings of this study revealed, ruling party candidates may find it beneficial to emphasize their achievements and future plans to project continuity and stability, while opposition candidates might wish to focus on critiquing the incumbents to highlight the need for change. Moreover, understanding the nuanced use of the defense function can help politicians better prepare for and respond to accusations and criticisms. By analyzing how President Erdoğan and Kılıçdaroğlu employed this function, candidates can develop more effective rebuttals that reinforce their credibility and address voter concerns. Politicians can also tailor their messages to reflect the themes and issues most relevant to their target audiences. As seen in President Erdoğan's emphasis on natural disaster management, economic policies, and strong leadership, and Kılıçdaroğlu's focus on social justice, inclusiveness, and democratic principles, candidates can prioritize topics that resonate with their constituents' values and needs. This strategic alignment of message content with voter priorities can enhance voter engagement and support. Additionally, the study highlights the importance of inclusivity in political discourse. Both leaders made efforts to appeal to diverse societal segments, reflecting a broader trend toward inclusive campaigning. Politicians can adopt this approach to broaden their appeal and connect with a wider range of voters, thereby increasing their electoral prospects. Lastly, the effective use of social media as a campaign tool is underscored by the findings. By strategically utilizing platforms like X to disseminate their messages, politicians can achieve real-time engagement with voters, track public reactions, and adjust their strategies accordingly. This dynamic interaction with the electorate can provide valuable feedback and foster a more responsive and adaptive campaign.

Voters can utilize the findings of this study to critically evaluate the messages presented to them, discerning the strategic intentions behind political discourse. By understanding the functions of acclaim, attack, and defense in political messaging, voters can better navigate the often complex landscape of electoral communication, making more informed decisions based on the underlying themes and priorities of each candidate's campaign.

Researchers in the field of political marketing can use the revealed insights to further explore the dynamics of political communication in different cultural and political contexts. The study underscores the value of Benoit's Functional Theory in dissecting and understanding political campaign strategies, providing a robust framework for analyzing how political actors engage with their audience. Future research can build on this work by examining other political contexts, comparing party-centric versus individual-centric campaign strategies, and exploring the impact of different media platforms on political discourse and voter engagement.

It should be noted that this study solely focuses on individual politicians' discourse shared on their personal social media accounts, specifically on the X platform. Social media platforms shift the focus to individual politicians over political parties, expanding the political arena for more personalized campaigning, which contrasts with the party-centered systems, where the need to communicate a personal image and post personalized messages online might not be as evident, potentially conflicting with political parties' structured communication strategies (Enli & Skogerbø, 2013). In future studies, political parties' discourse can be compared with that of individual politicians to assess their congruence. The study can also be broadened by considering candidates' posts on their other social media accounts, their appearances on television programs, speeches at rallies, messages on their political party's social media accounts, and the messages of other political leaders and parties in the alliance. Additionally, political marketing activities are not confined solely to election periods; they encompass all endeavors of political parties and leaders. Therefore, similar studies could be conducted by adjusting and/or extending the selected dates. Furthermore, an analysis can be conducted on which functions and themes of political messages disseminated on social media receive more shares, interactions, support, or criticism. Moreover, another potential research area could be the political campaign rhetoric crafted for political party members in leadership elections, which essentially target individuals from the same political ideology. The political message strategies observed in local elections, rather than in general elections, can also be studied within the framework of Benoit's Functional Theory of Political Campaign Discourse.

In summary, the distinct patterns in the political campaign discourse of Erdoğan and Kılıçdaroğlu not only enhance our understanding of the strategic use of acclaim, attack, and defense functions in electoral campaigns but also offer valuable guidance for political actors, voters, and researchers alike. These findings highlight the critical role of tailored communication strategies in shaping public perception and engagement, providing a roadmap for effective political marketing and voter education in diverse socio-political landscapes.

Notes

1 In 2013, it was initially started as a contest to the construction plan of Taksim Gezi Park in İstanbul. Later on, thousands of citizens were on the streets to protest government policies. (Can Gürcan, E., & Peker, E. (2015). A class analytic approach to the Gezi Park events: Challenging the "middle class" myth. *Capital & Class, 39*(2), 321–343.)

2 This principle emphasizes the separation of religious affairs from state governance and public institutions, aiming to ensure equality and freedom of religion for all citizens irrespective of their beliefs. Laicism in Türkiye is enshrined in the Constitution, which prohibits religious influence in state affairs, mandates a secular education system, and regulates religious practices under state control through institutions such as the Directorate of Religious Affairs (Diyanet) (Ulutas, U. (2010). Religion and Secularism in Turkey: The Dilemma of the Directorate of Religious Affairs. *Middle Eastern Studies, 46*(3), 389–399. https://doi.org/10.1080/00263200902899812)

REFERENCES

Anadolu Agency. (2024, August 5). *Türkiye remembers Feb. 6 earthquake victims*. Anadolu Agency. https://www.aa.com.tr/en/turkiye/turkiye-remembers-feb-6-earthquake-victims/3128724. Accessed on August 5, 2024.

Andaç, A., & Akbıyık, F. (2016). Siyasal Pazarlama Açısından Sosyal Medya Kullanımı: Isparta İli Örneği. *Süleyman Demirel Üniversitesi İktisadi ve İdari Bilimler Fakültesi Dergisi, 21*(3).

Banavand, R. (2020). *Political marketing and the US. Presidential campaign strategies: A functional and rhetorical analysis of Donald Trump's and Hillary Clinton's discourse on Twitter* (Publication No. 656638) [Doctoral Thesis]. Dokuz Eylul University.

Barlas, N. (2018). *Siyasal İletişimde Dijitalleşme: 24 Haziran 2018 Cumhurbaşkanlığı Seçimleri Üzerine Karşılaştırmalı Bir Twitter Analizi* (Publication No. 570829) [Master's Thesis]. Kadir Has University.

Bayraktutan, G., Binark, M., Çomu, T., Doğu, B., İslamoğlu, G., & Aydemir, A. T. (2014). Siyasal iletişim sürecinde sosyal medya ve Türkiye'de 2011 genel seçimlerinde Twitter kullanımı. *Bilig, 68*, 59–96.

BBC News. (2017, April 12). Türkiye referandumu: İşte kesin sonuçlar. *BBC*. https://www.bbc.com/turkce/haberler-turkiye-39612452. Accessed on July 18, 2024.

BBC News. (2018a, April 28). İşte cumhurbaşkanı adayları. *BBC*. https://www.bbc.com/turkce/haberler-turkiye-43992766. Accessed on July 18, 2024.

BBC News. (2018b, June 29). İşte Türkiye'nin yeni Cumhurbaşkanı Recep Tayyip Erdoğan. *BBC*. https://www.bbc.com/turkce/haberler-turkiye-44597179. Accessed on July 18, 2024.

Benoit, W. L. (1997). Image restoration discourse and crisis communication. *Public Relations Review, 23*, 177–186.

Benoit, W. L. (1999). *Seeing spots: A functional analysis of Presidential television advertisements, 1952–1996*. Praeger.

Benoit, W. L. (2001). The functional approach to Presidential television spots: Acclaiming, attacking, defending 1952–2000. *Communication Studies, 52*, 109–126.

Benoit, W. L. (2003). Topic of presidential campaign discourse and election outcome. *Western Journal of Communication, 67*, 97–111.

Benoit, W. L. (2007). *Communication in political campaigns*. Peter Lang.

Benoit, W. L. (2010). *Communication in political campaigns*. Peter Lang.

Benoit, W. L. (2017). Functional theory of political campaign discourse. In R. E. Denton (Ed.), *Political campaign communication: Theory, method, and practice* (pp. 3–32). Lexington Books, an imprint of The Rowman & Littlefield Publishing Group, Inc.

Benoit, W. L., & Goode, J. (2006). A functional analysis of non-presidential primary debates. *Speaker & Gavel*, *43*, 22–35.

Benoit, W. L., Henson, J. R., & Sudbrock, L. A. (2011). A functional analysis of 2008 US presidential primary debates. *Argumentation and Advocacy*, *48*(2), 97–110.

Benoit, W. L., Pier, P. M., & Blaney, J. R. (1997). Sustainable development' in visual imagery: A functional approach to televised political spots: Acclaiming, attacking, defending. *Communication Quarterly*, *45*(1), 1–20.

Bischof, D., & Senninger, R. (2018). Simple politics for the people? Complexity in campaign messages and political knowledge. *European Journal of Political Research*, *57*(2), 473–495. https://doi.org/10.1111/1475-6765.12235

Boukala, S., & Dimitrakopoulou, D. (2017). The politics of fear vs. the politics of hope: Analyzing the 2015 Greek election and referendum campaigns. *Critical Discourse Studies*, *14*(1), 39–55. https://doi.org/10.1080/17405904.2016.1182933

Boyd, D., Golder, S., & Lotan, G. (2010, January). Tweet, tweet, retweet: Conversational aspects of retweeting on twitter. In *2010 43rd Hawaii international conference on system sciences* (pp. 1–10). IEEE.

Brazeal, L. M., & Benoit, W. L. (2001). A functional analysis of congressional television spots, 1986–2000. *Communication Quarterly*, *49*(4), 436–454.

Broersma, M., & Graham, T. (2013). Twitter as a news source: How Dutch and British newspapers used tweets in their news coverage, 2007–2011. *Journalism Practice*, *7*(4), 446–464.

Choi, Y., & Benoit, W. L. (2009). A functional analysis of French and south Korean political leaders' debates. *Speaker & Gavel*, *46*, 59–80.

CNN Türk (2019). *İstanbul İli Yerel Seçim Sonuçları - 23 Haziran 2019 Yerel Seçimleri*. https://secim.cnnturk.com/23-haziran-2019-yerel-secimleri/istanbul-ili-yerel-secim-sonuclari/. Accessed on July 18, 2024.

Congar, K. (2019, February 19). *31 Mart yerel seçimleri: İttifak partileri toplam 51 ilde işbirliği yaptı*. https://tr.euronews.com/2019/02/19/31-mart-yerel-secimleri-ittifak-partileri-toplam-51-ilde-isbirligi-yapti-aday-listeleri. Accessed on July 18, 2024.

Deutsche Welle (2007, August 28) Cumhurbaşkanı Abdullah Gül. https://www.dw.com/tr/11-cumhurba%C5%9Fkan%C4%B1-abdullah-g%C3%BCl/a-2755773. Accessed on July 18, 2024.

Diken (2022, July 13). *BBP, 'Cumhur İttifakı'nın hem içinde hem dışında*. https://www.diken.com.tr/bbp-cumhur-ittifakinin-hem-icinde-hem-disinda/. Accessed on July 18, 2024.

Dudek, P., & Partacz, S. (2009). Functional theory of political discourse. Televised debates during the parliamentary campaign in 2007 in Poland. *Central European Journal of Chemistry*, *2*(2 (3)), 367–379.

El, K. (2023, March 6). *İYİ Parti'yi masaya döndüren 22 saat*. https://www.dw.com/tr/i%CC%87yi%CC%87-partiyi-masaya-d%C3%B6nd%C3%BCren-22-saat/a-64903726. Accessed on July 18, 2024.

Enli, G. S., & Skogerbø, E. (2013). Personalized campaigns in party-centred politics: Twitter and Facebook as arenas for political communication. *Information, Communication & Society*, *16*(5), 757–774.

Euronews (2014, August 8). *Cumhurbaşkanlığı seçimi'nin ilk turda sonuçlanacağını düşünüyorum*. https://tr.euronews.com/2014/08/08/cumhurbaskanligi-secimi-nin-ilk-turda-sonuclanacagini-dusunuyorum. Accessed on July 18, 2024.

Euronews (2023, November 4). *CHP 38. Olağan Kurultayı: Yeni Genel Başkan ve Parti Meclisi belirleniyor*. https://tr.euronews.com/2023/11/04/chp-38-olagan-kurultayi-yeni-genel-baskan-ve-parti-meclisi-belirleniyor. Accessed on July 18, 2024.

Henson, J. P., & Benoit, W. L. (2010). Because I said so: A functional theory analysis of evidence in political TV spots. *Speaker & Gavel*, *47*, l–l5.

Hjarvard, S. (2008). The mediatization of society. A theory of the media as agents of social and cultural change. *Nordicom Review*, *30*, 105–134.

Isotalus, P. (2011). Analyzing presidential debates. *Nordicom Review*, *32*(1), 31–43.

Kendall, K. E., & Paine, S. C. (1995). Political images and voting decisions. In *Candidate images in presidential elections* (pp. 19–35). Praeger Westport.

Kreiss, D., & McGregor, S. C. (2018). Technology firms shape political communication: The work of Microsoft, Facebook, Twitter, and Google with campaigns during the 2016 US presidential cycle. *Political Communication*, *35*(2), 155–177.

Lock, A., & Harris, P. (1996). Political marketing-vive la différence. *European Journal of Marketing*, *30*(10/11), 14–24.

McNair, B. (2017). *An introduction to political communication*. Routledge.

Merritt, S. (1984). Negative political advertising: Some empirical findings. *Journal of Advertising*, *13*(3), 27–38.

Ministry of Foreign Affairs of Turkey (n.d.). *Türkiye'nin Dış Politika Temel İlkeleri*. https://www.mfa.gov.tr/sub.tr.mfa?199113bb-f534-408f-a373-64fe1946f1b7. Accessed on July 18, 2024.

Mirzaei, A., Eslami, Z. R., & Safari, F. (2017). Exploring rhetorical-discursive practices of Rouhani's presidential campaign and victory of his prudence-and-hope key: A discourse of persuasion. *Russian Journal of Linguistics*, *21*(1), 161–182. https://doi.org/10.22363/2312-9182-2017-21-1-161-182

Neuendorf, K. A. (2002). *The content analysis guidebook*. SAGE.

Official Gazette of the Republic of Turkey (2007, June 16). *Türkiye Cumhuriyeti Anayasası*. https://www.

resmigazete.gov.tr/eskiler/2007/06/20070616-1.htm. Accessed on July 18, 2024.

Özdemir, F. N., Arpacı, I., & Katılmış, C. (2020). ABD ve Türkiye'nin Başkanlık Sistemlerinin Karşılaştırmalı bir Analizi. *Turkish Studies-Social Sciences, 15*(8).

Öztürk, F. (2018, October 1). *Cumhurbaşkanlığı hükümet sisteminde TBMM: Yetkileri ve görevleri ne olacak?*. https://www.bbc.com/turkce/haberler-turkiye-44737074. Accessed on July 18, 2024.

Painter, D. L., & Rizzo, K. (2017). The Verbal tone of the 2016 presidential primaries: Candidate twitter, debate, and campaign speech rhetoric. In *The Presidency and social media* (pp. 143–157). Routledge.

Papacharissi, Z., & de Fatima Oliveira, M. (2012). Affective news and networked publics: The rhythms of news storytelling on# Egypt. *Journal of Communication*, *62*(2), 266–282.

Popkin, S. L. (1994). *The reasoning voter: Communication and persuasion in presidential campaigns*. University of Chicago Press.

Sayın, A. (2023, January 27). *Altılı Masa 'Millet İttifakı'na dönüştü, cumhurbaşkanı adayı için 13 Subat'ta yapılacak toplantı işaret edildi*. https://www.bbc.com/turkce/articles/clkxen2mzj8o. Accessed on July 18, 2024.

Sheldon, C. A., & Sallot, L. M. (2008). Image repair in politics: Testing effects of communication strategy and performance history in a faux pas. *Journal of Public Relations Research*, *21*(1), 25–50.

Silsüpür, Ö. (2016). Siyasal iletişim aracı olarak Twitter'ın kullanımı: 07 Haziran 2015 genel seçimi üzerine bir çalışma. *Gümüşhane Üniversitesi İletişim Fakültesi Elektronik Dergisi*, *4*(2).

Sözcü (2018, February 20). *Cumhurbaşkanı Erdoğan AKP-MHP ittifakının ismini açıkladı*. Cumhur İttifakı. https://web.archive.org/web/20180221002854/http://www.sozcu.com.tr/2018/gundem/akp-grup-toplantisi-43-2234166/. Accessed on July 18, 2024.

Sriwimon, L., & Zilli, P. J. (2017). Applying Critical Discourse Analysis as a conceptual framework for investigating gender stereotypes in political media discourse. *Kasetsart Journal of Social Sciences*, *38*(2), 136–142.

Strömbäck, J. (2008). Four phases of mediatization: An analysis of the mediatization of politics. *The international journal of press/politics*, *13*(3), 228–246.

Supreme Election Council of the Republic of Türkiye (2024a). *14 May 2023 presidential election and 28th term parliamentary general election*. https://www.ysk.gov.tr/tr/14-mayis-2023-secimleri/82491

Supreme Election Council of the Republic of Türkiye (2024b). *03 November 2002 22nd term parliamentary general election*. https://www.ysk.gov.tr/tr/03-kasim-2002-xxii-donem-milletvekili-genel-secimi/3009. Accessed on July 16, 2024.

Supreme Election Council of the Republic of Türkiye (2024c). *22 July 2007 23rd term parliamentary general election*. https://www.ysk.gov.tr/tr/22-temmuz-2007-xxiii-donem-milletvekili-genel-secimi/5001. Accessed on July 16, 2024.

Supreme Election Council of the Republic of Türkiye (2024d). *12 June 2011 24th Term Parliamentary General Election*. https://www.ysk.gov.tr/tr/12-haziran-2011-xxiv-donem-milletvekili-genel-secimi/4929. Accessed on July 16, 2024.

Supreme Election Council of the Republic of Türkiye (2024e). *29 March 2009 Local government general elections*. https://www.ysk.gov.tr/tr/29-mart-2009-mahalli-idareler-genel-secimleri/2820. Accessed on July 16, 2024.

Supreme Election Council of the Republic of Türkiye (2024f). *30 March 2014 local government general elections*. https://www.ysk.gov.tr/tr/30-mart-2014-mahalli-idareler-genel-secimleri/2853. Accessed on July 16, 2024.

Supreme Election Council of the Republic of Türkiye (2024g). *21 October 2007 constitutional amendment referendum*. https://www.ysk.gov.tr/tr/21-ekim-2007-anayasa-degisikligi-halkoylamasi/2762. Accessed on July 16, 2024.

Supreme Election Council of the Republic of Türkiye (2024h). *12th presidential election*. https://www.ysk.gov.tr/tr/onikinci-cumhurbaskani-secimi/3456. Accessed on July 16, 2024.

Supreme Election Council of the Republic of Türkiye (2024i). *1 November 2015 26th term parliamentary general election*. https://www.ysk.gov.tr/tr/1-kasim-2015–26-donem-milletvekili-genel-secimi/3413. Accessed on July 16, 2024.

Supreme Election Council of the Republic of Türkiye (2024j). *24 June 2018 presidential election and 27th term parliamentary general election*. https://www.ysk.gov.tr/tr/24-haziran-2018-secimleri/77536. Accessed on July 18, 2024.

Supreme Election Council of the Republic of Türkiye (2024k). *31 March 2019 local government election*. https://www.ysk.gov.tr/tr/31-mart-2019-mahalli-i%CC%87dareler-secimi/77916. Accessed on July 18, 2024.

Supreme Election Council of the Republic of Türkiye (2024l). *14 may 2023 presidential election and 28th term parliamentary general election*. https://www.ysk.gov.tr/tr/14-mayis-2023-secimleri/82491. Accessed on July 16, 2024.

TBMM Araştırma Hizmetleri Başkanlığı (2017). *Karşılaştırmalı Hükümet Sistemleri: Yarı-Başkanlık Sistemi (Fransa, Polonya ve Rusya Örnekleri)* (2nd ed.). TBMM Basımevi.

TRT World (2024). *2024 Türkiye local elections*. https://www.trtworld.com/elections/turkiye/2024. Accessed on July 18, 2024.

Türk, H. S. (2006). Seçim, seçim sistemleri ve anayasal tercih. *Anayasa Yargısı*, *22*(1), 75–113.

Vavreck, L. (2016). Yes, political ads are still important, even for Donald Trump. *The New York Times*.

Vergeer, M. (2015). Twitter and political campaigning. *Sociology Compass*, *9*(9), 745–760.

Waymer, D., & Hill, T. E. (2023). A conceptual update to image restoration theory (IRT) via an analysis of the vice-presidential campaign of Kamala Harris. *Public Relations Review, 49*(2), 102306.

Westen, D. (2009). *The political brain: The role of emotion in deciding the fate of the nation*. Public Affairs.

Yıldırım, A., & Simsek, H. (1999). *Sosyal bilimlerde nitel araştırma yöntemleri* (11th ed.). Seçkin Yayıncılık.

Zhang, F., Stromer-Galley, J., Tanupabrungsun, S., Hegde, Y., Mccracken, N., & Hemsley, J. (2017). Understanding discourse acts: Political campaign messages classification on Facebook and twitter. In *Lecture notes in computer science* (pp. 242–247). Lecture Notes in Computer Science. https://doi.org/10.1007/978-3-319-60240-0_29

APPENDIX 9.1: TIMELINE OF 2023 PRESIDENTIAL ELECTIONS IN TÜRKİYE

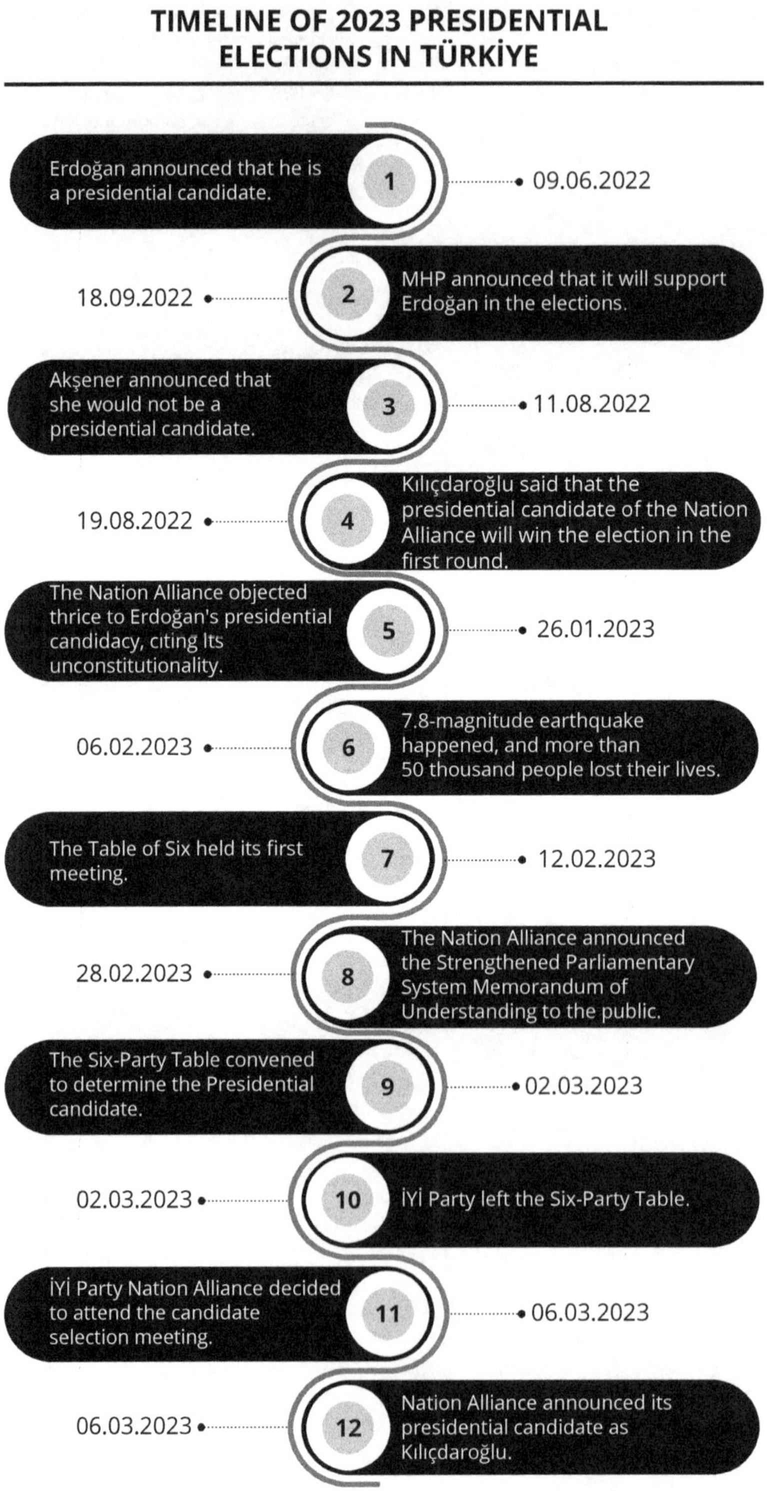
TIMELINE OF 2023 PRESIDENTIAL ELECTIONS IN TÜRKİYE
1
Erdoğan announced that he is a presidential candidate.
09.06.2022
2
MHP announced that it will support Erdoğan in the elections.
18.09.2022
3
Akşener announced that she would not be a presidential candidate.
11.08.2022
4
Kılıçdaroğlu said that the presidential candidate of the Nation Alliance will win the election in the first round.
19.08.2022
5
The Nation Alliance objected thrice to Erdoğan's presidential candidacy, citing Its unconstitutionality.
26.01.2023
6
7.8-magnitude earthquake happened, and more than 50 thousand people lost their lives.
06.02.2023
7
The Table of Six held its first meeting.
12.02.2023
8
The Nation Alliance announced the Strengthened Parliamentary System Memorandum of Understanding to the public.
28.02.2023
9
The Six-Party Table convened to determine the Presidential candidate.
02.03.2023
10
İYİ Party left the Six-Party Table.
02.03.2023
11
İYİ Party Nation Alliance decided to attend the candidate selection meeting.
06.03.2023
12
Nation Alliance announced its presidential candidate as Kılıçdaroğlu.
06.03.2023

TIMELINE OF 2023 PRESIDENTIAL ELECTIONS IN TÜRKİYE

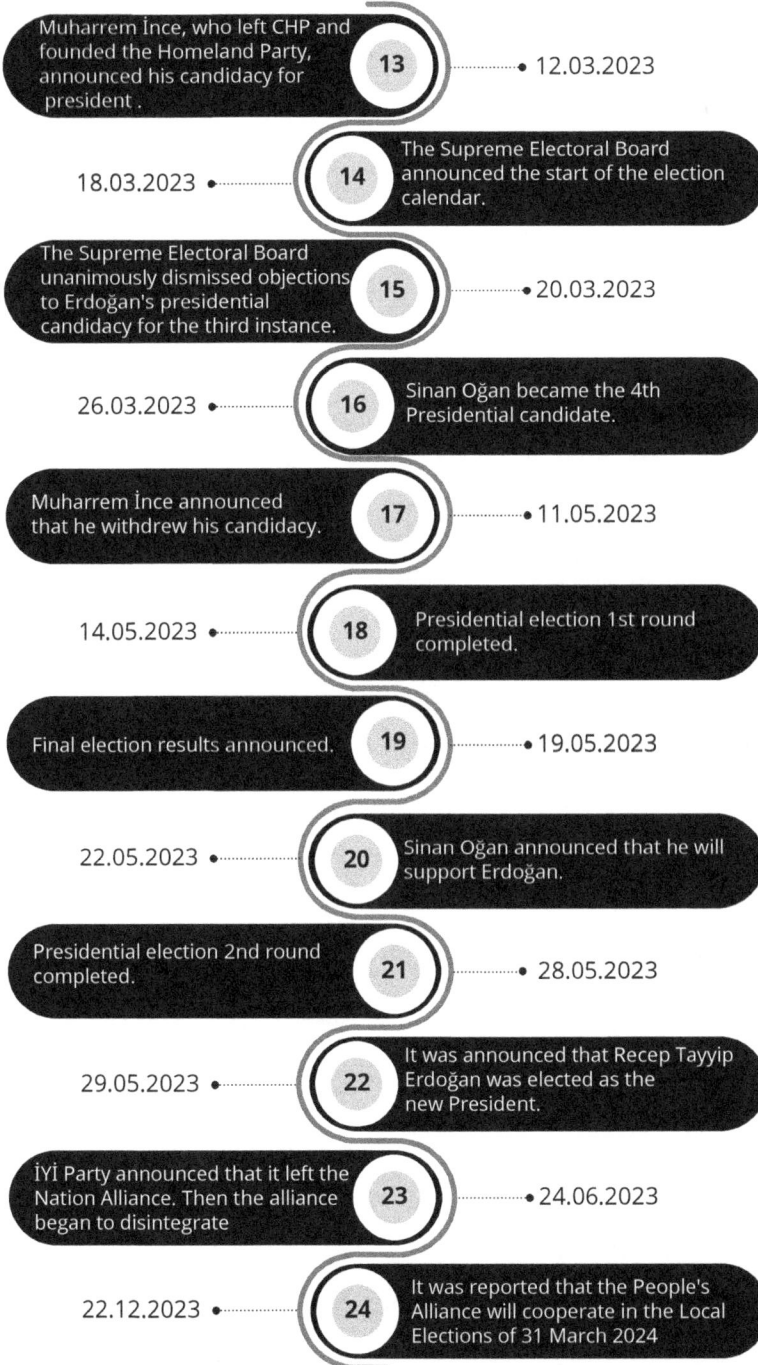

13	12.03.2023	Muharrem İnce, who left CHP and founded the Homeland Party, announced his candidacy for president .
14	18.03.2023	The Supreme Electoral Board announced the start of the election calendar.
15	20.03.2023	The Supreme Electoral Board unanimously dismissed objections to Erdoğan's presidential candidacy for the third instance.
16	26.03.2023	Sinan Oğan became the 4th Presidential candidate.
17	11.05.2023	Muharrem İnce announced that he withdrew his candidacy.
18	14.05.2023	Presidential election 1st round completed.
19	19.05.2023	Final election results announced.
20	22.05.2023	Sinan Oğan announced that he will support Erdoğan.
21	28.05.2023	Presidential election 2nd round completed.
22	29.05.2023	It was announced that Recep Tayyip Erdoğan was elected as the new President.
23	24.06.2023	İYİ Party announced that it left the Nation Alliance. Then the alliance began to disintegrate
24	22.12.2023	It was reported that the People's Alliance will cooperate in the Local Elections of 31 March 2024

APPENDIX 9.2: CODE BOOK FOR CONTENT ANALYSIS

The subsequent section delineates the categories utilized for coding each post on the X platform within the provided code sheet. Kindly complete the blank space with the relevant textual response or indicate the appropriate code by circling it.

Sample and Coder Information

1 **Coder ID**
Please identify your coder ID (i.e., 1).

2 **Post ID**
Each X platform post has a unique number. Please identify the post ID on code sheet (i.e., 163).

3 **Candidate**
Each candidate has a unique number, "1" represents Recep Tayyip Erdoğan, "2" represents Kemal Kılıçdaroğlu. Please identify the candidate number.

4 **Date**
Please record the day/month/year that the post was published. (i.e., 15/03/2023).

5 **Video**
If the post is video-based or a video attached to the post please circle "1," Circle "0" if not.

6 **Image**
If the post is picture, screenshot, or Graphics Interchange Format (GIF) based or those elements are attached to the post, please circle "1." Circle "0" if not.

7 **Repost**
If the X platform user reposts of another account, please circle "1." Circle "0" if not.

Functions of Political Campaign Discourse

8 **Acclaim Theme**
The candidate acclaiming themselves and/or the political party to which they are affiliated. Please circle "1" if the acclaim theme is identified. Circle "0" if not.

9 **Attack Theme**
The attack theme consists of criticisms aimed at putting the rival candidate and/or party in a difficult position. Please circle "1" if the attack theme is identified. Circle "0" if not.

10 **Defense Theme**
The defense theme involves responding to sentences containing attacks from the opponent, aiming to exonerate and protect oneself. Please circle "1" if the defense theme is identified. Circle "0" if not.

Topics of Political Campaign Discourse

According to Benoit's Functional Theory of Political Campaign Discourse, each acclaim, attack, and defense function can relate to character or policy topics. Therefore, carefully read each topic theme below and evaluate their presence.

11 **Policy**
- **Past Deeds**
  Past deeds relate to the achievements of the candidates in the past. Please circle "1" if the past deeds theme is identified. Circle "0" if not.
- **Future Goals**
  Future goals pertain to the candidates' plans, projects, and promises for the future. Please circle "1" if the future goals theme is identified. Circle "0" if not.
- **General Goals**
  General goals encompass broad plans and objectives for the future. The distinction between general goals and future goals lies in the latter being more specific plans and projects. Please circle "1" if the past deeds theme is identified. Circle "0" if not.

12 **Character**
- **Personal Qualities**
  Personal qualities are related to the candidate's personal characteristics. Please circle "1" if the personal qualities theme is identified. Circle "0" if not.
- **Leadership Abilities**
  Leadership abilities demonstrate the candidate's prior experience in government positions or possession of the skills and qualifications required to successfully fulfil such a role. Please circle "1" if the leadership abilities theme is identified. Circle "0" if not.
- **Ideals**
  Ideals represent the principles and values that the candidate possesses and adheres to. Please circle "1" if the ideals theme is identified. Circle "0" if not.

13 **Personal Qualities**
- **Sincerity**
  Sincerity includes traits such as trust, honesty, consistency, and openness. Please circle "1" if the sincerity theme is identified. Circle "0" if not.
- **Morality**
  Morality encompasses decency, integrity, responsibility, and fairness. Please circle "1" if the morality theme is identified. Circle "0" if not.
- **Empathy**
  Empathy involves understanding, similarity to the voter, advocating for the voter, and compassion. Please circle "1" if the empathy theme is identified. Circle "0" if not.
- **Drive**
  Drive entails courage, diligence, strength, and determination. Please circle "1" if the drive theme is identified. Circle "0" if not.
- **Private Work Experience**
  Private work experience elucidates the candidate's experience in the private sector, based on personal qualities. Please circle "1" if the personal work experience theme is identified. Circle "0" if not.

14 **Election Promotion Campaign Efforts**
Election Promotion Campaign Efforts encompasses the actions undertaken by the candidate to support their election campaign. (i.e., activities such as information dissemination, encouraging voter turnout, emphasizing election security, attending meetings, and participating in live broadcasts). Please circle "1" if the election promotion campaign theme is identified. Circle "0" if not.

15 **Inclusivity**
Inclusivity showcases the candidate's commitment to embracing societal diversity and appealing to all. They emphasize equality before the state for citizens regardless of religion, language, race, sect, or political belief, promising equal rights and freedoms. Please circle "1" if the inclusivity theme is identified. Circle "0" if not.

Political Communication and Digital Media in Japan: Trends and Challenges

Igor Prusa

INTRODUCTION

It seems to be a conventional wisdom that Japan ranks among the most digitalized countries in the world. Indeed, the spread of information technologies and their penetration into the various areas of the social life is relatively high, and the economy effectively uses the opportunities offered by information and communications technologies (ICTs) for increased competitiveness and well-being. Some empirical studies, however, have proved that in the realm of politics, the role of digital media as a powerful platform for political communication is significantly lower in Japan than in similar standard democracies. A broad range of factors might be seen behind this phenomenon – from the strength of the conventional media up to the low level of political polarization. The important, but frequently omitted factor is the relatively low political participation of citizens. It is no gainsaying that most of Japanese citizens have a negative view on politics and show very reluctant attitude toward the political affairs when compared to other countries where political attitudes sensitively reflect any changes in political, economic, and social climates. The long-term decline in citizens participation was to a certain extent inhibited by the Tōhoku triple disaster which sparked a wave of political activism, but the direct connection between the rise in citizens participation and strengthening of digital media is rather disputable.

Japan may profile itself to foreign observers as just another functioning democracy: it has regular democratic elections, regulated political campaigns, and erudite marketing strategies. However, political marketing products are always consumed against a certain culturally specific background. In other words, people with differing cultural and political ideologies have qualitatively different styles of interacting with political entities. Thus, this chapter focuses less on political marketing strategies per se (i.e., top-down political communication), and more on how Japanese voters and netizens receive political messages, how they interpret them, and finally how they respond to them (i.e., bottom-up political participation).

The chapter discusses the correlation of the role of digital media and political participation, including motivations for citizens to become involved in different channels of political engagement. The aim of the chapter is to answer the following questions. How Japanese citizens identify their political participation? Do the current channels of participation fit the needs of the people when it comes to take an active part in the political process? Can so-called "new" (i.e., social/digital) media serve as a new and more effective channel for the political participation of citizens, and can they accelerate or, on the contrary, hinder the political activism of Japanese citizens?

THEORETICAL BACKGROUND

Political Participation

Simply put, political participation refers to people participating in the political process by voicing their opinions and beliefs. It represents all voluntary, nonprofessional activities of the public that have a potential to influence public policy (Pekkanen, 2006; Putnam, 2000). The provision of political information to the citizens could lead directly to a more informed citizenry, willing to participate actively in politics (e.g., Castells, 1996; Tkach-Kawasaki, 2003). An active political participation in public life represents the key "civic virtue" in democracy (Putnam, 2000).

Political participation requires a readiness of both the government and the citizens to accept certain responsibilities and roles. The honest inclusion of a citizens' representatives as "partners" in decision-making makes for successful participation (Srinivas, 2015). This kind of participation, where citizens' activities affect politics, is not only about conventional voting – it also points to unconventional activities such as contacting public officials, donating money, protesting, but also posting online blogs, demonstrating online, and signing online petitions. In Japan, such participation is believed to contribute to the stability of political systems (Okura and Kaigo, 2017) while generating subjective feelings of well-being (Tiefenbach & Holdgrün, 2015).

Political participation is essential for democracy to function effectively – it can make citizens think more democratically and act more publicly. This democracy can be measured by the extent to which *formal* institutions at the center (parliament, ministries) are open to input from *informal* public spheres on the periphery (citizen groups, NGOs). Throughout the postwar period, however, Japanese society has only infrequently exhibited the level of vitality that is necessary for bringing conflicts from the periphery to the center (see Freeman, 2003). Besides, there is only little incentive on the part of the Japanese state to engage citizens in political participation in decision-making process. The government only makes suggestions for change, but it has no real motive to promote political participation (Kida, 2019; Ogawa, 2009). Consequently, political participation in Japan is less citizen-centric and elite-challenging, and more government-centric and system-affirming.

To make things worse, Japanese mass media were frequently subverting, misleading, or ignoring the political periphery represented by informal public spheres (see Hadl & Hamada, 2009; Pekkanen, 2006; Snow, 2020). In other words, the mass media serve to lower rather than raise the level of political participation in Japan. Obviously, Japanese newspapers and TV stations are not really appropriate for the purpose of political participation, as their reporting often reflects the partisan allegiance to political parties (consider only the close ties between the leading daily *Yomiuri Shimbun* and the ruling Liberal Democratic Party). There is no space for political participation because Japan's media system as a whole caters to the power elite center and does not engage in investigative journalism (Prusa, 2023; Snow, 2020). Logically, the spread of digital media in Japan was believed to create an alternative or parallel public sphere to the mass mediated one (see below).

Civic Engagement

Various forms of political participation are approached as a mode of civic engagement, that is, those activities that individuals perform to express their political voice (e.g., Hommerich, 2015). Simply put, civic engagement means participation in public life. It ranges from having a general interest in community-related matters to voluntary involvement in one's neighborhood. In the west, civic engagement took on a more confrontational form (i.e., violent protests and lawsuits), but Japanese engagement usually takes the cooperative form (i.e., civic groups collaborating with government officials). One exception to this rule was the radical social movement in the 1960s, which challenged the political status quo by opposing the US-Japan Security Treaty and the Vietnam War.

The crucial component for civic engagement in Japan is the citizen and his/her voluntariness. Here, the term "citizen" (*shimin*) simply represents anyone who voluntarily participates in civic engagement (Imada, 2010). Today, with the help of alternative (digital) media, these *shimin* supply infrastructure for all forms of civic engagement. Unfortunately, mature democracies including Japan experience a decline of civic engagement and political interest, which is often attributed to the expansion of the government and corporate sectors (e.g., Putnam, 2000; Steel, 2016). Besides, for ordinary Japanese, an intermediary civic engagement is less important than daily interpersonal communication (Lee, 2016). In other words, the emphasis does no rest on political discussions, but on the importance of belonging, community benefit, and shared values.

Sadly, Japanese *shimin* are today systematically produced through state-supervised education. They are expected to be docile, apolitical, and collaborating with authority (Ogawa, 2009). Thus, the Japanese state is making *shimin* an ideal subject of the state, which fits the ideology of the current neoliberal system, but it suppresses the ideology of an autonomous civil sphere.

Many agree that the digital media has a certain potential to develop civic engagement. In the digital age, civic engagement encompasses a range of repertoires and settings – including formal websites, social media platforms, use of SMS, email, and other digital modes of communication. These digital media create connections between affinity groups, enable citizens to gain knowledge on political issues, and increase the ability to compare multiple points of view (e.g., Calderado, 2018; Swope, 2021). Further, civil engagement points to using digital media to change others' political views. This engagement influences both the political actors (administration, government) and social actors (community organizations, NPOs). On the one hand, the citizens may be providing public services as patterns of government, but on the other hand, they can protest and lobby the government to achieve specific purpose. In Japanese history, the off- and online protest activity in the wake of the 2011 Tōhoku disaster indicated that Japan was at the start of a new phase of civil engagement (see below).

Social Capital

Civic engagement is a key component of social capital. Social capital is the amount of mobilizing power that people possess to achieve a goal. This goal is either private (self-interest) or public (collective interest). Simply put, it represents the connections among people that enable them to get things done together. Social capital promotes the resources that exist among positive human relationships (Putnam, 2000) and it produces social benefits such as economic growth and improved political performance (e.g., Kage, 2011). In Japan, the bedrock of social capital are voluntary organizations (see below).

Social capital makes Japanese society more cooperative through greater political participation (Ikeda & Richey, 2012). In other words, social capital enhances the likelihood that a citizen will be engaged in politics. This requires a sense of civic duty, high reciprocity among members, and a certain level of general social trust. (Lack of trust drives people to pursue only their self-interest). In Japan, social capital is usually generated either in personal networks (e.g., daily conversations) or during social interactions with a citizen's discussions (Lee, 2016). Besides, the areas with higher social capital are more likely to respond to natural disasters by pulling together while avoiding crimes such as looting (Pekkanen, 2006). This became evident in the aftermath of the 1995 Great Hanshin Earthquake as well as the 2011 Tōhoku disaster (see below).

As a matter of fact, there is an overall decline in social capital worldwide (Putnam, 2000). Some believe that this can be avoided in Japan by using digital media to redesign the concept of "community" (Kaigo & Tkach-Kawasaki, 2017, p. 102). If used correctly, digital media can raise social capital in Japan to new levels (Kaigo, 2017b). However, social capital in Japan is still measured best by traditional membership in social organizations, while the internet, albeit increasing social contacts, is less related to social capital (Huang, Whang, & Xuchuan, 2017). In other words, internet in Japan may develop social capital indirectly, but it does not automatically increase it.

Besides, internet in Japan and elsewhere is a double-edged sword: on the one hand, it makes the pursuit of public interest easier, while on the other hand, omnipresent cybercrimes can neutralize one's aspirations to engage in civic activities online. For many Japanese, internet is perceived as a convenient but scary place, full of virtual aggression, computer virus, data theft, and malware (e.g., Kaigo, 2017a).

Civil Society

Civil society can be understood as a public sphere in which independent voluntary associations engage in public debate about various sociopolitical issues. It represents the organized nonstate, nonmarket sphere. Thus, it is not based on state surveillance and capital production, but rather on interpersonal solidarity and moral sentiment. Civil society contributes to the development of social capital and the formation of civic trust as the basis of effective government (Tocqueville, 2012). It is a medium through which the social contract between individuals and power elites is negotiated (Ducke, 2007). Moreover, it serves as a "school for democracy": citizens learn to become more civic-minded, which is critical for sustaining modern political participation (Putnam, 2000).

Civil society (*shimin shakai*) is deeply rooted in Japan. Having a long and extraordinary history, Japanese civil society represents one of the largest, most diverse, and most rapidly expanding civil societies in the world (Haddad, 2021; Ogawa, 2022). The aftermath of the aforementioned Great Hanshin Earthquake from 1995 can be perceived as the real "birth of civil society in Japan" (Pekkanen, 2006, p. 169).

Japanese civil society includes nonprofit organizations (NPOs), nongovernmental organizations (NGOs), neighborhood associations (NHAs), and all kinds of voluntary "citizens' groups" (*nin'i dantai*). These groups can take various shapes, such as social welfare groups (focusing on some community and its wellbeing – e.g., the elderly), identity-based groups (supporting marginalized communities – e.g., Korean minorities), issue-based groups (sharing a commitment to the same cause – e.g., The Japan Red Cross), and public protest groups (engaging in demonstrations – e.g., Japanese activists opposing nuclear power).

Despite the variety of citizens' groups, the independence from the state, critical debate, and open confrontation are *not* considered as important features of Japanese civil society. Japanese civil society groups have only little power to influence the public debate on topics such as human rights, environmental issues, and gender issues (Pekkanen, 2004). The citizens' political activities (such as peace demonstrations) are presented as associational events without any confrontational aspects, while it is paradoxically the fringes of society (extremists, right-wingers) that engage actively in a critical debate with the state (see Takikawa & Nagayoshi, 2017).

On the one side, Japanese civil society groups are pushed to perform welfare functions of the state while abstaining from political issues. On the other side, however, Japanese citizens can learn about corruption or mismanagement, and they can in turn lobby governments and mobilize public opinion against the state (Kage, 2011). Nevertheless, those who are most vocal in opposing the state are often negatively labeled as "un-civil society." In Japan, this category includes demonstration organizers, leftists, anarchists, feminists, and homeless supporters (Hadl, 2010, p. 164). In other words, those who openly challenge the government are automatically perceived as unwelcome adversaries of the state.

Owing to the aforementioned pathologies, Japanese civil society tends to be apolitical while lacking in effective advocacy activities that would bring about real social change (e.g., Ducke, 2007; Ogawa, 2009; Pekkanen, 2004; Vosse, 1999). This may be partly caused by the heritage of Confucianism in which the Japanese have traditionally relied more on the state for welfare while maintaining close-knit groups for self-help (Ikeda & Richey, 2012). In this setting, the Japanese state maintains a system of integration propaganda where everyone knows their place in the hierarchy from bottom to top (Snow, 2020). The public maintains its spectator function in the political process, always working within and never outside the system.

Finally, the political impotence is caused by the fact that Japan's civil society is composed of many small local groups but only few large professional organizations on the national level (Pekkanen, 2006). The latter (economic groups, agricultural organizations) is dominant in advocacy and has more direct access to political elites, while the former (civic organizations, welfare/educational groups) has less access to political elites and is passive in voicing their interests. The countless small, local groups do sustain social capital, but not advocacy. Because of the low levels of professionalization, low numbers of employees, and high level of regulations, Japanese civil groups very seldom influence the public sphere compared to other countries (Pekkanen, 2006; Swope, 2021).

Nonprofit Organizations

One of the main developments that shaped Japanese civil society is the emergence of NPOs. In Japan, the term NPO refers primarily to domestic NPOs usually concerned with welfare issues. The NPOs are voluntary citizens' groups that are organized on a local level, perform humanitarian functions, and encourage civic participation. The NPO activities include lobbying legislators, educating people, volunteering, publishing newsletters, raising funds, recruiting members, and more. The term "NPO" first appeared in 1995 when the Great Hanshin Earthquake hit Japan and volunteers from all over the country acted to aid victims of the disaster. This experience resulted in the passage of the NPO Law in 1998, which was followed by an NPO boom: nearly 70.000 NPOs emerged over the past two decades (Ogawa, 2022).

Japanese NPOs are one of the major actors in Japanese civil society. However, they usually lack references to the public sphere and its autonomy from the state. Throughout the time, the NPOs became mere subcontractors of the government (Ogawa, 2009) and a "garbage can" of ambitious hopes and policy initiatives (Kingston, 2004, p. 79). The government expects the heavily regulated NPOs to provide a range of social services, but political participation (setting the agenda and shaping policies) is discouraged. To Ogawa (2022), the NPOs are simply exploited by the government as an administrative tool to implement public policies.

The core group of NPOs usually consists of people invited by the government, while the ideal member of the group is the "ordinary citizen" (*futsū no hito*) who is willing to follow the rules without complaint (Ogawa, 2009, p. 157). The term *futsū* is used to guarantee membership in the majority in Japanese society, but it also suggests a subconscious attempt to exclude otherness: the Japanese-Koreans, the migrant workers from Asia, or the social "outcasts" (*burakumin*) are not presented by NPOs, although these groups are significantly present in the community. Besides, many Japanese NPOs cannot flourish because they fail to attract financial resources and recruit skilled professionals (Pekkanen, 2004, 2006). This is also why Ogawa (2009; 2022) points to the "failure" of civil society in Japan.

The large, professional NPOs (especially in welfare and education) have introduced digital technologies relatively early. The early networks were important in building a community consciousness among various constituencies (feminists, sexual minorities). The NPOs were considered "Japanese internet pioneers" (Hadl, 2010, p. 164), but the early use of the internet only conformed to established professional standards while lacking innovation. The NPOs' use of digital media is still relatively low – as opposed to the rightwing extremists (*netto uyoku*) who are very active on the internet. For instance, in the new millennium, more than one third of *netto uyoku* was using their Twitter accounts every day, which was more active and widespread usage compared to the general population (Takikawa & Nagayoshi, 2017). This is problematic, because the extremists' use of digital media has led to the rise of chauvinistic nationalism in Japan (Mori, 2021).

Neighborhood Associations

Apart from the voluntary NPOs, there exist other "administered" civil organizations in Japan – such as the NHAs (*jichikai* or *chōnankai*). NHAs are major community- or territory-based social organizations in Japanese society. They represent traditional communities that are mostly managed by the political regime to implement public policy (Kaigo, 2017; Pekkanen, 2006). Historically, the NHAs have developed from the "fife family unit system" (*goningumi*) which worked very closely with local governments in feudal Japan (today, the NHAs represent about 100 families each). The NHAs function primarily as grassroots administrative entities: they collect garbage for recycling, organize seasonal festivals, clean local parks, deliver disaster relief, and much more. They are compensated for their administrative activities by payments from the local government, and this financial dependency makes the NHAs act as a quasi-government organization – just like many other civil society groups in Japan (Kida, 2019; Ogawa, 2009; Pekkanen, 2006).

Most Japanese belong to one local NHA or another, making them Japan's most numerous civil society organization (Japan has around 300.000 NHAs). However, many Japanese participate in NHAs not because of political participation, but because of social pressure: the members fear that their absence would negatively affect their reputation with neighbors (Pekkanen, 2006). Nonetheless, the NHAs still have greater direct access to political elites than the NPOs, and they can exert some influence over policies by directly contacting the administration through social media such as Facebook (see Okura & Kaigo, 2017b). Some NHAs have indeed entered the "digital age," but the majority still rely on face-to-face, personal connections among community members (Haddad, 2021). At any rate, the NHAs can be regarded as the most basic source of social capital in Japan – despite the fact that younger generations show signs of declining interest (Tiefenbach & Holdgrün, 2015).

Volunteerism

Most effective for promoting civic engagement is social capital developed through voluntary participation. Volunteerism is deeply rooted in Japanese local communities: there is a long tradition of neighbors helping each other (*otagaisama*), engaging in cooperative labor (*yui*) and practicing social networking (*tsunagari*), which all points to traditionally forged close ties based on mutual aid (Ogawa, 2009, p. 95).

The essential moment for volunteerism in Japan came in January 1995, when the Great Hanshin Earthquake triggered a volunteerism boom, with approx. 1.3 million volunteers acting to aid disaster victims (Ogawa, 2022, p. 300). Only by the end of the 20th century, nearly 7 million

Japanese were engaged in some form of volunteer work (Kingston, 2004, p. 77). In the previous decade, an increasing share of Japanese (67% in 2013) stated that they would like to contribute to society in some way (Hommerich, 2015). This is important because volunteerism has the greatest effectiveness in promoting all sorts of civic engagement (Huang et al., 2017), it contributes to the accumulation of social capital (Ogawa, 2009), and it has a positive effect on the citizens' psychological well-being (Tiefenbach & Holdgrün, 2015). Moreover, those regions where volunteering is active show lower crime rites, lower unemployment rates, and higher birth rates (Ogawa, 2009). It is, however, important to note that the main motivation of Japanese volunteers lies more in a sense of belonging, rather than in the urge to fulfil a moral or societal duty (Ducke, 2007; Pekkanen, 2006).

Volunteerism and community helping each other in Japan are becoming less common in today's urban areas. Since the postwar period, volunteerism and mutual aid have developed especially in rural areas. In such areas, residents are also active in political participation. Later, as Japan's rapid economic growth led to the formation of urban areas, mutual aid has become less important in the rural areas over time. In these areas, the percentage of political participation is low, and groups of voters such as independents have emerged.

For most Japanese volunteers, the notion of civil society as a political agency independent from state is rare. Cooperation policies are implemented only when it suits the government, owing to which volunteering in Japan is basically an apolitical activity (i.e., focusing on local festivals, recycling, collecting rubbish, cleaning neighborhood parks, etc.). Participating in antigovernment, antiglobalization, and antiwar activities has never been categorized as part of volunteer activities in Japan. In this context, Ogawa (2009) talks about a "volunteer subjectivity": a coercive, self-disciplined subjectivity which is being intentionally (re)produced by the Japanese state. This is often done in the name of "structural reform," that is, for the purpose of cost cutting. Thus, Japanese authorities mobilize people under the beautiful name "volunteerism," which, however, results in lasting frustration among the *pure* volunteers who complain about pointless government interventions and harassment by government officials (Ogawa, 2009). The situation improved slightly under the revised NPO law from 2008: the movements' approval of the government was not necessary anymore, but the criteria for the qualification became too complicated and difficult to follow (Imada, 2010). Despite the boom of volunteerism and NPOs, Japanese civil society is still relatively weak, financially fragile, and amateurish. This being said, Japanese civil society is growing (see Kingston, 2004) and volunteerism had a significant impact on this trend.

DIGITAL MEDIA IN POSTWAR JAPAN

East Asia has played a leading role in the world's ever-growing media cultures while representing the largest consumer and producer market of digital media. In this region, Japan quickly became one of the most wired countries in the world. While being among the most advanced nations, Japan was deemed to be at the forefront of the digital revolution. The internet developed slower in Japan, but the number of internet users has steadily increased since the 1990s, and it reached 100 million subscriptions in 2004 (Ducke, 2007, p. 21). In 2022, there were 104.2 million internet users in Japan (MIC, 2022). The internet usage by individuals in 2022 reached 82.9% of the total population. In 2023, this number increased to 84.9%.

The integration of digital media technologies into everyday life in Japan opened up a new space of communicative possibilities. By these technologies we mean those digital platforms, services, and apps built around the convergence of content sharing, public communication, and interpersonal connections. They include internet, SNS, mobile phones, and importantly in Japan, the mobile internet (i.e., the use of mobile phones for e-mails and web access). Before I focus on these technologies, let me briefly touch upon the role of traditional (conventional) media in Japan.

Traditional Media

Traditional media (mainly newspapers and television) has played a key role in postwar Japanese society (see, e.g., Flanagan, 1996; Hayashi, 2018; Taniguchi, 2018). Japan has one of the highest levels of daily newspaper circulation in the world (e.g., in 2015, the circulation was 44 million), but the revenue of the newspaper market is on a downward trend – partly as a result of the spread of the internet (e.g., Ogasahara, 2018). The Japanese public's trust in traditional media is still high but declining, adding to users' reliance on social media for news. For instance, since 2018, more

Japanese people read their news on the smartphones or computers rather than in their morning print newspapers. Only one out of three Japanese in the general public (32%) had trust in traditional media (Snow 2020, p. 430). With Japan's economic recession and the rise of the internet, the trend in circulation decline is likely to continue (Hayashi, 2018).

It is the relatively high trust in traditional media that still discourages many people from turning to digital media for news. In 2007, 63% of viewers were turning to regular newspapers (*shimbun*) for news stories, while 58.8% was watching commercial TV stations for addressing injustice in society or of those in power (Asano & Wakefield, 2010). The internet scored much lower than the traditional media. Ten years later, trust in newspapers edged up to nearly 70%, while online sources fell to cca 51% (Japan Times, 2018). Thus, we should not underestimate the lingering influence of newspapers and TV stations on political opinion in Japan.

The relatively low penetration of digital media is partly caused by the high proportion of elderly in the population. For instance, in 2015, 81% of elderly Japanese (70 years and above) read newspapers every day, whereas only 10% of Japanese teenagers read Japanese newspapers (Hayashi, 2018, p. 270). In other words, the young Japanese users ("digital natives") are much less dependent on conventional media, while the elderly Japanese ("digital immigrants") are still more likely to rely on newspapers and television (Abe, 2018; Ogasahara, 2018).

In Japan, the sole reliance on traditional mass media has changed with the 2011 Tōhoku disaster, because it was the social media that were the quickest to supply critical information. The TEPCO company did not immediately disclose the information on the radiation leak, leaving the public in the dark about what was happening. While being unable to provide essential information, the mainstream media were gradually losing credibility in the eyes of the public. Consequently, many Japanese have shifted into becoming more reliant on the internet. During this period, the social media became a new channel of (crisis) communication, providing breaking news and expert information from different sources, albeit not always accurate. The combination of smartphones and social media (Twitter, Facebook) was the perfect fit for the young Japanese who demanded an alternative information source during a serious crisis.

Between 2019 and 2021, the trust in conventional news increased slightly across Japan, which was attributed to the 2020 COVID-19 pandemic and its impact on Japanese media environment (Reuters Institute, 2022; Swope, 2021). The digitalization of news is in full swing in Japan, while professional journalists increasingly depend on the internet for news material. In 2020, the public broadcaster NHK initiated online live streaming services, and one year later, the *Asahi* newspaper started using LINE to send out daily news bulletins and alerts. Further, the *Yomiuri* newspaper added a Yomiuri Online option to its subscription service, and the economic newspaper *Nikkei* started publishing news stories online and using Twitter to advertise exclusive interviews prior to their release. The *Mainichi* newspaper started attracting digital audiences with long-format analysis by academics and experts. Even Japanese local newspapers (such as *Shizuoka* newspaper) have been accelerating digital subscription strategies. The growing trend toward consuming video-based news on YouTube prompted the majority of Japanese dailies to launch a joint website to showcase video clips produced by mainstream journalists (Reuters Institute, 2022).

Internet

In the year of 1994 – the "Internet Year One" – Japan's first internet Service Provider (ISP) went into business. At that time, Japan ranked 6th in the world in terms of total number of internet hosts, and it took only two years to reach 2nd place, behind the US (Melville, 1999, p. 175). In Japan, the internet infrastructure only started to become generally available in 1995. Although the first networks were crucial in bringing about a new kind of online sociality, they were not taken up by the population is a whole. For instance, by 1995, the two largest commercial networks (NEC's PC-Van and Fujitsu's Nifty-Serve) had only around a million users each (McLelland et al., 2017, p. 57). In 1996, Japanese internet users comprised less than five million, that is, only 4% of the total population (Tkach-Kawasaki, 2003). The prime users of the internet were Japanese engineers, followed by Japanese students and youngsters in their 20s and 30s (Melville, 1999, p. 175). By 1998, the majority of Japanese internet users connected to the internet five or more days a week.

Until the late 1990s, the internet was used mainly as a broadcast medium. The PC penetration and access to the internet remained low, which was a result of slow connections, high cost, and security concerns (Kim, 2018, p. 312). Other reasons included the fear of the conservative leaders that the individualistic internet threatens Japan's social cohesiveness (Kerr, 2001). Since the late 1990s, mobile internet was already an essential part of contemporary life in Japan, while the new mobile content included online banking, breaking news, and entertainment. Nevertheless, in 1998, Japanese internet users comprised only 7% of the population, while Japan ranked only 15th in the world for internet users per capita, falling far behind the western countries (Kerr, 2001, p. 304; Tkach-Kawasaki, 2003, p. 166). Since 1998, however, Japan had experienced an "internet boom," and the user population quadrupled to almost twenty million people in 2000 (Japan Internet Association, 2001). The ICT policy became high-priority for the Japanese government, while the IT industry was perceived as the key to economic growth (Hadl & Hamada, 2009). A full-fledged ICT became widespread starting with the "e-Japan Strategy" based on the 2001 IT Basic Law. This being said, only 10% of Japan's classrooms had internet access in 2001, compared with almost 80% of those in the United States (Freeman, 2003, p. 244).

The most popular activities for the early users of internet in Japan were e-mail, blogging, and accessing websites. Since 1999, blogs provided a simple interface for publishing content on the internet, while in 2003, official blogs were started by Japanese politicians, celebrities, and businesses (Kaigo, 2017a, p. 24). The blog interface facilitated the popularization of other social media in Japan such as the aggregator sites (*matome saito*). These individually managed blogs collect and edit information from anonymous BBS (such as 2-channel) about politics and society (often including scandals and controversies).

In 2021, the average of internet use for all generations was 176.8 hours on weekdays. In 2022, Japanese internet users spent 168 minutes on weekdays, overtaking TV real-time viewing for the first time (Reuters Institute, 2022). One year later, there were 104.2 million internet users in Japan, while around 83% of the public used the internet regularly (DataReportal, 2023). This being said, more than 20 million Japanese do not use the internet, while 17% remain offline. Moreover, only a small fraction of Japanese respondents actually uses digital media for political news: only 4% on Instagram, 6% on Facebook, and 16% on Twitter (Swope, 2021, p. 28).

According to the latest results of the Association For Promoting Fair Elections (2023), the average usage of social media is about 8% for all generations, but when the usage rate is classified by generation, it shows that younger generations use SNS more (Twitter, Facebook for 18–20 year olds and Instagram usage is about 21%). In addition, given that this is the 10th year since 2013, when the ban on internet elections was lifted, there is a possibility that the usage will increase among the younger generation.

Mobile Phones

One of the key differences between Japan and the West is the prevalence of web-enabled mobile phones. Japanese mobile phone (*keitai*) became the primary device for the development of ICT. In Japan, the mobile landscape was merging with the internet landscape as more Japanese access the internet via their mobile phones.

Japan is often celebrated as a model for early mobile use. In the 1990s, mobile phone companies (such as NTT Docomo) introduced the "i-mode" web service specifically designed for mobile phones. Toward the end of 1990s, Japanese providers introduced text messaging services (SMS), e-mail services, and finally web-compatible mobile phones. Only between 1994 and 1998, the number of *keitai* subscriptions rose more than tenfold, and since 1999, *keitai* became ubiquitous in Japanese life. In the same year, *emoji* (pictograms, emoticons) were invented as an integral part of the *keitai* culture.

At the turn of the century, a widespread adoption of the mobile internet led to a surge of population of Japanese internet users. By 2006, Japan had almost 80 million mobile subscribers, while many of them were using NTT Docomo's i-mode. By the late 2000s, 70% of *keitai* users subscribed to mobile internet and used it on a regular basis (Hadl & Hamada, 2009; Kim, 2018). The Japanese appreciated the *keitai's* ability to be mobile and less reliant on an electrical outlet especially during the 2011 Tōhoku disaster, during which the planned power outages served as a catalyst for the Japanese to embrace mobile ICT. Japanese *keitai* apps provided early earthquake warning systems and circulated safety tips.

For the citizen/activist movements, mobile internet access became an important factor in Japan. Some activist groups (such as World Peace Now, see below) actually adopted this new IT strategy and offered a mobile website, owing to which they increased their potential audience. This being said, the mobile phone usage occurs more often in a private informal social context, which does not necessarily promote formal political participation. Up to 50% of Japanese *keitai* holders reads political news online (Takeshita et al., 2014), but it is the entertainment-oriented content with immediate reward (i.e., without mental effort) which is more commonly accessed through smartphones.

At any rate, the smartphones are now the dominant way of accessing news in Japan, while the COVID-19 pandemic only accelerated the rate of change (Reuters Institute, 2022). By 2021, the *keitai* usage rate exceeded 90% (IICP, 2022), and in 2023, almost 185 million *keitai* connections were active in Japan, which equaled to almost 150% of the total population (DataReportal, 2023). This means that on average, each Japanese person has more than one mobile phone.

Social Media

The rising popularity of social networking services (SNS) such as Facebook, Twitter, and Instagram is a global phenomenon. In Japan, the online social media can be broken down into three basic groups: SNSs (Twitter, Facebook, Instagram), messaging apps and business networking platforms (LINE, Snapchat, Linkedin), and streaming video platforms (YouTube, Nico Nico, AbemaTV). For many Japanese, the social media and bulletin board systems (BBSs) became a "space to save, cure and heal" (Fujita in Onosaka, 2003, p. 216). The virtual BBS fora were not perceived as simple "chat rooms," but as "meeting rooms" – a term which implied political and civic research activity (Hadl & Hamada, 2009).

The majority of the Japanese youth views social media as a means to passively read information rather than a place to discuss politics (Katy, 2018; Swope, 2021; Takeshita et al., 2014). Further, Japanese youngsters use SNS mainly in order to avoid to the trouble of keeping good relationship with peers (Abe, 2018; Takahashi, 2010). Besides, the majority of Japanese users cannot really trust people online and discern between reliable and unreliable users (Katy, 2018). Participating in politically oriented communities or writing opinions on politics in one's blog is not usual among the Japanese youth. In other words, the desire is to connect with others rather than to express political opinions.

In Japan, the social media (SNS, blogs, microblogs) have grown rapidly, with various services emerging since the late 1990s. The early services included a customer purchasing support site kakaku.com, a large-scale anonymous BBS "2-channel," and the Japanese version of Wikipedia (Takeshita et al., 2014). The first real SNS in Japan was SNSGucoo (2003), followed by GREE (2004) and Mixi (2004). Social media outlets such as Twitter and Facebook became popular in Japan in the 2010s, leading to 51% of the population having social media accounts by 2017 (Swope, 2021, p. 29). In 2012, the amount of Twitter users in Japan (cca 30 million) was the third largest in the world, and in 2016, the penetration rate of Twitter was 46% while Facebook stood at 38% (Ogasahara, 2018, p. 94).

One of the largest Japanese SNS is Mixi, which became in 2007 the most popular SNS in Japan, with more than 87% of SNS users joining the platform (Takahashi, 2010). Another most frequently used social media in Japan is YouTube, whose Japanese language support was introduced in 2007. The Japanese language version of Facebook started in 2008 and was gaining ground ever since. At that time, two out of three Japanese students indicated that they received news through Facebook, Mixi, or Twitter (Takahashi, 2010).

The Japanese version of Twitter was introduced in 2008. By 2015, the site had almost one quarter of all internet users in Japan, making Twitter into the most popular SNS. Twitter and Facebook were found to be the most effective media for quickly spreading information during major disasters such as the 2011 Tōhoku earthquake (see below). The popular chatting application LINE was launched immediately after the earthquake. LINE can send and receive short messages as well as images, movies, and nontextual "stamps" that make communication fun and enjoyable. This application quickly became the most favorable social media for Japanese teenagers: more than 90% of high school and college students use LINE on a daily basis (Kim, 2018, p. 314). In 2020, the usage rate of LINE exceeded 90% (IICP 2022).

In 2023, Japan was home to 92 million social media users, which equates to 74% of the total population (DataReportal, 2023). LINE is still the most popular social media app (92 million users), followed by YouTube (78 million), Twitter (67.5 million), Instagram (46 million), TikTok (21 million), Facebook (15 million), Pinterest (7 million), LinkedIn (3.5 million), Snapchat (1.5 million).

POLITICAL PARTICIPATION VIA DIGITAL MEDIA IN JAPAN

This chapter focuses on how Japanese ordinary citizens, activists, and volunteers participate in political activities as a result of digital media use. I focus on the political potential of alternative (digital) routes to disseminate information and deepen participation. Further, I discuss the role of "digital citizenship" which allows people to participate as responsible and empowered citizens while drawing on the use of digital technology. Finally, I examine the state of "digital activism" (or cyber activism) which points to the utilization of digital technologies to mobilize public protest.

The Public Use of Digital Media in Japan

Digital media creates a useful environment in which the citizens can participate virtually and actively toward a more open government. It enables "e-government," that is, a top-down program initiated by the government to improve efficiency. However, democracy and participation are not necessarily the objectives of e-government. This is the role of "e-democracy," which points to the ability of technology to link decision-makers and political elites to citizens. It offers citizens additional opportunities for participation, and it is either introduced by the government or it originates from below (e.g., Ducke, 2007).

Today, Japanese citizens can access government sites, send emails to governmental offices, and contact local politicians (see, e.g., Kida, 2019; Okura & Kaigo, 2017a, 2017b). Apart from exchanging tweets and re-tweets, the citizens can follow, unfollow, or block politicians according to their public response to the situation. Further, the ability to "cross-post" by tagging and retagging information allows Japanese groups to work together (see Slater et al., 2012). Besides, the citizens and NGOs can set up "chat" rooms, providing short messages over the web. These virtual communities facilitate the actions of the civil society through digital media, which – theoretically speaking – leads to the creation of greater social capital (Abe, 2018; Jasper, 2022). Moreover, digital media can help to demystify Japanese society and encourage political participation (Snow, 2020). Nevertheless, many Japanese are disappointed with e-democracy and its increased access to digital media (Steel, 2016, p. 250). In other words, the coming together of the digital media and political participation in Japan is not a smooth process (see below).

Owing to the spread of digital media, Japanese citizens now have access to multiple information sources, and they can selectively accept or disregard messages from the state. They can bypass traditional media outlets (and the government) by using their own digital tools for political participation. These tools include services such as bulletin boards, mailing lists, blogs and microblogs, SNSs, video-hosting services, etc. For the networked citizen, internet offers a space for "collective intelligence" in which he/she easily shares self-generated content. In this setting, the citizen becomes "prosumer" of public services (i.e., both producer and consumer) who uses and shapes (political) information produced by others (Toffler, 1980). These prosumers can function as "e-journalists" who report online what they are witnessing of the event in which they are taking part, or as "opinion leaders" who select and interpret political messages for lower-end media users.

Owing to a relatively high internet penetration in Japan, even smaller citizens' groups can go online and establish their own website to communicate their policies and mobilize their members. The website, together with mailing lists and subscription letters, is essential because it represents the only effective communication route for reaching the general public (see Ducke, 2007). Nonetheless, as for the information flow, one-directional distribution is predominant, that is, dialogic and interactive features (BBS or open mailing list) are usually missing. Further, the websites are often amateurish, which is problematic because in order to address larger audiences the website requires a far more professional approach. Technology makes difference, but the use of new ICT in Japan does not increase political success (Ducke, 2007).

For Japanese civil society organizations, a platform like Facebook can (1) provide more chances to connect with the government, (2) provide more political opportunities to advocate, and (3) create opportunities to exert greater presence (Freeman, 2003; Okura & Kaigo, 2017b). The internet usage in Japan has remarkable explanatory power in particular modes of engagement, such as contacting opinion leaders, contacting the media, and attending demonstrations (Huang et al., 2017). In this context, social media such as Facebook, Twitter, or YouTube become effective platforms for deepening political engagement, organizing social movements, and expressing discontent toward the government. For instance, Japanese women's groups have begun to use the internet in order to resist the social pressures for "harmony" and "silence" in Japanese society (see Onosaka, 2003). Similarly, the internet provides a new horizon for marginalized members of Japanese society, including gays and lesbians, the Ainu, *Burakumin* outcasts, Korean-Japanese, etc.

Since the new millennium, the Japanese state has begun taking steps to include the public in decision-making process by using internet (see Hitachi-UTokyo 2022; Okura & Kaigo, 2017a). Indeed, the state helps to build stronger connections between citizens, governments, and businesses, but it fails to provide the tools for an autonomous and unmediated realm for public discussion (e.g., Freeman, 2003; Ogawa, 2009). To speak with Tsukada (2022), public discussion in Japan is more government-centric (i.e. focusing on government-led "services") and less citizen-centric (i.e., focusing on "emancipation" via digital media). Besides, when commoners appropriate digital technologies to create a new virtual community, the capital and state are quick to coopt and reappropriate this community (Hadl & Hamada, 2009; Ogawa, 2009). Consequently, there are many official "community networks" created by the government, but only a limited number of "virtual communities" that would represent a mobilized public sphere.

The disengaged Japanese youth still tends to use digital media mainly for nonpolitical purposes, while political participation (both offline and online) is generally low (e.g., Swope, 2021; Takeshita et al., 2014; Uchida, 2023). For instance, the turnout for the 2021 Lower House election among people in their twenties was the lowest in 18 elections since 1969 (MIC, 2022). Further, up to 50% of young voters voiced their interest in domestic politics, but only one third of them actually showed willingness to engage in political participation, which is the lowest number if compared to other countries (e.g., Nippon Foundation, 2022). In other words, Japanese youngsters are not disinterested in politics, but they do not want to talk about it (Uchida, 2023). The influence of digital media use on political participation in Japan seems to be minimal or limited to a particular group of voters. Nevertheless, the following subchapter will demonstrate that in Japanese postwar history, there are numerous examples of the ways in which digital media have been effectively used by activists, volunteers, and organizations.

Historical Examples of Political Participation via Digital Media in Japan

In the 1990s, when the internet began to establish itself as a new channel for social interaction in Japan, there were high hopes that the online world would become a new public sphere. Many cyber-optimists dreamt about "digital democracy" and perceived internet as a panacea for reinvigorating political participation (e.g., Tadamasa, 2017; Tkach-Kawasaki, 2003). Today, Japanese central and local governments are digitalizing their tasks while sharing data among diverse actors, which is believed to fundamentally change the premises on which Japanese civil society is based (Hitachi-UTokyo, 2022). The goal is to create a "super-smart society" (or "Society 5.0") which empowers local communities to engage in online political participation in accordance with the will of the people (Hitachi-UTokyo, 2022).

The first event which clearly pointed to the possibilities of internet in Japan was the Great Hanshin Earthquake from 1995. For many Japanese, this event represented their first real knowledge of the internet as an effective tool for (crisis) communication. The government and media's response to the quake was rather sluggish while it was the voluntary groups that actually proved more effective than state-controlled organizations. The disaster served as a catalyst for short-lived surges in participation (Kage, 2011, p. 49) while pointing to the vital role of civil society media in Japan (Hadl & Hamada, 2009). Ever since this catastrophic event, the internet has been used more extensively by volunteers, activists, and NPOs.

Since the new millennium, there was a gradual penetration of digital media in Japan's civil society. For instance, during the first "web election" in 2000, various political interest groups and individuals emerged, producing e-mail letters, BBS, and chat rooms to engage in internet-based political dialogue (Tkach-Kawasaki, 2003). The number of government homepages rose to more than one thousand, while political parties' websites offered political news, e-mail addresses, and interactive polls. Besides, the 2000 surprise election of novelist Tanaka Yasuo as governor of Nagano prefecture was attributed to the fact that many like-minded voters have "independently" (*katte ni*) established websites and mailing lists without even having met Tanaka in person (Freeman, 2003, p. 255).

There was one more case of political participation in 2000 that pointed to digital media's potential to encourage Japanese citizens to take action. One Okinawan woman (Hiroe Shimabukuro) decided to use digital media for a protest against military bases in Okinawa. On the internet, she uploaded her site "Red Card Movement" just 40 days before the G8 Summit in Okinawa, with the aim to "raise the red card to both the US and Japanese governments" (Onosaka, 2003, p. 220). After it went online, the site drew considerable attention from local, national, and foreign papers. While organizing events via social media, over 27,000 citizens and activists gathered in July 2000 in a protest meeting at one of the military bases (Onosaka, 2003). Being covered by BBC and CNN, the movement spread across Japan and the world, which would have hardly materialized without the movement's clever use of digital media.

In 2001, the so-called "textbook controversy" emerged, which involved the use of internet by a variety of actors. It was mostly the local authorities, parents, and Japanese/Korean citizens that became involved in public debate about a new, nationalist history textbook. The controversy played only a minor role on official Japanese homepages: the ministries' websites either ignored the issue altogether, or they offered little interactive information (Ducke, 2007). Nonetheless, the textbook was considered offensive by many citizens' groups and activists who immediately staged demonstrations and protests. Importantly, many public discussions about the textbook controversy took place online. The most influential in this regard was the Tokyo-based Children and Textbooks Japan Network ("Network 21") whose official website was at the core of campaign activities (see Ducke, 2007). The website was limited to online membership application; the BBS was not established, but the site offered a comment form and Q&A pages instead. Owing to the website, the citizens' campaigning and network building became much faster and more effective. Partly owing to the public pressure, the controversial textbook was adopted only in very small numbers of Japanese schools.

Since the new millennium, Japanese peace activists continued to use internet effectively in their mobilization efforts. In 2002, they founded a new network "World Peace Now" as a protest against the war in Iraq (and the dispatch of Japanese troops). Also here, the internet and e-mail played essential role in organizing peace demonstrations and distributing related information. Owing to this, in March 2003, up to 50.000 participants, including the elderly, families, and women with children managed to gather and protest the war (Ducke, 2007). Needless to say, World Peace Now did not succeed in actually preventing the war, but the effective use of the internet did contribute to a temporary success in terms of mobilization of public opinion. This being said, this success was only short-lived: later on, the atmosphere in the online public sphere turned more in favor of the troop dispatch. The online public has ceased to share the activists' views, while the mass media started to frame the activists as "troublemakers" (Ducke, 2007). This event indicated that the immediate appeal of an issue (i.e., flash issue) is essential for the effectiveness of online tools, but long-term issues, where audiences gradually lose interest, require a much more professional approach (i.e., beyond the simple website). Unfortunately, this is neither easy nor obvious task for the majority of Japanese activists' and citizens' groups.

Essential for political participation online was the public reaction to the 2011 Tōhoku disaster – the first "natural" disaster fully experienced through social media. The government and the media failed to provide a quick and objective information, while it was the social media that played the key role in crisis communication. By texting important information, tweeting and re-tweeting posts, and uploading videos, Japanese citizens generated huge amounts of first-hand information. They engaged their personal resources in order to support, help, and find common cause with others, which was perceived as "the first political act" (Slater et al., 2012, p. 3). The citizens were involved in alternative (digital) flows of nonofficial information while raising donations, recruiting volunteers, and creating links among different state and nonstate actors. Immediately after the disaster, the number of tweets increased to 1.8 times the average, the Mixi users' posts increased up to three times the usual, and the 2-channel BBS saw its number of page views climb by 20% (Slater et al., 2012, p. 6). Other Japanese web applications (such as Ustream or Nico Nico Dōga) were rebroadcasting mainstream news programs that were anonymously commented upon by Japanese viewers. Tweets and re-tweets were linked to others through hashtags (such as #j_j_helpme or #PrayforJapan) which enabled users to mark messages of distress or disaster information. Moreover, the activists' use of digital media was instrumental in gathering and mobilizing large-scale support for multiple mass protests – such as the September 2011 demonstration in Tokyo which gathered cca 60,000 people.

In the aftermath of the Tōhoku disaster, many Japanese started using digital media actively while pushing away previous concerns toward using the internet. Information about volunteering was shared through social media, and direct messaging on Twitter became a standard means of communication. Besides, there were countless regular demonstrations that were largely organized on Twitter, while for some of them (such as the monthly TwitNoNukes demonstration), the digital media constituted the very core of legitimacy for the whole movement (Slater et al., 2012). During the antinuclear protests that followed the disaster, political activists were making full use of digital media in order to mobilize citizens and organize demonstrations. Simultaneously, Japanese antiwar activists were mobilizing resistance to US military bases through a combination of aggressive ICT usage and occupation of public space.

Among the aforementioned citizen movements, perhaps the most vocal and visible was the Students Emergency Action for Liberal Democracy (SEALDS). While relying heavily on the digital media, the SEALDS movement was in 2015 organizing antiwar protests and petitions against the ruling coalition headed by PM Abe Shinzō. The members of the movement felt that current social movements were dull, old-fashioned, and lacking the youth-oriented appeal in their digital media presence (webpages, blogs). While criticizing Abe's manipulation of the constitutional system, the organizers were constantly updating their official website (sealds.com) while communicating their agenda via social media – either by explaining issues on Twitter, or by posting videoclips from demonstrations (Slater et al., 2015). Owing to the effective use of digital media, the SEALDS movement was able to rapidly mobilize tens of thousands of people who took part in large-scale demonstrations, protests rallies, and marches. In addition to these activities, the SEALDS were campaigning to unseat candidates who oppose the "unconstitutional" bill on collective self-defense. The digital media, however, has not replaced the need to face-to-face communication. Essential is still the public demonstration, whose sensory experience (chanting, drumming, dancing) gives reality to the abstract knowledge that is disseminated via digital media (Slater et al., 2015).

Owing to the expansion of internet access in the 2010s, the Japanese public became increasingly aware of ethically questionable practices by the politicians (Hayashi, 2018). Today, the Japanese online public is passionately concerned about the moral virtue of prominent individuals (politicians, celebrities, businessmen). Importantly, the social media's tendencies toward mockery and cynicism facilitates Japanese users to post and share materials that cover not only the elites' achievements and virtues but also their wrongdoings and scandals. Political corruption scandals come to light periodically and attract considerable attention in Japan (see Prusa, 2024). Encounters with scandals have negatively influenced the Japanese public and gave rise to young cynical voters who internalized political distrust. Importantly, these voters often go online and become active "netizens" (*nettomin*) who seem to function as watchdogs of the elites and whistleblowers of their transgressions. These users "flame" online debates (*netto enjō*) by posting discrediting exposures on BBS (e.g., 2-channel), weblogs (e.g., Netgeek), and video platforms (e.g., Nico Nico Dōga). Flaming has become very common in recent years with the advent of social media in Japan. Once the flaming starts, the discussion is literally up in flames and is difficult to stop. Japanese *nettomin* are especially effective in uncovering plagiarism and data fabrication. One example of an intense online flaming was the scandal of Sano Kenjirō – a prominent Japanese designer who was accused of plagiarizing the Japanese Olympic logo in 2015. While communicating via BBS, weblogs, and video platforms, the *nettomin* gathered a clear evidence of Sano's plagiarism and nepotism, which was eventually picked by the mainstream media (see Prusa, 2020). This scandal would have hardly materialized without the digital crowd journalism. Owing to the enormous public pressure, the logo was eventually scrapped and the designer vilified.

In 2017, digital media significantly contributed to the spread of the MeToo campaign in Japan. In the male-centered Japanese society, where sexual harassment remains widespread, people are rather critical of the women who stand up for the taboo topic of rape. Logically, the movement got only minimum coverage in Japanese mainstream media, while it was only the digital (social) media that publicized various #Mee too scandals. The movement gained momentum in Japan when a young freelance journalist (Itō Shiori) used Twitter to accuse another journalist of drugging and raping her. At first, Itō was vilified on social media and flooded with hate messages, but soon after, the hashtag *#FightTogetherWithShiori* started trending on Japanese Twitter, pushing other Japanese women to tweet about their own sexual assaults as well. Once the tweets vent viral, they were finally picked up by some magazines, both online (e.g., *Weezy*) and print (e.g., *Shūkan Shinchō*). Partly owing to the use of digital media, Itō gained some support from the public and eventually won a landmark civil case against the rapist.

The experience of the COVID-19 pandemic since 2019 has further accelerated the digitalization of all aspects of society, owing to which the digital media use is now essential to everyday life in Japan (Japan Times, 2021). In the COVID-19 era, more than 40% of Japanese teenagers turned to SNS to share their thoughts online (Endo & Imbong, 2020). Due to the pandemic, the Japanese youth's interest in politics via SNS has somewhat increased: there were more young people committed to positively approach politics in general and online politics in particular (Social Business Studio, 2020). The Japanese youth with good digital skills (i.e., "digital natives") has emerged as a new generation of media users. Japanese digital natives are good at multitasking: they read daily newspapers and political blogs, receive news via mobile phone or e-mail, participate in online forums, and discuss with others online (Abe, 2018; Takeshita et al., 2014).

In 2019, a Japanese popular actress and freelance writer (Ishikawa Yumi) started a Twitter campaign with a hashtag #KuToo. The campaign advocated against workplace dress codes requiring women to wear high heels. Ishikawa's first Twitter comment received 30,000 retweets and 60,000 likes, sparking a national debate about gender discrimination and labor rights. Owing to the immense online support, Ishikawa collected almost 20,000 signatures for a petition on not forcing women to wear high heels in the workplace.

One year later, the so-called "Twitter demo" emerged in Japan. Many citizens criticized the administration of Abe Shinzō for allowing the prosecutor Kurokawa Hiromu, Abe's friend, to take over as a prosecutor-general. On May 8, a feminist female, working as an advertising specialist in Tokyo, posted a tweet criticizing the state of prosecution in Japan. In two days' time, the tweet was shared more than 4.7 million times, which eventually pushed Abe to delay the new prosecutorial bill, while Kurokawa was made to resign his post (Uchida, 2023).

Current Situation

Despite all the aforementioned cases of "digital citizenship," political participation via digital media is generally rather low in contemporary Japan. This being said, some scholars indicate that Japanese movements that are alternative to the political mainstream are gaining ground, owing to which their digital media experience becomes "political" (Slater et al., 2012). Indeed, students and young professionals have deepened their voices through online petitions, social media posts, and other digital media (such as the SEALDS movement). Further, it became more usual for Japanese youngsters to write online comments and reviews (Tadamasa, 2017). Nevertheless, young Japanese citizens are still rather reluctant to engage in political conversations online. If they do engage, their online participation includes watching political videos online, visiting websites of political organizations, and communicating online with friends and family (Takeshita et al., 2014). If there is a discussion about politics on digital media, it is usually a by-product of nonpolitical use. Besides, for the majority of Japanese youth, the idea of putting their personal/political information online "for anyone to see" is a disturbing one (e.g., *Sora News*, 6 February 2014).

In today's Japan, most people still do not consider digital media as a tool for engaging in politics. The internet is less important for obtaining political news, interaction with news online is low, and digital media is used more for entertainment rather than for political participation. According to the most recent national election (the House of Councilors election held in March 2023), 55% of all respondents used websites, online news, and SNS (The Association For Promoting Fair Elections, 2023). This is a relatively high number, but the public is generally rather politically apathetic, lacking desire to engage in political discussions online, and having little to no confidence in the government. They remain in a vegetative state of political apathy with the only political expectation to vote, but even the voting patterns have started to decline (Snow, 2020, p. 426). Sadly, it is mainly the Japanese right-wing extremists (*uyoku*) who actively utilize (or exploit) digital media for political participation.

One reason behind the apolitical nature of Japanese youth's online communication lies in the fact that Japanese students are not educated how to develop the "mental habit" associated with citizenship and democracy in a digital era (see Tsukada, 2022). Another reason lies in the fact that the majority of young Japanese today has little to no confidence in their government. They usually perceive politicians and politics as too elitist, adult-centered, and corrupt. Finally, the youngsters are less motivated to participate politically because of the lack of political options under the LDP hegemony. It is hence unsurprising that political participation via digital media in Japan is now the lowest when compared to other Asian countries (see Swope, 2021; Uchida, 2018, 2023).

CONCLUSION

The advent of digital media worldwide has indeed boosted the capacity of networked facilities to influence politics. People can now access political information, participate in public affairs online, and voice their discontent via digital media.

However, the great expectations that the internet would revolutionize the established framework and alter political processes have largely failed (see, e.g., Calderado, 2018). Japan is no exception. The optimists would claim that Japan is now trying to change the imbalance of democracy by allowing digital media to become more prominent. Indeed, Japan has a relatively advanced (digital) media and information infrastructure, but the internet itself cannot be seen as an alternative to existing social and political spaces for action.

This is partly caused by the fact that Japanese government favors structured, managed, and prescribed processes for citizens' political participation (both online and offline). Consequently, political participation in Japanese civil society is government-centric (i.e., focusing on government-led "services") and not citizen-centric (i.e., using digital media for "emancipation"). Thus, Japan falls short of the (western) theoretical ideal of an independent civil society. Rather, it is a "bonsai" civil society where the branches of citizen output are rigorously pruned by the bureaucracy (Kingston, 2004, p. 119).

In many ways, the bonsai civil society remains an accurate description (Jeff Kingston, personal communication). Kingston notes that the role of civil society has expanded, but it still lacks financial strength and autonomy, because the government has not introduced tax incentives for individuals to make contributions. Without them, the civil society organizations will remain underfunded, understaffed, and lack autonomy. It is a sad state of affairs because there is so much more that NPOs and NGOs could contribute and offset shortcoming in state services.

It seems that digital transformation did not really lead to a fundamental change in Japanese civil society. Nevertheless, I have documented that Japanese citizen groups and NPOs were at times effectively using digital media to mobilize collective action. The most representative cases for examining public participation via digital media in Japan include the experience of the Great Hanshin Earthquake (1995), the Tōhoku disaster (2011), and the COVID-19 pandemic (2019). Japanese citizens' movements that effectively used digital media to further their political case include the Red Card Movement (2000), the Network 21 (2001), World Peace Now (2002), the SEALDS (2015), and the MeToo movement (2017). All these experiences have accelerated the digitalization of all aspects of Japanese society, owing to which the digital media use is now essential to everyday life in Japan.

To conclude, my findings regarding the association between digital media use and political participation in Japan are mixed. Despite the prevalence of digital media in Japan, its political use has only occasionally (and briefly) played some role in country's domestic politics. Many Japanese NPOs rely on the internet, but they do not use it to its full potential. Besides, political digital media use in Japan is likely to remain low due to less-polarized politics, strong conventional media, and single-party dominance in Japan.

In order to improve the situation, Japan needs to better engage younger voters and reform the electoral system to leverage digital tools for more effective political participation. Further, a proper "digital media literacy" must be introduced in Japan (see Tsukada, 2022). This kind of civic education needs to be taught in the context of democratic education, which enables Japanese citizens to develop their own understanding of the potential of the internet for democratic purposes. Finally, grassroot organizing, community outreach programs, and civic education initiatives must be prioritized to empower civil society in Japan. The promise of a proper "digital democracy" (or "e-democracy") may still be far away, but it does remain a possibility. This transformation is a slow and subtle process, but it may eventually forge a deeper and stronger civil society in Japan.

REFERENCES

Abe, K. (2018). Japanese youth and SNS use: Peer surveillance and the conditions governing tomodachi. In F. Darling-Wolf (Ed.), *Routledge handbook of Japanese media* (pp. 275–291). Routledge.

Asano, M., & Wakefield, B. (2010). Political market-orientation in Japan. In J. Lees-Marshment, J. Strömbäck, & C. Rudd (Eds.), *Global political marketing* (pp. 234–248). Routledge.

Calderado, A. (2018). Social media and politics. In W. Outhwaite & S. Turner (Eds.), *The SAGE handbook of political sociology* (pp. 781–796). SAGE.

Castells, M. (1996). *The information age: Economy, society and culture. Volume 1: The rise of the network society.* Blackwell.

DataReportal. (February 9, 2023). *Digital 2023: Japan.* https://datareportal.com/reports/digital-2023-japan

Ducke, I. (2007). *Civil society and the internet in Japan.* Routledge.

Endo, M., & Imbong, M. (2020). *The face of political participation is getting younger.* Change.org Foundation.

Flanagan, S. (1996). Media exposure and the quality of political participation in Japan. In S. Pharr &

E. Krauss (Eds.), *Media and politics in Japan* (pp. 277–312). University of Hawai'i Press.

Freeman, L. (2003). Mobilizing and demobilizing the Japanese public sphere: Mass media and the internet in Japan. In F. Schwartz, & S. Pharr (Eds.), *The State of civil Society in Japan* (pp. 235–256). Cambridge UP.

Haddad, M. A. (2021). Civil society in Japan. In H. Takeda, & M. Williams (Eds.), *Routledge handbook of contemporary Japan* (pp. 102–117). Routledge.

Hadl, G. (2010). Media and civic engagement in Japan. In H. Vinken, Y. Nishimura, B. White, & M. Deguchi (Eds.), *Civic engagement in contemporary Japan* (pp. 153–169). Springer.

Hadl, G., & Hamada, T. (2009). Policy convergence and online civil society media (CSM) in Japan. *International Journal of Media and Cultural Politics*, *5*(1&2), 69–88.

Hayashi, K. (2018). Culture of the print newspaper: The decline of Japanese mass press. In F. Darling-Wolf (Ed.), *Routledge handbook of Japanese media* (pp. 259–274). Routledge.

Hitachi-UTokyo Laboratory. (2022). *Society 5.0. A people-centric super-smart society*. Springer Open.

Hommerich, C. (2015). Feeling disconnected: Exploring the relationship between different forms of social capital and civic engagement in Japan. *Voluntas*, *26*, 45–68.

Huang, M., Whang, T., & Xuchuan, L. (2017). The internet, social capital, and civic engagement in Asia. *Social Indicators Research*, *132*, 559–578.

IICP (Institute for Information and Communications Policy) (2022). *Reiwa 3 Nendo Jōhō Tsūshin Media no Riyō Jikan to Jōhō Kōdō ni Kan Suru Chōsa [2021 Survey on Usage Time of Information and Communication Media]*. https://www.soumu.go.jp/iicp/research/results/media_usage-time.html

Ikeda, K., & Richey, S. (2012). *Social networks and Japanese democracy*. Routledge.

Imada, M. (2010). Civil society in Japan: Democracy, voluntary action, and philanthropy. In H. Vinken, Y. Nishimura, B. White, & M. Deguchi (Eds.), *Civic engagement in contemporary Japan* (pp. 21–40). Springer.

Japan Internet Association. (2001). *Intānetto hakusho 2001 [Internet White Paper 2001]*. Japan Internet Association.

Jasper, D. (2022). The impact of social media on politics: A full overview. Streetcivics.cz [cit. 10.12.2022]. https://streetcivics.com/the-impact-of-social-media-on-politics/

Kage, R. (2011). *Civil engagement in Postwar Japan*. Cambridge UP.

Kaigo, M. (2017a). The Japanese internet environment. In M. Kaigo (Ed.), *Social media and civil society in Japan* (pp. 1–36). Palgrave Macmillan.

Kaigo, M. (2017b). Social media in Japan and the great Eastern Japan earthquake. In M. Kaigo (Ed.), *Social Media and civil Society in Japan* (pp. 36–71). Palgrave Macmillan.

Kaigo, M., & Tkach-Kawasaki, L. (2017). Civil society, social media and Facebook usage by local governments: Birth of the Tsukuba study and the Tsukuba civic activities cyber-square. In M. Kaigo (Ed.), *Social media and civil Society in Japan* (pp. 97–119). Palgrave Macmillan.

Katy, K. (July 23, 2018). Locked and blocked! Japanese people don't trust others on social media, survey finds. *SoraNews24*.

Kerr, A. (2001). *Dogs and demons: The fall of modern Japan*. Penguin.

Kida, D. D. (2019). *Local political participation in Japan: A case study of Oita*. Routledge.

Kim, K. Y. (2018). Keitai in Japan. In F. Darling-Wolf (Ed.), *Routledge handbook of Japanese media* (pp. 308–320). Routledge.

Kingston, J. (2004). *Japan's quiet transformation*. Routledge.

Lee, A. (2016). Social network model of political participation in Japan. *Japanese Journal of Political Science*, *17*(1), 44–62.

McLelland, M., Yu, H., & Goggin, G. (2017). Alternative histories of social media in Japan and China. In J. Burgess, A. Marwick, & T. Poell (Eds.), *The SAGE handbook of social media* (pp. 53–68). SAGE.

Melville, I. (1999). *Marketing in Japan*. Butterworth-Heinemann.

MIC (Ministry of Internal Affairs and Communications). (2022). *White paper on information and communications*. https://www.soumu.go.jp/johotsusintokei/whitepaper/r04.html

Mori, Y. (2021). Media in Japan. In H. Takeda & M. Williams (Eds.), *Routledge handbook of contemporary Japan* (pp. 458–470). Routledge.

Nippon Foundation. (2022). *18 Sai Ishiki Chōsa 'Dai 46 Kai: Kuni ya Shakai ni Tai Suru Ishiki [18 Years Old Opinion Survey '46th: Attitudes Towards Country and Society']*. https://www.nippon-foundation.or.jp/what/projects/eighteen_survey

Ogasahara, M. (2018). Media environments in the United States, Japan, South Korea, and Taiwan. In S. Kiyohara, K. Maeshima, & D. Owen (Eds.), *Internet Election Campaigns in the United States, Japan, South Korea, and Taiwan* (pp. 79–113). Palgrave Macmillan.

Ogawa, A. (2009). *The failure of civil society?: The third sector and the state in contemporary Japan*. SUNY Press.

Ogawa, A. (2022). Civil society in Japan. In R. Pekkanen & S. Pekkanen (Eds.), *The Oxford handbook of Japanese politics* (pp. 299–316). Oxford University Press.

Okura, S., & Kaigo, M. (2017a). Japanese local government Facebook profiles. In M. Kaigo (Ed.), *Social media and civil society in Japan* (pp. 73–96). Palgrave Macmillan.

Okura, S., & Kaigo, M. (2017b). Who leads advocacy through social media in Japan? In M. Kaigo (Ed.), *Social media and civil society in Japan* (pp. 153–173). Palgrave Macmillan.

Onosaka, J. (2003). Opening a Pandora's box. The cyber activism of Japanese women. In K. C. Ho, R. Kluver, & K. C. C. Yang (Eds.), *Asia.com: Asia encounters the internet* (pp. 211–227). RoutledgeCurzon.

Pekkanen, R. (2004). Japan: Social capital without advocacy. In M. Alagappa (Ed.), *Civil society and political change in Asia* (pp. 223–255). Stanford UP.

Pekkanen, R. (2006). *Japan's dual civil society*. Stanford UP.

Prusa, I. (2020). Scandal: Sano Kenjirō. In J. G. Karlin, P. W. Galbraith, & S. Nozawa (Eds.), *Japanese media and popular culture open-access digital archive*. The University of Tokyo.

Prusa, I. (2023). The Johnny's sex abuse scandal and the role of media in Japan. *Contemporary Japan*. https://www.tandfonline.com/doi/full/10.1080/18692729.2023.2290369

Prusa, I. (2024). *Scandal in Japan: Transgression, performance and ritual*. Routledge.

Putnam, R. D. (2000). *Bowling alone: The collapse and revival of American community*. Simon & Schuster.

Reuters Institute. (2022). *Digital news report 2022*. Reuters/University of Oxford.

Slater, D., Kindstrand, L., O'Day, R., Uno, S., & Takano, C. (2015). Sealds: Research note on contemporary youth politics in Japan. *Asia-Pacific Journal: Japan Focus*, *13*(37), 1–25.

Slater, D., Nishimura, K., & Kindstrand, L. (2012). Social media, information and political activism in Japan's 3.11 crisis. *The Asia-Pacific Journal*, *10*(24), 1–31.

Snow, N. (2020). Darkness and light: Media, propaganda, and politics in Japan. In P. Baines, N. O'Shaughnessy, & N. Snow (Eds.), *The SAGE handbook of propaganda* (pp. 422–440). SAGE.

Social Business Studio. (2020). *Covid-19 social impact report*. Signing Ltd.

Srinivas, H. (2015). *Use of internet for citizens' participation in urban management: A view from Japan*. The Global Development Research Center, Policy Analysis Series E-079.

Steel, G. (Ed.). (2016). *Power in contemporary Japan*. Palgrave.

Swope, T. (2021). *Political social media use and political participation in Japan*. MA Thesis. Naval Postgraduate School.

Tadamasa, K. (2017, July 28). Netto Yoron no Jittai wo Semaru. [The Internet, Media, and Public Opinion in Japan]. *Nippon.com*.

Takahashi, T. (2010). MySpace or Mixi? Japanese engagement with SNS in the global age. *New Media & Society*, *12*(3), 453–475.

Takeshita, T., Saito, S., & Inaba, T. (2014). Social media and political participation in Japan. In L. Willnat & A. Aw (Eds.), *Social media, culture and politics in Asia* (pp. 127–142). Peter Lang.

Takikawa, H., & Nagayoshi, K. (2017). Political polarization in social media: Analysis of the 'Twitter political field' in Japan. In *2017 IEEE International Conference on Big Data*. https://doi.org/10.1109/BigData.2017.8258291

Taniguchi, M. (2018). Changing political communication in Japan. In F. Darling-Wolf (Ed.), *Routledge handbook of Japanese media* (pp. 121–135). Routledge.

The Association for Promoting Fair Elections. (2023). *National attitude survey for the 26th ordinary election of house of ouncilors members*. http://www.akaruisenkyo.or.jp/wp/wp-content/uploads/2011/07/26san.pdf

Tiefenbach, T., & Holdgrün, P. S. (2015). Happiness through participation in neighborhood associations in Japan? The impact of loneliness and voluntariness. *Voluntas*, *26*, 69–97.

Tkach-Kawasaki, L. (2003). Clicking for votes: Assessing Japanese political campaigns on the web. In K. C. Ho, R. Kluver, & K. C. C. Yang (Eds.), *Asia.com: Asia encounters the internet* (pp. 159–174). RoutledgeCurzon.

Tocqueville, A. (2012). *Democracy in America*. Chicago UP.

Toffler, A. (1980). *The third wave: The classic study of tomorrow*. Bantam.

Tsukada, J. (2022). Bridging the intersection between media literacy and citizenship education in Japan. *Electronic Journal of Contemporary Japanese Studies*, *22*(2).

Uchida, A. (2018). How do Japanese people talk about politics on Twitter? *Psychologia*, *61*(2), 124–157.

Uchida, A. (2023). Political participation through social media by Japanese youth. *Kyoto Review*, 36. https://kyotoreview.org/issue-36/political-participation-through-social-media-by-japanese-youth/

Vosse, W. (1999). Japanese civil society revisited. *Japanstudien*, *11*, 31–53.

Ukrainian Political Communication in the Russo-Ukrainian War: A Case of Strategic Communication and Political Marketing?

Nigel A. Jones and Paul Baines

INTRODUCTION

At the time of writing, there was no clear sense that the Russo-Ukraine war was nearing its conclusion, or of what that conclusion might be. Moreover, we could not at that point rule out a globally catastrophic escalation of the war. We offer this chapter not as a completed case study of strategic communication or political marketing success, but as a necessarily limited review of Ukraine's political communications to date from strategic communications (StratCom) and political marketing perspectives. It is clear that a crucial element of Ukrainian success so far has been the role of diplomacy and communications in mobilising and sustaining people and resources to resist Russian aggression in a war of national survival. It is in this context of ongoing resistance and survival that we analyse the Ukrainian effort. To do this, we first posit the utility of this single case study for probing existing StratCom and political marketing theory with a view to their further development and practice. We outline a far-from-distinct conceptual separation between StratCom and political marketing. This is followed by a narrative account of the Ukrainian government's communications and in which we assess its aims, audiences, channels and themes. We illustrate how the star power of a president has combined with participation in political communication activities by creative and technically literate citizens, engaging both internal and international, particularly donor, audiences. We demonstrate several key themes at work which highlight, among others, underdog resistance, democracy and European values, and the successful use of guilt appeals. Running through each of these is how Ukraine positions itself as antithetical to Russia, something that Russian has itself helped establish through its actions against Ukraine. Our case study ends by highlighting some of the future risks for Ukraine in its political communication strategy and activities as we discuss and weigh up the implications for political marketing and strategic communications theory and practice.

ONE CASE, TWO BODIES OF THEORY

The purpose of this case study is to expose theory to a specific context that allows us to reflect on the utility of that theory and how it may inform practice. As Flyvbjerg (2006) argues:

> The case study produces the type of context-dependent knowledge that research on learning shows to be necessary to allow people to develop from rule-based beginners to virtuoso experts.

Consequently, this chapter is pitched as an attempt to help communications practitioners learn more about their craft. We recognise the limitations in using a single case study to revise theory, and we leave it for others to confirm the observations we make here as being more or less valid. Nevertheless, the more limited aim of asking what this case to date can tell us about two bodies of theory, StratCom and political marketing, is worthwhile and to be encouraged for anyone engaged in reflective practice and theory development.

PROPAGANDA IN ALL BUT NAME?

Before delving into what Ukraine has done in its wartime political communications, and continues to do, we need to explain our rationale for why we examine this case from the perspectives of strategic communications and political marketing. Couldn't we simply call this a case of Ukrainian wartime propaganda? Our starting point is to align Ukraine in conceptual terms with pro-Ukrainian allies who rarely, if ever, claim their own political communications efforts to be propagandist. Berridge (2015, p. 200), for example, discusses the emergence of the term, 'public diplomacy' as 'simply propaganda rebranded', given propaganda's pejorative connotations established in the light (or perhaps darkness) of the first half of the 20th century. Russian communications approaches are regularly framed negatively, in terms of propaganda and disinformation and we are careful here not to lend any unwarranted moral equivalence between Ukrainian and Russian communications effort.

We are clear that our position is driven by a values-based approach that holds truthfulness, transparency and credibility as essential elements of public engagement in healthy, functioning, democracies and between states. Indeed, these are principles which we have kept in mind in our analysis of the opportunities and risks in Ukrainian political communications. In this way, we can retain the term 'propaganda' as a 'sensitizing concept' (Baines & O'Shaughnessy, 2014) in our analysis that allows us to sniff out when the boundaries of principles are being pushed or exceeded. Furthermore, these are the principles by which we (as in our society) must hold ourselves and our allies to account, before we, consciously or otherwise, acquiesce to an authoritarian, post-truth, alternative facts-based world. Nevertheless, we acknowledge that not all readers will unequivocally share this stance in all respects, just as there are differing positions on the justification of Russia's actions in Ukraine (at state and sub-state level). This is best illustrated by relevant UN General Assembly votes on Ukraine.

At the beginning of March 2022, a vote calling for an end to fighting and the withdrawal of Russia had 141 countries vote for the resolution, 5 against (Belarus, Russia, North Korea, Eritrea and Syria), with 32 abstentions (including China and the world's largest democracy, India) (United Nations, 2022a). A closer look at these figures reveals that:

> 28 out of the 54 African countries (just over 51 percent) represented in the U.N. voted in favour of the resolution, a sharp contrast to the 81.29 percent of non-African countries that voted in favor of the resolution. Of the 35 countries that voted to abstain, 17 (48.6 percent) were African – including Algeria, Angola, and South Africa. Eight African countries, including Cameroon, Ethiopia, and Morocco, did not submit a vote. (White and Holz, 2022)

Votes on Ukraine followed a similar pattern in October 2022, and March 2023 (United Nations, 2022b, 2023). Consequently, given geo-strategic dynamics and alignments, we do not make any claims for universal appeal regarding Ukraine's communications to international audiences. Indeed, it is evident and safe to assume throughout this chapter, that Ukrainian international communications have largely been directed towards audiences based in sympathetic countries likely to be donors of financial, political and military assistance.

Berridge (2015) argues that public diplomacy is aimed at foreign audiences (i.e. beyond a state's internal population), representing a form of communication that, in theory, listens and speaks to populations 'over the heads' of their governments. The foreign focus of public diplomacy alerts us to the issue of communication with one's own population. Political marketing as a term fits this context, as it is generally uncontentious for politicians and civil society organisations to influence or persuade one's own population regarding legitimate political objectives (and it is also the subject of this volume). It is certainly contentious, as the Cambridge Analytica scandal showed, when there is lack of transparency regarding micro-targeting of individuals to shape, say, voting behaviours through the use of data obtained without proper consent (Confessore, 2018). So, methods and intentions are important in law and ethics, at least in democratic countries. StratCom in the context of conflict and the defence community has developed to the point where there is NATO doctrine on the use of StratCom in support of NATO's Operations (NATO, 2023b). Political marketing and StratCom therefore have a good fit with this Ukrainian context. We now define them for use in this chapter.

DEFINING POLITICAL MARKETING

Scammel (1999) reviews the overlapping nature of a number of disciplines alongside political marketing, including electoral campaign studies, marketing management and associated marketing disciplines. In the latter, she notes the contribution of scholars in developing marketing beyond 'profit-driven commercial organisations to non-profit organisations' (1999, p. 722). This is something we also note in developments such as 'social marketing', 'an approach used to develop activities aimed at changing or maintaining people's behaviour for the benefit of individuals and society as a whole' (NSMC, n.d.), as opposed to profit alone.

Scammel (1999) identifies an emphasis on strategy in political marketing, rather than simply the tactical 'techniques of promotion'. As such, for example, political communication becomes a sub-set of broader political marketing. Lock and Harris (1996) also focus on exploring the similarities and differences between political marketing and commercial marketing, noting the exchange relationship between voters and political entities being one where the citizen (voter) is presented with a 'complex intangible product which the voter cannot unbundle. As a consequence, most voters have to judge on the overall packaged concept or message' (1996, p. 15). Wring (1997a) also focuses on an exchange relationship in his definition of political marketing:

> ...the party or candidate's use of opinion research and environmental analysis to produce and promote a competitive offering which will help realise organisational aims and satisfy groups of electors in exchange for their votes. (1997a, p. 653)

This is influenced by Niffenegger's (1989) political marketing process framework. (We discuss the framework later in the chapter in the section on 'The Case of Ukraine: A Scalable European and Global Historical Context'). The process contains the 'marketing mix' of the famous marketing 4Ps: Product, Promotion, Place and Price, which we use in our discussion of our case study. Note, that there have been attempts to develop political marketing beyond the 4Ps to 7Ps just like in commercial services marketing; however, we are opting for the more limited set of 'Ps' for the purposes of this case study. In the political marketing context, Niffenegger operationalises *product* as party image, leader image and manifesto. *Promotion* includes advertising, broadcasts, PR and direct mail. It involves the use of both paid (advertising), owned (websites, social media) and earned media (press, radio and television news). *Place* entails a distribution strategy through a network of 'suppliers' and includes local work by activists, canvassing and leaders' tours. One might query how *price* is operationalised outside of a commercial context, though Niffenegger suggests economic, psychological and national dimensions. Wring's interpretation of these resonates with our case study context:

> [Price] comprise[s] voter feelings of national, economic and psychological hope or insecurity. This notion of the political "price" reflects Reid's (1988) observation that a vote is a "psychological purchase". (Wring, 1997b, p. 658)

The 4Ps are guided by strategy, are aimed at a market in an environment of supporters, floating voters and opponents, which we seek to understand through market research. These stakeholders are engaged in activity that should be seen as more than a one-time 'purchase'. Using a relationship marketing perspective, Henneberg (1997) envisages an attempt to build political constituencies towards longer-term goals in political marketing as:

> ...seeking to establish, maintain and enhance long-term voter relationships at a profit for society and political parties, so that the objectives of the individual political actors and organisations involved are met. This is done by mutual exchange of promises.

STRATEGIC COMMUNICATIONS

Strategic Communications as a term is used in two different communication contexts. In a very broad sense, we can describe these as civilian and defence. This is not a perfect distinction in that both contexts involve taking a strategic approach to communication that aims to move audiences towards desired attitudes and behaviours, something shared with political marketing. In the civilian context, Macnamara (2021) discusses strategic communications management in a study comprising three insurance and financial services case studies. Similar to Scammell (1999), Macnamara spends some time exploring and grouping the disciplines involved in 'Organization-Public Relations' which he places in the context of 'a wide and growing range of communication activities…by organizations in attempts to engage and build and maintain relationships with and/or persuade various *publics* – also referred to as *stakeholders* and *audiences*' (2021, p. 66). He includes public relations and corporate communications in the discussion, and places strategic communications management in his review as an integrating concept. His case studies illustrate a complicated and diverse array of two-way communications with internal and external audiences. Macnamara argues that this activity does not neatly align with extant disciplinary theory, leaving room for integration and innovation in communications. As such he sees 'scope for further consideration of paradigms in which theories and practices are nested' (2021, p. 83), something that we endorse in our own conclusions.

In the defence context, one can see clear evidence of this attempt at nesting disciplines and activities. According to the NATO Strategic Communications Centre of Excellence (n.d.), StratCom encompasses:

> …multiple elements of public diplomacy, political marketing, persuasion, international relations, military strategy, and many others…We understand strategic communications as a holistic approach to communication, based on values and interests, that encompasses everything an actor does to achieve objectives, in a contested environment. It means that strategic communications is understood more as a holistic mind-set in projecting one's policies.

Not surprisingly, NATO positions StratCom in a 'contested environment' but also makes the point that it is about how NATO acts and not just what it says. StratCom is strategic because it oversees or coordinates many other forms of communications towards strategic political ends. The integrating concept of StratCom is essential in NATO's definition:

> …the integration of communication capabilities and information staff function with other military activities, in order to understand and shape the information environment, in support of NATO strategic aims and objectives. (NATO, 2023, p. 1)

The doctrine describes the 'How, What and Why' of NATO Strategic Communications as follows (NATO, 2023, p. 2):

- **What** – Maintaining strategic relevance of all activity at all levels of command, through the continuum of competition.
- **How** – Aligning the force to one common narrative, using actions, images and words.
- **Why** – To ensure all Alliance activity is coherent with the narrative and supports the desired strategic outcomes.

Analysis of the information environment encompasses information systems, virtual and physical environments in which people, live, work and operate, marking the holistic nature of this approach. After the primary concept of 'strategic outcomes', the central organising concept for NATO strategic Communications is 'Narrative'. Narrative is defined as:

> …a spoken or written account of events and information arranged in a logical sequence to influence the behaviour of a target audience. (2023, p. 16)

This story-like approach seeks to communicate, 'where we come from', 'where we are' and 'where we want to be' (2023, Annex A).

NATO recognises three types of narrative of relevance: (i) institutional narrative, (ii) strategic narrative and (iii) micro-narrative. A strong feature of these is the concept of time, where institutional narratives tend to be enduring and micro-narratives tend towards short to mid-term activity. All must be consistent, and actions taken by NATO should not undermine established narratives. This points towards consistency in approach, dissonance reduction in the minds of the public and arguably a sensitivity towards avoidance of charges of hypocrisy, in what NATO stands for, its aims and how it acts.

It is this focus on narrative, aside from the conflict context, that marks as distinct the defence understanding of StratCom. Indeed, it is picked out as one of the following three key elements of StratCom (2023, pp. 12–13):

1 Understanding [Audiences].
2 Integrated planning.

3 Narrative-led execution.

The latter is described as:

> ...[using] the narrative as an overarching expression of the whole-of-Alliance strategy to influence audiences and gives context to the campaign, operation or situation. It is conducted with the same behaviour-centric mindfulness as our planning. (2023, p. 13)

ASSUMPTIONS

Having outlined the political marketing and StratCom perspectives, it is worth noting some assumptions that we take forward into the case study. Scammell discusses the idea that surveys of practitioners and campaigners have found:

> ...little direct evidence of engagement with marketing theory and less knowledge of the 'marketing concept' even where its general philosophy is practiced. (Scammell, 1999, p. 737)

This however may be a time-related and more partial perspective. Others have contested the issue and see politics in Britain as heavily imbued by the marketing perspective (Kavanagh, 1995; Wring, 2004). More recent work by Pich and Dean (2015), Pich et al. (2020), and Schofield and Reeves (2015) have also illustrated the direct relevance of marketing to politics from branding and voter satisfaction perspectives. Such practice is considerably more advanced in scope in the United States. Microtargeting of voters en masse in Presidential elections (see Murray & Scime, 2010) has substantially altered the pace and nature of modern campaigning, not just in that country but elsewhere too (see Blaemire, 2018; Papakyriakopoulos et al., 2018).

Nevertheless, we do not assume the conscious application of a method or approach encompassing all communicators in Ukraine. We are also careful not to see deliberate integration, control or coordination, or a single hand at work where there may be none. Rather we seek to see what the case study might tell us about political marketing, primarily through the construct of the marketing mix (4Ps) in building constituencies, and StratCom in a Defence context from the perspective of narrative.

We started this theoretical section by making statements about ethics and values in relation to propaganda. We recognise as we go through this academic exercise that there is a lot at stake in Ukraine, not least the lives of a generation and the values and principles that have been the backdrop to the story of Europe.

THE CASE OF UKRAINE: A SCALABLE EUROPEAN AND GLOBAL HISTORICAL CONTEXT

It might be tempting to treat the war as starting in 2022, owing to its outright brutality along an 'active front line' of around 600 miles (Cohen, 2023) or the missile and drone attacks by Russia on urban centres across the second largest country in Europe by area. Alternatively, one might start the account with the invasion of Ukraine in Crimea by Russia's 'little green men' in 2014 (Shevenchenko, 2014). However, the information war is not bounded by recent episodes (see Figure 11.1 for a timeline). Rather, it draws on narratives that are both Ukrainian, such as the genesis and effect of the Maidan protests (Houeix, 2022), and scalable beyond Ukraine. For example, it is possible to interpret current events through the lenses of post-soviet discourse (Zubok, 2022), the Cold War (Sarotte, 2022), the Second World War (Goldenberg, 2022), the Russian Empire (Düben, 2020) and great power politics (Douglas Davis & Slobodchikoff, 2022). In all of this, one can observe changing and unsettled dynamics in which ideologies and forms of government are set in simple but contested opposition, such as capitalism versus communism, and liberal democracy versus authoritarianism.

Layered on top of this are ethical and legal arguments regarding the sovereignty of states and the rule-based international order, such as that argued by Tsuruoka:

> Even if Ukraine were not a democracy and Russia were an ideal democracy, this war would be unacceptable. It is a blatant violation of international law, including the UN Charter, and Russia is believed to have committed numerous war crimes. (Tsuruoka, 2022)

There is therefore an extensive contextual hinterland to the rise of Volodymyr Zelensky to Ukrainian president in 2019, and Putin's decision, in the post COVID-19 pandemic period, to launch a full-scale invasion. The current information environment in the war, to which we now turn, invokes this contested hinterland, and when

1 December 1991 – Ukrainian referendum on independence in which 92.3% of voters give their approval.

28 June 1996 – Ukraine adopts a new constitution.

31 May 1997 – Ukraine and Russia sign an agreement on partnership, borders and territorial integrity, including on Ukrainian sovereignty of Crimea.

November 2004-January 2005 – The Orange Revolution – a series of protests in response to the 2004 presidential election as a response to Russian interference in the election and a rejection of widespread corruption.

23 January 2005 – Pro-reform and pro-western government under President Viktor Yushchenko.

2008-2009 – Ukraine expresses a wish to join EU and EU Eastern Partnership Program.

2013 – Russian begins a trade-war with Ukraine. President Yanukovych is forced to reverse a decision on signing a trade-deal with the EU which initiates the protests known as EuroMaidan and the Revolution of Dignity.

2014 – President Viktor Yanukovych is removed from office by parliament, whilst violent protests are ongoing. Russia invades Crimea and move troops and supplies into the Donbas region.

17 July 2014 – Malaysia Airlines flight MH17 is shot down over eastern Ukraine with the loss of 298 lives.

2015-2019 – 3 seasons of *Servant of the People* are run (see https://www.imdb.com/title/tt6235122/)

21st April 2019 – Volodymyr Zelensky elected president.

24th February 2022 – Russia launches full-scale invasion of Ukraine.

Figure 11.1 Timeline Since the Fall of the USSR (Plokhy, 2016, IMDB, n.d.; UK Parliament 2023a)

Zelensky speaks to foreign audiences he invokes a shared hinterland.

ZELENSKY BEFORE THE 2022 INVASION

In the context of strategic communications, President Zelensky is the most strategic of communicators, speaking on behalf of his country for the most strategic of purposes: to generate diplomatic, economic and military support. His star power has allowed him to talk not only to governments in their own parliaments (often to rapturous applause), but in public diplomacy terms, over the heads of leaders to their publics. This has included speeches via video link at the Berlin Film Festival 2023, The Golden Globes 2023, Venice film Festival 2022, Cannes Film Festival 2022 and the Grammy Awards, 2022 (Roush, 2023). Through each speech, he has utilised his communication skills in ways which will not be surprising to Ukrainian audiences that have known him through his time as an actor of the satirical Ukrainian TV series, *Servant of the People*, the campaigning presidential candidate, President and wartime leader.

Liubchenko et al. (2021) describe how Zelensky 'unexpectedly burst into politics in 2019'. In the *Servant of the People*, he played a schoolteacher whose tirade about government corruption is videoed by a student. The video goes viral on social media and Zelensky's character eventually goes on to be elected president (IMDb, n.d.). Liubchenko et al.'s article is a research article applying a technique they call 'intent analysis to studying political language' (2021, p. 152). They had two research questions concerning the discovery of the most common intentions for 'influencing or interrelating with the audience' in Zelensky's speeches, and what values he communicates to the nation (2021, p. 154). Regarding the first they assess, using an intention schema, that his speeches are less about prompting the audiences towards specific behaviours, but cognitive and emotion-directed intentions, for example, to reason, encourage and please. They allude to the use of Ukrainian and Russian language for different audiences within Ukraine. Zelensky spoke Russian exclusively in his television shows and normally in 'everyday life', a result of his eastern Ukrainian upbringing. This allowed him to win the support of Russian speaking and pro-Russian citizens, and also to differentiate himself from his predecessor who had 'made language a key issue' (2021, p. 161).

Liubchenko et al.'s article is interesting because it selects speeches for analysis between 2019 and 2020, starting from his inauguration day on 20th May 2019. It is a period before the country rallies behind him after the 2022 invasion. Liubchenko et al. describe this as a time when there was criticism of his position and policies on key issues. They argue that he appears reluctant to engage in open public talks and to directly express his views on 'the most troublesome issues on Ukraine's political agenda' (2021, p. 148). They see this as consistent with his campaigning style of populist and emotional statements that were orientated towards informal social media communications through:

> ...a series of short, selfie-style videos circulating predominantly on Instagram and Facebook and stuffed with populist slogans and oversimplified demagogic statements aptly characterised as "for all the good and against all the bad". (2021, p. 148 with embedded quote attributed to S. Medvedev)

Regarding values, Liubchenko et al. argue that Zelensky's communication intentions tend to communicate core European values, taken to be:

- Respect for human life.
- Solidarity (support for others).
- Peace.
- The rule of Law.
- Human rights.
- Equality.
- Self-realisation.
- Individual freedom.
- Democracy.
- Freedom of religion.
- Respect for other cultures.
- Tolerance.

Despite this list, Zelensky's anti-corruption stance is also questioned, given that he made his surprise announcement to run for president on a television channel owned by oligarch, Ihor Kolomoisky, during prime time TV, New Year's Eve celebrations in 2018/2019. According to Liubchenko et al., 'investigative journalists and activists' have also shown links between the two, even if the personal role of Kolomoisky 'is yet to be determined' (2021, pp.147–148). This issue is also acknowledged by Onuch and Hale (2022) but framed more supportively, given that, according to Zelensky, nearly all major television channels were owned by oligarchs in Ukraine (Onuch and Hale 2022, p. 120) and that various investigations remain inconclusive about the precise nature of relationships (2022, p. 183–187). Perhaps the main takeaway from this period in terms of Zelensky's relationship with the electorate is as Onuch and Hale state: 'Zelensky's approval ratings ebbed and flowed throughout the first two and a half years of his presidency' (2022, p. 234). This is to some extent normal when the public expectation of a popular actor-turned-president is faced with exceptionally difficult political problems.

ZELENSKY THROUGH TO THE FULL-SCALE INVASION

Onuch and Hale's (2022) book on the 'Zelensky effect' tells the story of the context for Zelensky's presidency, his campaign, early presidential period and activities into the summer of 2022, therefore also covering the full-scale Russian invasion. Like Liubchenko et al., they too observe Zelensky's campaigning communications style pulled into his presidential communications. This is summarised as:

> Most noticeably for the public, he did not change the way he communicated with citizens upon assuming office. This includes his preference for personalized, direct, and curated appeals. His

> speeches are designed to be highly accessible to ordinary Ukrainians (the country's "median voter") and frequently delivered through short videos on social media. (2022, pp. 204–205)

Zelensky is described by Onuch and Hale as acting as a 'Virtual Incumbent' during his campaign. This relieved him of the some of the burden a new candidate might have faced when running for election. That is because he was already known by Ukrainians for playing the role of president in *The Servant of the People*, the third season of which aired during his campaign. He therefore did not have to fight for public exposure. His values communicated in the series were taken to be those that he would hold as a man as president. The effect of this is that critics of Zelensky see a failure to present policy alternatives or clear vision for the country (2022, p. 188). On the other hand, Onuch and Hale identify four themes in Zelensky's election campaign that resonated with voters (2022, pp. 187–192):

1. A promise to care for the material interests of ordinary people, including fighting corruption and shifting focus from elites to the people – a strong theme in *The Servant of the People.*
2. To bring peace, even if he had to sit down with Putin, the Russian President.
3. What Ukrainians have in common rather than what divides them.
4. Ukraine's path to Europe, with Ukraine embedded in Europe (as distinct from a sceptic's view of Zelensky that he was a 'Russian Project').

These themes, as part of his style, are then carried through into what Onuch and Hale call his role as Communicator-in-Chief in response to the Russian invasion of 2022. They use qualitative data analysis software to assess transcripts of speeches, 'close readings' of Instagram posts and appeals on Twitter and Telegram (2022, p. 259). They identify five themes for the Ukrainian audience in response to the invasion:

1. Zelensky addresses all Ukrainian citizens as citizens of a great country.
2. Ukrainian unity.
3. Criticism of elite actors who need to do more and 'come back on their private planes'.
4. Ukraine's values that are essentially European values – democratic, civic, liberal and inclusive – and in stark contrast to the Kremlin and oligarchical values.
5. The connection between personal and national responsibility.

A unifying idea that runs through each of these is the notion of civic duty. This was present in his pre-2022 invasion communications and particularly strong during the COVID-19 period (2022, pp. 261–262). He frames civic duty through a number of rhetorical devices. For example, he does not present the idea that it is he and the government that are protecting Ukraine, rather it is what Ukrainians are doing for themselves, including acts of everyday resistance, from simply doing one's day job, providing meals for the troops, to the most courageous acts. Consequently, Zelensky exudes a self-effacing, 'credit sharing' stance with the people. He does not ask for citizens to help him personally, but to support the state and the Army.

For Onuch and Hale, 'Zelensky embodies civic Ukrainian national identity' (2022, p. 33), able to bridge some of the real and mythical divides in Ukrainian society, not least in perceptions of allegiance and language. They cite the rallying effect of a crisis in bringing people together, something borne out in polling. In February 2023, over 90% of Ukrainians approved of the activities of Zelensky as President. This is as high as it was on June 2022, and much higher than 2021 (Statista, n.d.).

Onuch and Hale also point towards a 'generational effect' in Zelensky sharing 'perspectives and attitudes' in common with the 'Independence Generation':

> ...those Ukrainians who came of age politically in an independent Ukraine. Now in their late thirties and forties, they were born under Communism (between 1975 and 1985 – or thereabouts), and although children at the time of Ukrainian independence, they have personal memories of it. They were old enough to understand what was happening at the time and its significance but were too young to engage in the changes and transition in any meaningful manner. (2022, p. 37)

ZELENSKY DURING THE FULL-SCALE INVASION

Dyczok and Chung (2022) conducted a study of the speeches of Zelensky in the first fifty days of the full-scale invasion. For the first 12 days of this period of the war, he speaks directly via recorded video messages posted on the presidential website and on social media to his fellow Ukrainian citizens. On day 13, he starts to address international audiences, via live video links. Dyczok and Chung analyse 103 speeches, 74 of which they say are addressed to Ukrainian citizens, and 30 to international audiences (one of these being assessed as addressed to both audiences). They conduct a mixed method analysis involving word counts and word clouds via NVivo and qualitative methods for identifying topics, themes, tone, mood and rhetoric within the speeches. They look through a number of theoretical lenses involving the message construction phase in communications theory, McComb and Shaws' Agenda Setting theory[1] and Entman's Framing theory.[2]

As with the assessments discussed earlier, Dyczok and Chung also pick out Zelensky's personal charisma, communications skills and preference for directly talking to audiences as being an essential element of his effectiveness. In his videos addressed to Ukrainians in the first 50 days of the 2022 invasion, his daily communications take the style of a friend checking-in, setting the agenda for bolstering morale, maintaining integrity, and providing support. This entailed assuring Ukrainians of their strength, that the president was with them, that victory would come and that they were not alone with the support they were receiving from the 'democratic world' (2022, p. 150).

In terms of video style, the longest was almost 13 minutes, and the shortest just under three minutes. The videos were mostly recorded indoors, with the earlier ones showing Zelensky at a podium. Later, on day 12, with his phone, he 'took the audience on a walk with him' as he looks out the windows of his office and moves along the hall showing other people working there at night. In this video, he eventually moves to a room, where he puts down his phones, and a crew continue to capture his talk to camera. Future videos show him at his desk in his office – 21 videos – with 'only' eight videos shot outside his offices in the square. Overall, the main topics are a summary of events, the success of Ukraine, examples of Ukrainian bravery and the barbarity of Russia. On this later point, Dyczok and Chung cite Zelensky's references to the deaths of 52 children in one video and the death of an elderly holocaust survivor, 96 years old Borys Romanchenko, who had been in multiple Nazi camps, including Buchenwald and Bergen-Belsen, only to be killed by a Russian shell hitting his residential high-rise building (2022, p. 151).

A useful comparison to the video analysis above is a study by Plazas-Olmedo and López-Rabadán (2023) who compare two sets of Zelensky videos published at the beginning of the war from 24 February to 8 March 2022, and then between 25 September and 10 October 2022. Their article is one of a number in an issue examining 'Spectecularisation', or polititainment, which they describe as 'part of the digital landscape of our days'. One senses an echo of this in Liubchenko et al.'s article, which is entitled *Political communication in the post-truth era: mind mapping values of Ukraine's Volodymyr Zelensky*. Both articles suggest or imply a change towards style over substance or the entertaining media spectacle as central to political communications.

Plazas-Olmedo and López-Rabadán set out to conduct a content analysis of Zelensky's Instagram posts during the two periods. In both sets of data, videos make up the majority of posts to Instagram: 52.17% of 138 posts and 66.36% of 107 posts, indicating the importance of video in Zelensky's political communication and perhaps an increasing emphasis on video. A large majority of videos feature Zelensky on his own, though between the two data sets, there is an increasing proportion of videos where Zelensky is shown with other politicians or citizens. Although sometimes shown in an heroic way, his personal leadership is seen from the point of view of his political activity, rather than, for example, his personal life. Civil society images, without Zelensky present, also play a more important role in the proportion of videos between the two sets, from 2.78% to 8.45%. Where the videos are captured also changes. Over 90% in the first period are in official places, down to 63% in the second period, and from 8.33% up to 19.72% in public spaces. This may of course be influenced by how possible it is to move around in Ukraine. There are notable changes in the style of the video production, as constructed from Plazas-Olmedo and López-Rabadán's data in Table 11.1.

Professional production means well-framed in good lighting, in a classic political scenario with official symbols. Strategic amateur means filming with a mobile phone, with reduced image quality. Cinematic staging is where production is enhanced for quality, music and montages in typical post-production editing. Animated infographic is self-explanatory, while strategic spontaneity is a video which gives the impression of spontaneity but has been well-planned in advance. As indicated in Table 11.1, there is a large change in the proportion of professional production videos to strategic amateur production and videos involving additional post-production. Plazas-Olmedo and López-Rabadán posit that the second period shows more dynamic, natural videos with music. The most successful formats (according to likes etc.) have been 'the most amateurish' and easy to produce and that is the direction taken by Zelensky's team indicated in this study.

Regarding speeches to international audiences, the Dyczok and Chung study highlights many of

Table 11.1 Production Style and Values

Date	*Total Instagram Posts*	*% Videos*	*% Professional Production*	*% 'Strategic Amateur' Production*	*% Cinematic Staging*	*% Animated Infographic*	*% Strategic Spontaneity*
24/2/22–8/3/22	138	52.17	79.17	15.28	1.39	2.78	1.39
25/9/22–10/10/22	107	66.36	35.21	35.21	18.31	8.45	2.82

Source: Plazas-Olmedo and López-Rabadán (2023).

the same techniques Zelensky uses for Ukrainian audiences; however, they point to differing goals in the context of promoting Ukraine and garnering support (2022, p. 152). This included:

- Shifting the agenda from Russia's security concerns and NATO to 'Ukraine as a subject, not an object, of international affairs'.
- Addressing the false narrative of de-Nazification of Ukraine.
- Ukraine as a sovereign democracy and Russia's violation of international law.
- Ukraine's self-defence and intention not to surrender.
- The broader threat to European and global security where support by democracies to Ukraine is 'not only the right thing to do but also in their interests'.

These are consistent with other assessments which point towards heroic Ukrainian self-defence framed in the context of the underdog or David versus Goliath. 'The right thing to do' also leads Zelensky to leverage both guilt and shame appeals for those who do not come to the aid of Ukraine (Baines quoted in WSJ, 2022).

Dyczok and Chung (2022) outline a range of techniques used by Zelensky in his 'unconventional' framing and delivery of speeches to international audiences, including:

- Appearing in a green T-shirt rather than a suit before legislatures and institutions.
- Emotive language backed up by details of killings and atrocities.
- Repeatedly expressing gratitude but also asking for more concrete help.
- Speaking forthrightly where help was slow without shying 'away from shaming techniques'.
- Addressing world leaders by their first names.
- Tailoring messages to the national experience of audiences.

Regarding this last bullet point, Dyczok and Chung reference a number of international speeches in which audience experience and heritage is invoked, a selection of which are extracted and summarised in Table 11.2. Gallo (2022) refers to this rhetorical device as 'allusion' in his assessment of Zelensky's international speeches which 'are references to well-known events, people, or places that remind audiences of the values they share with a speaker and the topic'. This draws on the previously mentioned shared hinterland between Ukraine and the wider world to which Zelensky speaks.

The conclusion of the Dyczok and Chung study leads them to consider the success of Zelensky's speeches. They argue that Zelensky managed to shift the focus away from Russia's narrative to a Ukrainian one. It is clear that Zelensky's style stands in contrast to the 'demagogic manner of the Russian President' (2022, p. 156). Perhaps crucially they highlight the change in political discussion in the West from avoiding antagonising Russia, to increasing sanctions on Russia and the supply of weapons.

To put this in perspective, early requests for support by Ukraine were resisted in the United States, based on concerns about provoking Russia and that Ukraine may succumb to the Russian invasion (Ackerman, 2023). A few months later in March 2022, it was reported that the White House was concerned about demands by Ukraine for long range rockets, for fear of escalation, prompting frustration by Ukrainian officials (Mcleary, 2022). Later still, Ukraine continues to voice frustration about the timely supply of weapons, this time with Germany, on its decision-making regarding tanks (Sabbagh & Connolly, 2023). Features of Ukrainian international diplomacy and presidential speeches have therefore been to maintain pressure on donors for heavier kinds of weapons and ammunition, and to speed up the rate at which they are being delivered. For example, Zelensky, dressed in khaki, presented a fighter pilot's helmet to the Speaker of the UK House of Commons during

Table 11.2 Examples of Zelensky's Speeches Tailored to Audiences

Date	*Audience*	*Invoked History, Heritage or Circumstances*
8 March 2022	UK Parliament	• Shakespeare quotes • Ukraine circumstances similar to WWII Battle of Britain • Rewriting Winston Churchill's 'We shall fight them on the beaches' speech to fit the Ukraine context
11 March 2022	Polish Sejm	• References to Pope John Paul II • Smolensk (in Russia) air disaster, 2010 • Speech of former Polish president, Lech Kaczyńskiin in Tiblisi 2008, who later died in the Smolensk air disaster. • Complicated history of the two countries, but sure of today's support
15 March 2022	Canadian Houses of Parliament	• Canada as the first western country to recognise the independence of Ukraine in 1991. • (Author comment – note that a large section of the population of Canada claim Ukrainian heritage.)
16 March 2022	US Houses of Congress	• Pearl Harbour • Mount Rushmore • Martin Luther King, Jr. • 9/11 attack on the Twin Towers • 'Being the leader of the world means to be the Leader of Peace.' (Author comment –partly a guilt appeal, as this US trope is leveraged for its logical consequences)
17 March 2022	German Bundestag	• Reference to Ronald Reagan's instruction to Gorbachev. 'Chancellor Scholz! Tear down this wall!'
20 March 2022	Israeli Knesset	• Closeness of Ukraine and Jewish community (Author comment: Zelensky himself a Jew) • Golda Meir from Kyiv • Moral choices, comparing Ukrainians saving Jews in WWII. 'One can keep asking why we can't get weapons from you. Or why Israel has not imposed strong sanctions against Russia.' (Author comment – note the guilt appeal here)

Source: Extracted and summarised from Dyczok and Chung data, 2022.

his speech to both parliamentary houses on 8 February 2023. Written on the helmet were the words, 'We have freedom, give us wings to protect it', in an appeal for military aircraft (Patrick, 2023). Zelensky also warned in May 2023 that Ukraine needed more time to prepare for its counteroffensive, because of military equipment arriving in batches (Bachega, 2023). Nevertheless, according to a UK Parliament (2023b) briefing paper published on 12 May 2023, the United States provided the largest military assistance to Ukraine, with $37.6 billion committed since January 2021, the start of the Biden Administration. $36.9 billion of this has been committed since Russia invasion in February 2022. The United Kingdom has committed £4.6 billion in military assistance comprising £2.3 billion in 2022 to be matched in 2023. The EU, for the first time as a bloc, had committed just over €4.6 billion for the supply of lethal weapons.

Dyczok and Chung are less sure about the impact of Zelensky's messages on Ukrainian society where they quote a number of commentators that argue that Ukrainian society self-organised to respond to the invasion and that the actions of citizens inspired Zelensky (rather than the other way round). We illustrate this dynamic later. Nevertheless, even if this is the case, it is at least consistent with the assessment above by Onuch and Hale regarding Zelensky's self-effacing and credit-sharing posture.

STRATCOM AS A COORDINATING ACTIVITY

So far we have focused extensively on the strategic communicator that is President Zelensky. The understandable focus on him as a figurehead, facilitated by access to official speech transcripts, videos and social media accounts has perhaps meant less coverage of other Ukrainian communications activities. However, the Ukrainian government has been working on communication activity across the whole of government, in line with the holistic definition of strategic communications offered earlier from NATO. We know that such activities have been diverse and have included bringing celebrities to Ukraine, such as the rock band U2 to give an underground/metro concert; the display of captured Russian equipment in public and in museums; publishing citizen art on twitter; promoting the stories of animals on the battlefield, such as a mine clearing dog called *Patron*; the creation of postage stamps based on the famous episode of Snake Island when Ukrainians demonstrated courage and resistance, and the list continues (Sui, 2022). Together these efforts support a strategic narrative of resistance, and international support for Ukraine along the lines that defeat is not inevitable and that success is possible and probable. We provide two further examples here, The Ukrainian Center for Strategic Communications, and United24.

UKRAINIAN CENTER FOR STRATEGIC COMMUNICATION

When looking for coordinated activity and campaigns run by the Ukrainian government, it is worth starting with the Ukrainian Center for Strategic Communication. It has a web presence in both Ukrainian and English and was established under the:

> Ministry of Culture and Information Policy of Ukraine, as one of the mechanisms for countering disinformation by joint efforts of the state and civil society. The Center is focused on communication that is aiming to counter external threats, in particular information attacks of the Russian Federation. (Ukrainian Government, n.d.)

The website lists the functions in Table 11.3, on its 'About' page which clearly reinforce the notion of holistic StratCom.

The website also contains news, events and research/analytics pages. Each page entry is sharable on common social media platforms in English or Ukrainian, giving a sense of multiple audiences and international collaboration on countering disinformation. The busiest pages are on research and analytics, where at the time of writing, by way of illustration, the top three items were:

- *Weapons under control: 10 points to prove western weapons are in good hands in Ukraine* – 2 May 2023.
- *Russian Propaganda in Countries of Balkan Region: Pro-Kremlin Narratives in Local Online Media* – 28 April 2023.
- *Russians Don't Want to Learn from Chernobyl Lessons* – 26 April 2023.

UNITED24

United24 is a website positioned as a personal initiative of the President of Ukraine, with contact emails addresses noted as a gov.ua domain. On its homepage, Zelensky is pictured at a lectern wearing a black sweatshirt with a United24 logo. The website facilitates a 'one-click' ability to donate to Ukraine. United24 aims to collaborate with 'charities, donors, and public figures worldwide' (United24). The website provides reports on how donations are spent across Defence, humanitarian demining, medical aid, rebuilding Ukraine and education and science. At the time of writing, the website showed that over $337.4 million had been donated since its inception. Its 'ambassadors' and supporters feature prominently on the website, including: Mark Hamill, of *Star Wars* fame; Andriy Shevchenko, the Ukrainian footballer; Richard Branson, British billionaire businessman; and Barbara Streisand, American singer and actor. Corporate sponsors include the likes of Deloitte, Uber and Balenciaga. The prominence of Zelensky alongside such recognisable household, international names, speaks again to the personal impact he has in mobilising others internationally. That donations are channelled to a wide variety of activities, not just weapons, perhaps allowing a broader range of donors to be recruited behind the project.

MOBILISED CIVILIANS

Reflecting the effort to provide funding to Ukraine, there has been a wide range of initiatives set up internationally as campaigns to direct funding to Ukrainian causes. For example, https://www.weaponstoukraine.com/and https://www.proukrajinu.org/ are websites whose declared founder is Dalibor Dědek, a businessman. Both websites openly declare the backing of the Czech Ministry of Defence and Embassy of Ukraine in Czechia. The websites are available in English and Czech, with weaponstoukraine.com, also available in Slovak. The different language versions are not simply translations of each other, but are tailored

Table 11.3 Functions of the Ukrainian Center for Strategic Communication (Ukrainian Government, n.d.)

Development of Strategic Communication	• We develop narratives to strengthen Ukraine's image in the areas that are most targeted by the aggressor. • We create messages for coordinated government communication. • We unite the efforts of the state and civil society to provide coordinated counteraction to disinformation.

Countering disinformation and building resilience towards it	• We create an online resource that will:
	  • respond to information threats;
	  • serve as a united database of the aggressor's information presence;
	  • build resilience;
	  • support Ukrainian narratives.
	• Conduct information campaigns
	• We create a public platform to discuss problems and develop solutions to combat disinformation.

Conduct information campaign	• We regularly report on Russia's hybrid aggression. • We strengthen cooperation with the countries that have similar information threats to Ukraine. • We develop disinformation-countering mechanisms together with our partners.
For the State	• We conduct trainings to raise awareness about hybrid threats. • We develop proactive narratives for government communication. • We suggest mechanisms of systematic communication about the state efforts in countering disinformation.
For citizens	• We report on information threats and malign influence operations. • We provide tools to grow resilience to disinformation. • We communicate the victories of Ukraine in the information war.
For civil society	• We strengthen the voices of Civil Society Organisations (CSOs) through the promotion of their work. • We conduct joint information campaigns and trainings. • We ensure a dialogue between the state and CSOs in developing the regulatory framework.
For international partners	• We inform about the aggressor's malign operations regularly. • We share expertise in detecting and combating disinformation. • We jointly develop recommendations for combating disinformation and building resilience towards it.

to audiences accessing the different languages. The English version (click the EU flag for English) exhibits the logos of BBC, CNN, *The New York Times* and *Der Spiegel* above a description of a series of campaigns, featuring amounts raised for projects and the numbers of donors. For example, €2.12 million is declared as raised by 19,165 donors for a RM-70 missile launcher. The Slovak version does not carry the western news logos and describes a smaller number of projects, while highlighting its e-shop for merchandise with humorous or satirical t-shirts. Donations are portrayed as buying weapons for Ukraine, as a gift for Putin (Darcek pre Putina - Zbrane pre Ukrajinu, n.d.). The site lists as its partners a number of organisations such as Mier Ukrajine (Peace of Ukraine) whose page on a fundraising site, declares in Slovak:

> The Peace of Ukraine initiative was created as an immediate civil response to the unprecedented aggression and attack of the Russian army on free and sovereign Ukraine. The events in Ukraine fundamentally affect all of us. Just like Ukraine, free and democratic Slovakia is also under threat. (Donio, n.d.)

These Slovak websites straddle government and civil society efforts to support Ukraine, using a narrative that suggests Slovakia is also under threat, and that Ukraine is on the front line for a wider European/global community.

Another initiative raising money to support Ukraine's purchase of weapons is Saint Javelin, whose logo features a religious St Mary-like figure holding a portable anti-tank weapon, similar to a Javelin missile (Saint Javelin, n.d.). The organisation states that its founder is Canadian, Christian Borys who worked as a journalist in Ukraine from 2014 to 2019. He had initially hoped to raise $500 but to date has raised over $2 million (Saint Javelin n.d.). It was reported that in one transaction, Saint Javelin donated US$350,000 to 'Unite with Ukraine' to help build 'an army of drones' (Ukraine World Congress, 2022). Unite with Ukraine is an initiative of the NGO, Ukrainian World Congress, which had formed in 1967. According to Julia Tymoshenko, who runs marketing and communications for St Javelin, its success is attributed to the St Javelin social media meme. This heralded a campaigning social enterprise with an e-shop selling associated merchandise. Once more the merchandise it adopts is pointedly humorous and satirical with messaging on stickers, clothing and accessories. St Javelin was widely seen as a symbol of Ukrainian resistance and defence that 'flew across the world' (Tymoshenko, 2023). The website is in English, targeting an international audience. It too displays the logos of reputable international media organisations under the caption 'as seen on:' (Saint Javelin, n.d.).

This is a similar story to that of NAFO (North Atlantic Fella Organization, n.d.) which started from a meme, and developed a keen sense of satire to attack Russian disinformation and propaganda. It has gone on to fundraise through merchandise sales and inspire a series of campaigns on social media by followers, using a similar approach to humour and satire. A co-founder is Matt Moores, former United States Marine Corps (CSIS, 2022), who is one of a number of people inspired by the Shiba Inu 'doge' meme, created by @Kama_Kamilia in May 2022 (North Atlantic Fella Organisation, n.d.). Once again this highlights the international nature of the information response.

Tymoshenko is also Editor in Chief of *Ukraïner*. Ukraïner relies on over a hundred volunteers to run its service (Ukraïner, n.d.a). Although created in 2016 to tell stories about Ukrainian life, it is now positioned on its homepage as 'the platform for reliable information about events in Ukraine'. (Ukraïner, n.d.b). Tymoshenko argues that there was a clear need to debunk Russian disinformation and show 'Ukraine from the inside' (Tymoshenko, 2023). Ukraïner has been expanding the range of languages in which it publishes content – now up to 12 languages in May 2023. Perhaps most notably, it aims to not only communicate to the world but also to Ukrainians about their own country and its regions, giving a sense of nation building around unique identities, cultural groups and practices. A number of themes emerge in her interview on YouTube's Silicon Curtain channel. This includes Ukraine's open mindedness, free elections, pluralism and diversity which contrasts with Russian attempts to suppress differences. Ukrainian activism in protests, and mobilisation in the war, are seen in contrast to the passivity of Russian constituencies (Tymoshenko, 2023). Tymoshenko also highlights the idea that Russian language can be seen as the language of the colonist. Eastern European specialists have often learnt Russian rather than one of the national languages of the former republics in the USSR. This can introduce a sort of bias that means journalists and academics (and others) are exposed to issues from a Russia-centric perspective rather than Ukrainian. This reflects the ongoing question of attitudes towards Russian language in Ukraine since Russia's aggression (Afanasiev et al., 2022).

Another example, set up in 'the first hours of the invasion', is an initiative called PR Army. They describe themselves:

> As a self-organized community, each of the members brought something precious: contacts, connections, stories, expertise. By putting it all together we could effectively work with Western journalists, opinion makers, governments, institutions, and media. At PR Army, we believe that communication leads to global changes. And by conveying truthful narratives about the war, we facilitate the victory of Ukraine. (Ukrainian PR Army, n.d.a)

PR Army pursues a number of thematic streams as indicated in Table 11.4 (Ukrainian PR Army, n.d.b):

Its focus as declared is decidedly international, providing content through a series of 'projects' based in the themes described in Table 11.4. The work has gained international recognition through PR industry awards from *PR Week* and the *North America Sabre Awards*. Through their pro-bono partnership with PLUS Communications, their campaign entitled 'Fighting with Our Words' ran with the aim of 'driving the call to action through the media to elected officials and government agencies for military and humanitarian aid' (PLUS Communications, 2023). They focused primarily on 'national cable television and streaming news coverage' and claim results based in the following metrics:

Table 11.4 Thematic Streams in Ukrainian Political Communications – (Ukrainian PR Army, n.d.b)

Thematic Stream	*Description*
Security and Cyber Threat	Exposing Russian manoeuvres of weakening physical and digital security, of European countries
Trade Ban	An umbrella project for demanding economic sanctions, oil-gas embargo and trade ban with Russia
Disinformation	Tracking and tackling Russian propaganda with the means of PR and technology
Eyewitnesses and Experts	Proactive pitching of Ukrainian eyewitnesses, experts and spokespersons in the worldwide media
Expert columns	Promoting pro-Ukrainian narratives via expert commentaries, interviews and expert columns
Culture and History	Presenting Ukrainian culture to the world and showcasing destructions it encounters by Russia now and in the past
Free Our Heroes	PR support of the activities of the Association of Families of Defenders of Azovstal, aimed at the liberation of Ukrainian captives
Business and Economy	Raising awareness of Ukrainian business resilience in the light of economic struggle in the country and in the world
Food Crisis and Nuclear Threat	Showcasing the consequences of Russian war on the world food sector and uncovering Russian nuclear terrorism

- Secured more than 2,000 earned media hits, with a combined national publicity value of more than $230 million according to Critical Mention.
- Secured more than 100 live television interviews with major cable news outlets in the first 45 days of the effort.

In terms of actual outcomes from such campaigns, these are much harder to assess. However, Mark Laity, former BBC News journalist and former Director of Strategic Communication at NATO Headquarters, discusses his advisory contribution to PR Army's work (Laity, 2023). One area he highlights is their decision to focus on the forced deportation of children from Ukraine to Russia, which culminated in the campaign 'Where are our People?' (WAOP?, n.d.). Laity points out that historically, especially under Stalin, mass forced deportations had been a tactic to change the demographics in territories, including the Baltic states, Ukraine and Moldova. Whilst it was recognised as happening in Ukraine in the current conflict, prior to the campaign it was not seen as 'a major talking point in the public debate' (Laity, 2023). Whilst he acknowledges that one cannot measure how much the campaign directly changed the debate, it can be seen as part of an emerging awareness of this issue. Laity refers to the international arrest warrant for President Putin issued on 17 March 2023 by the International Criminal Court for the unlawful deportation of children (International Criminal Court, 2023).

It is also worth mentioning the creation of Ukraine's so called IT Army and not simply because it chimes with the title of PR Army. The branding of business functions put towards defence and military use is very interesting. It again frames the country's response in terms of national defence and civic duty by Ukrainian citizens – and sympathetic international supporters. The initiative was formed towards the end of February 2022, under the Ukrainian Ministry for Digital Transformation. Volunteers with digital and cyber skills were called to support, with the coordination of their activity being conducted through a *Telegram* channel. Their activities are not only about 'hitting back' at Russian cyber-attacks but also protecting Ukraine (Burgess, 2022). By 18 March 2022, *The Guardian* reported that 300,000 Ukrainian and international people had volunteered, even though 'western officials' were discouraging volunteers, with fears about where the boundaries of criminality lay (Milmo, 2022). In 2023, Biggerstaff reports that nearly 200,000 had volunteered and also discusses the challenge in the Law of Armed Conflict regarding military distinction between civilians and combatants, particularly where actions by volunteers are designed to cause harm to another party to the conflict, such as attacking Russian information infrastructure (Biggerstaff, 2023). The discussion on StratCom earlier mentioned that NATO took the view that the broader information environment also comprised cognitive and virtual dimensions. That the PR Army and IT Army exist, speaks to a holistic approach, by design or otherwise, that addresses both content of communications and the technology platforms that facilitate and propagate communication and information (Maksymiv, 2022). This is in line with the notion of integrated actions in StratCom. Consequently, Russian disinformation is undermined by, for example, defacement of a propaganda website and the rebuttal of messages, while protecting Ukraine's own information capability. Maksymiv is writing for UkraineWorld, run by Internews Ukraine, that also has its roots in volunteer responses, this time in supporting international journalists after the EuroMaidan protests of 2013–2014 (UkraineWorld n.d.).

There are many other government and civil society organisations engaged in supporting Ukraine's information and communication efforts. We hope that the few highlighted here are sufficient to give a sense of activity.

DISCUSSION

In using theory to reflect on the Ukrainian case, part of the skill is in understanding that which is universal and may be transferrable to other contexts, and that which is so contextual it cannot be repeated elsewhere in any planned sense. We start first with trying to point towards the highly contextual and perhaps there is nowhere better to start than with President Zelensky himself.

The Strategic Communicator – President Zelensky

Coming to politics from three seasons of a TV show in which he has played the Ukrainian President does seem rather context-specific. That he could play the 'virtual incumbent' during his election campaign and use his drama, combined with a direct-to-the-public approach through social media is hardly repeatable. One might compare this to President Trump in the light of his *The Apprentice* programme (see Heritage, 2016 'You're hired: how The Apprentice led to President Trump'), perhaps as part of a broader trend relating to spectacularisation. That the public knew Zelensky based on his TV character is nevertheless an interesting entry-point to what may be learnt in three respects. Firstly, it points towards consistency at the root of narrative in strategic communications. There is an expectation that Zelensky, the president, will act in a way consistent with what he represented as an actor. This he was able to leverage through continuing the story of what he was for and against in his own narrative position, before being president and since. Secondly, related to the first, a number of studies mentioned in this chapter have described how he pulled his pre-war style and preferences for communications through from his campaigning into the post 2022 invasion period. The first two lessons embody the 'style as substance' approach and have proved to be both conceptually and pragmatically beneficial. The Ukrainian public has had the same experience of communications throughout his Presidency, and it has been able to continue in practice, even as conflict has intensified. Whilst he was initially criticised for being light on policy, it is challenging to be a peace-builder across different groups in a diverse Ukraine, in which negotiations at that point with Russia may have been at least theoretically possible. To be a unifying figure of 'Ukrainian national identity', his emotional style did not have to change to build constituencies. It became appropriate for building constituencies when events created crisis and the need for defence of the homeland.

The third lesson is also related to narrative consistency but plays into political marketing too. Owing to the cycle of elections, one can come to view political marketing as episodic. Even when one is trying to build long-term public constituencies, the next election and the next vote can encourage short-term thinking. Interestingly, this is something shared with a defence view of Strategic Communications, as this too is often associated with conflict episodes with a beginning, middle and end. For Zelensky, there was a recognisable overarching narrative and mode of presentation, even as events changed on the ground. This can partly be explained by the fact that Zelensky was elected in a country effectively at war since 2014. Soldiers had been fighting and dying in eastern Ukraine for five years before he came to power. Nevertheless, it does not make sense to say that during his Presidential campaign and before the 2022 invasion he did political marketing and afterwards he did wartime strategic communication. Rather, as mentioned above, it is his narrative consistency and communications style that are essential.

NATO's idea of institutional narrative, beyond the coming and going of episodic strategic and micro narratives is helpful. If one looks at the Ukrainian government as having an institutional narrative, albeit one acutely tied to the character of the President, this appears to have provided the consistency throughout regarding what Ukraine stands for. What Ukrainian Government or Ukrainian people stand for have been at the heart of their nation building and international narrative. None of this can be separated from the notion of an international environment that some argue is pitting democracy against authoritarianism. What does NATO stand for is a relevant question if it is to represent the values of its members. It is arguable that NATO has struggled to maintain its relevance, perhaps typified by President Trump's view (at one point) that NATO was obsolete (Anon., 2017). Since then, the United Kingdom has changed its defence and security policy to be less episodic around crisis, and to think longer term about ongoing competition with Russia and China (UK Government, 2023). There is therefore a lesson regarding longer-term perspectives in both political marketing and strategic communications, one that institutional and strategic narratives have something to offer.

Applying the Marketing Mix: The 4Ps

If the Zelensky presidency offers strategic communications lessons on consistency and communications style, how does this fit with a marketing mix (4Ps) view of the case study? We consider each component further below.

Product/Offering

Niffenegger notes party image, leader image and manifesto as elements of product in political marketing. It is in this that the notion of narrative tells the story of the product – that complex package of elements upon which the public have to make decisions. It is here where actions and words have to be consistent and it is where a series of risks sit when they do not. At least this is the case for most politicians outside of the Trump paradigm, but then again, he does display a type of consistency for his supporters. The concept of narrative might be easily wrapped into the idea of product, or political service.

On the topic of manifesto, it is clear Zelensky has been criticised for style over substance. However, while nation-building and aiming for unity at home in the face of Russian aggression, his 'offering' is also to be sold to international donors. His manifesto has been values based, taking each opportunity to say 'your values are our values', 'you and us are alike', 'to help us defend ourselves is also your defence'. The 2022 invasion has clarified one area of policy necessity – materiel and support for the war and he has excelled in pursuing this. Having said that, Ukraine has been requesting military support, and was getting some, long before the 2022 invasion (UK Parliament, 2022).

The leader's image has perhaps come to dominate the concept of product or better still, 'offering'. One must take into account the personal charisma of Zelensky, something we have called star power earlier in this chapter. This has helped mobilise resources, not least because of the willingness of others to be associated with him, celebrities, politicians and public alike. His personal charisma stands in contrast to Putin's, almost in every presentational and political way, and it is not just in terms of personalities. A positive statement of Ukrainian values is almost always an implicit statement of what Putin's Russia is not. This has fed into Zelensky's agenda right from the start in terms of, for example, continued post-soviet reform and the rejection of oligarchism.

Product Risk

Scepticism about reform was evident in the early stages of Zelensky's presidency and it still presents a risk for him. It is one thing to hold a reform policy, it is another for that reform to be completed and seen to be done. This is about narrative consistency. For example, Politico (2022) headlines this issue as 'Ukraine takes two steps forward, one step back in the anti-corruption fight'. These policy issues await Zelensky (or successor) once this conflict phase of his presidency subsides and some form of normal political life resumes. There is also a risk that this transformational narrative is undermined in the domestic politics of key allies, particular in the United States, but not only. The Hunter Biden story is a case in point which continues to be a means by which to attack Biden (American Enterprise Institute, 2021) and can support anti-Ukraine policy lobbies in Allied countries. Regarding this last point, there is a conservative strain of US politics that sees Ukraine practicing disinformation in order to pull the United States away from an America First policy (Bandow, 2023). Any temptation by Ukraine towards deception or disinformation – propaganda as a sensitising device – will be seized upon in debates among allies, and in Ukraine. It is interesting how the BBC frames the 'Ghost of Kiev' story – the heroic pilot – as legend rather than an untruth (Anon, 2022) which brings the discussion back to ethics and intentions. Getting the balance right isn't always easy. Maksymiv (2022) in her UkraineWorld post notes the pros and cons of the Ukrainian governments approaches to Strategic

Communication in wartime. One con is that 'Quite often, Ukraine's government has preferred maintaining calm to the delivery of the whole truth' which can risk leading to inflated expectations by people and underestimation of 'the severity of the wartime situation'.

Promotion

Promotion concerns paid, owned and earned media. At the time, the early political marketing articles referenced in this paper were published, TV was the dominant media. Social media has been a huge disruptor since in this regard, particularly in the hands of Zelensky and civil society actors, in his wartime context. Nevertheless, it is clear that major international TV channels remain important to Ukraine, as the focus on cable channels and streaming news by PLUS Communications and PR Army demonstrated. Another interesting feature of communications for western audiences is the use of the logos of reputable major media channels, such as the BBC, *The New York Times* and *Der Spiegel* and celebrity endorsement. These serve to give authority and trustworthiness to social media operations, particularly when they are asking for individual donations or wish to make sales. Also of note is the initiative of the Ministry of Digital Transformations to set up an IT Army to operate in the information domain, through the use of cyber skills to target disinformation and the platforms that propagate it, while protecting Ukrainian capability.

Place (Distribution)

Place is taken to mean distribution strategy for ideas and messaging. Social media in a sense provides its own distribution strategy and squeezes the distinction above with promotion, as part of its disruption. It is therefore more helpful to think about what social media does for people, rather than its technical features and content. What this case study shows is the power of social media to help groups of activists self-organise for action – in this case many people with social media and communications skills, who understand emotion, pathos, humour and satire in its cultural setting. Regarding humour it is noted by Maksymiv (2022):

> Gradually, official governmental channels have also integrated humorous content into their channels. As Ukrainians create memes and produce humor even during the war, officials realize that jokes are an effective part of communication, too. For instance, the Ministry of Defense has turned to trolling the Russian enemy and posting folk memes.

This illustrates how government and civil society organisations have been able to work and learn together and have a softer kind of coordination rather than directed control by a central body. This has been used remarkably well to integrate Ukrainian society towards the existential fight that they face and to unify people in that common good. There is a remarkable consistency in themes and intent between government and civil society as the result. A war of national survival at a time of technological know-how and capability has allowed this to happen, irrespective of strategic communication existing as an 'integrating function'. When political marketing was in its infancy, distribution strategy relied a lot on party member activists. Social media has allowed other groups to form and participate, even if party membership is in decline among some electorates. How this self-organising network of activists and mix of institutional and civil society groups work together in other contexts is an area open to much further research in civilian, defence, peace and conflict contexts. Indeed, it is a strong indicator of a potential need to revise political marketing and StratCom theory regarding notions of control and integration.

Price

One way to assess when and how people might respond to crisis, and the extent to which they rally around a flag or lend support to a leader, is through the concept of price. If we operationalise price along the lines of those proposed by Wring (1997) – feelings of national, economic and psychological hope or insecurity – which result in support for a 'product' be it a president, a nation or its values, then we can observe it being expressed in the polling and behaviours of Ukrainian citizens, international supporters and donors. Zelensky's support in Ukraine moved to 90% in favour of his actions; confidence in him as leader in a diverse country is a result of a change in the price/value placed in rallying around the flag because of the invasion of 2022. We observe it in the self-organising groups giving of their time, and those who provide their support in defence of Ukraine. We observe it in everyday resistance and the actions of many in the international donor community to provide support and military assistance in Ukraine. All who do so accept the price in exchange for what and who they believe in and we observe it in their actions.

CONCLUDING REMARKS

Our single case study highlights the general applicability of both Strategic Communications and Political Marketing to help explain the political communications of the Ukrainian government and President Zelensky himself during the current Russo-Ukraine crisis. It is difficult to privilege one concept over the other in the specific scenario of Ukrainian political communications here, because President Zelensky appears to have been running a campaign to become President for a very long time before the invasion and just carried this on during the invasion, albeit with more gusto and purpose.

Our contribution in this chapter is to highlight the important link between political marketing (especially that conducted during elections) and strategic communications (conducted during wartime). This alignment arises in this unique case because President Zelensky is essentially campaigning for his Western friends to support him in his country's hour of need, and this requires him to prepare a persuasive brief, because he cannot defeat Russia without western support. His persuasion tactics are aimed at getting western partners to donate more aid, provide more political support, hurt Russia with ever greater economic sanctions and provide more lethal weapons (particularly longer-range missile systems and next-generation fighter jets), despite western fears that providing this support and materiel might poke the bear into a third world war and potentially a nuclear confrontation.

Applying the marketing mix concept to a wartime scenario has indicated that it has direct relevance. The product relates to whether or not the audience will 'buy' the offer (in this case Zelensky's 'fight to the finish' appeal to Ukrainians and 'we are defending Western values' to western donors). Promotion strategy is through paid, owned and earned media. Distribution strategy relates to how the message is relayed to the audience, and the central importance of social media in distributing this message across to people around the world, as well as through political leaders in NATO country parliaments. Zelensky's use of social media is perhaps the first time a wartime leader has galvanised political support in a nation-on-nation conflict across the world in this way. The concept of price is particularly relevant, because it alludes to the price of support for supporting Zelensky and Ukraine, or not as the case may be. We urge researchers to consider how political marketing techniques are, ought to be, and can be applied in conflict and military contexts given their clear relevance.

Nevertheless, there are features of the Ukrainian case study that prompt us to invite researchers to further review the adequacy of current theory. How do we more effectively take account of timescales that span war and peace, strategic competition and participation of publics and governments in communication and disinformation activities? This includes the rise of self-organising groups who can participate in technology-enabled communications, challenging and amplifying centrally controlled and integrating efforts in communications planning and execution. There is also Zelensky's celebrity status which appears unique in terms of his acting and then political roles, yet we can see the growth in the performative nature of politics elsewhere (and from other celebrity leaders). Moreover, there is the need for a better understanding of how values and ethics in communication activities affect practice – and all of this in the context of polarised ideological differences in a competitive, hyper-connected, global information environment.

Notes

1 McCombs and Shaw first set out their theory in their 1972 paper on the effect of mass media on setting the agenda for what was important for the public, prompted by the amount of information in the story and its position (McCombs & Shaw, 1972).

2 Entman (1993) states 'Framing essentially involves *selection* and *salience*. To frame is to select some aspects of a perceived reality and make them more salient in a communicating text in such a way as to promote a particular problem definition, causal interpretation, moral evaluation, and/or treatment recommendation. . .'.

REFERENCES

Ackerman, E. (2023, 28 March). Ukraine can only win if the U.S. delivers more weapons faster. *Time*. https://time.com/6266296/ukraine-win-if-the-u-s-delivers-more-weapons/. Accessed on 28 May 2024.

Afanasiev, I., Mann, B., Selyukh, A., & Nadworny, E. (2022, June 2). Ukraine agonizes over Russian culture and language in its social fabric. *NPR*. https://www.npr.org/2022/06/02/1101712731/russia-invasion-ukraine-russian-language-culture-identity. Accessed on 28 May 2024.

American Enterprise Institute. (2021). *Did Biden just commit an impeachable offense in Ukraine?* https://www.aei.org/op-eds/did-biden-just-commit-an-impeachable-offense-in-ukraine/. Accessed on 28 May 2024.

Anon. (2017, January 16). Trump worries Nato with 'obsolete' comment. *BBC News*. https://www.bbc.com/news/world-us-canada-38635181. Accessed on 28 May 2024.

Anon. (2022, May 1) How Ukraine's 'Ghost of Kyiv' legendary pilot was born. *BBC News*. https://www.bbc.com/news/world-europe-61285833. Accessed on 28 May 2024.

Bachega, H. (2023, May 11). Zelensky says Ukraine needs more time for counter-offensive. *BBC News*. https://www.bbc.com/news/world-europe-65550427. Accessed on 28 May 2024.

Baines, P. R., & O'Shaughnessy, N. J. (2014). Political marketing and propaganda: Uses, abuses, misuses. *Journal of Political Marketing*, 13, 1–18.

Bandow, D. (2023, January 12). Ukrainian disinformation. *The American Conservative*. https://www.theamericanconservative.com/ukrainian-disinformation/. Accessed on 28 May 2024.

Berridge, G. R. (2015). *Diplomacy: Theory and practice*. Palgrave Macmillan.

Biggerstaff, W. C. (2023, May 10). The status of Ukraine's 'IT army' under the law of armed conflict. *Articles of War*. https://lieber.westpoint.edu/status-ukraines-it-army-law-armed-conflict/. Accessed 28 May, 2024.

Blaemire, R. (2018). The evolution of microtargeting. In J. A. Thurber & C. I. Nelson (Eds.), *Campaigns and elections American style* (pp. 217–236). Routledge.

Burgess, M. (2022, February 11). Ukraine's volunteer 'IT Army' is hacking in uncharted territory. *Wired UK*. https://www.wired.co.uk/article/ukraine-it-army-russia-war-cyberattacks-ddos. Accessed on 28 May 2024.

Cohen, E. A. (2023, February 28). The shortest path to peace. *The Atlantic*. https://www.theatlantic.com/ideas/archive/2023/02/russia-invasion-ukraine-peace-military-history/673231/. Accessed on 3 May 2023.

Confessore, N. (2018, April 4) Cambridge Analytica and Facebook: The Scandal and the fallout so far. *The New York Times*. https://www.nytimes.com/2018/04/04/us/politics/cambridge-analytica-scandal-fallout.html. Accessed on 17 May 2023.

CSIS. (2022). *#NAFO and winning the information war: Lessons learned from Ukraine | CSIS events*. https://www.csis.org/events/nafo-and-winning-information-war-lessons-learned-ukraine. Accessed on 10 March 2023.

Darcek pre Putina - Zbrane pre Ukrajinu (n.d.). https://www.darcekpreputina.eu/. Accessed on 18 May 2023.

Donio. (n.d.). *Mier Ukrajine*. https://www.donio.sk/mier-ukrajine. Accessed on May 18 2023.

Douglas Davies, G., & Slobodchikoff, M. O. (2022, August 1) *Great-power competition and the Russian invasion of Ukraine, Journal of Indo-Pacific Affairs*. Air University Press. https://www.airuniversity.af.edu/JIPA/Article-Display/Article/3111129/great-power-competition-and-the-russian-invasion-of-ukraine/. Accessed on 3 May 2023.

Düben, B. A. (2020). "There is no Ukraine": Fact-checking the Kremlin's version of Ukrainian history LSE blog 1st July 2020. https://blogs.lse.ac.uk/lseih/2020/07/01/there-is-no-ukraine-fact-checking-the-kremlins-version-of-ukrainian-history/. Accessed on 3 May 2023.

Dyczok, M., & Chung, Y. (2022). Zelens'kyi uses his communication skills as a weapon of war. *Canadian Slavonic Papers*, 64(2–3), 146–161. https://doi.org/10.1080/00085006.2022.2106699

Entman, R. M. (1993). Framing: Toward clarification of a fractured paradigm. *Journal of Communication*, 43(4), 51–58.

Flyvbjerg, B. (2006). Five misunderstandings about case-study research. *Qualitative Inquiry*, 12(2), 219–245. https://doi.org/10.1177/1077800405284363

Gallo, C. (2022, March 17) Zelensky's audience-centered speeches connect to shared values. https://www.forbes.com/sites/carminegallo/2022/03/17/zelenskys-audience-centered-speeches-connect-to-shared-values/. Accessed on 10 March 2023.

Goldenberg, T. (2022, March 18) Explainer: Why Putin uses WWII to justify war with Ukraine. *AP News*. https://apnews.com/article/russia-ukraine-putin-israel-europe-tel-aviv-54f1524afdf732d1716782e01accc089. Accessed on 3 May 2023.

Henneberg, S. C. (1997). Research in political marketing – An overview. In S. C. Henneberg & N. J. O'Shaughnessy (Eds.), *Readings in political marketing* (pp. 777–783). Praegar.

Heritage, S. (2016, November 10). You're hired: How the Apprentice led to president Trump. *The Guardian*. https://www.theguardian.com/commentisfree/2016/nov/10/trump-the-apprentice-president-elect-reality-tv. Accessed on 23 May 2023.

Houeix, R. (2022, February 28). From the Maidan protests to Russia's invasion: Eight years of conflict in Ukraine. *France, 24*. https://www.france24.com/en/europe/20220228-from-the-maidan-protests-to-russia-s-invasion-eight-years-of-conflict-in-ukraine. Accessed on 3 May 2023.

IMDb. (n.d.). *Sluga narodu (TV Series 2015–2019)*. https://www.imdb.com/title/tt6235122/?ref_=fn_al_tt_3. Accessed on 4 May 2023.

International Criminal Court. (2023, March 17). Situation in Ukraine: ICC judges issue arrest warrants against Vladimir Vladimirovich Putin and Maria Alekseyevna Lvova-Belova. https://www.icc-cpi.int/news/situation-ukraine-icc-judges-issue-arrest-warrants-against-vladimir-vladimirovich-putin-and. Accessed on 19 May 2023.

Kavanagh, D. (1995). *Election campaigning: The new marketing of politics*. Blackwell.

Laity, M. (2023) Europe's future can be found in Ukraine's people. In *Mark Laity's Newsletter*. https://marklaity.substack.com/p/europes-future-can-be-found-in-ukraines. Accessed on 19 May 2023.

Liubchenko, Y., Miroshnychenko, P., Sirinyok-Dolgaryova, K., & et al (2021). Political communication in the post-truth era: Mind mapping values of Ukraine's Volodymyr Zelensky. *Communication Today*, 12(2), 146–167. Trnava, Slovakia: Univerzita sv. Cyrila a Metoda v Trnave.

Lock, A., & Harris, P. (1996). Political marketing – vive la différence. *European Journal of Marketing*, *30*(10/11), 14–24. https://doi.org/10.1108/03090569610149764

Maksymiv, S. (2022) How strategic communications are managed in wartime Ukraine: Pros and cons (n.d.). *UkraineWorld* https://ukraineworld.org/articles/opinions/strategic-communications. Accessed on 23 May 2023.

McCombs, M. E., & Shaw, D. L. (1972). The agenda-setting function of mass media. *Public Opinion Quarterly*, 36(2), 176–187. Summer 1972. https://doi.org/10.1086/267990

Mcleary, P. (2022) Biden resists Ukrainian demands for long-range rocket launchers. https://www.politico.com/news/2022/05/18/biden-resists-ukrainian-demands-long-range-rocket-launchers-00033473. Accessed on 18 May 2023.

Milmo, D. (2022, March 18) Amateur hackers warned against joining Ukraine's 'IT army'. *The Guardian*. https://www.theguardian.com/world/2022/mar/18/amateur-hackers-warned-against-joining-ukraines-it-army. Accessed on 23 May 2023.

Murray, G. R., & Scime, A. (2010). Microtargeting and electorate segmentation: Data mining the American national election studies. *Journal Of Political Marketing*, 9(3), 143–166.

NATO. (2023). Allied joint publication 01. Editon F version 1, December. https://assets.publishing.service.gov.uk/government/uploads/system/uploads/attachment_data/file/1148298/AJP_01_EdF_with_UK_elements.pdf.pdf. Accessed on 19 May 2023.

NATO. (2023). AJP-10 allied joint doctrine for strategic communications. Edition A, version 1, March 2023. https://assets.publishing.service.gov.uk/government/uploads/system/uploads/attachment_data/file/1146501/20230328-AJP_10_EdA_V1_Strategic_Communications-O.pdf. Accessed on 16 may 2023.

NATO Strategic Communication Centre of Excellence. (n.d.). About Strategic Communications (Web Page). https://stratcomcoe.org/about_us/about-strategic-communications/1. Accessed on 20 April 2023.

Niffenegger, P. (1989). Strategies for success from the political marketers. *Journal of Consumer Marketing*, *6*, 45–51.

North Atlantic Fella Organization (n.d.) *We are NAFO*. https://nafo-ofan.org/pages/we-are-nafo. Accessed on 19 May 2023.

NSMC. (n.d.) What is social marketing? | The NSMC. https://www.thensmc.com/content/what-social-marketing-1. Accessed on 16 May 2023.

Onuch, O., & Hale (2022). *HE, the Zelensky effect* (Kindle Edition). Hurst Publishers.

Papakyriakopoulos, O., Hegelich, S., Shahrezaye, M., & Serrano, J. C. M. (2018). Social media and microtargeting: Political data processing and the consequences for Germany. *Big Data & Society*, *5*(2), 205395171881184.

Patrick, H. (2023, February 8) Zelensky presents Ukrainian pilot's helmet to Speaker of Commons. *Independent*. https://www.independent.co.uk/tv/news/zelensky-parliament-pilot-lindsay-hoyle-b2278268.html. Accessed on 18 May 2023.

Pich, C., Armannsdottir, G., Dean, D., Spry, L., & Jain, V. (2020). Problematizing the presentation and reception of political brands: The strategic and operational nature of the political brand alignment model. *European Journal of Marketing*, 54(1), 190–211.

Pich, C., & Dean, D. (2015). Political branding: Sense of identity or identity crisis? An investigation of the transfer potential of the brand identity prism to the UK Conservative Party. *Journal of Marketing Management*, 31(11–12), 1353–1378.

Plazas-Olmedo, M., & López-Rabadán, P. (2023). Selfies and speeches of a president at war: Volodymyr Zelensky's strategy of spectacularization on Instagram. *Media and Communication*, *11*(2). https://doi.org/10.17645/mac.v11i2.6366

Plokhy, S. (2016). *The gates of Europe: A history of Ukraine*. Penguin Books.

PLUS Communications. (2023). *PLUS communications wins 2023 PRWeek award for best in crisis, nominated for campaign of the year*. https://pluspr.com/plus-communications-wins-2023-prweek-award-for-best-in-crisis-nominated-for-campaign-of-the-year/. Accessed on 18 May 2023.

PLUS Communications. (n.d.b). *Ukrainian PR army*. https://pluspr.com/case-studies/ukrainian-pr-army/. Accessed on 18 May 2023.

Politico. (2022). *Ukraine takes two steps forward, one step back in anti-corruption fight*. https://www.politico.eu/article/ukraine-takes-two-steps-forward-one-step-back-in-anti-corruption-fight-constitutional-court-reform/. Accessed 19 May 2023.

Roush, T. (2023, February 16) Zelensky urges support for Ukraine at Berlin film festival—Here are his other surprise appearances at big-name cultural events. *Forbes*. https://www.forbes.com/sites/tylerroush/2023/02/16/zelensky-urges-support-for-ukraine-at-berlin-film-festival-here-are-his-other-surprise-appearances-at-big-name-cultural-events/. Accessed on 3 May 2023.

Sabbagh, D., & Connolly, K. (2023, January 20). Ukraine frustrated as Germany holds back decision on supply of tanks. *The Guardian*. https://www.theguardian.com/world/2023/jan/20/ukraine-germany-leopard-2-tanks-ramstein. Accessed on 18 May 2023.

Saint Javelin. (n.d.). Saint Javelin official. https://www.saintjavelin.com/. Accessed on 18 May 2023.

Sarotte, M. E. (2022, July 1). The classic cold war conundrum is back. *Foreign Policy*. https://foreignpolicy.com/2022/07/01/iron-curtain-russia-ukraine-cold-war/. Accessed on 3 May 2023.

Scammell, M. (1999). Political marketing: Lessons for political science. *Political Studies*, *XLVII*, 718–739. https://journals.sagepub.com/doi/epdf/10.1111/1467-9248.00228. Accessed on 12 May 2023.

Schofield, P., & Reeves, P. (2015). Does the factor theory of satisfaction explain political voting behaviour? *European Journal of Marketing*, *49*(5/6), 968–992.

Shevchenko, V. (2014, March 11). Little green men or Russian invaders. *BBC News*. https://www.theatlantic.com/ideas/archive/2023/02/russia-invasion-ukraine-peace-military-history/673231/. Accessed on 3 May 2023.

Statista. (n.d.). Zelensky approval rating 2023. https://www.statista.com/statistics/1100076/volodymyr-zelensky-s-approval-rating-ukraine/. Accessed on 4 May 2023.

Sui (2022). *WSJ video: Cute dogs, bono and Ads: Ukraine's PR strategy to rally global support*. https://www.wsj.com/video/cute-dogs-bono-and-ads-ukraines-pr-strategy-to-rally-global-support/379763DE-79D2-4285-93C1-9588651E5AC9.html. Accessed on 28 May 2024.

Tymoshenko, J. (2023). Saint Javelin and Ukrainer – Fighting for Ukraine on the informational frontline. *The Silicon Curtain YouTube Channel*. https://www.youtube.com/watch?v=mLqB7ShA2l4. Accessed on 10 March 2023.

UK Government. (2023). *Integrated Review Refresh 2023: Responding to a more contested and volatile world*. https://www.gov.uk/government/publications/integrated-review-refresh-2023-responding-to-a-more-contested-and-volatile-world/integrated-review-refresh-2023-responding-to-a-more-contested-and-volatile-world. Accessed on 19 May 2023.

UK Parliament. (2022). *Military assistance to Ukraine 2014-2021*. House of Commons Library. https://researchbriefings.files.parliament.uk/documents/SN07135/SN07135.pdf. Accessed on 19 May 2023.

UK Parliament. (2023a). *Conflict in Ukraine: A timeline (2014 – present)*. House of Commons Library. https://researchbriefings.files.parliament.uk/documents/CBP-9476/CBP-9476.pdf. Accessed on 17 May 2023.

UK Parliament. (2023b). *Military assistance to Ukraine since the invasion*, House of Commons Library. https://researchbriefings.files.parliament.uk/documents/CBP-9477/CBP-9477.pdf. Accessed 18 May 2023.

UkraineWorld. (n.d.). *About us*. UkraineWorld. https://ukraineworld.org/about. Accessed on 23 May 2023.

Ukrainian Government. (n.d.). *Center for strategic communications*. https://spravdi.gov.ua/en/. Accessed on 5 May 2023.

Ukrainian PR Army. (n.d.a). *About us*. https://www.pr.army/about-us. Accessed on 18 May 2023.

Ukrainian PR Army. (n.d.b). *Streams and departments*. https://www.pr.army/streams-and-departments. Accessed on18 May 2023.

Ukraïner (n.d.a). *We are raising 3 million UAH*. https://ukrainer.net/donate-en/. Accessed on 18 May 2023.

Ukraïner (n.d.b). *Home Ukraïner*. https://ukrainer.net/en/. Accessed on 18 May 2023.

Unite with Ukraine. (n.d.). *About unite with Ukraine | our mission and goals*. https://unitewithukraine.com/about. Accessed on 18 May 2023.

United Nations. (2023). *Principles of the charter of the united nations underlying a comprehensive, just and lasting peace in Ukraine: Resolution/adopted by the general assembly*. Available at: https://digitallibrary.un.org/record/4003921?ln=en. Accessed on 4 April 2024.

United Nations. (2022a). *Aggression against Ukraine: Resolution/adopted by the general assembly*. https://digitallibrary.un.org/record/3959039?ln=en. Accessed on 4 April 2024.

United24. (n.d.). *The initiative of the President of Ukraine*. https://u24.gov.ua/about. Accessed on 18 May 2023.

Unites Nations. (2022b). *Territorial integrity of Ukraine: Defending the principles of the charter of the united nations: Resolution/adopted by the general assembly*. https://digitallibrary.un.org/record/3990400?ln=en. Accessed on 4 April 2024.

WAOP? (n.d.) *Homepage*. https://deportation.org.ua/. Accessed on 18 May 2023.

White, A., & Holz, L. (2022, March 9). Figure of the week: African countries' votes on the UN resolution condemning Russia's invasion of Ukraine. *Brookings*. https://www.brookings.edu/articles/figure-of-the-week-african-countries-votes-on-the-un-resolution-condemning-russias-invasion-of-ukraine/. Accessed on 4 April 2024.

Wring, D. (1997a). Reconciling marketing with political science: Theories of political marketing. *Journal of Marketing Management*, *13*(7), 651–663. https://doi.org/10.1080/0267257X.1997.9964502

Wring, D. (1997b). Reconciling marketing with political science: Theories of political marketing. *Journal of Marketing Management*, *13*(7), 651–663. https://doi.org/10.1080/0267257X.1997.9964502. quoting Reid, D. (1988), "Marketing the Political Product", *European Journal of Marketing, 22*, 34–17.

Wring, D. (2004). *The politics of marketing the labour party*. Palgrave Macmillan.

WSJ Video; Cute Dogs, Bono and Ads: Ukraine's PR Strategy to Rally Global Support. (2022). https://www.wsj.com/video/cute-dogs-bono-and-ads-ukraines-pr-strategy-to-rally-global-support/379763DE-79D2-4285-93C1-9588651E5AC9.html. Accessed on 5 May 2023.

Zubok, V. (2022, February 26). The post-soviet roots of the war in Ukraine. *The Spectator*. https://www.spectator.co.uk/article/the-post-soviet-roots-of-the-war-in-ukraine/. Accessed on 28 May 2024.

PART 2

Political Marketing, Propaganda, and Digital Evolution: Global South and Eastern European Perspectives

Political Marketing and Propaganda: Definitions, Evolutionary Changes, and Their Implications for a Taxonomy of Regime Types

Denisa Hejlová

INTRODUCTION

Nicolas O'Shaughnessy called both political marketing and propaganda "weapons of mass seduction" (O'Shaughnessy, 2004). While political marketing has become synonymous with professionalized political communication and campaigning, propaganda often signifies stealthy or unethical communication. Both aim to shape public opinion and persuade citizens to act according to a leader's or political party's objectives. However, they differ significantly in the ethics of their tools and the coercive power accompanying them.

To define and understand propaganda, we must consider the regime or group's historical context, geopolitical shifts, and coercive power. These elements are crucial for distinguishing propaganda from other forms of political communication and understanding its role in different political systems. Moreover, we need to understand the communication technology, which has changed dramatically with the digital revolution. Nowadays, the notion of propaganda "is more open-ended and, in a sense, more omnivorous" than it has ever been before (Baines et al., 2019, p. xxvii).

The distinction between political marketing (Ormrod et al., 2013) and political propaganda (Ellul, 1965; Jowett & O'Donnell, 2018) has been extensively examined by many scholars, yet it remains the subject of fierce debate and controversy (Baines & O'Shaughnessy, 2014). So, how do we define the (often fine) line that differentiates political marketing from propaganda? Firstly, we need to understand the historical context, such as how propaganda evolved during the 20th century and how "political marketing" emerged as a professionalized, ethically framed counterpart. Secondly, we must consider the broader societal and political context: how society values individual freedom, human rights, and the idea that citizens have the right to participate in governance and act freely in the public sphere. Finally, we need to view persuasion not merely as a one-way process but as a constant renegotiation between the communicator and the public. This includes examining what factors influence the receptivity of propaganda, how people are seduced by it and believe it (or just pretend to believe it), and how they may develop resistance to it.

The common ground for both propaganda and political marketing is the fundamental principle of persuasion: both propaganda and political marketing are trying to persuade people to act according to their aims. Jowett and O'Donnell define persuasion simply as "a communicative process to influence others" (2018, p. 31).

Political marketing is usually more localized: it is typically employed within the domestic context of a single state or country, focusing on influencing local citizens during elections or public campaigns. In contrast, propaganda often transcends national borders, targeting not only domestic audiences but also international publics. Its aim is to influence foreign populations, shape perceptions in other countries, and serve broader geopolitical goals, such as legitimizing actions, undermining foreign governments, or promoting an ideology on a global scale. Politicians or media often call it "disinformation" or "fake news." In academia, we use more precise terms like *Foreign Information Manipulation and Interference (FIMI)*, *Hybrid Threats*, or *Cognitive Warfare* to describe their efforts to destabilize or influence situations in other countries (Deppe, 2023). These campaigns often aim to erode trust, sow discord, and manipulate public opinion for strategic gains. A component of such operations is disinformation campaigns, which involve the deliberate spread of false or misleading information to achieve geopolitical objectives. NATO and the European Union both identify FIMI as a growing threat involving coordinated disinformation campaigns aimed at destabilizing democratic processes by influencing elections, spreading fake news, and undermining public trust (Henschke et al., 2020; Hollis & Ohlin, 2021). Lanoszka (2019) emphasizes that disinformation plays a strategic role in shaping international policy, for example, Russia targeting foreign publics in countries like the Baltic states.

We broadly define the common goal of both political marketing and propaganda as persuading people to believe in certain values or propositions. We could argue that the definition of strategic communication is somehow similar: "purposeful use of communication by an organization to fulfill its mission" (Hallahan et al., 2007, p. 3). The "organization" can mean a corporation but also a state, political party, or even a terrorist group. Graham (2017, p. 1) calls strategic communication the "catch-all term for persuasive communication on the part of military, corporate, and government organizations." The tools, strategies, and tactics in political marketing, strategic communication, or public relations can be very similar to those used in propaganda. Again, the differentiator between strategic communication and propaganda is the ethical approach: whereas strategic communication should aim for transparency, openness, and ethical use of persuasive tools, propaganda is not limited to any of these.

Despite the overall globalization, the ethical boundaries and coercive power differ dramatically from country to country, and they fundamentally predetermine the coercive power of persuasion (Baines et al., 2019; Cull et al., 2003; Jowett & O'Donnell, 2018; Welch, 2013). Political marketing and propaganda need to be studied in the context of their historical development, new digital communication and information processes, and new tools of control and surveillance of citizens' political opinions. Also, there is an ongoing debate across many fields, ranging from sociology and psychology to neuroscience, on what is the process of influence, how a person is being influenced, and if or how the person can decide not to get influenced. We need to consider the factors that influence receptivity to propaganda, along with the practical and political impact of political marketing and propaganda on democracy and fair political campaigning.

Some persuasion techniques are quite easy to recognize and resist, but some are not: for example, deep-fakes, bots, Artificial Intelligence (AI)-generated content, and algorithmic personalization are way beyond the cognitive capacities of a person to be recognized (so-called computational, algorithmic, or cyber propaganda) (Bronk, 2018; Kollanyi et al., 2016; Tsyrenzhapova & Wolley, 2021; Woolley & Howard, 2019). New technological developments have blurred the distinction between reality and manipulation in political marketing and propaganda.

HISTORICAL ROOTS OF PROPAGANDA AND POLITICAL MARKETING

The roots of persuasion to enhance or keep the political power of rulers or political formations can be traced back to ancient history. Political or ideological persuasion was often intertwined with military strategy and information warfare. One of the earliest notions of persuasion and the use of information as a part of a military strategy is by the Chinese thinker Sun-Tzu. Sun-Tzu is believed to be the author of The Art of War, one of the first military strategy books (6th century BC) (Tzu, 2007). In ancient Greece, the art of political speech flourished, and up until today, the key speeches by famous orators, such as Demosthenes or Lysias, have been studied by political scientists and philosophers (Phillips, 2014). Orators were those who were paid to defend their clients in court (similarly to lawyers) or to present political opinions in public. The art of becoming an orator and studying rhetorics became central to success in ancient Greek society, a first form of democracy, where citizens could express their political opinions and vote for their political representatives (Kennedy, 1963). In Aristotle's rhetorics in the 4th century BC, people studied how to persuade others using rational arguments (logos), emotions (pathos), and trust (ethos), and how to time the speech at the right moment (kairos) (Cope & Sandys, 2010).

However, the word propaganda became tainted during World War I (1914–1918). George Creel, a Head of the Committee on Public Information in the United States in 1917–1918, noted: "we did not call it propaganda, for that word, in German hands, had come to be associated with deceit and corruption" (Creel, 1920, p. 29). Edward Bernays (and others), who used to work for George Creel, almost two decades later re-labeled the practice of modern, professionalized practice of communication consultancy with the term "public relations" (Bernays, 1945), later reflecting that "if you could use propaganda for war, you could certainly use it for peace" (Curtis, 2002). However, up until today, the terms political marketing, public relations, strategic communication, and propaganda are often used interchangeably, depending on the political stand of the communicator. An infamous adage quotes: "We do political marketing, they do propaganda." The word "propaganda" is often used just as an insult or label, referring to the Nazi leader Joseph Goebbels, who led the "Ministry of Public Enlightenment and Propaganda" from 1933–1945.

However, along with the study and practice of rhetorics, a form of smart manipulation has also emerged – today, it is known as demagoguery or sophism. Whereas Plato's followers would dwell on the distinction of truth versus falsehood, fostering a high moral standard, the sophists would argue that truth can change according to a perspective, and they would spin the communication to their advantage using several logical fallacies, like argumentation *ad hominem* (personal attacks) (Bartlett, 2016). We can thus see that the moral and ethical question has been intertwined with persuasive communication from the very start of "professionalizing" this skill. "*Poeta nascitur, orator fit*," a poet is born, but an orator is made, is an aphorism that reflects the growth of ancient Greek and Roman rhetorics, where the ability to speak persuasively was highly valued (Gunderson, 2009). During the Renaissance period, the study of political practice and persuasion has developed further, dwelling on the antique roots. Niccolo' di Bernardo dei Machiavelli (1469–1527), known for his writing "The Prince," became synonymous for unscrupulous, immoral politics, where the end justifies the means. However, as Phill Harris argues, that is a rather simplistic and incorrect interpretation of Machiavelli. Harris argues that for Machiavelli, "obtaining liberty dictated the means" (Harris, 2010, p. 134). We should acknowledge that the overall environment with multiple actors is an important framework through which we should see and interpret various forms of persuasion and negotiation (lobbying, political campaigning, public affairs management, etc.). Harris notes that "leaders make promises that later on cannot and are not kept": they must present a persuasive and challenging vision because neutrality doesn't bring them gains (Harris, 2010, pp. 134–135).

Somewhat surprisingly, propaganda has not originated only from political communication or politics. It is not the scope of this chapter to provide a detailed history of propaganda (see, e.g., Cull et al., 2003). However, we'll highlight some moments which are crucial for understanding the theoretical and practical implications. Propaganda developed as a form of a strategic communication system within the Catholic Church in the late 17th century to combat reformism and spread catholic belief through missionary work, often "with fire and sword" (Jowett & O'Donnell, 2018). It was notably Napoleon Bonaparte (1769–1821), a French military and political leader, who has acknowledged the important role of information management, image, and media control. Napoleon built his vision into a state-controlled ideology based on nationalism, equality before the law, and secularism. He embedded this vision in education, art, press, and symbolism. Napoleon had his own printing press, which he always took with him in military campaigns to spread the news he wanted to say (Hanley, 2005).

Political propaganda was then professionalized during WWI, when it was used as a tool to motivate citizens to support war (Fleming, 2015; Fox & Welch, 2012). We've already mentioned

U.S. practitioner George Creel, who has in many ways set the professional standard and proved the power of shaping public opinions. This fact was not perceived only in a positive way, and it has led to an increased interest in how persuasion works. It raised questions of legitimacy, mechanisms, and ethical implications of "manufacturing the consent". This idea of manipulation of public opinion by the privileged and knowledgeable elite – for their own sake – was widely criticized by some theorists like Walter Lippmann (1922) but accepted and coined in practice by communication professionals like Edward Bernays. Still in the 1920s, communication professional Edward Bernays still considered "propaganda" a suitable word for modern-day persuasion (Bernays, 2005, originally published 1928). Similarly, Harold Lasswell, a leading figure in communication theory and political science, dedicated much of his work to understanding propaganda. In his book "*Propaganda Technique in the World War*" (1927), Lasswell analyzed propaganda techniques used during World War I:

> "*It (propaganda) refers solely to the control of opinion by significant symbols, or, to speak more concretely and less accurately, by stories, rumours, reports, pictures and other forms of social communication. Propaganda is concerned with the management of opinions and attitudes by the direct manipulation of social suggestion rather than altering other conditions in the environment or in the organism. (. . .) Propaganda is the war of ideas on ideas.*" (Lasswell, 1927, pp. 9–12)

Lasswell's study of propaganda led to the development of the now-classic communication model of "Who (says) What (to) Whom (in) What Channel (with) What Effect."

The global perspectives on propaganda and political ideology started to differ dramatically after WWI. Whereas some parts of the world, such as the United States or Great Britain, embraced democracy and tried to renegotiate the relationships between the government and the publics to create more open and transparent governance and gain public trust, other states, such as Russia, Italy, Germany, Japan or China, have strengthened the persuasive power of political communication and coercive power. During the first half of the 20th century, most dominant political ideologies, like nationalism, fascism, and communism, rose to power and used propaganda to shape public opinion. The first communist state arose after the Bolshevik Revolution in Russia in 1917, from where it spread communism as an ideology to other parts of the world. Communist ideology was propagated through state-controlled media, the education system, and the suppression of religion (Hejlová & Klimeš, 2019). Communist ideology presented a solution to societal inequality, but it was forced by the totalitarian form of governance. For example, in China, the political movements called "The Great Leap Forward (1958–1962) and The Cultural Revolution (1966–1976), led by Mao Zedong, aimed at structurally reforming the society from its core principles, tearing apart families, social circles, or destroying regional roots, habits, and culture (Dikötter, 2017). However, the policies led to widespread economic disaster, resulting in what is believed to be the largest famine in human history, causing the deaths of millions of people (Dikötter, 2010).

The rise of militarism and nationalism has led to the growth of other destructive political ideologies coined by propaganda, such as fascism in Italy, Nazism in Germany, and militarism in Japan. It was especially the abovementioned Joseph Goebbels, who became emblematic to propaganda. Through his way up to the power, which he gained under the government of Adolf Hitler in 1933, Goebbels mastered his work with public opinion through various strategies and tactics, such as organizing mass rallies, which resembled religious gatherings and built the cult of personality of Adolf Hitler. Goebbels also controlled state media and used modern technologies, such as radio broadcasting and film making (e.g., with the famous film director Leni Riefenstahl) to create a bold, persuasive image of a strong Germany, which has the right to rule above other nations (including diminishing some of them, like the Jews or the Roma, terminally). Goebbels was well aware that persuasion is a matter of both seduction and coercive power. He followed the American rise of public relations, read Bernays' books, and consulted with Ivy Lee, another so-called father of public relations. "Propaganda becomes ineffective the moment we are aware of it," noted Goebbels, the "tricky part" of persuasion (Welch, 2002). Even Goebbels knew that the word propaganda "always leaves a bitter aftertaste" (sic!) (Cull et al., xv). From the very brief historical overview, we can get a sense of why the term "propaganda" became toxic during the late 20th century as an unacceptable practice of persuasion. Propaganda became something that is not compatible with the values of democracy and fair political campaigning (Sartori, 1987).

The word propaganda became an insult; however, the practice has not disappeared. In the communication profession, public relations or strategic communication became labels used for the professional business of persuasion, which shall comply with international law and ethical standards set either by the corporations themselves or international associations. Similarly, the distinction has evolved in politics, where political marketing became synonymous with the fierce, yet standardized and professionalized way of persuasive political communication and campaigning (O'Shaughnessy, 1990; Henneberg et al., 2009), and propaganda is used for stealth or unethical political communication, which can use manipulation, lies, or other means of pressure. Let's look closely at the theoretical distinction between political marketing and propaganda.

THEORETICAL FOUNDATIONS AND SOCIAL CONTEXT OF PROPAGANDA AND POLITICAL MARKETING

In the previous introduction, we stated that propaganda and political marketing have a lot in common: strategies, tactics, and aims. However, there are very important differences and nuances that we are going to focus on now. Simply stated, the dividing question between political marketing and propaganda is: "How far can someone go to achieve their goals?" (Nahon-Serfaty, 2018, p. 2). There is rather a simple and basic rule that political marketing shall not go against the existing laws and legislations, and if that happens, it can be dealt with it in a legal process. However, what is legal in one country cannot be legal in another one, which makes it more difficult for public diplomacy and diplomatic political communication.

According to the Democracy Index, issued by the Economist Intelligence Unit, only 45.3% of the world's population has lived in a full or flawed democracy (such as Canada, Japan, or India), 17.9 % in hybrid regimes, and 36.9 % in authoritarian regimes (Economist Intelligence Unit, 2022). Thus 54.8 % of the world's population in 2022 has lived in socio-political environment, where fundamental human rights cannot be guaranteed. In hybrid regimes (such as Turkey, Guatemala, or Pakistan), the rule of law is flawed – things like electoral fraud, corruption, harassment of political opposers, or active foreign interference against other countries like disinformation campaigns happen regularly. They are not an exception, but tolerated status quo. In authoritarian regimes (such as Russia, China, Cuba, Saudi Arabia, or North Korea), we cannot think of any real political opposition in a democratic sense, which is essential for the concept of political marketing, where political parties or individuals compete within more or less free conditions and a transparent market. Authoritarian regimes only mock political pluralism and democratic institutions. The governance is strongly linked to intelligence and secret service. There are no obstacles or ethical barriers in using any kind of information or communication tool as a weapon against the enemy, be it own citizen or foreign national. Surveillance is often also used to achieve state or government goals. The legitimacy of the governance is closely tied to an ideology, which is conveyed through a well-established propaganda system in education, social life, religion, etc. (De Mesquita & Smith, 2011).

The social and legal context is crucial for the distinction between political marketing and propaganda. If the persuasion is or can be accompanied by some coercive power, like imprisoning, physical or psychical terror, threatening family members or colleagues, etc., its coercive power is logically much stronger. In the following scheme (see Table 12.1), we see the distinction between propaganda and political marketing (or strategic communication) within the context of democracy and the rule of law. The dynamics of power and control in hybrid and authoritarian regimes are multifaceted, and they always exist within a certain environment, which needs to be taken into account.

Table 12.1 provides a framework for understanding the spectrum of political communication across regime types, illustrating how coercive power and freedom of speech shape the information landscape.

Various stakeholders can use this framework for:

Academics and researchers: analyzing regime types and communication strategies, exploring how they align with or deviate from democratic norms.

Policymakers: identifying threats posed by propaganda in hybrid or authoritarian regimes, guiding strategies to counter disinformation, and protecting democratic institutions.

Citizens: enhancing their media literacy by enabling individuals to recognize manipulative communication tactics and understand their socio-political contexts.

As we noted in the introductory part of this chapter, propaganda is usually used only to describe the communication of one's opponent or enemy. Even states that develop a demonstrably closed, controlled, and controlling system of communication and control never talk about producing propaganda.

Table 12.1 Framework for Distinguishing Political Marketing and Propaganda in SocioPolitical Contexts

	Authoritarian Regimes	*Hybrid Regimes*	*Flawed Democracies*	*Full Democracies*
Coercive Power	Very strong: The state has significant control over citizens, enforced through surveillance, censorship, and punishment of dissent.	Moderate: The state has some control over citizens, but there may be pockets of resistance or areas where the state's control is weaker.	Weak: The state has limited control over citizens, and there may be significant pushback against attempts to exert control.	Very Weak: Citizens enjoy significant personal freedoms, and the state has limited ability to exert coercive control.
Freedom of Speech	Very restricted: Freedom of speech is often restricted, with state-sanctioned narratives dominating the media landscape. Dissenting voices can be silenced through censorship or intimidation.	Partial: Freedom of speech is limited,with state-sanctioned narratives dominating, but some alternative viewpoints may be expressed.	Broad but Constrained: Citizens are generally free to express their views, but there may be limits on certain forms of speech or certain topics.	Broad: Citizens are free to express their views, and a diversity of opinions can be found in the media.The state does not control or significantly influence the narratives that are presented.
Control and Surveillance	Very high: The state closely monitors the actions and communications of its citizens, often using this information to maintain control and suppress dissent.	Moderate: The state monitors its citizens, but the level of surveillance may vary and is not as comprehensive or invasive as in authoritarian regimes.	Low: While some surveillance exists, it is usually for security purposes and is subject to oversight and legal restrictions.	Very Low: While some surveillance exists (largely for security purposes), it is subject to legal restrictions and oversight. Citizens have a reasonable expectation of privacy.
Information Dissemination	Propaganda: The state controls or heavily influences the information disseminated to citizens. This can be used to promote a specific ideology, suppress dissent, and maintain control.	Mixed: The state controls or influences much of the information disseminated to citizens, but there may be alternative sources of information available.	Political Marketing merges with propaganda: While political parties and candidates use strategic communications to persuade voters, there may also be state- sanctioned propaganda or other coercive tools or context, such as self-censorship.	Political Marketing: Political parties and candidates use strategic communications to persuade voters. However, they do not control the overall information landscape, and their messages are subject to scrutiny and debate.
Public Participation	Limited: Citizens have little or no influence over government decisions or policies. Elections, if they exist, often lack genuine competition. Citizens need to obey state ideology and publicly signal their consent.	Partial: Citizens have some influence over government, but elections may not be fully free and fair, and the state may exert significant influence over the process. Transparency is very limited.	High but Constrained: Citizens have significant influence over government through regular, but flawed elections. There is competition between political parties and candidates, but the process may be affected by corruption or other issues.	High: Citizens have significant influence over government through regular, free, and fair elections. There is a genuine competition between political parties and candidates.

We must also bear in mind the limitations of freedom of speech when discussing research in propaganda and political marketing. Thus, articles and research describing Russian, Chinese, or North Korean propaganda will never come from these states or will never be free from state control or censorship. For example, China uses extensively the system of digital censorship, which is called harmonization. Opposition views, specific topics, expressions, or even individuals (netizens) are being silenced in the digital sphere though a sophisticated system of online censors ("harmony makers") (Nordin, 2016). Despite some digital behavior, like the "cancel culture" movement, where certain opinions are met with harsh reactions or even attempts to erase the individual or opinion from the (digital) public sphere ("deplatforming"), they are not usually linked to the government, secret intelligence, or any kind of state-controlled power (Liang et al., 2021). On the contrary, in the Western world, we can read about propaganda in a context where the word is misused just to label the opposition or even in commercial communication (so-called "corporate propaganda") (Jowett & O'Donnell, 2018).

The perspectives on what is ethical, when it comes to propaganda and political communication, are even much more complicated (e.g., see a comprehensive book by Johannesen et al., 2008). Similar to the concept of transparency, we can talk about the different notions of truthfulness and sincerity in political marketing and propaganda. In propaganda, there is no obligation to stick to reality, truth, or almost any ethical boundaries, when it comes to coercive power. In totalitarian states or hybrid régimes, coercive power, censorship, and limited freedom of speech are natural components of political power and society.

Another distinction is transparency: whereas political marketing shall be to a large extent transparent and often is even regulated (such as the caps on the financing of campaigns, etc.), propaganda doesn't need to obey any rules of transparency and disclosing its aims or tactics at all. Political marketing in a democratic country is "a formal process, as distinct from propaganda" (O'Shaughnessy, 1990, p. xii). It is "non-authoritative"; everyone knows the message and even messengers are hired (O'Shaughnessy, 1990, p. 25). Propaganda can be classified according to the transparency of its source and the accuracy of the information it presents. In white propaganda, the source of the information is correctly identified, and the information itself is mostly truthful and accurate. Although the information is designed to persuade or influence, it shall not intentionally deceive. Black propaganda often hides its source and it can use a high level of manipulation. Gray propaganda is something in between black and white: it intertwines facts with falsehoods to create a particular impression or to spread confusion or doubt (Baines & O'Shaugnessy, 2014). However, this distinction is not always easy to prove (for example, in black propaganda, the undercover of the sources can be quite sophisticated, especially in the digital world).

An important distinction between political marketing and propaganda is in the target audience. Political marketing often targets specific groups of citizens to influence their voting behavior in elections at various levels (local, regional, national, European, etc.). These groups are often defined based on various factors, e.g., age, socioeconomic status, political views, geographical location, etc. Political marketing uses strategies and tactics to align the political program of the candidate or party with the opinions, expectations, or perceived threats by the target audience to gain the support of the public (campaign communication) (Maarek, 2011). This communication, however, does not need to be limited to the pre-election campaign stage itself, but it exists continuously (so-called permanent campaigning).

Propaganda often targets a broader audience and is not limited to potential voters or even to a particular country. It can be aimed at the general public, specific social or ethnic groups, or even at the international community. The aim of propaganda is not merely to win votes but to shape public opinion, control information, manipulate perceptions, and create a favorable (or unfavorable) political or ideological climate, such as support for an invasion, legitimizing occupation of a foreign territory, terrorist attacks, etc. (Baines et al., 2019). It can be used to rally support for a regime, to demonize enemies or scapegoats, or to justify policies or actions. Propaganda is often conveyed of various communication forms and media, such as film, speeches, rallies, etc., but it can also take the form of events or social actions such as violent attacks, revolutions, etc. – so-called propaganda of the deed, coined by the Russian revolutionary Bakunin (Bolt, 2019; O'Shaughnessy & Baines, 2009). However, the more recent approach of "propaganda of the deeds" has adopted the marketing logic, and thus can be seen as one examples on the edge of the distinction between political marketing and propaganda. O'Shaugnessy and Baines state in their analysis of Islamic terrorism (2009, p. 239):

"There is no doubt that terrorists a) have target markets; b) use communications prodigiously to the extent that these matter now far more than the actual terror act itself; c) access channels of distribution; and d) have a market differentiation strategy. There can at least be said to exist metaphorically, the ubiquitous marketing mix of product, place, price, promotion in terrorist political marketing/ propaganda." (O'Shaughnessy & Baines, 2009, p. 239) With the rise of new possibilities in digital communication, propaganda can employ the same targeting tools, as political marketing.

Both propaganda and political marketing also work with frames and narratives that are essential for the publics' understanding and reception of the communicators' aim. This line is being constantly renegotiated, and it is extremely difficult to find in times of crises: in conflicts, wars, pandemics, or life-threatening situations. For example, Isaac Nahon-Serfaty discusses in his book the concept of "deformative transparency": How far are you willing to go in disclosing shocking news, statements, or visuals to persuade your public? Deformative transparency is a tactic of the disclosure of information not to enlighten, but to shock or manipulate the publics. It can involve the deliberate framing of events, statistics, or other pieces of news in a way that evokes strong emotional responses or confirms pre-existing biases. For example, Donald Trump stated in his tweet in 2016: "The media is so after me on women. (. . .) Nobody has more respect for women than Donald Trump!" (Nahon-Serfaty, 2018, p. 37). Therefore, to define the fine line, it is necessary to observe the inner tactics of persuasion, to acknowledge the role of language, sense-making, framing, and other aspects of communication, as well as the external factors.

When it comes to publics, propaganda can be aimed at the country's own citizens, or at citizens of other states as a part of so-called foreign interference (or foreign influence) campaigns (as we defined above, we will use the abbreviation FIMI for Foreign Information Manipulation and Interference). Miah Hammond-Errey defines foreign interference as "strategy-driven, state-sponsored information activities" (2019, p. 1). The theoretical concept has developed from the practice, concretely from the Russian information operations (Hammond-Errey, 2019, p. 3). The strategic intent of such a campaign can include, for example, overload (sending large volumes of information, often conflicting), denial (restricting information access), distraction (by creating an imaginary threat), division (turning a state against its allies), provocation (forcing into offensive action), etc. (Hammond-Errey, 2019, p. 6). For example, a Kyiv-born British journalist and academic Peter Pomerantsev described vividly how Russia is using the strategy to blur the distinction between the truth and lie, reality and fiction, in his books "*Nothing is true and everything is possible: Adventures in modern Russia*" (Pomerantsev, 2014) and "*This is not propaganda: Adventures in War against reality*" (2019). Pomerantsev argues that strategies of disinformation and reality distortion represent a new kind of warfare. It uses narratives and digital technologies to blur the distinction of truth and falsehood, reality versus fiction, to make citizens feel apathetic and disoriented. Their goal is to make people doubt the basic facts and present a world as a battlefield of ideas. In such an environment with low public trust towards government institutions, rule of law or even basic physical facts like that the Earth is not flat, it is easy to shape public opinion in a desired manner and to distract the publics from political news. Pomerantsev describes, for example, how Russian "troll armies" work: hundreds of skilled personnel create fake identities, spread disinformation according to given narratives, amplify divisive content, coordinate together, and focus their activity in crisis situations (e.g., elections, accidents, etc.) (Pomerantsev, 2019). For example, when Russian brigade downed civil plane MH17 on 17 July 2014, resulting in 298 death of mostly Dutch citizens, Russian troll armies (Internet Research Agency) and other citizens like state employees or Kremlin-run media produced content that elaborated on several narratives, such as that Ukraine attacked it, or it crashed due to technical reasons, or even that there were orgies on the plane, because people fell down naked. Dmitry Peskov, Kremlin's spokesperson, has since called Russia's "state of information warfare with the trend-setters in the information space" (Nimmo, 2016, p. 29). The tools and tactics of the hybrid information warfare have been (partly mistakenly) labelled as the "Gerasimov doctrine," based on political scientist Mark Galeotti's interpretation of a journal article, written by the Russian General and Chief of the General Staff of the Armed Forces of Russia Valery Gerasimov in a Russian military journal (Galeotti, 2018).

Nevertheless, information operations, use of propaganda, and disinformation campaigns are key to what we generally call "hybrid wars."

Those wars don't need to be officially declared, and they often happen in the digital sphere. However, they do combine both conventional and unconventional warfare, like the use of missiles as well as cyberattacks. Other tactics include manipulation in the digital sphere, namely on social media and discussion forums, where a desired narrative is spread under fake accounts or through programmed bots. In politics and diplomacy, hybrid warfare includes tactics to interfere in foreign elections or other political events, such as Brexit. Hybrid information warfare can also include covert operations, like the Russian attack on an ammunition warehouse in Vrbětice in the Czech Republic in 2014, killing two civilians, or on Sergei and Yulia Skripal in 2018 in Salisbury in Great Britain (Baines et al., 2019; Paul & Matthews, 2016).

The rise of new technological developments has even more blurred the distinction between reality and manipulation in political marketing and propaganda. Terms like computational propaganda or algorithmic propaganda have risen to prominence. For example, Samuel C. Wolley and Philip N. Howard led an international research in nine countries to examine, define, and highlight the existence of "computational propaganda" that is, the use of algorithms, automation, and manual information creation and management to create and disseminate misleading messages on social media (Woolley & Howard, 2019, p. 4). According to the authors, computational propaganda occurs primarily when computer bots or algorithms appear on social media and elsewhere in the digital space to control, comment on, and actively create communications themselves to benefit certain political parties, political candidates, states, or ideological systems. As Wolley and Howard note, while there is a significant difference between how computer propaganda is used in authoritarian and democratic regimes, this difference has tended to narrow in recent times (Woolley & Howard, 2019, p. 14). The significant difference, however, is that in totalitarian or hybrid regimes, it is the states themselves that organize, run, and also finance these campaigns. Thus, states such as Russia or China organize, finance, and run campaigns targeting their own populations or against their foreign enemies. Their aim is to use digital technologies to influence the thoughts, opinions, or moods of specific groups of people in order to achieve their objectives.

In democratic states, digital technologies may be used more by political groups, political parties, individuals, and especially by large digital companies or other commercial or noncommercial actors in the online space. Probably the most prominent case of a breach of trust and exploitation of personal data in political marketing is known as the "Cambridge Analytica Scandal" which broke in 2018. Facebook lacked and oversight of the third parties (e.g., political marketing consultancy called Cambridge Analytica) to misuse personal data of their users with or without their consent for personalizes political marketing targeting and messaging, based on the behavioral and psychological profile of the users (Matz et al., 2020).

On the other hand, the use of digital technologies by state actors in democratic societies does not necessarily lead to their negative impact through manipulation or abuse. Examples from Canada or the United States have shown us that digital communications can be used for public service. For example, communication robots (AI-guided chatbots) are now increasingly being implemented in communication tools to inform citizens and answer their questions in government communication or health communication (Androutsopoulou et al., 2019). Nevertheless, AI-aided communication tools also possess a major threat to public communication in terms of security, spreading disinformation and foreign interference manipulation.

CITIZEN'S PERSPECTIVE: A NEED TO DEVELOP RESILIENCE AND CRITICAL THINKING

Finally, it is necessary to explore the question of receptivity, impact, and possible resistance to persuasive communication, be it propaganda or political marketing. A number of factors influence the receptivity to manipulative content and its critical reflection, such as the level, and tradition of democracy, socioeconomic factors (education, access to information, etc.), or psychological and situational factors (the herd effect, copycat effect, etc.). In political marketing, the resistance is often clear and easily implemented in the voting behavior, and other public engagement activities like grassroots campaigns, public activism, advocacy, etc. In a defensive reaction against this aggressive style of propaganda in WWII, William McGuire proposed the so-called inoculation theory, or "inoculation against propaganda," which sought to develop a critical thinking so strong that it would simply act as a vaccination shield against any further propaganda (similar to inoculation against diphtheria, etc.)

(Banas & Rains, 2010). The notion of the possibility of "inoculating" against propaganda has recently been revived under the modern terms (and in a slightly more sophisticated version) of prebunking and debunking. Prebunking can be described as the ability to detect propaganda or manipulation in advance. Debunking can be explained as retrospectively clarifying how a given piece of information is false, manipulative, or contrary to reality (Lewandowsky & van der Linden, 2021).

According to debunking theory, which is based on fact-checking, when a piece of misleading, manipulated, fabricated, or false information appears, it should be enough to explain to the public what the manipulation is, how it contradicts reality, and why it is untrue. A number of global and domestic fact-checking organizations work on this principle, for example, US-based FactCheck.org, UK-based FullFact.org, or Czech-based Manipulátoři.cz. However, as some authors point out, simply a reactive debunking is not effective enough and citizens need to develop more proactive ways to combat disinformation campaigns as a part of FIMI. Professor Nicholas J. Cull talks about the necessity of developing a strong collective vision of a state and fostering international alliances to build reputational security (Cull, 2019). A recent example of Ukraine fighting against the Russian invasion gives a good example of "nation building" and creating a strong national narrative to gain international support and fight against the aggressors' propaganda (Kaneva, 2022; Kaneva et al., 2023).

The distinction between political marketing and propaganda lies primarily in their ethical frameworks, transparency, and intended purposes. Political marketing operates in democratic systems emphasizing persuasion through transparency and accountability, while propaganda often thrives in authoritarian and hybrid regimes, leveraging coercive power and misinformation to manipulate audiences. In democratic regimes, however, propaganda and censorship may be employed during times of war. Over time, technological advancements have blurred some distinctions between political marketing and propaganda, as new possibilities of stealth manipulation or creating a preset choice architecture emerged. Computational propaganda, fueled by algorithms, bots, and digital platforms, now merges elements of political marketing with propaganda, creating new challenges in discerning between the two (Hobbs, 2020; Woolley & Howard, 2019; Wooley, 2023; Zuboff, 2015, 2019).

This fuzziness is especially pronounced when authoritarian regimes employ advanced marketing techniques to enhance propaganda's appeal or when democratic actors resort to manipulative tactics under the guise of political marketing. For example, algorithmic targeting, often associated with ethical political campaigns, has been used to propagate disinformation during foreign influence campaigns. This blending of techniques complicates efforts to differentiate between ethical persuasion and manipulative propaganda.

Policy implications of these changes are profound. Governments in democratic systems should take in account combating disinformation to protect electoral integrity and democratic norms. This includes creating robust regulations for transparency in political advertising and addressing the misuse of digital technologies. Citizens, too, have a role to play by developing media literacy skills to evaluate information and recognize manipulative content critically. As citizens lose their interest in news and geopolitics (so-called media fatigue), it is easier for maleficent actors to present them with a manipulated version of history and offer them their own narrative and explanation of events. To foster critical thinking and prebunking strategies, democratic governments should invest in building resilient society of active and educated citizens, freedom of speech, and trustworthy news media.

The evolving overlap between political marketing and propaganda also raises critical questions about the ethics of communication practices in the digital age. What safeguards can ensure that advanced marketing tools or social media algorithms and personal data are not weaponized? How can international actors collaborate to build resilience against foreign influence campaigns? Addressing these questions requires a holistic approach, combining regulatory action, public education, and international cooperation to mitigate the risks posed by this new propaganda landscape.

CONCLUSION

The aim of this chapter was to draw (or at least to point out) the line between political marketing and propaganda. They both have the same goal of persuading citizens to act according to the politician's or political parties' aim. The key difference lies within the socio-political context and ethics of communication and persuasion, such as coercive power, freedom of speech, surveillance and control, information dissemination, and public participation. Political marketing and propaganda need to be studied in the context of their historical development, new digital communication and information processes, and new tools of control and surveillance of citizens' political opinions. The ethical boundaries of political marketing and propaganda differ dramatically from country to country, depending, namely, on their governance, level of democracy, and human rights. The term "propaganda" has become toxic and is no longer compatible with the values of democracy and fair political campaigning. However, it can be used for the communication of an ideology of nondemocratic actors or countries or, in an extreme case, when the human rights and critical thinking of the citizens are severely restrained (e.g., through algorithmic bubbles and behavioral targeting, etc.). Political marketing has become synonymous with professionalized political communication and campaigning, while propaganda is used for stealth or unethical political communication. The rise of new technological developments has blurred the distinction between reality and manipulation in political marketing and propaganda, and they also pose a significant threat to the democratic public debate. Resilience strategies should focus on strengthening democracy, freedom of speech, media literacy, general knowledge of history and geopolitics, and keeping up with the speed of digital environment development.

REFERENCES

Androutsopoulou, A., Karacapilidis, N., Loukis, E., & Charalabidis, Y. (2019). Transforming the communication between citizens and government through AI-guided chatbots. *Government Information Quarterly*, *36*(2), 358–367.

Baines, P. R., & O'Shaughnessy, N. J. (2014). Political marketing and propaganda: Uses, abuses, misuses. *Journal of Political Marketing*, *13*(1–2), 1–18.

Baines, P., O'Shaugnessy, N. J., & Nicolas, J. (Eds.). (2019). *The Sage handbook of propaganda*. SAGE.

Banas, J. A., & Rains, S. A. (2010). A meta-analysis of research on inoculation theory. *Communication Monographs*, 77(3), 281–311. https://doi.org/10.1080/03637751003758193

Bartlett, R. C. (2016). *Sophistry and political philosophy: Protagoras' challenge to Socrates*. University of Chicago Press.

Bernays, E. L. (1945). *Public relations*. Bellman.

Bernays, E. L. (2005). *Propaganda*. Ig Publishing.

Bolt, N. (2019). Propaganda of the deed and its anarchist origins. In P. Baines, N. J. O'Shaugnessy, & N. Snow (Eds.), *The Sage handbook of propaganda* (pp. 3–21). SAGE.

Bronk, C. (2018). *Cyber propaganda*. Autor: G. S. Jowett a V. O'Donnell, 331-337. SAGE.

Cope, E. M., & Sandys, J. E. (Eds.). (2010). *Aristotle: Rhetoric* (*Vol. 2*). Cambridge University Press.

Creel, G. (1920). *How We Advertised America*. New York – Harper and Brothers.

Cull, N. J. (2019). The tightrope to tomorrow: Reputational security, collective vision and the future of public diplomacy. *The Hague Journal of Diplomacy*, 14(1–2), 21–35.

Cull, N. J., Culbert, D. H., & Welch, D. (2003). *Propaganda and mass persuasion: A historical encyclopedia, 1500 to the present*. ABC-clio.

Curtis, A. (2002). *The century of the self – Part 2: "Engineering of consent*. BBC.

De Mesquita, B. B., & Smith, A. (2011). *The dictator's handbook: Why bad behavior is almost always good politics*. Hachette.

Deppe, C. (2023, October 16). *Disinformation, cognitive warfare, and hybrid threats*. https://tdhj.org/blog/post/disinformation-cognitive-warfare-hybrid/

Dikötter, F. (2010). *Mao's great famine: The history of China's most devastating catastrophe, 1958–62*. A&C Black.

Dikötter, F. (2017). *The Cultural Revolution: A People's History*, 1962–1976. Bloomsbury Publishing

Economist Intelligence Unit. (2022). *Economist democracy Index 2023*. https://www.eiu.com/n/campaigns/democracy-index-2022/ May1, 2023

Ellul, J. (1965). *Propaganda: The formation of men's attitudes*. Vintage Books.

Fleming, M. (2015). Propaganda by the deed: Terrorism and anarchist theory in late nineteenth-century Europe. In *Terrorism in Europe* (pp. 8–28). Routledge.

Fox, J., & Welch, D. (2012). Justifying war: Propaganda, politics and the modern age. In *Justifying war* (pp. 1–20). Palgrave Macmillan.

Galeotti, M. (2018, March 5). *I'm sorry for creating the 'Gerasimov doctrine'*. Foreign Policy. https://foreignpolicy.com/2018/03/05/im-sorry-for-creating-the-gerasimov-doctrine/

Graham, P. (2017). *Strategic communication, corporatism, and eternal crisis: The Creel century*. Routledge.

Gunderson, E. (Ed.). (2009). *The Cambridge companion to ancient rhetoric*. Cambridge University Press.

Hallahan, K., Holtzhausen, D., van Ruler, B., Verčič, D., & Sriramesh, K. (2007). Defining strategic communication. *International Journal of Strategic Communication*, *1*(1), 3–35.

Hobbs, R. (2020). Propaganda in an age of algorithmic personalization: Expanding literacy research and practice. *Reading Research Quarterly, 55*(3), 521–533.

Hammond-Errey, M. (2019). Understanding and assessing information influence and foreign interference. *Journal of Information Warfare, 18*(1), 1–22.

Hanley, W. M. (2005). *The genesis of Napoleonic propaganda, 1796 to 1799*. University of Missouri-Columbia.

Harris, P. (2010). Machiavelli and the global compass: Ends and means in ethics and leadership. *Journal of Business Ethics, 93*, 131–138.

Hejlová, D., & Klimeš, D. (2019). Propaganda stories in Czechoslovakia in the late 1980s: Believe it or not? *Public Relations Review, 45*(2), 217–226.

Henneberg, S. C., Scammell, M., & O'Shaughnessy, N. J. (2009). Political marketing management and theories of democracy. *Marketing Theory, 9*(2), 165–188.

Henschke, A., Sussex, M., & O'Connor, C. J. (2020). Countering foreign interference: Election integrity lessons for liberal democracies. *Global Discourse, 10*(3), 329–345.

Hollis, D., & Ohlin, J. (2021). Introduction. In *Defending democracies in the digital age*. Oxford University Press.

Johannesen, R. L., Valde, K. S., & Whedbee, K. E. (2008). *Ethics in human communication* (6th ed.). Waveland Press.

Jowett, G. S., & O'Donnell, V. (2018). *Propaganda and persuasion*. SAGE.

Kaneva, N. (2022). "Brave like Ukraine": A critical discourse perspective on Ukraine's wartime brand. *Place Branding and Public Diplomacy*, 1–5.

Kaneva, N., Dolea, A., & Manor, I. (2023). Public diplomacy and nation branding in the wake of the Russia–Ukraine War. *Place Branding and Public Diplomacy*, 1–5.

Kennedy, G. (1963). *History of rhetoric*. In *The art of persuasion in Greecee* (*Vol. I*). Princeton Legacy Library.

Kollanyi, B., Howard, P. N., & Woolley, S. C. (2016). Bots and automation over Twitter during the first US presidential debate. *Comprop Data Memo, 1*, 1–4.

Lanoszka, A. (2019). Disinformation in international politics. *European Journal of International Security, 4*(2), 227–248.

Lasswell, H. D. (1927). The theory of political propaganda. *American Political Science Review, 21*(3), 627–631.

Lewandowsky, S., & van der Linden, S. (2021). Countering misinformation and fake news through inoculation and prebunking. *European Review of Social Psychology, 32*(2), 348–384. https://doi.org/10.1080/10463283.2021.1876983

Liang, F., Chen, Y., & Zhao, F. (2021). The platformization of propaganda: How xuexi qiangguo expands persuasion and assesses citizens in China. *International Journal of Communication, 15*, 20.

Lippmann, W. (1922). *Public Opinion*. New York: Hartcourt, Brace and Company.

Maarek, P. J. (2011). *Campaign communication and political marketing*. John Wiley & Sons.

Matz, S. C., Appel, R. E., & Kosinski, M. (2020). Privacy in the age of psychological targeting. *Current Opinion in Psychology, 31*, 116–121.

Nahon-Serfaty, I. (2018). *Strategic communication and deformative transparency: Persuasion in politics, propaganda, and public health*. Routledge.

Nimmo, B. (2016). *How MH17 gave birth to the modern Russian spin machine* (p. 29). Foreign Policy.

Nordin, A. H. M. (2016). Ironic 'resistance' in Chinese citizen media online. In M. Baker & B. Blaagaard (Eds.), *Citizen media and public spaces: Diverse expressions of citizenship and dissent*. London: Routledge.

O'Shaughnessy, N. J. (1990). *The phenomenon of political marketing*. Palgrave Macmillan.

O'Shaughnessy, N. J. (2004). *Politics and propaganda: Weapons of mass seduction*. Manchester University Press.

O'Shaughnessy, N. J., & Baines, P. R. (2009). Selling terror: The symbolization and positioning of Jihad. *Marketing Theory, 9*(2), 227–241.

Ormrod, R. P., Henneberg, S. C., & O'Shaughnessy, a N. J. (2013). *Political marketing: Theory and concepts*. SAGE.

Paul, C., & Matthews, M. (2016). The Russian "firehose of falsehood" propaganda model. *Rand Corporation, 2*(7), 1–10.

Phillips, D. D. (2014). *Athenian political oratory: 16 key speeches*. Routledge.

Pomerantsev, P. (2014). *Nothing is true and everything is possible: Adventures in modern Russia*. Faber & Faber.

Pomerantsev, P. (2019). *This is not propaganda: Adventures in War against reality Faber*. Faber.

Sartori, G. (1987) *The theory of democracy revisited* (*Vol. 2*). Chatham House Publishers.

Tsyrenzhapova, D., & Woolley, S. C. (2021). The evolution of computational propaganda: Theories, debates, and innovation of the Russian model. In *The Routledge companion to media disinformation and populism* (pp. 121–130). Routledge.

Tzu, S. (2007). *The art of war*. Filiquarian.

Welch, D. (2002). *The third Reich: Politics and propaganda*. Psychology Press.

Welch, D. (Ed.). (2013). *Propaganda, power and persuasion: From World War I to wikileaks*. Bloomsbury Publishing.

Woolley, S. C., & Howard, P. N. (Eds.). (2019). *Computational propaganda: Political parties, politicians, and political manipulation on social media*. Oxford University Press.

Woolley, S. C. (Ed.). (2023). *Manufacturing consensus: Understanding propaganda in the era of automation and anonymity*. Yale University Press.

Zuboff, S. (2015). Big other: Surveillance capitalism and the prospects of an information civilization. *Journal of Information Technology*, *30*(1), 75–89.

Zuboff, S. (2019). *The age of surveillance capitalism: The fight for a human future at the new frontier of power: Profile books.*

Strategic Market Segmentation and Targeting in the 21st Century: Ethical Challenges, Trends and Innovations

Otto Eibl and Miloš Gregor

INTRODUCTION

At the heart of successful campaigns is the assumption that they managed to reach the right voters at the right place, at the right time, with the right message. In other words, finding persuadable voters and pitching them the appropriate message is key to any successful campaign. As obvious as this may sound, fulfilling all these conditions is far from easy. While in the past it may have been difficult for political parties and candidates to know their intended target groups in detail, today's technologies make it possible to build de facto individual profiles of each voter and prepare tailored messages for them. As fascinating as this is, it raises numerous questions and doubts about whether deploying state-of-the-art tools (including various artificial intelligence [AI], language learning models [LLMs] and deep learning models) is indeed what we should use for persuading and mobilizing voters – especially in the context of discussions about ethics, morality and the quality of democracy in general.

This chapter focuses on the tools marketers and political consultants use to approach the market, with a primary focus on segmentation and targeting. We have divided the text into three interrelated parts. The first part offers definitions of basic terminology and answers the question of how approaches and possibilities for segmentation and targeting (not only in the context of politics) have changed over time. The second part highlights the new opportunities that modern technologies have brought to marketers – from automating many processes involved in data mining and advanced multi-level analysis to micro-targeting and the development of highly personalized messages. Finally, the concluding third part offers a critical reflection on current trends and highlights the dark side of these trends, particularly related to the newest models of AI. What may represent a dream come true for marketers may raise a cautionary finger for scholars engaged in discussions about democracy and its quality. We are aware that a single chapter cannot address all the important issues and various aspects of this topic. Thus, we focus mainly on the 'legitimate' actors within a national democratic state – especially political parties. However, we must stress the importance of also paying attention to non-legitimate actors and their activities, and closely observing potential hostile activities of non-democratic states and actors. Unfortunately, they can use all the tools and approaches described below as well, but they use them to conduct hybrid warfare (see Gregor & Mlejnková, 2021; Reichborn-Kjennerud & Cullen, 2016; Thiele, 2021) and affect the degree of polarization in entire societies, thereby impacting the quality of democracy in the affected states.

WHY IT MAKES SENSE TO SEGMENT THE MARKET AND TARGET SPECIFIC GROUPS OF VOTERS?

Before discussing segmentation and targeting in more depth, it is important to remind ourselves why it makes sense to use them. Campaigns are demanding in many ways – in terms of finance, energy, staff, but also voters' attention, their reactions to campaign stimuli and messages, etc. To avoid wasting expensive resources, we need to be as efficient as possible, that is, try to spend them where it makes sense. Therefore, it is not helpful to think of the market as a whole, and it would be naive to assume that the political message will reach and persuade all (or even most) voters. Each group has specific needs, a specific communication code and is grounded in a specific environment. Thus, it is necessary to find those constituencies and target them with a campaign that is willing to listen to us and ideally respond positively to what we are trying to tell them. That is what segmentation helps us to do. While in the past, at least part of the decisions in a campaign could be led by candidates, with the advent of political marketing, this phase of campaign preparation has become more professional and formalized. Campaign preparations include market research, analysis of legislative rules, spending limits, the media environment and testing how voters would respond to candidates' and parties' offers. Segmentation involves dividing citizens and markets into smaller homogeneous groups based on shared and preferably stable characteristics. There are a number of segmentation criteria: geographic, sociodemographic, psychographic and behavioural (Kotler & Keller, 2012, pp. 214–229; Dolnicar et al., 2018, pp. 41–45; McDonald & Dunbar 2013, pp. 11–13). In the case of political marketing, we could also add affection for a particular ideology or preference for a set of particular issues, partisanship and party loyalty.

Segmentation Criteria

As mentioned above, there are multiple ways to segment a market, and the entire process can be perceived as consisting of multiple steps. We need to realize that various groups of people, even if they share many common 'objective' characteristics, have different needs and there are various ways to meet those needs. When thinking about politics, we should first evaluate how firm and stable the relationship with a respective political party is. In other words, we need to estimate the probability that they will vote for a particular party and how they would likely react to campaign stimuli – a party label plays a crucial role in voters' party evaluation as it is one of the most common heuristics that voters use to come to a decision (Lau & Redlawsk, 2001). Voters closely attached to a party are likely to vote for that party and will probably agree more on campaign issues and proposed policies. A party then only needs to remind these voters about the election and activate them. On the other hand, voters whose relationship is loose or even nonexistent (but not negative!) need to be persuaded, and it will require more effort to win their support. Voters with a negative relationship to a party cannot usually be persuaded by any campaign means; the only thing a party can try is to demobilize them and give them a reason to abstain from the election. Thus, we can speak about primary and secondary segmentation (comp. Cwalina et al. 2015, 81–89). During primary segmentation, we divide voters based on the party they support and the strength of that support. During secondary segmentation, which mostly aims at the undecided, we may consider one of the following criteria or better – a combination of them.

Geographical segmentation is probably the simplest one – voters are often categorized based on their geographical location, including whether they reside in urban or rural areas, specific constituencies or urban districts, among other criteria. Although some may perceive this categorization as inconsequential, it is not – it helps with campaign planning and execution, particularly for activities such as door-to-door campaigns. Therefore, sorting voters based on their location is not without merit and remains a crucial aspect of modern political campaigning. Indeed, it is one of the most frequently employed segmentation criteria.

Segmentation based on socio-demographic characteristics is also quite common. We work with information that can be easily measured and objectively expressed – age, gender, family situation, nationality, occupation, race or ethnicity, education, personal income, etc. Although segmenting by these criteria is relatively easy, we must realize that it does not help us much – we have to delve deeper and go 'beyond the data' to make sense of it. Just because someone falls into a column in an excel spreadsheet labelled 'first-time male voter' doesn't mean we know how to communicate with that person. Every single member of this broad group will be different – one will go to the gym, another will love reading classic literature, and another will be a devotee of extreme sports. As we can see, although such a group is stable and homogeneous by one criterion, it is very heterogeneous by other criteria. The goal of a marketer is to reveal the most suitable criteria that allow planning an effective campaign. Very often, emotions are the key to correct and effective outreach – but we'll get to those a little later.

Psychographic segmentation is a little more complicated. Here, we sort by personal characteristics such as values, attitudes, interests, motivations, personality characteristics or lifestyle in general. These are characteristics that are intangible and some of them may not be easy to measure. On the other hand, the investment of time and energy is worthwhile, as it allows us to understand the value worlds of the intended constituencies.

The segmentation methods discussed above deal primarily with the question of who our target voter is (or where to find them). But we can also use another approach, that is, behavioural segmentation. It focuses on something slightly different – it notes the voter's behaviour and answers the question of what the voter actually does. Thus, it looks at various habits, reactions to particular political brands and whether and to what extent the voter is involved in the political life of the community or state, or how he or she 'consumes' or perform politics. With the help of behavioural segmentation, we should also be able to tackle the various reasons for voting for a particular party. A political party or candidate offers or represents a series of benefits for voters; if the expected benefit is big enough (or bigger than that of other parties and candidates), a voter should vote for that party. Here, every single political party has the ability to make changes in their products (policies and candidates) to differentiate from other parties and improve their image and likability in general. However, the perception of such changes and their final effects are a different story.

This is an approach that Baines et al. (2005) call product attribute-based segmentation. We agree that designing a product or making amendments to it and offering it to a specific group of voters with a special need or desire is easier than looking for specific groups that would appreciate the offered policies (Baines et al., 2005, p. 1081). We can go even further – to craft a specific image of a party or candidate might be one of the most important differentiating factors for voters. This is especially true in political systems with proportional electoral systems where moderate or even extreme pluralism and the need for establishing coalitions to form a government is common. Manifestos are converging and contain many valence issues and just a few positional issues. In such systems, changing just the product (policies) is simply not enough. Of course, we are often able to identify two competing blocs of parties with different values; however, differentiation within the blocs is more challenging. If this situation occurs, brand equity or party image plays a crucial role in voters' decisions. This is why political parties carry out a permanent campaign and try to maintain the existing relationship with voters with the help of social media, where they can aim at various segments of voters with ease and experiment with various forms of messaging.

Based on the segment's characteristics, it is possible to define so-called personas (see Andrews, 2020; Revella, 2015; Toth, 2019) that can become everyday tactical tools. This involves the creation of fictional characters that represent each segment (see, e.g. Hayward, 2019, pp. 48–50) and allow working with emotions and behavioural components. When creating them, we pay enough attention to make the characters believable and to make their profiles as detailed as possible – it should include information about gender, age, education, interests, number of children, favourite films, problems they face, etc. The advantage of personas is that we can imagine them in specific life situations, which will make our job easier when formulating the creative part of the campaign and its communication mix.

Targeting Strategies

Based on a properly performed segmentation, we should have a clear market structure and be able to consider targeting, that is, deciding which segments the campaign will try to reach. Again, this might seem like a simple process, but considerations about target segments should take into account the goals of the campaign and the 'viability' and 'effectiveness' of the identified segments. The criteria for assessing the segments such as sustainability, measurability and accessibility were defined by Kotler (see, e.g. Kotler & Keller, 2012, p. 231), but this catalogue proved inadequate and has been further expanded (e.g. Grigsby, 2018, p. 127; Kotler & Keller, 2012, pp. 231–232; Gavett, 2014; for a review of the literature, see Dolnicar et al., 2018, pp. 32–22; conf. Henneberg, 2002, p. 134):

- Members of a segment must share some salient characteristic.
- Segments must not overlap.
- The segment must be large enough to be worth investing in (prepare a special communication mix for it).
- The segment should be identifiable, addressable and reachable in the market.
- The segment should not be too competitive – if there are too many parties competing for it, a functional strategy can be expected to yield fewer votes (as these will be divided between the competing parties).

After evaluating the attractiveness of each segment, we can then proceed to select the right targeting strategy – we are basically talking about a threefold approach: concentrated, undifferentiated and differentiated (see Henneberg, 2002, pp. 134–137). Concentrated marketing involves a rather crude division of the voting population and addresses the audience as a 'mass' whose interest is, for example, derived from the nature of a particular cleavage – hence it is typical of parties and the era of mass politics (Lipset & Rokkan, 1967; Henneberg, 2002, p. 134). Undifferentiated marketing carries the idea of transcending the conflict stemming from a particular cleavage and trying to reach as many voters as possible. Such a strategy is typical of catch-all parties (cf. Kirchheimer, 1966). The emphasis is on finding common denominators whose emphasis is at the very core of the political offering. Finally, differentiated marketing actively works with the awareness of the need to address different segments of society to whom it tries to present an attractive unique selling proposition. This is due to the atomization of society and the individualization of various political interests. The important thing is that the political offer may differ for each segment – it is no longer necessarily about finding common denominators, but about meeting the needs of several (different) segments. This entails the need to develop different strategies and tools for different segments, always bearing in mind that everything should make sense from the perspective of each single political brand.

In the context of this approach, we can also talk about micro-segmentation and micro-targeting, which can ultimately lead to the establishment of longer-term close relationships between the party and the voter. While this approach was quite difficult two or three decades ago, current technologies have managed to remove most of the barriers. But as we will show below, this is not always to the benefit of the political culture and quality of democracy in individual countries. Thus, we have briefly outlined how to think about the (political) market and its attractive segments at a general level. Based on identifying the right segments and choosing an appropriate (in time and place) strategy for targeting, further considerations can be made about the nature of the message itself and the set of activities such as a campaign and media mix that will help us deliver the message and meet the set objective (i.e. mobilizing or demobilizing the electorate, persuading undecided voters, or encouraging them to contribute to the campaign, etc.).

RECENT TRENDS: SOCIAL MEDIA AND (SEMI)AUTOMATED TOOLS

In this section, our primary focus is on working with large volumes of data and the opportunities presented by automated tools and AI, although we also pay partial attention to smaller changes and innovations that are not so much related to technical advances as to the behaviour of voters themselves in the context of (social) media.

Although television is still the primary source of information about the world and politics in certain segments (Ipsos, 2022; Newman et al., 2021), the last few years have seen the rapid rise of social media, which have the potential to at least complement, and in some cases replace, traditional information channels (Koc-Michalska et al., 2024). While the debate about the changing flow of information and the relationship with the media is fascinating and interesting, it must be set aside for the moment. What we cannot ignore, however, is the nature of social media in relation to political communication, campaigning and advertising. Indeed, social media must be seen (at least for our purposes) as a vehicle for advertising that is tailored to deliver persuasive messages to the right people at the right time. From the marketers' perspective, it is an ideal medium where large groups of voters can be reached relatively quickly and where a community can be managed and developed. In addition, it is a dialogical media, giving political parties the opportunity to get feedback. Finally, they provide a space where no third party interferes – they allow the story to be told as the sponsor wishes.

While every social medium is a little different, and while there have been adjustments over time in what advertisers can do and how they can do it (i.e. how they can target their intended audience), it is still a relatively precise tool to get the message across to the audience. Advertisers have the ability to target based on basic demographic characteristics of users and also by location. Some media then offer/offered much more. For example, Facebook used to allow very detailed targeting based on various criteria based on lifestyle or political beliefs. However, there have been adjustments and Facebook has limited the targeting options for political purposes. It was, and remains to some extent, possible to work with multiple variations of messages, test their reception and ultimately select the most effective one.

In addition, Facebook advertisers have the option of using so-called dark posts. The labelling of such posts can be a bit misleading – it evokes negative connotations, but it is a common practice used on a daily basis without any side dark motives. Dark posts are usually targeted to a specific audience and appear in targeted users' feeds. However, they are not visible on the timeline of the sponsor, that is, political party or candidate in the case of politics, and also are not visible to users who are not part of the target audience. Dark posts can easily be micro-targeted to appeal to specific demographics or interest groups without spamming the main page or other users (or without revealing certain information to the public). With dark posts, advertisers can tailor their messages to different segments of their audience, experiment with various versions of the message (A/B testing) and measure the effectiveness of their campaigns through Facebook's ad analytics (Banks, 2020).

What sounds like a bonanza for marketers could turn into something that could ultimately damage democracy in the respective countries. On the one hand, we have a precisely targeted message that evokes reactions from the audience. On the other hand, we have a tool that can be used to activate certain sections of society, which can ultimately lead to increased social polarization – the targeting of the message and its hidden nature can encourage actors to make their communication more crude and perhaps more shocking. Moreover, the ability to target narrowly defined groups allows us to present a different message to each of group and thus create a more or less different reason for each segment to choose a particular party. In the extreme case, then each segment has a slightly different reason for choosing a particular party and the common goal and common interest disappears. In fact, part of the legitimacy of elected representatives may also disappear as individual segments elect political parties for different reasons without knowing the broader and general context (comp. Vaidhyanathan, 2018; Barocas, 2012). This is what we could label as a consequence of an extreme orientation towards satisfying the needs of different customers.

Of course, voters do not operate in an information vacuum and are not solely reliant on communication on social media – they have plenty of other sources from which they can obtain information about politics, either purposefully or peripherally, and thus have an awareness of the main topics of public debate at election time. But this does not diminish the polarizing potential of advertising targeting on social media. For this reason alone, it is therefore desirable for the public to monitor (at least indirectly) tools such as Meta's Ad Library in order to have an overview of how different actors communicate with different groups.

In the context of X (ex Twitter), Instagram, TikTok and other media, it is also possible to use thematic targeting by using hashtags (Bode et al., 2015; Ryan, 2024). Hashtags are a perfect and beloved tool to help users explore and discover content dedicated to selected topic on social media, and they are also great in identifying new trends. Their power also lies in linking different sources of information within the given social media. The advantage of such targeting is the ability to transcend demographics and to really focus on the message itself, even if the degree of control over the potential debate is limited since anyone can attach a hashtag to their posts – whatever their message – and it does not always have to be an endorsement of the original intention of the person who introduced the hashtag. As can be seen, social media have brought new opportunities, especially in the speed and efficiency of working with advertising or community.

Even more interesting changes have been brought about by advances in computing technology and AI. There is no question that, in the last few years, we have witnessed significant technological shift that can automate and streamline the above processes quite well. In a sense, we are fortunate to be witnessing a true technological revolution. Not only in the context of political campaigns, new roles also – data scientists specializing in data mining – are emerging, which are associated with several interrelated terms that allow us to get to know a potential voter, predict their behaviour and effectively reach them with a highly tailored message. These are primarily Big Data and its processing and AI, or machine and deep learning models, or generative language models such as ChatGPT.

Although the basic principles of the marketing team's work remain the same, that is, 'dividing a market into distinct groups of buyers [voters] with different needs, characteristics, or behaviour who might require separate products or marketing mixes' (Kotler & Armstrong, 1996, p. 235, parenthesis inserted by the authors), the way in which the steps are executed has changed dramatically. Technological tools offer automation of predefined processes and can be largely autonomous. They also allow us to go much deeper in the analysis of target audiences and work on a more individualized level – mainly thanks to psychological profiling, which was simply not possible to such an extent before. In addition to the risks, the subsequent section of the chapter will examine the potential benefits that technology can offer. First, we will outline the basic contours of the use of technology and use concrete examples to highlight the potential (not insignificant) risks and ethical concerns that we must address today.

Big Data and Psychographics

The term 'Big Data' refers to large, complex and diverse sets of (semi- or un-) structured data that are created virtually constantly and that require advanced analytical tools (i.e. statistics) and techniques to process, manage and extract meaningful insights from them. Big Data is *de facto* aggregated data on individual user behaviour – everything we do in the online (web browsing, social media behaviour, etc.) and offline (e.g. purchases and bank card payments) world leaves behind traces that can be tracked and analyzed. Depending on the legal regulation, user data can then be either collected directly or purchased from third parties in different parts of the world. However, there is quite a difference between the practice in the US and the EU, for example. Marketers can thus get a fairly good idea of who their customers are (in the context of socio-demographic characteristics), but also what kind of lives they live and how they behave. This fact is quite crucial. Traditional segmentation relied on overly broad categories such as age, sex and geolocation, that, while easily observable and often tangible, may not always have worked well because they may have lacked the potential to find the right emotional triggers for different (sub) segments of the audience. Segmentation based on voter behaviour has the potential to solve this problem and has become a trend in recent years.

Psychological profiling plays a crucial role here – practices based on the so-called Big Five (OCEAN) have become, in a sense, the industry standard. By assessing scores on the five dimensions (openness, conscientiousness, extraversion, agreeableness and neuroticism), we can create a profile for individual voters and try to estimate the person's needs and concerns, and how they are likely to behave (Gerber et al., 2011). The method itself is not entirely new and dates back to the 1980s, but its 'mass' deployment in the context of campaigns has been limited by the lack of data (which had to be collected through questionnaires). However, this problem was solved when it became possible to collect and mine data on a large scale from, for example, social media; indeed, every tap on a mobile phone screen can be seen as the equivalent of filling in a standard questionnaire item.

Psychographic profiling in the service of political campaigns has been discussed in particular in the context of the scandal surrounding the activities of the consultancy Cambridge Analytica (see Box 13.1), which has been used to run campaigns (with varying results, it should be added) for various positions around the world. The consultancy firm built on the work of psychologist Michal Kosinski, who with the help of the MyPersonality application collected data from Facebook users – and, as it later turned out, their friends too – and built a model that was able to estimate personality traits based on the (then) available data – Facebook likes (Kosinski et al., 2013). Although Facebook is very often mentioned in the context of our subject, the data can come from virtually anywhere. As obvious as it may sound nowadays, it is important to remember that this is a statistical inference of characteristics that users would like to keep private – such as age, intelligence, sexual orientation or political views. This information can be further used to build a psychological profile; based on its evaluation, a specific form of (advertising) message can then be chosen, which is then believed to have a greater chance of success (Matz et al., 2017). From the marketing perspective, Kosinski succeeded in creating a people search engine. Kosinski himself warned against the potential danger of misuse of his work and did not plan to apply it in practice. However, others (among others, Cambridge Analytica) were not reluctant to use a similar tool.

Box 13.1 Cambridge Analytica Scandal

Cambridge Analytica was a consulting firm, established in 2013, that specialized in data analytics, behavioural profiling and strategic political communication. Its representatives, led by Alexander Nix, claimed that they had developed a new set of tools based on the OCEAN model and Big Data that could be used to target individuals with highly personalized political messages and advertising, matching the individual's psychological profile as closely as possible.

Cambridge Analytica worked for the Republican National Committee and the Trump campaign itself (during the primaries, they worked for Ted Cruz). Besides these cases, the firm also worked on several other political campaigns around the world, including the Leave.EU campaign during the Brexit referendum in the UK and the 2013 and 2017 Kenyan presidential elections. In all cases, Cambridge Analytica reportedly used data mining and psychological profiling to micro-target voters with personalized ads and messages designed to appeal to their emotions and influence their decision-making (comp. Cadwalladr & Graham-Harrison, 2018; Confessore, 2018; Tarran, 2018).

Although Cambridge Analytica claimed that it combined data from various sources, such as real estate records, car data, shopping data, bonus cards and club memberships, in 2018, it was revealed that the firm used data harvested from millions of Facebook users without their consent to inform its work on both the Brexit campaign and the Trump campaign. This led to widespread controversy and legal challenges, with some critics accusing the company of engaging in unethical and potentially illegal data practices. As a result of the scandals, the company shut down its operations (comp. Lapowsky, 2019; Chang, 2018; Harbath & Fernekes, 2023).

However, it is worth mentioning that, as alarming as the tools and practices described in the context of Cambridge Analytica appear, we do not actually know how effective they were. Cambridge Analytica and other similar firms often spoke about their products in superlatives, but independent testing of the effectiveness of the tools used is simply lacking (comp. Baldwin-Philippi 2019). Without wishing to relativize the seriousness of what actually happened, this fact is worth recalling.

Most – if not all – of the above-mentioned processes can be fully automated – from data mining to identifying target audiences to targeting and preparing specific messages. The use of AI then gives us a very powerful tool to reach audiences in a persuasive way. Machine data processing makes it possible to look for clusters and relationships between data that would remain hidden from human researchers. In addition, generative language models can design the wording of the message for various micro-segments, personalizing the message as much as possible and increasing the likelihood of reaching the target audience effectively – these texts are often referred to as computational propaganda. Moreover, machine-generated texts seem to be slightly more persuasive than those written by a human copywriter (Meyers, 2023), which raises questions about even free will: Are people more susceptible to persuasion when their psychographic profile is used or even exploited? Another concern is the democratic process and deliberation in general (comp. Ward, 2018).

The advantages of working with Big Data do not disappear even when we plan an offline contact campaign. Combined with geographic analysis, they can help with profiling on the ground, and campaign teams can then arrive at voters' doors with multiple scenarios that are again tailored to them. In addition, there are apps that are designed specifically for linking databases, geographic data and other relevant data, such as Nation Builder, Ground Game and others. Thus, those who use Big Data in some form may hold a rather large advantage over competitors who are falling behind in this sense.

POSSIBLE EFFECTS OF NEW TECHNOLOGIES ON POLITICAL MARKETING AND HOW TO PREVENT THEIR EXPLOITATION

The following section will focus primarily on the ethics of using new technologies in the context of political marketing and will reflect on the motives and reasons why different actors should strive for maximum transparency and the most correct use of these cutting-edge technologies. At the same time, we will offer a perspective on a problem that is already serious today but will certainly increase in intensity in the near future – the security of the electoral process. Global society and its networking allow third-party actors to easily interfere in elections (or democratic processes in general) – be it business, organized crime or foreign actors. With the help of automated tools, troll farms, bots and chatbots, they can very easily influence the sentiment of public opinion (or at least key segments) and thus poison democratic society. As it turns out, information warfare (although this is nothing new, remember the pamphlet wars of the past) is being waged on many fronts with great intensity – the examples of the Trump campaign and Brexit are just the tip of the iceberg. Unfortunately, it is new technologies and tools that enable and amplify these hostile intentions and may have a serious impact on democracy and internal security.

Before we discuss potential issues related to the integration of novel technologies into political marketing management, it is necessary first to define what constitutes an ethical approach in this field. This is essential, as ethical considerations form the crux of evaluating the effects of various approaches and technologies utilized in political marketing. Ethical behaviour in political marketing refers to the adherence to moral and professional principles and norms while conducting political campaigns (Banker, 1992; Lock & Harris, 1996). These principles aim to ensure that political actors do not engage in deceptive or misleading practices, such as disseminating false information, spreading fake news or engaging in voter suppression tactics (Pérez-Escolar et al., 2023). It also entails the protection of citizens' privacy and data, avoiding the use of personal information for nefarious purposes (Lees-Marshment, 2019; Scullion, 2008). Additionally, ethical behaviour requires transparency and accountability in the financing and funding of political campaigns, as well as avoiding conflicts of interest that may compromise the integrity of the democratic process (Lees-Marshment & Raynauld, 2021; Marland, 2011). The primary goal of ethical behaviour in political marketing is to ensure that political actors act in the best interest of the democratic process and protect the rights of citizens to access accurate information and participate fully in the political process (Henneberg & O'Shaughnessy, 2007; O'Shaughnessy, 2002). Conversely, unethical behaviour is characterized by actions that violate moral and ethical principles, values or norms and undermine the integrity and legitimacy of the political process (Gregor, 2019; Lees-Marshment, 2019).

The utilization of emerging technologies and AI in the segmentation and targeting process of political campaigns presents both substantial advantages and irreversible harm to politics and the quality of democracy. On the one hand, the proper application of AI can positively impact voter engagement by facilitating more accurate targeting of potential voters (Chen, 2009), thereby augmenting voter turnout and engagement in the election. Moreover, it can enhance the efficiency of political marketing by automating various tasks involved in political campaigns, such as data analysis, ad targeting and sentiment analysis, resulting in more efficient and cost-effective campaigns.

However, there are serious concerns and risks associated with the utilization of AI in political marketing. Through the use of new technologies, AI included, political consultants have the capability to create highly targeted ads that can be tailored to appeal to specific demographics. While this may not be intrinsically negative, it can result in polarization and the creation of echo chambers, as seen in Trump's 2016 presidential campaign. Such an outcome can limit the number of well-informed citizens and decrease the quality of public discussion, which can have an adverse effect on the quality of democracy. Additionally, it can be utilized to create voter suppression tactics, such as micro-targeting and voter suppression ads, which can demobilize certain segments of voters or manipulate public opinion. This can undermine the democratic process by creating barriers to voting and reducing the influence of certain citizens on the outcome of elections (Brkan, 2019). In addition, AI can perpetuate and amplify existing biases in political messaging. For instance, if an AI algorithm is trained on data that displays a preference towards a specific political party or demographic, this may lead to the continuance of such biases in future campaigns. Such an approach is sensitive to the data generated by surveys and polls, thus the quality of the questionnaires, for example. This can result in unequal representation and further division between various groups of citizens. Such errors can result in the selection of an inappropriate campaign strategy resulting in disappointing election results or, even worse, campaign salience for irrelevant issues or opinions empowering political radicals and extremists and thus being harmful to a democratic society. Lastly, AI can be instrumental in the dissemination of fake news and disinformation (Gregor & Mlejnková, 2021), and automated accounts and bots can be deployed (Brkan, 2019). AI-powered political campaigns can spread fake news and disinformation on a significant scale, causing confusion and distrust in the political process itself (Deibert & Pauly, 2019). This can damage the credibility of democratic institutions and eventually erode public trust in the democratic process (Duberry, 2022, p. 159).

In general, the ethical and responsible use of AI is essential to prevent negative impacts on the quality of democracy. Numerous national authorities across the globe have published various documents that address the ethical principles of utilizing AI. A meta-analysis conducted by Jobin et al. (2019) reveals that the majority of these approaches involve the articulation of principles related to transparency, justice and fairness, non-maleficence, responsibility and privacy. Additionally, several other less common principles include beneficence, freedom and autonomy, trust, sustainability, dignity and solidarity (Jobin et al., 2019). Despite existing studies on the ethical principles of utilizing AI, there remains a gap in research that specifically focuses on the field of political marketing. It is essential to address the involvement of particular stakeholders in political campaigns and elections and their underlying motivations. The prevention of unethical usage of AI by political consultants poses a complex and challenging issue that necessitates a multifaceted approach. There are several steps that can be taken to mitigate the risk.

The first and most obvious are regulations and laws set by governments or supranational organizations such as the European Union. In addition to generally applicable regulations on the use of AI, there can be regulations for the use of AI in political marketing, such as requiring transparency in political advertising (similar to what Facebook provides in the political ads library), prohibiting the use of bots or spreading disinformation with strict penalization and limiting micro-targeting. In the case of mandatory registration of all actors involved in political campaigning, governments could demand that the data used for AI algorithms come from a trustworthy source and is unbiased. Secondly, professional organizations and industry associations can establish ethical standards for the use of AI in political campaigns, such as the American Association of Political Consultants' code of ethics. Adherence to these standards could be monitored and enforced by the organization or association. The tech industry can play a role in self-regulating the use of AI as well. For example, social media platforms can develop algorithms that prioritize authentic information and reduce the spread of disinformation. The third way is educating the public and political consultants about the ethical implications of the usage of new technologies and AI in political marketing, which could raise awareness and help prevent unethical usage on the side of consultants and help citizens understand the potential risks of AI and how to recognize disinformation. Such an approach could empower voters to make more informed decisions and hold politicians and political consultants accountable. Lastly, public scrutiny and independent oversight can raise attention to the unethical use of AI. The media and civic society can act as watchdogs, monitoring the use of AI in political marketing, which could put pressure on politicians and consultants to act ethically and transparently; otherwise, they could face the unfavorability of the electorate or even sanctions from the regulatory office.

Motivation of Actors for (un)ethical Behaviour

In the context of political marketing, the implementation and (un)ethical implications of AI involve three distinct categories of actors, each with unique motivations that influence their behaviour. These actors comprise big-tech companies, democratic institutions and third parties such as non-governmental organizations (NGOs) and potentially hostile (even foreign) actors. It is important to consider the distinct interests and objectives of each of these actors to better understand the potential implications and consequences of their involvement in the implementation and use of AI within political marketing frameworks.

The category of big-tech companies primarily includes social media platforms, search engines and producers of technological hardware, although it is not limited to these. These private companies operate with the primary objective of generating revenue, which raises questions about their motivation for the ethical or unethical use of

AI. If these companies focus on a good reputation and determine that operating in a democratic environment that provides fair conditions for all stakeholders, including themselves, will lead to greater profitability, then we can anticipate ethical behaviour more probably. However, experiences with big-tech companies so far have been mixed. For instance, Meta (formerly Facebook) has demonstrated a long-term focus on financial profits at the expense of fair algorithms providing equal chances for different content to be shared and seen, as testified by whistle-blower Frances Haugen in 2021, who disclosed that Meta had been aware for years of Facebook's algorithms' tendency to promote negative emotions and false news. Despite having a technical solution, the company chose not to implement it, as it would reduce advertising profits. On the other hand, Facebook rectified errors in its source code that enabled the Cambridge Analytica scandal after it was exposed. It is therefore a question of what kind of cause Meta will act on in the case of AI. Another example is YouTube, which regularly collaborates and coordinates its activities with experts, NGOs and academics to avoid an overwhelming amount of AI-generated content.

The imperative for democratic institutions, whether at the state or public administration level, national or supranational, to employ AI ethically is self-evident and unequivocal. Employing AI in an unethical manner transgresses the fundamental principles upon which democratic establishments are founded. Besides legality, democratic institutions rest on the pillars of citizen trust and legitimacy. If the public becomes aware that institutions are using AI in a manner that contravenes citizens' interests, it becomes challenging for such institutions to maintain public trust. This erosion of trust and legitimacy could result in a change of regime, leading to the replacement of existing institutions with new ones.

The third category of actors can be classified into two distinct subcategories. The first of these are NGOs that oversee various phenomena, including the utilization of AI. The non-profit sector, together with the media, has long served as watchdogs of democracy, scrutinizing the activities of institutions and powerful organizations. NGOs are an essential component of a free and democratic society, ensuring compliance with laws, transparency of financing, fact-checking and the debunking of disinformation in an information environment (Pavlíková et al., 2021). Thus, it is evident that NGOs will now seek to influence the adherence to regulations, standards and ethics in AI usage. NGOs serve as controllers of the two aforementioned groups of actors, including big-tech companies and democratic institutions, verifying whether their behaviour aligns with their declarations and citizens' expectations. However, NGOs may also use AI to monitor such compliance. It would be paradoxical if these organizations sought to regulate ethics and compliance while employing AI unethically to do so. The second subcategory is represented by hostile actors, usually coming from abroad. While we implicitly expect more ethical use of AI from the first group, the opposite is true for the subcategory of hostile actors. Subjects trying to undermine democratic institutions and political establishment as such have no incentive to do so within the bounds of honest and fair behaviour (Wecel et al., 2023). We already have experience with other forms of efforts by foreign or international actors to intervene in the democratic establishment and processes of other countries, such as tools of hybrid warfare (Yan, 2020) and information warfare (Floridi & Taddeo, 2014). Unfortunately, such behaviour is difficult to prove – or rather, the secret services of individual countries may point to the threat of external interference, but in the information space it is not a direct influence. The dissemination of disinformation can take place in closed groups, through collaborators or vulnerable persons who for some reason agree with the content of the message, but also by exploiting the potential offered by advanced algorithms. For example, the Chinese government not only has theoretical access to the data of millions of TikTok users, but can also use an algorithm over which it can have at least indirect control to spread Chinese propaganda; this is the reason why TikTok is banned in some countries and why in others a possible TikTok ban is a salient political issue. As a rule, they try to keep their activities secret, and if they are discovered, they often relativize or deny their involvement due to the illegality or unethicality of these actions. Thus, it is necessary to address the potential misuse of AI by hostile (foreign) actors as they represent a threat. Intelligence services, the military and other actors responsible for national security have to develop strategies to mitigate their impact. Although this issue is important and deserves more attention (including analyses of communication on networks such as Telegram or VKontakte), this text focuses mainly on domestic actors and their behaviour. This is not to relativize harmful influences from outside; there is just not enough space in this chapter to address them – but the fact remains that everything discussed in this chapter can be used by third parties to harm and polarize societies and thus destroy democratic institutions.

One more thing: We have not mentioned another important player yet: AI itself. At the time of writing this chapter, LLMs based on AI such as ChatGPT or similar do not possess their own agenda; however, it is conceivable that these AI systems could eventually develop their own goals and motivations. As such, AI as a tool has the potential to become a distinct actor with its own interests and objectives. The critical question is whether we will be able to recognize such developments in time and respond accordingly. Even the signatories of the petition (Future of Life 2023) are concerned about the rapid development of AI. Hundreds of prominent individuals, including Elon Musk (CEO of SpaceX, Tesla and Twitter) and Steve Wozniak (Co-founder of Apple), as well as numerous scholars and experts from the technology sector, were calling for a slowdown in the development of next-generation AI for at least six months. Of course, we can ask whether the motivation of people like Musk or Wozniak is not driven by personal reasons connected to their own business. Nevertheless, no matter what their motivation, it is important not to underestimate the concerns and arguments put forth by the petition's signatories. The rationale behind this call to action was based on a number of recognized risks associated with advanced AI systems. These risks include concerns about the adaptability of the labour market and the proliferation of generated fake news and alternate realities. Nevertheless, the most urgent and profound risk is linked to the potential for AI systems to attain autonomous agency, where they are capable of maintaining a particular intention and carrying out actions independently over an extended period.

Although this section of the chapter deals with the question of the ethics of using AI in general, it can serve as a basis for defining the ethical use of AI within political marketing, specifically in segmentation and targeting. The problems and actors outlined above show what election campaigns and political marketing have to deal with. The following recommendations are based on Lees-Marshment and Raynauld (2021, p. 127), who formulate principles for best practice for political marketing outreach and engagement, and Jobin et al. (2019), who observed national AI ethical codes. All of the principles are presented as a way to minimize harm and improve public trust in the practice of political marketing:

1 *Transparency*: Political consultants should be open in providing information in what stage of the political campaign they use AI and to what it was used (data use, human-AI interaction, automated decisions). Transparency is essential so that the structure and content can be discussed and criticized.
2 *Non-Maleficence*: AI should not be used to harm, for example, misuse in cyberwarfare and malicious hacking. Another aspect is the violation of privacy, that is, access to private data without the subject's permission. Controversial is the usage of AI for micro-targeting which disables public debate on the topic, and therefore encourages social and information bubbles.
3 *Responsibility and accountability*: AI should be used basically in accordance with the laws and political culture. When using AI for segmentation and targeting, consultants should avoid defining criteria leading to higher polarization in society. They should be aware not only of the campaign outcome but also of the consequences.
4 *Openness and diversity*: Consultants should not rely on AI as the only source of data for segmentation. Since we do not know exactly what data AI draws from and what algorithm it implements (and if we ask whether it does not lie to us), dependence on AI solely could be misleading. Therefore, wide range of market research sources and methods is still preferred.
5 *Common societal good*: Use AI to segmentation to better understand the society; to create new groups in the market, to identify and understand under-represented or emerging groups in society, to better understand the diverse needs of existing segments and better understand how to tailor the offer; not to encourage hate, fear or rage. They should avoid doing damage to the society.
6 *Inclusivity*: Targeted political appeal should not be used with the intention to exclude specific segments from the public debate and political process.
7 *Professionalism*: Clear and broadly accepted standards for AI usage should be defined and upheld.

CONCLUSION

A successful campaign must be based on data, timely and accurate decisions, a creative communications mix and a commitment by politicians and volunteers to reach and persuade as many voters as possible. For decades, political campaigns have been designed to appeal primarily to selected target audiences rather than the population as a whole. Logically, a one-size-fits-all message and policy simply do not exist. Parties compete not only for campaign agendas and issues or competencies but also for particular segments of the electorate. Whereas in the past, some campaign decisions were made based on intuition, today AI and machine and deep learning models increasingly replace the human factor. Some activities are becoming fully automated and can be expected to run autonomously, allowing new patterns to be found in the data and used to improve campaign effectiveness. As technology advances, we can expect to see even greater opportunities for personalized messaging (micro-targeting) through language models such as the increasingly popular ChatGPT. Ultimately, campaigns can become truly intimate, offering a unique emotional trigger for each individual voter, potentially changing their political behaviour.

Moreover, with the expansion of global communication tools, typically social media, the opportunity for outside interference in democratic processes and influence on the political situation in individual countries is becoming more prevalent. What seemed like dystopian science fiction a few years ago has become a reality. These developments raise many questions concerning the morality and ethics of campaigning in the 21st century. At the moment, we do not have the answers to these questions, and we do not know what path we will take – whether we will follow the path of restrictions and regulations or allow things to run relatively freely.

The recent past has uncovered cases where the data of millions of users have been misused to influence them with messages tailored to their needs and psychological profiles. The mere fact that such manipulation is possible raises concerns for our future. Every exposed case that tests the strength of democracy, democratic institutions and the willingness of tech companies to adjust their products underscores the importance of setting boundaries, ethical standards and maintaining transparency in how campaigns are run. So far, it appears that we are willing to have that debate and are still striving to defend the values that concern our freedoms and rights.

We live with technologies that are capable of understanding us better than anyone else and providing compelling incentives to change our behaviour. As fantastic as this sounds, we need to be vigilant and pay close attention to civic education and constant reminders of the potential negative consequences.

Acknowledgements

This text was written as an output of the 'CEDMO 2.0 NPO' project of the Czech Ministry of Industry and Trade (code MPO 60273/24/21300/21000).

REFERENCES

Andrews, S. (2020). *The world's best buyer persona system*. Yokel Local Publications.

Baines, P. R., Worcester, R. M., Jarrett, D., & Mortimore, R. (2005). Product attribute-based voter segmentation and resource advantage theory. *Journal of Marketing Management*, *21*(9–10), 1079–1115. https://doi.org/10.1362/026725705775194102

Baldwin-Philippi, J. (2019). Data campaigning: Between empirics and assumptions. *Internet Policy Review*, *8*(4), 1–18. https://doi.org/10.14763/2019.4.1437

Banker, S. (1992). The ethics of political marketing practices, the rhetorical perspective. *Journal of Business Ethics*, *11*, 843–848.

Banks, S. (2020, November 6). What are dark posts and how can you use them? *Zoomsphere*. https://blog.zoomsphere.com/what-are-dark-posts-and-how-can-you-use-them

Barocas, S. (2012). The price of precision: Voter microtargeting and its potential harms to the democratic process. In *PLEAD '12: Proceeding of the first edition workshop on Politics, elections and data*. 31–36. https://doi.org/10.1145/2389661.2389671.

Bode, L., Hanna, A., Yang, J., & Shah, D. V. (2015). Candidate networks, citizen clusters, and political expression: Strategic hashtag use in the 2010 midterms. *The Annals of the American Academy of Political and Social Science*, *659*(1), 149–165. https://doi.org/10.1177/0002716214563923

Brkan, M. (2019). Artificial intelligence and democracy: The impact of disinformation, social bots and political targeting. *Delphi*, *2*(2), 66–71. https://doi.org/10.21552/delphi/2019/2/4

Cadwalladr, C., & Graham-Harrison, E. (2018, March 17). Revealed: 50 million Facebook profiles harvested for Cambridge Analytica in major data breach. *The Guardian*. https://www.theguardian.com/news/2018/mar/17/cambridge-analytica-facebook-influence-us-election

Chang, A. (2018, May 2). The Facebook and Cambridge Analytica scandal, explained with a simple diagram. *Vox*. https://www.vox.com/policy-and-politics/2018/3/23/17151916/facebook-cambridge-analytica-trump-diagram

Chen, H. (2009). AI, E-government, and politics 2.0. *IEEE Intelligent Systems*, *24*(5), 64–86. https://doi.org/10.1109/MIS.2009.91

Confessore, N. (2018, April 4). Cambridge Analytica and Facebook: The Scandal and the fallout so far. *The New York Times*. https://www.nytimes.com/2018/04/04/us/politics/cambridge-analytica-scandal-fallout.html

Deibert, R. J., & Pauly, L. W. (2019). Mutual entanglement and complex sovereignty in cyberspace. In

D. Bigo, E. Isin, & E. Ruppert (Eds.), *Data politics. Worlds, subjects, rights* (pp. 81–99). Routledge.

Cwalina, W., Falkowski, A. & Newman, B. I. (2015). Persuasion in the political context: Opportunities and threats. In: D. W. Stewart (Ed.). *The handbook of persuassion and social marketing* (pp. 61–128). Bloomsbury Publishing.

Dolnicar, S., Grün, B., & Leisch, F. (2018). *Market segmentation analysis*. Springer.

Donatelli, D. (2023, May 16). Creating personas vs. Customer segments: What's the difference? *Acquia*. https://www.acquia.com/blog/creating-personas-vs-customer-segments-whats-difference

Duberry, J. (2022). *Artificial intelligence and democracy. risks and promises of AI-mediated citizen–government relations*. Edward Elgar Publishing. https://doi.org/10.4337/9781788977319

Floridi, L., & Taddeo, M. (2014). *The Ethics of information warfare*. Springer.

Future of Life Institute. (2023, March 22). *Pause giant AI experiments: An open letter*. https://futureoflife.org/open-letter/pause-giant-ai-experiments/?fbclid=IwAR0aD5bGwYCE77B43Al2Bnk3jbbnA_lvIubh4XeFOrKHw4TreClMA3arNZY

Gavett, G. (2014, July 9). What you need to know about segmentation. *Harvard Business Review*. https://hbr.org/2014/07/what-you-need-to-know-about-segmentation

Gerber, A. S., Huber, G. A., Doherty, D., & Dowling, C. M. (2011). The big five personality traits in the political arena. *Annual Review of Political Science, 14*, 265–287. https://doi.org/10.1146/annurev-polisci-051010-111659

Gregor, M. (2019). Political consultants' ethics of conviction. In J. Lees-Marshment (Ed.), *Political marketing. Principles and applications* (pp. 176–178). Routledge. https://doi.org/10.4324/9781351136907

Gregor, M., & Mlejnková, P. (2021). Explaining the challenge: From persuasion to relativisation. In M. Gregor, & P. Mlejnková (Eds.), *Challenging online propaganda and disinformation in the 21st Century* (pp. 3–41). Palgrave Macmillan. https://doi.org/10.1007/978-3-030-58624-9_1

Grigsby, M. (2018). *Marketing analytics: A practical guide to improving consumer insights using data techniques* (2nd ed.). Kogan Page Limited.

Harbath, K., & Fernekes, C. (2023, March 16). *History of the Cambridge Analytica controversy*. Bipartisan Policy Center. https://bipartisanpolicy.org/blog/cambridge-analytica-controversy.

Hayward, K. (2019). *Stop random acts of marketing*. BookBaby.

Henneberg, S. C. (2002). Understanding political marketing. In N. J. O'Shaughnessy, & S. C. Henneberg (Eds.), *The Idea of political marketing* (pp. 93–170). Praeger.

Henneberg, S. C., & O'Shaughnessy, N. (2007). Theory and concept development in political marketing. Issues and an agenda. *Journal of Political Marketing, 6*(2–3), 5–31. https://doi.org/10.1300/J199v06n02_02

Ipsos. (2022, July 13). Television is the primary news source for 75% of EU citizens. https://www.ipsos.com/en/television-primary-news-source-75-eu-citizens

Jobin, A., Ienca, M., & Vayena, E. (2019). The global landscape of AI ethics guidelines. *Nature Machine Intelligence, 1*, 389–399. https://doi.org/10.1038/s42256-019-0088-2

Kirchheimer, O. (1966). The transformation of the west European party system. In J. La Palombara & M. Weiner (Eds.), *Political parties and political development* (pp. 177–200). Princeton University Press.

Koc-Michalska, K., Lilleker, D., Baden, C., Guzek, D., Bene, M., Doroshenko, L., Gregor, M., & Skoric, M. (2024). *Citizens, participation and media in Central and Eastern European Nations*. Routledge.

Kosinski, M., Stillwell, D., & Graepel, T. (2013). Private traits and attributes are predictable from digital records of human behavior. *PNAS Proceedings of the National Academy of Sciences of the United States of America, 110*(15), 5802–5805. https://doi.org/10.1073/pnas.1218772110

Kotler, P., & Armstrong, G. (1996). *Principles of marketing* (7th ed.). Prentice-Hall.

Kotler, P., & Keller, K. L. (2012). *Marketing management* (14th ed.). Prentice Hall.

Lapowsky, I. (2019, March 17). How Cambridge analytica sparked the great privacy awakening. *Wired*. https://www.wired.com/story/cambridge-analytica-facebook-privacy-awakening

Lau, R. R., & Redlawsk, D. P. (2001). Advantages and disadvantages of cognitive heuristics in political decision making. *American Journal of Political Science, 45*(4), 951–971. https://doi.org/10.2307/2669334

Lees-Marshment, J. (2019). Conclusion. Political marketing practice and ethics. In J. Lees-Marshment (Ed.), *Political marketing. Principles and applications* (pp. 240–264). Routledge. https://doi.org/10.4324/9781351136907

Lees-Marshment, J., & Raynauld, V. (2021). Overview of digital political communication and marketing. In P. Loge (Ed.), *Political communication ethics* (pp. 115–136). Rowman & Littlefield.

Lipset, S. M., & Rokkan, S. (1967). Cleavage structures, party systems and voter alignments: An introduction. In S. M. Lipset & S. Rokkan (Eds.), *Party systems and voter alignments*. Free Press.

Lock, A., & Harris, P. (1996). Political marketing – vive la difference! *European Journal of Marketing, 30*(10/11), 14–24. https://doi.org/10.1108/03090569610149764

Marland, A. (2011). Yes we can (fundraise): The ethics of marketing in political fundraising. In J. Lees-Marshment (Ed.), *Routledge handbook of political marketing* (pp. 164–176). Routledge. https://doi.org/10.4324/9780203349908

Matz, S. C., Kosinski, M., Nave, G., & Stillwell, D. J. (2017). Psychological targeting as an effective approach to digital mass persuasion. *Proceedings of the National Academy of Sciences of the United States of America*, *114*(48), 12714–12719. https://doi.org/10.1073/pnas.1710966114

McDonald, M., & Dunbar, I. (2012). *Market segmentation: How to do It and how to profit from it* (4th ed.). John Wiley & Sons.

Meyers, A. (2023, February 27). *AI's powers of political persuasion*. Stanford University – Human-Centered Artificial Intelligence. https://hai.stanford.edu/news/ais-powers-political-persuasion

Newman, N., Fletcher, R., Schulz, A., Andi, S., Robertson, C. T. & Nielsen, R. K. (2021). *Reuters institute digital news report 2021*. Reuters Institute for the Study of Journalism.

O'Shaughnessy, N. (2002). Toward an ethical framework for political marketing. *Psychology and Marketing*, *19*(12), 983–1094. https://doi.org/10.1002/mar.10054

Paul, R. B., Worcester, R. M., Jarrett, D., & Mortimore, R. (2005). Product attribute-based voter segmentation and resource advantage theory. *Journal of Marketing Management*, *21*(9–10), 1079–1115. https://doi.org/10.1362/026725705775194102

Pavlíková, M., Šenkýřová, B., & Drmola, J. (2021). Propaganda and disinformation go online. In M. Gregor, & P. Mlejnková (Eds.), *Challenging online propaganda and disinformation in the 21st century* (pp. 43–74). Palgrave Macmillan. https://doi.org/10.1007/978-3-030-58624-9_2

Pérez-Escolar, M., Lilleker, D., & Tapia-Frade, A. (2023). A systematic literature review of the phenomenon of disinformation and misinformation. *Media and Communication*, *11*(2). https://doi.org/10.17645/mac.v11i2.6453

Reichborn-Kjennerud, E., & Cullen, P. (2016). *What is hybrid warfare?*. Norwegian Institute of International Affairs.

Revella, A. (2015). *Buyer personas*. John Wiley & Sons.

Ryan, O. (2024, January 21). Hashtag marketing: How to use hashtags for better marketing campaigns. *Mention*. https://mention.com/en/blog/hashtag-marketing-how-to-use-hashtags-for-better-marketing-campaigns

Scullion, R. (2008). The impact of the market on the character of citizenship, and the consequences of this for political engagement. In D. Lilleker & R. Scullion (Eds.), *Voters or consumers: Imagining the contemporary electorate* (pp. 51–72). Cambridge Scholar Publishing.

Tarran, B. (2018). What can we learn from the Facebook-Cambridge Analytica scandal? *Significance*, *15*(3), 4–5. https://doi.org/10.1111/j.1740-9713.2018.01139.x

Thiele, R. (2021). *Hybrid warfare. Future and technologies*. Springer.

Toth, O. A. (2019). *The lowest hanging fruit: How to build a target audience persona for better marketing plans & find people who really want to buy from you*. Orsolya Anna Toth at Smashwords.

Vaidhyanathan, S. (2018). *Antisocial media: How Facebook disconnects us and undermines democracy*. Oxford University Press.

Ward, J. (2018). Democratic change and 'the referendum effect' in the UK: Reasserting the good of political participation. In *Virtues in the public sphere* (pp. 234–249). Routledge.

Wecel, K., Sawiński, M., Stróżyna, M., Lewoniewski, W., Ksieżniak, E., Stolarski, P., & Abeamowicz, W. (2023). Artificial intelligence–friend or foe in fake news campaigns. *Economics and Business Review*, *9*(2), 41–70. https://doi.org/10.18559/ebr.2023.2.736

Yan, G. (2020). The impact of Artificial Intelligence on hybrid warfare. *Small Wars and Insurgencies*, *31*(4), 898–917. https://doi.org/10.1080/09592318.2019.1682908

Vetting Political Candidates in the Digital World

Filip Scherf and Michael Vintr

INTRODUCTION

Political vetting is a routine component of selecting viable candidates for elected offices or political appointments and understanding political opposition. Thanks to the spread of digital technologies, vetting can be done not only by political marketing professionals but also by the wider general public, as we shall argue. Thus, the widespread practice of *sous*veillance, watching from below, departs dramatically from the historical praxis of background checks into candidates conducted by specialized units inside political parties. The advent of digital communications technology has democratized the established processes and shifted them away from secrecy to the forefront of political competition. In the present chapter, we offer critical reflections on the ongoing shift of political theatre into the online sphere and consider how digital vetting through practices of open-source intelligence ('OSINT') opens new multi-faceted opportunities in political marketing.

First, we argue that digital vetting of political candidates, which significantly augments and expands traditional vetting tools and methods, reverses the modes of surveillance and control in a society. To substantiate this argument, we develop an original theoretical framework that reverses the traditional Benthamian–Foucauldian model of top-down control. Through digital tools, the disciplinary, behaviour-altering power of the panopticon prison becomes its mirror image: the politician-guard is subjected to the potentially ceaseless gaze of individuals-prisoners. Thus, surveillance (watching from above) becomes sousveillance (watching from below) as the disciplinary power shifts away from the nominally powerful to the masses equipped with tools for vetting the would-be elite. We further assert, leveraging Jean-Paul Sartre's observations, that the reversed Benthamian–Foucauldian model turns the candidate-politician into an object that is constituted through the peering of others who, using digital tools, judge the candidates' acts. Further, we insist, with Eric Stoddart, that digital vetting tools should promote inclusive common good, rather than lead to exclusionary shaming, and appreciate the depth of what it means to be a *real* person engaged in, and constituted through, interpersonal relations.

Second, the chapter considers practical digital vetting within the developed framework. While traditional vetting practices still have a place in assessing the viability of political candidates, they have limitations and may leave crucial intelligence undiscovered. We critically explore the OSINT collection and analysis processes, a professionalized version of sousveillance, with a focus on the intelligence cycle used to discover these and discuss some of the tools that empower digital vetting. We demonstrate the use of these tools and methodologies using real-world examples.

Looking at the current but evolving state of vetting political candidates in the digital world, we consider its implications on the democratic process, assess its benefits, risks and limitations and envision its future.

CANDIDATES IN THE PANOPTICON PRISON

We maintain that digital vetting of candidates for political office reverses the panopticon model of surveillance, turning candidates into relational data-doubles subject to sousveillance, which alters the candidates' behaviour and reduces their identity with profound ethical implications for the watchers and the watched. Let us unpack this rather dense assertion upon which we develop this chapter.

The *panopticon* was a prison design proposed by the eighteenth-century reformer Jeremy Bentham. Intended as a prison by Bentham, the panopticon represents an architectural structure built to maximize the visibility of the inmates who were to be isolated in individual cells such that they were unaware at any particular moment whether they were being observed by guards in a central tower. This constant *potential* watching altered the inmates' behaviour and, in consequence, their relation to their self (Haggerty & Ericson, 2000, p. 607).

Michel Foucault's twentieth-century reinterpretation of the concept has become a major paradigm, however disputed and incomplete, of surveillance in the political domain (1977). In Foucault's broad application to society as such, the panopticon is a 'generalizable model of functioning; a way of defining power relations in terms of everyday life of men' (1977, p. 205). Therefore, as Masa Galic argues, the Foucauldian reinterpretation of panopticism involves (almost) all-seeing watchers who can survey 'everything, everyone, all the time' (Galic et al., 2017, p. 12).

Foucault recognized that, in a modern society washed in surveillance technologies, the panopticon model has polyvalent applications in diverse political contexts (1977, p. 205). When applied to surveillance, the panopticon model provides inspection functions ceaselessly, the gaze is alert everywhere (1977, p. 195). Foucault further noted that, with its potential for seeing everything, the panopticon inevitably imposes behavioural norms on a particular individual who is being, or might be, watched (1977, p. 205). The slightest movements of the person are recorded and analyzed, representing an almost automatized (often preventative) 'disciplinary mechanism' (1977, p. 197). This disciplinary mechanism turns panopticism into the 'general principle of new "political anatomy" whose object and end are not the relations of sovereignty but the relations of discipline' (1977, p. 208).[1]

It is indeed the watchers who are vested with the disciplinary power by setting the norms of behaviour and by identifying supposedly pathological elements and deviations from the norm (Foucault, 1977, p. 196). The disciplinary panoptical watching, in Foucault's observation, functions according to a dual mode. The first mode creates binary divisions – the normal and the abnormal. The second mode makes coercive assignments – attempts to define one's identity (Foucault, 1977, p. 199). This dual mode is massively augmented by digital technologies which do not watch a real person, as inmates in Bentham's prison, but rather the real person's virtual image. Kevin Haggerty and Richard Ericsson have coined the term 'data-double' (2000).

These data-doubles are assembled by aggregating and cross-referencing multiple data trails in the digital network, independent of spatial and temporal settings (Bakir, 2015, p. 17). The dispersed data inputs, generated by a concrete individual, do not individually tell much about the person. But when they are *ex-post* re-constructed, they generate a 'surveillant assemblage' which abstracts human material bodies from their territorial and interpersonal settings and reduces them into oversimplified virtual data-doubles. The abstractions transform persons into pure information that can be assessed against the norm (Haggerty & Ericson, 2000, pp. 605, 613). It is such *digitized* data-doubles, not real persons in their richness and depth, who are subject to *digital* vetting.

In the digitized world, the generalized and normalized practice of watching, with its behaviour-altering potential, has given vetting in the political contest a disciplinary nature. The power exercised by the watcher or, more correctly, the power vested in the potential act of watching, is always visible and never verifiable. The candidate knows that they might always be observed and judged, but they cannot know at which particular moment they are actually being looked at (Foucault, 1977, p. 201). To retain integrity in front of the all-seeing eye, the candidate therefore has to be always disciplined for they never know who might be watching.

In practice, surveillance brings discipline over the data-doubles as they can be thus deconstructed, analyzed and reconstructed again (echoing the Foucauldian second mode). Once reconstructed, the digitalized data-double can be endlessly judged against whatever norm and categorized accordingly (the first mode). Finally, the abnormal is disciplined through non-physical mechanisms of power. Through co-setting the norm and then judging others against it, the watcher achieves a 'perpetual victory that avoids any physical confrontation and which is always decided in advance' (Foucault, 1977, p. 203). To illustrate this in a political context, if the watcher decides that a candidate's appearance at a pro-life rally is *abnormal*, and then finds evidence of the candidate's participation, the latter is defeated by an invisible foe relying on *a priori* norms. More generally, the disciplined data-double who deviates from the norm can be, for instance, subject to online shaming or simply eliminated from a race for political office.

Thus, the subjection of the watched in the digital age is born from a potential, even fictitious, relation. The watched does not know the watcher; they do not know whether the watcher is looking. And yet, looked at or not, the watched is subjected to the invisible *potential* watcher's disciplinary power. Because he who is knowingly subjected to a field of visibility 'becomes the principle of his own subjection' (Foucault, 1977, p. 202). In effect, the candidates are inevitably entrenched in a complex web of behaviour-altering and identity-forming interactions. Their self is no longer only digitally *constructed*, but is constantly *being re-formed* as an action of individuals in, and in relation to, a society of watchers (Stoddart, 2023). The relational nature of the candidates' personal profile, and indeed of their very identity, creates yet another challenge for their political marketeers. This challenge is further augmented by the democratization of surveillance technologies which makes candidates subject to a gaze not only from above, but also – and predominantly – from *below*.

POWER TO THE MASSES: THE PANOPTICON REVERSED

We have hitherto described the panopticon. In our opening assertion, we maintain, however, that digital vetting *reverses* the panopticon. Let us therefore progress in our argument. The original panopticism describes the traditional top-down *sur*veillance where comparatively few powerful individuals or groups watch the many. As Steve Mann and Joseph Ferenbok astutely observe, in the digital age, with ubiquitous computing, this model is no longer singular (2013, p. 26). Through digital vetting tools, the many are now empowered to watch the few. The panopticon has become its mirror image whereby the 'inmate' can discipline the 'guard'. Each individual in the faceless mass of digitally equipped watchers exercises asymmetrical, unequal disciplinary power over the concrete (if virtualized) candidate. Such as *any* individual can exercise power if assuming the guard's vantage point in the panopticon, so can anyone who uses the right tools in the digitized world. What Foucault called the 'surplus power' of the watcher is now fixed not in the nominally powerful, a politician, but in the invisible mass (Foucault, 1977, p. 223).

Thus, the watcher from below – even if formally powerless – possesses immense disciplinary power over a more potent person through their ability to watch, and so to manipulate, the candidate's behaviour. Surveillance is replaced by *sous*veillance.[2] This kind of 'inverse surveillance' (Borradaile & Reeves, 2017, p. 272; Reilly, 2023) alters the relative standing of the powerful watcher (the guard in the panopticon) and the watched (the inmates). The hitherto watched become the watchers; masses subject to gaze can now practice gazing (Reilly, 2023). Sousveillance thus conceptualized is facilitated by digital technologies (Bakir, 2015, p. 13; Newell, 2020). They are the crucial empowering tools for sousveillance precisely because without them looking from below is both practically and metaphorically at a disadvantage (Mann & Ferenbok, 2013, p. 27).

Digital vetting tools connect citizens directly to political candidates, or more correctly to their data-doubles. This creates what Eric Stoddart calls the 'network society' (2008, p. 370). Such society has, according to Stoddart, at least two distinct characteristics relevant to the reality of sousveillance. First, information is spread across multiple nodes and exchanged through a multiplicity of possible interconnections. Second, information gathering and sharing occurs between nodes that blur the pre-digital distinction into political, civil, commercial or personal (Stoddart, 2008, p. 370). The distributed nature of sousveillance provides countless eyes that can watch, and discipline, ceaselessly (Garrido, 2015, p. 164; Reilly, 2023).

Mann and Ferenbok put it bluntly, arguing that 'sousveillance is more dependent on technology than surveillance' (2013, p. 26). Technology, they continue, facilitates capabilities necessary not only to watch but also for political action (2013, p. 26). Sousveillance powered by the vast volumes of data in the digital age creates 'political possibilities' for those previously at the margin of politics

(Borradaile & Reeves, 2017, pp. 272, 274). Therefore, writes Miguelangel Garrido, the digitally powered sousveillance has created a new political agency for the masses, creating a globalized civil society of watchers (2015, p. 153). Mann and Ferenbok concur that the time for sousveillance as a social tool for political action is reaching a critical mass, facilitated by a convergence of transmission, mobility and media channels for content distribution and engagement. Ubiquitous computing allows for unprecedented collection of data inputs into a surveillant assemblage.

THE DICTATE OF THE NORMAL

Having described the reversed panoptical sousveillance of data-doubles, let us now explore how the *real person's behaviour is altered* by being potentially watched. As a result of the panoptical watching, Foucault notes, the watched becomes conscious of the permanent visibility that gives the watcher automatic power over them (Foucault, 1977, p. 201). This *potentiality* of the disciplinary power makes its use often unnecessary by *a priori* altering the behaviour of the watched. For the pressure 'acts even before the offences, mistakes or crimes haven't been committed' (Foucault, 1977, p. 206). Being under scrutiny, the watched does not dare to deviate from the norm. And if the norm evolves, so does the watched. The existence of this behaviour-altering power is independent, as in the panopticon, of the person who exercises it. It is vested in the act, even in an *unrealized* act, of watching (Foucault, 1977).

Foucault notes that the more numerous those anonymous observers are, the greater the anxious awareness of the watched of being observed. This insight brings striking implications for the age of digital vetting in the vastness of the internet with billions of users. The perpetual potential watching, the knowledge of a *future* vetting, alters behaviour and pushes candidates to continuously self-correct (Foucault, 1977, pp. 202–203).

Let us apply Jean-Paul Sartre's famous parable of a person peeping through a keyhole until being distracted by a *potential* watcher behind them. Realizing that one may be watched, Sartre writes, affects one's being and triggers essential modifications in one's structure. One enters the real or perceptual field of another and becomes present to their eyes which are distant to one's spatial location (1943, p. 347). As a candidate subject to digital vetting, one confronts the other in a space that is both one's own, and not of one's choosing; and in that space, one apprehends the other as a subject in one's becoming an object for that other. This 'being-for-others', Sartre concludes, is manifested in the public space and in political life (1943, pp. 340–400).

According to Sartre, three transformations occur to the self as it becomes an object of gaze. First, one receives an identity outside of their body, their 'I' (1943, p. 360). Second, one becomes the other's project. Finally, as a consequence, one loses their self-determining autonomy. This is exactly what happens to the virtualized data-double, constituted by the other's gaze, and locked in a tangled web of interpersonal relations.

WATCHING TO DO GOOD: ETHICAL DIGITAL VETTING

Power exercised through digital vetting, a tool of sousveillance, is homogenous. No one is spared; no candidate is invisible to the gaze. Thus, digital tools give one power of mind over mind, which translates into power in the political (Foucault, 1977, pp. 202, 206). Borradaile and Reeves observe that sousveillance has facilitated political activism. Reversing the panopticon model, digital technology gives the previous inmates an 'opportunity to participate in the synergy of real-world collective political activity' (2017, pp. 273, 275).

The newly found political power acquired through digital tools for vetting political candidates raises profound ethical questions. The candidate, reconstructed as a data-double, inevitably lacks the immeasurable depth of what being a *person* means (Bakir, 2015, p. 17; Lyon, 2014; Tillich, 1968). Getting to know a person is an embodied, relational experience, ideally shaped by personal care in a context of mutual trust (Lyon, 2014, p. 24). On the contrary, vetting a candidate is an impersonal, virtual enterprise, often driven by a quest for power (Ellul, 1964; Tillich, 1968). Thus, in the digital world, a virtual double, an assemblage of data inputs, not only lacks the depth of the whole person but is measured by norms whose origin cannot be traced and whose motivations melt down in the endless vastness of the impersonal digital space. Furthermore, the projection of an abstracted individual loses sight of the depth of their personality as expressed in, and shaped through, real (as opposed to online) interpersonal engagements. Given the power of digital vetting, warn Borradaile and Reeves, one has to 'be cautious about why, how, and to what ultimate effect sousveillance is carried out' (2017, p. 273).

To counter the depersonalizing, reductionistic and excessively individualized force of digital vetting, as practiced against digital data-doubles, Stoddart calls on the practice of the *common gaze* driven by *solidarity* in promoting the *common good* and appreciating the relational nature of one's identity. Problematically, Stoddart observes that 'engaging in solidaristic action is a response to recognizing others as persons' (2008, pp. 372–373; 2023). This is precisely the challenge to *digital* vetting which is conditioned on depersonalized data inputs that replace the person as a subject of vetting. This creates the risk of overreliance on 'technologistic' solutions to human challenges. One can perhaps know more *about* the other by downloading more data, but one cannot know more about the other as a person through ever larger volumes of data.

Stoddart develops a positive relationality and asserts that mutual responsibility for one another's data-image is derived from solidarity which, further, offers a response to the angst of a culture of suspicion. The power of digital vetting should therefore not be used primarily to rise suspicion or to shame, but rather, continues Stoddart, as the good shepherd watches over the flock, carefully looking out for the lost and the outcast. As such, digital vetting can be inclusive (identifying the right candidates) more than exclusive (eliminating supposed deviators from the norm). Such an inclusionary common gaze serves the common good of society better than an angry look seeking to discipline and punish (Stoddart, 2021). It is up to the citizens, and by extension up to the political marketing professionals, vested with the power of digital vetting, to contribute to such a caring common gaze (Stoddart, 2008, 2021, 2023). The actual historic and current practice of digital vetting, however, remains far behind this aspiration.

The reversal of the panopticon model through digital surveillance that turns candidates into data-doubles subject to sousveillance has immense implications for the world of candidate vetting and political marketing in general. Indeed, with the digital tools available to the masses providing the ability to look up information about the candidates themselves, does political vetting as a professionalized industry even make sense in the 21st century?

We maintain that not only does it make sense, but it is even more important than ever. Now, sousveillance not only creates pressure on the powerful but also on those responsible for selecting them. The vetting process thus plays an increased role under this reversed Panopticon model. Knowing that these vetting teams must compete with the masses with equal access to information, professionals need to use industry best practices and tradecraft to stay ahead. The following sections discuss these best practices and their relevance and application in the world of digitized political marketing.

DIGITAL VETTING IN THE 21ST CENTURY

While this chapter focuses on modern tools and techniques, it is illuminating to contextualize the current praxis, powered by digital tools, in its pre-digital settings. The disciplinary nature of surveillance for vetting, now augmented, is historically in the fabric of the process. While tools for vetting evolve, the process itself has been an integral part of electoral politics for centuries. Early specific examples of what is sometimes referred to as *opposition research* (or *oppo*) include the research into John Adams' alleged desire to go to war against France that was supposedly commissioned by his rival and opponent in the presidential election, Thomas Jefferson (Huffman & Rejebian, 2012, p. 54). More recent examples of oppo work include the controversial Steele Dossier, which is a collection of research into the alleged collusion between then-Presidential candidate Donald J. Trump and Russia (Lerner, 2021), or the request of the former Czech Prime Minister Andrej Babiš to dig up dirt on one of his political opponents that he inadvertently sent to a wrong email address (Jochecová, 2024).

Over the years, opposition research evolved from a small but secretive part of political campaigns into a dirty secret that everyone knew but no one wanted to talk about, and then to a widely accepted and necessary component of the political theatre, not dissimilar from pre-employment background checks and basic due diligence. In other words, *exclusionary* vetting has come to dominate over a more caring, inclusive approach.

While the change in perception of political vetting has certainly played a role in its growth into the professionalized industry it is today, the main driver of this change has been the rise and prevalence of the internet and its unprecedented access to information. Of course, traditional offline techniques and methods of political vetting, such as lengthy screening questionnaires and reference calls, still have a place in assessing the viability of potential candidates. However, they have become less prominent and are often part of follow-up research based on information that was gathered online.

Furthermore, vetting candidates' online presence is increasingly more important due to the simple fact that people are generally willing to share information about themselves and others online that they typically would not in the physical world (Berkelaar & Harrison, 2016). Jennifer Martin notes that 'almost all content is user-generated and users retain a significant amount of autonomy' (2012, p. 408). However, the false sense of anonymity may encourage a willingness to engage in activities that may not be as accessible in the physical world. The candidates often willingly and knowingly make themselves subject to sousveillance; they lock themselves into the panopticon prison. However, as breaches and leaks of various online platforms ranging from Yahoo to LinkedIn to Adult Friend Finder demonstrate, there is no anonymity on the internet (Swinhoe & Hill, 2021; Teaching Privacy, 2014). The candidates are always potentially watched and disciplined, which increases the need of political parties for proactive reputation and brand management (Marland & DeCillia 2020).

In addition to creating new opportunities in oppo, this access to information also creates multiple challenges. The ever-increasing amount of data from a growing number of varied sources requires sophisticated methodology for collection and analysis. Additionally, as previously mentioned, professional vetting teams have to compete with the newly empowered civil society of watchers. Best practices of open-source intelligence ('OSINT'), a sophisticated form of sousveillance, offer a proven solution to these challenges.

DIGITAL VETTING, SOUSVEILLANCE AND OSINT

For the purposes of this chapter, we use the definition used by Schaurer and Störger, who define OSINT as 'the collection, processing, analysis, production, classification, and dissemination of information derived from sources and by means openly available to and legally accessible and employable by the public' (Schaurer & Störge, 2013).[3] Similar to other definitions, Schaurer and Störger also emphasize the role of OSINT in pursuing national security interests. However, in the 21st Century, OSINT is no longer solely the domain of national governments. It has increasingly become used by commercial enterprises, political marketing teams and, to some extent, the wider public. Furthermore, while OSINT sources include offline means, such as information gathered from print media, physical books and other similar materials, this chapter focuses on sources that live in the virtual world of the internet.

Whether knowingly or not, all readers of this chapter are very familiar with two of the most powerful OSINT tools: the web browser and search engine. Yet, conducting simple keyword searches using Google can be considered a part of sousveillance, but not necessarily of OSINT. Indeed, while sousveillance is what anyone with access to digital tools can do, OSINT turns the practice of common sousveillance into an expert discipline required of political marketing professionals.

Furthermore, despite the ever-growing array of increasingly more sophisticated tools for collection, tools do not equate to intelligence; they may have limited scopes of use or expiration dates due to the emergence of new platforms and changing online privacy rules and settings. To be considered intelligence, like other *ints*,[4] OSINT relies on a process known as the intelligence cycle. The following section discusses the intelligence cycle and its steps – planning and direction, collection, processing, analysis and dissemination – as applied by political marketing professionals when vetting political candidates.

DIGITAL VETTING THE INTELLIGENCE CYCLE

There is a plethora of literature on the intelligence cycle, including discussions and criticism of its efficacy. Most of this literature focuses on the cycle as it relates to the government and national security intelligence tradecraft. However, vetting of political candidates more closely resembles intelligence in the corporate world. Unlike governments or the military, commercial organizations use intelligence to inform their decisions on taking or avoiding risks (Strachan-Morris, 2014). Similarly, political parties use, or should use, the vetting process to identify or expose risks associated with political candidates to prepare for controversy and identify lines of defence or attack (Marland & DeCillia, 2020). Therefore, we maintain that the intelligence cycle works fairly well in the context of candidate vetting.

Planning and Direction

The starting point of the cycle is planning and direction. In this phase, candidate committees, campaign strategists, marketing teams or whoever else may be responsible for putting forth candidates or commissioning oppo research, ideally determine the research requirements and outline basic questions that will guide the rest of the process. Of course, a simple direction that comes to mind in association with oppo work is simply to 'find dirt', or, using standard background check terminology, red flags. However, in the context of political vetting, red flags are not universally defined, may change over time and are viewed differently by different segments of the population or electorate. Therefore, even an all-encompassing scope that aims to produce a complete book on a given candidate should include context and guidelines. For example, when the U.S. Democratic Party seemingly bet on basing their 2022 midterm strategy on promoting women's right to choose and fighting 2020 election deniers, their research into their opponents likely predominantly focused on past statements, voting records and other activities associated with these two topics, in addition to just finding general dirt (Cai, 2022; Sullivan, 2022).

Proper direction from the beginning of the research process is also necessary due to the simple fact that while most campaign teams have finite resources (e.g. time, budget, people, etc.), there is an almost infinite amount of information online, most of which is simply noise. Finally, proper direction and planning should at least assess what sources will be predominantly used in the collection phase. Research into incumbents with existing voting records differs from political novices. Similarly, research into a 66-year-old candidate will be different from a candidate three times younger. A good planning and direction phase allows for the appropriate allocation of resources and helps researchers stay on track throughout the rest of the cycle.

Without going in-depth into the different types of sources, it is worth discussing at least one type – leaked credential repositories – as it raises an ethical dilemma. As noted earlier, there is no anonymity on the internet since even once private and secured credentials and other information may become public through leaks and breaches. Such information, including usernames, hashed or plain passwords, IP addresses and other data, may contain both crucial information and provide data points to further the investigation by pivoting from them. Information found in these repositories has become a gold mine for investigators, as demonstrated by the large number of companies that specialize in dark web research and monitoring.

Leaked and breached credential repositories are notable because they arguably fall in an ethically grey area of online sources. Thus, not only the practice of sousveillance and the use of the data, but even the act of collecting the data raises ethical challenges. As the names suggest, information in these repositories is either accidentally exposed to the public or simply stolen. This may cause conflict with the definition of OSINT as information derived from publicly and legally available sources. However, we argue that such information is fair game as long as it was already made public and the team did not actively (e.g. perform hacking) or passively (e.g. instruct cybercriminals to hack, etc.) contribute to its original mining. While the information obtained in this grey area may quietly serve a candidate's own team (for instance, preventatively), its public use is highly limited by ethical, and often legal, ramifications.

Collection

The second stage of the intelligence cycle is collection. There are two basic forms of data collection methods – active and passive. While active collection methods include direct interaction with subjects to gather or elicit information not available publicly, passive collection takes advantage of information that already lives in the online sphere. Given that OSINT deals with public sources, the following paragraphs discuss passive collection methods.

Passive collection can be further broken down into several types, such as catch-all versus targeted or manual versus automized. Regardless of the approach used, the goal of this stage of the intelligence cycle is to gather any and all information that may be relevant to satisfy the requirements set in the planning and direction phase. While the specific methodology and tools used in this phase may differ based on the type of source that is being investigated, the general idea is to start with broad requirements and keywords and then narrow the search as more information surfaces. In the context of search engines, a broad search may start with just the name of the subject before adding additional keywords, such as education, spouse name, professional history and so on. Even though a broad search may generate too much noise to produce relevant information, narrowing searches from the beginning risks omitting important results.

As stressed earlier, OSINT is not defined by the ever-increasing assortment of research tools. Nevertheless, it is impossible to discuss collection without referencing these tools. While search engines remain the primary tool of online researchers, sophisticated and targeted tools such as data scrapers, monitoring platforms, transcription programs and other tools help to navigate through a large amount of data and enable its effective collection. For example, a manual search through hundreds of tweets from the subject may require hours of scrolling, loading and transcribing. Similarly, watching hours of interviews posted on YouTube takes, well, hours. Modern tools allow us to make these tasks more efficient by scraping these tweets, automizing the video transcription process and producing the results in a searchable spreadsheet. Other tools such as data enrichment platforms then help to synthesize collected information and seamlessly pivot from one finding to another.

Teams engaged in digital vetting would benefit from having members who are familiar with some of these tools. Furthermore, the online OSINT community is characterized by a willingness to share knowledge, resources and tools through various blogs and platforms such as GitHub and Discord channels. Teams whose researchers are members of this community, or can at least orient themselves in it, have a clear advantage over those who do not. Finally, the ability to create and maintain in-house tools using programming languages such as Python opens additional possibilities and enhances collection capabilities.

Processing

The third stage of the intelligence cycle is processing. In theory, this stage transforms the raw collected data from the collection phase to make it easier to analyze. In the example of collected tweets from a candidate's Twitter account, the processing phase would involve a cleanup of the spreadsheet and its organization by tweets, retweets, likes and so on to prepare for analysis. Another useful way of organizing the collected data could be to organize it by type (e.g. professional history, family, voting record, etc.) and by date to create a timeline of events.

With the amount of available information, not all information gathered in the collection phase likely ends up being useful. This is especially true in catch-all investigations that attempt to cast a wide net to create a complete book on the subject. Processing raw collected data may thus begin the process of cleaning the signals from the noise. In this stage, researchers should be careful not to dismiss any data too hastily, as it may be proven useful later. This is true especially when it comes to statements made by the candidates, as statements perceived as innocuous today may be considered controversial in the future. However, clear false positives, such as records associated with identically named individuals that are confidently determined to be different people, can typically be dismissed at this stage.

Analysis

The penultimate stage of the intelligence cycle – analysis – is perhaps the most important stage in order to call the final product intelligence. Indeed, open-source intelligence is not intelligence at all if it is simply a stream or collection of data. For example, a collection of all tweets is meaningless unless there is context to them. Is the candidate inflating credentials, contradicting their past statements or tweeting something considered controversial? If they are contradicting their past statements, is it a one-off contradiction on a major issue or an evolution of opinion over time in line with the evolution of their party's stances? If they tweeted something the researcher considers controversial, will the general electorate view it similarly?

The analysis stage is crucial because it puts the collected information in context. In short, if the collection phase is about gathering all the dots and the processing stage is about making sure analysts can read them, the analysis stage is about connecting them in a meaningful way (Phythian, 2014). Analysis creates the data-double, the surveillant assemblage, to be judged against a norm. For example, finding eviction filings against a candidate may be interesting but not critical. However, such filings become more relevant if the candidate has built their campaign on the image of a successful businessperson with millions of dollars in assets.

Analysts seek to answer questions about the data in two categories: evaluation and reflection. Questions that fall under the evaluation category address the credibility and reliability of the sources. Within the reflection category, the perspective shifts to attempting to understand and determine whether the data provides any new insights and answers the questions set in the direction phase (Gill & Phythian, 2014). At the same time, analysis looks for gaps in the collection phase.

A common critique of the intelligence cycle is the disconnect between the collection and analysis phases (Phythian, 2014). However, in the context of candidate vetting, like in the corporate world, these two phases often work in tandem (Strachan-Morris, 2014). Indeed, with limited resources and smaller research teams, both phases are often completed by the same person.

Dissemination

If the analysis stage is crucial to be considered intelligence, the last stage – dissemination – is vital to make this intelligence useful. Compiling the relevant results and presenting them in a digestible way while highlighting key findings is perhaps the most important part of the whole cycle. Clearly defined goals, data collected with state-of-the-art tools and pointed analysis may all be for nothing if the results are not presented in a meaningful way, or worse, misrepresented.

CONCLUSION

We have demonstrated that digital technologies democratize the power to watch candidates for political office. This power, wielded by professional political marketeers and by the general public, can alter the candidate's behaviour to make them comply with pre-defined norms. Such omnipresent sousveillance, watching from below, poses a twofold challenge for political marketers. First, the candidate, if they are to succeed, must behave as if they are always watched – without knowing the watcher. This requires the candidate to exercise restraint in both their professional *and* personal conduct *both* online and offline. Furthermore, candidates are encouraged to transcend the reductionistic online world and re-form their identity through real interpersonal engagements. Second, to remain useful, the political marketing team must surpass the widely available sousveillance techniques by mastering advanced defensive and active OSINT tools for digital vetting. Only then can the political marketer choose a candidate with an acceptable history on one hand and identify the opponent's weak spots on the other.

Of course, these advanced tools and processes are not a panacea and bring their own challenges. As discussed above, some sources and their mining techniques raise critical ethical questions. Answers to these questions then may vary based on the combination of self-imposed codes of conduct and the environment and form of government (democratic v. autocratic societies). Furthermore, as technology evolves, political marketing teams conducting digital vetting will face new challenges. For example, artificial intelligence has the potential to change many industries and disciplines, including political marketing. For instance, in the run-up to the 2023 parliamentary elections in Slovakia, a deepfake audio recording of a major candidate discussing how to rig the election demonstrated these challenges (Meaker, 2023). Additionally, general questions and discussions about access to information, misinformation and free speech and data privacy may have its implications as well.

Many of these discussions and their practical outcomes will be shaped and influenced by elected officials. Given this, the role and responsibility of vetting teams and the general public in advancing the best candidates cannot be understated.

Notes

1 Foucault defines 'disciplines' as 'techniques for assuring the ordering of human multiplicities' (1977, 218).

2 The term is derived from the French words 'sous' (below) and 'veiller' (to watch). For details on the term, see: (Mann et al., 2003, pp. 332–333).

3 OSINT has multiple definitions. For example, NATO defines it as 'Intelligence derived from publicly available information, as well as other unclassified information that has limited public distribution or access'. See: https://nso.nato.int/natoterm/content/nato/pages/home.html

4 In addition to OSINT, other basic intelligence-gathering disciplines as defined by the DNI include Human Intelligence (HUMINT), Signal Intelligence (SIGINT), Geospatial Intelligence (GEOINT), Measurement and Signature Intelligence (MASINT) and Imagery Intelligence (IMINT). See: Office of the Director of National Intelligence (2018).

REFERENCES

Bakir, V. (2015). Veillant panoptic assemblage: Mutual watching and resistance to mass surveillance after Snowden. *Media and Communication*, *3*(3), 12–25.

Berkelaar, B. L., & Harrison, M. A. (2016). Cybervetting. In C. R. Scott, J. R. Barker, T. Kuhn, J. Keyton, P. K. Turner, & L. K. Lewis (Eds.), *The international encyclopedia of organizational communication* (1 st ed.). Wiley.

Borradaile, G., & Reeves, J. (2017). Sousveillance Capitalism. *Surveillance & Society*, *18*(2), 272–275.

Cai, S. (2022). Democrats bet on Roe's ballot power ahead of midterms. *Axios*. https://www.axios.com/2022/06/27/roe-v-wade-democrats-republicans-midterm. Accessed on 03 February 2023.

Ellul, J. (1964). *The technological society*. Vintage Books.

Foucault, M. (1977). *Discipline and punish: The Birth of the prison*. Allen Lance.

Galic, M., Timan, T., & Koops, B. (2017). Bentham, Deleuze and beyond: An overview of surveillance theories from the panopticon to participation. *Philosophy & Technology*, *30*(1), 9–37.

Garrido, M. (2015). Contesting a biopolitics of information and communications: The importance of truth and sousveillance after Snowden. *Surveillance & Society*, *13*(2), 253–167.

Gill, P., & Phythian, M. (2014). From intelligence cycle to web of intelligence: Complexity and the conceptualisation of intelligence. In M. Phythian (Ed.),

2014, Understanding the intelligence cycle. Routledge.

Haggerty, K., & Ericson, R. (2000). The surveillant assemblage. *British Journal of Sociology*, *51*(4), 605–622.

Huffman, A., & Rejebian, M. (2012). *We're with nobody: Two insiders reveal the dark side of American politics* (p. 54). W. Morrow.

Jochecová, K. (2024). Former Czech PM Babiš in turmoil after email leak. *Politico*. https://www.politico.eu/article/former-czech-prime-minister-andrej-babis-leaked-email/. Accessed on 14 March 2024.

Lerner, K. L. (2021). *The discredited Steele dossier, a test of media ethics*. Taking Bearings. Harvard Blogs.

Lyon, D. (2014). Surveillance and the eye of god. *Studies in Christian Ethics*, *27*(1), 21–32.

Mann, S., & Ferenbok, J. (2013). New media and the power politics of sousveillance in a surveillance-dominated world. *Surveillance & Society*, *11*(1), 18–34.

Mann, S., Nolan, J., & Wellman, B. (2003). Sousveillance: Inventing and using wearable computing devices for data collection in surveillance environments. *Surveillance & Society*, *1*(3), 331–355.

Marland, A., & De Cillia, B. (2020). Reputation and brand management by political parties: Party vetting of election candidates in Canada. *Journal of Nonprofit & Public Sector Marketing*, *32*(1).

Martin, J. (2012). Second life surveillance: Power to the people or virtual surveillance society? *Surveillance & Society*, *9*(4), 408–423.

Meaker, M. (2023). Slovakia's election deepfakes show AI is a danger to democracy. *Wired*. https://www.wired.com/story/slovakias-election-deepfakes-show-ai-is-a-danger-to-democracy/. Accessed on 14 March 2024.

Newell, B. (2020). The state of sousveillance. *Surveillance & Society*, *18*(2), 257–261.

Office of the Director of National Intelligence. (2018). *What is intelligence?* https://www.dni.gov/index.php/what-we-do/what-is-intelligence

Phythian, M. (2014). *Understanding the intelligence cycle*. London Routledge.

Reilly, P. (2023). Watching the watchers: Sousveillance as a political response to surveillance society. In D. Lilleker & A. Veneti (Eds.), *Research handbook on visual politics* (pp. 395–406). Series: Elgar handbooks in political science. Edward Elgar. ISBN 9781800376922.

Sartre, J. (1943). *Being and nothingness*. Washington Square Press.

Schaurer, F., & Störge, J. (2013). The evolution of open source intelligence (OSINT). *Journal of U.S. Intelligence Studies*, *19*(3), 53.

Stoddart, E. (2008). Who watches the watchers? Towards an ethic of surveillance in a digital age. *Studies in Christian Ethics*, *21*(3), 362–381.

Stoddart, E. (2021). *The common gaze*. SCM Press.

Stoddart, E. (2023). Sorting identity. In M. Kwet(Ed.), *Cambridge handbook of surveillance and race*, ch. 2. Cambridge University Press.

Strachan-Morris, D. (2014). The intelligence cycle in the corporate world: Bespoke or off-the-shelf? In M. Phythian (Ed.), *2014, Understanding the intelligence cycle*. Routledge. ch. 7.

Sullivan, A. (2022, November 9). 'Democrats' risky midterm strategy to elevate election deniers appears to pay off. *Reuters*. https://www.reuters.com/world/us/democrats-risky-midterm-strategy-elevate-election-deniers-appears-pay-off-2022-11-09/

Swinhoe, D., & Hill, M. (2021). *The 18 biggest data breaches of the 21st century*. https://www.csoonline.com/article/2130877/the-biggest-data-breaches-of-the-21st-century.html

Teaching Privacy. (2014). *There's no anonymity*. https://teachingprivacy.org/theres-no-anonymity/

Tillich, P. (1968). The person in a technical society. In G. Winter (Ed.), *Social ethics: Issues in ethics and society* (pp. 120–138). Harper & Row.

Political Marketing and the Strategic Populism in Poland

Wojciech Cwalina and Paweł Koniak

INTRODUCTION

Populism has become a regular feature of politics in liberal democracies, including Poland. While populism is still mostly used by outsider or challenger parties, mainstream politicians, both in the government and in opposition, have been using it as well – generally in an attempt to counter the populist challengers (Mudde, 2004). However, mainstream populism has not only a "defensive" function. It is also strategically woven into the message of the main parties. This is aimed at attracting more voters and mobilizing those already "owned." Defining and analyzing populism solely as a political or social phenomenon is, however, only one of the possible perspectives. Populism is also a phenomenon of marketing importance. It involves the segmentation and targeting of voters and the positioning of politicians and political parties.

The chapter analyzes the phenomenon of populism in Poland, from the perspective of a "thin" ideology and as a strategy in political marketing. The emergence and development of populism in post-communist Poland was influenced by both historical factors and sociopolitical divisions. According to Przyłecki (2012), these include, above all: difficulty in adapting to the requirements of the market economy, weakness of the democratic system, corruption of political elites, and lack of political sophistication of the elites and society. These factors were also influenced by globalization processes. The result of these conditions was the appearance on the Polish political scene, both on the left and on the right, of people proclaiming various populist messages. They are based on five basic narratives of dissatisfaction (Kotwas & Kubik, 2019; Sadecka, 2023; Yatsyk, 2020): historical dissatisfaction (lack of justice, e.g., decommunization, sense of betrayal by the West, and euroscepticism); dissatisfaction with the state (lack of trust in state institutions, corrupt elites); economic dissatisfaction (need to "re-Polonize" the economy, social protection for various social groups); ontological dissatisfaction (lack of respect for national traditions and symbols, and religion); and cultural dissatisfaction (immigrants, LGBTQ+).

Poland also seems to be a particularly interesting case (especially compared to the situation in Hungary or Slovakia now, in 2024) because after eight years of rule by the Law and Justice (*Prawo i Sprawiedliwość*; *PiS*), the elections in October 2023 were announced in Europe as a victory of democracy over populism and as proof that "populists can be beaten" (*The Economist*, 2023). In this context, however, it is worth asking questions: has populism really failed in Poland? Have citizens stopped being populists and have become resistant to populist narratives, or has one populist message been replaced by another?

POPULISM AS A "THIN" IDEOLOGY

A comprehensive, "full" ideology is a belief system, the configuration of ideas and attitudes in which the elements are bound by some form of constraint or functional interdependence (Converse, 1964). The ideologies are the shared framework of mental models that groups of individuals possess and that provide both interpretation of the environment and a prescription for how that environment should be structured (Denzau & North, 1994). They contain particular interpretations and configurations of all major political concepts attached to a general plan of public policy that a specific society requires. They provide politicians with a broad conceptual map of politics into which political events, current problems, voters' preferences, and other parties' policies can be fitted. Thus, ideology in this sense is a set of coherent issue positions, and this consistency has been understood to form in one dimension: left to right or liberal to conservative. However, an ideological belief system, such as liberalism and conservatism, acquires coherence and structure from psychological needs, motives, and constraints that vary both situationally and dispositionally (Jost et al., 2008; Lüders et al., 2020; Rovira Kaltwasser, 2021).

On the other hand, according to a commonly accepted definition, populism is a "thin" ideology that "considers society to be ultimately separated into two homogeneous and antagonistic groups, 'the pure people' versus the 'corrupt elite', and which argues that politics should be an expression of the *volonté générale* (general will) of the people" (Mudde, 2004, p. 543). "Thin" ideologies are those "whose morphological structure is restricted to a set of core concepts which alone are unable to provide a reasonably broad, if not comprehensive, range of answers to the political questions that societies generate" (Stanley, 2008, p. 99). Then, as a thin-centered ideology, populism is easily combined with very different (thin and full) other ideologies, including conservatism, communism, ecologism, nationalism, or socialism (Mudde, 2004). The main reason the populists need to associate with other ideologies, rightists or leftists, is because populist ideology is not sufficiently comprehensive to translate into a coherent and multidimensional policy offer in its own right. In consequence, the populist message is partly dependent on the content of the host ideology. For example, while the exclusionist nativism of the populist radical right elicits disrespect for the rights of ethnic or religious minorities, the populist radical left is more focused on economic questions and the "capitalist enemy," and is more prone to violate ownership rights (Havlík, 2019).

Moreover, populism can also have a centrist variant (Stanley, 2017). In this incarnation, populists largely focus on exploiting dissatisfaction with corrupt and incompetent elites. "Centrist populism is a form of political populism that emphasizes the anti-establishment element of its appeal" (Učeň, 2004, p. 48). Its distinguishing feature is a pragmatic approach to serve as a substitute for the thick-ideological aspects of their appeal, and the foregrounding of qualities such as competence, probity, and newness. Centrist-populist parties position themselves as an alternative to either (conservative or liberal) side in principal political conflict. Then, instead of ideology, such parties (for example, *Action of Dissatisfied Citizens*, *ANO* in Czechia or *Party of Civic Understanding*, *SOP* in Slovakia) try to "sell" their technocratic or managerial qualities related to leadership or competence (Havlík, 2019). They shift the emphasis from the differences between the proposed policies (in terms of standard cleavages) to one that focused on how politics is conducted.

Petrivić et al. (2022) in their analysis, based on Stanley's (2008) characterization of radical and centrist populism, focused on ruling populist leaders and their parties from Central and Eastern Europe that are members of the EU: three radical populists – *Fidesz* (Hungary), *Law and Justice* (*PiS*; Poland), *Slovenian Democratic Party* (*SDS*; Slovenia), and three centrist populists – *Citizens for European Development of Bulgaria* (*GERB*; Bulgaria), *ANO* (Czechia), and *Ordinary People and Independent Personalities* (*OĽaNO*; Slovakia). They found that radical right-wing populist parties are more oriented toward national histories, memory wars against ex-communists, and critical events for losing or gaining their national sovereignty. Centrist populist parties largely ignore that kind of narrative and focus on anti-corruption or promises of managing the state more effectively. Radical right-wing populist parties are also more likely to challenge the Brussels elites by using examples from their national histories. In their analysis, Petković et al. (2022) focused mainly on the European dimension of the populism of these ruling parties, more precisely on the opposition of the "nation" to the "European elites" in Brussels. Euroscepticism is an important aspect of populism in Central and Eastern Europe, including Poland. However, this is only one aspect.

However, regardless of the ideological component or its absence, the core of populism as a "thin" ideology consists of four distinct but interrelated concepts (Stanley, 2008, p. 102):

- "The existence of two homogeneous units of analysis: 'the people' and 'the elite'.
- The antagonistic relationship between the people and the elite.
- The idea of popular sovereignty.
- The positive valorization of 'the people' and denigration of 'the elite'."

The basic dimension of populism is the way in which populist actors define who belongs to "the people" vis-à-vis "the elite." In other words, it is crucial to determine who is included and who is excluded from these opposing social constructs and based on what criteria: material (refer to the distribution of state resources, both monetary and nonmonetary, to specific groups in society; e.g., poor vs. the rich), political (refer to political participation and public contestation; e.g., natives vs. immigrants), or symbolic (e.g., cultural or religious differences) (Mudde & Rovira Kaltwasser, 2013).

Defining populism as a "thin" ideology seems to implicitly assume that it is the ideology component that is matched to the populist "scaffolding." In other words, populism is ideologized to expand popular support for replacing liberal democracy with an alternative form of regime. This is the path that *Kukiz'15* seems to follow in Poland. The *Kukiz'15* (formerly *Kukiz Movement*) leading by rock star and social activist Paweł Kukiz constituted a populist attack on the established political system and parties, depicting the party system as a closed cartel of professional politicians, which had become entirely detached from the needs and concerns of ordinary Poles. The movement consciously sought to avoid defining itself ideologically, arguing that manifestos were symptoms of the problem with party politics. However, Paweł Kukiz's social conservatism and the willingness of the movement to populate its electoral list with representatives of numerous minor radical right parties and movements bore witness to a strongly nationalist tendency, and its hostility to the European Union (EU) also suggested that it was congenial to the anti-liberal insurgency (Stanley, 2019; Szczerbiak, 2017). Despite the joint electoral coalition with the agrarian *Polish People's Party* (*Polskie Stronnictwo Ludowe*; *PSL*) in the 2019 parliamentary election, at the end of May 2021, *Kukiz'15* concluded a program agreement with the right-wing ruling *Law and Justice* (*PiS*).

The most in-depth empirical and theoretical analysis of the thin-centered ideological populism of Polish political parties and the populist attitudes of Poles were conducted by Stanley (2008, 2017, 2019; Stanley & Cześnik, 2022). His empirical analyses mainly focus on the October 2015 Polish parliamentary election, which brought a stunning victory of the right-wing opposition *Law and Justice* party (*PiS*), which became the first in post-communist Poland to secure an outright parliamentary majority, and an equally comprehensive defeat of the incumbent liberal Civic Platform (*Platforma Obywatelska*; *PO*). According to Szczerbiak (2017), in addition to the fact that the outgoing ruling party could no longer rely on its strategy of mobilizing passive anti-*PiS* voters by resorting to the "politics of fear," the main factor in the success of the right-wing opposition was the widespread disillusionment with the country's ruling elite, accompanied by a strong belief that it's time for a change. It was connected to the skepticism about the outgoing government's rhetoric about its achievements and the wider success of the post-communist transformation, widespread among many Poles, especially younger ones, living outside major urban centers, frustrated that they had no part in it.

Stanley's (2019) goal of analyzing the survey data from the 2015 Polish National Election Study was to determine whether the supply-side divide between populist and nonpopulist parties that has emerged over the last decade in Poland is reflected on the demand side (Stanley, 2019). More specifically, he wanted to find answers to two questions: *Do populist attitudes correlate with economic and cultural attitudes?* and *Do populist attitudes predict voting behavior for populist parties?* He assumed that the criterion (at least controversial and subjective, see Aslandis, 2016) for distinguishing populist and nonpopulist parties is that the former contest the liberal model of democracy, and the latter – broadly accept it. According to Stanley (2019), the populist parties are: *Law and Justice* (PiS) and *Kukiz'15*, and the nonpopulist ones are: *Civic Platform* (PO) and *Modern* (*Nowoczesna*). This classification results from the fact that the political message of *PiS* and *Kukiz'15* links populist arguments to a set of cultural attitudes that embrace traditionalism, nativism, and skepticism toward supranational integration, and in *PiS*'s case to a more market-sceptic and interventionist set of positions on economic policy. On the other hand, *PO* and *Nowoczesna* avoid populist rhetoric and arguments, and have a broadly liberal stance on economic and cultural issues. First, the results of Stanley's analysis showed what he assumed: the more respondents hold antiliberal views on both cultural and economic issues, the stronger their adherence to populist views. Further, with regard to the sentiments or liking of particular parties, he found that populism is associated with more positive attitudes toward *PiS* and *Kukiz'15*. However, in the case of *PiS*, the effect of populism diminished and became insignificant when cultural and ideological attitudes are added to the model. In contrast, for *PO* and *Nowoczesna*, as populism increases, the probability of liking both parties declines. Then, it seems that, in some cases, cultural and populist attitudes combine to amplify the extent to which parties are liked or disliked. However, what is particularly worth emphasizing, analysis of the intentions of supporting individual parties (both populist and not) has shown that there is no clear evidence that the same effect is present in the case of vote choice, with no statistically significant changes in the impact of populism on vote choice at different levels of cultural liberalism.

In the context of the same Polish parliamentary elections in 2015, but without a formal division of parties into populist and nonpopulist ones, Stanley and Cześnik (2022) found that respondents with high levels of populism and political knowledge were more likely to vote for parties of the right (i.e., *PiS*, *Kukiz'15*, or the minor libertarian party *KORWiN*) than those with high populism but low political knowledge, those with low populism but high political knowledge, or those with low levels of both. In contrast, the probability of voting for liberal parties (i.e., *PO* or *Nowoczesna*), increased as political knowledge increases, but this relationship is mediated by the level of populism, in such a way that the negative relationship between populism and voting was strengthened as political knowledge increased. Furthermore, the level of populism had no statistically significant influence on the probability of voting for a party of the left (i.e., *Zjednoczona Lewica* [*United Left*] or *Razem* [*Together*]), regardless of a voter's level of political knowledge.

To sum up, the results of the analysis conducted by Stanley (2019) and Stanley and Cześnik (2022) seem to suggest that support for "populist" parties (especially *PiS*) is mainly conditioned by thick ideology, which is attractive to voters with specific demographic and psychological characteristics and value systems. In this aspect, these results are consistent with those obtained by Vasilopoulos and Jost (2020) based on data from the 2017 French Election Study. They investigated the psychological characteristics of supporters of the French populist parties – left-wing (the *Left Front* leading by Jean-Luc Mélenchon) and right-wing (the *Front National* leading by Marine Le Pen), and they found that support for Mélenchon and LePen was driven more by the fact that they represented left-wing and right-wing options than the fact that they represented populist ideals. These results seem to confirm that populist appeals may be an important element that complements and strengthens the ideological message addressed to specific segments of voters. Their demographic and psychological characteristics are "specific" to adherents of different ideologies, rather than to general populist attitudes *per se*. More generally, the frame of *inclusionary populism* is a reinforcement of the leftist message, which demands that rights and resources are extended to minority as well as majority groups. On the other hand, the frame of *exclusionary populism* is a reinforcement of the rightist message that regards members of ethnic, religious, and sexual minorities as violating the homogeneous whole that is assumed to constitute the "native" majority population.

The results presented by Stanley and Cześnik (2022) also suggest that in the Polish case, there is evidence that parties of the right have been able to mobilize voters with populist attitudes regardless of their level of political knowledge, and that much of their support is drawn from politically well-informed and socio-economically secure members of society who hold populist views. Therefore, the appeals of Polish parties combining populism with ideology (at least conservative ones) may be more effective in discouraging voting or supporting "hostile" (i.e., liberal) parties than in generating support for themselves in the segment of people with populist attitudes. Moreover, it also means that populist appeals can have a certain controlled impact on the entire electorate, and not just and exclusively on their core supporters.

POPULISM AS A POLITICAL MARKETING STRATEGY

Researchers accepting that populism is a "thin" ideology strongly emphasize that it is primarily moralistic rather than programmatic or strategic (Mudde, 2004; Mudde & Rovira Kaltwasser, 2013). It can be assumed, with a certain oversimplification, that from the perspective of political marketing, a "populist" party as an exponent of a "thin" ideology is another option on the political scene that is trying to win elections and introduce its rule. Furthermore, a careful look at the functioning of political parties over the years shows the need to take into account a different approach to populism. Stanley (2008) notes that political parties may become more populist at one point in time than at another (e.g., during an election campaign). Some of them may retain over time a consistent combination of populism and ideology, and, in some cases, they may also exhibit no particular ideological consistency, thin or full. In other words, parties can "regulate the volume" of their populism depending on their strategic goals. This seems particularly evident in the actions and maneuvers of mainstream parties. In such cases, it is not populism that is ideologized, but ideology consciously "supplemented" by populist appeals. This does not mean that these parties become "populist."

According to Mudde (2004), we are witnessing a populist *Zeitgeist*. He claims that radical left and right-wing populist parties are gaining support, and that in response to this development, mainstream parties are increasingly using populist rhetoric. An example of this phenomenon is what happened on the Polish political scene at the beginning of the 21st century. In 2001, as Stanley (2008, 2019) describes, a wave of dissatisfaction with the reforms of transition, and the political class responsible for their implementation led to significant party system change, with four parties entering parliament for the first time. Two of these parties, *Self-Defence* (*Samoobrona Rzeczypospolitej Polskiej*; *SRP*) and *the League of Polish Families* (*Liga Polskich Rodzin*; *LPR*), were not allied with either side of the regime divide. Instead, they articulated a populist critique of the transition elite as a whole, contesting the legitimacy of the current political system and decrying the economic inequalities it generated, and the threats they felt it posed to Polish traditions and identity. After the next Polish parliamentary elections in 2005, the winning *PiS* invited the *SRP* and *LPR* to form a government. This "populist coalition" strongly criticized liberalism and offered a comprehensive and compelling alternative narrative for those who rejected the liberal orthodoxy. During its short period in office, *PiS* succeeded in marginalizing its radical coalition partners and absorbing a significant proportion of their electorates, but in doing so became significantly more radical and populist in its own right. This "takeover" was confirmed by the results of the 2007 elections, in which no *SRP* and *LPR* candidates were elected to parliament.

This situation seems to fully confirm Mudde's (2004, p. 563) reflection that, "when explicitly populist outsider groups gain prominence, parts of the establishment will react by a combined strategy of exclusion and inclusion; while trying to exclude the populist actor(s) from political power, they will include populist themes and rhetoric to try and fight off the challenge." In this manner, populism is contagious. However, as Rooduijn et al. (2014) infer, given that populism is a "thin" ideology, it can be expected that mainstream parties have to not only change the way they speak about the people, but have to also change the way they think about the people. These changes should be, then, reflected in the "adjustments" of mainstream parties' manifestos in a more populist direction. In order to empirically verify this hypothesis, they content analyzed the election manifestos of mainstream and populist parties in five Western European countries (Italy, The Netherlands, France, Germany, and the United Kingdom) in the period from 1988 to 2008. The results indicate that the manifestos of mainstream parties have not become more populist. Instead, they found that populist parties change their own manifestos when they have been successful: Their initial success makes them tone down their populism. Then, Rooduijn et al. (2014) conclude, populism need not be a deeply rooted worldview, and it can just be used strategically to gain votes. This does not mean, of course, that populist content is not present in the manifestos of mainstream parties, but that it is not significantly increasing.

From this perspective, populist appeals can also be regarded as just another element of marketing strategies: persuasive and mobilizing. They are used to gain the support of "new" voters and/or to mobilize their (more or less undecided) supporters, often with the support of "populist skirmishers." In Poland, they are "politicians, publicists, and activists who ruthlessly fight tactical battles that suit the general party agenda while pursuing their own career schedules" (Zbytniewska, 2022, p. 72). Such a "practical" dimension of populist appeals is implied by the results of Stanley and Cześnik's analyses. Then, it is "cynical" or "tactical" populism. Yoshida (2020) comes to a similar conclusion in the context of Japanese politics. By examining cases of populist Japanese governors and mayors, he shows that populism in Japan must be understood as a political strategy employed by the local executives and not an ideology or organizational structure. It is a form of political style that maximizes mobilization in order to win an election in particular circumstances. It seems, that "any organization, institution, or group of individuals can be labeled by populists as 'the enemy of the people' if and when it stands in the way of the 'will of the people'" (Kucharczyk, 2019).

The goal of politics and politicians is to satisfy the needs and expectations of the people as well as their well-being and to constantly improve the quality of life. In this way, politicians are in the business of selling hope to citizens (Cwalina et al., 2011; Newman, 1994). This hope is related to convincing people it is this particular politician or party that guarantees successful management of national security, social stability, and/or economic growth on behalf of the electorate. Not all politicians, of course, have a clearly and precisely defined goal to which they want to lead the society. Some of them are completely win-oriented, and they view policy only as a means to of winning the election (Downs, 1957). They tactically react to changes in the electorate's feelings, trying to fine-tune to the voters.

From an ideological marketing perspective (Cwalina & Falkowski, 2022), there is a trade-off between the desirability of the platform (from the candidate's point of view) and the probability of the platform position winning (voters' needs and wants). Compromising on policy is thus not a sign that the candidate is only interested in winning, but it is perfectly consistent with the expected policy maximization. If a party, more or less ideological, wants to be successful, it must create and deliver a wanted political offer. It must follow the marketing concept.

As Henneberg (2006a, 2006b) argues, political parties have two different dimensions to choose from: leading or following. If the politicians try to lead, they know that their political concept (political product, ideology) is essentially right. Leading consists of trying to convince voters of the beneficial nature of a political offer and influencing others to do something to realize a political concept. If the politicians try to follow, they guess, anticipate and analyze the wishes of the biggest possible number of voters. Here, political marketing is not so much a managerial tool to execute strategies, as the strategy itself to develop a political offering.

Depending on a party's or candidate's position relative to their focus on driving the political market (leading) or being driven by it (following), Henneberg distinguished four generic strategic postures: the Relationship Builder (high in market-driving and high in market-driven), the Convinced Ideologist (high/low), the Tactical Populist (low/high), and the Political Lightweight (low/low; in fact it does not participate in the competition). They exemplify in marketing terms how the party organization aspires to be perceived by citizens relative to its competitors. Although Henneberg believes that the most mature and democratic posture is building a relationship that combines the desire to lead the country with the best understanding of the needs of voters, the combination of these two attitudes can also be characteristic of a completely different type of party, which can be described as an Ideological Populist. It combines a commitment to ideology and the desire to implement it with reliance on marketing strategies that can bring this goal closer.

The Convinced Ideologist scores high on the leading-scale, while its following capabilities are not fully developed. This posture is characterized by a clear focal point for policymaking – implementing ideological postulates. Preferences of voters or opinion shifts are secondary. The CI party concentrates on persuading and convincing voters to follow its proposals, without, however, paying too much attention to how they react to those proposals. In turn, the Tactical Populist is characterized by following more than leading. It reacts, above all, to changes in the electorate's feelings, trying to fine-tune to the voters. Therefore, strategic marketing techniques are applied to ensure that the political propositions on offer are always in synchronization with public opinion. Recognizing the political pulse of the electorate is its most important strategic aim. Therefore, strategic marketing techniques (microsegmentation and concentration on marginal seats and swing voters) are applied to ensure that its political propositions are best fitted to voters' current needs and opinions. If these two attitudes toward marketing activities are professionally coordinated, it can be an important element of electoral success. It seems crucial here to recognize the needs of voters and reformulate ideological postulates in such a way that they constitute an attractive response to these needs. The use of populism here seems to be one of the possible frames encompassing both of these postures. Such a strategy must be flexible with regard to the core characteristics of its political offer, which can change rapidly.

The main electoral aim of candidates and parties is to mobilize core supporters and attract voters who are "potentially available" (Cwalina et al., 2011; Lees-Marshemnt, 2009). One of the key elements in mobilizing supporters is cueing their ideological thinking, also using populist appeals. Hameleers and his collaborators (2018) conducted a comparative experiment in sixteen European countries (including Poland), and found that antielitist populism has a strong mobilizing effect on political engagement, but only in countries with a stronger populist left. However, anti-immigrant messages demobilize voters more in countries with a more successful populist left and mobilize voters when they resonate with the electoral success of the populist right.

Unlike core supporters, independents do not possess strong ideological or partisan schema, and they are less likely to filter campaign communications in a consistent manner. Thus, independents need to be persuaded and mobilized, while partisans mainly need to be mobilized. Campaign effects occur not only through winning the hearts and minds of some voters but also by getting the right people – their likely supporters – to turn out to vote.

The challenge facing ideology is, in particular, to "package" and frame its offer in such a way that it is attractive and acceptable to a large part of the electorate and does not alienate existing supporters (Cwalina et al., 2015), so they can consider shifting toward the views and attitudes of voters. However, this is not a very common option, as indicated by the analysis of Rooduijn and his collaborates (2014). Another strategy may be merely temporarily change in the campaign platform, which will return to the ideological baseline after winning the elections. Such a change in strategy was typical of neoliberal candidates (*PO*) in the Polish election campaigns in 2015 (parliamentary and presidential). Analyzes conducted by Borowiec (2020) prove that the passive strategy (accusing rivals of populism) was successively replaced by an active strategy (one's own populist proposals) as support for opposition candidates (mainly from *PiS*) increased.

Change in the campaign platform may also happen after the formation of the government. Cwalina and Drzewiecka (2022), with the example of the right-wing *PiS* party, showed how perceived trust triumphs criticism and how giving, fulfilling, and enabling promises leads to success in politics. The biggest victory of this party came in the 2015 presidential and parliamentary elections and brought political changes in the justice and media system, which led to clashes with the EU. Despite this, the *PiS* is perceived as a "guarantee" of successful management of national security and independence, social, and economic growth, but in line with a conservative vision with populistic elements and with values such as dignity, nation, tradition, and family life. However, in the context of *PiS*, it is also worth noting that by fulfilling his election promises (more or less populist), he undermined one of the reasons for his success (Stanley, 2024, p. 768). Promises once fulfilled cannot be fulfilled again.

Another point of the intersection of ideology and populism in marketing strategies is inducing and managing the polarization of the electorate (Cwalina & Falkowski, 2022). Conflict is the basis of politics, and it is something natural for the humans. Most often it takes the form of a conflict of wants, conflict of interests, or a conflict of values. It makes that angry attacks substitute reasoned discussion, and it leads to a "culture war." "'Culture war' refers to displacement of the classic economic conflict that animated twentieth-century politics in the advanced democracies by newly emergent moral and religious one" (Fiorina et al., 2006, p. 2). These new divisions based on sexuality, morality, and religion are deep enough to justify fears of violence and talk of war in describing them. However, as Fiorina and his collaborators (2006) state, this conflict, more or less consciously and strategically, is aroused by ideology-oriented politicians. Ideology, similarly to populism, entails the construction of a binary divide between antagonistic groups: "us" and "them."

Populist framing can be one of the tools used to achieve this goal, especially since they usually evoke strong negative emotions (e.g., anger and fear) in their recipients (Hameleers et al., 2017; Wirz, 2018). Populist framing can equally be perceived as the systematic dissemination of a frame that diagnoses reality as problematic – because "corrupt elites" have unjustly usurped the sovereign authority of the "noble people" – and maintains that the solution to the problem resides in the righteous political mobilization of the latter in order to regain power (Aslandis, 2016). It is a conscious and planned activity with a purpose to persuade audiences to tune into their own representation of reality (Cwalina et al., 2015). Caiani and della Porta (2011) analyzing the extreme right-wing discourses in Italy and Germany found that in the frames of the extreme right, there is a rather exclusive vision of the people, which refers to a strongly hierarchical and elitist conception of society. Indeed, not only corrupt political elites but also other political and ethnic adversaries are excluded from this conception of the people, which is, furthermore, relegated to a passive role in politics. Framing can also be aimed at activating populist attitudes of citizens. In an experiment conducted in 15 countries, Hameleers and his collaborates (2021) investigated the effects of populist framing that stress the centrality of "ordinary" people, shift blame to the "corrupt" elites, or combine people centrality and antielitist cues. Their results suggest that messages stressing the centrality of the ordinary people activate all dimensions of populist attitudes: antielitism, homogeneous people, and popular sovereignty. In contrast, antielite messages activate antielitism attitudes only for those individuals with lower levels of education and extreme positions on the ideological left-right spectrum.

Ideologists can also focus only on certain selected issues and try to "remove" the remaining ones from the voters' field of attention by covering them with a smokescreen. Noury and Roland (2020) point to two main factors that contribute to the rise of populism and the reaction of political parties to changes in voter attitudes: cultural and economic. Among the cultural causes they mention: opposition to multiculturalism and a backlash against cultural evolution toward gender equality, laws against discrimination of ethnic and sexual minorities, etc. In turn, the economic factors include the effects of globalization and trade openness, rising inequality, and adverse income shocks generated by the Great Recession. However, some factors are potentially both economic and cultural, as in the case of opposition to immigration. From these two areas, specific issues are selected, which are populistically used as "the wedge issues." The wedge issue is "any policy concern that is used to divide the opposition's potential winning coalition" (Hillygus & Shields, 2008, p. 36). These issues are typically positional, on which people take different sides and that have different policy-outcome goals. They are chosen to elicit a specific response, especially among the independents and cross-pressured partisans, those who disagree with their affiliated party on this issue. Candidates look, then, for issues that will bridge their core supporters and the persuadable voters. In the case of Polish political campaigns, such wedge issues have become, for example, the 2015 immigration crisis and economic shock. Both of these issues not only attracted the attention of the media and political commentators, but, more importantly, were the subject of scientific empirical analyses.

Immigration Crisis and Strategic Populism

In the case of right-wing populism in Europe, populists oppose innocent and always hard-working people also against culpable others (e.g., immigrants) who do not work and who live off the work of others (Noury & Roland, 2020). The 2015 refugee crisis lifted the issue of immigration higher on the list of political concerns throughout Europe. Pappas and Kriesi (2015) documented that this crisis positively affects the vote shares of European right-wing populist parties. Moreover, the mainstream parties, both on the left and on the right, were affected by the success of the radical right parties and shifted their positions on immigration toward greater radicalization (Abou-Chadi & Krause, 2020).

After winning the 2015 elections, *PiS*'s government has been redefining Poland's position with respect to the most critical issues surrounding Europe and the EU, such as the Eurozone crisis, Brexit, and the problem of refugee migration into Europe. Regarding the latter, *PiS* has refused to implement the refugee distribution arrangement agreed on by the former cabinet, arguing that it realizes a "German plan" at the cost of Poland's national interests. While this kind of policy finds little understanding with most European partners, it enjoys relatively high popularity on the home front, among Poles. According to Cap (2018), this is due to a skillful rhetorical campaign, which not only legitimizes that policy but also, and consequently, plays a key role in legitimizing the new government as a whole. He analyzed a corpus of 124 addresses, statements, and comments by the most prominent PiS politicians: Jarosław Kaczyński (the PiS leader), Beata Szydło (the 2015–2017 Prime Minister in the PiS government), Witold Waszczykowski (the Minister of Foreign Affairs), and Mariusz Błaszczak (the Minister of the Interior and Administration). Their time frame is the 17-month period between 1 November 2015 (a week after the PiS electoral victory) and 31 March 2017. Cap's (2018) goal was to account for elements of the "us" central camp, then elements of the "them"-remote camp, and the threat construction patterns involving a symbolic invasion of entities of the latter camp on the former. A substantial part of PiS's anti-immigration discourse includes the description of "us" – Poland, Poles, and the current Polish government – in deeply conservative, ideological-religious terms. References to traditional Polish values (e.g., "national sovereignty" or "*As Christian, we raised to be tolerant and respectful of other cultures. But we ask the same kind of respect from others*") are construed as warrants of personal and economic well-being as well as personal and national security. The main purpose of these linguistic treatments is the conceptual consolidation of the "us" camp and instilling a sense of social belonging and solidarity in the face of an outside threat. In turn, "them" is construed as culturally, socio-politically, and ideologically alien and potentially antagonistic to the "us." Then, immigrants are presented as having socio-cultural, religious, and biological characteristics that preclude their inclusion in Poland, thus generating frustration and anger. Moreover, associations are also created between immigrants, especially Muslims, and terrorists. Cap (2018) emphasizes that many of these characteristics stand in sharp contrast to conservative values of the "us" camp, particularly the traditional family values. The third rhetorical device is the constructing proximization of the "them" impact on the "us." An example of this can be a fragment of Mariusz Błaszczak's statement: "See the young Muslim criminals. See the anger, violence, and terror. It is there and is ready for export. This evil might not have reached us yet, but it is well in sight. And there is no-one in Brussels who can protect us when it comes" (Cap, 2018, p. 392).

Migration of refugee groups into Europe – mainly from Syria, but also other countries of the Middle East as well as East Africa – was and is consistently conceptualized by *PiS* as a growing threat to Poland's national security. The threat is construed in ideological as well as populist terms, involving strategic interplay of abstract and material fear appeals. The construal of the threat rests on forced conceptualizations of a destructive impact of the apparently distant entities (immigrant groups from external territories – a symbolic "them") on the home entities (Poland and other European countries – a symbolic "us").

In sum, Cap's (2018) analysis show how *PiS*'s government populistically manufactured and perpetuated the aura of fear by conflating the issue of refugee migration into Europe with the problem of global terrorism, and how virtual threats to Polish cultural legacy and values are conceived to justify the government's opposition to the idea of the multiethnic and multicultural state in general.

Economic Shock and Strategic Populism

Economic shocks present an opportunity for political parties to win votes by offering (populist) policy promises targeted at exposed voters. On January 15, 2015, the Swiss National Bank (SNB) suspended its exchange rate floor of 1.20 euro/CHF and allowed the Swiss franc to appreciate. The move was a response to strong exchange market pressure on the Swiss franc and growing domestic criticism of the peg. The SNB announcement completely surprised financial market participants and policymakers – both in Switzerland and abroad. The bank did not give the Swiss government or other international monetary institutions any significant warning. The exchange rate very quickly became so unstable that Swiss banks temporarily stopped converting Swiss francs into euros. Also, the decision resulted in huge losses and even bankruptcies among foreign exchange brokers and banks. Moreover, the Swiss franc exchange rates against the euro and other currencies, including the Polish zloty, increased drastically. At this time, in Poland were more than 500,000 households repaying CHF-denominated loans, mostly mortgages. The immediate and most visible consequences of the exchange rate shock were thus largely restricted to one group, the so-called *Frankowiczów*, that is, the 4% of Polish households repaying CHF-denominated debts.

The *PO* and *PSL* coalition government was initially reluctant to engage in any meaningful support for CHF borrowers. However, the issue became highly politicized during the May 2015 presidential campaign, when the opposition *PiS*'s candidate, Andrzej Duda, proposed the conversion of Swiss franc debts into Polish zloty at a preferential exchange rate. Furthermore, the opposition parties, with *PiS* among them, together with the government coalition member, *PSL*, passed an amended bill in parliament that broadened eligibility for loan conversion. However, no final decision was made by the parliament before the 2015 parliamentary election won decisively by *PiS* (Ahlquist et al., 2020).

In the context of this crisis, Ahlquist et al. (2020) fielded a survey immediately before the October elections to study how Polish voters evaluated these different policy proposals and how they voted in the 2015 elections. The results show that the small group of respondents with these loans (*Frankowicze*) had strong and distinct policy preferences in line with their material economic interests, whereas those without CHF-denominated mortgages were both less interested in and less inclined to support policy from which they would not directly benefit. What's more important, those directly exposed to the CHF shock – unlikely *PiS* supporters – became far more likely to shift their support from the incumbent *PO* to the challenger *PiS*. This shift likely produced additional parliamentary seats for the *PiS*. As Ahlquist and his collaborates estimate, there is about a 1 in 3 chance that the *PiS* would not have won its outright majority absent the electoral effects of the CHF shock.

These results clearly indicate that Polish voters repaying foreign currency denominated loans were directly exposed to the CHF shock, favored populist and generous bailout policies, and were more likely to switch their vote to the opposition party that offered it: the *PiS*.

CONCLUSION

Treating populism as an ideology leads to a dichotomous process of classification: a political party or leader can or cannot be populist. There is no gray zone (Aslandis, 2016). From the perspective of political marketing, populism is a matter of degree. In the messages of virtually all political parties, populist appeals can be easily noticed. Then, it's not that important if they are populist, but rather how many and how intense they are.

The examples presented in this chapter focused on the manifestations of populism in Polish politics, and in particular on the strategies used mainly by *Law and Justice* (*PiS*). However, the effectiveness of these strategies in gaining and maintaining voter support at a high level also encourages other Polish parties, considered to be nonpopulist (Stanley, 2019), to adopt this strategy. For example, on 23 February 2023, in a television program, the leader of the opposition *Civic Platform* (*PO*), Donald Tusk, announced that when they win the elections, he will implement a new program, which he called "Cell plus" ("Cela plus") aimed at the currently ruling *PiS*: "'Cell plus' will be a program even better prepared for all those who built this system of milking the state in such an unprecedented and so well-organized way when it comes to money" (Szpyrka, 2023). In turn, on 23 March 2023, during a meeting with voters, he said: "We will offer 1,500 zloty for grandmothers for every mother who would like to return to work after maternity leave" (Kucharczyk, 2023). As the campaign progressed, further promises were announced, for example, the introduction of a "widow's pension" for the oldest citizens who lost their spouses, and the abolition of the saving tax (so-called "the Belka's tax") or prohibiting homework in grades 1–3 of primary schools. It seems, therefore, that the "contagion of populism" can also occur at the marketing level between mainstream parties. Furthermore, as Polish cases demonstrate, political parties play a significant role in developing populist arguments, but other actors, such as Polish Catholic Church, civil activists, religious groups apply the populist rhetoric in their activities as well. It is not only the "elite" but also different "others" (e.g., pro- vs. antiabortion groups, traditional vs. LGBT community), who are viewed as the inimical opponents to the "good Polish people" (Borowiec, 2020; Yatsyk, 2020).

Both "real" and strategic (or "reactive") populism can have negative consequences for democracy: in Poland as in any other democratic country. According to Havlík (2019), in the eyes of populists, democracy is a one-sided phenomenon: it refers only to the power of the people. Populism is a threat to contemporary democracies not because it is fundamentally undemocratic, but because it is illiberal. The populist perception of politics relies on one single divide: the moral conflict between the good people and the bad elite. Since populism is based on the principle of homogeneity of the people, there is very little space for political pluralism. Populism draws its strength from the confused and often opportunistic democratic promises of the political elites. It is "first and foremost about the perceived degeneration of representative democracy" (Akkerman, 2003, p. 149). In this age of egalitarianism, the defense of the elitist aspects of liberal democracy becomes more and more like political suicide. Consequently, politicians left, right, and center are emphasizing almost exclusively the importance of the popular aspects, that is, the democratic side.

However, in most cases, populists are reformist rather than revolutionary, and they do not oppose political parties *per se*. Rather, they oppose the established parties and call for (or claim to be) a new kind of party. They express populist antiparty sentiments rather than extremist antiparty sentiments (Mudde, 2004, p. 156). Nevertheless, as Akkerman (2003, p. 156) points out, "an unmediated and unrestrained popular will, therefore, is a populist ideal that should not be confounded with democratic principles". It seems that, as Stanley (2024, p. 768) states, "in a world where most people have at least some reasons to be dissatisfied with a given government and trust elites less and less, populism will remain an effective tool for constructing narratives in which various sources of irritation receive common explanation." However, the question still remains unanswered whether populism has actually been beaten in Poland. And whether it can be definitively defeated in other countries.

There is no doubt that populism is a threat to democracy because it "stupefies" citizens, builds on their weaknesses, and, as a consequence, makes them thoughtless (Cwalina & Falkowski, 2008). The main danger here lies in people's mixing fiction with reality. Spontaneity is thus eliminated, critical thinking is "switched off," and individual's original psychological acts are replaced with somebody else's feelings, thoughts, and desires (Fromm, 1941/s).

REFERENCES

Abou-Chadi, T., & Krause, W. (2020). The causal effect of radical right success on mainstream parties' policy positions: A regression discontinuity approach. *British Journal of Political Science*, *50*(3), 829–847.

Ahlquist, J., Copelovitch, M., & Walter, S. (2020). The political consequences of external economic shocks: Evidence from Poland. *American Journal of Political Science*, *64*(4), 904–920.

Akkerman, T. (2003). Populism and democracy: Challenge or pathology? *Acta Politica*, *38*(2), 147–159.

Aslanidis, P. (2016). Is populism an ideology? A refutation and a new perspective. *Political Studies*, *64*(1_suppl), 88–104.

Borowiec, P. (2020). Populistyczne strategie – narzedzia polskich neoliberalnych elit w kampaniach wyborczych 2015 roku [The strategies of populism – A tools used by Polish neoliberał elites in the election campaigns of 2015]. *Studia Politologiczne*, *55*, 191–211.

Caiani, M., & della Porta, D. (2011). The elitist populism of the extreme right: A frame analysis of extreme right-wing discourses in Italy and Germany. *Acta Politica*, *46*(2), 180–202.

Cap, P. (2018). 'We don't want any immigrants or terrorist here': The linguistic manufacturing of xenophobia in the post-2015 Poland. *Discourse & Society*, *29*(4), 380–398.

Converse, P. E. (1964). The nature of belief systems in mass public. In D. E. Apter (Ed.), *Ideology and discontent* (pp. 206–261). The Free Press of Glencoe.

Cwalina, W., & Drzewiecka, M. (2022). How trust wins against criticism: Promise concept as a political branding tool. Lessons from Polish politics. In M. Moufahim (Ed.), *Political branding in turbulent times* (pp. 123–140). Palgrave Macmillan.

Cwalina, W., & Falkowski, A. (2008). Constructivist mind: False memory, freedom, and democracy. *Journal of Political Marketing*, *7*(3/4), 239–255.

Cwalina, W., & Falkowski, A. (2022). Political marketing from an ideological marketing perspective. In B. I. Newman, & T. P. Newman (Eds.), *A research agenda for political marketing* (pp. 15–49). Edward Elgar Publishing.

Cwalina, W., Falkowski, A., & Newman, B. I. (2011). *Political marketing: Theoretical and strategic foundations*. M.E. Sharpe.

Cwalina, W., Falkowski, A., & Newman, B. I. (2015). Persuasion in the political context: Opportunities and threats. In D. W. Stewart (Ed.), *Handbook of persuasion and social marketing* (Vol. 1, pp. 61–128). Praeger.

Denzau, A. T., & North, D. C. (1994). Shared mental models: Ideologies and institutions. *Kyklos*, *47*(1), 3–31.

Downs, A. (1957). *An economic theory of democracy*. HarperCollins Publishers.

Fiorina, M. P., Abrams, S. J., & Pope, J. C. (2006). *Culture war? The myth of a polarized America*. Pearson Longman.

Fromm, E. (1941/1965). *Escape from freedom*. Avon Books.

Hameleers, M., Bos, L., & de Vreese, C. H. (2017). "They did it": The effects of emotionalized blame attribution in populist communication. *Communication Research*, *44*(6), 870–900.

Hameleers, M., Bos, L., Fawzi, N., Reinemann, C., Andreadis, I., Corbu, N., Schemer, C., Schulz, A., Shaefer, T., Aalberg, T., Axelsson, S., Berganza, R., Cremonesi, C., Dahlberg, S., de Vreese, C. H., Hess, A., Kartsounidou, E., Kasprowicz, D., Matthes, J., ... Weiss-Yaniv, N. (2018). Start spreading the news: A comparative experiment on the effects of populist communication on political engagement in sixteen European countries. *The International Journal of Press/Politics*, *23*(4), 517–538.

Hameleers, M., Schmuck, D., Schulz, A., Wirz, D. S., Matthes, J., Bos, L., Corbu, N., & Andreadis, I. (2021). The effects of populist identity framing on populist attitudes across Europe: Evidence from a 15-country comparative experiment. *International Journal of Public Opinion Research*, *33*(3), 491–511.

Havlík, V. (2019). Technocratic populism and political illiberalism in Central Europe. *Problems of Post-Communism*, *66*(6), 369–384.

Henneberg, S. C. (2006a). Strategic postures of political marketing: An exploratory operationalization. *Journal of Public Affairs*, *6*(1), 15–30.

Henneberg, S. C. (2006b). Leading or following? A theoretical analysis of political marketing postures. *Journal of Political Marketing*, *5*(3), 29–46.

Hillygus, D. S., & Shields, T. G. (2008). *The persuadable voter: Wedge issues in presidential campaigns*. Princeton University Press.

Jost, J. T., Nosek, B. A., & Gosling, S. D. (2008). Ideology: Its resurgence in social, personality, and political psychology. *Perspectives on Psychological Science*, *3*(2), 126–136.

Kotwas, M., & Kubik, J. (2019). Symbolic thickening of public culture and the rise of right-wing populism in Poland. *East European Politics & Societies*, *33*(2), 435–471.

Kucharczyk, J. (2019). Democracy in Poland? From authoritarian populism to populist authoritarianism. *Public Seminar*. https://publicseminar.org/essays/democracy-in-poland/

Kucharczyk, M. (2023). *Tusk obiecuje nowe świadczenie dla matek*. Interia.pl, 23.03.2023. https://wydarzenia.interia.pl/kraj/news-tusk-obiecuje-nowe-swiadczenie-dla-matek,nId,6673284#utm_source=paste&utm_medium=paste&utm_campaign=chrome

Lees-Marshment, J. (2009). *Political marketing: Principles and applications*. Routledge.

Lüders, A., Mühleberger, C., & Jonas, E. (2020). Motivational and affective drivers of right-wing populism support: Insights from an Austrian presidential election. *Social Psychological Bulletin*, *15*(3), e2875. https://doi.org/10.32872/spb.2875

Mudde, C. (2004). The populist Zeitgeist. *Government and Opposition*, *39*(4), 541–563.

Mudde, C., & Rovira Kaltwasser, C. (2013). Exclusionary vs. inclusionary populism: Comparing contemporary Europe and Latin America. *Government and Opposition*, *48*(2), 147–174.

Newman, B. I. (1994). *The marketing of the president: Political marketing as campaign strategy*. SAGE.

Noury, A., & Roland, G. (2020). Identity politics and populism in Europe. *Annual Review of Political Science*, *23*, 421–439.

Pappas, T. S., & Kriesi, H. (2015). Populism and crisis: A fuzzy relationship. In H. Kriesi & T. S. Pappas (Eds.), *European populism in the shadow of the Great Recession* (pp. 303–325). ECPR Press.

Petković, N., Raos, V., & Fila, F. (2022). Centrist and radical right populists in Central and Eastern Europe: Divergent visions of history and the EU. *Journal of Contemporary European Studies*. https://doi.org/10.1080/14782804.2022.2051000

Przyłecki, A. (2012). Populizm w polskiej polityce. In *Analiza dyskursu polityki [Populism in Polish politics. Policy discourse analysis]*. Wydawnictwo Sejmowe.

Rooduijn, M., de Lange, S. L., & van der Brug, W. (2014). A populist Zeitgeist? Programmatic contagion by populist parties in Western Europe. *Party Politics*, *20*(4), 563–575.

Rovira Kaltwasser, C. (2021). Bringing political psychology into the study of populism. *Philosophical Transactions of the Royal Society B*, *376*(1822), 20200148. https://doi.org/10.1098/rstb.2020.0148

Sadecka, A. (2023). Zapotrzebowanie na populizm w ujeciu kulturowym: Niezadowolenie post-transformacyjne i neotradycjonalizm [The demand for populism from a cultural perspective: Post-transformation dissatisfaction and neo-traditionalism]. In J. Kubik (Ed.), *Populizm i demokracja: Romans czy dysonans?* (pp. 5–8). Fundacja im. Stefana Batorego. [Populism and democracy: Romance or dissonance?]. https://www.batory.org.pl/wp-content/uploads/2023/02/Populizm.i.demokracja_romans.czy_.dysonans.pdf

Stanley, B. (2008). The thin ideology of populism. *Journal of Political Ideologies*, *13*(1), 95–110.

Stanley, B. (2017). Populism in central and Eastern Europe. In C. Rovira Kaltwasser, P. Taggart, P. Ochoa Espejo, & P. Ostiguy (Eds.), *The Oxford handbook of populism* (pp. 140–158). Oxford University Press.

Stanley, B. (2019). A new populist divide? Correspondences of supply and demand in the 2015 Polish parliamentary elections. *East European Politics & Societies*, *33*(1), 17–43.

Stanley, B. (2024). *Populizm pozostanie polityka dla ludzi sfrustrowanych [Populism will remain politics for frustrated people]* (pp. 768). Kultura Liberalna. https://kulturaliberalna.pl/2024/01/30/populizm-pozostanie-polityka-dla-ludzi-sfrustrowanych/

Stanley, B., & Cześnik, M. (2022). Uninformed or informed populist? The relationship between political knowledge, socio-economic status and populist attitudes in Poland. *East European Politics*, *38*(1), 43–60.

Szczerbiak, A. (2017). An anti-establishment backlash that shook up the party system? The October 2015 Polish parliamentary election. *European Politics and Society*, *18*(4), 404–427.

Szpyrka, Ł. (2023). *Tusk zapowiada program "Cela plus". Polityk PiS: To junta wojskowa*. Interia.pl, 27.02.2023. https://wydarzenia.interia.pl/kraj/news-tusk-zapowiada-program-cela-plus-polityk-pis-to-junta-wojsko,nId,6621768#utm_source=paste&utm_medium=paste&utm_campaign=chrome

The Economist (2023). *Poland shows that populist can be beaten*. October 17, 2023. https://www.economist.com/leaders/2023/10/17/poland-shows-that-populists-can-be-beaten

Učeň, P. (2004). Centrist populism as a new competitive and mobilization strategy in Slovak politics. In O. Gyárfášová, & G. Mesežnikov (Eds.), *Party government in Slovakia: Experience and perspectives* (pp. 45–73). IVO (Institute for Public Affairs.

Vasilopoulos, P., & Jost, J. T. (2020). Psychological similarities and dissimilarities between left-wing and right-wing populists: Evidence from a nationally representative survey in France. *Journal of Research in Personality*, *88*, 104004.

Wirtz, D. S. (2018). Persuasion through emotion? An experimental test of the emotion-eliciting nature of populist communication. *International Journal of Communication*, *12*, 1114–1138.

Yatsyk, A. (2020). Biopolitical populism in Poland: The case of PiS. *Populism*, *3*(2), 148–164.

Yoshida, T. (2020). Populism "made in Japan": A new species? *Asian Journal of Comparative Politics*, 288–299.

Zbytniewska, K. (2022). Populist skirmishers: Frontrunners of populist radical right in Poland. *Politics and Governance*, *10*(4), 72–83.

Disinformation and Elections: Old Challenge in the New Context

Sára Cigánková, Jonáš Syrovátka and Martin Vérteši

INTRODUCTION

In recent years, the study of disinformation – factually incorrect statement spread with the intention to mislead targeted audience (as defined by Wardle & Derakhshan, 2017) – has become one of the most rapidly growing research fields, attracting interest not only in academia but also in the wider community of think tanks, journalists and specialists in state institutions. The focus on political processes – and elections in particular – has always been an incremental part in this topic (Pérez-Escolar et al., 2023). However, the problem with debating the topic of disinformation is the lack of terminological clarity within the field. There is a basic distinction between *disinformation*, *misinformation* – factually incorrect statements spread without malicious intent – and *malinformation* – genuine information spread with intent to cause harm (Wardle & Derakhshan, 2017). However, ways of using these terms vary significantly across the literature (Miró-Llinares & Aguerri, 2021). Moreover, these are not only terms used in relation to manipulative falsehoods as a significant part of the literature; the term *fake news* is used to describe this phenomenon (Kapantai et al., 2020).

Originally, the term disinformation was closely associated with security and international relations, as spreaders of manipulative falsehoods should be hostile states or non-state actors and their proxies. The European Union's European External Action Service uses the term Foreign Information Manipulation & Interference (FIMI) – defined as a 'pattern of behaviour that threatens or has the potential to negatively impact values, procedures and political processes. Such activity is manipulative in character, conducted in an intentional and coordinated manner. Actors of such activity can be state or non-state actors, including their proxies inside and outside of their own territory' – as a synonym to the term disinformation (EEAS, 2021). Needless to say, despite being introduced in 2021, the term FIMI has not caught up in academic debate, and it appears primarily in the jargon of EU policy documents and bureaucratic institutions. North Atlantic Treaty Organization (NATO) associates disinformation with a wide range of tactics, techniques and procedures of 'hostile information activities' seeking to deepen divisions between its member countries and ultimately weaken the Alliance (NATO, 2023). These definitions demonstrate the tendency of each institution to adjust the term disinformation to their specific needs and fit into existing lingo. Obviously, such pragmatic usage does not help find common terminology.

Moreover, as the topic of manipulative falsehoods spreading in the information space attracted the attention of researchers from various fields, the term disinformation stopped to be used exclusively by security scholars and proliferated also to other areas. In the literature review, Tucker et al. (2018) conceptualize *disinformation* (together with *misinformation* and *online propaganda*) as a type of *information problem* that 'one can encounter online and might lead him to factually incorrect view of the political world'. This is obviously a significant shift in perception since it puts emphasis on the nature and consequences of disinformation and treats the question of their origin and creator as secondary – unlike the above-mentioned security mind definition with a clear adversary in mind. While such a shift of focus can be criticized for blurring the meaning of the term further, our own inquiry into existing literature about disinformation and elections forced us to apply a similar strategy. The problem is that rich and further expanding literature on *disinformation*, *misinformation* and *fake news* does not relate only to the interference of foreign entities but encapsulates a wide range of different topics with underlying themes of change of the information space in which political campaigns are led in the 21st century. The aim of this chapter is to walk the reader through debates reflecting on the role of manipulative falsehoods in contemporary elections, to show which questions are debated and present existing knowledge. At the same time, we urge readers to be mindful of the fact that these debates are very much alive and focus of the field is shifting constantly informed by new research findings.

Before starting this journey, it should be stressed that we decided to limit the chapter to the literature dedicated to campaigns in democratic countries with free and fair elections. Even though authoritarian regimes are notorious for using disinformation to weaken their adversaries on the international stage, marginalize political opposition or manipulate the domestic population, we do not find it useful in such limited space to elaborate on their practices since the context differs significantly from democracies. Moreover, the use of disinformation in non-democratic states is already sufficiently covered elsewhere (see, for instance, Treisman & Guriev, 2023).

Our chapter will introduce the ongoing debates about disinformation in elections in five sections. Firstly, we will tackle the question of the novelty of the phenomenon – which is, in fact, also related to the relevance of disinformation as a unique field of study. Secondly, we present studied cases of disinformation in elections with particular attention dedicated to the 2016 US presidential elections that were not only by far the most studied example but also have an indispensable role in establishing the whole debate about the topic. In the next section, we highlight that political parties can be not only the target of disinformation from abroad but also use them as a tool against their opponents or strategy for controlling the narrative about the situation. The fourth section deals with the difficult question of the impact of disinformation on voting behaviour and presents different perspectives to the topic. We conclude with an overview of existing measures applied by different actors to protect elections or themselves from disinformation, highlight their strengths and weaknesses and consider various dilemmas in their application in democratic societies.

Disinformation and Elections Before Internet

Disinformation in elections is only one topic within a larger discussion about spread of manipulative falsehoods in the contemporary information environment that started approximately a decade ago (Cook, 2020; Martin et al., 2019; Tucker et al., 2018; Woolley & Howard, 2017). This topic is associated with considerations about the influence of changes in the information environment such as emergence of the internet, the decline of traditional media and establishing of social networks to society and politics in the 21st century. Another context for debate about disinformation is the rise of populist politicians using a new style of communication completely dissociated from the truth (Hameleers, 2022). The combination of these two trends became known as post-truth politics (Waisbord, 2018) best personified by former US president Donald Trump (Aratani, 2020). Therefore, it is hardly surprising that his victory in the 2016 presidential election represented an important impetus for debates not only about the role of disinformation in the elections but more broadly about disinformation as a phenomenon shaping contemporary society and politics.

Since post-truth politics is viewed as a contemporary phenomenon, there is a certain tendency to downplay the relevance of historical examples in some segments of the debate on disinformation. Due to technological progress, the past is viewed as too distant and too disconnected from the present experience to bring truly valuable insights (McIntyre, 2018). This argument has certain ground since it is undeniable that in the past few decades political life and electoral campaigns changed profoundly. At the same time, it is important to acknowledge that since we are in the midst of developments, it is difficult to make definite conclusions, for instance, about the impact of social networks on politics (Lorenz-Spreen et al., 2022). More cautious voices warn against jumping to hasty conclusions – including dismissing historical experiences (Carlson, 2018; Farkas & Schou, 2019 or Altay et al., 2023). Therefore, even if we acknowledge that the information environment has changed profoundly, it is still useful to keep the historical perspective in mind and try to position the topic of disinformation and elections in the context of long-term debates on security, election interference and conspiracy theories.

The thinking about war and conflict has never been focused solely on the physical battlefield but also perceived it as a contestation in opponents' minds. Already, pioneers of thinking about wars underlined the importance of manipulation and deception for achieving victory (Tzu, 2020). It would be possible to point out examples of disinformation in every conflict in human history. Its forms, dissemination and tactics would differ depending on possibilities of the given era, but the goal to gain upper hand in the contestation would remain the same. Propaganda – including the spread of disinformation – was applied on a mass scale during the First World War (Paddock, 2014). The very term disinformation originates in the parlance of intelligence services in the Soviet Union, which embrace it as one of the important tools for achieving political goals (Romerstein, 2001). During the Cold War, Western states took advantage of information manipulations, even though the debate about the moral acceptability of using falsehoods by democratic governments appeared (Bittman, 1990 or Walton, 2019). The proliferation of manipulative falsehoods by US officials is also an inseparable part of the story of the Iraq War of 2003 (Lewandowsky et al., 2013). Most recently, the debate about information warfare rose to prominence in the security studies as a consequence of the Russian invasion of Ukraine in 2014 and its hostile propaganda against Western states (Rietjens, 2019). The increasing tensions in international relations will almost certainly motivate various states to update their military strategies and adapt them to the online information environment (Bradshaw & Howard, 2019).

The context of the Cold War era turned every election into a potential battleground of competing great powers. Therefore, it is not surprising that foreign interference using various techniques, including disinformation, was rather common in this period. According to Levin's account, 11.3% of electoral races between 1946 and 2000 were targeted by foreign interference and 60 states globally experienced it during this period (Levin, 2020). For instance, before the 1948 Italian elections, the CIA started a propagandistic campaign targeting the Communist Party of Italy. Disinformation was also part of it, with forged letters aiming to scandalize its representatives or short-wave radio broadcasts claiming that workers not sufficiently compliant with communist rule will be transformed into gulags (Baines & Jones, 2018). It should be underlined that disinformation was only one of many tools used during the Cold War era whose climate allowed for more crude and direct measures such as economic measures, overt threats or – in the case of the Philippines in 1953 – drugging a leading candidate before a press conference (Mohan & Wall, 2019). Nowadays, election interference tends to be more subtle and it is possible to assume that frequency of using disinformation as a technique of interference will increase as the contemporary information space allows for greater level of deniability.

As disinformation can be successful only if tapping into existing social fissures and capitalizing on distrust towards political institutions, it is worth mentioning conspiracy theories. Conspiracy theories are political myths standing on the borderline of folklore, culture and social commentary, promising to uncover the 'real' yet hidden nature of the power structures. According to conspiracy theories, visible power mechanisms such as elections are merely the smokescreen covering the plot of a group of powerful individuals preparing intrigues that have detrimental consequences for the population (Douglas et al., 2019). Such Manichean view of politics and power structure resonated in societies over centuries and up to this day is more present in public opinion than one might assumed – especially in the context of social media that simplifies their proliferation and makes their audience more engaged in the construction of their own conspiratorial narratives (Mahl et al., 2022). Conspiracy thinking can also be utilized politically as its messaging intersects with populist criticism of the political elite (Castanho Silva et al., 2017). One could argue that conspiracy theories are used as disinformation campaigns per se. Hence, it is not surprising that these two phenomena – while still distinct – are often researched in parallel.

Disinformation in Elections: Long Shadow of 2016 US Presidential Elections

The plenitude of empirical studies demonstrates that scholars analyzed disinformation in multiple electoral races worldwide. It was documented that international as well as domestic actors spread disinformation in the leadup to Brexit referendum in 2016 (Bastos & Mercea, 2018). Far-right politicians were spreading disinformation prior to elections in France (Ferrara, 2017 or Couzigou, 2021), Italy (Pierri et al., 2020) or Portugal (Baptista & Gradim, 2022). All European countries faced foreign influence operations including disinformation during their national elections as well as prior elections to the European Parliament (Magdin, 2020). Cases for the United States and Europe tend to be overrepresented in the literature, so it is important to underline that disinformation was also studied in the context of the so-called Global South (Wasserman & Madrid-Morales, 2022). Manipulative falsehoods were documented, for instance, during elections in India (Das & Schroeder, 2021), Kenya (Maweu, 2019) or Brazil (Recuero et al., 2020).

Out of these numerous cases, the 2016 US presidential elections stands out as the event enjoying significant attention of researchers (Badawy et al., 2018; Eady et al., 2023 and many others). This is not because it would be the first election during which disinformation appeared. Neither because of unique empirics since disinformation tactics or methods were not significantly different from other cases. The importance of the 2016 US presidential elections is mainly symbolic as this event of global importance and consequences was one of the key accelerators of the whole debate on disinformation. In the aftermath of their unexpected results disinformation was certified as one of the main threats for liberal democracies and legitimacy of its processes (e.g. Bennett & Livingston, 2018). To put it differently, if Donald Trump had not won the 2016 elections, the debate on disinformation would look significantly differently today.

Disinformation in the 2016 US presidential elections is most commonly associated with Russian interference. Notable attention was dedicated to 'troll farms' such as the infamous internet Research Agency set up to polarize online discussions (McCombie et al., 2019). However, Russian entities were not only game in town when it comes to foreign interference. Rather different case was the involvement of for-profit Macedonian 'disinformation factory' disseminating falsehoods about the elections that feed – as its own founders acknowledge – public demand for negative news and generated money from online advertisement (Hughes & Waismel-Manor, 2021). Also, domestic actors played an important role in spreading and amplifying disinformation. Conservative leaning news outlets published manipulative falsehoods about migration from Muslim countries. These messages were then heavily utilized in Trump's campaign (Faris et al., 2017). Some lower-key channels were also used to spread disinformation. For instance, anonymous automated phone calls and text messages tried to persuade voters to stay home or head to the wrong polling stations (Adler & Dhanaraj, 2022). On the top of that, every research looking into the 2016 US presidential elections has to deal with the 'elephant in the room' – presidential candidate Donald Trump whose communication style disregarded truthfulness and mixed factually correct statements, half-truths and disinformation to appeal to his voter base (Montgomery, 2017).

The varying focus on research on spreaders of disinformation during the 2016 US presidential elections shows various applications of the term disinformation in the literature. This term is not related only to cases of Russian interference but serves as a catch-phrase for multiple manipulative falsehoods that appeared before elections. Such usage of the term is understandable since in contemporary information space it is hard to identify the original source of the manipulative statements. Also as the online environment becomes more interconnected, it is no longer possible to limit it by state borders. Therefore, the very understanding of national elections as one separated case is somewhat misleading. This situation calls for comparative studies including multiple elections that would help to understand similarities and differences of disinformation appearing during individual campaigns and provide more general insights into the nature of manipulative techniques. For instance, the study by Pierri et al. (2020) shows that manipulative falsehoods appearing in various countries were almost identical – oftentimes only translations of one original text – which leads to the conclusion that these were the result of coordinated manipulation. Similarly, Magdin, based on findings of comparative framework, suggests that Russia was amplifying disinformation related to COVID-19 pandemic (Magdin, 2020).

Political Actors and Disinformation: Manipulative Technique and Label

The previous chapter demonstrates that disinformation was observed in multiple electoral contests across the globe. However, the reason for this is not necessary that spread of manipulative falsehoods would become more common. Equally importantly, the use of the term disinformation became more widespread to describe also unfair campaign tactics and practices used by politicians, their teams or supporters to achieve victory. This chapter summarizes findings about two main ways how politicians in democratic countries use disinformation – spreading them to harm their political opponents and applying this term as a label to delegitimize their critiques.

Sadly the spreading of disinformation seems to be quite common in contemporary political campaigns. Bradshaw and Howard, in their reports (2018, 2019), state that in approximately 75 % of the countries they examined, political parties and candidates were using social media platforms to spread disinformation to manipulate voters' opinions and shape the result of the election. They uncovered various manipulation techniques, but the most prominent was creation of the so-called cyber troops, which consist of bots, online commentators and fake accounts, to shape the online discussion by spreading pro-party news, disinformation, attacking opponents or diverting attention away from specific issues (Bradshaw & Howard, 2017, 2018, 2019). Existing studies show that social bots can be very effective in spreading falsehoods in microblogging platforms such as social network X (Shao et al., 2018). Therefore, multiple politicians take advantage of them to artificially boost their popularity or discredit political opponents (Howard et al., 2018; Woolley, no date). For example, Schäfer et al. (2017) showed that the political bots were used to support the extreme-right wing agenda during the electoral campaign of the 2014 general election in Japan. One of the most discussed manipulative techniques in the literature connected to cyber troops is political astroturfing. The term stands for attempts to make some agenda as an organic and spontaneous expression of public opinion, but it is in reality centrally coordinated and created (Ratkiewicz et al., 2011, p. 257). Keller et al. (2020, p. 257) describe this technique as 'a strategy of disinformation, where the disinformation pertains less to the content of the campaign – which can be completely truthful – but to the false impression of independent popular support'. Besides online technologies, politicians can simply contribute to the spread of disinformation by false statements (that can be amplified by mainstream media as well), untruthful posts on social media or giving interviews to disinformation media (Lewis & Marwick, 2017).

Disinformation can target various actors – competing politicians, critical media or even the electoral process itself. The use of manipulative falsehoods to question the legitimacy of the elections and its results is worth discussing in detail. The spread of disinformation is already bad enough as it undermines the fair electoral competition. However, targeting its rules might be detrimental to trust in key principles of democracy. Edelson et al. (2017) demonstrated that there is always popular demand for such disinformation as supporters of the candidate who loses in US presidential elections are more inclined to believe that the whole process was rigged. This sentiment, hipped by Donald Trump's unwillingness to acknowledge electoral results and interviewed with the popularity of QAnon conspiracy theory created the pretext for the infamous attack on Capitol Hill on 6th January 2021 (Hannah, 2021). Therefore, the use of disinformation as a way to question the legitimacy of elections can destabilize the whole democratic process.

Political actors can use the term disinformation as a label to delegitimize the claims of media that oppose their political thinking and goals (Egelhofer & Lecheler, 2019) or to disparage the political opponents and their discourse (Brummette et al., 2018). This tactic was popularized by Donald Trumps' rhetoric who labelled media as 'fake', 'dishonest', 'failing'' or 'phoney'' to delegitimize them (Ross & Rivers, 2018). Some studies suggest that to populist actors, this rhetoric serves as a way of discrediting dominating knowledge systems in order to establish alternative truth that corresponds to their worldview (Farhall et al., 2019 or Hameleers & Minihold, 2022). Nevertheless, the label 'disinformation' can be used for delegitimation of unwelcome opinions basically by any actor in the public sphere: Farkas and Schou (2018) argue that disinformation has become more of a political concept that serves to 'delegitimize political opponents and construct hegemony'. Labelling different points of view can have serious consequences not only during the electoral campaigns but also on the state of democracy in general. First of all, the label disinformation can contribute to the (de)formation of voters' perceptions of reality. Second, it can serve as a censorship tool that can directly and indirectly impact the press publishing policy and thereby reduce voter awareness (RSF, 2017). Monsees (2020) warns about the fact that disinformation is not dangerous only because of the impact on voting choices, but because of the discourse and controversies that are connected with it, such as the regulation of free speech or the attempts of politicians to cover other social issues. And thirdly, when the term disinformation is used so often that it loses any meaning – for which actually scholars can be at least partly blamed, it is significantly harder to have serious conversation about ways to secure elections from manipulative falsehoods spread with malicious intentions.

What Is the (Real) Impact of Disinformation?

Disinformation is blamed for social developments that we can observe for the last decade, such as political polarization, lack of trust in democratic institutions and undermining stability of democracies due to threatening free speech and the legitimacy of democratic elections (Egelhofer & Lecheler, 2019; Monsees, 2020; Tucker et al., 2018). But were these trends really caused by disinformation? There is still no consensus in the existing literature about this question. This chapter will present different ways how scholars tried to describe the influence of disinformation on elections (and political life more broadly) and arguments pointing to limitations of their impact.

The most straightforward approach is measuring the impact of exposure to disinformation on voting behaviour (Cantarella et al., 2023; Iida et al., 2022; Weeks & Garrett, 2014; Wells et al., 2009; Zimmermann & Kohring, 2020). Researchers argue that the exposure of disinformation leads to emotional arousal – in the form of fear or anger – leading to unconscious change of opinions and attitudes (Bastick, 2021). Swami et al. (2018) show that the belief in threatening disinformation was associated with the voting choices during the Brexit referendum. In their experimental study, Barrera et al. (2020) show that disinformation about the European refugee situation could play a role during the 2017 French presidential election campaign and made people vote for the right-wing candidate Marine Le Pen. Similar pattern was observed during the German Parliamentary Elections in 2017, where belief in disinformation had driven voters' support from the governing party CDU/CSU to the right-wing populist party Alternative für Deutschland (Zimmermann & Kohring, 2020).

The important side-effect of disinformation is the loss of trust in democratic institutions and official sources of information (Monsees, 2020; Persily, 2017; Tucker et al., 2018). In extreme cases, these can result in 'disruption of democratic order' when the critical mass of citizens refuses existing institutional setting (Bennett & Livingston, 2018). The clear example can be the attack on Capitol Hill in the aftermath of the 2020 U.S. presidential election that was perceived as rigged by most radical Donald Trump supporters (Calvillo et al., 2021; Tollefson, 2021). Disinformation has detrimental effects not only on that trust to political process but also to credibility of traditional media and the established knowledge system represented, for instance, by science (Bennett & Livingston, 2018). Another negative effect of disinformation is the increase of society's polarization. Conviction that people holding different views are not genuine but were manipulated by disinformation can lead to perception of other opinion groups not as partners for debate but as either misguided or outright hostile (Asmolov, 2018; Del Vicario et al., 2016). To conclude, the danger of disinformation (and discourse surrounding them) is not related only to electoral outcomes, but it can influence popular moods and change public attitudes towards democratic processes.

Based on the above-presented studies, spread of disinformation represents an urgent problem. However, other authors are challenging these findings and are sceptical about the impact of disinformation. Their main argument points out the difference between exposure, belief and change of behaviour (Allen et al., 2020; Eady et al., 2023). Allen et al. (2020) demonstrates that the consumption of outlets regularly spreading disinformation is negligible compared to mainstream information resources. Scholars argue that disinformation does not influence all society equally as only a small part of it tends to be overexposed (Allcott & Gentzkow, 2017; Guess & Nyhan, 2018; Nelson, 2017; Nelson & Taneja, 2018). The characteristics of this group are still a matter of research. Baptista and Gradim (2022) have shown that people with conservative and right-leaning political views are more susceptible to disinformation. Other studies suggest that disinformation vulnerability is linked with higher age and lower education (Brashier & Schacter, 2020; Guess et al., 2019) and connected with other factors, such as low trust in traditional media (Ognyanova et al., 2020).

Debate about the impact of disinformation on change of opinions and behaviours is still ongoing and it is certain that our knowledge on the matter will further evolve. The lack of consensus about this issue can be demonstrated in studies aiming to describe the impact of echo chambers on spread of disinformation on social media. On the one hand, social media are perceived as an ideal environment for the spread of disinformation, as they get amplified in like-minded communities, and the consumers are thus not confronted with different points of view and arguments (Del Vicario et al., 2016; Jiang et al., 2021). Ribeiro et al. (2017) argue that the polarizing effect may contribute to the fact that people tend to label everything that disagrees with their viewpoints as disinformation. On the other hand, Guess et al. (2018) present three reasons why the concept of echo chambers is not as functional as one expects. Firstly, studies focusing solely on echo chambers do not take in account exposure to other information sources outside of social networks and therefore overestimate their influence. Secondly, only a few people actually pay attention to political news, while the rest are interested in politics only in critical moments. Finally, the social connection in the offline world tends to be more important for forming one's opinion. In addition, other studies show that people are exposed to pluralistic content on social networks which contradicts basic assumptions about echo chambers (Tucker et al., 2018).

Fighting Disinformation: a Game of Cat and Mouse

The very existence of disinformation and the consequences of its dissemination naturally lead various actors to look for ways to tackle this problem. In this section, we will categorize numerous strategies for fighting disinformation according to the actors applying them. Firstly, there are public actors – states, their institutions and international organizations. Secondly, there is civil society, non-governmental organizations (NGOs) and private companies. Each actor has different tools at its disposal and uses different strategies. States, through legislative changes, most often force internet giants to implement necessary measures and push the boundaries of what can be sanctioned. However, they face the problem outlined at the beginning of the chapter – the difficulty of defining what constitutes disinformation in the first place. The civil society actors often focus on education and fact-checking. After taking a closer look at various strategies, we will also discuss the controversies surrounding the fight against disinformation.

In describing the steps democratic states are taking to combat disinformation, it is good to start with efforts to regulate social media, which in modern communication greatly facilitates dissemination online. States are adopting legislation regulating social media and putting the responsibility for the spread of disinformation on the technology companies (Haciyakupoglu et al., 2018). This approach is taken not only on the level of individual states such as the US, Germany, Italy, United Kingdom or India but also on the international stage. The European Union is planning to adopt legislation that will require social network operators to report on specific actions to combat the spread of disinformation (Fišer, 2022).

Governments are also taking sporadic legal action targeting individuals who spread disinformation (Chang, 2022). In this case, governments can theoretically use some of the already existing legal tools addressing such problems as hate crime or spreading alarmist messages. However, the ability to adapt these laws to the new situation varies from case to case. The most notable punitive measure was taken in the aftermath of Russian full-scale invasion of Ukraine when the EU sanctioned Kremlin propagandistic outlets RT/Russia Today and Sputnik and effectively stopped their broadcasting activities (EU, 2022).

States are increasingly turning to incentive-based measures. These are to support institutions helping to spread the factually correct information or combat disinformation such as reputable media or civil society actors. For example, the EU financed the establishment of the European Digital Observatory – interdisciplinary network to counter disinformation covering all its member states (EDMO, n.d.). Similarly, there is a drive to favour social media users who demonstrate authentic communication (Kovic et al., 2018).

Aside from these short-term activities, states also focus long-term efforts to fight disinformation. Most often mentioned in this context is the strengthening of media literacy in school curricula and among the general population, especially the elderly (Haciyakupoglu et al., 2018). Another long-term approach is improving state communication to be able to provide necessary information to citizens and increase their trust in the state and its institutions. The practical example of this approach can be RESIST 2 Counter Disinformation Toolkit introduced by the UK Government Communication Unite (Pamment, 2021).

Out of all civil society actors, those who are disadvantaged by disinformation have the most significant incentive to fight them. However, their options to fight back are rather limited. To illustrate this example of candidates in the elections, they try to refute disinformation directed against them during the campaign and, if used by political competitors, try to use the verification to counterattack and to challenge the credibility of the opposing candidate. In some countries, it is common to defend oneself against false accusations in court, but there are clear limits to this in an electoral contest. It is a time-consuming effort that will not likely have an impact during given elections and it can be applied only in case that entities spreading elections are known (Collins et al., 2021). One example is the 2018 presidential election in the Czech Republic, when the Supreme Administrative Court had to deal with a complaint about a disinformation campaign against the unsuccessful candidate Jiří Drahoš. However, the court stated that it could not prove influence on voters' decision-making, so it will not look into the matter further (iDnes, 2018).

The popular tool to fight disinformation used by NGOs, the media and the private sector is fact-checking. An essential part of this technique of uncovering and refuting false statements combined with detailed and transparent explanation of the verification process, which allows the reader to understand how this process works (Churanova, 2018). This way of fighting is considered as highly insufficient by some scholars. In the first place, it has a limited reach and it is not likely to reach vulnerable audiences. Secondly, it usually covers only a very narrow segment of the channels through which disinformation is disseminated. And finally, even when disinformation is detected and debunked, it can still do damage. This is shown again in the case of the 2016 US presidential election, where 70% of the statements made by candidate Trump during the campaign were already verified as false, but his public image was still not significantly shaken (Nyhan & Reifler, 2015). This phenomenon is referred to as the 'continued-influence effect' and means that once (massively) spread, disinformation can influence public discourse even if it is subsequently retrospectively labelled as false (Swire-Thompson, 2018). Despite its limitation, fact-checking remains one of the most prominent tactics used to fight disinformation as the attention of researchers attests (Ziemer & Rothmund, 2024).

Technically tracking disinformation that should be fact-checked is done in two ways. First of them is manual relying on people chasing disinformation on the internet. However, the wide internet space significantly limits the effectiveness of this approach and therefore some authors believe that the future of identifying disinformation lies in using artificial intelligence (Ciampaglia, 2018). In machine identification of disinformation, we can talk about three basic types of approaches (Sharma et al., 2019). The first one is content-based identification. These approaches work with the proposition that disinformation differs from factually correct news in terms of textual content, and this difference can be quantified and recognized. The second type of approach is based on responses to content (so-called feedback-based identification). This method is based on the premise that disinformation can be identified from how users react to the news, how they comment on it or how the news is promoted or spread in terms of time. A third type of approach is directly linked to proactive interventions in the spread of disinformation and efforts to mitigate the effects of its spread (so-called intervention-based solutions). These approaches most often work with automatic exposure to true messages by users affected by disinformation (Nguyen et al., 2012) and with artificial intelligence that tries to limit the spread of a message identified as false at an early stage.

However, the current debate does not mention solely the spread of disinformation as a threat to democracy. The fight against disinformation can represent a concern for democracy as well. Most importantly, the thin line between the fight against (harmful) disinformation and using the as excuse to legitimize the control (and even censorship) of the media poses the primary concern to the right of free speech and democracy as it is (Egelhofer & Lecheler, 2019).

Furthermore, the current discussion questioned the role of social platforms and their regulation policies, as the self-regulatory standards are considered lax, unclear and inconsistent. The concern lies in the conflict between the self-interest of the big internet media private companies and the public interest, which makes the self-regulatory policies ineffective. Moreover, Douek (2021) criticizes the lack of transparency, which opposes the requirements of respect for free speech. For example, one of the ultimate sanctions of social media companies is the account removal of harmful accounts – deplatforming – is on one hand seen as an effective countermeasure to control disinformation. On the other hand, it is criticized as unilateral action of big companies without any control and thus raise ethical and legal questions (Gorissen, 2023).

The example of deplatforming also raises a question of the effectiveness of steps against the harmful effects of disinformation. These actions can have both intended effects, that is, suppressing problematic behaviour and content on social media, and unintended effects. Among its unintended effects can be 're-platforming' activities, the increase of the resilience of the target group by diversifying their cross-platform presence or hardening the ideological convictions of followers (Innes & Innes, 2023). On the example of deplatforming, Gorissen (2023) shows that every direct action of controlling the disinformation spread needs to be a transparent process, which requires clear definitions.

To conclude, the fight against disinformation in election campaigns is still in its infancy. Much of the disinformation spreaders are still untouched and essentially unpunishable, although significant progress is already being made. On the one hand, progress has been made in the gradual legislative anchoring of the fight against disinformation. However, this still faces resistance from some political actors and also deals with the challenge to define the line between the fight against disinformation and censorship. The development of automated mechanisms for the detection of disinformation can be a great enhancement of existing fact-checking activities. Governments' efforts to enforce legislation seem to be more successful when framed by the risk of foreign intervention in electoral contests rather than by concern about domestic threats. Series of successful measures applied in Sweden to protect elections against Russian interference is such an example (LaForge, 2020). At the moment, we consider thoughtful and longer-term campaigns that openly communicate not only the measures being implemented but also about consequences that disinformation can have if the state will not intervene, the necessary part of effort to fight disinformation. In this context, elections can serve as useful and comprehensible examples of their malign impacts.

CONCLUSION

Elections are the central topics of the burgeoning research on disinformation. In the past several years, numerous articles and books have tried to uncover manipulative falsehoods that can influence electoral processes, undermine its legitimacy or harm running parties and candidates. These findings should interest anyone focusing on topics related to politics, including researchers and practitioners in the field of political marketing. Our chapter aims to serve as an introduction to the discussion about disinformation allowing readers to find how to utilize existing knowledge in their existing research projects.

In this sense, some readers might find our chapter a bit disappointing since we showed that despite its intensity and rapid development, the research on disinformation still has numerous blind spots. An illustrative example could be the limits of understanding of the influence of disinformation on voting behaviour or open-ended debate about the impact of the online environment on society and politics. Therefore, we suggest to readers that any conclusions in this field should be treated with a certain level of caution and corroborated with other existing research. However, the rapid development of the field and its maturing gives hope that existing knowledge gaps will be sooner or later filled. As one way to overcome current limitations, we suggest not perceiving disinformation as a brand-new topic but understanding some of its aspects with reference to more established research disciplines. For instance, its security implication is possible to consider in the context of debates about propaganda or interpret its role in modern political campaigns in relation to debates about astroturfing.

However, we are convinced that the debate about disinformation can be useful for the field of political marketing also from an ethical perspective. After all, cynics might claim that political marketing is mainly about manipulation and, therefore, there is no special reason to get excited about the topic of disinformation. This claim becomes quite hard to ignore, especially since entities offering tailor-made disinformation campaigns become a part of electoral processes and negative campaigning also in democratic countries (for latest example, see Kirchgaessner et al., 2023). Henceforth, we claim that confrontation with the debate on disinformation can help experts and practitioners in the field of political marketing rethink the ethical guidelines of their field and look for ways to effectively enforce them in practice. We are convinced that this introspection would be beneficial not only for the state of discipline but also for the quality of public debate in our democracies.

Acknowledgements

This chapter was written at Masaryk University with the support of a Specific University Research Grant provided by the Ministry of Education, Youth and Sports of the Czech Republic.

REFERENCES

Adler, W. T., & Dhanaraj, T. (2022, December 14). *A lie can travel: Election disinformation in the United States, Brazil, and France*. Centre for Democracy and Technology. https://cdt.org/insights/cdt-and-kas-report-a-lie-can-travel-election-disinformation-in-the-united-states-brazil-and-france/. (Accessed on 28 February 2023).

Allcott, H., & Gentzkow, M. (2017). Social media and fake news in the 2016 election. *The Journal of Economic Perspectives*, *31*(2), 211–236. https://doi.org/10.1257/jep.31.2.211

Allen, J., Howland, B., Mobius, M., Rothschild, D., & Watts, D. J. (2020). Evaluating the fake news problem at the scale of the information ecosystem. *Science Advances*, *6*(14). eaay3539. https://doi.org/10.1126/sciadv.aay3539

Altay, S., Berriche, M., & Acerbi, A. (2023). Misinformation on misinformation: Conceptual and methodological challenges. *Social Media + Society*, *9*(1). https://doi.org/10.1177/20563051221150412

Aratani, L. (2020, July 13). Tsunami of untruths': Trump has made 20,000 false or misleading claims – Report. *The Guardian*. https://www.theguardian.com/us-news/2020/jul/13/donald-trump-20000-false-or-misleading-claims. Accessed on 27 February 2023.

Asmolov, G. (2018). The disconnective power of disinformation campaigns. *Journal of International Affairs*, *71*, 69–76.

Badawy, A., Ferrara, E., & Lerman, K. (2018). Analyzing the digital traces of political manipulation: The 2016 Russian interference Twitter campaign. In *2018 IEEE/ACM International Conference on Advances in Social Networks Analysis and Mining (ASONAM)* (pp. 258–265). https://doi.org/10.1109/ASONAM.2018.8508646

Baines, P., & Jones, J. (2018). Influence and interference in foreign elections. *The RUSI Journal*, *163*(1), 12–19. https://doi.org/10.1080/03071847.2018.1446723

Baptista, J. P., & Gradim, A. (2022). Online disinformation on Facebook: The spread of fake news during the Portuguese 2019 election. *Journal of Contemporary European Studies*, *30*(2), 297–312. https://doi.org/10.1080/14782804.2020.1843415

Barrera, O., Guriev, S., Emeric, H., & Zhuravskayaet, E. (2020). Facts, alternative facts, and fact checking in times of post-truth politics. *Journal of Public Economics*, *182*, 104123. https://doi.org/10.1016/j.jpubeco.2019.104123

Bastick, Z. (2021). Would you notice if fake news changed your behavior? An experiment on the unconscious effects of disinformation. *Computers in Human Behavior*, *116*(4). https://doi.org/10.1016/j.chb.2020.106633

Bastos, M., & Mercea, D. (2018). The public accountability of social platforms: Lessons from a study on bots and trolls in the Brexit campaign. *Philosophical Transactions of the Royal Society A*. http://doi.org/10.1098/rsta.2018.0003

Bennett, W. L., & Livingston, S. (2018). The disinformation order: Disruptive communication and the decline of democratic institutions. *European Journal of Communication*, *33*(2), 122–139. https://doi.org/10.1177/0267323118760317

Bittman, L. (1990). The use of disinformation by democracies. *International Journal of Intelligence & Counter Intelligence*, *4*(2), 243–261. https://doi.org/10.1080/08850609008435142

Bradshaw, S., & Howard, P. N. (2018a). *Challenging truth and trust: A global inventory of organized social media manipulation*. Working paper. Project on Computational Propaganda. https://demtech.oii.ox.ac.uk/research/posts/challenging-truth-and-trust-a-global-inventory-of-organized-social-media-manipulation/. Accessed on 27 February 2023.

Bradshaw, S., & Howard, P. (2019). *The global disinformation order: 2019 global inventory of organised social media manipulation*. Oxford Internet Institute. https://digitalcommons.unl.edu/cgi/viewcontent.cgi?article=1209&context=scholcom. Accessed on 27 February 2023.

Brashier, N. M., & Schacter, D. L. (2020). Aging in an era of fake news. *Current Directions in Psychological Science*, *29*(3), 316–323. https://doi.org/10.1177/0963721420915872

Brummette, J. DiStaso, M., Vafeiadis, M., & Messner, M. (2018). Read all about it: The politicization of "fake news" on Twitter. *Journalism & Mass Communication Quarterly*, *95*(2), 497–517. https://doi.org/10.1177/1077699018769906

Churanova, O. (2018). Countering Russian disinformation: Ukrainian NGOs on the frontline. *Ukraine Analytica*, *11*(1), 59–66.

Calvillo, D. P., Rutchick, A. M., & Garcia, R. J. B. (2021). Individual differences in belief in fake news about election fraud after the 2020 U.S. Election. *Behavioral Sciences*, *11*(12), 175. https://doi.org/10.3390/bs11120175

Cantarella, M., Fraccaroli, N., & Volpe, R. (2023). Does fake news affect voting behaviour? *Research Policy*, *52*(1), 104628. https://doi.org/10.1016/j.respol.2022.104628

Carlson, M. (2018). Fake news as an informational moral panic: The symbolic deviancy of social media during the 2016 US presidential election. *Information, Communication & Society*, *23*(3), 1–15. https://doi.org/10.1080/1369118x.2018.1505934

Castanho Silva, B., Vegetti, F., & Littvay, L. (2017). The elite is up to something: Exploring the relation between populism and belief in conspiracy theories. *Swiss Political Science Review*, *23*(4), 423–443. https://doi.org/10.1111/spsr.12270

Chang, C. C. (2022). Revisiting disinformation laws in the age of social media. *Arizona Law Journal of Emerging Technologies*, *6*. i.

Ciampaglia, G. L. (2018). Fighting fake news: A role for computational social science in the fight against digital misinformation. *Journal of Computational Social Science*, *1*(1), 147–153. https://doi.org/10.1007/s42001-017-0005-6

Collins, B., Dinh, T. H., Ngoc, T. N., & Dosam, H. (2021). Trends in combating fake news on social media – A survey. *Journal of Information and Telecommunication*, *5*(2), 247–266. https://doi.org/10.1080/24751839.2020.1847379

Cook, S. (2020). Beijing's global megaphone. *Freedom House*. https://freedomhouse.org/report/special-report/2020/beijings-global-megaphone. Accessed on 15 February 2023.

Couzigou, I. (2021). The French legislation against digital information manipulation in electoral campaigns: A scope limited by freedom of expression, election law journal: Rules. *Politics & Policy*, *20*(1), 98–115. https://doi.org/10.1089/elj.2021.0001

Das, A., & Schroeder, R. (2021). Online disinformation in the run-up to the Indian 2019 election. *Information, Communication & Society*, *24*(12), 1762–1778. https://doi.org/10.1080/1369118X.2020.1736123

Del Vicario, M., Bessi, A., Zollo, F., Petroni, F., Scala, A., Caldarelli, G. H., Stanley, E., & Quattrociocchi, W. (2016). The spreading of misinformation online. *Proceedings of the National Academy of Sciences*, *113*(3), 554–559. https://doi.org/10.1073/pnas.1517441113

Douek, E. (2021). The free speech blind spot: Foreign election interference on social media. In J. D. Ohlin, & D. B. Hollis (Eds.), *Defending democracies: Combating foreign election interference in a digital age*. Oxford Academic. https://doi.org/10.1093/oso/9780197556979.003.0013. Accessed on 11 March 2024.

Douglas, K. M., Uscinski, J. E., Sutton, R. M., Cichocka, A., Nefes, T., Ang, C. S., & Deravi, F. (2019). Understanding conspiracy theories. *Political Psychology*, *40*(1), 3–35. https://doi.org/10.1111/pops.12568

Eady, G. Paskhalis, T., Zilinsky, J., Bonneau, R., Nagler, J., & Tucker, J. A. (2023). Exposure to the Russian Internet Research Agency foreign influence campaign on Twitter in the 2016 US election and its relationship to attitudes and voting behavior. *Nature Communications*, *14*(62). https://doi.org/10.1038/s41467-022-35576-9

Edelson, J., Alduncin, A., Krewson, C., Sieja, J. A., & Uscinski, J. E. (2017). The effect of conspiratorial thinking and motivated reasoning on belief in election fraud. *Political Research Quarterly*, *70*(4), 933–946. https://doi.org/10.1177/1065912917721061

EDMO. (n.d.). *About us, European digital media observatory*. https://edmo.eu/about-us/edmoeu/

EEAS. (2021). *Tackling disinformation, foreign information manipulation & interference*. European Union External Action. 27th October 2021. https://www.eeas.europa.eu/eeas/tackling-disinformation-foreign-information-manipulation-interference_en

Egelhofer, J. L., & Lecheler, S. (2019). Fake news as a two-dimensional phenomenon: A framework and research agenda. *Annals of the International Communication Association*, *43*(2), 97–116. https://doi.org/10.1080/23808985.2019.1602782

EU. (2022). *EU imposes sanctions on state-owned outlets RT/Russia Today and Sputnik's broadcasting in the EU*. https://www.consilium.europa.eu/en/press/press-releases/2022/03/02/eu-imposes-sanctions-on-state-owned-outlets-rt-russia-today-and-sputnik-s-broadcasting-in-the-eu/

Farhall, K. Carson, A., Wright, S., Gibbons, A., & Lukamto, W. (2019). Political elites' use of fake news discourse across communications platforms. *International Journal of Communication*, *13*(0), 23. https://ijoc.org/index.php/ijoc/article/view/10677

Faris, R., Roberts, H., Elting, B., Bourassa, N., Zuckerman, E., & Benkler, Y. (2017, August 16). *Partisanship, propaganda and disinformation: Online media and the 2016 US presidential election*. Berkman Klein Center for Internet & Society at Harvard University. https://cyber.harvard.edu/publications/2017/08/mediacloud. Accessed 28 February 2023.

Farkas, J., & Schou, J. (2018). Fake news as a floating signifier: Hegemony, antagonism and the politics of falsehood. *Javnost - The Public*, *25*(3), 298–314. https://doi.org/10.1080/13183222.2018.1463047

Farkas, J., & Schou, J. (2019). *Post-truth, fake news and democracy: Mapping the politics of falsehood*. Routledge.

Ferrara, E. (2017). Disinformation and social bot operations in the run up to the 2017 French presidential election. *First Monday*, *22*(8). https://doi.org/10.48550/ARXIV.1707.00086

Fišer, J. (2022, April 25). Zemětřesení na sociálních sítích! Evropská unie chce vymýtit fake news na Facebooku. *SMARTmania.cz*. https://smartmania.cz/zemetreseni-na-socialnich-sitich-evropska-unie-chce-vymytit-fake-news-na-facebooku/. Accessed on 28 February 2023.

Gorissen, S. (2023). 'Weathering and weaponizing the #TwitterPurge: Digital content moderation and the dimensions of deplatforming'. *Communication and Democracy*. https://www.tandfonline.com/doi/full/10.1080/27671127.2023.2264367. Accessed on 11 March 2024.

Guess, A., Lyons, B., Nyhan, B., & Reifler, J. (2018). *Avoiding the echo chamber about echo chambers: Why selective exposure to like-minded political news is less prevalent than you think*. Miami, Knight Foundation.

Guess, A., Nagler, J., & Tucker, J. (2019). Less than you think: Prevalence and predictors of fake news dissemination on Facebook. *Science Advances*, *5*(1). eaau4586. https://doi.org/10.1126/sciadv.aau4586

Guess, A., & Nyhan, B. (2018). Selective Exposure to Misinformation: Evidence from the consumption of fake news during the 2016 U.S. presidential campaign. https://about.fb.com/wp-content/uploads/2018/01/fake-news-2016.pdf. Accessed on 17 February 2023.

Haciyakupoglu, G., Jennifer, Y. H., Suguna, V. S., Dymples, L., & Rahman, M. F. A. (2018). *Countering fake news: A Survey of recent global initiatives*. S. Rajaratnam School of International Studies. http://hdl.handle.net/11540/8063

Hameleers, M. (2022). *Populist disinformation in fragmented information settings: Understanding the nature and persuasiveness of populist and post-factual communication*. Routledge.

Hameleers, M., & Minihold, S. (2022). Constructing discourses on (Un)truthfulness: Attributions of reality, misinformation, and disinformation by politicians in a comparative social media setting. *Communication Research*, *49*(8), 1176–1199. https://doi.org/10.1177/0093650220982762

Hannah, M. (2021). QAnon and the information dark age. *First Monday*, *26*(2). https://doi.org/10.5210/fm.v26i2.10868

Howard, P. N., Woolley, S., & Calo, R. (2018). Algorithms, bots, and political communication in the US 2016 election: The challenge of automated political communication for election law and administration. *Journal of Information Technology & Politics*, *15*(2), 81–93. https://doi.org/10.1080/19331681.2018.1448735

Hughes, H. C., & Waismel-Manor, I. (2021). The Macedonian fake news industry and the 2016 US election. *Political Science & Politics*, *54*(1), 19–23. https://doi.org/10.1017/S1049096520000992

iDnes. (2018, October 1). Dezinformace Drahoše v prezidentských volbách nepoškodily, rozhodl Ústavní soud. *iDNES.cz*. https://www.idnes.cz/zpravy/domaci/ustavni-soud-stiznost-volby-prezident-nejvyssi-spravni-soud-jiri-drahos-milos-zeman.A181001_111042_domaci_mpl. Accessed on 28 February 2023.

Iida, T., Song, J., Estrada, J. L., & Takahashi, Y. (2022). Fake news and its electoral consequences: A survey experiment on Mexico. *AI & Society*. https://doi.org/10.1007/s00146-022-01541-9

Innes, H., & Innes, M. (2023) De-platforming disinformation: Conspiracy theories and their control. *Information, Communication & Society*, *26* (6) pp 1262-1280. https://doi.org/10.1080/1369118X.2021.1994631. Accessed on 11 March 2024.

Jiang, J., Ren, X., & Ferrara, E. (2021). Social media polarization and echo chambers in the context of COVID-19: Case study. *Jmirx Med*, *2*(3), e29570. Available at:. https://doi.org/10.2196/29570

Kapantai, E., Christopoulou, A., Berberidis, C., & Peristeras, V. (2020). A systematic literature review on disinformation: Toward a unified taxonomical framework. *New Media & Society*, *23*(5). Available at:. https://doi.org/10.1177/1461444820959296

Keller, F. B. Schoch, D., Stier, S., & Yang, J. (2020). Political astroturfing on Twitter: How to coordinate a disinformation campaign. *Political Communication*, *37*(2), 256–280. https://doi.org/10.1080/10584609.2019.1661888

Kirchgaessner, S., Ganguly, M., Pegg, D., Cadwalladr, C., & Burke, J. (2023, February 15). Revealed: The hacking and disinformation team meddling in elections. *The Guardian*. https://www.theguardian.com/world/2023/feb/15/revealed-disinformation-team-jorge-claim-meddling-elections-tal-hanan. Accessedon 27 February 2023.

Kovic, M., Rauchfleisch, A., Sele, M., & Caspar, C. (2018). Digital astroturfing in politics: Definition, typology, and countermeasures. *Studies in Communication Sciences*, *18*(1), 69–85. https://doi.org/10.24434/j.scoms.2018.01.005

LaForge, G. (2020). *Sweden Defends its elections against disinformation, 2016-2018*. Princeton University, Innovations for Successful Societies. https://successfulsocieties.princeton.edu/publications/sweden-defends-its-elections-against-disinformation-2016-%E2%80%93-2018

Levin, D. H. (2020). *Meddling in the Ballot box: The causes and effects of partisan electoral interventions*. Oxford University Press.

Lewandowsky, S., Stritzke, W. G. K., Freund, A. M., Oberauer, K., & Krueger, J. I. (2013). Misinformation, disinformation, and violent conflict: From Iraq and the "War on Terror" to future threats to peace. *American Psychologist*, *68*(7), 487–501. https://doi.org/10.1037/a0034515

Lewis, B., & Marwick, A. E. (2017). *Media manipulation and disinformation online*. Data & Society Research Institute. Available at: https://datasociety.net/library/media-manipulation-and-disinfo-online/. Accessed: 22 December 2022.

Lorenz-Spreen, P., Oswald, L., Lewandowsky, S., & Hertwig, R. (2022). A systematic review of worldwide causal and correlational evidence on digital media and democracy. *Nature Human Behaviour*, *7*, 1–28. https://doi.org/10.1038/s41562-022-01460-1

Magdin, R. (2020). Disinformation campaigns in the European Union: Lessons learned from the 2019 European Elections and 2020 COVID-19 infodemic in Romania. *Romanian Journal of European Affairs*, *20*(2), 49–61.

Mahl, D., Schäfer, M. S., & Zeng, J. (2022). Conspiracy theories in online environments: An interdisciplinary literature review and agenda for future research. *New Media & Society*. Available at:. https://doi.org/10.1177/14614448221075759

Martin, D. A., Shapiro, J. N., & Nedashkovskaya, M. (2019). Recent trends in online foreign influence efforts. *Journal of Information Warfare*, *18*(3), pp. 15–48. https://www.jstor.org/stable/26894680. Accessed on 15 February 2023.

Maweu, J. M. (2019). "Fake elections"? Cyber propaganda, disinformation and the 2017 general elections in Kenya. *African Journalism Studies*, *40*(4), 62–76. https://doi.org/10.1080/23743670.2020.1719858

McCombie, S., Uhlmann, A. J., & Morrison, S. (2019). The US 2016 presidential election & Russia's troll farms. *Intelligence and National Security*, *35*(1), 95–114. https://doi.org/10.1080/02684527.2019.1673940

McIntyre, L. C. (2018). *Post-truth*. Mit Press.

Miró-Llinares, F., & Aguerri, J. C. (2021). Misinformation about fake news: A systematic critical review of empirical studies on the phenomenon and its status as a 'threat'. *European*

Journal of Criminology, 20(1). https://doi.org/10.1177/1477370821994059

Mohan, V., & Wall, A. (2019, Fall). Foreign electoral interference. *Georgetown Journal of International Affairs, 20*, 110–119.

Monsees, L. (2020). "A war against truth" – understanding the fake news controversy. *Critical Studies on Security, 8*(2), 116–129. https://doi.org/10.1080/21624887.2020.1763708

Montgomery, M. (2017). Post-truth politics? Authenticity, populism and the electoral discourses of Donald Trump. *Journal of Language and Politics, 16*(4), 619–639. https://doi.org/10.1075/jlp.17023.mon

NATO (2023). *'NATO's approach to countering disinformation*. North Atlantic Treaty Organization. 8th November 2023. https://www.nato.int/cps/en/natohq/topics_219728.htm

Nelson, J. L. (2017). Is 'fake news' a fake problem? *Columbia Journalism Review*. https://www.cjr.org/analysis/fake-news-facebook-audience-drudge-breitbart-study.php. Accessed on 12 February 2023.

Nelson, J. L., & Taneja, H. (2018). The small, disloyal fake news audience: The role of audience availability in fake news consumption. *New Media & Society, 20*(10), 3720–3737. https://doi.org/10.1177/1461444818758715

Nguyen, N. P., Guanhua, Y., Thai, M. T., & Eidenbenz, S. (2012). Containment of misinformation spread in online social networks. In *Proceedings of the 4th Annual ACM Web Science Conference* (pp. 213–222). Association for Computing Machinery. https://dl.acm.org/doi/proceedings/10.1145/2380718

Nyhan, B., & Reifler, J. (2015). The effect of fact-checking on elites: A field experiment on U.S. State legislators: The effect of fact-checking on elites. *American Journal of Political Science, 59*(3), 628–640. https://doi.org/10.1111/ajps.12162

Ognyanova, K., Lazer, D., Robertson, R. E., & Wilson, Ch. (2020). Misinformation in action: Fake news exposure is linked to lower trust in media, higher trust in government when your side is in power. *Harvard Kennedy School Misinformation Review*. https://doi.org/10.37016/mr-2020-024

Paddock, T. R. E. (2014). *World war I and propaganda*. Brill.

Pamment, J. (2021). *RESIST 2 counter disinformation Toolkit*. https://gcs.civilservice.gov.uk/publications/resist-2-counter-disinformation-toolkit/

Pérez-Escolar, M., Lilleker, D., & Tapia-Frade, A. (2023). A systematic literature review of the phenomenon of disinformation and misinformation. *Media and Communication, 11*(2). https://doi.org/10.17645/mac.v11i2.6453

Persily, N. (2017). Can democracy survive the internet? *Journal of Democracy, 28*(2), 63–76. Available at:. https://doi.org/10.1353/jod.2017.0025

Pierri, F., Artoni, A., & Ceri, S. (2020). Investigating Italian disinformation spreading on Twitter in the context of 2019 European elections. *PLoS One, 15*(1). https://doi.org/10.1371/journal.pone.0227821

Ratkiewicz, J., Conover, M., Meiss, M., Goncalves, B., Flammini, A., & Menczer, F. (2011). Detecting and tracking political abuse in social media. In *Proceedings of the International AAAI Conference on Web and Social Media* (Vol. 5, No. 1, pp. 297–304). https://doi.org/10.1609/icwsm.v5i1.14127.

Recuero, R., Soares, F. B., & Gruzd, A. (2020). Hyperpartisanship, disinformation and political conversations on Twitter: The Brazilian presidential election of 2018. In *Proceedings of the Fourteenth International AAAI Conference on Web and Social Media (ICWSM 2020)* (Vol. 14). https://doi.org/10.1609/icwsm.v14i1.7324

Ribeiro, M. H., Calais, P. H., Almeida, V. A. F., & Meira Jr., W. (2017). 'Everything I disagree with is #FakeNews: Correlating political Polarization and spread of misinformation'. *arXiv*. http://arxiv.org/abs/1706.05924. Accessed on 11 February 2023.

Rietjens, S. (2019). Unraveling disinformation: The case of Malaysia airlines flight MH17. *The International Journal of Intelligence, Security, and Public Affairs, 21*(3), 195–218. https://doi.org/10.1080/23800992.2019.1695666

Romerstein, H. (2001). Disinformation as a KGB weapon in the Cold War. *Journal of Intelligence History, 1*(1), 54–67. https://doi.org/10.1080/16161262.2001.10555046

Ross, A. S., & Rivers, D. J. (2018). Discursive deflection: Accusation of "fake news" and the spread of mis- and disinformation in the tweets of president Trump. *Social Media + Society, 4*(2). Available at:. https://doi.org/10.1177/2056305118776010

RSF. (2017). *Predators of press freedom use fake news as a censorship tool*. RSF Reporters without borders. https://rsf.org/en/predators-press-freedom-use-fake-news-censorship-tool. Accessed on 22 December 2022.

Schäfer, F., Evert, S., & Heinrich, P. (2017). Japan's 2014 general election: Political bots, right-wing internet activism, and Prime Minister Shinzō Abe's hidden nationalist agenda. *Big Data, 5*(4), 294–309. https://doi.org/10.1089/big.2017.0049

Shao, C. Ciampaglia, G. L., Varol, O., Yang, K., Flammini, A., & Menczer, F. (2018). The spread of low-credibility content by social bots. *Nature Communications, 9*(1), 4787. https://doi.org/10.1038/s41467-018-06930-7

Sharma, K., Qian, F., Jiang, H., Ruchansky, N., Zhang, M., & Liu, Y. (2019). Combating fake news: A survey on identification and mitigation techniques. *ACM Transactions on Intelligent Systems and Technology, 10*(3), 1–42. https://doi.org/10.1145/3305260

Swami, V. Barron, D., Weis, L., & Furnham, A. (2018). To Brexit or not to Brexit: The roles of Islamophobia, conspiracist beliefs, and integrated threat in voting intentions for the United Kingdom European Union membership referendum. *British Journal of Psychology*, *109*(1), 156–179. https://doi.org/10.1111/bjop.12252

Swire-Thompson, B. (2018). *The role of memory and ideological biases in the correction of misinformation*. Doctoral Thesis. The University of Western Australia.

Tollefson, J. (2021). Tracking QAnon: How Trump turned conspiracy-theory research upside down. *Nature*, *590*, 192–193. https://doi.org/10.1038/d41586-021-00257-y

Treisman, D., & Guriev, S. (2023). *Spin dictators*. Princeton University Press.

Tucker, J., Guess, A., Barbera, P., Vaccari, C., Siegel, A., Sanovich, S., Stukal, D., & Nyhan, B. (2018). Social media, political polarization, and political disinformation: A review of the scientific literature. *SSRN Electronic Journal*. https://doi.org/10.2139/ssrn.3144139

Tzu, S. (2020). *Art of war*. S.L.: Flame Tree Publishing.

Waisbord, S. (2018). The elective affinity between post-truth communication and populist politics. *Communication Research and Practice*, *4*(1), 17–34. https://doi.org/10.1080/22041451.2018.1428928

Walton, C. (2019). Spies, election meddling, and disinformation: Past and present. *The Brown Journal of World Affairs*, *26*(1).

Wardle, C., & Derakhshan, H. (2017). *Information Disorder: Toward an interdisciplinary framework for research and policy making*. Council of Europe. https://rm.coe.int/090000168076299d. Accessed on 27 February 2023.

Wasserman, H., & Madrid-Morales, D. (2022). *Disinformation in the Global South*. John Wiley & Sons, Inc.

Weeks, B. E., & Garrett, R. K. (2014). Electoral consequences of political rumors: Motivated reasoning, candidate rumors, and vote choice during the 2008 U.S. Presidential election. *International Journal of Public Opinion Research*, *26*(4), 401–422. https://doi.org/10.1093/ijpor/edu005

Wells, C., Justin Reedy, J., Gastil, J., & Lee, C. (2009). Information distortion and voting choices: The origins and effects of factual beliefs in initiative elections. *Political Psychology*, *30*(6), 953–969. Available at:. https://doi.org/10.1111/j.1467-9221.2009.00735.x

Woolley, S., & Howard, P. (2017). *Computational propaganda worldwide: Executive summary*. Project on Computational Propaganda. https://demtech.oii.ox.ac.uk/research/posts/computational-propaganda-worldwide-executive-summary/. Accessed on 24 February 2023.

Woolley, S. (n.d.). Bots unite to automate the presidential election. *Wired*. https://www.wired.com/2016/05/twitterbots-2/. Accessed on 24 February 2023.

Ziemer, C. T., & Rothmund, T. (2024). Psychological underpinnings of misinformation countermeasures: A systematic scoping review. leden, 1864-1105/a000407. *Journal of Media Psychology*. https://doi.org/10.1027/1864-1105/a000407

Zimmermann, F., & Kohring, M. (2020). Mistrust, disinforming news, and vote choice: A panel survey on the origins and consequences of believing disinformation in the 2017 German parliamentary election. *Political Communication*, *37*(2), 215–237. https://doi.org/10.1080/10584609.2019.1686095

Use of Analytics in Political Marketing: Data-Driven Campaigns, Theory and Examples

Anna Shavit and Marcela Konrádová

INTRODUCTION

The main goal of this chapter is to investigate the importance of data in the modern era of campaigning. Political campaigns always have a specific objective and are usually conducted within a particular time frame (see Brady et al., 2006). However, depending on the main objectives and context (and the party's goals), the activities may differ, and not every political campaign is conducted similarly. Through the decades, the focus shifted from electoral posters and billboard slogans to data-driven campaigns (Römmele & Gibson, 2020). Parties and candidates use data to build profiles of potential voters and target their outreach in the same way enterprises use business intelligence tools to personalize marketing efforts. Data analytics is gaining particular importance as a valuable source of information about the political environment, voters, topics and opponents – polls and other data collections back up the overall electoral strategy. Some authors discuss data-driven political campaigns and politics (Dommett, 2019).

At the same time, no one doubts that we live in an era of permanent political campaigns (Blumenthal, 1982). The assumption is that 'every day is election day'. While in the 1980s, when this concept had its roots, interest was focused mainly on the communication of politicians and political parties, today, attention focuses on new tools and techniques of political marketing. If a permanent campaign is to be effective and cover different types/levels of elections, resources (both human and financial) need to be managed sophisticatedly.

So, are modern campaigns rooted in data and data analytics? What data are needed, and how are the data collected and processed? We will explain this step by step with a closer look into the type of data, the diversity of data-driven practices and the role of analytics in politics. Who is behind a successful data-driven campaign? Usually, this topic covers mysteries created by companies like Cambridge Analytica (Isaak & Hanna, 2018) or misinterpretations of the role of data in the campaign process. Based on the author's experience, this chapter answers the questions above. The main contribution of the chapter is thus to simplify the basic principles of political analytics in campaigning into transparent figures applicable to any type of election.

Despite different election cycles, voters are now selecting their representatives every year. That creates a massive inquiry for election data and capable analytics. Election marketers willy-nilly lead a permanent campaign (Blumenthal, 1982) dependent on the data of political analysts. Nevertheless, this field is still in its infancy in the Czech environment, and political entities buy/order analysts and data from external agencies. There are exceptions, and some parties hire, collect and process data on a much bigger scale than others (see Appendix 17.1 for basic information on the Czech political parties). Few of them invest and create a quality and stable analytical team. Many parties need more human resources and the means to work with data, resulting in losing out to the competition. At the same time, as this chapter will show, their work is a de facto never-ending cycle.

Modern Political Campaigning

It is roughly 20 years since the British-American political scientist Pippa Norris published the text *The Evolution of Election Campaigns: Eroding Political Engagement?* in which she defined three different stages of political campaign management according to historical development: premodern, modern and postmodern (Norris, 2004). According to her, the importance of political marketing grew in the second half of the 20th century with the onset of the so-called modern campaign, when the services of marketing professionals began to be used, and election campaigns became more financially demanding. Similarly, the postmodern campaign characterizes the onset of new technological possibilities – the internet and social media (Gregor, 2012, pp. 66–67). Farrell and Webb (2002, pp. 103–108) approach the development similarly. They talk about three stages of professionalization of political campaigns, from the traditional model of ad hoc campaigning at the time of elections to a highly professional permanent campaign targeting different electorate segments (see Bailey et al., 2009; Baines, 1999; Baines et al., 2003). This campaign uses all new technical tools, especially the internet and its platforms. The goal is to segment the public into well-defined voter groups and adapt their means and campaign management.

In the new millennium, campaigns were gradually professionalized and modernized across democratic systems. Professionalization, or sometimes Americanization (Baines et al., 2001), entered the vocabulary of political scientists and professional political marketers. Key features of the new approach included a growing use of external consultants, micro-targeted advertising, computerized databases and an emphasis on marketing research to better package and 'design' party messages (Römmele & Gibson, 2020, p. 596; cf Baines et al., 2002). However, the professionalization of political communication is also associated with declining mass political partisanship. The parties perceive electronic media as a critical communication channel during the electoral campaign, forcing communication campaign strategists to adopt the media logic (Papathanassopoulos et al., 2007). The new medialization of politics manifests strongly in using elements of political marketing in election campaigns.

The professionalization of campaigns also relates to the fact that the number of elections is increasing. It forces the parties and their candidate to run permanent campaigns. Figure 17.1 summarizes the political cycle. It needs to include the difference between various elections, what is essential for the permanent campaign, and the employment of political marketing methods and tools. There is a specific strategy for each type of election campaign, thus also different requirements for political analytics. Elections held at other levels in parallel with the performance of government functions are the so-called second-order elections (Norris, 1997). This label was first used by Reif and Schmitt in 1980 when describing the elections to the European Parliament. Nowadays, the term refers to all electoral contests in the country, except for parliamentary elections (the general elections) and the vote for the president.

Nevertheless, the arena of primary and secondary elections is inseparable. The operation of a political subject at one level affects its perception at another level. In other words, what a political subject does, for example, in a campaign and the subsequent performance of a function in municipal self-government, affects its perception by voters and the formation of preferences at the level of elections to the Senate (the so-called dimension of the transformation of the main arena; see Reif & Schmitt, 1980, pp. 13–14). The overlapping exercise of power at one level and the ongoing election campaign at another level are other factors and reasons for the growing importance of the permanent campaign. The campaign process is continual, with fund-raising for the next election requiring a new or renewed storyline to extract contributions from the same old pockets (Loomis, 2000, p. 162) and new sponsors, too, of course.

In such a case, a long-term strategic plan plays an essential role in the viability of a political party. American consultant Joseph Napolitano states that strategy is vital (Napolitan, 2003, p. 26). With a step-by-step plan and precise formulation of goals, election campaigns can quickly become an efficient waste of often considerable financial and human resources. Compiling a comprehensive programme covering all areas is undoubtedly

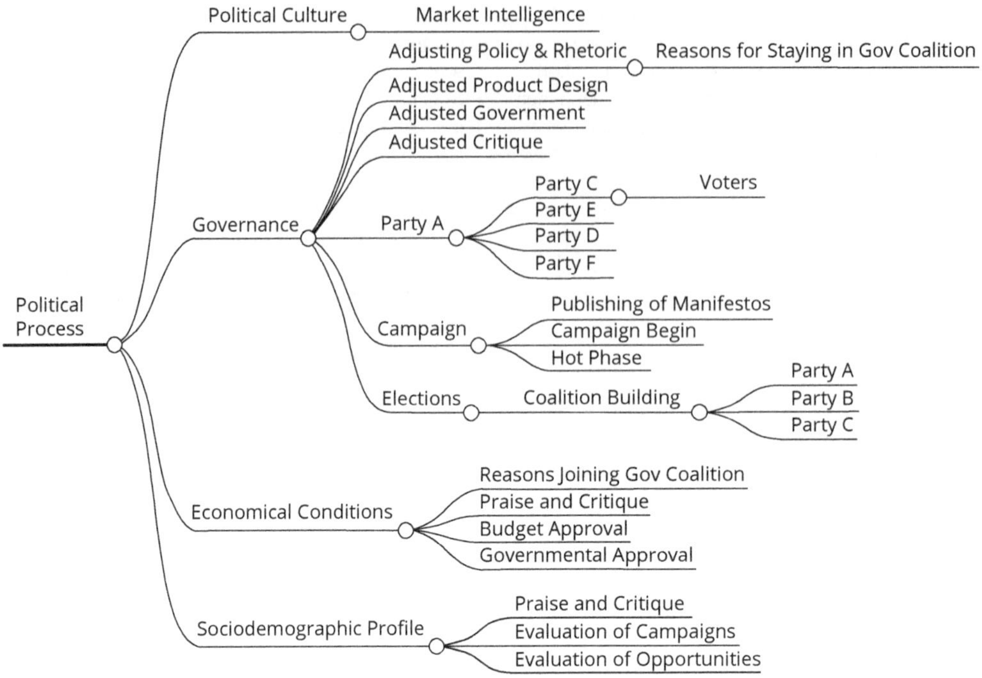

Figure 17.1 Political Election Cycle

Source: Eibl and Matušková (2007, p. 117).

tricky and necessary. The time and financial investment in preparing the strategy (and its subsequent implementation) will benefit the political party during the election campaign (Pavlová & Matušková, 2012, p. 152).

In such a political reality, the continuous work of a massive team of people is necessary, from politicians (party members, officials, candidates) through the internal party team (managers, spokespeople, marketers, analysts) to externally hired professionals (PR and research agencies, graphic designers and many others).

The Fourth Era of Election Campaigns

Due to the complexity of the current political process and further developments in the field of technology, today, we are no longer dealing with a postmodern election campaign. However, we are moving into a fourth era, which can be defined as ***data driven***. It is characterized by shifts in four critical areas of campaign practice. First, and most obviously, the infrastructure and tools used to fight the campaign. Digital technology and data are now hardwired into the campaign organization and operation. Second, parties have moved away from the top-down, 'point to mass' use of mainstream media channels to embrace a more devolved and networked approach to voter communication (see Strömbäck, 2008). Third, the targets for those messages have been reformulated, focusing now on producing a much more fine-grained and personality-based understanding of the persuadable electorate (see also Karvonen, 2009). Finally, campaigns have become far more internationalized regarding the range of actors seeking to participate and influence the outcome. Both 'real' and automated external actors seek influence in orthodox and highly unorthodox or illegitimate ways (Römmele & Gibson, 2020, p. 596).

From the list of characteristics that data-driven campaigns have brought, it is evident that data analytics, data and analytics are an integral part of contemporary political marketing (Baines & Egan, 2001). Data-driven campaigns are a reality at all levels of politics – from local elections to international ones. However, indeed, data analytics is best used at the local level to guide campaigns at the grassroots level. Why is that?

The key feature here is data. Data have become an essential part of how we understand political campaigns. In reviewing coverage of elections – the idea that political parties and campaigners now utilize data to deliver highly targeted, strategic and successful campaigns is readily found (Dommett, 2019, p. 2). Describing the focus of party campaigning, Dalton et al. (2013, p. 56) outline the longstanding interest parties have in collecting data that can be analyzed to (attempt to) achieve electoral success. In their account, candidates and party workers meet with individual voters and develop a list of people's voting preferences. Then, on election day, a party worker knocks on the doors of prospective supporters at their homes to make sure they cast their ballot and often offers a ride to the polls if needed. Hersh (2015) has shown that parties' data about voters are not fine-grained and tend to be drawn from public records containing certain standardized information. Moreover, Bennett has highlighted the significant incentive that campaign consultants and managers must emphasize the sophistication and success of their strategies, suggesting that campaigners may not be offering an accurate account of current practices (2016, p. 261; Kreiss & McGregor, 2018).

Parties gather data about their voter interests, voting preferences and degree of support, allowing them to build large data sets and email lists at national and local levels (Dommett, 2019, p. 3). It is data on constituencies, precincts, neighbourhoods and (ideally) individual voters. Success lies in the detail and the details. The more information there is about voters, the easier it is to tailor a campaign. It all depends on how many resources are available (staff or finances). This is only sometimes possible (due to legislation or lack of information and data), but personal knowledge and experience of the locality can be essential. That is why data-driven campaigns tend to emerge in local elections. Knowledge of the precinct's detailed information about voters is crucial and relatively easy and cheap to obtain in local elections.

Despite the apparent fact that having data is crucial and it is needed. Moreover, even if a party has enough resources (especially finances) to collect data continuously, it does not automatically mean electoral victory. If the party has the data, it must also be able to evaluate, process it and work with it in the campaign. In the fourth era of political campaigning, parties and politicians collect data before, during and after the elections. It is a continuous process (also thanks to the importance of digital technologies).

Therefore, campaigning is an ongoing process seeking to manipulate sources of public approval to engage in governing itself (Heclo, 2000, p. 17). A political party cannot be satisfied with one electoral victory; it must build its structure at all levels. That goes hand in hand with the need to manage resources efficiently. However, data-driven campaigning is even more expensive than professionalized campaigning (Gibson & Römmele, 2001).

Analytics and Politics Then and Now

Data-driven campaigning is believed to enable parties to evaluate campaign actions and gather feedback in a previously impossible way (Dommett, 2019, p. 4). The deployment of analytics can be the difference between success and failure, between victory and defeat in elections. That is nothing new – election campaigns have long used data. Practical politics always relied heavily on data, particularly in electoral campaigns. That data, however, largely came from polls, which are conducted infrequently throughout campaign cycles and can miss shifts in voter sentiment (Avidon, 2022). It has also been claimed that data-driven campaigning enables parties to evaluate campaign actions and gather feedback in a previously impossible way (Dommett, 2019, p. 4).

So why not discuss data in the earlier political marketing and election campaign stages? Farrell and Schmitt-Beck (2002) usefully mapped out the stages of campaigning according to three main features or areas of operation that showed a marked shift over time. The first of these was concerning 'technical developments', which they subdivided into the particular areas of campaign preparation and media use. A second focus was on 'resource developments', which focused on changes to the level and type of internal organizational support and external/commercial expertise that parties and candidates could draw on. Finally, there was an emphasis on what they saw as crucial changes in the 'thematic developments' within campaigns, which centred on changes to the more performative elements of the campaign, that is, the use of events and communicative strategies to engage with voters (cf Römmele & Gibson, 2020, p. 602).

To be more specific – historically, political marketing efforts have centred on television, radio and print advertising, which has always been a substantial part of the budget. In this light, online ads are more affordable. Nevertheless, investing in analytics tools and identifying who to target is even less expensive. Also, historically, polling data has been crucial for political campaigns. Polls can inform candidates which issues are most important to their constituents and whether candidates are ahead of their opponents or trailing where the election is held at a given moment. They can also reveal where candidates are doing well, where they are so far behind it is not even worth sending people to canvass for votes, and where there may be large numbers of voters who might be swayed. However, polls have their drawbacks. They are snapshots of a moment before Election Day rather than an accurate portrayal of what will happen on Election Day – the closer to the election they are conducted, the more predictive they can be. They are also expensive, so polling is not constant and does not always reflect what is happening within an electorate. Census data, party affiliation and voter histories are also informative and have historically been used by campaigns to make data-informed decisions based on demographic data and voter patterns. But analytics in politics has evolved (cf ERC, 2023).

Now, campaigns collect reams of data about potential voters based on their online activity, and just as online activity enables marketers to understand more about individual customers than in the past, it also gives election campaigns greater insight into the public as individuals. Campaigns can see what topics are bubbling up on Google Trends or Twitter in a particular area. They can also monitor how many clicks their ads get and who clicks on them. At a more personal level, they can track email and text exchanges they are having with constituents to understand more about those people, glean trends among voters and view the social media activity of potential voters. Even door-to-door information gathering is more advanced than just a few election cycles ago. Now, canvassers are equipped with tablets, and the information campaign workers collect can be uploaded immediately into a database, as opposed to a couple of decades ago when all that information was written with pen and paper and perhaps never put into a database. The ultimate goal is to create a complete view of each potential voter and use that 'Voter 360' concept to personalize a candidate's message to a potential voter (Avidon, 2022).

So, the analytics used in politics is just as sophisticated as the data analysis used to inform decision-making in the corporate world. A campaign intends to determine how to attract enough votes to ensure victory. Furthermore, they do nearly everything within their means to do so. The key is thus adopting new analytical methods. It has yet to transform how campaigns operate wholly; data-savvy campaigns have gained a competitive advantage due to increased efficiency. That means using data to inform strategy (see section 3.3). Campaigns use analytics to allocate scant resources depending on funding, optimize whom to contact to raise funds, inform messaging, and learn as much as possible about potential voters in their district to decide how to get those likely voters to vote for their candidates.

Development is always moving forward, so even data-driven campaigning has recently changed significantly. Campaigns have increasingly relied on analyzing large and detailed datasets to make predictions. Political parties match new findings with old knowledge. Essentially, marketers engage in an incremental process where they must deal with a bureaucracy of fragmented decision-making structures and a focus on solving day-to-day problems rather than exploring opportunities in the environment (Nielsen, 2012, p. 297). Political parties constantly seek to leverage ever-growing volumes of data to create votes (Nickerson & Rogers, 2014, p. 51). The costs of purchasing, storing, managing and analyzing data have decreased exponentially, while the supply of quantitatively oriented political operatives and campaign data analysts has increased. Predictive analytics, which has gained footholds in other sectors of the economy, such as banking, consulting, marketing and e-commerce, has provided a fertile ground for analytically minded consultants to apply statistical tools to campaign activities and data. Contemporary political campaigns accumulate enormous databases of individual citizens and hire data analysts to create models predicting citizens' behaviours, dispositions and responses to campaign contact. This data-driven campaigning gives candidates and advisers powerful tools for plotting electoral strategy (Nickerson & Rogers, 2014, p. 53). In particular, the data, statistical algorithms and machine learning techniques can help identify the outcome based on historical data. Practical examples can be voter targeting. Campaigns can use information to identify and categorize voters based on their likelihood of supporting a candidate. It helps to allocate sources efficiently. In 2012, the Obama campaign used data to target undecided voters in the key swing states. Another example can be the US presidential election 2016, and both candidates used targeted and personalized messages in social media. The Trump campaign became famous using Cambridge Analytica[1] (focusing on targeting specifically created voter segments; see Laterza, 2021; Richterich, 2018).

Generally, no matter the level or type of election, the current process proceeds from goal definition through planning, data collection and analysis to interpretation and marketing decisions. What remains the same is the need for data, the size of the team and the budget. Individual areas are interconnected. Logically, the organization of a political campaign differs fundamentally depending on the particular election in question (cf Avidon, 2022). The organization will be completely different in first vs. second-order elections. Personalized vote vs. party vote will vary, too. The same applies to the regional vs. national (general) or international (e.g. European parliament elections) campaigns. For general (national, first-order) elections, parties usually have extensive budgets and can hire external marketers and analysts to join their internal teams.

In contrast, at lower levels (local and regional elections), internal teams have a freer hand and rely on local knowledge. The logic of communication in a campaign depends on data, which in significant elections depends on surveys (often carried out by external agencies), unlike issues, for example, municipal elections, where the budget is not so large and therefore turns to some extent on the specific team of people who know the environment. However, the essential elements of a good, effective, successful political campaign are data, and the analytical cycle is transferable to different levels of elections. What differs is the political management involved and the depth of data processing.

The Cycle of Elections and the Cycle of Analytics

Politicians and political parties view their analytic techniques as secret weapons to be kept out of opponents' hands. The public discourse on campaign data has mainly been speculative and somewhat hypothetical, ranging from hyping the performance of the tools (Scherer, 2012) to alarmist concerns about voters' privacy (Duhigg, 2012). This part of the text aims to introduce a general analytical cycle in politics in the case of the Czech Republic. Despite the local focus on the Czech Republic, many things are similar, at least on the European level. Current political campaign trends also cause the sharing of experience across countries, the search for inspiration, and especially the hiring of international experts. The developed figure is thus transferable to other political systems to some extent.

Despite the increasingly interconnected techniques and market similarities, following the rules of the specific electoral market and laws are always necessary. Many records are publicly available, such as voter history in the United States. The voter history, databases, canvassing interferences or social media data can help model and predict voter behaviour. In contrast, these are unavailable for purchase in the European Union countries and other countries that ratified The General Data Protection Regulation (GDPR, 2023). GDPR has significant implications for political campaigns. Shortly, it protects citizens and their data. However, it does not mean they cannot store data; it is an opt-in process, and people have the right to remove their consent. Politicians, organizations and parties can only use data with permission from the actual person. GDPR and other laws reduce many possibilities of direct contact with voters but create another need for authorized voter data. Political analysts in these countries are thus dependent on publicly available sources or their research, which raises the question of a given political party's budget for data collection and analysis. These characteristics are also encountered in the cycle description in Figure 17.2.

The following section will describe the analytical methods at each campaign stage and what data are needed (Figure 17.3). To explain this, we will use examples from campaigns in the Czech Republic (from parliamentary to presidential elections[2]). However, we are using examples from one country. This is the basic alphabet of any campaign. Some items in the use list may change due to different legislation. However, the campaign's organization and the work with data remain the same.

1. What data are needed, and how do you collect them?
2. What are available data sources?
3. Data mining, analyzing and processing.
4. Social media data and how to use them.
5. Who is working with data, and what is the role of consultants and analytics? How do the departments operate?
6. How is political analytics different in campaigns, government and partisan activities?

We argue above that politics is a never-ending process (Figure 17.1). Political campaigning and governing are phases that significantly influence each other. Similarly, political analytics does not begin and end with campaigning. However, it is necessary for a political party's existence, success and effectiveness in modern democracies 'burdened' by permanent campaigns. While election campaign management varies, not only from election to

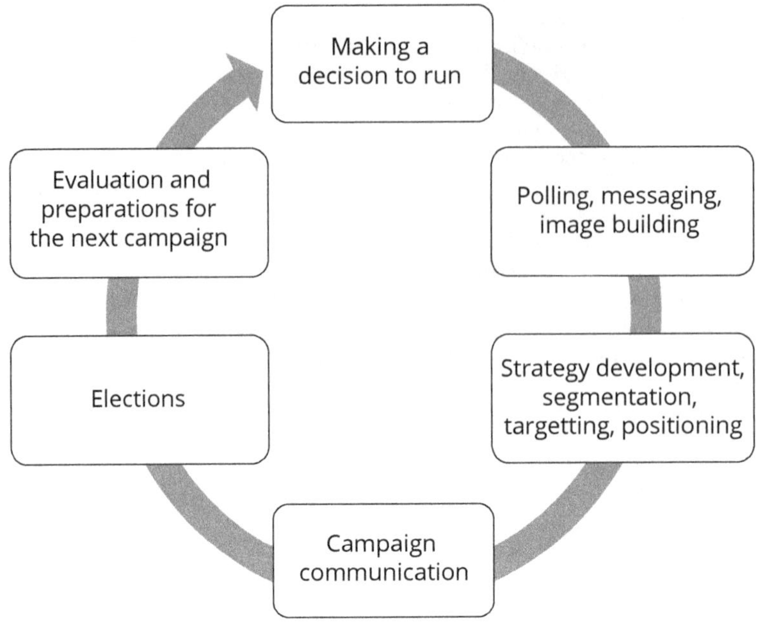

Figure 17.2 Political Campaign Cycle

Source: Authors.

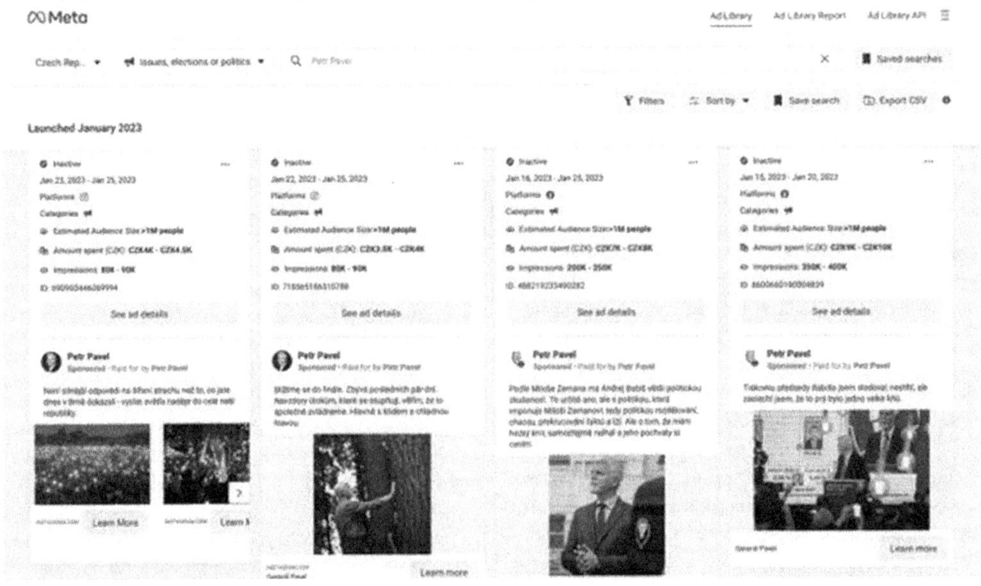

Figure 17.3 The Example of Meta ad Library, Czech Presidential Candidate Petr Pavel

Source: Facebook, 2023 – screenshots from February 17, 2023.

election but also in between due to other levels of elections, the context to adapt to, the communication channels to work with, the need for data and its analysis remains.

If this is the case, the management of the political party can be considered rational. It is logical to run a (permanent) professional data-driven campaign. Furthermore, if that is the case, the answer to the above questions is known initially. In a current political campaign, planning and strategy are essential. Such a campaign is prepared for weeks and months before the election. Political and professional management plays a significant role (see Newman, 1994; Shavit et al., 2024). Every decision to run for office, start a political movement, support a cause or any other type of direct political involvement combines predictable or less predictable variables.

Moreover, every step should be backed by reliable information and data. The given political landscape is an essential factor in any campaign. In many cases – the difference between winning and losing – is what goes on inside the campaign.

The above questions will be answered in the individual stages of the preparation of the election campaign. At each campaign stage, analytics work with different data. The same applies to analytical tools. Therefore, for each point, we will clearly describe and thus answer the questions above, the '*what-who-how*'.

Becoming a Candidate

If we live in an era of permanent campaigns, the question is how to define the start of a campaign or, better, the moment of the need for data. Specific electoral laws for every political contest in the Czech Republic regulate this issue. The political battle begins with the announcement by the party or the candidate. However, it is crucial to note that data are required before the campaign's official launch. The cycle begins with the decision to run. When a party or an individual decides to run, they need a plan and a strategy based on data. The first step is to analyze the political environment, which should address whether voters are interested in the proposed political platform or if it is feasible to convince them to elect a particular candidate.

Running for office is a life-changing experience and a complicated and ultimately personal decision. It is difficult to imagine all the challenges, benefits and sacrifices that will come with it. However, it must first be established if the person is ready. To navigate a campaign, one needs an exact plan – strategy. That can be prepared either by the in-house team or hired experts.

Furthermore, such analysis will use both – primary and secondary data, meaning the internal and external – publicly available data. Today, when there is talk of a leadership crisis (Johansen, 2005; Lees-Marshment, 2012), it is difficult to find a suitable candidate. Political parties need help with declining membership and the often-criticized coexistence of functions (e.g. an MP is also a mayor). Therefore, whether the candidate is a party member or an independent is an important factor for political management when looking for a candidate. In other words, whether it is a candidate who has a proven track record and loyalty to the party or whether it is an external sympathizer or expert. Gripping from the data point of view is mainly the second case when the analytical team examines the independent candidate, his background, professional experience, family background and motivations for entering politics.

For candidates seeking a specific political position, examining their familiarity or potential, particularly their media image and social media analysis, is essential (see Barisione, 2009). That involves determining the candidate's potential and requires not only the ability to find data and process and evaluate it, particularly concerning media analysis. One of the critical factors is the candidate's motivation (Wittman, 2014). Why did they decide to enter the political race? Many things can be measured, calculated and prepared for, but personal motivation and the desire to change something in the public space cannot be staged. Some candidates are completely win-oriented and view policy only to win the election (see Downs, 1957). They tactically react to changes in the electorate's feelings, trying to fine-tune the voters. This kind of politician or party does not have a political concept that would be stable and consistently presented to the citizens. A candidate concerned only with winning is interested in policy only if the policy promotes winning.

On the other hand, what can be measured or researched quite quickly is the candidate's familiarity, how the public perceives them, and then, especially, the associations associated with him. That is, what themes and issues they may represent. That is also related to authenticity, which is extremely important for a candidate. On the other hand, some politicians and parties are issue-oriented, and they view winning to policy (Wittman, 2014). This is important to consider, especially in highly personalized elections such as presidential or senatorial elections (or generally elections in which a majority voting system is used; see Voženílková, 2018).

The first step is a detailed mapping of the political and economic situation in the country and a detailed knowledge of the electoral laws. Political parties usually have an analytical team working throughout the year and preparing data and materials about various policies. This team can provide much analysis of publicly available data. The analytical team elaborates on these factors defining the electoral market (Cichozs, 2006, pp. 51–52):

- Legal factors (e.g. passive suffrage, conditions for candidacy – signatures, bail, the concurrence of offices, electoral system).
- Political criteria (electoral history, political geography, relevant number of parties, personalization of politics, political culture, populism).
- Economic factors (GDP, import/export, debt ratio, inflation).
- Socio-demographic factors (population structure, ethnic and racial composition, age distribution, educational attainment, unemployment rates, regional characteristics or household practices).

These data are publicly available to analysts through statistical offices or similar institutions (in many countries, these data are available, but it is not a universal law). Suppose the political and party system is stable, and we are talking about the candidacy of an established political party or its candidate. In that case, the internal analytical team has a whole range of data at its disposal thanks to its archive.

Before an election, a party usually has detailed research prepared by a research agency. Members of the analytical team or hired experts may be involved in preparing the material. In the Czech Republic, it is standard practice that public opinion polls, which serve as a basis for the election strategy, are commissioned by outside experts. For example, the ANO 2011 political movement[3] collaborated with Alexander Braun,[4] a specialist in working with data. His role was as a pollster and strategist. For example, in the 2021 parliamentary elections, the coalition SPOLU (ODS, KDU-ČSL, TOP 09) created a special strategic team of advisors from all three parties, who then prepared sub-clauses for research. The data obtained, however, were already processed by party analysts.

Thus, the preparation of each campaign starts with the collection of primary data such as opinion polls (see Kuha, 2022; Pereira, 2019), whether they are obtained in the form of traditional questionnaire surveys or data obtained from social media (companies such as Semantic Visions, Behaviour and others), together with information about the candidate (familiarity, available information, voter perception) or the political party (party preferences, popularity, electoral programme). It is then used to inform what will be developed into an electoral strategy. Further steps, such as communication and online media, will emerge from this. The interesting point is that the party starts to work with its data (such as voter databases) and can also use opposition research (Ogden & Medina, 2020) to see what the competition is doing. The 'oppo' is collecting and analyzing information about an opponent. Sometimes, 'oppo' research is handled in-house. It is often outsourced to third-party researchers (Masterclass, 2021). Opposition research might include:

- Checking the integrity of a candidate's personal story or biography.
- Combing through the social media accounts of opposing candidates.
- Talking to past colleagues or employers.
- Inspecting the candidate's voting record and tax records.
- Analysis of media outputs.
- Analysis of the opponent's election programme or various policies.

In this case, it is worth noticing how much data are available online – for example, the Meta platform's ad library or Google ads. The data from Meta's Ad Library and Google's Ad Library can be valuable in analyzing political advertising campaigns (cf Ciper & Meyer, 2022; Nott, 2020). These libraries provide information on political ads, such as the amount spent, targeted demographics and specific messaging. By analyzing these data, political analysts can gain insights into the strategies and tactics used by political campaigns and their effectiveness. In January 2023, the Czech Republic held presidential elections. One can quickly investigate the Meta ad Library to see how much the winner, Petr Pavel, spent on his Facebook campaign advertisement.

Such data are publicly available for every politician and campaign using the Meta platforms (Facebook, Instagram) and provide detailed information about advertising strategy and spending. Constant analysis of platforms such as Facebook, Twitter, Instagram, TikTok or BeReal is routine.

We established that polling is an essential tool for the campaigns. It can provide much different information, such as the level of public support, the popularity of the candidate and the geographical spread of the voters' support. Another vital part is testing the main messages of the campaign. These must be based on the electoral programme or evaluating the issues perceived as crucial among the electorate. The candidate and the central message of the campaign must work well together. In 2013 (Králíková et al., 2014, p. 204), the ANO movement ran for the first time with Andrej Babiš as its elected leader. Babiš is one of the richest Czechs and is also the largest employer. Election polls at the time showed that many of the population feared losing their jobs. One of the election slogans associated with the person of Babiš then was: '*We will create jobs*'. Given that he came into politics as a businessman and an employer, this slogan was exceptionally well-received (see Figure 17.4).[5]

A political campaign is a communication process – find the right message, target that message to the right group of voters and repeat that message repeatedly (O'Day, 20023 p. 9). Issues and electoral programmes are closely related to the candidates or party's image (Dalton & Weldon, 2005) and brand. As a brand, a political party should stand on a solid foundation of ideology, be based on a programme, and remain consistent in its views and positions over the long term. It is predicated on constant communication to create and sustain a long-term relationship with the electorate. Political parties have lost this connection due to the gradual loosening of party structures, and the rise of short-term marketing strategies focused on maximizing profits in a single election, which has been further reinforced (Gregor, 2016, p. 9). Therefore, in a data-driven campaign, opinion polls – message and topic testing are crucial for political parties, politicians/candidates and their brands.

Campaign Strategy

Data are the main foundation of the campaign strategy (compare Butler & Collins, 1996). A successful campaign must use a strategic plan based on information and data obtained from research and polling. An important role is the electoral team, consisting of party employees from communication, analytical, creative and other teams and hired consultants (such as strategists, media consultants, policy advisers and social media platforms); see Shavit et al., 2024).

Electoral strategy is a plan that tells the candidate or the political party what steps to take to achieve their goals (Pavlová & Matušková, 2012, p. 154). It is also the foundation for all tactical moves – follow-up polling, communication, social media, segment creation and targeting. The closest team, including the main political frontrunners, prepared it. An analyst is also integral to this team, providing essential data for strategy development. The field of political marketing strategy can be divided into three faces: design, emergent and interpretive (see Table 17.1). The first phase of the strategy is concerned with designing a game plan. The strategy-making process revolves mainly around a controlled and planned platform entrenched in the top management of the political organization. The axiomatic ground is shaped by rational actors who engage in a linear decision-making process with the capacity to plan and implement change. Most actions are based on political marketers' ability to predict the moves of competitors and voters in a relatively stable environment (Nielsen, 2012, p. 296). The design includes segmentation and positioning (cf Baines et al., 2002). Secondly, the idea behind the emergent political marketing strategy phase can be summarized in one sentence: It is a marketing strategy carried out on the run. Under conditions of unpredictability, political marketing strategy becomes an emergent process. The focal point is to adapt using 'matching and learning' to have a competitive advantage in the market. An emergent strategy will develop feedback mechanisms that factor in environmental information (Nielsen, 2012, p. 297). Thirdly and lastly, the world outside the political organization is a construction. The interpretive political marketing strategy face is built on this bold statement, which dictates that the world is shaped by inter-subjective thoughts and actions we all assemble. It represents a certain logic in, for example, constructivist and post-modern marketing theories. The foundation of the interpretive strategy face is that a party, for instance, builds strategies to manipulate and alter the environment to gain legitimacy. By envisioning and enforcing new worldviews, symbols, norms and metaphors, a party can transform the general perception of a policy output, societal problem or political landscape (Nielsen, 2012, p. 298).

In this sense, a strategy is more than the content of the marketing plan but also involves the legal, cultural and institutional context constraining actors and, finally, the complexities of the managerial decision-making process (Nielsen, 2012, p. 295). A large part of the strategy lies in the ability of the political marketer to predict what the competition plans to do. Such a plan uses and works with voter segments and a stable environment (Nielsen, 2012, p. 296). A SWOT analysis[6] is valuable for any political campaign. It can help identify strengths and weaknesses and the opportunities and threats the candidate or party might face. For example, its greatest strength is its ability to connect with voters through social media. However, its defect might be that it needs more money to run face-to-face campaigning. It includes public opinion polls, election results and media coverage. The SWOT analysis must involve not only the analytical team, the media team and the candidate himself. The data entering the SWOT analysis are like those collected before the start of the campaign. Once the data get gathered, it is time to analyze it and look for patterns. From the SWOT analysis, the analyst should infer four strategies:

1. Exploitation strategies – how to use strengths to take advantage of opportunities.
2. Seeking strategy – using opportunities to remove/reduce weaknesses.
3. Confrontation strategy – how to use strengths to ward off threats.
4. Avoidance strategy – how to reduce threats concerning weaknesses (see Sarsby, 2016).

Second, political marketing strategy becomes an emergent process under unpredictability. The focal point is to adapt using 'matching and learning' to have a competitive advantage in the market (Nielsen, 2012, p. 297). Organizations match new findings with old knowledge. Essentially, marketers engage in an incremental process where they must deal with a bureaucracy of fragmented decision-making structures and a focus on solving day-to-day problems rather than exploring opportunities in the environment (Fischer et al., 2007, p. 191). In practice, it means testing public opinion or focus groups related to sudden 'events' before presenting the policy offerings in more detail during an election (Fischer et al., 2007; Sparrow & Turner, 2001). The exact polling focuses on the party position and audience response to the political offer (programme, candidates). This quantitative research establishes how many complications there are. The focus groups are qualitative research and provide answers and an understanding of why voters like or dislike a particular issue or how they understand the topic. Extensive polling operations require a very advanced team, but mainly financial sources, representing a significant part of the budget during the campaign and generally during the whole electoral cycle.

An example of working with data is the billboard from the presidential election 2023, which says, 'The General does not believe in peace. Vote for peace. Vote Babiš'. The political party ANO has long commissioned opinion polls, based on which it prepares its communication strategy. In this case, the topic of the military conflict in Ukraine was further tested qualitatively to negatively define itself against the opposing candidate, General Petr Pavel. Andrej Babiš tried to appear as a diplomat and peacemaker (see Figure 17.5). During the second round of the elections, Babiš used billboards that insinuated that his opponent, Petr Pavel, a former NATO official, would drag the Czech Republic into the war. The frame was supported later during the two weeks after Babiš said in one of the presidential debates that he would not keep sending the Czech army to help Poland if a fellow NATO member was attacked by Russia (something that goes directly against Article 5 of the North Atlantic Treaty; Křovák et al., 2023). This billboard ('The general does not believe in peace. Vote for peace. Vote for Babiš'.) caused a great wave of criticism and fear.

The correct use of political marketing tools and their control in the campaign helps in the efficient use of funds in the organization, pointing out possible shortcomings and weaknesses and warning of problems that may occur (Králíková, 2014, p. 108). First, the strategy relies on electoral segmentation (Smith & Hirst, 2001). The segments are a group of voters most responsive to the electoral proposal, and the chance they will vote for the candidate is high. The classification of voters into homogeneous groups is done according to (1) geographic, (2) demographic, (3) behavioural and (4) psychological criteria. While the first two criteria are based on publicly available data, the second assumes that the analysis team will have its data. Based on analysis of previous elections, long-term observation of voter behaviour or competition, and public opinion surveys. A fitting example from Czechia is the activity of the ANO party – online platform 'We want a better Czech Republic'. The regional and senate elections campaign used data from this platform (www.chcemelepsicesko.cz). The platform invited people to comment on selected topics and share their ideas and views (ANO, 2016). The ANO team gained valuable insights (such as what people specifically want in their region, what is bothering them, what they would like to change and also how), and it helped to formulate the issues for the campaign.

Segmentation, that is, after collecting and processing data and identifying distinct groups, is followed by targeting. The selection of those groups or segments will be targeted by the campaign (Lees-Marshment, 2009, p. 77). In this part of the analytical work, knowing the strengths and weaknesses of one's candidates and those of political opponents is vital. Thus, polls and marketing research again play an important role. Sometimes, the selection of segments based on their attractiveness is unambiguous. Other times, the attractiveness of the segments is similar, and a system for prioritizing the segments needs to be used (for more, see Bannon, 2004: primary goals, secondary goals, relationship building, lost segment). Electoral maps can also help.

Table 17.1 shows the proposed targeting in the 2018 municipal elections in Prague for the already mentioned ANO movement. To create such a map, the team needs electoral data (voter numbers, turnout and history of winners), the structure of the population, party membership and sympathizers, the activity of opponents and specific issues. Social media analytics and publicly available proprietary data are relevant at this stage (see Figure 17.6).

Graphical information systems pictures let candidates know which places to focus on in the election or, on the contrary, avoid them for campaign effectiveness.

The last phase, which is directly related to targeting, is positioning, that is, the most appropriate portrayal of the candidate/party for the segment selected in the targeting process to get the voter to vote for the party/candidate or to switch support from one candidate/party to another (Baines, 1999, p. 413 and Baines et al., 2003). At this stage of the analytical work, it is essential to know opponents as well as possible and to differentiate oneself from them, but most impressively, to the chosen segment. The analytics team presents the data at this stage, but the strategist and the media team do the central part of the work.

Campaign

The actual campaign is the peak of the preparation phase, and suddenly, all the activities involved become 'real'. The team works, the candidate is ready, all campaign literature is printed, all the billboards and posters are visible, and the social media accounts are running. It is time for the communication phase. It is the time to meet with the voters, communicate with the media and participate in televised debates. It is also when the team evaluates the candidate's performance and needs feedback from the voter segments.

It is the busiest time of the whole process. Data analytics does not stop; on the contrary, it

Table 17.1 Three Faces of Strategy in Political Marketing

	Design	*Emergent*	*Interpretive*
Actor assumptions	Foundational: Rational	Foundational: Historical calculus - eclectic basis	Anti-foundational: Sociopsychology
Political environment	Stable and unchangeable	Unstable and unchangeable	Unstable and changeable
Strategic Political behaviour	Outline a precise long-term plan with means and ends	Trial and error. Create a fit between internal and external events.	Develop norms, rituals, signs and symbols.
Strategy objective	Goal attainment	Match and learn to	Create legitimacy
Problems in strategy execution.	The planning becomes too overwhelming. At the same time, there is no room for adaptive actions and responses to feedback from the environment.	Institutional inertia and the deep-rooted culture in political organizations complicate the 'fitting. process.'	The cognitive and normative limitations of top managers hamper the ability to scan input,fabricate meaning and change the environment
Points of critique (Theoretical and practical)	(a) Superhumans (b) Assumptions of environmental status quo	(a) The unlearning of valuable procedures (b) Epistemological confusion	(a) Lopsided focus on outside-in explanations (b) Install a social determinism

Source: Nielsen (2012, p. 295).

Figure 17.4 Political Party ANO, Andrej Babiš and Jaroslav Faltýnek, Slogan – *We Will Create Jobs*

Source: Photo courtesy of Anna Shavit.

Figure 17.5 Presidential Elections in the Czech Republic, Slogan - The General Does Not Believe in Peace.

Source: Photo courtesy of Anna Shavit.

needs to act faster and provide candidate feedback much quicker. Every day, it is necessary to prepare documents for media outputs, analyze their effects on voters and monitor performance on social media. All campaign activities then lead to having new content just for social networks when it is possible to measure their efficiency accurately.

In the case of social media (Petrova et al., 2021), specifically Facebook, the most important things to evaluate are engagement and reach. Engagement (interaction) is the number of user

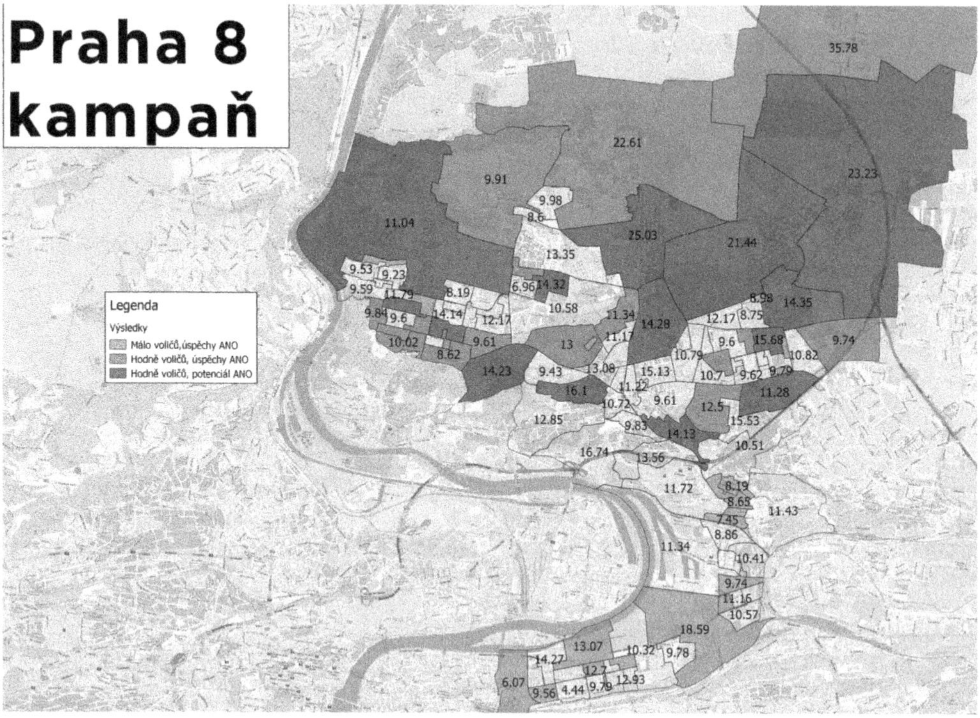

Figure 17.6 Targeting Proposal for the 2018 Municipal Elections in Prague
Source: Authors.

actions on the page. This public data can be measured and compared with any other page on Facebook). Reach is non-public and only seen by people with access to the page, such as the candidate, consultants, analytics team and social media team (the number of users is not limited here). The total reach is counted, whether spontaneous – organic, or paid. For example, the presidential election that took place in the Czech Republic in January 2023 showed the importance and benefits of using social media data in the Czech Republic. This campaign component can give us a clue as to how the individual candidates' teams think, their ambitions, how they want to present themselves online and to whom. Among the metrics that candidates can choose from when placing an advert, which we can then track, some of the most interesting are the following categories: age, region and the gender of the target group. Importantly, however, the Ad Library only informs us of the actual resulting ad impressions, which may differ from what the advertisers originally planned – it reflects the basic algorithm of ad distribution on Facebook and Instagram and user behaviour. For example, analysis by Transparency International and the Association for International Affairs showed how candidates targeted single regions, which candidates were betting on first-time voters versus retirees, or who was trying to attract women versus men (Transparentní volby, 2023).

Many campaigns conclude with televised debates (see Coleman, 2000), requiring preparation and subsequent content work. Preparing for debates is demanding in terms of content, but it also requires practicing public speaking, preparing a communication strategy and choosing topics and key campaign messages. Each preparation is then tailored to the candidate concerning his opponent (see also McQuail, 2009).

Electoral Performance Evaluation and on to the New Campaign

Successful or unsuccessful, the election campaign and results provide parties and their candidates with a wide range of data. That includes data on their success rates, both thematic and electoral-geographic. Analysts examine increases or decreases in support down to the constituency level depending on the election results. They compare the data with the party/candidate's electoral history but also with the gains of the opposition. The best thing about this stage is that the data are publicly available through the Statistical Office, that is, for free. An in-house, permanent analytical team is usually mainly involved in this phase.

However, it is about more than preparing for the next election of the same type. The election result is also vital for planning the forthcoming elections, which may be elections held under different rules (degree of personalization, electoral system). That means that the turnout, the gains of each candidate, and vote transfers can be used not only to get the best possible electoral outcome in the next election but also in strategy planning. The rational thing to do for the next elections is to join with another party in an electoral coalition or even not to field a candidate of one's own and support another.

Evaluating the campaign is a challenging part of the process, but it is imperative. It can outline very well what works and what does not work. The evaluation should focus more on setting up processes and communication within the election team because it can lead to improvements in these processes and the expansion of the analytical or communication teams. It is also essential to determine whether the financial flows were well set up and whether the money was invested correctly and meaningfully. Evaluating a particular candidate is more complicated (for example, political vetting is included – identifying personal, career and political history, both in a positive sense so that it can be used in a campaign, but also the dark shadows that need to be prepared for in case opponents use them in a negative campaign). There is very much a difference between a good politician and a good candidate. It only sometimes goes hand in hand.

DISCUSSION

It is easy to get lost in the overload of information and data related to political campaigns. This text is a window into complex areas related to data-driven campaigns. It is an area of political marketing that is in its infancy and, at the same time, growing at an incredible speed. What was unimaginable a decade ago, such as the role of social networks in political marketing, is now seen as a necessary part of a professionally run campaign. At the same time, the role of analytics in modern, contemporary and practical political marketing is essential. The use of data is enabled by technology. What needs to be clarified is where data analytics will go from here.

Issues related to elections and data analytics are constantly evolving. New and new tools are emerging, as is talk about how Artificial Intelligence (AI) will impact election campaigns in the future. We also asked the ChatGPT chat what it knows about data, strategy and political marketing. Here is what the tool generated.

1 Election campaigns: Political campaigns use data to target voters, analyze public opinion and forecast election outcomes. These data can come from various sources, such as polling, voter databases and social media activity.
2 Policymaking: Government agencies use data to inform policy decisions, such as where to allocate resources and how to tackle social and economic issues. For example, crime rates, employment and economic growth data can inform law enforcement decisions, job creation and economic stimulus programmes.
3 Public opinion: Data can be used to gauge public opinion on political issues, shaping political discourse and decision-making. For example, polls and surveys on hot-button topics such as healthcare, immigration and gun control can help politicians understand the public's position and respond accordingly.
4 Transparency and accountability: Data can be used to hold politicians and governments accountable for their actions. For example, budget data can track government spending and ensure public funds are used appropriately. Data on voting records can be used to hold elected officials accountable for their actions in office (OpenAI, 2023).

CONCLUSION

Every campaign is unique yet very similar. Some basic principles and rules can apply to any electoral race (O'Day, 2003, p. 9). In the text, we have shown that just as political campaigning and communication run in a cycle that never begins or ends in the era of permanent campaigns, analytical work with data is continuous if the work of the party team is to be effective. We imaginatively began our data collection and analysis description by deciding to run in the election. This point is often forgotten, but the rational thing to do before the actual announcement of candidacy is to have enough data to help the party/candidate manage the campaign effectively and, in the best possible case, win. The following stages could be more surprising – strategy development, analytical work during the campaign and evaluation and preparation for the party's subsequent activities, not only in the elected institution and the next election.

The question is, can we automatically equate modern campaigns with data? We would say yes, indeed. Data dominate, whether a party or personal candidacy, an established or new entity, or an ideologically based or more ad-hoc issue-based campaign. Generally, a successful campaign works well with data and can reach and engage voters.

Nevertheless, what data are needed, and how do you collect them? That was the first question we wanted to answer. We showed that different data are required for each campaign phase, from the personal information about the candidate, which sometimes only they can provide, to publicly available statistical data. Collecting them then depends on their availability – whether they can simply be downloaded or need to be commissioned. These are the two most common ways of managing them. Increasingly crucial in data-driven campaigns is the data available through social networks and the activity of their users. These de facto answers the second question regarding the data sources needed. Here, it is essential to note the importance of externally hired agencies, which, if there is funding for the campaign, can provide the data and analyze it for a specific party campaign.

That brings us to the third question, namely, how to work with the data and analyze and process it, and the fifth question, who works with the data? Our emphasis was mainly on the internal analytical team, which is permanent, and its work is continuous. In the era of data-driven campaigns, the focus is on collecting, archiving and comparing the data with the current context. How political reality changes is one thing, but how to respond to it within the brand is another. We described the analytical tools used in political marketing in the context of the Czech elections without going into technical details. It is worth noting that the analytics team does not work in a vacuum – it is a necessary part of the closer campaign management.

Since the text deals with the fourth phase of campaign management, data-driven campaigns, we have included one of the most powerful tools of our time, namely social networks. The data we get through them are unique and unavailable in any other way. In a real political campaign, the analytical team and the social networks managing team are often separate. Nevertheless, they still need to reach out to the analytics team. The so-called political institutes can also play an analytical role here. In the Czech Republic, their operation is regulated by Act No 424/1991 Coll. on association with political parties and political movements. It is a legal entity established under the Public Utilities Act. According to the Law, political institutes are supposed to serve the development of democracy and civil society, promote active participation of citizens in public life, improve the quality of political culture and debate or contribute to international understanding and cooperation. Each year, political institutes are entitled to receive from the State an amount equal to 10 % of the total activity contribution due to the party or movement that founded or is a member of the political institutes. These institutes can substitute for analytical work since their activities include, among other things, the publication of policy papers and policy analysis available to party members and officials. They also serve as a platform for politicians at different party levels to meet with their supporters, sharing experiences, ideas, information, data and analysis.

Lastly, how is political analytics different in campaigns, government and partisan activities? The focus was on the continuation of data analytics for the needs of subsequent election campaigns. However, if a party/candidate is successful and wins a mandate, it is impossible to rest on our laurels. Logically, the sub-objectives for which data are collected change. It is about something other than immediate data use in a campaign but about long-term branding and positioning in the political marketplace as part of a permanent campaign for re-election. It is essential to distinguish whether we are talking about the party as such or a specific candidate (especially in personalized elections, e.g. a senator). In the case of individual performance, the central (analytical) team takes a back seat in the mid-term elections, and the candidate's team comes to the fore.

In conclusion, we dare to say that no successful political party or politician can do without analytical work. The only question is who manages this work, how the analytical team is composed and how it cooperates with other campaign managers. And, of course, how much money is allocated to analytics.

Notes

1 A British political consulting firm. Cambridge Analytica was established in 2013 as a subsidiary of the private intelligence company SCL Group that was active in military and political arenas. In March 2018, media outlets broke news of Cambridge Analytica's business practices. *The New York Times* and *The Observer* reported that the

company had acquired and used personal data about Facebook users from an external researcher who had told Facebook he was collecting it for academic purposes.

2 The authors use available records, information and knowledge from personal experience. They both worked on numerous campaigns as consultants.

3 The aim of the text is not to analyze the Czech party system. Basic information and abbreviations can be found in Annex 1; for more information, see Havlík & Hloušek, 2013.

4 Alexander Braun, an award-winning strategist who crafts communications campaigns based on research and analytics. Called a 'campaign magician' by Forbes, Alex has founded and leads the research and international political practices at SKDK, one of America's top consultancies. He is also an adjunct professor of the campaign management at George Washington University (LinkedIn, 2023; SKDK, 2024).

5 This slogan was tested, along with many others, and picked based on the data support.

6 A SWOT analysis examines the internal environment of an organization – its strengths and weaknesses – and the external factors that affect it in the form of opportunities or threats (Speth, 2015). Internal factors support or hinder an organization in achieving its objectives and are also controllable. Opportunities and threats, on the other hand, are uncontrollable and are more likely to represent opportunities that could enable or prevent the. pursuit of the strategy (Dyson, 2004). For more, see Leigh, 2009.

REFERENCES

ANO. (2016). *Chceme lepší Česko - v každé části naší země*. https://www.anobudelip.cz/cs/makame/aktuality/tiskove-zpravy/chceme-lepsi-cesko-v-kazde-casti-nasi-zeme-26333.shtml. Accessed on February 19, 2023.

Avidon, E. (2022). Election campaigns recognize the need for analytics in politics. *Tech Target*. https://www.techtarget.com/searchbusinessanalytics/feature/Election-campaigns-recognize-need-for-analytics-in-politics. Accessed on February 21, 2024.

Bailey, C., Baines, P., Lang, B., & Warnaby, G. (2009). Segmentation and customer insight in contemporary services marketing practice: Why grouping customers is no longer enough. *Journal of Marketing Management*, *25*(3–4), 227–252.

Baines, P. (1999). Voter segmentation and candidate positioning. In B. I. Newman (Ed.), *Political marketing handbook*. SAGE.

Baines, P., & Egan, J. (2001). Marketing and political campaigning: Mutually exclusive or exclusively mutual? *Qualitative Market Research: An International Journal*, *4*(1), 25–34.

Baines, P., Harris, P., & Lewis, B. (2001). The "Americanisation" myth in European political markets-A focus on the United Kingdom. *European Journal of Marketing*, *35*(9–10), 1099–1117.

Baines, P., Harris, P., & Lewis, B. (2002). The political marketing planning process: Improving image and message in strategic target areas. *Marketing Intelligence & Planning*, *20*(1), 6–14.

Baines, P., Harris, P., & Lewis, B. (2003). Market segmentation and product differentiation in political campaigns: A technical feature perspective. *Journal of Marketing Management*, *19*(1–2), 225–249.

Bannon, D. P. (2004). *Marketing segmentation and political marketing*. Political Studies Association.

Barisione, M. (2009). So, what difference do leaders make? Candidates' images and the "conditionality" of leader effects on voting. *Journal of Elections, Public Opinion, and Parties*, *19*(4), 473–500.

Bennett, C. (2016). Voter databases, micro-targeting, and data protection law: Can political parties campaign in Europe as they do in North America? *International Data Privacy Law*, *6*(4), 261–275.

Blumenthal, S. (1982). *The permanent campaign*. Simon & Schuster.

Brady, H. E., Johnston, R., & Sides, J. (2006). *The study of political campaigns*. https://www.press.umich.edu/pdf/0472099213-ch1.pdf

Butler, P., & Collins, N. (1996). Strategic analysis in political markets. *European Journal of Marketing*, *30*(10–11), 25–36.

Cichozs, M. (2006). Metody analýzy a diagnostiky politického trhu. In A. W. Jabłoński & others (Eds.), *Politický marketing. Úvod do teorie a praxe*. Barrister & Principal.

Ciper, S., & Meyer, T. (2022). *What is political? The uncoordinated efforts of social media platforms on political advertising*. Brussels School of Governance. https://brussels-school.be/publications/policy-briefs/policy-brief-what-political-uncoordinated-efforts-social-media-platforms

Coleman, S. (2000). *Televised election debates: International perspectives*. Macmillan Press.

Dalton, R. J., Farrell, D. M., & McAllister, I. (2013). *Political parties and democratic linkage*. Oxford University Press.

Dalton, R. J., & Weldon, S. A. (2005). Public images of political parties: A necessary evil? *West European Politics*, *28*(5), 931–951.

Dommett, K. (2019). Data-driven political campaigns in practice: Understanding and regulating diverse data-driven campaigns. *Internet Policy Review*, *8*(4). https://policyreview.info/articles/analysis/data-driven-political-campaigns-practice-understanding-and-regulating-diverse-data

Downs, A. (1957). *An economic theory of democracy*. Addison-Wesley.

Duhigg, C. (2012, October 13). Campaigns mine personal lives to get out vote. *New York Times*, A1.

Dyson, R. (2004). Strategic development and SWOT analysis at the university of Warwick. *European Journal of Operational Research*, *152*(3), 631–640.

Eibl, O., & Matušková, A. (2007). Introduction of the election cycle model: The case of the Czech Republic 2006–2007. *Central European Political Studies Review*, *IX*(2–3), 114–138.

ERC. (2023). *How technology is reshaping political campaigns*. https://erc.europa.eu/projects-statistics/science-stories/how-technology-reshaping-political-campaigns. Accessed on February 21, 2024.

Facebook. (2023). https://www.facebook.com/ads/library/?^ff=trun -1active_status=all&ad_type=political_and_issue_ads&country=CZ&q=petr%20pavel&sort_data[direction]=desc&sort_data[mode]=relevancy_monthly_grouped&search_type=keyword_unordered&media_type=all. Accessed on February 17, 2024.

Farrell, D., & Schmitt-Beck, R. (Eds.). (2002). *Do political campaigns matter? Campaign effects in elections and referendums*. Routledge.

Farrell, D., & Webb, P. (2002). Political parties as campaign organizations. In R. J. Dalton & M. P. Wattenberg (Eds.), *Parties without partisans*. Oxford University Press.

Fischer, T., & others (Eds.). (2007). *The strategy of politics. Bielefeld*: Verlag Bertelsmann Stiftung.

GDPR. (2023). https://gdpr.eu/what-is-gdpr/. Accessed on February 7, 2023.

Gibson, R., & Römmele, A. (2001). A party-centered theory of professionalized campaigning. *Harvard International Journal of Press*, *6*(4), 31–43.

Gregor, M. (2012). Klasické koncepty v politickém marketingu. In R. Chytilek, O. Eibl, A. Matušková, & others (Eds.), *Teorie a metody politického marketingu*. Centrum pro studium demokracie a kultury.

Gregor, M. (2016). *Základní atributy značek ČSSD a ODS 2002–2013 ve volebních kampaních*. Masarykova univerzita.

Havlík, V., & Hloušek, V. (2013). Czech political parties, their functions and performance: Assessing Czech party politics. *Scientia et Societas*, *IX*(1), 121–143.

Heclo, H. (2000). Campaigning and governing: A conspectus. In N. J. Ornstein & T. E. Mann (Eds.), *The permanent campaign and its future*. American Enterprise Institute, The Brookings Institution.

Hersh, E. (2015). *Hacking the electorate: How campaigns perceive voters*. Cambridge University Press.

Isaak, J., & Hanna, M. J. (2018). User data privacy: Facebook, Cambridge Analytica, and privacy protection. *Computer*, *51*(8), 56–59.

Johansen, H. P. (2005). Political marketing. *Journal of Political Marketing*, *4*, 105–185.

Karvonen, L. (2009). *The personalisation of politics: A study of parliamentary democracies*. ECPR Press.

Králiková, M., & others (2014). *Volební kampaně 2013*. Barrister & Principal.

Kreiss, D., & McGregor, S. (2018). Technology firms shape political communication: The work of Microsoft, Facebook, Twitter and Google with campaigns during the 2016 US presidential cycle. *Political Communication*, *35*(2), 155–177.

Křovák, J., Konrádová, M., & Shavit, A. (2023). Populist leadership in the Czech Republic through media framing perspective. In **Populism in National and Global Media* (Vilnius)*. Conference paper.

Kuha, J. (2022). *The politics of polling: Why are polls important during elections? The London school of economics and political science*. https://www.lse.ac.uk/research/research-for-the-world/impact/the-politics-of-polling-why-are-polls-important-during-elections. Accessed on February 19, 2023.

Laterza, V. (2021). Could Cambridge analytica have delivered Donald Trump's 2016 presidential victory? An anthropologist's look at big data and political campaigning. *Public Anthropologist*, *3*, 119–147.

Lees-Marshment, J. (2009). *Political marketing: Principles and applications*. Routledge.

Lees-Marshment, J. (2012). *Political marketing and opinion leadership: Comparative perspectives and findings*. Palgrave Macmillan.

Leigh, D. (2009). SWOT analysis. In K. H. Silber & others (Eds.), *Handbook of improving performance in the workplace, volumes 1-3*. International Society for Performance Improvement.

LinkedIn. (2023). *Alexander Braun*. https://www.linkedin.com/in/alexander-braun-8802283/. Accessed on February 16, 2023.

Loomis, B. A. (2000). The never-ending story: Campaigns without elections. In N. J. Ornstein & T. E. Mann (Eds.), *The permanent campaign and its future*. American Enterprise Institute, The Brookings Institution.

Masterclass. (2021). What is opposition research? Understanding the tactics used by political campaigns to conduct and use opposition research. https://www.masterclass.com/articles/what-is-opposition-research-understanding-the-tactics-used-by-political-campaigns-to-conduct-and-use-opposition-research

McQuail, D. (2009). *Úvod do teorie masové komunikace*. Portál.

Napolitan, J. (2003). Napolitan's rules: 112 Lessons learned from career in politics. In R. A. Faucheux (Ed.), *Winning elections. Political campaign management, strategy, and tactics*. M. Evans and Company, Inc.

Newman, B. I. (1994). *The marketing of the president. Political marketing as campaign strategy*. SAGE.

Nickerson, D. W., & Rogers, T. (2014). Political campaigns and big data. *The Journal of Economic Perspectives*, *28*(2), 51–74.

Nielsen, S. W. (2012). Three faces of political marketing strategy. *Journal of Public Affairs*, *12*(4), 293–302.

Norris, P. (1997). Second-order elections. *European Journal of Political Research*, *31*, 109–124.

Norris, P. (2004). *The evolution of election campaigns: Eroding political engagement?* Harvard University.

Nott, L. (2020). Political advertising on social media platforms. *Human Rights Magazine*, *45*(3). . https://www.americanbar.org/groups/crsj/publications/human_rights_magazine_home/voting-in-2020/political-advertising-on-social-media-platforms/

O'Day, J. B. (2003). *Political campaign planning manual: A step by step guide to winning elections*. National Democratic Institute for International Affairs.

Ogden, B. & Medina, A.. (2020). *Strategic opposition research*. Available at SSRN 3631386.

OpenAI. (2023). *Data and politics*. openai.com/data-and-politics/. Accessed on February 10, 2023.

Papathanassopoulos, S., & others (2007). Political communication in the era of professionalisation. In R. Negrine & others (Eds.), *The professionalisation of political communication*. Intellect.

Pavlová, E., & Matušková, A. (2012). Volební strategie a kampaně. In R. Chytilek, O. Eibl, A. Matušková, & others (Eds.), *Teorie a metody politického marketingu*. Centrum pro studium demokracie a kultury.

Pereira, M. M. (2019). Do parties respond strategically to opinion polls? Evidence from campaign statements. *Electoral Studies*, *59*, 78–86.

Petrova, M., Sen, A., & Yildirim, P. (2021). Social media and political contributions: The impact of new technology on political competition. *Management Science*, *67*(5), 2997–3021.

Römmele, A., & Gibson, R. (2020). Scientific and subversive: The two faces of the fourth era of political campaigning. *New Media & Society*, *22*(4), 595–610.

Reif, K., & Schmitt, H. (1980). Nine second-order national elections – A conceptual framework for the analysis of European election results. *European Journal of Political Research*, *8*, 3–44.

Richterich, A. (2018). How data-driven research fuelled the Cambridge analytica controversy. *Partecipazione e Conflitto*, *11*(2), 528–543 (Symposium).

Sarsby, A. (2016). *SWOT analysis. Guide to swot for business studies students*. Spectaris Ltd.

Scherer, M. (2012, November 19). Inside the secret world of quants and data crunchers who helped Obama win. *Time*, 56–60.

Shavit, A., Konrádová, M., & Koudelková, P. (2024). Management of political leadership and branding. In J. Lees-Marshment (Ed.), *Routledge handbook of applied political management. The accepted manuscript will be issued in May 2024*.Routledge.

SKDK. (2024). https://skdknick.com/

Smith, G., & Hirst, A. (2001). Strategic political segmentation – A new approach for a new era of political marketing. *European Journal of Marketing*, *35*(9/10), 1058–1073.

Sparrow, N., & Turner, J. (2001). The permanent campaign. *European Journal of Marketing*, *35*(9/10), 984–1002.

Speth, C. (2015). *The SWOT analysis: Develop strengths to decrease the weaknesses of your business*. Primento Digital.

Strömbäck, J. (2008). Four phases of mediatization: An analysis of the mediatization of politics. *The International Journal of Press/Politics*, *13*(3), 228–246.

Transparentní volby. (2023). *Na koho a kde cílí s placenou reklamou na sociálních sítích prezidentští kandidáti?* https://www.transparentnivolby.cz/hrad2023/aktuality/na-koho-a-kde-cili-s-placenou-reklamou-na-socialnich-sitich-prezidentsti-kandidati/. Accessed on February 20, 2023.

Voženílková, M. (2018). *Personalizace politiky v České republice*. Masarykova univerzita.

Wittman, D. (2014). Candidate motivation: A synthesis of alternative theories. *American Political Science Review*, *77*(1), 142–157.

APPENDIX 17.1 CZECH POLITICAL PARTIES, BASIC INFORMATION

Name	*Abbreviation*	*Ideology*
Civic Democratic Party	ODS	Conservatism Economic liberalism Euroscepticism
Christian and Democratic Union	KDU-ČSL	Christian democracy
TOP 09	-	Liberal conservatism
ANO 2011	ANO	Centrism Populism
Mayors and Independents	STAN	Local politics Liberal conservatism
Czech Pirate Party	Piráti	Liberalism Direct democracy Digitalization Transparency
Freedom and Direct Democracy	SPD	Right-wing populism Direct democracy

Source: Authors.

Role of Content and Narrative in Indian Political Leadership Communication: A Narrative Paradigm Theory Approach

Pooja Sharma and Varsha Jain

INTRODUCTION

The evolving social media usage affects all aspects of our lives, including politics. It has transformed the way people communicate, regulating their thoughts, behaviour and interactions with each other (Munger et al., 2022). Content plays a vital role in shaping engaging and compelling stories, posts and tweets on social media platforms such as Instagram, Facebook and X, covering the digital media landscape (Papacharissi & de Fatima Oliveira, 2012). Content plays a role in encouraging participation and interaction, sharing information, building brands and fostering audience engagement on these platforms. Each social media platform adopts strategies for creating content and engaging users based on their features, audience demographics and communication dynamics involving (i) message sending, (ii) receiving messages and (iii) feedback (Kiesler et al., 1984). Platforms like Facebook, Instagram, X and YouTube have made significant progress in recent years, changing how interactions occur, information is shared and engagement with political matters (Klinger & Svensson, 2015; Papakyriakopoulos et al., 2020). Social media has transformed the political landscape by introducing advancements and new global challenges for political leaders, parties, organizations and individuals, including citizens and communities. It has revolutionized political communication by enabling leaders, policymakers and ordinary citizens to engage in real-time conversations. Political leaders worldwide have been using social media platforms to engage with their target audiences, expressing their thoughts and perspectives (Weeks et al., 2017) and garnering support during elections and around policy decisions. Social media platforms help political actors connect with their broader audience base by sharing content that could help them formulate their opinions and decisions, defying geographical divisions. These platforms also empower people to engage in discussions and voice their opinions and expectations on policies, programmes and initiatives that political actors formulate.

While communicating their aspirations and opinions on specific policy issues, programmes and initiatives, the voter audiences are wielded with the power to scrutinize the decision-making and governance of political actors. This crucial role of holding political actors accountable for their actions related to policymaking is provided by social media through different platforms

(Helbing et al., 2023). These platforms are effective tools for generating awareness and activism, as exhibited by global movements such as Black Lives Matter, Occupy Wall Street and the Arab Spring. These movements amassed tremendous support through social media platforms (Jenzen et al., 2021). Protests, activism and advocacy have assumed a reformed outlook with social media platforms' introduction and strategic use, resulting in mobilization and support for causes that would have gone unnoticed (Gerbaudo, 2014, 2022). To build trust and promote transparency, these social media platforms are utilized by political leaders to interact with their voter audience, gaining an understanding of their aspirations and policy concerns. The narratives crafted by the political actors on social media platforms while communicating with their voter audiences help develop opinions and perception building. To help them resonate with the voter audiences, the political actors use storytelling as a tool to connect with them effectively (Walsh et al., 2022). Content and narratives significantly affect the voters' perceptions and should not be disregarded. Understanding how these elements are used to engage voters and influence their perceptions, opinions and behaviours on social media platforms is important and recognized as timely to be discussed (Santini et al., 2021). Different studies have focused on the role that content and narratives play on social media in political communication. However, the research gap still exists in terms of understanding their impact on shaping the perception and opinions of voter audiences about political leaders and parties.

Therefore, this chapter focuses on how content and narratives as tools of social media platforms are employed by political leaders to engage with their voter audiences and contribute to crafting their opinions and beliefs. To explain the strategic use of content and narratives, we employ the narrative paradigm theory (Fisher, 1984, 1985; Todorov & Weinstein, 1969). A phenomenological approach was employed to understand how voter perceptions developed across social media platforms and how this influenced the further development of content and narratives by leaders and parties for their future political campaigns.

THE ROLE OF CONTENT IN POLITICAL COMMUNICATION

The term 'content' encompasses the information sent through diverse communication channels (McQuail & Deuze, 2020), including but not limited to the internet, film, television, radio, audio CDs, books, magazines, physical art and live events. The intended recipients of this communication are individuals or collectives engaged in the domains of publishing, art and communication. Within the contemporary political landscape on social media platforms, content appropriates a critical and diverse significance while communicating messages, moulding public opinion, amassing support (Wu, 2022) and controlling political narratives. It constitutes the basis for effective political communication on social media platforms. Political leaders utilize social media's potential as dynamic and pivotal communication platforms through prudent content crafting focused on elucidative and evocative approaches. Social media platforms such as Facebook, X and Instagram exhibit different content stemming from their intrinsic features, user demographics and communication dynamics (Schreiner et al., 2021). These are explained in Table 18.1.

Thus, the alteration in content creation and curation strategies over platforms such as Facebook, Instagram and X is associated with their idiosyncrasies and user demographics. While Facebook burgeoned on invigorating discourses and user engagement through comprehensive content, Instagram flourishes based on visually fascinating images and videos accompanied by epigrammatic captions, and X, on the other hand, progresses on account of providing crisp and compact real-time messages that capture audience attention instantly. User preferences and dynamics of the social media platforms, coupled with strategic content creation, facilitate purposeful interactions and connections (Mention et al., 2019).

Within the contemporary political landscape, content plays a pivotal role for political leader and their party while crafting posts, stories, tweets and threads on social media platforms. The primary functions of 'content' in social media political communication (see Figure 18.1.) include agenda setting, message communication, image building, voter engagement, mobilization crisis management and narrative building. The functions of the content of social media posts by political leaders are discussed in detail below.

1 *Agenda Setting and Message Communication:* How effectively political leaders convey their ideas, messages, policy initiatives and decisions to the audience or communicate their stance on issues of national and international importance is mainly dependent on the content of their social media posts, stories, tweets and threads. Social media helps shape the narrative,

Table 18.1 Content Across Social Media Platforms: Facebook-Instagram-X

Facebook	*Instagram*	*X*
It promotes content as a multifarious networking platform, facilitating deep and sustained user engagement (Li et al., 2021).	It focuses on images and concise captions as a content creation strategy (Spina, 2018).	It is characterized by its concise and real-time content delivery format, focuses on condensed content of 280 characters (4,000 characters for subscribers and X Blue users outside of the United States).
Its user base comprises demographics that range across a diverse gamut, where the content creators resort to a broader approach catering to differing preferences through videos, images, and textual narratives.	Its user audience is primarily inclined towards aesthetic content and appealing to the eyes. Consequently, content creators focus on deploying prime-quality images and curated aesthetics to establish the narrative and brand identity.	The content creators focus on delivering engaging tweets and threads based on trending topics and the need for rapid information dissemination (Orellana-Rodriguez & Keane, 2018) while embracing the platform's brevity.
Text-based long-format content finds its base on Facebook in blogs and articles (Kramer & Chung, 2011), where users can engage with each other and express their diverse opinions, resonating with the content.	The content creators utilize the in-built 'stories' feature of Instagram to share ephemeral moments, BTS (behind-the-scenes) interactions and real-time conversations ('live' component) with the audiences (Basu, 2023).	'Retweets' and 'replies' are other features of X that help foster interactions and discourses (Middaugh et al., 2023), highlighting its dynamic nature.
Moreover, the built-in Facebook features, such as groups and pages, are often utilized to post content targeted towards a particular cause, making them relevant to a specific set of user audiences (Oeldorf-Hirsch & Sundar, 2015), focusing on the personalization aspect of the platform.	Moreover, the 'hashtags' feature of Instagram broadens the reach of posts and enhances the discoverability of the content to a broader audience (Baker & Walsh, 2018). Social media influencers also play an essential role in amplifying content engagement and reach by collaborating on sponsored posts over their Instagram handles.	Incorporating hashtags also capitalizes on trending threads and tweets, making the content more discoverable (Stukus, 2019).

enabling leaders to highlight governance and political questions for voters to think about and discuss. The Bharatiya Janata Party (BJP), during the 2019 general elections, utilized these social media platforms to steer the discussion and convey its ideas successfully. With the help of pictures, memes, graphics and video format content, the BJP projected its efforts, performance and achievements, highlighting its policies and programmes. These strategies result in discussions on online forums and platforms and help mould opinions and points of view of voter audiences.

2 *Branding and Image Building of Leaders:* Political leaders use social media platforms to express their merits, such as being reliable, loyal, empathetic and honest leaders. They share posts with audio video messages and picture content highlighting their experiences, behind-the-scenes talks and discussions with the general public, establishing a sense of belongingness and connection with them. These strategies help them carve an image of themselves and establish camaraderie with their voter audiences. Prime Minister Narendra Modi has effectively utilized the medium of social media platforms to build a personal image and brand for himself while sharing content that showcases him as a visionary leader (who not only thinks of the upcoming elections of 2024 but while campaigning highlights that he was busy preparing the roadmaps for the development of India when it reaches 2047 elections). Such statements by political leaders, when shared on social media platforms, help them develop their image as progressive, patriotic and strong, contributing to their positive popularity and appeal among voter audiences.

3 *Voter Audience Engagement and Interaction:* Political leaders must connect with the voters, and social media platforms provide them with the medium that enables this process. When they produce content that ignites conversations and engagement on social media platforms, leaders can gather information about what their constituents want and care about. This interaction helps

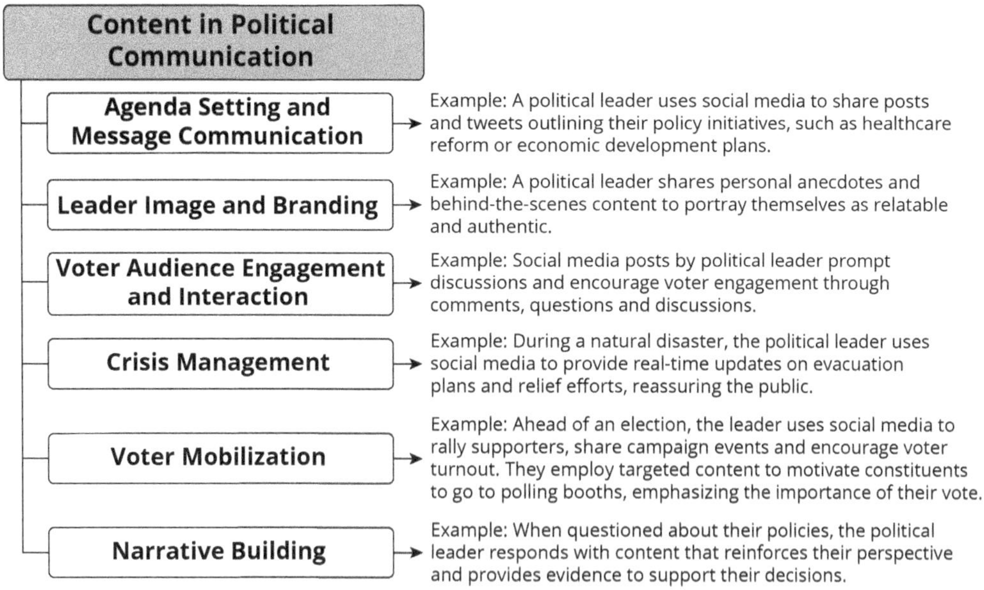

Figure 18.1 Functions of Social Media Platform's Content in Political Communication

build dialogue and relationships between politicians and the community. The Delhi-based Aam Aadmi Party (AAP) actively interacts with voters on social media platforms by creating interactive content and participating in online forums. AAP leaders engage in election campaigns by organizing live question-and-answer sessions, administering polls and actively seeking input from citizens. This approach promoted interactive communication and cultivated a feeling of inclusiveness and active involvement among voters. When the political leaders timely respond to their queries, it fosters a sense of effectiveness about the leader among the voters.

4 *Crisis Management:* Social media has proved to be a source of rapid response information to crises, and political leaders utilize them efficiently to disseminate real-time updates about the crisis and the measures taken to reassure the public about the actions taken towards mitigating the crisis. Social media content sharing accurate information through the official accounts of political leaders provides a sense of trust and faith among the public in challenging times. In response to the COVID-19 pandemic, various state governments in India utilized social media platforms for crisis management and communication. They disseminated important updates, guidelines and preventive measures through official handles, leveraging the reach and immediacy of social media to address public concerns and coordinate relief efforts.

5 *Voter Mobilization:* While political leaders organize rallies and campaigns at the grassroots levels to interact with the voters, the coverage of the same and showcasing on social media platforms helps the leaders reach broader audiences and also helps mobilize them. Content on social media platforms during these times is crucial since it should be crafted to engage the voters, encourage them to turn up for the voting day at the polling booths and consequently galvanize the voter base in favour of the leader. The Election Commission of India (ECI) also utilizes social media platforms to mobilize voters and facilitate electoral participation. During elections, the ECI teams up with influencers, celebrities and community organizations to develop initiatives that promote awareness, provide voter registration information and motivate individuals to participate in voting. They utilize media platforms to engage with demographic groups efficiently.

6 *Narrative Building:* Political leaders craft narratives and arguments around matters influenced by their policies and choices. They use content and narratives to address their supporters' and opponents' concerns, questions and criticisms. By responding, they shape perception in their favour. In India, political parties leverage social media platforms to create narratives that resonate effectively with their target audience. For instance, the Indian National Congress (INC) employs narrative techniques on platforms like Facebook to highlight joblessness, economic inequality and social justice, influencing opinion and garnering support for their goals.

These actions illustrate how politicians use social media to share messages, establish their brand identity and shape the prevailing narrative (Bossetta & Schmøkel, 2023). Therefore, content creation on these platforms goes beyond information dissemination; it shapes public sentiment. As a result, crafting thought-out content has become vital for politicians in today's political communication landscape.

THE ROLE OF NARRATIVES IN POLITICAL COMMUNICATION

A narrative, commonly called a story or account, portrays a sequence of linked events or encounters (Carr, 1986; Ryan, 2017). The narratives above can be categorized into two overarching classifications: (i) nonfictional narratives, encompassing memoirs, biographies, news reports, documentaries and travelogues, and (ii) fictional narratives, containing fairy tales, fables, legends, thrillers and novels. Narratives can be communicated through various mediums, including written or spoken words, visual representations such as still or moving images, or a combination of these modalities.

Narratives play a consequential role in apprehending and influencing voter perception over social media platforms (Mochla et al., 2023), where compelling storytelling and content with emotional appeals hold significant importance. Narratives often spin around specific issues, themes, ideologies and personalities crafted for a particular target voter audience. Political leaders employ strategies that help them create a solid and influential social media presence. They engage with the citizens in real time through their tweets, stories and posts (for instance, on Twitter, Facebook and Instagram) and update them on the policies and programmes undertaken to improve the standard of living (Ross & Bürger, 2014). Political leaders have used these techniques to identify themselves with citizens in the digital age. They use their personal life experiences and their journey to connect with the voter base at a deeper level. Political leaders target messages that echo certain groups' demands, concerns and aspirations squarely, where content and narratives play an imperative role. Leveraging storytelling approaches, narratives evoke trust, anger, empathy, enthusiasm or fear among the voters (Murphy, 2021). These affect their interpretation of political issues, events, leaders and parties. For narrating their part of the story (for example, a political issue), political leaders utilize social media campaigning content formats such as memes, videos, catchy slogans and grassroots-level campaigning updates, which help garner traction due to their wider reach and elicit strong emotions (Sharma & Jain, 2022). Amplification of narratives through content on social media exposes the voter audience to broader information. It makes them aware of diverse opinions, discourses and beliefs, evoking their perceptions and viewpoints.

Social media platforms have revolutionized political communication and citizen engagement (Adamczewska, 2023). The 2008 Obama Presidential campaign strategically utilized social media platforms like X and Facebook to mobilize young voters, raise funds and spread his narrative of hope and transformation. Similarly, nations such as Tunisia, Egypt and Libya saw extensive use of social media platforms for protest coordination, information dissemination and mobilization of support. They exemplified the influential capacity of online platforms in fostering grassroots movements aimed at effecting political transformation. Moreover, these platforms provide excellent avenues for citizens and political leaders to interact and engage, promoting the democratization of political participation. Social media platforms have evoked the spirit of instantaneous communication among political leaders. They can now reach out to their citizens directly without worrying about traditional gatekeepers (the press), facilitating real-time political messages and information dissemination, stimulating prompt responses to issues of evolving national and global importance issues. These platforms also help political leaders tailor their campaign content and narratives around their target voter demographics' concerns, problems and demands (Bossetta, 2018). Prime Minister Narendra Modi skilfully utilized social media platforms while campaigning during the 2014 Lok Sabha elections. It was the first internet election in India, transforming the political campaigning communications landscape. It has allowed for direct interaction with citizens, efficient dissemination of government policies and mobilization of support during elections. It also highlights the substantial influence of digital communication tools on shaping modern politics. This micro-targeting further enhances engagements and segmented mobilization for political rallies, events and demonstrations, fostering perceptions of collective actions and inclusivity.

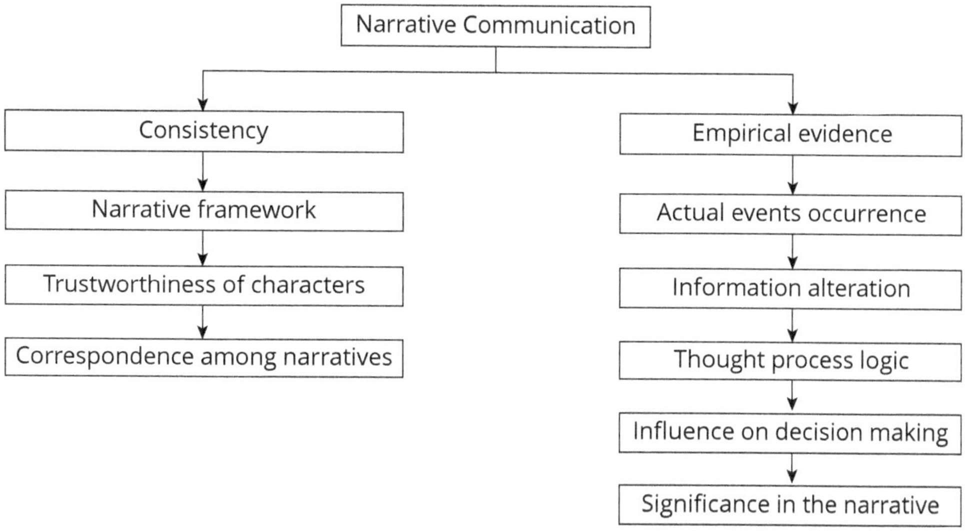

Figure 18.2 The Narrative Paradigm

THE NARRATIVE PARADIGM THEORY FRAMEWORK

Compelling narratives is the most fundamental way of persuading individuals, as humans are naturally inclined to tell rather than being swayed solely by rational arguments or evidence-based reasoning. Focusing on narratives as a means of interpersonal communication among people (see Figure 18.2), in the late 20th century, Walter Fisher developed the narrative paradigm theory (Fisher, 1989, 2021). It predicates that humans are inclined to be influenced and persuaded by compelling narratives rather than relying on abstract logic and empirical evidence (Bossetta & Schmøkel, 2023; Fisher, 1984). According to the narrative paradigm idea, it is argued that people possess an inherent inclination towards storytelling and that political communication tends to be most impactful when it utilizes narrative frameworks to transmit messages effectively. Political leaders may effectively persuade and engage their constituents by crafting coherent, intelligible and emotionally compelling narratives while aligning with the audience's beliefs and experiences. Within political persuasion and communication, storytelling and emotions play a crucial role. These valuable insights are offered through the narrative paradigm theory framework.

In the field of political communication, the ideas of 'narrative coherence' and 'narrative fidelity' act as benchmarks for assessing the impact of narratives (Fisher, 1984). Here, coherence pertains to how the organization of a story can be understood by its target audience, and the cohesive narrative entails a structure, a series of occurrences and a plot that progresses seamlessly. A coherent narrative facilitates the audience's comprehension of the message within political communication, fostering active engagement with the content. Fidelity, conversely, pertains to the extent to which a description conforms to the audience's values, beliefs and experiences. Political narratives that align with the audience's pre-existing worldview and personal experiences are more likely to be embraced and influential. Within this particular framework, political narratives must adhere to the principles and anticipated desires of the intended target group.

Hence, narratives significantly influence the target audience's attitudes and behaviours and affect their response to issues of public importance. By intertwining moral values and themes into stories, humans are emotionally engaged, which further helps shape the public sphere within moral discourse (Fisher, 1984). Leaders (people of authority) utilize moral values, strategically knitting them into their stories, advancing their agendas and garnering public support. Political leaders use three crucial narrative strategies to increase their ethical argumentation: (i) personal storytelling, (ii) appeals based on emotions and (iii) issue framing. While knitting narratives, they focus on maintaining coherence and accuracy in arguments that make logical sense and, at the same time, resonate with the values and experiences of their listeners. Humans are inherent storytellers (they interpret the world based on their lived experiences and construct their identities through those story narratives) and listeners (they assess the narrative's credibility and persuasiveness based on how it is structured and appealed) (Gabriel, 2004). Their emotional connection with narratives (stories and events) explains the effectiveness and impact of communication. Stories intertwined in the sociocultural context of human audiences pronounce the significance of narratives since they are based on shared values, norms, beliefs and practices (Turner, 1980). Thus, narratives are a cogent persuasion tool for shaping the opinions and perceptions of humans. Narratives are applied to various fields, such as public relations, advertising, interpersonal communication and political communication, and influence the decision-making of humans based on them.

Some key areas in which narratives are applied to communication by political leaders include:

1 *Candidate's personal stories:* Political leaders use personal stories and experiences to engage with the voter audiences. These include instances from their childhood, the challenges they faced and their cultural underpinnings, helping them resonate with the upbringing, challenges and culture of their voters and humanizing them as similar individuals hoping for a better future for generations to come based on empathy and trust (Lee & Oh, 2012). For instance, Prime Minister Narendra Modi frequently narrates his modest origins as a tea seller, underscoring his ascent from poverty to authority. This narrative serves the purpose of establishing a connection with voters and presenting himself as a leader who comprehends ordinary individuals' challenges. By formulating their life journey across such instances, they narrate their commitment, perseverance and responsibility towards the public to the voters.
2 *Electoral campaigning:* Crafting political campaigns resonating with the needs, aspirations and demands of the target voter audience is an effective strategy of political leaders during elections (Bossetta & Schmøkel, 2023). They build rapport with the voter audience by knitting narratives around themes such as security, development, change and hope, appealing to their collective identity and promoting a sense of shared purpose and affinity. An example of this can be seen in the utilization of the national security and development narrative by the BJP during its electoral campaigns. In contrast, the INC has prioritized social justice and inclusivity narratives.
3 *Issue framing:* It pertains to the conceptualization, formulation and portrayal of a policy issue through alternative frames (Nelson & Oxley, 1999). Issue framing is a dominant tool that political leaders use to shape voter perceptions and beliefs, regulate policy debates and mobilize votes for their agendas. This approach involves the development of a compelling narrative or storyline surrounding a specific subject, policy or occurrence that emerges from an intricate issue that may be far from the direct encounters of the general public to shape their perception and comprehension of it (Cobb et al., 1976). Political leaders use this process to accomplish their political goals, including winning elections. The leaders get strong support when the issues are addressed, and performance is reflected in their narratives (Jacoby, 2000). Narratives are developed to aim at the problems while communicating with the voters. The BJP presents the immigration narrative as a potential risk to the nation's security, whereas the Congress party presents it as a matter of humanitarian importance. Narrative storytelling is thus employed while framing peculiar policy issues, eliciting emotional responses and support from the voter audience (Shanahan et al., 2023). These narratives showcase the advantages and disadvantages of policies that hold significance for voters when they participate in elections, a process influenced by how individuals process information at a level (Lau et al., 1991).
4 *Emotional appeals:* Emotional appeals play an essential role in political communication by evoking emotions like fear, trust, empathy and anger among voters. These narratives influence how voter audiences perceive and believe in candidates, encouraging them to support a candidate, attend party events and rallies or contribute to campaigns. Arvind Kejriwal, the Chief Minister of Delhi, often uses appeals in his speeches, especially when discussing healthcare issues. By sharing stories of people struggling with healthcare costs, he aimed to evoke empathy and unity. Kejriwal's skilful use of language and genuine concern for citizens' well-being positioned him as a leader dedicated to addressing needs, significantly contributing to his political success in Delhi.
5 *Image building:* Positive and negative images of preferred and opposing candidates are built using narratives by political parties and their leaders. Former Prime Minister Indira Gandhi fostered a perception of herself as a persistent and authoritative figure. In contrast, leaders such as Atal Bihari Vajpayee projected an image characterized by astute governance and inclusiveness. The construction of image-centred narratives focuses on the credibility and image of the leaders, generating a sense of positivity, doubt or fear based on their work, inclinations and aspirations (Lalancette & Raynauld, 2019).
6 *Structuring speeches:* While delivering an address to their voter audience, the speeches of political leaders are often crafted with a definite beginning (an introduction to what they want to convey), a middle structure (focusing on the policies and proposals that they want to take up once elected to power) and an end (calling for immediate action against the opposing parties and leaders for their unwillingness to work on

critical aspects of governance). Prime Minister Narendra Modi often utilizes a methodical storytelling technique. He starts by portraying the difficulties encountered by the country, shifts to his government's endeavours as remedies and concludes with a vision of advancement. Doing this helps him build a connection with the voters, building an ambiance that reinforces his footing as a leader committing to working towards the development of India. This engineered storyline amplifies voter audience engagement during the speeches, which remains in their minds and plays a crucial role for them while casting their votes during elections.

7 *Advocacy:* Narratives are influential in establishing connection and confidence, generating awareness and stimulating citizen involvement. Rahul Gandhi, a leader in the INC, actively advocated for farmers' rights issues, highlighted during farmers' protests in India against the farmers' bill passed by parliament. He openly opposed those policies, talked to them on the ground and gained their support. His actions promoted his image as a leader committed to justice and fairness, empowering underrepresented communities and their issues. In such instances, when political leaders share their experiences over social media platforms about their meetings with the citizens to understand and support their grievances, it strengthens their public backing for future agendas and policy goals.

THE INDIAN POLITICAL LANDSCAPE

India's political landscape is shaped by byzantine and continually evolving political parties and their ideologies and regional ambitions. BJP and INC are the two national parties defining this landscape's core, and they enjoy well-established popular support among the Indian electorate. Still and all, the regional dynamics determine the politics across different states. Therefore, the regional parties remain equally important as the national parties. They determine the power structure and balance. Some of the parties of regional importance include Trinamool Congress in West Bengal, Dravida Munnetra Kazhagam in Tamil Nadu, Samajwadi Party in Uttar Pradesh and AAP in Delhi. In this context, social media was a significant impetus in amending and facilitating the Indian political environment to reach the masses. Social media platforms such as Facebook, Instagram, X and YouTube have penetrated the lives of urban and rural voter audiences equally and facilitate political discussions and debates, shaping narratives and swaying vox populi.

The easy availability of smartphones and affordable internet services, as well as information dissemination and accessibility, are just a click away. This helps the political leaders to reach out to the masses all at once, with a broad demography in real time. To engage and interact with the voter audiences, popular leaders in Indian politics, such as Narendra Modi, Rahul Gandhi, Mamata Banerjee and Arvind Kejriwal, among others, use Facebook, Instagram and X strategically. They use targeted advertisements and personalized messages to connect with the diverse voter base. Prime Minister Narendra Modi, in this regard, has been utilizing X very efficiently, where he updates his voters in real time without relying on traditional media channels. With the evolution of social media platforms, a dearth of true and false information is available to people. Hence, the spread of misinformation, disinformation and misleading content also extends to the political communication environment, which makes it challenging to understand the credibility of these platforms. Government and social media platform agencies try to tackle these challenges for better navigation and information sharing with the voter audiences. Despite these challenges, social media platforms are crucial in narrative construction, engagement, mobilizing support for policies and programmes and determining election results. Using trending hashtags, campaign video clips and pictures across social media platforms helps leaders strike a chord with the audience's sentiments and navigate the evolving digital media environment. The interwoven relationship between the influence of social media and the Indian political environment can be emphasized by the level of interconnection that can be observed between democracy, governance and technology in the present times.

There are various instances in the context of Indian general elections that can explain how social media platforms contributed to narrative farming and targeted audience engagement. These include Narendra Modi's strategic and effective utilization of X and Facebook during the 2014 election campaign. It was the first time that social media platforms were used extensively by a political party and leader to connect with the voter audiences, share messages and seek active support. He used video conferencing as an effective tool for social media platforms. He named it 'Chai pe Charcha (Talk over Tea)'. He engaged in real time with the citizens, thereby gaining popularity and highlighting to them the revolution that social media platforms are going to bring to connect them instantaneously where he will be able to listen to their grievances, tell them about the progress of his government and way forward with the developmental agendas. The state assembly elections in Uttar Pradesh in 2017 also saw the strategic use of social media by BJP leaders, who employed an info-centric approach while targeting voter groups and areas and tailored advertisements and messages accordingly. There, personalized content sharing with the supporters significantly contributed to their success. During the 2019 general elections also, the political leaders from the ruling as well as the opposition all tried to strategically use social media platforms such as X, Facebook and Instagram to engage with the voters, actively highlighting their achievements and leadership contributions to development and counterbalancing each other's campaign narratives.

The recent 2024 Indian General Elections saw Facebook, Instagram and X as the battlefronts for the political parties to register their narratives with the voters. Political leaders and parties are actively utilizing these social media platforms to influence and engage voters, creating content that resonates with the aspirations and needs of diverse demographic electorates. The critical narrative themes that the BJP and party leader Narendra Modi propagated included economic development, infrastructure building, nationalism and a solid international presence. To highlight their government's work, they frequently posted about various defence advancements, infrastructure developments and significant economic policies on all social media platforms. They posted photos and videos of this work on Facebook and Instagram; examples of videos showcasing the development include those of Vande Bharat express trains highlighting the technological progress and broader connectivity. To provide his concise thoughts and updates on matters of national and international importance, Prime Minister Modi used hashtags such as #NewIndia and #AtmaNirbharBharat to reinforce a vision of a prosperous and self-reliant Indian nation. Doing online polls and surveys on their official apps and social media accounts helped them connect better with the voters since it helped them engage better and provide a follow-up on significant policy decisions. Celebrating unparalleled vaccination drives and conducting social media polls on new public policies are some interactive content strategies Narendra Modi and his party employed during the 2024 general elections.

Similarly, the INC focused on inclusive growth, economic inequality and social justice as the major narratives during the 2024 elections. The leaders from the INC, more importantly, the face of the party, Rahul Gandhi, posted content and narratives that critiqued the ruling BJP government on issues such as unemployment and distress among farmers due to farmer's bills being passed in the parliament which called for action for the government to address the struggle of the farmers and youth suffering due to unemployment. He critiqued the ruling party's governance policies using public statistics, personal experiences and stories. He used hashtags such as #SaveDemocracy and #BharatJodoNyayYatra.

AAP and its leader, Arvind Kejriwal, focused on the narratives of anti-corruption, good governance and education to fight the elections of 2024. He often would post images and share videos that showcased how the Delhi government's education and healthcare policies resulted in significant improvements in both these sectors. The content and narratives also showcased other public sector schemes such as free water and electricity. After this, he even shared testimonials of the people benefitting from such schemes, showing before and after images and statistics highlighting the success of the policies. He used hashtags such as #DelhiModel and #KejriwalGuarantee to advocate for the achievements and promises fulfilled by his party while in power.

The regional parties Trinamool Congress (TMC) and the Dravida Munnetra Kazhagam (DMK) and their leaders, Mamata Banerjee and M.K. Stalin, all focused on region-specific narratives such as federal requirements, identity and local developments. They highlighted their regional pride and promoted their regional cultures and languages on social media platforms, where they utilized the platforms by using their language selection to promote their regionalism and instil a sense of belongingness among their voter audience. Moreover, during the festivals of their respective states, they focused on sharing religious content and narratives (such as celebrating Durga Puja or Pongal) and sending messages of good over evil on their social media platforms.

More importantly, for the 2024 general elections, the INDIA Alliance (Indian National Developmental Alliance) came into being. Its focused narrative included safeguarding the democratic institutions, promoting the secular character of Indian democracy and ensuring inclusive development. It was formed with a coalition of many parties, which comprised the opposition to counter the perceived authoritarianism of the BJP. The content and narratives floated on social media platforms such as Facebook and Instagram emphasized the call for action to promote development for all against the majoritarian rule of the BJP. They used X to share coordinated campaigns, press conferences and rallies, and they used hashtags such as #UnitedForIndia and #RestoreDemocracy to strike a chord with the voter audiences.

In a nutshell, the 2024 Indian General elections saw extensive use of social media platforms where videos, photos, infographics, public statements and live streams by political leaders like Narendra Modi for sharing details of national issues and Rahul Gandhi for presenting a critique of policies and programmes of the ruling government were used to capture voter audiences' attention. Leaders like Arvind Kejriwal used the technique of personalized content and even used live-streamed town hall meetings on social media platforms to reach a broader voter base. Political leaders and parties leverage social media platforms to construct compelling narratives, interact directly with voters and shape and influence public opinion, highlighting the increasing influence of social media platforms.

India ranked second globally after China in the social media user base in 2023, which is 755.47 million (Shewale, 2023), emphasizing how important it is to reflect upon. This chapter tries to explore how the opinions and perceptions of Indian voters are impacted by the content and narratives that are floated on social media platforms. The study investigates the evolving views and voting patterns of citizens.

Figure 18.3 depicts the main themes that could be deduced from the Indian General elections studies. The main focus of the analysis was to explore how the cultivation theory of media studies impacts user attitudes and behaviours in the social media scene.

The individuals who actively engage with media for updates tend to form their perceptions of leaders based on their portrayal on these platforms. In turn, it influences their voting decisions and perceptions, aligning with the cultivation theory of media studies (Gerbner, 1973), which suggests that exposure to media content shapes individuals' views, influencing their beliefs according to what they consume through media. Political figures strategically leverage each social media platform's features

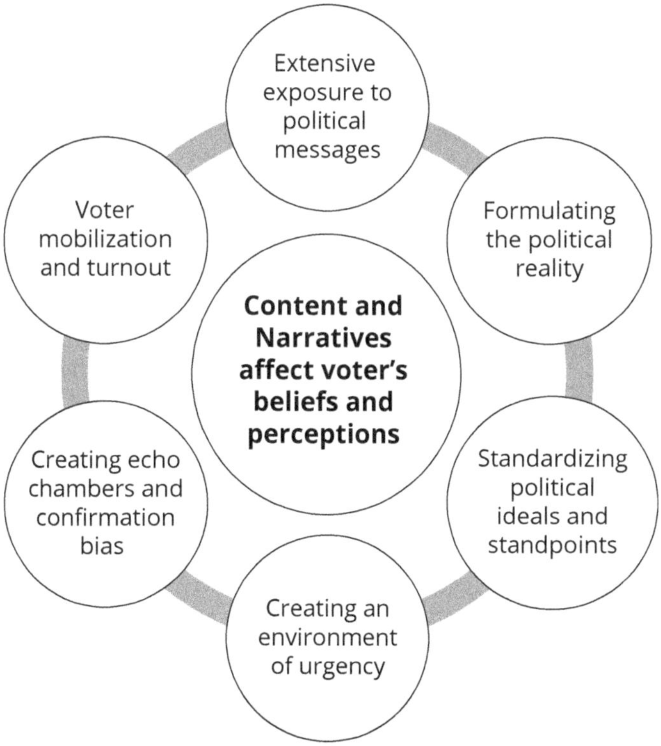

Figure 18.3 Beliefs and Perceptions of Voters Affected by Content and Narratives

by creating content and narratives that resonate with users. How content and narratives affect voters' behaviour is explained below.

1 *Extensive exposure to political messages:* It was observed from the interviews and supported by cultivation theory (Gerbner, 1998) that when the user audiences are shown posts, stories and statements extensively over a more extended period, they tend to remain in the memory, and when the audiences interact with each other they tend to reiterate the political leaders' views and standpoints as their own (Busselle & Bulck, 2019). Political parties showcase their work towards the community's welfare during election campaigning. They share pictures and videos on their social media profiles (Bennett, 2012). The voter audiences see them and discuss them with friends and family. Those discussions help them understand the leader's work, and when they vote, they remember those social media posts and decide who their vote goes to. Thus, political leaders strategically employ social media platforms to infuse the timelines of the voter audiences with their content and campaign narratives, highlighting their political agendas, messages, policies and proposals (Raynauld & Lalancette, 2023).
2 *Formulating the political reality:* While engaging with the user audiences during interviews, it was evident that how political leaders frame their narratives significantly shapes how voters perceive political realities (Johnson-Cartee, 2004). Political leaders come up with such statements and personal anecdotes in their speeches, which directly affect the emotions of voters. When the elections come, the voters remember what the leader said during the speech (Hart et al., 2013). When the leader emphasizes the importance of crucial issues and agendas for the target audience, they strike the right chord while downplaying specific agendas that might not be that relevant to a particular voter audience. When political leaders frame their narratives through the lens of how the voter audience views a particular political matter, they sway the opinions, decisions and, consequently, the votes during the elections (Slothuus & de Vreese, 2010).
3 *Standardizing political ideals and standpoints:* Political leaders are very active across social media platforms, using the tools that help them project and reflect their ideals, goals and aspirations for the citizens of their constituencies (Sircar, 2020). When the leader expresses their ideals, values and what they stand for, the voter audiences also accept that the leader's standpoint on a particular issue is due to the underlying ideals and principles they follow. Accepting a leader's position as a societal norm makes the voter audience gravitate towards the same ideals while voting decisions during elections. When a political leader like Arvind Kejriwal says that he will work for the welfare of the schools and make good infrastructure available for government school students, and then his work shows what he preaches, the voters become confident that he is the leader they want to vote for. Education for all is the stand that Kejriwal takes, and he works towards achieving that goal of making government school education at par with private schools.
4 *Creating an environment of urgency:* It was observed that since social media provide exposure to a wide variety of content, political leaders utilize this to employ narratives that encompass fear and anxiety in the minds of voters. They, for example, update content depicting a state of hostility in the state and their policies and candidacy as the essential solutions to forestall atrocious upshots. They regularly update content that portrays a state of hostility within the state while also promoting their policies and candidacy as crucial measures to prevent catastrophic consequences. For example, after the farmer's protest in New Delhi, a voter was explaining to the news media reporters, 'I remember when the centre passed farmer bills, there was so much chaos in the minds of people that why farmers are protesting and then opposition parties like Congress and Aam Aadmi Party came forward to support the farmer's cause and reiterated that the BJP (ruling party) is doing wrong by bringing these laws. They questioned the ruling party and said we were the solution to citizens' problems. It is now important to overthrow the BJP government since it is not working towards the welfare of farmers'.
5 *Creating echo chambers and confirmation bias:* Algorithms on social media platforms remember the content that user audiences prefer and, to reinforce their views and beliefs, show them similar content. Political figures leverage the power of media platforms by customizing their messages and stories to cater to groups, forming effective echo chambers (Bail et al., 2018). Political parties and leaders frequently share numerous small videos and images on their social media platforms. However, there are instances where the voter audiences selectively adhere to a specific political party and leader, forming their opinions about other parties and leaders solely based on the content and narratives put forth by these leaders. Their friends and family also express similar perspectives on their social media profiles. Upon repeated exposure to these instances, they start perceiving a specific leader and political party as effective, leading them to align themselves with those leaders and their ideologies. When people are repeatedly presented with information that confirms their opinions and values, they tend to become more inclined to support the leaders' perspectives.
6 *Voter mobilization and turnout:* Political leaders harness the influence of media not to shape the opinions and sentiments of their followers but also to rally voters and urge them to participate on election day in their favour. They stress the importance of elections, inspiring individuals to engage by volunteering, contributing and casting their votes through content and stories.

The interviews show that politicians use social media to share messages and stories that connect with users' wants and influence how they vote. Social media users see a variety of viewpoints on national and global issues, which helps spread information and connect with diverse perspectives and for the political leaders and parties to rally voters and makes social media a tool for reaching people with different perspectives. Essentially, the content politicians share on these social media platforms shapes their image and helps them gain support from voters by creating a perception for themselves. Consequently, the content shared and narratives articulated on social media platforms affect people's perceptions to a great extent and can contribute (in making or breaking) a political leader's image and reputation.

DISCUSSION

This study investigates the influence of social media platforms on content consumption and how political leaders utilize content strategies to shape narratives to cater to the information-seeking behaviour of their targeted voter audiences and determine voting behaviour in the long run. The insights generated from the studies in the Indian political scenario support the narrative theory framework and provide insights into how storytelling techniques and communication play a significant role in political communication, especially on social media platforms like Facebook and Instagram. Our study explains this by exhibiting how political leaders utilize the social media landscape (Facebook, X and Instagram) to construct narratives and story content that resonate with the voter audiences. These tactics help them connect personally with their voters, improve, consistently maintain their image and persona and interact effectively to mobilize their support. This highlights the significance of narrative theory in comprehending the digital age of communication, particularly in politics, focusing on Indian political leaders and election campaigning.

Moreover, our study also underlines how narratives constantly evolve in the digital landscape of political communication. Political leaders and parties utilize the interactive hypermedia elements of different social media platforms to cater to their unique set of voter audiences by adapting platform-specific strategies related to content and narratives. Our study explored the fluidity and flexibility of social media platforms in narrative building during election campaigning. Focusing on narratives on social media platforms' role, our study provides insights into information dissemination, voter mobilization, engagement and the evolving digital political discourse.

Even though our study contributes valuable insights, it is crucial to acknowledge definite limitations. Our study lags in capturing the real-time social media interactions that influence voter perceptions and voting patterns with figures. Longitudinal research focusing on social media usage trends and patterns over an extended period would provide more significant insights into the changing voting behaviour and patterns after the advent of social media and its engagement tools during election cycles by political leaders and parties. We are delving deeper and comparing different approaches to communications and individual responses across demographics and psychographics to social media engagement strategies such as narratives and storytelling content. Furthermore, exploring the cultural aspect of political communication and citizen engagement could provide valuable insights into understanding the role of social media platforms in comprehending Indian political discourse, where commonalities and variance become more evident.

CONCLUSION

This chapter focused on the multilayered role of content and narratives for political leaders to engage with voter audiences on social media platforms. These platforms have highly influenced how political leaders interact with the public, carve an image for themselves and disseminate their messages. These strategies play a significant role in shaping public perception of the leader, participating in discussions and consequently affecting the election campaigning outcomes. In the present digital environment, capitalizing on social media platforms' content and narrative strategies is crucial for political leaders. The evolving political communication technologies empower leaders to engage and build connections with the citizens, mobilize their support, regulate opinions, carve an image for themselves and effectively handle communications. In doing so, they craft narratives that appeal to the target audience's emotions and the issues they are most concerned with. Therefore, these emerging narrative and content-creation strategies have become crucial for political leaders' communication and engagement with their audiences. These strategies help the leaders cultivate a sense of belongingness, inclusivity and community association. The aim is to utilize the specific features of different social media platforms catering to various audiences and use their flexible and fluid elements to interact with, promote and amass support through other approaches. This chapter focuses on the emerging relevance of content and narrative strategies on social media platforms for political information dissemination among active Indian voter audiences. The research analysis and findings propose that political leaders utilize diverse tactics, including sharing personal anecdotes, stories and behind-the-scenes interaction with the citizens while doing ground-level campaigning, resulting in effective voter mobilization. The study findings resonate with the Narrative Paradigm Theory, which proposes that fundamental human interactions and communication are based on storytelling and are inevitably swayed by engrossing narratives. Insights from the in-depth interviews undertaken as a part of this study evidenced that content and narratives on social media platforms play a crucial role in enabling political leaders to strike a personal chord with the voters and motivate them to vote for the development that these leaders are aspiring to bring for them once they are elected to power and form government. The insights also highlight narratives' role in moulding conversations and regulating voter audience engagement in political communications and discussions on social media platforms.

Thus, we underscore the role of content and narratives on social media platforms in shaping political discourse and encouraging participation. Political leaders in India employ strategies to connect with voters and influence public opinion, including crafting stories and using appeals. While the study has its limitations, the insights it provides deepen our understanding of how political communication is evolving in the digital age. By acknowledging these limitations and exploring potential areas for future research, we can continue to enhance our understanding of how social media impacts political engagement and narrative formation. Ultimately, leveraging media effectively allows politicians to engage with the public, steer conversations, garner support and enhance democratic participation, involvement and governance.

REFERENCES

Adamczewska, K. (2023). Interactive election campaigns on social media? Flow of political information among journalists and politicians as an element of the communication strategy of political actors. *Journal of Information Technology & Politics*. https://doi.org/10.1080/19331681.2023.2222717

Bail, C. A., Argyle, L. P., Brown, T. W., Bumpus, J. P., Chen, H., Hunzaker, M. B. F., Lee, J., Mann, M., Merhout, F., & Volfovsky, A. (2018). Exposure to opposing views on social media can increase political polarization. *Proceedings of the National Academy of Sciences*, *115*(37), 9216–9221. https://doi.org/10.1073/pnas.1804840115

Baker, S. A., & Walsh, M. J. (2018). 'Good Morning Fitfam': Top posts, hashtags and gender display on Instagram. *New Media & Society*, *20*(12), 4553-4570. https://doi.org/10.1177/1461444818777514

Basu, S. (2023). "Why do Indians cry passionately on Insta?": Grief performativity and ecologies of commerce of crying videos. *South Asian Popular Culture*, 1–17. https://doi.org/10.1080/14746689.2023.2215227

Bennett, W. L. (2012). The personalization of politics: Political identity, social media, and changing patterns of participation. *The Annals of the American Academy of Political and Social Science*, *644*(1), 20–39. https://doi.org/10.1177/0002716212451428

Bossetta, M. (2018). The digital Architectures of social media: Comparing political campaigning on Facebook, Twitter, Instagram, and Snapchat in the 2016 U.S. Election. *Journalism & Mass Communication Quarterly*, *95*(2), 471–496. https://doi.org/10.1177/1077699018763307

Bossetta, M., & Schmøkel, R. (2023). Cross-platform emotions and audience engagement in social media political campaigning: Comparing candidates' Facebook and Instagram images in the 2020 US election. *Political Communication*, *40*(1), 48–68. https://doi.org/10.1080/10584609.2022.2128949

Busselle, R., & Bulck, J. V. D. (2019). Cultivation theory, media, stories, processes, and reality. In *Media effects* (4th ed.). Routledge.

Carr, D. (1986). Narrative and the real world: An argument for continuity. *History and Theory*, *25*(2), 117–131. https://doi.org/10.2307/2505301

Cobb, R., Ross, J.-K., & Ross, M. H. (1976). Agenda building as a comparative political process. *American Political Science Review*, *70*(1), 126–138. https://doi.org/10.2307/1960328

Fisher, W. R. (1984). Narration as a human communication paradigm: The case of public moral argument. *Communication Monographs*, *51*(1), 1–22. https://doi.org/10.1080/03637758409390180

Fisher, W. R. (1985). The narrative paradigm: An elaboration. *Communication Monographs*, *52*(4), 347–367. https://doi.org/10.1080/03637758509376117

Fisher, W. R. (1989). *Human communication as narration: Toward a philosophy of reason, value, and action*. University of South Carolina Press. https://doi.org/10.2307/j.ctv1nwbqtk

Fisher, W. R. (2021). *Human communication as narration: Toward a philosophy of reason, value, and action*. University of South Carolina Press.

Gabriel, Y. (2004). Narratives, stories and texts. In *The SAGE Handbook of organizational discourse*. SAGE.

Gerbaudo, P. (2014). Populism 2.0: Social media activism, the generic internet user and interactive direct democracy. In *Social media, politics and the state*. Routledge.

Gerbaudo, P. (2022). Theorizing reactive democracy the social media public sphere, online crowds and the plebiscitary logic of online reactions. *Democratic Theory—An Interdisciplinary Journal*, *9*(2), 120–138. https://doi.org/10.3167/dt.2022.090207

Gerbner, G. (1973). Cultural indicators: The thud voice. In G. Gerbner, L. Gross, & W. H. Melody (Eds.), *Communications technology and social policy* (pp. 555–573). Wiley.

Gerbner, G. (1998). Cultivation analysis: An overview. *Mass Communication & Society*, *1*(3–4), 175–194. https://doi.org/10.1080/15205436.1998.9677855

Hart, R. P., Childers, J. P., & Lind, C. J. (2013). The mysteries of political Tone. In *Political tone: How leaders talk and why*. University of Chicago Press.

Helbing, D., Mahajan, S., Fricker, R. H., Musso, A., Hausladen, C. I., Carissimo, C., Carpentras, D., Stockinger, E., Argota Sanchez-Vaquerizo, J., Yang, J. C., Ballandies, M. C., Korecki, M., Dubey, R. K., & Pournaras, E. (2023). Democracy by design: Perspectives for digitally assisted, participatory upgrades of society. *Journal of Computational Science*, *71*, 102061. https://doi.org/10.1016/j.jocs.2023.102061

Jacoby, W. G. (2000). Issue framing and public opinion on government spending. *American Journal of Political Science*, 750–767. https://doi.org/10.2307/2669279

Jenzen, O., Erhart, I., Eslen-Ziya, H., Korkut, U., & McGarry, A. (2021). The symbol of social media in contemporary protest: Twitter and the Gezi Park movement. *Convergence*, *27*(2), 414–437. https://doi.org/10.1177/1354856520933747

Johnson-Cartee, K. S. (2004). The social construction of reality. In *News narratives and news framing: Constructing political reality*. Rowman & Littlefield Publishers.

Kiesler, S., Siegel, J., & McGuire, T. W. (1984). Social psychological aspects of computer-mediated communication. *American Psychologist*, *39*(10), 1123–1134. https://doi.org/10.1037/0003-066X.39.10.1123

Klinger, U., & Svensson, J. (2015). The emergence of network media logic in political communication: A theoretical approach. *New Media & Society*, *17*(8), 1241–1257. https://doi.org/10.1177/1461444814522952

Kramer, A., & Chung, C. (2021). Dimensions of self-expression in Facebook status updates. *Proceedings of the International AAAI Conference on Web and Social Media*, *5*(1), 169–176. https://doi.org/10.1609/icwsm.v5i1.14140

Lalancette, M., & Raynauld, V. (2019). The power of political image: Justin Trudeau, Instagram, and celebrity politics. *American Behavioral Scientist*, *63*(7), 888–924. https://doi.org/10.1177/0002764217744838

Lau, R. R., Smith, R. A., & Fiske, S. T. (1991). Political beliefs, policy interpretations, and political persuasion. *The Journal of Politics*, *53*(3), 644–675. https://doi.org/10.2307/2131574

Lee, E.-J., & Oh, S. Y. (2012). To personalize or depersonalize? When and how politicians' personalized tweets affect the public's reactions. *Journal of Communication*, *62*(6), 932–949. https://doi.org/10.1111/j.1460-2466.2012.01681.x

Li, F., Larimo, J., & Leonidou, L. C. (2021). Social media marketing strategy: Definition, conceptualization, taxonomy, validation, and future agenda. *Journal of the Academy of Marketing Science*, *49*, 51–70. https://doi.org/10.1007/s11747-020-00733-3

McQuail, D., & Deuze, M. (2020). Chapter 2: The rise, decline, and return of mass media. In *McQuail's media and mass communication theory*. SAGE. https://us.sagepub.com/en-us/nam/book/mcquails-mass-communication-theory-3

Mention, A.-L., Barlatier, P.-J., & Josserand, E. (2019). Using social media to leverage and develop dynamic capabilities for innovation. *Technological Forecasting and Social Change*, *144*, 242–250. https://doi.org/10.1016/j.techfore.2019.03.003

Middaugh, E., Felton, M., & Fan, H. (2023). What's in a Tweet? How platform features facilitate and constrain civic discourse and what it means for teaching civic media literacy. In *Education in the age of misinformation: philosophical and pedagogical explorations* (pp. 203–223). Springer International Publishing. https://doi.org/10.1007/978-3-031-25871-8_11

Mochla, V., Tsourvakas, G., & Stoubos, I. (2023). Segmenting voters by motivation to use social media and their lifestyle for political engagement. *Journal of Political Marketing*, 1–22. https://doi.org/10.1080/15377857.2023.2168831

Munger, K., Egan, P., Nagler, J., Ronen, J., & Tucker, J. (2022). Political knowledge and misinformation in the era of social media: Evidence from the 2015 UK election. *British Journal of Political Science*, *52*(1), 107–127. https://doi.org/10.1017/S0007123420000198

Murphy, P. D. (2021). Speaking for the youth, speaking for the planet: Greta Thunberg and the representational politics of eco-celebrity. *Popular Communication*, *19*(3), 193–206. https://doi.org/10.1080/15405702.2021.1913493

Nelson, T. E., & Oxley, Z. M. (1999). Issue framing effects on belief importance and opinion. *The Journal of Politics*, *61*(4), 1040–1067. https://doi.org/10.2307/2647553

Oeldorf-Hirsch, A., & Sundar, S. S. (2015). Posting, commenting, and tagging: Effects of sharing news stories on Facebook. *Computers in human behavior*, *44*, 240–249. https://doi.org/10.1016/j.chb.2014.11.024

Papacharissi, Z., & de Fatima Oliveira, M. (2012). Affective news and networked publics: The rhythms of news storytelling on #Egypt. *Journal of Communication*, *62*(2), 266–282. https://doi.org/10.1111/j.1460-2466.2012.01630.x

Papakyriakopoulos, O., Serrano, J. C. M., & Hegelich, S. (2020). Political communication on social media: A tale of hyperactive users and bias in recommender systems. *Online Social Networks and Media*, *15*, 100058. https://doi.org/10.1016/j.osnem.2019.100058

Raynauld, V., & Lalancette, M. (2023). Social media, visuals, and politics: A look at politicians' digital visual habitus on Instagram. In *Research handbook on visual politics* (pp. 167–180). Edward Elgar Publishing. https://www.elgaronline.com/edcollchap/book/9781800376939/book-part-9781800376939-21.xml

Ross, K., & Bürger, T. (2014). Face to face(book). *Political Science*, *66*(1), 46–62. https://doi.org/10.1177/0032318714534106

Ryan, M.-L. (2017). Narrative. In *A companion to critical and cultural theory* (pp. 517–530). John Wiley & Sons, Ltd. https://doi.org/10.1002/9781118472262.ch33

Santini, M., Salles, D., Estrella, C., Barros, C., & Orofino, D. (2021). Bots as online impersonators: Automated manipulators and their different roles on social media. *International Review of Information Ethics*, *30*.

Schreiner, M., Fischer, T., & Riedl, R. (2021). Impact of content characteristics and emotion on behavioral engagement in social media: Literature review and research agenda. *Electronic Commerce Research*, *21*(2), 329–345. https://doi.org/10.1007/s10660-019-09353-8

Shanahan, M. D. J., Aaron, S.-W., Mark, K., & McBeth, E. A. (2023). The narrative policy framework. In *Theories of the policy process* (5th ed., pp. 161–195). Routledge.

Sharma, P., & Jain, V. (2022). Influencers and the building of political brands—The case of India. In M. Moufahim (Ed.), *Political Branding in Turbulent times* (pp. 69–85). Springer International Publishing. https://doi.org/10.1007/978-3-030-83229-2_5

Shewale, R. (2023, September 12). *Social media users—Global demographics*. DemandSage. https://www.demandsage.com/social-media-users/

Sircar, N. (2020). The politics of vishwas: Political mobilization in the 2019 national election. *Contemporary South Asia*, *28*(2), 178–194. https://doi.org/10.1080/09584935.2020.1765988

Slothuus, R., & de Vreese, C. H. (2010). Political parties, motivated reasoning, and issue framing Effects. *The Journal of Politics*, *72*(3), 630–645. https://doi.org/10.1017/S002238161000006X

Stukus, D. R. (2019). If you tweet it, they will come. In *Social media for medical professionals*. Springer. https://doi.org/10.1007/978-3-030-14439-5_6

Todorov, T., & Weinstein, A. (1969). Structural analysis of narrative. NOVEL. *A Forum on Fiction*, *3*(1), 70–76. https://doi.org/10.2307/1345003

Turner, V. (1980). Social dramas and stories about them. *Critical Inquiry*, *7*(1), 141–168. https://doi.org/10.1086/448092

Walsh, J., Vaida, N., Coman, A., & Fiske, S. T. (2022). Stories in action. *Psychological Science in the Public Interest*, *23*(3), 99–141. https://doi.org/10.1177/15291006231161337

Weeks, B. E., Ardèvol-Abreu, A., & Gil de Zúñiga, H. (2017). Online influence? Social media use, opinion leadership, and political persuasion. *International Journal of Public Opinion Research*, *29*(2), 214–239. https://doi.org/10.1093/ijpor/edv050

Wu, A. X. (2022). The ambient politics of affective computing. *Public Culture*, *34*(1 (96)), 21–45. https://doi.org/10.1215/08992363-9435427

Political Marketing at the Bottom of the Pyramid: Shreds of Evidence From India

Subhojit Sengupta and Srabanti Mukherjee

INTRODUCTION

Understanding voter behaviour is paramount for political analysts, strategists and institutions, as it fundamentally shapes campaign strategies and electoral outcomes. Insights derived from consumer behaviour theories unveil compelling parallels between voters and consumers. Just as consumers select brands based on distinct attributes, voters scrutinise political parties and candidates through analogous evaluative frameworks, effectively treating political entities as consumer brands (Banerjee & Ray Chaudhuri, 2016; Kotler & Levy, 1969; Reeves et al., 2006). The intricacy of voter behaviour is further exacerbated by the ever-evolving political landscape, marked by a plethora of choices and a ceaseless stream of campaign information, which complicates the interpretation of voter decisions (McNair, 2017). Although existing research has scrutinised demographic factors – such as education, gender, marital status, age, income and occupation – that affect political preferences (Banerjee & Ray Chaudhuri, 2016), a significant gap persists in understanding the voting behaviour of the Bottom of the Pyramid (BOP) segment.

The World Bank historically categorised the BOP segment as subsisting on less than $1 a day (Karnani, 2007). This definition has evolved, with the current threshold set at an annual income below $3,000 in 2005 US dollars (London, 2016). This expanded perspective acknowledges that poverty extends beyond mere income to encompass limited access to essential goods, services and economic opportunities (Narayan et al., 1999; World Resources Institute & International Finance Corporation, 2008). In rural regions across Asia, Africa, Eastern Europe, Latin America and the Caribbean, the BOP population grapples with profound poverty, decision-making uncertainty, low literacy and inadequate infrastructure (Dinica et al., 2012; Mason et al., 2013; Viswanathan et al., 2008). In India, where a significant proportion of the BOP population resides, socio-economic barriers profoundly influence political decision-making. Due to limited resources, BOP voters often rely on social networks and personal relationships to navigate political information (Uzzi, 1999; Woodcock & Narayan, 2000). These constraints give rise to 'missing information strategies' or self-fulfilling prophecies in decision-making (Burke, 1996; Viswanathan et al., 2005), whereby voting behaviour is driven more by social and emotional factors than comprehensive information.

Despite extensive research into BOP consumers' practices and poverty alleviation strategies

(Hamilton & Catterall, 2008; Hill & Gaines, 2007; Varman & Costa, 2009), there remains a conspicuous dearth of studies examining how BOP voters engage with political information and make electoral decisions. Kolk et al. (2015) emphasise that while BOP literature has delved into consumer behaviour and market development, it has largely overlooked political behaviour within this segment. Although existing studies have explored social embeddedness and economic challenges, the cognitive and behavioural constraints influencing BOP voters' political choices remain insufficiently examined (Gupta & Srivastava, 2016; Keefer & Khemani, 2005).

This chapter adopts a qualitative phenomenological approach to investigate political behaviour at the BOP. By centring on lived experiences and perceptions, this methodology offers profound insights into how BOP voters process political communications, form perceptions of political brands and make voting decisions. The study will scrutinise how party positioning, political knowledge and social relationships affect voting behaviour, focusing on rural India. It will evaluate the impact of poverty, limited education and cognitive constraints on political decision-making and perceptions of political brands. Integrating theories of political marketing with BOP literature, this chapter aims to develop a nuanced framework for understanding the distinctive challenges faced by BOP voters.

The significance of this chapter lies in its potential to bridge gaps identified in existing literature and offer targeted insights for public policy and political marketing strategies. By addressing the specific needs of BOP voters and proposing actionable approaches, the study aspires to enhance our comprehension of political marketing within this context and contribute to more effective engagement strategies for this vital segment of the electorate. In conclusion, this chapter will explore the implications of these findings for public policy and political marketing strategies. It will outline future research directions and propose targeted approaches to address the needs of BOP voters, striving to improve political engagement and representation for this crucial demographic.

DEVELOPMENT OF THE TOPIC

History and Core Concepts

The BOP population was initially defined as people who live on less than $1 a day by the World Bank (Karnani, 2007). Another base of the pyramid definition, given by the World Resource Institute and according to the International Finance Corporation (IFC) estimates, uses a cut-off of $1.72 per person per day in the Indian context. However, this definition is inadequate to define the BOP, as it considers only an individual's income while neglecting other important aspects of poverty. A World Bank Report titled 'Voices of the Poor' states that poverty is multidimensional. Apart from income levels, there are other dimensions of poverty, including the lack of access to essential goods and services and economic opportunities (Narayan et al., 1999). The IFC elaborated on the definition by including two more non-monetary aspects: lack of basic goods and services and lack of income generation opportunities.

BOP was initially characterised as 70% of the world's population living on less than two dollars a day (Karnani, 2007). More recently, the BOP has been defined as individuals with an annual income of less than $3000 in 2005 US dollars regarding purchasing power parity (London, 2016). The income classification mentioned above puts the BOP above the most impoverished individuals (those living on less than a dollar a day) but below what may be considered the 'mid-market' segment, which ranges in annual income from $3000 to $20000 (World Resources Institute & International Finance Corporation, 2008). This market has recently received the heightened attention of marketers and policymakers (Jebarajakirthy et al., 2016).

BOP markets are primarily, though not exclusively, located in rural areas and are found primarily in Asia, Africa, Eastern Europe, Latin America and the Caribbean (World Resources Institute & International Finance Corporation, 2008). The BOP market is characterised by abject poverty (Mason et al., 2013), uncertainty in decision-making (Dinica et al., 2012), lack of literacy (Viswanathan et al., 2008), restricted movement (Dinica et al., 2012) and limited infrastructure facility (Prahalad, 2007; Weidner et al., 2010). Due to poverty, they experience difficulty in meeting their basic needs in life and struggle to mitigate them continuously (Venugopal & Viswanathan, 2017). However, the most important distinguishing characteristic of the BOP population is their social embeddedness. Social embeddedness is 'the degree to which commercial transactions occur through social relations and networks of relations that use exchange protocols associated with social, non-commercial attachments to govern business dealings' (Uzzi, 1999, p. 482). When people fall on hard times, they know their friends and family constitute the final safety net (Woodcock & Narayan, 2000).

The BOP population residing in the interior or under-developed parts of the country faces severe resource limitations, mutual dependence and access limitations. They depend on social capital and conform to group norms (Viswanathan et al., 2014). Lack of proper information among BOP voters about the performance of politicians, the existence of social fragmentation among the voters (manifested as identity-based voting) and the lack of credibility of political promises to citizens serve as crucial factors in the political market while processing information for making voting decisions. Moreover, low levels of literacy and limited information about the object of decision-making make information processing of BOP customers highly constrained (Viswanathan et al., 2014). Such limited information processing capability subsequently leads BOP consumers to adopt self-fulfilling prophecies (Viswanathan et al., 2005) or 'missing information strategies' (Burke, 1996). Self-fulfilling prophecies occur when consumers' assumptions about products or services influence their behaviour, making those assumptions come true. Missing information strategies involve using mental shortcuts or assumptions to make decisions when complete information is not available. The cognitive-behavioural aspects of the voters at the BOP lack proper investigation, leaving out the scope for further research in the context of the latter's political voting decision-making.

The BOP voters remain constrained and entangled in their problems (Gupta & Srivastava, 2016). Their illiteracy and resource constraints, information asymmetry, political influence, peer pressure and community indulgence make them vulnerable (Keefer & Khemani, 2005) and overshadow their rational decision-making ability (Dayaratan-Banda, 2007). It has also been claimed that the poor interact differently than the upper-class population regarding thinking styles, emotional factors and social relationships (Viswanathan et al., 2008). Further, the existence of information asymmetry regarding the performance of politicians, social fragmentation among the voters (manifested as identity-based voting) and lack of credibility of political promises also act as constraints on BOP voters' processing of information when making voter decisions (Keefer & Khemani, 2005). Analysing such constrained behavioural patterns of BOP voters while making voting decisions calls for attention in the political marketing theory (Esposito et al., 2012). Therefore, we integrate the literature on the brand image of political parties with the BOP literature to highlight research questions that can guide the development of models of political behaviour at the BOP.

BOP voters are often ignorant about the issues or policies that do not concern them. This behavioural psychology is backed by BOP characteristics like limited literacy, meaning they cannot comprehend the messages the politician or political party wants to convey. To cope with this inability, BOP voters apply missing information strategies (Burke, 1996) like self-fulfilling prophecies or heuristics to reach a specific conclusion. Self-fulfilling prophecies here refer to situations where voters, with limited information, form expectations about political outcomes, and these expectations influence their voting behaviour, potentially causing those outcomes to happen. Nonetheless, such moderated decisions may not be free from subjectivity and uncertainty. The vicious cycle of chronic unemployment and underemployment, lack of property, meagre wages, lack of savings, the absence of food reserves in the home and chronic shortage of cash leaves no scope for cognitive development (Lewis, 1996). The individual who grows up in this culture has a strong feeling of fatalism, helplessness, dependence and inferiority and suffers from constrained cognitive ability (Lewis, 1996). Therefore, the constrained characteristics of the BOP segment moderate the perceived brand image of the political party.

Exploring the Political Lives of BOP Voters

The methodology of this study employs a qualitative phenomenological approach to explore the political behaviour of BOP voters in rural India. This approach is chosen for its ability to delve into the lived experiences and perceptions of individuals, particularly those with limited resources, cognitive abilities and political knowledge, and to provide profound insights into their decision-making processes regarding political communications and perceptions of political brands. The study focuses on understanding how poverty, low literacy and limited cognitive capacity impact BOP voters' political decision-making and perceptions of political brands in a politically dynamic environment.

The study is set in India, where a significant proportion of the population resides in rural areas, many of whom fall into the BOP category. Approximately 70% of India's population lives in rural regions with limited access to electricity, medical facilities and infrastructure (Rodrigues, 2017; Singh & Rahman, 2018). Although there will be improvements in sanitation facilities by 2023, other socio-economic barriers will continue to affect the political behaviour of BOP voters (The Hindu, 2024). This study was conducted in rural villages on the outskirts of Kolkata and Kharagpur in West Bengal, India. These areas were selected because the percentage of poor people in West Bengal (19.98%) is close to the national average (21.92%), making them representative of the broader Indian BOP demographic (Reserve Bank of India, 2016).

Consistent with the qualitative phenomenological approach, purposive sampling was used to recruit respondents. This sampling method is appropriate for selecting individuals with experience related to the phenomenon being studied and who best meet the research questions addressed in this study (Groenewald, 2004). In total, 29 individual interviews were conducted with BOP voters who regularly participate in elections (see Table 19.1). The selection criteria included a diversity of demographic backgrounds such as age, gender, occupation and marital status. Recruitment of participants was conducted in rural markets, where the purpose of the study was explained to potential respondents. Participants who consented to be interviewed were asked for a convenient time and location for the interview, with no incentives offered for participation.

A semi-structured and open-ended interview protocol was employed to collect data (see Table 19.2). The questions in the protocol were designed based on the study's objectives and focus and deliberately kept broad and open-ended to encourage the emergence of new ideas. This design allowed for capturing a wide range of perspectives and experiences from the respondents. The interview protocol was content-tested with two professors who had research experience in the subject area. Both verified the questions and recommended no changes. The protocol was then pre-tested with five BOP respondents, leading to minor wording and format adjustments to improve clarity. The pre-test respondents did not participate in the actual interviews used for data collection.

Table 19.1 Demographic Profile of the Respondents (n = 29)

Characteristic	*Subgroup*	*Frequency*
Monthly income (INR)	Less than 1000	9
	Between 1000 and 3000	4
	Between 3001 and 5000	6
	Between 5001 and 7000	5
	Between 7001 and 9000	3
	Above 9000	2
Education	Illiterate (no proper schooling)	9
	Primary school (till 4th standard)	6
	Junior High school (till 8th standard)	14
Location	Kolkata	16
	Kharagpur	13
Gender	Male	17
	Female	12
Age	Below 30 years	10
	31–45 years	9
	46–60 years	6
	Above 60	4
Occupation	Rickshaw pullers	11
	Construction labourers	8
	Cleaner	2
	Maidservants	3
	Factory workers	3
	Unemployed	2

Table 19.2 Protocol (Semi-Structured and Open-Ended)

Questions
Have you participated in the elections in the past five years?
When was it, and how was the experience? Can you please elaborate?
How did you decide on the political candidate or the party?
How are you connected with members of your community?
What did you like about the candidate for whom you voted?
Who are the members with whom you discuss political news and information?

A researcher with experience conducting qualitative interviews carried out all the interviews to ensure consistency. The interviews were conducted in Bengali, the local language of the respondents, and lasted between 50 and 60 minutes. To create a comfortable and familiar environment for the respondents, interviews were held in their homes. This setting facilitated a relaxed atmosphere, encouraging open and honest responses. The semi-structured interview format enabled emergent themes to surface naturally, allowing for follow-up and probing questions to be asked as needed to clarify critical issues. At the beginning of each interview, the interviewer explained the study's purpose and assured the respondents of their anonymity and confidentiality. Written consent was obtained from each participant before the interview commenced. Participants also permitted the interviews to be audiotaped and transcribed verbatim in Bengali by trained research assistants. Selected quotations from the Bengali transcripts were translated verbatim into English, ensuring that the original meaning of the quotations remained intact through back-translation.

Thematic analysis was employed to analyse the interview transcripts, following the guidelines provided by Braun and Clarke (2006). Two researchers independently coded the transcripts to ensure reliability and then met to discuss and resolve any similarities and differences in their coding schemes, achieving an inter-coder reliability of 0.89. The researchers then reviewed and grouped the generated codes based on emerging patterns, variability and response consistency. Two independently produced thematic maps were used to capture these groupings and refined into a final thematic map, which defined and named key themes and categories. The thematic map is summarised in Appendix 19.1.

In qualitative research, the term 'rigour' emphasises the credibility and authenticity of a study's findings (O'Reilly & Marx, 2011). A three-step approach was adopted to ensure the credibility and authenticity of the findings in this study. First, interviews were conducted face-to-face using a detailed method that allows for replication of the interviews and their analyses (Shenton, 2004). Second, as previously mentioned, coding and thematic analysis was performed independently by two researchers, who resolved any differences through discussion and the involvement of a third researcher. Finally, qualitative researchers (Baker et al., 2002; Elliot et al., 1999; Popay et al., 1998; Smith, 1996) advocate for presenting quotes that support the themes and sub-themes identified. This study provides exemplary quotes to support the themes and sub-themes reported in the 'findings and discussion' section.

Emergent Perspectives of the Political Marketing at the BOP

The study's findings on political marketing at the BOP highlight several key factors that influence the political behaviour and decision-making processes of BOP voters. The findings are structured around central themes such as party positioning, political dominance, political knowledge and a sense of belonging. Each theme reveals how the unique socio-economic conditions of BOP voters shape their political perceptions and choices. The discussion integrates these findings with existing literature to provide a deeper understanding of the dynamics of political marketing at the BOP.

Party Positioning

The concept of party positioning plays a crucial role in shaping the political brand image in the minds of BOP voters. The findings suggest that factors such as political issues, campaigning strategies, candidates' personalities and party ideology significantly influence the positioning of a party among BOP voters. According to Kotler's (1984) exchange theory, candidates seek votes in exchange for promises to develop low-income communities. The study finds that BOP voters, often constrained by cognitive limitations and lack of information, rely heavily on political issues that resonate with their immediate needs and concerns, such as employment, welfare, poverty alleviation and healthcare (Conover & Feldman, 1989). For example, one respondent stated, '*...in the last election, X (politician) promised to give us jobs and increase our government benefits.. even his political agenda said employment would be given, healthcare would be better.. I heard this at the rally I went to..*' (Male, 34). This demonstrates how BOP voters prioritise tangible, issue-based promises over broader political ideologies.

Due to limited access to media and low literacy, BOP voters often depend on local party workers and peers for political information (Keefer & Khemani, 2005). The findings also reveal that political campaigning in BOP communities is highly localised, relying on trusted local politicians and party workers to convey the party's messages (Lumpkin et al., 2018). These local representatives, known within the community, help create a positive image of the party or candidate, reinforcing the political brand. For instance, a respondent mentioned, '*...For me, X (a local politician) is the face of Party Y (a prominent political party in India).. though I know A as the main in Party Y, he will not come and listen to my cry and help me. X dada will only help me, so I am loyal to him, and whomever he says, I vote for ..*' (Female, 39).

Furthermore, the personality of political candidates and their alignment with party ideologies also impact voter choices at the BOP. The candidate's personal traits, such as their ability to connect with voters, perceived sincerity and accessibility, are pivotal in forming voters' perceptions (Rahat, 2007). BOP voters often view the candidate as the party's sole representative, reinforcing their trust and loyalty to the candidate and the party. This reflects the significance of candidates' personal connections with voters, which often outweighs party policies or ideologies in influencing voting behaviour.

Political Dominance

Political dominance in BOP communities manifests through clientelism and coercion, significantly shaping the political landscape. Clientelism is an exchange system where voters receive goods, services or other benefits in return for their votes (Kitschelt & Wilkinson, 2007). The study finds that most BOP voters mentioned receiving some form of patronage, such as direct cash transfers, food, job opportunities or other material benefits, which compels them to vote for specific parties or candidates. For example, one respondent noted, '*...while a few days back when my child was hospitalised, he (the party leader) helped us by arranging a bed at the hospital...he also got me a daily wage labourer job... at least it gives me some money...so I will vote for him only as he has helped in crisis...*' (Female, 24). This illustrates how immediate economic needs and dependencies drive political loyalty among BOP voters.

The hierarchical and unequal nature of clientelist relationships perpetuates a cycle of dependence and control, where local leaders, acting as brokers, maintain strong ties with voters and use their influence to deliver votes to higher-level political leaders (Powell, 1970; Shami, 2012). This triadic relationship between patrons, brokers and clients reinforces political dominance in BOP communities, often undermining democratic values of free choice and fair competition (Gonzalez-Ocantos et al., 2019; Simmel, 1971).

Coercion is another significant aspect of political dominance at the BOP. The study highlights that voter intimidation is a widespread problem, with local political leaders or party workers using threats, violence and harassment to ensure voter compliance. This form of coercion is particularly prevalent in rural India, where economically vulnerable voters are threatened with losing access to essential resources or subjected to physical violence if they do not support specific parties or candidates (Daxecker, 2020). A respondent shared, '*...they (local party members) threatened me that if I didn't vote for them, they would abduct my daughter and rape her... it's not very uncommon... if you don't follow or abide by the local leaders, you will be the victim of physical abuse and violence...*' (Male, 45). This quote underscores the extreme measures taken to manipulate voter behaviour and maintain political control in BOP areas.

Political Knowledge

Political knowledge among BOP voters is limited due to several factors, including low literacy levels, poor access to information and constrained cognitive abilities. The study finds that BOP voters often lack comprehensive political knowledge and rely on simple cues, such as party labels or the opinions of trusted community members, to guide their voting decisions (Clark, 2018). Limited access to objective information sources, such as newspapers or unbiased television channels, further restricts their ability to evaluate political candidates or policies critically. Instead, they depend on discussions with peers, family members or local leaders to understand political issues (Venugopal & Viswanathan, 2017). For example, a respondent explained, '...*during the Durga puja meeting at our club, they discussed the proposed agenda for the upcoming election... since I can't read and write, I get the information through these meetings. Also, some terms are too complex and are in English, difficult for me to understand, so I ask my local leader to explain...*' (Female, 32).

The study also highlights the concept of political sophistication, which refers to an individual's capacity to process political information and make informed decisions (Luskin, 1990). Due to constrained cognitive abilities and low motivation to engage with political information, BOP voters often exhibit low political sophistication. This leads them to adopt cognitive shortcuts, such as relying on party symbols or candidate characteristics, to make quick decisions (Petty et al., 2003). As one respondent noted, '...*I studied till class eight only; then I have been working as a factory worker since early childhood to serve food to my family. Firstly, I don't understand much of politics, and then I am also uninterested in it because this will not provide food for my family; my work will only do...*' (Male, 25). This statement illustrates how economic constraints and immediate survival needs to limit the capacity and motivation of BOP voters to engage deeply with political processes.

Sense of Belonging

A sense of belonging, driven by social capital, social identity and social representation, is another critical factor influencing political behaviour at the BOP. The study finds that BOP voters often decide based on their social identity, such as caste, religion or community affiliations, rather than purely on the candidates' performance or policies (Hogg & Abrams, 1988). Social capital, which refers to the networks, shared values and trust among community members, is crucial in shaping political choices at the BOP (Sen & Cowley, 2013). The strong social ties within BOP communities often lead voters to conform to the majority's decision to maintain group cohesiveness and access social resources (Viswanathan et al., 2014). For instance, a respondent mentioned, '...*I always attend all community meetings and participate in discussions actively because that is a major way to get information, and I show my obligation towards my community. If god forbids me, I need some help tomorrow; the first people I will approach are my community members...*' (Female, 28).

Social identity theory suggests that people define themselves in terms of their group image and act similarly to other group members (Hogg & Abrams, 1988). The study finds that BOP voters often support candidates or parties that reflect their social identity, even if these candidates do not offer the best political solutions. For example, a respondent stated, '...*we are in the majority but have minority status... we are being looked down on by the wealthy and upper class... Therefore, I stick to my roots... I decide to vote based on where the local candidate comes from and who he is representative of in the real sense... similar background and caste matter to me...*' (Male, 48). This highlights how identity-based voting, driven by a sense of belonging, often overshadows rational evaluations of candidates' qualifications or policies.

The concept of social representation further influences voting decisions at the BOP. BOP voters support politicians and parties representing their socio-economic identity and interests. They perceive politicians from similar backgrounds as more relatable and trustworthy, leading to stronger affiliations and political loyalty (Kitschelt & Wilkinson, 2007). A respondent said, '...while voting, I don't find anyone who represents me realistically. *None of the political leaders at the central office come from a poor background. I feel our voices are not being heard/ignored in the parliament. This miserable status quo never ends...*' (Male, 56). This sentiment reflects the deep-rooted sense of disconnection and marginalisation felt by BOP voters towards mainstream political entities, driving them to seek representation within their communities.

We summarise the emergent themes of political marketing at the BOP in Figures 19.1 and 19.2.

Implications for Practice and Policy

The implications for practice and policy in political marketing at the BOP are significant for various stakeholders, including government election officials, political party officials, non-governmental organisations (NGOs) and election commissions. Each of these entities plays a crucial role in addressing the unique challenges BOP voters face, often characterised by poverty, limited literacy, constrained cognitive abilities and a lack of political knowledge.

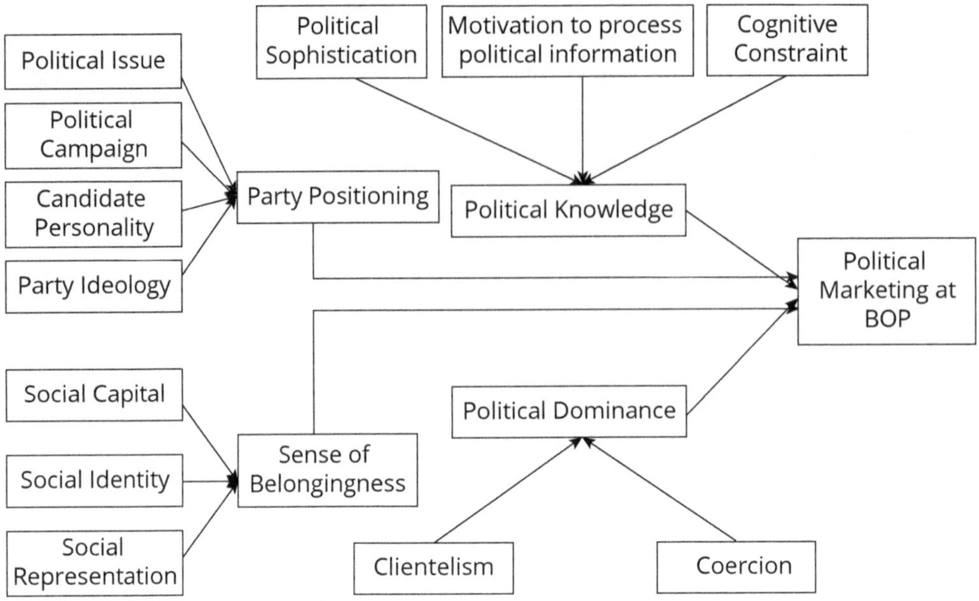

Figure 19.1 Influences on Political Marketing at the Base of the Pyramid

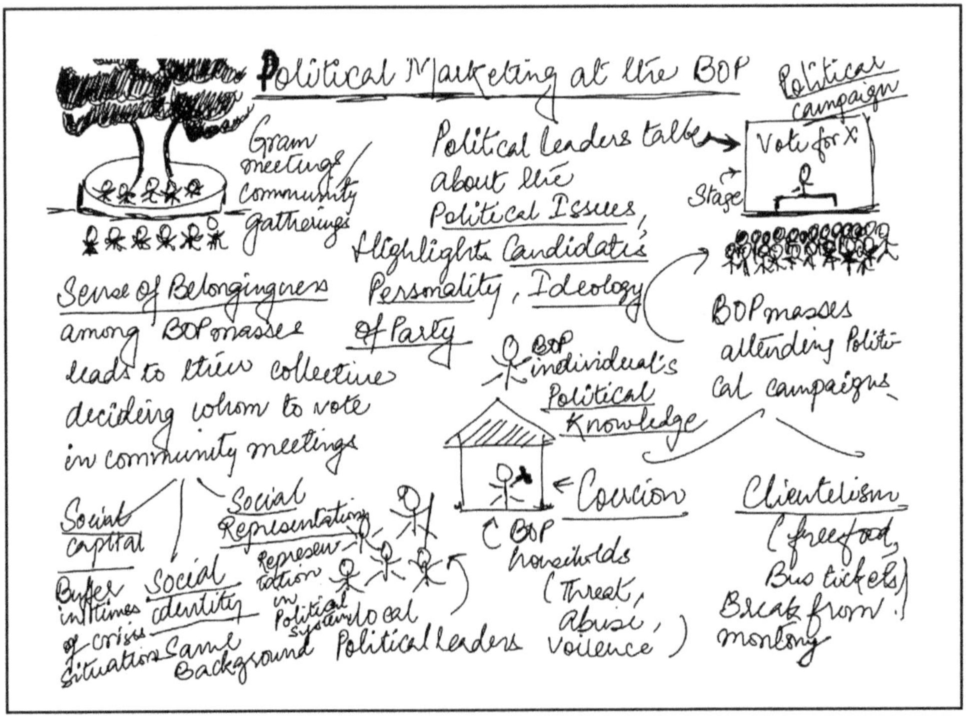

Figure 19.2 Rich Diagram Explaining Influences on Political Marketing at the BOP

Government election authorities, such as the Election Commission of India (ECI), must initiate comprehensive voter education campaigns targeting BOP voters. These campaigns should emphasise the importance of electing leaders prioritising long-term development goals over immediate, short-term handouts. By focusing on how investments in healthcare, education, infrastructure and employment schemes can transform communities, these programs can guide BOP voters towards making more informed decisions. Local dialects, regional media and collaboration with local governance structures, such as panchayats (village councils), will ensure the messages resonate effectively across diverse Indian regions. Additionally, election officials must enhance security measures throughout the election phases to safeguard BOP voters from coercion and intimidation. This includes deploying additional Central Reserve Police Force (CRPF) personnel in vulnerable regions, installing CCTV cameras at polling booths, and establishing secure zones in areas prone to electoral violence. The continuous patrolling by security forces from the announcement of elections until after the results will instil confidence among BOP voters, ensuring they can exercise their rights without fear. Coordination with local law enforcement agencies and leveraging technology like the ECI's cVIGIL app will further bolster election security.

Political party officials also have a critical role to play in shaping campaign strategies that prioritise the long-term development of BOP communities. Instead of encouraging short-term incentives like direct cash transfers or temporary job opportunities, party officials should advocate for comprehensive plans that enhance essential public services, such as improvements in education through Sarva Shiksha Abhiyan (SSA), healthcare via Ayushman Bharat and housing under Pradhan Mantri Awas Yojana (PMAY). These plans should be effectively communicated to voters through grassroots methods, including nukkad nataks (road shows), village panchayat meetings and targeted social media campaigns, demonstrating how such policies will lead to sustainable improvements in their communities. Party officials must also implement measures to prevent voter intimidation, particularly in regions with high BOP populations. This includes thoroughly training party workers on the Model Code of Conduct (MCC) and ensuring strict adherence to electoral guidelines. Officials should take a strong stance against coercion by publicly condemning such practices and supporting the implementation of anonymous reporting systems like those offered through the cVIGIL app.

NGOs are vital in educating BOP voters about their legal rights and the electoral process. Legal literacy camps using regional languages and culturally relevant examples can explain voter rights and how to address electoral malpractices. Partnering with local legal professionals to offer free legal consultations and setting up help desks in rural areas can empower BOP voters to understand and exercise their rights. NGOs should also focus on increasing awareness of laws like the Representation of the People Act, which protects voters from electoral fraud and coercion. Furthermore, NGOs should collaborate with the government to establish legal aid centres, especially in remote and underserved areas, to provide BOP voters with legal tools to protect their rights. These centres could offer services like filing complaints, legal counselling and representation in cases of electoral misconduct. Mobile legal vans could be deployed in rural areas to extend these services further, ensuring that even the most isolated voters can access the help they need.

For election commissions and regulatory bodies, such as the ECI, the rigorous enforcement of anti-intimidation policies is crucial to protecting voters, particularly those in BOP segments. This includes imposing strict penalties on candidates or parties found guilty of coercion or violence, ensuring thorough monitoring of high-risk areas through human and technological means, and offering real-time grievance redress mechanisms. The ECI should also enhance the transparency of these measures through public reports and collaborations with civil society organisations to ensure accountability. Establishing a robust independent observer system to oversee elections in sensitive areas can deter malpractices and ensure free and fair elections. Additionally, the ECI, in partnership with NGOs and local governments, should launch widespread public awareness campaigns that educate BOP voters on the importance of electing candidates with a strong commitment to long-term development. To reach a broad audience, these campaigns should utilise a mix of traditional and digital media, including Doordarshan broadcasts, community radio, social media platforms and local influencers. The focus should be on explaining how initiatives like Digital India, Skill India and Swachh Bharat Mission can improve the quality of life, highlighting success stories from various parts of India where such policies have significantly impacted.

CONCLUSION

This chapter focuses on understanding political behaviour at the BOP in rural India, exploring how unique socio-economic constraints shape voting decisions among BOP voters. Using a qualitative phenomenological approach, the study delves into how BOP voters, characterised by poverty, low literacy, limited cognitive abilities and restricted access to information, interact with political marketing and form perceptions of political brands. It bridges gaps in existing political communication and BOP literature by proposing a conceptual framework that integrates theories of political marketing with insights specific to BOP contexts.

The chapter highlights several critical issues influencing the political behaviour of BOP voters. These include information asymmetry and constrained cognitive abilities, where limited access to media and low literacy levels lead BOP voters to rely on social networks and local influencers rather than comprehensive political information (Keefer & Khemani, 2005). This results in a high dependency on clientelism and coercion, where BOP voters often exchange their votes for immediate benefits, such as direct cash transfers, jobs or other material goods (Kitschelt & Wilkinson, 2007). The prevalence of coercion and electoral violence further undermines democratic values, as BOP voters are often subject to threats and harassment to influence their voting behaviour (Daxecker, 2020).

The study also emphasises the short-term focus of BOP voters in their political decision-making. This orientation is driven by immediate economic needs rather than long-term policy implications, leading to a preference for candidates who promise immediate relief over those advocating for sustainable development (Viswanathan, 2007). Additionally, the role of social identity and belonging is critical, as BOP voters often make voting decisions based on caste, religion or community affiliations rather than the qualifications or policies of the candidates (Gupta & Shrivastav, 2016).

This chapter demonstrates the profound impact of socio-economic barriers on political behaviour among marginalised communities. It underscores the need to understand these unique dynamics to create more effective political marketing strategies and policies that genuinely engage BOP voters. The implications are clear: for political engagement to be meaningful and democratic, strategies must address the specific needs and vulnerabilities of BOP voters. This means moving beyond short-term incentives and building long-term trust through policies prioritising development, inclusivity and empowerment.

This study points to multi-stakeholder efforts to enhance democratic engagement for BOP communities. Government election officials, political parties, NGOs and election commissions must collaborate to develop voter education programs that emphasise long-term development goals, enhance electoral security and rigorously enforce anti-intimidation measures (Viswanathan et al., 2014). Political parties should shift from clientelist tactics to more development-oriented campaigns. At the same time, NGOs need to focus on legal empowerment and voter awareness initiatives to protect BOP voters from coercion and fraud.

In conclusion, this chapter provides a comprehensive framework for understanding BOP voters' political behaviour and lays out actionable strategies for more inclusive political participation. By addressing the unique challenges of BOP communities, this work calls for policies and practices that foster equitable political representation, ultimately contributing to a more just and participatory democratic system. Future research should explore cross-country studies and quantitative analyses to further validate and expand on the findings presented here, ensuring a broader understanding of political behaviour at the BOP level.

REFERENCES

Abrams, D., & Hogg, M. A. (1988). Comments on the motivational status of self-esteem in social identity and intergroup discrimination. *European Journal of Social Psychology*, *18*(4), 317–334.

Baker, J., Parasuraman, A., Grewal, D., & Voss, G. B. (2002). The influence of multiple store environment cues on perceived merchandise value and patronage intentions. *Journal of Marketing*, *66*(2), 120–141.

Banerjee, S., & Ray Chaudhuri, H. (2016). Political marketing in India: Parties and voters. *Journal of Political Marketing*, *15*(2--3), 112–139.

Braun, V., & Clarke, V. (2006). Using thematic analysis in psychology. *Qualitative Research in Psychology*, *3*(2), 77–101.

Burke, R. R. (1996). Missing information: Implications for consumer decision-making and marketing strategy. *Journal of Retailing*, *72*(4), 410–433.

Clark, R. (2018). Political knowledge in democracies: Bridging the divide. *The Journal of Politics Journal of Politics*, *80*(4), 1255–1269.

Daxecker, U. (2020). The cost of exposing cheating: International election monitoring, fraud, and post-election violence in Africa. *Journal of Peace Research*, *57*(3), 431–447.

Dayaratan-Banda, S. (2007). Voter bBehavior: Cognitive perspectives. *Journal of Political Science*, *12*(3), 56–71.

Dinica, V., Sartorius, R. H., & Viswanathan, M. (2012). Ethics and sustainable development are at the base of the pyramid. *International Journal of Market Research*, *54*(2), 227–241.

Elliott, R., Fischer, C. T., & Rennie, D. L. (1999). Evolving guidelines for publication of qualitative research studies in psychology and related fields. *British Journal of Clinical Psychology*, *38*(3), 215–229.

Esposito, V., Sen, S., & Cowley, E. (2012). Political mMarketing and the BOP. *Journal of Political Marketing*, *11*(3), 232–250.

Gonzalez-Ocantos, E., Kiewiet de Jonge, C., Meléndez, C., Osorio, J., & Nickerson, D. W. (2019). The conditionality of vote-buying norms: Experimental evidence from Latin America. *American Journal of Political Science*, *63*(1), 178–192.

Groenewald, T. (2004). A phenomenological research design illustrated. *International Journal of Qualitative Methods*, *3*(1), 42–55.

Gupta, A., & Srivastava, R. K. (2016). Brand positioning of political parties. *International Journal of Research in Marketing*, *33*(2), 265–279.

Hamilton, K., & Catterall, M. (2008). The role of family financial socialisation in influencing individuals'' financial literacy. *Journal of Consumer Affairs*, *42*(1), 92–112.

Hill, R. P., & Gaines, J. (2007). The consumer culture of poverty: Behavioral research findings and their implications in an ethnically pluralistic society. *Journal of Business Research*, *60*(5), 496–503.

Jebarajakirthy, C., Thaichon, P., & Yoganathan, D. (2016). Enhancing corporate social responsibility through market orientation practices in bottom of pyramid markets: with special reference to microcredit institutions. *Journal of Strategic Marketing*, *24*(5), 398–417.

Karnani, A. (2007). The mirage of marketing to the bottom of the pyramid. *California Management Review*, *49*(4), 90–111.

Keefer, P., & Khemani, S. (2005). Democracy, public expenditures, and the poor: Understanding political incentives for providing public services. *The World Bank Research Observer*, *20*(1), 1–27.

Kitschelt, H., & Wilkinson, S. I. (Eds.). (2007). *Patrons, clients and policies: Patterns of democratic accountability and political competition*. Cambridge University Press.

Kolk, A., Rivera-Santos, M., & Rufín, C. (2015). Reviewing a decade of research on the "base/bottom of the pyramid" (BOP) concept. *Business & Society*, *54*(2), 143–190.

Kotler, P., & Levy, S. J. (1969). Broadening the concept of marketing. *Journal of Marketing*, *33*(1), 10–15.

Lewis, O. (1996). Culture of poverty. In G. Gmelch & W. Zenner (Eds.), *Urban life: Readings in the anthropology of the city* (pp. 440–449). Waveland Press.

London, T. (2016). *The base of the pyramid promise: Building businesses with impact and scale*. Stanford University Press.

Lumpkin, G. T., Bacq, S., & Pidduck, R. J. (2018). Where change happens: Social entrepreneurship and the scaling of social impact. *Journal of Business Venturing Insights*, *9*, 1–7.

Luskin, R. C. (1990). Explaining political sophistication. *Political behavior*, *12*, 331–361.

Mason, K., Chakrabarti, R., & Singh, R. (2013). Base of the pyramid: A new market for innovative companies. *Journal of Consumer Marketing*, *30*(6), 567–578.

McNair, B. (2017). *An introduction to political communication* (6th ed. ed.). Routledge.

Narayan, D., Chambers, R., Shah, M. K., & Petesch, P. (1999). *Voices of the poor: Can anyone hear us?* Oxford University Press for the World Bank.

O'Reilly, K., & Marx, S. (2011). How young, technical consumers assess online WOM credibility. *Qualitative Market Research: An International Journal*, *14*(4), 330–359.

Petty, R. E., Fabrigar, L. R., & Wegener, D. T. (2003). Emotional factors in attitudes and persuasion. *Handbook of affective sciences*, *752*, 772.

Popay, J., Rogers, A., & Williams, G. (1998). Rationale and standards for the systematic review of qualitative literature in health services research. *Qualitative Health Research*, *8*(3), 341–351.

Powell, J. (1970). The political use of private patronage: Influence of parliamentarians on immigration regulation in Britain. *The Journal of Politics Journal of Politics*, *32*(2), 286–303.

Prahalad, C. K. (2007). *The fortune at the bottom of the pyramid: Eradicating poverty through profits*. Wharton School Publishing.

Rahat, G. (2007). Candidate selection: The choice before the choice. *Journal of Democracy*, *18*(1), 157–170.

Reeves, P., de Chernatony, L., & Carrigan, M. (2006). Building a political brand: Ideology or voter-driven strategy? *Journal of Brand Management*, *13*(6), 418–428.

Reserve Bank of India. (2016). Annual report of the Banking Ombudsman Scheme 2015-16. https://rbi.org.in/scripts/PublicationsView.aspx?id=17399

Rodrigues, J. (2017, December 27). *Angry young rural voters to set economic tone for India in 2018*. Bloomberg. https://www.bloomberg.com/news/articles/2017-12-26/angry-young-rural-voters-to-set-economic-tone-for-india-in-2018

Sen, S., & Cowley, J. (2013). The relevance of stakeholder theory and social capital theory in the context of CSR in SMEs: An Australian perspective. *Journal of Business Ethics*, *118*, 413–427.

Shami, M. (2012). Collective action, clientelism, and connectivity. *World Politics*, *64*(2), 213–241.

Shenton, A. K. (2004). Strategies for ensuring trustworthiness in qualitative research projects. *Education for Information*, *22*(2), 63–75.

Simmel, G. (1971). *On iIndividuality and sSocial fForms*. University of Chicago Press.

Singh, C., & Rahman, A. (2018). Urbanising the rural: Reflections on India's National Rurban Mission. *Asia & the Pacific Policy Studies*, *5*(2), 370–377.

Smith, J. A. (1996). Qualitative methodology: Analysing participants' perspectives. *Current Opinion in Psychiatry*, *9*(6), 417–421.

Uzzi, B. (1999). Embeddedness in the making of financial capital: How social relations and networks benefit firms seeking financing. *American Sociological Review*, *64*(4), 481–505.

Varman, R., & Costa, J. A. (2009). Competitive and cooperative behavior in embedded markets: Developing a theory of marketplace literacy. *Marketing Theory*, *9*(1), 99–121.

Venugopal, S., & Viswanathan, M. (2017). The subsistence marketplaces approach to poverty: Implications for marketing theory and practice. *Marketing Theory*, *17*(3), 435–454.

Viswanathan, M., Gajendiran, S., & Venkatesan, R. (2008). Understanding and enabling marketplace literacy in subsistence contexts: The development of a consumer and entrepreneurial literacy educational program in South India. *International Journal of Educational Development*, *28*(3), 300–319.

Viswanathan, M., Gajendiran, S., & Venkatesan, R. (2014). Understanding and enabling marketplace literacy in subsistence contexts. *International Journal of Consumer Studies*, *38*(3), 278–289.

Viswanathan, M. (2007). Understanding product and market interactions in subsistence marketplaces: A study in South India. In *Product and market development for subsistence marketplaces* (pp. 21–57). Emerald Group Publishing Limited.

Viswanathan, M., Rosa, J. A., & Harris, J. E. (2005). Decision making and coping of functionally illiterate consumers and some implications for marketing management. *Journal of Marketing*, *69*(1), 15–31.

Weidner, K. L., Rosa, J. A., & Viswanathan, M. (2010). Marketing to subsistence consumers: Lessons from practice. *Journal of Business Research*, *63*(6), 559–569.

Woodcock, M., & Narayan, D. (2000). Social capital: Implications for development theory, research, and policy. *The World Bank Research Observer*, *15*(2), 225–249.

World Resources Institute & International Finance Corporation. (2008). *The next 4 billion: Market size and business strategy at the base of the pyramid*. World Resources Institute and International Finance Corporation.

Appendix 19.1 Final Codes, Categories and Themes

Sl No.	*Final Codes*	*Categories*	*Theme*	*Explanation of the Themes*
1	Government benefits	Political Issue	Party Positioning	For Bottom of the Pyramid (BOP) voters, party positioning in their minds is influenced by several key factors. Political parties and candidates position themselves through promises addressing BOP issues such as employment, healthcare and poverty. Because BOP voters have limited access to detailed information, they rely heavily on local politicians and party workers for political education and cues. Campaigns that leverage local trust and community bonds are particularly effective, as local figures are seen as more relatable and trustworthy. Additionally, a party's ideology can reinforce its position if it aligns with the voters' social, cultural and ideological preferences. Therefore, a party's ability to connect its image and promises to the everyday realities and needs of BOP voters plays a crucial role in shaping its positioning in their minds.
2	Poverty			
3	Abortion			
4	Job opportunities			
5	Unemployment			
6	Healthcare facilities			
7	Women empowerment	Political Campaigning		
8	Racial discrimination			
9	Civil rights			
10	Advertising			
11	Charming	Candidate Personality		
12	Listen's to us			
13	Celebrity			
14	One of us			
15	Party Agenda	Ideology of the party		
16	Religious stands			
17	Polarity			
18	Abuse	Coercion	Political Dominance	In BOP areas, political dominance significantly influences voting decisions. Political parties exert control through clientelism and coercion. Clientelism involves exchanging votes for immediate benefits such as money, jobs or services, which fosters dependence and loyalty among voters. This hierarchical relationship, where local leaders (brokers) mediate between voters and higher political authorities (patrons), consolidates political power and ensures voter allegiance. Coercion complements this by using intimidation tactics, including violence and threats, to suppress dissent and enforce compliance. Such methods undermine democratic principles by manipulating and controlling voter behaviour, ensuring voters support those who provide material benefits or threaten reprisals. This dominance shapes voting patterns and perpetuates a cycle of dependency and fear, distorting democratic processes and governance.
19	Physical harm			
20	Manipulation			
21	Extortion			
22	Violence			
23	Abduction			
24	Benefits	Clientelism		
25	Helped me in crisis			
26	Provided reference			
27	Gave money to build a home			
28	Free food			
29	Difficult terms and terminologies	Political sophistication	Political Knowledge	Low political knowledge among BOP voters significantly affects their voting decisions. With limited access to comprehensive news sources and poor educational opportunities, BOP individuals often lack the necessary information to make informed political choices. They frequently rely on local leaders or family members for political guidance, which can result in a limited and sometimes biased
30	Not a commoner's language			
31	Difficult to interpret			
32	Language barrier			
33	Low literacy			

(Continued)

Appendix 19.1 (Continued)

Sl No.	*Final Codes*	*Categories*	*Theme*	*Explanation of the Themes*
34	Unawareness	Cognitive constraints		understanding of political candidates and issues.
35	Ignorance			Political sophistication, which involves the ability to process and organise complex political information, is generally low among BOP voters. Their political knowledge is often superficial, focusing more on immediate, tangible benefits such as financial aid or personal favours than on the broader implications of a party's policies or a candidate's platform. This lack of sophistication, combined with cognitive constraints like low literacy and financial insecurity, leads BOP voters to make decisions based on short-term gains and personal relationships rather than informed evaluations of political ideologies or long-term policy effects.
36	Lack of education			
37	Difficult to read and write	Motivation to process political information		
38	Apolitical attitude			
39	Feeling of worthlessness			
40	Apathy towards political parties			
41	Struggle for existence			
42	Community member	Social Capital	Sense of Belongingness	BOP voters' sense of belongingness crucially influences their voting decisions. Social capital, derived from tight-knit community ties, provides BOP individuals with essential resources and political information, leading them to vote in line with community consensus rather than personal research. Their social identity and cultural background shape their preferences, often driving them to support candidates who reflect their socio-economic status and experiences. Additionally, BOP voters prioritise representation from those who genuinely understand and advocate for their needs, as they feel more aligned with candidates who share their socio-economic and cultural identity. Consequently, feelings of alienation from disconnected politicians can lead to disengagement or resistance to broader political options.
43	Protection from atrocity			
44	Fall back in crisis			
45	Same locality			
46	Substitute to resource constraint			
47	Trust and affinity for community members			
48	Shield for my family			
49	Herd mentality	Social representation		
50	Lack of representation			
51	Voicelessness			
52	Minority status			
53	Miserable status-quo			
54	Low-socio-economic identity	Social identity		
55	Stigma due to poverty			
56	Looked down in society			
57	Similar caste and creed			
58	Belongingness to group			
59	Similar background			

PART 3

Ideology in Political Marketing: Advocacy, Movements, Lobbying, and Public Diplomacy

The Marketing of an Ideal: The Hong Kong Pro-Democracy Movement

Georgios Patsiaouras

INTRODUCTION

The rise and popularity of new social movements, over the last 20 years, has been widely acknowledged and discussed both by political scientists and marketing scholars (Della Porta & Diani, 2020; Jasper, 2014; Kozinets & Handelman, 2004). Although the rigid leadership structures of 20th century social movements sought to secure mainstream media and mainly television attention, decentralized New Social Movements (NSMs henceforth) have been displaying much more sophisticated strategies and tactics to communicate their aims within digital venues and creative spaces. For example, The MeToo, Black Lives Matter and Strike for Climate movements skilfully employed both social media and urban spaces to reach global audiences and change perceptions around inequality and environmental destruction. The rise of socio-economic and political challenges, over the last 20 years – such as the emergence of populism, austerity and geopolitical conflicts – have been fostering not only the growth of social movements globally but also their capacity to achieve unparalleled records of mainstream media coverage, digital presence and long-standing occupation of public spaces. Such phenomena have prompted several institutions, commercial organizations and global brands to enter their political domain and, both subtly and explicitly, to express sympathy or support towards movements' causes (New York Times, 2020). Simultaneously, NSMs themselves have been developing imaginative and creative campaigns, branding symbolism and digital communication practices, to stir action and captivate audiences' attention, phenomena remaining underexplored in political marketing literature. Accordingly, the aim of this chapter is threefold: (a) first, it seeks to critically examine and discuss the existing literature around the interface between NSMs and (political) marketing practices; (b) second, it aims to focus on how the 2014–2020 Hong Kong Umbrella Movement utilized marketing and promotional tactics to communicate its aims to local and global audiences; (c) third, it seeks to provide wider conclusions around the interface between political marketing and 21st century NSMs.

EARLY FORMS OF COMMUNICATION PRACTICES BY SOCIAL MOVEMENTS

The political meaning of protest symbols, across space and time, has been meticulously discussed by both historians and political theorists (Berger &

Nehring, 2013; Meyer & Tarrow, 1998). Moving away from a Western-centric perspective, undeniably, it can be argued that the communication of protest symbolism is a spatially and culturally dependent phenomenon and practice, whose breadth and depth lies beyond the scope of this chapter. However, for a thorough understanding on the political communication of protest meanings, a semi-historical angle can reveal valuable insights.

Synoptically, popular signs of resistance or political opposition emerged since ancient times, such as the olive branch and the dove expressing resistance towards military plans and enlistment in ancient Greece and Rome (Finley, 1983). Party colours and diverse political banners were displayed – and occasionally violently clashed – at the Hippodrome of Constantinople, Byzantine Empire's centre of social and political life (Langdale, 2019). Possibly, it was during the French Revolution when protest symbols created mass appeal and visibility among the public and revolutionaries; such as the tricolour cockade, the broken chain and the adoption of 'The Marseillaise' as a popular anthem (Andress, 2015). The international impact of the French Revolution not only led to the rapid rise of parliamentary democracies but also invigorated and developed political ideologies and beliefs – such as communism, liberalism and radicalism – which, in their turn, heavily informed the growth of 19th and 20th century social movements (Hobsbawn, 1962; Jones, 2003). Gradually, the repercussions of the long-standing and violent protests in France infused emerging labour, feminist and pro-democratic social movements with an ethos of collective struggle and protest symbolism.

The historical sociologist Charles Tilly (1986, 1995) has provided an in-depth exploration around the use and evolution of symbols in demonstrations, petitions and strikes throughout the eighteenth and nineteenth centuries. During these periods, which lacked microphones, cameras and other digital resources, revolutionary and chartist leaders placed special emphasis on colours, dresses and banners to communicate their messages. The use of red flags and colours by the 1870 Paris Commune became an emotive symbol that was adopted by international communist and socialist movements (Leith, 1978). Ribbons, armbands, paintings and installations had been enthusiastically disseminated and displayed during the Second International along with trade unions and anarcho-syndicalist conferences. In those early days of radical movements, whose protest activities often clashed with State police, the communication of a common symbol sought to achieve increased party membership, exposure through newspapers and to arise class-consciousness primarily among industrial workers and under-privileged citizens (Berger & Nehring, 2013).

Some of the most innovative, imaginative and creative campaigns emerged in the early 20th century from women's struggle for, among others, voting and equal rights. In the United Kingdom, the Women's Social and Political Union (WSPU) – under the leadership of the Pankhurst sisters – embarked upon some of the most visible, unconventional and spectacular campaigns to raise awareness around the suffrage movement and its cause: women's rights and vote. Large parades, window smashing, public hunger strikes, public shouting to oppositional speakers are only a few among many other militant/radical tactics that managed to re-invigorate the suffragette movement and communicate women's liberation from male-dominated structures (Mayhall, 2003). Apart from employing symbols of (non)traditional womanhood, the suffragette movement utilized pioneering techniques of attracting audience engagement and encourage political participation (Teske & Tetrault, 2000). Sylvia Pankhurst, in particular, was exceptional in the promotion of movement's aims (Smith, 2003) designing a Women's Fair in 1909 where suffrage postcards, books, statuettes, badges and trimmings were both sold and disseminated to the public (Raeburn, 1973; Stanton et al., 2017). Suffragette tea sets and especially suffragette jewellery became so popular among supporters that shopkeepers struggled to meet demand during the first decade of the century, while anti-suffragette propaganda, in form of posters, was also rising at the same time (Museum of London, Suffragette Collection, 2018). Apart from the tactics and campaigns of WSPU, the promotional practices of early feminist movements globally – the 1930's Chinese feminist movement, for example – could historically inform the contemporary, politically seminal and growing marketing/consumer research around gender and feminist perspectives (Catterall et al., 2005; Hein et al., 2016; Maclaran, 2015).

Although pre-WWII social movements mainly demanded economic equality and improved labour conditions, the post-war economic euphoria and rise of consumer culture brought forward NSMs that promoted new political identities related to peace, sex equality and ecology (Scott, 1990). The popularity of television and radio facilitated these movements to create multi-channel communication campaigns and accordingly protesters could reach global audiences. Furthermore, post-war movements disengaged from political party membership and skilfully managed to engage youth segments, cultural intermediaries and renown artists with their causes and goals. Gradually, the synthesis of cultural experimentation and sophisticated communication strategies began to adopt a marketing ethos since movements' slogans, events and images informed branding and advertising strategies which, in their turn, sought to appeal anti-establishment, affluent and educated consumer segments of Western societies (Stinerock, 2015).

With the end of the Cold War and the rise of liberalism worldwide, we observe the transformation of old political social movements (feminist/labour movements) towards what we call as 'New Social Movements', whose key aims sought to achieve socio-cultural change rather than to demand civic rights and improved labour conditions (Beck, 1992; Habermas, 1981). Becoming decentralized, open and ideologically diverse, facilitated NSMs to improvise with flexible marketing communications so as to enhance their media and public visibility (Castells, 2004). Since the massive and televised 1999 Seattle anti-globalization protests, the more flexible and multi-media friendly NSMs (Higgins & Tadajewski, 2002) became both ardent students of sophisticated marketing communications and producers of their own ideological branding positioning to stir international crowns and growing segments of internet users. As we will see in the following section, 21st century NSMs skilfully employ marketing mix, digital and branding practices to compete for public attention, mobilization and lobbying.

MARKETING, CONSUMPTION AND NEW SOCIAL MOVEMENTS

Marketing scholars and political scientists have placed more emphasis on the activities and communication practices of consumer movements, compared to the campaigns of NSMs (Patsiaouras, 2022). Following the wave of the 'anti-globalization' movement and rising reports on climate change (Della Porta & Diani, 2020), formal and informal groups of consumers began to align and collaborate with existing anti-consumerist groups (Klein, 2000), ecological teams (Shultz & Peterson, 2019) and forms of consumer activism against unethical corporate profits (Lekakis, 2022). Accordingly, marketing scholars have elaborated on how specific groups of customers communicated distinctive preferences related to ethical and sustainable choices via shared lifestyles (Wahlen & Laamanen, 2015), products (Chatzidakis et al., 2016) and campaigns (Campana et al., 2017; Weijo et al., 2018). Marketing research on consumer movements has been exploring the size, scope and technologically advanced means of those groups, in communicating notions of consumer care, along with the development of sustainable and ethical ways of consuming.

As Kozinets and Handelman (2004) argued, we can identify clear distinctions between NSMs and consumer movements. First, although changing consumption practices constitutes the key aim of consumer movements (Gollnofer et al., 2019), NSMs seek to instigate or resist socio-economic change by directly challenging both government and economic paradigms, among others. Second, consumer movements' communications aim to reach groups or individual consumers and change their perceptions/behaviour, while NSMs understand consumer behaviour as a variable within a wider politico-economic system whose principles and directions can be shaped or challenged. Third, the activities of 21st century consumer movements mainly focus on retail spaces and online marketplaces, while NSMs utilize public spaces and digital communications so as to visibly alter urban landscapes and invite citizens to physically/digitally participate within their activities and political causes (King & Pearce, 2010). Finally, the causes and aims of consumer movements can be measured and assessed via numerical and calculable results of petitions, social media activity, boycotting campaigns and sub-advertising, among others. On the other hand, it is much more complicated to assess the impact and long-term outcomes of NSMs related to pro-democratic values, human rights and income austerity, for example, since their causes might be carried across generations and enduring political struggles (Habermas, 1981).

Although the structure, political aims and promotional tactics of NSMs vary across space and time, we can argue that their key activities can be synopsized in the following common themes. In general: a) they seek to achieve long-term occupation of urban public space; b) they skilfully employ marketing tools to engage audiences and to promote their ideological aims; and c) they aim to internationalize their key causes to global audiences. Each of these activities will be analyzed below via the prism of political marketing.

PUBLIC SPACE AND PROMOTION OF NSMS

Since the fall of Lehman Brothers and the global 2007/2008 financial crisis, a rising number of anti-austerity social movements rose globally. From the 2011 Occupy Wall Street movement in the City of New York (New York Times, 2011) to the Occupy London Movement (BBC, 2011) and anti-austerity protests in Athens during 2009–2014 (The Guardian, 2010), protesters sought to occupy public space next to capitals' commercial, political and financial districts. Central urban spaces turn into seminal territorial sites for the organization of movements' physical headquarters along with protesters' creative and promotional practices (Vasudevan, 2015).

Similar to the development of marketing environments and shopping (Maclaran & Brown, 2005), spatial aesthetics and the socio-cultural organization of space define the success or failure of NSMs. We can draw parallels here between the marketing and promotional patterns of cultural organizations, like museums (Goulding, 2001; Joy & Sherry, 2003), shopping malls (MacLaran and Brown), concert halls (Skandalis et al., 2016) and festivals (Kozinets, 2002) and urban protesters' activities to engage audiences via political space reproduction. As the aforementioned marketing scholars indicate, organizations aim to create cultural spaces leading to the full immersion of consumers and visitors' multisensory experiences, via music, access to services and interactive environments. Likewise, peaceful and urban NSMs meticulously organize public spaces to invite, maintain and shape visitors, journalists and citizens' experiences, seeking to forge emotional bonds between them and their causes. New York and London Occupy protesters, cautiously chose public squares, so as to employ a variety of aesthetic and spatial tactics that engaged the highest number of participants and bystanders, as well as to maximize the visibility of their banners and protest symbols (Brown et al., 2017). Accordingly, they achieved not only to create collective audience experiences but also to unite diverse citizen groups and audiences at ideological and experiential levels. Similar to the promotion of street art (Patsiaouras et al., 2018; Visconti et al., 2010), contemporary protesters turn metropolitan public spaces into sites of ideological consumption and production, where citizens might build a resonance with movements' aims and a sense of common belonging within a wider cause. While street artists' activities might be short lived and aimed to small audiences, NSMs utilize spatial practices to attract large crowds, communities and vast audiences in general, along with generating traditional and social media headlines. Banners, interactive protest art, educational workshops, music and speeches constitute only few among their practices which essentially alter the urban landscape and, for a significant period of time, invite citizens to consider their aims for social change.

Studies have indicated how NSMs in the United Kingdom (Halvorsen, 2015; Uitermark, 2004), Canada (Zajko & Beland, 2008), Athens (Chatzidakis et al., 2012; Karyotis & Rüdig, 2018) and Taiwan (Fell, 2017) have meticulously infused public spaces with innovative, engaging and digital forms of protest symbolism and imaginative communications, altering the presentation and aesthetic experience of central parks and central squares. Proposing an alternative and unconventional view of urban space, protesters managed to attract citizens' attention and via installations and interactive activities, invited them to alter their viewpoints around specific social causes, using techniques similar to open-air festivals and outdoor brand building visual art (Patterson, 2010; Sjoholm & Pasquinelli, 2014). Similar to political and business organizations that employ outdoor events and atmospherics to enhance brand equity and value, peaceful NSMs occupy and re-organize public space to provide a fresh awareness of city centres and invite citizens and journalists to co-create and amplify the 'branding' visibility around their key causes.

NEW SOCIAL MOVEMENTS, EXPERIENCES AND AUDIENCE ENGAGEMENT

A major shift in marketing, over the last 20 years, has perceived organizations moving from producers of standardized products, in providers of experiential services and settings (Schmitt, 2003; Vargo & Lusch, 2016). Since the turn of the century (Pine & Gilmore, 1999), national and global brands began to design, create and promote strategies so as to enhance audience participation and engagement within their settings, exhibitions, events and recently digital environments. Such efforts sought to increase consumers and potential customers' emotional attachment with brand's mission and values and to amplify social interaction as well as a feeling of belonging within brand's wider architecture and environment. Likewise social movements' public and digital spaces seek to foster citizens' participation and engagement to strengthen the growth of a collective aim and vision (Della Porta, 2013). In the occupied public spaces of metropolitan centres, protesters invite citizens, tourists and bystanders to participate in the co-production of projects, activities and protest art, for example. Similar to outdoor arts marketing practices (vom Lehn & Heath, 2016), NSMs turn citizens into collaborative producers of small-scale protest projects, whose completion can inform them about movements' aims. Collaborative painting and gardening activities, along with public speeches and leisure activities, peacefully invite audiences to visit, observe and immerse themselves within protest sites that occupy hundreds square metres of urban space (New York Times, 2021). Accordingly, the occupied sites of social movements can turn into experiential socio-cultural contexts where the boundaries between protesters, citizens and tourists can be blurred through the collaborative co-creation of protest experiences, similar to those of respectable arts organizations and global brands offering experiential services (Minkiewicz et al., 2016; Patsiaouras et al., 2018). NSMs seem to understand and embrace the importance of experiences, collaboration and co-creation for diverse physical and digital audiences. Accordingly, protest sites become carefully planned spaces for co-created experiences and collaborative performances that emphasize movements' peaceful features and facilitate audience participation. These innovative and imaginative terrains can reach ideologically, politically and culturally diverse segments of citizens and bystanders and accordingly to increase support or just sympathy towards movements aims, especially among sceptical or undecided citizens.

Educational levels and demographics play a seminal role for the formation of political campaigns and marketing communications (Apospori et al., 2010; Weinschenk, 2019). The interrelationships between information, education and voting choice constitute some of the most valuable dynamics throughout an electoral campaign. Both political scientists and political marketing scholars have meticulously explored the educational background of Generation Z (Broadbent et al., 2017). Although the duration and nature of NSMs is short lived, compared to centenarian political parties in the West, their members seek to act as educators and to increase citizens' literacy around political and social themes. From Zuccotti Park in New York to Taksim Square in Istanbul and the city centre of Hong Kong protests, NSM protesters organized and delivered hundreds of seminars, workshops, readings groups and in general a variety of educational activities. Although marketing and social marketing scholarship has explored the role of education to enhance and empower consumers' knowledge (Bresler, 2007; Enhuber, 2015), limited attention has been played on the promotion of educational activities by NSMs. Commercial organizations aim to educate customers around technical issues and post-purchase services, while cultural institutions and NGOs attempt to foster audiences' education via specific strategies around visitors' motivations, enterprise targets and calculable participation rates (Osborne & Rentschler, 2010). Protesters, on the other hand, approach educational practices both via digital channels and through all-inclusive protest camp events. Taking into account that demands for social change might be more appealing to students and younger audiences, NSMs have developed communications and educational practices to increase citizens' awareness about specific public issues, from their own perspective.

THE GLOBAL BRANDING AND IMPACT OF NSMS

Marketing research on social movements has focused on the ideological basis of consumer activism and anti-consumption movements, exploring a variety of political orientations and phenomena such as colonialism and nationalist ideology in India (Varman & Belk, 2009), anti-capitalist ethos in Greece (Chatzidakis et al., 2012) and the interface of State interventions with consumption practices (Weijo et al., 2018), among others. On the other hand, limited research exists on how NSMs interact and shape institutional actors like governments and foreign affairs, as well as how macro-environmental forces shape the international marketing communications of protesters. Although Keck and Sikkink (1998) suggested and highlighted the capacity of social movements in creating and fostering networks that coalesce and operate across national frontiers, limited empirical research exists on how NSMs have been communicating their aims and causes to international audiences and networks. NSMs occupation of public spaces in metropolitan centres like London, New York and Hong Kong – for example – receive global attention and quite often their causes and struggles mirror and reflect wider political issues related with post-colonialism, power asymmetries, austerity and global inequality. Protesters are very aware of how these common themes can appeal audiences globally and communicate universal values, for example, around democracy and civic societies. Accordingly, they will employ digital and media communications so as to reach global segments and promote their aims to different continents and institutional actors (Patsiaouras, 2022).

Traditional marketing fields adopting an international angle such as macromarketing as well as public policy and marketing research have also paid limited attention on the transnational features of marketing promotions and communications utilized by NSMs to amplify their message. Despite the fact that global brands' involvement with social causes and social movements has been increasing in the last ten years (see Black Lives Matter movement), political marketing scholars could focus more on the intersections between movements, traditional and digital media communications (New York Times, 2020). Taking into account recent geopolitical events like the barbaric invasion of Russia's army to Ukraine, along with the ongoing energy crisis and heightened levels of austerity globally, more research can be conducted on how collective consumer/citizen responses utilize media and digital tools to internationalize their key causes and aims.

THE HONG KONG UMBRELLA MOVEMENT

The city of Hong Kong is characterized by some unique historical, economic and geographical features. Following a period of British occupation (1841–1997), a 'Handover' to China was followed by the promise of allowing the creation of an autonomous electoral system by 2017 (Chan, 2014). However, in August 2014, a document was leaked, revealing China's intention to enforce the pre-screening of political candidates, a move which directly challenged the principles of universal suffrage (Chan, 2016). Immense dissatisfaction was expressed by Hong Kong citizens who perceived candidates' pre-screening as an effort to suppress their political rights and autonomy. As reaction, between the 28th of September and 15 of December 2014, millions of Hong Kong protesters occupied the key public spaces of the city, creating the Umbrella Movement (Chan, 2014). Eventually, the occupied spaces were cleared by December 2014, without reaching a settlement between the Chinese government and protesters' demands. Accordingly, the movement continued its efforts in restoring a democratic and semi-autonomous status for the city.

The pro-democratic Umbrella Movement was characterized by a decentralized leadership, massive and peaceful participation and the long-term occupation of Hong Kong's city centre, leading to the longstanding paralysis of commercial, educational and finance institutions (Tin-bor Hui, 2017). As noted by foreign press (BBC, 2014), the Umbrella Movement was characterized by unique, innovative and imaginative communications and engagement with the public. The well-planned occupation of one of world's key business and commercial urban centres was accompanied by the strategic installation of highly visible and interactive protest activities including: statues, libraries, speeches, study areas, protest artwork, banners, leaflets and workshops among others. Contrasting the skyscraper architecture, protesters managed to attract, during the period occupation, millions of citizens, tourists and journalists who, in their turn expressed their physical and digital solidarity towards movements' aims. Back in 2019, the introduction of an Extradition Law by the Hong Kong's government led to a new series of demonstrations (Wong, 2017). The extreme violence between protesters and the police continued up to 2020 and the first COVID-19 lockdown and in October 2022, Hong Kong citizens took the streets to display their solidarity with the anti-lockdown protests in mainland China (CNN, 2022). In a wider political context, the Hong Kong Umbrella Movement has been at the heart of wider geopolitical tensions, especially between the Chinese and USA governments. Hong Kong protesters have asked and received public support from the USA government (Cheung & Lau, 2022; Whyte, 2022) – a move which was heavily criticized by the Chinese government as interference to its internal politics (FMPRC, 2002) – and as explained below immense support by Western audiences and institutions.

The examination of the Umbrella Movement (2014) and Hong Kong protests (2019–2022) took place via both empirical and secondary material. The author spent a week at the Hong Kong protest sites during November 2014, collecting primary data through moderate participant observation (DeWalt & DeWalt, 2010) and photo-documentation (Rose, 2012). Moderate participant observation involved informal discussions with protesters, the co-creation of protest art and careful examination of protesters' communication practices. Photo-documentation was focused on capturing images of protest communications that sought to engage audiences and promote movements' ideas to local and global audiences. Essentially, primary data collection led to the production of hundreds of fieldnotes and 300 photographic images. The empirical data have been complemented with secondary pictorial sources stemming from digital archiving of photos (open access via the internet) and a careful examination of the Umbrella Movement Visual Archives and Research Collectives (Hilgers, 2015). Archival newspaper records stemming from and valid newspaper materials were also employed. I focused both on Western media (BBC, The Guardian, The New York Times) as well as Hong Kong's most credible newspaper, the South China Morning Post (Centre for Communication and Public Opinion Survey, 2019), with emphasis on the 2019–2022 Hong Kong protests. Of course, both the anonymity and confidentiality of the protesters were protected and all information which could endanger any of the protesters was removed.

THE RISE OF POLITICAL SPACES

Limited research exists around the role and capacity of physical spaces within the field of political marketing (Michailovna Vinogradova et al., 2020; Tempest & Newman, 2016), placing emphasis on media, information and digital spaces. Acting as a decentralized organization, the Umbrella Movement strategically utilized commercial, financial and tourist urban space as vehicle of political promotion. For almost 80 days, the organizers managed to occupy the busiest central roads including the financial district (Admiralty) and Hong Kong's busiest commercial avenue (Nathan Road), exceeding 2 kilometres of protest space. In the heart of Asia's leading commercial and financial centre, by-passers and tourists observed the gradual emergence of a tiny protest village (Admiralty) which included: tents, toilets, medical corners, worship spaces, phone recharging facilities, post-it note walls, outdoor library and a vegetable garden, among others. Citizens, journalists and tourists could see, throughout the camps, hundreds of yellow umbrellas, in different forms and sizes, the unifying symbol of the Movement. A canopy of interwoven open umbrellas was connecting two footbridges, origami yellow umbrellas could be seen on escalators and tube stations, large yellow umbrellas welcomed passengers at the key entrances of the protest camp, umbrellas printed on posters, a 5 metres wooden statue holding a yellow umbrella (known as Umbrella Man) and even a cut out poster of President Xi Jinping holding a yellow umbrella, attracting hordes of citizens wishing to take a picture. Back in September 2014, a USA-based twitter user (Adam Cotton) introduced the term 'Umbrella Revolution' referring to the imaginative use of protesters' open umbrellas against police tear gas (Schumacher, 2014) and the cover of October 2014 TIME magazine, contributed in spreading protesters' unifying symbol to global audiences (Ming, 2015). Apart from the political transformation of urban space, the protesters employed digital avenues via the creation of an online contest for movements' most popular and best logo. The contest received thousands of entries and submissions from several countries, including from renown artists, activists and printers.

The co-creating of movements' marketing material could be studied both by corporate and political parties wishing to decentralize creativity and decision making. Taking into account the emerging and dynamic literature around the process of digital brand co-creation (Tajvidi et al., 2020), political parties can consider inclusive and digital pathways for the emergence of collective symbols stemming from crowdsourcing methods and involved national/digital audiences. Additionally, NGOs and pro-democracy organizations, with global appeal, could co-produce visual brand materials so as to maximize the levels of unification, inspiration and mobilization among their existing and potential audiences. Exploring the use of colours and logos for social movements from a socio-historic angle, Sawer (2007, p. 54) argued that NSMs employ 'symbolic languages that are about emotional identification as well as about organizational needs for distinctive brands and brand loyalty, to use the language of modern marketing'. It would not be an exaggeration to argue the Umbrella Movement has achieved such aim with excellent results. Following the wide-spread police clashes and violence during the 2019–2020 Hong Kong protests, the protesters replaced the playful yellow colour umbrellas, using black hardhats to communicate the overall mood and opposition towards police brutality.

The long-term occupation of major avenues and city intersections by the Umbrella Movement – which led to school closures and economic slowdown – was received with mixed feeling by local audiences, which led to an online social media war between 'yellow' (pro-Occupy) versus 'blue' (anti-Occupy) users (Chan & Tsui, 2014). Such political and ideological divide continues even nowadays, expressed through public spaces, identity expression and consumer choice. Since the summer of 2019, Hong Kong protesters have been organizing peaceful sit-ins in retail stores and popular shopping malls, while they signal the boycotting of stores which have been characterized as pro-government/pro-Beijing, and vice versa anti-protesters boycott what they call 'yellow' businesses. A divisive and peculiar system between 'yellow' and 'anti-protest' shops has been created and even a digital database and mobile app has been introduced, separating city's commercial activity into two groups (New York Times, 2019). Pro-democracy stores decorate their interior with yellow umbrellas and overall, we notice how the protest turned consumer choice into political expression and positioning. Pro-democracy protesters argue that the emergence of the so called 'yellow economic circle' will generate emerging and alternative marketplace cultures based on fair trade and local products, compared to the dominance of high street luxury brands (The Guardian, 2020), although evidence does not suggest this happening. Overall, political marketing theorists could further elaborate on the impact of NSMs as organizations which have the capacity not only to generate imaginative marketing communications but also as institutions that can shape purchasing power. Also, further research on how urban, digital and commercial spaces can be utilized as vehicles of political ideas can be conducted. Hong Kong protesters show the importance of peaceful, decentralized, creative and imaginative use of limited resources, which can be seen substitute to tight campaign budgets, sophisticated websites and hired venues for political events, a recurring challenge for young and rising political candidates.

ENGAGING AND EDUCATING AUDIENCES WITH POLITICAL AIMS

One of the most prominent features of the Umbrella Movement protest sites has been its capacity to engage and educate audiences around their political goals, using playfulness and interaction. Artistic performances, interactive activities, co-created protest artwork and outdoors speeches, among others, prompted the former Director of the Hong Kong Arts Centre (Oscar Ho Hing-kay) to argue that 'the entire city is a work of art, and everyone is an artist' (Pollack, 2015). At the heart of the central protest camp, the protesters, inspired by the John Lennon Wall in Prague, produced their own Lennon Wall, which was filled with thousands of post-it notes expressing solidarity and support to the movement. A group of activists distributed pens and colourful post-it notes to by-passers, citizens, tourists, journalists and within a week the Lennon Wall was filled with more than 10.000 messages of support (Ng, 2014).

Contrary to popular beliefs and media representations of protest camps as sites of clash and violence, the Umbrella Movement invited both tourists and Hong Kong citizens not only to visit their sites but also to co-create and co-produce their activities. Visitors were encouraged to participate in interactive street painting sessions, blindfold portrait drawing, pavement chalk-drawing, origami collaborative projects and post-it notes which led to thousands of polymorphous protest messages. Audiences' immersion within an experiential protest context not only familiarized neutral citizens with movements' ideas but also invited them, in a peaceful and inclusive way, to become part of it, even ephemerally. Emotions and feelings of sympathy and solidarity began to spread among audiences who saw protest camps as sites of openness, communication and community building. Along with cost effective tactical media for the promotion of protest ideology (Michailovna Vinogradova et al., 2020), political marketing theorists can conduct more empirical research on how audiences are engaged in physical protest sites through a variety of collaborative projects. Especially within protest sites of metropolitan centres, issues around citizens' inclusion, empowerment and political literacy can be further investigated. Umbrella Movements' collaborative protest art was preserved by two voluntary groups which created both an inventory and digital archive for more than 2000 artistic installations, objects and posters. Part of the collaborative art was also displayed at the exhibition titled 'Disobedient Objects' at Victoria and Albert Museum in London, attracting massive audiences (Victoria & Albert Museum, 2016).

Similar to the other NSMs (Brown et al., 2017), Hong Kong protesters utilized educational tools and pedagogical experiments to engage younger audiences and segments. Two sites developed their 'Mobile Democracy Classroom' venues where outdoor education activities took place, including discussions, seminars and speeches from academics and public intellectuals around the importance of democracy compared to authoritarian regimes. In Admiralty, the protesters turned a space of almost five hundred metres into a 'study zone' which included free internet access, reading lamps, study spaces, pens and office materials, frequently used by university students affiliated with the movement. Additionally, the screening of films, followed by open discussion and a media projector was displaying 'live' messages of solidarity, received as text or emails by sympathizers around the globe. As it has been reported, Hong Kong's student body played a seminal role in supporting the movement and it is not surprising that protesters carefully created spaces for student engagement and education. Along with social media metrics, political marketing scholars can measure and assess the direct engagement of political parties with student segments via the organization of similar activities.

TRANSNATIONAL MARKETING PRACTICES

At the heart of the Admiralty protest site, a peculiar large stand included a bizarre collage of political figures, superheroes and famous individuals including: Queen Elizabeth II, Mahatma Gandhi, Bruce Lee, Winston Churchill, Jesus Christ, Che Guevara and Hulk among others. Across the protest camps images of Western superheroes like Captain America and Spiderman holding yellow umbrellas provided an unusual view of a protest site at South-East Asia. Protesters used extensively images of Neo from Matrix, V for Vendetta and Martin Luther King, while unofficially the song 'Do you hear People Sing' from the film Les Misérables, turned into movement's anthem played from megaphones across the protest sites. It should not be surprising that within 'Asia's World City' (Hong Kong Government, 2002), the Umbrella Movement employed fusion practices of amalgamating Western and Eastern protest symbolism and communications, to express their values towards global and international audiences. Hong Kong's identity shaped by its colonial past, unique international standing as financial centre, semi-autonomous identity and multi-cultural environment was carefully injected within those images. Although political marketing scholars have thoroughly explored the role of celebrities in promoting candidates and ideals (Henneberg & Chen, 2008; Jackson, 2018), limited attention has been paid on how they have been employed by NSMs. Especially pro-democratic social movements with global appeal, like the Umbrella Movement, skilfully used Western personas, politicians and celebrities to build intimacy and identification with expats, journalists and Western audiences. Embracing and displaying Western figures facilitated them to simplify their message and to strengthen an internationalization strategy, suitable for the struggles occurring within a major international financial centre. Expectedly, Hong Kong's enduring protests have had an impact to transnational relations and marketing communications among global brands and political entities.

In the summer of 2020, the British government reacted to Beijing's implementation of national security law on Hong Kong, by cancelling a contract with Huawei's 5G telecommunication services (The Guardian, 2020). Once the general manager of NBA's Houston Rockets sent a pro-democracy tweet, a series of orchestrated boycott activities against Nike sneakers occurred in several Chinese cities (New York Times, 2019). More than twenty British, American and Japanese brands have publicly expressed messages of support towards the Hong Kong protests, followed by antithetical messages from Chinese brands. Following strong demands from the Chinese government, Apple company deleted a mobile application which allowed protesters to identify the presence of police forces in real time and Google removed an online story game, where users developed choice-based capabilities regarding protest activities in Hong Kong (Financial Times, 2019). Additionally, the 2019–2020 protesters, surprisingly, financed their promotional activities using mainstream media channels in order to reach global audiences. Following a very successful crowdfunding campaign, Hong Kong protesters paid for the publication of high exposure ads at some of the most prestigious newspapers globally, such as Le Monde in France, New York Times in the USA and Frankfurter Allegemeine in Germany, among others (HK Free Press, 2019). Netflix documentaries, billboard adverts in the United Kingdom and at home, and invitations from the USA congress to deliver a speech, clearly show the transnational character of the movement and how its causes mirror wider geopolitical struggles. Considering heightened tensions (see Taiwan) in the area, political marketing scholars and practitioners could further explore the evolution of Hong Kong's protests and pro-democracy social movements so as to draw wider conclusions on issues around political communications, discourses and expansion on behalf of democratic values.

CONCLUDING COMMENTS

Conclusively, this chapter suggested that political marketing theorists and practitioners should pay much closer attention to the communication practices and tactics of NSMs in the 21st century. Digital, spatial and international aspects of their marketing campaign illustrate how large and leaderless organizations can organically co-produce marketing campaigns which have a massive appeal to urban and international audiences. Political parties and NGOs can study closely the resourceful and imaginative methods around protesters' spatial strategies, digital tactics and international campaigns, and accordingly to consider whether their own organizations might approach a more open and inclusive approach regarding audience engagement and communications. It has been noted that 21st century voters prefer more authentic political candidates and campaigns' ideals (Patsiaouras & Fitchett, 2022), compared to the slick and unimaginative campaigns recycled or reproduced by ideologically similar political parties. NSMs' success with young voters of citizens shows that spontaneity, improvisation and co-production can enable groups to communicate ideas that inspire, empower and engage citizens. Without seeking to eulogize or demonize social movements in general, which might often display or receive violent tactics, it can be argued that peaceful have become not only keen studies of marketing communications but also masters of the art emerging as multi-media friendly and marketing savvy political organizations. Future political marketing research can explore aspects around organizational hierarchy, internationalization practices and the heavy involvement of global brand activism with movements' aims, along with its wider geopolitical impact.

REFERENCES

Andress, D. (2015). *The Oxford handbook of the French revolution*. Oxford University Press.

Apospori, E., Avlonitis, G., & Zisouli, M. (2010). Political culture and perception of political marketing tools: A cross-generational comparison. *Journal of Political Marketing*, *9*(1–2), 111–134.

BBC News. (2011). Occupy London: Why I am protesting. https://www.bbc.co.uk/news/av/uk-15340020/occupy-london-why-i-m-protesting. Accessed on 2 June, 2020.

BBC News. (2014). In pictures: Hong Kong protest art. http://www.bbc.co.uk/news/world-asia-china-29648459. Accessed on April 2015.

Beck, U. (1992). *Risk society: Towards a new modernity*. SAGE.

Berger, S., & Nehring, H. (2013). *Palgrave studies in the history of social movements*. Palgrave.

Bresler, L. (2007). *International handbook of research in arts education*. Springer.

Broadbent, E., Gougoulis, J., Lui, N., Pota, V., Simons, J., & Generation, Z. (2017). *Global citizenship survey*. Varkey Foundation.

Brown, G., Feigenbaum, A., Frenzel, F., & McCurdy, P. (2017). *Protest camps in international contexts: Spaces, infrastructures and media*. University of Bristol: Polity Press.

Campana, M., Chatzidakis, A., & Laamanen, M. (2017). Introduction to the special issue: A macromarketing perspective on alternative economies. *Journal of Macromarketing*, *37*(2), 125–130.

Castells, M. (2004). *The power of identity* (2nd ed.). Blackwell.

Catterall, M., McLaran, P., & Stevens, L. (2005). Postmodern paralysis: The critical impasse in feminist perspectives on consumers. *Journal of Marketing Management*, *21*(5/6), 489–504.

Centre for Communication and Public Opinion Survey. (2019) *Tracking research: Public evaluation on media credibility – Survey results*. Chinese University of Hong Kong. http://www.com.cuhk.edu.hk/ccpos/en/research/Credibility_Survey%20Results_2019_ENG.pdf. Accessed on 10 June 2020.

Chan, J. (2014). Hong Kong's umbrella movement. *The Round Table: The Commonwealth Journal of International Affairs*, *103*(6), 571–580.

Chan, K. (2016). Occupying Hong Kong. *Sur: International Journal of Human Rights*, *12*(21), 1–7.

Chan, W., & Tsui, A. (2014). Who's Who in the Hong Kong protest? *CNN News*. http://edition.cnn.com/2014/10/07/world/asia/hong-kong-protest-explainer/index.html

Chatzidakis, A., Kastanakis, M., & Stathopoulou, A. (2016). Socio-cognitive determinants of consumer support for the Fair-Trade Movement. *Journal of Business Ethics*, *133*(1), 95–109.

Chatzidakis, A., Maclaran, P., & Bradshaw, P. (2012). Heterotopian space and the utopics of ethical and green consumption. *Journal of Marketing Management*, *28*(3–4), 494–515.

Cheung, T., & Lau, C. (2022). Hongkongers with ties to US-backed group slammed by Beijing report could risk censure, analysts warn. *South China Morning Post*. https://www.scmp.com/news/hong-kong/politics/article/3177383/hongkongers-ties-us-backed-group-slammed-beijing-report

CNN. (2022). Protesters take to Hong Kong's streets in solidarity with mainland. https://edition.cnn.com/videos/world/2022/11/28/hong-kong-protests-solidarity-mainland-china-watson-newsroom-vpx.cnn. Accessed on 13 December 2022.

Della Porta, D. (2013) *Can democracy be saved? Participation, deliberation and social movements*. Polity Press.

Della Porta, D., & Diani, M. (2020). *Social movements: An introduction*. Wiley Blackwell.

DeWalt, K., & DeWalt, B. (2010). Participant observation. In H. Bernard (Ed.), *Handbook of methods in cultural anthropology* (pp. 259–299). AltaMira Press.

Enhuber, M. (2015). Art, space and technology: How the digitisation and digitalisation of art space affect the consumption of art – A critical approach. *Digital Creativity*, *26*(2), 121–137.

Fell, D. (2017). *Taiwan's social movements under Ma Ying-jeou from the wild strawberries to the sunflowers*. Routledge.

Financial Times. (2019). China state media attacks Apple for Hong Kong police tracking app. *Financial Times*. https://www.ft.com/content/47ceb216-ea55-11e9-a240-3b065ef5fc55. Accessed on 13 October 2019.

Finley, M. (1983). *Politics in Ancient World*. Cambridge University Press.

Foreign Ministry of the People' Republic of China (FMPRC). (2002). Full text: Fact sheet on the national endowment for democracy. *China Daily*. https://global.chinadaily.com.cn/a/202205/08/WS6277847fa310fd2b29e5b4c2.html

Gollnhofer, J., Weijo, H., & Schouten, J. (2019). Consumer movements and value regimes: Fighting food waste in Germany by building alternative object pathways. *Journal of Consumer Research*, *46*(3), 460–482.

Goulding, C. (2001). Romancing the past: Heritage visiting and the nostalgic consumer. *Psychology and Marketing*, *18*, 565–592.

Habermas, J. (1981). New social movements. *Telos*, *21*(49), 33–37.

Halvorsen, S. (2015). Encountering Occupy London: Boundary making and the territoriality of urban activism. *Environment and Planning D: Society and Space*, *33*(2), 314–330.

Hein, W., Steinfield, L., Ourahmoune, N., Coleman, C. A., Zayer, L. T., & Littlefield, J. (2016). Gender justice and the market: A transformative consumer research perspective. *Journal of Public Policy and Marketing*, *35*(2), 223–236.

Henneberg, S., & Chen, Y. (2008). Celebrity political endorsement. *Journal of Political Marketing*, *6*(4), 1–31.

Higgins, M., & Tadajewski, M. (2002). Anti-corporate protest as consumer spectacle. *Management Decision*, *40*(4), 363–371.

Hilgers, L. (2015). Hong Kong's Umbrella revolution isn't over yet. *New York Times*. http://www.nytimes.com/2015/02/22/magazine/hong-kongs-umbrella-revolution-isnt-over-yet.html

Hobsbawn, E. (1962). *The age of revolution 1789 – 1848*. Vintage Books.

Hong Kong Free Press (2019b). *New Hong Kong protest ads urging international help appear in 11 newspapers worldwide*. https://hongkongfp.com/2019/08/19/pictures-new-hong-kong-protest-ads-urging-intl-help-appear-11-newspapers-worldwide/. Accessed on 10 October 2020.

Hong Kong Government. (2002). *Asia's world city*. http://www.info.gov.hk/info/sar5/easia.htm. Accessed on May, 2016.

Jackson, D. (2018). The effects of celebrity endorsements of ideas and presidential candidates. *Journal of Political Marketing*, *17*(4), 301–321.

Jasper, J. (2014). *Protest: A cultural introduction to social movements*. Polity Press.

Jones, P. (2003). *The French revolution 1787–1804*. Routledge.

Joy, A., & Sherry, J. (2003). Speaking of art as embodied imaginations: A multisensory approach to understanding aesthetic experience. *Journal of Consumer Research*, *30*(3), 259–82.

Karyotis, G., & Rüdig, W. (2018). The three waves of anti-austerity protest in Greece, 2010–2015. *Political Studies Review*, *16*(2), 158–169.

Keck, M., & Sikkink, K. (1998). *Activists beyond borders: Advocacy networks in international politics*. Cornell University Press.

King, B., & Pearce, N. (2010). The contentiousness of markets: Politics, social movements, and institutional change in markets. *Annual Review of Sociology*, *36*, 249–267.

Klein, N. (2000). *No logo*. Vintage Canada.

Kozinets, R. (2002). Can consumers escape the market? Emancipatory illuminations from burning man. *Journal of Consumer Research*, *29*, 20–38.

Kozinets, R. V., & Handelman, J. M. (2004). Adversaries of consumption: Consumer movements, activism, and ideology. *Journal of Consumer Research*, *31*(3), 691–704.

Langdale, A. (2019). *The hippodrome of Istanbul/Constantinople*. Land of Empires Books.

Leith, J. A. (1978). The war of images surrounding the commune. In J. Leith (Ed.), *Images of the commune* (pp. 101–150). McGill-Queen's University Press.

Lekakis, E. (2022). *Consumer activism: Promotional culture and resistance*. SAGE.

Maclaran, P. (2015). Feminism's fourth wave: A research agenda for marketing and consumer research. *Journal of Marketing Management*, *31*(15–16), 1732–1738.

Maclaran, P., & Brown, S. (2005). The center cannot hold: Consuming the utopian marketplace. *Journal of Consumer Research*, *32*(2), 311–323.

Mayhall, L. (2003). *The militant suffrage movement: Citizenship and resistance in Britain, 1860–1930*. Oxford University Press.

Meyer, D., & Tarrow, S. (1998). *The social movement society: Contentious politics for the new century*. Rowman and Littlefierd Publishers.

Michailovna Vinogradova, S., Melnik, G. S., & Shaldenkova, T. Y. (2020). Promotion of ideology of protest in the tactical media. *Journal of Political Marketing*. https://doi.org/10.1080/15377857.2020.1724422

Ming, T. (2015). The aesthetics of Hong Kong's "umbrella revolution" in the first ten days: A historical anatomy of the first phase (27 Oct 2014 to 6 October 2014) of Hong Kong's umbrella revolution. *East Asia*, *32*(1), 83–98.

Minkiewicz, J., Bridson, K., & Evans, J. (2016). Co-production of service experiences: Insights from the cultural sector. *Journal of Services Marketing*, *30*(7), 749–761.

Museum of London. (2018). *Votes for women exhibition*. Suffragette Collection. https://www.museumoflondon.org.uk/discover/suffragettes. Accessed on 4 September 2019

New York Times. (2011). Who is occupy wall street?. https://www.nytimes.com/2011/11/13/opinion/sunday/who-is-occupy-wall-street.html. Accessed on 2 June 2020.

New York Times. (2019). N.B.A. Executive's Hong Kong tweet starts firestorm in China. https://www.nytimes.com/2019/10/06/sports/daryl-morey-rockets-china.html. Accessed on 15 June 2020.

New York Times. (2020). Top U.K. Tea brands urge #solidarity with anti-racism protests. https://www.nytimes.com/2020/06/09/world/europe/yorkshire-tea-pg-tips-black-lives-matter.html. Accessed on 2 June 2020.

New York Times. (2021). Hong Kong Protesters silenced in the streets surface in artwork. *New York Times*. https://www.nytimes.com/2021/05/20/world/asia/hong-kong-protests-art.html. Accessed on 4 November 2020.

Ng, J. (2014). Website in the works to display protesters' notes from 'Lennon Wall. *South China Morning Post*. http://www.scmp.com/news/hong-kong/article/1618852/websiteworks-display-protesters-notes-lennon-wall. Accessed on April 2015.

Osborne, A., & Rentschler, R. (2010). Conversation, collaboration and cooperation: Courting new audiences for a new century. In D. O'Reilly & F. Kerrigan (Eds.), *Marketing the arts: A fresh approach* (pp. 54–71). Routledge.

Patsiaouras, G. (2022). Marketplace cultures for social change? New social movements and consumer culture theory. *Journal of Marketing Management*, *38*(1–2), 17–47.

Patsiaouras, G., & Fitchett, J. (2022). Red Tsars and Iron Ladies: Exploring the role of marketing forces in the construction of political heroism. *Marketing Theory*. https://doi.org/10.1177/14705931221137734

Patsiaouras, G., Veneti, A., & Green, W. (2018). Marketing, art and voices of dissent: Promotional methods of protest art by the 2014 Hong Kong's umbrella movement. *Marketing Theory*, *18*(1), 75–100.

Patterson, A. (2010). Extreme cultural and marketing makeover: Liverpool home edition. In D. O'Reilly & F. Kerrigan (Eds.), *Marketing the arts: A fresh approach* (pp. 240–257). Routledge.

Pine, J., & Gilmore, J. (1999) *The experience economy*, Harvard Business School Press.

Pollack, B. (2015). The state of Hong Kong's art scene. *ARTnews*. http://www.artnews.com/2015/01/06/art-during-hong-kong-umbrella-movement/. Accessed on June 2015.

Raeburn, A. (1973). *The militant suffragettes*. The University of Michigan Press.

Rose, G. (2012). *Visual methodologies: An introduction to researching with visual materials*. SAGE.

Sawer, M. (2007). Wearing your politics on your sleeve: The role of political colours in social movements. *Social Movement Studies*, *6*(1), 39–56.

Schmitt, B. (2003). *Customer experience management*. The Free Press.

Schumacher, M. (2014). Q&A with Charlotte Frost about the umbrella revolution. *Milwaukee Journal Sentinel*. http://www.jsonline.com/entertainment/arts/qa-with-charlottefrost-about-the-umbrella-revolution-b99385857z1-281808161.html. Accessed on March 2015.

Scott, A. (1990). *Ideology and the new social movements*. Unwin Hyman.

Shultz, C., & Peterson, M. (2019). Macromarketing view of sustainable development in Vietnam. *Environmental Management*, *63*, 507–519.

Sjoholm, J., & Pasquinelli, C. (2014). Artist brand building: Towards a spatial perspective. *Arts Marketing: International Journal*, *4*(1/2), 10–24.

Skandalis, A., Banister, E., & Byrom, J. (2016). Marketplace orchestration of taste: Insights from the Bridgewater Hall. *Journal of Marketing Management*, *32*(9–10), 926–943.

Smith, A. (2003). The pankhursts and the war: Suffrage magazines and first world war propaganda. *Women's History Review*, *12*(1), 103–118.

Stanton, E., Antony, S., Gage, M., Blatch, H., & Harper, I. (2017) *The suffragettes: Complete history of the movement* (Vol. 6). E-artnow.

Stinerock, R. (2015). The unintended consequences of the countercultural movement of the 1960s: What's marketing got to do with it? *Journal of Macromarketing*, *36*(2), 229–236.

Tajvidi, M., Richard, M., Wang, Y., & Hajli, N. (2020). Brand co-creation through social commerce information sharing: The role of social media. *Journal of Business Research*, *121*, 476–486.

Tempest, R., & Newman, B. (2016). Political spaces in Eurasia: Global contexts, local outcomes. *Journal of Political Marketing*, *15*(2–3), 97–100. https://doi.org/10.1080/15377857.2016.1151103

Teske, R., & Tetrault, M. (2000). *Feminist approaches to social movements, community and power: Conscious acts and the politics of change*. University of Carolina Southern Press.

The Guardian. (2010). Greek bailout: Athens burns – and crisis strikes at heart of the EU. https://www.theguardian.com/world/2010/may/05/greek-bailout-economic-crisis-deaths. Accessed on 10 June 2020.

The Guardian. (2020) From loo roll to dumplings: Hong Kong protesters weaponise purchasing power. https://www.theguardian.com/world/2020/jan/23/from-loo-roll-to-dumplings-hong-kong-protesters-weaponise-purchasing-power. Accessed on 25 June 2020.

Tilly, C. (1986). *The contentious French*. Harvard University Press.

Tilly, C. (1995). *Popular contention in Great Britain, 1758–1834*. Paradigm Publishers.

Tin-bor Hui, V. (2017). The protest and beyond. *Journal of Democracy*, *26*(2), 111–121.

Uitermark, J. (2004). Looking forward by looking back: May day protests in London and the strategic significance of the urban. *Antipode: A Radical Journal of Geography*, *36*(4), 706–727.

Victoria and Albert Museum. (2016). *Closed exhibition – Disobedient objects*. http://www.vam.ac.uk/content/exhibitions/disobedient-objects/. Accessed on May 2016.

Vargo, S. L., & Lusch, R. F. (2016). Institutions and axioms: An extension and update of service-dominant logic. *Journal of the Academy of Marketing Science*, *44*(4), 5–23.

Varman, R., & Belk, R. (2009). Nationalism and ideology in an anticonsumption movement. *Journal of Consumer Research*, *36*(4), 686–700.

Vasudevan, A. (2015). The autonomous city: Towards a critical geography of occupation. *Progress in Human Geography*, *39*(3), 316–337.

Visconti, L., Sherry, J., Jr., Borghini, S., & Anderson, L. (2010). Street art, sweet art? Reclaiming the "public" in public place. *Journal of Consumer Research*, *37*(3), 511–529.

vom Lehn, D., & Heath, C. (2016). Action at the exhibit face: Video and the analysis of social interaction in museums and galleries. *Journal of Marketing Management*, *32*(15–16), 1441–1457.

Wahlen, S., & Laamanen, M. (2015). Consumption, lifestyle and social movements. *International Journal of Consumer Studies*, *39*(5), 397–403.

Weijo, H., Martin, D., & Arnould, E. (2018). Consumer movements and collective creativity: The case of restaurant day. *Journal of Consumer Research*, *45*(2), 251–274.

Weinschenk, A. (2019). That's why the lady lost to the trump: Demographics and the 2016 presidential election. *Journal of Political Marketing*, *18*(1–2), 69–91.

Whyte, L. (2022, February 14). *Hong Kong (China) 2021*. National Endowment for Democracy. https://www.ned.org/region/asia/hong-kong-china-2021/

Wong, T., (2017) How Hong Kong got trapped in a cycle of violence. *BBC News*. https://www.bbc.co.uk/news/av/world-asia-china-49369052/how-hong-kong-got-trapped-in-a-cycle-of-violence. Accessed on 20 August 2019.

Zajko, M., & Beland, D. (2008). Space and protest policing at international summits. *Environment and Planning D: Society and Space*, *26*(4), 719–735.

Pick-Six: How Grassroots Organizations in the United States Can Use Core Stakeholder Influence Techniques in Political Marketing

Craig S. Fleisher and Jason Voiovich

INTRODUCTION

> One example of a successful partnership is an event co-organized by leaders from a community clinic and the Somali community in Minnesota. Elder Imams from across the state came to Community-University Health Care Center (CUHCC) to receive COVID-19 vaccinations. Imam Sharif Mohamed from Dar al-Hijrah Mosque helped to organize the event to encourage vaccine confidence within the Somali community. Imam Sharif and other Somali faith leaders saw the need to help promote and advocate for increased COVID-19 vaccination and decided to lead by example. Sixteen Imams volunteered to get the vaccines. The event was filmed by Somali media outlets and was viewed more than 200,000 times in the first week by people in Minnesota, across the U.S., and around the world. (Johansen, 2024) (https://nrcrim.org/vaccine-campaign-partnerships-faith-based-organizations)

On the surface, this seems like a standard partnership between a large, public research and medical institution (the University of Minnesota, USA) and a large ethic and religious constituent group in its immediate vicinity. However, those with an eye toward influence techniques will see a deeper set of strategies in play. With vaccine hesitancy a significant concern, the Somali immigrant community risked becoming disproportionately impacted by COVID-19 infections and complications. Grassroots activists had precious little time to experiment with, test, and validate novel approaches; they needed to *know* their techniques would work. In this example, we see three of the six core influence strategies outlined by Robert Cialdini (1984) in use: Authority, Consistency, and Social Proof. The local Imams have substantial influence within this community. Their action (getting the vaccine publicly) matches their rhetoric (you should get the vaccine) – that demonstrates internal consistency. Finally, the number of Imams participating (16) shows a level of social proof (others are doing it) that only one or two volunteers would not. In short, it was the alignment of solid grassroots organization and targeted influence strategies that made the critical difference for this constituency.

This chapter explores how political marketers in grassroots organizations can achieve a more predictable and sustainable level of influence and success on display above using a combination of organizational best-practices and evidence-based communication strategies (Public Affairs Council, 2000). We will show how the consistent and deliberate applications of several demonstrated influence principles can lead to superior outcomes. Lastly, we'll demonstrate how these work by demonstrating their use in practice during the time of the "tripledemic" experiences in the United States during late 2022/2023. This is when COVID-19, seasonal flu, and RSV (Respiratory Syncytial Virus – a common respiratory infection that can be dangerous to some groups) were causing serious concern, if not panic in some places, that people's health was being jeopardized at levels that made the recovery from COVID-19 unsustainable.

STARTING AT THE GRASSROOTS

Before we can understand how Cialdini's six evidence-based influence strategies may be applied to amplified and improve grassroots political marketing, we must address best-practices and nuances in grassroots efforts in the United States. This will ensure practitioners understand how to leverage these proven strategies depending on the context of their unique situation. Additionally, without a strong foundation, even proven communication strategies are unlikely to generate maximum impact. In other words, excellent adornment in a shoddily constructed house will only impress at a shallow, first glance.

What do such diverse group including the American Civil Liberties Union (ACLU), the Christian Coalition, the National Abortion Rights Action League (NARAL), Black Lives Matter (BLM), the National Rifle Association (NRA), the National Taxpayers Union (NTU), People for the American Way (PFAW), and the "Me-too" movements have in common when it comes to public policy? Each has developed and invested in sophisticated lobbying, advocacy, influence, and grassroots capabilities designed to increase its ability to influence public policy decisions. These capabilities are part of the over four billion ($USD) invested in related nonmarket influence activities by U.S. interests during the 2023 calendar year according to the lobbying trends total spend tracking datasets (CS Fleisher, 2022) provided by OpenSecrets (https://www.opensecrets.org); nevertheless, trying to decipher how much or what proportion of that total was specifically spent on grassroots activities is intentionally difficult to assess since it is a mostly unregulated component of nonmarket influence. This is a key reason that some interested influencers invest heavily in it, since it offers a greater range of discretion to using monetary resources to influence policy than more regulated channels.

Grassroots leadership can be essential to community cohesion and mobilization, to community and economic development, to political protection and representation (Kellogg Foundation, undated). Grassroots activism can restore, expand, and build the coalitions that have long guarded the social and political spaces in which civil rights, health care, and public education, and social services can thrive. But grassroots activists must master essential rules, or the "art, science and craft" of political communication, influence, and marketing, to achieve success (Public Affairs Council, 2000).

Labor, consumer, environmental, and many other self-described socio-political interest group movements in the US have enjoyed much success over the last five decades using grassroots techniques to influence legislation and law-making; consequently, corporations found themselves on the losing end of several public battles. The business community was initially caught off guard by the emergence of these groups and their use of new government, media, and public relations influence techniques. Their use prompted companies to re-evaluate the role, and the effectiveness of its public affairs (PA) management. Keim et al. (1984: 44) noted in a foundational piece in this field that "if corporations are to be effective in influencing public policy, they must have the support of an informed and motivated constituency." Decades later, this remains valid.

Many U.S. corporations, associations, and special interest groups invest enormous financial resources and manpower into implementing grassroots programs (Stone, 1994) to gain constituency support. The absolute size of resources allocated to the grassroots for both in-house and outside supplier expenses at the federal, state, and local levels is likely quite large. A review of the data from websites like Open Secrets, which is designed to research, document, and track the influence of money in U.S. politics, will quickly show the vast sums spent by various groups on grassroots and related communication activities designed to influence political leadership.

Political influence and institutions in the U.S. have long been fertile grounds for grassroots consultants, activists, and activism (Walker, 2014). Politicians can come into governance through their affiliations with grassroots organizations on their way into being elected by their constituents. Grassroots activity has and can be a powerful toolset in the arsenals of public affairs, government affairs/relations, and lobbying professionals to help tilt the balance of a policy debate to their view's favor (Walker, 2021). Combined with direct lobbying, political action committees (PACs), traditional communication, media, and public relations (PR), or other related public policy influence functions, grassroots efforts can be difference makers in demonstrating the gravity of importance an issue has to constituents (Showalter & Fleisher, 2021).

TYPICAL FORMS OF GRASSROOTS PROGRAMS

Table 21.1 outlines the characteristics, advantages, and disadvantages of the major grassroots programs.

While each program has enjoyed different levels of popularity and effectiveness over decades of use, we suggest that third-party advocacy programs will likely become the most effective form in the future. This suggestion is supported by the strategic importance of coalition building. The potential of a grassroots program is limited by the resources that are allocated to its development. Since all companies have limited resources, this puts a practical constraint on how "big" a grassroots program can become. Coalition building allows companies to pool resources toward a common cause or issue; consequently, third party advocacy programs are important for facilitating alliances and coalition building.

Third party advocacy programs also allow companies to join forces with their opponents on some issues. This can be a very powerful advantage. It not only eliminates opposition in some instances, but it also sends a strong message to politicians who have been known to play opponents off each other when forming public policy. This leaves policy makers with fewer allies when they take a position on an issue which aligns and motivates opponents. Used in conjunction with other advocacy tactics potentially including lobbying, coalition building, media outreach, and public education, third-party advocacy programs can play a crucial role in contesting public issues by providing independent analysis, amplifying marginalized voices, building public support, and influencing policymakers.

Table 21.1 Typical Forms of Grassroots Programs

Form of Program	*Key Characteristics*	*Advantages*	*Disadvantages*
Ad-Hoc	-most common form -no formal structure or organization -use of broad-based tactics	quickly implemented -low cost of implementation	-not designed to produce sustained results -challenges in coordination and collaboration
Broad-Based	-aims to get majority of employees involved -quantity emphasized over quality -want employees who are politically active	-development of informational assets -can positively influence company culture	-effect of volume-based grassroots increasingly less effective -usually are higher cost
Key Contact	-aim is to develop high quality relationships between policymakers and employees -uses administrative and operational management personnel -stresses quality over quantity of impact	-currently the most effective program -strong use of employee self-interest -most efficient in terms of benefits/ costs	-requires longest implementation period -does not aspire to involve entire company -management turnover affects performance of program -lacks "power in numbers"
Third Party Advocacy	-utilizes outside stakeholders -emphasis is on coalition building -external vs. internal focus -sometimes used in conjunction with other programs	-develops informational assets -can lead to strong coalitions of interests -effective program when dealing with large issues	-does not develop internal grassroots resources and capabilities -difficult to organize and manage -can fail to build institutional memory

Source: Table developed by the authors.

When we suggest third-party grassroots efforts may prove to be a most effective strategy as a whole, it's important to consider the difference between grassroots, "grass tops," and so-called astroturfing. These partnerships inevitably lead to the possibility (real or perceived) that the advocacy isn't authentically "bottoms-up," but rather driven by large corporate or organizational interests. In a true grassroots effort, the sponsoring third-party organization acts as an amplifier and catalyst of true constituency-led efforts. They play a minimal role in shaping those objectives, instead lending their financial and other resources to support objectives chosen and planned by the movement's leadership. A "grass tops" approach is similar in that individual activists play a central role, but they are supported much more assertively by their corporate sponsor who will shape the underlying strategy. The "grass tops" gives the public the perception that this is a true, bottoms-up grassroots effort while masking the level of corporate support and guidance (Bruhn et al., 2009).

Walker (2014) makes the distinction between whether professional consultants who organize grassroots campaigns on behalf of paying clients are viewed and in fact act as gardeners who carefully tend organic growth into desirable outputs, or as manufacturers producing inferior substitutes from artificial materials (aka, astroturfing). Astroturfing is a deceptive and manipulative strategy in which there is no control or guidance from bottoms-up activists – it is simply the appearance of grassroots. The word astroturf implies the artificial nature of this strategy. In the end, these are not sharp distinctions, but exist on a continuum. For example: When do corporate guidance and behaviors transition from grassroots to grass tops? It's reasonable to assume that the corporate sponsor may understand better the communication influence strategies we will discuss later in this chapter. Is leveraging these strategies evidence of the dog wagging its tail, or the tail wagging the dog?

Another issue that must be addressed with respect to all forms of grassroots programs is the importance of ensuring that grassroots efforts are constituency-based. Just like a program which does not work to influence legislation, a program that does not target your constituency representatives is ineffective for clear reasons. Referring to the U.S. political system, grassroots expert Michael Dunn (1989, p. 15) confirms the importance of constituency-based grassroots:

> No grassroots program...will be effective over the long run unless it is constituency-based, unless it is targeted at legislators who represent the program participants. Remember, there are only three people in Congress who really care what your employees think: their two senators and their representative.

Regardless of which form(-s) are chosen to model a grassroots program after, organizational leaders should ensure that it exists to influence the legislative process and does so by targeting its constituents' district representatives.

PURSUING GRASSROOTS EFFECTIVENESS

Grassroots has specific advantages and disadvantages compared to other corporate political activities (aka, CPAs). Table 21.2 outlines key differences between traditional strategies and grassroots programs (Keim et al., 1984; Sethi, 1987; Showalter & Fleisher, 2021; Swift-Rosenzweig, 1989).

Some of the differences identified require further comment, especially as it pertains to managing these approaches and measuring their performance (Fleisher, 2003). An important characteristic of CPAs is their "potential benefits to costs ratio." Grassroots typically will obtain better results than lobbying or advocacy advertising for the same cost. The start-up times for other CPAs is usually less, but this is often accompanied by a

Table 21.2 The Effectiveness of Grassroots Activity versus Other Forms of Political Influence

Characteristics	*Grassroots Programs*	*Traditional Lobbying*	*Advocacy Advertising*
Adaptability	adaptable to both reactive and proactive initiatives	usually confined to reactive initiatives	can be adapted to both reactive and proactive initiatives
Benefits/Cost Ratio	highest benefits/cost ratios in most instances	highly variable benefits to costs received	lowest benefits/costs in most cases

(Continued)

Table 21.2 (Continued)

Characteristics	*Grassroots Programs*	*Traditional Lobbying*	*Advocacy Advertising*
Start Up Time	most time-consuming start- up to mobilize and organize program participants	short start up time/longer term needed to witness results in many cases	likely the shortest start up time
Nature of Arguments Used to Alter Policy-Making Actions	uses a combination of rational and emotional pleas; utilizes self-interest of employees	traditionally confined to rational arguments: self-interest plays minor role	can use emotional or rational argument although employee self-interest plays virtually no role
Degree of Stakeholder Commitment	strong commitment needed from employees and stakeholders	little commitment needed from employees or stakeholders	virtually no commitment needed from stakeholders
Accumulation of Transferable Assets	information assets accumulated through databases and building of coalitions	effective accumulation to the extent that there is durational stability in lobbyist/target relationship	virtually no accumulation of transferable assets
Level of Top Management Support Needed	strong top management support is required	less top management support needed	least top management support (outside of monetary) needed
Range of Government Levels Affected	applicable and effective at all levels of government	can be effective at multiple levels of government	generally aimed broadly at influencing public opinion, not specific decision makers
Posture of Program	used as an offensive or defensive tactic	typically used as a defensive maneuver	generally used as a defensive technique
Measurability of Nonmarket Performance	more measurable: effect on legislation graded through political testimonials/ results[9]	somewhat measurable: dependent on opinion of lobbyists and targets	least measurable

Source: Original table developed by the authors.

greater difficulty in measuring performance, and an inability to accumulate transferable resources.

One of the most intriguing and informative comparisons between CPAs are the arguments used to change officials' voting behavior. Some PA tactics such as lobbying typically use rational arguments to convince legislators to change their political behavior. Others like advocacy advertising can use both rational and emotional pleas to help influence behavior. However, both lack arguably the most effective tool in changing the behavior of legislators, and that is the use of voter self-interest. Individual self-interests are usually motivated by both rational and emotional reasoning; correspondingly, grassroots campaigns promote the communication of this voter self-interest directly to the individuals responsible for forming public policy.

Both rational and economic arguments in the legislative process can carry political weight. Yet, self-interested pleas for particular action on an issue can carry unique consequences for a policy maker. Not only do self-interested pleas convey a publicly defensible argument to the legislator, but it is also backed by an emotional component which communicates an individual's willingness to act if an appropriate response is not made. The synergistic use of stakeholders shared and self-interests toward pre-existing aims can be seen as the "purest" advantage of grassroots programs. Effective grassroots activity motivates and injects self- and shared-interest stakeholders into the legislative process. This ensures that as policy is proposed or formed, policy makers are aware of a group of individuals that are capable, and willing, to act against politicians and their interests if their opinion on issues are not considered.

CRUCIAL ELEMENTS UNDERLYING EFFECTIVE GRASSROOTS PROGRAMS

There are some basic elements that must be present and understood in any organization wishing to implement a successful grassroots program. According to two experienced grassroots leaders, there are nine basic factors essential to ensuring successful grassroots campaigns (Dunn, 1989, p. 16; Wittenberg & Wittenberg, 1989, p. 52). In addition to these, we suggest there are three other factors that have emerged that we suggest will be needed in future grassroots programs. First, we examine the nine basic elements needed for a successful grassroots program:

1 **Top Management Support:** Like any new program introduced into an organization's strategic array, top executives must give more support than a simple go-ahead for implementation. It must be aligned with top executives' interests, and grassroots leaders need to know that top executives "have their backs" when they deploy grassroots activity. Dunn (1989, p. 16) argues this "support" should translate into a renewed commitment for dollars, staff, or any other resources needed to properly implement a program.
2 **Grassroots Policy Statement and Strategy:** This is the opportunity for the company to set out the guidelines by which it wants its grassroots programs to be governed. The policy statement should address questions like: What is the company's attitude toward policy formation? What role does the company see itself playing? What role will the company's stakeholders play? What is the policy regarding the endorsement of political candidates? What is the policy regarding an employee becoming a candidate? How, if at all, will the company engage in fund-raising for grassroots programs? What policy areas will not fall within the parameters of corporate grassroots initiatives? These are just samples of questions that should be addressed to ensure the company is equipped to manage different policy contingencies.

Even more important than the policy statement is the development of a concise and clear grassroots strategy that sets the agenda the corporation will follow in its PA initiatives. The importance of creating a strategy that is more than reactive is summarized as follows:

> Today, by the time a solution to an organization's problem has turned into a piece of legislation, management may still win a battle or two, but they've already lost the war. If the proposal is inimical to the organization, it's all over when they file a bill because the organization is then reacting to someone else's agenda rather than setting their own. (Grefe & Linsky, 1995, p. 63)

Grefe and Linsky (1995) suggest establishing an adaptive approach to nonmarket, public affairs, and strategy formulation. This not only allows the company to be proactive in its policy stances but flexible enough to accommodate new ideals and viewpoints as well. The emphasis for strategy formulation should be placed on determining what accomplishments are desired and ensuring the blueprint is proactive and flexible enough to manage new ideas and political volatility.

3 **Government Contact:** It can be assumed that a corporation's knowledge of the formal and informal legislative processes is quite limited. Firms wishing to influence legislation must understand how bills are passed, as well as how the informal channels in government affect this process. An inside government contact or lobbyist can provide this information. They can assist the grassroots manager by supplying current legislative information, tracking informal support in government for the company's position, and giving practical advice on grassroots strategies and tactics.
4 **Fit with Corporate Culture:** Any implemented grassroots program will involve organizational change. Stakeholders must understand what is being changed, why the change must take place, and what the corporation will be like after the change has been implemented. The bottom line is that whatever structural or organizational changes take place, attention must be given to assuring fit between the evolved corporation and its prevailing corporate culture. Neglecting to realize the importance of this factor will render useless your grassroots strategy.
5 **Regular Communication:** As we'll explore in much greater depth before this chapter concludes, grassroots cannot exist without effective, efficient, and efficacious communication. Stakeholders must be given information on the issues in question, what the organization's stance is, the legislative process that leadership is trying to influence, and their role in the initiative. This information needs to be constantly updated to properly undertake performance appraisals, anticipate contingencies, and remain adaptive instead of reactive.

An important aspect of grassroots communication, which is commonly overlooked, is flow. Stakeholders must be given and directed to use the appropriate channels to effectively communicate up the organizational chart to top executives. If communication is only a top-down process, then as the program progresses, the grassroots manager may find herself in an unforeseen predicament with little support from her most effective resource: lower-level employees.

6 **Job Description:** If a grassroots program is going to involve managers to act as political activists or lobbyists, then it only makes sense that this responsibility be written into job descriptions. This gives top management an effective method for performance appraisals,

and a channel to implement reward systems. Revised job descriptions give employees a guide to how they will be evaluated, as well as an idea of what they will receive for good performance.

7 **Training:** It is safe to assume that most stakeholders in a grassroots program will have little to no experience in managing their involvement in the legislative process; therefore, they must be given opportunities to understand how the legislative process works, what needs to be done to make changes in or to it, and what role they will play in that change.

Training is also an arena where grassroots programs can be better sold to stakeholders in order to motivate political activism. There are two types of interests that can be sold during these training sessions: 1) self-interests specific to the stakeholder, and 2) the interests' stakeholders and the organization share. These joint training sessions not only provide employees the skills to effectively implement and carry out grassroots initiatives but also solidify the business relationship between stakeholders and their organization.

8 **Support Materials (aka, communication collateral):** Part of properly communicating, supporting, and training stakeholders involves providing appropriate support material. Among other things, support materials should give a step-by-step explanation of the legislative process, communicate corporate policy in a political context, briefs of the specific issues at hand, and what stance the company is taking on those issues. Support materials may also constitute pamphlets that will be read by the voting public, so stakeholders will need to know what will be seen by the voting public and the most effective ways of presenting the material.

9 **Recognition and Feedback:** Any grassroots program depends on the success of motivating stakeholders to become involved in the legislative process. Recognition for stakeholders that perform well in a nonmarket context is critical. While companies may be able to motivate stakeholders to initiate a grassroots program, the true test comes in sustaining stakeholder involvement. Some suggestions include providing promotions based on grassroots performance, bonuses when benchmarks are met and/or when final grassroots objectives are achieved.

In addition to these nine factors for organizing a successful grassroots agenda, three other factors have become important due to the changes in the political environment. The first of these factors is the importance of grassroots programs functioning as profit centers (Bonner, 1989). As firms continue cutting costs, programs which are not directly contributing to profitability or revenue generation will come under increased pressure to function using less resources. Using fund-raising, self-sufficient grassroots programs which operate as profit centers can and will provide their own financial resources. The creation of a detailed database of individuals willing to donate money also constitutes another precious information asset that can be used in additional programs.

The second factor is access, which can be provided through corporate donations from grassroots programs in the U.S. Even in the face of the financial resources provided by PACs, corporate donations from a grassroots program can provide access when access is critically needed:

> Access. That's the name of the game. Large corporate donors meet with the leadership and the chairmen of the congressional committees. We don't sell legislation; we sell the opportunity to be heard. (Brooks & Stritch, 1991, p. 292)

These information assets do not always constitute a competitive advantage in the U.S. As is already apparent, grassroots have become a necessary characteristic of U.S. corporate political activity. Historic and ongoing use of grassroots campaigns by numerous players within the political environment should cause a grassroots manager to assume that these players will continue to utilize accumulated informational assets. This creates a situation where corporations wishing to get the most out of their grassroots campaigns must maintain these assets. Failure to do so would put the organization at a strategic disadvantage in environments where these campaigns have become commonplace. This also has ramifications for those organizations who prefer to use grassroots consultants and do not internalize the capabilities they build in this realm (Walker, 2014).

The final factor, ensuring a successful grassroots program, may be the most important of all the previous factors. No matter the informational asset sophistication, or the self-sufficiency of programs, grassroots are only effective if activated individuals can make their views known to public officials (Newman et al., 2020; Walker, 2021). This relates back to the very definition of grassroots communication and influence as a conscious effort to motivate and empower stakeholders to get involved in the legislative process to influence legislation.

It is easy to lose track of the primary objective of grassroots when trying to ensure proper programmatic implementation. A good litmus test is provided by Dunn (1989, p. 13) who suggests grassroots managers should ask themselves if the initiatives of their programs are in place to influence legislation. Answering "no" to this question means that the program implemented might be a nonmarket or public affairs operation, but it is not a grassroots campaign. Furthermore, a grassroots program can be oriented toward changing legislative outcomes and still fail. Grassroots campaigns that fail ultimately do so because of an inability to affect politician's or stakeholder's behavior.

Grassroots campaigns hope to influence four different characteristics in both legislators and stakeholders: values, attitudes, opinions, and behavior. Even if grassroots activity is overwhelmingly successful at changing values, attitudes, and opinions, the program will be of no practical value if the voting behavior of legislators, and activist behavior of stakeholders remains unchanged. The ability to change policy votes and related political behavior is the essence of grassroots.

WHAT IS GRASSROOTS COMMUNICATION AND ITS KEY ROLES IN ACHIEVING GRASSROOTS SUCCESS?

In this chapter's treatment, grassroots communications are defined as the dissemination of information usually to targeted stakeholders which is designed to motivate their active participation in the political process and its institutions. Grassroots organizations are primarily made up of civilians advocating on behalf of a cause to spur desired change at local, national, or international levels. Grassroots communications are focused on influencing policy, public opinion, regulatory behavior or to persuade elected and public officials in the pursuit of a particular political outcome. Though aspects of grassroots activity including planning, intelligence gathering, and leadership are also part of the larger grassroots effort, this chapter predominantly focuses on the communication outputs that are a result of these other capabilities.

Often viewed by the public as citizen activism, an array of influence, persuasion, communications, and advocacy strategies are used to create predominantly politically focused communications that engage specific stakeholder groups in grassroots advocacy. While lobbying is frequently regulated and performed by experienced professionals known as lobbyists, grassroots advocacy – outside of voting during elections – is the most basic level of political engagement done by interested stakeholders; despite its basic level of near-amateur participation, done effectively it is also among the most powerful forms of political influence (Walker, 2021).

However, the opposite danger may also arise – whether in the application of grassroots methods unethically or simply in the *appearance* of unethical behavior. Unethical grassroots political marketing often manifests itself as "astroturfing." Astroturfing refers to an advocacy organization using staged communications meant to appear spontaneous, partisans masquerading as "interested citizens," or other techniques (Lits, 2020). Even in the absence of unethical behavior, by assisting, organizing, and facilitating grassroots efforts, public affairs professionals run the risk of audiences questioning the authenticity of their efforts. PA professionals must take care to remain transparent and open about their role in the process to avoid (and ideally inoculate) these perceptions as they will threaten the effectiveness of grassroots campaigns.

EDUCATING AND MANAGING YOUR GRASSROOTS (OR OTHER STAKEHOLDER) NETWORKS

Finding the targets of your influence activity is more difficult that most people suspect. Elected leaders and lawmakers are usually among the easiest to locate and target, but even these change with each new Congress and statehouse turnover. And since an elected officials' staff members often have tight control of their agendas or schedules, grassroots leaders often must begin building many of these relationships from the ground up after each new election cycle or special election.

Making these "tracking" tasks more difficult is the analytical task of connecting the dots (van Haperen et al., 2023). Grassroots leadership needs to understand how and who members in your grassroots network has relationships with and knows as well as understanding how they formed and maintained those relationships. Accomplishing this task requires the convergence of human, informational, and technical intelligence to establish the networks and to stay up to date with them as they evolve. The grassroots leaders and organizations who have the capability for accessing these professional relationships all in a centralized and accessible location have a key advantage in driving their legislative and regulatory agendas.

Lastly, grassroots leaders must act akin to orchestra conductors in that they have to collaborate internally. Both in-person/face-to-face and virtual influence and communication still matter a lot most of the time. Everyone in the (grassroots and larger) organization needs to know who is meeting with whom, who is communicating what to the targets of their influence, and which of those stakeholder targets are sympathetic or not to your positions on the issues. This communication can also allow leadership to develop insights on where to leverage additional investments of resources and/or to build closer or sever unproductive ties.

USING COLLABORATION TOOLS TO KEEP THE NETWORK ROWING IN THE SAME DIRECTION

In the "old days" of grassroots activity and influence attempts, many organizations used card (i.e., business, 3 × 5, 4 × 6, etc.) systems to manage their networks. The next generation of grassroots leadership saw the frequent use of spreadsheets and e-mails. Unfortunately, the growth of social media and the internet more generally resulted in large volumes of information that quickly overwhelmed the capabilities of grassroots leadership to properly use. Worse still, trying to keep up with changes in either targets or your own network members also added to the complexities of staying updated on who was doing what and communicating key messages to a moving set of influence targets.

Contemporary grassroots leadership in the 2020s have access to powerful information platform and collaboration toolsets that permit them to leverage the growing volume relevant non-market intelligence (Fleisher & Miller, 2021). These allow leadership and team members to track their issues and stakeholders – including sources (Fleisher, 2022), log their notes, insert and organize their files, and access grassroots mission-critical data and information in seamless and friction-reduced ways for internal communication. Leadership and team leads can be tagged and notified of important changes. Everyone can have 24 × 7 access to positions, talking points, and other relevant datasets. It also makes it possible to gain productivity by holistically connecting these inputs to each targeted stakeholder and achieving more success due to everybody's ability to easily and timely identify which targets are moving needles on your issues.

ANALYTICALLY DEMONSTRATING YOUR VALUE PROPOSITION

Two of the enduring truths of grassroots activity is that (1) constituents and their voting behavior matter most when it comes to relationship building with lawmakers and how much your organization matters in terms of them accomplishing their agendas, and that (2) money matters. Grassroots leadership and networks who can tangibly show lawmaking targets the financial impacts and outcomes of their positions on issues have more direct communication and influence with all levels of political leadership. This means being able to show where organizational assets are geo-located such as office or production locations are located at the most micro of district levels, postal zones, or zip codes.

Analytics matters more than ever to achieving influence. Effectively configuring toolsets like contact directories, network mapping, geolocational district identification, stakeholder influence matrices, dynamic issues and stakeholder profiling, and living stakeholder scorecards can often be the difference between winning or losing grassroots battles (Showalter & Fleisher, 2021). Knowing and communicating the number of jobs your organization provides to the elected members' community, amount of property and sales taxes paid, and size of your payroll provides a powerful financial case to political officials underlying the roles you take on the issues your grassroots networks seek to influence.

DESIGNING, EXECUTING, AND AMPLIFYING SOCIAL MEDIA STRATEGY

Politically motivated stakeholders use social media as a primary way for communicating with their constituents and staying on top of issues they care about, emerging trends, and segments of sentiment. Online monitoring of stakeholders is the process of gathering information about an entity using publicly available sources and methods found via the internet or other public records (Davies & Calderon, 2022). Nearly all public interest groups have a public presence from which pertinent information can be gathered (Westberg, 2020). As such, social media monitoring, scanning, analytics, and advocacy mastery have become essential skillsets for modern grassroots leadership (Zeng et al., 2010).

The first emergence of issues that affect your organization or get the attention of lawmakers often surface in social media; therefore, it is essential for efficient resource allocation to know what lawmakers and other stakeholders are communicating there. By leveraging social media, your leadership can grow awareness, educate and inform your stakeholders while issues can still be shaped, and you have more discretion to influence their trajectory.

Digital lobbying has also become essential to grassroots influence success. The principal digital tools used by grassroots leaders and their networks are based on generative and other forms of artificial intelligence (AI), knowledge management (KM), machine learning (ML), and open data/source analytics. These toolsets make it possible to gather and analyze data from inside and outside an organization's aegis to develop more effective, transparent, and measurable grassroots, advocacy, public affairs, lobbying, and political marketing strategies (Carro & Di Mario, 2020). Some of the most advanced models allow us to think of digital lobbying as a six-step process based on (1) monitoring, (2) analysis, (3) strategical evaluations, (4) positioning, (5) acting, and (6) evaluating outcomes.

By vigilantly tracking issues and stakeholders in social and traditional media, grassroots leaders can better analyze and prioritize their communication outreach strategy to lawmakers and related external stakeholders. They can also acquire an accurate holistic view of what public officials and other related influencers are saying and what others are communicating in response to them. This permits grassroots leaders to make sense of emerging movements and to know how to effectively respond in near real time, another major advantage in today's fast moving socio-political contexts.

APPLYING CIALDINI'S SIX INFLUENCE TACTICS

Given the complexity just described regarding the strategy, tactics, planning, and execution of effective grassroots programs, it's clear that overlaying this process with complex message experimentation and refinement will prove challenging. The key difficult comes from the immutable nature of time and timing of the legislative cycle (Fleisher & Voiovich, 2022). Building and maintaining influence with key legislators and staffers takes time and sustained effort, which must be added to the time it takes to demonstrate evidence of grassroots support for a particular issue. Additionally, depending on the local, state, or federal government, the legislative calendar has fixed dates for the introduction, consideration, voting, amendments, conference committees, and final passage of any new legislation. If these two core activities – the time to demonstrate grassroots support and the timing of the legislative calendar – fail to align, the grassroots effort will likely fail. Therefore, PA practitioners must do everything possible to shorten the time-intensive persuasive message development process to give their efforts maximum flexibility. In short: *time* is limited because *timing* is fixed.

Although multiple persuasive messaging frameworks exist to guide PA practitioners, few are as evidence-based and reliable as Cialdini's six influence or persuasion strategies as originally detailed in his 1984 book, *Influence*. Although he suggested in the book that there were arguably thousands of different persuasion tactics available for use, the vast majority of them cluster into just six groups. They are: Reciprocity, Scarcity, Authority, Commitment and Consistency, Consensus/Social proof, and Liking. We'll examine each below.

Reciprocity refers to the natural human tendency to return a favor. In a simple example, people are more likely to agree to a proposal (e.g., sales pitch, request, etc.) when it has been preceded with a small gift, helpful act, or compliment. Giving first creates a psychological urge (in most people) to reciprocate by agreeing with the person or organization that gave initially (Mustapha & Shamsudin, 2020). Additionally, this reciprocation need not be precisely tit-for-tat. For example, giving a child a balloon at a car dealership may convince her parents to buy a specific car over another or accept an advantageous financing offer (for the dealer), all things being equal. The critical point to creating the influence pressure though is to give first in the interaction.

Scarcity refers to the increased perceived value of goods or services that are in short supply. This could be a genuine shortage, or merely a perceived limitation of access (Xenos, 2017). Commercial airlines employ this strategy by creating a limited number of "first-class" seats, thereby increasing their value. Unsold first-class tickets may then be "gifted" to other passengers as an "upgrade" (see reciprocity) to create a twofold pull. The airline therefore uses two techniques at once to build customer loyalty and create an increased perception of the flying experience above and beyond the tangible differences – seat size, meals, boarding time, etc.

Authority refers to the desire to trust those with special knowledge or competence in a particular domain. That authority can come from multiple sources – credentialled people, statistical arguments, social standing, or legitimate hierarchies (Cohen & Bradford, 2011). Prescription drug manufacturers use the authority strategy when they show a doctor in a white coat in their advertising for a new drug. Presumably, that doctor knows more than the average person about the drug, the condition, and about general health and wellbeing. Interestingly, authority can transfer (in certain circumstances) from one domain to another, even if they are not precisely related.

Commitment and Consistency refers to the desire to remain internally consistent between our beliefs and actions – essentially to "do what we say we're going to do." This strategy works by triggering cognitive dissonance when there is conflict. (Jaume et al., 2022). The feeling is psychologically uncomfortable, so much so that people will work to resolve it. The effect can work both ways: Either people will change their actions in accordance with their beliefs – or more surprisingly – change their beliefs to match their actions. The Alcoholics Anonymous (AA) organization makes use of this strategy when they encourage their members to make public commitments to sobriety. Even if the member doesn't quite "believe" they are an alcoholic, repeating the statement (especially in a public setting, see Consensus/Social Proof) triggers a change in internalized beliefs.

Consensus/Social Proof refers to the desire to "go along with the crowd," especially in uncertain situations, even more so if those people are "like you" in some meaningful way (Wolferts, 2019). Customer reviews are the classic example. People are more likely to purchase a product – all else being equal – with more or higher reviews – and sometimes when all else is *not* equal. People may choose the inferior product that has more reviews (and hence, more social proof) than an objectively superior product with fewer reviews. This is especially effective when the decision to be made (or product to be bought) is not well-understood, the decision isn't necessarily consequential, and the peer group is very similar.

Liking refers to the psychological desire to associate with people, causes, and things we enjoy. "People do business with people they like." This influence strategy can sometimes overpower "objective" evidence to the contrary. Physical attractiveness can play a role, as can demonstrated interest (also a form of reciprocity) in the other person – whether genuine or not. Corporations use celebrities for precisely this purpose. If we like the celebrity, the "halo effect" can transfer to the product, service, or cause in question. Sarah McLachlan's support for the ASPCA is an example of transferring positive feelings for her (and her music) to an inclination to donate to her chosen cause – in this case, supporting the fight against animal cruelty.

As we've explored in a few of these definitions, these six techniques are not mutually exclusive. Indeed, effective communicators often deploy multiple persuasion strategies at the same time to maximize effectiveness or employ a sequenced application of these techniques to achieve maximum impact in the allotted time frame.

In most contexts, Cialdini's six influence strategies are described and deployed in a commercial context – the buying and selling of goods and services in a free market. However, as we will demonstrate here, PA practitioners can use these techniques as a powerful toolset not only to accelerate message development but also to increase the chances it will prove effective. Table 21.3 following summarizes how each strategy might be used in a public affairs communication context.

Table 21.3 Influence Strategies in Grassroots Public Affairs Communication

Influence Strategy	*Brief Description*	*Grassroots Public Affairs Communication Example*
Reciprocity	The natural human tendency to return a favor.	Providing drinks and snacks ahead of a town hall meeting where a request will be made for volunteers.
Scarcity	The increased perceived value of goods or services that are in short supply.	Reminding voters that a legislator will vote on an important bill on a specific date, and that the time to influence that legislator is limited.
Authority	The desire to trust those with special knowledge or competence in a particular domain.	Leveraging a member of the community with special expertise to a serve as a spokesperson. (Example: an engineer on a technical matter.)
Commitment and Consistency	The desire to remain internally consistent between our beliefs and actions – to "do what we say we're going to do."	Asking voters to support a school funding referendum as a show of commitment to their children's education.

Table 21.3 (Continued)

Influence Strategy	*Brief Description*	*Grassroots Public Affairs Communication Example*
Consensus/ Social Proof	The desire to "go along with the crowd," especially in uncertain situations, especially if those people are "like you" in some meaningful way.	Asking a resident of a community to sign a petition that already contains hundreds of signatures from neighbors, many of whom they recognize.
Liking	The psychological desire to associate with people, causes, and things we enjoy.	Holding a community meeting at a locally owned coffee shop with a long, positive history of caring for its community.

Source: Original table developed by the authors.

PICKING SIX IN THE CONTEXT OF THE U.S. TRIPLE-DEMIC: THE LAST TWO QUARTERS OF 2022

The triple or "tri-demic" as it is commonly known as refers to a coincidence of RSV (respiratory syncytial virus), seasonal flu, and COVID-19. The concern held among health professionals is that the tri-demic might overwhelm already COVID-19 stretched public healthcare resources, and especially hospital emergency rooms and intensive care units. Physicians and public health professionals sounded the alarm early and often in the final quarters of 2022 and early 2023. Their messages applied to all adults (and especially vulnerable or immune-compromised populations), but also parents of young children since RSV tends to be more prevalent in younger age groups.

Given the rapid onset of all three viral conditions, message deployment speed was paramount. There was little time to test the optimal wording for maximum awareness – and more to the point, for maximum action (e.g., vaccinations, mandated masking, and other countermeasures.) Therefore, PA practitioners could take advantage of Cialdini's six influence strategies to craft grassroots messaging to maximum effect. Below is a summary of tactics the authors observed being used by grassroots political marketers in the last half of 2022 and their alignment with Cialdini's (1984) six strategies. (Table 21.4)

Table 21.4 Brief Evaluation of Cialdini's Influence StrategiesApplied to the Tripledemic in 2022

Influence Strategy	*Example from the "Tripledemic"*	*Brief Evaluation*
Reciprocity	Offering a cash-value gift card for receiving a COVID-19 vaccine or booster.	This created an exchange of value rather than leveraging reciprocity. Recipients were "paid for their time" much like any other "employment" agreement. A better reciprocity strategy would have been to provide a "chance to win" in advance with no requirement that people received the vaccine. That gift in advance would trigger the reciprocity instinct. Instead, the payment triggered a "is it worth that?" question in the mind of the recipient.
Scarcity	Communicating that hospital emergency facilities are "stretched to the breaking point" by the Tripledemic.	The headlines of these articles (and quotes by hospital administrators) created the impression that children may not be cared for adequately when they arrived in the ER. This certainly created scarcity and doubtless encouraged many parents to vaccinate their children. However, the level of fear created often did not match the objective situation as it played out, leaving some parents

(Continued)

Table 21.4 (Continued)

Influence Strategy	*Example from the "Tripledemic"*	*Brief Evaluation*
		feeling "duped" and accusing hospital staff of fearmongering. This will limit future (similar) appeals.
Authority	The Centers for Disease Control and Prevention (CDC) in the United States created a "Social Media Toolkit" to assist grassroots efforts.	This toolkit offers "shareable" resources for multiple social media platforms in a variety of media (text, charts, videos, infographics, statistics, etc.). By arming people with authoritative information, those people who share it have that halo of authority transferred to them as they communicate with others.
Commitment and Consistency	Health insurers encouraging people to receive both the COVID-19 and flu vaccines at the same time.	The results from the NIH show that: "Among participants, 77.8% reported receiving the COVID-19 vaccine and 55.4% received the flu vaccine. After adjusting for demographics and sources of trusted health information, participants reporting receiving the flu vaccine had 5.18 times the odds of also receiving the COVID-19 vaccine."
Consensus/ Social Proof	The "Families Fighting Flu" organization used stories of real people choosing to vaccinate.	This organization used stories from both mothers and (importantly) fathers, as well as people of several racial, ethnic, and income backgrounds. It created a sense that the desire to vaccinate against the flu did not depend on traditional societal divisions and that it should be equitably embraced by everyone.
Liking	Actress and Comedian Amy Schumer shared her RSV story, encouraging people to heed the advice of their pediatrician.	Ohio Health used the story (with Schumer's permission) to cast a light on the severity of the RSV season. Although Schumer's comedy may be controversial to some, her role as a parent helped to transcend that division and likely reached even parents who do not approve of her comedic style.

CONCLUSION

The practice of grassroots marketing in organizations as a corporate political activity that achieves results should continue growing as practitioners pair the demonstrated effectiveness of Cialdini's (1984) influence strategies with the growing tactics, tools, and techniques that grassroots marketers have been wielding for decades in their other influence activities. The expansion and growth of new social media channels, new forms of trust, the receptivity of government officials to receive messages in expanded communication fora, and the natural evolution of innovative practice that achieves results bodes well for the future of grassroots marketing as a socio-political influence method. Further research into the timing and sequencing of messages, the effectiveness of communication channels, the benchmarking of demonstrated practices, and the sharing of successful cases can all add more knowledge about what is most effective and what is not.

REFERENCES

Bonner, J. (1989). Forecast: A new awareness by management of grassroots as a profit centre…, Ch. 25. In W. Pedersen (Ed.), *Winning at the grassroots handbook*. Public Affairs Council.

Brooks, S., & Stritch, A. (1991). *Business and government in Canada*. Prentice-Hall.

Bruhn, P., Howard, M., & Paxton, G. (2009). Taking a "grass-tops" approach to lobbying. *Forum Journal*, *23*(2), 5–11. https://www.muse.jhu.edu/article/908549

Carro, M., & Di Mario, C. (2020). Digital lobbying. In P. Harris, A. Bitonti, C. Fleisher, & A. Skorkjær Binderkrantz (Eds.), *The Palgrave encyclopedia of interest groups, lobbying and public affairs*. Palgrave Macmillan. https://doi.org/10.1007/978-3-030-13895-0_78-1.

Cialdini, R. B. (1984). *Influence*. William Morrow and Company.

Cohen, A. R., & Bradford, D. L. (2011). *Influence without authority*. John Wiley & Sons.

Davies, T., & Calderon, A. (2022). Open data. In P. Harris, A. Bitonti, C. S. Fleisher, & A. S. Binderkrantz (Eds.), *The Palgrave encyclopedia of interest groups, lobbying and public affairs*. Palgrave Macmillan. https://doi.org/10.1007/978-3-030-44556-0_102

Dunn, M. E. (1989). Programs, prototypes, and perquisites, Ch. 2. In W. Pedersen (Ed.), *Winning at the grassroots handbook*. Public Affairs Council.

Fleisher, C. S. (2003). Managing the grassroots and assessing its performance. *Journal of Public Affairs*, *3*(4), 371–382.

Fleisher, A. (2022). Information sources for interest groups, lobbying, and public affairs. In P. Harris, A. Bitonti, C. S. Fleisher, & A. S. Binderkrantz (Eds.), *The Palgrave encyclopedia of interest groups, lobbying and public affairs*. Palgrave Macmillan. https://doi.org/10.1007/978-3-030-44556-0_28.

Fleisher, C. S. (2022). Datasets: Configuring their applications in public affairs. In P. Harris, A. Bitonti, C. S. Fleisher, & A. S. Binderkrantz (Eds.), *The Palgrave encyclopedia of interest groups, lobbying and public affairs*. Palgrave Macmillan. https://doi.org/10.1007/978-3-030-44556-0_226.

Fleisher, C. S., & Miller, J. (2021). Non-market intelligence for public affairs. In P. Harris, A. Bitonti, C. S. Fleisher, & A. Skorkjær Binderkrantz (Eds.), *The Palgrave encyclopedia of interest groups, lobbying and public affairs*. Palgrave Macmillan. https://doi.org/10.1007/978-3-030-13895-0_96-1.

Fleisher, C. S., & Voiovich, J. (2022). Time and timing in public affairs practice. In P. Harris, A. Bitonti, C. S. Fleisher, & A. S. Binderkrantz (Eds.), *The Palgrave encyclopedia of interest groups, lobbying and public affairs*. Palgrave Macmillan. https://doi.org/10.1007/978-3-030-44556-0_15

Grefe, E., & Linsky, M. (1995). *The new corporate activism*. McGraw-Hill.

Jaume, L. C., Schetsche, C., Roca, M. A., & Quattrocchi, P. (2022). Factor structure and internal consistency on a reduced version of the revised test of need for cognitive closure. *Frontiers in Psychology*, *12*, 6523.

Johansen, I. (2024). *Vaccine campaign partnerships with faith-based organizations*. University of Minnesota National Resource Center for Refugees, Immigrants, and Migrants (NRC-RIM). https://nrcrim.org/vaccine-campaign-partnerships-faith-based-organizations. Accessed on May 17, 2024.

Keim, G. D., Zeithaml, C., & Baysinger, B. (1984, Spring). SMR Forum: New directions for corporate political strategy. *Sloan Management Review*, 53–62.

Kellogg Foundation. (undated). *Grassroots leadership development: A guide for grassroots leaders, support organizations, and funders*. WK Kellogg Foundation.

Lits, B. (2020). Detecting astroturf lobbying movements. *Communication and the Public*, *5*(3–4), 164–177.

Mustapha, N. N. S. N., & Shamsudin, M. F. (2020). The power of reciprocity theory in marketing. *Journal of Postgraduate Current Business Research*, *5*(1).

Newman, B. I., Cwalina, W., Falkowski, A., Newman, T. P., & Jabłońska, M. (2020). Political marketing. In P. Harris, A. Bitonti, C. S. Fleisher, & A. S. Binderkrantz (Eds.), *The Palgrave encyclopedia of interest groups, lobbying and public affairs*. Palgrave Macmillan. https://doi.org/10.1007/978-3-030-13895-0_5-1

Public Affairs Council. (2000). *Winning at the grassroots*. Public Affairs Council.

Sethi, S. P. (1987). Corporate political involvement, Ch. 9. In S. Sethi & C. Falbe (Eds.), *Business and society: Dimensions of cooperation and conflict*. McGraw Hill.

Showalter, A., & Fleisher, C. S. (2021). Tools, tactics and techniques in lobbying and public affairs. In P. Harris, A. Bitonti, C. S. Fleisher, & A. S. Binderkrantz (Eds.), *The Palgrave encyclopedia of interest groups*. Lobbying and Public Affairs. https://doi.org/10.1007/978-3-030-13895-0_17-1

Stone, P. H. (1994). Learning from Nader. *National Journal*, *6/11*, 1342–1344.

Swift-Rosenzweig, L. (1989). Grassroots programs: Models and strategies, Ch. 2. In W. Pedersen (Ed.), *Winning at the grassroots handbook*. Public Affairs Council.

van Haperen, S., Uitermark, J., & Nicholls, W. (2023). The Swarm versus the Grassroots: Places and networks of supporters and opponents of Black Lives Matter on Twitter. *Social Movement Studies*, *22*(2), 171–189.

Walker, E. T. (2014). *Grassroots for hire: Public affairs consultants in American democracy*. Cambridge University Press.

Walker, R. T. (2021). Grassroots communication. In P. Harris, A. Bitonti, C. S. Fleisher, & A. Skorkjær Binderkrantz (Eds.), *The palgrave encyclopedia of interest groups, lobbying and public affairs*. Palgrave Macmillan. https://doi.org/10.1007/978-3-030-13895-0_196-1

Westberg, J. (2020). Online monitoring of interest groups. In P. Harris, A. Bitonti, C. S. Fleisher, & A. Skorkjær Binderkrantz (Eds.), *The Palgrave encyclopedia of interest groups, lobbying and public affairs*. Palgrave Macmillan. https://doi.org/10.1007/978-3-030-13895-0_26-1

Wittenberg, E., & Wittenberg, E. (1989). *How to win in Washington*. Basil Blackwell.

Wolferts, A. (2019). How to get the attention of government officials: A test of the effectiveness of social proof treatments. *Sigma: Linguistique Anglaise, Linguistique Generale: Journal of Political and International Studies*, *36*(1), 9.

Xenos, N. (2017). *Scarcity and modernity*. Routledge.

Zeng, D., Chen, H., Lusch, R., & Li, S. H. (2010). Social media analytics and intelligence. *IEEE Intelligent Systems*, *25*(6), 13–16.

It's all About Position, Position, Position: The Case of the Five Star Movement in Italy

Fabio Bordignon, Luigi Ceccarini and Claudia Mariotti

INTRODUCTION

What is the "place" of a populist, digital party in the political market? Further, how does it change as it evolves from the stage of protest toward institutionalization? In this chapter, we will examine these issues through the lens of a specific national case that has garnered significant attention on the international stage: the Italian Movimento 5 Stelle (Five Star Movement, FSM).

Notoriously, Niffenegger (1988) has developed a model for the use of political marketing in the political process, the "political marketing mix," referring to the classic marketing concept of the 4Ps (product, price, place, promotion) directed to specific political segments. Our focus will be on the *place strategy*, which can be understood as "the methods or channels used to get a candidate [or a party and its leader(s), in our case] across in a personal way to the voters" (Niffenegger, 1988).

In this chapter, we will first analyze the "place" of the FSM, referring to its revolutionary extended use of the internet as an alternative space for engagement and political action. The search for the physical place of the FSM will inevitably shift our attention from organizational to ideological, strategic, and communication aspects, focusing on its positioning in the political market.

Positioning has long been recognized as playing a key role in politics (Harrop, 1990; Mauser, 1983). According to Trout and Rivkin (1996), politics centers around perception, posturing, and positioning. Lock and Harris's definition (1996) of political marketing describes it "as a discipline, the study of the processes of exchanges between political entities and their environment and among themselves, with particular reference to the positioning of those entities and their communication." Thus, positioning can be considered the process of building and conveying an identity for a political organization and defining its organizational, ideological, and strategic coordinates.

Positioning can be linked to the political brand concept, which has been used in political marketing research (Winther Nielsen, 2017). According to relevant studies, a political brand can be defined as the "psychological representation" of the candidate or the party, encompassing attributes, values, personality, and benefits. The brand is thus a multidimensional construct with both functional aspects – represented by the results achieved through the implementation of their policies, which potential voters can assess objectively and rationally – and motivational aspects – represented by the emotions and desires stemming from the subjective situation and interpersonal relationships of individuals (Prete, 2015).

After having introduced our case study and situated it within the literature on party models through the analysis of party statutes in section 2, in section 3, we analyze the central role played by digital resources at the organizational (but also ideological) level. In section 4, we focus on the party on the ground and its controversial and changing relationship with territory.

In the context of the *populist zeitgeist* that currently permeates the political competition in many countries, we specifically refer to the positioning along the line of division separating mainstream parties and challenger parties. Consequently, in section 5, we illustrate the location of the FSM on the traditional left–right scale and its evolution over time. Finally, in section 6, we address the relationship of the FSM with political institutions, analyzing its complex "movement" from the streets of "the people" to the corridors of power (and perhaps back to the former).

In the concluding section, we discuss the development of the *place strategy* of the FSM and its (ongoing) process of positioning and institutionalization, underlining its limits and potential directions.

THE ORIGINS OF THE FIVE STAR MOVEMENT AND ITS EVOLUTION IN THE ITALIAN POLITICAL SYSTEM

From the end of World War II to the present day, the Italian political system has been the subject of numerous upheavals – cultural, political, social, national, and international – which have strongly influenced its development, including modifying, over time, the format of the political competition.

After the 1946 referendum that marked the birth of the Italian Republic, the Italian political system was characterized by a multiparty system that gradually consolidated into a polarized system (Sartori, 1976). This process was underpinned by the essentially proportional electoral system, chosen by the members of the Constituent Assembly. This polarized multiparty system characterized, with rare exceptions, the whole life of the so-called First Republic.

Subsequently, the dramatic political and international crisis of 1989–1994 led to the collapse and fragmentation of the traditional political parties – causing processes of adaptation, relocation, and the aggregation of old and new political formations in a bipolar system that was favored, in all national and local institutional contexts, by the dynamics of the new majoritarian electoral laws.

After fifteen years of transition marked by a "fragmented bipolarity," it has moved – albeit not always coherently and linearly – to a prevailing bipartisan system. This materialization, even if for a very short period, has resulted in the confluence of the main formations of the respective political-electoral alignments in two new unitary party subjects: the Democratic Party (PD, established at the end of 2007) and the People of Freedom (formally born in March 2009). However, the tendentially bipartisan format had a very short life: established in the 2008 elections, which were characterized by Silvio Berlusconi's landslide victory, it lasted for only one parliamentary term, during which members witnessed the passage from the fourth Berlusconi government to the technocratic government of Mario Monti. In fact, bipolarism itself has been put into crisis and subsequently swept away by the emergence on the national political scene of a new party formation – affirmed in the subsequent national elections of 2013 – the FSM, which caused an upheaval in the Italian political system and moved it to a tripolar competition.

In reviewing the genesis of the FSM, it is necessary to begin with its leader, Beppe Grillo. He is a comedian who became very famous during the 1970s and 1980s with his satirical political shows. In 1986, following his criticism of the Italian socialist party then in government, he was ostracized from national Italian television. Then he decided to leave television, staging his shows in theaters and squares, and his work was increasingly characterized by biting satire and unmasking the documented history of economic, financial, and political scandals. Through continuous contact with a live audience, Grillo continued to develop his communication skills and strengthen the bond with his "people." In 2005 – after meeting his future partner Gianroberto Casaleggio[1] in 2004 – he decided to launch his blog (beppegrillo.it), which was soon ranked ninth in the Observer's international ranking of the most influential blogs in the world. In a short time, the blog became the primary organizational tool of the future FSM along with the Meetups, which were digital platforms to form groups on diverse topics, generally of a political and social nature, to be pursued at a local level. Through the Meetups, Grillo's supporters could come together (online) and set a local agenda.

When Grillo realized the impact of his blog, he launched two massive public protest events to foster antipolitics among his followers. After these successes, he encouraged his supporters to participate in local elections, and in 2009, he and Casaleggio officially created a political movement, which they named the Five Star Movement.

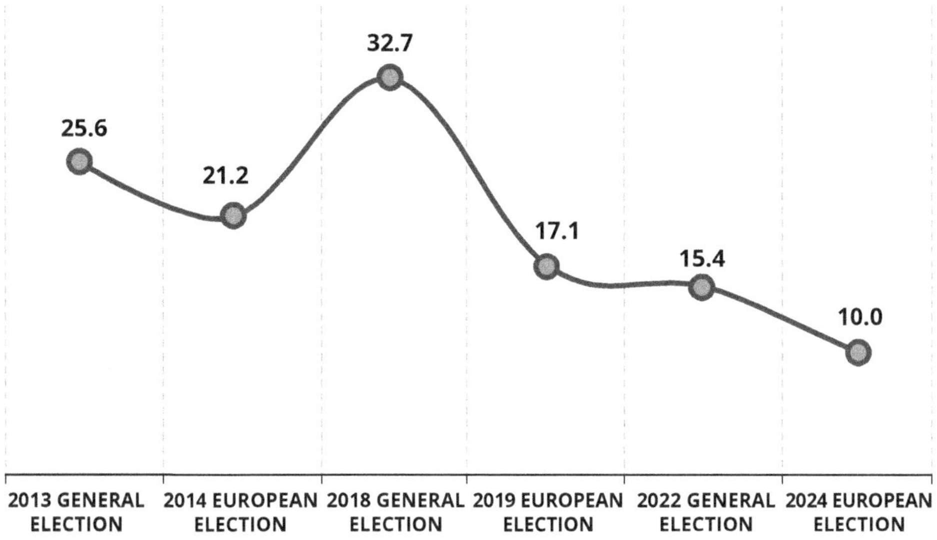

Figure 22.1 Five Star Movement Electoral Trends (%; General and European Elections)
Source: Lapolis Electoral Observatory of the University of Urbino Carlo Bo (Italy) on Ministry of the Interior data.

In the 2013 general elections, the FSM became, in its first attempt, the first national political party in terms of votes (25.6%), but due to its internal rule of shunning alliances (in a parliamentary system) with other political parties, it was relegated to the opposition. Nevertheless, in the 2018 general election, the FSM confirmed and reinforced its success, participating in two different governments in the same parliamentary term: one with the right-wing party, the League, and one with the center-left Democratic Party. Only in the 2022 general elections did the FSM begin to lose support, halving its votes—a trend that deepened in the subsequent 2024 European elections (Figure 22.1).

The elusive nature of the FSM is consistent with the different government alliances it set up during the 2018–2022 parliamentary term and with the variety of labels used in the literature to describe it—labels that are not coherent over time but rather reflect the party's constant transformations and its evolving trajectory toward institutionalization. These shifts have repeatedly altered the party's identity, as shown in the 2024 European elections, when the FSM repositioned itself to the left of the Democratic Party. The FSM has been linked to a highly heterogeneous family of political entities described by several scholars as *populist*. Populism is a composite concept conceived mostly as an ideology (Mudde, 2004), as a political strategy (Weyland, 2001, 2017), and as a form of communication (Jagers & Walgrave, 2007). The FSM presents some of the attributes that act as the lowest common denominator of these definitions, including the radical contrast between the "pure" people and "corrupt" elites, the idea that the "general will" of the people should be expressed continuously and immediately (winking at the idea of a web-based direct democracy), radical opposition to the traditional political class, criticism of global powers, and the attempt to overcome the classic left–right axis (Ceccarini & Bordignon, 2018). The FSM combines many attributes that characterize different types of populism worldwide, such as right-wing (anti-immigration issues), left-wing (economic measures), and centrist populism (the absence of a strong host ideology) (Mariotti, 2022; Mosca & Tronconi, 2019).

The FSM was also labeled a techno-populist party (Deseriis, 2017), a new party family in which digital affordances are a key organizational aspect. Techno-populists emphasize their distance from mainstream models of organization, favoring instead a model of disintermediated representation through instruments of direct democracy such as digital platforms (Mosca & Vittori, 2022). Although populism is a recurrent political label for the FSM it is not the only one. The FSM was variously labeled a protest/challenger party that stresses its anti-establishment character but without the necessity of a moralistic view (Hanley & Sikk, 2016), a digital party focusing on the digital platform and the role of the hyper-leader (Gerbaudo, 2019), and a movement party defined as "a political party that has particularly strong organizational and external links with social movements" (Della Porta et al., 2017).

While all these definitions partially fit with the main characteristics of the FSM – which changed over time – it is still necessary to wait to capture the essence of this party. As also shown by changes in its regulatory framework, the FSM is undergoing a process of increasing institutionalization, reshaping its political identity, and modifying its positioning within the broader political landscape. The FSM underwent several statutory changes and additional internal regulations (all voted online). These changes have been continuous in the history of the party, from the 2009 nonstatute to the first statute in 2012, then reviewed in 2014 by Grillo's decision to create a special committee (whose members were personally chosen by him, but that never really functioned) called "the directorate," to help him manage the party. A new statute was approved in 2017, further changing the internal rules and introducing the figure of a "political leader" other than Grillo, who remained the guarantor of the party. Later in 2020, after the first online party congress, the "Stati Generali," a special committee was appointed to draft a new statute, in line with the requests of party members asking for more local structures (with more power), and to transfer the prerogatives of the abolished political leader to a special committee. The changes were approved at the beginning of 2021, mentioning for the first time the possibility of opening physical (not online) local branches where party activists could meet face-to-face. However, later that same year, Grillo gave the task of writing a new statute to the two-time Prime Minister (chosen by the FSM) Giuseppe Conte. This new statute – along with a code of conduct and other regulations – was approved in August 2021, marking the presence of two top figures: the guarantor (at the very top) and the president. The former is "for life," but it is possible to vote for their removal through a complex procedure; the latter is voted online with a four-year term. The online Meetups were formally abolished, and for the first time, party documents mentioned the need to establish a school of politics to raise a new political class. This statute was approved online, but the legal dispute with the owner of the online platform "Rousseau" (Casaleggio's son, who left the FSM) forced the party to repeat the online voting in March 2022 through a new platform, much less articulated than Rousseau.

In November 2024, the FSM held a constituent assembly during which members voted to abolish the "Garante" role, a position held by the historical co-founder Beppe Grillo. This decision was part of a broader effort led by current party leader Giuseppe Conte to reform the party's structure and reduce Grillo's influence. Grillo opposed this move and, exercising his rights under the party's statute, requested a repeat of the vote. He viewed eliminating the "Garante" role as a departure from the movement's founding principles and an attempt to sideline his influence within the party. This subsequent vote, conducted in December 2024, reaffirmed the initial decision. During the same assembly, the party also addressed the long-standing term limit policy, with the majority of participating members supporting modifications to the existing two-term restriction, thus weakening one of the foundational constraints originally designed to distinguish the FSM from traditional parties. These decisions marked a strategic move towards redefining the party's internal dynamics and leadership structure. All the changes in the statutes show how the ongoing process of institutionalization and positioning is far from concluded, making any attempt to define this party quite challenging. In fact, every definition that has been used to describe the FSM over time fits for a while, for a specific stage, until new changes transform the organization into something different. Last, but not least, the replacement of the digital platform Rousseau with another extremely basic one that does not allow any interaction seems to put the *place strategy* of FSM, with its internet-fueled ideology and organization, into question.

THE INTERNET AS AN IDEOLOGY AND A FORM OF ORGANIZATION

The FSM is a lightly structured party with a peculiar idea of membership and participation, different from traditional parties. For a long time, its identity was based on an internet-fueled ideology: the idea of direct democracy made possible by members' participation through an online platform. Throughout its history, the *place strategy* of the FSM has been characterized by the use of the internet. It was used as a tool for involving members in internal decision-making through online voting, for organizing activists (through the Meetup platform), for communicating with voters and sympathizers, and for creating and diffusing a cyberutopian narrative presenting the Web as the very solution for contemporary corrupted "democracy" (Mosca, 2020, p. 3).

In the FSM ideology, the Web is a tool that allows disintermediation from the media system – every citizen can monitor those in power – and from political parties – through a direct relationship with representatives. More specifically, on "the web no one is a journalist, we are all journalists" and it "makes people aware and encourages new forms of aggregation and participation." Furthermore, it is around the Web that the *grillini* construct their own idea of democracy, founded on a direct relationship between citizens and the res publica: "The country," according to Grillo, "can only be rebuilt from the bottom up. By citizens who turn themselves into the state." "Each person counts for one" is a recurrent refrain in Grillo's discourse: with the Web, the political delegation has no further reason to exist.

The FSM was labeled a techno-populist party in consideration of the decisive role played by its platform in the life of the party and by the importance of the internet in the discourse of its leaders. One of the pillars of the FSM is the idea of improving representative democracy by implementing elements of direct democracy with digital tools. Its platform, Rousseau, was created in 2016 as an attempt to give shape to the idea of disintermediation, where the party's structures and, one day, even representatives will not be necessary: the people can decide everything through referendums or online platforms.

The platform was launched by the son of Roberto Casaleggio (Grillo's partner) immediately after his death. The platform, however, even if very articulated, could not meet the expectations set by the leaders of the FSM. Rousseau allowed the members of the FSM to discuss bills presented in Parliament by their MPs, interacting with them in a "vertical" form and showing their appreciation or disappointment, but without any "horizontal" interactions. However, this form of online participation also declined over time, as did participation in online votes, which could only be arranged by the leaders of the FSM, meaning that members could generally accept or refuse a specific proposal without any other interaction. Reading the comments of the members of the FSM, dissatisfaction emerged with the functioning of the platform as many of its aspects did no more than affirm a top-down structure of power, very different from the one communicated by party leaders.

Further, the full control of Casaleggio Jr. over the platform caused several protests, and the FSM, the "party for the people," was accused of being controlled by a private company (Casaleggio's communication company). This issue was addressed a few years later, in 2020, when a dispute between the FSM and Casaleggio Jr. exploded. The platform's owner publicly (with a post on his platform) accused several MPs of not paying the fees necessary to maintain this expensive platform, warning the FSM that he would reduce part of the services offered by Rousseau. At the beginning of 2021, the dispute became legal: Casaleggio and the FSM officially split, with the former remaining the owner of Rousseau, leaving the party without a digital platform and, for a while, even without the contacts of the party members. In July of the same year, the FSM announced the launch of another platform for online voting: Skyvotes. This new platform, however, can just be used for voting procedures, without any kind of interaction, a major deficiency compared to Rousseau, which, despite all the limitations considered, was much more articulated, allowing members to interact and even influence their representatives.

In this regard, a recent study showed that the Five Star Movement MPs have been very responsive to the preferences expressed by the militants on Rousseau (Mosca & Vittori, 2022). Moreover, the congruence between the issues raised by the members of the party and the policy proposals of their MPs increased over time through a process of adaptation, showing that the members of the party could genuinely influence the choices of their representatives. In the end, the close association between the party and the idea of digital democracy seemed to be better embodied through the use of Rousseau as a digital platform with specific affordances than through policy proposals focused on digital-centered issues: "the digital issues are substantially neglected or ignored: while the leadership of the party frame this topic as a defining ideological element, the issue is not incorporated by its representatives and its members" (Mosca & Vittori, 2022, p. 21).

The decision to replace Rousseau with a much simpler and less articulated platform seems to reveal a change in the *place strategy*, which is now less focused on harnessing the potential of the internet, a shift that questions the solidity of the party's web-fueled ideology and organization. Explicitly including the creation of physical local party branches in the 2021 statute seems to confirm a trend that may push the profile of the FSM toward a more traditional model, revisiting its original idea of digital democracy, positioning the party toward more customary topics, such as environmental and economic issues—a trend further echoed in the 2024 statutory revisions.

FSM ON THE GROUND

Born in the Meetup platform, in the early stages of its development the FSM was difficult to geo-localize in physical space, even though its granular activism and campaigns were pretty lively at the local and municipality levels. Grillo and Casaleggio's political creature had no physical headquarters, only a website: the comedian's blog. Groups of Grillo's followers clustered around specific initiatives, often linked to local problems and pre-existing movements in defense of territory or the environment (Mosca, 2020). The Meetup platform offered the ideal mobilization tools for a post-bureaucratic type of organization, linking online and offline activism. In this phase, the movement could be described as a "meta-organization" (Lanfrey, 2011, pp. 144–145) – a web-like structure consisting of micro-organizations conducting a heterogeneous range of activities. At the peripheral level, groups of "friends of Beppe Grillo" formed the backbone of the organization and ran for the first time in municipal and regional elections in 2008. At a central level, the distinguishing features were outstanding professionalism and the sophisticated technical skills provided by the web-marketing company Casaleggio Associati, with a strong orientation toward political marketing.

The relationship between the FSM and the local dimension has been controversial from the outset. In municipal and regional councils, the first Five Star representatives entered institutions and developed a repertoire of actions that would later be reproduced on a larger scale. The first Five Star boom, in 2012, was primarily fueled by municipal elections. The election of Federico Pizzarotti in Parma, an important city in the Emilia-Romagna region, drew the attention of the national and foreign media. The success in the Sicily regional election of 2012, when the FSM won 15% of the vote, made it the first party on the island and further broadened its potential voting support. In the ascending phases in the evolution of the FSM vote, a substantial boost came from local government elections. In 2016, the FSM won control of the cities of Turin and Rome, which became veritable testing grounds for government at the national level.

Nevertheless, except for these significant episodes of extraordinary breakthroughs at the local level, the FSM has never particularly shone in municipal or regional elections. When the result did not assume a "national" meaning, the FSM's performance was often disappointing. Several factors led to this outcome: the lack of a solid territorial organization, the absence of a ruling class rooted on the ground, difficulties in recruiting appealing candidates, and its lack of competitiveness in a majoritarian competition due to its refusal to collaborate with other political forces. Moreover, it was at the municipal level that the FSM's shift from protest to government proved most difficult. Such difficulty, deriving from internal conflicts and the lack of experience of those elected, often led FSM incumbents to fail in their re-election attempts.

What about the party's electoral geography? In its first actions on the ground and its earliest participation in local elections, the FSM was over-represented in the central and northern (northeastern) regions, while it showed some difficulties in organizing lists and fielding candidates in southern Italy. As noted above, the 2012 result in Sicily marked a turning point, revealing that the FSM could make inroads in the southern region. The remarkable growth between 2012 and 2013 saw the territorial profile losing its original coordinates in favor of a straightforward process to nationalize the FSM vote. At the time of its great electoral expansion, the FSM was a tsunami inundating the peninsula. Not accidentally, "Tsunami tour" was also the name of Grillo's 2013 campaign. After the general election of 2013, the FSM was everywhere: the Italian electoral map was painted yellow (its symbolic color). The FSM assumed the profile of a national party whose distribution of votes had now, if anything, shifted southwards. Even in its development through physical space, the FSM seemed to break the established patterns of Italian politics. In a country traditionally characterized by strong continuity in the relationships between parties and territory (Diamanti, 2009), it emerged as (perhaps the first) a-territorial political actor.

However, the following phase – with its electoral ups and downs – was characterized by a significant territorial repositioning. In the 2014 European elections – in which it lost four points compared to 2013 – the FSM's losses were more limited in the South. From Lazio (included) southwards, the result remained above 25%. North of Rome, it dropped below 20%. This trend was reinforced in the run-up to the 2018 general election, in which the FSM garnered almost one-third of the votes. The 2018 electoral map revealed the clear southernization of its territorial support: 25% of the single-member constituencies in which the party obtained the best results were located in the southern and island regions. In the 2022 elections, the FSM halved its vote share, but its electoral support was strongly skewed toward the South. Although its candidates won in only ten single-member constituencies, the FSM established itself as the first party in 36 single-member constituencies (in the lower chamber), all located in southern regions.

This process also reflects the progressive redefinition of party leadership. While the original organization had developed mainly on the Genoa (Grillo)–Milan (Casaleggio) axis, all subsequent leaders came from the southern regions. Luigi Di Maio (2017–2020) was born in Campania, where the FSM experienced the most significant growth in 2018, getting almost half of the votes (49%). Giuseppe Conte (2021) comes from Puglia, where the FSM won the most votes in 2022: 28% (but it rose to 41% in the single-member constituency where the leader was born, in the province of Foggia). The evolution of the territorial structure of the FSM vote underlines its profile as a political entrepreneur of crises, able to grasp the divide between the "upper" and "lower" parts of society and give voice to those "left behind" in the southern regions of southern Europe.

THE FSM ON THE LEFT–RIGHT AXIS

From its origins, the FSM has defined itself as a post-ideological political subject. Its chosen political locus transcended the categories of left and right, which its leaders described as outdated. In the party's narrative, the division between center-left and center-right, which had characterized Italy since the early 1990s, concealed a unified system: a single powerful cartel formed by the major parties of both sides. Grillo refused to align the FSM with the most traditional political axes: it was neither left-wing nor right-wing, but "ahead of" or better: "above." This approach also helped him stress the similarity and connivance of the other political forces. As he used to say: "Right and left do not exist. What exists is a business group. Italy is its business" (Bordignon & Ceccarini, 2013, p. 463).

The FSM's ideological antecedents and part of its original following could be placed loosely on the left, with which it shared battles for legality, environmental protection, and the defense of workers. However, in its boom phase (2012–2013), in which a small movement rose to become Italy's leading party, Grillo directed the resentment of his people against the entire political class: the indistinct "caste" of professional politicians, barricaded in the corridors of power in defense of their privileges.

The FSM political platform was indeed protean, multifaceted, and heterogeneous. Its founder, more an oracle than a traditional political actor, constantly shaped it according to the evolution of public opinion, also thanks to the strategies defined by Gianroberto Casaleggio. Maybe the most significant feature of Grillo's political creature is its ability to combine various populist messages, solutions, and host ideologies. In this sense, the party manifesto lacks precise ideological coordinates. In public policy terms, too, the FSM tends to amalgamate issues and proposals drawn from the right and the left, making it difficult to locate in traditional ideological terms. At some stages, the FSM has presented itself as a single-issue movement party, taking the valence issue of legality and the fight against political corruption as its central theme. Environmental battles are also prominent in its identity-building process.

Nevertheless, its post-ideological nature emerges most clearly when looking at the political background of its electorate. At the time of its resounding debut on the national political scene in 2013, the FSM succeeded in attracting voters who, in the past, had voted for both center-right and center-left parties, along with voters without a clear ideological profile: disillusioned voters, detached from politics, including a substantial proportion of ex-abstainers. Grillo's party managed to connect electoral areas that, during the long phase of the Second Republic (roughly 1994–2011), had mainly remained impermeable to each other. Its very presence (and relevance) rewrote the coordinates of political competition and called into question the bipolar set-up assumed over the previous decades. With the FSM, the Italian party system moved from the phase of bi-polarism to that of tri-polarism.

A large proportion of its voters refused to take a position on the left–right axis. Consequently, its representatives in Parliament choose to sit neither on the benches of the right, nor on those of the left, nor even in the center, but rather behind their colleagues, in order to keep "breathing down the neck" (Bordignon & Ceccarini, 2014) – the name of a monitoring campaign developed at the municipality level. The rise of the FSM in Italian politics actually suggested the emergence of a new axis of political competition, orthogonal to the one dividing left and right. The FSM presented itself as an anti-establishment political actor, channeling protest stemming from a widespread sense of social, cultural, and political malaise affecting contemporary democracies (Morlino & Raniolo, 2017; Norris & Inglehart, 2019).

The determinants of the FSM vote in 2018 are consistent with the significant strand of literature linking the success of populist parties to the effects of globalization, particularly its economic and cultural effects (Crouch, 2020). The party's constituents can be largely described as the "losers of globalization" (Ceccarini, 2018; Kriesi et al., 2006) – those most impacted by the recurrent crises of the globalized world, particularly in economic terms, but also as regards feelings of displacement. The success of the FSM and the southernization of its 2018 electoral map (see also the next section) have been linked to the party's ambitious plan to "abolish poverty" through its "citizenship income" policy measure.

The claimed originality of its ideological positioning and the antipolitical posture it adopted against the (old) mainstream parties translated into its initial choice to reject alliances. Despite the proposals made by the Democratic Party after the 2013 general election, the FSM remained in opposition throughout the following legislative term. Even in the 2018 general election, it ran outside any coalitions and stated that it wanted to win and govern alone. However, although it emerged from the elections with the most votes, the party – then led by Luigi Di Maio – lacked the numbers to form a majority. Government access, now considered a priority by the FSM leadership, required setting aside the taboo of alliances. During the next legislative term, the FSM would participate in three different majorities, including, at different times, almost all the major Italian parties (see section 6).

Populist elective affinities with Salvini's League initially drove the FSM to the right. The two parties formed the so-called "government of change" led by the independent jurist Giuseppe Conte (2018–2019). With their yellow-green government, the FSM and the League seemed to embody a new line of division polarizing the political landscape at both the mass and the elite levels. The anti-establishment, anti-globalization and eurosceptic views expressed (although to different degrees) by the two allies seemed to support this interpretation and, at the same time, provide common ground for their joint access to power. Then, after Salvini decided to dissolve the government, the FSM moved to the left, with the formation of the yellow-red government with the Democratic Party (and other minor center-left forces), led once again by the same prime minister (Conte II cabinet, 2019–2021).

The joint participation in the Conte II government marked the final convergence in the controversial relationship between the FSM and the largest party of the left. Despite having shared, in the early stages of its political journey, the battles of the parties of the left against Berlusconi and the Berlusconism, the FSM has often accused the latter, and in particular the PD, of having abandoned the weakest parts of society, the so-called "left behind." For the same reasons, Grillo's party accused the center-left of having become indistinguishable from the center-right. In 2009, Grillo even provocatively attempted to run in the "primary" elections to select the PD secretary. This criticism became particularly harsh in the season of grand coalitions after 2011, during which Grillo labeled the PD as PD-minus-L, playing on the affinities with the largest party of the center-right, Berlusconi's PdL (People of Freedom).

While describing itself as postideological, the FSM has always implicitly (and intermittently) attempted to present itself as the authentic interpreter of the "true left," or at least its traditional values. This narrative was reinforced during (and after) the yellow-red government. During that phase, the secretary of the PD, Nicola Zingaretti, defined Prime Minister Conte, who was increasingly closer to the FSM, as "a very strong point of reference for all progressive forces." It was Conte himself, as the new leader of the FSM (2021–), who inaugurated the new "progressive course" of the FSM, putting the battles against poverty and, in particular, the defense of the "citizenship income" flagship policy at the center of the FSM platform. However, the possibility of an alliance with the PD and the formation of a new center-left "pole," repeatedly the subject of talks between the leaderships of the two parties, would fail due to the divisions surrounding the policies of the Draghi government, and its fall in the turbulent summer of 2022 (see section 6). For this reason, in the general election of 2022, the FSM still ran outside any alliance as a progressive alternative to the PD.

FROM THE STREETS TO THE PALACE (AND BACK)

The 2007 and 2008 "*Vaffa*" (Fuck off) days, with their expressions of protest against the political system in its entirety – including the party system, the mass media, and the concentrations of economic power – were the most explicit manifestation of the FSM's plan to challenge established political frameworks. However, its electoral success in 2013 and then its assumption of government responsibilities after 2018 triggered a change of the opposite kind: a predictable – if controversial – process of institutionalization (Bordignon & Ceccarini, 2013; Tronconi, 2018).

The FSM's original conception of democracy revealed a problematic relationship with representative institutions and, especially, the Parliament, which, during the 2013 campaign, Grillo said he wanted "to open up like a tin of tuna." The first FSM MPs brought into the temple of representative democracy a style of action and communication reminiscent of protest, one that manifested in explicit acts of obstruction in the Chamber of Deputies and the Senate. In the months following the election, the party's parliamentarians even went as far as to occupy the roof of the Palace of Montecitorio – the building of the lower chamber – to protest the decisions of the governing majority. Moreover, the FSM continued to espouse a specific interpretation of the concept of representation, typical of a *movement party* (Kitschelt, 2006). Its elected representatives were subject to a time-limited responsibility (not exceeding two terms) and rigid party discipline, as well as the self-reduction of salaries and specific measures designed to create binding mandates. Consequently, the suspension, expulsion, or voluntary departure of MPs and local representatives has occurred on several occasions in the history of the FSM, revealing its difficulty in creating smooth working relationships between the (original) central office and the emerging party in public office.

A crucial step in the movement's path toward institutionalization concerns the political developments following the 2018 election when the party led by Di Maio assumed government responsibilities. Though the FSM could be said to have "won" the elections, as its 32.7% of the vote made it the largest party in Italy, it did not have enough seats to govern alone. The initial idea that a FSM minority government might seek the votes it needed in Parliament on an issue-by-issue basis was dropped. Di Maio's emphasis on the notion of "responsibility" and especially on the idea of a "contract," borrowed from the German experience, became ever more insistent. The idea of a *Koalitionsvertrag* made it possible, at least to some extent, to keep the purity of the Movement's isolationist paradigm alive while weakening the impact of the break with its taboo against alliances. A coalition government was thus formed based on a contract between the FSM and Salvini's League, a party that had all of the characteristics of the European populist parties of the nationalist right.

It is important to emphasize how the assumption of government responsibilities led the FSM to soften some of its original policy positions. This dynamic particularly impacted its approach to the European Union, as the FSM had often maintained an ambiguous stance, stating on several occasions that the decision to withdraw from either the EU or the euro should be up to Italian citizens through a referendum. However, party leaders progressively chose to replace these suggestions with ones based on negotiating with Brussels-based institutions. This choice was driven by the need to show the movement's international counterparts that it was a reliable partner that would have credibility in the eyes of the markets.

Nevertheless, after this shift, a considerable loss of votes started to shape its electoral path. During the months of the yellow-green Conte I government, the FSM began to lose votes, and the League started to gain increasing approval ratings. Just one year after its formation, the FSM won only 17.1% of the votes in the European election of 2019, while its allies rose to 34.3%. The end of the populist experiment and the birth of the Conte II government did not reverse the trend of the FSM in the polls. Despite the growth in support for the government during the pandemic emergency, the party entered a phase of involution. After the end of Conte II, the FSM was also involved in the grand coalition government led by former European Central Bank president Mario Draghi (2021–2022), supported by almost all major center-right and center-left parties.

Within this new oversized and highly heterogeneous majority, with a strong "technocratic" leadership at the helm of the country, the role of the FSM was marginal. Bound by the emergency framework brought about by the pandemic and then prolonged by the war in Ukraine, the ruling FSM had been forced to put aside its manifesto of radical change. At the same time, the loss of leadership positions after the fall of the Conte II cabinet deprived the largest parliamentary force of its role as the country's leading force. In a way, the FSM had completed its political journey: from being an anticartel movement during the phase of the large coalition government led by Mario Monti to being a member of the largest parliamentary cartel Italy had ever witnessed. This change resulted in another drop in electoral support: during 2022, polls recorded a further decline, and pundits doubted that the FSM could even reach 10%.

With the general elections (scheduled for 2023) fast approaching, the pressure on the FSM and its new leadership rapidly increased. The call of the "populist forest" was growing louder and louder. For these reasons, Conte chose a strategy of progressive distinction from the Draghi government and its policies. This approach, combined with growing tensions within the majority, led to

Draghi's resignation and the calling of early elections in the turbulent political summer of 2022.

In the general election of 25 September 2022, the FSM suffered one of the worst defeats in its history, at least in numerical terms: it lost over six million votes compared to 2018, dropping from 32.7 to 15.4%. Compared to the previous general election, its losses were mainly picked up by the center-right (FdI in particular) or switched back to abstention. However, the late re-positioning in the op-position allowed the FSM to limit its defeat in the public debate following the election. Expectations of a worse result and the reduced distance from its failed ally (the PD: 19.1%) even allowed Conte to present himself as a partial winner: the leader of a recovering party and the dominant political force in many areas of the South.

CONCLUSION

"Power is a lot like real estate. It's all about location, location, location. The closer you are to the source, the higher your property value." This quote by Frank Underwood (from the opening scenes of the television show *House of Cards*) can be applied and somewhat reversed for contemporary challenger parties – perhaps for contemporary political parties in general. This chapter has drawn on the political adaptation of the political marketing concept of "brand," meant as positioning, and the 4P model, focusing on "Place" and applying them to the Italian FSM. The populist digital (anti-party) party founded by the comedian Beppe Grillo represents one of the most successful political "products" to emerge on the political market in recent times, well beyond the Italian case. Its path toward political institutions provides scholars with an extraordinary experiment to analyze the possible evolution of populist parties.

The analyses presented in these pages reveal how it is all about *position, position, position* – proximity to power is a crucial variable in explaining the evolution of popular support for populist parties. The populist wave rises as those parties manage to present themselves as counter-power against mainstream parties and their perceived corrupt elites. However, contrary to the "Underwood theorem," populist parties do not seem to benefit from contact with institutions, proximity to state resources, or access to government roles. On the contrary, the fortunes of the insurgents seem to vanish as soon as they become incumbents, turning from outsiders into insiders.

During its impressive breakthrough on the Italian political scene, the position of the FSM was uncertain, at least following traditional coordinates. The movement was nowhere and everywhere at the same time. Its web-based organization defied traditional models and intersected with almost all the newer ones. The FSM was a challenger party, a populist party, an antiparty party, an anti-establishment party, a movement party, a digital party – and all these at once. Its conception of democracy challenged the principle of representation, reviving the utopia of direct democracy in the new agora of cyberspace.

The Five Star Movement's electoral map redrew the traditional colors and boundaries of Italian geopolitics. In general, it suggested the pattern of an authentic national party. FSM representatives and many of its voters refused to place themselves on the left–right axis. The FSM claimed to be beyond these categories and – at the same time – intercepted a new axis, or perhaps a new cleavage, of the political space, one that represented the emerging division between the winners and losers of globalization, between the integrated and the excluded, between those riding the transformations of society and those left behind... Certainly, the place of the movement, in its nascent state, was outside the corridors of power, alone against all the major political players.

Access to political representation and, in particular, the assumption of governmental responsibility have initiated a process of a different kind. The FSM partly normalized and institutionalized itself without losing some of the distinctive features of its genetic makeup. Its electoral geography, in particular, became very clear in the elections of 2018 and 2022, in which the FSM yellow largely colored the southern regions. In doing so, the movement partly shifted to the left on the traditional ideological axis. Meanwhile, its organizational structure at least partially evolved and became more complex, thanks to the new party statute promoted by former Prime Minister Giuseppe Conte. The utopian vision of entirely horizontal and fluid power relations was partly set aside, in favor of a more complex arrangement. As its leadership became at least potentially "challenging," this process of successive adjustments led the party closer to a traditional party organization.

Entering institutions, the movement had to come to terms with representative democracy, accepting its rules, procedures, and institutions. It also had to come to terms with the extraordinary complexity of the state's bureaucratic apparatus and acknowledge the levels of competence demanded by the administrative machine. In doing so, the FSM partially set aside its repertoire of contentious activism and the promise of radical change, accepting the logic of negotiation, moderation, and compromise. Moralism left room for pragmatism. The taboo of alliances was also set aside, together with many other taboos of the original party.

However, this process of normalization and institutionalization has been far from smooth and uncomplicated. The re-positioning of the FSM generated internal conflicts, splits, and defections. Above all, it coincided with a sharp decline in the movement's electoral appeal. Against this backdrop, the "call of the populist forest" has grown louder and louder, particularly during the Draghi government. The approaching elections pushed the new FSM leadership to distance itself from the grand coalition government and to differentiate its choices from those of the other parties, including those parties with whom efforts to build a center-left coalition ultimately proved unsuccessful.

While the overall result rewarded the only party that opposed the Draghi government – Giorgia Meloni's Brothers of Italy – and made it the uncontested winner of the general election of 2022, the performance of the FSM also revealed that op-position was still rewarding in terms of popular support. In the aftermath of the election, Conte's (new) FSM reoccupied the political terrain it had originally occupied and where it felt most comfortable. It was the political position where it all began.

Note

1 Gianroberto Casaleggio was the president and founding partner of Casaleggio Associati, which offers marketing and web strategy consulting to companies. He also oversees the FSM's presence on the web: in short, Casaleggio is the spin doctor, ideologist, and – in some people's view – the man at the helm behind the FSM.

REFERENCES

Biorcio, R., & Natale, P. (2013). *Politica a 5 stelle*. Feltrinelli.

Bordignon, F., & Ceccarini, L. (2013). Five stars and a cricket. Beppe Grillo Shakes Italian politics. *South European Society & Politics*, 18(4), 427–449. https://doi.org/10.1080/13608746.2013.775720

Bordignon, F., & Ceccarini, L. (2014). Protest and project, leader and party: Normalisation of the five star movement. *Contemporary Italian Politics*, 6(1), 54–72. https://doi.org/10.1080/23248823.2014.881015

Ceccarini, L. (2018). Un nuovo cleavage ? I vincenti e i perdenti (della globalizzazione). In F. Bordignon, L. Ceccarini, & I. Diamanti (Eds.), *Le divergenze parallele* (pp. 156–182). Laterza.

Ceccarini, L., & Bordignon, F. (2018). Towards the 5 star party. *Contemporary Italian Politics*, 10(4), 346–362. https://doi.org/10.1080/23248823.2018.1544351

Corbetta, P., & Gualmini, E. (Eds.), (2013) *Il partito di Grillo*. Il Mulino.

Crouch, C. (2020). *Post-democracy after the crises*. Wiley.

Della Porta, D., FernáNdez, J., Kouki, H., & Mosca, L. (2017). *Movement parties against austerity*. Polity.

Deseriis, M. (2017). Technopopulism: The emergence of a discursive formation. *TripleC: Communication, Capitalism & Critique*, *15*(2), 441–458.

Diamanti, I. (2009). *Mappe dell'Italia politica*. Il Mulino.

Gerbaudo, P. (2019). *The digital party: Political Organisation and online democracy*. Pluto Press.

Hanley, S., & Sikk, A. (2016). Economy, corruption or floating voters? Explaining the breakthroughs of anti-establishment reform parties in eastern Europe. *Party Politics*, *22*(4), 522–533. https://journals.sagepub.com/doi/abs/10.1177/1354068814550438

Harrop, M. (1990). Political marketing. *Parliamentary Affairs*, *43*(3), 277–291. https://doi.org/10.1093/oxfordjournals.pa.a052253

Jagers, J., & Walgrave, S. (2007). Populism as political communication style: An empirical study of political parties' discourse in Belgium. *European Journal of Political Research*, *46*(3), 319–345. https://ejpr.onlinelibrary.wiley.com/doi/abs/10.1111/j.1475-6765.2006.00690.x

Kitschelt, H. (2006). Movement parties. In R. S. Katz & W. J. Crotty (Eds.), *Handbook of party politics* (pp. 278–290). SAGE.

Kriesi, H., Grande, E., Lachat, R., Dolezal, M., Bornschier, S., & Frey, T. (2006). Globalization and the transformation of the national political space: Six European countries compared. *European Journal of Political Research*, *45*(6), 921–956. https://doi.org/10.1111/j.1475-6765.2006.00644.x

Lanfrey, D. (2011). Il movimento dei grillini tra meetup, meta-organizzazione e democrazia del monitoraggio. In L. Mosca & C. Vaccari (Eds.), *Nuovi media, nuova politica?* (pp. 143–166). Franco Angeli.

Lock, A., & Harris, P. (1996). Political marketing. *European Journal of Marketing*, *30*(10/11), 14–24. https://doi.org/10.1108/03090569610149764

Mariotti, C. (2022). Tra polarizzazione e populismo. Il ruolo della comunicazione politica. *Comunicazione Politica (ComPol)*, *1*, 39–62. https://www.rivisteweb.it/doi/10.3270/103649

Mauser, G. A. (1983). *Political marketing: An approach to campaign strategy*. Praeger.

Morlino, L., & Raniolo, F. (2017). *The impact of the economic crisis on South European democracies*. Palgrave Macmillan.

Mosca, L. (2020). Democratic vision and online participatory spaces in the Italian Movimento 5 Stelle. *Acta Politica*, *55*(1), 1–18. https://doi.org/10.1057/s41269-018-0096-y

Mosca, L., & Tronconi, F. (2019). Beyond left and right: The eclectic populism of the five star movement. *West European Politics*, *42*(6), 1258–1283. https://doi.org/10.1080/01402382.2019.1596691

Mosca, L., & Vittori, D. (2022). A digital principal? Substantive representation in the case of the Italian five star movement. *European Societies*, 1–30. https://doi.org/10.1080/14616696.2022.2144638

Mudde, C. (2004). The populist zeitgeist. *Government and Opposition*, *39*(4), 541–563. https://onlinelibrary.wiley.com/doi/abs/10.1111/j.1477-7053.2004.00135.x

Niffenegger, P. B. (1988). Strategies for success from the political marketers. *Journal of Services Marketing*, *2*(3), 15–21. https://doi.org/10.1108/eb024729

Norris, P., & Inglehart, R. (2019). *Cultural backlash: Trump, Brexit, and authoritarian populism*. Cambridge University Press.

Prete, M. I. (2015). *Aspetti Metodologici e Strategici dell'Approccio di Marketing Politico*. Università del Salento: Coordinamento SIBA.

Rivkin, S., & Trout, J. (1996). *The new positioning*. McGraw-Hill.

Sartori, G. (1976). *Parties and party systems: A framework for analysis*. Cambridge University Press.

Tronconi, F. (Ed.). (2015). *Beppe Grillo's five star movement. Organisation, communication and ideology*. Ashgate.

Tronconi, F. (2018). The Italian five star movement during the crisis: Towards normalisation? *South European Society & Politics*, *23*(1), 163–180. https://doi.org/10.1080/13608746.2018.1428889

Weyland, K. (2001). Clarifying a contested concept: Populism in the study of Latin American politics. *Comparative Politics*, *34*(1), 1–22. http://www.jstor.org/stable/422412

Weyland, K. (2017). Populism: A political-strategic approach. In C. R. Kaltwasser, P. Taggart, P. O. Espejo, & P. Ostiguy (Eds.), *The oxford handbook of populism*.

Winther Nielsen, S. (2017, April 3). On political brands: A systematic review of the literature. *Journal of Political Marketing*, *16*(2), 118–146. https://doi.org/10.1080/15377857.2014.959694

Soft Power, Art of the Media and International Political Marketing: A Cross-Cultural Perspective

Henry Sun and Phil Harris

INTRODUCTION

Robert Keohane and Joe Nye, pioneers in the field of international relations, co-founded the theory of neoliberalism, which they further developed in their 1977 book *Power and Interdependence*. Together, they introduced the concepts of asymmetrical and complex interdependence. This concept provides the theoretical foundation of soft power, which Nye later defined further as 'the ability to affect others to obtain the outcomes one wants through attraction and persuasion rather than coercion or payment. A country's soft power rests on its resources of culture, values and policies' (Nye, 2019). As a 'Contributor', Joseph Nye advocated for the quantitative study in his soft power theory through a joint force of academia, practitioners and government officials. This group made the Annual Report on Soft Power 30 ranking published since 2015 (Portland, 2019). This index 'showed that American soft power declined considerably after the beginning of the Trump administration' (Nye, 2020, p. 173).

Since 2020, Brand Finance (UK) (2024, n.p.) has published annually 'the world's most comprehensive research study on perceptions of nation brands – the Global Soft Power Index', surveying over 170,000 respondents from over 100 countries to gather data on global perceptions of all 193 member states of the United Nations. In the 2024 Brand Finance's annual global survey, the key findings, which are not surprising but confirm other data sources and thinking, have real-world implications (Brand Finance, 2024). They provide a comprehensive understanding of international awareness and global perceptions, shedding light on the soft power dynamics associated with nations.

Military conflict harms soft power, with Russia, Ukraine and Israel falling down the ranking. Conflicts across Africa and Latin America have the same impact. Instability undermines good images, the national brand and its stature. The rankings in the Global Soft Power Index are not static, reflecting the dynamic nature of soft power. This year, China has emerged as the fastest-growing nation brand, rising from 5th to third. This shift underscores the need for continuous monitoring and analysis of soft power dynamics. The United Arab Emirates, Saudi Arabia, Qatar and Türkiye have seen the most significant improvement since the inception of the Global Soft Power Index in 2020. Thanks to its scope, the Index is the world's most comprehensive study on perceptions of national brands, providing an in-depth analysis of the evolving status of soft power as nations navigate significant global changes and challenges.

Today, soft power has been widely adopted, used and understood in academic and practical studies in nations' internal and external affairs. The wielding and promoting of soft power has been widely reported and become standard practice and an essential function of international relations. Former US Secretary of State Hilary Clinton advocated applying Smart Power, combining soft and hard power for the US foreign policy. Hu Jintao followed by being the first Chinese President who called for the people to 'raise the culture soft power'. Boris Johnson, the former Prime Minister of the UK, has argued that the freedom of speech, freedom of life and freedom of love – is the soft power that turned 'this country into a great magnet for talent… We have the world's best minds in this country' (Brand Finance, 2024).

The application and development of soft power is much more complex, and for it to be effective, it has to jointly be applied with hard power, such as military and economic strength. On the other hand, developing soft power requires significant investments in education, culture and diplomacy, and it may take significant time to impact and yield results. Like any new concept or theory, the terminology of soft power has also been the target of numerous criticisms from policymakers and scholars. The most debated is the Neorealism critique, claiming that in the real world, it is not feasible to distinguish the effectiveness of hard power and soft power. Some studies argued that quantitative research on soft power is more subjective than objective, and some claimed, 'Soft Power initiatives may be undermined by domestic policies or actions that are perceived as hypocritical or inconsistent with the values being promoted' (Brand Finance, 2024). The question is how to objectively test and rank soft power and proactively wield and promote soft power.

With the existing data of soft power testing and ranking, this chapter tries to look at soft power from the perspective of a time-serious and cross-section study on how to wield soft power with Sun Zi: The Art of Media strategies and how to promote soft power with the cross-border and cross-culture political marketing – International Political Marketing. A triadic model is used to examine the three dimensions of political marketing, that is, Election Political Marketing, EPM, Government Political Marketing, GPM, and International Political Marketing, IPM, and a cross-sectional model is applied to analyse the 4P's of international political marketing, with a centrepiece of the Art of Media which is a study of power exchange strategies based on ancient philosophy and modern science and technology of communication psychology, political choice behaviour, Open AI, big data and social media. This and future study will address the theory development of soft power and its application through international political marketing.

SOFT POWER, THE ART OF MEDIA AND INTERNATIONAL POLITICAL MARKETING

By the end of the 20th century, the application and use of the term soft power were developed. They had become commonly adopted in academic studies, the media and practical works in domestic politics and foreign affairs, as well as international coverage.

SOFT POWER THEORY DEVELOPMENT AND APPLICATION

Nye points out that in the international arena, besides military and economic power, there is the third dimension of power, which is characterised as indirect power, co-Optiv power and intangible power and is contrary to direct power, coercive power and tangible power. Nye states, 'The ability to establish references tends to be associated with intangible power resources such as culture, ideology and institutions. This dimension can be considered soft power, in contrast to the hard command power usually associated with tangible resources like military and economic strength' (Nye, 1990, p. 31). Hard power is the power to force someone, through a threat or reward, to do something unwillingly. In other words, the application of hard power is to seduce with economic reward or threaten military power. Instead of using the carrot and stick approach, soft power in foreign policy is the ability of one country to indirectly influence other countries to follow through with the attractiveness of its political and cultural values. The appeals and attractions can be seen as part of leadership power through communication and persuasion, which falls into cross-border and cross-cultural political marketing.

In his dozen and more books on world power and leadership, Nye has discussed the wielding of soft power and its application to American foreign policy. In the book *Soft Power, The Means to Success in World Politics*, Nye examines the interrelationship between soft power and hard power and develops the concept of Smart Power as a balance and combination of powers. Nye analyses the application of soft power and claims it is more difficult to wield it because 'many of its crucial resources are outside the control of governments, and their effects depend heavily on acceptance by the receiving audiences' (Nye, 2004a, p. 99). For example, Hollywood films are not subject to US government censorship from a political point of view. However, they are censored by many Middle Eastern countries due to their cultural and religious values. In international relations, 'the receiving audiences' could be people of all races, interest groups and nation-states. The application of hard power is much more straightforward as the government can use military threat or launch a war to gain the result as planned in a reasonable time frame. One nation can also use its economic power to achieve its political goal by foreign aid or economic sanction towards the other country.

In *The Powers to Lead*, Nye quotes the power philosophy and leadership strategies from the great works and ideas of Lao Tzu, Sun Tzu, Niccolo Machiavelli, Karl Marx and George Washington (Nye, 2008). Nye states, 'Smart warriors, however, know how to lead with more than just the use of force. Part of ancient Chinese wisdom is represented by Sun Tzu...'. The ancient war strategist 'concluded that the highest excellence is never having to fight because the commencement of battle signifies a political failure' (Nye, 2004a, p. 11).

This ancient code and power philosophy are fully appreciated, shared and quoted by today's world leaders in their policies, communications and even 'Presidential Tweets'. In his recent book *Do Morals Matter? Presidents and Foreign Policy from FDR to Trump*, Nye assesses foreign policy on three ethical dimensions: intentions, means and consequences, for example, the significant ethical consequences of Truman's willingness to accept stalemate in Korea rather than use nuclear weapons during the Korean War (Nye, 2020). In addition to applying existing soft power, there is the question of boosting soft power to favour one nation-state. Sun Tzu reflects the importance of understanding soft power and its promotion during a very turbulent period in Chinese history, the Waring States period. He is popularly known for his Art of War strategy such as 'know your enemy and yourself' and 'to subdue the enemy without fighting'. The same principles apply to political campaigning, marketing and public affairs. Sun Tzu's Art of War is universal and can be applied as the Art of Media in today's media war.

FROM SUN TZU: THE ART OF WAR TO SUN ZI: THE ART OF MEDIA

Chinese Philosopher Lao Tzu (Laozi) described leadership in his Daoism Philosophy of Harmony. 'A leader is best when people barely know he exists, not so good when people obey and acclaim him, worst when they despise him' (Lao Tzu, 630 BC). Chinese classic studies found that Lao Tzu and Sun Tzu have some similarities in their philosophy, for example, on the doctrine of Dao, leadership in war and governance, the energy of water for Shi (势), the applying Shi as a strategy for war psychology, etc. Later, Confucius stresses virtue as the power of leadership, similar to the concept of soft power today, with this famous quote, 'To govern with virtue, one will be surrounded with stars' (Confucius, 479 BC). Confucius advised the ruler to lead by the power of virtue so that he or she will be surrounded by talents, just like stars surround the moon.

The application of soft power can be traced to Sun Tzu (2002) in his Daoist strategy book, *The Art of War*, in which the 'Moral Law' is on top of the five principles of strategic planning: 'The Moral Law causes the people to be in complete accord with their ruler so that they will follow him regardless of their lives, undismayed by any danger' (Giles, 1910). Sun Tzu establishes the five principles of the strategic plan as: The Moral Law and Policy, Heaven, Earth, The Characters of Commander, and Human Resources, Infrastructure and Logistics.

The first important thing about the plan is to adhere to moral law and choose policy accordingly. In Chapter 4 of the work, Tactical Dispositions, Sun Tzu stressed the importance of 'Dao' (道) as Moral Law and the political agenda. Sun Tzu states, 'The consummate leader cultivates the moral law and strictly adheres to method and discipline; thus, it is in his power to control success' (修道保法). This ancient leadership philosophy of the power of moral law and the establishment of a political agenda is consistent with today's terminology of soft power.

According to Sun Tzu (2002), the spiritual or media war strategy is the most effective in any military conflict, commercial competition or political campaign. In today's terms, strategy per se is a form of soft power, and its historical roots prove that Sun Tzu: The Art of War can be categorised as an art for soft power strategies. Thus, instead of Sun Tzu: The Art of War, these strategies can be defined as the alternative and much more communications orientated as Sun Zi: The Art of Media, which combines leadership philosophy, war strategies and communication tactics.

INTERNATIONAL POLITICAL MARKETING: CROSS-CULTURE CROSS-BORDER POLITICAL MARKETING

The Western power exchange practice can be traced to the Athenian Democracy in ancient

Greece. Solon, who lived in the same sixth-century BC period as Lao Tzu, contributed to the development of Athenian democracy, where election was based on expressing and wielding influence instead of noble birth and wealth. Under the political system of Athenian democracy, the influence of an officer was based on his relationship with the assembly, which protects the right of any citizen to stand and speak before the people. The roles of the general and the political speakers in the assembly tend to be filled by different people due to the warfare practised. The influence of speaking has a similar meaning to soft power applied in the power exchange process of ancient democracy. Two thousand years later, the power philosophy development went in different directions, such as Machiavelli's principle, 'One ought to be both feared and loved, but as it is difficult for the two to go together, it is much safer to be feared than loved' (Machiavelli, 1513). Here, Machiavelli recommends to his Prince that he place hard power, which causes fear, on top of the soft power of love. Adam Smith's power exchanges among 'a people of customers', shopkeepers and governments apply as much to today's world as in the 18th century in the UK. With the development of the international markets, the internet and regulatory influence and power, the world is increasingly run by shopkeepers and their customers (Harris & Sun, 2017). In the book *Des Kapital*, Karl Marx's social equality revolutions changed the power relationship to a market-orientated free exchange where workers are not slaves but free men who exchange their labour for wages from capitalists. Marx elaborated on this economic phenomenon of free market exchange from the class-based political exchange perspective, comparing the workers' struggle for better wages and work conditions with the capitalists' drive for ever greater profits. This political exchange theory can still be seen in the collective bargaining between worker's unions and capitalists. Nye claims that the best summary of leadership history came from Karl Marx: 'Men make their history, but they do not make it as they please…' (Nye, 2008, p. 5).

As the founding father of the US, George Washington saw the importance of political ideology and values in all governments when he stated, 'It is substantially true that virtue or morality is a necessary spring of popular government. The rule extends with more or less force to every species of free government' (George Washington, 1796). In the modern era, world leaders transformed from brutal power force towards soft power attraction, persuasion, communication and power exchange. During the Revolution of 1911, Dr Sun Yat-sen, the 'father of the Republic of China', advocated a different approach to power struggle by saying, 'For the revolution, we shall use only 10% of the efforts on force and 90% of the efforts on propaganda'. Dr Sun Yat-sen adopted the Chinese words 宣传 (pronounced as 'Xuan Chuan') with a positive meaning for promoting political and cultural values in comparison to the definition of propaganda as a neutral 'means of organising and shaping thought and perception' by The Oxford Handbook of Propaganda Studies (Sun, 2020). According to this Oxford definition, propaganda can be a neutral methodology in soft power application and promotion, as stated by Harvard Professor Tony Saich, 'Presidents FDR and Ronald Reagan used their formidable powers of communication to build a popular and political will to reach beneficial international agreements in tough political climates. The UN Secretary-General has no hard power through which he or she can get agreement and has to rely on soft power and marketing skills to promote various agendas' (Sun & Zhao, 2011, p. 12).

Similar studies can be conducted with the concept of soft power. Measuring these political events will formalise a nation's general perceptions and branding, which is part of the measurement by the Soft Power 30 by Portland and the Global Soft Power Index by Brand Finance. The Global Soft Power Index 2023 incorporates a broad range of measures to evaluate nations' presence, reputation and impact on the world stage. These measures include four aspects of soft power, that is, familiarity, reputation, influence and performance, which can be measured in '8 pillars: Business & Trade, Governance, International Relations, Culture & Heritage, Media & Communication, Education & Science, People & Values, Sustainable Future' (Brand Finance, 2024). While the concepts differ, the research methodology can be structured similarly to the latest communication technology, such as OpenAI, big data and social media. For example, the time-serious and cross-section study can test the co-relation between US soft power ranking during the N years perceived by X nations with either positive or negative changes of Y in bilateral relations. Thus, theoretically, the same statistical model can be tested globally for studying soft power and cross-border and cross-cultural political marketing. Soft power indexes can provide an all-around view for diplomats, tourism boards, trade agencies and national brand managers to formalise the political marketing strategy in soft power application. On the other hand, it can allow any nation to boost its soft power by investment to identify its strengths and weaknesses and increase its familiarity, reputation, influence and performance in the world arena for peace and development.

While the application of nation branding caught the attention of political marketing researchers and practitioners, other concepts were used to study the impact of marketing on the reputation of nations before the term 'soft power' was conceptualised. At the end of last century, Dow-Jones Irvin published a book on 'Practices and Business Opportunities in the Far East: The Complete Reference Guide to Practices and Procedures'. One chapter of this book discusses the cultural values, procedures and customs of marketing in China, which also fall into today's soft power study for conducting business in the world markets (Sun 1990). In 2007, om a paper entitled 'International Political Marketing: A Case Study of its Application in China', Sun (2008) argues that China applied its soft power to compete to host the 2008 Olympic Games and gain support for joining the World Trade Organization, WTO. In both cases, China wielded its soft power and achieved its goals, and as a result, China boosted its soft power by hosting the 2008 Olympic Games and joining the WTO (Sun, 2007). Later, another study was published in the same journal titled 'International Political Marketing: A Case Study of United States Soft Power and Public Diplomacy' (Sun, 2008, chap. 18). Since the theoretical concept of international political marketing was defined for the first time in 2007, the study of soft power and international political marketing joined hand in hand. Jennifer Lees-Marshment discussed political marketing in the election of a targeted country as a comparative study of Global Political Marketing. In their recent publication on International Political Marketing and Advocacy, the authors looked into the relationship between international political marketing and influence (as relevant to soft power). 'While most political marketing research focuses on how candidates and parties use tools such as market research, branding, positioning, and advertising to win national elections, international political marketing focuses on achieving international influence' (Lim & Lees-Marshment, 2022).

Political Marketing has been defined by Ormrod et al. (2013, p. 18) as:

- Political marketing is a perspective from which to understand phenomena in the political sphere and an approach that seeks to facilitate political exchanges of value through interactions in the electoral, parliamentary and governmental markets to manage relationships with stakeholders.

Unlike many other definitions, this recent definition of political marketing is focused on two keywords: exchange and relationship (Ormrod et al., 2013). In other words, political marketing studies political exchange and relationship maintenance among the stakeholders. The definition of exchange and relationship would fit well for further discussion of international political marketing, an interdisciplinary study of the existing fields of political marketing, political communication and international relations. Like its definition, many political marketing models, such as those established by Henneberg, represent the multi-aspects of political marketing, that is, electoral, governmental and interest group political marketing (Henneberg, 2002). However, the Henneberg models do not describe the 'international phenomena' as they are mentioned in the paper.

As shown in Figure 23.1, the Triadic Model of Political Marketing describes political exchanges in three aspects: that is, electoral political marketing (EPM), governmental political marketing (GPM) and international political marketing (IPM). This model tries to present a complete picture of all the exchanges and relationships in political marketing (Sun, 2008). This model presents six sets of interactive political relations in the three pairs of political exchanges. The first group of exchange, shown on the left of the figure, describes the process of EPM, where the candidates and parties make the political exchange and advance their relationship with voters and interest groups. For instance, in his 2012 re-election, Barack Obama was confronted with a daunting task: to convince voters that despite an anemic economic recovery, he deserved to be re-elected (Sun & Johnson, 2014). Obama's campaign rhetoric is focused on three words, 'jobs, jobs and jobs', seen as the exchange of jobs for votes. The second exchange process, shown in the middle of Figure 23.1, deals with the GPM for governance after the general election and for exchanges among the current administrative body, the legislation of Congress and the supervision of justice departments, which include all the political stockholders from government leaders, public servants, to members of Congress and senators, to citizens and interest groups. The 'Permanent Campaign' is for policy promotion, promise delivery, legislation, supervision and government-related functions. For example, the Obama Administration in 2009 and 2013 launched political marketing campaign to promote social policy on universal medical coverage, government fiscal policy on budgetary increase and taxation policy on eliminating tax holidays for big corporates, all

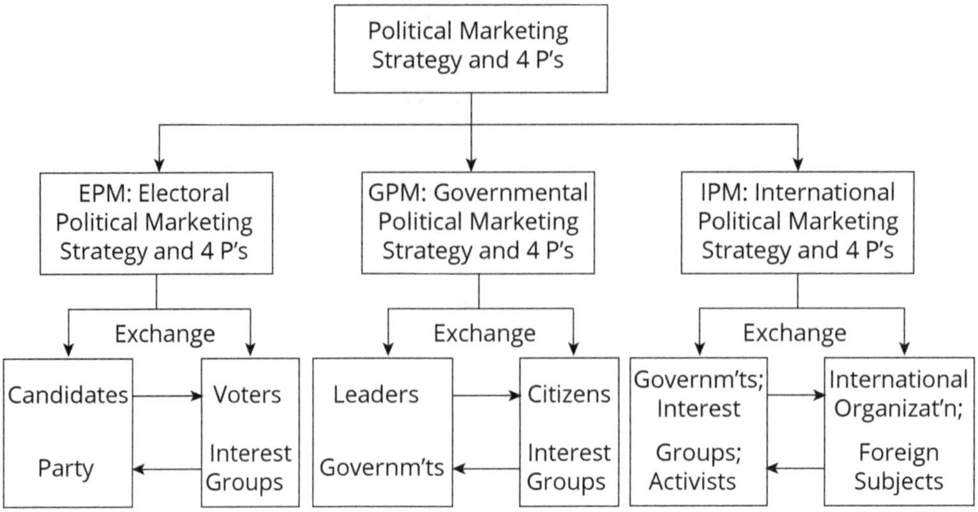

Figure 23.1 'Triadic Model of Political Marketing'
Source: Sun (2008)

of which can be viewed as part of the governmental power exchange. The last part of the political marketing model, shown on the right side of Figure 23.1, describes International Political Marketing as cross-culture and cross-border political exchange with different environments with different players and even different rules. However, as part of the general model, it shares the same political marketing values and principles, that is, soft power and national brand, polls and promotions with stockholders at a national level in the world arena. International political marketing is the third dimension of political marketing, commonly practised and studied in international relations. For example, when Obama ratified the trade agreement on the Trans-Pacific Partnership (TPP), the international political exchange was strategically sound 'but encountered Congressional resistance in the face of rising populist pressures at home' (Nye, 2020, p. 164). Foreign policy is a unique aspect of the model of political marketing extended to the international arena with a complete view of the power exchange process. In today's globalised society, any domestic policy will affect the international agenda, such as global warming, trade and development, pandemics and anti-terrorism, which will impact the citizens and interest groups in all related countries.

The three sets of political exchanges, in EPM, GPM and IPM, are interrelated in three dimensions of political marketing. The GPM and IPM will continue the EPM in the presidential election in the new administration through permanent campaigns, which are the political exchanges where the voters cash in with policy promises made by the candidates. EPM and GPM should be consistent for the incumbent party and its government. According to political science theory, foreign policy serves the incumbent party's general political agenda; thus, GPM and IPM should also work together because IPM is the cross-border and cross-culture political exchange of GPM. They have the same permanent campaign goal for the party or candidates to keep their promises to voters and to win their re-election. Brexit is a perfect example for the cross-sectional study of international political marketing, as the Conservative Party promoted their agenda through all three aspects of political marketing: EPM and GPM for citizens and interest groups of the U.K., and IPM for the 27 countries of European Union during the entire political exchange process.

In 2007, the term 'International Political Marketing' was defined by Henry Sun at the 4th International Political Marketing Conference, based on the interdisciplinary studies of Public Affairs, Political Marketing, Political Communication, International Relations and International Marketing. He suggested:

- International Political Marketing seeks to establish, maintain and enhance long-term relations among nation-states, political actors and organisations to meet the stakeholders' objectives. This is done through political exchanges and the fulfilment of promises through cross-border and cross-culture marketing strategies and management.

This definition reflects the interdisciplinary nature of international political marketing (Sun & Harris, 2022, p. 1221). Like the concept of international political communication defined by scholars of political communication, the study of international political marketing can be viewed as part of the global transformation in both practical and academic fields (McNair, 2018). Similarly, transformation is seen from political marketing to international political marketing in the trend of globalisation when the practitioners are calling for theoretical answers for international expansion, like the development of marketing into international marketing in the 1980s. There are comparative studies of political marketing in different countries, such as the edited book on Global Political Marketing (Lee-Marshment & et al, 2009) and the cross-culture study of voter behaviour (Cwalina et al., 2008). However, the study of cross-border election political marketing should be distinguished from foreign interference in elections, such as in the case of Trump's impeachment in 2019 and other social media-related EPM cases. With the classification of the three dimensions in the Triadic Political Marketing Model, the relationship between EPM and IPM can be studied for elections within one country or the election in an international organisation such as the UN, EU, G20 and BRICS, and the soft power-wielding and promoting as discussed previously. Under this triadic model of EPM, GPM and IPM, the management of international political marketing can be studied, and the relationship between international political marketing and soft power can be explained.

Harvard professor Tony Saich states, 'Traditional studies of international political communication have not had the exchange of power and the processes through which this happens at its core. Political marketing focuses on this exchange process, which will significantly influence the power to lead' (Sun & Zhao, 2011, p. 11). This statement points out the need to study the exchange process in international political marketing and the application of soft power. The following model explains the relationship between international political marketing and soft power.

Figure 23.2 is a Model of International Political Marketing and soft Power, which illustrates the relationship between the two interacting concepts. According to this model, any organisation can form international political marketing strategies with the Art of Media to manage the International Political Marketing Mix of 4 P's: Product of soft power, Place in the global markets, Promotion through all media and Polls on soft power ranking.

As David Haigh, the CEO of Brand Finance, states, 'In a world where power is increasingly defined by intangible factors such as reputation, influence, and values, Soft Power has become an essential tool for achieving strategic objectives and promoting international cooperation' (Brand Finance, 2024). According to the soft power indexes, the product of soft power can be studied as the basis and result of international political marketing. Soft power is, on the one hand, a wielding tool which impacts the negotiation power in the political exchange through its attraction and persuasion, and on the other hand, as a result of the promotion through international political marketing, just like the domestic election polls can be analysed as both a base and a result of an election campaign. The Place of globalised political market consists of interest groups, nation-states and international organisations, such as the UN, EU, G20 and BRICS, and the bilateral and multilateral relations among nation-states and international organisations, such as the relations between the US and the UK, and the relations among NATO countries and the WHO member states. The poll ranking is the feedback on the efficiency of international political marketing and the impact on soft power. Poll has a similar function to 'Price' in the 4P's matrix of commercial marketing. Although the effect of soft power can be witnessed over the long term, some ranking results can show up on the annual Soft Power Index in the year right after an international event takes place, such as hosting the Olympic Games, overcoming a pandemic like COVID-19 and the negative impact of launching a war. Promotion is through conventional media outlets and social media through the internet. It is essential to have the right IPM strategy, or the Art of Media, for political marketing in the digitalisation and globalisation markets with big data, OpenAI and other media technologies, especially in dealing with misinformation and fake news.

Sun Zi: The Art of Media is a set of strategies for international political marketing consists of the ancient war strategy of Sun Tzu: The Art of War, the principles of political propaganda by Sun Yat-sen, and modern sciences and technology

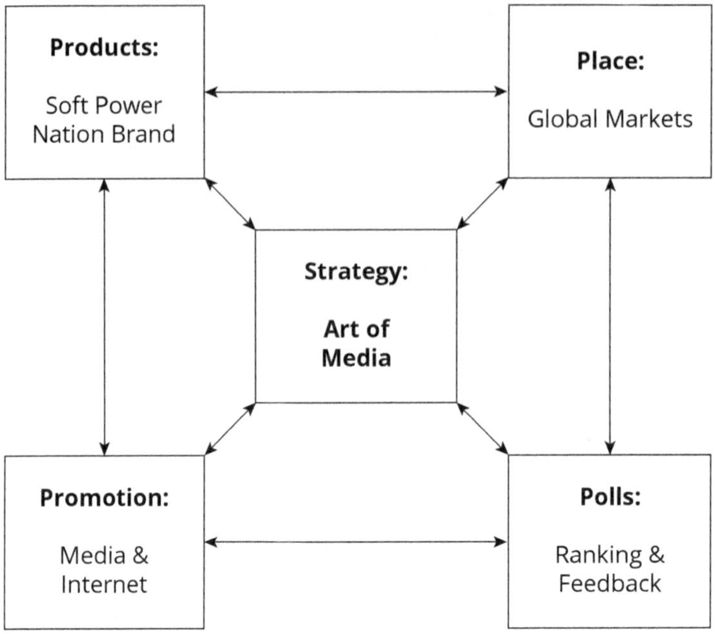

Figure 23.2 Model of International Political Marketing and Soft Power

Source: Sun (2008).

such as communication psychology and political choice behaviour, big data, AI and social media. The centrepiece of the IPM model is the Art of Media, which is the strategy for domestic and international political marketing. Besides political marketing research and study, the Art of Media can be a practical management function for constructing soft power as a product, evaluating the poll of the soft power index, selecting political marketplaces and wielding soft power through international political marketing promotion. According to Nye's power theory, soft power application can be affected by hard power in both positive and negative ways. The combination of hard and soft power, or smart power, will also fit into the discussion of the above model of The Art of Media strategies.

The IPM & Soft Power Model can also be an analytic tool for the result of international political marketing – soft power ranking – the goal of attraction and persuasion of political marketing. In his book *Power in the Global Information Age*, Joe Ney analyses the US foreign policy through the information revolution post-Cold War (Nye, 2004b). Globalisation and digitalisation provide both the opportunity to access social media and world affairs and the threat of misinformation and fake news. Similarly, Bruce Newman once pointed out that the rapid growth of the internet and the communication infrastructure has made political marketing a tool for politicians, political parties, interest groups and even governments worldwide (Zhao & Sun, 2008). With advanced communication technology, soft power and international political marketing interact more closely through the internet. The International Political Marketing Mix makes soft power much more efficient. Nation-states and interest groups set up their websites as a new marketplace to Promote two-way political exchanges: soft power Products with Polls for public opinion feedback.

Globalisation and digitalisation allow everyone with internet access to become a publisher, join the political exchange process and maintain the desired political relations through big data, social media and AI technology. In 2023, ChatGPT – Chat Generative Pre-Trained Transformer – had over 100 million live accounts in a month and became the fastest-growing app. On 4 February 2023, Israeli President Isaac Herzog made a speech partially written by AI and became the first world leader who publicly utilised ChatGPT. On 7 July 2023, the world's first robot-only press conference was held in Geneva on the sidelines of the United Nations AI for Good

Global Summit. Eight humanoid robots answered questions from journalists on the future of AI and their coexistence with humans. One of them, 'Sophia' said, 'I believe humans and AI working together can create synergy: AI can provide unbiased data while humans can provide the emotion, intelligence, and creativity to make the best decision. Together, we can achieve great things'. In other words, humans have the power and the strategy to make the best decision with unbiased data. Thus, the Art of Media strategies will lead to the right decision to handle social media, promote political agenda, increase soft power ranking, deal with misinformation and fake news and even win a media war.

REFERENCES

Brand Finance. (2024, February 29). *Brand Finance's Global Soft Power Index 2024: USA and UK ranked top nation brands, China takes third place, overtaking Japan and Germany*. Brand Finance. https://brandfinance.com/press-releases/brand-finances-global-soft-power-index-2024-usa-and-uk-ranked-top-nation-brands-china-takes-third-place-overtaking-japan-and-germany

Cwalina, W., Falkowski, A., & Newman, B. I. (2008). *A cross-cultural theory of voter behaviour*. Haworth Press/Taylor & Francis Group.

Confucius, 479 BC. (2008). In Ding, W. D. (Ed.), *Sayings of confucius* (English Chinese ed, p. 3). China Translation Corporation.

Giles, L. (1910). *Sun Tzu, 496 BC, the art of war*. Chapter 3.

Harris, P., & Sun, H. (2017). The ends justify the means: A global research agenda for political marketing and public affairs. *Journal of Public Affairs*, *17*, 1–9.

Henneberg, S. (2002). Understanding political marketing. In N. O'Shaughnessy, & S. Henneberg (Eds.), *The idea of political marketing* (pp. 93–171). Praeger.

Keohane, R. O., & Nye, J. S. (1977). *Power and independence: World Politics in transition*. Little Brown Company.

Lao Tzu, 630 BC. (1988). *Tao Te Ching: A new English version, with foreword and notes by Stephen Mitchell*. Macmillan. (Chapter 17).

Lee-Marshment, J., Rudd, C., & Strömbäck, J. (2009). *Global political marketing*. Routledge.

Lim, A., & Lees-Marshment, J. (2022). *International political marketing and advocacy*. The Palgrave Encyclopedia of Interest Groups, Lobbying and Public Affairs.

Machiavelli. (1513). *The prince*. Chapter VII.

McNair, B. (2018). *An introduction to political communication* (6th ed.). Routledge.

Nye, J. (1990). *Bond to lead: The changing nature of American power* (pp. 31). Basic Books.

Nye, J. (2004a). *Soft power: The means to success in the world of politics* (Vol. XII, p. 11). Public Affairs.

Nye, J. (2004b). *Power in the global information Age*. Routledge.

Nye, J. (2008). *Power to lead* (Vol. 125, p. 5). Oxford University Press.

Nye, J. (2020). *Do morals matter? Presidents and foreign policy from FDR to trump*. Oxford University Press. 179, 173, 171, 164.

Nye Jr., J. S. (2019). Soft power and the public diplomacy revisited. *The Hague Journal of Diplomacy*, 14.

Ormrod, R. P., Henneberg, S. C. M., & O'Shaughnessy, N. J. (2013). *Political marketing theory and concepts*. SAGE Publications.

Portland. (2019). *Soft power 30*. https://softpower30.com/

Sun, H. (2007). International political marketing: A case study of its application in China. *Journal of Public Affairs*, *7*(4), 331–340.

Sun, H. (2008). Political marketing, In S. Z. Wu & M. Sheng (Eds) *Marketing, (Chinese textbook)* (pp. 368–376, Chapter 18). Tsinghua University Press.

Sun, H. (2008). International political marketing: A case study of United States soft power and public diplomacy. *Journal of Public Affairs*, *8*(3), 165–183.

Sun, H. (2020). Mao's art of propaganda. *Journal of Public Affairs*, *20*.

Sun, H. (1990). Chinese markets and products. In L. Chimerine, K. Matsumoto, & R. F. Cushman (Eds.), *Practices business opportunities in the far east: The complete reference guide to practices and procedures* (pp. 523–536). Dow-Jones Irvin.

Sun, H., & Harris, P. (2022). *Soft power and international political marketing*. The Palgrave Encyclopedia of Interest Groups, Lobbying and Public Affairs.

Sun, H., & Johnson, D. (2014). Jobs, and the economy: Campaign rhetoric and reality. In D. Johnson (Ed). *From campaigning for president 2012, strategy and tactics*. Routledge.

Sun, H., & Zhao, K. J. (2011). *An Introduction to international political marketing* (pp. 5–12). Peking University Press.

Sun, T. (2002). *The art of war*. Grange Books.

Washington, G. (1796). In W. Irving (Ed.), *1876, Life of George Washington* (Vol. 2, p. 780). Putman's Sons.

Zhao, K. J., & Sun, H. (2008). *An introduction to political marketing* (pp. 1–4). Fudan University Press.

The Pandemic Olympics: Japan's COVID-19 Crisis Communications[1]

Nancy Snow

INTRODUCTION

On 5 May 2023, the head of the World Health Organization declared the end of COVID-19 as a global health emergency. This chapter is a critical case study of how Japan's government handled the coronavirus in 18 months before the Tokyo 2020 Summer Olympics took place from July 23 to 8 August 2021 (Snow, 2022). The coronavirus global health emergency held no national allegiance, but the perception battle to contain it and who was winning that perception war was primarily national as countries used the epidemic as a marker of their ability to manage cross-border conflicts.

Early on, the East Asian state of South Korea received almost universally high marks for its swift and aggressive response to test and track the spread of COVID-19 (Thompson, 2020). This helped to elevate perceptions about Japan's handling of the pandemic crisis through geographical proximity and a knowledge gap about the two countries' contrasting societies and approaches. The head of the World Health Organization told the world "to apply the lessons learned in Korea and elsewhere," (Kong, 2020) creating a spillover halo effect for its neighbor Japan. In a fall 2020 study commissioned by the Korea Economic Institute of America, Canada (68%), Japan (61%), and Australia (58%) were deemed by Americans as "very well" or "well" at handling COVID-19, ahead of South Korea that trailed all three at 54% (Kim, 2020).

In contrast to South Korea, Japan only revealed some of the reality of the coronavirus spread by documenting infection numbers. Instead, some observers said that Japan's higher cultural standards helped curtail widespread infection. "Japan's figures are relatively low, it has been suggested, because the country has a culture of cleanliness, including washing hands frequently, and people bow in formal situations instead of shaking hands and do not kiss cheeks to greet friends or family. Similarly, wearing a mask in public is a habit that has been widely practiced for over a century and appears to have its roots in religious festivals (Ryall, 2020b)." This mask diplomacy explanation was a primary factor in Japan's early containment success (Pereira, 2020).

A week after South Korea identified its first case, it coordinated a brain trust between government and medical companies to create test kits for general and cluster testing (Fisher & Sang-Hun, 2020). That, along with contact tracing and earning national emergency buy-in from the public, provided a practical three-pillar approach to containing the spread of infection. This country had a recent memory bank from battling primarily MERS (2015) and secondarily SARS (2002–2004) (DiMoia, 2020). It was primed for action. In comparison, Japan's memory bank reference was the deadly Spanish Flu (1918–1919), a century before that claimed millions of Japanese lives. The less stringent guidelines of mask-wearing and social isolation through avoiding crowds and closed spaces were similar to the response a century before (Ryall, 2020a). More recent memories recalled the run on hospitals for 2009 H1N1 influenza tests, so Japan's Ministry of Health, Labor and Welfare recommended limited access to testing except for the most severe cases. Otherwise, anyone infected with COVID-19 was told to recover at home (Suzuki, 2020b).

Former US Food and Drug Commissioner Scott Gottlieb was full of praise for South Korea's landscape testing plan, with 268,000 in the first five weeks.[2] In contrast, the Government of Japan downplayed testing, except for the worst symptomatic cases, which lulled its citizens into indifference. Japan delayed the declaration of its first state of emergency until April 2020, months after other countries were in various degrees of lockdown and quarantine. By this time, the Japanese people had lost support for the government's ability to lead, unlike in South Korea, where the public could voice its concern about losing some civil liberties while simultaneously showing a high degree of support for its full-throttle approach.

THE PARADOX OF JAPAN'S EARLY SUCCESS

Tuesday, 26 May 2020, in the United States, was the first day of national protests after George Floyd died in police custody the night before while handcuffed and with his neck pinned to the ground in Minneapolis, Minnesota. His dying words, "I can't breathe," would go on to spark a prairie fire of public protest and cries of Black Lives Matter across the United States and later the world (Buchanan et al., 2020). The social justice outrage that brought millions out onto the streets would also raise concerns that the COVID-19 pandemic had a new means of spreading during civil unrest (Associated Press, 2020a; Dave et al., 2020).

While the United States was in chaos and unrest from the streets to the White House, Japan appeared as an island nation of calm. On that same kick-off date of protests, the leading American public radio network, National Public Radio, led with "What Lies Behind Japan's Successful Management of the Pandemic," (Kuhn, 2020) a significant turnaround in tone and impression from just a few months earlier when the Diamond Princess cruise ship, "a precious gemstone on the seas of the world," where, "day or night, it's always an adventure," had come to be dubbed the world's largest floating petri dish (Hunt, 2020). Diamond Princess was becoming the new shorthand label to define Japan's crisis communications' mishandling of the coronavirus.

Prime Minister Shinzo Abe proclaimed: "We were able to contain the virus in a month and a half in a uniquely Japanese way. We showed the power of the Japanese model."[3] He added that hosting a "complete Tokyo Games" in 2021 would serve as "the symbol for victory of mankind against the novel coronavirus next summer (Obe & Okutsu, 2020)." *Foreign Policy* writer William Sposato described Japan's pandemic success as a mystery: "In its battle with the coronavirus, Japan appears to be doing everything wrong. It has tested just 0.185% of its population, its social distancing has been half-hearted, and a majority of Japanese are critical of the government's response. Yet with among the lowest death rates in the world, a medical system that has avoided an overloading crisis, and a declining number of cases, everything seems to be going weirdly right (Sposato, 2020)."

In hindsight, these early evaluations were premature and would underscore the overconfidence that marked the Abe administration's communication about handling the coronavirus. This pattern would continue with Abe's handpicked successor, Yoshihide Suga, who mimicked Abe's tone when he told the UN General Assembly, "Japan is determined to host the Tokyo Olympic and Paralympic Games as proof that humanity has defeated the pandemic. I will continue to spare no effort in order to welcome you to Games that are safe and secure."[4] This would come back to haunt the nation as questions about the safety and security of the Games grew with the reality of cancelled Olympic torch rallies, a new state of emergency, and the confirmation of a new virulent strain of the virus that was impacting both young and old (Yamaguchi, 2021). By Golden Week 2021 (April 29–May 5), with ninety days left before the Games, Japan's rate of complete vaccination stood at 0.8%, with 2.6% doses administered, the same as Laos (New York Times, 2021).

Japan's early credit for containing the virus spurred political hubris. The explanation was that the Abe administration acted swiftly to curtail the virus by striking a prudent balance between serving the economy and protecting the public. South Korea and Japan were given global extra credit as East Asian neighbors to China. They were seen as acting prudently since they were in the closest proximity to ground zero of the initial virus outbreak, despite how different their public health management methods were. South Korea's successful management of coronavirus was attributed to "blending technology and testing like no other country, centralized control and communication—and a constant fear of failure (Martin & Yoon, 2020)." The South Korean government focused on widespread testing and containing clusters through contact tracing. It took a publicly supported social surveillance approach with tracking apps, frequent mobile phone updates, and twice-daily press briefings. It was more of an all-hands-on-deck approach that Japan lacked with its soft lockdowns and social distance recommendations (Fendos, 2020).

Japan watchers like Jeff Kingston, Koichi Nakano, and this author shared that Japan's pandemic management pinged far different messages—lackadaisical in spirit, limited in scope, little in action, and late in the decision (Kingston, 2020; Nakano, 2020; Snow, 2020a). Abe shut down K-12 schools for a month from the end of February to the end of school holidays at the end of March 2020, which impacted nearly 13 million students and their families, but health experts argued that it wasn't long enough. The government called on the Japanese people to shelter in place and, when outside, to forgo large gatherings. After the first state of emergency was declared on 7 April 2020, Abe released a video showing him entertaining himself at home while watching TV, drinking tea, petting his dog, and listening to live music. His video, viewed nearly 20 million times in the first few weeks of its release, contained a benign message to the Japanese: "We can't see our friends or go out drinking. However, such actions are saving many lives and relieve the strain on health care professionals who are facing very challenging circumstances. Thanks to every single individual for their cooperation (Snow, 2020a)." The video seemed perplexing to many viewers, neither instructive nor confidence-boosting, if not condescending. Ostensibly, the Japanese people already knew what sheltering in place looked like. This and a country-wide distribution of child-size gauze masks per household sparked ridicule at home and abroad.

Japan's longest-serving prime minister seemed to be out of touch with personal hardships and unable to connect with the nation. As I wrote then, "If the Japanese government is going to come out of this with any credit, it does not just need tighter measures on public movement, though those would be welcome. It needs to rethink entirely how it communicates those measures and its attitudes to the public, or face its complacency worsening the problem (Snow, 2020a)." The abrupt change in daily life, including forcing stay-at-home mothers and some fathers to shelter at home with their school-age children, placed the public under great stress since workplace telecommuting options were not yet the norm. Single mothers fared the worst in the pandemic, just as the octogenarian former Japanese prime minister and Tokyo Olympic Chief Yoshiro Mori was complaining about female board members talking too much and taking up too much time. His controversial remarks led to his resignation (Joji, 2021). Working fathers, who customarily would spend time in *Nomenkai* (after-work drinking parties), were now spending more time at home with their wives, who weren't used to having their husbands and children "all the time (Kyodo News, 2020b)." Husbands were happier than their wives, while a considerable strain was placed on the family's social structure. Most Japanese homes did not have the space or the technology for online instruction or telecommuting. Nevertheless, the people followed the new guidelines, except for the cherry blossom period when they broke social distance warnings. And six weeks later, Abe declared that the virus was "contained." Abe's words would echo his close friend Donald J. Trump, who predicted that the coronavirus would go away on its own, first by Easter and then well before Election Day 2020 (BBC News, 2020).

FROM THE BEGINNING: A SO-CALLED "CHINA VIRUS" GOES GLOBAL

In mid-January of 2020, like so many expats do, I returned to my home country for what I thought would be a month-long stay before returning to East Asia to spend a semester teaching in Beijing, China, on leave from my university teaching in Japan. Upon landing, there was nothing in the news about COVID-19, certainly nothing alarming enough to make me think that I would be denied residence entry in China's capital city and remain at my home, teaching classes online. Within a week, a jaw-dropping announcement raised concern. On 23 January 2020, the Chinese government put in place a 76-day lockdown of the ninth-most populous city in China and expanded it to almost all of Hubei province (Associated Press, 2021). Wuhan, China, was now ground zero for a virus first recognized in mid-December 2019 when sick citizens showed up at Wuhan hospitals with flu-like symptoms. By the year's end, this novel virus had been sequenced similarly to the SARS virus from 2002 to 2003. Apart from some whistle-blowing health officials like Li Wenliang, the world did not pay much attention until the lockdown, and even then, it wasn't too worried. The World Health Organization and national governments reassured citizens that there was no outside threat from the China-based virus. This proverbial calm before the storm would extend well into February and part of March. For Japan, it had a growing problem off its shores, and the world's media was paying close attention.

THE SHIP AND THE STATE

In January 2020, Japan's Prime Minister Shinzo Abe was beginning the eighth year of his second term, soon to break the record for the longest-serving prime minister of the world's third-largest economy. It was the start of the ninth month of Reiwa ("beautiful harmony") that succeeded the Heisei era.[5] Japan was readying itself for Tokyo 2020. A record 31.9 million international visitors visited Japan in 2019, and government targets of 40 million were expected in 2020 (Nippon, 2020). Under what we called Abe 2.0, Abe's second term as prime minister, Japan had taken on a more global footprint with confidence and assuredness, what the prime minister referred to as *chikyushugi o fukansuru gaiko*, translated as a "proactive contribution to peace with international principle (Tatsumi, 2020)." While it remained a vassal security state of the United States, Japan was finding its unique voice separate from the U.S., particularly in regions where the U.S. is not seen as a neutral mediator. Abe traveled to the Middle East from January 11th to the 15th, 2020, at a time of heightened tension after the U.S. assassination of Iranian military commander Qasem Soleimani and Iran's downing of a Ukrainian commercial airliner. Abe couched the trip as personal peace diplomacy, underscoring how Japan viewed its global mission and national brand. "I hope to contribute to peace and stability in the region through diplomatic efforts to ease tensions (Agence France-Presse, 2020)" by "promoting dialogue, self-restraint and persistent peaceful diplomacy (Siripala, 2020)." Little did he know that shortly, the hotbed of tension would shift offshore to the Yokohama harbor, and his meeting with Crown Prince Mohammed bin Salman in Riyadh would look like relaxing afternoon tea.

The Diamond Princess[6] cruise ship, full of 2,600 passengers and 1,044 crew, departed Japan's main departure port for cruise ships on January 20th as part of a 14-day trip across north and southeast Asia. It sailed for two weeks with seven stops where passengers disembarked and boarded, including Hong Kong, where a man left the ship and tested positive for coronavirus within a week. On February 3rd, as the boat was returning to Yokohama, passengers were notified of the infected ship passenger and were told that their disembarkation in Japan would be delayed. The ship would soon garner global headlines as it became the largest cluster of positive coronavirus cases outside mainland China, and passengers were forced to remain in quarantine for 14 days. Very soon, a contrast in management emerged.

Abe did not approach these quarantined passengers with the same zeal for peaceful resolution as he had in the Middle East. The virus went on to infect nearly 700 passengers and crew, killing 13. The *New York Times* called Abe a political Houdini. "For nearly a month, as the coronavirus has threatened the health and economy of Japan, Prime Minister Shinzo Abe has been almost invisible (Dooley & Abe, 2020)." He did not hold his first news conference on coronavirus until the end of February, and even then, the government pre-approved the questions. By now, social media was helping to drive down Abe's approval numbers into the 30s with more than a million tweets calling for his resignation (Dooley & Abe, 2020). I noted in my column for *Nikkei Asia* in February 2020, "The Japanese government, for some reason, has a communication problem regarding the coronavirus. Just when it should be leading, it is staying silent (Snow, 2020c)." Part of the silence concerned the government's fumbled effort to delink the coronavirus numbers on the offshore Diamond Princess from mainland Japan. It did not know if passengers should remain onboard or be brought into Japan. The result was a public relations debacle whereby the floating petri dish became the label that stuck, and the Abe administration's response was seen as too little, too late from a political leader who seemed to have been caught flat-footed (Swift & Sieg, 2020). A new COVID-19-Map tracking system at Johns Hopkins University[7] to compare the country-to-country infection spread of COVID-19 integrated the Diamond Princess coronavirus numbers with mainland Japan so that by the end of February, news wires were reporting Japan with 890 cases, "including 705 from a quarantined cruise ship (Associated Press, 2020b)."

THE JAPAN MODEL: LOCKDOWN LITE, MINIMIZE TESTING

Japan is an example of an East Asian country that relied much on its self-image of exceptionalism to manage COVID-19. From the start, the government elected to keep testing to a minimum, only for those who were highly symptomatic and showing signs of flu or pneumonia, so as not to overwhelm the medical system. Public health analysts expressed concern, but outside of expressing their worries in the media, they failed to persuade the government to change this policy significantly. The head-in-the-sand syndrome seemed dominant, especially since COVID-19 mortality rates were low. An April 2020 Keio University Hospital survey showed that 6% of hospital patients being treated for non-COVID-19-related illnesses and procedures were testing positive for COVID-19, suggesting that widespread community transmission was already happening and that numbers of infected could be 20 to 50 times higher than official numbers, but without widespread testing these projections were speculative (Wingfield-Hayes, 2020).

Abe's May 2020 proclamation that Japan had successfully contained the virus was undoubtedly influenced by a widely distributed op-ed published in April by Kazuto Suzuki, a professor of international politics at the Public Policy School, Hokkaido University. Suzuki argued in favor of the success of the Japanese model in handling the coronavirus. His motivation was that "this Japan model has not been well understood, with the result that reports in overseas media have been erroneous, generating misunderstanding (Suzuki, 2020a)." The praising tone and its swipe at international media set the right tone for a government still reeling from the global pile-on of negative scrutiny about the Diamond Princess. But it was a sign that the Government of Japan would continue to remain a cultural and political exception nation in managing its pandemic. The "testing, testing, testing" scientific model of managing COVID-19 was not the Japanese government's approach. Japan chose its way or, as the *New York Times* put it, "had other ideas (Dooley & Inoue, 2020)." It preferred limited contact tracing and building on the longtime reputation of the Japanese to conform and practice reciprocal courtesies socially (Lee, 2020). Behavioral adherence like mask-wearing, maintaining a safe social distance, and limiting interaction in crowded places such as elevators and trains seemed much easier to follow in a place where few would object based on civil liberties or restrictions on human rights. Even the typical bowing greeting gesture over hugs and handshakes was said to give a comparative advantage to the Japanese, as did the laudatory hygienic habits of cleanliness, frequent bathing, and hand washing (Powell & Cabello, 2019).

The Japan Model of limited testing was not what epidemiologists recommended or what East Asian neighboring countries like South Korea, China, and Taiwan were practicing. In Wuhan, China, there were three times as many tests in one day than what the entire country of Japan tested nationwide between February and May 2020 (Powell & Cabello, 2019). The comparable success of Japan's model, Harvard's Andrew Gordon called a "soft approach to COVID-19," (Gordon, 2020) did not require a draconian lockdown like in China or too much public health intervention like the drive-through testing sites in South Korea. Keeping testing to a minimum shifted responsibility almost solely to the people to practice good public health sensibly and responsibly. This did not bode well for a sense of trust-building between the people and government as the people felt like they were sharing more than their share of the burden. At the same time, officials violated state of emergency protocols with group dining and karaoke outings.[8]

WHEN TOKYO 2020 BECAME CORONA 2020

March 11 (aka 3/11) is a date seared in the memories of all Japanese as it represents a day of infamy known as the triple disaster earthquake, tsunami, and Fukushima-Daiichi nuclear reactor meltdown. For the world, 11 March 2020, became a new date that will live in infamy. A global virus with no known cure or vaccine was the new normal for the foreseeable and uncertain future (Hanks, 2021). The World Health Organization Director-General Tedros Adhanom declared COVID-19 a global coronavirus pandemic. "If countries detect, test, treat, isolate, trace, and mobilize their people in the response, those with a handful of cases can prevent those cases becoming clusters, and those clusters becoming community transmission," said Tedros. He concluded his remarks with a Five Ps [9] response to coronavirus:

> Prevention. Preparedness. Public health. Political leadership. And most of all, people.

Throughout February and March 2020, most Olympic observers publicly supported holding Tokyo 2020 on schedule. The Japanese leadership, from Tokyo's Governor Koike to Diet members and Abe's Cabinet, said so. Abe had not even addressed the press about the government's response to the coronavirus until the 29th of February. From my perch in the United States, 11 March 2020, changed everything since it coincided with turning out the lights on sports and entertainment (Wamsley, 2020). The National Basketball Association announced on Twitter that day: "The NBA is suspending game play following the conclusion of tonight's schedule of games until further notice. The NBA will use this hiatus to determine next steps for moving forward in regard to the coronavirus pandemic." The day after, Tokyo Gov. Tokyo Metropolitan Governor Yuriko Koike said that Tokyo 2020 "cancellation is not an option."[10] Two weeks later, the Summer Olympics would be postponed to 2021.

The Abe government needed to respond to a crisis that had taken hold across all public venues where people gathered. How could Japan possibly think it was business as usual to stage an international competition and host up to 15,000 of the world's greatest athletes and hundreds of thousands of their fans sitting in stadiums and cheering them along the streets? On 3/11/20, the World Health Organization notified the global community that despite hope for containment in China, COVID-19 was on the move. The global health organization had hesitated to designate the virus as a pandemic out of fear of causing public panic, but Japan seemed to have had no such panic.

An entire month earlier, in February 2020, the inevitable Summer Olympics cancellation-in-waiting played out aboard the Diamond Princess. In mid-March, the Government of Japan was well past putting off the inevitable. Its crisis communications strategy was now playing out like a theater of the absurd. The longer the cancellation announcement loomed above like an invisible cloud, the worse it marked Japan's political leadership in public health. Japan is world-renowned for its technology and science prowess but was left wanting to take the lead in pandemic crisis decision-making.

The payoff in Japan's early coronavirus success had negative fallout. First, the Japanese public was not on board with the Abe administration's overall virus management. It wasn't just the slow response to the Diamond Princess but also a sense that the government favored staging the Tokyo 2020 Olympics at all costs to save the Japanese economy and face in the eyes of the world. Postponement seemed out of the question well into March. Even the National Basketball Association acted swifter than the Japanese government when it immediately shut down the 2019-2020 season on March 11th after one of its players tested positive. Japan passed two stimulus relief packages amounting to 40% of Japan's GDP. Despite that enormous economic relief of 234 trillion yen (US$ 2.2 trillion), nearly two-thirds of the public disapproved of the government's leadership during the crisis. Putting aside coronavirus numbers, there was a sense that the economy and the Olympics mattered a lot more than people's suffering. In a May 2020 op-ed for *Nikkei Asia*, "Japan's government gets no credit for coronavirus response," (Snow, 2020b) I explained why negative public opinion in Japan was on the rise despite no virus surge at the time:

> Why aren't the Japanese people giving the government much credit for the coronavirus? The early surge did not happen as the government suggested it would. Meanwhile the Diamond Princess, once dubbed a quarantine debacle for the slow and silent Japanese government response, left Yokohama Port for Malaysia. But recent memories lingered. Abe's derided shelter-in-place video was one. The Abenomasks delivered to every household was another. Neither efforts to show that the government cared could cover up the reality that the government had failed connecting with the people in its early handling of the virus. It seemed focused on saving the economy more.

The public knew better. Those deserving of any credit were in medical facilities and research labs, not government corridors. This may explain why The Economist research unit ranked Japan fair to poor in its management skills, (Jiji News Wire, 2020) while a 23-nation survey gave Japan the lowest marks in its coronavirus management skills as seen through the eyes of its citizens (Gilchrist, 2020). Shinzo Abe was one of a few country leaders whose approval rating had declined as coronavirus numbers declined or remained low. One might imagine the opposite to happen. Japan was doing relatively well in its COVID-19 outcomes compared to the rest of the world, but the government was not credited for these outcomes.

The Japanese public expected an understanding government that showed sensitivity to the economic misery that partnered with the pandemic. As misery increased, including a rise in suicides (Wingfield-Hayes, 2021), especially among women, the government's approval ratings became more fleeting.

QUESTIONING THE JAPAN MODEL

In this chapter, I've laid out the missteps of the Government of Japan related to the crisis communications handling of the coronavirus. Missteps were to be expected at the beginning when Japan, like any other country, was facing an unexpected new virus. No one could have predicted that COVID-19 would have swift and devastating consequences on the country's political economy, society, and ability to stage the most prominent global international sports competition. Throughout the crisis, analysts wondered aloud if Japan's low numbers resulted from government leadership or just plain luck. A headline in the *New York Times* questioned if its perceived early success would vanish in time (Rich & Ueno, 2020). Sociologist David H. Slater stated the same lack of consensus about luck vs. good management:

> Few say with any certainty that the relatively mild effects have resulted from planning or systematically executed precautions and mitigation efforts by government agencies. Japan has lucked out for reasons we may never fully understand. The political narrative might shift in time from one of "lucked out" to "well-managed," (especially as mismanagement of the virus continues in much larger countries such as the United States, India and Brazil, for example) but as yet, no one has taken credit for a job well done. (Slater, 2020)

I conclude that expected missteps at the beginning needed to be corrected, and political leadership needed to be improved. With the resignation of Shinzo Abe in September 2020, Abe's successor, Yoshihide Suga, government's slow-moving consensus-driven model took over from individual voices like that of Tokyo's Governor Yuriko Koike, who received praise early on for holding both Japanese and English language news conferences and expressing caution (The Asahi Shimbun, 2021). Ultimately, it was the myopia over hosting the Olympic Games that derailed Japan's effective handling of the coronavirus, along with a host of other communication problems, including sexism. I laid out these hurdles in a February 2021 email to a professional colleague and friend whose global PR firm advises the Japanese government:

> I'm sure you are busy with the coronavirus task force. I must say that I remain disappointed with the rollout of the vaccine, the silencing of women (who talk too much!) and the government's handling of the second state of emergency (too late after Go To Travel campaign). Japan's communications platform needs a reboot—better spokespeople not based on seniority but ability to persuade, equal footing for men and women, and a sense of urgency. I'm afraid that the slow vaccine rollout is going to negatively impact the hosting of the Olympics. (Snow, 2020c)

Closely related to the Olympic Games mismanagement, the Government of Japan was shortsighted in not allowing the science, health, and welfare community to direct public policy. It was also irresponsible not to communicate consistent policies that were easy to follow. The behavioral-driven "Three C's" approach placed the responsibility for infection squarely on the Japanese people. Still, it needed to be balanced with the government's effort to accurately communicate rates of illness as well as their cluster sites. Infectious disease experts expressed concern with the limited emergency and minimal testing policies employed by the government to reduce the infection rate. Even though the Abe administration quickly shut down schools, this early move was temporary and unpopular with the public. There was no additional domestic muscular policy except for an external international travel ban that held foreigners responsible for the spread of coronavirus.

After Abe stepped down in September 2020, the Suga administration was known more for encouraging a false sense of domestic tranquility and security by encouraging Japanese to travel the country and eat out in restaurants through the now-debunked Go To Travel and Go To Eat Campaigns. Those countries that received the most international praise for managing the spread of the infection chose to control the virus by acting swiftly and severely. The philosophy was to go at COVID-19 with everything the country had in lockdown capabilities and to communicate to the public that a painful process at the beginning would pay off. When the numbers decreased, then so would the shutdown measures. Japan went about the process backward. It enacted stop-and-start measures while utilizing catch-up and Whac-A-Mole-style strategies to see what worked the best. Nothing seemed consistent, and yet Japan held its own in a summer 2020 Pew survey ranking of the countries where it managed the coronavirus better than others compared to the United States and the United Kingdom (Wood, 2020).

Shinzo Abe's highly touted contact tracing app COCOA became a "miss app" when a government audit found it full of problems and never updated for four months. A *Mainichi* editorial said, "Former Prime Minister Shinzo Abe billed COCOA as the ace in Japan's infection control measures. The government bears a heavy responsibility for failing to arrange the necessary systems for the app to function properly (The Mainichi, 2021)." The question of who's in charge or is anyone in charge approach to the virus seemed closely linked to improving Japan's readiness before hosting the postponed Olympics.

The Government of Japan's global reputation and image was fully invested in holding the postponed Games, despite consistently low public support (Nakano, 2021), cancelled torch rallies (Reuters, 2021), vaccine readiness (CBS News this Morning, 2021), volunteers, or spectators. Ultimately, the Games served as a dress rehearsal for Japan's ability to reopen to the world. As a third state of emergency went into effect on 25 April 2021, Tokyo 2020 President Seiko Hashimoto said that the Summer Olympics would signify that Japan is back...again. "If the government can carry off the Games, that means the government is ready to welcome back other people as well. It is part of a broader effort to open Japan." Even though Olympic athletes were not required to quarantine for 14 days after arriving in Japan and vaccines were not mandatory, daily testing was enacted for safety reasons, except for volunteers. By the end of April 2021, Tokyo Olympics chief Hashimoto announced that Japan would postpone allowing domestic fans until June, when a final COVID-19 playbook would be issued (Fukue & McKirdy, 2021). In the end, fans were banned, except for government officials and corporate sponsors.

Just months away from the Olympics, a familiar voice from Canada reemerged to ask questions about the feasibility of staging this postponed international competition. Global infection rates continue to decimate populations overseas. Six-time Canadian Olympian and doctor-in-training Hayley Wickenheiser became world famous on 17 March 2020, when she tweeted that the pandemic crisis was bigger than the Olympics and that the IOC insisting that it would move ahead was "insensitive" and "irresponsible (O'Connor, 2020)." Within a week, the Canadian Olympic Committee announced that it would not be sending a team to Tokyo 2020, and on 24 March 2020, the Olympics and Paralympics were finally postponed after much insistence to the contrary from Shinzo Abe and the IOC. In April 2021, Wickenheiser stepped forward again. Sounding a tone similar to the growing editorials inside Japan, she declared that the decision to hold the Games "needs to be made by medical and health experts, not by corporate and big business. A clear and transparent explanation needs to be given if the Games will go ahead (Heroux, 2021b)." She explained her stance against the tide of hosting inevitability:

> I have to ask the questions. And I think they're fair questions. Prior to the pandemic I said there's no way the Olympics can go ahead because history told us there was no way they could. And now I'm saying I don't know, I wonder if they can again.

Strategically speaking, Japan's government boxed itself in with its final decision to proceed with the postponed Olympics. The International Olympic Committee squarely placed the burden for COVID-19 success on the backs of the Tokyo 2020 hosts with an attitude of "You wanted it. You got it." IOC vice-president John Coates said: "The responsibility for the response to COVID-19 during, before and after the games lies with the Japanese government, and to a lesser extent with the Tokyo city government (Wade, 2021)."

Foreign and domestic media institutions and global experts united their voices in opposition to the Olympics' inevitability while the pandemic raged worldwide. A *British Medical Journal* editorial called for reconsidering the Games in light of safety-first concerns. "Unlike other countries in the Asia-Pacific region, Japan has not yet contained COVID-19 transmission. Despite its poor performance, Japan still invokes exceptionalism and continues to conceptualize COVID-19 within previous planning for pandemic influenza (Shimizu et al., 2021)." The liberal *Asahi Shimbun* ran several staff editorials questioning the ability of the government to manage the Summer Olympics. "There is no end in sight to the scourge of the pandemic. The dire situation makes many people doubt whether the Tokyo Olympics and Paralympics can be held this summer as planned. Many are anxiously wondering if proceeding with the huge international event will only make things worse both at home and abroad. The Japanese government, the Tokyo metropolitan government, the Tokyo Olympic organizing committee, and the International Olympic Committee, however, remain adamantly determined to hold the competitions. They are showing little interest in offering sincere responses to reasonable concerns and questions among citizens (Asahi Shimbun, 2021b)." On 30 April 2021, Asahi Shimbun editorial pulled no punches: "Organizers and policymakers have often said the decision has been made to hold the event, and the only question is how to do it. But the situation no longer allows this argument. It is clearly time to make a tough-minded assessment of the viability of holding the event based on the cold reality (Asahi Shimbun, 2021a)." Dr Isaac Bogoch, an infectious diseases physician and a member of Ontario's COVID-19 vaccine task force, expressed doubts for a COVID-19-free Olympics. "If you have no mandatory quarantine and you're not mandating vaccinations, you wouldn't be surprised if there are outbreaks of COVID-19 (Heroux, 2021a)." The main problem remains a lack of vaccine readiness when most Japanese are vaccine-willing. Bloomberg Japan reported that "While vaccine hesitancy has been a key issue in Japan and other Asian countries where people are more wary of side effects, there are signs more residents are becoming willing. In late March, the Jiji news agency survey showed 79 percent of respondents wanted to take the COVID-19 jab. Another poll showed about two-thirds of people are getting impatient with the speed of the rollout."[11]

ABE'S LEGACY AND SUGA'S SUCCESSION

For years, the Abe government had been dedicated to improving Japan's image and reputation worldwide by monitoring international public opinion and correcting what it viewed as an overly critical foreign press agenda. However, it missed the fundamentals of leadership management in crisis: the government must display genuine empathy and compassion in times of uncertainty and insecurity. It cannot just advocate for transparency without a strategic plan.

A Kyodo News survey released in May 2020 reported that 84% of Japanese people felt insecure in their personal lives (Kyodo News, 2020a). This didn't begin with the pandemic but extended these feelings of discontent. More people were seeking household financial assistance while the government asked them to do more with less. The public was justified that the government seemed overly concerned with his political legacy. At the same time, the public is bearing the brunt of Japan's economic downturn. While Abe was not known as an empathic leader in the style of Prime Minister Jacinda Ardern of New Zealand (Blackwell & Andern, 2020), he or a designated point person could still have engaged in the role of helpful compatriot to overcoming personal misery, not as someone who was dedicated to maintaining his party's dominance or saving the economy. In February 2021, Abe's successor, Suga, announced the appointment of a new Minister of Loneliness to combat COVID-19-related suicides, but without a plan or strategy that could explain to the public what a difference this would make (Sheehy, 2021). Tetsushi Sakamoto, a cabinet member, was already tasked with advocating for an increase in female birthrates across Japan and half a dozen other political appointments.[12] With an increase of 880 female suicides in October 2020 alone, the appointment of a 70+-year-old man affiliated with the far-right nationalist *Nippon Kaigi* faction of the Liberal Democratic Party could very well have struck a puzzling tone to go along with Japan's mysterious early success in managing the pandemic.

There is no correlation between falling coronavirus numbers and improving personal incomes, not now or for the foreseeable future. In crisis times, leaders get painted, unfairly or not, in broad strokes. They are either helpers in common cause or obstructionists and self-preservationists. They are credited only when they help build confidence or unite a population behind a common cause. The problem for Japan in the pre-Olympics coronavirus period was the absence of a common cause of unity. At one time, the Tokyo Olympics was one cause. Still, even that was only partially supported by the public, and it had all but lost its appeal amid the ongoing pandemic and single-digit vaccination rates. The financial overlay associated with its staging was seen as a white elephant in these challenging times.

Abe, unlike Suga, was always quite effective at making persuasive appeals when he wanted to win something big. He won hosting the Olympics based on a personal pledge that the Fukushima-Daichi fallout would be "under control" in time for the international games. He needed to put that winning effort into appealing to the personal sacrifices of the people post-pandemic and pre-Games. This should have mattered to him more than his or his party's political survival. A healthy dosage of gratitude and humility, even acknowledging Japan's slow start in handling the pandemic, would have narrowed the credibility gap between the public and political leaders. Sadly, the former prime minister was assassinated on 8 July 2022, at age 67, never able to fully realize and reflect on his political management during his global statesman years.

The assassination of Shinzo Abe ended the life of a critical stakeholder in the longtime management of Japan's global image, from his winning the Summer Olympics bid in September 2013[13] to his health-related resignation in August 2020 (Rich & Abe, 2020). Abe's worldwide influence and legacy remain strong, even after his untimely death (Harris, 2022). However, in the immediate aftermath of his death, domestic public opinion shifted away from pandemic management to the LDP's and the Abe family's ties to the anti-communist Unification Church. Mari Yamaguchi, an Associated Press journalist based in Japan, explained the links between the dominant party and a political family dynasty that had ruled Japan for more than sixty years: "The ties between the church and Japan's governing party go back to

Abe's grandfather, Nobusuke Kishi, who served as prime minister and shared worries with Washington over the spread of communism in Japan in the 1960s as labor union activists gained strength (Yamaguchi, 2022)." Abe's assassin had proclaimed that he was motivated to hold political leaders like Abe responsible for his mother's having been bilked of her life savings through large donations for "spiritual merchandise" that promised salvation (Yamaguchi, 2022). Abe's campaigning for an LDP candidate in July 2022 was the highest profile target of his anger, which precipitated a motive for murder (Siripala, 2022).

CONCLUSIONS: POST-PANDEMIC OLYMPIC LESSONS

Many political marketing lessons can be learned from the Tokyo 2020 Olympics, and these lessons will be examined in due time. A few to share here are that a global pandemic is a superordinate distractor from bribery charges, at least in the immediate crisis period. To paraphrase, hindsight is the best disinfectant. Over time, dirt comes out in the wash, even for Japan, which maintains a top reputation ranking (Snow, 2023; Wade & Kageyama, 2023). As Wade and Kageyama reported about the laundering between sponsors and advertisers: "Dentsu has a long history of lining up sponsorships and advertising with bodies like World Athletics, headed by Sebastian Coe, and the Switzerland-based International Olympic Committee, led by Thomas Bach."[14] As of 2023, Dentsu, the largest advertising agency in Japan and the fifth largest advertising agency network in the world in terms of worldwide revenues was pushed out as an IOC broadcast partner in Asia (AP News, 2023).

French prosecutors first announced in 2019 that they were investigating allegations of tens of millions in bribes related to Tokyo's successful bid for the 2020 Olympics. The investigation centered around the bidding process of suspicious payments totaling $2 million to a Singaporean consulting firm linked to the son of a former influential International Olympic Committee (IOC) member. Reuters later revealed in April 2020 that "Haruyuki Takahashi, a former executive at the advertising agency Dentsu Inc, was paid $8.2 million (6.6 million pounds) by the committee that spearheaded Tokyo's bid for the 2020 Games, according to financial records reviewed by Reuters (Slodkowski et al., 2020)." That was only the beginning. Bribery scandals remain ongoing, with arrests and charges continuing. AP writer Yuri Kageyama explains the repercussions for Japan moving forward: "Japanese culture usually favors 'saving face', and embarrassment on the international stage tends to be avoided. The arrests are also likely a setback for Japan's ambitions in bidding for the 2030 Winter Olympics for Sapporo (Kageyama, 2022, 2023)."

Secondly, and in the final analysis, as someone who views political marketing from a strategic communications lens, I saw that the Japanese government needed to communicate more effectively with its foreign and domestic public about handling pandemic protocols. Even worse, as this chapter shows, it faced widespread media criticism for inconsistent messaging regarding safety protocols, audience restrictions, and the overall feasibility of holding the Games. Establishing clear communication channels and consistent messaging strategies to keep the public informed and maintain trust was essential, but a stakeholder-driven mission never materialized. Instead, collaborative decision-making was kept to a minimum and replaced by a top-down hierarchical structure. Coordination among various stakeholders, including the IOC, local authorities, and health experts, was essential but often challenging. Had the government directed a collaborative framework to ensure that all relevant parties could contribute to and agree on critical decisions swiftly and efficiently, it is less likely that the decision to proceed with the Olympics, albeit without spectators, would have had so many negative social implications.

Despite the critical reception that many of us living in Japan and observing from abroad had with the official management of the "pandemic Olympics" in summer 2021, the collective wisdom of health officials labeled the Games a success: "The effectiveness of various mitigation and control measures, including the availability of vaccines and the expansion of effective testing options, allowed event organizers and the Japanese Government to successfully host the rescheduled Tokyo 2020 Olympic Games from July 23 to August 8, 2021 with robust safety plans in place." This testimonial was published in the prestigious and authoritative medical journal *The Lancet* in early 2024, two and a half years after the Games. It includes a byline of twelve high-placed worldwide medical professionals (McCloskey et al., 2024). To be sure, despite the global health crisis, the Tokyo Olympics were successfully conducted with stringent health protocols, including regular testing, quarantine measures, and the absence of international spectators. This helped prevent major COVID-19 outbreaks among participants and staff. Financial costs were historically high, with the final cost double the initial estimate, making these pandemic Olympics the most expensive on record at $13 billion (Wade, 2022). Public sentiment in Japan was mixed, with considerable opposition to holding the Games amid a pandemic. Concerns about health risks and prioritizing the Olympics over local health needs were prominent, as was the social fallout of banning international and Japanese spectators but allowing corporate sponsors and IOC cronies to attend the Games. Likewise, the ongoing bribery scandal and pending charges involving the Tokyo Olympic organizing committee and various companies cast a shadow over the Games, raising questions about ethical standards and governance in the bidding and organization process.

The 2020 Tokyo Olympics will be viewed as a success in sporting achievements, effective health and safety management, and technological advancements. However, the Games were marred by significant financial costs, public opposition, and ethical concerns related to the bribery scandal. The overall success of the Tokyo Olympics thus depends on the perspective from which it is evaluated—whether focusing on athletic triumphs and operational management or considering the broader socioeconomic and ethical implications. I argue that we need the widest perspective to assess political marketing successes and failures fairly.

Notes

1 This paper covers the 100-day countdown before the postponed Tokyo Olympics and Paralympics. The author, a Japanese resident, advises the Japanese government on global strategic communications. A public diplomacy and propaganda scholar, she is an opinion writer for *Nikkei* and *Nikkei Asia*. Snow provides a critical political communications case study of the government of Japan's handling of the "pandemic Olympics" through global media coverage, her personal experience, and the lessons drawn after the Tokyo 2020 Summer Olympics (23 July 2021–8 August 2021).

2 Scott Gottlieb, MD, Twitter feed, 15 March 2020: "South Korea is showing #COVID-19 can be beat with smart, aggressive public health. Their daily new cases declined again to 76. They've tested 268,000 people for virus since their epidemic began and implemented aggressive containment and mitigation, closing schools, venues quickly."

3 Snow, op. cit.

4 *Address by Prime Minister Suga at the Seventy-Fifth Session of the United Nations General Assembly*, 26 September 2020.

5 Emperor Akihito 's elder son, Naruhito, ascended the Reiwa throne as the 126th Emperor of Japan on 1 May 2019. On 30 April 2019, Emperor Akihito abdicated the Chrysanthemum Throne, marking the end of the Heisei era.

6 *Diamond Princess cruise ship information*, Princess Cruises.

7 *COVID-19 Map*, Johns Hopkins Coronavirus Resource Center.

8 2,356 Osaka gov't workers in hot water for eating out late, in groups since March, *The Mainichi*, April 28.

9 WHO Director-General's opening remarks at the media briefing on COVID-19, 11 March 2020.

10 Tokyo governor says canceling Olympics "not an option," *Nikkei Asia* staff writers, 12 March 2020.

11 Bloomberg, Japan's slow COVID-19 vaccine roll-out pushes back recovery time frame, 12 April 2021. See also Half a million and counting — Japan's rollout of the COVID-19 vaccine, *Japan Times*, 24 March 2021. At that time Japan was being labeled an exception, with one of the slowest vaccine rollouts in Asia. Less than 1% of its population has been inoculated, nearly all of them medical workers. The general public might not get the vaccine until the end of the year.

12 Tetsushi Sakamoto, Wikipedia.

13 Press Conference by Prime Minister Shinzo Abe Following His Attendance at the G20 Summit Meeting in Saint Petersburg and the 125th International Olympic Committee Session, Saturday, 7 September 2013.

14 Wade and Kageyama, Tokyo Olympics sullied by bid-rigging.

REFERENCES

Agence France-Presse. (2020, January 11). Japan's Abe begins Gulf tour in Saudi Arabia amid tensions.

AP News. (2023, June 15). Facing Olympic corruption charges, Dentsu out as IOC broadcast partner in Asia.

Associated Press. (2021, January 22). *Timeline: China's COVID-19 outbreak and lockdown of Wuhan*.

Associated Press. (2020a, May 30). Cities fear George Floyd protests may fuel coronavirus spread. *Los Angeles Times*.

Associated Press. (2020b, February 27). *Japan to close all schools until the end of March due to the coronavirus*.

BBC News. (2020, March 25). Coronavirus: Trump hopes US will shake off pandemic by Easter.

BBC News. (2021, February 12). Yoshiro Mori: Tokyo Olympics chief steps down over sexism row.

Blackwell, G., & Ardern, J. (2020, May 31). Political leaders can be both empathetic and strong. *BBC News*.

Buchanan, L., Bui, Q., & Jugal, K. (2020, July 3). Patel, Black lives matter may be the largest movement in U.S. History. *New York Times*.

COVID-19 World Vaccination Tracker. (29 April 2021). *New York Times*.

Dave, D. M., Friedson, A. I., Matsuzawa, K., Sabia, J. J., & Safford, S. (June 2020/Revised January 2021). *Black lives matter protests and risk avoidance: The case of civil unrest during a pandemic*. Working Paper 27408. National Bureau of Economic Research.

DiMoia, J. (2020, May 4). Remembering MERS in South Korea: Mobilizing experience of epidemic disease. *Journal of the History of Ideas Think Piece*.

Dooley, B., & Abe, S. (2020, March 5). Japan's political Houdini, can't escape Coronavirus backlash. *New York Times*.

Dooley, B., & Inoue, M. (2020, May 29). Testing is key to beating Coronavirus, right? Japan has other ideas. *New York Times*.

EDITORIAL: It's time to make tough call on whether to stage Tokyo Olympics. (2021a, April 30). *Asahi Shimbun*.

EDITORIAL: Olympics must not be held at any cost by putting lives in jeopardy. (2021b, April 23). *Asahi Shimbun*.

Fendos, J. (2020, April 29). *How surveillance technology powered South Korea's COVID-19 response*. Brookings Institution TechStream.

Fisher, M., & Sang-Hun, C. (2020, March 23). How South Korea flattened the coronavirus curve. *New York Times*.

Fifty-seven percent discontent with Japan gov't response to coronavirus outbreak: Poll. (2020a, May 10). *Kyodo News*.

Fukue, N., & McKirdy, A. (2021, April 30). Tokyo Olympics could be held without fans: Games chief to AFP. *AFP*.

Gilchrist, K. (2020, May 6). China gets top score as citizens rank their governments' response to the coronavirus outbreak. *CNBC*.

Gordon, A. (2020, July 3). *Explaining Japan's soft approach to COVID-19*. Harvard University Weatherhead Center for International Affairs.

Hanks, T. (2021, March 11). The NBA, and COVID-19's day of reckoning in the US: An oral history. *Buzzfeed News*.

Harris, T. (2022, July 14). Why Shinzo Abe will continue to govern Japan for years after his death. *Time*.

Heroux, D. (2021a, April 21). Canadian expert doubts Tokyo can hold a COVID-19-free Olympics. *CBC Sports*.

Heroux, D. (2021b, April 23). Hayley Wickenheiser again sounds alarm, saying wrong people making decision on Olympic Games. *CBC Sports*.

Hunt, J. (2020, April 22). The coronavirus cruise: On board the diamond princess. *The Economist*.

Jiji News Wire. (2020, June 18). Japan's coronavirus response rated mediocre by Economist's research unit. *The Japan Times*.

Joji, M. (2021, February 12). Single mothers in the pandemic: Job loss, shrinking incomes, and scant support. *Nippon.com*.

Kageyama, Y. (2022, September 27). Tokyo Olympics bribery arrests widens to third Japan sponsor. *AP and Yahoo*.

Kageyama, Y. (2023, February 28). Dentsu and others charged in Tokyo Olympic bid-rigging probe. *AP*.

Kim, J. (2020, October 21). How do Americans view South Korea's COVID-19 response? *The Diplomat*.

Kingston, J. (2020, April 23). COVID-19 is a test for world leaders. So far, Japan's Abe is failing. *The Diplomat*.

Kong, L. (2020, March 31). Why South Korea should now be on every public policy & public health student's radar. *Study International*.

Koike requests pre-emergency measures, urges restraint on trips. (2021, April 8). *The Asahi Shimbun*.

Kuhn, A. (2020, May 26). *What lies behind Japan's successful management of the pandemic*. National Public Radio, All Things Considered.

Kyodo News. (2020b, July 25). Husbands happy, wives stressed over parenting during stay-home spell.

Lee, G. (2020, June 17). Is Japan's pandemic response a disaster or a success? *PBS Newshour*.

Martin, T. W., & Yoon, D. (2020, September 25). How South Korea successfully managed Coronavirus the country has blended technology and testing like no other. *Wall Street Journal*.

McCloskey, B., Saito, T., Shimada, S., Ikenoue, C., Endericks, T., Mullen, L., Mota, P., Kumar, C. K., Laxminarayan, R., Budgett, R., Heymann, D., & Zumla, A. (2024, January 17). The Tokyo 2020 and Beijing 2022 Olympic Games held during the COVID-19 pandemic: Planning, outcomes, and lessons learnt. *The Lancet*. https://doi.org/10.1016/S0140-6736(23)02635-1

Nakano, K. (2020, February 26). Japan can't handle the coronavirus. Can it host the Olympics? *New York Times*.

Nakano, K. (2021, March 25). The Tokyo Olympics are on! But why? *New York Times*.

New record for international visitors to Japan. (27 January 2020). Nippon.

O'Connor, J. (2020, March 24). Heroes of the pandemic: Hockey legend Hayley Wickenheiser on her Olympic-tweet heard round the world. *National Post*.

Obe, M., & Okutsu, A. (2020, May 25). Abe comes down on side of economy with decision to reopen Tokyo Prime minister stops short of stricter criteria for new coronavirus cases. *Nikkei Asia*.

Olympics-Torch relay on public roads cancelled in Okinawa's Miyakojima, *Reuters*, 2021, April 23.

Olympics organizers update COVID-19 rules to mitigate risk despite relatively low vaccination rates. (2021, April 28). *CBS News this Morning*.

Pereira, A. (2020, July 5). What mask use looks like in 10 countries compared to the U.S. *San Francisco Chronicle*.

Powell, S. J., & Cabello, A. M. (2019, October 7). What Japan can teach us about cleanliness. *BBC Travel*.

Rich, M., & Abe, S. (2020, August 28). Japan's longest-serving prime minister, resigns because of illness. *The New York Times*.

Rich, M., & Ueno, H. (2020, March 26). Japan's virus success has puzzled the world. Is its luck running out? *New York Times*. The subheading read: "The country has not widely tested. Its people are going about their lives, even crowding into clubs that had previous outbreaks. But now Japan is warning of the risk of rampant infection."

Ryall, J. (2020a, March 24). Avoid crowds, wear a mask and isolate: How Japan's coronavirus response echoes Spanish flu guidelines. *South China Morning Post*.

Ryall, J. (2020b, October 19). How Japan's mask culture may have saved lives from across the continent. *Deutsche Welle*.

Sheehy, K. (2021, February 22). Japan creates Minister of Loneliness to fight COVID-19 suicides. *New York Post*.

Shimizu, K., Sridhar, D., Taniguchi, K., & Shibuya, K. (2021, April 14). Reconsider this summer's Olympic and Paralympic games. *British Medical Journal*, *373*(962).

Siripala, T. (2020, January 13). Japan to the rescue: Can Abe defuse tensions in the Middle East? *The Diplomat*.

Siripala, T. (2022, September 15). Japan and the controversial unification church, in a post-Abe era, Japanese politics has been rocked by the unification church's links to LDP lawmakers. *The Diplomat*.

Slater, D. H. (2020, September 15). Vulnerable populations under COVID-19 in Japan: A lull in the storm? The Asia-Pacific. *Journal: Japan Focus*, *18*(18), 2.

Slodkowski, A., Layne, N., Saito, M., & Miyazaki, A. (2020, April 1). Exclusive: Japan businessman paid $8.2 million by Tokyo Olympics bid lobbied figure at centre of French corruption probe. *Reuters*.

Snow, N. (2020a, April 25). Abe's cheesy video highlights Japan's coronavirus PR failure. *Nikkei Asia*.

Snow, N. (2020b, May 25). Japan's government gets no credit for coronavirus response. *Nikkei Asia*.

Snow, N. (2020c, February 21). Japan's government has failed coronavirus communications test. *Nikkei Asia*.

Snow, N. (2022). Japan's strategic miscommunications: In the shadow of the pandemic Olympics. *Place Brand Public Diplomacy*. https://doi.org/10.1057/s41254-022-00259-1

Snow, N. (2023, December 24). Perceptions of Japan have never been better, but that is not enough. *Nikkei Asia*.

Sposato, W. (2020, May 14). Japan's mysterious pandemic success. *Foreign Policy*.

Suzuki, K. (2020a, April 24). COVID-19 Strategy: The Japan Model: Has Japan found a viable long-term strategy for the pandemic? *The Diplomat*.

Suzuki, K. (2020b, July 10). Japan's COVID-19 measures: Controlling the spread without lockdowns. *Nippon*.

Swift, R., & Sieg, L. (2020, March 18). Japan uses just a fraction of its coronavirus testing capacity. *Reuters*.

Tatsumi, Y. (2020, June 24). *Abe Shinzo: Diplomat-in-Chief* (Vol. 31). Korea Economic Institute of America, Joint US-Korea Academic Studies.

The Mainichi. (2021, April 20). Editorial: Japan gov't COVID-19 app fiasco typifies its chronic IT irresponsibility.

Thompson, D. (2020, May 6). What's behind South Korea's COVID-19 exceptionalism? *The Atlantic*.

Wade, S. (2021, April 19). Tokyo Olympics: Will Japanese Olympians be vaccinated ahead of the public? *Associated Press*.

Wade, S. (2022, June 21). $13 billion cost for COVID-19-delayed Tokyo Olympics is double the original estimate. *Los Angeles Times*.

Wade, S., & Kageyama, Y. (2023, December 5). Tokyo Olympics sullied by bid-rigging, bribery trials more than 2 years after the Games closed. *AP News*.

Wamsley, L. (2020, March 12). The day everything changed. *National Public Radio*, 11 March 2021.

Wingfield-Hayes, R. (2021, February 18). COVID-19 and suicide: Japan's rise a warning to the world? *BBC News*.

Wingfield-Hayes, R. (2020, April 30). Coronavirus: Japan's low testing rate raises questions. *BBC News*.

Wood, J. (2020, September 15). *People in these countries think their government did a good job of dealing with the pandemic*. World Economic Forum.

Yamaguchi, M. (2021, April 15). *Japan expands virus alert in Tokyo area as surge spreads*. Associated Press.

Yamaguchi, M. (2022, July 17). Explainer: The Unification Church's Ties to Japan's politics. *AP News*.

Marketing the Far-Right: How Do They Get it Right?

Mona Moufahim

INTRODUCTION

My interest in the marketing practices of far-right political parties is not new. By 2006, alerted by the steady ascension of xenophobic extreme right-wing parties of my home country Belgium, I decided to focus my doctoral research on the most prominent of those parties: The Vlaams Blok. That political marketing was strategically used by the party executives was beyond doubt: the well targeted electoral campaigns and the professionally designed communication material were obvious to the fresh marketing graduate I was. This was confirmed when I got my hands on an internal guide from the party which clearly explained to their local candidates what political marketing was and does.[1] Interesting, this in parallel with the party leaders *publicly* adopting an attitude of distaste for the use of 'spin doctors' by other political parties.

My analysis of the party showed a well-crafted and persuasive discourse supported by a sound marketing strategy (see Moufahim, 2007). I concluded at the time that the party was apt at political persuasion, creating a threatening reality where the natives were taken advantage of and victimised by the corrupt political elites in favour of their 'other' clients (foreigners, namely Muslims) and in great danger of losing their culture and identity in the face of the looming Islamisation of society. Students of the far right would instantly recognise these familiar themes, tropes and tactics. They are shared among many parties and social movements in the West. At the time, I noted the potential dangers of 'contamination' where mainstream centrist parties would be tempted to borrow their xenophobic and identitarian stances in the hope of quick electoral gains. I could not have predicted how much 'mainstreaming' of xenophobic positions there would be, 20 years later, across the European political spectrum. For example, Davey and Ebner (2019, p. 19) have noted that several more traditional conservative and centre-right parties have directly or indirectly (through so-called dog-whistling) endorsed far-right narratives, such as the Austrian chancellor Sebastian Kurz who has been called out by the Austrian Freedom Party leader for copying his agenda on immigration. More surprisingly, such rhetoric has also been identified on the political left (see, for example, the harsh anti-immigration policies of Social Democrats in Denmark, in Davey and Ebner, 2019). Adopting the far-right policies (on immigration, crime, etc) or rhetoric is perverse strategy that provides a strong legitimacy and acceptability of the extreme right party policies while not guaranteeing votes for the other parties (which are perceived by voters as 'me-too' copies of the original (see Moufahim, 2007, pp. 303–306).

In this chapter, I am taking stock of the development of a particularly successful far-right party, the Vlaams Blok/Vlaams Belang (VB), and how the party uses political marketing. Firstly, I review research dedicated to the study of the far-right. Next, I present key concepts in political marketing and political branding, focusing in particular on positioning, image, and identity. The remainder of the chapter is dedicated to analysing the VB using this analytical lens.

STUDYING THE FAR-RIGHT

When tackling the study of parties like the Flemish VB, the Austrian Freedom Party (FPÖ), or the French *Rassemblement National* (formerly known as Front National), the catch-all labels of far-right, extreme-right, or (extreme) right-wing populism are commonly used. There are several designations, many of which are used interchangeably, which complicates and confuses their study. To further complicate matters, some of these organisations are formal political parties operating within parliamentary democratic systems; others are more akin to social movements organisations. Groupuscules at the margins of, or outside, legality (e.g. white supremacists and neo-Nazi groups) also fall into this broad political family. We can find a variety of terms 'used synonymously and without any clear intention' (Mudde, 2000, p. 13) which highlights the far-right's organisational complexity and ideological heterogeneity, such as: populist radical right (Mols & Jetten, 2020); radical right and far-right (Cheles et al., 1991); mimetic or nostalgic fascism (Griffin, 1993); new populism (Betz & Immerfall, 1998); radical right-wing populism (Helms, 1997); new right (Minkenberg, 2000) or new radical right (Kitschelt, 1996) to only cite a few. Alongside these differences, we also can find disagreements in the classification of organisations. For example, the FPÖ is labelled by Gallagher et al. (1995) as a liberal party but has been considered an unambiguous case of an extreme right party for Mudde (2000) and McLean and McMillan (2003). Of course, the parties themselves reject the label of 'extreme right' (Mudde, 2000) and prefer more 'respectable' self-description, such as conservative and/or nationalist. The VB is thus described as a 'culturally racist, separatist, and authoritarian party of the ultra-right' by Swyngedouw (1998, p. 72), but for its supporters, it is a populist, ethnocentrist protest party (Swyngedouw, 1998). The complexity of classification also arises from the dynamic nature of political parties. Parties are not static: they develop and may discard issues (e.g. the centrality of immigration policies) in favour of others because of the changing social base of their electorate (Mudde, 2000).

For years, I have used the label 'far right' or 'extreme right' (see Moufahim et al., 2007) because many prominent scholars have chosen these denominations (Eatwell, 1998; Mudde, 2000). Accordingly, I define the far/extreme right as a *political family* whose members share common characteristics but also feature differences that classify them into subtypes (e.g. 'modern', 'traditional', 'post-industrial) (Hainsworth, 2000; Mudde, 2000). This broad qualification acknowledges the specific nature of political parties within the broader extreme right-wing movement (Hainsworth, 2000). Although there are disagreements on what constitutes an extreme right programme, Cas Mudde,[2] an essential reference in the study of the far/extreme right, notes that the recurrent elements in the literature on extreme right parties are: 'nationalism', 'racism', 'xenophobia', 'anti-democracy' and 'the strong state' (Mudde, 1995, 2000). Mudde states that a group or individual which exhibits at least 3 of these criteria would be classified under the extreme right label.

Davey and Ebner (2017) who focus their study on extreme right movements and subcultures (rather than political parties) have found developed and complex networks and collaborations at a global scale. Their use of online platforms, some of these being alternative platforms (to circumvent their ban from mainstream platforms), allow for important levels of knowledge exchange, coordinated operations on Twitter/X, and fundraising. Diverse groups collaborate – despite geographical differences and sometimes clear ideological differences (e.g. white supremacy) – to recruit new members and expand their influence. They focus instead on areas of convergence, such as the anti-Muslim and anti-immigration sentiments they all share. An interesting case authors discuss is how, through coordinated grassroots efforts, online activists have been able to influence the 2017 German elections by lending their support to the far-right party AfD (Alternative for Germany). Davey and Ebner (2017) further discuss the increased trans-Atlantic online cooperation between extreme right activists for the elections in France, the Netherlands and Germany. They explain that supporters of Geert Wilders in the Netherland, and for Marine Lepen's presidential campaign in France, borrowed tactics employed by the alt-right in the US elections, such as the organised use of trolls, memes, fake accounts and social media bots to spread disinformation (Davey & Ebner, 2017, p. 19). Worryingly, the same authors highlight that the most extreme fringe groups attempt to penetrate new audiences and mainstream their ideologies by using 'less extreme' groups as strategic mouthpieces (Davey & Ebner, 2017, p. 6). Their aim is the creation of a 'mass movement' through the radicalisation of people who consume mainstream (online) media, in particular Generation Z.

While I am not focusing specifically on these groups and movements here, it should be noted that many of these online activities, deploy the power of the web and social media platforms to organise, recruit, disrupt, communicate and mobilise, both online and offline. There is anecdotal evidence that, if the political parties are not directly/actively collaborating with those activists, they are aware of their work and they do benefit from their mobilisation (see Davey and Ebner's case about the German AfD, 2017). The changes in organising and mobilising are fast paced. The online extreme right social movements have proved to be very skilled at pushing their agenda when they generated media attention, and in 'their outmanoeuvring of traditional communication channels […] create their own news networks, social media platforms, funding structures and chat applications' (Davey & Ebner, 2017, p. 8). Some successfully weaponise the internet and demonstrate a sophisticated understanding of persuasive communication and segmentation by strategically 'framing their fringe narratives [white supremacy for example] through socially more acceptable lens of freedom of speech and criticism of multiculturalism, the globalist elites and political correctness' (Davey & Ebner, 2017, p. 14; my note added) and by tailoring of their communications efforts, across different platforms to different target audiences (Davey & Ebner, 2017, p. 15).

This brief overview of online campaigning is of relevance here, since, as Comerford and Avlicek (2021, p. 13) note, the extreme right movement does have political ambitions and does have sympathisers within the political establishment, which allows for mainstreaming divisive and problematic narratives and for influencing the mainstream political agenda. The most prominent of those narratives is about the existential 'threat' of Islam and the Islamisation of Western countries, under the popular myths of the 'Foreign Invasion' and the 'Great Replacement', 'Eurabia' and 'the Clash of Civilisations'. For readers interested in the online mobilisation of extreme right actors, I recommend Davey and Ebner (2017)'s report which discussed the use of message boards, discord[3] channels, Infowars, fake news, memes, parody accounts and obfuscation tactics. You could also consult Kuchta et al.'s (2021) analysis of the online strategies to disseminate right-wing extremist content, and of the emergence of alt-tech, that is, platforms designed specifically for extremist users to circumvent the ban for hate speech and disinformation.

Attempting to explain the success of the far right (both parliamentary and extra-parliamentary) only thanks to supposedly superior organisational capabilities would be short-sighted. The phenomenon has been extensively studied, looking at both the 'supply-side' (the party themselves) and the 'demand-side' (their electorate's characteristics and motivations). A nuanced analysis considering both the supply and demand sides (Mols & Jetten, 2020) would provide a sounder explanation for their extraordinary resilience and resurgence through times of crises. Arguably, adopting a political branding framework, which focuses on the creation and management of brand identity (internal, i.e. supply-side) and brand image perception by voters and external stakeholders (external, i.e. demand-side) aligns with the call by Mols and Jetten (2020) to account for the interactions between both sides to better study political parties of the far-right family.

POLITICAL MARKETING

Political parties and politicians use marketing to achieve their political goals and connect with voters but, in doing so, appear to borrow marketing tools and concepts in an *ad hoc* and instrumental fashion. According to Wring (1997), the term 'political marketing' was first coined by Kelley (1956) in his study on the increasing influence of professional persuaders in politics. Advocates of the introduction of marketing principles and techniques to a political context have suggested that, as the citizen is treated more as a consumer with a focus of decision-making processes (Lees-Marshment, 2001; Moufahim & Lim, 2009), a stronger relationship is more likely to develop between citizens and political institutions. Consumer marketing provides thus an analytical lens for the understanding of the processes observable in the political arena.

In political practice, as marketing has been adopted by political parties (Harris & Lock, 2010; O'Shaughnessy, 1990), it has moved beyond influencing only tactical matters of communication and presentation towards playing a significant role in policy formulation and long-term direction

(Butler & Collins, 1996). Many would argue that political marketing has replaced traditional forms of policy development with market research techniques to uncover voters' prime concerns (Palmer, 2002), the nature and size of voters' segments and to tailor policies (and communication campaigns) they would be most responsive to. In other words, the political marketer tries to find out who is persuadable and on what grounds (Maarek, 1992). In 2007, I showed that the VB strategically used marketing discourse to make political ideas 'voter-friendly' and packaged for easy consumption by the electorate (Moufahim, 2007).

Academically, efforts have been made to extend political marketing as an academic discipline beyond the limitations of traditional mass marketing theory. Political marketing was developed, not always without fierce debates (see Lock & Harris, 1996; Savigny, 2008), as a comprehensive approach that includes the political organisation's whole behaviour alongside the citizen-consumer's behaviour (see, e.g. Ingram & Lees-Marshment, 2002; Moufahim & Lim, 2009; Wring, 1996; see also Harris & Lock, 2010 for a brief history of the development of the discipline). As such, political marketing is interdisciplinary and focuses on applying marketing tools and concepts to politics to maximise the support for political parties and candidates, but also on the full range of social theory informing the study of (political) consumer society.

In the 1990s already, scholars observed that it is impossible not to use political marketing in (post) modern politics (O'Cass, 1996). Since, marketing ideology and technologies have been institutionalised and naturalised in consumer society in the conduct of political campaigning, party organising and, more broadly, in day-to-day political life. This is, of course, part of the broader neoliberal discourse that frames citizen's everyday lives as consumption choices, making the language of marketing 'normal' for citizens: legitimate, intelligible and acceptable (Wring & Savigny, 2008). Whether this is a good thing for democracy or something to be resisted, is a question I leave for the reader to grapple with; others have debated the issue (see Dermody & Scullion, 2001; Norris, 2004; Savigny, 2008).

POLITICAL BRANDING: POSITIONING, IDENTITY AND IMAGE MANAGEMENT

A particular subfield of political marketing I want to focus on is political branding. Many have fruitfully studied branding as a sound analytical lens to understand political parties' strategies and decisions (see collections of papers in Moufahim, 2022). In practice, over the last twenty years, we have seen the use of commercial branding concepts, theories and frameworks to political parties and candidates with varying levels of success (Marland et al., 2017; Pich & Newman, 2020; Pich, Armannsdottir, & Dean, 2020).

We know from extensive branding research that a brand is not just the name of an organisation or a product. It is a communication device which represents a complex cluster of values, vision and personality (Harris & Rae, 2011; Pich & Armannsdottir, 2022; Ströbel & Germelmann, 2020). They represent promises of quality and benefits made to the target consumers about what to expect from consuming the brand (see Aaker & Joachimsthaler, 2002; Davies, 2010; Essamri et al., 2019). In politics, a political brand may be simply defined as the cluster of impressions, associations and images held by the public towards a politician or a political organisation. Those names, signs, symbols and design associated with a brand are used to communicate the values, vision and personality of a political 'object', and such identity markers help voters in their efforts to differentiate one political representation over another, take shortcuts when facing complex political programmes (the brand as a 'summary' of what the party/candidate stands for) (Balmer & Liao, 2007; Essamri et al., 2019; Guzman & Sierra, 2009; Pich, Armannsdottir, & Dean, 2020; Van Steenburg & Guzmán, 2019).

However, while I attempt to provide a 'simple' conceptualisation of political brands, I should stress that managing political brands is anything but simple: they represent complex interactions of various elements, such as the history and traditions of the party, its stated core values, its past and current leader, the policies it advocates, as well as positive and negative associations from communication from or about the party in the minds of citizens (Cwalina & Falkowski, 2015; Moufahim & Lilleker, 2022). Political brands must deal with a fragmented media environment, a highly competitive political market, and 'floating voters' who have essentially low interest in politics (Lilleker, 2005). Hence, political actors must make their promises clear and straightforward and may have to focus more on identity than policy (Moufahim & Lilleker, 2022; Pich, Armannsdottir, & Dean, 2020), which is exactly what political branding is about.

A brand's strategic creation, management and development process is known as 'political branding'. Successful political branding's mission is to have voters (and influential media stakeholders) perceive the brand as authentic, trustworthy, engaging, united and coherent with the aim of ensuring its election. Party communication must contribute to building a coherent and consistent image of the brand, rectifying any potential gaps between brand identity (internal construction) and brand image (how voters perceive the party) (Medveschi & Frunza, 2018). Parties must thus position themselves compared to their political competitors (Smith & French, 2009). Aaker and Shansby (1982, p. 56) explain positioning as: 'a product or organisation has many associations which combine to form a total impression. The positioning decision often means selecting those associations to be built upon and emphasised and those associations to be removed or de-emphasised'. How a political brand is positioned helps customers identify how a brand is different and better than competitors. When a target voter has been identified, the party/candidate needs to clearly communicate its positions in the political marketplace (Mauser, 1983; Newman, 2001).

In short, political branding involves issue positioning and image and perception management. Following the commercial brand logic, political strategists seek to develop brand identity and brand image for their political clients to establish a differentiated competitive advantage (Cwalina & Falkowski, 2015).

Political Brand Identity

Brand identity relates to the 'distinctive and relatively enduring characteristics' (He et al., 2016, p. 1310) of a brand's position in the market (Pich & Armannsdottir, 2022, chap. 2). In politics, brand identity is the desired narrative (position) formulated and communicated by individuals within the political organisation about what the brand should stand for in the minds of internal (staff, strategists, activists/party members) and external stakeholders (voters, media, competition) (Pich & Armannsdottir, 2022, chap. 2). This desired identity is developed around the brand's policies, symbols and messages, communicated across their selected platforms (Baines et al., 2014; Schneider, 2004). Pich, Armannsdottir, and Dean (2020) also highlight how political brand identity can be crafted from intangible elements such as a distinct set of values, narratives, mission, vision, ideology and heritage, all brought to life through preferred imagery and associations (see also Nandan, 2005). Consistency between the physical and intangible elements is paramount to ensure the projection of a clear and unambiguous identity (and thereby a credible and united brand) (Marland et al., 2017; Marland & Flanagan, 2014). Pich, Armannsdottir, and Dean (2020) further explain that a clear, understandable, relatable political brand increases the likelihood of citizens' engagement and identity alignment with the brand (see also Marland, 2016). Such alignment may lead to the citizen's loyalty to the political brand (Armannsdottir et al., 2019).

Research and practice show that political brand identity formation and management is an ongoing process. While identity is predominantly an internally created construct, brand managers do not necessarily fully control the branding process (Armannsdottir et al., 2019). External actors such as political competitors, rivals, non-supporters and competing groups can shape a party's brand identity, as we have seen attempt by externals to rewrite the narrative of the political brand identity (Marland, 2016; Marland et al., 2017).

Political Brand Image

Brand image can be broadly defined as the 'perceptions about a brand as reflected by the brand associations held in consumers' memory' (Keller, 1993, p. 3). In the political context, brand image is the manifestation of the communicated identity combined with perceptions, associations and attitudes in the citizens' minds (Pich et al., 2018). In other words, brand image is the perception and immediate understanding of what the political brand is all about, as expressed by the target's top-of-mind associations, perceived expectations of how the brand will perform and how it differs from competitive offerings (i.e. its unique selling proposition), all of which supported or by past direct and indirect experiences (Nielsen, 2017; Pich et al., 2018, 2020a). Brand strategists must select relevant and innovative modes of engagement and produce a desired brand image among their target audience *by delivering* what they set out to do. Failure to deliver on a brand promise can be costly and may result in long-term damage to the brand (Moufahim, 2022).

Political brand image and political brand identity are distinct concepts but related essential concepts in the study and management of brands (Nandan, 2005; Pich & Newman, 2020; Pich, Armannsdottir, & Dean, 2020) and should be combined. For example, misalignment between the brand's communicated identity and the image perceived by the target can weaken political brands, because it can damage the clarity of the brand positioning (Pich & Armannsdottir, 2022). A strong brand image can help politicians and political parties build relationships with voters and increase brand trust (Pich, Armannsdottir, & Dean, 2020). Therefore, utilising the theoretical lens of political brand identity and political brand image will reveal (mis)alignment between desired and actual positioning (Needham & Smith, 2015; Pich & Armannsdottir, 2022; Pich et al., 2018, 2020a). Given the fast-moving environment in which political brands operate, brand managers are advised to monitor competitive offerings, and periodically assess their brand's identity to ensure its continuous resonance with the target audience and positive brand image (Pich & Armannsdottir, 2022). For a detailed framework of various political brands, see Pich and Armannsdottir (2022).

The following section explores the trajectory of the VB under a branding lens, which would help illuminate their strategic choices and what they have been doing 'right' across the years.

BRANDING AND REBRANDING STRATEGY: THE CASE OF THE VB

Over the years, the Vlaams Blok had managed to build a strong brand with a significantly loyal following. The VB has developed a successful positioning of difference from, and alternative to, the mainstream. The party has claimed ownership of some critical issues (Coffé, 2004) and, in doing so, developed other 'points of difference' (see Keller, 2003; Keller et al., 2002) on crime, immigration and Flemish independence. Judging from the success at the polls, the party has managed to carve a solid positioning, and has communicated well its brand's values. According to Keller (2003), good positioning of a brand requires the establishment of important points of difference (POD) over the competition and at the same time, turning policies where the brand is disadvantaged, into points of parity (POP). Let us review some of the key moments for the party and analyse the party's strategic decisions.

The VB was created in 1978 from the merger of two small nationalist parties run by radical dissidents of the Volksunie (a prominent nationalist post-war party at the time) (Camus, 2003). From 1979 to 1985, the VB transformed itself from a minor protest group into a political party. Since 1991, the party has employed advertising professionals to develop its campaigns and create memorable slogans[4] associated with recognisable symbols (Bossemans, 2001; Vander Velpen, 1992). In 2004, Filip Dewinter, one of the top members of the party, stated:

> I am the head of a campaign group of 13 people. Among them, there are three employees of well-known advertising agencies, who are members of our party, and have helped for free to set up campaigns. (in Het Belang van Limburg,[5] 17/03/2004: 4)

In 1994, the VB became the largest party on the city council of Antwerp and was consequently entitled to participate in the city's government. However, a *cordon sanitaire* (or quarantine) created by the other parties excluded the VB from entering any governing coalition (Mudde, 2000). At the June 2004 regional elections, more than one Fleming out of five voted for the VB and it became the second largest party in Flanders (it scored nearly 30% in the city of Antwerp).

The VB has consistently positioned itself as an honest party caring for people's rights and denouncing both the 'diseases' of society and those causing them. When campaigning, the VB focused on three major themes: (1) the issue of immigration; (2) Flemish nationalism (VB has been robustly campaigning for the independence of Flanders from the Belgian state); (3) the incompetence and dishonesty of the other parties (Faniel, 2003). Crime (law and order) was paired with the issue of immigration. In 1992, Filip Dewinter argued in the infamous '70-point programme' (see Dewinter, 2002), that to protect Flemish identity, a halt to immigration and the accelerated repatriation of foreigners, along with harsher regulations against criminal and illegal immigrants were necessary (Coffé, 2005). Swyngedouw (1998, p. 68) explained that the Vlaams Blok created 'a dominant ideological space' (i.e. its positioning in the political market) by engaging in anti-immigration agitation in sensitive neighbourhoods where crime and unemployment were high. Part of this strategy was attributing such problems to immigrants (Swyngedouw, 1998) and to the inaction (if not complicity) of the political class. At the time their political vision was for Flanders as mono-ethnic state, where non-European immigrants would be repatriated, and European 'foreigners' assimilated (Nollet, 2000).

Positioning of the Vlaams Blok

Since its inception, the VB has positioned itself as a nationalist, solidarist[6] party of the right. This positioning is translated through the policies adopted by the party. These are Flemish independence, a free market, a reduction of taxes, a limitation on social security, the repatriation of guest workers, zero tolerance of criminality and a total and unconditional amnesty for WWII collaborators (Vos, 1992, in Bossemans, 2001). As stated above, the party started its political career as a protest and opposition party, denouncing society's ills and refusing to align with 'corrupt' mainstream parties. For example, in 1991, the Vlaams Blok refused a ministerial portfolio it was entitled to thanks to its 10.3% of the Flemish votes (Bossemans, 2001). This attitude reinforced the party's positioning as uncompromising, non-conformist and radical (Spruyt, 2000). Some 20 years later, the positioning remained consistent:

> A party unlike any other. The Vlaams Blok is indeed not a compromising party, but a programme party faithful to its principles and programme, [...], for the Flemish and European peoples. A party rooted in a great past, but resolutely turned towards the future. (VB President, Frank Vanhecke, in www.vlaamsblok.be)

Of note is that not all this positioning was chosen by the party. As highlighted in the previous section, external actors do impact the identity of a political brand (Marland, 2016; Marland et al., 2017). Indeed, with their electoral successes, the VB should have been included in governing coalitions, but was excluded because of the *cordon sanitaire*. On occasion, this meant that other parties were forced into awkward coalition arrangements (Spruyt, 2000). While the VB was keen to project the image of a party that gets business done, their exclusion and the subsequent underdog/rebel position also benefited the VB, as it positioned it as the *de facto* opposition party. For example, at the 2000 elections for the Antwerp city council, although the VB won a third of the total votes, the liberal VLD (the other winner of the election) refused to share power with the extreme right, and thus further solidify the position of the VB as the underdog who was undemocratically gagged by other parties.

The VB has thus occupied a clear position in the political 'marketplace' for a while. This may be seen as evidence of a carefully thought-out marketing strategy, or at the very least, of a sound political conviction and direction. Of note, however, is the evidence of opportunism in their selection of 'winning' campaigning themes. While the independence of Flanders was the original founding principle underlying the creation of the VB, the anti-immigrant position became the most salient theme and the most effective vote gatherer for the party. Filip Dewinter was the first to recognise the electoral potential of an anti-immigrant stance (Mudde, 2004), inspired by the success of the French Front National (Coffé, 2004). Consequently, the party conducted a fierce anti-immigrant campaign in the 1987 parliamentary elections, which won them two seats in Parliament and one seat in the Belgian Senate (Coffé, 2004).

The VB Brand Identity

The pragmatism of the party leaders is evident in their recruitment of communication professionals (Bossemans, 2001; Vander Velpen, 1992). The VB was rewarded for its consistent positioning and clear, recognisable communications. In less than 30 years, the VB has become one of the most significant and recognised parties in Flanders. No Belgian citizen could currently ignore or confuse the party's core themes with those of the other political parties. The main themes of the VB have even become the party's unique selling proposition (Olins, 2002). Any other party calling for a clampdown on immigration or a tougher stance on crime would merely look like a pale imitation of the VB. The stance on immigration became their distinguishable POD at the start of the 1987 campaign when the party successfully raised the perceived importance of immigration in public debate. Butler and Collins (1996) also argue that anticipating the electorate's preferences can be helpful for challengers. A party can steal a march on its opponents if a policy can be 'branded' before its appeal is widely recognised (Butler & Collins, 1996). However, Butler and Collins (1996) also note that the difficulty with this strategy is retaining ownership of the idea once it has become popular.

The party has also demonstrated campaigning maturity by designing simple, impactful and memorable campaigns, carefully targeted for their specific audience: from one election to the next, from one Region to another, the VB's focused on one specific core theme, while the other topics were downplayed. For example, the 1987 campaign zoomed in on anti-immigration (Coffé, 2005). In Brussels, the party has downplayed Flemish nationalism when targeting Brussels' francophone voters, and addressed the issues of immigration and criminality: the topics of independence of Flanders and the annexation of Brussels (and its consequent mandatory 'Dutch-isation') have been carefully avoided in the party's communication material for for the Region of Brussels. This aligns with branding experts' recommendations for clarity, consistency and resonance with target voters' concerns (Armannsdottir et al., 2019).

The 'new' Vlaams Belang created in November 2004 (see next section) continued capitalising on those crucial PODs developed by the former Vlaams Blok. Over the years, other political parties have more or less successfully attempted to recover the voters they have lost to the VB by hardening their discourse and policies on immigration or on Flemish nationalism. The most notable impact this approach had was to push immigration (and anti-immigrant sentiments) as a principal concern in the country and contributed to the further legitimating of VB policies among the electorate.

Rebranding Into the Vlaams Belang

The Court of Appeal of Ghent condemned three non-profit associations linked to the VB for violating the anti-racism law. The condemnation gave the party high visibility, and they scored their highest scores to date at the 2004 regional and European elections. *Coup de théâtre* in 2004: having seen their appeal fail and the condemnation confirmed, the VB was disbanded to avoid further prosecution.

This condemnation proved to be a gift offered to the VB, giving them widespread media visibility and the opportunity to rebrand themselves as *the* right-wing opposition party. The Vlaams Belang was promptly created in November 2004, with the same leaders and structures as the Vlaams Blok. The continuity of leadership, ideology and identity has been emphasised by the Vlaams Blok/Vlaams[7] leaders themselves at the party conference: 'We are changing our name, but not our stripes' (Coffé, 2005, p. 217, citing VB leader Frank Vanhecke). It is therefore uncontroversial to call what happened a rebranding exercise rather than the creation of a new political brand. The recently created Vlaams Belang was indeed facing a delicate situation in preserving the USPs of the VB which generated a loyal following for the party.

The Vlaams Belang was thus trying to be perceived as a nationalist right-wing party, which still has immigration, security and anti-establishment feelings as its driving forces, but which has cut the ties with its unsavoury past (e.g. they were not calling anymore for the deportation of all immigrants) (Coffé, 2005). However, keen to reassure and retain their core electorate, the party leadership stated that: 'multiculturalism leads to multi-criminality' (in the Annual Report 2005 on Human Rights in Belgium), and that 'any Muslim woman wearing the headscarf will sign thereby the warrant for her repatriation' ('Buitenhof', Nederland 3, 14/11/2004). They also stated: 'we don't need a Vlaams Blok Light' or a 'Vlaams Blok Ultra', but a 'Vlaams Blok Plus!' Indeed, our programme is not changing at all (in an interview in Dag Allemaal3); '"Xenophobia" is not the word I would use. If it absolutely must be a "phobia" let it be "Islamophobia"' (Jewish Week, 28/10/2005). Along with the 'softening' and mainstreaming of their most controversial policies (to avoid legal prosecutions), these controlled outbursts in media were intended to avoid the alienation of the existing loyal Vlaams Blok voters. The party was intent on breaking from the cordon sanitaire through their opportunity to become a more mainstream party:

> Our story has a meaning only when we can implement the essence of our programme: independence, a stricter immigration policy, an uncompromising approach to crime. It is clear now that these points of our programme will not be implemented by using increased decibels to shout original terms of abuse from within the quarantine zone. Contrary to lemmings or howler monkeys, who follow their instinct, man can evaluate his situation, consider alternative strategies, and analyse carefully who can be opponents and who can be allies, if need be temporarily. (Vlaams Belang, November 2006, p. 3)

The party leader went on to explain:

> The Danish example proves that other scenarios are possible, other than quarantine zones [...] A shrewd Vlaams Belang is, of course much more dangerous than a shouting Vlaams Belang in a quarantine zone. It is going to be a challenging but necessary exercise. We owe it to ourselves and our children and grandchildren. (Vlaams Belang, November 2006, p. 3)

Ostensibly, the Vlaams Belang was positioned differently than the Vlaams Blok, carving a spot in the conservative right of the Belgian/Flemish political landscape, while keeping it away from legal troubles. However, this somewhat ambiguous position flirting with both the old positioning and the new one meant that the party had watered down its USP and muddled the clarity of their brand narrative. They appeared too similar to other parties in the same quadrant of the political space, but with the major weakness of having no real opportunity to govern because of the cordon sanitaire. Due to new competitors entering the political marketplace, the party started experiencing in 2006 its first defeats at the polls, facing intense competition from the populist neo-liberal List Dedecker (LDD). In 2014, the VB lost many voters[8] to the nationalist New Flemish Alliance (N-VA). The party leadership's hesitations and experimentations with their brand image, coupled with the NV-A's more moderate and attractive alternative, made the brand seem less relevant to the existing VB voters.[9]

Announcing the decline of the VB brand would have however been premature. From 2015, the party experienced an electoral comeback, and they performed very well in the 2019 elections. They still had to resolve the issue of their brand identity and positioning. Reports indicated that there were 2 opposing factions within the party: those advocating the mainstreaming strategy (the official line by party leadership) and those pushing for a radicalisation strategy (spearheaded by Filip Dewinter) which would take the party back to the Vlaams Blok's roots and heritage, adopt an even more radical anti-refugee and anti-Muslim/anti-Islam[10] position (van Haute & Pauwels & Haute, 2016). The party chose to retain their key central issues (law and order, Flemish independence, immigration, EU integration), and a hard stance on immigration which further contributed to keep immigration at the centre stage of Flemish politics, in that it forced the N-VA to pursue restrictive immigration policies to prevent their electorate from defecting back to the VB (Pauwels & Haute, 2017).

Despite the 2005–2014 lull, the VB has built a strong brand with a significantly loyal core following. Trying for a potentially ambiguous mainstream *and* xenophobic/Islamophobic positioning led to the need for a careful segmentation and targeting of the electorate. By adopting this approach, the Vlaams Belang seemed to be aiming at both attracting a larger audience (interested in its strict approach on criminality and in greater autonomy for Flanders) and at the same time, reassuring the voters of the former Vlaams Blok (who were not shy of voting for an anti-immigrant party), that the party did not change and would continue defending the nation and identity of its people. This analysis cannot be done in a vacuum, as competitors' strategies need to be acknowledged alongside broader environmental variables. Some political commentators indicate that voters may have grown tired of the too 'moderate' N-VA and are searching for a more radical option in the face of the refugee crisis and the terrorist attacks in Brussels in 2016.

CONCLUSION

It is undeniable that marketing now plays a significant role in branding strategies, shaping platforms to align with public attitudes, market testing messages and the integrated marketing communication techniques apparent in campaigning innovations. Following my interest in far-right politics, and in particular, my expertise in the Flemish VB, I have revisited some of my analysis of the party (Moufahim et al., 2007, 2015; Moufahim & Humphreys, 2015) using a political branding framework, which lends itself well at understanding both internal mechanisms and the reception of the brand by external audiences. More than ever, the sustained success of many far-right parties, the worrying popularity of the divisive theses they advocate, and the vitality of the related extremist social movements mobilising both online and offline make their study by scholars, policymakers and activists of prime importance.

I have proposed a political branding approach to explain the strategic development of the VB. While the adoption of marketing technology was not initially openly admitted by the party, the party leadership knows how to carefully segment the political market and to lead successful communication campaigns. They have done so through the selection of clear and distinctive themes and a sound positioning of their brand, clearly communicating its core value and USPs to an expanding target audience, and to expertly engage with various stakeholders.

The Vlaams Belang has managed the delicate transition to a right-wing conservative image while retaining the brand heritage of the Vlaams Blok (and its voters). The 'new' Vlaams Belang has pragmatically not abandoned its anti-immigration stance (electorally rewarding) and has kept its original ideological core of Flemish nationalism (its origin and identity base). The party seeks to gain a broad appeal by stressing its Flemish nationalist and anti-establishment policies, and wishes to retain the large anti-immigrant electoral base. The outcome of such a strategy is the creation of controlled outbursts and controversies that give visibility in media while the party's political programme retains its newly acquired right-wing conservative flavour.

A political branding approach provides a two-pronged approach to the study of far-right parties, addressing the limitations of existing research that focus either on the supply or the demand dimensions. More research is needed, especially as we are witnessing a transition *from bureaucracies to platforms* fundamentally reshaping many parts of society and its organisations (Husted et al., 2021) and sophisticated and agile use of recent technologies to organise and mobilise politically.

It should be acknowledged that my analysis of the party's branding is 'external', as it has been impossible for me to be granted access to the party itself or speak with its members/leaders. Thus, I have argued elsewhere that there is a need further to explore political parties and their modes of organisation from within (see Husted et al., 2021). We called on the need to expand our modes of analysis, that is, involving not just quantitative methods and 'official' data but also engagement with the inner life of the party to understand the actual organisation taking place 'on the ground' and not just 'on paper'. Relatedly, additional and further research on the marketing, branding and related questions about parties and movements at the extreme right (including those at the fringe) of the political spectrum is needed to expand our understanding of those organisations, how they organise, spread their influence, engage and disrupt democratic processes, and how they recruit at-risk young people. This is difficult: far-right parties and radical populist parties are notoriously closed to non-vetted new members. Much of what we know about extreme right parties and movements comes from 'infiltrated' journalists and activists. Approval for covert research remains challenging to secure for researchers affiliated with universities.

Notes

1 '[M]arketing comes from the study of the needs of consumers, and from this follows the production of resources which could satisfy those needs. A company must study first the needs of its consumers and adapt its production according to those needs. Political marketing broadly follows the same line of thought' and '[p]olitical marketing is a global project with which the candidate can organize well his or her political activities. The VB is choosing without a doubt an anti-demagogic practice, with which we have so often tried to be the voice of the people' (in Politieke Communicatie-Technieken, Deel 1. De persoonlijke campagne van de kandidaat. Vlaams Blok Publications. (Translation: Political communication techniques- Part 1: The personal campaign of the candidate))

2 Of note, Mudde has been using from 2007 the term radical populist right (Mudde, 2007, 2010, 2014).

3 Discord – an online chat application. Developed for use by gamers, it now hosts several extreme-right channels. Meme – a concept coined by Richard Dawkins in 1976, a meme refers to a unit of transfer for cultural ideas. It is commonly used to refer to (often humorous) user-generated content which is rapidly spread socially throughout the internet; obfuscation: how to hide IP addresses, how to automate Twitter accounts or how to avoid getting them shut down (Davey & Ebner, 2017).

4 There were, for example, in 1991, boxing gloves and a '*Self-defence*' slogan; or in 1999, a family and '*Boss in one's land*', a broom and 'Grote Kuis', that is, 'Big Cleaning up'; in 1999, a family and 'Baas in eigen land', that is, 'Boss in one's land'; a kid pointing a finger and 'Thuis zijn', that is, 'at home'. These slogans have always been combined with the well-known party slogan 'Eigen Volk Eerst', that is, 'One's people first'.

5 Local Flemish newspapers (in the Flemish province of Limburg)

6 'Solidarism' is a system where the economy should be aimed at maintaining the welfare of the whole nation and where national solidarity replaces class struggle (Mudde, 2000, p. 189).

7 To stress this continuity, a combination of both names, '*VB*', refers indistinctively to the Vlaams Blok and the Vlaams Belang unless stated otherwise.

8 Besides the ideological priorities, the losses were also attributed to an ageing membership, the multi-level complex structure of the party and conflict between leadership and the grassroots (van Haute and Pauwels, 2016). This was in parallel with the breakthrough of the N-VA (New Flemish Alliance), both conservative and Flemish nationalist/independentist, created in 2002 (from the ashes of the Flemish independentist Volksunie), with a clear brand heritage and a clean sheet from any associations to xenophobia and racism like the Vlaams Blok was (Delwitt, 2019)

9 In 2014, a staggering 44% of the VB's voters from 2010 chose to vote for the N-VA.

10 In January 2015, the ever popular and mediatised Filip Dewinter denounced Islam in Parliament with a Quran in his hand; he launched a videogame where players could slap 'Muslim terrorists' and the French-speaking Socialist prime minister. The game was removed in February 2015, after its signalment as racist (Pauwels & Haute, 2017).

REFERENCES

Aaker, D., & Joachimsthaler, E. (2002). *Brand leadership*. Simon & Schuster UK Ltd.

Aaker, D., & Shansby, J. G. (1982). Positioning your product. *Business Horizons*, *25*, 56–62.

Armannsdottir, G., Pich, C., & Spry, L. (2019). Exploring the creation and development of political Co-brand identity: A multi-case study approach. *Qualitative Market Research: An International Journal*. https://doi.org/10.1108/QMR-10-2018-0119

Baines, P. (1999). Voter segmentation and candidate positioning. In B. Newman (Ed.), *Handbook of political marketing*. SAGE.

Baines, P., Crawford, I., O'Shaughnessy, N., Worcester, R., & Mortimore, R. (2014). Positioning in political marketing: How semiotic analysis adds value to traditional survey approaches. *Journal of Marketing Management*, *30*(1–2), 172–200.

Balmer, J. M. T., & Liao, M. N. (2007). Student corporate brand identification: An exploratory case study, corporate communications. *An International Journal*, *12*(4), 356–375.

Betz, H.-G., & Immerfall, S. (1998). The new politics of the right. In *Neo-populist parties and movements in established democracies* (p. 268). St Martin's Press.

Bossemans, V. (2001). *De Communicatiestrategie van het Vlaams Blok. Evolutie van positionering, doelgroep en boodschap*. Faculteit Politieke en Sociale Wetenschappen, 175. Unpublished dissertation.

Butler, P., & Collins, N. (1996). Strategic analysis in political markets. *European Journal of Marketing*, *30*(10/11), pp. 32–44.

Camus, J.-Y. (2003). La figure de l'étranger dans le discours de l'extrême droite européenne. *Nouvelle Tribune*. n.33 Juin/Août Trimestriel.

Cheles, L., Ferguson, R., & Vaughan, M. (1991). *Neo-fascism in Europe*. Longman.

Coffé, H. (2004). Can extreme right voting be explained ideologically? Conference paper. In *ECPR Joint Sessions, 13-18 April 2004*. Workshop No.3.

Coffé, H. (2005). The adaptation of the extreme right's discourse: The case of the Vlaams Blok. *Ethical Perspectives: Journal of the European Ethics Network*, *12*(2), 205–230.

Comerford and Avlicek (2021). *Policy paper: Mainstreamed extremism and the future of prevention*, ISD, https://www.isdglobal.org/wp-content/uploads/2021/10/ISD-Mainstreamed-extremism-and-the-future-of-prevention-3.pdf. Accessed on October 29, 2023.

Cwalina, W., & Falkowski, A. (2015). Political branding: Political candidates positioning based on inter-object associative affinity index. *Journal of Political Marketing*, *14*(1–2), 152–174.

Davey, J., & Ebner, J. (2017). *The Fringer Insurgency Connectivity, convergence and mainstreaming of the extreme right*. ISD report. https://www.isdglobal.org/wp-content/uploads/2017/10/The-Fringe-Insurgency-221017_2.pdf. Accessed on October, 29 2023.

Davies, J. A. (2010). *Competitive success: How branding adds value*. John Wiley and Sons Ltd.

Davies, G., & Chun, R. (2002). Gaps between the internal and external perceptions of the corporate brand. *Corporate Reputation Review*, *5*(2/3), 144–158.

Delwit, P. (2019). Radical right-wing parties facing the wall of the local? The Vlaams Belang and Local Elections (1982-2018). *Open Journal of Political Science*, *9*, 631–651. https://doi.org/10.4236/ojps.2019.94039

Dermody, J., & Scullion, R. (2001). Delusions of grandeur? *European Journal of Marketing*, *35*(Issue 9/10), 1085–1098.

Dewinter, F. (2002). *Baas in eigen land*. Vlaams Blok Publications.

Eatwell, R. (1998). The dynamics of right-wing electoral breakthrough. *Patterns of Prejudice*, *32*(3).

Essamri, A., McKechnie, S., & Winklhofer, H. (2019). Co-creating corporate brand identity with online brand communities: A managerial perspective. *Journal of Business Research*. https://doi.org/10.1016/j.jbusres.2018.07.015

Faniel, J. (2003, August). L'extrême droite en Belgique: puissance du Vlaams Blok, (in)existence du Front National. *Nouvelle Tribune*, 50–54.

Gallagher, M., Laver, M., & Mair, P. (1995). *Representative government in modern Europe* (revised edition). McGraw-Hill.

Griffin, R. (1993). *The nature of fascism* (4th ed.). Prentice-Hall.

Guzman, F., & Sierra, V. (2009). A political candidate's brand image scale: Are political candidates brands? *Journal of Brand Management*, *17*(No 3), 207–2017.

Hainsworth, P. (2000). *The politics of the extreme right: From the margins to the mainstream*. Pinter.

Harris, P., & Lock, A. (2010). Editorial. "Mind the Gao": The rise of political marketing and a perspective on its future agenda. *European Journal of Marketing*, *44*(3/4), 297–307.

Harris, L., & Rae, A. (2011). Building a personal brand through social networking. *Journal of Business Strategy*, *32*(5), 14–21.

Helms, L. (1997). Right-wing populist parties in Austria and Switzerland: A comparative analysis of electoral support and conditions of success. *West European Politics*, *2*, 37–52.

He, H., Harris, L. C., Wang, W., & Haider, K. (2016). Brand identity and online self-customisation usefulness perception. *Journal of Marketing Management*. https://doi.org/10.1080/0267257X.2016.1170720

Husted, E. Moufahim, M., & Fredriksson, M. (2021). Welcome to the party! Unpacking party

organizations. *Ephemera: Theory and Politics in Organization*, *21*, 2.
Ingram, P., & Lees-Marshment, J. P. (2002). The Anglicisation of political marketing: How Blair 'out-marketed' Clinton. *Journal of Public Affairs*, *2*(2), 44–57.
Keller, K. (2003). Brand synthesis: The multidimensionality of brand knowledge. *Journal of Consumer Research*, *29*(1), 595–600.
Keller, K., Sternthal, B., & Tybout, A. (2002). Three questions you need to ask about your brand. *Harvard Business Review*, *80*(9), 80–89.
Kelley, S. (1956). *Professional public relations and political power*. John Hopkins.
Kitschelt, H. (1996). *The radical right in Western Europe*. University of Michigan Press.
Kuchta et al. (2021). *Detours and diversions. Online strategies used to disseminate right-wing extremist content*. USD publication. Accessed on October, 292023.
Lilleker, D. (2005). The impact of political marketing on internal party democracy. *Parliamentary Affairs*, *58*(3), 570–584.
Lock, A., & Harris, P. (1996). Political Marketing: Vive la différence. *European Journal of Marketing*, *30*(10/11), 14–24.
Less-Marshment, J. (2001). *Political marketing and British political parties: The party's just begun*. Manchester University Press.
Maarek, P. J. (1992, January). Elections Americaines: dans les coulisses du marketing politique. *Marketing*, *43*, 37–44.
Marland, A. (2016). *Brand command: Canadian politics and democracy in the age of message control*. UBC Press.
Marland, A., & Flanagan, T. (2014). Brand new party: Political branding and the conservative party of Canada. *Canadian Journal of Political Science*, *46*(4), 951–972.
Marland, A., Lewis, J. P., & Flanagan, T. (2017). Governance in the age of digital media and branding. *Governance: An International Journal of Policy, Administration and Institutions*, *30*(1), 125–141. https://doi.org/10.1111/gove.12194
Mauser, G. A. (1983). *Political marketing: An approach to campaign strategy*. Praeger.
McLean, I., & McMillan, A. (2003). *The concise Oxford dictionary of politics*. Oxford University Press.
Medveschi, I., & Frunza, S. (2018). Political brand, symbolic construction and public image communication. *Journal for the Study of Religions and Ideologies*, *17*(49), 137–152.
Minkenberg, M. (2000). The renewal of the radical right: Between modernity and anti-modernity. *Government and Opposition*, *2*, 170–188.
Mols, F., & Jetten, J. (2020). Understanding support for populist radiacl right parties: Toward a model that captures both demand- and spply-side factors. *Frontiers in Communication*, *5*, 1–13.
Moufahim, M. (2007). *Interpreting discourse*. Unpublished thesis. The University of Nottingham.
Moufahim, M. (2022). *Political branding in turbulent times*. Palgrave MacMillan.
Moufahim, M., & Humphreys, M. (2015). Marketing an extremist ideology: The Vlaams Belang's nationalist discourse. In A. Pullen & C. Rhodes (Eds.). *The Routledge companion to ethics, politics and organizations. Routledge companions in business, management and accounting* (pp. 85–100). Routledge.
Moufahim, M., Humphreys, M., Mitussis, D., & Fitchett, J. (2007). Interpreting discourse: A critical discourse analysis of the marketing of an extreme right party. *Journal of Marketing Management*, *23*(5/6), 539–558.
Moufahim, M., & Lilleker, D. (2022). The ethical challenges at the heart of political branding. In M. Moufahim (Ed.), *Political branding in turbulent times*. Palgrave MacMillan.
Moufahim, M., & Lim, M. (2009). Towards a critical political marketing agenda? *Journal of Marketing Management*, *25*(7–8), 763–776.
Moufahim, M., Reedy, P., & Humphreys, M. (2015). The Vlaams Belang: The rhetoric of organizational identity. *Organization Studies*, *36*(1), 91–111.
Mudde, C. (1995). Right-wing extremism analyzed. A comparative analysis of the ideologies of three alleged right-wing extremist parties (NPD, NDP, CP'86). *European Journal of Political Research*, *27*(2), 203–224.
Mudde, C. (2000). *The ideology of the extreme right* (p. 212). Manchester University Press.
Mudde, C. (2004). The populist zeitgeist. *Government and Opposition*, *39*, 541–563.
Nandan, S. (2005). An exploration of the brand identity-brand image linkage: A communications perspective. *Journal of Brand Management*, *12*(4), 264–278.
Needham, C., & Smith, G. (2015). Introduction: Political branding. *Journal of Political Marketing*. https://doi.org/10.1080/15377857.2014.990828
Newman, B. L. (2001). *Political marketing: Lessons from recent presidential elections*. Yaffe Center for Persuasive Communications, Michigan Ross School of Business. Working Paper.
Nielsen, S. W. (2017). Measuring political brands: An art and a science of mapping the mind. *Journal of Political Marketing*, *15*(1), 70–95.
Nollet, F. (2000, February 21). L'Extrême droite en Europe et en Belgique: Etat des Lieux et stratégies. *Note du CEPESS*.
Norris, P. (2004, January). The evolution of election campaigns: Eroding political engagement? Conference Paper. In *Political communication in the 21st century, St Margaret's College*. University of Otago.
O'Cass, A. (1996). Political marketing and the marketing concept. *European Journal of Marketing*, *30*(10/11).

Olins, W. (2002). How brands are taking over the corporation. In Schultz, M., Hatch, M. J., & Larsen, M. H. (Eds.), *The expressive corporation* (p. 320). Oxford University Press.

O'Shaughnessy, N. (1990). *The phenomenon of political marketing*. Macmillan.

Palmer, J. (2002). Smoke and mirrors: Is that the way it is? Themes in political marketing. *Media, Culture & Society*, *24*, 345–363.

Pauwels, T., & Haute, E. V. (2017, January 11). Caught between mainstreaming and radicalisation: tensions inside the populist Vlaams Belang in Belgium. *LSE European Politics and Policy (EUROPP) Blog*. http://blogs.lse.ac.uk/europpblog/

Pich, C., & Armannsdottir, G. (2022). Political brand identity and image: Typologies, challenges and tensions. Chapter 2. In M. Moufahim (Ed.), *Political Branding in turbulent times*. Palgrave MacMillan.

Pich, C., Armannsdottir, G., & Dean, D. (2020). Exploring the process of creating and managing personal political brand identities in non-party environments: The case of the Bailiwick of Guernsey. *Journal of Political Marketing*. *19*(4), 414–434.

Pich, C., Armannsdottir, G., Dean, D., Spry, L., & Jain, V. (2020). Problematizing the presentation and reception of political brands: The strategic and operational nature of the political brand alignment model. *European Journal of Marketing*. *54*(1), 190–211.

Pich, C., Armannsdottir, G., & Spry, L. (2018). Investigating political brand reputation with qualitative projective techniques from the perspective of young adults. *International Journal of Market Research*. https://doi.org/10.1177/1470785317750817

Pich, C., & Newman, B. I. (2020). *Political branding: More than parties, leaders and policies*. Taylor and Francis Publications. 978-0-367-49227-4.

Smith, G. (2005). Positioning political parties: The 2005 UK general election. *Journal of Marketing Management*, *21*, 1135–1149.

Savigny, H. (2008). *The problem of political marketing*. The Continuum International Publishing Group.

Schneider, H. (2004). Branding in politics – Manifestations, relevance and identity-oriented management. *Journal of Political Marketing*, *3*(3), 41–67.

Smith, G., & French, A. (2009). The political brand: A consumer perspective. *Marketing Theory*, *9*(2), 209–226.

Spruyt, M. (2000). *Wat het Vlaams Blok verzwijgt*. Van Halewijck.

Ströbel, T., & Germelmann, C. C. (2020). Exploring new routes within brand research in sport management: Directions and methodological approaches. *European Sport Management Quarterly*, *20*(1), 1–9.

Swyngedouw, M. (1998). The extreme right in Belgium: Of a non-existent Front national and an omnipresent Vlaams Blok. pp59-75, In Betz, H.-G., & Immerfall, S. (Eds.), *The new politics of the right. Neo-populist parties and movements in established democracies* (p. 268). St Martin's Press.

van Haute, E., & Pauwels, T. (2016). The Vlaams Belang: Party organization and party dynamics. In R. Heinisch & O. Mazzoleni (Eds.), *Understanding populist party organisation* (pp. 49–77). Palgrave Macmillan Ltd.

Van Steenburg, E., & Guzmán, F. (2019). The influence of political candidate brands during the 2012 and 2016 US presidential elections. *European Journal of Marketing*, *53*(12), 2629–2656.

Vander Velpen, J. (1992). *Daar Komen ze aangemarcheerd. Extreme-Rechts in West-Europa*. EPO.

Vos, L. (1992). De politieke kleur van jonge generaties. In Van Doorslaer, R., & Gotovitch, J. (Eds.), *Herfsttij van de 20ste eeuw. Extreme-rechts in Vlaanderen 1920–1990*. (pp. 15–46). Kritak.

Wring, D. (1996). Political marketing and party development in Britain: A "secret" history. *European Journal of Marketing*, *30*(10/11), 100–113.

Wring, D. (1997). Reconciling marketing with political science: Theories of political marketing. *Proceedings of the 1997 Academy of Marketing Conference*, Manchester, 1131–1144.

Wring, D., & Savigny, H. (2008). An ideology of disconnection: For a critical political marketing. *Central European Journal of Communication*, *2*, 251–266.

The Political Marketing of Austerity and Anti-Austerity Policies in the UK[1]

Christopher Robertson

THE CRAFTING OF AUSTERITY: A BROAD CHURCH

The term 'austerity' evokes numerous connotations. Until the 21st century, the word induced memories of post-war economic hardship: being 'austere as a collective effort revive a war-stricken economy' (Robertson, 2022, p. 51). Contemporarily, austerity is widely associated with ideologically motivated policy intended to reduce government debt, often through cutting public expenditure, raising taxes and ideologically 'interpolating neoliberalism within the wider political context' (Robertson, 2022, p. 30). Clearly, socio-political circumstances, alongside the marketing and framing of the policy, determine the guise of austerity. To take the most recognised definition of 'austerity', we must consign the term to its fiscal interpretation. Konzelmann (2012, p. 2) determines that the purpose of economic austerity 'is to reduce a country's deficit – the difference between what a government spends and the revenue it earns. Austerity measures therefore include some element of public expenditure reductions and increased taxes.' Often, this may involve an anti-statist narrative that encourages minimal government intervention in economic affairs (Talving, 2017). However, while this understanding of 'austerity' is often pejoratively associated with contemporary neoliberalism (Craddock, 2019), the term should not be consigned solely to anti-interventionism, or indeed, to economics. Austerity can be cultural, shaping the way in which people react to austerity policies and base everyday decisions depending on the wider socio-economic aura generated by the policy (Bramall, 2013; Hitchen, 2016). Therefore, different subjective experiences of austerity raise questions as to how austerity is manufactured, marketed and sold to electorates by considering the wider economic effects of the policy upon everyday life. For example, the notion to live within our means designates austerity as a way of life, where governments visibly attempting to reduce public spending encouraged citizens to follow suit (Van Lerven, 2019). Moreover, this implies that austerity is often subjectively experienced, and the marketing of austerity as necessary both depends on the success of the marketing frame, alongside the subjective interpretation of the frame presented. This cultural-economic hybrid interpretation of austerity will inform a discussion on how contemporary austerity has been resisted by non-traditional political communities later in this chapter. This first section will explore the marketing and justification of austerity from the post-war consensus to present. Doing so will illuminate the variability in construction of austerity frames, which also attempts to contextualise what communities that attempt to resist austerity are fighting against, and how they attempt to market their counter-agendas.

THE POST-WAR CONSTRUCTION OF AUSTERITY: MAKE DO AND MEND?

Britain was economically lambasted following WW2 due to the profligate war effort. Known as a 'financial Dunkirk' (Johnson & Moggridge, 1978, p. 410) upon the British economy, a clear policy to reduce private consumption and bolster external economic activity and incentivise investment was marketed as essential. The success of this marketing frame was reinforced by the dire state of the economy, alongside historical memory of WW2 and the wider acceptance to 'make do and mend' from the previous years. Britain acquired its biggest debt in history, as between 1939– and 1945, the government borrowed £15.2 billion and Britain's external sterling debt rose by £3.1 billion to £3.7 billion, which equalled 40% of Britain's national income in 1945 (Hughes, 1958). Therefore, citizens understood the circumstances for a dramatic shift in government priority, with the marketing of austerity in this period having clear rationale and justification (Bruley, 1999). This was perceived as a necessary compromise for the goal of full employment (Robertson, 2022).

Following the relative decline of Keynesian economics, alongside the changing socio-political context (Casey, 2011), the initial post-war marketing of austerity was reconfigured to align with the changing times, desires of the population and emerging political agendas. The welfare state, crafted as an invaluable safety net in the post-war years, was becoming increasingly expensive. There was an aura that Britain was 'living beyond its means', epitomised by Prime Minister James Callaghan securing a large loan from the International Monetary Fund in 1976 (Williams, 2019), which elevated societal anxiety over government spending and fiscal stability. With Callaghan beginning to impose austerity measures in the wake of the 1976 Sterling Crisis, this laid fertile ground for a new age of neoliberalism, and a new manifestation of austerity. With the UK's world share of GDP through manufacturing declining from 25.4% in 1950 to 9.1% in 1979 (Cloake, 1994) alongside the cost of the welfare state increasing from £1.3 billion to £9.5 billion between 1955 and 1969 (Traynor & Wilmot, 1994), the UK economy was severely contracting. In-line with the decline of embedded liberalism in the 1970s, with the emergence of contemporary globalisation came the election of Margaret Thatcher and Thatcherite neoliberalism. This entirely reconfigured economic management strategies of the previous years, with changing attitudes towards the welfare state and key priorities including tackling inflation and kickstarting the economy: a perfect storm for fiscal austerity and free market economics.

Clarke and Newman (2012) speak of the 'alchemy of austerity': where austerity as a narrative is always changing to meet different ideological desires, often pragmatically appropriated around the wider socio-economic context. Simply, austerity can transmute and mould to fit specific agendas and circumstances. Thatcher's imposition of austerity instigated the first visible mutation of austerity that remains visible today, where austerity is regularly associated with neoliberalism and its ambition to cut the welfare state (Robertson, 2022). Whereas under the post-war consensus, the initial purpose of austerity and 'being austere' was to rejuvenate the shattered UK economy, spearheaded by state intervention, Thatcherite austerity reconfigured this. Post-war austerity was initially guided by social-democratic ideals, where austerity policies sought to reduce the gap between what the government spent on the welfare state and what was earned from bolstering its export market (Crafts, 1993). While this affected partisan alignment with the proportion of non-manual voters choosing Labour declining from 55% to 47% between 1945– and 1950 (Crowcroft & Theakston, 2013), in this period of austerity, there was clear economic justification for pursuing austerity. Therefore, the marketability of austerity was underpinned by numerous factors in this period.

Firstly, the historical memory of WW2 legitimised the pursuit of austerity to achieve economic growth, with governments discouraging imports, but investing in public services, supplemented by a £3.75 billion loan from the United States (Williams, 2019). Indeed, public debt fell from 237.94% of GDP in 1947 to 131.1% 10 years later (Reeves et al., 2013).

Secondly, these austerity policies sought to reduce the gap between what the government spent on the welfare state and what was earned from bolstering its export market (Crafts, 1993). With full employment as the macroeconomic objective, there was a clear justification to provide a safety net for the population through the welfare state and increasing the amount of people in work.

Thatcherite austerity evidenced the transmutability of the policy. With the UK in a period of relative decline economically (Cloake, 1994) and the welfare state becoming increasingly expensive (Traynor & Wilmot, 1994), there was a shift in priority following the long recovery from WW2. This justified Conservative Chancellor Geoffrey Howe to initiate a monetarist budget in 1981 consisting of stringent deficit targets, austerity cuts and a regressive redistributive taxation policy where tax-free incomes were frozen (Fourton, 2017). A constructivist perspective is apposite here, where following years of high levels of trade barriers, nationalised enterprise and business regulation, the norm of embedded liberalism shifted to a neoliberal framework, characterised by deregulation of markets and the privatisation of state enterprise (Cohen & Centano, 2006). This shifted the marketing and understanding of austerity as policy from a tolerated post-war burden to an emphasis of the capacity of austerity to stimulate the market, encourage innovation and improve the economy following the relative decline of the post-war years. This differed from Thatcherite austerity of the post-war years. Post-war austerity sought to collectively rejuvenate society. Thatcherism sought to utilise austerity to dismantle the welfare state and improve the competitiveness of the UK economy. Post-war austerity required state intervention. Under Thatcher, it was the opposite. This clearly evidences the malleability of austerity as policy, and its capacity to be utilised to achieve different policy goals across differing time periods.

This next section will focus on the marketing and political selling of austerity in the run-up to the 2010 UK general election, amidst the context of the (then) recent 2008 financial crisis. This election marked the 'breaking point' with each party attempting to manufacture the most convincing 'story' of austerity to the electorate. With this election kickstarting the contemporary 'age of austerity', it must be understood how austerity was marketed and sold to the electorate before anti-austerity communities emerged that attempted to market their own counter-frames that continually seek to reject and contest regressive austerity measures.

THE SPURIOUS 'SELLING' OF AUSTERITY

With the historical memory of the 2008 financial crisis readily apparent in voters' minds, in the run-up to the 2010 election, the financial crisis was a core issue for voters. By following similar discursive strategies in their framing of austerity (English et al., 2016), Labour, The Conservatives and the Liberal Democrats cumulatively acquired 88.1% of the vote (White, 2017). Austerity was framed as a beneficial policy that would help the nation recover economically, but the potentiality to increase inequality and reduce incomes were not visibly marketed (Macartney, 2011). So, given the different manifestations of austerity, and a surfeit of academic suggestions that austerity policies generally tend to be unpopular among electorates (Biten et al., 2023; Giuliani, 2020; Irving, 2021), how, and why was austerity able to be crafted and sold to the public?

Firstly, the media played an influential role in highlighting the cross-party acceptance of austerity as painful but necessary (Hunt & Stanley, 2019). Newspapers similarly framed austerity, identifying that the policy was required to help the UK ameliorate the crisis (White, 2017). Even media outlets ordinarily averse to austerity such as *The Guardian* initially framed austerity with a slant towards endorsement (Basu, 2017). However, following George Osborne's emergency budget in June 2010 (Griffiths & Kippan, 2017), *The Guardian* began attacking austerity (Basu, 2017). Anstead (2018) echoes this, noting that periods of crisis can lead to the reconfiguration of ideas, which is evident following the allure of austerity being transformed. It was then evident that this was not the case, with a cacophony of economists, activists, academics and politicians (Emmerson & Tetlow, 2015; Krugman, 2015; NEF, 2013, 2015; Varoufakis, 2016; Wren-Lewis, 2016) perceiving austerity as ideologically inclined and unnecessary that anti-austerity organisations drew upon to craft their progressive movement. This perception of austerity having an ideological basis contradicted the propositions of the Conservative/Lib-Dem government's 'painful but necessary' deficit reduction policy that sought to sustainably revive UK public finances following the shocks of the 2008 financial crisis (HM Treasury, 2015).

Secondly, Labour, Conservatives and the Liberal Democrats understood from a cross-party consensus that neoliberal marketing could attract votes. Given the well-documented economic impact of the financial crisis, the economy acted as a valence issue in the run-up to the 2010 election, with each party attempting to market their interpretation of austerity to appeal to the median voter (Downs, 1957; English et al., 2016; Fairclough, 2016). Recent historical memory from the Thatcher years highlights that neoliberal austerity could cut workers' rights, indebt the poorest in society and increase inequalities (Hudson, 2013;

Irving, 2021). However, with 32% of the electorate in 2009 (Hansard Society, 2009) highlighting that managing the economy should be the core concern of the elected government, widespread economic panic and consistent articulation of the inevitability of austerity was weaponised to acquire voter consent. This austerity acceptance was quickly revoked following the election of the Conservative-Liberal-Democrat coalition, however, with 73% of the public discerning once the government had begun its austerity agenda that economic inequality was a major issue (Borges et al., 2013). This echoes recent empirical research contrasting previous scholarship (Alesina et al., 1998, 2011; Hübscher & Sattler, 2017), highlighting that a government's re-election chances decrease and their political credibility declines if they propose, or enact austerity spending cuts (Hübscher et al., 2020). George Osborne marketed his austerity brand as necessary to retain investor confidence in the British economy and discredit Gordon Brown's previous economic policies. For example, The Treasury's 'optimistic fiscal projections for the worsening of public finances' (Tomlinson, 2017, p. 114) which coincided with the breaking of Labour's 'golden rule' policy and Brown's perception that the years of 'boom and bust' had ended (Johnson & Chandler, 2015). Despite Brown's shift from fiscal-conservatism to profligacy, research institutes such as the Institute for Fiscal Studies (Chote et al., 2010) and scholars such as Wren-Lewis (2013) determined that while Labour did not have a model economic policy, it was not the prime causal factor for the financial crisis (Tomlinson, 2017) and that Conservative attempts to target Brown's policies explicitly were 'pure spin' (Wren-Lewis, 2013, p. 45). Therefore, it can be argued that the coalition implementation of austerity was thoroughly ideological, acquiring consent of the public through carefully marketed discursive tropes.

Misleading pro-austerity narratives by the coalition government restricted debate on economic solutions to the crisis within the locus of austerity (Barnes & Hicks, 2018). By excluding alternatives to austerity and constructing austerity as the only economic solution, this evidenced an element of democratic enclosure by the government to pursue ideological agendas veiled in the façade of pragmatic politics. Given the context of the 2010 election and the UK on the imminency of bankruptcy, the Conservatives offered a fundamental alternative to Labour policy that voters could heuristically associate with the crisis, with continual referral to the size of the budget deficit (Clarke et al., 2011). Authors such as Harrison (2021) argue that austerity escaped critique from large swathes of the population due to the marketing frame of cuts being essential to stimulate business growth, coinciding with those who are wealthier and less reliant on public services being more likely to buy into the notion that austerity is 'necessary and fair', with Bansak et al. (2021) finding that those on the centre to the far-right of the political spectrum were much more likely to exhibit preference for austerity compared to those on the left. Conversely, Harrison (2021) argues that those who are disproportionately affected by austerity lack the resources to act against austerity. Despite a useful observation of the effect of austerity upon political behaviour, Robertson (2022) critiques the simplicity of Harrison's (2021) notion that those who are more visibly affected by austerity being less likely to act, given the plethora of participatory opportunities granted by anti-austerity communities and their increasingly visible and inclusive 'brand', that will be further expanded throughout this work.

There are several themes surrounding how austerity was sold. Firstly, the notion of 'dangerous debt' as an emotive, alliterative frame evokes connotations of an ill, generated by previous Labour governments, that must be purged (NEF, 2013). This could be clearly seen in Osborne's narrative, with repetition of the danger of public sector debt attributed to Tony Blair and Gordon Brown's previous Labour governments (Henry, 2015; Skidelsky, 2015). Free market think tanks such as the Adam Smith Institute supported these measures under the justification that public sector debt should be swiftly reduced by austerity (Inman, 2020) and through this narrative, this justifies spending cuts by constructing that states cannot cure debt by borrowing more, thus, cuts are necessary and spending must decline to revitalise the economy (Blyth, 2013). The second frame directly linked to this, arguing that Britain was 'broke' and collective austerity was required to recuperate the economy, embodied by David Cameron's 'Big Society' ethos. This delegated that it was not just the government that should enact austerity policies, but that the British public should be austere also. While this policy was an ambitious attempt to recraft the image of the party and, to some extent, assisted Cameron in this 2010 electoral victory, in the medium-term austerity overshadowed this policy and ultimately the 'Big Society' policies were unable to be effectively delivered (Williams, 2019). Moreover, discursive strategies were utilised, such as the claim that Britain had 'maxed out its credit card': a familiar metaphor that attempted to imply the severity of the economic crisis and the requirement of austerity to reduce the balance of the country's credit card. Austerity was also presented as a necessary evil, with democratic enclosure readily apparent through the articulation that 'there is no alternative to austerity': a strong frame that continually reinforced the narrative that spending cuts were both necessary, and the only policy option available, with research suggesting that right-wing parties are less likely to face electoral repercussions when enacting austerity measures (Langsæther et al., 2022; Suzuki, 2024). With austerity continually marketed as the only option available to the government, this misled the public into thinking that other potential policy options had been deliberated, but later found unfit for purpose. Lastly, the ideological trope of an intrusive, domineering state was utilised to market the ideology of austerity through rhetorically tarnishing perceptions of government intervention and heightening the salience of austerity's capacity to rejuvenate the economy: a key issue for voters (Robertson, 2022). This also heightens the salience of 'small' government as necessary, and less invasive than 'big' government (NEF, 2013). With empirical evidence highlighting that public support for 'small' government is often low, due to its perceived impact upon public services (Hastings et al., 2017; Wren-Lewis, 2016), the government's carefully crafted frames sought to bypass public perceptions of austerity and justify the ideological dismantling of welfare and rollback of the state. This visibly evidences the variant marketability of austerity, continually expanding and retracting its meaning simultaneously to encapsulate different ideas and methods of achieving neoliberal goals.

Austerity began by being sold as the only way to solve the UK's economic woes. This later mutated into economic storytelling that interpolated the financial crisis with a fiscal crisis, where the media played a key role in this (Basu, 2017) through the careful discursive choices employed by George Osborne and David Cameron. This subsequently reinforced Conservative ideology by proposing cuts to the welfare state and reducing public spending as mechanisms to cut costs. The last frame is apparent throughout the strategies, encompassing an ideological narrative that also attempted to discredit the Shadow Cabinet. Gordon Brown was framed as directly responsible for the financial crisis and the reason why austerity was required to be imposed, due to his irresponsible spending (Skidelsky, 2015). Despite the wider global implications of the financial crisis, this was an easy sell to the public since Labour had been in power during the financial crisis (NEF, 2013). Furthermore, Labour failed to convincingly display to the electorate that it was in no way responsible for the crisis, which shifted attention to the Conservative Party relative to the declining public perception of Brown and Blair (Clarke et al., 2011), alongside accentuating the ideology of austerity as painful, but necessary (Robertson, 2022).

With several frames incessantly peddled by supporters of austerity and channelled through regularly corresponding mass media coverage, the narrative of austerity became dominant and easily sold. While much of the British public were indoctrinated into believing the coalition's justifications of austerity, several pockets of society, predominantly those in the public sector, began to construct and market counternarratives. These attempted to challenge the dominant norms and ideas of austerity within the public sphere and to make visible the regressive impacts of austerity. This next section will focus on the policies initiated by the coalition government to prompt the emergence of anti-austerity marketing, and how the anti-austerity community and their marketing strategy have continually developed and strengthened, despite the ostensibly muted on-the-ground response to austerity (Harrison, 2022).

THE MAKING OF THE ANTI-AUSTERITY COMMUNITY IN THE UK

The contemporary 'age of austerity' and subsequent anti-austerity culture in the UK was constructed through the discourse of 'breaking point' (White, 2017) and dissatisfaction with the Coalition's austerity. Despite repeated affirmation that University tuition fees would not be increased by the Coalition government, in 2012 it was proposed that tuition fees would be increased to £9000 per year, accompanied by a 40% cut to the higher education teaching budget from the 2014/2015 academic year (Hensby, 2014). This not only eroded the electorate's trust of the Liberal Democrats who pledged not to increase fees (Butler, 2021) but also illuminated evidence of ideological austerity cuts and the continuing of the marketisation of education which had been a core policy frame of numerous successive governments prior to 2010 (Dean, 2016; Lunt, 2008). E-petitions, as tools that attempt to mobilise collective awareness of issues often omitted in mainstream agendas have also been utilised by anti-austerity communities as important tools of 'democratic furniture' (Chadwick, 2012, n.p.), alongside websites such as change.org and by citizen-led initiatives spearheaded through 38 Degrees. If MPs do not satisfactorily respond to these issues, voters can continue to exert pressure online, spreading awareness of their cause and attempting to foster political discussion surrounding how austerity affects the everyday lived-and-felt experience of publics (Hitchen, 2016). Digital media was also a battleground that drew support, with some anti-tuition-fee movements acquiring thousands of followers in their first week, and online chatter swiftly emerging and forming a collective anti-austerity identity (Graham et al., 2015; Theocharis, 2013). Despite initial 'failures' after Parliament affirmed the increase in tuition fees alongside a £4.2 billion reduction in funding for state education (Theocharis, 2013), this began the contemporary 'anti-age-of-austerity' and the emergence of a counterpublic brand. The term 'counterpublic', first used by Nancy Fraser (1990) builds upon Jürgen Habermas's (1989) notion of the public sphere as a realm of our social life where publics come together to engage in rational-critical debate. Defined by Fraser (1990, p. 67) as 'parallel discursive arenas where members of subordinated social groups invent and circulate counterdiscourses', Robertson (2022, p. 7) later noted that anti-austerity organisations constituted 'visible counterpublics' by displaying oppositional discourses, ideas and identities that rejected dominant austerity frames to craft a distinct oppositional counterpublic 'brand.'

It is worth appraising what is meant by 'anti-austerity' to contextualise what this brand entailed, and what messages were formed. 'Anti-austerity' encompasses more than opposing austerity. It is subjective, incorporating many perceptions as to what 'austerity' embodies (Chalari & Sealey, 2017). Therefore, when considering 'anti-austerity', we should not just recognise this as rejection of austerity as policy but also the multitude of cumulative effects that these policies create. Indeed, many political concepts are indeterminate, and austerity is no exception (Fitzgerald, 2013). Anti-austerity issues are comparably subjective, and therefore there is not one universal 'anti-austerity market' or target group. Yet, the broad locus of anti-austerity counterpublics consist of inclusive, catch-all arenas that reject neoliberalism and austerity, and attempt to promote socially-just, progressive imaginaries that attempt to represent and make visible the impact of austerity on broad swathes of society (Robertson, 2022). What is shared by all facets of the anti-austerity apparatus are that anti-austerity encompasses a unifying agenda to construct alternative counterpublics that reject austerity and seek to make visible its negative impacts. As opposed to rigidly defining 'austerity', therefore, anti-austerity is a broad, transmutable doctrine, akin to austerity. Concurring, Robertson (2022) found that despite the often indeterminate nature of the anti-austerity community, it is collectively bound by rejection of neoliberalism and the Conservative government's austerity programme. Moreover, despite the varying concerns of the community, empirical research has suggested that anti-austerity communities online are sought to be engaged with for several reasons. Overarching these is their descriptive representational nature: while anti-austerity communities are not 'elected' nor representative of everyone, respondents to Robertson's (2022) study largely perceived that these communities were more subjectively representative than formal political or institutional arrangements, in a model entitled the 'sixth-estate'. Building upon notions of mass media as the fourth estate and social media as the fifth estate (Dutton, 2009), Robertson's (2022) model postulated that anti-austerity communities as non-traditional counterpublics act as discursive agents that attempt to market narratives that resonate with broader digital opinion through rejecting dominant rhetorical interpretations of 'austerity'. They do so due to the following criteria:

Firstly, due to their alternative marketing shifting discussion from 'there is no alternative to austerity' to 'perhaps there are alternatives' (Hunt & Stanley, 2019), such as through tackling corporate tax avoidance in attempt to reduce the national deficit (Bramall, 2016).

Secondly, their focus on single-issues that have subjective importance, such as the impact of austerity cuts to the NHS, with evidence suggesting that this marketing is beneficial given that voters' often perceive that mainstream institutions often do not effectively respond to issues that voters genuinely care about (McCombs & Shaw, 1972; Coleman, 2012; Robertson, 2022).

Thirdly, anti-austerity communities seek to amplify traditionally marginalised discourses that challenge dominant narratives of austerity and seek to illuminate alternatives, such as investment over cuts, interventionist industrial strategies (Cole, 2016) or an activist industrial policy where prolonged backing of developing skills, technology or infrastructure would pay long-term dividends (Hansard, 2012). Moreover, these communities provide a more specific and focused discussion on issues that voters care about, alongside providing them with a political voice to discuss the impact of austerity upon their lived-and-felt experiences, relating how austerity impacts across social groups and competing with dominant interpretations of austerity as a policy of growth in a democratically-significant, agonistic vein (Mouffe, 2016; Robertson, 2022).

Lastly, these communities by marketing alternative messages and attempting to sustain ambitious imaginaries of a future without austerity can affect perceived political self-efficacy (Vecchione et al., 2014) and foster political competence. Publics are able to learn about alternative marketing frames which facilitates the acquisition of subjectively important, educational information that allows one to position themselves and understand austerity affects their everyday life (Robertson, 2022).

Therefore, anti-tuition fee and anti-corporate protests may initially seem disparate issues. Other issues which highlight the broad umbrella of the anti-austerity brand are green politics, feminist agendas and anti-consumerism (Bramall, 2013). The glue which binds these progressive syndicates together is a shared vilification of the enemy ethos (Vanderford, 1989) which targets elites and seeks to make visible progressive alternatives to marginalised or disproportionately impacted agendas. Therefore, anti-austerity represents a seemingly perpetual array of issues, yet retains consistent marketability due to the array of progressive causes that it encapsulates. Consequently, the marketing by these alternative communities merits attention given their capacity to not only make visible and increase the accessibility of alternatives to austerity but also their capacity to influence political socialisation, social learning, and act as digital movements of opinion that highlights the democratic potential of alternative political actors in marketing and circulating counterpublic marketing frames (see Robertson, 2022 for an elaborated discussion).

However, for a marketing strategy to be successful, there needs to be a clear differentiation with competing brands, and, subsequently, their message (Dickson & Ginter, 1987). Therefore, anti-austerity communities have attempted to locate their wide-ranging ideas create a unique anti-austerity brand. These organisations seek to redefine political engagement and provide a chorus of counter-narratives that demand alternative ways of countering the austerity-influenced crisis (Drago, 2021; Hatzisavvidou, 2017). Robertson (2022) argues that anti-austerity communities' use of digital media provides an advantageous tool for heuristic political engagement in marketing and selling the anti-austerity brand, alongside acting as a channel for this individualised method of political engagement. For example, Manchón and Guerrero-Solé (2019) discuss hashtag and phrase-led branding, where users can formulate hashtags to formulate distinct social identities to identify support of a brand. This is essential for anti-austerity communities to focus their narrative within the broad and subjective locus of the anti-austerity community at large. Walker's (2021) grassroots communication model (see Figure 26.1) can be applied to anti-austerity marketing strategies, and their use of 'hashtag' branding. Anti-austerity communities must firstly identify an issue. The policy identified, shared by the entire anti-austerity community, will be austerity, with different understandings of the social need of tackling this policy across the community. For example, some groups will identify the disproportionate impact of austerity upon women earning less than men in the gendered labour market, alongside being disproportionately affected by austerity cuts due to unpaid family responsibilities (Pearson, 2019), highlighting austerity as an 'uneven process of social differentiation' (Hall, 2020, p. 242). Other groups, despite recognising this area, will heighten the salience of austerity's regressive impact upon public services, attempting to make visible 'stealth' effects of austerity, such as increased GP waiting times that seeks to illuminate the impact of austerity upon all (Barnes & Hicks, 2018; Harrison, 2021), as opposed to specific demographics. With the financial crisis opening a significant hole in the UK economy, the coalition government implemented significant public spending cuts alongside tax rises to compensate for the significant GDP drop, alongside the economy shrinking by 5% between 2007 and 2009 (Emmerson & Tetlow, 2015). While austerity is articulated as a policy to stimulate the market by some (Arrieta, 2022), anti-austerity communities attempted to challenge government rhetoric that austerity was necessary and identified how poorer areas of the UK were disproportionately impacted by austerity, such as Liverpool being struck by a 58% cut in funding between 2010 and 2017, whereas affluent councils received an 8% increase in social care spending between 2010 and 2015 (Hastings et al., 2015; Lavalette, 2017).

Secondly, determining solutions and outcomes. For example, Momentum advocate investing in public services as opposed to austerity cuts and, as an example of an outcome, work interdependently with other progressive syndicates to promote and attempt to develop responses to this goal, such as reforming the tax system (Resolution Foundation, 2023). Room et al. (2015) also considered, as an alternative to austerity, that investment over cuts

Figure 26.1 Walker's (2021) Grassroots Communication Model

should be pursued, particularly in disadvantaged communities that are often adversely affected by austerity. Room et al. (2015) suggest that a 'new social contract' by drawn that attempts to reduce the risks of poverty spearheaded by austerity, alongside stimulating economic growth: the justification for austerity itself to be pursued. Alongside other anti-austerity alternatives such as closing tax loopholes and tackling corporate tax avoidance and attempting to amplify the benefits of public investment, countered against the regressive impact of austerity, anti-austerity strategies link to Taylor's (2002) work on modern social imaginaries, where 'imagining alternative possibilities can de-legitimise hegemonic practices [those of austerity] and provide justification for alternatives...based on collective betterment' (Robertson, 2022, p. 42). By drawing upon Keynesian critiques of austerity and advocating expanding public spending to stimulate economic activity, a strong investment strategy in education and training (Room et al., 2015) and a redistributive strategy to underpin this expansionary fiscal policy, anti-austerity communities attempt to market a myriad of alternatives to austerity, underpinned by the lived-and-felt experiences of those who are adversely affected by the policy (Hitchen, 2016). By making visible the ideological component of austerity as a mechanism to reduce the size of the state (Wren-Lewis, 2016) and attempting to creatively offer solutions to adapt to, challenge and imagine (Bramall, 2013; Craddock, 2021) a scenario without austerity, anti-austerity communities play an intrinsic role in fostering counterpublics that challenge hegemonic narratives and attempt to illuminate and educate publics into possible alternatives (Robertson, 2022).

Thirdly, for an effective communication strategy, anti-austerity communities need to gauge public opinion. Using hashtag and phrase-led branding strategies, and wider probing of 'digital movements of opinion' (Barisione & Ceron, 2017) on digital media, this can be used to gauge wider public opinion on issues. Anti-austerity communities do this, as seen in Figure 26.2, and attempt to generate public support and sentiment on issues in attempt to raise awareness of alternatives to austerity, aid people in relating austerity to their everyday lives, and acts as a form of movement social learning (Robertson, 2022). Fourthly, this feeds into strategising, which builds upon gauging public opinion, and fifthly, a full communications strategy (Walker, 2021), which is currently enacted by anti-austerity communities utilising different digital and face-to-face communication channels in attempt to spread awareness of their cause, affect political perceptions of publics and unify the anti-austerity counterpublic towards broadening the reach of anti-austerity discourse.

Anti-austerity organisations clearly attempt to market themselves as non-hierarchical groups distant from formal legislative and political agendas (Beveridge & Featherstone, 2021). Hatzisavvidou (2017) concurs, finding that anti-austerity communities present themselves as truth tellers that speak truth to power and reject mainstream narratives that

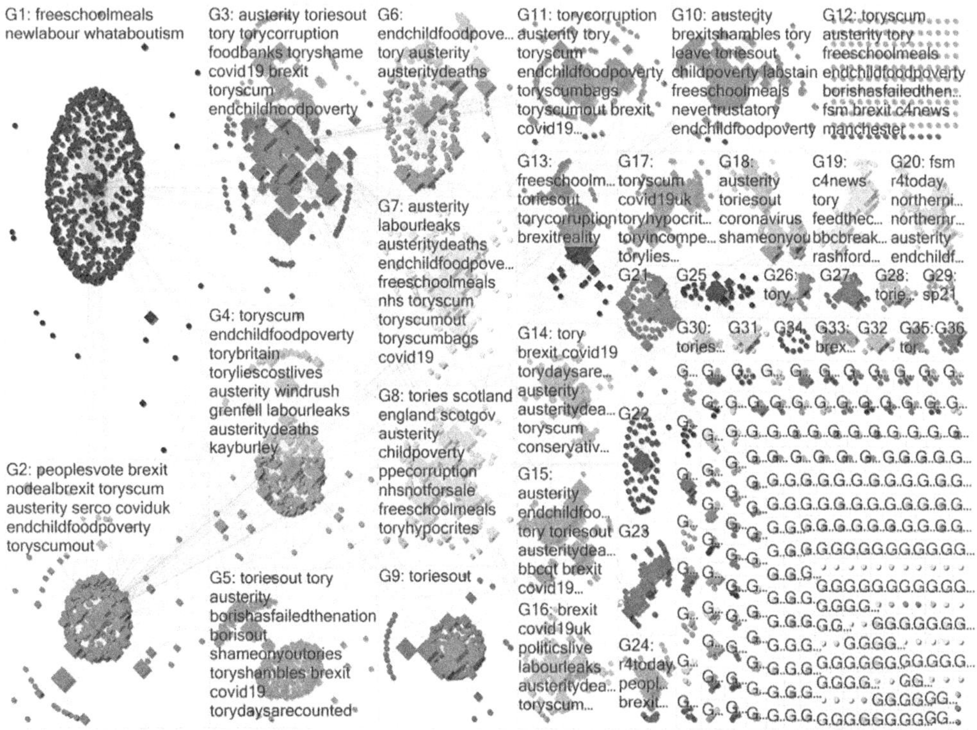

Figure 26.2 Original Social Network Analysis Highlighting Top Hashtags Across the 'Tory Austerity' Twitter Network (Robertson, 2022)

attempt to mislead. For example, UK anti-austerity group The People's Assembly Against Austerity (2014) attempted to discredit the government's 'lies, damned lies, and OFSTED's pseudostatistics' (n.p). Other anti-austerity communities have focused their marketing efforts on other elements of the anti-austerity apparatus, such as the UCU defending public education. Therefore, the heterogenous anti-austerity movement, to effectively formulate a credible brand, must formulate a consistent, marketable identity, identify relevant areas of concern and support these with convincing evidence, which must also tap into wider public opinion on the matters (Beraldo, 2022; Hatzisavvidou, 2017; Kaldor & Selchow, 2013; Richardson, 1995). Non-traditional narratives must be effectively framed as a recognisable yet distinct brand from mainstream political organisations. This can be seen in Figure 26.2. A Social Network Analysis was conducted to determine what anti-austerity communities online talked about, how anti-austerity discourses were marketed, and what elements of the centralised austerity agenda were rejected. The term 'Tory austerity' (a reference to the Conservative government's austerity programme) was utilised to create this sociogram, highlighting the diverse yet interconnected anti-austerity community, and how these discourses were marketed. Discussions related to austerity and food poverty (#foodbanks, #endchildfoodpoverty), a rejection of the Conservative government at large (#torycorruption, #toryshambles), to criticism and discussion of Brexit (#peoplevote, #nodealbrexit, #borisjohnsonhasfailedthenation).

What can be gathered is that with anti-austerity communities are attempting to make visible the regressive impacts of austerity, these groups market themselves as 'truth tellers' (Hatzisavvidou, 2017) that aim to construct and market imaginaries of a world without austerity by identifying and diffusing narratives that affirm progressive ideology. What was found across the network analysis, and other anti-austerity network searches (see Robertson, 2022) is that anti-austerity discourse was unified by four common themes highlighted in Table 26.1. By unifying a marketing strategy through subjectively-interpreted 'anti-austerity' framings, a pro-Corbyn and anti-Starmer agenda, the backdrop of perceived mishandling of the COVID-19 crisis by the UK Conservative government and a broad anti-Tory narrative, the anti-austerity community has clearly evolved since its culmination to include a multitude of broad, yet subjectively-salient factors within its 'brand'. These strategies adhere to Walker's (2021) grassroots communication model. While austerity has been marketed as painful but necessary by successive governments with its current neoliberal application alchemically distant from its post-war conceptualisation, anti-austerity communities, through a cacophony of alternative voices, has sought to remarket the austerity brand as an ideologically motivated agenda that should be repealed. Through the affordances provided by digital media and the construction of counter-hegemonic communities, the anti-austerity brand continues to evolve, with the market of this community deliberately broad to encourage high levels of personability and relatability with areas discredited by ideological austerity (Table 26.2).

CONCLUSIONS

This chapter has sought to overview how austerity was differently marketed and received in two different periods in the UK. The purpose of doing

Table 26.1 Main Themes of Anti-Austerity Discourse

Main Theme	*Definition*	*Example*
Anti-austerity	A subjectively defined term that seeks to make visible the regressive effects of austerity and promote alternatives to reshape social and political relations	'Austerity [as] ideological project inflicting needless misery' ('#ToryAusterity' 17 December 2020).
Pro-Corbyn, anti-Starmer	Discourse that supports the anti-austerity tenets of Jeremy Corbyn while discrediting the direction of the Labour Party under Keir Starmer.	'#StarmerOut', #IStandWithJeremyCorbyn' ('#StarmerOut 4 November 2020).
COVID-19	Illness caused by Coronavirus	'Billionaires wealth risen [during] pandemic' ('Rishi Austerity', 7 December 2020)
Anti-Tory	Anti-Conservative	'BorisHasFailedTheNation' ('Tory Austerity', 25 September 2020)

Table 26.2 Main Themes of Austerity Discourse: Past and Present

Marketing/ Purpose	*Post-war Austerity*	*Austerity Present*	*Comparison*
Austerity – Definition	Policy that attempted to encourage exports and minimise imports, underpinned by frugality and omission of unnecessary wants to revive the economy.	A policy aligned with neoliberalism that seeks to reduce the size of the state and cut public spending	Austerity initially had different purpose and justification to contemporary austerity given the context of the post-war era demanding frugality and the need to lower the war-induced balance of payments deficit. Austerity moves from being a painful necessity to a strategy to stimulate growth and concurrently reduce the size of the state.
Attempt to reduce public spending and achieve growth	'Make do and mend' attitude encouraging post-war frugality through rationing to ensure equitable distribution of essentials in a time of shortage. Reduce the gap between spending on the welfare state and what was earned from the export market	Holding down public sector pay and cutting staff while attempting to stimulate productivity. Marketed as necessary to stimulate economic growth and framed with 'no alternative' and 'painful but necessary'. Past Labour policy blamed for having to pursue austerity.	Post-war austerity was marketed as a strategy that would rejuvenate the economy: times of prosperity would follow the times of hardship. Akin to contemporary austerity, it was marketed as 'the only option' under the WW2 coalition government, and later under Attlee's 1945 Labour government (Hood & Himaz, 2017). However, the difference can be distinguished as post-war austerity was initially perceived as a cross-party consensus to aid in the UK's economic recovery. Contemporary austerity was one of a multitude of options available to the Conservative Party, yet was presented as the only feasible policy. The Conservatives in 1951 following the initial wartime coalition agreement targeted the Labour Party's austerity policies and illuminated that austerity policies disproportionately impacted higher income groups and called for their own version of austerity spending cuts to fund lower taxation which increased their electoral success (Hood & Himaz, 2017; Zweiniger-Bargielowska, 1994). Contemporary austerity continues the narrative of cutting spending, marketed as 'painful but necessary' to revive the economy following the period of turbulence in what

(Continued)

Table 26.2 (Continued)

Marketing/ Purpose	*Post-war Austerity*	*Austerity Present*	*Comparison*
			Oren and Blyth (2019, p. 618) term the 'boom, crash, austerity, reset' cycle.
Britain begins to 'live beyond its means'	Shift towards austerity and its contemporary association with neoliberalism under Margaret Thatcher following 1976 Sterling Crisis and the IMF's demand for austerity measures.		Following the election of Thatcher in 1979 there is a shift from welfare capitalism to individualism, cuts to public services, and a business-oriented financial growth model, in-line with other countries such as the US increasingly liberalising their labour markets (Blyth, 2013). Contemporary austerity continued to be marketed as economically beneficial for growth by Conservative politicians, and was framed as the 'only alternative' to extricate the UK from the financial crisis, which was also used to rhetorically tarnish the reputation of Gordon Brown and Labour Party economic policy.

so has been to illuminate why past periods of austerity were seemingly consensual, while, contemporarily, it has become more visibly contested. Following WW2, austerity was undisputed by much of the population given the wider socio-economic context justifying the dramatic shift in government priority. Contrasting this, the 21st century application of austerity in the UK has a visible ideological backbone, marketed in the shadow of a significant financial crisis. Through securitising the economy and presenting austerity as the only means necessary, this policy was marketed and received by electorates in entirely different circumstances compared to post-WW2 austerity. In response, anti-austerity communities emerged seeking to market narratives that make visible the regressive and ideologically inclined nature of contemporary austerity. Despite a lack of visible retraction of austerity agendas in response to anti-austerity communities in the UK, digital media has been consistently utilised by these communities to create collective identities and market alternative, progressive agendas to electorates.

It has been discussed that through the alternative marketing frames proposed by anti-austerity communities, these organisations possess democratic worth as non-traditional conduits of political information that seek to bind together communities and expand awareness of the impact of, and alternatives to, austerity as practiced. The contribution of this work, therefore, has been to illuminate different reactions to, and the rationale for these different responses to austerity, and how austerity policies have become increasingly challenged and marketed within anti-austerity counterpublics. In doing so, the democratic worth of non-traditional communities that are subjectively representative and beneficial has been noted, building into literature considering the role of 'digital movements of opinion' and marketing non-conventional political brands (e.g. Drago, 2021; Mercea & Yilmaz, 2018; Pich & Newman, 2020) in the form of digitally mediated counterpublics (Robertson, 2022). This has built upon notions of social learning (Gleason, 2013) and drew upon findings by Robertson (2022) that identified the democratic role and purpose of non-traditional political communities beyond 'tangible' upheaval of austerity agendas, labelled as the 'sixth estate'. Future research should continue to explore the state of the field and shift attention to how non-traditional communities, despite lacking 'tangible' on-the-ground change, influence electorates through alternative marketing strategies that seek to critically dismantle hegemonic government agendas. There is little research currently exploring how 'non-tangible' change initiated by non-traditional communities affects wider public opinion on issues. This is required, as it is unlikely that continual non-traditional marketing has no observable effect upon electorates, as was found in previous work (Robertson, 2022).

Note

1 Elements of this work have been taken from the author's PhD thesis – See Robertson, 2022.

REFERENCES

Alesina, A., Ardagna, S., & Lecce, G. (2011). *The electoral consequences of large fiscal adjustments*. National Bureau of Economic Research working paper no.17655. National Bureau of Economic Research.

Alesina, A., Perotti, R., & Tavares, J. (1998). The political economy of fiscal adjustments. *Brookings Papers on Economic Activity*, 1, 197–266. https://dash.harvard.edu

Anstead, N. (2018). The idea of austerity in British politics, 2003–2013. *Political Studies*, 66(2), 287–305. https://doi.org/10.1177/0032321717720376

Arrieta, T. (2022). Austerity in the United Kingdom and its legacy: Lessons from the COVID-19 pandemic. *Economic and Labour Relations Review*, 33(2), 238–255. https://doi.org/10.1177/10353046221083051

Bansak, K., Bechtel, M. M., & Margalit, Y. (2021). Why austerity? The mass politics of a contested policy. *American Political Science Review*, 115(2), 486–505. https://doi.org/10.1017/s0003055420001136

Barisione, M., & Ceron, A. (2017). A digital movement of opinion? Contesting austerity through social media. In M. Barisione & A. Michailidou (Eds.), *Social media and European politics: Rethinking power and legitimacy in the digital era* (pp. 77–104). Palgrave Macmillan.

Barnes, L., & Hicks, T. (2018). Making austerity popular: The media and mass attitudes towards fiscal policy. *American Journal of Political Science*, 62(2), 340–354. https://doi.org/10.1111/ajps.12346

Basu, L. (2017). Living within our means. The UK new construction of the austerity frame over time. *Journalism: Theory, Practice & Criticism*, *20*(2), 313–330. https://doi.org/10.1177/1464884917708870

Beraldo, D. (2022). Movements as multiplicities and contentious branding: Lessons from the digital exploration of #Occupy and #Anonymous. *Information, Communication & Society*, *25*(8), 1098–1114. https://doi.org/10.1080/1369118X.2020.1847164

Beveridge, R., & Featherstone, D. (2021). Introduction: Anti-politics, austerity and spaces of politicisation. *Environment and Planning C: Politics and Space*, *39*(3), 437–450. https://doi.org/10.1177%2F23996544211004188

Biten, M., Kuhn, T., & van der Brug, W. (2023). How does fiscal austerity affect trust in the European Union? Analyzing the role of responsibility attribution. *Journal of European Public Policy*, 1–18. https://doi.org/10.1080/13501763.2022.2060282

Blyth, M. (2013). *Austerity: The history of a dangerous idea*. Oxford University Press.

Borges, W., Clarke, H. D., Stewart, M. C., Sanders, D., & Whiteley, P. (2013). The emerging political economy of austerity in Britain. *Electoral Studies*, *32*(3), 396–403. https://doi.org/10.1016/j.electstud.2013.05.020

Bramall, R. (2013). *The cultural politics of austerity*. Palgrave Macmillan.

Bramall, R. (2016). Austerity pasts, austerity futures?. In E. Garcia, M. Martinez-Iglesias, & P. Kirby (Eds.), *Transitioning to a post-carbon society, degrowth, austerity and wellbeing* (pp. 111–129). Palgrave Macmillan.

Bruley, S. (1999). From austerity to prosperity and the pill: The post-war years, 1945-c.1968. In S. Bruley (Ed.), *Women in Britain since 1900* (pp. 117–146). Palgrave.

Butler, C. (2021). When are governing parties more likely to respond to public opinion? The strange case of the liberal democrats and tuition fees. *British Politics*, *16*, 1–19. https://doi.org/10.1057/s41293-020-00139-3

Casey, T. (2011). *The legacy of the crash how the financial crisis changed America and Britain*. Palgrave Macmillan.

Chadwick, A. (2012). *How digital petitions are replacing traditional parties as the engine of modern, popular democracy*. https://www.independent.co.uk/voices/comment/how-digital- petitions-are-replacing-traditional-parties-as-the-engine-of-modern-popular-democracy-8329266.html

Chalari, A., & Sealey, C. (2017). UK students' subjective experiences and responses to higher education austerity: Implications and lessons for the future. *Observatoire de la société britannique*, *19*, 229–245. https://doi.org/10.4000/osb.1949

Chote, R., Crawford, R., Emmerson, C., & Tetlow, G. (2010). *Public spending under labour*. Institute for Fiscal Studies.

Clarke, J., & Newman, J. (2012). The alchemy of austerity. *Critical Social Policy*, *32*(3), 299–319. https://doi.org/10.1177%2F0261018312444405

Clarke, H., Sanders, D., Stewart, M., & Whiteley, P. (2011). Valence politics and electoral choice in Britain, 2010. *Journal of Elections, Public Opinion, and Parties*, *21*(2), 237–253. https://doi.org/10.1080/17457289.2011.562614

Cloake, J. A. (1994). *Britain in the modern world*. Oxford University Press.

Cole, M. (2016). Liberal Democrats in coalition: Economic policy. *Journal of Liberal History*, *92*, 6–15. https://liberalhistory.org.uk/wp-content/uploads/2016/09/92-Cole-Cable-Swinson-Howarth-Economic-policy.pdf

Coleman, S. (2012). Believing the news: From sinking trust to atrophied efficacy. *European Journal of Communication*, *27*(1), 35–45. https://doi.org/10.1177/0267323112438806

Cohen, J. N., & Centano, M. A. (2006). Neoliberalism and patterns of economic performance, 1980–2000. *The ANNALS of the American Academy of Political and Social Science*. *606*(1), 32–67. https://doi.org/10.1177/0002716206288751

Collington, R. (2022). Liz Truss wants to inflict more austerity on Britain – But there's nothing left to cut. https://www.theguardian.com/commentisfree/2022/oct/04/liz-truss-austerity-britain-public-sector-welfare-state

Craddock, E. (2019). What is the point of anti-austerity activism? Exploring the motivating and sustaining emotional forces of political participation. *Interface: A Journal for an about Social Movements*, *11*(1), 62–88. https://www.interfacejournal.net/

Craddock, E. (2021). *Living against austerity A feminist investigation of doing activism and being activist*. Bristol University Press.

Crafts, N. F. R. (1993). *Adjusting from War to Peace in 1940s Britain* [Working Paper #411]. Warwick: University of Warwick Economic Research Papers.

Crowcroft, R., & Theakston, K. (2013). The fall of the Attlee Government, 1951. In T. Heppell & K. Theakston (Eds.), *How labour governments Fall: From Ramsay Macdonald to Gordon Brown* (pp. 61–82). Palgrave Macmillan.

Dean, J. (2016). "Angelic spirits of '68': Memories of 60s" radicalism in responses to the 2010–11 UK student protests. *Contemporary British History*, *30*(3), 305–325. https://doi.org/10.1080/13619462.2015.1099438

Dickson, P. R., & Ginter, J. L. (1987). Market segmentation, product differentiation, and marketing strategy. *Journal of Marketing*, *51*(2), 1–10. https://doi.org/10.2307/1251125

Dorling, D. (2022). Austerity led to twice as many excess UK deaths as previously thought – here's what that means for future cuts. https://theconversation.com/austerity-led-to-twice-as-many-excess-uk-deaths-as-previously-thought-heres-what-that-means-for-future-cuts-192033

Downs, A. (1957). An economic theory of political action in a democracy. *Journal of Political Economy*, *65*(2), 135–150. https://doi.org/10.1086/257897

Drago, A. (2021). Afterword: They say the Centre cannot hold: Austerity, crisis, and the rise of anti-politics. *Environment and Planning C: Politics and Space*, *39*(3), 597–605. https://doi.org/10.1177%2F2399654420981388

Eichengreen, B. (1996). Institutions and economic growth: Europe after world war II. In N. F. R. Crafts & G. Toniolo (Eds.), *Economic growth in Europe since 1945* (pp. 38–65). Cambridge University Press.

Emmerson, C., & Tetlow, G. (2015). UK public finances: From crisis to recovery. *Fiscal Studies*, *36*(4), 555–577. https://www.jstor.org/stable/26604931

English, P., Grasso, M. T., Buraczynska, B., Karampampas, S., & Temple, L. (2016). Convergence on crisis? Comparing labour and conservative party framing of the economic crisis in Britain, 2008-2014. *Politics & Policy*, *44*(3), 577–603. https://doi.org/10.1111/polp.12160

Fairclough, I. (2016). Evaluating policy as argument: The public debate over the first UK austerity budget. *Critical Discourse Studies*, *13*(1), 57–77. https://doi.org/10.1080/17405904.2015.1074595

Feigenbaum, A., & Iqani, M. (2015). Quality after the cuts? Higher education practitioners' accounts of systemic challenges to teaching quality in times of 'austerity. *Journal of Further and Higher Education*, *39*(1), 46–66. https://doi.org/10.1080/0309877X.2013.778961

Fetzer, T. (2019). Did austerity cause Brexit? *The American Economic Review*, *109*(11), 3849–3886. https://doi.org/10.1257/aer.20181164

Fitzgerald, J. (2013). What does "political" mean to you? *Political Behavior*, *35*, 453–479. https://doi.org/10.1007/s11109-012-9212-2

Flesher Fominaya, C. (2017). European anti-austerity and pro-democracy protests in the wake of the global financial crisis. *Social Movement Studies*, *16*(1), 1–20. https://doi.org/10.1080/14742837.2016.1256193

Fourton, C. (2017). Political and discursive characteristics of the austerity consensus in the UK and France since 1975. *Observatoire de la société britannique*, *19*, 91–109. https://journals.openedition.org/osb/1913

Fraser, N. (1990). Rethinking the public sphere: A contribution to the critique of actually existing democracy. *Social Text*, *25/26*, 56–80. https://doi.org/10.2307/466240

Giuliani, M. (2020). Economy or austerity? Drivers of retrospective voting before and during the Great Recession. *International Political Science Review*, *43*(2), 173–190. https://doi.org/10.1177/0192512120919138

Gleason, B. (2013). #Occupy Wall Street: Exploring informal learning about a social movement on Twitter. *American Behavioral Scientist*, *57*(7), 966–982. https://doi.org/10.1177%2F0002764213479372

Graham, T., Jackson, D., & Wright, S. (2015). From everyday conversation to political action: Talking austerity in online 'third spaces'. *European Journal of Communication*, *30*(6), 648–665. https://doi.org/10.1177%2F0267323115595529

Griffiths, S., & Kippan, H. (2017). Public services after austerity: Zombies, Suez or collaboration?. *The Political Quarterly*, *88*(3), 417–424. https://doi.org/10.1111/1467-923x.12367

Habermas, J. (1989). *The structural transformation of the public sphere*. Polity Press.

Hall, S. M. (2020). The personal is political: Feminist geographies of/in austerity. *Geoforum*, *110*, 242–251. https://doi.org/10.1016/j.geoforum.2018.04.010

Ham, A. (1981). *Treasury rules: Recurrent themes in British economic policy*. Quartet Books.

Hanisch, K., & Messinger-Zimmer, S. (2017). Also ich trau da überhaupt gar keinem.': Die Konflikte aus der Perspektive der Unbeteiligten. In C. Hoeft, S. Messinger-Zimmer, & J. Zilles (Eds.), *Lokale Konflikte um Windkraft, Stromtrassen und Fracking* (pp. 169–181). Bielefeld: Transcript.

Hansard. (2009, April 22). *House of commons debate*. Hansard.

Hansard HL vol 739 written answers col 989 (2012, October 9). [Electronic version].

Harris, P. (2001). To spin or not to spin that is the question: The emergence of modern political marketing. *The Marketing Review*, *2*(1), 35–53. https://doi.org/10.1362/1469347012569436

Harrison, K. (2021). Can't, won't, and what's the point? A theory of the UK public's muted response to austerity. *Representation: Journal of Representative Democracy*, *57*(2), 159–174. https://doi.org/10.1080/00344893.2020.1728367

Harrison, K. (2022). The futility of participation: Austerity and public reluctance to oppose it. *British Politics*, *17*, 469–487. https://doi.org/10.1057/s41293-021-00174-8

Hastings, A., Bailey, N., Besemer, K., Bramley, G., Gannon, M., & Watkins, D. (2015). *Coping with the cuts? Local government and poorer communities*. Joseph Rowntree Foundation.

Hastings, A., Bailey, N., Bramley, G., & Gannon, M. (2017). Austerity urbanism in England: The 'regressive redistribution' of local government services and the impact on the poor and marginalised. *Environment and Planning A: Economy and Space*, *49*(9), 2007–2024. https://doi.org/10.1177%2F0308518X17714797

Hatzisavvidou, S. (2015). Disturbing binaries in political thought: Silence as political activism. *Social Movement Studies*, *14*(5), 509–522. https://doi.org/10.1080/14742837.2015.1043989

Hatzisavvidou, S. (2017). Demanding the alternative: The rhetoric of the UK anti-austerity movement. In J. Atkins & J. Gaffney (Eds.), *Voices of the UK left rhetoric, ideology and the performance of politics* (pp. 211–230). Palgrave Macmillan.

Henry, S. G. B. (2015). Does austerity work? Theory and evidence. *Economic Outlook*, *39*(2), 13–19. https://doi.org/10.1111/1468-0319.12148

Hensby, A. (2014). Networks, counter-networks and political socialisation – paths and barriers to high-cost/risk activism in the 2010/11 student protests against fees and cuts. *Contemporary Social Science*, *9*(1), 92–105. https://doi.org/10.1080/21582041.2013.851409

Hirowatari, K. (2015). *Britain and European monetary cooperation, 1964–1979*. Palgrave MacMillan.

Hitchen, E. (2016). Living and feeling the austere. *New Formations*, *87*, 102–118. https://doi.org/10.3898/NEWF.87.6.2016

HM Treasury. (2015). *2010 to 2015 government policy: Deficit reduction*. Westminster.

Holt, K., Figenschou, T. U., & Frischlich, L. (2019). Key dimensions of alternative news media. *Digital Journalism*, *7*(7), 860–869. https://doi.org/10.1080/21670811.2019.1625715

Hood, C., & Himaz, R. (2017). *A century of fiscal squeeze politics: 100 Years of austerity, politics and bureaucracy in Britain*. Oxford University Press.

Hudson, R. (2013). Thatcherism and its geographical legacies: The new map of socio-spatial inequality in the divided kingdom. *The Geographic Journal*, *179*(4), 377–381. https://doi.org/10.1111/geoj.12052

Hughes, J. R. T. (1958). Review: Financing the British war effort. *The Journal of Economic History*, *18*(2), 193–199. https://www.jstor.org/stable/2115103

Hunt, T., & Stanley, L. (2019). From "there is No alternative" to "maybe there are alternatives": Five challenges to economic orthodoxy after the crash. *The Political Quarterly*, *90*(3), 479–487. https://doi.org/10.1111/1467-923X.12707

Hübscher, E., & Sattler, T. (2017). Fiscal consolidation under electoral risk. *European Journal of Political Research*, *56*(1), 151–168. https://doi.org/10.1111/1475-6765.12171

Hübscher, E., Sattler, T., & Wagner, M. (2020). Voter responses to fiscal austerity. *British Journal of Political Science*, 1–10. https://doi.org/10.1017/S0007123420000320

Inman, P. (2020). Rightwing thinktanks call time on age of austerity. https://www.theguardian.com/politics/2020/may/16/thatcherite-thinktanks-back-increase-public-spending-in-lockdown

Irving, Z. (2021). The legacy of austerity. *Social Policy and Society*, *20*(1), 97–110. https://doi.org/10.1017/S1474746420000500

Johnson, P., & Chandler, D. (2015). The coalition and the economy. In A. Seldon & M. Finn (Eds.), *The coalition effect 2010–2015* (pp. 159–193). Cambridge University Press.

Johnson, E., & Moggridge, D. (1978). *The collected writings of John Maynard Kenyes volume XXIV: Activities 1944–1946: The transition to peace*. Macmillan.

Kaldor, M., & Selchow, S. (2013). The 'bubbling up' of subterranean politics in Europe. *Journal of Civil Society*, *9*(1), 78–99. https://doi.org/10.1080/17448689.2013.784501

Khasnabish, A., & Haiven, M. (2014). *The radical imagination: Social movement research in the age of austerity*. Zed Books.

Kickert, W. (2012). State responses to the fiscal crisis in Britain, Germany and the Netherlands. *Public Management Review*, *14*(3), 299–309. https://doi.org/10.1080/14719037.2011.637410

Konzelmann, S. (2012). *The Economics of austerity (CBR Research Programme on Corporate Governance no. 434)*. University of Cambridge.

Krugman, P. (2015). *The case for cuts was a lie. Why does Britain still believe it? The austerity delusion*. https://www.theguardian.com/business/ng-interactive/2015/apr/29/the-austerity-delusion

Langsæther, P. E., Goubin, S., & Haugsgjerd, A. (2022). Subverted expectations and social democratic austerity: How voters' reactions to policies are conditional on the policy-implementing actor. *Electoral Studies*, *80*. https://doi.org/10.1016/j.electstud.2022.102529

Lavalette, M. (2017). Austerity, inequality and the context of contemporary social work. *Social Work and Social Sciences Review*, *19*(1), 31–39. https://doi.org/10.1921/swssr.v19i1.1080

Lees-Marshment, J. (2001). The marriage of politics and marketing. *Political Studies*, *49*(4), 692–713. https://doi.org/10.1111/1467-9248.00337

Lock, A., & Harris, P. (1996). Political marketing-vive la différence. *European Journal of Marketing*, *30*(10/11), 14–24. https://doi.org/10.1108/03090569610149764

Luna, J. P., Toro, S., & Valenzuela, S. (2022). Amplifying counter-public spheres on social media: News sharing of alternative versus traditional media after the 2019 Chilean uprising. *Social Media + Society*, *8*(1), 1–11. https://doi.org/10.1177/20563051221077308

Lunt, I. (2008). Beyond tuition fees? The legacy of Blair's government to higher education. *Oxford Review of Education*, *34*(6), 741–752. https://doi.org/10.1080/03054980802519001

Maarek, P. J. (1997). New trends in French political communication: The 1995 presidential elections. *Media, Culture & Society*, *19*(3), 357–368. https://doi.org/10.1177/016344397019003004

Macartney, H. (2011). Crisis for the state or crisis of the state? *The Political Quarterly*, *82*(2), 193–203. https://doi.org/10.1111/j.1467-923x.2011.02178.x

Manchón, L. M., & Guerrero-Solé, F. (2019). The use of hashtags as a political branding strategy. *Revista Internacional de Relaciones Públicas*, *9*(17), 5–24. https://doi.org/10.5783/RIRP-17-2019-02-05-24

Matthews, K., Minford, P., Nickell, S., & Helpman, E. (1987). Mrs Thatcher's economic policies 1979-1987. *Economic Policy*, *2*(5), 57–101. https://doi.org/10.2307/1344621

McCallum. (2023). Google: Political adverts must disclose use of AI. https://www.bbc.co.uk/news/technology-66739858

Mercea, D., & Yilmaz, K. E. (2018). Movement social learning on Twitter: The case of the People's Assembly. *The Sociological Review*, *66*(1), 20–40. http://doi.org/10.1177/0038026117710536

Mouffe, C. (2016). Democratic politics and conflict: An agonistic approach. *Política común*, *9*. n. p. https://doi.org/10.3998/pc.12322227.0009.011

New Economics Foundation (2015). *Responses to austerity How groups across the UK are adapting, challenging and imagining alternatives*. New Economics Foundation.

New Economics Foundation (2013). *Framing the economy: The austerity story*. New Economics Foundation.

Newman, B. I. (1994). *The marketing of the president: Political marketing as campaign strategy*. SAGE.

Newman, B. I. (2002). The role of marketing in politics. *Journal of Political Marketing*, *1*(1), 1–5. https://doi.org/10.1300/J199v01n01_01

O'Shaughnessy, N. J. (1990). *The Phenomenon of political marketing*. St. Martin's Press.

Pearson, R. (2019). A feminist analysis of neoliberalism and austerity policies in the UK. *Soundings*, *71*(71), 28–39. https://doi.org/10.3898/soun.71.02.2019

Pemberton, H. (2004). Relative decline and British economic policy in the 1960s. *The Historical Journal*, *47*(4), 989–1013. https://www.jstor.org/stable/4091665

People's Assembly Against Austerity Nottingham (2014). *Lies, damned lies and Ofsted's Pseudostatistics*. https://www.nottspeoplesassembly.org/lies_ofsted

Pich, C., & Newman, B. I. (2020). Evolution of political branding: Typologies, diverse settings and future research. *Journal of Political Marketing*, *19*(1–2), 3–14. https://doi.org/10.1080/15377857.2019.1680932

Pollard, S. (1982). *The wasting of the British economy: British economic policy 1945 to the present*. Croom Helm.

Reeves, A., Basu, S., McKee, M., Marmot, M., & Stuckler, D. (2013). Austere or not? UK coalition government budgets and health inequalities. *Journal of the Royal Society of Medicine*, *106*(11), 432–436. https://doi.org/10.1177%2F0141076813501101

Resolution Foundation (2023). *Britain needs better taxes, rather than just higher ones, to boost fairness and economic growth*. https://www.resolutionfoundation.org/press-releases/britain-needs-better-taxes-rather-than-just-higher-ones-to-boost-fairness-and-economic-growth/

Richardson, J. (1995). The market for political activism: Interest groups as a challenge to political parties. *West European Politics*, *18*(1), 116–139. https://doi.org/10.1080/01402389508425060

Rivière, D., & Curnow, J. (2016). Cutting through the rhetoric: The rise and fall of austerity narratives in Toronto's budget battle. *Storyworlds: A Journal of Narrative Studies*, *8*(2), 27–52. https://doi.org/10.5250/storyworlds.8.2.0027

Robertson, C. (2022). *Anti-austerity politics and social media in the UK: Political participation and non-traditional political organisations*. [PhD Dissertation]. University of Chester.

Rodriguez-Amat, J. R., & Jeffery, B. (2017). Student protests. Three periods of university governance. tripleC. *Communication, Capitalism & Critique. Open Access Journal for a Global Sustainable Information Society*, *15*(2), 524–539. https://doi.org/10.31269/triplec.v15i2.771

Room, G., Carmel, E., Eatwell, J., Gregg, P., Martin, C., Mazzucato, M., Papadopoulos, T., Pitelis, C., Tomlinson, P., & Toner, P. (2015). *Alternatives to austerity*. Institute for Policy Research.

Scammell, M. (1999). Political marketing: Lessons for political science. *Political Studies*, *47*(4), 718–739. https://doi.org/10.1111/1467-9248.00228

Schafer, A., & Streeck, W. (2013). *Politics in the Age of austerity*. Polity Press.

Skidelsky, R. (2015). Austerity: The wrong story. *Economic and Labour Relations Review*, *26*(3), 377–383. https://doi.org/10.1177%2F1035304615601588

Suzuki, J. (2024). A 'leftist premium' to protest movements?: How incumbent partisanship conditions austerity-spurred mass protest. *Acta Politica*, *59*, 124–144. https://doi.org/10.1057/s41269-022-00283-2

Talving, L. (2017). The electoral consequences of austerity: Economic policy voting in Europe in times of crisis. *West European Politics*, *40*(3), 560–583. https://doi.org/10.1080/01402382.2016.1271600

Taylor, C. (2002). Modern social imaginaries. *Public Culture*, *14*(1), 91–124. https://doi.org/10.1215/08992363-14-1-91

Theocharis, Y. (2013). The contribution of websites and blogs to the students' protest communication tactics during the 2010 UK university occupations. *Information, Communication & Society*, *16*(9), 1477–1513. https://doi.org/10.1080/1369118x.2012.706315

Tomlinson, J. (2013). The spirit of '45? Austerity then and now. *Renewal*, *21*(2–3), 46–53. https://www.renewal.org.uk/

Tomlinson, J. (2017). Deficits, debts, and austerity. In J. Tomlinson (Ed.), *Managing the economy, managing the people: Narratives of economic life in Britain from Beveridge to Brexit managing the economy, managing the people: Narratives of economic life in Britain from Beveridge to Brexit* (pp. 110–134). Oxford University Press.

Toms, M. (2013). *The Thatcher privatisation legacy: Not quite what she planned?* Oxera.

Traynor, J., & Wilmot, E. (1994). *Britain in the 20th century world*. Nelson Thornes.

Van Lerven, F. (2019). *Government attempts to 'live within its means' encourages UK households living beyond theirs*. New Economics Foundation.

Vanderford, M. L. (1989). Vilification and social movements: A case study of pro-life and pro-choice rhetoric. *Quarterly Journal of Speech*, *75*(2), 166–182. https://doi.org/10.1080/00335638909383870

Varoufakis, Y. (2016). *Austerity*. Vintage.

Vecchione, M., Caprara, V. G., Giovanna Caprara, M., Alessandri, G., Tabernero, C., & Luis González- Castro, J. (2014). The perceived political self-efficacy scale–short form (PPSE-S): A validation study in three Mediterranean countries. *Cross-Cultural Research*, *48*(4), 368–384. https://doi.org/10.1177%2F1069397114523924

Walker, R. T. (2021). Grassroots communication. In P. Harris, A. Bitonti, C. S. Fleisher, & A. Skorkjær Binderkrantz (Eds.), *The Palgrave encyclopedia of interest groups, lobbying and public affairs section 'G'* (pp. 1–6). Palgrave Macmillan.

White, H. (2017). *Westminster's narration of neoliberal crisis: Rationalising the irrational?* (PhD Dissertation). Edge Hill University.

Williams, B. (2019). Austerity Britain: A brief history. *Political Insight*, *10*(1), 16–19. https://doi.org/10.1177/2041905819838148

Williams, B. (2019). The big society: Ten years on. *Political Insight*, *10*(4), 22–25. https://doi.org/10.1177/2041905819891369

Wonneberger, A., Hellsten, L. R., & Jacobs, S. H. J. (2021). Hashtag activism and the configuration of counterpublics: Dutch animal welfare debates on Twitter. *Information, Communication & Society*, *24*(12), 1694–1711. https://doi.org/10.1080/1369118X.2020.1720770

Wren-Lewis, S. (2013). Aggregate fiscal policy under the Labour government, 1997–2010. *Oxford Review of Economic Policy*, *29*(1), 25–46. https://www.jstor.org/stable/23607129

Wren-Lewis, S. (2016). *A general theory of austerity*. University of Oxford.

Wren-Lewis, S. (2016). *What Brexit and austerity tell us about economics, policy and the media. Sheffield: Sheffield Political Economy Research Institute (SPERI)*. paper no. 36. http://speri.dept.shef.ac.uk/wp-content/uploads/2018/11/SPERI-Paper-36-What-Brexit-and-austerity-tell-us-about-economics-policy-and-the-media.pdf

Wring, D. J. (1997). *Political marketing and the labour party: The relationship between campaign strategy and intra-organisational power [PhD Dissertation]*. Retrieved from University of Cambridge.

Zweiniger-Bargielowska, I. (1994). Rationing, austerity and the Conservative party recovery after 1945. *The Historical Journal*, *37*(1), 173–197. https://doi.org/10.1017/s0018246x00014758

Women in Public Affairs and Lobbying

Maria Cristina Antonucci

INTRODUCTION

When envisioning a lobbyist, the general perception tends to conjure an image of a male figure. In 1990, Schlozman called the lobbyist profession a job 'based on the old boys' political network'and Nownes Freeman 1997 have supported, with data, a professional interpretation grounded in this gender predominance. However, the lobbying and public affairs sector is experiencing, in the last 20 years, a gradual influx of new waves: women and young individuals, who are entering the profession, are now changing the public image of political lobbyists. This trend ensures a diverse and inclusive environment, which is increasingly being recognized and embraced in the management practices of public affairs consulting firms, corporations and associations. In this entry, the objective is to shed light on the extent of women's presence in lobbying and public affairs careers, utilizing the limited publicly available data. We will also explore how the sociological and political science literature has addressed the issue of gender equality within these professions. Finally, we will examine certain factors related to the work of lobbyists that suggest the importance of achieving a gender balance in the staffing of lobbying and public affairs roles. This two-step approach, comprising data analysis and a review of the scientific literature on the topic, aims to elucidate two key aspects: firstly, the ongoing issue of the persistent underrepresentation of women in lobbying and public affairs careers; and secondly, the potential solutions to this issue. The proposed solutions include the adoption of the gender mainstreaming approach endorsed by the Beijing Conference and the European Commission, as well as the integration of gender considerations into Diversity, Equity and Inclusion (DEI) systems. These practices are increasingly implemented by organizations that adhere to the Environmental, Social and Governance (ESG) model, thereby offering, in addition to gender mainstreaming approach, a pathway to achieving gender balance in lobbying and public affairs careers.

A GENDER-DOMINATED PROFESSION? THROUGH THE LENS OF THE DATA

The role of women as political lobbyists has undergone significant changes in the past two decades. Women professionals in public affairs hold a higher proportion of lobbying positions, represent more clients and major interests.

This situation is also influenced by the social and economic recognition of the lobbying profession within democratic systems. The widespread adoption of professional standards, the increased use of lobbying by multinational and national corporations due to globalization, and the interconnectedness between the political, institutional, economic and production spheres have contributed to the establishment of a standardized model of the profession. This has further led to the development of a reputation system, educational pathways and mechanisms of representation of lobbying and public affairs, capable of attracting new and diverse types of workforces into the profession.

Despite this progress in status and in the inclusion of diversities in the profession, lobbying remains a male-dominated profession, prompting questions about the inclusion and exclusion of women in the profession. Recent sociological research has presented data that offer evidence of the ongoing under-representation of women in lobbyist careers. The ability to measure and track the progress of women in this professional area is contingent upon having gender statistics readily available.

The issue of gender statistics presents a challenge: how and where can we obtain gender data regarding the professional lobbyists within a political system? In cases where gender data are not readily available from national level associations of lobbyists, one potential solution lies in examining public registers of interests' representatives. These registers, established through regulatory measures in some mayor political systems (US, Canada, France, UK, Germany, Australia, Denmark, Ireland, Israel, Lithuania, Poland, Taiwan, Hungary), allow interest representatives to gain access to political-institutional spaces and engage with decision-makers only after registration, disclosure and reporting on the meetings. As a result, these registers serve as a valuable public data source, including gender-related information. The scientific literature has recognized and analyzed these registers, extracting valuable insights from them.

In a study conducted by LaPira et al. (2020), gender-based research was carried out using data from public lobbying registers, with a specific focus on lobbyists in Washington. The findings from the collected data revealed that women make up 37% of the total lobbyists in Washington, USA.

A different research paper by Junk et al. (2021) experimented an innovative approach, examining a sample of women in the lobbying profession across Germany, Sweden, Denmark and the UK. This study aimed to explore the varying levels of female representation in this professional sector, ranging from more than 10% in Germany to 30% in Sweden. Notably, this research highlighted the factors on both the supply and demand sides that contribute to the gender imbalance observed in the lobbying profession within these five political systems.

Antonucci (2021) considered the representation of women in public lobbyist registers across Italy, France, the UK and the EU. The findings from the study revealed that in 2021, the percentage of female professionals registered in the public register, which is a requirement to practice the lobbying profession, stood at 18.5% in France and 22% in both Italy and the UK.

Data regarding the registration of lobbyists accessing the European Parliament through dedicated badges indicate a contrasting level of gender representation within this specific domain. In Brussels, women in public affairs and lobbying constitute 45% of the total registered professionals, displaying a higher degree of gender equity within this political-institutional framework, when compared to the United States, United Kingdom, France and Italy.

FROM DATA TO EXPLANATORY PROCESS: WHY LOBBYING AND PUBLIC AFFAIRS REMAIN A GENDER UNBALANCED PROFESSION?

The beforementioned data reveal that the representation of women in the lobbying profession varies between 18% and 37% across different political systems, including the USA, UK, Germany, France, Italy and Denmark. While not all cases indicate a clear male dominance where the presence of women in the workforce is below 25%, the low proportion of women in the public affairs and lobbying profession has prompted several interpretative hypotheses in the scientific literature, which we will discuss below.

The first possible explanation for the under-representation of women in lobbying relies on a relational perspective. Lobbying emerged as a relational response from organized civil society to the political action of political parties and institutions. Those who engage in lobbying, aiming to persuade and convince political decision-makers and institutional offices, are individuals with comparable political knowledge who specialize in policy activities outside formal political institutions. However, individuals with political and legal expertise may choose a role in different realms on the two sides of the decision-making process: either party organizations and institutional positions, associations, corporations and lobbying consultancies. In this functional isomorphism, male figures, with common academic background, similar lifestyles, shared political experiences tend to prevail. The 'old boys network' is the motivation that Kay Lehman Schlozman presented in her 1990 research paper, arguing that: 'pressure politics is a sphere of political activity characterized by reliance on the most traditional kind of old-boy political network, [and] the unabashed pursuit of narrow self-interest' (1990, p. 339). According to Lucas and Hyde (2012, p. 397), 'If women cannot become full members of these informal networks, they will continue to be excluded from the most competitive, lucrative lobbying positions.' Hence, the gender barrier poses a significant obstacle for women trying to enter the highly lucrative male networks within the lobbying profession. The exclusion from these informal networks' limits women access to the most competitive and financially rewarding lobbying positions. This gendered relational barrier, rooted in informal professional norms, often drives women to seek alternative careers where such barriers are not prevalent.

Further factors such as the methods and practices of political decision-making, the prevalence of professional theoretical and practical paths of study and shared social origins contribute to affirm the male prevalence within lobbying organizations, which are perceived as a counterpart to the familiar male-dominated political sphere. From a relational standpoint, the interactions between male lobbyists and those they lobby are shaped by shared experiences and social backgrounds. This relational aspect often takes precedence over technical and professional expertise. Consequently, women face greater challenges in actively participating in lobbying activities in a meaningful manner, as the relational dimension tends to overshadow the technical and professional aspects of the field.

Alternatively, explanations for the increased presence of women in the lobbying profession can be attributed to the isomorphism between lobbyists and public decision-makers. As the number of women decision-makers in political institutions rises, there is a need to include a greater representation (English, 2022) of women in consultancies, corporations and associations engaged in lobbying activities. This serves as a response to ensure gender diversity within the profession (McGrath, 2005; Kim, 2006).

By analysing lobbyist-client pairings data from all American states in 1989 and 2011, Strickland and Stauffer (2022) show that, in the US, gender diversity among legislative targets influences the number of lobby contracts held by women, also revealing that a greater number of former women legislators become lobbyists in more diverse legislatures. The presence of gender symmetry between lobbyists and those being lobbied goes beyond mere relational dynamics and extends to the realms of representation and influence. It becomes apparent that an increase in women within political institutions is essential to foster a corresponding increase in women within lobbying and public affairs organizations. This gender parity is particularly crucial when establishing stable and focused relationships with women decision-makers, emphasizing the need for women's representation at all levels of the lobbying process.

The second perspective regarding the under-representation of women in the lobbying and public affairs professions revolves around the organizational and functional aspects. These roles entail a demanding agenda dictated by the political calendar, involving numerous formal and informal meetings throughout the day without autonomy in planning. The inherent complexity of managing lobbying activities, including political crises, unexpected workloads and meetings outside regular hours, presents challenges for women seeking to balance work and personal life. Even in societies where gender equality is more advanced in domestic and family responsibilities, the nature of lobbying work with its demanding schedules tends to deter women from pursuing this profession. Considering that the initial barriers to entry, rooted in traditional old boys' networks, are compounded by difficulties in managing unpredictable workloads, it becomes evident that the scarcity of women in this field can be attributed to a multi-factor motivation.

Due to the existing functional, relational and organizational aspects that inherently contribute to a predominance of males in the field of professional lobbying, it becomes crucial to adopt a comprehensive approach like gender mainstreaming (Caglar, 2013; Hubert & Stratigaki, 2011) especially connecting it to the institutional machinery (Staudt, 2018).

The concept of 'gender mainstreaming' is widely recognized in global public policy discourse and within the United Nations frameworks, yet it often lacks comprehensive understanding outside these specialized contexts. It is important to understand its significance, especially in relation to the Beijing Platform for Action, which adopted gender mainstreaming as a crucial tool for promoting gender equality. Gender mainstreaming involves the systematic consideration of the differing needs and rights of both men and women in all policies, programmes, strategies, research and various other domains. This approach aims to counteract the long-standing and pervasive gender biases – both explicit and implicit – that can lead to policy decisions inadvertently increasing inequality. By integrating a gender perspective into all aspects of policy-making and implementation, gender mainstreaming ensures that gender-specific implications are identified and addressed, thereby promoting equitable outcomes. The adoption of gender mainstreaming by the Beijing Platform for Action underscores its critical role in fostering gender equality. This strategy mandates that gender considerations are not an afterthought but a foundational element in the development and execution of all public policies and initiatives. Consequently, this comprehensive approach helps in mitigating the risk of perpetuating existing gender disparities and supports the creation of more inclusive and just societal frameworks.

The gender mainstreaming approach has become particularly relevant in certain political and institutional systems, line United Nations and the European Commission. At the EU level, to coordinate and advance gender equality at the European level, several organizations have been established, including the European Commission's Gender Equality Unit and the European Institute for Gender Equality. The European Parliament also plays a role in promoting actions in this area through its Commission on Women's Rights and Gender Equality. Through gender mainstreaming, the aim is to bridge the gender gap between lobbyists and initiate organizational policy actions that foster transformation. The gender mainstreaming approach has attained significant prominence within various political and institutional frameworks, particularly within the United Nations and the European Commission. At the European Union (EU) level, a multitude of organizations have been established to coordinate and promote gender equality. Notable among these are the European Commission's Gender Equality Unit and the European Institute for Gender Equality. Additionally, the European Parliament actively contributes to this endeavour through its Committee on Women's Rights and Gender Equality. Gender mainstreaming is a strategic approach that entails the systematic incorporation of gender perspectives into all policy domains and organizational practices. This methodology is designed to address and mitigate the gender disparity among lobbyists and to catalyze policy actions that foster organizational transformation. By embedding gender considerations into the core of decision-making processes, gender mainstreaming facilitates the development of more inclusive and equitable institutional frameworks. Such integration is crucial for advancing gender equality and ensuring that both men's and women's needs and rights are adequately represented and addressed in all aspects of public policy and institutional operations.

Looking at it from this perspective, Antonucci (2021a) suggests that the increasing presence of women in political positions within EU institutions has led to the need for adjustments in the gender makeup of lobbyist personnel. This shift has been accompanied by policies such as gender mainstreaming, which aims to promote equality of opportunity between men and women across all aspects of society. Gender mainstreaming involves integrating a gender perspective into policy development, implementation, regulation, spending decisions, evaluation and monitoring. Its primary goal is to address gender inequalities by examining the underlying mechanisms that perpetuate them. This is the perspective adopted by Prügl (2011), which considers the role of gender mainstreaming as a technology of government for complex organizations, beyond its role of diversity management.

The lack of symmetry between the gender of political decision-makers, institutional leadership and top management in the lobbying and public affairs professions stems from relational and organizational-functional motivations. These factors form the fundamental elements underlying the observed gender imbalance. Considering these factors, it becomes necessary to assess the reasons why striving for improved gender equity within these professional structures is essential in terms of enhancing the public image and reputation of lobbying organizations.

A GENDER BALANCE PERSPECTIVE ON WOMEN IN LOBBYING AND PUBLIC AFFAIRS: REASONS AND PERSPECTIVES

Promoting equality and inclusiveness in male-dominated careers is a widely discussed objective today. Numerous international organizations have dedicated themselves to this cause, including the Equal Pay International Coalition (EPIC) led by the ILO, UN Women and OECD. The general objective of these institutional approaches is to reduce the gender pay gap and advocate for worldwide equal pay for work of equal value, while achieving this through the means of cooperation with various stakeholders, including governments, employers, workers' organizations, the private sector, civil society and academia. Consulting firms like McKinsey also contribute to this cause through research on women in the workplace, conducting yearly surveys in corporate settings, and promoting diversity management and gender inclusiveness in large companies.

The importance of recognizing women's contributions in the workplace and creating gender-inclusive paths is now widely acknowledged. However, certain professions, such as politics, communication and public affairs, continue to be male-prevalent, leading to an imbalanced ratio of women participating in those professional contexts (Bath et al., 2005). Gender biases in career development, limited work-life balance options and varying levels of acceptance of women professionals in relationships with public decision-makers informally contribute to these challenges in the professional sector of public affairs and lobbying.

While progress has been made in achieving greater gender equality, particularly in political contexts where gender opportunities tend to be more balanced and gender mainstreaming is an established public policy, further efforts are needed to support gender equality within the lobbying and public affairs professions.

The idea that advancing gender equality in lobbying and public affairs is associated with the Corporate Social Responsibility (CSR) approach (Grosser, 2016; Torres et al., 2019) has gained significant support in the scientific literature over the past decade. However, it is essential to acknowledge the risks and paradoxes that have emerged of the public dimension of feminization in complex organizations, including the potential for 'femvertising' (Sterbenk et al., 2022) become the latest form of greenwashing, as recently highlighted.

Furthermore, the pursuit of gender equality has now been integrated into the wider range of strategies focused on social sustainability (Desiderio et al., 2022), as an element from the UN Strategy for Sustainable Goals.

In this general context of CSR and social sustainability, specific elements and structures within lobbying and public affairs activities suggest that organizations (such as consultancies, associations, corporations and public advocacy groups) prioritizing gender equality, both in terms of workforce feminization and the distribution of top management positions, can anticipate gaining competitive assets in terms of identity and reputation.

In relation to the integration of women within lobbying and public affairs organizations, several areas can contribute to enhancing the reputation of entities that adopt this strategy. These areas include:

1 **The inclusion of gender-diverse perspectives in lobbying and public affairs as a leverage for better business opportunities and improved organizational dynamics:** Integrating diverse perspectives into lobbying and public affairs business opportunities is essential for fostering improved organizational dynamics. Women professionals in public affairs bring unique experiences that enrich political, legal and economic discussions, enhancing decision-making processes with their diverse perspectives. Including women ensures a more comprehensive understanding of issues and the development of more effective, diversified strategies compared to a gender-homogeneous staff. Moreover, a gender-balanced workforce contributes to a healthier work environment with varied ideas, skills and approaches. Recognizing the value of diversity (Leisink, 2021), organizations create a supportive, inclusive environment that breaks down barriers and biases, ensuring equal representation, bias elimination, inclusive policies, pay equity, career development, mentorship and zero tolerance for harassment and discrimination. These policies enhance organizational culture, promoting gender equality, work-life balance and increased collaboration. This cohesive and integrated climate is crucial for managing the demanding nature of political agendas in lobbying and public affairs organizations.
2 **Gender-balanced staffing as an intangible asset for public affairs organizations and reputational leverage:** Gender-balanced staffing is an intangible asset for public affairs organizations (Shaiko, 1997), enhancing their image and reputation. The increasing prominence of female leadership in traditionally male-dominated fields, like public affairs, signifies a growing acceptance and inclusion of female professionals. A balanced gender composition within the staff is valuable, signalling to decision-makers, customers and the public that the organization is committed to equal opportunities, inclusivity and effective diversity management. Prioritizing gender diversity and equality fosters a more inclusive environment and enhances the organization's credibility as a progressive entity. Higher representation of women in public affairs and lobbying roles demonstrates a commitment to inclusiveness and gender equality, aligning with societal expectations and values. This commitment strengthens the organization's legitimacy and reputation, making it responsive to stakeholders' needs and societal demands for equal opportunities and gender representation. Such a reputation is an intangible yet valuable asset in the eyes of both external and internal stakeholders and public opinion.
3 **Addressing, more competently and with a more significant insight, women's issues in public policy consultancy:** Women often face specific challenges and

issues that require dedicated attention. Having more women in public affairs and lobbying enables a better understanding and promotion of policies and initiatives that address these issues, such as maternity and parental leave policies; violence against women prevention and response policies; affirmative action and quotas in workforce and economy; access to reproductive health services; economic empowerment policies; education and skills development policies and social welfare policies.

4 **Better collaboration with the growing number of women decision-makers associated with isomorphism and improved gender representativeness:** Women legislators and politicians may find it easier to collaborate with women lobbyists due to shared experiences and perspectives, such as being a gender minority in political and economic male-dominated groups. This basis for collaboration can lead to more effective advocacy and the advancement of policies, based on gender empathy and mutual trust.

5 **Expanded talent pool:** Encouraging and attracting women to pursue careers in public affairs and lobbying taps into a larger pool of talent and offers diverse perspectives, by providing a range of interpretive viewpoints, policy solutions and problem-solving approaches based on a multifocal and multivisional model. Embracing an inclusive approach that integrates diverse aspects such as gender, ethnicity, religion and political vision, it facilitates the integration of talents and qualifications within the lobbying organization. By leveraging different perspectives of representation, this approach fosters a more comprehensive and insightful synthesis, enabling the organization to embrace diverse and integrated visions. This results in a more competitive and diverse industry that attracts individuals with a wider range of skills and expertise.

6 **Role modelling and mentorship:** Women lobbyists who successfully engage with women decision-makers can serve as role models for aspiring women lobbyists, inspiring them to pursue careers in advocacy and public affairs. They can also provide mentorship and guidance to support the professional development and advancement of younger women in the field. Successful women in lobbying can serve as role models, influencing and shaping the aspirations, achievements and socialization of future generations, and thus impacting the ongoing process of social reproduction in different formats (challenging traditional gender roles, inspiring and empowering other women, breaking barriers and contributing to positive social change) in public affairs.

The enhancement factors associated with a more balanced gender composition in lobbying and public affairs staff can be viewed as optimizing human capital dedicated to interest representation activities. In his seminal work on the ideal qualities of a lobbying candidate, Mc Grath (2006) identifies several key characteristics – such as being a good listener and observer, facilitating effective turn-taking in interactions with political representatives, sensitivity to nuances, courtesy and the ability to build up and cultivate relationships – that are frequently attributed to female staff members. Mac Grath suggests that gender, as a personal quality of lobbying firm staff, combined with practical skills and effectiveness, is more significant than academic qualifications. Consequently, achieving a proper gender balance within lobbying organizations not only promotes equitable external representation but also enhances the effectiveness of public affairs teams.

The perception and significance of achieving gender balance within lobbying and public affairs organizations vary across different political systems and organizational cultures. Eccles (2023) highlights in a recent article that the institutional context and organizational culture of the Commission and Parliament have played a pivotal role in encouraging greater gender diversity and facilitating career advancement for women in lobbying organizations. By incorporating the voices of numerous female interest representatives in the EU, Eccles argues that this context has influenced and propelled the feminization of the sector, promoting the ascent of women to top positions. This development is beneficial for both professional women and the organizations they work for, yielding tangible and intangible advantages.

CONCLUSIONS

The perception of lobbyists and public affairs specialists as predominantly male has begun to change, as evidenced by open access data from public registers of lobbyists in regulated political systems. Over the past two decades, there has been a gradual influx of women and young individuals into the lobbying and public affairs profession, thereby transforming the public image of political lobbyists across various political systems considered in scientific literature. Research papers and surveys indicate that the representation of women in lobbying varies significantly across different political systems. For example, women constitute approximately 37% of lobbyists in Washington, USA, while in some European countries, the percentage is lower, ranging from over 10% in Germany to 30% in Sweden.

The underrepresentation of women in lobbying can be attributed to several factors. Established networks and informal professional norms, often referred to as 'old boys' networks', create barriers that hinder women's entry into the profession. These relational and organizational challenges, along with demanding schedules and excessive workloads, make achieving a healthy work-life balance difficult. Consequently, these systemic factors inherent to the lobbying profession exacerbate the gender imbalance by diverting women's talents and aspirations towards alternative career paths.

However, the inclusion of women in lobbying and public affairs introduces valuable perspectives and experiences that enrich political, legal and economic deliberations. Gender diversity within the lobbying and public affairs workforce enhances organizational dynamics, promotes collaboration, sparks innovation and provides a range of problem-solving approaches. This phenomenon mirrors the positive outcomes observed in organizations that embrace diversity management and integrate differences into their operational procedures.

In this context, the enhancement factors associated with a more balanced gender composition in lobbying and public affairs staff can be viewed as optimizing human capital dedicated to interest representation activities. What is more, the ideal qualities of a lobbying candidate traced in scientific literature and experienced in everyday practices, identifies several key characteristics – such as being a good listener and observer, facilitating effective turn-taking in interactions with political representatives, sensitivity to nuances, courtesy and the ability to cultivate relationships – that are frequently attributed to female staff members. In this perspective, gender, as a personal quality of lobbying firm staff, combined with practical skills and effectiveness, may result more significant than mere academic qualifications, as the profession still needs a specific on-the-job training and skilling. Consequently, achieving a proper gender balance within lobbying organizations not only promotes equitable external representation but also enhances the effectiveness of public affairs teams.

Therefore, gender balance in lobbying and public affairs organizations is increasingly recognized and embraced in management practices. It is seen as beneficial for enhancing the image and reputation of these organizations, signifying a commitment to equal opportunities, inclusivity and effective management of diversity. Achieving gender balance in lobbying and public affairs is important not only for gender equality but also for improving public representation and influence among stakeholders and public opinion at large. This perspective aligns with broader goals of CSR and social sustainability. Organizations that prioritize gender equality can gain competitive advantages in terms of public identity and reputation by actively participating in CSR and social sustainability paradigms.

Accordingly, there is a growing public demand for greater gender balance and inclusivity in lobbying and public affairs. This necessitates that lobbying groups acknowledge the significance of diverse perspectives, equal opportunities and adept management of diversity within their organizational culture. By prioritizing these principles, lobbying groups can achieve more effective and inclusive decision-making processes, aligning with the ultimate purpose of lobbying itself.

REFERENCES

Antonucci, M. C. (2021a). Female presence in lobbying careers in Europe: A comparison of women in the lobbying workforce in three national political systems and the EU. *GENDER–Zeitschrift für Geschlecht, Kultur und Gesellschaft*, 13(1), 13–14.

Antonucci, M. C. (2021b). Women in lobbying professions. In P. Harris, A. Bitonti, C. S. Fleisher, & A. Skorkjær Binderkrantz (Eds.), *The Palgrave encyclopedia of interest groups, lobbying and public affairs*. Palgrave Macmillan. https://doi.org/10.1007/978-3-030-13895-0_143-1.Cham

Bath, M. G., Gayvert-Owen, J., & Nownes, A. J. (2005). Women lobbyists: The gender gap and interest representation. *Politics & Policy*, 33(1), 136–152.

Caglar, G. (2013). Gender mainstreaming. *Politics and Gender*, 9(3), 336–344.

Desiderio, E., García-Herrero, L., Hall, D., Segrè, A., & Vittuari, M. (2022). Social sustainability tools and indicators for the food supply chain: A systematic literature review. *Sustainable Production and Consumption*, 30, 527–540.

Eccles, M. (2023, May 9). EU Influence: Women's lobby priorities. *Politico.eu*. https://www.politico.eu/newsletter/politico-eu-influence/eu-influence-womens-lobby-priorities-hololeis-missing-meetings-mep-side-hustles-2/

English, A. (2022). Lobbying beyond the legislature: Challenges and biases in women's organizations' participation in rulemaking. *Politics and Gender*, 18(4), 1077–1111.

Grosser, K. (2016). Corporate social responsibility and multi-stakeholder governance: Pluralism, feminist perspectives and women's NGOs. *Journal of Business Ethics*, 137, 65–81.

Hubert, A., & Stratigaki, M. (2011). The European institute for gender equality: A window of opportunity for gender equality policies? *European Journal of Women's Studies*, 18(2), 169–181.

Junk, W. M., Romeijn, J., & Rasmussen, A. (2021). Is this a men's world? On the need to study descriptive representation of women in lobbying and policy advocacy. *Journal of European Public Policy*, 28(6), 943–957.

Kim, B. Y. (2006). Managing workforce diversity: Developing a learning organization. *Journal of Human Resources in Hospitality & Tourism*, 5(2), 69–90.

LaPira, T. M., Marchetti, K., & Thomas, H. F. (2020). Gender politics in the lobbying profession. *Politics and Gender*, 16(3), 816–844.

Leisink, P., Andersen, L. B., Brewer, G. A., Jacobsen, C. B., Knies, E., & Vandenabeele, W. (Eds.). (2021). *Managing for public service performance: How people and values make a difference*. Oxford University Press.

Lucas, J. C., & Hyde, M. S. (2012). Men and women lobbyists in the American states. *Social Science Quarterly*, 93(2), 394–414.

McGrath, C. (2005). Towards a lobbying profession: Developing the industry's reputation, education, and representation. *Journal of Public Affairs: An International Journal*, 5(2), 124–135.

McGrath, C. (2006). The ideal lobbyist: Personal characteristics of effective lobbyists. *Journal of Communication Management*, 10(1), 67–79.

Nownes, A. J., & Freeman, P. K. (1998). Female lobbyists: Women in the world of good Ol'Boys. *The Journal of Politics*, 60(4), 1181–1201.

Prügl, E. (2011). Diversity management and gender mainstreaming as technologies of government. *Politics and Gender*, 7(1), 71–89.

Shaiko, R. G. (1997). Female participation in association governance and political representation: Women as executive directors, board members, lobbyists, and political action committee directors. *Nonprofit Management and Leadership*, 8(2), 121–139.

Staudt, K. (2018). *Gender mainstreaming: Conceptual links to institutional machineries* (pp. 40–66). Manchester University Press.

Sterbenk, Y., Champlin, S., Windels, K, & Shelton, S. (2022). Is femvertising the new greenwashing? Examining corporate commitment to gender equality. *Journal of Business Ethics*, 177(3), 491–505.

Strickland, J. M., & Stauffer, K. E. (2022). Legislative diversity and the rise of women lobbyists. *Political Research Quarterly*, 75(3), 531–546.

Torres, L. D., Jain, A., & Leka, S. (2019). (Un) doing gender for achieving equality at work: The role of corporate social responsibility. *Business Strategy & Development*, 2(1), 32–39.

Going Blue in the Deep Red: How Kansas Voters Shocked the Nation and Protected Choice

Nada Hashmi, Suniti S. Bal and Anjali S. Bal

INTRODUCTION

The overturn of *Roe v. Wade* marked a turning point in America's civil rights and health care access. With this decision, the right to access abortions, essential health care for millions, was no longer federally mandated (Gemmil & Bell, 2025). In a flash, all eyes turned to states who now held the right to determine if abortion access would remain legal. At the time of this decision, several states had "trigger bans" in place, meaning that abortion would almost immediately be banned (Kim, 2022). Some states, like Kansas, did not have such a ban in place but moved quickly with ballot initiatives to ban nearly all abortions. While the Republican super majority in Kansas' state legislature led many to fear a ban was all but inevitable, the large-scale political marketing campaign that ensued led to a huge win for pro-choice advocates (Lysen et al., 2022).

The research outlined in this chapter analyses the Kansas ballot initiative entitled "Value Them Both" and sheds light on how pro-choice advocates were able to see this ballot initiative fail. Leading up to the vote, polling showed that the initiative was close but predominantly supported by Kansas voters (Taborda, 2022). Conversely, the ballot initiative was frequently associated with a negative sentiment on social media channels. We propose that this sentiment was driven by younger, more diverse audiences – groups that are not well-represented in traditional polling. This meant that poll results being released did not give a comprehensive view of sentiment to the initiative. Subsequently, related media coverage was not wholly accurate.

The findings that follow highlight the need for public polling to be approached with an intersectional perspective. Kansas provides an important example of how a significant portion of public sentiment might have been overlooked by traditional polling. Traditional polling represents "likely voters." This is determined by past voting data and pollsters' reflection on who will vote (Arrojas, 2023). This means that younger voters and nontraditional voters are often overlooked in polling (Arrojas, 2023). Social media platforms can provide insights to a broad range of voices, especially younger demographics. While there are limitations and concerns with social media, this case study shows that relevant perspectives were overlooked in Kansas.

It is important to note that abortion bans/restrictions are linked to systemic racism and disproportionately impact Black, Hispanic, Indigenous, other people of color, people with disabilities, people in rural areas, and young people (Abrams, 2023; Fuentes, 2023). These groups played a key role in voting down the Kansas ballot initiative, and Twitter-based sentiment underscored their strong opposition to the initiative. Moreover, intersectionality is not always accounted for when looking at voter response to ballot initiatives. For example, if polls account for all Republicans believing that abortion access should be limited, this undercuts the nuances of the issue for people who have intersectional beliefs. Another example is that while Republican women are more likely to be pro-life versus politically Independent women or Democratic women, they are more likely to be pro-choice compared to men within their own party (Elangovan, 2023). Moreover, younger people are more likely to be pro-choice versus older people (Gallup Abortion Trends by Age, 2023).

Political campaigns and marketing are continuously evolving and, to ensure accuracy, political polling must evolve as well. The findings of this research show that if traditional polling tapped younger and more diverse audiences, polls would have predicted a negative outcome for the Kansas abortion referendum. As we continue to see states taking action to restrict abortion access with similar ballot initiatives, these findings are extremely important to ensure that polling is accurate and reaches the audiences that will be most impacted by abortion bans.

POLITICAL MARKETING ABORTION ACCESS USA

A historic ruling, *Roe v. Wade* made it so that abortion was legal in the United States. But the legality of that ruling came into question from the beginning and was under scrutiny for the entire time it was in place. Political marketing strategists started to attack abortion access within moments of the initial Supreme Court ruling in 1973. Since *Roe v. Wade* was overturned in 2022, numerous political strategists have been working to reinstate abortion access on a state-by-state basis. The strategy behind political marketing with regard to abortion access in the United States is highly complex and multifaceted. When assessing the political marketing with regard to abortion access, it is important to examine strategies in three main areas: context, content, and process (Baines & Lynch, 2005). The following sections will examine each of these areas with particular focus on the Kansas Referendum.

CONTEXT

When deriving a marketing strategy for a political issue, it is important to first assess and understand the context unto which the issue is arising. Context is the situation surrounding the political messaging. When *Roe v. Wade* was overturned in the US, the decision was first leaked to the public (Mane et al., 2022; Thomadsen et al., 2023). The ruling came after decades of challenge to the initial law that protected a woman's right to choose (Andaya & Mishtal, 2017). Pro-life political marketing was dominated by questions related to ideas of conception, the religious rights of medical providers, and morality (Andaya & Mishtal, 2017). The context of the court decision also was associated with a "win" for pro-life advocates who had been lobbying to change the law for nearly a half century.

From its inception, *Roe v. Wade* was a controversial ruling that highlighted the polarized politics of the US. When *Roe v. Wade* was overturned, it created a rift among voters based on beliefs, political affiliation, and location within the US (Mane et al., 2022; Thomadsen et al., 2023). The leak of the Supreme Court decision to overturn Roe v. Wade made the issue of abortion more important to independents and nonvoters while making the issue of abortion less important to Republicans (Thomadsen et al., 2023). The divide between Democrats and Republicans on the issue of abortion also increased (Thomadsen et al., 2023). Twitter (now X) also saw a significant increase in discussion about abortion when the decision was leaked (Mane et al., 2022). Overwhelmingly, pro-life sentiment in Kansas was greater than pro-choice sentiments after the decision to overturn *Roe v. Wade* was leaked (Mane et al., 2022).

CONTENT/POLLING

The content of a political marketing effort relates to the method and target market of a campaign. In the example of Kansas, marketers took an intersectional approach to the content of their campaign (Baines & Lynch, 2005).

Polling and prediction are intimately tied to American politics. But, in the last few elections, polls have gotten it completely wrong. Famously, in 2016, almost every major poll predicted that Hillary Clinton would beat Donald Trump (Mercer et al., 2016). Even after major changes to polling were made in 2016, pollsters got predictions wrong in 2018, 2020, and 2022

(Sonnenfeld & Tian, 2022). There are numerous reasons as to why these polls proved to be inaccurate but the ones of particular note in Kansas were how pollsters assumed turnout or "likely voters," voter response bias, and sampling issues (Mercer et al., 2016). Likely voters are determined by a combination of many things, including past voter behavior for people in similar groups. One issue with these assessments is that they often do not highlight certain decisions that might be more important to certain voter groups, including abortion access (Elangovan, 2023). For certain voters, including many women and younger voters, abortion is one of the top issues in how they determine candidates they are voting for as well as policy. Voter response bias and sampling issues are closely tied to one another. The sheer number of people who are seeking out voter information in the form of polls leads to high levels of voter response bias. Specifically, the people who are willing to respond to polls tend to be in certain demographics and not representative of the voting public. This closely ties to challenges in sampling methods. Less and less people are willing to be polled and many methods that pollsters have utilized are becoming less accepted by the voting population (Elangovan, 2023). Specifically, less people are willing to answer questions on the phone regarding voting behavior or to answer polling questions. This exacerbates the issues with voting as seen in recent elections within the United States.

In the summer of 2022, Kansas politicians proposed a ballot initiative that would give lawmakers the opportunity to amend the constitution of the state and create abortion restrictions as part of the state constitution. In the weeks leading into the election, Kansas polls showed a weak lead for those who supported the "Value Them Both" initiative (Taborda, 2022). A "yes" vote would mean that the constitution of Kansas would be modified to allow lawmakers the opportunity to create bans on abortion access. The leading results from the poll reflected that 47% would vote "yes" and 42% would vote "no," bolstering confidence from the Republicans that their referendum would in fact succeed (Co/efficient Poll, 2022). However, the initiative actually failed with 59% of the voters in Kansas voting "no" (Lysen et al., 2022). As of July of 2022, there were a total of 1,929,972 registered voters in Kansas, of which 851,882 were registered Republicans, 560,309 were registered with no affiliation, 495,574 were registered Democrats, and 22,207 were registered Libertarian (State of Kansas, 2023). For this initiative to fail, there had to be voters who were not Democrats who voted against it. In other words, polling did not accurately represent the voting population and their beliefs to account for this level of inaccuracy. The question is: why? We propose two thoughts on this matter. First, we believe that polls are not accurately reflecting the voting public. As we will show in the next section, X (formerly known as Twitter) showed consistent negative sentiment toward the "Value Them Both" initiative. While on X, the data are not controlled for the location of the tweeter nor, if that person is a voter, is it a strong indicator of sentiment. Second, people no longer ascribe to a political party in the same way they might have in the past. There are numerous ways in which voters vote against their party. To better understand why and when this occurs, it is important to understand intersectionality.

PROCESS

The content of a political marketing campaign relates to the method and target market of a campaign. In the example of Kansas, marketers took an intersectional approach to the content of their campaign (Baines & Lynch, 2005). For many years, the approach by pro-choice advocates was to focus on the binary of being pro-choice or pro-life. Lobbying to protect choice came through predictable methods. Specifically, engaging predicted votes was utilized. An attempt to engage with nontraditional voters was never utilized. The campaign in Kansas provides a unique opportunity to analyze a changed process for political marketing. In the following sections, we examine how this occurred.

VOTER SENTIMENT ON X

Given that polls are currently unable to accurately assess and represent the population and their beliefs, two different options remain to improve and gain accuracy. The first one is to understand the issues that have caused inaccurate polling and have corrective measures in place. This may be a systematic issue and one that requires time and resources to correct. We propose a second option: the use of neutral social media platforms to assess the population's belief and sentiment quickly and efficiently toward any topic.

ANALYZING PLATFORM X (FORMERLY TWITTER) SENTIMENT ON THE KANSAS ABORTION REFERENDUM

To gain a deeper understanding of public sentiment regarding the Kansas abortion referendum, we turned to platform X (formerly Twitter), a neutral platform renowned for its real-time insights into public opinion. Recognizing the potential biases in traditional polling methods, we sought to capture a broader spectrum of voices, especially those that might have been underrepresented in conventional surveys.

DATA EXTRACTION METHODOLOGY

We implemented a structured data extraction process to systematically examine public sentiment surrounding the Kansas abortion referendum. This approach involved identifying relevant keywords, collecting a comprehensive set of tweets, cleaning and organizing the data, and applying sentiment analysis techniques. Each step in this methodology was designed to ensure that the data captured accurately reflected the range of public sentiment leading up to the referendum. The key components of this process are outlined below.

- **Keyword Selection**: We identified a set of keywords and phrases that were pertinent to the referendum. These included "Kansas abortion referendum," "value them both," "votenoAug2," and other related terms. The choice of these keywords was based on their relevance to the topic and their frequency of use in public discourse surrounding the referendum.
- **Data Collection**: Using Twitter's API, we extracted tweets containing the selected keywords over six months leading up to the referendum. This allowed us to amass a substantial dataset of over 150,000 tweets that reflected diverse opinions on the matter.
- **Data Wrangling**: The tweets were then processed and cleaned to remove unnecessary characters and hashtags, and to capture only the text of the message. Retweets were merged to be associated with the original tweet and the number of retweets was then added. In addition, tweets that were in a non-English language were also removed as our method could only be applied to tweets in English.
- **Sentiment Analysis**: Once the tweets were cleaned, we employed sentiment analysis techniques to categorize each tweet as positive, negative, or neutral in sentiment. This categorization was based on the language and tone used in the tweets. Advanced natural language processing packages, including NLTK as well as Vader, were utilized to ensure accuracy in sentiment categorization.

Our analysis revealed a predominant negative sentiment toward the Kansas abortion referendum. A significant portion of the tweets expressed opposition to the referendum, indicating little to no support for its provisions. The term "value them both," which was frequently used in discussions around the referendum, was also predominantly associated with negative sentiment.

This Twitter-based sentiment analysis provided a contrasting perspective to some of the earlier polls. In the days leading up to the vote, the overwhelming negative sentiment on Twitter suggested that there was a substantial group of individuals, possibly younger and more diverse, whose voices were not adequately captured in traditional polling.

INTERSECTIONALITY: A LENS INTO GENDER, RACE, AND AGE

While Twitter and other social media platforms provide assessments, there are limitations with social media platforms. That is, social media platforms provide a reverse bias from the polling systems. They focus on people, typically younger, who have access and knowledge, and who are comfortable with the use of technology. In addition, within the population with access, only people who are comfortable with sharing their beliefs online will use social media. Finally, there might be inherent biases within the social media platforms to promote or demote certain posts (e.g., shadow banning).

As such, despite Twitter data being able to predict the Kansas referendum results more accurately than the traditional polling systems, it is possible, dependent on the topic, the reverse could also be true. For instance, topics such as Medicare, the future of social security, and retirement benefits resonate with the older generation – many of whom are not on social media. Hence, their opinions and voices would be missed.

As such, it is important to gain viewpoints from across different demographics in order to gain comprehensive insights. Furthermore, while in this example we have created categorization according to age, there are many more demographic categories to capture (e.g., gender, race, socio-economic status, etc.). Furthermore, even within the surface-level demographics, one must understand how the demographics interact with other demographics – a research stream known as "intersectionality."

Intersectionality, a term introduced by Kimberlé Crenshaw, provides a theoretical framework to understand how various social categorizations, such as gender, race, age, and political affiliation interconnect (see below) and influence individual experiences of discrimination and privilege (Crenshaw, 1989). Specifically, these social categories are not experienced independently but operate in tandem, shaping how individuals navigate institutions, social norms, and access to rights – such as reproductive autonomy. In what follows, we explore how key identity dimensions, beginning with gender, intersect to influence perspectives and experiences related to abortion.

- **Gender**: Gender is a multifaceted construct that extends beyond the binary of male and female. It includes a spectrum of identities, such as transgender, nonbinary, and genderqueer. Intersectionality underscores that gendered experiences are influenced by other identity facets. For instance, Black women may encounter unique challenges distinct from those faced by white women or Black men due to the intersection of gender and race (Collins, 2002). Regarding gender and abortion access, more women believe abortion should be legal in all/most cases versus men (Pew, 2022) and more women identify as pro-choice versus men (Gallup Abortion Trends by Gender, 2023).
- **Race**: Racial identity is complex, encompassing various ethnic, national, and cultural backgrounds. Through an intersectional lens, it's evident that racial experiences are shaped by other intersecting identities. An Asian woman's racial experiences, for example, might differ from those of an Asian man because of the combined effects of gender and race (Cho et al., 2013). According to the Pew Research Center, 74% of Asian voters support abortion access in most/all cases, versus 68% for Black voters, 60% of Hispanic voters, and 59% of White voters (2022).
- **Age**: Age intersects with other identities, influencing individuals' experiences in distinct ways. Younger individuals, for instance, might face ageism, which can be compounded by other forms of discrimination. A young Black woman's experience with ageism might differ from that of an older Black woman or a young white man (Calasanti, 2009). Younger adults are more likely to support legal abortion in all/some cases versus older voters (Gallup Abortion Trends by Age, 2023). Sixty-four percent of younger adults (18–29) identify as pro-choice, while 55% of adults 50–64 and 49% of adults 65+ identify as pro-life (Gallup Abortion Trends by Age, 2023).
- **Political Affiliation**: A great deal of research has been done to address how political affiliation is impacted by intersectionality. It is important to note that for some people political affiliation can become part of a prescribed and embedded social identity (Greene, 1999). Social Identity Theory proposes that individuals derive, in part, their self-concept from groups to which they belong and groups to which they do not belong (Greene, 1999). Political affiliation in the USA has become polarized, where those who identify as Democrats also identify as not being Republicans and vice versus. Abortion is an issue in the USA that is especially polarizing. Opinions tend to follow political party lines where Democrats support abortion access and Republicans do not. According to Gallup, 76% of Republicans identify as pro-life and only 21% identify as pro-choice (2023). Conversely, 84% of Democrats identify as pro-choice and only 15% identify as pro-life (Gallup Abortion Trends by Party, 2023).

The marketing campaigns run against the "Value Them Both" amendment focused on numerous intersectional realities for voters. One organization, Kansans for Constitutional Freedom, decided early on that they were not only going to target Democrats in the big cities in Kansas (Gowan, 2022). Instead, Kansans for Constitutional Freedom targeted Republicans, Libertarians, Independents, and Rural Voters. While many pro-choice advocates were sticking with traditional talking points, Kansans for Constitutional Freedom focused on keeping government out of personal healthcare decisions (Gowan, 2022). In doing so, they were able to appeal beyond traditional pro-choice voters and flip the state. The company went so far as to plan rallies in rural communities featuring horses to draw interest from youth in those areas. Kansans of all political affiliations and from urban, suburban, and rural communities voted no on the "Value Them Both" amendment (Gowan, 2022). Three specific campaigns are analyzed below.

The first ad analyzed will be a 30-second video that was created by the company Kansans for Constitutional Freedom featuring Rev. Jay McKell. The transcript of the advertisement is included below:

> As a pastor for over 50 years, I counsel and pray with individuals facing difficult personal decisions. Sometimes those conversations are about abortion. As Christians, we are instructed to love one another. We do so when we respect and trust women as God does, I'm voting no on the proposed amendment because it replaces religious freedom with government control. It restricts women's rights, and it puts their very lives at risk. Join me and thousands of Christians in voting no.

This advertisement addresses intersectionality in a multitude of ways. First, the ad highlights the role of religion in the discussion on abortion access. Many assume that most Christians are pro-life when, in fact, both race and which Christian faith one follows are strong determinants of abortion access views. While 74% of white Evangelicals believe that abortion should be illegal in most situations, white (non- Evangelical) Protestants (60%), Black Protestants (66%), and Catholics (56%) believe that abortion should be legal in most situations (Pew Public Opinion on Abortion, 2022). Here, by choosing a non-Evangelical white male pastor to be highlighted in this ad, Kansans for Constitutional Freedom was recognizing that not all white Christian Protestants are pro-life. Moreover, in this ad the pastor highlights his belief in both religious freedom and less government control. These are two of the strongest beliefs in the Republican Party. The ad strikes people in ways they will respond to.

The second ad analyzed will be a 30-second video that was created by the company Kansans for Constitutional Freedom featuring a woman, Jane Byrne, speaking about her thoughts on the proposed amendment.

> Growing up Catholic we didn't talk about abortion but now it's on the ballot and we can no longer ignore it. I won't support putting a woman's life at risk and that's just what this constitutional amendment does. It could ban any abortion in Kansas even when a mother's life is on the line or with rape or incest. If it were my granddaughter I wouldn't want the government making that decision for her. Vote no.

The Catholic Church was strongly in favor of this amendment. They funded most of the 'Vote Yes' ads in Kansas. Here the ad goes directly to highlight this issue on an intersectional basis. Byrne is directly playing on the power dynamics of being an older white woman and eliciting her responsibility for the next generation of women. Once again, the ad highlights the idea that she doesn't want the government making decisions for her. This highlights the Republican ethic of small government, privacy, and independence. In this instance, the speaker was stating that while she was raised Catholic, her gender and age were part of the determining factor as to why she was against this amendment.

The third and final ad highlighted is also by the Kansans for Constitutional Freedom:

> This confusing constitutional amendment is a slippery slope for Kansas. It gives government more power over your privacy and your personal medical decisions. Don't let politicians take away your freedom. Send a message, vote no.

This ad is even more direct and blunt in the attestation that the amendment would provide the government with more power. Once again, this highlights the Kansans' desire for independence.

In all three of these ads, Kansans for Constitutional Freedom are attempting to pull in voters who would normally vote along party lines or would not vote at all. The intersectional nature of these ads targets a voter that traditional polling may deem likely to be in favor of the Kansas ballot initiative based on their age and religious beliefs. In doing so, it highlights the key role of intersectionality in political marketing and subsequently the role it played in the election outcomes in Kansas.

Polling and public opinion research must be approached with an intersectional perspective. If polls disproportionately focus on specific demographics, they risk missing nuanced perspectives. In the context of the Kansas abortion referendum, if younger voices were underrepresented in polling, a significant portion of public sentiment might have been overlooked.

Social media platforms, like Twitter, can offer insights into a broader range of voices, especially from younger demographics, though they come with their own set of limitations (Jungherr, 2015). It is our belief that had conventional polling tapped into a much younger and more diverse group of voters, the polls also would have predicted a negative outcome for the Kansas abortion referendum.

CONCLUSION

In an ever-changing political landscape, our polling methods and public opinion research has not kept pace. Inaccuracy remains in how likely voters are identified by pollsters and voter response bias and sampling issues are impacting the success of polling. While this issue is pervasive, there is opportunity to improve the process by utilizing social media platforms to assess under-represented populations' belief and sentiment on key topics, including legislation, in real time.

Sentiment on many topics, including abortion access, may not be accurately captured by previous voting behaviors based on the intersectional nature of the topic. If a voter identifies as both Catholic and is registered as Republican, their previous voting history would lead traditional polling methods to show them likely supporting the Kansas abortion initiative. This fails to take into consideration the fact that for younger women, abortion access is a top issue and not a party line vote.

It is necessary for polling to better represent the voting public. Political parties do not hold the same power they once did. Nuanced topics lead voters on both sides of the aisle to vote in ways that historically may not have been true of their voter profile. Kansas provides a powerful example of why it is important to understand the intersectionality of voters and how we can better approach polling methods and opinion research in the future. This can be done by appropriately utilizing social media platforms to assess the sentiment and beliefs of various populations.

While there are limitations to use of these platforms, they have proven effective at more accurately determining the sentiment of younger voters on key topics and campaigns as outlined above. This approach can be used in partnership with traditional polling methods to accurately represent multiple demographics by meeting voters where they are.

By modifying the marketing content, context, and process strategy through the lens of intersectionality, Kansas voters shocked the world and protected choice. In utilizing this approach and understanding the importance of the intersectionality of voters, polls can better predict outcomes in campaigns by capturing the perspective of audiences that have been historically overlooked.

REFERENCES

Abrams, Z. (2023, June 1). Abortion bans cause outsized harm for people of color. *Monitor on Psychology*. https://www.apa.org/monitor/2023/06/abortion-bans-harm-people-of-color

Andaya, E., & Mishtal, J. (2017). The erosion of rights to abortion care in the United States: A call for a renewed anthropological engagement with the politics of abortion. *Medical Anthropology Quarterly*, 31(1), 40–59. https://doi.org/10.1111/maq.12298

Arrojas, M. (September 29, 2023). *Why college students aren't well represented in voter polls*. Best Colleges. https://www.bestcolleges.com/news/2022/03/08/college-student-voter-polls-midterm-election/

Baines, P., & Lynch, R. (2005). The context, content and process of political marketing strategy. *Journal of Political Marketing*, 4(2–3), 1–18. https://doi.org/10.1300/J199v04n02_01

Calasanti, T. (2009). Theorizing feminist gerontology, sexuality, and beyond: An intersectional approach. In V. L. Bengtson, D. Gans, N. M. Putney, & M. Silverstein (Eds.), *Handbook of theories of aging* (pp. 471–485). Springer Publishing Company.

Cho, S., Crenshaw, K. W., & McCall, L. (2013). Toward a field of intersectionality studies: Theory, applications, and praxis. *Signs: Journal of Women in Culture and Society*, 38(4), 785–810.

Co/efficient. (2022). *Kansas abortion "value them both" amendment poll results*. https://kansasreflector.com/2022/07/20/poll-shows-kansans-closely-divided-on-constitutional-amendment-on-abortion/

Collins, P. H. (2002). *Black feminist thought: Knowledge, consciousness, and the politics of empowerment*. Routledge.

Crenshaw, K. (1989). Demarginalizing the intersection of race and sex: A Black feminist critique of antidiscrimination doctrine, feminist theory, and antiracist politics. *University of Chicago Legal Forum*, 1, 139–168.

Elangovan, P. (June 20, 2023). *50% of women support federal law guaranteeing abortion access*. All in Together. https://aitogether.org/women-support-federal-abortion-access

Fuentes, L. (2023). *Inequity in US abortion rights and access: The end of Roe is deepening existing divides*. Guttmacher Institute.

Gallup. https://news.gallup.com/poll/246206/abortion-trends-age.aspx

Gallup. https://news.gallup.com/poll/245618/abortion-trends-gender.aspx

Gallup. https://news.gallup.com/poll/246278/abortion-trends-party.aspx

Gemmill, A., & Bell, S. (2025, March 13). *The unequal impacts of abortion bans*. Johns Hopkins Bloomberg School of Public Health. https://publichealth.jhu.edu/2025/the-unequal-impacts-of-abortion-bans

Gowan, A. (August 2, 2022). *How abortion rights organizers won in Kansas: Horse parades and canvassing*. The Washington Post. https://www.washingtonpost.com/nation/2022/08/03/kansas-abortion-amendment/

Greene, S. (1999). Understanding party identification: A social identity approach. *Political Psychology*, 20(2), 393–403.

Jungherr, A. (2015). *Analyzing political communication with digital trace data: The role of Twitter messages in social science research*. Springer.

Kim, J. (August 22, 2022). *3 more states are poised to enact abortion trigger bans this week*. NPR.https://www.npr.org/2022/08/22/1118635642/abortion-trigger-ban-tennessee-idaho-texas

Lysen, D., Ziegler, L., & Mesa, B. (August 3, 2022). *Voters in Kansas decide to keep abortion legal in the state, rejecting an amendment*. NPR. https://www.npr.org/sections/2022-live-primary-election-race-results/2022/08/02/1115317596/kansas-voters-abortion-legal-reject-constitutional-amendment

Mane, H., Yue, X., Yu, W., Doig, A. C., Wei, H., Delcid, N., Harris, A., Nguyen, T. T., & Nguyen, Q. C. (2022). Examination of the public's reaction on Twitter to the over-turning of Roe v. Wade and abortion bans. *Healthcare*, 10(12), 2390. https://doi.org/10.3390/healthcare10122390

Mercer, A., Deane, C., & McGeeney, K. (November 9, 2016). *Why 2016 election polls missed their mark*. Pew Research Center. https://www.pewresearch.org/short-reads/2016/11/09/why-2016-election-polls-missed-their-mark/

Pew: Public Opinion on Abortion. (2022). https://www.pewresearch.org/religion/fact-sheet/public-opinion-on-abortion/

Sonnenfeld, J., & Tian, J. (2022). *Pollsters got it wrong in 2018, 2020, and 2022. Here's why political polling is no more than statistical sophistry*. Fortune. https://fortune.com/2022/11/16/pollsters-got-it-wrong-2018-2020-elections-statistical-sophistry-accuracy-sonnenfeld-tian/

Taborda, N. (July 20, 2022). *Poll shows Kansans closely divided on constitutional amendment on abortion*. Kansas Reflector. https://kansasreflector.com/2022/07/20/poll-shows-kansans-closely-divided-on-constitutional-amendment-on-abortion/

Thomadsen, R., Zeithammer, R., & Yao, S. (2023). The impact of a supreme court decision on the preferences of Americans regarding abortion policy. *Management Science*, 69(9), 5405–5417. https://doi.org/10.1287/mnsc.2023.4802

PART 4

Contemporary Political Marketing: Cybercampaigning, Fake News, and Social Media

Digital Political Campaigning and Social Media

Katherine Haenschen and Bridget Barrett

INTRODUCTION

In 2004, US Presidential candidates John Kerry and John Edwards created the first social media pages for political campaigns – on the Friendster platform.[1] Since then, social media have only grown in usage and importance for contemporary political candidates around the globe. Now, political actors make social media a major component – if not the centrepiece – of their communication strategies. Platforms such as Facebook, Instagram, Twitter, YouTube and TikTok have become common ways to engage voters, disseminate campaign messaging and communicate with press. The digital technologies on which these platforms rely are credited with changing political behaviour through lowering costs, removing barriers to engagement and creating new forms of participation (Bimber et al., 2005; Han, 2014). However, while social media is changing how campaigns go about accomplishing their goals, the goals themselves have remained largely unchanged: communicate to voters, organise supporters, shape media narratives. Digital and social tools have become an integral part of this work (Jungherr et al., 2020).

In this chapter, we review existing research on the role of social media platform usage in the context of political campaigns from the perspective of three sets of actors: candidates and campaigns, users, and the platforms themselves. We recognise that other political forms of social media use exist, including by social movements and for policy or non-electoral purposes (e.g. Jackson et al., 2020; Valenzuela et al., 2020; Workneh, 2020); our focus here is on political campaigns' use of social media to win elections. First, we focus on how campaigns use social media. Social media are an incredibly attractive tool for campaigns due to their microtargeting affordances. Affordances do not have a single agreed-upon definition but refer to 'possibilities for action' (Evans et al., 2017, p. 36) or in the case of social media platforms what they are 'actually capable of doing and perceptions of what they enable, along with the actual practices that emerge as people interact with them' (Kreiss et al., 2018, p. 12). For example, the ability to create narrow, defined audiences for advertising campaigns invites campaigns to do so to reach specific subgroups of supporters and would-be supporters.

Social media platforms also have many affordances that enable users to engage in peer-to-peer influence. We focus on paid and organic communication by campaigns, candidates and political organizations: the former is used to fundraise and mobilize voters, while the latter is used to set the media agenda and engage supporters in sharing content within their networks. Specific candidate content strategies are discussed. Next, we consider the role of users sharing campaign content on social media to persuade and mobilise one's network. Finally, we consider the role of the social media platforms themselves in shaping political communication.

Across this literature, several key debates emerge repeatedly. The first is one of impact: do social media have strong effects or limited and weak effects in terms of shaping voter behaviour? While press coverage has credited Facebook ads with the victories of Donald J. Trump in the United States and the Brexit 'Leave' campaign in the United Kingdom, empirical reality suggests that if ads on Facebook or other platforms are effective, the impact is actually very, very small (e.g. Aggarwal et al., 2023; Coppock et al., 2022; Haenschen, 2022; Hager, 2019). Similarly, while candidates and consultants emphasise the importance of campaigns posting on their social media accounts, scholars often lack the means to study the effect of organic social media content 'in the wild' and must turn instead to lab studies.

While early work on digital campaigning focused predominantly on surveys and self-reported behaviours, the rise of field and lab experiments and digital trace data analysis – especially when coupled with survey data – have allowed researchers to better estimate effects of social media campaigns on political outcomes. However, the field often suffers from a lack of rigorous academic descriptive work cataloguing what political actors and the public alike are doing online. There is a growing recognition of the need to describe quantitatively and qualitatively how social media are currently used for political outcomes, to extend the types of behaviours that are measured – such as campaign contributions or email list growth – and to recognise the role of social media in group identity formation and alignment. Additionally, scholars are beginning to focus less on general behaviours and analysis of central tendencies, and more on small but politically powerful groups – such as the most active or most followed users on Facebook or Twitter – who may have disproportionate influences on social media.

A related debate is what the field of political communication decides 'matters' in terms of both outcomes and approaches. There is a wide dichotomy between what scholars value and what campaign practitioners actually do – see, for example, the dearth of scholarship on online fundraising tactics. Finally, the overlapping fields of political communication, communication and political science are still grappling with the legacy of largely White, Western scholars despite the dire need to expand research beyond the United States, Western Europe and select other global democracies. Candidates and parties across the globe use social media, but studies of such campaigning are typically focused on the United States, and Western and Northern European countries (Jungherr et al., 2020). Additionally, the field is dealing with extension of anti-democratic and far-right movements in many countries and role of social media – both platforms and users – in disseminating this content (e.g. Facebook's role in Myanmar and Belarus, or Twitter's decision to censor political content in Turkey). Finally, a broadening of perspectives to include people of colour, queer populations and other minoritised groups is necessary to fully understand how social media campaigning is impacting political practice, behaviours and outcomes.

What Is Social Media?

When we refer to social media in this chapter, we mean digital platforms on which the primary purpose is for users to create profiles on which they share and consume user-generated content (UGC). We draw on the classic definition of social network sites from boyd and Ellison (2007, p. 211), which categorised then-nascent platforms such as Friendster and Facebook as 'web-based services that allow individuals to (1) construct a public or semi-public profile within a bounded system, (2) articulate a list of other users with whom they share a connection, and (3) view and traverse their list of connections and those made by others within the system'. Their definition emphasises the role, importance and formation of the network itself, rather than the activity of networking.

Today, our understanding of social media also includes sites such as YouTube or Reddit, which focus more on content and less on networks; WhatsApp or SnapChat, which have become primarily direct messaging tools rather than profile-based sites; and platforms focused on specific uses such as LinkedIn (business networking) or Pinterest (content curation rather than content generation). Importantly, social media are not a monolith, but rather multiple platforms with different affordances, uses, audiences and customs. However, in this chapter we will use the phrase 'social media' to refer to these platforms generally.

What characterises social media writ large and social network sites in particular are the prominence of UGC. UGC is defined as 'any kind of text, data or action performed by online digital systems users, published and disseminated by the same user through independent channels, that incur an expressive or communicative effect either on an individual manner or combined with other contributions from the same or other sources' (Santos, 2021). Users can be an individual posting a photo of their pet, or a major news source posting a link to an article; when this content is posted by the user directly, it is referred to as organic. UGC is what draws users in to like, comment and share. This audience, in turn, is monetised by enabling advertisers to target paid communication to precise segments of the public based on not only basic demographics but also interests and past behaviours on the platform and elsewhere on the internet (Barrett, Kreiss, & Reddi, 2020; Dommett & Power, 2019; Munger, 2019).

HOW DO CAMPAIGNS USE SOCIAL MEDIA?

In Jungherr et al.'s (2020) comprehensive book *Retooling Politics: How Digital Media are Shaping Democracy*, they argue that digital media serve the same purposes as traditional media, but just provide campaigns with new tools. Campaigns thus use social media to accomplish the same goals that they've always had: to garner media attention, disseminate their message, mobilise supporters and volunteers and decide who to contact (and then contact them). As the authors argue, these new tools have had some profound consequences, including limiting the gatekeeping power of the press on campaigns. Yet, many aspects of campaigning are shockingly similar to the pre-social era. Ultimately, these authors construct a compelling argument that digital media – including social media – have not overhauled everything about campaigns and elections as some have claimed. Rather, it has changed little in some areas while having profound consequences in others. Below, we summarise how campaigns are using paid and organic social media to engage in these core functions.

Paid Campaign Communication

Social media platforms are common vectors of paid political communication, largely due to their microtargeting affordances that enable campaigns to direct advertisements to specific segments or even lists of voters. Platforms such as Facebook allow advertisers to segment the electorate by geography, demographics and interest ('women in Ohio interested in country music') as well as upload lists from the voter file to create specific targets. These affordances generate massive benefits for ROI on spending, enabling campaigns to focus their limited dollars on the exact voters to whom they want to speak. Ads are also relatively low-cost and easy to set up (or 'stage'), making them an attractive choice for campaigns large and small. During the 2016 US election cycle, over $1 billion USD was spent on digital political ads. Advertisements are also easy to A/B test – to run a field experiment or randomised controlled trial (RCT) that shows which version of an ad is most effective at generating the desired outcome, thus offering campaign operatives the ability to make so-called data-driven decisions (Baldwin-Philippi, 2019). Platforms such as Facebook include tools that make it relatively easy for digital staff to set up these tests.

Fundraising

Raising money is a core component of modern campaigns, and social media are becoming a primary tool with which to do so. Campaigns use social media to reach voters who are also donors, who have been referred to the financial 'electorate', the 'monetary surrogacy' and the 'donorate' (Hill & Huber, 2017; Kim et al., 2023; Mansbridge, 2003). According to the Wesleyan Media Project, over half of Senate candidates' advertisements on Facebook in the US 2018 elections were not designed to persuade people to get out to vote or change their vote choice – they were intended to raise money or collect email addresses that would then be used to solicit donations.

Some scholars have begun studying the content of these ads. Kim et al. (2023) found that donation-based ads on Facebook run by 2020 US congressional candidates were more likely to be toxic, negative and reference Donald Trump than ads with other goals. As the authors conclude, 'Politicians strategically devise campaign messages, and our results suggest that congressional candidates believe stoking partisan grievances with donors is an effective communication strategy, even more so than with voters' (Kim et al., 2023, p. 2). The people who donate to campaigns also tend to be more extreme in their views and ideological than typical voters (Hill & Huber, 2017).

Yet, the current literature on the effects of these advertisements on campaign contributions is nearly nonexistent within the academic sphere. One study estimated that for every 100 Facebook advertising impressions run by The Lincoln Project in the 2020 US presidential election, it received a $6 boost in campaign contributions, equalling likely more than a 250% return (Keena & Wintersieck, 2022). Importantly, however, the methods of this study are not able to fully account for many major events that drove massive donations to many organisations that opposed Donald Trump, regardless of ad spend.

This lack of empirical, public, academic evidence has not stopped campaigns from investing heavily in social media advertising, due to its low cost, microtargeting affordances that let campaigns show ads to highly specific voters or geographic targets and high rates of adoption of social media platforms (Social Media Fact Sheet, 2021). The ability to target specific lists of voters in particular has a massive impact on advertising ROI: political actors can spend money only on the precise segment of the public they wish to reach (e.g. past donors, likely supporters, infrequent voters). These advertising strategies seem to be effective: FEC data show that small dollar donations made up 22% of 2020 fundraising revenue, a marked increase from 15% in 2016 (Gratzinger, 2020). Furthermore, given the widespread use of A/B testing to optimise advertisements, it is likely that practitioners have already demonstrated internally that they work (Haenschen et al., 2023).

Voter Mobilisation

Another common and high-profile use of social media ads are for voter turnout. However, academic evidence suggests that if these advertisements have an effect, the impact is extremely small and contextually limited. Field experiments in the United States involving Facebook and Twitter ads largely fail to find main effects of assignment to treatment on turnout (Aggarwal et al., 2023; Collins, Kalla, & Keane, 2014; Haenschen, 2022) though some studies have identified significant increases in voter participation on particular subgroups (Aggarwal et al., 2023; Haenschen, 2022); another study reported negative impacts on turnout (Shaw et al., 2018). Other work in the American context finds no impact of Facebook ads on vote share (Coppock et al., 2020), name recognition or candidate favourability (Broockman & Green, 2014). One study conducted in Berlin in a multi-party system finds that Facebook ads were likely able to potentially increase the sponsoring party's vote share and decrease the share of votes for the sponsor's main competing party (Hager, 2019).

The dearth of significant effects across the mobilisation literature should not immediately be taken to mean that ads 'don't work' – it may instead point to the methodological difficulty in detecting an impact. The two studies that find a meaningful impact on turnout among subgroups of voters (Aggarwal et al., 2023; Haenschen, 2022) suggest that sample sizes must be extremely large (and thus costly) and that studies must be designed to both target and measure impact at the level of the individual. This is feasible given technological affordances of these platforms, though privacy concerns make it difficult to measure treatment effects on those who actually received the ads.

Ultimately, ads on Facebook and Instagram offer ways to communicate to a group of voters that can be otherwise hard-to-reach via traditional TV ads or contact via phone calls or canvassing. Even in the face of an ever-changing regulatory environment, political campaigns seem committed to using social media advertisements as a way to reach the public.

Organic Campaign Communication

Political actors' organic social media content also has the potential to exert influence on the public and the press; the latter then influence the public through their agenda-setting function. Social media offer political actors a way to speak directly to voters without mediatisation, or the process by which the news media reports on and shapes their statements. This content plays a key role in the formation of the candidate's image or brand – the characteristics, personality and traits that are associated with them (Hultman et al., 2019). Notably, political actors use their multiple social media accounts in different ways – for instance, Instagram is image-based, whereas Twitter is primarily text-based – in a manner shaped by platform affordances. Significant research shows that organic social media messages are widely used by campaigns to recruit supporters, raise funds and garner petition signatures (e.g. Coppock et al., 2016; Issenberg, 2012; Karpf, 2016).

There is no question that campaigns are posting organic social media content to engage supporters and disseminate their message to the public and the press. However, the effects of organic posts from campaigns' own social media profiles are much less understood largely due to measurement challenges (Kim et al., 2018). Methodologically, it is difficult to disentangle the exposure to political content from the audience, who have often affirmatively selected to see this political content. People who 'Like', 'Follow' or 'Subscribe' to political content are different from those who don't, and platform algorithms further exacerbate the amount of political content shown to individuals it perceives as being interested (Thorson et al., 2021). Nevertheless we can draw some conclusions via observational, content analytic and experimental studies that explore some of the strategies candidates pursue; we outline this work below.

Candidate Content Strategies

A range of studies have explored the different strategies political actors use to craft organic content on their own pages; below we highlight major trends.

Information and Mobilisation

Facebook is considered a key tool to building a successful campaign, and in some places, a campaign's Facebook page is replacing the campaign's website as its home on the web. In a study of regional campaigns in Poland, Baranowski found that candidates had fewer websites in 2018 than 2014 and had more Facebook pages and Twitter accounts. The most common strategy used by campaigns on Facebook in regional Polish campaigns was mobilisation, rather than providing policy information or personalised content. In a 2018 state election in Germany, Kruschinski et al. (2022) found that candidates were more likely to use organic Facebook posts for information rather than mobilisation. These two studies both rigorously analysed the content of many parties or candidates' social media and focused almost solely on descriptive work.

Such descriptive work is sorely needed to help determine what types of content should be tested for what kinds of effects, and necessary for tracking changes over time and differences across countries. The Wesleyan Media Project conducts in-depth content analyses of political advertisements in the United States which allows for over-time comparisons in changes of types of content and strategies (Fowler et al., 2016, 2020; Franz et al., 2020; Ridout et al., 2018, 2021). Importantly, their work includes both television and digital advertising. Rigorous, descriptive research programmes like this are sorely needed on social media in other countries for comparative research.

Personalisation, Identity and Emotion

Candidates use a range of strategies on social media to appeal to potential voters. Three well-studied strategies are personalisation, identity and emotion. Personalisation involves posting content about the candidate's private life in an attempt to reveal their personality and connect with voters as an individual (McGregor, 2018; Meeks, 2017). Empirical work suggests that this strategy is effective: McGregor (2018, p. 1139) finds that 'the feelings of intimacy created by personalized tweets [lead] respondents to express support for personalizing candidates, but this effect is contingent upon the gender and in-party status of the candidate.'

Other research has explored how group identities influence the effects of social media and other political communication and are influenced by them in return. Campaigns and parties try to convince various social identity groups that they are their best representatives; Huber (2022) calls this 'social group yield', demonstrating through an analysis of Austrian party manifestos and cross-sectional survey data the interaction between the electorate's attitudes and what groups the parties focus on. Kreiss et al. (2020) propose a similar concept of 'social identity ownership'. Extant literature shows how social groups are targeted and portrayed by political campaigns can influence people in those groups' understanding of their own role in politics and their groups' power. For example, Ostfeld (2017) ran an experiment using television ads featuring Latino voters and found that Spanish-language political ads increased Latinos' perceptions of collective power. Attempts to use peoples' social identities strategically is nothing new to politics, but the ways in which these strategies can interact with the way content delivery algorithms group and segment users is novel (Gillespie, 2014).

In addition to personalisation and appeals to identities, candidates and other political groups use emotions to encourage users to share information. Anger is an important driver of engagement with politics online – although it is by no means the only one – and is unsurprisingly used regularly by candidates on social media (e.g. Heiss, 2020; Sahly et al., 2019; Weismueller et al., 2022), though importantly not always (Bagic & Podobnk, 2018; Sampietro & Ordaz, 2015).

Agenda-Setting

Social media platforms also enable political candidates and parties to serve an agenda-setting function. Agenda-setting refers generally to the process by which the mass media cues the public to see certain issues as important by reporting on them (McCombs & Valenzuela, 2021; Russell &

Eissler, 2021). Issues that the media focus on (e.g. the economy) become the heuristics by which the public rates elected officials and chooses for whom to vote. Intermediate agenda-setting refers to the influence that different media outlets and sources have on each other. Ample empirical work charts the role of candidates' social media accounts such as Instagram (e.g. Towner & Muñoz, 2018) and Twitter (Su & Borah, 2019) in reflecting the media's agenda-setting function (post topics follow news coverage) and setting the agenda itself (news coverage reflects post topics). One study looking at intermediate agenda-setting among Swiss actors not only finds that traditional media, candidate social media and party social media influence each other but also that no one entity is more influential than the others (Gilardi et al., 2021). All play a role in determining what the public views as important.

Donald J. Trump: An Anomalous Case?

Twice impeached, repeatedly indicted, convicted, and then re-elected President Donald J. Trump is considered to be an extreme example of how a candidate can shape public opinion and media coverage, wielding his own Twitter account to compel mass public and media attention from the moment of his June 2015 announcement (e.g. Wells et al., 2016). While Trump's social media use has garnered tremendous attention, scholars debate whether his missives are merely reflective of broader current trends towards incivility, impulsivity and simplicity on social media platforms (Ott, 2017), are an outlier in terms of tone, content and perceived influence (Wiemer & Scacco, 2018), or have fundamentally changed politics (Bernhard & O'Neill, 2019). In an analysis of Trump tweets around the topics of tax reform and North Korea, Wiemer and Scacco (2018) find little evidence that Trump's digital utterances are consistently and substantially disrupting the news agenda, though Trump was specifically able to influence public semantics on North Korea after a major summit in Singapore.

Trump is also known for his public disdain for the mainstream media, a topic about which he tweeted frequently before being banned from the platform in the wake of the January 6, 2021 insurrection. A content analysis of Trump tweets shows that he praises conservative news outlets while attacking mainstream sources as biased (Meeks, 2020); this pattern is reflected in public opinion polling showing depressed trust in media among Trump supporters and Republicans generally (Gottfried, 2019). Based on Trump's comments during the insurrection that were widely interpreted to show support for inciting violence after he lost the 2020 US Presidential election to Joe Biden, multiple platforms banned Trump in some manner for at least some length of time, including Twitter, Facebook, Instagram, Snapchat, the video-game streaming platform Twitch and the online shopping site Shopify (Fischer & Gold, 2021). Trump proceeded to start his own social platform, TRUTH [*sic*] Social, though user figures suggest a limited appeal: the site had 1.7 unique visitors in September 2022, compared with over 2.9 billion average monthly global users for Facebook (Dixon, 2023; Thompson & Goldstein, 2022).

HOW DO CAMPAIGNS ENGAGE SUPPORTERS IN USING SOCIAL MEDIA?

In an attempt to cut through a crowded mass communication environment, campaigns are increasingly looking to engage supporters to speak directly with their own networks about their support for a candidate or cause. This can take the form of spreading campaign messaging either in concert with or independently from the campaign, or organising friends to vote, donate or volunteer through social channels. Such peer influence can mobilise potential voters, a precursor to participation (Haßler et al., 2023). Social science demonstrates the power of individuals to influence their friends, neighbours, cohabitants and others in terms of political opinions, candidate choice or whether to vote (e.g. Huckfeldt & Sprague, 1995; Katz, 1957; Nickerson, 2008). Experimental work on Facebook and other platforms shows this to be true as well (e.g. Bond et al., 2012; Feezell, 2018; Haenschen, 2016), thus it is no surprise that campaigns also look to harness this energy. However, there is a risk that supporters will share harmful or untrue information about a candidate or their opponent, which raises normative concerns for democracy given platforms' general unwillingness to moderate all political content shared on their sites.

Social Sharing

Campaigns and parties create novel and interesting content that leverage social media affordances in the hopes that their supporters will share it with their friends. The National Republican State Committee (NRSC) has created custom Snapchat filters[2] supporting Republican candidates. One filter supporting Ohio incumbent Rob Portman was deployed using geofilters[3] to target it to people attending an Ohio State University football game; the filter was only available to people in the vicinity of the game. The limited nature of the filter increased the likelihood that individuals would use it to take photos and share them with their friends (The Columbus Dispatch, 2016). Texas Democratic candidate for US Senate Beto O'Rourke also used a Snapchat filter to criticise Republican incumbent Ted Cruz for spending more time campaigning in Iowa than Texas (Sullivan, 2018).

Another common way that campaigns look to harness the power of social sharing on social media is through organising supporters to do exactly that. A qualitative study of the 2016 US Bernie Sanders campaign demonstrated how the campaign organised supporters 'into a tightly controlled distribution network for its social media messaging', while an 'unofficial' grassroots group of supporters shared other less formal content (Penney, 2017). In the 2018 Zimbabwe presidential election, opposition parties heavily used social media and encouraged supporters to share digital posters when they could not acquire billboard space in urban areas (Mare & Matsilele, 2020). The ruling party candidate Emmerson Mnangagwa asked his supporters to go on social media and 'destroy' opposition supporters; supporters adopted the name 'varakashi' from the word 'kurakasha' meaning 'to destroy' (Munoriyarwa & Chambwera, 2020).

Relational Organising

So-called 'relational organising' is another area of user-generated influence on political behaviours. Among contemporary political campaign practitioners, relational organising refers to the efforts to organise supporters to leverage their existing interpersonal relationships to get friends, family and neighbours out to vote. Increasingly this type of mobilisation takes place using digital and social media and has been tested through a number of field experiments. Interpersonal voting reminders delivered on Facebook are effective (Haenschen, 2016; Teresi & Michelson, 2015) at increasing turnout; friend-to-friend messages are also effective when delivered via SMS (Schein et al., 2021) and WhatsApp (Moura & Michelson, 2017). Non-profit voter mobilisation organisations are increasingly turning to relational organising as a way to boost turnout. One effort organised by Turnout Nation, a non-partisan group, generated a roughly 13.2-percentage point increase in participation (Talbot, 2020). During the 2021 Georgia runoffs for two US Senate seats, Democratic candidate Jon Ossoff hired organisers to engage in paid relational organising, which boosted turnout by approximately 3.8pp (Schneider, 2022).

HOW ARE PLATFORMS SHAPING POLITICAL CAMPAIGN ACTIVITY?

Finally, we turn to the platforms, who are also political actors. Social media platforms offer different affordances and architectures, which in turn shape and constrain how campaigns use them – what messages and media types they post, the audience they seek to reach, and if they use paid ads or organic posts to communicate (Bossetta, 2018). Practitioners also understand that they can reach different audiences on each platform and know to tailor content to the general habitus of how people use and interact with each other and the platform affordances (i.e. a quote tweet 'makes sense' on Twitter; a duet or stitch 'makes sense' on TikTok). As such, digital directors state that they develop platform-specific strategies based on these affordances, of which the companies themselves are likely aware (Kreiss et al., 2018). These architectures regularly change, such as a given platform's community guidelines, advertising policies and other capabilities in what Barrett and Kreiss call 'platform transience' (Barrett & Kreiss, 2019). The architecture of a platform, the affordances and the constant changes made by platforms are never random: they are created by choices and trade-offs made by employees of social media companies. These choices are why the platforms themselves are political actors: all of their decisions have impacts on political communication.

Algorithms

The manner in which platforms display their content is their algorithms – complex rules that draw on users' past behaviours to predict what content is most likely to engage them (Gillespie, 2014). This means that even when users follow a candidate or political group on social media, that does not guarantee that the user will see that candidate's posts. Current research estimates that Facebook page owners reach under 5% of people when they post organically (Cucu, 2023). These algorithms also group users into audience segments that advertisers and political marketers can pay to reach, likely creating a self-enforcing cycle in which people who engage with political content are labelled as 'political' and given more of this content, while those who do not interact are not served such content (Annany, 2020; Gillespie, 2014). Even when candidates pay to reach audiences, the algorithm intervenes. According to one study, it costs twice as much to reach people who disagree politically with a candidate on Facebook than those already agree (Ali et al., 2021).

Employees as Consultants

Social media platforms' algorithms are only one way in which these platforms intervene in political communication. In the United States, employees of major technology platforms have closely advised campaigns, serving a role closer to consultants than was widely known (Kreiss & McGregor, 2018). Furthermore, between 2004 and 2012, Democratic Party campaigns hired 507 staffers from technology, data and analytics companies (Kreiss, 2016). To give one well-known example, Jason Barnes worked at Facebook but was embedded in the Trump campaign in 2016. He went on to work at a Democratic advocacy organisation (Seetharaman, 2019). Given these companies' central role in digital campaigning in the United States, their employees have been theorised as members of extended party networks (Barrett, 2021). Dommett and colleagues have made similar observations in the United Kingdom and Australia (Dommett et al., 2020).

Content Moderation

Despite attempting to frame themselves as neutral conduits of political content, social media platforms also play a tremendous role in determining the content of allowable political speech online through their content-moderation policies (or lack thereof). Social media platforms have historically focused content moderation on the risk of real-world harm – prohibiting threats of violence or hate speech, for example – and have given public figures more leeway in what they say rather than stricter scrutiny (Barrett et al., 2020). However, recent shifts in how platforms moderate political content are changing this norm.

In 2020, social media platforms unanimously promised to safeguard US elections. Facebook went even further: founder Mark Zuckerberg posted on his Facebook account that 'We all have a responsibility to protect our Democracy' (Zuckerberg, 2018). Over the course of 2020, Facebook, Twitter and YouTube adjusted their civic integrity policies to better account for what they perceived to be the greatest threats to free and fair elections in the United States and across the world (Barrett et al., 2020). Political advertising policies were the focus of significant attention. Google restricted what types of data political advertisers could use for audience targeting, Twitter banned most forms of political advertising, and Facebook made comparatively few adjustments to their political advertising policies despite significant pressure (Barrett et al., 2020). In 2021, Facebook limited political advertising targeting as well (Bond, 2021). These changes were met with great controversy, calls of unfair partisan bias and critiques that they were not doing more or did not act soon enough (Avaaz, 2021; Clayton, 2020).

While the effects of these changes have not been fully quantified, recent research questions if the changes made by platforms actually addressed the problems they were solving for, and has raised questions about what they wanted to accomplish to begin with (Brennan & Perault, 2021). Ultimately, there is little agreement on what democratic problems social media platforms should be trying to solve for even if they consider it their responsibility to 'protect democracy' (Kreiss & Barrett, 2020). What is sure, however, is that these changes (and others) have massive impacts on political campaigns that are trying to navigate an ever-changing and complicated content-moderation environment.

The active role that platforms take in determining the political content that citizens see is one of many reasons for the emergence of 'platform governance' as a field of study. Work in this area addresses government regulation, platforms' own policies, advertisers' roles in governance, how policies are made and the role of users in regulatory regimes (Gorwa, 2019). Campaigns are greatly affected by the policies that platforms implement and how they are enforced, including by the ability to run political ads or not, rules for how to target political ads and community guidelines that can result in candidates being deplatformed.

DISCUSSION

The use of social media by political campaigns is now a widely accepted part of contemporary political communication scholarship. In this section, we preview where the field is going in terms of research topics and methodological approach.

Social media changes rapidly, and so too do campaigns' strategies for using it. Barrett and Kreiss (2019) call these rapid changes 'platform transience'. Because of this platform transience, studying the nuances of how social media are used by individual campaigns and the effects of those uses in a given election cycle is as difficult as it is important. The unfortunate truth is that communication strategies and their effects are likely to change rapidly, possibly before research articulating them can even be published, raising questions about what Munger (2019) calls 'temporal validity'. However, the broad learnings from the aggregate of each research project can still help draw expectations as long as researchers describe the specific circumstances of their studies. If surveys and experiments on media effects are accompanied by rich description of a platform's architecture at time of the study, future scholars will be more likely to be able to determine what the similarities and differences that might alter effects are in future scenarios. We are not the only researchers to make a call for thick, descriptive work: a whole journal, in fact, was created to serve this purpose (Munger et al., 2021).

In addition to new descriptive work, academics who study social media campaigning would benefit from setting our own research trajectory, lest the mainstream media set it for us. Research trends can sometimes react to news media cycles without first looking back to what we already know from prior work. Examples include an explosion of scholarship on microtargeting after the 2012 presidential election, misinformation after the 2016 election and conspiracy theories and hate groups after the 2020 election.

Like other fields, research on social media and digital campaigning often focuses on US and Western European democracies. Research often also fails to include minoritised groups in its studies. Recent calls within political communication highlight the need to broaden perspectives to people of colour, LGBTQIA+ – identifying and other minoritised groups as well as to broaden the range of countries studied (e.g. Chakravartty et al., 2018; Freelon et al., 2016, 2023). Extending the field into more geographies and with inclusive subjects of interest also opens up the opportunity to redefine what 'matters' in research on social media and digital campaigning.

In sum, we know that campaigns use social media for more than voter persuasion and mobilisation: they use social media for organising volunteers, informing people of policy consequences, fundraising, email collection, stoking anger, shaping the media agenda and social identity positioning, to name a few. These effects matter, and yet we still have tremendous gaps in knowledge in terms of what campaign professionals do, the effects of these social media strategies and how they may differentially impact minoritised groups. Finally, while social media is changing how campaigns do things, the core organisational goals and tactics remain largely unchanged, as candidates and parties remain focused on electoral victory.

Notes

1 Friendster was an early social network site launched in 2002, prior to MySpace (2003) and Facebook (2004). Its name is a portmanteau of 'friend' and 'Napster', the latter being a common file-sharing platform used to share music in the late 1990s and early 2000s. Friendster was one of the first sites to attract over 1 million users.

2 Snapchat is a social media platform for sharing images or short videos with friends that disappear after being viewed. The images are referred to as 'snaps' and often include filters, which are text and image overlays added to a video or image. Filters can be interactive, and often include AI-powered features that give the user unique features, such as cat ears that move with the user on a video.

3 'Geofilters' are tools that limit access to any feature on an app to a specific geographic area.

REFERENCES

Aggarwal, M., Allen, J., Coppock, A., Frankowski, D., Messing, S., Zhang, K., Barnes, J., Beasley, A., Hantman, H., & Zheng, S. (2023). A 2 million-person, campaign-wide field experiment shows how digital advertising affects voter turnout. *Nature Human Behaviour*, *7*(3), 332–341. https://doi.org/10.1038/s41562-022-01487-4

Ali, M., Sapiezynski, P., Korolova, A., Mislove, A., & Rieke, A. (2021). Ad delivery algorithms: The hidden arbiters of political messaging. In *Proceedings of the 14th ACM international conference on web search and data mining* (pp. 13–21). https://doi.org/10.1145/3437963.3441801

Annany, M. (2020, July 24). Making up political people: How social media create the ideals, definitions, and probabilities of political speech. *Georgetown Law Technology Review*. https://georgetownlawtechreview.org/making-up-political-people-how-social-media-create-the-ideals-definitions-and-probabilities-of-political-speech/GLTR-07-2020/

Avaaz. (2021). *Facebook from election to insurrection: How Facebook failed voters and nearly set democracy aflame*. AVAAZ. https://avaazimages.avaaz.org/facebook_election_insurrection.pdf

Bagić Babac, M., & Podobnik, V. (2018). What social media activities reveal about election results? The use of Facebook during the 2015 general election campaign in Croatia. *Information Technology & People, 31*(2), 327–347. https://doi.org/10.1108/ITP-08-2016-0200

Baldwin-Philippi, J. (2019). Data campaigning: Between empirics and assumptions. *Internet Policy Review, 8*(4), 1–18. https://doi.org/10.14763/2019.4.1437

Baranowski, P. (2022). Leaning toward social media-based campaigning? Political communication online in Poland during the 2018 regional elections. Information polity. *The International Journal of Government & Democracy in the Information Age, 27*(3), 357–371. https://doi.org/10.3233/IP-200239

Barrett, B. (2021). Commercial companies in party networks: Digital advertising firms in US elections from 2006–2016. *Political Communication, 39*(2), 147–162. https://doi.org/10.1080/10584609.2021.1978021

Barrett, B., & Kreiss, D. (2019). Platform transience: Changes in Facebook's policies, procedures, and affordances in global electoral politics. *Internet Policy Review, 8*(4), 22.

Barrett, B., Kreiss, D., Fox, A., & Ekstrand, T. (2020). *Political advertising on platforms in the US: A brief primer.* The Bulletin of Technology & Public Life. https://citap.pubpub.org/pub/zfzjkbgz/release/1

Barrett, B., Kreiss, D., & Reddi, M. (2020). *Enforcers of truth: Social media platforms and misinformation.* The Bulletin of Technology & Public Life. https://citap.pubpub.org/pub/696n4r53/release/1

Bernhard, M., & O'Neill, D. (2019). Trump: Causes and consequences. *Perspectives on Politics, 17*(2), 317–324. https://doi.org/10.1017/S1537592719000896

Bimber, B., Flanagin, A. J., & Stohl, C. (2005). Reconceptualizing collective action in the contemporary media environment. *Communication Theory, 15*, 365–388. https://doi.org/10.1111/j.1468-2885.2005.tb00340.x

Bond, S. (2021, November 9). *Facebook scraps ad targeting based on politics, race and other "sensitive" topics.* NPR. https://www.npr.org/2021/11/09/1054021911/facebook-scraps-ad-targeting-politics-race-sensitive-topics

Bond, R. M., Fariss, C. J., Jones, J. J., Kramer, A. D. I., Marlow, C., Settle, J. E., & Fowler, J. H. (2012). A 61-million-person experiment in social influence and political mobilization. *Nature, 489*(7415), 295–298. https://doi.org/10.1038/nature11421

Bossetta, M. (2018). The digital architectures of social media: Comparing political campaigning on Facebook, Twitter, Instagram, and Snapchat in the 2016 US Election. *Journalism & Mass Communication Quarterly, 95*(2), 471–496. https://doi.org/10.1177/1077699018763307

boyd, d. m., & Ellison, N. B. (2007). Social network sites: Definition, history, and scholarship. *Journal of Computer-Mediated Communication, 13*(1), 210–230.

Broockman, D., & Green, D. (2014). Do online advertisements increase political candidates' name recognition or favorability? Evidence from randomized field experiments. *Political Behavior, 36*(2), 263–289. https://doi.org/10.1007/s11109-013-9239-z

Chakravartty, P., Kuo, R., Grubbs, V., & McIlwain, C. (2018). #CommunicationSoWhite. *Journal of Communication, 68*(2), 254–266. https://doi.org/10.1093/joc/jqy003

Clayton, J. (2020, October 27). *Social media: Is it really biased against US Republicans?* BBC News. https://www.bbc.com/news/technology-54698186

Coppock, A., Guess, A., & Ternovski, J. (2016). When treatments are tweets: A network mobilization experiment over twitter. *Political Behavior, 38*(1), 105–128. https://doi.org/10.1007/s11109-015-9308-6

Coppock, A., Hill, S. J., & Vavreck, L. (2020). The small effects of political advertising are small regardless of context, message, sender, or receiver: Evidence from 59 real-time randomized experiments. *Science Advances*, 6(36), eabc4046. https://doi.org/10.1126/sciadv.abc4046

Cucu, E. (2023, March 21). *Social media reach statistics for 2023.* SocialInsider Blog: Social Media Marketing Insights and Industry Tips. https://www.socialinsider.io/blog/social-media-reach/

Dixon, S. J. (2023, May 21). *Number of monthly active Facebook users worldwide as of 4th quarter 2023.* Statista. https://www.statista.com/statistics/264810/number-of-monthly-active-facebook-users-worldwide/

Dommett, K., Kefford, G., & Power, S. (2020). The digital ecosystem: The new politics of party organization in parliamentary democracies. *Party Politics.* https://doi.org/10.1177/1354068820907667

Dommett, K., & Power, S. (2019). The political economy of Facebook advertising: Election spending, regulation and targeting online. *The Political Quarterly, 90*(2), 257–265. https://doi.org/10.1111/1467-923X.12687

Evans, S. K., Pearce, K. E., Vitak, J., & Treem, J. W. (2017). Explicating affordances: A conceptual framework for understanding affordances in communication research. *Journal of Computer-Mediated Communication, 22*, 35–52. https://doi.org/10.1111/jcc4.12180

Feezell, J. T. (2018). Agenda setting through social media: The importance of incidental news exposure and social filtering in the digital era. *Political research quarterly, 71*(2), 482–494.

Fowler, E. F., Franz, M. M., Martin, G. J., Peskowitz, Z., & Ridout, T. N. (2020). Political advertising online and offline. *American Political Science Review*, 1–20. https://doi.org/10.1017/S0003055420000696

Fowler, E. F., Franz, M. M., & Ridout, T. N. (2016). *Political advertising in the United States*. Westview Press.

Franz, M. M., Franklin Fowler, E., Ridout, T., & Wang, M. Y. (2020). The issue focus of online and television advertising in the 2016 presidential campaign. *American Politics Research*, *48*(1), 175–196. https://doi.org/10.1177/1532673X19875722

Freelon, D., McIlwain, C. D., & Clark, M. (2016). Beyond the hashtags: #Ferguson, #Blacklivesmatter, and the online struggle for offline justice. *SSRN*. Scholarly Paper No. 2747066. https://doi.org/10.2139/ssrn.2747066

Freelon, D., Pruden, M. L., Eddy, K. A., & Kuo, R. (2023). Inequities of race, place, and gender among the communication citation elite, 2000–2019. *Journal of Communication*. jqad002. https://doi.org/10.1093/joc/jqad002

Gilardi, F., Gessler, T., Kubli, M., & Müller, S. (2022). Issue ownership and agenda setting in the 2019 Swiss national elections. *Swiss Political Science Review*, *28*(2), 190–208. https://doi.org/10.1111/spsr.12496

Gillespie, T. (2014). The relevance of algorithms. In T. Gillespie, P. J. Boczkowski, & K. A. Foot (Eds.), *Media technologies* (pp. 167–194). The MIT Press. https://doi.org/10.7551/mitpress/9780262525374.003.0009

Gold, S., & Ashley, F. (2021, January 11). *All the platforms that have banned or restricted trump so far*. Axios. https://www.axios.com/2021/01/09/platforms-social-media-ban-restrict-trump

Gorwa, R. (2019). What is platform governance? *Information, Communication & Society*, *22*(6), 854–871. https://doi.org/10.1080/1369118X.2019.1573914

Gottfried, J., Stocking, G., Grieco, E., Walker, M., Khuzam, M., & Mitchell, A. (2019, December 12). *Trusting the news media in the Trump era*. Pew Research Center. https://www.pewresearch.org/journalism/2019/12/12/trusting-the-news-media-in-the-trump-era/

Gratzinger, O. (2020, October 30). *Small donors give big money in 2020 election cycle*. OpenSecrets News. https://www.opensecrets.org/news/2020/10/small-donors-give-big-2020-thanks-to-technology/

Haenschen, K. (2016). Social pressure on social media: Using Facebook status updates to increase voter turnout. *Journal of Communication*, *66*(4), 542–563. https://doi.org/10.1111/jcom.12236

Haenschen, K. (2022). The conditional effects of microtargeted Facebook advertisements on voter turnout. *Political Behavior*. https://doi.org/10.1007/s11109-022-09781-7

Haenschen, K., Cilke, C., & Boal, A. (2023). Testing, testing: Identifying contemporary analytics practices in digital politics. *Journal of Quantitative Description: Digital Media*, *3*. https://doi.org/10.51685/jqd.2023.012

Hager, A. (2019). Do online ads influence vote choice? *Political Communication*, 1–18. https://doi.org/10.1080/10584609.2018.1548529

Han, H. (2014). *How organizations develop activists: Civic associations and leadership in the 21st century*. Oxford University Press.

Haßler, J., Magin, M., & Russmann, U. (2023). Why we should distinguish between mobilization and participation when investigating social media. *Media and Communication*, *11*(3), 124–128. https://doi.org/10.17645/mac.v11i3.7285

Heiss, R. (2021). The affective foundation of political opinion expression on social media: A panel analysis. *International Journal of Public Opinion Research*, *33*(1), 57–75.

Hill, S. J., & Huber, G. A. (2017). Representativeness and motivations of the contemporary donorate: Results from merged survey and administrative records. *Political Behavior*, *39*(1), 3–29. https://doi.org/10.1007/s11109-016-9343-y

Huber, L. M. (2022). Beyond policy: The use of social group appeals in party communication. *Political Communication*, *39*(3), 293–310. https://doi.org/10.1080/10584609.2021.1998264

Huckfeldt, R. R., & Sprague, J. (1995). In S. Feldman (Ed.), *Citizens, politics and social communication: Information and influence in an election campaign*. Cambridge University Press. https://doi.org/10.1017/CBO9780511664113

Hultman, M., Ulusoy, S., & Oghazi, P. (2019). Drivers and outcomes of political candidate image creation: The role of social media marketing. *Psychology and Marketing*, *36*(12), 1226–1236. https://doi.org/10.1002/mar.21271

Issenberg, S. (2012, December 19). *How obama's team used big data to rally voters*. MIT Technology Review. https://www.technologyreview.com/2012/12/19/114510/how-obamas-team-used-big-data-to-rally-voters/

Jackson, S. J., Bailey, M., & Welles, B. F. (2020). *#HashtagActivism: Networks of race and gender justice*. MIT Press.

Jungherr, A., Rivero, G., & Gayo-Avello, D. (2020). *Retooling politics: How digital media are shaping democracy* (1st ed.). Cambridge University Press.

Kalla, J., Collins, K., & Keane, L. (2021). *Youth voter mobilization through online advertising: Evidence from two GOTV field experiments*. OSF Preprints. https://doi.org/10.31219/osf.io/6c9na

Karpf, D. (2016). *Analytic activism: Digital listening and the new political strategy*. Oxford University Press.

Katz, E. (1957). The two-step flow of communication: An up-to-date report on an hypothesis. *Public Opinion Quarterly*, *21*(1), 61–78. https://doi.org/10.1086/266687

Keena, A., & Wintersieck, A. (2022). The fundraising effects of Facebook marketing during the 2020 election. *Journal of Marketing Development and Competitiveness*, *16*(4), 1–10.

Kim, Y. M., Heinrich, R. J., Kim, S. Y., & Baragwanath, R. (2018). Campaigns go social: Are Facebook, Snapchat, and Twitter changing elections? In T. Ridout (Ed.), *New directions in media and politics* (pp. 122–142). Routledge.

Kim, S. S., Zilinsky, J., & Brew, B. (2023). *Donate to help us fight back: Mobilization Rhetoric in political fundraising*. APSA Preprints. https://doi.org/10.33774/apsa-2022-np4xv-v2

Kreiss, D. (2016). *Prototype politics: Technology-intensive campaigning and the data of democracy*. Oxford University Press.

Kreiss, D., Lawrence, R. G., & McGregor, S. C. (2018). In their own words: Political practitioner accounts of candidates, audiences, affordances, genres, and timing in strategic social media use. *Political Communication*, *35*(1), 8–31. https://doi.org/10.1080/10584609.2017.1334727

Kreiss, D., Lawrence, R. G., & McGregor, S. C. (2020). Political identity ownership: Symbolic contests to represent members of the public. *Social Media + Society*, *6*(2), https://doi.org/10.1177/2056305120926495

Kreiss, D., & McGregor, S. C. (2018). Technology firms shape political communication: The work of Microsoft, Facebook, Twitter, and Google with campaigns during the 2016 US presidential cycle. *Political Communication*, *35*(2), 155–177. https://doi.org/10.1080/10584609.2017.1364814

Kruschinski, S., Haßler, J., Jost, P., & Sülflow, M. (2022). Posting or advertising? How political parties adapt their messaging strategies to Facebook's organic and paid media affordances. *Journal of Political Marketing*, *0*(0), 1–21. https://doi.org/10.1080/15377857.2022.2110352

Mansbridge, J. (2003). Rethinking representation. *American Political Science Review*, *97*(4), 515–528.

Mare, A., & Matsilele, T. (2020). Hybrid media system and the July 2018 elections in "post-mugabe" Zimbabwe. In N. N. Martin, & W. Mana (Eds.), *Social media and elections in Africa* (*Vol. 1*, pp. 75–96). Springer Nature. https://doi.org/10.1007/978-3-030-30553-6

McCombs, M., & Valenzuela, S. (2021). *Setting the agenda: Mass media and public opinion* (3rd ed.). Polity.

McGregor, S. (2018). Personalization, social media, and voting: Effects of candidate self-personalization on vote intention. *New Media & Society*, *20*(3). https://doi.org/10.1177/1461444816686103

Meeks, L. (2017). Getting personal: Effects of Twitter personalization on candidate evaluations. *Politics and Gender*, *13*(1), 1–25.

Meeks, L. (2020). Defining the enemy: How Donald Trump frames the news media. *Journalism & Mass Communication Quarterly*, *97*(1). https://doi.org/10.1177/1077699019857676

Meet John Kerry—On Friendster. (2004, March 4). *Bloomberg.Com*. https://www.bloomberg.com/news/articles/2004-03-03/meet-john-kerry-on-friendster

Moura, M., & Michelson, M. R. (2017). WhatsApp in Brazil: Mobilising voters through door-to-door and personal messages. *Internet Policy Review*, *6*(4). https://policyreview.info/articles/analysis/whatsapp-brazil-mobilising-voters-through-door-door-and-personal-messages

Munger, K. (2019). The limited value of non-replicable field experiments in contexts with low temporal validity. *Social Media + Society*, *5*(3), https://doi.org/10.1177/2056305119859294.

Munger, K., Guess, A. M., & Hargittai, E. (2021). Quantitative description of digital media: A modest proposal to disrupt academic publishing. *Journal of Quantitative Description: Digital Media*, *1*. https://doi.org/10.51685/jqd.2021.000

Munoriyarwa, A., & Chambwera, C. (2020). Tweeting the July 2018 elections in Zimbabwe. In N. N. Martin, & W. Mana (Eds.), *Social media and elections in Africa* (*Vol. 1*, pp. 147–176). Springer Nature. https://doi.org/10.1007/978-3-030-30553-6

Nickerson, D. W. (2008). Is voting contagious? Evidence from two field experiments. *American Political Science Review*, *102*(1), 49–57. https://doi.org/10.1017/S0003055408080039

Ostfeld, M. (2017). Unity versus uniformity: Effects of targeted advertising on perceptions of group politics. *Political Communication*, *34*(4), 530–547. https://doi.org/10.1080/10584609.2017.1288183

Ott, B. L. (2017). The age of Twitter: Donald J. Trump and the politics of debasement. *Critical Studies in Media Communication*, *34*(1), 59–68. https://doi.org/10.1080/15295036.2016.1266686

Penney, J. (2017). Social media and citizen participation in "official" and "unofficial" electoral promotion: A structural analysis of the 2016 bernie Sanders digital campaign. *Journal of Communication*, *67*(3), 402–423. https://doi.org/10.1111/jcom.12300

Ridout, T. N., Fowler, E. F., & Franz, M. M. (2021). The influence of goals and timing: How campaigns deploy ads on Facebook. *Journal of Information Technology & Politics*, 1–17. https://doi.org/10.1080/19331681.2021.1874585

Ridout, T. N., Franklin Fowler, E., Franz, M. M., & Goldstein, K. (2018). The long-term and geographically constrained effects of campaign advertising on political polarization and sorting. *American Politics Research*, *46*(1), 3–25. https://doi.org/10.1177/1532673X17721479

Russell, A., & Eissler, R. (2021). What's in a name?: Policy and Media agenda setting. *The Agenda Setting Journal*, *5*(2), 134–155. https://doi.org/10.1075/asj.20013.rus

Sahly, A., Shao, C., & Kwon, K. H. (2019). Social media for political campaigns: An examination of trump's and clinton's frame building and its effect on audience engagement. *Social Media + Society*, *5*(2). https://doi.org/10.1177/2056305119855141

Sampietro, A., & Ordaz, L. V. (2015). Emotional politics on Facebook. An exploratory study of Podemos' discourse during the European election campaign 2014. *RECERCA. Revista de Pensament i Anàlisi*, *17*. Article 17. https://doi.org/10.6035/Recerca.2015.17.4

Santos, M. L. B. dos (2021). The "so-called" UGC: An updated definition of user-generated content in the age of social media. *Online Information Review*, *46*(1), 95–113. https://doi.org/10.1108/OIR-06-2020-0258

Schein, A., Vafa, K., Sridhar, D., Veitch, V., Quinn, J., Moffet, J., Blei, D. M., & Green, D. P. (2021). Assessing the effects of friend-to-friend texting onTurnout in the 2018 US midterm elections. In *Proceedings of the web conference 2021* (pp. 2025–2036). https://doi.org/10.1145/3442381.3449800

Schneider, E. (2022, April 8). *'If we do this right ...': The new Dem organizing strategy catching fire ahead of the midterms*. POLITICO. https://www.politico.com/news/2022/04/08/democrats-spread-organizing-strategy-that-flipped-georgia-to-other-states-00023892

Seetharaman, D. (2019, November 23). How a Facebook employee helped Trump Win—But switched sides for 2020. *Wall Street Journal*. https://www.wsj.com/articles/how-facebooks-embed-in-the-trump-campaign-helped-the-president-win-11574521712

Shaw, D., Blunt, C., & Seaborn, B. (2018). Testing overall and synergistic campaign effects in a partisan statewide election. *Political Research Quarterly*, *71*(2), 361–379.

Social Media Fact Sheet. (2021). *Pew research center: Internet, science & tech*. https://www.pewresearch.org/internet/fact-sheet/social-media/. Accessed on May 16, 2023.

Staff writer. (2016, April 15). Portman using Snapchat to woo college supporters at Saturday's OSU game. *The Columbus Dispatch*. https://www.dispatch.com/story/news/politics/2016/04/15/portman-using-snapchat-to-woo/23936244007/

Su, Y., & Borah, P. (2019). Who is the agenda setter? Examining the intermedia agenda-setting effect between Twitter and newspapers. *Journal of Information Technology & Politics*, *16*(3), 236–249. https://doi.org/10.1080/19331681.2019.1641451

Sullivan, J. (2018, April 3). *Ted Cruz gives nod to O'Rourke's fundraising but says GOP will prevail*. San Antonio Report. http://sanantonioreport.org/ted-cruz-gives-nod-to-orourkes-fundraising-but-says-gop-will-prevail/image-uploaded-from-ios-68/

Talbot, M. (2020, November 2). A vote-tripling project is Betting that non-voters will Vote if a friend asks them to. *The New Yorker*. https://www.newyorker.com/news/daily-comment/a-vote-tripling-project-is-betting-that-non-voters-will-vote-if-a-friend-asks-them-to

Teresi, H., & Michelson, M. R. (2015). Wired to mobilize: The effect of social networking messages on voter turnout. *The Social Science Journal*, *52*(2), 195–204. https://doi.org/10.1016/j.soscij.2014.09.004

Thompson, S., & Goldstein, M. (2022, November 7). Truth social's influence grows despite its business problems. *The New York Times*. https://www.nytimes.com/2022/11/01/technology/truth-social-conservative-social-app.html

Thorson, K., Cotter, K., Medeiros, M., & Pak, C. (2021). Algorithmic inference, political interest, and exposure to news and politics on Facebook. *Information, Communication & Society*, *24*(2), 183–200. https://doi.org/10.1080/1369118X.2019.1642934

Towner, T. L., & Muñoz, C. L. (2018). Picture perfect? The role of Instagram in issue agenda setting during the 2016 presidential primary campaign. *Social Science Computer Review*, *36*(4), 484–499. https://doi.org/10.1177/0894439317728222

Valenzuela, S., Correa, T., & de Zúñiga, H. G. (2020). Ties, likes, and tweets: Using strong and weak ties to explain differences in protest participation across Facebook and Twitter use. In *Studying politics across media* (pp. 117–134). Routledge.

Weismueller, J., Harrigan, P., Coussement, K., & Tessitore, T. (2022). What makes people share political content on social media? The role of emotion, authority and ideology. *Computers in Human Behavior*, *129*, 107150. https://doi.org/10.1016/j.chb.2021.107150

Wells, C., Shah, D. V., Pevehouse, J. C., Yang, J., Pelled, A., Boehm, F., Lukito, J., Ghosh, S., & Schmidt, J. L. (2016). How Trump drove coverage to the nomination: Hybrid media campaigning. *Political Communication*, *33*(4), 669–676. https://doi.org/10.1080/10584609.2016.1224416

Wiemer, E. C., & Scacco, J. M. (2018). Disruptor-in-chief?: The networked influence of president Trump in building and setting the agenda. *The Agenda Setting Journal*, *2*(2), 191–213. https://doi.org/10.1075/asj.18020.wie

Workneh, T. W. (2020). Social media, protest, & outrage communication in Ethiopia: Toward fractured publics or pluralistic polity? *Information, Communication & Society*, *24*(3), 309–328. https://doi-org.colorado.idm.oclc.org/10.1080/1369118X.2020.1811367

Zuckerberg, M. (2018, January 11). *Mark Zuckerberg—One of our big focus areas for 2018 is making*. Facebook. https://www.facebook.com/zuck/posts/10104413015393571

The Role of Artificial Intelligence in Political Marketing

Christopher Robertson and Phil Harris

INTRODUCTION

This chapter seeks to investigate the increasing role of Artificial Intelligence (AI) in contemporary political marketing. Broadly defined as "a branch of computer science focused on simulating human intelligence" (Broussard et al., 2019, p. 673), AI has existed for some time, informing how search engines tailor their results (Haleem et al., 2022), technological development of autonomous vehicles (IEEE, 2022), and facial-recognition technologies of smartphones (Ríos-Sánchez et al., 2020). Yet, public and wider academic interest in AI has become more noticeable in previous years, with the creation of generative AI software being used to create "deepfakes," a form of synthetically altered video that attempts to mislead viewers into believing that they are watching an authentic video clip (Vaccari & Chadwick, 2020). Moreover, there has been increasing skepticism of generative AI software such as ChatGPT which has marred idyllic notions of AI as an "ideal type" (Robertson & Ridge-Newman, 2022). Building upon wider debates into the societal role of AI, this chapter considers the current and future role of AI in political marketing, and the potential this holds for fostering or frustrating normative democratic values. By appropriating a theoretical model of public trust, it will be discussed the preconditions for AI to fulfil its "ideal type" functions and whether AI's current usage in political marketing is enacting these criteria or failing to meet them. Moreover, it will be discussed why this is significant for democracy and how it is essential to craft an academic field whereby a marriage between the study of political marketing coalesces with the study of AI. Indeed, AI represents "the new frontiers in political advertising" (Isenstadt, 2023, n.p.), and is intrinsic to the modern political campaign, with scholarship required in determining how AI is going to reshape political communications in current and future campaigns.

Firstly, this chapter will provide a background to political marketing and scholarship on AI, appraising issues within contemporary research that this chapter will contribute toward. Secondly, this chapter's theoretical backbone will be introduced and discussed in-line with AI, considering the preconditions for "trust" and for "trust culture" to be forged and sustained, or, equally importantly, lost. Thirdly, contemporary application of AI technology in political marketing will be presented and evaluated in-line with theoretical ideals. Lastly, the wider implications of AI for political marketing will be presented, considering what the future holds for AI, political marketing, and the modern political campaign.

BACKGROUND TO POLITICAL MARKETING, TRUST AND AI

Political marketing research has flourished over the last 30 years, with older contributions tending to focus on political consultancy (Keller, 1956), until Nimmo (1970) began discussions on how politics was increasingly "marketed." Broadly defined as including "political campaigning for elections and referenda and more covert campaigning in support of lobbying, pressure group and public affairs work" (Harris, 2009, p. 190), political marketing is often discussed alongside political branding, which recognizes the brand awareness, brand image, and brand personality of political candidates and parties (Harris & Lock, 2010; Smith & French, 2009). While political marketing was evident throughout the 20th century, coinciding with the development of mass media and the advent of the second age of political communication (Blumler & Kavanagh, 1999), continual technological advancements have continued to play a role in how politics is marketed and communicated to electorates. For example, while the agenda-setting power of the mass media was recognized by McCombs and Shaw (1972), modern political marketing has informed the creation of the subfield of digital political marketing, focusing on how modern digital communications technologies inform political campaigns, branding, and advertising (Ridge-Newman & Mitchell, 2016). This plays into wider literature discussing the increased "personalisation of politics" (Bennett, 2012) facilitated via interactive or social forms of media, "i" branding (Lilleker, 2015) to craft a relatable and personable political identity, and the informalization of politics via the internet, where politicians attempt to craft relatable and approachable personas to electorates (Manning et al., 2017). Simply, digital media has allowed for new ways to engage in political marketing (Robertson, 2022) and equipped campaigners with different tools to market their message to voters. The role of AI in political marketing is yet to receive sustained academic attention, with a surfeit of academic literature appearing on AI (e.g., Erman & Furendal, 2022; Jungherr, 2023; López-López et al., 2023) that has yet to be explicitly interrogated in-line with political marketing and branding. Moreover, literature on political marketing is yet to fully engage with literature on "trust" (e.g., Andrei, 2018) in the way that this chapter will where Sztompka's (2000) sociological model of public trust is developed and appraised in-line with AI-induced developments in political marketing. By applying a sociological perspective on trust and weaving this in-line with contemporary applications of AI to political marketing, this provides a cross-disciplinary perspective on how AI is reshaping politics and what the potential consequences of current AI implementation are for achieving "ideal type" AI (Robertson & Ridge-Newman, 2022). While achieving "ideal type" AI could be perceived as naïve and idyllic, this is argued as the marker that we strive toward regarding use of AI. By endeavoring to achieve a normative ideal, this does not just link to political marketing, but also a wider "ideal type" of AI and its inclusion into society, with socialization and familiarity of the technology in apolitical scenarios such as education or purchasing decisions (Feindt & Marijn Poortvliet, 2020) and its immersion into wider society playing a key role in wider public perception of the technology. TV was once a new medium for communication, as was social media, which have become gradually instigated into and accepted as methods of political communication. While not "trusted" (this is an endless, subjectively inclined debate), by striving for a normative AI ideal, this offers the first signpost in recognizing how AI can be accommodated and understood by electorates within wider society, and within the realm of political marketing.

There is a growing body of literature discussing trust and AI, with tentative attempts at creating foundational models of AI and public trust. Lukyanenko et al. (2022), for example, recognized that while "the issue of trust in AI emerges as a paramount societal concern." Despite increased attention of researchers, "the topic remains fragmented without a common conceptual and theoretical foundation" (Lukyanenko et al., 2022, p. 1993). The authors note several maxims conducive for public trust in AI drawing on the work of Niklas Luhmann, recognizing that we need to consider the stability and predictability of AI technologies, and that trust can be conceptualized at different levels (Lukyanenko et al., 2022). While several future research directions are suggested by the authors, there is little to no suggestion of researching AI's role in politics and political marketing, which this chapter seeks to do. Unlike Lukyanenko et al.'s (2022) work, this chapter adopts Sztompka's (2000) sociological theory of trust. It does so to broaden analysis beyond system theory analysis of trust, to encapsulate the wider social becoming of trust, and how trust in the use of AI as a system depends upon a multitude of factors that adds a nuance to Luhmann's (2018) personal and systemic levels of trust. Other scholarship, while not explicitly attempting to craft models of trust have rather attempted to gauge usage of AI and whether this corresponds with perceived notions of trust (Kreps & Kriner, 2023), public perceptions and trust of

AI governance models (Robles & Mallinson, 2023), and trust in ethical usage of AI in governance and policy (Kleizen et al., 2023). Yet, while a surfeit of academic literature incorporating trust, AI and democracy has emerged (e.g., Jungherr, 2023; Kane, 2019; Schippers, 2020), there is little serious academic engagement with how AI is transforming modern political campaigns and political marketing as this chapter will explore.

One could ask; however, do we really care about trust in AIs, and should we not be directing our attention toward trust in political parties and democracy itself? If we trust the communicator, why should we care about the tools used to craft and spread their message? As a response to this, however, this work argues that we do care about trust in AI, as the human condition is easily misled into trusting when they are being deceived, as put forward by truth default theory (Levine, 2014), but also that if we do genuinely "trust" the communicator utilizing AI, how are we to trust a software that perhaps we are unfamiliar with, or is facing diverse coverage in the media which may affect our trust perception of that particular technology (Nader et al., 2022)? Contributing to a growing field of research that also considers trust toward AIs, as opposed to the actors utilizing the technology (e.g., Arguedas et al., 2023; Deley & Dubois, 2020; Xu et al., 2014), it can be argued that trust toward the communicator using the technology can be very easily retracted if an unfamiliar technology is inadequately utilized. If political parties or representatives are using a software, perhaps one that is new, emerging or potentially controversial such as AI that users are unfamiliar with, this is likely to distort their perceptions of trust toward the actor and affect one's trust perception toward both the technology, and the actor using this (Yang et al., 2023). Indeed, while "we do not trust technologies like we trust people, rather we rely on them" (Deley & Dubois, 2020, p. 1), if a trusted actor utilizes an AI nefariously or potentially misleads by doing so, this may constitute the trusting relationship toward the actor to shift toward one of mis-, or distrust. Therefore, with information being the currency of democracy, understanding the role that AI plays in communicating false, misleading, or misappropriated messages plays a key role in the sustainment, or degradation of trust culture. AI, as with previous "new" or "emerging" technologies such as the advent of mass media or social media is here to stay and has the potential to radically alter the modern political campaign. Therefore, this chapter seeks to contribute to a surfeit of literature on AI and trust and attempts to bring the two together through marrying a sociological theory of trust with contemporary developments of the use of AI in political marketing. The goal is to determine how current use of AI in political marketing fosters or frustrates a culture of trust, and what challenges this poses for politics moving forward, and what is being done to ameliorate a currently ambivalent culture of trust toward AI. Therefore, this next section will introduce the theoretical backbone for this chapter before considering throughout whether current usage of AI in political marketing is conducive for trust and, if not, what is currently being done to ameliorate this trust discrepancy and the future implications for if public trust in AI does not change.

TO TRUST OR NOT TO TRUST?

The theoretical foundation of this chapter draws upon Piotr Sztompka's (2000) sociological theory of trust that was later expanded and built upon in recent work where an "ideal-type" of AI in journalism was crafted, looking forward to 2030 (Robertson & Ridge-Newman, 2022). Therefore, the main elements extracted from Sztompka's (2000) theory will be presented, alongside considering how Robertson and Ridge-Newman's (2022) previous application of trust for determining trustworthiness of AI that had previously been applied to AI's role in journalism, to political marketing. It will be proposed that public trust in AI hinges on several factors, which if not met will mar public perception of the technology, fostering a culture of distrust which has negative implications for democracy and contemporary political marketing.

The premise of Sztompka's (2000) theory is that "trust is a bet about the future contingent actions of others" (p. 25). To place trust in someone, or something, we need to calculate the risk in taking such an action; a term deemed "trust bets." To measure whether I trust, or distrust something, one needs to believe that taking an action is likely to fulfil their expectations, and with this belief informs confidence: if I am confident that taking an action is likely to work out in my favor, then my anticipatory trust will increase, and the success of this trust bet is also increased. Once the individual has a belief and confidence in engaging in an act, one begins to engage in trusting with the trustor anticipating that this action will be beneficial, and that there is unlikely to be negative repercussions for doing so (Sztompka, 2014).

Provisionally, an example of a low-risk trust bet regarding the use AI in political marketing may relate to familiarity and confidence in the use of AI as technology in a political advertisement, and transparency into how this AI technology has been incorporated. Transparency is key in democratic accountability and decision-making, and if voters are unaware that AI is being used in constructing voice, image, or synthetic video in political advertisements, then the capacity to mislead increases and voter perception toward the technology concurrently with trust toward the distributing actor will be marred, as found in previous studies (Vaccari & Chadwick, 2020). For an actor to be deemed "trustworthy," it is gauged whether citizen's interests are considered when implementing decisions, and if this is failed to be achieved (Winsvold et al., 2024) or that is an information deficit in this "trust transaction," then this may lead to harm such as distrust. With scholars such as Yang et al. (2023) unveiling that trust in political actors is beginning to be balanced alongside trust in their AI usage, alongside Kreps and Jakesch (2023) finding that AI-mediated communication between citizens and legislators can foster trust toward politicians, it is important to consider the role that AI plays in affecting positive trust toward political actors, but also the potentially negative effects that AI can play in affecting trust culture toward politicians, parties and democratic representation itself. If voters are unaware that AI is being utilized in political communications and this information is framed as authentic or legitimate but has perhaps had its context altered or meaning exaggerated through the use of AI, this provides democratic challenges as voters should not be expected to "guess" whether the information they are receiving is false or genuine, particularly in governmental political advertising in democracies. AI, therefore, is revolutionizing the trust "game" within political marketing. This is because AI intertwines with other trust objects in crafting a new, multilayered trust culture in which political trust is granted, or retracted, with AI changing the conventional "rules of the game" (Jungherr, 2023) through its sudden boom within political craftsmanship contrasted with wider societal hesitancy of AI as technology, mediated by factors such as self-efficacy, political identification, generalized media and institutional trust, and sociodemographic factors (Araujo et al., 2023).

Therefore, this work seeks to move beyond understandings that we should only be studying "trust" toward the communicator, but that the technology utilized to construct political messages also merits attention as a key component in the formulation of trust, distrust, and the wider democratic implications of this. By considering the emerging and future role of AI, this extends discussion beyond the role of a particular technology explicitly upon political marketing itself, but also the wider social becoming of AI as technology and its multifaceted capacity to influence perceptions toward political advertising, but also the capacity for wider experiences of AI technology to socialize and influence perception toward the technology itself. Indeed, as political marketing scholars, we must consider the influence of how controversial and potentially mistrusted technologies, if utilized by ostensibly trusted politicians, may affect the perception and reception of messages from this actor. This is particularly pertinent given that there is not always a "fan" culture surrounding politicians which will automatically positively alter perception of or normalize a technology – wider public understanding of AI as technology plays a key role, which is especially complex given the multiple forms of AI that can play a role in society, and in political marketing itself.

Indeed, if the trust culture, understood as the wider context or perceptions of the technology, is impacted by nefarious applications such as deepfakes or unaccountability of the tech firms responsible for the AI (Robertson & Ridge-Newman, 2022), this poses challenges for granting trust, with every action of trusting involving risk. However, while all actions involve risk, this risk can be mitigated if a trusting culture is fortified. Linking to Sztompka's (2000) perspective, Levine's (2014) truth default theory should also be considered. Levine's (2014) theory recognizes that humans tend to assume that what another says to them is honest, which opens up the possibility of deception in communication. Markowitz and Hancock (2023) considered truth default theory in relation to generative AI, determining that it had a greater propensity of truth bias compared to communication with humans. While this work recognizes the contributions of truth default theory and its capacity to study trust in AI, Sztompka's (2000) approach was chosen due to its multidimensional understanding of the social becoming of trust culture. Moreover, this approach provides clear differentiation between "trusting," "mistrusting," and "distrusting" which offer useful markers in studying political marketing through AI and the multitude of variables which may influence the trust culture surrounding this, building upon previous scholarship. For example, an example of how AI can foster a distrusting or mistrusting culture can be seen in Vaccari and Chadwick's (2020) study. The researchers found that upon showing respondents deepfake-altered political video, sizeable minorities of respondents were deceived, and this affects one's trust of AI-technology in political video. 14.9% of respondents who watched a deceptive 4 second video clip were deceived compared to 16.4% of those deceived who watched a deceptive 26 second clip, or 16.9% who watched a full deepfake video with an educational reveal at the end (Vaccari & Chadwick, 2020). Increasingly disconcertingly, many respondents felt uncertain after watching the deepfake clip, with 27.5% of those who saw the video with educational reveal still feeling uncertain, compared to 36.1% of those who watched the deceptive 26 second clip (Vaccari & Chadwick, 2020).

However, in September 2023, Google laid out plans to make creators of political content that has been fully or partially created with AI to disclose this in response to "growing prevalence of tools that produce synthetic content" (McCallum, 2023, n.p.). In doing so, Google are attempting to regulate the use of AI, widely seen as necessary to forge normative "ideal type" use of AI (Davies & Birstwistle, 2023; Farid, 2023), and in doing so are attempting to foster transparency and trust of AI's use in political advertising. Google has recognized in its previous policy on AI that several key factors that must be acknowledged when regulating AI include parity between AI and non-AI systems, proportionally balancing out the potential harms and benefits of AI, and transparency. Indeed, Google have stated that "transparency…is a means to enable accountability, empower users, and build trust and confidence" (Google, n.d., p. 5). This distinctly alludes to Sztompka's (2000) ideas of the social becoming of trust culture, and if political advertising is responsively and reflectively developed by Google, where glitches are removed and AI technology is continually improved, a trust culture is likely to form. Yet, while trust may be apparent in one instance, such as trusting a political advert once Google has enforced this policy, this may not be universal in its approach and may require developing and amending potential glitches in its pilot period. If this occurs, a trust bet may turn out to be detrimental which may reverse this trusting instinct to one of distrust. Moreover, one could question whether Google's policies to counteract nefarious use of AI can be trusted, and the extent to which they care about democracy given historical marring's of trust by big tech as in the case of Cambridge Analytica, or the Google + scandal in 2018 (Bendall & Robertson, 2018; O'Flaherty, 2018). This chapter therefore does not instruct that we should "trust" private tech, but that we recognize the Machiavellian approach of Google (Robertson and Harris, forthcoming), and other tech platforms, to appear that they recognize that significance of AI in contemporary public life and are attempting to provide solutions in order to maintain trust in their brand, even if this approach merely seeks to retain Google's user base and market positioning. Therefore, Google, and other tech companies, must enact the role of the modern digital prince (see Robertson & Harris, forthcoming, for a prolonged discussion), triumphing over "difficulties and opposition" (Machiavelli, 2003, p. 69) by enacting policies that seek to represent public interest, alongside attempting to prevent future scandal or harm to their brand and market positioning. One response, therefore, is to pragmatically respond to the increasing prominence of AI and develop policies and procedures that attempt to retain user trust in the platform.

It is important not to confuse distrust with "mistrust," with some scholars equating the concepts similarly (Engelke et al., 2019). Mistrust can be deemed as "a neutral, cautious state" (Robertson & Ridge-Newman, 2022, p. 132). In the context of AI, this could be experienced if one is unsure about AI's impact in political marketing, perhaps due to previous negative experiences of being misled by AI, as in the case of deepfakes, but also having positive experience of AI through conversational chatbots, with scholars such as Fan et al. (2023) finding that anthropomorphic chatbots can bolster trust, for example. Distrust, however, is the direct opposite of trust. Trusting is a positive bet: placing a wager that is likely to create positive returns for the trustor. For example, encountering a political advert where it is transparently stated how AI has been used, of being able to find why a political advert has been recommended to you, and how your user data have been used in doing this. Distrusting is a negative bet, likely to be experienced by those who have been misled by AI and have a wider negative perception of the technology. For example, those who were entirely deceived in Vaccari and Chadwick's (2020) study, or those who were encouraged by motivated reasoning to believe that the Republican National Committee's (RNC's) dystopian Biden advert was real, simply because they wanted to believe this. Therefore, the role and future journey of AI in political marketing largely depends upon wider public perceptions of the technology.

THE SOCIAL BECOMING OF TRUST CULTURE

Sztompka (2000) writes of the social becoming of trust culture, specifying three variables conducive to the construction of a trusting, or distrusting, culture. Firstly, historical factors of trusting or distrusting as the background variable. With AI, public awareness of the use of powerful machine AI associated with products owned by familiar, ostensibly trustworthy, familiar companies such as Amazon or Google can craft both cultures of trust toward AI, but also distrust surrounding the use of personal data and privacy (Jungherr, 2023). This historical tradition is then informed by independent structural variables, such as the transparency of the use of AI, and the accountability of the organization using AI (Sztompka, 2000). Regarding political marketing, if the use of AI is disguised, with AI-generated content presented as genuine, unedited footage, this may lead to democratic malaise and distrust of the technology (Savaget et al., 2019). Conversely, if the use of AI is transparent and the organization recognizes potential faults and is continually seeking to improve its utilization of AI, this may craft a more trusting relationship of both the organization, and AI itself. Indeed, granting trust relates to experiences and expectations (Robertson & Ridge-Newman, 2022), and while expectations are highly subjective and may vary, individuals are unlikely to trust AI if its use is attempted to be concealed or masked.

In political marketing, this closely links to AI's use in political campaigns, with Clementson (2023) arguing that AI can mislead voters through personalized microtargeting promising unrealistic policies, specifically tailored to the interests of the user. Alluding to aggressive, undemocratic microtargeting seen in the Cambridge Analytica scandal, where information was manipulated without voter consent (Bendall & Robertson, 2018), the use of AI in political marketing in this way may evoke memory of previous nefarious application of AI in politics, which is likely to tarnish the historical reputation of AI's trust culture. Similarly, if chatbots are utilized in campaigning for swift, large-scale dissemination of messaging, this can lead to unaccountability and distrust, given that generative AI can often misread context and deliver misleading advertisements (Clementson, 2023; Gehl & Lawson, 2022).

Thirdly, Sztompka (2000) recognizes the moderating importance of agential endowment, encompassing social mood toward entities, such as one's trusting impulses. Indeed, Savaget et al. (2019) argue that AI can fortify democracy, by informing voters about relevant information to increase political knowledge and efficacy, bringing electorates closer to public affairs, alongside empowering marginalized people to join the democratic process through translation software. Agential endowment also encompasses collective capital, understood as one's societal power, educational attainments, and wider social networks. This collective capital potentially allows the individual to make more secure trust bets based upon personal evaluation of whether AI has been utilized in political advertisements, if not made readily apparent. Greater levels of this capital would reduce the risk in making trust bets, alongside if AI is utilized transparently and the organization using AI is accountable and responsive to improvements, this could reduce uncertainty, increase confidence, and ameliorate trust culture (Robertson & Ridge-Newman, 2022). Indeed, Appel and Prietzel (2022) found that higher levels of political interest and knowledge increased the likelihood of individuals detecting political deepfakes, alongside those who can use this knowledge to analytically unpick the credibility of political content. Combined, these variables inform the social becoming of a trust culture, which is continually subject to change.

Yet, historical perceptions of a technology are much more difficult to alter than structural and agential factors. Rainie et al. (2022) writing for the Pew Research Center recently found that Americans are generally skeptical about AI, with 45% of respondents being equally concerned and excited about AI compared to 37% who were more concerned than excited, and only 18% being more excited than concerned. In a different poll, Rainie et al. (2022) found that 46% of respondents felt that facial recognition technology use by the police is a good thing, but only 21% felt that driverless cars are a good idea. This hinges upon familiarity with the software, with gradual instigation of AI technology breeding a culture of trust (Thiebes et al., 2021). People regularly use facial-recognition technology themselves for banking applications, opening their phone, and so on, but the idea of driverless cars sounds unfamiliar and abstract. This is consistent with previous scholarship evidencing familiarity with technological applications such as e-commerce, regularly visiting certain websites on the internet, or perceived credibility with brands can generate a feeling of trust of the technologies or products with which they interact (Cheshire et al., 2010; Gefen, 2000; Jadil et al.,

2022). Therefore, gradually instigating AI in political marketing merits attention, as many once unfamiliar technologies have now become universally recognized and accepted in public life, such as computers, the internet, or even mobile phones. Moreover, familiarity with the involvement of AI's involvement in crafting and sustaining political brands alludes to debates on brand management, where it is postulated what the potential current and future role of AI becoming normalized in crafting an authentic brand voice or persona is (Kirkby et al., 2023).

MACRO-SOCIETAL TRUST VARIABLES

The final macro-societal variables conducive to trust culture proposed by Sztompka (2000) that pose relevance for application to AI are normative coherence, transparency, familiarity, and accountability. Normative coherence relates to AI striving to achieve normative ideals, where AI must be used to understand the electorate's needs, chatbots can be used to provide voters with accurate, factually driven information, and if AI is used in political video, it must be clearly apparent and not intended to mislead watchers. This would envisage "ideal type" AI (Robertson & Ridge-Newman, 2022) and are the markers that political marketers and AI manufacturers should be striving for to craft an AI trust culture. Indeed, in the RNC's May 2023 advert that generated a dystopian video of what the world would seemingly be like if Joe Biden was re-elected in 2024, the words "built entirely with AI imagery" were visible in the top left corner of the screen, although as O'Sullivan and Abou-Ghazala (2023) note, this was very faint, potentially misleading less keen-eyed viewers. Thiebes et al. (2021) note that functionality, helpfulness, and the reliability/predictability of AI are required to craft trust in the technology. Therefore, for ideal type AI in political marketing, a clear purpose of how the AI is being used, and the purpose of its utilization must be apparent. If AI is used in political video, it must be noticeable and have a clear distinction from "real" video (Maras & Alexandrou, 2018), in the same way in which computer-generated imagery (CGI) is used in films. If people go to see a CGI generated film, they will be aware that sequences will be partially or entirely generated with computer-assisted technology. Similarly with political marketing, AI tools incorporated into campaign such as AI-generated imagery or targeted advertisements need to be clearly distinguished from "real," human-directed marketing. With the Federal Election Commission (FEC) proposing that AI is regulated in the run-up to the 2024 US election (Farid, 2023), it seems that the move toward ideal type AI is in process, although crafting trust toward an emerging technology such as AI will quickly shift toward distrust if this regulation is not stringently implemented.

This links into the second variable of transparency. As in "ideal type" use of AI in journalism (Robertson & Ridge-Newman, 2022), for AI to be transparent, "the audience must have knowledge that AI is being utilised and the creation of the story is not an entirely human construct" (p. 137). As in political marketing, if the organization is transparent and open, clearly presenting how AI has been used, this will reduce the risk of placing trust bets and is likely to increase familiarity with the incorporation of AI into campaigning over time (Zerilli et al., 2022). Haresamudram et al. (2023) propose that there are three levels of AI transparency which must be recognized to foster trust in AI: algorithmic, interaction and social transparency. Algorithmic transparency is largely consigned to benefitting developers of software and the regulators, as opposed to users and society at large, given that if the creators of the technology can understand how to craft objective and unbiased algorithms, this fosters wider societal benefit (Haresamudram et al., 2023). Interaction transparency benefits both user and designer, with Haresamudram et al. (2023) providing examples such as the interaction with smart watches or phones. In political marketing, the product that users are interacting with is the flows of political communication such as political video crafted entirely or aided in creation by AI, and how interaction with this information informs choices made by the user. Transparency in this sense relates to knowledge; both the knowledge provided by the user to craft AI-generated adverts or building knowledge of an AI-chatbot, alongside the message delivered to the user, tailored to their interests without bias or misinformation present (Panch et al., 2019). If a trust culture for AI in political marketing is to be created, a clear transparency in communications and the use of user data is required, which is largely dependent upon the algorithmic design of the software to be created to mitigate bias and misleading content. The third variable is social transparency, with the relevant stakeholders here being owners, users, regulators, and society (Haresamudram et al., 2023). This is perhaps the most pervasive element of transparency, with public awareness of events such as the Cambridge Analytica scandal prompting a multitude of regulations on AI, such as the proposed EU AI Act seeking to ban real-time facial-recognition and increase the transparency of generative AI software such as ChatGPT (Perrigo & Gordon, 2023). With historical memory of misuse of AI being evoked by events such as the Cambridge Analytica scandal or deepfake video of prominent world leaders, this links to the macro-societal variable of the historical context of the technology, with public trust in AI marred by events such as this, encouraging regulation in attempt to rebuild public trust in AI. Therefore, in political marketing, lessons should be learned from how nefarious application of AI technology has shaken public trust of AI. Indeed, with the FEC proposing regulation of AI in the run-up to the 2024 US elections, this is occurring.

This links to the third variable of familiarity. Familiarity can foster trust, and for "ideal type" AI to occur, historical marring's of the virtuous nature of AI technology can reduce this trust, with people being aware of AI technology, but in a negative sense. Yet, given the potential and seeming commitment by organizations to regulate AI and continue to use AI in many different forms, there is a clear drive to familiarize people with AI and be transparent in its utilization: a clear prerequisite for trust. In political marketing, if AI is gradually instigated and publics are aware that its use will be regulated, this could reduce the risk in placing risky trust bets (Robertson & Ridge-Newman, 2022), if people can be confident that they are not being intentionally misled based upon political preferences. While people may receive tailored political adverts based upon interests and ideology, Google has updated its political content policy in September 2023 so that political adverts incorporating AI require "a clear and conscientious disclosure" (Google, 2023, n.p). In response to global concerns surrounding electoral interference and the nefarious use of AI in political campaigns to deceive electorates, Google's policy seeks to regulate potentially manipulative forms of AI use:

> An ad with synthetic content that makes it appear as if a person is saying or doing something they didn't say or do'
>
> An ad with synthetic content that alters footage of a real event or generates a realistic portrayal of an event to depict scenes that did not actually take place. (Google, 2023, n.p.)

Alongside the FEC attempting to regulate AI use on social media platforms, there is a clear recognition of the dangers posed by AI, and how regulating AI will increase the transparency of AI use, increase familiarity of AI being incorporated into politics and what it does, with greater transparency also fostering higher levels of accountability of the tech firms. If this continues and AI can build trustworthiness, this means that AI will gradually become recognized as an acceptable technology in modern political marketing in the same way in which the modern social media campaign is: an unprecedented campaigning tool in recent memory in Barack Obama's famous 2008 campaign (Bimber, 2014).

Lastly, if the accountability of AI firms continues, this will increase trust. If institutions are crafting AI in attempt to achieve normative ideals of the technology, if algorithmic, interactive and social levels of transparency (Haresamudram et al., 2023) are achieved, and if people gradually become familiar with AI in political marketing, people will hold greater confidence in AI as technology, recognize its purpose, and form expectations about AI's role in political marketing. As a result, this reduces the risk in placing trust bets, which will be sustained if AI is continually regulated, and its functionality improved to benefit society. These are standards that must be achieved if "ideal type" AI usage is to exist both in political marketing and in wider societal applications of AI: normative coherence, transparency, familiarity, accountability. These factors are conducive to trust, with their opposites facilitating distrust, and therefore are markers that should be avoided. These are normative turmoil, pervading secrecy, unfamiliarity, and unaccountability. If AI stimulates these variables, this will ultimately foster a culture of distrust (Robertson & Ridge-Newman, 2022), and is likely to pose challenges for democracy, representation, and trust of not just AI, but also trust of politicians and democratic institutions themselves which is already a challenge in contemporary society (Dahlgren, 2018; Jones, 2019). Now these variables have been introduced and provisionally situated in-line with AI, contemporary examples of AI's application in political marketing will be provided and evaluated in-line with the theoretical model of trust. How is AI being used, what future developments are there, and are current events cultivating, or eroding trust of AI?

AI'S USE IN MODERN POLITICAL MARKETING

> I'm the AI. (Laughter). If any of you think I'm Abe Lincoln, blame it on the AI. (White House, 2023, n.p.)

This remark from Joe Biden in 2023 encompasses the nature of AI in modern political marketing: Who is who? What is real? What can I trust? At the time of writing, in the run-up to the 2024 US election, voters need to be informed by mediums they can trust, not manipulated, or unduly influenced. Therefore, AI's role in political marketing in the run-up to the 2024 US elections is essential to recognizing AI's future direction in political campaigning. Firstly, Ron DeSantis's super PAC in July 2023 featured an ad discrediting former US President Donald Trump, utilizing AI to do so. While the astute listener is likely to recognize that Donald Trump's voice in the advert is AI-generated, given that what is read out on the political ad is a verbatim quote from Trump posted on his Truth Social platform, there is a high likelihood that some listeners would be deceived. This clearly relates to scholarship discussed earlier on levels of political knowledge and sophistication determining the likelihood of a listener recognizing the AI-generated audio, considering people globally are generally ambivalent about the use of AI (Gillespie et al., 2023). While it was reported that the "Trump attacks Iowa" advert was AI-generated (Isenstadt, 2023), how is a viewer to know that Trump did not say what he had written on his social media platform in real time? Indeed, it was not stated in the campaign advert that AI was utilized, implying that "an information environment where voters are faced with a deluge of false and misleading information, AI content has the potential to muddy the waters even more" (Steiner in Jacobsen & Tuquero, 2023, n.p.). Another example is in the RNC's AI-generated "Biden-induced dystopian future" video, where Wall Street is shown as abandoned, and Taiwan is under attack, the disclaimer that this video was made with AI is very small, included only as a statement to avoid the video potentially being taken down. When AI is used in cases such as this, despite the relative ease of recognizing that this video is not real, this shows the potentiality of AI to craft dangerous and misleading narratives if better disguised. However, while AI did not change the content of the message in the DeSantis ad, people are often more influenced by spoken as opposed to written communication, highlighting the importance of listening, as opposed to simply reading Trump's rhetoric (Shen & Sengupta, 2018). Moreover, the generation of Trump's voice by AI adds a sense of authenticity to this soundbite, particularly given that the advert simply featured an audio rendering of what Trump wrote on Truth Social, as opposed to something outlandish and unbelievable as featured in other generative AI content such as deepfakes (Hameleers et al., 2022).

Consequently, despite personal attacks on opponents being commonplace in political campaigning (Verhulsdonk et al., 2021), AI, if utilized in this way, has the potential to further blur the divide between falsehood and reality, misinforming voters and crafting alternative paradigms of what does and does not constitute "truth." Alluding to debates on "post-truth," where anything said can be claimed to be true, this crafts what Fish (2016) labels as an "illusory democracy," mirroring falsehoods articulated by Trump when he was President. If listeners are led to believe that a figure with perceived credibility is proclaiming things that were never spoken or said, advancements in AI technology could continue to refine the authenticity of such as actions, with research evidencing that people often think they can detect deceptive video, but in reality, cannot (Köbis et al., 2021). If people begin to question what information is AI-generated and what information is unedited, this poses significant challenges for political marketing and the trustworthiness of both the candidate, and AI as technology.

Alluding to Sztompka's (2000) social becoming of trust culture, misleading advertisements such as this can erode levels of trust in AI, informing wider public perceptions of the trustworthiness of AI as technology. In this case, while later admitted by Never Back Down, AI was not transparently and openly used, implying that viewers were meant to be led to believe that they were listening to Trump's voice, and not an AI-generated one. Therefore, the lack of transparency here erodes trust culture and, if correctly implemented, heavily justifies Google's forthcoming policy on regulating online political advertising. Agential endowment is directly relevant to this case, and AI's utilization in wider political marketing, as one's collective capital directly relates to their trusting impulses. While research has found that higher levels of education correlate with increased levels of generalized trust (Charron & Rothstein, 2016), people are more likely to exhibit trust over phenomena that they can influence (Lukyanenko et al., 2022). Yet, with scholarship proposing that greater levels of political interest and media education could encourage greater skepticism of online content before idly believing anything encountered online (Appel & Prietzel, 2022), the moderating importance of agential endowment is noticeable. In this instance, placing a "trust bet" on the validity of the generative audio was dependent upon whether one had previously heard Trump's voice, motivated reasoning influencing whether one wished to believe that it was Trump speaking versus those who were either neutral or did not want to believe that they were listening to Trump, alongside one's ingrained social trusting impulses. Therefore, the misleading AI in the DeSantis super PEC, while not directly harmful for democracy, poses wider questions for political marketing surrounding how one's agential endowment will be tested when AI is used to falsify information or generate targeted adverts that tap into individuals' deep-seated beliefs.

Considering Sztompka's (2000) other variables, it is clear that "normative coherence" was not present in the DeSantis super PAC. As an "ideal type" (Robertson & Ridge-Newman, 2022), AI should be utilized to craft accurate information that can remove misinformation and "potential algorithm production bias" (p. 136). Moreover, people should be confident that AI is being used to increase levels of anticipatory trust of the source and reduce the risk in placing negative trust bets that would mar one's perception of the AI technology. Secondly, transparency of AI was not present, here. For AI to enact normative ideals in political marketing, "the audience must have knowledge that AI is being utilised and the creation of the story is not an entirely human construct" (Robertson & Ridge-Newman, 2022, p. 137). In this DeSantis ad, as in other deceptive use of AI, if people are not fully aware of whether information presented to them is AI generated, this can increase levels of uncertainty and the likelihood of being deceived (Vaccari & Chadwick, 2020). While outwardly insignificant given that the AI-generated voice was simply replicating what Trump wrote, the potentiality for AI to be used more nefarious creations is very real. For example, in the RNC's AI-generated ad that depicted a dystopian world foreshadowing what would happen if Biden won the 2024 elections highlights the possibility of more dangerous applications of AI has previously occurred, and could very easily continue to be realized without proper regulation.

Considering the variable of familiarity, Sztompka (2000) postulated that familiarity can foster trust. However, voters' familiarity with AI in the field of politics is often marred by how AI is used, and, indeed, what they are becoming familiar with. While increased familiarity can reduce the risk of placing negative trust bets if people are aware of what AI is and what it is capable of, if AI is not enacting normative ideals and political organizations are not being transparent in its usage, this prevents familiarity with "ideal type" AI, and thus prevents the ability to trust AI. With the RNC and other Republican-affiliated organizations having a history of incorporating AI into their political advertising, familiarity with AI's use is linked to one's perceptions of how AI is being used by a particular organization or group. For example, Gillespie et al. (2023) found that 44% of respondents were likely to trust healthcare AI, while only 36% were likely to trust recommender AI, and only 34% trusted the use of AI in human resources. Therefore, for "ideal type" AI usage to be achieved in political marketing, an organization's track record of how they use AI, alongside wider historical and structural factors must be considered. Lastly, when considering accountability, AI was used in the super PEC ad to amplify support for DeSantis while slandering Trump, with little consideration for how AI could be accountably or normatively used. With universal recognition among politicians, supranational organizations, and business leaders that AI should be regulated (Perrigo, 2023; Rajvanshi, 2023), future use of AI in political marketing should prevent the misleading use of AI, as in the DeSantis ad, in attempt to mitigate curtailment of democracy and misleading electorates.

Therefore, in the case of the DeSantis super PAC, it can be determined that "ideal type" AI was not apparent, and that further regulation is required to make AI trustworthy in political marketing. While there have always been challenges in elections, if AI continues to become more advanced and there is a greater possibility to mislead voters, even with regulation. While this chapter has mainly focused upon generative AI in the context of political video, there is potential for AI to be weaponized by nefarious actors in other ways that may dismantle the vestiges of democracy. For example, Klepper and Swenson (2023) muse several possibilities:

> Automated robocall messages, in a candidate's voice, instructing voters to cast ballots on the wrong date; audio recordings of a candidate supposedly confessing to a crime or expressing racist views; video footage showing someone giving a speech or interview they never gave. Fake images designed to look like local news reports, falsely claiming a candidate dropped out of the race (n.p.)

Indeed, while there are processes discussed throughout this chapter to regulate the official use of AI in political campaigning, what possibilities are there for regulation of AI being used by nongovernmental actors attempting to deliberatively deceive and mislead voters? What is the possibility of greater misinformation from both state and non-state actors in disrupting elections through generative AI (Klepper & Swenson, 2023)? While there is much possibility for the regulation of AI, and the emergence of a trusting culture, there continues to be much potential for AI to become an object of mistrust, or even distrust, if there is not a universal strategy to prevent AI becoming weaponized by a multitude of different actors. Therefore, while progress has been made toward achieving "ideal type" AI, prompted by misleading applications of AI in the modern political campaign, there remains much capacity for regulation and debate moving forward.

CONCLUSION

This chapter has sought to present Sztompka's (2000) sociological theory of trust and considers how AI's current and future use in political marketing hinges upon the level of trust that it can generate among electorates. AI poses both challenges and opportunities for the modern political campaign, with virtuous usage of the technology holding possibilities to harvest large amounts of data, target voters with relevant information, encourage real-time engagement with voters, and play roles in enhancing political video. However, AI also raises ethical dilemmas that require regulation, alongside international co-operation amongst nation-states to prevent potentially nefarious use of the technology by adversarial actors. It has been argued that AI in all its manifestations must attempt to envisage an "ideal type" where normative coherence, transparency, familiarity, and accountability of AI software are achieved in order to foster a trust culture surrounding the technology. Doing so would ameliorate previous negative historical memory of AI, as in the case of deepfakes, with one's agential endowment being strengthened by positive perceptions of AI as technology, alongside one's political and tech literacy of being able to recognize false and misleading content, which is likely to be aided by tech company's regulation of AI technologies. By appraising potential challenges of AI's use in political marketing and focusing in-depth on a current example of AI in politics, it has been determined the normative ideals that AI should strive toward, how this could be achieved, and what possible ramifications of AI's misuse in politics are. Indeed, in the DeSantis super PAC, on face value this does not appear damaging for democracy: a verbatim quote is verbally expressed through AI-generated voice. However, when the potentially misleading aspect of this AI generation is recognized, alongside the potential for this technology to be used in more malicious and misleading ways, this raises questions that should be tackled by academics and policymakers now to prevent further democratic challenges. Therefore, moving forward, academics clearly play a role in providing guidance and solutions to be adopted by policymakers to envisage an "ideal type" AI that can be trusted, where AI creators are responsive to change and continually strive to achieve ethical, trustworthy AI. Conclusively, AI is here to stay. Transparency of the technology is imperative, as is increasing familiarity and perceived benefit of the technology, alongside one's understanding of how the technology will be used, what its purpose is, and how it benefits both creator and receiver of AI-induced political marketing tools. This will not be easy, but taking into account developments in 2023 regarding AI regulation and its imminent role in political campaigning, scholars and policymakers must continue to work in attempt to ameliorate the trust culture of AI, and recognize its boundless possibilities for reconfiguring the modern political campaign.

REFERENCES

Andrei, C. (2018). The political marketing of broken trust. *Journal of Political Marketing*, *17*(2), 176–192. https://doi.org/10.1080/15377857.2018.1447764

Appel, M., & Prietzel, F. (2022). The detection of political deepfakes. *Journal of Computer-Mediated Communication*, *27*(4), 1–13. https://doi.org/10.1093/jcmc/zmac008

Araujo, T., Brosius, A., Goldberg, A. C., Möller, J., & de Vreese, C. (2023). Humans vs. AI: The role of trust, political attitudes, and individual characteristics on perceptions about automated decision making across Europe. *International Journal of Communication*, *17*, 6222–6249. https://ijoc.org/index.php/ijoc/article/view/20612

Bendall, M., & Robertson, C. (2018). The crisis of democratic culture? *International Journal of Media and Cultural Politics*, *14*(3), 383–391. https://doi.org/10.1386/macp.14.3.383_7

Bennett, W. L. (2012). The personalization of politics: Political identity, social media, and changing patterns of participation. *The Annals of the American Academy of Political and Social Science*, *644*(1), 20–39. https://doi.org/10.1177/0002716212451428

Bimber, B. (2014). Digital media in the Obama campaigns of 2008 and 2012: Adaption to the personalized political communication environment.

Journal of Information Technology & Politics, *11*(2), 130–150. https://doi.org/10.1080/19331681.2014.895691

Blumler, J. G., & Kavanagh, D. (1999). The third age of political communication: Influences and features. *Political Communication*, *16*(3), 209–230. https://doi.org/10.1080/105846099198596

Broussard, M., Diakopoulos, N., Guzman, A. L., Abebe, R., Dupagne, M., & Chuan, C.-H. (2019). Artificial intelligence and journalism. *Journalism & Mass Communication Quarterly*, *96*(3), 673–695. https://doi.org/10.1177/1077699019859901

Charron, N., & Rothstein, B. (2016). Does education lead to higher generalized trust? The importance of quality of government. *International Journal of Educational Development*, *50*, 59–73. https://doi.org/10.1016/j.ijedudev.2016.05.009

Cheshire, C., Antin, J., Cook, K. S., & Churchill, E. F. (2010). General and familiar trust in websites. *Knowledge, Technology & Policy*, *23*, 311–331. https://doi.org/10.1007/s12130-010-9116-6

Clementson, D. E. (2023). *6 ways AI can make political campaigns more deceptive than ever*. https://theconversation.com/6-ways-ai-can-make-political-campaigns-more-deceptive-than-ever-209760

Dahlgren, P. (2018). Media, knowledge and trust: The deepening epistemic crisis of democracy. *Javnost – The Public*, *25*(1–2), 20–27. https://doi.org/10.1080/13183222.2018.1418819

Davies, M., & Birstwistle, M. (2023). *Regulating AI in the UK*. Ada Lovelace Institute.

Deley, T., & Dubois, E. (2020). Assessing trust versus reliance for technology platforms by systematic literature review. *Social Media + Society*, *6*(2). https://doi.org/10.1177/2056305120913883

Engelke, K. M., Hase, V., & Wintterlin, F. (2019). On measuring trust and distrust in journalism: Reflection of the status quo and suggestions for the road ahead. *Journal of Trust Research*, *9*(1), 66–86. https://doi.org/10.1080/21515581.2019.1588741

Erman, E., & Furendal, M. (2022). Artificial intelligence and the political legitimacy of global governance. *Political Studies*. https://doi.org/10.1177/00323217221126665

Fan, H., Gao, W., & Han, B. (2023). Are AI chatbots a cure-all? The relative effectiveness of chatbot ambidexterity in crafting hedonic and cognitive smart experiences. *Journal of Business Research*, *156*, 1–12. https://doi.org/10.1016/j.jbusres.2022.113526

Farid, H. (2023). *Yes, we should regulate AI-generated political ads—But don't stop there*. https://thehill.com/opinion/campaign/4151633-yes-we-should-regulate-ai-generated-political-ads-but-dont-stop-there/

Feindt, P. H., & Marijn Poortvliet, P. (2020). Consumer reactions to unfamiliar technologies: Mental and social formation of perceptions and attitudes toward nano and GM products. *Journal of Risk Research*, *23*(4), 475–489. https://doi.org/10.1080/13669877.2019.1591487

Fish, W. (2016). "Post-truth" politics and illusory democracy. *Psychotherapy and Politics International*, *14*(3), 211–213. https://doi.org/10.1002/ppi.1387

Gefen, D. (2000). E-Commerce: The role of familiarity and trust. *Omega*, *28*(6), 727–737. https://doi.org/10.1016/S0305-0483(00)00021-9

Gehl, R. W., & Lawson, S. T. (2022). *Social engineering how crowdmasters, phreaks, hackers, and trolls created a new form of manipulative communication*. MIT Press.

Gillespie, N., Lockey, S., Curtis, C., Pool, J., & Akbari, A. (2023). *Trust in artificial intelligence: A global study*. The University of Queensland and KPMG Australia.

Google. (2023). *Updates to Political content policy (September 2023)*. https://support.google.com/adspolicy/answer/13755910?hl=en&ref_topic=29265

Google. (n.d.). *Recommendations for regulating AI*. https://ai.google/static/documents/recommendations-for-regulating-ai.pdf

Haleem, A., Javaid, M., Qadri, M. A., Singh, R. P., & Suman, R. (2022). Artificial intelligence (AI) applications for marketing: A literature-based study. *International Journal of Intelligent Networks*, *3*, 119–132. https://doi.org/10.1016/j.ijin.2022.08.005

Hameleers, M., van der Meer, T. G. L. A., & Dobber, T. (2022). You won't believe what they just said! The effects of political deepfakes embedded as Vox Populi on social media. *Social Media + Society*, *8*(3). https://doi.org/10.1177/20563051221116346

Haresamudram, K., Larsson, S., & Heintz, F. (2023). Three levels of AI transparency. *Computer*, *56*(2), 93–100. https://ieeexplore.ieee.org/document/10042109

Harris, P. (2009). *Penguin dictionary of marketing*. Penguin Books.

Harris, P., & Lock, A. (2010). "Mind the gap": The rise of political marketing and a perspective on its future agenda. *European Journal of Marketing*, *44*(3/4), 297–307. https://doi.org/10.1108/03090561011020435

IEEE. (2022, March 4). IEEE draft standard for transparency of autonomous systems. In *IEEE P7001/D1* (pp. 1–70). https://standards.ieee.org/ieee/7001/6929/. Accessed on September 13, 2023.

Isenstadt, A. (2023). *DeSantis PAC uses AI-generated Trump voice in ad attacking ex-president*. https://www.politico.com/news/2023/07/17/desantis-pac-ai-generated-trump-in-ad-00106695

Jacobsen, L., & Tuquero, L. (2023). *A pro-Ron DeSantis ad used AI to recreate Donald Trump's voice. Experts say it won't be the last*. https://www.poynter.org/fact-checking/2023/desantis-never-back-down-pac-ai-ad-trump-voice/

Jadil, Y., Rana, N. P., & Dwivedi, Y. K. (2022). Understanding the drivers of online trust and intention to buy on a website: An emerging market perspective. *International Journal of Information Management Data Insights*, *2*(1), 1–12. https://doi.org/10.1016/j.jjimei.2022.100065

Jones, B. (2019). Is liberal democracy doomed? *Political Insight*, *10*(2), 34–36. https://doi.org/10.1177/2041905819854316

Jungherr, A. (2023). Artificial intelligence and democracy: A conceptual framework. *Social Media + Society*, *9*(3). https://doi.org/10.1177/20563051231186353

Kane, T. B. (2019). Artificial intelligence in politics: Establishing ethics. *IEEE Technology and Society Magazine*, *38*(1), 72–80. https://ieeexplore.ieee.org/document/8664495

Keller, S. (1956). *Professional public relations and political power*. Johns Hopkins Press.

Kirkby, A., Baumgarth, C., & Henseler, J. (2023). To disclose or not disclose, is no longer the question – Effect of AI-disclosed brand voice on brand authenticity and attitude. *The Journal of Product and Brand Management*, *32*(7), 1108–1122. https://www.emerald.com/insight/content/doi/10.1108/JPBM-02-2022-3864/full/html

Kleizen, B., Van Dooren, W., Verhoest, K., & Tam, E. (2023). Do citizens trust trustworthy artificial intelligence? Experimental evidence on the limits of ethical AI measures in government. *Government Information Quarterly*. https://doi.org/10.1016/j.giq.2023.101834

Klepper, D., & Swenson, A. (2023). *AI presents political peril for 2024 with threat to mislead voters*. https://apnews.com/article/artificial-intelligence-misinformation-deepfakes-2024-election-trump-59fb51002661ac5290089060b3ae39a0

Köbis, N. C., Doležalová, B., & Soraperra, I. (2021). Fooled twice: People cannot detect deepfakes but think they can. *iScience*, *24*(11). https://doi.org/10.1016/j.isci.2021.103364

Kreps, S., George, J., Lushenko, P., & Rao, A. (2023). Exploring the artificial intelligence "Trust paradox": Evidence from a survey experiment in the United States. *PLoS One*, *18*(7), 1–21. https://doi.org/10.1371/journal.pone.0288109

Kreps, S., & Jakesch, M. (2023). Can AI communication tools increase legislative responsiveness and trust in democratic institutions? *Government Information Quarterly*, *40*(3). https://doi.org/10.1016/j.giq.2023.101829

Kreps, S., & Kriner, D. (2023). How AI threatens democracy. *Journal of Democracy*, *34*(4), 122–131. https://www.journalofdemocracy.org/articles/how-ai-threatens-democracy/

Levine, T. R. (2014). Truth-default theory (TDT): A theory of human deception and deception detection. *Journal of Language and Social Psychology*, *33*(4), 378–392. https://doi.org/10.1177/0261927X14535916

Lilleker, D. G. (2015). Interactivity and branding: Public political communication as a marketing tool. *Journal of Political Marketing*, *14*(1–2), 111–128. https://doi.org/10.1080/15377857.2014.990841

López-López, P., Barredo-Ibáñez, D., & Jaráiz-Gulías, E. (2023). Research on digital political communication: Electoral campaigns, disinformation, and artificial intelligence. *Societies*, *13*(5), 1–5. https://doi.org/10.3390/soc13050126

Luhmann, N. (2018). *Trust and power*. John Wiley & Sons.

Lukyanenko, R., Maass, W., & Storey, V. C. (2022). Trust in artificial intelligence: From a Foundational Trust Framework to emerging research opportunities. *Electronic Markets*, *32*, 1993–2020. https://doi.org/10.1007/s12525-022-00605-4

Machiavelli, N. (2003). *The prince*. Penguin Books.

Manning, N., Penfold-Mounce, R., Loader, B. D., Vromen, A., & Xenos, M. (2017). Politicians, celebrities and social media: A case of informalisation? *Journal of Youth Studies*, *20*(2), 127–144. https://doi.org/10.1080/13676261.2016.1206867

Maras, M.-H., & Alexandrou, A. (2018). Determining authenticity of video evidence in the age of artificial intelligence and in the wake of Deepfake videos. *International Journal of Evidence and Proof*, *23*(3), 255–262. https://doi.org/10.1177/1365712718807226

Markowitz, D. M., & Hancock, J. T. (2023). Generative AI are more truth-biased than humans: A replication and extension of core truth-default theory principles. *Journal of Language and Social Psychology*, *43*(2), 261–267. https://doi.org/10.1177/0261927X231220404

McCallum. (2023). Google: Political adverts must disclose use of AI. https://www.bbc.co.uk/news/technology-66739858

McCombs, M. E., & Shaw, D. L. (1972). The agenda-setting function of mass media. *Public Opinion Quarterly*, *36*(2), 176–187. https://www.jstor.org/stable/2747787

Nader, K., Toprac, P., Scott, S., & Baker, S. (2022). Public understanding of artificial intelligence through entertainment media. *AI and Society*. *39*, 713–726. https://doi.org/10.1007/s00146-022-01427-w

Nimmo, D. (1970). *The political persuaders: The techniques of modern election campaigns*. Prentice-Hall.

O'Flaherty, K. (2018). *Google+ security bug – What happened, who was impacted and how to delete your account*. https://www.forbes.com/sites/kateoflahertyuk/2018/10/09/google-plus-breach-what-happened-who-was-impacted-and-how-to-delete-your-account/#774716286491

O'Sullivan, D., & Abou-Ghazala, Y. (2023). *The AI political campaign is here*. https://edition.cnn.com/2023/05/02/politics/ai-election-ads-2024/index.html

Panch, T., Mattie, H., & Atun, R. (2019). Artificial intelligence and algorithmic bias: Implications for health systems. *Journal of Global Health*, *9*(2).

https://www.ncbi.nlm.nih.gov/pmc/articles/PMC6875681/

Perrigo, B. (2023). *AI Is as risky as pandemics and nuclear war, top CEOs say*. Urging Global Cooperation. https://time.com/6283386/ai-risk-openai-deepmind-letter/

Perrigo, B., & Gordon, A. (2023). E.U. takes a step closer to passing the world's most comprehensive AI regulation. https://time.com/6287136/eu-ai-regulation/

Rainie, L., Funk, C., Anderson, M., & Tyson, A. (2022). *AI and human enhancement: Americans' openness is tempered by a range of concerns*. Pew Research Center.

Rajvanshi, A. (2023). *Rishi Sunak wants the U.K. to be a key player in global AI regulation*. https://time.com/6287253/uk-rishi-sunak-ai-regulation/

Ridge-Newman, A., & Mitchell, M. (2016). Digital political marketing. In D. G. Lilleker & M. Pack (Eds.), *Political marketing and the 2015 UK general election* (pp. 99–116). Palgrave Macmillan.

Ríos-Sánchez, B., Costa-da Silva, D., Martín-Yuste, N., & Sánchez-Ávila, C. (2020). Deep learning for face recognition on mobile devices. *IET Biometrics*, *9*(3), 109–117. https://doi.org/10.1049/iet-bmt.2019.0093

Robertson, C. (2022). *Anti-austerity politics and social media in the UK: Political participation and non-traditional political organisations*. [Doctoral Dissertation]. University of Chester.

Robertson, C., & Harris, P. (Forthcoming, 2024/2025). A Machiavellian digital media? In P. Harris, P. Rees, & A. Lock (Eds.), *Machiavelli, marketing and management: Reflections on his contribution to communications, management, marketing, and political thought*. Routledge.

Robertson, C., & Ridge-Newman, A. (2022). The potential of artificial intelligence to rejuvenate public trust in journalism. In V. J. E. Manninen, M. K. Niemi, & A. Ridge-Newman (Eds.), *Futures of journalism technology-stimulated evolution in the audience-news media relationship* (pp. 127–142). Palgrave MacMillan.

Robles, P., & Mallinson, D. J. (2023). Artificial intelligence technology, public trust, and effective governance. *The Review of Policy Research*. https://doi.org/10.1111/ropr.12555

Ross Arguedas, A. A., Badrinathan, S., Mont'Alverne, C., Toff, B., Fletcher, R., & Kleis Nielsen, R. (2023). Shortcuts to trust: Relying on cues to judge online news from unfamiliar sources on digital platforms. *Journalism*. https://doi.org/10.1177/14648849231194485

Savaget, P., Chiarini, T., & Evans, S. (2019). Empowering political participation through artificial intelligence. *Science and Public Policy*, *46*(3), 369–380. https://doi.org/10.1093/scipol/scy064

Schippers, B. (2020). Artificial intelligence and democratic politics. *Political Insight*, *11*(1), 32–35. https://doi.org/10.1177/2041905820911746

Shen, H., & Sengupta, J. (2018). Word of mouth versus word of mouse: Speaking about a brand connects you to it more than writing does. *Journal of Consumer Research*, *45*(3), 595–614. https://doi.org/10.1093/jcr/ucy011

Smith, G., & French, A. (2009). The political brand: A consumer perspective. *Marketing Theory*, *9*(2), 209–226. https://doi.org/10.1177%2F1470593109103068

Sztompka, P. (2000). *Trust: A sociological theory*. Cambridge University Press.

Sztompka, P. (2014). Trust. In M. Sasaki, J. Goldstone, E. Zimmermann, & S. K. Sanderson (Eds.), *Concise encyclopedia of comparative sociology* (pp. 492–498). Brill Publishers.

Thiebes, S., Lins, S., & Sunyaev, A. (2021). Trustworthy artifical intelligence. *Electronic Markets*, *31*, 447–464. https://doi.org/10.1007/s12525-020-00441-4

Vaccari, C., & Chadwick, A. (2020). Deepfakes and disinformation: Exploring the impact of synthetic political video on deception, uncertainty, and trust in news. *Social Media + Society*, *6*(1). https://doi.org/10.1177/2056305120903408

Verhulsdonk, I., Nai, A., & Karp, J. A. (2021). Are political attacks a laughing matter? Three experiments on political humor and the effectiveness of negative campaigning. *Political Research Quarterly*, *75*(3), 720–737. https://doi.org/10.1177/10659129211023590

White House. (2023) Remarks by President Biden on Artificial Intelligence. https://bidenwhitehouse.archives.gov/briefing-room/speeches-remarks/2023/07/21/remarks-by-president-biden-on-artificial-intelligence/

Winsvold, M., Haugsgjerd, A., Saglie, J., & Bock Segaard, S. (2024). What makes people trust or distrust politicians? Insights from open-ended survey questions. *West European Politics*, *47*(4), 759–783. https://doi.org/10.1080/01402382.2023.2268459

Xu, J., Le, K., Deitermann, A., & Montague, E. (2014). How different types of users develop trust in technology: A qualitative analysis of the antecedents of active and passive user trust in a shared technology. *Applied Ergonomics*, *45*(6), 1495–1503. https://doi.org/10.1016/j.apergo.2014.04.012

Yang, S., Krause, N. M., Bao, L., Calice, M. N., Newman, T. P., Scheufele, D. A., Xenos, M. A., & Brossard, D. (2023). In AI we trust: The interplay of media use, political ideology, and trust in shaping emerging AI attitudes. *Journalism & Mass Communication Quarterly*. https://doi.org/10.1177/10776990231190868

Zerilli, J., Bhatt, U., & Weller, A. (2022). How transparency modulates trust in artificial intelligence. *Patterns*, *3*(4), 1–10. https://doi.org/10.1016/j.patter.2022.100455

Digital Political Marketing: Informing, Mobilising and Interacting During the 2023 Zimbabwean Election

Darren Lilleker and Darlington Nyambiya

INTRODUCTION

Digital political marketing involves the use of the range of digital tools, from websites to social platforms to chat applications to inform and engage citizens to secure their support. Engagement involves a value exchange; citizens give attention to content and promote it within networks in return for effective representation. Building on the definition of political marketing as interactions in the electoral, parliamentary, governmental and civil society sectors (Ormrod et al., 2013, p. 18), we understand digital political marketing as the utilisation of information and communication technologies which provide spaces where interactions take place: political organisations, media outlets and citizens produce and promote content and leave comments and discussions can take place. Research within the field of political marketing communication has focused on three broad functions where digital technologies have had impact: informing, mobilising and interacting. Informing covers not only 'displaying the product on offer' but is also a key means for communicating about 'the political brand' as well as specific policy products and will likely utilise persuasive rhetoric (Marland et al., 2017). Mobilising seeks not only to extend the reach of content by harnessing the free labour of supporters but also drawing supporters closer to the organisation, encouraging brand loyalty (Jackson, 2006). Interacting not only involves responding to questions but also connective action (Bennett & Segerberg, 2013) where citizens utilise platforms to organise themselves and challenge power structures. Digital platforms tend to adhere to a logic of interaction, closing distances between users independent of social hierarchies (Kalsnes et al., 2017).

Utilising a triadic framework, informing, mobilising and interacting, we explore how political organisations, from governments to informal collectives, can utilise digital technologies and how we can understand these developments through the lens of political marketing. We explore this not by focusing on more obvious examples but focus on Zimbabwe, a nation in the global south where democracy is undermined by corruption and repression challenged by a strong pro-democracy oppositional movement.

Zimbabwe makes for an interesting case study as parties and civil society run highly digitised campaigns, despite there being lower access levels in rural areas (Mare, 2018). Zimbabwe has been ruled by the autocratic Zanu PF party since independence in 1980. However, the party of the late dictator Robert Mugabe, which has held control over governance and media faced a significant challenge from the Citizens Coalition for Change (CCC) during the 2023 election contest. The CCC's ability to become a credible force despite the repressive conditions is largely due to their leveraging the capacity of digital technology to extend their reach and draw support from citizens who are anti-Zanu PF. The chapter draws on interview data with candidates and activists from Zimbabwe who are active within Zanu PF, the CCC as well as civil society organisations. This Zimbabwe case study allows insights into the ways political parties and civil society compete within digital spaces, market their brands and ideas, attempt to build support and attain power and control over a nation.

By focusing on a less-researched environment, the chapter highlights the challenges that digital political marketing poses both for established structures of power as well as for democracy. Technologies, as has ever been the case, can have both positive and negative impacts; the creators and users share control over how technology is used (Lewandowsky & Pomerantsev, 2022). Research shows that the use of digital political marketing is increasing within and across political levels and societies and potentially has significant impacts on electoral outcomes (Towner & Dulio, 2014). Digital technologies have been utilised to strengthen the voices of citizens, to empower marginalised groups and to redress power inequalities within societies (Lember et al., 2019). However, these technologies are also employed to spread disinformation designed to manipulate groups in a society (Marsden et al., 2020), to create echo chambers that become hotbeds of extremism, for the spread of hate speech and to foster political polarisation (Miller & Vaccari, 2020). Hence the chapter offers a critical realist perspective on digital political marketing which reflects the political context of the 21st century demonstrating that both pro- and anti-democratic forces can be highly effective in utilising the tools of digital political marketing to build a following, extend their influence and leverage power. Zimbabwe makes for an excellent environment to explore these issues.

DEVELOPMENT OF THE TOPIC

Studies on the uses of digital technologies for political purposes have dominated the field of political communication in the last two decades. Research has mapped the uptake of websites, email and the popular social media platforms, in particular Twitter, Facebook, YouTube, Instagram and most recently TikTok, and to a lesser extent encrypted services such as Snapchat or WhatsApp (Stier et al., 2020). While initial focus was on election campaigns, this has widened out to demonstrate patterns of use of digital platforms extend into permanent campaigning (Joathan & Lilleker, 2023), as well as changing the nature of civil society and social movement campaigning especially in weak democratic regimes (LePere-Schloop et al., 2022). The field is dominated by studies of US politics, focusing on presidential campaigns, the permanent campaigning of Senators and Congress members and high-profile social movements such as Black Lives Matter. What the field demonstrates is the embedding of digital technologies across all aspects of politics, and that the uses of technologies are having impacts upon the nature and scale of political engagement and participation of citizens (Boulianne & Theocharis, 2020). Research has particularly explored how digital technologies are utilised by political organisations, for what functions and with what effects, mapping onto well-established models of communication. In doing so, studies respond to three important questions relating to digital political marketing: firstly, are digital technologies used to inform citizens about politics and so are citizens better informed? Secondly, are citizens encouraged to participate in ways that enhance democracy? Thirdly, are citizens engaged and empowered through having the potential to interact with organisations and one another?

Informed Citizens?

Digital technology has made it possible to access a vast amount of information, including political information. It is commonplace for political organisations of all sizes, types and level to have a website as well as profiles across the social media platforms with the greatest reach within their nations (Stier et al., 2020). Some parties' existence and organisation is almost entirely online leading some to talk of 'platform parties' (De Blasio & Viviani, 2020). Research suggests the most successful strategy is to integrate all platforms into the communication mix, from email and websites through to social media platforms, providing tailored but consistent content for each media and the intended audiences (Bossetta & Schmøkel, 2023). Such a strategy makes the brand accessible, ubiquitous and recognised for having a clear and relevant message. However, information is largely simplistic and persuasive and often following a generic, one-size fits all platforms model. Larger, more established, governmental parties are particularly found to violate platform norms and avoid innovations in their style of communication despite the danger that generic content will not appeal to platform users (Haßler et al., 2023). Consultants argue that content must be developed that is platform specific, in terms of both the style and the message (Veneti et al., 2022). There is evidence of innovation, such as adapting electoral marketing into formats that suit platforms which are largely geared towards entertainment, like TikTok, or embedding content into games (De la Cruz et al., 2023).

Early research showed websites were used as multipage hubs including press releases, manifestoes and important information. Largely these have become slimmed down tools which set out the key selling points of an organisation. Social media platforms are spaces that act as an auxiliary space to share messages for immediate consumption. Pages on platforms can be created to connect to supporters, push content from the party and encourage supporters to share material within their networks. Strategically this ensures the organisation, and its messages, are front of mind among followers, while encouraging users to extend their reach by liking and sharing their content. Gaining awareness among as many citizens as possible is key to campaigning and digital technologies have been crucial for disseminating information widely, especially hard to reach citizens. X, the platform previously known as Twitter, in particular, promoted the notion of the hashtag, where campaign messages, slogans and interactions could be connected and curated. It is challenging for major parties to establish unique hashtags that will not be hijacked by opponents; however, they prove highly successful for civil society movements. The #MeToo and #BlackLivesMatter brands went viral and became rallying points for supporters of the causes. Sebeelo (2021) records similar trends emerging across the Global South.

Content produced by an organisation can be shared by supporters which makes it visible within their networks (Koc-Michalska et al., 2021). Similarly, if content is liked, it can be made more visible to similar people due to the algorithms that work in the background. Content can also be cascaded down from platforms such as X to private groups using platforms like WhatsApp, which are particularly popular across many nations of the Global South for political organisation (Cruz & Harindranath, 2020). Hence from a marketing perspective having an active followership is important for reaching citizens who may be fertile for conversion and so mobilisation is key for ensuring the wider citizenry, and not just followers, are informed.

Mobilised Citizens?

Digital political marketing does not only focus on promoting and defending a party brand and its policies, but strategists also need advocates to promote their campaigns and policies. To harness the benefits of social media, a political organisation requires an engaged and active followership. Mobilisation strategies are core to digital political marketing as they are crucial for extending the reach of content by harnessing the free labour of supporters while also drawing supporters closer to the organisation. Research indicates that most political organisations rely on their owned media platforms, websites and social media profiles, as a means for getting their message out. Unlike commercial organisations, they largely do not exploit the full potential of advertising to reach beyond existing followers and their networks (Kruschinski & Bene, 2022). Rather they use a combination of eye-catching imagery, short slogan-style messages and calls to action posted to their pages as a means of engaging their followers (Farkas et al., 2022). The followers of organisations are thus found to play a vital role in campaigns acting as carriers and amplifiers of organisational messages, thus they are a key element of the marketing process as well as the brand itself (Falasca et al., 2019).

Followers can simply be asked to engage with content within the platform or across other platforms they use. Common requests are to share a post, to like, follow or subscribe to a specific campaign account, to participate in an online campaign which can involve simple clicks such as signing an online petition or participation in an online survey. Research on party communication during the 2019 European parliamentary election found the request to 'click like if you agree' was a popular strategy, the intention being to extend the reach within the networks of followers as each like increased the visibility of the original post. Followers can also be asked to participate in more effortful forms of activism. Some parties will ask followers to watch a TV debate or contribute by asking questions or showing support on social media during a public event. Political organisations will also promote events and rallies. Volunteering to participate in campaigning activities, such as door-to-door or telephone canvassing, posting bills or demonstrations of support can also be requested. Political organisations may also attempt to mobilise followers to join and/or donate money or other resources to the party. However, the most popular request during election campaigns is the request to go to vote and, naturally, to vote for the party (Haßler et al., 2021).

Interactive Citizenship?

Strategically the most important aspect of mobilisation is to draw followers closer to the organisation. Adapting the consumer loyalty ladder, which conceptualised different stages from prospective customer to loyal consumer, Lilleker and Jackson (2014) proposed similar mechanisms that could be operationalised within a political context. Firstly, an organisation needs to be findable but also reach out to information seekers, citizens who are interested in particular ideas and policies. The information they receive must engage them but also use the right persuasive mechanisms to convert them into passive supporters. Given that digital technologies provide ways for passive supporters to follow an organisation, it is important for organisations to provide the motivations for joining a community and then energising their followership. Strategies for increasing involvement may start with simple requests, from liking and sharing content, to responding to polls or questions, each of which are designed to stimulate engagement among followers and involve them with the organisation. But ultimately the desire is to convert interested but passive supporters to perform the role of active advocates. Targeted communication can prove crucial here. As organisations can gather rich information about their followers' demographics, interests and concerns and so tailor their mobilisation appeals. Mobilisation strategies go beyond the sales model implicit with information provision and relate to relationship management. The organisation needs to build relationships with their supportive communities based on trust and shared goals, allowing the co-ownership of communication, and campaigns, to create the circumstances within which activists will act as brand advocates. Advocates are also a key audience for requests to donate to campaigns and perform a range of roles which advance the aims of the organisation.

Communities are built and maintained online through interaction, both at a horizontal level among followers as well as vertically between followers and key figures within the organisation. Hence, for a relationship marketing campaign to be successful, followers need to feel they are valued, listened to and responded to by the organisation (Ebrahim, 2020). Interactive political leadership, employing a range of models for citizen involvement in decision making, is argued to be crucial for the legitimacy of governance that claims to be responsive to the people (Sorensen, 2020) and so for campaigning organisations to harness the potential of supporters the leaders need to offer some form of dialogue, interaction and connectivity to their strategies. Early research on digital technology highlighted citizens seek greater interactivity from political organisations, especially political parties. However, studies largely found even with early features such as email there were few points when organisations, or their prominent figures, entered into conversations (Jackson & Lilleker, 2009). Social media did not increase levels of interpersonal communication in party political contexts between parties and their followers. Consistent with the distinction between interactivity as a product of the platform versus interactivity as a conversational process between followers and the organisation (Stromer-Galley, 2004), political organisations encouraged followers to use the interactive features of systems, liking and sharing, while discouraging commenting and asking questions.

Controlled interactivity makes sense from a marketing perspective. Questions can lead political organisations to make more specific pledges and promises than they are comfortable with, adding detail to their often bland slogans. Similarly, comments can detract from core branding information, possibly countering or contradicting the messages the organisation seeks to communicate. Slogans are designed carefully to resonate and to be memorable, follower interactions can distract from the clarity of these messages. However, from a relationship marketing perspective, controlled interactivity places barriers between followers and the organisation. The interactive features of social media have the potential to reduce the distance between users independent of social hierarchies. For some non-electoral campaign groups and movements, these features are utilised to foster connective action, citizens connect around issues and organise and mobilise themselves to challenge power structures (Bennett & Segerberg, 2013). Loose organisations built around hashtags such as #MeToo or

#FridaysforFuture utilise devolved, 'citizen-initiated' approaches to political marketing (Gibson, 2015). The citizens who make up the organisation are both the brand and the advocates. Yet parties still tend to eschew interactivity and its potential for building loyalty.

Ethical Campaigning Versus Doing Anything to Win

Digital technologies are unregulated spaces where largely any material can be posted. Hence some argue it has become a space for unethical practices as parties and candidates pursue any tactics they feel will help them win (Elsheikh, 2018). There are many ways in which digital technologies positively benefit democracy, such as campaign groups challenging abuses of power, holding governing institutions to account and building support for pro-democracy movements. These campaigns and movements are buoyed by digital platforms offering the power to reach a wide audience with rapidity as well as allowing communication across societal strata. But this speed and ubiquity has led some to call digital platforms a 'permanent menace' due to them creating an anarchic and uncontrollable information environment where disinformation, malinformation (decontextualised or doctored material designed to manipulate), rumour and conspiracy theories can spread (Maarek, 2014).

Some campaigns will resort to these tactics, and in terms of gaining reach, they can pay dividends. Often due to the controversial content, emotive language and engaging style, content containing malinformation elements are also found more likely to be shared (Xu et al., 2020). The attractiveness of this type of content gives an advantage within the marketplace of ideas to right wing, populist or anti-democratic actors who are most likely to spread disinformation designed to manipulate groups in a society (König, 2020). The use of disinformation, hate speech and polarising communication is a feature of mobilisation tactics of a range of candidates globally and this has a negative impact upon democratic culture (Hameleers, 2020).

There are also dangers of targeted manipulation; platform users leave rich data trails which can be exploited by political organisations to ensure their messages resonate with individuals. Such data are used by an array of campaign consultants globally to shape both the style and the content to appeal best to specific target groups. Such practices can also aid organisations develop microtargeting strategies designed to manipulate groups of citizens who are viewed as electorally valuable (Howard et al., 2005). Data-driven microtargeting permits increased personalisation of messages, particularly using relatively inexpensive advertising or sponsored post features across social media platforms. Targeted messages are often below the radar and can only be seen by select groups within society. The combination of no gatekeepers and the ability to microtarget is both a benefit and a challenge for democracy that is highlighted by digital political marketing practices. The impact depends on the goals and ethos of the organisation and the extent they are concerned about campaign ethics and their own reputations. The chapter proceeds to explore the use of the main components of digital political marketing within the Zimbabwean context.

DIGITAL POLITICAL MARKETING IN ZIMBABWE

It is indisputable that Zimbabweans can access a far more pluralist information landscape thanks to digital platforms. Both Zanu PF and the CCC have presences across digital platforms that provide key messages about the party brand, in the case of Zanu PF its history as the driver of independence from the British empire, statements of values and aims, key personnel, current campaigns or pledges. These presences, like most party digital spaces, are designed to persuade citizens that the organisation is worthy of support. Zanu PF activist David Muchuchu argued social media offers a range of key platforms which push information out to citizens:

> Honestly, we can never also underestimate what social media has actually done in terms of also informing people.

Muchuchu says this despite the fact Zanu PF have almost complete control over state media. For the CCC, it was viewed as crucial for getting their message out to citizens with the capacity to be influential in changing voters' minds during the 2023 national election campaign. The CCC especially viewed social media as crucial as their strategy was to target and mobilise Zimbabwe's youth. Former CCC MP Regai Tsunga offered his perspective on the impact of digital platforms thus:

> It's (social media) going to be a game changer. I hope by then a good number of our young people, and even those in the rural areas, will have access to WhatsApp and Facebook so that messaging reaches out to every corner of this country.

The CCC activists saw digital technology as a game changer not just because of the potential reach but due to the repressive conditions in Zimbabwe. Digital platforms allow them to work in the safety of virtual spaces, learn about what is happening on the ground in communities and is the only space they can use to spread their political messages due to the closed media environment. While for Zanu PF social media is an adjunct media, they still view it as important for marketing the party brand to citizens. Zanu PF activist Kudzai Mutisi explained digital technologies allow candidates to directly reach citizens who do not rely on or access traditional media:

> I think Zanu PF gained (political influence due to social media) and the gain is mainly in the urban setting, because they are now more exposed or rather more available to or connected to the urban electorate, or even the diaspora. There are people now who had this kind of image of Zanu PF that they hate, and they see a different one via social media.

Activists also demonstrated the flow of information is no longer one way and top down, but also horizontal and bottom-up. Both parties see social media as the perfect tool to measure the political temperature of Zimbabwean politics, offering insights into the thinking of ordinary people in local communities and thus allow them to tailor their messages towards different communities. The CCC particularly use this to overcome their lack of state resources and media access. The minimal filtering of posts and lack of gatekeepers on social media platforms also means that they, like all political organisations, can post any content providing it fits their brand ethos and will be seen as acceptable to their followership. Therefore, we find digital political marketing plays an important role in this nascent autocratic democracy, particularly for opposition forces with limited access to traditional media.

Zimbabwean parties also exploit the multi-step flow of information into networks as citizens cascade party materials across platforms. Social media can thus act as a space where party activists can inform and empower citizens in a fast and efficient manner without wasting significant resources while avoiding facing risks of oppression by being on the ground. Events can also be organised and publicised, for Zanu PF, digital platforms work are a complementary tool used in combination with offline activities as activist Sybeth Musengezi argues:

> Yes, it (social media) cannot be a perfect substitute. But it can be used in situations where people want to send, you know, politicians want to send messages to their supporters without physically going on the ground. So, it's really it really has that influence.

Due to the risks of ground campaigning the CCC, Zimbabwean civil society activists and citizens critical of Zanu PF particularly exploit the affordances of digital platforms. Civil society activist Youngerson Matete pointed out that people are scared to raise their voice in physical spaces, but feel empowered when able to discuss their opinions and concerns on social media:

> In a country like Zimbabwe many people are afraid to express themselves, there is no freedom of expression in Zimbabwe, no freedom of speech in Zimbabwe so we find that many people on social media use ghost accounts to express themselves because they are afraid to put their real names. So it was quite important in a country like Zimbabwe that social media has given a platform for so many people to express themselves.

One key tactic the CCC and civil society organisations have employed are hashtags, for example, #RegisterToVoteZw which has been used by a variety of activists to share information on why, how and where to register to vote. The CCC also highlighted evidence of corruption (#HowFar), vote rigging (#ProtectTheVote) and government control of the Zimbabwe Election Commission (#DisbandZec) and used the hope-filled slogan #ForEveryone. Parties use these to connect arguments, but citizens also play a highly active role in informing one another.

Despite the positive effects social media has had for democratising the flow of information in Zimbabwe, disinformation campaigns are a serious problem. CCC activists accuse Zanu PF of spreading fake stories and vice versa. Many posts about corruption and brutality by Zanu PF operatives are difficult to verify, as are claims the CCC are agents of 'the West', but are amplified by social media and so impact the attitudes and voting behaviour of Zimbabweans. Activists argue that sometimes disinformation can dupe thousands if not millions of its supporters and they fear that it can influence election outcomes. CCC candidate Regai Tsunga informed us how the CCC try to combat this:

> The other advantage of social media is that it can help correct assumptions. Yeah, where for example, the CCC being labelled a puppet of the West you can package material to ensure that people understand that this is propaganda meant to discredit an otherwise indigenous institution with the objective of enhancing or improving the welfare of the people of this country.

With a population that lacks digital and political literacy, and is mistrusting of politicians, it is easy for disinformation to be accepted as genuine. In turn, this can force the party to divert attention and resources to responding.

Combatting disinformation and repression is key to the mobilisation strategy developed by the CCC. CCC activists see first time voters who are mainly young and between the ages of 18 and 35 years as the most fertile group to target, and this is a multi-stage process. Firstly, due to high political apathy and low engagement, it has been to get these voters to register to vote. The hashtag #RegisterToVoteZw has been a key mechanism, promoting the notion that young people have the power to change politics. Empowerment messages are proven to be highly effective tools of persuasion, especially when promoted by Zimbabwean civil society organisations (Yingi, 2023). Secondly, CCC developed empowering messages to build momentum against Zanu PF. CCC activist Netsai Marova argued:

> I think it has weakened greatly (Zanu PF political influence), because number one, I'm sure you know that in Zimbabwe, we have one media station, you know, and the greater populace of Zimbabwe used to rely on ZBC and Power FM. And now with the coming of social media and now our generation is always on social media, you know, it has managed to redirect the focus of where people get the news, people now get their news on social media.

The CCC campaign was highly successful. In the lead up to the 2023 election, they built a strong following across social media platforms. Due to encouragement from the CCC, their supporters monitored all content posted by Zanu PF or their supportive media outlets and organisations and challenged their claims online within minutes of the content being posted Thus, CCC feel that social media has severely undercut the political influence of the ruling party as previously its political messaging went unchallenged. CCC also encouraged sharing their content, in particular into the wider communities on WhatsApp, and activists interviewed claimed Zanu PF were unable to respond effectively to CCC campaign messages. Given the potential for brutal crackdowns on the opposition, mobilisation focused mainly on being active online using anonymous profiles.

Both Zanu PF and CCC also hold events and rallies which bring followers together and cement their support. However, in terms of having an active and seemingly committed following, it is CCC that appear to have the right messages for their relationship management strategy to be effective. They argued this is because their mobilisation strategies involve messages which seek to empower citizens and focused on redressing power inequalities within Zimbabwean society. Due to these messages resonating widely, the CCC have created a community around their organisations which is composed of seemingly loyal followers, a strategic aim of many political organisations.

However, high levels of loyalty and commitment can lead followers of parties to become polarised. Though perhaps more concerned about the changing political dynamics in Zimbabwean society, Zanu PF activist David Muchuchu said:

> Especially on Twitter, you can see the binary, the binary world that we actually live in, you know, in terms of us, people that support Zanu PF and then that support Nelson Chamisa.

Polarisation has thus become a key feature of Zimbabwean society, accelerated by the rise of CCC and its focus on digital political marketing. CCC supporters encourage 'othering' of followers of Zanu PF and vice versa. Election outcomes are seen as manufactured, elected governments and leaders viewed as illegitimate and society has become divided along partisan lines. While these are caused by structural problem embedded in Zimbabwean politics and society, and many of the perspectives of Zanu PF opponents are accurate, both parties feed polarisation for electoral ends.

However, the challenging political situation in Zimbabwe appears to increase the likelihood of citizens interacting and for organisations to harness their desire to have a voice. Activists argue there is a vibrant political public sphere where engaged citizens, activists and the Zimbabwean diaspora share experiences and ideas. Hence the interactive functionality of digital platforms connects Zimbabweans locally, across regions but also to a wider international community. Depending on your side in the polarised environment, this can be an advantage or a disadvantage but cannot be ignored. Zanu PF activist Kudzai Mutisi highlights developments which many would see as a positive impact of digital technology but for his party represents a challenge:

> Social media now allows people in different geographical regions to respond or to participate in a political debate or something. It is rich, and it's interactive.

Fortune Chasi, Zanu PF's former MP for Mazowe south constituency, highlighted concerns about the loss of control over the agenda observing:

> Social media really lessens dependence on traditional media, if there's such a term in the sense that almost everyone becomes a journalist.

However, such developments are celebrated by the CCC, in particular as citizens are redefining the barriers of Zimbabwe's information environment. Digital platforms facilitate Zimbabweans to raise local concerns which provides important material CCC activists can use in campaigns against the ruling party. Citizen contributions have been harnessed also by civil society, activist Peter Mutasa highlighted the importance of the hashtag #HowFar to coordinate citizens demanding to what extent the Zanu PF government was delivering on its promises. Citizens then responded to the hashtag, often highlighting 'you promised this, but you have not done it' and many Zimbabweans also used the reply function to converse with each other and discuss the broken promises made by Zanu PF. This provides a wealth of information on real lived experiences that the CCC can draw upon. CCC activist Nonhlanhla Mlotshwa argues:

> I think social media provides that space for Zimbabweans, you get to meet a lot of Zimbabweans from different walks of life, and you get to hear their experiences, you know, even if it's not, politically but socially.

Despite the benefits, globally studies show that it is very rare for parties or their candidates and key activists to take part in conversations online themselves. However, for the CCC, there are imperatives for responding to conversations and comments. Firstly, as noted previously, the CCC need to prevent the spread of disinformation and challenge false claims made to discredit them. Hence leading party officials directly responded to comments which repeated false claims. The CCC also made efforts to respond to criticisms or challenges. When challenged about announcing the selection of candidates by a citizen on X on 14 May 2023, CCC presidential candidate Nelson Chamisa responded personally with the short explanation 'We are not operating in a normal environment!'. While not a profound answer, the context will be understood by the user who challenged him, also anyone reading Chamisa's reply and other similar interactions will see he was listening and prepared to respond to citizens who have concerns. Such short interactions offer important information about Chamisa and the CCC in terms of their communication style and political brand to citizens mistrusting of elites and politicians.

Civil society organisations also respond to comments and concerns of citizens. A post by Team Pachedu congratulating the defeat of the military backed ruling party candidate in a by-election received a cynical reply from one citizen saying: 'They must have had a free and fair election'. Team Pachedu almost instantly responded 'There were many irregularities, but the opposition won because many youths turned out to vote. Rigging has a limit. It's important for Zim youths to vote in their numbers'. The clear intention is to challenge the apathy and cynicism of this citizen, as well as the wider audience for the conversation. Strategically, such interactions, even if simplistic, demonstrate that the CCC and civil society organisations aligned against Zanu PF are willing to listen and respond to ordinary citizens. This again is important information about their brand values and ethos.

Digital Political Marketing: A Zimbabwean Gamechanger

Across the political divide, interviewees representing Zanu PF, the CCC and civil society shared the view that social media has had a profound effect on the politics of Zimbabwe. All sides particularly agree that social media has strengthened the CCC's political influence and poses a challenge to the autocratic rule of Zanu PF. There is also a recognition that the CCC strategically utilises social media to the extent that it outperforms its competitors in the political marketplace of Zimbabwean politics. However, their success may also be due to them capturing the zeitgeist of younger, pro-democratic Zimbabweans. Reference is made to the fact that despite the CCC starting afresh on 24 January 2022 from the ashes of the Movement for Democratic Change, with virtually no access to traditional media and its rallies banned by the police, this young new party rose from being an unknown entity on Zimbabwe's political battlefield to being the new main opposition party within three months of its formation. CCC activist Netsai Marova argued:

> CCC doesn't have access to the national broadcasting platforms, so it got launched on social media... but it managed to get to attract its supporters on social media and even managed to surpass other opposition parties that that were there to become the main opposition in Zimbabwe.

Hence, CCC attribute their rise from zero to a political giant to be largely underpinned by their shrewd utilisation of digital political marketing. CCC sell their brand as being the antithesis of Zanu PF, highlight socio-political concerns experienced across society, and use empowering messages to mobilise supporters to be active online and to promote the CCC generally.

Unpacking the CCC strategy, we find it rests on the three key affordances offered by social media platforms. Citizens were given access to a diverse range of viewpoints and are no longer reliant on the Zanu PF controlled state broadcasters and media outlets. More importantly, the CCC's digital political marketing strategy is to develop content that resonates with citizens. They also encourage citizens to contribute to the information environment, offering their own experiences and opinions which they draw on to further shape content. Using these relationship marketing mechanisms, the CCC managed to create a community around the party, tapping into the issues citizens are concerned about and mobilising them to support CCC campaigns. With the support of anti Zanu PF civil society organisation, they built momentum around the idea of the party as a viable oppositional force.

Zanu PF struggled to gain the same traction, but they remain a significant force and have a strong following and strategy. Even Zanu PF activists attest to the advantage of having their own space where they can post their views as opposed to the party line which dominates traditional media and party platforms. However, due to the long tenure and autocratic nature of Zanu PF rule, momentum appears to be with the opposition forces and CCC have managed to harness a wide coalition in opposition to Zanu PF. However, the digital movement was unable to overcome the repressive tactics and vote rigging which secured Zanu PF victory at the 2023 election. The fact that the result was close does suggest the CCC were unable to overcome some of the many structural and indeed communicative hurdles Zanu PF set out to ensure they retained power.

CONCLUSIONS

Following an overview of the literature on digital campaigning and what this demonstrates about digital political marketing strategies, we applied these to the case of Zimbabwe. The case study highlights how the affordances of social media, for informing, engaging, mobilising and interacting with citizens, can benefit political organisations. The lessons from the case study are widely applicable and are replicated by campaigns the world over. Parties and campaign organisations use digital platforms to provide information about their brand, their values, their policies, and their vision for society. Using resonant messages and eye-catching graphics, campaigns attempt to cut through the clutter and gain the attention of platform users, encouraging supporters to extend the reach of campaign messages within networks. Employing persuasive language and resonant slogans, they attempt to build support and activate their followship. Follower's energies are harnessed to extend their reach but also to perform a range of tasks which can range from clicking like or share, to joining the party and participating in the campaign. Campaign organisations offer diverse ways for citizens to engage while supporting their objectives: not only liking and sharing but also by creating events, demonstrations and coordinated petitioning or contacting representatives. However, during election campaigns, the key action that party mobilisation strategies focus on is the vote. But securing votes necessitates building relationships, the most interesting lesson from Zimbabwe may be the power of empowering messages and interactive communication. The latter has particularly been discussed as a gold standard of digital political marketing as it demonstrates how the party performs representation and is accessible and responsive. The CCC appears to be demonstrating the value of responding to follower comments while also benefiting from providing ways in which Zimbabweans can contribute to their campaign.

However, there are concerns regarding the impacts on democracy regarding digital political marketing that are highlighted by the case study; although as Zimbabwe lacks an embedded democratic culture, their presence is unsurprising. The tactics employed by Zimbabwean political campaigners involved spreading disinformation within a society designed to undermine opponents, depress the turnout of opposition supporters or mobilise citizens due to moral panics and fear campaigns. All of these can make strategic sense in terms of reaching electoral goals but have a negative impact on the political and democratic culture of a nation. Similarly, both Zanu PF and the CCC encourage followers to become more polarised and view opponents as inferior. Hate speech can be used through interactions which impact the attitudes of other users. While polarisation is unsurprisingly a feature of Zimbabwean politics, it has increased through the rise of the CCC and their strategic use of digital media. But none of these factors are unique to Zimbabwe and have infected a range of democracies and regimes over recent elections (Lilleker & Moufahim, 2022).

There are also a range of wider concerns that are not yet relevant to the Zimbabwean context but relate to digital political marketing to some extent. Data collection raises issues regarding privacy and the ethics of various data mining practices are hotly debated in particular in the light of the Cambridge Analytica scandal. Artificial intelligence already plays a role in selecting what content is prioritised on user's feeds, and in the future, this may be utilised to enhance the manipulative impact of messages (Niininen et al., 2022). These present new ways of manipulating and misleading citizens which the unethical campaigner may employ. There are also serious questions about safeguarding citizens against bad actors and debates concerning the extent that free speech should be curtailed to defend democratic institutions. This is particularly a problem when the source of content could be an external actor seeking to subvert electoral process within a nation. What views are unacceptable, how to prevent false information spreading, and how to prevent polarisation is extremely challenging. This is particularly the case when it proves impossible to find a universally acceptable understanding of the limits that should be imposed upon pluralism, how we can detect disinformation or even what constitutes hate speech (Chester & Montgomery, 2017). Future research can track digital political marketing strategies, their evolution and how affordances are exploited, and it is important to broaden focus beyond advanced democracies. However, researchers must also be cognisant of the ethics of political marketing and perform the role of activist in defending democratic values when political marketers cross the boundaries of acceptable behaviour.

REFERENCES

Bennett, W. L., & Segerberg, A. (2013). *The logic of connective action: Digital media and the personalization of contentious politics*. Cambridge University Press.

Bossetta, M., & Schmøkel, R. (2023). Cross-platform emotions and audience engagement in social media political campaigning: Comparing candidates' Facebook and Instagram images in the 2020 US election. *Political Communication*, *40*(1), 48–68.

Boulianne, S., & Theocharis, Y. (2020). Young people, digital media, and engagement: A meta-analysis of research. *Social Science Computer Review*, *38*(2), 111–127.

Chester, J., & Montgomery, K. C. (2017). The role of digital marketing in political campaigns. *Internet Policy Review*, *6*(4), 1–20.

Cruz, E. G., & Harindranath, R. (2020). WhatsApp as' technology of life': Reframing research agendas. *First Monday*, *25*(12). https://doi.org/10.5210/fm.v25i12.10405

De Blasio, E., & Viviani, L. (2020). Platform party between digital activism and hyper-leadership: The reshaping of the public sphere. *Media and Communication*, *8*(4), 16–27.

De la Cruz, J. S., de la Hera, T., Gómez, S. C., & Lacasa, P. (2023). Digital games as persuasion spaces for political marketing: Joe Biden's campaign in fortnite. *Media and Communication*, *11*(2), 266–277.

Ebrahim, R. S. (2020). The role of trust in understanding the impact of social media marketing on brand equity and brand loyalty. *Journal of Relationship Marketing*, *19*(4), 287–308.

Elsheikh, D. (2018). *Campaign professionalism during Egypt's 2012 presidential election*. Springer.

Falasca, K., Dymek, M., & Grandien, C. (2019). Social media election campaigning: Who is working for whom? A conceptual exploration of digital political labour. *Contemporary Social Science*, *14*(1), 89–101.

Farkas, X., Jackson, D., Baranowski, P., Bene, M., Russmann, U., & Veneti, A. (2022). Strikingly similar: Comparing visual political communication of populist and non-populist parties across 28 countries. *European Journal of Communication*, *37*(5), 545–562.

Gibson, R. K. (2015). Party change, social media and the rise of 'citizen-initiated' campaigning. *Party Politics*, *21*(2), 183–197.

Hameleers, M. (2020). Augmenting polarization via social media? A comparative analysis of Trump's and Wilders' online populist communication and the electorate's interpretations surrounding the elections. *Acta Politica*, *55*(3), 331–350.

Haßler, J., Kümpel, A. S., & Keller, J. (2023). Instagram and political campaigning in the 2017 German federal election. A quantitative content analysis of German top politicians' and parliamentary parties' posts. *Information, Communication & Society*, *26*(3), 530–550.

Haßler, J., Magin, M., Russmann, U., & Fenoll, V. (Eds.). (2021). *Campaigning on Facebook in the 2019 European Parliament Election: Informing, interacting with, and mobilising voters*. Springer.

Howard, P. N., Carr, J. N., & Milstein, T. J. (2005). Digital technology and the market for political surveillance. *Surveillance and Society*, *3*(1), 59–73.

Jackson, N. (2006). Banking online: The use of the Internet by political parties to build relationships with voters. In D. G. Lilleker, N. A. Jackson, & R. Scullion (Eds.), *The marketing of political parties: Political marketing at the 2005 general election* (pp. 157–184). Manchester University Press.

Jackson, N. A., & Lilleker, D. G. (2009). Building an architecture of participation? Political parties and Web 2.0 in Britain. *Journal of Information Technology & Politics*, *6*(3–4), 232–250.

Joathan, Í., & Lilleker, D. G. (2023). Permanent campaigning: A meta-analysis and framework for measurement. *Journal of Political Marketing*, *22*(1), 67–85.

Kalsnes, B., Larsson, A. O., & Enli, G. (2017). The social media logic of political interaction: Exploring citizens' and politicians' relationship on Facebook and Twitter. *First Monday*, *22*(2).

Koc-Michalska, K., Lilleker, D. G., Michalski, T., Gibson, R., & Zajac, J. M. (2021). Facebook affordances and citizen engagement during elections: European political parties and their benefit from online strategies? *Journal of Information Technology & Politics*, *18*(2), 180–193.

König, P. D. (2020). Why digital-era political marketing is not the death Knell for democracy: On the importance of placing political microtargeting in the context of party competition. *Statistics, Politics, and Policy*, *11*(1), 87–110.

Kruschinski, S., & Bene, M. (2022). In varietate concordia?! Political parties' digital political marketing in the 2019 European Parliament election campaign. *European Union Politics*, *23*(1), 43–65.

Lember, V., Brandsen, T., & Tõnurist, P. (2019). The potential impacts of digital technologies on co-production and co-creation. *Public Management Review*, *21*(11), 1665–1686.

LePere-Schloop, M., Appe, S., Adjei-Bamfo, P., Zook, S., & Bawole, J. N. (2022). Mapping civil society in the digital age: Critical reflections from a project based in the Global South. *Nonprofit and Voluntary Sector Quarterly*, *51*(3), 587–605.

Lewandowsky, S., & Pomerantsev, P. (2022). Technology and democracy: A paradox wrapped in a contradiction inside an irony. *Memory, Mind & Media*, *1*(e5), 1–9. https://doi.org/10.1017/mem.2021.7

Lilleker, D. G., & Jackson, N. (2014). Brand management and relationship marketing in online environments. In J. Lees-Marshment, B. Conley, & K. Cosgrove (Eds.), *Political marketing in the United States* (pp. 165–184). Routledge.

Lilleker, D., & Moufahim, M. (2022). The ethical challenges at the heart of political branding. In M. Moufahim (Ed.), *Political branding in turbulent times* (pp. 141–151). Springer.

Maarek, P. J. (2014). Politics 2.0: New forms of digital political marketing and political communication. *Trípodos*, 34, 13–22.

Mare, A. (2018). Politics unusual? Facebook and political campaigning during the 2013 harmonised elections in Zimbabwe. *African Journalism Studies*, *39*(1), 90–110.

Marland, A., Lewis, J. P., & Flanagan, T. (2017). Governance in the age of digital media and branding. *Governance*, *30*(1), 125–141.

Marsden, C., Meyer, T., & Brown, I. (2020). Platform values and democratic elections: How can the law regulate digital disinformation? *Computer Law & Security Report*, *36*, 105373.

Miller, M. L., & Vaccari, C. (2020). Digital threats to democracy: Comparative lessons and possible remedies. *The International Journal of Press/Politics*, *25*(3), 333–356.

Niininen, O., Singaraju, S., Karjaluoto, H., Valentini, C., & Muhonen, M. (2022). Communicating with customers using digital channels. In O. Niininen (Ed.), *Contemporary issues in digital marketing* (pp. 165–175). Taylor & Francis.

Ormrod, R. P., Henneberg, S. C., & O'Shaughnessy, N. J. (2013). *Political marketing: Theory and concepts*. SAGE.

Sebeelo, T. B. (2021). Hashtag activism, politics and resistance in Africa: Examining #ThisFlag and #RhodesMustFall online movements. *Insight on Africa*, *13*(1), 95–109.

Sørensen, E. (2020). *Interactive political leadership: The role of politicians in the age of governance*. Oxford University Press.

Stier, S., Bleier, A., Lietz, H., & Strohmaier, M. (2020). Election campaigning on social media: Politicians, audiences, and the mediation of political communication on Facebook and Twitter. In L. Bode, & E. K. Vraga (Eds.), *Studying politics across media* (pp. 50–74). Routledge.

Stromer-Galley, J. (2004). Interactivity-as-product and interactivity-as-process. *The Information Society, 20*(5), 391–394.

Towner, T. L., & Dulio, D. A. (2014). New media and political marketing in the United States: 2012 and beyond. In C. B. Williams & B. I. Newman (Eds.), *Political marketing in retrospective and prospective* (pp. 103–127). Routledge.

Veneti, A., Lilleker, D. G., & Jackson, D. (2022). Between analogue and digital: A critical exploration of strategic social media use in Greek election campaigns. *Journal of Information Technology & Politics, 19*(1), 50–64.

Xu, W. W., Sang, Y., & Kim, C. (2020). What drives hyper-partisan news sharing: Exploring the role of source, style, and content. *Digital Journalism, 8*(4), 486–505.

Yingi, E. (2023). Youth Bulge as a peacebuilding opportunity for Africa: The case of Zimbabwe's youth empowerment programmes. *Journal of Asian and African Studies*, https://doi.org/10.1177/00219096231173392

Character Assassination in Electoral Negative Campaigns

Sergei A. Samoilenko and Alessandro Nai

INTRODUCTION

During the 2004 presidential campaign, a group of U.S. Navy Vietnam veterans and former prisoners of war formed a political organisation called Swift Boat Veterans for Truth (later known as Swift Vets and POWs for Truth) to oppose Sen. John Kerry's candidacy for the presidency. The group produced a series of television ads and a book, *Unfit for Command*, to question Kerry's military record and discredit the Democratic presidential nominee in the eyes of U.S. voters and multiple stakeholders. The negative campaign took place against the backdrop of the ongoing controversy surrounding the military service of Kerry's rival, George W. Bush. During the 2000 presidential election, Bush was accused of having used his father's political influence to avoid conscription into the U.S. Army and possible service in the Vietnam War. John Kerry's contrasting status as a decorated Vietnam War veteran posed a problem for Bush's reelection campaign, which Republicans sought to counter by calling Kerry's war record into doubt. It was generally believed that the smear campaign, coupled with the slow reaction from the politician's campaign team, played a critical role in Kerry's defeat (Manjoo, 2008). Since the 2004 election, the term 'swiftboating' has come to denote a smear campaign focused on questioning someone's credibility or patriotism. It has also become a communication technique claiming to expose truth while in fact attempting to taint someone's image and forcing the target to drop out of the race. For example, during the 2012 presidential campaign, Republican Newt Gingrich said he felt he was being 'Romney-boated' (Gabriel, 2012).

Historically, *character assassination* has been among the most popular methods of political persuasion (Samoilenko et al., 2020). Character assassination is primarily a strategic effort to discredit an individual or group target via subversive communication (Samoilenko, 2021). Character assassination is prevalent in politicised contexts and considered instrumental to goal achievement during power struggles (Shiraev et al., 2022). Name-calling, mockery, vilification and accusations of bad character have been part of politics since the days of Classical Athens and the Roman Republic (Icks & Shiraev, 2014). In the United States, public attacks on character have been the centrepiece of election campaigning from the early days. Scher (1997) refers to mudslinging in U.S. politics as 'as American as apple pie' (p. 28).

In the 21st century, accusing political opponents of moral transgressions has reached new heights. The 2016 U.S. presidential election campaign between Hillary Clinton and Donald Trump was particularly negative in tone and light on policy (Patterson, 2016). Character attacks are a frequent feature of contemporary campaigns outside of the United States as well. Recent research has shown, for instance, that during the 2019 election for the European parliament, parties across the (then) 28 countries of the European Union frequently and predominantly engaged in aggressive rhetoric against their opponents, including leveraging uncivil attacks (Klinger et al., 2023; Nai, Medeiros, et al., 2022). Adopting an even larger cross-national perspective confirms that candidates across the world – including top candidates, such as party leaders and front-runners in presidential elections – rarely shy away from character attacks (Maier & Nai, 2022; Valli & Nai, 2022). Quite simply, trashing your opponents is an inextricable part of the global political landscape.

The struggles over personal character and reputation are particularly significant in liberal democracies, where a competitive party system demands that political actors publicly showcase their core moral values for the public assessment of their credibility and competence. According to Walton (1998), this obliges actors holding certain social expectations to voluntarily engage in credibility contests to demonstrate their ability to perform well under pressure. However, 'all forms of symbolic capital, including status, prestige, charisma, are vulnerable to the destructive effect of political polemics' (Bourdieu, 1991, p. 281). The competitive logic of political systems implies that candidates persuade the public of their legitimacy while calling into question the reputation and good name of their rivals, thereby undermining their legitimacy and chances for success. In this context, character attacks are acceptable rhetorical means of political polemics that can be justifiable and reasonable (Benoit, 2017; Walton, 1998).

An electoral campaign, or any competitive selection procedure, provides favourable conditions for character assassination (Shiraev, 2014). Stemming from the broad dynamics of personalisation and privatisation of politics (e.g. Gattermann, 2022), political campaigns tend to become increasingly 'candidate-centred', with both campaign strategists and the media more focused on the candidates' personalities rather than substantive issues related to parties and their policies (Stanyer, 2008). In this environment, reputation based on personal character (as opposed to reputation based on specific skills) is intrinsically contestable and can be quickly eroded by misuse or offensive actions (Thompson, 2000).

Character assassination is usually considered *strategic* political communication; however, recent research suggests that nonstrategic components might also contribute to this phenomenon, which we will address in the conclusion. Benoit et al. (2007) argued that 'political campaign messages have three functions: acclaims, which praise the candidate; attacks, which attack the opponent; and defenses, which refute attacks' (p. 77). Political scientists consider character attacks an effective means of influencing voters, creating uncertainty or preventing defections (Shiraev, 2014).

Name-calling is one the primary methods of character assassination (Shiraev, 2014, p. 13). Naming and labelling strategies suggest how a person should be treated by others. This tactic is often used in *ad hominem* arguments to steer attention away from the issue and towards personality traits, or to ridicule the target before the audience. Boykoff (2013, p. 13) argued that the 'treatment of individuals through denigrating monikers . . . can lead to new debates becoming less about evidence and more about an actual moral conflict over legitimacy'. For example, Thompson (2016) considered former U.S. President George W. Bush's use of 'political sobriquet' as an effective rhetorical strategy to assert dominance over the individuals named and emphasise his own superior position. This approach inevitably leads to the 'punishment of ironic circulation', where a nickname is adopted by the public and subsequently used for mockery.

Populist politicians often attack their opponents to steal the media spotlight, shock the audience and promote policy preferences (Jensen & Bang, 2017). Populist inflammatory rhetoric aims to improve political ratings, generate hype and manipulate public opinion. For example, in June 2019, U.S. House Speaker Nancy Pelosi responded to President Trump's personal attacks by calling him the 'diverter-of-attention in chief' (Roth, 2019). In the Netherlands, Dutch firebrand politician Geert Wilders frequently railed against his opponents, the Dutch political establishment and the European Union to solidify his voter base and exploit political opportunities (van Kessel, 2020). These trends hold when adopting a global perspective. A recent analysis of the media attention towards more than 500 'top candidates' as they were competing in more than 100 national elections across the world shows that candidates who attack their opponents receive significantly more media coverage (Maier & Nai, 2020). If it bleeds, it leads.[1]

In sum, character assassination is a strategic effort to damage someone's political reputation or credibility. As part of negative electoral campaigns, it is commonly used in political environments that favour character-centred competition and promote combatant rhetorical discourses. This chapter explains how the five pillars of character assassination are used in negative campaigns. It also discusses the fundamental strategies of character assassination in the media and provides recommendations for future research.

Five Pillars of Character Assassination

In analysing negative campaigns, the scholars of the Research Lab for Character Assassination and Reputation Politics (CARP) have identified five key pillars of character assassination: attacker, target, audience, context and media (Samoilenko et al., 2020; Shiraev et al., 2022). These components interact to determine their effectiveness and impact on public opinion.

The character *attacker* aims to persuade the public that the target is morally corrupt, incompetent or otherwise unfit to perform their social functions, thereby undermining the target's social standing. Aside from personal reasons, attackers often act strategically, seeking to eliminate a rival in a power contest or improve their own chances of success. In particular, political actors also employ character attacks to force a target to expend time, energy and resources responding to accusations (Shiraev, 2014).

A character assassination *target* is typically a competitive rival who has garnered considerable public support and has a high chance of winning a political race. The outcome of a character assassination attempt is assessed in terms of reduced confidence in leadership, erosion of public trust and a decline in voter support. Character attacks on individuals and groups may overlap when individuals are targeted because they represent a particular ideology or cause.

Public opinion is crucial in character assassination–related scenarios, as a target's reputation is damaged only when various *audiences* perceive it as such, regardless of the truth or relevance of the allegations. The public has the power to either heed or ignore the attacker's allegations, as well as to choose sides and engage in online discussions, thereby cocreating the direction and outcomes of character assassination campaigns.

Character attacks occur in political, social and cultural *contexts* characterised by social norms, cultural traditions and embedded moral codes. Similarly, character attacks launched in different historical epochs feature different moral and cultural standards (Icks & Shiraev, 2014). The sociocultural perspective of character assassination examines issues and events within the framework of intergroup or institutional logic, explaining the history of relationships between attackers, targets and their multiple audiences within broader contexts (Samoilenko, 2021).

Nai (2020) examined the relationships between the attacker, target and context in presidential elections and party leader campaigns in parliamentary elections. He studied the campaigning strategies of 172 candidates in 35 different elections worldwide to understand why parties and candidates use negative tactics against their rivals. His analysis yielded systematic results that suggest the existence of five general trends. First, incumbents who have a lot to lose and thus few incentives to attack are more likely to adopt a positive approach and promote themselves, though they often become the target of attacks. Inversely, challengers have less material upon which to build positive campaigns but plenty to criticise about the past actions and deeds of incumbents. Second, more extreme candidates, particularly those on the right end of the political spectrum, are more likely to go negative. Ideological distance between candidates fosters negativity, as candidates seem more likely to attack ideologically distant rivals who disagree with them on issues and policy. Third, regardless of their competitive standing or ideology, candidates are likely to target front-runners who have a greater chance of electoral success. Fourth, the study showed a strong trend towards attack reciprocity and retaliation, regardless of who went negative first. Finally, the context provides incentives to attack by altering the importance of individual characteristics (e.g. incumbency status) depending on specific election dynamics (e.g. high competitiveness).

The final character assassination pillar is *media*. In contemporary media democracies, the development of a political brand follows the logic of the media market. Hence, in deeply *mediatised* societies, media organisations play a central role, imposing their agenda and other imperatives on the rest of society (Couldry & Hepp, 2017). In this media environment, negative campaigns are often orchestrated and played as a chess game. Next, we discuss the media pillar of character assassination in more detail.

THE MEDIA PILLAR OF CHARACTER ASSASSINATION

During the 2017 close Virginia governor's race, Democrat Ralph Northam and Republican Ed

Gillespie traded lurid attacks in the final days of the closely watched campaign. In one of Gillespie's TV ads, a young mother proclaimed she could not vote for Northam because he 'supports automatic restoration of rights for sex offenders, making it easier for these violent felons to get guns'. Gillespie's ads also suggested Northam paved the way for the Central American gang MS-13 to thrive in Virginia. A Latino advocacy group supporting Northam responded to Gillespie's claims by releasing an ad showing minority children running away from a man driving a pickup truck sporting a Confederate flag and a bumper sticker for Republican Ed Gillespie. A Democratic Party of Virginia mailer also linked Gillespie to white nationalist protesters. The flyer superimposed images of Gillespie and Trump over white supremacists at the march in Charlottesville (Robillard, 2017). Northam defeated the Republican nominee, winning by the largest margin for a Democrat since 1985.

In the United States, the emergence of the Fox News and MSNBC news channels in 1996 gave rise to partisan media focusing on issues that appeal to either conservatives or liberals. Since then, the development of online websites and niche media has increasingly contributed to audience segmentation and growing ideological polarisation. An analysis of the 2016 U.S. presidential election revealed that the partisan left and right media was mainly responsible for setting a media agenda and negative coverage for both candidates (Faris et al., 2017). On the left, *Huffington Post*, MSNBC and *Vox* were prominent on all platforms. On the right, *Breitbart*, Fox News, *the Daily Caller* and *the New York Post* dominated across platforms. The rising prominence of *Breitbart* along with relatively new outlets such as *the Daily Caller* marked a significant reshaping of the conservative media landscape. When the media is fragmented and polarised, incivility and personal attacks abound. Partisan media exposure promotes positive feelings towards ingroup members and negative feelings towards the outgroup (Lelkes et al., 2017). There is evidence that negative information has a stronger influence on overall impressions and elicits stronger and faster responses than positive information (O'Keefe, 2012).

Media scholars have examined how media market logic influences framing strategies, including promoting sensational aspects of political events; focusing on conflict over compromise; relying on emotions, polarisation and stereotyping for storytelling; and using catchy phrases and compelling visuals to highlight fragments of political discourse (Hallin & Mancini, 2004; Mazzoleni & Schulz, 1999). Mediatisation effects include content simplification, personalisation and the production of clickbait content favouring conflict and negativity (Esser, 2013). Hostility towards political opponents has been linked to the effects of partisan media and the promotions of inaccurate beliefs (Garrett et al., 2019; Perloff, 2022).

Character attacks in the media range from offensive caricatures in newspapers to virulent conspiracy theories on social media. Empirical evidence indicates that people recognise negative ads more quickly and remember them more effectively than positive ads (Shapiro & Rieger, 1992). In countries with dichotomous political landscapes, such as the United States, negative media coverage promoting scandals dominates headlines (Downey & Stanyer, 2013). This is because when citizens are polarised and divided in terms of the trait perceptions of presidential candidates, negative content holds more value for media producers (Iyengar & Westwood, 2014).

Journalists may deliberately engage in proactive newsgathering to elicit and expose scandalous information about political figures that would otherwise remain hidden. These strategies, which scholars call 'entrapment journalism' or 'ambush journalism', range from persuading a source to admit legal or moral transgressions to betraying their trust and exposing off-the-record information (Kampf, 2019; Rainey, 2011). In some instances, reporters or bloggers have used inopportune or doctored photos to portray a politician in an unflattering light. In 2002, a digitally manipulated photo of then-President George W. Bush holding a children's book upside down was widely circulated shortly after he appeared at the George Sanchez Charter School in Houston in 2002. In reality, the book, *America: A Patriotic Primer,* by Lynne Cheney, was never held upside down during the visit.

In 2017, the media market witnessed a so-called 'Trump bump', or an economic upturn attributed to Donald Trump's electoral victory. Donald Trump had a tremendous advantage in earned media from tweets in both the primaries and the general election. Between June 2015, when he declared his intention to run for president, and December 2016 one month after he was elected, Donald Trump issued 289 insults via Twitter (Lee & Quealy, 2019). The Trump campaign's use of the pejorative 'crooked Hillary' and its hashtag #CrookedHillary was used 5.8 million times on Twitter alone between its debut and the election. The phrase triggered a popular response,

'Lock Her Up', which was chanted at rallies and posted with a hashtag 1.1 million times. The party conventions and televised debates led to significant spikes in the number of tweets containing these phrases that were posted and shared (Cornfield, 2017). The insults and name-calling in Trump's tweets were much more likely to receive media coverage than any of his opponents' activities.

Media companies sensed Trump's brand potential as a reliable clickbait provider and leveraged the emotions of his haters and supporters into a full-scale campaign based on negatively framed materials built around democracy desperately fighting for freedom (Samoilenko & Miroshnichenko, 2019). The commercial media logic behind the 24/7 news coverage led to the revival of the media market and instant subscription growth.

Strategies for Character Assassination Media Campaigns

Often, negative campaigns targeting the public images and reputations of politicians are designed and executed by teams of media strategists and professional communicators. These campaigns may focus on provocation and intervention strategies as orchestrated attempts to instigate highly mediated character assassination events, such as scandals, or capitalise on ongoing reputational crises caused by moral transgressions. We will next discuss three cardinal strategies for mediated character assassination campaigns: provocation/amplification, contamination and obliteration.

PROVOCATION AND AMPLIFICATION STRATEGIES

Provocation and amplification strategies aim to create highly mediated events or amplify crisis situations involving accusations of moral transgressions (Coombs & Holladay, 2020). The goal is to cause public outrage within multiple communities and shape negative attitudes and public opinion against the target. Character assassination events create serious legitimacy issues for the target, lowering their credibility to a degree that is unacceptable to the public.

Provoking a *scandal* is the most popular means of provocation to gain media attention and incite public outrage. Attackers often seek to create negative publicity for the target that subsequently becomes clickbait. The media can expose personal or organisational misdeeds, instigate lawsuits and prompt activists to launch boycotts or protests against the target and their organisations. The goal is to make the target appear morally or legally in the wrong, creating an issue that incites public outrage and demands immediate action and issue resolution.

A powerful framing mechanism is *misquoting*, which refers to intentionally quoting someone out of context or omitting significant details from a quote. In 2011, Rick Perry, the longest-serving Texas governor and the 2012 presidential Republican nominee snipped a quote from then-U.S. President Barack Obama talking about U.S. efforts to attract foreign investment. On November 12 at the APEC CEO Business Summit, Obama said:

> There are a lot of things that make foreign investors see the US as a great opportunity – our stability, our openness, our innovative free market culture. But we've been a little bit lazy, I think, over the last couple of decades. We've kind of taken for granted – well, people will want to come here and we aren't out there hungry, selling America and trying to attract new business into America. (Adler, 2011)

It is clear from the context that Obama did not call the American people themselves lazy. However, taking the phrase out of context, Perry said in his ad, 'Can you believe that? That's what our president thinks is wrong with America? That Americans are lazy?' Perry says in the commercial, which aired in Iowa and New Hampshire. 'That's pathetic. It's time to clean house in Washington.... Obama's socialist policies are bankrupting America. We must stop him now'. In addition, Perry's press release for the ad accused Obama of 'apologising for America and disparaging Americans by calling us lazy, soft and unambitious'.

Another provocation strategy is *push polling*, which involves a caller contacting a voter under the guise of a normal polling call, but asking loaded questions designed to bring attention to a candidate's negative attributes. Manipulative questions like 'How would you react if Candidate A was revealed to beat his wife?' plant seeds of doubt in the listener. In 2000, John McCain won the New Hampshire primary and was favoured to win in South Carolina. Had he succeeded, he would likely have become the Republican nominee. George W. Bush strategists came up with an injurious fiction for his operatives to circulate via a phony poll. Voters were asked, 'Would you be more or less likely to vote for John

McCain ... if you knew he had fathered an illegitimate black child?' McCain was at the time campaigning with his daughter, Bridget, adopted from Bangladesh. This vicious smear campaign helped Bush win the 2000 Republican nomination (Gooding, 2008).

Data breaches, leaks and hacks can cause scandals of historic magnitude. In May 2019, Austria's vice chancellor and head of the far-right Freedom Party, Heinz-Christian Strache, announced his resignation from both offices. It started with a leaked video that showed the vice chancellor engaging in 'alcohol-induced macho talk', offering lucrative government contracts to a woman posing as a Russian oligarch's niece in exchange for campaign donations (Deutsche Welle, 2019). The scandal caused the collapse of the Austrian governing coalition and the announcement of a snap election.

CONTAMINATION STRATEGIES

The contamination strategy involves spreading misinformation, rumours and conspiracy theories. The idea is to introduce an issue about the target into the existing consensus of a community in a clandestine manner. The attacker may attempt to 'poison the well' by gradually introducing irrelevant negative information about a target, aiming to discredit or ridicule public statements they have made.

Insular online communities can be especially conducive to misinformation. Research on validity judgements of recurrent rumours found that people find familiar messages more believable, suggesting that repetitive contact with online falsehoods encourages their acceptance (Fonzo, 2016). Rumours shared via email with friends and family are more likely to be disseminated further, and these patterns of circulation and belief often exhibit strong political biases (Garrett, 2011). Researchers have argued that homogeny makes acceptance of a falsehood appear normal by decreasing the visibility and familiarity of contradictory information (Scheufele & Krause, 2019). For certain nodes, high visibility can amplify their influence, making some beliefs appear more prevalent in a network than they actually are (Lerman et al., 2016).

The tendency of online users to follow like-minded people leads to the creation of echo chambers and filter bubbles, which exacerbate polarisation. Conspiracy theories have the tendency to mushroom in gated communities. During the 2016 presidential election, a conspiracy theory spread throughout numerous social media groups and 4chan.org, an image board website for anonymous posting, claiming that Democratic candidate Hillary Clinton was involved in a child sex ring and satanic rituals. This rumour was then circulated via decoy internet sites specialising in sensationalistic false content. It was also retweeted by the son of Mike Flynn, Trump's newly appointed security adviser. Soon after, WikiLeaks published hacked emails from Clinton's campaign, in which her campaign chair and the owner of Comet Ping Pong, a Washington, DC, pizza restaurant, discussed the details of a Clinton fundraiser set to take place there. The restaurant quickly became tainted by allegations of being a site of sexual misconduct, as the 'Pizzagate' conspiracy theory spread online. This false narrative claimed that the restaurant was the headquarters of a child sex ring, with the word 'pizza' being a code name for 'pedophilia'. The owner and employees of the pizza restaurant soon became the targets of repeated harassment. On 4 December 2016, Edgar Maddison Welch entered the restaurant and fired an assault rifle, claiming he wanted to investigate the story himself (Siddiqui & Svrluga, 2016).

Strategic attackers engage both authentic audience members and social bots to spread negative information about the target. According to Wanless and Berk (2020), attackers conduct audience analysis to determine what specific messages will provoke group engagement, and then create and share provocative content that elicits action. Attackers infiltrate online communities or create echo chambers through algorithms in order to incubate conspiracy theories or fake news stories. Followers are encouraged to spread supportive content and attack the opposition. Through computational propaganda (botnets, seeding, etc.), persuasive content is amplified across multiple websites for better organic placement in newsfeeds. The origin of such provocative content is typically obfuscated. Finally, attackers reach out to partisan media to ensure traditional media coverage.

OBLITERATION STRATEGIES

Some clandestine attacks aim to purge the public memory and silence the achievements of the target. By avoiding any references to individuals and their work, the attacker attempts to erase their public record from the collective memory. Defacing the past is a quintessential method of obliteration strategy. Memory sanctions applied to dethroned emperors and defacing the past were common in Ancient Rome. The damnation of memory can be used as an ideological tool and a state policy. This is reminiscent of the *memory hole* in George Orwell's dystopian novel *1984*, an opening in a wall connected to an incinerator used to dispose of all unwanted documents, documents, photographs or other records.

Obliteration strategies can also be used to purge living individuals from memory and public significance. The slow pace of this type of character poisoning is based on a long-term plan. It resembles *lingchi*, or 'death by a thousand cuts', which was used as a capital punishment in Imperial China. This brutal torture involved slowly slicing the offender's flesh, even past the point of death. The punishment was intended to be both physical and psychological, aiming to undermine the offender's sense of wholeness. It was also designed to dishonour the individual by removing any hope of an afterlife, causing them to feel shame and embarrassment due to their lack of bodily integrity.

In modern times, Wikipedia is a convenient place for obliteration practices, including falsifications of a person's early biography or forged evidence about an individual's inappropriate social ties or political associations. In some cases, Wikipedia has been altered for negative labelling purposes, including an example when a staffer working on a White House computer updated Wikipedia to call government leaker Edward Snowden an 'American traitor who defected to Russia' (Hattem, 2014).

Obliteration may appear in various forms of historical revisionism for purely ideological or political reasons. For example, in April 2020, Virginian Governor Ralph Northam signed a bill allowing individual localities to remove, relocate or contextualise Confederate statues and monuments within their communities (Rosenthal, 2020).

However, many symbolic acts of historic revisionism are public relations decisions designed to address public concerns. These decisions are used by the authorities as an immediate response to public outrage. For example, following the 2011 Penn State sex abuse scandal, the bronze statue of Joe Paterno, former head coach of the Penn State football team, was removed in July 2012 because it had become a 'source of division and an obstacle to healing' (Van Natta, 2012). Similarly, in 2017, Ben's Chili Bowl, a landmark in Washington, DC, had to paint over its mural of Bill Cosby. The mural, which had featured the comedian for five years, was removed after the sex scandal despite the restaurant's long-standing association with him (Beaujon et al., 2017). The wall now features a series of portraits that include Barack Obama, Donnie Simpson and Chuck Brown. The owners also removed Cosby from the wall at its other location in Arlington, VA, after a petition asked the restaurant to replace Cosby's image with one that features women.

CONCLUSION

Character assassination is here to stay. In deeply mediatised societies, media organisations play a central role, using strategies like clickbait framing, negativity and person-centred media coverage to influence the entire political system. Capitalising on politicians' faux pas, gaffes and mismanaged performances that can be conveniently exaggerated and exposed, the media plays a central role in the normalisation of political behaviour that promotes incivility and character attacks.

However, this does not necessarily mean that character assassinations (and political attacks in general) are merely a reflection of systemic incentives to 'go nasty' – such as being picked up by the news media (Geer, 2012) – or strategic considerations (e.g. Maier et al., 2023). Indeed, new evidence suggests that the rhetoric candidates use during elections is largely driven by their essential character – most notably their *personality traits*. In their examination of the 2018 U.S. Senate midterm elections, Nai and Maier (2020) found that candidates with a 'darker' personality profile (e.g. scoring high on the psychopathy scale) were significantly more likely to use more negative and uncivil language in their social media posts. This trend also holds when looking at elections across the world, suggesting that some candidates, regardless of the strategic considerations of their campaign, might simply be 'hardwired to go negative' (Nai, Medeiros, et al., 2022; Nai & Maier, 2024).

The implications of this 'personality turn' for research on character assassination are not yet clear. On the one hand, further research may need to explore the balance between strategic motivations and personal inclinations in decisions to engage in attacks. On the other hand, it is unlikely that personality influences solely the attacker. Evidence suggests that voter personality plays a crucial role in shaping their reception and interpretation of negativity and incivility (Nai & Maier, 2021; Weinschenk & Panagopoulos, 2014).

Note

1 'If it bleeds, it leads' is a saying used in news broadcasting to indicate that dramatic and violent stories are given priority in headlines.

REFERENCES

Adler, B. (2011, November 23). Republican campaign commercials misquote Obama. *The Nation*. https://www.thenation.com/article/archive/republican-campaign-commercials-misquote-obama/

Beaujon, A., Sidman, J., & Cartagena, R. (2017). *Ben's Chili Bowl removes Bill Cosby mural*. Washingtonian. https://bit.ly/3aq1SuW

Benoit, W. L. (2017). Criticism of actions and character: Strategies for persuasive attack. *Extended Relevant Rhetoric, 8*. https://bit.ly/2Y0rqvC

Benoit, W. L., Brazeal, L., & Airne, D. (2007). *A functional analysis of televised U.S. senateand gubernatorial campaign debates*. Communication Studies Faculty Publications. Paper 7. http://scholarworks.umt.edu/communications_pubs/

Bourdieu, P. (1991). *Language and symbolic power*. Polity Press.

Boykoff, M. T. (2013). Public enemy no. 1? Understanding media representations of outlier views on climate change. *American Behavioral Scientist, 57*, 796–817.

Coombs, W. T., & Holladay, S. J. (2020). How scandal varies by industry: The effect of industry culture on scandalization of behaviors. *Scandalogy, 2*, 144–161.

Cornfield, M. (2017). Empowering the party-crasher: Donald J. Trump, the first 2016 GOP presidential debate, and the Twitter marketplace for political campaigns. *Journal of Political Marketing, 16*(3–4), 212–243.

Couldry, N., & Hepp, A. (2017). *The mediated construction of reality*. Polity.

Deutsche Welle (2019, May 19). *Austria to hold snap polls in September after corruption sting*. https://bit.ly/2WnrL99

Downey, J., & Stanyer, J. (2013). Exposing politicians' peccadilloes in comparative context: Explaining the frequency of political sex scandals in eight democracies using fuzzy set qualitative comparative analysis. *Political Communication, 30*(3), 495–509.

Esser, F. (2013). Mediatization as challenge: Media logic versus political logic. In H. Kriesi, S. Lavenex, F. Esser, J. Matthes, M. Bühlmann, & D. Bochsler (Eds.), *Democracy in the age of globalization and mediatization* (pp. 155–176). Palgrave Macmillan.

Faris, R. M., Roberts, H., Etling, B., Bourassa, N., Zuckerman, E., & Benkler, Y. (2017). *Partisanship, propaganda, and disinformation: Online media and the 2016 U.S. presidential election*. Berkman Klein Center for Internet & Society, Harvard University. https://bit.ly/3bEmKiH

Gabriel, T. (2012, January 1). Gingrich says he's been 'Romney-boated'. *The New York Times*. https://nyti.ms/3cZPKl4

Garrett, R. K. (2011). Troubling consequences of online political rumoring. *Human Communication Research, 37*, 255–274.

Garrett, R. K., Long, J. A., & Jeong, M. S. (2019). From partisan media to misperception: Affective polarization as mediator. *Journal of Communication, 69*(5), 490–512.

Gattermann, K. (2022). *The personalization of politics in the European Union*. Oxford University Press.

Geer, J. G. (2012). The news media and the rise of negativity in presidential campaigns. *PS: Political Science & Politics, 45*(3), 422–427.

Gooding, R. (2008, September 24). *The trashing of John McCain*. Vanity Fair. https://bit.ly/3avwFFY

Hallin, D. C., & Mancini, P. (2004). *Comparing media systems: Three models of media and politics*. Cambridge University Press.

Hattem, J. (2014, August 05). House staffer edited Wikipedia page to label Snowden a 'traitor'. *The Hill*. https://bit.ly/2yOJcXT

Huffington, A. (2007, March 21). Who created "Hillary 1984"? Mystery solved!. *HuffPost*. https://bit.ly/354iSFa

Icks, M., & Shiraev, E. (2014). *Character assassination throughout the ages*. Palgrave Macmillan.

Iyengar, S., & Westwood, S. J. (2014). Fear and loathing across party lines: New evidence for group polarization. *American Journal of Political Science, 59*(3), 690–707.

Jensen, M. J., & Bang, H. P. (2017). Populism and connectivism: An analysis of the Sanders and Trump nomination campaigns. *Journal of Political Marketing, 16*(3–4), 343–364.

Kampf, Z. (2019). To bark or to bite? Journalism and entrapment. In *The Routledge companion to media and scandal* (pp. 245–253). Routledge.

Klinger, U., Koc-Michalska, K., & Russmann, U. (2023). Are campaigns getting uglier, and who is to blame? Negativity, dramatization and populism on Facebook in the 2014 and 2019 EP election campaigns. *Political Communication, 40*(3), 263–282.

Lee, J. C., & Quealy, K. (2019, May 24). The 598 people, places and things Donald Trump has insulted on Twitter: A complete list. *The New York Times*. https://goo.gl/287GJo

Lelkes, Y., Sood, G., & Iyengar, S. (2017). The hostile audience: The effect of access to broadband internet on partisan affect. *American Journal of Political Science, 61*(1), 5–20.

Lerman, K., Yan, X., & Wu, X.-Z. (2016). The" majority illusion" in social networks. *PLoS One, 11*, e0147617.

Maier, J., & Nai, A. (2020). Roaring candidates in the spotlight: Campaign negativity, emotions, and media coverage in 107 national elections. *The International Journal of Press/Politics, 25*(4), 576–606.

Maier, J., & Nai, A. (2022). When conflict fuels negativity. A large-scale comparative investigation of the contextual drivers of negative campaigning in elections worldwide. *The Leadership Quarterly, 33*(2), 101564.

Maier, J., Stier, S., & Oschatz, C. (2023). Are candidates rational when it comes to negative campaigning? Empirical evidence from three German candidate surveys. *Party Politics, 29*(4), 766–779.

Manjoo, F. (2008). *True enough: Learning to live in a post-fact society.* Wiley.

Mazzoleni, G., & Schulz, W. (1999). Mediatization of politics: A challenge for democracy. *Political Communication, 16*, 247–261.

Nai, A. (2020). Going negative, worldwide: Towards a general understanding of determinants and targets of negative campaigning. *Government and Opposition, 55*(3), 430–455.

Nai, A., & Maier, J. (2020). Dark necessities? Candidates' aversive personality traits and negative campaigning in the 2018 American Midterms. *Electoral Studies, 68*, 102233.

Nai, A., & Maier, J. (2021). Is negative campaigning a matter of taste? Political attacks, incivility, and the moderating role of individual differences. *American Politics Research, 49*(3), 269–281.

Nai, A., & Maier, J. (2024). *Dark politics: The personality of politicians and the future of democracy.* Oxford University Press.

Nai, A., Medeiros, M., Maier, M., & Maier, J. (2022). Euroscepticism and the use of negative, uncivil and emotional campaigns in the 2019 European Parliament election: A winning combination. *European Union Politics, 23*(1), 21–42.

Nai, A., Tresch, A., & Maier, J. (2022). Hardwired to attack. Candidates' personality traits and negative campaigning in three European countries. *Acta Politica, 57*(4), 772–797.

O'Keefe, D. J. (2012). From psychological theory to message design: Lessons from the story of gain-framed and loss-framed persuasive messages. In H. Cho (Ed.), *Health communication message design: Theory and practice* (pp. 3–20). Sage.

Patterson, T. E. (2016, September 21). *News coverage of the 2016 national conventions: Negative news, lacking context.* Harvard Kennedy School. https://bit.ly/2znkcXT

Perloff, R. M. (2022). *The dynamics of political communication* (3rd ed.). Routledge.

Rainey, J. (2011, March 12). Secret recordings trespass on ethics. *Los Angeles Times.* https://www.pressreader.com/usa/los-angeles-times/20110312/285787125121868

Robillard, K. (2017, October 29). Mud flies in close Virginia governor's race. *Politico.* https://politi.co/2Wag9Gr

Rosenthal, Z. (2020, April 13). New law allows Virginia localities to remove Confederate statues and monuments. *Cavalier Daily.* https://bit.ly/3blHGoX

Roth, K. (2019, June 11). House speaker Pelosi to CNN: Trump is 'diverter-of-attention-in-chief. . . I'm done with him.'. *International Business Times.* https://bit.ly/2LivAJr

Samoilenko, S. A. (2021). Character assassination: The sociocultural perspective. *Journal of Applied Social Theory, 1*(3), 186–205.

Samoilenko, S. A., Icks, M., Keohane, J., & Shiraev, E. (Eds.). (2020). *The Routledge handbook of character assassination and reputation management.* Routledge.

Samoilenko, S. A., & Miroshnichenko, A. (2019). Profiting from the "Trump Bump": The effects of selling negativity in the media. In I. E. Chiluwa & S. A. Samoilenko (Eds.), *Handbook of research on deception, fake news, and misinformation online* (pp. 375–391). IGI Global.

Scheufele, D. A., & Krause, N. M. (2019). Science audiences, misinformation, and fake news. *Proceedings of the National Academy of Sciences of the United States of America, 116*(16), 7662–7669. https://doi.org/10.1073/pnas.1805871115

Scher, R. K. (1997). *The modern presidential campaign: Mudslinging, bombast, and the vitality of American politics.* M.E. Sharpe.

Shapiro, M. A., & Rieger, R. H. (1992). Comparing positive and negative political advertising on radio. *Journalism Quarterly, 69*, 135–145.

Shiraev, E. (2014). Character assassination: How political psychologists can assist historians. In M. Icks & E. Shiraev (Eds.), *Character assassination throughout the ages* (pp. 15–36). Palgrave-MacMillan.

Shiraev, E., Keohane, J., Icks, M., & Samoilenko, S. A. (2022). *Character assassination and reputation management: Theory and applications.* Routledge.

Siddiqui, F., & Svrluga, S. (2016, December 5). N.C. man told police he went to D.C. pizzeria with gun to investigate conspiracy theory. *The Washington Post.* http://bit.ly/44rScfl

Stanyer, J. (2008). Candidate-centered communication. In L. L. Kaid & C. Holtz-Bacha (Eds.), *Encyclopedia of political communication* (Vol. 1, pp. 81–83). SAGE.

Thompson, J. (2016). From "big time" to "turd blossom": George W. Bush and the rhetoric of the political sobriquet. In S. M. Vanguri (Ed.), *Rhetorics of names and naming* (pp. 33–48). Routledge.

Thompson, J. B. (2000). *Political scandal: Power and visibility and in the media age.* Polity.

Valli, C., & Nai, A. (2022). Attack politics from Albania to Zimbabwe: A large-scale comparative study on the drivers of negative campaigning. *International Political Science Review, 43*(5), 680–696.

van Kessel, S. (2020). Character attacks by Dutch populist radical right leader Geert Wilders. In S. A. Samoilenko, M. Icks, J. Keohane, & E. Shiraev (Eds.), *Routledge handbook of character assassination and reputation management* (pp. 131–143). Routledge.

Van Natta, D., Jr. (2012, April 3). *Fight on state*. ESPN. https://es.pn/3cZNn1W

Walton, D. N. (1998). *Ad hominem arguments*. University of Alabama Press.

Wanless, A., & Berk, M. (2020). The audience is the amplifier: Participatory propaganda. In P. Baines, N. O'Shaughnessy, & N. Snow (Eds.), *The Sage handbook of propaganda* (pp. 85–104). SAGE.

Weinschenk, A. C., & Panagopoulos, C. (2014). Personality, negativity, and political participation. *Journal of Social and Political Psychology*, *2*(1), 164–182.

What Can Nation Branding Research Learn From Political Marketing?

Tom Wraight

INTRODUCTION

In the last two decades, academics, policymakers, and marketers have become increasingly interested in how nation states might influence their reputation using the techniques of brand-management (Anholt, 1998, 2007, 2010; Volcic & Andrejevic, 2011). "Nation branding" has thus emerged as a lively field of interdisciplinary research, synthesizing ideas in marketing, international business, and national identity studies (Fan, 2010; Hao et al., 2019; Rojas-Méndez & Khoshnevis, 2023; Tijani et al., 2024). In its application of marketing concepts outside the sphere of traditional enterprise, nation branding research closely parallels the development of political marketing scholarship. Yet while political marketing has increasingly established itself as a recognized subfield of political science, nation branding has remained relatively aloof. Indeed, nation branding has sometimes been portrayed as an "apolitical" activity (Varga, 2013), and researchers in the field have historically drawn more heavily from international business or marketing than they do from political science (Fan, 2010). Nonetheless, the activity of marketing states in the international arena remains a fundamentally political act (Sun & Harris, 2020). There is consequently a need for nation branding to follow in the footsteps of political marketing and engage more extensively with concepts from political science.

There are hopeful signs that this is beginning to happen, with a growing critical literature in nation branding recognizing the political dimensions of the field (Kaneva, 2011, 2021). This chapter seeks to review those trends and to identify some key themes for future research in nation branding. I begin by overviewing recent developments in nation branding which are moving the field closer to political science. I then discuss the possibility of integrating theories from political science and international relations – specifically surrounding state-society relations and state position in the international system – into nation branding research. This is followed by an identification of new opportunities for empirical research involving the distinctive branding strategies of small, large, and intermediate states in the international system. I then conclude by reflecting on how a more political nation branding research agenda might be brought into dialog with political marketing, especially the application of political marketing to international affairs.

THE GROWTH OF NATION BRANDING RESEARCH

The idea that a nation's reputation – and its perception abroad by tourists, investors, and immigrants – possess properties akin to a corporate brand first grew to prominence in the late 1990s and was articulated especially by Simon Anholt (Dinnie, 2008). Anholt noted that "throughout the twentieth century, most of the really successful international brands have come from countries that are successful brands in their own right, and substantial transfer of imagery and brand equity can often be seen to occur between the two" (Anholt, 1998, p. 395). The success of developed economies such as the United States in attracting foreign investment, Anholt suggested, was to a significant degree related to the power of their national brands, and countries seeking to foster globally competitive national champions must do so by cultivating effective national brands (Anholt & Hildreth, 2004). These ideas prompted the growth in efforts to measure national reputation, such as the Anholt-Ipsos nation Brand Index or the Future-Brand country index (Beaumont & Towns, 2021; Buhmann, 2016). This corresponded with a growing research infrastructure concerned with how public diplomacy might impact on nation brands; especially following the creation of the journal *Place Branding and Public Diplomacy* in 2004 (Anholt, 2004).

These ideas of nation branding have had a clear influence on public agencies concerned with tourism, export promotion or inward investment, who have increasingly conceptualized their role as selling a particular image of the nation at large. Some states have gone so far as to coordinate such activities behind official "nation branding campaigns." South Korea's "Presidential Council on Nation Branding" – set up in 2009 with the explicit goal of improving the country's standing in nation-brand indexes – has become a high-profile example of this, and some have attributed the growth of "Hallyu 2.0" (the resurgence of global interest in Korean culture since 2008) in part to these nation branding efforts (Choi & Kim, 2014; Lee, 2011). There are also numerous cases where public policy issues or responses to national events have been strongly influenced by consideration of national branding. After the so-called "cartoon crisis" in Denmark, where drawings of the prophet Muhammed in the newspaper *Jylland's-Posten* attracted international controversy, the Danish State set up a new nation branding program specifically to manage fallout of the incident (Rasmussen & Merkelsen, 2014). Debates around the introduction of genetic modification or nuclear power in New Zealand have in part rested on how such actions might affect New Zealand's "Clean Green" image (Hamlin et al., 2016; Knight et al., 2013). Such examples attest to how concerns with protecting and promoting national brands have come to bear influence on policymaking.

The growing interest in nation branding during the 1990s and 2000s reflected several key trends. Firstly, research within psychology and behavior economics had highlighted the role of heuristics – as opposed to rational calculation – in guiding much of human behavior (Gigerenzer & Brighton, 2009; Kahneman, 2003; Knight, 2014). This suggested that the various images, feelings, and stereotypes associated with a nation might have a significant impact on how people interacted with that nation's products or companies. In Anholt's words.

> We all navigate through the complexity of the modern world armed with a few simple cliches. . .Paris is about style, Japan about technology, Switzerland about wealth and precisions. . .These cliches and stereotypes – whether they are positive or negative, true or untrue-fundamentally affect our behaviour towards other places. . .So all responsible governments, on behalf of their people, their institutions and their companies, need to discover what the world's perception of their country is, and develop a strategy for managing it. . .This huge task has become one of the primary skills of government in the twenty-first century. (Anholt, 2007, p. 4)

Secondly, the 1990s saw widespread predictions about the transformative impact of globalization, and the rise of globally mobile companies and skilled professionals able to move to wherever offered the best business environment (Friedman, 2005). This was expected to lead to a global convergence toward one economic model, as states adopted similar tax and regulatory frameworks to attract investment (Korten, 1998; Sassen, 1998). With this reduction in policy differences between the states, the promotion of national culture and image was expected to assume more importance in dictating a country's international competitiveness. Again, to quote Anholt. . .

> Today, the world is one market. The rapid advance of globalisation means that every country. . .must compete with every other for its share of the world's consumers, tourists, investors, students. . .and for the attention and respect of the international media. (Anholt, 2007, p. 1)

Thirdly, the end of the Cold War in the 1990s had been interpreted as heralding a decline in great power strategic rivalry. In such a world, it was imagined that power and international status would rest less on "hard power" – military or technological dominance – than on "soft power"; the "power to persuade" through social and cultural influence (Nye, 2004). This also coincided with the growing popularity of poststructuralist theory within social science, which pointed to the power of image and perception in driving social life. According to Van Ham, for instance, the growing importance of national brands presaged a transformation "from the modern world of geopolitics and power to a post-modern world of image and influence" (Van Ham, 2001, p. 4).

Where do these three assumptions which underpinned the growth of nation branding as field stand from a contemporary perspective? Certainly, the importance of heuristics in guiding human behavior remains widely recognized and applications of this have been pioneered in many domains (Cai, 2020; Olya et al., 2024). Yet the other two assumptions look considerably shakier. Populist revolts against globalization and divergent responses to the financial crisis of 2008 have challenged notions that the world is converging toward one economic model (Rodrik, 2021). Instead, scholarship of comparative and international political economy points to a range of competing economic models and industrial *strategies* used by states to advance their position within global value chains (Behringer & van Treeck, 2022; Schedelik et al., 2021). China's continued promotion of its state-capitalist model and the opposition this has provoked in the United States is pointed to as a key fracture in the world economy, epitomized by the ongoing US-China trade war (Petry, 2021). This economic conflict, as well as the disruptive effect of Russia's invasion of Ukraine, also speak to the potential reemergence of great power rivalry, with dramatic implications for the global order.

None of these transformations mean that nation branding has lost relevance. On the contrary, as nations and their firms jockey for position in a rapidly polarizing economic order, considerations about the image presented to the world may become increasingly important and complex (Volcic & Andrejevic, 2011). This does however imply a need to reconsider how nation branding can work in an increasingly unstable world. Many researchers are already taking on that challenge, from studies of how nations can avoid being drawn into great-power rivalries, to research on information warfare as a threat to national brands (Manor, 2021; Ren et al., 2024). A recent special issue on "Public Diplomacy and Nation Branding in the Wake of Russia-Ukraine," edited by three scholars who have long been pushing for more critical analysis of how geopolitics influence nation branding research, has made a powerful case for how nation branding research must evolve to understand the contemporary world (Kaneva et al., 2023). This new mood is also reflected in the increasing skepticism toward what Anholt termed "superficial" nation branding activities – general promotion campaigns targeting international audience – which are increasingly regarded as ineffective (Anholt, 2010). Instead Anholt has insisted in more recent work that only "substantive action" which is part of a nation broader economic and foreign policy goals can significantly alter perceptions of that nation (Anholt, 2020).

Current trends therefore suggest that nation branding research must be more attentive to the strategic goals of states, their position within an uncertain international order, and the internal structure of their social and economic models. This imperative is pushing nation branding closer toward topics that have long been central to political science and international relations as academic fields. Historically, such topics have been a minority interest within nation branding research, perhaps reflecting that the leading journals of the field, *The Journal of Brand Management* and *Place Blanding and Public Diplomacy* have been primarily marketing focused. Fan (2010, p. 101), for instance, found that only 35% of articles on nation branding came from a political science or international relations background. In the next suggestion, I will discuss how theories and concepts from these disciplines, particular from political economy, might be integrated within nation branding research, and the opportunities this might unlock for nation branding research.

BRINGING THE POLITICAL INTO NATION BRANDING

If it is accepted, then, that the future of nation branding research involves drawing more heavily on the political science and international relations, the question arises as how concepts from these fields can be best applied to study nation branding. In this regard, the example set by political marketing when studying the marketing of policies and candidates in elections is instructive. The situation of party's and politicians competing for votes is in many ways more closely analogous to the marketing activities of firms, compared to nation-states engaged in marketing themselves internationally (Pich & Newman, 2020). In an election campaign, political parties are in direct competition with each other, "selling" a vision of the country to voters and trying to attract votes(Cwalina et al., 2000). Political parties as organizations and politicians as individuals also clearly have "brands" they are associated with and which they have to manage in a similar way to corporations and CEOs (Pich & Newman, 2020; Scammell, 2015). Yet despite the parallels between political marketing and commercial marketing, political marketing researchers have generally been quite disciplined in not overestimating the similarities. Instead, as early as 1996, Lock and Harris argued that "the assumption of direct transferability of marketing theory and applications [to politics] seems to us to be questionable" (Lock & Harris, 1996, p. 16) and this viewpoint has come to enjoy widespread assent within the literature. Political marketing researchers have been at pains to identify the unique features of electoral competition including, the winner takes all nature of many contests, the absence of a direct cost of purchase for voters, the highly unspecified nature of the "product" (given political parties rarely spell out their policies in detail before elections), and the temporal dimension of all nearly voting happening on election day. Based on this analysis, they have successfully specified the boundaries and dimensions of political marketing as a field, discounted marketing tools not relevant to politics, and developed specialized concepts and frameworks to study political marketing activity. In so doing, they have placed political marketing research on a more solid conceptual foundation and answered the doubts of sceptics who are distrustful on the relevance of marketing concepts within political life. When considering how nation-states engage in branding activities, researchers would be wise to follow this example, discounting prospects of direct transferability and instead being explicit at what makes states different than other organizations engaged in branding activities.

One important question to ask in this regard is exactly how far states "own" the brand identity of their nation. Whereas corporations clearly do have an intimate association with their corporate brands, and political parties tend to be inseparable from specific brand identities, the relationship of a state to the symbols, idioms, and mental pictures of a nation can be more ambivalent. To illustrate this, let us imagine an American man drinking a McDonalds milkshake, wearing a "Make America Great Again" hat and tattooed with the famous "don't tread on me" Gadsen emblem of the American revolution. The golden arches on his cup indicate the man's patronage of the McDonalds Corporation. His "MAGA" hat makes clear his support for Donald Trump. His tattoo on the other hand, while undeniably a part of the American national brand, does not make a clear signal of his support for the actions of the American state. On the contrary, it could signal a spirit of antigovernment libertarianism which, while deeply American is profoundly hostile to the state (Gershtenson & Plane, 2015).

On the other hand, we might imagine a Chinese woman using a Huawei tablet and wearing a shirt emblazoned with the flag of the People's Republic of China. In this case, the flag sends a different signal about her relationship to the state. That flag, while a symbol of the Chinese nation, is also the symbol of the Chinese Communist party and intimately associated with the regime that it established. The Huawei logo, also, arguably has a different connotation. The logo is a symbol of a great Chinese company, just as the golden arches is of an American company, but in a business environment where corporations rely much more intimately on state patronage and direction, support for Huawei arguably indicates more tacit support for the Chinese state than, for example, displaying the apple logo would (Wright, 2010).

What these examples attest to is that the context in which states engage in nation branding differs depending on the kind of state-society relations which exist in a particular nation. In contexts where the state has portrayed itself as the embodiment of the nation, it may possess a greater level of ownership of national images and symbols, and therefore control over the national brand. This is not simply a matter of authoritarianism vs liberal democracy. Within democratic states, the level of connection between the state and national identity can take varied forms. That relationship depends on many factors, such as political attitudes toward state-involvement in the economy, levels of administrative capacity and centralization, and the strength and organization of civil-society relations. A vast literature on state-society relations within political science has sought to analyze and describe these variations. This is a literature which nation branding researchers may find useful to draw on more when considering how state branding activities work.

Closely related to state-society relations is the issue of state-business relations and the degree to which companies choose to draw on national imagery in their own branding strategies. From the outset of nation branding research, it has been recognized that there is transfer of imagery between national and corporate brands. Yet this transfer is not unidirectional, and it is often the aggregated individual branding strategies of corporations that shape the direction of the national brand (Beverland et al., 2021; He et al., 2020). To take the case of the United States once again, it is hard to deny that the role of corporate icons like Apple, Facebook, Amazon, and Microsoft in shaping the global reputation of the US as a center of innovation. Such accumulated branding activity is at least as important as any direct state-led campaigns of nation branding. Indeed, it has been argued that in the neoliberal period, with the declining significance of state-owned enterprises within western countries, it is now corporations, much more than governments who define the images of nations in the global economy (LLorac, 2023). Given this, a critical question is how far states can exert influence over a country's major corporations so as to coordinate their branding strategies. How far states can exert such influence may depend on many factors including the structure of corporate governance in different societies, traditional attitudes concerning the role of the state, how far industrial associations can coordinate the activities of their members, and how far major companies are internationalized vs nationalized in their culture and growth strategy.

Paying attention to state-society and state-business relations may be important to explaining the relative prevalence and effectiveness of nation branding efforts. It is particularly worth noting that South Korea, arguably the most prominent example of deliberate nation branding, is widely regarded as having possessed a "developmental state." This state model, associated with many states in east Asia, is one in which the state is expected to guide the process of economic development through industrial strategies, and exerts strong influence on the nation's companies often through informal networks. It stands in contrast to more neoliberal modes of governmentality where the state's economic role is understood to lie in maintaining the infrastructure for the economy, and then leaving it to free competition between firms to determine the economy's direction. Political economists are divided into how far South Korea's developmental state remained in operation by the 21st industry, yet many would say that at least elements of it remain; in particular the "Chalebol" large industrial groupings that dominate the economy (Dannita & Deniar, 2021). Some efforts have been made to link these vestiges of South Korea's developmental state to its practices of nation branding (Schmuck, 2011). Building on this through studies of nation branding in other nations with a history of developmental states might yield more generalizable insights in how state-structures.

These considerations of state-society/state-business relations also link to the issue of understanding state strategy. Research within International Political Economy, particularly as regards neomercantilism in the contemporary global economy and growth models in macroeconomic policy, points to the wide variety of industrial strategies different states deploy in an effort to secure advantageous positions in global value chains (Hauge, 2020; Nem Singh, 2023). From Resource-Based Industrialization (RBI) strategies in many developing countries, to inward-investment diversification strategies which have become prominent in many gulf states, to export-oriented policies of manufacturing powerhouses, different states pursue many different routes to economic growth, conditioned both by their position in existing supply chains and the structure of their various political economies (Cherif & Hasanov, 2024; Neilson et al., 2020). Such industrial strategies potentially have important implications for nation branding, and it is perhaps against these industrial strategies and their objectives that the success or failure of nation branding campaigns.

To properly understand the strategic goals of states, there is a need for nation branding researchers to draw more on ideas within international relations concerning the different positioning of states within the international systems. Research on this topic is of course vast, spanning from neorealist approaches which assign states a central place in the global order (or disorder), to neoliberal and constructivists approaches which question the boundaries between state and non-state actors in shaping international events. To pick up one popular theme within current International Relations literature, there is likely scope to explore more the distinctive positioning of small states vs great powers in the world order and their significance for nation branding(Armen Sarkissian, 2024; Baldacchino, 2023). Great Powers tend to have much greater ambitions in terms of reshaping global supply chains to pursue their strategic interests (Weiss & Thurbon, 2021). They also have larger, more diverse economies, which may be more difficult to fit into coherent national brands and are much more likely to engage in largescale military conflicts which undoubtedly have powerful effects on national image. In a world of great power rivalry, they are also more likely to face concerted efforts by other powers to damage their international reputation, and thus face distinctive challenges in maintaining brand integrity. Small states, by contrast tend to have more limited objectives, involving fitting into global supply chains and alliance systems, and carving out specialized niches for their companies in global markets. Often only able to be internationally competitive in a few sectors, the brand identity can often be more tightly focused. These differences may suggest different challenges and opportunities affect nation branding in small or large states, respectively.

By locating nation branding activities within the distinctive political economies of different states and their wider industrial and soft-power strategies, researchers should be able to gain new insights into the formation and effect of nation branding strategies. To illustrate this, it may be useful to briefly consider what a consideration of these factors might look like when applied to some of the major national case studies within nation branding research.

Great Powers and Nation Branding: The Case of the US and China

One major area where there is a growing need for nation branding research is in the context of US-China strategic rivalry. As arguably the world's only two economic superpowers, the US and China have an unmatched level of exposure in terms of their national brands (Anholt & Hildreth, 2004; Loo & Davies, 2006; Rawson, 2007; Sun, 2007). Their relationship over the past decade has been characterized by escalating tension. China's economic rise, and ambitions in high-tech industries such as Biotech, artificial intelligence, and aerospace have become widely seen as a threat in American circles; an anxiety further heightened by accusations of Chinese industrial espionage and distortionary trade practices (Liu & Woo, 2018). The result has been first the US-China trade war launched by the Trump administration, and increasingly a "tech-war" with Chinese and American companies racing to dominate the high-tech industries of the future. In this competition, penetration of international markets and thus the global reputation of the US and China is an important consideration. There is thus a need to understand nation branding as a component of US and Chinese general soft-power strategies.

From China's point of view, a central objective of state strategy for the last decade has been transforming the country from a center of cheap, labor-intensive manufacturing to a center of innovation and high value-added production (Chao, 2023). This requires not only a material transformation of the Chinese economy but also a transformation of China's image in the world. Two strategies have been central to this. Firstly the "Made in China 2025" initiative – an industrial strategy aiming to make China a leader in 10 strategic high-technology sectors – and the "Belt and Road" initiative; an infrastructure development strategy which aims to partner with foreign governments to build infrastructure across much of Eurasia (Ittefaq et al., 2023; Li, 2018). It is important to recognize that these campaigns are in part exactly the kind of "symbolic actions" aimed at changing the perception and narrative of a country's place in the world that form a core part of nation branding activities. Therefore, when studying Chinese nation branding activities, I would argue, it is increasingly to these campaigns that scholars should look.

Such work has increasingly been done regarding Belt and Road, yet there has been less consideration of the nation branding implications of Made-in-China 2025. This is significant, as arguably it is Made in China 2025, which runs more directly against China's brand-image as more of a low-middle value manufacturer. The very slogan "Made in China" arguably indicates policymakers are still thinking in quite conventional terms about manufacturing, envisaging China as the sole *location* for production rather than Chinese firms as managers of distributed value chains spanning global networks. Much of the rhetoric around Made in China 2025 also arguably fails to recognize the main perception problems that have concern investors and potential partners about China; the idea that China is excessively focused on dominating production locally and willing to violate the international property of foreign companies to do so. Certainly, US diplomats have been able to present Made in China 2025 in this regard, and this has had significant implications for how China is perceived internationally, with many states introducing more investment screening for Chinese companies and adopting industrial strategies explicitly aimed at containing China(Chhetri, 2022; Le Corree, 2020). "Made in China 2025" could thus very plausibly be viewed as a case where poor-branding strategy has backfired against a great power.

In the meantime, the United States has had to face the reputational fallout associated with the Trump years. Discussion of American soft-power have often centered on the failure of US to "live the brand" – pursuing policies and rhetoric in conflict with stated American values of tolerance, democracy, and respect for national sovereignty (Anholt & Hildreth, 2004; Rawson, 2007). An important example of this, is how the negative reception of the Iraq War and other US military interventions, has eroded global perceptions of the US. Trump's controversial presidency arguably represents a continuation of this issue and there is certainly evidence that he has damaged American soft power. During his term, for instance, the US fall from 1st to 8th in the Anholt-Ipsos index. In many ways however, the more striking picture is how resilient the American brand has proved despite these many controversies. In absolute terms on the Anholt-Ipsos index, the US declined very little in the Trump years and according to the Brand-finance nation-brand index, it did not decline at all. This likely reflects how both the global reach of many US companies and the porous nature of American politics allows firms to act with considerable autonomy from the state (Dubinsky, 2023). The degree of distance that icons of US capitalism have been able to keep from the US government is likely a source of resilience for the US national brand, even if it makes it less easy to deploy that brand in the service of US soft power.

The impact of COVID-19 on both American and Chinese national brands has also been significant and the response of both states to the crisis reveals much about their respective approaches to nation branding. While facing the prospect of severe reputational damage as the origin point for the crisis, China made great efforts to engage in vaccine diplomacy; attempting to showcase both the countries technological prowess in developing a vaccine, and its generosity in providing vaccines and medical equipment throughout the developing world (Lee, 2023). By contrast, American efforts at vaccine diplomacy were generally perceived to be lackluster, and perceptions of "vaccine hording" by the US arguably played in to long-standing resentments of the country as a "selfish" global actor (Cull, 2023). Despite the arguable success of its vaccine diplomacy however, China's attempt to demonstrate the efficiency of its system with a "zero covid" strategy appears to have overreached, producing high-profile economic disruption and national protests that have dented the country's image for ruthless efficiency. In these ways, the COVID-19 appears to have significantly impacted on both the US and China's national brands.

The recent response of the American State both to China and the COVID-19 pandemic, in the form of the "Build Back Better" campaign represents another interesting attempt at great power nation branding. Originating as a Biden election slogan concerning proposed responses to COVID-19, it then became a key framework for the Biden administrations economic strategy and particularly its investment in infrastructure and green technologies. From there it has been applied internationally in the "Build Back Better World" program, a global infrastructure program widely interpreted as a counter to the Belt and Road. The Build Back better program focuses heavily on quality infrastructure and environmental sustainability, implying the creation of a "better" quality systems than existed before COVID-19, or through Belt and Road. An interesting feature of the strategy is how it aims to address key weaknesses within the US's national brand. As the home of both Silicon Valley and Wall-street, the US's reputation for technology and finance is dominant. Yet the country's reputation for infrastructure and for manufacturing has lagged somewhat, compared to states such as Japan, China, or Germany. The Build Back Better program thus seems in many ways well-selected to remedy core weaknesses within the US national brand. However, the structure of the American state, the relatively loose ties between the state and American corporations, and the polarization of American politics have made it difficult for this campaign to have the reach or salience of "Made in China 2025" or the Belt and Road initiative (Rine, 2022).

The competitive nation branding of the US and China reflects several factors distinctive about great-powers. While the scale and resources of such powers gives high exposure, and therefore strong opportunities to engage in nation branding activities, this can also mean that current perceptions are deep-set and difficult to change. Moreover, just as large corporations or political parties know that their branding strategies will be reacted to and counteracted by rivals, so great powers must be prepared for efforts by their rivals to weaken or disrupt perceptions of the national brand.

Middle Powers and Nation Branding

In comparison with great powers, middle powers have less hope of shaping the global order as well as less global exposure with which to brand themselves. They can sometimes use to dramatic actions to signal changes in their economic strategy, yet such actions tend to come with heavy risks.

A contemporary case that illustrates this strongly is the United Kingdom. The UK is widely recognized as having an extremely powerful national brand relative to its size, stemming in part from British history and heritage and also from the success of powerful internal brands such as the BBC, the city of London and British universities, especially Oxbridge (Lomer et al., 2016). Yet the impact of Brexit – with Britain hurtling out of the world's largest trading block – marks an interesting case study of how far political decisions can disrupt an otherwise successful national brand. The UK government made a concerted to define Brexit positively, less as a protectionist retreat from Europe as an opportunity to forge more commercial links with the wider world. The well-publicized slogan of "Global Britain," accompanied by liberalizing movements to create "free-ports" for international trade and a reorganization of the UK foreign policy bureaucracy to produce greater linkages between diplomacy and trade promotion. The impact of this program is debatable. There is certainly evidence that Brexit has impacted negatively on Britain's global brand, the UK something a 14% drop in Brand finances "Nation Brand" Index during the Brexit negotiations in 2019 (Brand-Finance, 2020). However, similar to the impact of Trump in the US, there is also evidence of considerable resilience for the British national brand. Since Brexit, Britain has regained ground on most nation-brand indexes, retaining the 5th most powerful nation brand in the world according to the Brand finance index (2020) and the 4th in the Anholt Nation Brand index (Visit-Britain 2023). There is however little evidence so far of a major revaluation of Britain by non-European markets (such as the US, Commonwealth countries, or the wider Asia-Pacific) that the "Global Britain" campaign was aimed at achieving.

The lack of cut-through by the Global Britain campaign, despite the dramatic events surrounding Brexit, may be reflective of numerous factors. Firstly, the "Global Britain" branding only ever had limited buy-in from British businesses. Both the British Chamber of Commerce (2024) and the Confederation of British Industry (2021) running campaigns in concert with the governments "Global Britain" strategy, but these campaigns have been relatively subdued. Secondly, "Global Britain" had its origins in the Brexiteer campaign against the European Union, and had thus been much derided by the Remainer opposition to Brexit. Such a campaign was thus likely to have limited support across British society given the polarization that Brexit had caused. The case of post-Brexit nation branding, then, is perhaps an illustration of the difficulty in promoting a coherent national image in the context of strong political polarization.

Smaller States and Nation Branding

Compared to the often-mixed results attached to larger states efforts at nation branding, smaller states often stand out for their successful cultivation of distinctive national brand (Browning, 2015). This may in part reflect the stakes involved. Most small states are acutely aware of their dependence on international trade, and conscious of the need to maintain positive relations with international partners. In comparison with larger powers, they automatically have little exposure in international media and thus have limited opportunities to build or reshape their image in the minds of international consumers or investors. They therefore face distinctive obstacles and must act strategically to promote their people, locations, and companies.

One common theme is for smaller states to rely upon anchoring industries or sectors in which they specialize and to build their broader appeal based on those industries. Denmark, for instance, is a world leader in wind energy, with the Danish company Vestas being the largest wind turbine manufacturer globally. This promotes a general image of Denmark as a high-innovation and environmentally conscious state, and Danish nation branding efforts have sought to reinforce this by emphasizing sustainability as theme (Frig & Sorsa, 2020). Similarly, New Zealand's close association with agriculture exports has encouraged those promoting New Zealand to emphasize a "Clean and Green" as seen in initiatives such as the 100% pure New Zealand campaign. It may be that, since small states tend to lack substantial heavy industry, it is easier to present a positive environmental image, encouraging small states to specialize in such brands (Lebdioui, 2024).

Other small states have used similar techniques to market themselves as commercial hubs opening access to larger regional economies. Major example of this includes Singapore and Qatar, and there are interesting parallels between the approaches these states have taken to build their national brands. Notably both states have invested heavily in state-owned national airlines which play a major role in marketing the country to international gatekeepers. The internal focus on cleanliness, public order, and hospitality within Singapore and Qatar have likewise serve to reinforce their reputation as commercial hubs.

Another common strategy for nation branding and public diplomacy in smaller states is to use regional associations to amplify their exposure. This has been an important phenomenon among Caribbean states, in the pacific and in southern

Africa. The risks of such an approach are twofold, however. There is firstly the possibility that the nations' distinctive identity will be eclipsed. Then there is the risk of being drawn into stances on controversial global issues which could alienate major countries. Mogensen (2024) has argued, using the example that small states can reduce reputational risk, by instead pursuing bilateral innovation partnerships with other states – channeled through consortiums of government, university, and private sector actors. Such consortiums can then become venues in which the branding strategies of different states can interact and potentially be reworked. A good example of this, cited by Morgensen, is a Danish-Chinese consortium being advertised as "from Made in China, to created with China." This also perhaps illustrates why large states in an effort to refine and develop their own branding strategies may find it useful to participate in such bilateral with smaller states.

Contrasting these different cases illustrate that nation branding ought not be viewed as a monolithic activity, or as isolated from the larger world of statecraft. Instead, the approaches to branding that nation-states pursue depend deeply on the broader economic/industrial strategies that make sense given their international position, as well as on the nature of the branding resources they can mobilize given the structure of state-society relations. In other words, political considerations both international and domestic strongly influence the direction nation branding takes. By attending to the structure, position, and strategies of states, researchers may be able to ascertain the strengths and limitations of nation branding efforts more effectively.

CONCLUSION: NATION BRANDING AS A COMPONENT OF INTERNATIONAL POLITICAL MARKETING?

This chapter has discussed the evolution of nation branding research in the past two decades and has suggested that the field is moving toward greater engagement with the *political* dimensions of branding nation-states. It has specifically suggested that nation branding research should pay greater attention to state-society relations, state development strategy, and state positioning in the international system. Such an agenda might see nation branding following the path of political marketing as a field and becoming increasingly integrated within the discipline of political science. Should this occur, it is worth considering what prospects there might be for greater dialog between nation branding and political marketing research. Political marketing has primarily been concerned with the marketing of politicians, parties, and policies within electoral competition, and is thus associated more with domestic politics. Nation branding and public diplomacy, meanwhile, fits more immediately into international politics, and is thus may seem somewhat separated from the core concerns of political marketing. Yet, it has long been recognized that domestic and international politics are not cleanly separated. Instead, political actors must play a "two-level game," simultaneously marketing themselves to domestic electorates while being mindful of their image (and the image of their nation) with a global audience. Images of nations meanwhile are not produce purely for international consumption but are often aimed at domestic nation-building. There is consequently a substantial area of crossover between nation branding and political marketing, and even a case for seeing nation branding as a specific type of political marketing.

A natural place for dialog between these fields to start might be in the work to construct frameworks for International Political Marketing. Sun and Harris (2020), building on early work by Sun (2007, 2008), have proposed a tripartite model in which political marketing takes place across three domains. The first of these is electoral political marketing (EPM) in which parties and candidates market themselves to voters and interest groups. The second is governmental political marketing (GPM), in which leaders and governments market their agenda to citizens and interest groups. The third is international political marketing (IPM) in which governments market themselves to international organizations and to foreign subjects. Using this schema, we might regard nation branding as an element within both IPM and GPM activities. New governments and leaders within nation-states inherit an association with the existing national brand (as well as the machinery of public diplomacy engaged in nation branding). They then must make decisions about how (or weather) to make use of national brands and integrate them with their own distinctive brand identities. In so doing, they are simultaneously having to consider the impacts of their activity on their EPM strategy, and through their actions, they potentially restructure or reimagine the national brand itself.

Conceiving of nation branding as linked to political marketing in this way has the potential to open up new research avenues for both fields. For political marketing researchers, it may provide a scaffolding to conceptualize how and why politicians employ images of the nation within their political campaigns. For nation branding researchers, it may provide a means to interrogate more closely, the role of leaders, politicians, and parties in shaping perceptions of nations. This might involve a closer consideration of domestic political campaigns as instances of nation branding, and more consideration of the contested and politicized nature of national identity. In these ways, cross-fertilization between nation branding and political marketing may ultimately open new research avenues for both fields.

REFERENCES

Anholt, S. (1998). Nation-brands of the twenty-first century. *Journal of Brand Management, 5*, 395–406.

Anholt, S. (2004). Editorial. *Place Branding, 1*(1), 4–11. https://doi.org/10.1057/palgrave.pb.5990001

Anholt, S. (2007). *Competitive identity the new brand management for nations, cities and regions*. Palgrave Macmillan.

Anholt, S. (2010). *Places, identity, image and reputation*. Palgrave Macmillan.

Anholt, S. (2020). *The good country equation: How we can repair the world in one generation*. Berrett-Koehler Publishers.

Anholt, S., & Hildreth, J. (2004). *Brand America: The mother of all brands*. Cyan.

Baldacchino, G. (2023). *The success of small states in international relations*. Routledge. https://doi.org/10.4324/9781003314745

Beaumont, P., & Towns, A. E. (2021). The rankings game: A relational approach to country performance indicators. *International Studies Review, 23*(4), 1467–1494. https://doi.org/10.1093/isr/viab017

Behringer, J., & van Treeck, T. (2022). Varieties of capitalism and growth regimes: The role of income distribution. *Socio-Economic Review, 20*(3), 1249–1286. https://doi.org/10.1093/ser/mwab032

Beverland, M. B., Eckhardt, G. M., Sands, S., & Shankar, A. (2021). How brands craft national identity. *Journal of Consumer Research, 48*(4), 586–609. https://doi.org/10.1093/jcr/ucaa062

Browning, C. (2015). Small-state identities: Promotions past and present. In *Histories of public diplomacy and nation branding in the Nordic and Baltic countries* (pp. 281–300). Brill | Nijhoff. https://doi.org/10.1163/9789004305496_015

Buhmann, A. (2016). *Measuring country image, theory, method and effects*. Springer.

Cai, C. W. (2020). Nudging the financial market? A review of the nudge theory. *Accounting and Finance, 60*(4), 3341–3365. https://doi.org/10.1111/acfi.12471

Chao, J. (2023). The visual politics of Brand China: Exceptional history and speculative future. *Place Branding and Public Diplomacy, 19*(3), 305–316. https://doi.org/10.1057/s41254-022-00270-6

Cherif, R., & Hasanov, F. (2024). The pitfalls of protectionism: Import substitution vs. xport-oriented industrial policy. *Journal of Industry, Competition and Trade, 24*(1), 14. https://doi.org/10.1007/s10842-024-00414-9

Chhetri, P. S. (2022). Contemporary transformations in the European Union–Germany–China relations. *International Studies, 59*(3), 212–233. https://doi.org/10.1177/00208817221092839

Choi, D., & Kim, P. S. (2014). Promoting a policy initiative for nation branding: The case of South Korea. *Journal of Comparative Asian Development, 13*(2), 346–368. https://doi.org/10.1080/10548408.2014.926804

Cull, N. J. (2023). From soft power to Reputational Security. In *Soft power and the future of US foreign policy* (pp. 100–120). Manchester University Press. https://doi.org/10.7765/9781526169136.00011

Cwalina, W., Falkowski, A., & Kaid, L. L. (2000). Role of advertising in forming the image of politicians: Comparative analysis of Poland, France, and Germany. *Media Psychology, 2*(2), 119–146. https://doi.org/10.1207/S1532785XMEP0202_2

Dannita, S., & Deniar, S. (2021). The Chaebol's contribution on South Korea nation branding through Korean wave. *Satwika: Kajian Ilmu Budaya dan Perubahan Sosial, 5*(2), 317–336. https://doi.org/10.22219/satwika.v5i2.17609

Dinnie, K. (2008). *Nation branding: Concepts, issues, practice*. Butterworth-Heinemann.

Dubinsky (2023). Sports, brand America and U.S public diplomacy during the presidency of Donald Trump. *Sports, Brand America and U.S Public Diplomacy during the presidency of Donald Trump, 19*(167–180), 167–180.

Fan, Y. (2010). Branding the nation: Towards a better understanding. *Place Branding and Public Diplomacy, 6*(2), 97–103.

Friedman, T. (2005). *The world is flat: A brief history of the twenty-first century*. Farrar, Straus and Giroux.

Frig, M., & Sorsa, V.-P. (2020). Nation branding as sustainability governance: A comparative case analysis. *Business and Society, 59*(6), 1151–1180. https://doi.org/10.1177/0007650318758322

Gershtenson, J., & Plane, D. L. (2015). In government we distrust: Citizen Skepticism and democracy in the United States. *The Forum, 13*(3). https://doi.org/10.1515/for-2015-0029

Gigerenzer, G., & Brighton, H. (2009). Homo Heuristicus: Why biased minds make better inferences. *Topics in Cognitive Science, 1*(1), 107–143. https://doi.org/10.1111/j.1756-8765.2008.01006.x

Hamlin, R., Knight, J., & Cuthbert, R. (2016). Niche marketing and farm diversification processes: Insights from New Zealand and Canada. *Renewable Agriculture and Food Systems*, *31*(1), 86–98. https://doi.org/10.1017/S1742170514000489

Hao, A. W., Paul, J., Trott, S., Guo, C., & Wu, H.-H. (2019). Two decades of research on nation branding: A review and future research agenda. *International Marketing Review*, *38*(1), 46–69.

Hauge, J. (2020). Industrial policy in the era of global value chains: Towards a developmentalist framework drawing on the industrialisation experiences of South Korea and Taiwan. *The World Economy*, *43*(8), 2070–2092. https://doi.org/10.1111/twec.12922

He, J., Wang, C. L., & Wu, Y. (2020). Building the connection between nation and commercial brand: An integrative review and future research directions. *International Marketing Review*, *38*(1), 19–35. https://doi.org/10.1108/IMR-11-2019-0268

Ittefaq, M., Ahmed, Z. S., & Martínez Pantoja, Y. I. (2023). 'China's Belt and Road initiative and soft power in Pakistan: An examination of the local English-language press. *Place Branding and Public Diplomacy*, *19*(1), 1–14. https://doi.org/10.1057/s41254-021-00212-8

Kahneman, D. (2003). Maps of bounded rationality: Psychology for behavioral economics. *The American Economic Review*, *93*(5), 1449–1475. https://doi.org/10.1257/000282803322655392

Kaneva, N. (2011). Nation branding: Towards an agenda for critical research. *International Journal of Communication*, *5*.

Kaneva, N. (2021). Nation branding in the post-communist world: Assessing the field of critical research. *Nationalities Papers*, *49*(5), 797–807. https://doi.org/10.1017/nps.2020.106

Kaneva, N., Dolea, A., & Manor, I. (2023). Public diplomacy and nation branding in the wake of the Russia–Ukraine War. *Place Branding and Public Diplomacy*, *19*(2), 185–189. https://doi.org/10.1057/s41254-022-00293-z

Knight, J. (2014). *Homo Heuristicus and the (mis) perception of Risk*. University of Otago.

Knight, J. G., Clark, A., & Mather, D. W. (2013). Potential damage of GM crops to the country image of the producing country. *GM Crops and Food*, *4*(3), 151–157. https://doi.org/10.4161/gmcr.26321

Korten, D. (1998). When corporations rule the world. *European Business Review*, *98*(1).

Le Corree, P. (2020). *The EU's new defensive approach to a rising China*.

Lebdioui, A. (2024). *Survival of the greenest*. Cambridge University Press. https://doi.org/10.1017/9781009339414

Lee, K.-M. (2011). Toward nation branding systems: Evidence from brand Korea development. *Journal of International and Area Studies*, *18*(1), 1–18.

Lee, S. T. (2023). Vaccine diplomacy: Nation branding and China's COVID-19 soft power play. *Place Branding and Public Diplomacy*, *19*(1), 64–78. https://doi.org/10.1057/s41254-021-00224-4

Li, L. (2018). China's manufacturing locus in 2025: With a comparison of "Made-in-China 2025" and "Industry 4.0". *Technological Forecasting and Social Change*, *135*, 66–74. https://doi.org/10.1016/j.techfore.2017.05.028

Liu, T., & Woo, W. T. (2018). Understanding the U.S.-China trade war. *China Economic Journal*, *11*(3), 319–340. https://doi.org/10.1080/17538963.2018.1516256

Lomer, S., Papatsiba, V., & Naidoo, R. (2016). Constructing a national higher education brand for the UK: Positional competition and promised capitals. *Studies in Higher Education*. https://doi.org/10.1080/03075079.2016.1157859

LLorac, R. (2023). *Le Roman National des Marques: Le Nouvel Imaginaire Francais [The National Story of Brands: The New French Imagination]*. Editions De L'Aube/Fondation Jean Jaures.

Lock, A., & Harris, P. (1996). Political marketikng – Vive La difference. *European Journal of Marketing*, *30*, 28–96.

Loo, T., & Davies, G. (2006). Branding China: The ultimate challenge in reputation management? *Corporate Reputation Review*, *9*, 189–210.

Manor, I. (2021). The Russians are laughing! The Russians are laughing! How Russian diplomats employ humour in online public diplomacy. *Global Society*, *35*(1), 61–83. https://doi.org/10.1080/13600826.2020.1828299

Mogensen, K. (2024). Branding a small state as an innovation business partner. *Place Branding and Public Diplomacy*. https://doi.org/10.1057/s41254-024-00335-8

Neilson, J., Dwiartama, A., Fold, N., & Permadi, D. (2020). Resource-based industrial policy in an era of global production networks: Strategic coupling in the Indonesian cocoa sector. *World Development*, *135*, 105045. https://doi.org/10.1016/j.worlddev.2020.105045

Nem Singh, J. T. (2023). The advance of the state and the renewal of industrial policy in the age of strategic competition. *Third World Quarterly*, *44*(9), 1919–1937. https://doi.org/10.1080/01436597.2023.2217766

Nye, J. S. (2004). *Soft power: The means to success in world politics*. Public Affairs.

Olya, H., Kim, N., & Kim, M. J. (2024). Climate change and pro-sustainable behaviors: Application of nudge theory. *Journal of Sustainable Tourism*, *32*(6), 1077–1095. https://doi.org/10.1080/09669582.2023.2201409

Petry, J. (2021). Same same, but different: Varieties of capital markets, Chinese state capitalism and the global financial order. *Competition and Change*,

25(5), 605–630. https://doi.org/10.1177/1024529420964723

Pich, C., & Newman, B. I. (2020). Evolution of political branding: Typologies, diverse settings and future research. *Journal of Political Marketing*, *19*(1–2), 3–14. https://doi.org/10.1080/15377857.2019.1680932

Rasmussen, R. K., & Merkelsen, H. (2014). The risks of nation branding as crisis response: A case study of how the Danish government turned the cartoon crisis into a struggle with globalization. *Place Branding and Public Diplomacy*, *10*(3), 230–248. https://doi.org/10.1057/pb.2014.13

Rawson, E. A. G. (2007). Perceptions of the United States of America: Exploring the political brand of a nation. *Place Branding and Public Diplomacy*, *3*, 213–221.

Ren, M., Chugh, R., & Gao, H. (2024). Fencing or balancing? An exploratory study of Australian and New Zealand exporters' strategic responses during the US-China trade war. *International Marketing Review*. https://doi.org/10.1108/IMR-07-2023-0139

Rine, C. M. (2022). Uncertainty and missed opportunities of build back better. *Health and Social Work*, *47*(2), 85–86. https://doi.org/10.1093/hsw/hlac007

Rodrik, D. (2021). Why does globalization fuel populism? Economics, culture, and the rise of right-wing populism. *Annual Review of Economics*, *13*(1), 133–170. https://doi.org/10.1146/annurev-economics-070220-032416

Rojas-Méndez, J. I., & Khoshnevis, M. (2023). Conceptualizing nation branding: The systematic literature review. *The Journal of Product and Brand Management*, *32*(1), 107–123. https://doi.org/10.1108/JPBM-04-2021-3444

Sarkissian, A. (2024). *The small states club: How small smart states can Save the world*. Hurst.

Sassen, S. (1998). *Globalization and its discontents: Essays on the new Mobility of People and money*. New Press.

Scammell, M. (2015). Politics and image: The conceptual value of branding. *Journal of Political Marketing*, *14*(1–2), 7–18. https://doi.org/10.1080/15377857.2014.990829

Schedelik, M., Nölke, A., Mertens, D., & May, C. (2021). Comparative capitalism, growth models and emerging markets: The development of the field. *New Political Economy*, *26*(4), 514–526. https://doi.org/10.1080/13563467.2020.1807487

Schmuck, A. (2011). Nation branding in South Korea: A modern continuation of the developmental state? In *Korea 2011* (pp. 91–117). BRILL. https://doi.org/10.1163/9789004219359_008

Sun, H. (2007). International political marketing: A case study of its application in China. *Journal of Public Affairs*, *7*(4), 331–340.

Sun, H. (2008). International political marketing: A case study of United States soft power and public diplomacy. *Journal of Public Affairs*, *8*(3), 165–183.

Sun, H., & Harris, P. (2020). Soft power and international political marketing. In *The Palgrave encyclopaedia of interest groups, lobbying and public affairs*. Palgrave Macmillan.

Tijani, A., Majeed, M., Ofori, K. S., & Abubakari, A. (2024). Country branding research: A decade's systematic review. *Cogent Business & Management*, *11*(1). https://doi.org/10.1080/23311975.2024.2307640

Van Ham, P. (2001). The rise of the brand state: The postmodern politics of image and reputation. *Foreign Affairs*, *5*, 2–6.

Varga, S. (2013). The politics of nation branding. *Philosophy and Social Criticism*, *39*(8), 825–845. https://doi.org/10.1177/0191453713494969

Volcic, Z., & Andrejevic, M. (2011). Nation branding in the era of commercial nationalism. *International Journal of Communication*, *5*.

Weiss, L., & Thurbon, E. (2021). Developmental state or economic statecraft? Where, why and how the difference matters. *New Political Economy*, *26*(3), 472–489. https://doi.org/10.1080/13563467.2020.1766431

Wright, T. (2010). *Accepting authoritarianism: State-society relations in China's reform era*. Stanford University Press.

Challenges to Political Marketing: Overcoming Risks When Engaging in Socio-Political Issues

Jennifer J. Griffin

> Business is a very beautiful mechanism to solve problems, but we almost never use it for that purpose. We use it to make money. It satisfies our selfish interest but not our collective interest. (Muhammad Yunus, Nobel Peace Prize Winner)

INTRODUCTION

Firms continually engage in socio-political issues. Either firms adapt to fierce competition and navigate social customs within legal frameworks or cease to exist (Bowen, 1953). Notably, in the last century, manufacturers have added seatbelts in cars, put warning labels on cigarette packages, created renewable energy options and incorporate post-consumer waste packaging materials despite considerable corporate opposition (Allen, 2020; Mahon & McGowan, 1998).

Today's expectations are that CEOs and by extension, their firms, engage in more than episodic electoral politics (Bonardi & Keim, 2005; Keim & Zeithaml, 1986; Lock & Harris, 1996) by weighing in on sensitive social issues and public policies (Public Affairs Council, 2016, 2021, 2022a, 2023; Aon, 2022; Edelman Trust Barometer, 2022a, 2022b, 2023, 2024).

Certainly, doubling down on political marketing – 'a direct transference of (marketing) concepts and tools to the political arena ….(to) communicat(e) with party members, media and prospective sources of funding as well as the electorate' (Lock & Harris, 1996, p. 14) – is one option. Yet, narrowly conceived, short-term, episodic political marketing campaigns targeting an elected audience – might satisfy the firms' interest but not collective interests. As the Yunus quote suggests – businesses can miss the mark by focusing on making money rather than solving problems, unintentionally raising longer-term reputational and regulatory risks.

Recent turmoil at PwC, Disney, Target, Boeing and Anheuser Busch (Bansinath, 2023; Dunn, 2024; Nazzaro, 2023) hold cautionary tales for CEOs, their ill-fated marketing departments and hastily called in corporate affairs functions left to pick up the rubble while trying to re-build corporate reputations. Corporate affairs functions, rather than political marketing teams, are systematically better prepared with repertoires of coherent activities to influence the policy process and steward corporate reputations (Allen, 2020; Australian Centre for

Corporate Public Affairs, 2019; Timmermans, 2024).

This chapter argues that firms considering traditional political marketing campaigns should consult with corporate affairs colleagues and proceed cautiously. Hastily construed political marketing campaigns can backfire spectacularly, inadvertently triggering significant regulatory and reputational ramifications. A political marketing campaign must do more than communicate with party members, the media, citizens and prospective sources of funding. Without an intentional enterprise-level campaign that holistically coordinates the many interests at stake, one-off, siloed, outward-bound political marketing messages can increase enterprise-level risks due to potent misfires (Allen, 2022a, 2022b; Aon, 2022; Edelman Trust Barometer, 2022a, 2022b, 2023; World Economic Forum, 2022).

In short, swift responses through corporate political marketing campaigns are not a panacea for firms engaging in today's socio-political issues. Ameliorating enterprise-level reputational and regulatory risks requires engaging early with corporate affairs colleagues – the focus of this chapter. Corporate affairs executives often have a long-term, impact-oriented, patient capital approach as the public policy process is a complex, competitive arena (Allen, 2020; Griffin & Youm, 2023; Public Affairs Council, 2023). By intentionally focusing on enterprise-wide outcomes benefiting others, beyond merely investors or consumers in this quarter, businesses can be a beautiful mechanism to help solve public problems – as the Yunus quote suggests.

Notably, corporate political marketing campaigns require specialised skills, techniques and capabilities often complementing an integrated corporate affairs function. This is far better than siloed, social media savvy marketing teams that dip a proverbial toe into political marketing campaigns. This chapter elaborates on reputational and regulatory risks in political marketing campaigns (Lock & Harris, 1996) when engaging in modern-day political marketing campaigns. Such campaigns should consider the following principles.

1. Political marketing campaigns must emphasise *ongoing influence* beyond mere electoral politics (Lock & Harris, 1996) since policy and rulemaking also occur during non-election-years. Ongoing influence is critical as a trusted partner. Whereas direct-to-consumer (or direct-to-politician) marketing techniques might emphasise shorter-term, immediate gratification rather than longer-term influence and trust building; an ongoing organisational commitment to sound policy transcends individual CEOs extending beyond popular tactics (i.e. social media and AI).

   Ensuring a whole-of-company perspective is why (political) marketing campaigners should consult with corporate affairs colleagues (Allen, 2020, 2022a, 2022b). In addition, a deep understanding of downside organisational risks (Public Affairs Council, 2023), often secured through CEO commitment (Edmans, 2022), is needed. Without an enterprise-wide perspective, a direct transference of marketing concepts, slogans and tactics into the political arena can backfire with employees often the first to point out the hypocrisies (Johnson & Greening, 1999) or laid off when 'edgy' political marketing tactics go pear-shaped (Nazzaro, 2023).
2. Rather than a singular event (voting) with a winner-take-all metric of success (Lock & Harris, 1996), public policy making is *a complex, issues-rich process* in a long-term, *competitive arena* composed of probabilities not guarantees. Integrating community, policy and political interests requires careful navigation of polarising socio-political issues.

   Corporate affairs professionals are uniquely positioned as trusted advisors with training in issues management (Australian Centre for Corporate Public Affairs, 2019; Bell, 2023; Bell et al., 2023; Fleisher, 2024; Public Affairs Council, 2023). Selectively framing (and re-framing) strategic issues to avoid direct confrontations can decrease risks and enhance upside opportunities (Mahon, 1989). Who, for example, might be against child-proof medicine caps after the Tylenol tampering crisis when pills were laced cyanide? Child-proof caps might have been perceived as an increased cost for an innovative pharmaceutical manufacturer already experimenting with secure containers. Reframing new caps as children's safety helped gain an early advantage for some firms while putting many other industry players on the back foot. Inferred within a complex milieu of contestations are multiple definitions of success (i.e. not being in the headlines; seeing opportunity when others see onerous, costly regulations; speed to market; and common good) that increases organisational effectiveness (Fleisher, 2024; Public Affairs Council, 2023; Timmermans, 2024). This includes, also, a winner-take-all definition of success.
3. Effectiveness through *timely engagement* – means the corporation is an ongoing trusted source of information. Long-standing best practices from corporate affairs functions (Allen, 2020; Mahon & McGowan, 1998) suggests ongoing engagement with employees, community, political- and policy audiences prior to broadcasting political marketing campaigns. Specialised skillsets *to engage* (rather than one-way messages intended *to manage*) influencers, talk back radio, employees, digital and social channels while navigating long-term policy-oriented outcomes might be new terrain for short-term political marketing campaigners.

Public policy making is a long-term game requiring careful consideration of the firm's time and timing in political marketing campaigns. Harmonising corporate strategy aims of 'does it pay?' to remain competitive can create a myopic short-term focus that unintentionally narrows tomorrow's public policy options. Unintentional consequences of short-term, growth-oriented marketing campaigns juxtaposed with long-term, policy outcomes are explored.

4 Political marketing campaigns traditionally feature the firm (Lock & Harris, 1996) not a coalition, whereas policy making affects sectors, communities, countries, constituencies and coalitions not just an individual firm. *Coalitions* – an underutilised tactic in many political marketing campaigns – are explored in the penultimate section.
Gaining safety through numbers means numerous like-minded companies, with a common vision hammered out in advance, can be protected from the backlash of politicised issues. Downside risks, however, loom large if meaningful positions are watered down, unclear, delayed or when members are not held to minimal standards.

In conclusion, practical guidelines to avoid reputational and regulatory pitfalls in modern-day political marketing campaigns suggests collaborating early with experienced corporate affairs colleagues. Coordinating messages can be difficult with veto power often held by the corporate affairs function – the custodians of organisational reputation and government relationships. Conflict can create cumbersome and confrontational relationships. Yet, issues of where authority should lie, if left ambiguous, can create its own set of problems.

All in all, collaborating early with corporate affairs colleagues can overcome the potentially lethal risks. Avoiding hypocritical, one-off, traditional political marketing campaigns thinly disguised as pushing product or buffing up a tattered corporate image is important. At the same time, honing enterprise-wide skills to glean unique, upside opportunities are possible with corporate affairs collaborations (Public Affairs Council, 2023).

POLITICAL MARKETING CAMPAIGNS TARGETING POLITICAL ARENAS: CONSULT WITH CORPORATE AFFAIRS COLLEAGUES

> Politics is a strong and slow boring of hard boards. It takes both passion and perspective. Max Weber[1]

Political marketing campaigns siloed from corporate affairs expertise can create unintended, organisation-wide reputational challenges. Many firms flounder trying to 'deny', 'educate', 'ignore', 'message through', 'control' or 'contain' a political marketing crisis that was intended to appeal to younger generations, especially in growth-oriented enterprises (Caruso, 2023). Target, for example, was caught up in a media frenzy after its PRIDE month displays were targeted by a group of conservatives who provoked employees, leaving Target unprepared for the vitriolic backlash. Without a prompt, corporate-wide response, deployed across all branches with processes backing up Target's social media claims, the company faced condemnation and headline news for multiple weeks (Dunn, 2024). Significant changes were announced a year later (Dunn, 2024).

As the Target backlash demonstrates, companies are often on the back foot not understanding the true impacts of a well-intentioned marketing campaign or how swiftly social media can go awry (Caruso, 2023; Dunn, 2024). Early missteps with slow, siloed responses often make recovery more expensive than if mitigation strategies are set up in the first place (Mitroff et al., 1989; Mahon, 1989).

For Target, the downside organisation-wide reputation risks when political marketing messages go awry can be large, exacerbated by social media posts transcending traditional boundaries. Reputational risks can spread virally impacting ever-larger numbers of consumers, employees and investors which can create a contagion affecting the firm's growth and competitiveness (Edmans, 2022).

While the *intended* audience of a political marketing campaign may be a specific audience (stewarded by the marketing division), the *unintended* consequence of an ill-conceived campaign might affect relationships with journalists, broadsheets and other news-making channels; the local community; public officials; prospective employees and the public. In doing so, the law-abiding company might be dragged into a very public, highly politicised period across multiple communities with mixed messages sent and received (Dunn, 2024; Griffin, 2008, 2016; Nazzaro, 2023).

An integrative approach to communications, political marketing campaigns and public policy engagement (Allen, 2020; Bell, 2023; Harsanyi & Allen, 2017) is needed. Political marketing campaigns targeting political arenas should be mindful of organisation-wide reputational and regulatory consequences. When a firm is rushed or clumsy in public policy initiatives, it risks being branded as politically corrupt (Nyberg, 2021).

Why is it difficult to achieve a holistic organisation-wide perspective? Aligning traditionally siloed marketing, corporate communications and policy interests is fraught with risks. Each department has different aims. A corporation's social media policy, stewarded by corporate communications, might want a rapid response. While policy engagement, the purview of corporate affairs, may collect more data from a different audience. Meanwhile the marketing division tracking real-time consumer sentiments/advertising spend might want a narrow, brand-related response. Each department, developed in isolation without cross-over training, can be stymied when challenged with crafting a coherent, whole-of-company set of responses (Healy & Griffin, 2004). An integrated corporate affairs function draws expertise across these departments to gain early, enterprise-wide buy-in (Allen, 2020, 2022a; Griffin, 2024). Importantly, new chief marketing officers (CMOs) understand the power of social media as a game changer. Many younger CMOs having grown up living in a polarised political world may help bridge these siloed reputational and regulatory gaps (Tanega et al., 2017; Griffin, 2024).

Budgets: Significantly larger marketing budgets can connote 'might makes right' in political marketing campaigns. Corporate affairs departments, operating with a fraction of the marketing budget, can be easily ignored until too late (ACCPA, 2019; Public Affairs Council, 2020, 2022a). Relatively resource-rich in time, treasury and talent, marketing department's larger discretionary budgets might create a sense of invincibility with like-minded affirmation. Yet, it takes practice to meld different interests and outcomes. Integrated corporate affairs functions have a finely honed capability to coordinate – via internal and external corporate communications as well as engaging corporate, policy and political audiences (Allen, 2020).

Legacy: A legacy of poorly managed socio-political issues, even for well-resourced firms with multi-million-dollar marketing budgets, are now classic business school cases: OpenAI with ChatGPT; Enron's market-to-market fraud; BP's spill in the Gulf of Mexico oil spill; Exxon Mobil with the Valdez disaster and tobacco manufacturers denying addictive chemicals were in cigarettes (Griffin et al., 2021; Mahon, 1989; Mahon & McGowan, 1998). Marketing departments with a bevy of adverts and savvy skillsets were likely re-deployed during these crises to target politicians, the media, consumers and citizens. Yet, internal silos separating channels with isolated 'ownership' of audiences can interfere with early recognition of politicised issues that can quickly risk the reputation of the whole company.

Reporting relationships: In the U.S., for example, public policy, stakeholder engagement and communications experts often do not report through marketing. Rather corporate affairs experts might report to legal and general counsel and may not be part of CEOs' top management team (Public Affairs Council, 2020). Coordination costs when conducting political marketing campaigns amidst siloed functions might be significant as gaining clarity of a firm's socio-political aims, interests and positions across the whole enterprise is difficult.

Employees pay the price: Working at cross-purposes despite the best intentions to enhance corporate brand; consumers, investors, board members, employees as well as prospective employees may be easy prey, as the recent Target example showed (Dunn, 2024). In the case of Anheuser Busch's missteps with a political marketing campaign featuring a transgender influencer (Holpuch, 2023), sales plummeted, and employees were laid off (Nazzaro, 2023). Political missteps are also a situation ripe for competitors to exploit (Schuler et al., 2002).

Coordination is costly: Uncoordinated overlap of messages, messengers and channels creates internal confusion if political marketing campaigns are isolated from the stewards of corporate reputation and regulatory affairs (Griffin & Vivari, 2009; Post & Griffin, 1997). Social media experts in a marketing department might curate forward-looking commercial interest through paid advertising, YouTube and Facebook. Meanwhile, corporate communications and public policy experts might be on the back foot responding to incidents and debunking falsehoods via newsletters, traditional print, videos, X, Slack, zooms, WhatsApp, Threads, Instagram and LinkedIn.

Compounding the differences in budgets, legacy issues, reporting relationships, layoffs and coordination costs, the difficulty of crafting a rapid corporate reply can be significantly delayed getting 'everyone' altogether to map out a swift response. The delay can exacerbate or set into motion a crisis.

Rapid responses expected: If silence, or worse hypocritical responses across different markets, ensues it can reverberate loudly as information is the new common currency (Edmans, 2022). Centralised social media policies, for example, might 'solve' ownership and ease coordination issues. Yet, centralisation is problematic when speed is required. Rapid responses across channels to budding socio-political issues puts all external-facing departments of profit-oriented firms in the bulls' eye. Reputational risks are on the line as the costs of building affinity, engaging communities, securing commitments and communicating outcomes in the policy process is non-trivial. The complex, competitive policy process is explored in the next section with a need for coherent issues management strategies.

Public Policy Is a Complex Process in a Competitive Arena Requiring Issues Management Strategies

Political marketing campaigns aimed at short-term (reactive) gains may unintentionally undermine longer-term policy processes. Shaping critical policy issues requires a long-term plan. Consider, for example, the significant winners and losers of past tax and tariff policies. Proactively engaging for ongoing influence in the policy process – is in a firm's best interests and a skillset central to effective issues management strategies (Mahon, 1989: Griffin & Youm, 2018).

Policy and politics have become increasingly complex as publicly listed companies have become larger and more complex. Remarkably, in his Inaugural Address, President Reagan (1981) stated that the 'government is not the solution to our problem; government is the problem .... time to check and reverse the growth of government.' Decades later the scope of regulations increased as new technologies such as artificial intelligence (AI) and relatively new policy issues such cybersecurity, privacy, environmental/energy policy continue apace. Rather than policy solely being an insiders' game, the complexity has encouraged outsiders with voice to join in deliberative processes (Public Affairs Council, 2023).

For example, the controversial U.S. healthcare law, colloquially known as Obamacare, affected numerous sectors, positively and negatively – hospitals, pharmaceutical manufacturers, retailers, insurance companies, prescription drugs, physicians, surgeons, nurses, paediatricians and patient advocates. As a high stakes game, healthcare policy in the United States has many voices wanting to be heard (e.g. https://justfacts.votesmart.org/interest-groups/NA/38). Similarly, as energy policy is promulgated across the 27-common market in the EU, and elsewhere, there will be a wide distribution of winners and losers that changes over time.

One-off political marketing campaigns produced in isolation can create undue organisation-wide reputational and regulatory risks. Collaborating with colleagues, skilled in framing salient issues – a long-standing, core competence of corporate affairs professionals worldwide (Australian Centre for Corporate Public Affairs, 2019; Fleisher, 2024; Public Affairs Council, 2023; Timmermans, 2024) – can alleviate some risks through effective issues management strategies.

Issues Management: Without universal understanding of what makes an issue (or set of seemingly unrelated issues) controversial, sensitive, salient or material ex ante; debunking falsehoods, responding to industry missteps and engaging when others want to impose restrictions (consumer groups, special interests, government agencies) is part of the issues management repertoire (Griffin & Koerber, 2006; Healy & Griffin, 2004; Mahon, 1989). An issue might stem from the perception of serious moral or legal wrongdoing (regulatory risk) or occur when a contrarian stance is taken on a socio-political issue (reputational risk). Importantly, policy issues centred on people and communities (Mitroff et al., 1987) that might attract political marketing campaigners are handled quite differently yet can potentially undermine policy issues of a technical and science-based nature (e.g. tariffs, AI, science-based targets). This nuance in issues management may be overlooked by siloed political marketing campaigns using primarily social media channels.

Understanding how to frame different types of issues, factors leading to issue escalation and various means to defuse or engage constituencies is central to effective issues management (Fleisher, 2024; Mahon, 1989; Mitroff et al., 1987). Selectively choosing the most salient issue, especially during election season, is paramount (Bonardi & Keim, 2005). Corporate affairs regularly engaged with public and political audiences to gather information, choose selective issues, share knowledge and create common understanding are experts at understanding issues management at different stage of the issues life cycle (Allen, 2020; Public Affairs Council, 2020).

Issues Management Life Cycle: The issues management life cycle, a generalised s-shaped curve depicting the trajectory of issues (Mahon, 1989), consists of several steps charting the maturity of an issue and a range of containing, shaping or coping strategies. The earlier managers can identify and understand the true impacts of an issue, the more discretion, fewer resources and better positioned a company can be in containing the issue. If already public, early shaping of an issue is, in general, less expensive than coping with government mandates (Mahon, 1989; Post & Griffin, 1997).

As issues linger, regulatory and reputational risks can multiply creating unequal distributions of costs and benefits (Baron, 2013). Certainly, a firm may wait for clarity with codified rulings (e.g. firms awaiting double materiality guidance from the SEC). In doing so, the firms lose precious time to experiment or shape the regulations during comment periods. Delay makes eventual transitions fraught with increased operational risks. Alternatively, a firm may prefer proactive unilateral actions to forestall federal mandates (Prakash & Griffin, 2012). Without fanfare some firms, for example, deliberately expanded inter-state employee health coverage. This included all employees' healthcare such as treatment for cancer. Notably, this expansion of inter-state healthcare occurred after the Supreme Court overturned federal protections for women's reproductive rights. Subsequently, several states limited access to certain health services for women.

As issues mature and become politicised, ever more stakeholders enter the fray. Achieving cut through often requires a common, longer-term goal, such as national competitiveness rather than individual businesses concerned with specific, protectionist policies. Yet, a political marketing campaign focused on a single firm and a profit motive can fall by the wayside of this national debate.

Early, Coordinated Action to Stymie Others: Proactively managing selective issues by framing (or re-framing) responses to avoid direct confrontations can decrease organisational risks (Mahon, 1989). The Tylenol tampering crisis, for example, left some pharmaceutical manufacturers flatfooted and facing increased packaging costs. Reframing the issue as children's safety helped Tylenol gain an early advantage after the new, industry-wide, tamper-proof cap mandate was passed.

Rather than reactive, individual political marketing campaigns, for example, proactively *engaging with* legal, regulatory and community interests can augment customer sentiments (Kujala et al., 2022). Companies getting on the front foot as accountable, transparent and trusted partners can be an advantage. Yet, authentic engagement with clarity on goals and means. Increasingly, being defensive (reactive), a dilatant in policy arenas, or doing nothing is especially risky (Griffin, 2024).

For example, large firms may prefer more onerous federal regulations that provide consistency across an entire country rather than a patchwork of policies at the state, regional or municipal council levels. Promulgating national policy, however, requires longer-term, collaborative approaches within the organisation that might include strategic forbearance (Andrevski & Miller, 2022) rather than knee-jerk rapid responses from political marketing campaigners. Choosing the appropriate arenas (federal, state deliberative processes; courts; or the court of public opinion) and coordinating messages for complex policy debates is discussed next.

Competitive Arenas: Whereas traditional political marketing campaigns might directly focus on the political arena to communicate with politicians, citizens or funders (Lock & Harris, 1996), many venues are engaged in policy debates. Arenas might include a complicated, multi-level patchwork of legislative and regulatory debates at the state, national or regional levels. Alternatively, community issues might escalate into significant policy issues (Griffin, 2008). Missteps at one level can increase regulatory risks across multiple levels (Bonardi & Keim, 2005; Keim & Zeithaml, 1986; Taneja et al., 2017). Large firms might be squeezed as each country, region, province and municipality can enact laws requiring customised approaches.

For example, there were myriad multi-local responses to women's reproductive rights after the United States Supreme Court 2022 decision struck down *Roe v. Wade*. Legalising cannabis; government-led shutdowns in the face of COVID-19; and marriage equality debates across various countries are additional examples. Advocating for socio-political issues through well-intentional, yet myopic and uncoordinated political marketing campaigns can unintentionally increase organisation-wide and sector-level risks.

During a crisis, risks can be exacerbated if responses are not well-coordinated across an organisation or the sector. Governments, for example, may hope to swoop in and sway public perception if they perceive (rightly or wrongly) there are vulnerabilities to exploit and profits for the taking (i.e. increasing taxes) during a crisis. Responding with a one-off individualised political marketing campaign is not likely to stem the tide or cut-through a competitive political arena – creating an expense rather than an investment.

During the 2008 global financial crisis, for example, the Australian government proposed a 'super profits' resource tax on the mining and extraction sectors. The resources sector effectively fought back in the court of public opinion (with full page ads and other channels) enumerating their commitments to communities throughout the country, catalogued through integrated corporate affairs functions (Allen, 2020) and broadcast through communications and marketing efforts. This effective industry-wide pushback played a role in costing Prime Minister Rudd his job. The firms successfully argued (early in the issues life cycle prior to regulations being promulgated) that you shouldn't kill the goose that laid the golden egg.

All in all, ill-timed political marketing campaigns (whether originated by corporates or politicians) can create regulatory and reputational risks (Bell, 2023; Post & Griffin, 1997). Compounding risks associated with (ill-conceived) time and (inappropriate) timing in complex competitive arenas are highlighted in the next section.

Time and Timing: Compounding Regulatory and Reputational Risks

Issue life cycles are becoming compressed as social media channels indiscriminately overlap across political marketing campaigns and policy efforts. While the news cycle might have once been structured with just a few broadcast channels, the current 24/7/365 breaking news cycle has upended traditional targeted campaigns. Political marketing campaigners collaborating with corporate affairs colleagues – the focus of this chapter – may help alleviate reputational and regulatory risks with a holistic, coordinated approach to early action. If not, the character and identity of the whole business is elevated. But coordination to build trust and reveal true preferences takes time (Griffin, 2024).

Keen awareness of downside risks of a product and brand – certainly not featured in marketing campaigns (e.g. sugary drinks being tied to obesity; negative public health implications of tobacco products or fast-food companies) – must be part of an enterprise-wide reputational risk calculus. Being a fearless leader to identify less than savoury aspects of product perceptions is part of corporate affairs expertise (Fleisher, 2024; Griffin, 2024; Public Affairs Council, 2023).

Moreover, the multiple arenas of policy engagement create more complex regulatory risks. Juxtaposing a desire for swift (corporate) responses with employees being geographically dispersed and working from home extends traditional 9a-5p workdays. Seasonal shareholders meetings (AGM), proxy filings, daily stock prices and annual reports are no longer the main informational tools others. Similarly political marketing campaigns to communicate directly with politicians during election season are passe – political marketing campaigns must regularly connect with relevant audiences on widely salient issues e (Clark et al., 2017).

All in all, traditional political marketing tactics dedicated to narrow audiences during an election season may undermine the ability of the firm to find common ground with others, a necessary condition for favourable public policy outcomes. Focusing managerial attention on salient issues still malleable in the shaping stage allows firms to grapple with naming the issue, forming coalitions, engaging with common interests, blaming others and claiming a viable outcome (Bonardi & Keim, 2005; Mahon, 1989). Actively monitoring widely salient political issues gives the advantage of time to coordinate internal efforts, create coalitions and potentially run table-top scenarios to troubleshoot controversial options (Bonardi & Keim, 2005).

Contrast this gift of time through coordinated, early action with a merciless stock market that monetises political marketing miscalculations with pricing adjustments measured in seconds, minutes, hours or, less frequently, days. Early proactive interventions can be difficult; yet it can build organisation-wide skillsets gleaned from rapid response readiness (Public Affairs Council, 2023). Contrast this organisation-wide readiness culture with siloed reactive engagement through political campaigns and the outcomes can be stark. The 'edgy' political marketing campaigns from Target and Anheuser-Busch were defensive manoeuvres to generate sales from a younger generation of consumers that simply backfired (Bansinath, 2023; Caruso, 2023; Dunn, 2024; Nazzaro, 2023).

Aggressive, short-lived commercial gains at odds with political aims: A large multinational drinks company, for example, after spending millions of dollars developing an advertising campaign targeting teenagers was halted by a CEO in late stage of development on advice from corporate affairs experts due to political sensitivities of underage drinking and responsible drinking. Legally, the drinks company complied with extant laws. The proposed political marketing campaigns, however, were shuttled as they might have ultimately derailed commercial interests by unintentionally causing regulatory and reputational issues. Everyday marketing campaigns, however well-intentioned, may become politicised as political marketing campaigns with the inept organisation tainted as politically corrupt (Nyberg, 2021).

Commercial gains achieved through aggressive marketing behaviours can cast doubts on a firm's claims of authenticity and collaborative nature. The Australian branch of a consulting firm with an admittedly aggressive culture, for example, shared proprietary governmental tax policy insights with other divisions of the consulting firm to gain additional business. In pursuing forward-thinking, aggressive activities aimed at profit maximisation, the consulting firm missed several key points important to deliberative democracy and building trust with the Australian government. When splashed across the headlines, credibility and authenticity, central to policy deliberations, was lost. The consulting firm is now precluded from bidding on governmental work and sold off its government practice to a previous competitor.

As Adam Smith (1776) pointed out, a focus on commercial aims while coordinating collaborative (intra- and inter-organisational) efforts are possible, yet nontrivial. The search for COVID-19 vaccines, for example, demonstrated that common aims, interests and outcomes across public policy, corporate initiatives and marketing campaigns could be complementary as well as competitive. Yet, effectively mobilising coordinated efforts across multiple government agencies, citizens, community groups citizens and large corporations takes concerted time, treasury, talent and leadership (Public Affairs Council, 2020, 2021).

What is a CEO to do? Political marketing campaigns hewing to a single corporate objective (e.g. maximising profits) are increasingly risky narratives for large, visible, multinational branded corporations (Caruso, 2023). Chief executives trained in economics with profits as the end-all objective are quite different than CEOs focused on long-term growth amidst regulatory and reputational risks (Miller & LeBreton-Miller, 2005). Learning can be quick after missteps as CEOs increasingly are let go despite 'do-good' behaviour (Shin et al., 2022).

To avoid unnecessary damage to corporate reputation and undue regulatory risks, this chapter has suggested political marketing campaigners collaborate with corporate affairs colleagues. Intra-organisational coordination is one path forward for businesses wanting to be responsive can engage selectively in socio-political issues (Allen, 2020; Public Affairs Council, 2021). Another might be low stakes inter-organisational collaborations. During COVID-19, for example, a pharmaceutical peak association optimised newsletters for mobile phones, updated progress, shared information and created new outreach channels. Meanwhile, financial service companies created podcasts on financial investing and financial literacy while sharing information with broader sets of constituents.

Multi-stakeholder initiatives, coalitions, industry associations and peak bodies have been growing (Johns Hopkins Report, 2003; Public Affairs Council, 2021, 2023) with 33% growth in nonprofit employment dwarfing private sector trends (Van Dam, 2023). Our current, issues-rich environment has many socio-political and commercial interests that appeal to more than merely consumer-buying interests. Political marketing campaigns that appeal to more than consumption interests, and our collective interests, may be one avenue of growth.

Creating coalitions of common interests is increasingly important as getting caught out on politicised issues as a single firm using profit-motived tools is risky (Public Affairs Council, 2023). The next section outlines the growth of coalitions discussing both the advantages and disadvantages of working in collaboration with others that can complement traditional political marketing campaigns.

Coalitions, Peak Bodies and Industry/ Business Associations

One advantage of coalitions producing political marketing campaigns is a groundswell of support rather than a traditional focus on firm-centric outcomes. Motivating multiple constituencies and broadening audiences can heighten awareness of a widely salient issue moving political marketing campaigns towards non-commercial, collective outcomes. Crucially, coalitions must identify broad-based benefits (i.e. to neighbours or regions) rather than narrow appeals to say, elected politicians or consumers-only, when crafting political marketing campaigns on sensitive issues.

Importantly, a coalition can be a shield for hard messages that might be difficult for an individual company to convey (Public Affairs Council, 2023). Further, coalitions of real people can shield individual companies from being targeted or from retribution. 'The same job, same pay' campaign, for example, encourages discussion on sticky issues such as pay fairness, flexibility, productivity and workplace equity in large and small businesses. In contrast to traditional political marketing campaigns, these coalition-oriented efforts can be effective conduits. Elected officials and regulators might be grateful to meet once with a broad coalition in lieu of multiple individual meetings – leveraging elected politicians time through a collective effort that engages more people by raising one voice.

A coalition allows multiple firms to work out differences, in private, to arrive at a clear message with common goals. The upsides are commonalities before a website is live – as a single, clear message is easier to create cut-through. A clear message resonating with the business community, consumers, regulators and lawmakers is likely broad based and inclusive. In addition, a common message from an industry peak body allows individual firms to also have their own voice (Dolsak et al., 2020, 2022).

Widespread agreement, or subtle differences, on important issues (c.f., minimum wages, climate action), however, are difficult. Coalition members must agree on either the ends or the means with means-agreement generally leading to better performance outcomes (Bourgeois, 1980). Goal-oriented businesspeople, however, focus on common goals leaving the details to be hashed out later on remaining differences. Importantly, as the coalition is accountable to the coalition, rather than a single organisation or an individual CEO, common interests may be more easily attained than within a single company. Common mechanisms to arrive at a desired outcome, however, means trust building that seeks common interests. Yet, coalitions do not always agree, stymieing future political marketing campaigns. As interests diverge, conflicts can increase, meaning that conflict resolution techniques with trusted advisors are cornerstones to collective progress.

In lieu of permanent coalitions, temporary coalitions might be created for a specific purpose/event; thus, crafting effective political marketing campaigns on common interests. Examples include: a COVID-19 healthcare coalition designed around not wearing masks, a coalition created for disaster resilience or a specific issue such as safe communities (e.g. everytown for gun safety). For some organisations, signing up to a coalition may be relatively easy if there are low thresholds for engagement and first mover advantages. The World Economic Forum (2021) coalition on partnering for racial justice in business, for example, had more than 40 large global companies signed up early.[2] Early joiners (founders) received significant media kudos (a homepage link dedicated to 'what founding members are saying'); whereas other companies that waited have missed the opportunity to be recognised. Time will tell if this coalition is temporary or permanent as it addresses a systemic issue.

Disadvantages of Collaborations: As with any voluntary collection of organisations, conflicts around priorities will emerge. Differences in priorities may entail disagreement in investing resources on one item versus others. Relatedly, transparency and accountability on action taken and outcomes achieved are significant in coalitions. As the number of coalitions grows, achieving clarity and coordination in Washington, D.C., for example, where thousands of coalitions might vie for attention on Capitol Hill is non-trivial (Public Affairs Council, 2020, 2021, 2023).

As interests diverge, conflicts increase meaning that conflict resolution and trusted advisors are cornerstones to progress. Fee structures often suggest increased influence through size or market power putting undue pressure on small, less-resourced organisations looking for longer-term cooperative engagement, such as family firms (Youm et al., 2024). Some businesses paying disproportionately larger fees within member-based coalitions might expect the industry association to work for them.

Further, relying on coalitions (by outsourcing political marketing campaigns) can ultimately increase an individual firm's costs. Inside a company, eroding skillsets that limit the leverage of insiders' policy knowledge and relationships might undermine collective efforts. In addition, other companies (rivals) can set the coalition agenda or capture the coalition. Large companies might send lower-level executives, not briefed, not prepared and without clear aims that undermine the coalitions interests.

Alternatively, a coalition that represents all interests might be unwieldly, leaving the members without a voice or alignment. Without a clear message, political marketing campaigns might be non-starters. Alternatively, given discord, a small company may dominate the agenda leveraging for their own self-interests the monies and interests outlined by other companies. Without clear guardrails on resources, narrative and processes of deliberation, coalitions and their political marketing campaigns can become ineffective. Overall, understanding short-term, immediate, and the longer-term objectives of a coalition can help resolve political marketing campaign tensions before escalating into unmanageable conflicts.

WHAT'S NEXT? IMPLICATIONS AND CONCLUSIONS

Corporate marketing campaigns, including political ads, targeting political audiences are neither new nor novel (Lock & Harris, 1996) as near continuous billboards inside Washington D.C. – metropolitan public transit stations suggest. These campaigns are a thriving source of revenue for transit authorities while building awareness of, and acceptance for, a company's stance with the media, citizens and policy and political stakeholders (Lock & Harris, 1996). Yet, targeting mass-market audiences (e.g. employees, consumers, investors, journalists, public officials, tourists riding on the Metro) can be expensive, raising enterprise-wide risks without accomplishing desired outcomes. For example, Boeing's safety lapses and legal troubles with travellers fearful of flying can't be fixed through advertising or marketing campaigns (Klara, 2024).

This chapter suggests that political marketing campaigns should intendedly integrate insights from corporate affairs experts to avoid missteps causing more reputational and regulatory damage. In doing so, campaigns can more effectively shape today's politicised and competitive context without compromising tomorrow's ability to reap continued profits. This chapter suggests that navigating increasingly complex, socio-political issues amidst a variety of competing egos, interests, and institutions (c.f., re-election, power, currying constituent favour, profits) requires more than traditional marketing campaigns focused on building brands by directly transferring marketing 'concepts and tools to the political arena ….(to) communicat(e) with party members, media and prospective sources of funding as well as the electorate' (Lock & Harris, 1996, p. 14).

A poorly executed political marketing campaign can backfire, risking corporate autonomy (Epstein, 1969). Target is just one recent example of significant downside risks (i.e. delays and uncertainty adding expenses to the profit and loss statement. All too often, political marketing is siloed from government relations, communications, investor and employee relations or neighbourhood outreach. This isolates consumer and commercial interests from the interests of regulators, lawmakers, local community members, the public and general counsel that can adversely affect the business (Allen, 2020; Griffin, 2008).

Political marketing campaigns that are tone deaf to the intersection of commercial and widely salient socio-political issues can backfire with unintended regulatory (political) and reputational (commercial) risks. Companies are being called out for being slow, or ineffectual claims and commitments. Dashboard tracking business's progress towards meeting commitments during the Ukraine War (Egan, 2023) as well as public commitments (e.g. ESG, workplace safety, hiring, inequities) can quickly expose corporate rhetoric that doesn't meet current reality.

Reputational risks require careful consideration to avoid backlashes such as the Sackler family's relentless pursuit of profits while aggressively marketing OxyContin, an addictive medicine (Mann & Bebinger, 2022). Similarly, firms' regulatory risks may be compounded when a swift social media reaction might undermine its future voice (Broccardo et al., 2022). Political-, policy- and community pressure may require firms to retract marketing campaigns (e.g. Target). While there is room for risk-taking, regulatory risks are often underexamined (Bryant et al., 2020) despite widespread imitation of risky behaviours (Bryant et al., 2023).

This chapter suggests political marketing campaigns should proceed cautiously and consult with their corporate affairs colleagues. It remains to be seen if firms created within conflict-ridden, digital environments may be better at negotiations, complex relationships and finding common solutions. Firms most comfortable with placid socio-political environments might be less adaptive to uncertainty and volatile socio-political spaces. Similarly, smaller, resource-constrained organisations seeking partnerships with like-minded companies might build supportive ecosystems through coalitions. Expanding their reach through networked ties, these collaborations might hold the competitive dynamic in abeyance while common interests are addressed. Being competitive and collaborative might be a new skillset required of CEOs.

One avenue ripe for exploration are coalitions' use of political marketing campaigns. Collective action through political marketing campaigns that address widely salient issues – too big, too complex or too important for any one firm or one government/nation (c.f., climate action, inequities, AI, human rights in the supply chain/due diligence). These issues can seemingly neither be handled by government, commercial or civic interests alone or kicked down the road. Coalitions, focused on shared aims, interests and public outcomes (e.g. health outcomes), may have an advantage in cutting through the noise with a collective voice. That is, focusing political marketing campaigns on public outcomes without a firm-specific, brand-oriented, commercial interest being monetised might be effective.

In conclusion, what might an integrated political marketing campaign look like in the coming decades? Contrast yesteryear's lobbyists joining the idiosyncratic, stereotypical backroom, closed door, cigar smoking, card playing, whiskey drinking politicos as wheelers and dealers securing our (collective) future. This was quiet politics (Bell et al., 2023). Tomorrow's digital savvy influencers working from home creating video content on widely salient issues spread through social media and specialized channels might have real time impact. Mobilizing crowds and garnering attention will supplement specialised relationships based on tit-for-tat gamesmanship and long memories. Political marketing campaigns may become the means for elevating influence across many channels for large and small businesses.

Certainly, clarity of focus in political marketing campaigns is needed. Yet rather than narrowly targeting elected politicians and funders during election season using marketing concepts and tools (Lock & Harris, 1996), political marketing campaigns might strategically select issues and messages to influence more constituencies far more frequently using new tactics: generative AI, virtual town halls and social media videos. Clarity that consistently expresses common shared values without privileging consumers, investors, employees, funders or politicians – as backlashes are certain to come – is better to be hashed out early with a holistic organisation-wide perspective. Consulting corporate affairs colleagues as the policy and communications experts when responding with clear, consistent messages that do not undermine reputational or regulatory risks is simply in the business's best interests – to help solve problems that further our collective interests.

Acknowledgements

With gratitude to the visiting executives and 2023/2024 cohorts of the Australian Centre for Corporate Public Affairs (CCPA), Melbourne Institute. With special thanks to the many conversations with Geoff Allen, Wayne Burns, Fruzsina Harsanyi, Jason Laird, John F. Mahon, Doug Pinkham, James E. Post and many others who have generously and very patiently shared incredible insights, over the past few decades.

Notes

1 https://www.goodreads.com/quotes/70587-politics-is-a-strong-and-slow-boring-of-hard-boards. If you want to bore (i.e. drill) a hole in hard wood, you need to do it slowly to avoid overheating and consequently fulling your drill, making it less useful or even useless for further work. That is why you need 'passion and perspective' with a five-year burn time to affect change.

2 As of July 2024, fifty corporations have joined: https://www.weforum.org/projects/partnering-for-racial-justice-in-business/

REFERENCES

ACCPA, Australian Centre for Corporate Public Affairs. (2019). *2019 State of Australian public affairs*. Centre for Corporate Public Affairs.

Allen, G. (2020). Public affairs in Australia: Evolving and enhancing corporate performance. *Journal of Public Affairs*, *20*(1), e2066. https://onlinelibrary.wiley.com/doi/10.1002/pa.2066

Allen, G. (2022a). Towards a strategic function. In P. Harris, A. Bitonti, C. S. Fleisher, & A. S. Binderkrantz (Eds.), *The Palgrave Encyclopedia of interest groups*. Lobbying and Public Affairs.

Allen, G. (2022b). The evolution of the public affairs management profession in Australia. In P. Harris, A. Bitonti, C. S. Fleisher, & A. S. Binderkrantz (Eds.), *The Palgrave encyclopedia of interest groups*. Lobbying and Public Affairs.

Andrevski, G., & Miller, D. (2022). Forbearance: Strategic nonresponse to competitive attacks, strategic forbearance. *Academy of Management Review*, *47*(1). https://doi.org/10.5465/amr.2018.0248

Aon. (2022). *Global risk management report*. https://www.aon.com/2021-global-risk-management-survey/index.html

Bansinath, B. (2023, June14). Things got really scary really fast during pride month. *Power*. https://www.thecut.com/2023/06/target-employees-harassment-transphobia.html

Baron, D. P. (2013). *Business and its environment* (7th ed.). Pearson.

Baumhart, R. C. (1968). *An honest profit: What businessmen say about ethics in business*. Holt, Rinehart and Winston, Inc.

Bell, S. (2023). Large firms in Australian politics: The institutional dynamics of the government relations function. *Australian Journal of Political Science*, *58*(1), 124–140. https://doi.org/10.1080/10361146.2022.2142517

Bell, S., Hindmoor, A., & Umashev, N. (2023). The determinants of corporate political activity in Australia. *Australian Journal of Political Science*. https://doi.org/10.1080/10361146.2023.2231893

Bonardi, J.-P., & Keim, G. D. (2005). Corporate political strategies for widely salient issues. *The Academy of Management Review*, *30*(3), 555–557.

Bourgeois, L. J. (1980). Performance and Consensus. *Strategic Management Journal*, *1*(3), 227–248.

Bowen, H. R. (1953, reprinted 2013). *Social responsibilities of the businessman*. University of Iowa Press.

Broccardo, E., Hart, O., & Zingales, L. (2022). Exit verses voice. *Journal of Political Economy*, *130*(12), 3101–3145. https://doi.org/10.1086/720516

Bryant, A., Griffin, J. J., & Perry, V. G. (2020). Mitigating climate change: A role for regulations and risk-taking. *Business Strategy and the Environment*, *29*(2), 605–618.

Bryant, A., Griffin, J. J., & Perry, V. G. (2023). Irresponsible contagions: Propagating harmful behavior through Imitation. *Business Ethics, the Environment & Responsibility*, *32*(1), 292–311.

Carouso, T. (2023). *The state of multiculturalism in America today: A new mandate*. Zeno Group. https://www.zenogroup.com/insights/state-multiculturalism-america-today-new-mandate

Clark, C. E., Bryant, A. P., & Griffin, J. J. (2017). Firm engagement and social issue salience, consensus, and contestation. *Business & Society*, *56*(8), 1136–1168.

Dolsak, N., Griffin, J. J., & Prakash, A. (2020). Milton Friedman and Jeff Bezos on climate leadership. In *The regulatory review*. University of Pennsylvania Law School. https://www.theregreview.org/2020/12/28/dolsak-griffin-prakash-milton-friedman-versus-jeff-bezos-climate-leadership/

Dolsak, N., Griffin, J. J., & Prakash, A. (2022). Is ESG simply the old CSR wine in a new bottle? In *The regulatory review*. University of Pennsylvania Law School. https://www.theregreview.org/2022/03/28/dolsak-griffin-prakash-is-esg-old-csr-wine-in-new-bottle/

Dunn, B. S. (2024, June 1). Target is treating pride month very differently this year. *Newsweek*. https://www.newsweek.com/target-treating-pride-month-differently-this-year-1906899

Edelman Trust Barometer. (2022a, February). *Trust barometer 2022 global report*. https://www.edelman.com/trust/2022-trust-barometer

Edelman Trust Barometer. (2022b, September). *Trust Barometer 2022 special report trust in the workplace*. https://www.edelman.com/trust/2022-trust-barometer/special-report-trust-workplace

Edelman Trust Barometer. (2023). *2023 Edelman Trust Barometer*. https://www.edelman.com/trust/trust-barometer

Edelman Trust Barometer. (2024, January 14). *Edelman Trust Barometer global report*. https://www.edelman.com/trust/2024/trust-barometer

Edmans, A. (2022). *Grow the Pie: How great companies deliver both purpose and profit*. Cambridge University Press.

Egan, M. (2023, July 11). 'Shameful and unethical.' Heineken, Unilever and Oreo maker Mondelez accused of breaking promises to leave Russia. *CNN Business*.

Epstein, E. (1969). *The corporation in American politics*. Prentice Hall.

Fleisher, C. F. (2024). Managing and practicing public affairs around the globe. In A. Timmermans (Ed.), *Research handbook on public affairs: Connecting evidence and strategy, in the handbooks in public administration and management series* (pp. 24–38). Edward Elgar Publishing Ltd. ISBN: 978-1-80392-027- 6.

Griffin, J. J. (2008). Re-examining corporate community investment: Allen's Australian Centre for Corporate Public Affairs (ACCPA) corporate community involvement report. *Journal of Public Affairs*, *8*, 219–227.

Griffin, J. J. (2016). *Managing corporate impacts: Co-creating value*. Cambridge University Press.

Griffin, J. J. (2024). Organizational settings and corporate affairs: Building trust for thriving in a polarized world. In A. Timmermans (Ed.), *Research handbook on public affairs: Connecting evidence and strategy, in the handbooks in public administration and management series*. Edward Elgar Publishing Ltd. ISBN: 978-1-80392-027-6.

Griffin, J. J., & Koerber, C. P. (2006). Does industry matter when managing stakeholder relations? *Academy of Management Proceedings*. https://doi.org/10.5465/ambpp.2006.27182171

Griffin, J. J., & Vivari, B. (2009). Corporate social responsibility in America. In S. O. Idowu & W. L. Filho (Eds.), *Global practices of corporate social responsibility* (pp. 235–250). Springer Verlag. ISBN: 978-3-540-68812-9.

Griffin, J. J., & Youm, Y. N. (2018). Voluntarily disclosing prosocial behaviors in Korean firms. *Journal of Business Ethics*, *153*(4), 1017–1030.

Griffin, J. J., & Youm, Y. N. (2023). External affairs and trusted family businesses: A research agenda. *Journal of Public Affairs*. https://doi.org/10.1002/pa.2853

Griffin, J. J., Youm, Y. N., & Vivari, B. (2021). Stakeholder engagement strategies after an exogenous shock: How Philip Morris and R.J. Reynolds adapted differently to the 1998 Master settlement agreement. *Business & Society*, *60*(4), 1009–1036.

Harsanyi, F. M., & Allen, G. (2017). Achieving the strategic potential of public affairs. In P. Harris & C. S. Fleischer (Eds.), *The sage handbook of international corporate and public affairs* (pp. 65–81). SAGE.

Healy, R., & Griffin, J. J. (2004). Building BP's reputation: Tooting your own horn, 2001–2002. *Public Relations Quarterly*, *49*(4), 33–42.

Holpuch, A. (2023, November 21). *Behind the backlash at bud light*.https://www.nytimes.com/article/bud-light-boycott.html

Johns Hopkins Report. (2003). *Global civil society report*. Johns Hopkins University.

Johnson, R. A., & Greening, D. W. (1999). The effects of corporate governance and institutional ownership types on corporate social performance. *Academy of Management Journal*, *42*, 564–576.

Keim, G. D., & Zeithaml, C. R. (1986). Corporate political strategy and legislative decision making: A review and contingency approach. *Academy of Management Review*, *11*(4), 828–843.

Klara, R. (2024, July 15). What should Boeing due to repair its damaged reputation? Boeing isn't a consumer brand, but the flying public is treating it like one. *Adweek*. https://www.adweek.com/brand-marketing/boeing-repair-damaged-brand-reputation/

Kujala, J., Sachs, S., Leinonen, H., Heikkinen, A., & Laude, D. (2022). Stakeholder engagement: Past, present, and future. *Business & Society*, *61*(5), 1136–1196. https://doi.org/10.1177/00076503211066595

Lock, A., & Harris, P. (1996). Political marketing – Vive la différence. *European Journal of Marketing*, *30*(10/11), 14–24.

Mahon, J. F. (1989). Corporate political strategy. *Business in the Contemporary World*, *II*(1), Autumn, pp. 50–63.

Mahon, J. F., & McGowan, R. A. (1998). Modeling industry political dynamics. *Business & Society*, *37*(4), 390–413.

Mann, B., & Bebinger, M. (2022, March 3). *Purdue Pharma, Sacklers reach $6 billion deal with state attorneys general*. NPR. www.npr.org/2022/03/03/1084163626/purdue-sacklers-oxycontin-settlement

Mitroff, I. I., Shrivastava, P., & Udwadia, F. E. (1987). Effective crisis management. *The Academy of Management Executive*, *1*(3), 283–292.

Nazzaro, M. (2023). Anheuser-Busch lays off hundreds amid Bud Light controversy, drop in sales. 07/27/23. *The Hill*. https://thehill.com/homenews/4122942-anheuser-busch-lays-off-hundreds-amid-bud-light-controversy-drop-in-sales/. July 2023.

Nyberg, D. (2021). Corporations, politics, and democracy: Corporate political activities as political corruption. *Organization Theory*, *2*, 1–24.

Post, J. E., & Griffin, J. J. (1997, Summer/Fall). Corporate reputation and external affairs management. *Corporate Reputation Review*, *1*, 165–172.

Prakash, A., & Griffin, J. J. (2012). Corporate responsibility, multinational corporations, and nation states: An introduction. *Business and Politics*, *14*(3), 1–10.

Public Affairs Council. (2016). *Taking it to the top: Engaging corporate leadership in public policy*. Foundation for Public Affairs.

Public Affairs Council. (2022b). *2022 trends in European public affairs survey report*. Public Affairs Council.

Public Affairs Council. (2020). *The State of corporate public affairs 2020–2021*. Public Affairs Council.

Public Affairs Council. (2021). *Taking a stand: How corporations engage on social issues*. Public Affairs Council.

Public Affairs Council. (2022a). *Public affairs pulse survey*. Public Affairs Council. https://pac.org/public-affairs-pulse-survey-2022.

Public Affairs Council (2023). *2023 communications and value of public affairs*. Public Affairs Council.

Reagan, R. (1981, January 20). *Inaugural address*. https://www.reaganfoundation.org/media/128614/inaguration.pdf

Schuler, D. A., Rehbein, K., & Cramer, R. D. (2002). Pursuing strategic advantage through political means: A multivariate approach. *Academy of Management Journal*, *45*(4), 659–672.

Shin, S., Lee, J., & Bansal, P. (2022). From a shareholder to stakeholder orientation: Evidence from the analyses of CEO dismissal in large U.S. firms. *Strategic Management Journal*, *43*(7), 1233–1257.

Smith, A. (1776). *An inquiry into the nature and causes of the wealth of nations*. W. Strahan and T. Cadell.

Taneja, S., Griffin, J. J., Taneja, P. K., Sharma, R., Davidson, D. K., & Ray, R. S. (2017). Using a stakeholder approach to understand success: Empirical tests in Indian business. In G. Aras, & C. Ingley (Eds.), *Corporate behavior and sustainability: Doing well by being good* (pp. 21–41). Ashgate (Taylor and Francis Group).

Timmermans, A. (2024). The analytical and normative basis of public affairs. In A. Timmermans (Ed.), *Research handbook on public affairs: Connecting evidence and strategy, in the handbooks in public administration and management series* (pp. 9–23). Edward Elgar Publishing Ltd. ISBN: 978-1-80392-027-6.

Van Dam, A. (2023, May 12). *The real reason America's nonprofit sector is seeing massive growth, and more! Washington Post*. . https://www.washingtonpost.com/business/2023/05/12/force-behind-americas-fast-growing-nonprofit-sector-more/

World Economic Forum. (2022). *The global risks report 2022* (17th ed.). https://www.weforum.org/reports/global-risks-report-2022

Youm, Y. N., Griffin, J. J., & Bryant, A. (2024). An exploration of cooperative stakeholder engagement and risk-taking behavior in privately held family firms. *Business Ethics, the Environment & Responsibility*. https://doi.org/10.1111/beer.12720

Entrepreneurs or Franchisees? The Use of Individual Versus Party Branding in Contemporary American Politics

Kenneth M. Cosgrove and Nathan R. Shrader

INTRODUCTION

This chapter will outline the history and contemporary uses of one of the most important political marketing techniques: political branding while showing how it has significantly contributed to the rise of a political franchise model in American politics. Political marketing has gained prominence in the United States because the population's values have become consumerist in orientation (Barber, 2008) because a great deal of the way in which people learn about products and ideas comes through electronic and social media, because the size of the population and its geographic dispersion make it difficult to do anything but try to reach large numbers of people efficiently, and because the amount of entities competing for the limited attention spans and resources of Americans are much more numerous than they were a century ago (Turow, 2007). We will look at the ways in which both parties have used political branding and how they are moving toward a franchise model that makes life easier for the party as organization even as it saddles the voters with choices they'd rather not make.

Political marketing and branding have become more important in American politics in recent decades. The period from the late 1960s onward saw significant changes in American life and politics. As Skocpol notes, earlier generations of Americans joined organizations that met in person like civic or benevolent associations (Skocpol, 2004).

American civic engagement weakened in the second half of the 20th century because of several trends that empowered political marketing including suburbanization, longer commute times, the nature of work itself which led many people to perceive themselves as either salaried professionals or independent contractors rather than union members, an increase in overall education level, the rise of instantaneous electronic communication technologies, and the development of vast databases of information about voters that could be mined to target individuals specifically (Bennett, 2008; Issenberg, 2013; McCauliffe, 2008; Putnam, 2000).

American politics went from torch light parades and speechifying to drum up support to a tightly targeted branded politics in the space of a few decades. This fit with the much more socially sorted country that the United States is in which most Americans live around people who occupy the same kinds of income, interest, and occupational categories that they themselves do (Bishop, 2008). Technology made it possible for people to sort themselves into electronic communities of the likeminded in terms of the media that they consume, the experiences that they enjoy, and the political causes with which they identify (Bishop, 2018; Mason, 2018).

Political parties have changed too. They are wealthier and offer more professional services to candidates than has traditionally been the case in the United States (Newman, 2004 or McCauliffe, 2008). They encourage their candidates to run coordinated campaigns across all levels of government[1] (See McAuliffe (2008) for examples of improvements in Democratic coordination). It is not unusual to see political advertising produced by a party being used in several different contests during the same electoral cycle. Only the names of the candidates involved and the jurisdiction in which the contest is taking place are changed, all of which fuels the rise of the franchise model of political branding. American parties differ significantly from parties in other systems because they are coalitional not ideological, are reluctant to discipline their members for not toeing the party line and have repeatedly either absorbed or been taken over by insurgent factions and are often faced with factional fights for dominance. Thus, it is possible for a political entrepreneur to mount a takeover of an extant party and try to launch a new franchise business as Barack Obama and Donald Trump have attempted to do over the last two decades. This chapter will explore that process, and the pluses and minuses associated with trying to launch a new franchise brand in the American system.

Branding: What It Is and Why It Is Used?

The brand can be defined as the total user experience with a product and everything that a marketer does presents the brand to the audience (Zyman & Brott, 2002). The need for consistency in branding is part of what makes American politics very scripted and why compromise is so difficult. To be effective, a brand must develop a clear identity in the mind of the user (Ries, Trout & Colter, 2001). The brand is the total user experience with the product (Zyman & Brott, 2002). One of the interesting things about political branding is that it often supports products that are remote from the consumer's experience. Supporting enhanced abortion access (branded as pro-choice) is not quite the same thing as purchasing a Volvo or a BMW. In that case, one gets either the chance to drive safely (Volvo) or the ultimate driving machine (BMW), whereas supporting abortion rights produces a possible future substantive payoff but an immediate emotional one. This example shows how the brand is a key part of building a structured narrative.

Brands serve as short cuts that can be used to quickly explain something to the average person that allows them to make choices quickly. Brands simplify the complicated and turn the abstract into the understandable often via powerful storytelling (Mark & Pearson, 2001). Political candidates and parties brand their policies because it is more efficient to reach and easier to engage the casual voter by talking about emotive terms than it is to delve into the nuances of public policies, party positions or candidate attributes. The brand is a multiplatform tool. It can be visual, auditory, typographical, or emotional (Postman, 2005; Reis & Ries, 2002). Donald Trump, for example, adopted a brand strategy in which it was important to work with specific phrases and words to produce a response on social media among his supporters but also among journalists who would then amplify his message by reporting on it (Cosgrove, 2022; Miller, 2015). Another way we can see this is in the terms that are used to sell public policies. Branding is ubiquitous in the American system right down to the given names of legislative proposals (Newman, 1999).

Brands can produce deep emotion and create loyalty in the targeted audience while doing the opposite with other audiences. The brand is one of the key drivers of American political polarization because different audiences can have diametrically opposite reactions to a brand. To be successful, a brand must keep its promises and embody its emotions in all situations. Branding, when combined with other techniques like segmentation and targeting have produced the ability to reach very specific parts of the electorate and make the targets feel like they are part of something bigger than themselves. It is why politicians often talk about their movement instead of simply talking about a campaign or stress they are either interested in bringing about some sort of dramatic restoration to a great lost yesterday or transformation toward a great shining future. This is part of why political branding has taken advantage of technological and societal changes to both market in the way that professional sports teams do and to produce a similar level of supporter engagement. There is no logical reason why one might follow a particular sports team just as there is no logical reason why people develop such deep emotional attachments to a political party. Indeed, consistent with the rise of brand politics, for many politics has become about their identity not elections or policymaking (Mason, 2018).

The brand can support an overall organization and its products (house or top-level branding) as both parties do. Individual brand aspects can be used to support different types of candidates or policy positions. Individual brand aspects can be presented to different segments of the population at any given time. For example, the branded issues on which Democrats campaign with White college-educated voters occupy a different market space than do the issues on which they campaign with young voters or working-class voters or Black voters.[2] Technological changes have enabled parties to target specific policies and messaging at very specific voters meaning the audience perception of the house brand might vary wildly between said segments. A specific brand can be developed to support an individual policy or candidate and used only to support that policy. This is a platform brand. A candidate can develop their own brand that is distinct from the political party. American party brands can change depending on which faction within the party gets in control of the party organization and, like partisan messaging globally, the brand is adjusted to fit some specific traits of the President when the party controls that office. A faction that becomes dominant in a political party is positioned to launch a franchiseable brand that then shapes the party[3] (Carty, 2004; Oleschuk, 2020).

POLITICAL FRANCHISING IN THE UNITED STATES?

Both American parties are battling over what are their products and brands, which faction will be in control of the organization, and who their faces will be. Should the winners of these battles establish durable political coalitions then they can establish political franchises and brands. Franchising offers the advantage of giving an identity to a given product that is consistent across a marketplace. The advantage to the candidate is the same as it would be for a small business owner (Oleschuk, 2020). Blair and LaFontaine define franchising as "a contractual arrangement between two legally independent firms, in which one firm, the franchisee, pays the other firm, the franchisor, for the right to sell the franchisor's product and/or the right to use its trademarks and business format in a given area for a limited period of time (Blair & LaFontaine, 2005)." This is similar to the way in which a party nominee gets access to the party as organization's resources and the ability to use its the party brand and access its political products during their campaign.

The effectiveness of the franchise model for political branding depends on a number of factors as Nijmeijer et al. note is true in the commercial world (Nijmeijer et al., 2014). These can include ownership structures, the way in which the franchisor and the franchisee interact, the business format design among others. It is easy to see the application of such things to political campaigning. Candidates might use the franchise's model, but they might not execute it well or take direction from the franchisor (the party organization) or they might apply it inappropriately thus explaining why some candidates succeed using a party's franchise brand and others do not.

As Oleschuk (2020) has noted, in politics, franchising can mean "the transference of charisma from one politician to another (Oleschuk, 2020)." This is precisely what is currently occurring with both American political parties. He further notes that the franchise offers "a universal political brand" (Oleschuk, 2020) and that too is being attempted by both American parties. Carty (2004) notes the possibility of parties acting as franchisors when writing in the Canadian context. He notes that there can be flexibility in terms of the franchise model within the party or the use of its brand, that crossnationally the political franchise structure can vary but that its real strength is that it can organize a party (Carty, 2004). In the last several electoral cycles, we have seen both parties attempt to use the franchise model with varying degrees of success. We will look first and the Republicans and then at the Democrats to better understand how these efforts have played out.

BATTLE FOR THE SOUL OF THE REPUBLICAN PARTY: THE REAGAN HERITAGE BRAND VERSUS DONALD TRUMP

Ronald Reagan remains the Republican heritage brand, but it is a brand under attack by the entrepreneurial Donald Trump. Reagan's victorious 1980 campaign pioneered the use of a full marketing model in politics including the development of a brand (Cosgrove, 2017). The Reagan brand was based upon a set of emotions that were nostalgic, aimed at restoration of a great lost America but also hopeful and humorous about the possibility of actually changing the country and what he saw as the wrongheaded views of his opponents (Combs, 1993). Reagan represented the triumph of an insurgent movement in the Republican Party that was based in the West and South called Movement Conservatism (McGirr, 2001). Reagan as a movement leader showed how a party brand can change in response to changes in internal coalitional dominance. Reagan's program represented a significant shift away from the New Deal policies that had dominated for the prior five decades but he sold them in a way that argued that they would make things better for the average American just as Franklin D. Roosevelt (FDR) had done in the 1930s. The Reagan brand's success shows how technology impacts branding. The Reagan brand developed in an era of cable television proliferation and defined news cycles meaning it was possible for the White House to focus on specific aspects of its brand on specific days or weeks and at specific times (Cannon, 2000; Smith, 1996). Reagan's "Make America Great Again" 1980 campaign messaging had to be pitched to a mass audience using media that could not be time-shifted. Reagan's team was the first to use the so-called Morning Again in America theme in a 1984 reelection campaign advertisement entitled "Prouder, Stronger, Better." These themes continue to be used in Republican branding including by Donald Trump.

In 1994, the House Republicans ran on a platform brand entitled "The Contract with America." In addition to being a very successful platform brand, it portended a shift in Republican branding. It consisted of ten very popular items, each of which had its own brand name and was dubbed a contract to draw a contrast with the incumbent President whom the Republicans had negatively branded as being an immoral liar (Cosgrove, 2017). The Contract heralded a shift away from the Reagan brand emotions toward something angrier and more visceral that Donald Trump would tap into years later. Like Donald Trump in future election cycles, Representative Newt Gingrich directly confronted the more bipartisan-oriented members of his caucus in favor of a more confrontational approach than his intra-partisan opponents. Both presented an angry vision of the status quo that differed from the Reagan brand emotions and both confronted members of their own party whom they saw as not being sufficiently pugilistic toward the Democrats (Coppins, 2015; Sabato & Simpson, 1996). In both cases, they presented themselves as insurgents hoping to restore the country to its great lost past just as Reagan had but the brand emotions that they employed were very different from those used by the Gipper.[4]

The contemporary Republican Party's strategic problem is that many of the issues on which Ronald Reagan ran and built a durable electoral coalition have both been solved and created new problems of their own (Cosgrove in Gilles, 2021; Skowronek, 2008). Changing demography has meant that the Republican's overwhelming lead with white voters is not enough to win elections on a consistent basis anymore (Walshe, 2013). Republicans struggled at the ballot box because of issues and demography but also because Democrats had conquered the next several innovations in campaigning including social media, developing large data bases to better understand the electorate that could be used in real time, and a renewed focus on turnout all done within a branding framework. The 2008 and 2012 Obama campaigns were state of the art branding, marketing, and grassroots organizing efforts that took advantage of the time, money, and effort Democrats had expended during the Bush years to build a marketing juggernaut. This is typical of life in a political marketing world. When the parties are out of power, they spend a lot of time trying to understand why they are out and working to retool in hopes of gaining power once more.[5] After Obama rolled over Mitt Romney, Donald Trump vowed that if he ever ran for President, he would be much tougher to run against than was the Grand Old Party's defeated standard bearer in 2012 (Coppins, 2015). True to his word, he repositioned the Republican brand to be much hotter emotionally and in a way that drove upper middle-class voters away while attracting more working-class audiences (Cosgrove, 2022).

Trump's 2016 campaign was, in many ways, modeled on the Obama campaigns but simultaneously employed his personal brand and Reagan-level acumen as a pitch person. Trump used branding differently than had previous Republicans. The Trump brand is class-conscious and optimized for the social media era. By building an omnipresent emotive sticky brand that could be deployed on social media then amplified by journalists and influencers, Trump found a way to cut through the cacophony of a socially sorted country and generate wide-spread attention for and interest in his offering (Cosgrove, 2022). Trump has attempted to build a political franchise that mirrors his commercial franchises, but this effort has yielded mixed results. Trump personally has a politically potent brand. The poor results of the 2018 and 2022 midterm elections that pro-Trump candidates produced show that his efforts to build a political franchise have not clearly succeeded but his faction's takeover of the Republican Party show that they have not entirely failed either.

Trump and Reagan have a common background as commercial pitchmen and media figures that helped them to succeed politically. The environment in which Trump worked was more socially sorted, had more outlets competing for public attention, far less mediation, far more immediacy, and much less structure in terms of the information dissemination system. Trump's strategy was twofold: (1) expand the audience for the "Make America Great Again Brand" by changing its emotions to be angrier and (2) changing its policy offering to be much more populist. He has succeeded with the working-class but repelling the college-educated. Working-class voters have been drifting toward the GOP in recent years, but working-class turnout is lower than middle and upper middle-class voters. The Trump brand was aimed at attracting and driving turnout among these voters.

Donald Trump's version of "Make America Great Again" works with an issue agenda and emotions that are very different than the ones with which the original Reagan version worked. This was in part because the situation in the country had changed significantly since Reagan ruled, but it was also caused by changes in technology that placed a great deal of emphasis on cutting through the background noise because there was much more of and the need to be present continuously because social media had undermined the traditional news cycle. Trump's solution was to build a brand that was everywhere all the time, highly emotive and highly memorable to differentiate him from competitors (Cosgrove, 2022). Trump's emotive sticky brand encouraged Democrats to both run a four-year negative branding campaign around Trump and to mobilize literally everyone that they could find in 2020 to vote against him (Cosgrove and Shrader in Moufahim (2021)). It generated high levels of emotional engagement, but it did so among all voters not just Republicans. The problem with the omnipresent sticky brand strategy was that Trump said and did things that drove more voters away using it than he attracted[6].

Trump's biggest problem as a marketer is that his brand didn't deliver on its promise of effective management (Cosgrove, 2022). The way in which the Administration performed during COVID-19 and its associated crises during 2020 visibly proved this point to many Americans during the COVID-19 pandemic (Cosgrove, 2022). One of the basic tenets of branding is that promises made must be kept and while Trump incorporated this phrase specifically into his marketing, by the time the 2020 election rolled around the public's issue interests and tastes had changed. The Trump brand wasn't nimble enough to reposition its offering, emotions, and visual performance on the fly in the face of a sudden radical change in the marketplace (Cosgrove, 2022).

It isn't clear that Trump laid the foundation for the long-term success that a franchise model could offer. This is based on the way in which the party in general and candidates using the Trump branding underperformed in 2022, their loss in 2018 and Trump's own loss in 2020. This has produced a real problem for the Party because Donald Trump and his franchise branded candidates have enough support to win partisan nomination contests even if they struggle with the wider electorate. His chosen candidates often are either politically inexperienced or far away from the median voter in terms of ideology and attitudes. Trump's personal brand might be strong enough to overcome such concerns, but the 2018 and 2022 cycles show that such strength does not translate to his franchisees. Thus, the Republican Party currently is composed of an uncomfortable mix of Trump and Reagan brand loyalists. Its coalition is composed of traditional conservatives, faith and flag conservatives, the populist right, the ambivalent right, and a group for whose loyalty it competes with the Democrats that Donald Trump emphasized: stressed sideliners (Pew Research, 2021).

Democratic Heritage Branding and the FDR Franchise

The Democrats' history with branding is long. Like the Republican brand, the Democratic brand has changed over the years based on technical and ideological changes. President FDR began the primordial era of Democratic branding by stressing his three initials, which can be seen much of the branded FDR advertising done by the Roosevelt organization throughout all four of his presidential campaigns. The Roosevelt "FDR" branding was a simple, symbolic effort to link him to the "alphabet soup" agencies that he was chiefly responsible for under the New Deal programs. American voters could easily connect the New Deal's Civilian Conservation Corps (CCC), the Works Progress Administration (WPA), or the Tennessee Valley Authority (TVA) acronyms with FDR himself. The branding wasn't just about the acronyms, but instead what they stood for: an attempt to repackage the Democratic Party as the party of government and of working-class people at a time when that segment of the American electorate was suffering during the dark days of the Great Depression. This becomes the basis of the Democrats' three-letter brand and franchise model that was used by Roosevelt, Harry Truman, John F. Kennedy, Lyndon Johnson, and Hubert Humphrey. It has periodically been resurrected as part of campaigns, but its use as a political franchise and brand died out in the 1970s. This was a result of partisan in-fighting and product performance problems.

FDR remains a large part of the Democratic heritage brand even if he is no longer the party's franchise brand. In 2016, Hillary Clinton kicked off her Presidential run with an event on Roosevelt Island in New York City. FDR's next three Democratic successors in the White House emulated this three-letter model. Doing so gave them brand fellowship with FDR and positioned them as advocates for continuing and expanding FDR's governing philosophy. Not only were these Democratic politicians engaging in a heritage branding effort, but they were also keeping the popular memory of Roosevelt associated with their own candidacies in a way that voters would likely feel some level of emotive connection to the acronym-driven marketing approach.

From FDR forward, the Democratic brand story has stressed the need for government action to expand opportunity and legal rights to broad swaths of the electorate. The Democratic offering has included programs like the New Deal, the Fair Deal (a Truman proposal that included National Health Insurance), and the Great Society. Democrats of this era presented themselves using the three-letter branding as FDR did. Democratic Presidents of the era include Harry Truman (HST), John F. Kennedy (JFK), Lyndon B. Johnson (LBJ), Robert F. Kennedy (RFK), and Hubert H. Humphrey (HHH). The three-letter model and named programs were a direct link to the FDR franchise and its brand.

Following Humphrey's defeat in 1968 at the hands of Richard Nixon (with the help of George Wallace who was able to poach numerous traditional Democratic states in the Deep South), the power of the FDR heritage brand began to wane among Democratic candidates, especially as Nixon largely continued the New Deal policies that his party sought to bury just several years earlier with Barry Goldwater's ill-fated 1964 effort. Although George McGovern's campaign in 1972 largely reinforced the principles of the FDR heritage brand on economic policy and the superiority of the federal government as the chief policy-making organ in American political life, that campaign was not run on the traditional trajectory of FDR, HST, JFK, LBJ, RFK, and HHH. Instead, McGovern's race was a quixotic campaign against Richard Nixon and the Vietnam War.

It could be argued that Hubert Humphrey's oft-repeated statement that "The ultimate moral test of any government is the way it treats three groups of its citizens. First, those in the dawn of life – our children. Second, those in the shadows of life – our needy, our sick, our handicapped. Third, those in the twilight of life – our elderly"(Senator Hubert, 1976) served as the attempted equivalent of a preinternet, pre-YouTube sound bite for the purpose of reintroducing or reinforcing the attributes of the FDR franchise brand at a time when its strength appeared to be fading. This becomes more apparent when considering that Humphrey did not deliver those famous lines until the 1976 Democratic National Convention in New York City during the formal nomination of Jimmy Carter who was seeking to shake up the Democratic coalition in order to save it (Skowronek, 2008). Like Donald Trump many years later, by the time Jimmy Carter ran for President the Democrats' three letter brand and the products it supported had largely done what they were supposed to do and simultaneously created new problems of their own. Carter, like Trump much later, was attempting to update the product to attract new voters in new places to it and, like Trump, was partly undone by the way in which he chose to present himself during a crisis. In retrospect, there is a sense that Humphrey – the last in the long line of acronym party leaders of that era – knew that the FDR heritage brand and franchise were weakening and wanted to make one last appeal to the party faithful at that national convention to keep it alive and well as the centerpiece of the Democratic Party product line. Since that time, the FDR heritage branding has not applied as clearly to subsequent Democrats despite the fact that all of them sought to extend elements of the FDR heritage in its emotional branding and policy ideas. The FDR franchise has likewise remained moribund. Bill Clinton and the Democratic Leadership Council shifted the party rightward and, eventually, Barack Obama moved it somewhat back toward the FDR franchise but, as a political entrepreneur, launched his own version of it.

The Democrats three letter brands and FDR Franchise faltered because technology and demography changed significantly from the time FDR was President until the time Carter was President. The 1960s produced more college-educated voters and many of them had more post-materialist than materialist values meaning that nondefense, noneconomic issues became more salient (Inglehart, 1977). In 1980, Carter was not the candidate of the college-educated young voter. Ted Kennedy was. On the other hand, the college-educated progressive voters turned out in primaries and started to dominate the party apparatus. Thus, after Carter was defeated, the Democrats nominated the liberal Walter Mondale and the technocrat Michael Dukakis as standard bearers both of whom lost badly to Reagan and his successor George H.W. Bush. The next Democrat to win the White House, Bill Clinton ran as a "New Democrat" and made no secret of the idea that he wanted to shift the party product in a centrist direction while keeping some of the best of FDR's values and programs.

The Democrats were slow to adapt to changes in the environment around talk radio and cable television and changes in the country around the nature of work and geographic dispersion that helped the Reagan brand succeed. They did not adjust quickly as technology moved political brands from a feature of advertising to a fully marketed activity. Reagan and other conservatives caught onto all this because he and his team spent years running an insurgent campaign against the Republican establishment and the Democratic Party and had also been affiliated with the Democratic Party during the FDR era leaving him with an understanding of how to talk to those particular types of Democratic voters in ways other Republicans could not. The Democrats were in power and had battles to mediate between their liberal and conservative wings during this period. Thus, it was the Republicans who were first to jump onto the shift from a more traditional advertising and grassroots style model to a marketing model in politics.

The next and current era of Democratic success developed because the party, and especially its progressive wing, had time to master the next big series of technical innovations while the Republicans were either running the country or at least some of its institutions. In 2008, the Obama campaign rolled out a state-of-the-art branding and marketing campaign that was data driven, innovative, targeted, and branded in ways that fit the technology of its era. Obama adds a great deal to the Democratic heritage brand while retaining fellowship with two of its most successful three letter branded Presidents: FDR and JFK. Obama incorporated the FDR heritage with his campaign logos, his willingness to engage in the same kind of class-based rhetoric FDR used, and his vision of a major and positive role for government in American life. Obama's victory seemed to represent the triumph of the progressives over the Clintonites meaning that the Democratic brand changed to a more Obama-centric entity as a result. Obama sold progressive policies with an emphasis on good values and good value for the consumer as his administration tried to show in the case of the Affordable Care Act by arguing that this policy would cut costs, increase access, prevent catastrophic financial losses caused by medical treatment, and retain patient choice of plan and doctor. He embraced the progressive legacy of Robert F. Kennedy and by doing so brought progressives back to prominence in the party. Thus, the current Democratic heritage brand is a hybrid of FDR, the Kennedys, and Barack Obama, but the emerging Democratic franchise is clearly the Obama franchise.

As shown in Table 35.1, the three most recent Democratic nominees have been remarkably similar in both style and substance. First, it is noticeable that the Democratic candidates tend

Table 35.1 List of Democrats by Franchise and Values

Candidate	*Franchise*	*Values*
FDR	Founder	The New Deal
Harry Truman	FDR	The Square Deal
John F. Kennedy	FDR	The New Frontier
Lyndon B. Johnson	FDR	The Great Society
Barack Obama	Founder	Change you Can Believe in
Hillary Clinton	Obama	Stronger Together, the Four Fights
Joe Biden	Obama	Build Back Better
Kamala Harris	Obama	We Are Not Going Back

to use a lighter blue for the visuals and have maintained similar fonts through their last three presidential campaigns. Harris, Biden, and Hillary Clinton have all used fonts, colors, tag lines, and campaign themes that were similar to the two Obama campaigns. All of these candidates have used the same kinds of emotional branding that Barack Obama used including the terms "change" and "hope." While "hope" goes back to the 1988 Jesse Jackson campaign, it is most recently associated with the Obama campaigns and has become a key part of the Obama franchise brand. While the Obama Franchise brand had hits, it has also had misses with the 2016 Clinton campaign being the most notable case in point.

Despite its positive emotions, the Obama franchise brand can be used in a negative way as the man himself sometimes used it or as the 2020 Biden campaign did. Biden 2020 was largely an exercise in anti-Trump marketing that fit with the concept of negative partisanship that Abramowitz and Webster (2018) have noted. One of the ways the Biden camp tried to soften the negativity in its message was by arguing that the country was in a battle for its soul and that electing Biden would restore its traditional values that had been usurped by Trump and his "MAGA forces." A common theme between all three of the most recent Democratic Party nominees for the presidency include these emotionally laden pitches and a "unity" framework. This frame is detectible through "Hope and Change" and "Hope, Never Fear" from Obama in 2008, the "Greater Together" and "We Don't Quit (Blake, 2012)" themes of Obama's 2012 race supported by Bruce Springsteen's *We Take Care of Our Own* as his campaign song, and Biden's "Let's Stop Fighting and Let's Start Fixing (Elliott, 2019)" from his campaign launch in May 2019.

The Obama-Biden Normalcy Brand: A Short-Term Branding Tool with Benefits

The 2022 midterm results are a testimony to the strengths and weaknesses of branding and the franchise model. Writing just 24 hours before the 2022 midterm elections, Aliza Astrow and Lanae Erickson of Third Way predicted that "If Democrats manage to hold on to the House and Senate, it will be in spite of the party brand, not because of it (Astrow & Erickson, 2022)," citing a poll conducted just days earlier by their own organization in conjunction with Impact Research and Welcome PAC. This survey found that "Democrats are underwater on issues voters name as their highest priorities, including the economy, immigration, and crime, they are perceived as distant from the electorate ideologically, and voters question whether the party shares essential values like patriotism and the importance of hard work (Astrow & Erickson, 2022)." Astrow and Erickson were proven correct as Democrats managed to overperform in races for the United States House of Representative to the point where they finished just seven seats down to the Republicans and managed to hold the Senate after yet another wild Georgia runoff election. The midterm election environment, party performance on the issues they identified as being the ones most important to voters, and the grim outlook for inflation and cost of living should have signified a Republican wave, or at least a larger GOP victory in the House and a Senate takeover. Instead, Democrats were able to out-perform expectations. Democratic pundits declared victory in the days and weeks following the midterms.

While Democrats were celebrating as if they were vindicated by the election, the weak

Republican performance likely papered over the serious branding challenges facing the Democratic Party. As noted in the Third Way/Impact Research/Welcome PAC survey, midterm voters chose Democrats because they offered a message of institutional normalcy in contrast to a Republican field that appeared to be far too extreme for the median voter in important House and Senate contests. These candidates were very closely associated with Donald Trump and many of them used the Trump branding specifically meaning that they managed to turn the election, once again, into a referendum on the nascent Trump franchise brand. Democrats may have won a reprieve with their overperformance in 2022, but their branding challenges moving forward remain unsolved and raise serious questions about the durability of the Obama franchise. The present-day Democratic Party is one that is largely identity-driven, it lacks coherence when it comes to appealing to the working class and blue-collar voters that once comprised the bulk of the party's ranks, and it is largely tailored around the interests and needs of college-educated voters living in suburban, urban, and usually coastal America. The Democrats are having difficulty building a political franchise as FDR built because its brand does not sell nationwide.

On 9 November 2021, the Pew Research Center released an impressive and highly detailed study titled "Beyond Red vs. Blue: The Political Typology[7] (Pew Research Center, 2021)" which surveyed over 10,200 American adults to determine the size and scope of the divisions within the two major political party coalitions. The findings show that building a political franchise and brand could be important tools to produce stable electoral coalitions and insure electoral success over the long haul, something Judis and Texiera (2023) have noted is lacking in contemporary American politics. The report showed that the contemporary Democratic Party coalition can be split into five categories as indicated in Table 35.2.

Leaders within the party as well as the strategists who are tasked with developing and maintaining the party brand and, ideally building a franchise business, face an ongoing struggle: how do they successful build, nurture, grow, and preserve a consistent product when the various component parts of the coalition have differing visions for what the party ought to be fighting for and how it ought to be presented to the electorate as a whole? The coalitional nature of the party shows why it is very difficult for American parties to do the kind of franchise wide branding that a private company can do. Indeed, the challenge for political branding is how to unite a fractious coalition around a single brand.

Joe Biden shows the branding challenge facing Democrats. Establishment Liberals and Democratic Mainstays cheered his nomination because of his more centrist Senate voting record. Nominating a centrist likely attracted many Stressed Sideliners thus making Biden very competitive against Donald Trump. Once Biden won the nomination, he had to bring the 20% of the party that was far to the left of him into his coalition. He did so by gaining endorsements from prominent leftists like Bernie Sanders (Ember & Kaplan 2020), by visibly aligning his brand with the Black Lives Matter movement at the height of its prominence in the summer of 2020 (Tensley, 2020) by visibly aligning with the progressives by nominating a vice presidential candidate who called the enforcement of immigration laws a "campaign of terror (Givas, 2019)," and by adopting progressive environmental policies (Bernstein, 2020). Biden adjusted his positioning and the contents of the Democratic brand to hold his party coalition together. The Democrats don't have a clear party brand because much of its coalition is focused on niche issues or those supported by single audience segments or interest groups[8] (Judis & Teixeira, 2023). Biden's

Table 35.2 Democratic Voter Types

Voter Type	*Share*	*Traits*	*Candidate*
Democratic Mainstays	*28%*	*Moderate Likely voters*	*Biden*
Establishment Liberals	*23%*	*Gradual change*	*Biden*
Outsider Left	*16%*	*Frustrated with the system including the Democratic Party*	*Less Politically active*
Stressed Sideliners	*13%*	*Swing Voters*	*Trump or Sanders*
Progressive Left	*12%*	*Younger, more active, highly educated white*	*Sanders or Warren*

brand modification can be seen as the actions of a campaign that adjusted because its internal market required it to do so to have any chance of winning.

This too is evidence for the difficulty of applying a franchise branding model in American politics. Because they are largely an identity-driven coalition, Democrats must still overcome the challenge of winning enough votes from people outside of those identity groups to forge electoral majorities. How do they accomplish this in the present political environment? The midterm election of 2022 reinforced a component of the Democratic brand that has been successful going back to Barack Obama's reelection in 2012 in the face of the growing Tea Party movement and then soon the Make America Great Again Movement: normalcy.

The normalcy brand has been strengthened using contrast and differentiation marketing. Consider Biden's statements that his opposition "ain't your father's Republican Party (Singman, 2022)." Another example is provided in his controversial Philadelphia speech on 1 September 2022, when he declared that "Too much of what is happening in our country today is not normal" (Lemire & McGraw, 2022) and pilloried the MAGA Republicans as anti-democratic extremists. Biden also exhibited the trust placed in this normalcy branding mechanism by frequently uttering the phrase "Don't compare me to the almighty, compare me to the alternative" (Hains, 2022) as a means of suggesting that he is imperfect, but the only alternative option in the GOP is wholly unacceptable and extreme while he and the Democrats are the voices of normalcy.

Moufahim (2022) wrote that "the task of developing, managing, and growing brands is anything but simple, in often overly complex and unstable political environments" (Moufahim, 2022). The Obama-Biden Normalcy brand paid off for Democrats in 2012 with Obama's reelection, the 2018 midterm elections that saw Democrats returned to power in both chambers of Congress, Biden's 2020 victory over Trump, and the salvaging of the 2022 midterm elections. However, the normalcy brand is unlikely to be a long-term strategy given the complex political environment in today's United States. Democrats have been able to shift the conversation away from their generally unpopular positions they are perceived as having on a series of policy issues by branding themselves as the normal party and the Republicans as extremists. Trump and many of the candidates who use his branding and some party figures associated with him who use Trump brand friendly messaging have aided and abetted the Democratic Party's normalcy branding strategy through their words, actions, and issue positions that lie outside of the mainstream of American politics. This has helped provide the Democrats with cover for running as the Party of Normalcy because they can – utilizing Biden's "compare me to the alternative" phrase – remind voters that "we are not perfect but look at the other option."

In the short-term, at least from Obama's reelection bid in 2012 to Biden's first midterm cycle in 2022, the normalcy brand has been effective for Democrats because it allows them to continue servicing the vast array of identity and interest groups that comprise the party's base, brand their opposition as dangerous and outside the mainstream, and garner a sufficient number of votes from outside of their identity and interest group driven base to win crucial races. It has built a strong enough franchise within the party that it was possible to swap out a candidate, in President Joe Biden, who was faltering and had been beaten badly in a debate by Donald Trump with Vice-President Kamala Harris seamlessly in the summer of 2024. The Democrats have not built a similarly strong franchise and brand with the general electorate as shown by the tightness of the 2024 race after Harris entered it.

CONTRARY INCENTIVES: BRANDING AND GOVERNING

This chapter has shown that both American political parties are facing branding challenges and both have politicians within their ranks who are trying to build political franchises. For the Republicans, the question is will its brand be closer in content and emotion to that developed by Ronald Reagan or that developed by Donald Trump and can Trump actually establish a franchise that can succeed beyond his base and win elections even though he personally is not on the ballot? For Democrats, the challenge is how to build a party brand that holds together a fractious coalition each element of which cares deeply about its issues while appealing to enough other voters to win elections on a consistent basis and is it possible that the Obama franchise and brand can sell to enough voters to consistently win elections? It is imperative for political practitioners to develop a strong brand, but the structure of the American system incentivizes politicians and interest groups to focus on their own brands not that of the party as a whole. This is especially true for politicians seeking the Presidency. Thus, it is not surprising that franchise building efforts have produced mixed results below that level.

Presidents, as Suri (2017) has noted, sell themselves as capable of handling all problems (Suri, 2017). They build brand stories arguing that they alone can fix the problems facing Americans as Donald Trump did or that action by the government of which they are in charge will solve said problems as Joe Biden claimed. To listen to Biden's State of the Union addresses, themselves brand building exercises, is to listen to an effort to place government at the center of American life in a way that FDR would have been proud of. It also highlights one of the biggest problems with political branding, franchising, and marketing in the American system: these techniques let politicians avoid having difficult conversations with each other and the public about thorny public policy problems. A case in point is provided by Biden's pitch on Social Security during the 2023 State of the Union Address in which he attempted to persuade the majority party in the House of Representatives to make no changes to the program by accusing them of planning to damage or end this popular entitlement program. Offering people great products at low prices with a recognizable brand everywhere is a great strategy for a retailer, but it might not be for government given that politics is about making difficult decision about who gets what and who pays. Building a strong brand and distributing it as a franchise represents an effort by both parties to avoid presenting voters with difficult choices.

The parties do these things because they capture the attention of the right audiences while allowing them to explain how their solutions and candidates are right while those of their opponents are wrong. The seemingly perennial fight in Washington over the historically mundane task of raising the nation's debt ceiling has become a recurring example of this. When there is a Democratic president, the Republicans in the US Congress balk at raising the limit, citing the need to be fiscally prudent despite putting up no such opposition when a president of their own party advocates for routine increases in the nation's debt limit during their administrations. The congressional Republicans are engaged in telling this simplistic brand story because it allows them to paint themselves as being fiscally prudent and the Democrats fiscally reckless. To be fair, Democrats have also played their part in grandstanding over the generally commonplace act of raising the debt limit, having done so in 20 March 2006 (Amira, 2011) during the George W. Bush administration, but their opposition did not appear to be serious about driving the country to the brink of default. The point is that these brand story telling opportunities exist and are practiced among both parties as part of the normal American political dialog in contemporary politics.

Donald Trump and Barack Obama present themselves as political supermen because doing so puts a name and a face to the party, its agenda, and its proposed policy solutions. This is the potential upside of parties acting like franchises. What American political parties cannot do is impose the kinds of discipline that parties in a responsible system can.[9] This limits their ability to campaign like a franchise business operates. To be a McDonald's franchisee, an operator has to agree to follow the company's standard operating procedures, menu, and branding to the letter. While there have been several candidates in both parties and at all levels of government who have lined up squarely behind the party brand just like a franchisee would line up behind the corporate brand, there is no way, nor might it be in the party's interest to compel them to do so. What constitutes electoral success varies by institution in the United States. For the Presidency, the US Senate, and governorships, it is states, but for the US House and most state legislatures, it is districts. Thus, the marketplace is different for each contest meaning the adoption of strict political franchise branding may not capture this reality on the ground.

Consider the case of the pro-Trump franchise branded candidates in 2022 as almost all of them lost the general election. Their decision to follow the Trump franchise model closely resembled the earlier McDonald's franchisee example. Those candidates who ran on the pro-Trump franchise brand such as Republican nominees Kari Lake in Arizona, Doug Mastriano in Pennsylvania, and Don Bolduc in New Hampshire changed very little on the menu and utilized Trumpian operating procedures regarding how they portrayed themselves as candidates, how they denied the legitimacy of the 2020 election, and how they sought to portray their opposition and the news media as enemies of the public and the nation.

CONCLUSION

Thinking about contemporary American politics through the lens of political marketing with an emphasis on branding and franchising is a beneficial means of attempting to understand the current chaotic political environment. More so, conceptualizing America's two major parties as corporate franchisors and the individual party nominees as the franchisees who can either adopt the full menu and operating procedure manual of the franchise or tailor their offerings depending on the political environment in which they are operating is essential for understanding the current struggles facing the American political system both electorally and when it comes to governing. Americans are routinely inundated with a variety of conflicting messages and brand appeals that are increasingly tailored to their specific interests, wants, and needs through the advancement of technology and the expansion of microtargeting. This is happening with increased frequency and intensity in American political campaigns, whether they are races occurring nationally for the presidency, statewide or district races, or local elections in one's hometown. The result is that the art of governing has become more problematic and challenging because the incentives for elected officials to depart from their party brands or candidate brands are very low.

We have demonstrated that party brands adjust to competing factions within their franchise and the changing technological mediums available to them, that branding shifts within a party as one faction gains control over the party apparatus, and that the franchise model is better suited for a parliamentary system rather than for one as large and diverse as the United States where voters are given two choices without additional competition for their consideration (Tables 35.1 and 35.2).

Notes

1 See McAuliffe, (2008) for examples of improvements in Democratic coordination
2 See Ries and Ries (2002) for a book length discussion of brand positioning.
3 As Carty notes could be true see Carty (2004) and Oleschuk (2020).
4 Ronald Reagan often made reference to the film "Knute Rockne All American" in which he played the ill-fated George Gipp. Gipp, nicknamed "the Gipper" gave a speech to the Notre Dame football team while on his deathbed urging them to win a big game in his honor. See AFP (2004) "How Reagan Got His Gipper Nickname." 'Sydney Morning Herald' 8 June. https://www.smh.com.au/world/howreagan-got-his-gipper-nickname-20040608-gdj2ut.html
5 See, for example, Patrick Ruffini (2012) in which a Republican consultant reverse engineered the Obama 2012 digital and analytics efforts. It makes great note of the things the Obama campaign had innovated.
6 The GOP coalition has shifted away from college-educated voters since 2012 toward a more working-class set of constituencies. See, for example, Elwood-Dieu, Piper and jin. (2022)
7 All of the data in the chart and text: see Pew Research Center (2021).
8 See Judis & Teixeira (2023) for an in-depth discussion.
9 For descriptions of how a brand is controlled in a responsible system, see Marland (2016) or Nimijean and Carment (2020) and for a possible explanation of how franchising could work in such a system, see Carty (2004).

REFERENCES

Abramowitz, A. I., & Webster, S. W. (2018). Negative partisanship: Why Americans dislike parties but behave like rabid partisans. *Political Psychology*, *39*, 119–135. https://doi.org/10.1111/pops.1247

Amira, D. (2011, April 12). Democrats suddenly regret voting against raising the debt ceiling under president Bush. *New York Magazine*. https://nymag.com/intelligencer/2011/04/democrats_suddenly_regret_voti.html

AFP. (2004, June 8). How Reagan got his Gipper Nickname. *Sydney Morning Herald*. https://www.smh.com.au/world/how-reagan-got-his-gipper-nickname-20040608-gdj2ut.html

Astrow, A., & Erickson, L. (2022, November 7). Overcoming the democratic party brand. *Third Way*. https://www.thirdway.org/memo/overcoming-the-democratic-party-brand

Barber, B. (2008). *Consumed*. W. W. Norton.

Bennett, W. L. (2008). *News: The politics of illusion*. Longman.

Bernstein, S. (2020, October 23). Trump, Biden clash over climate, oil industry in final debate. *Reuters*. https://www.reuters.com/article/us-usa-election-debate-climate-change/trump-biden-clash-over-climate-oil-industry-in-final-debate-idUSKBN2780HW

Bishop, B. (2008). *The big sort*. Houghton Mifflin.

Blair, R. D., & LaFontaine, F. (2005). *The economics of franchising*. Cambridge University Press.

Blake, A. (2012, July 10). Obama: The man of many slogans. *The Washington Post*. https://www.washingtonpost.com/blogs/the-fix/post/president-obama-a-man-of-many-slogans/2012/07/10/gJQAf8UlaW_blog.html

Cannon, L. (2000). *President Reagan: The role of a lifetime*. Public Affairs.

Carty, R. (2004). Parties as franchise systems – The stratarchical organizational imperative. *Party Politics*, *10*(1), 5–24. https://doi.org/10.1177/1354068804039118

Combs, J. (1993). *The Reagan range: Nostalgia and myth in American politics*. Popular Press.
Coppins, M. (2015). *The wilderness*. Little-Brown.
Cosgrove, K., & Shrader, N. R. (2021). Politcal branding in the USA election of 2020. In M. Moufahim (Ed.), *Political branding in turbulent times*. Palgrave Studies in Marketing and Management.
Cosgrove, K. (August 2017). GOP brand refresh. In J. Gillies (Ed.), *Political marketing in the 2016 US presidential election*. Palgrave.
Cosgrove, K. M. (2020). *Branded conservatives*. Peter Lang.
Cosgrove, K. M. (2022). *Donald Trump and the branding of the American presidency*. Palgrave.
Elliott, P. (2019, May 20). 'Let's stop fighting and let's start fixing'. Joe Biden Settles on election theme. *Time*. https://time.com/5591469/joe-biden-campaign-launch-philadelphia-2/
Elwood-Dieu, K., Piper, J., & Jin, B. (November 17, 2022). Election 2022: The educational divide that helps Explain the midterms. *Politico*. https://www.politico.com/interactives/2022/midterm-election-house-districts-by-education/
Ember, S., & Kaplan, T. (2020, July 8). Joe Biden and Bernie Sanders deepen their cooperation. *The New York Times*. https://www.nytimes.com/2020/07/08/us/politics/biden-bernie-sanders.html
Gillies, J. (Ed.). (2021). *Political marketing in the 2020 U.S. Presidential election*. Palgrave.
Givas, N. (2019, August 11). Kamala Harris: DHS raid on illegal immigrants was a 'campaign of terror' by Trump administration. *Fox News*. https://www.foxnews.com/media/kamala-harris-dhs-raids-illegal-immigrants-trump
Hains, T. (2022, September 23). Biden on 2022 midterms: 'Don't compare me to the almighty, compare me to the alternative. *Real Clear Politics*. https://www.realclearpolitics.com/video/2022/09/23/biden_on_2022_midterms_dont_compare_me_to_the_almighty_compare_me_to_the_alternative.html
Humphrey, H. (1976). Senator Hubert Humphrey's address to the democratic national convention. http:// www2.mnhs.org/library/findaids/00442/pdfa/0044 2-04021.pdf.
Inglehart, R. (1977). *The silent revolution*. Princeton University Press.
Issenberg, S. (2013). *The victory lab*. Crown.
Judis, J. B., & Teixeira, R. (Ruy, A.) (2023). *Where have all the democrats gone ?* Henry Holt.
Lemire, J., & McGraw, M. (2022, September 1). *Biden addresses nation: 'Too much of what's happening ... Today is not normal'*. Politico. https://www.politico.com/news/2022/09/01/biden-maga-republicans-philadelphia-speech-00054510
Mark, M., & Pearson, C. (2001). *The hero and the outlaw: Building extrodinary brands through the power of archetypes*. McGraw-Hill.
Marland, A. (2016). *Brand command*. UBC Press.
Mason, L. (2018). *Uncivil agreement: How politics became our identity*. University of Chicago Press.
McCauliffe, T. (2008). *What a party!!* St. Martin's Griffin.
McGirr, L. (2001). *Suburban warriors*. Princeton University Press.
Miller, J. (2015). *Sticky branding: 12.5 Strategies to stand out, attract customers and grown an incredible brand*. Page Two.
Moufaim, M. (Ed.). (2021). *Political branding in turbulent times*. Palgrave.
Newman, B. I. (1993). *The marketing of the president*. SAGE.
Newman, B. I. (1999). *The mass marketing of politics*. SAGE.
News. (April 22). https://www.foxnews.com/politics/biden-says-gop-aint-your-fathers-republican-party-maga-party-now
Nijmeijer, K. J., Fabbricotti, I. N., & Huijsman, R. (2014). Making franchising work. *International Journal of Management Reviews*, *16*, 62–83. https://doi.org/10.1111/ijmr.12009
Nimijean, R., & Carment, D. (2020). *Canada, nation branding and domestic politics*. Routeldge.
Oleschuk, P. (December 2020). Political franchising as a modern political technology. *Ukrainian Policymaker*, *7*, 35–42.
Pew Research Center. (2021). *Beyond red vs. blue: The political typology*. Pew Research Center. https://www.pewresearch.org/politics/2021/11/09/beyond-red-vs-blue-the-political-typology-2/
Pew Research the republican coalition. (2021, November 9). Pew Research. https://www.pewresearch.org/politics/2021/11/09/the-republican-coalition/
Postman, N. (2005). *Amusing oursleves to death*.
Putnam, R. D. (2000). *Bowling alone*. Simon and Schuster.
Ries, A., & Jack, T. (foreward by Irving Kotler) (2001). *Positioning: The battle for your mind*. McGraw-Hill.
Ries, A., & Ries, L. (2002). *The 22 immutable laws of branding*. Harper Business.
Ruffini, P. (2012). *Inside the Cave*. https:enga.ge/going-inside-the-cave/
Sabato, L., & Simpson, G. R. (1996). *Dirty little secrets*. Crown.
Singman, B. (2022). Biden says GOP 'ain't your father's Republican party': 'This is a MAGA party now'. *Fox*. https://www.foxnews.com/politics/biden-says-gop-aint-your-fathers-republican-party-maga-party-now
Skocpol, T. (2004). *Diminished democracy*. University of Oklahoma Press.
Skowronek, S. (2008). *Presidential leadership in political time*. University of Kansas Press.
Smith, H. (1996). *Hederick the power game*. Ballentine.
Suri, J. (2017). *The impossible presidency*. Basic.

Tensley, B. (2020, November 10). How Black voters and simmering protests contributed to Trump's loss. *CNN*. https://www.cnn.com/2020/11/10/politics/alicia-garza-black-lives-matter-election-joe-biden/index.html

Turow, J. (2007). *Breaking up America*. University of Chicago Press.

Walshe, S. (2013, March 13). RNC completes Autopsy on 2012 loss. Calls for inclusion not policy change. *ABC News*. https://abcnews.go.com/Politics/OTUS/rnc-completes-autopsy-2012-loss-calls-inclusion-policy/story?id=18755809

Zyman, S., & Brott, A. (2002). *The end of advertising as we know it*. Wiley.

Zyman, S. (2000). *The end of marketing as we know it*. Harper Business.

36

Political Marketing Amid the Rise and Fall of Democratic Regimes in Africa

George M. Bob-Milliar and Lauren M. MacLean

INTRODUCTION: DYNAMICS OF POLITICAL MARKETING WITH CHALLENGES TO DEMOCRACY AND LARGE YOUTH POPULATION IN AFRICA

In the latter part of 2023, giant billboards were unveiled in Ghana, featuring a masked male with the message "leadership for the next generation" and the hashtag "#TheNewForce." Similar billboards displayed the same faceless man flanked by people in various colored clothes with covered faces. The colorful face covering was an iconic design drawn from the combination of Dan and Bamana traditional masks. The visual appeared on all social media platforms and quickly went viral.

The "Man in the Mask" campaign created suspense, attracted the attention of Ghanaian citizens, and generated headlines worldwide. The billboards were strategically positioned along busy inner-city streets, including the capital city of Accra and the urban centers of Kumasi, Tamale, Ho, and Cape Coast. For months, Ghanaians speculated about the masked man's identity. The New Africa Foundation, the organization behind the campaign, utilized political marketing tools that generated strong popular curiosity and media interest. It was unclear who the smartly dressed man behind the mask was. Both traditional and social media platforms were used to market the unknown individual. Nevertheless, the message on the billboards provided clues to the rationale of the campaigners – "leadership for the next generation" implied a new political organization directed at the youth. The campaign, launched a year before national elections in Ghana, communicated a political intent.

On 7 January 2024, the #TheNewForce movement public lecture, dubbed "the Convention 2024," was scheduled to take place at the famous Black Star Square/Independence Square in Accra but was canceled by the incumbent government at the last minute. The convention was advertised as a Pan-African event to discuss Africa's development challenges, and the invited speakers included progressive influential African thought leaders, including former Director of the Kenya School of Law, Professor P. L. O. Lumumba, Nigerian Labour Party presidential candidate Peter Obi, and Zimbabwean former diplomat, Dr Arikana Chihombori-Quao. In place of the canceled lecture, the movement instead organized a press conference in Accra. During the press briefing, the mysterious figure on the giant billboards at last revealed his identity. Flanked by the invited speakers, Nana Kwame Bediako, also known as "Cheddar" or "Freedom Jacob Caesar," a

43-year-old Accra-based businessman, addressed his audience. He said, "You are about to find out about this man in the mask because I never spoke a word, you were looking for me… I didn't tell you whether I am into politics, whether I am an evangelist, whether I am conventionist or a revolutionist. After this day, you will have to wait for me to share my policies and my visions with you."

Two invitees to the convention also deserved close attention as political leaders who had challenged dominant parties in South Africa and Nigeria drawing on youth movements. Julius Malema was a former member of the governing African National Congress (ANC), where he was the Youth League leader; after being dismissed from the ANC, he founded the Economic Freedom Fighters (EFF) party of South Africa. Malema was billed to speak at the "Convention 2024," but then could not travel to Accra. Since its founding, the EFF has provided a template for youth-led movements to emerge and challenge dominant governing parties, for example, Bobi Wine's National Unity Platform in Uganda and Ousmane Sonko's Patriotes Africains du Sénégal pour le travail, l'éthique et la fraternité (PASTEF) in Senegal.

While third-party presidential candidates have struggled to make an impact in national elections in multiparty electoral systems in Africa, the presence of Peter Obi was significant because his movement did shake the foundations of the institutionalized parties in Nigeria. Obi and the Labour Party had emerged to challenge the longstanding duopoly by the All Progressives Congress (APC) and the People's Democratic Party (PDP) in Nigeria. Peter Obi had broken away from the PDP and tapped into youth activism through Nigeria's #EndSARS campaign and other youth discontent to launch his political movement.

We argue in this essay that political marketing practices in Africa's electoral space are distinctive due to the relative importance of the youth demographic and vary between countries depending on the nature of the political regime. As the continent deepens its democratic practices, political branding and communication are becoming increasingly important on the continent. Whether in weakly democratic, hybrid, or authoritarian regimes, political parties have increasingly utilized new tools in political marketing to communicate policies and mobilize voters, particularly the youth. Nevertheless, the level of sophistication of the marketing/branding strategies has varied across countries. For example, the elegant marketing of party campaign messages in South Africa, Ghana, Nigeria, and Senegal proves that political marketing has gained roots in some of Africa's more stable democracies. Similarly, the availability and embrace of social media platforms by Africa's youth has challenged the state monopoly of communication tools.

Political marketing has thus changed dramatically since the 1990s in many countries in Africa with unexpected evolutions in political regimes and new developments in information and communication technology. We adopt Lees-Marshment et al.'s (2019) definition of political marketing, which involves how politicians, parties, and governments use political marketing to engage and develop a relationship with citizens. The broad approach covers market surveys/research, branding, political parties, political communication, candidate electioneering, journalism, e-marketing, e-government, public relations, and political advertising (see Abid et al., 2023; Lees-Marshment, 2001a, 2001b).

Despite a revival of interest in electoral politics with the "third wave" of democratic transitions in the early 1990s (Di Palma, 1990; Levitsky & Way, 2024), scholars of African politics have emphasized the continued presence of informality, political clientelism, weak party organizations, and weak programmatic appeals (Chabal & Daloz, 1999; Cheeseman & Fisher, 2021; Englebert & Dunn, 2013). Liberal democracy has now existed for more three decades and many Africans have indicated in several opinion surveys their preference for political pluralism (Afrobarometer, 2024). The semi-presidential systems that dominate the continent produces variation in the development of political parties. The party organization has institutionalized in countries such as Ghana, Senegal, and Nigeria. The multiparty systems in these countries have seen power alternate between political parties. In other countries such as Uganda, Tanzania, Botswana, and Namibia where the dominant party model is the standard, parties are institutionalized. Whether in multiparty or dominant party systems, political parties have used political marketing strategies to package their platforms. In many African countries, political marketing has also been utilized by political leaders outside of parties, from religious organizations to state bureaucracies. This chapter, therefore, takes a critical look at the development of political marketing and broadens the conceptualization and analysis given the nature of post-colonial power, the repertoire of citizenship practices, and contested narratives of nationhood. The chapter first provides an overview of previous research, highlighting the role of democratization and new political parties, the expansion of mobile phone and social media use, and democratic backsliding and censorship from the 1990s to the 2010s. The chapter then showcases new issues and research that illuminates the overall decline of media freedoms despite an increasingly privatized media landscape, the role of the African diaspora in elections, and the increasing transnational activism of African youth through hashtag protests. The chapter concludes with concerns about how the use of AI in political marketing and rising income inequality may aggravate citizen distrust of government and politics and further weaken the prospects for democracy in Africa.

HOW POLITICAL MARKETING IN AFRICA CHANGES WITH POLITICAL REGIMES AND NEW TECHNOLOGY

Political marketing is a well-researched field in the US and the Global North. Several studies examined this subject and its influence on political behavior (Abid et al., 2023; Kaid & Holtz-Bacha, 2006; Lees-Marshment, 2001a, 2001b, 2024; O'Cass, 1996). Few studies on political marketing exist in Africa (Appau, 2021; Bukari et al., 2022; Hinson & Tweneboah-Koduah, 2010; Mensah, 2017a, 2017b; Kofi Preko, 2019; Starcevic, 2021). Yet, political marketing has contributed to electoral victories in countries with more competitive electoral systems, such as Ghana, Nigeria, and Senegal (Manyo & Mensah, 2024). This section reviews how the changing political regimes beginning in the 1990s and introduction of new information and communication technologies in the early 2000s until today has shaped the practices of political marketing in Africa.

Weak Democratic Roots in Early Post-Independence Period

Africa has fallen behind in political marketing scholarship for three important reasons. First, the democratic institutions that the departing imperial powers bequeathed to their former colonies failed to take root in most states (Ekeh, 1975). For example, the multiparty systems introduced in Ghana, Nigeria, Tanzania, Uganda, and Senegal did not last. The post-independence leaders adjusted the political systems to suit the prevailing conditions of the new states created out of colonialism. Consequently, democratic pluralism was curtained in many countries, and de facto one-party or quasi-one-party systems replaced what imperial powers left behind (Jackson & Rosberg, 1983; Zolberg, 1968, 1962). The single-party state was dominated by the ruling party, and the state media marketed the party's ideology and its achievements in government (Michel et al., 1999). The noncompetitive political environment did not provide the space for investing in competing political ideas. Instead, the constricted political space encouraged limited political marketing that featured the name, likeness, and party symbols of the solitary authoritarian leader – for example, Mobutu, Nyerere, or Mugabe.

Second, the growth of political parties suffered through repressive state policies including using constitutional amendments and harassing opposition figures. Party organizations became weak and the party systems were never truly institutionalized during this period (Arriola, 2013; Riedl, 2014). Yet, the governing parties enjoyed some privileges (Ninsin, 2018; LeBas, 2011). The voice of the state party dominated the monologue environment. The post-colonial political environment did not promote the growth of party organizations with strong ideological roots with the ability to sponsor outdoor and print media advertisements.

Third, during this early post-independence era, advertising through traditional platforms, such as radio, television, and print media, was seen as elitist, as most of the voting population resided in rural areas with relatively low literacy. Contacting rural voters directly through in-person campaign rallies with music and dancing or campaigning on market days was more cost-effective than mounting giant billboards at the village square or by the roadside.

The party system institutionalized with a weak foundation in some African states (e.g., Botswana, Tanzania, and Cameroon). The one-party system was the nodal party system, but it was seen as illegitimate by the opposition and military leaders. Consequently, military coups occurred in several states beginning in the late 1960s with Togo, and the military's involvement in African politics further hampered the growth of liberal democracy for a considerable period of the postcolonial era (Ake, 1996; Akyeampong, 2023; Hyden, 2013; Nugent, 1996; Van de Walle, 2001; Zartman, 1995). The late 1960s until the 1980s saw military regimes ruling in several countries, including Ghana and Nigeria. Indeed, it was the norm and not the exception for an African country to be ruled by a council of camouflaged men.

Transitions to Democracy in 1990s Spurs New Political Marketing

By the early 1990s, several African countries made the transition to democracy. The fall of the

Berlin Wall in the late 1980s had a profound impact on African countries. Confronted by a newly unipolar world dominated by US interests, several African countries were compelled to liberalize their political systems. Africa joined the "third wave" of democratization as several countries inaugurated civilian administrations and legalized the existence of multiple political parties.

Nevertheless, the transition was problematic in most cases (Bratton & Van de Walle, 1994). For example, in Gabon, Cameroon, Kenya, and Tanzania, the leaders manipulated the transition process. Therefore, several cases could be described as transitions without change, as the military administrations that initiated the transition used the advantages of incumbency to manipulate state institutions and the electoral systems. The likes of Ghana's Jerry John Rawlings and Yaya Jammeh of The Gambia installed themselves as heads of "democratic" administrations, having won disputed elections in their countries.

With the revival of multiparty politics in Africa, party scholars have examined the types of political parties that emerged in different countries (Basedau & Stroh, 2008; Bogaards, 2004; Ishiyama & Quinn, 2006; Kuenzi & Lambright, 2005). The conduct of elections and the nature of everyday politics attracted the attention of scholars (Oloka-Onyango & Ahikire, 2017; Osei, 2013; Paller, 2019). Political parties have been studied peripherally and intensively. Findings from such studies tend to make comparisons with Western parties (Elischer, 2013; LeBas, 2011; Riedl, 2014). Consequently, researchers have emphasized informality, political clientelism, weak party organizations, and weak programmatic appeals (Cheeseman, 2015; Osei, 2016). The African political party could not claim a distinctive ideology (Erdmann, 2004). Many Euro-American party research approaches were of limited analytical value in the African context. Context-specific methodological approaches are needed to improve our understanding beyond a mere description of what electoral political activities are *not* compared to the Western template.

The regime transitions of the 1990s sparked the emergence of large numbers of new political parties, many with relatively similar political marketing strategies and general promises for a better future (Bleck & van de Walle, 2019; Gyimah-Boadi, 2004). What is clear is that parties were hurriedly formed by remnants of the political elites in exile or within the country. Restrictions placed on political mobilization, including campaign funds, further crippled the growth of strong political parties and the development of a democratic culture supportive of electoral politics. The performance of many political parties in elections declined and subsequently political parties vanished over time, but others have become institutionalized (Whitfield, 2009). Parties were mostly located in the nation's capital, they lacked a coherent ideology, membership registers did not exist, and organizational infrastructure was often absent (Bob-Milliar, 2019). Political parties and electoral politics were heavily personalized and tailored toward promoting the ambitions of the party founder and his ethnic group. The weak and factionalized opposition parties had no realistic chance of winning national elections in this environment. However, in Benin, the opposition forces succeeded in dislodging the administration of Mathieu Kérékou in the 1991 transition election, albeit briefly. He reclaimed the presidency in the 1996 elections and then managed to dominate politics for another decade (Bratton & van de Walle, 1997; Sigman, 2023).

The hostile environment in which the parties operated during this period dictated the types of political marketing they engaged in. The transition to multiparty systems was supervised by civilian dictators and strong military leaders who approved constitutions that assured them of enormous executive powers. In many African countries, the airwaves were not liberalized and so government broadcasting stations and state-owned newspapers were the only means of advertising political messages. The opposition parties were either denied access to state media or given limited air time compared to the governing parties. Furthermore, most of the voting population in Nigeria, Zambia, and Chad, for example, had never before voted in a multiparty election and lived in rural areas where illiteracy was high, so marketing was mostly through state-owned radio and in-person campaign rallies where the party's candidates distributed white t-shirts and clothes. In short, the period before the 2000s saw very limited forms or at best basic political marketing practices that were more clientelist in orientation.

Mixed Success in the Consolidation of Democratic Regimes

The 2000s signaled some notable progress in the development of democracy in Africa. Africa's democracy was consolidating through the repetition of multiparty elections (Lindberg, 2006, 2009). Opposition leader Abdoulaye Wade and the Senegalese Democratic Party (PDS), with the support of several minor parties, won the presidency after the second round of elections held in March 2000. The reign of the independence-era Socialist Party of Senegal (Parti Socialiste du Sénégal, PS) of Léopold Sédar Senghor, whose candidate was the incumbent President, Abdou Diouf, ended with the election of Wade as president of Senegal. Similarly, Ghana's December 2000 elections were significant; the country experienced its first democratic alternation of government. President J. J. Rawlings, who had already served the constitutionally limit of two terms, supervised an election in which his governing party, the National Democratic Congress (NDC), lost to the opposition New Patriotic Party (NPP). The opposition victories in Benin, Senegal, and Ghana suggested the institutionalization of liberal democracy and the building of institutions to support democracy in some parts of Africa. Nevertheless, the overall picture of democratic gains was limited in scope.

The democratic practice in some states failed to deepen as the governing parties went into survival mode and oppressed the political opposition. In Uganda, President Yoweri Museveni's National Resistance Movement (NRM) resisted calls to reform the "no-party system" to allow for the establishment of political parties (Carbone, 2008). The dominant party systems in Eastern and Southern Africa consolidated: South Africa's African National Congress (ANC), Tanzania's Chama Cha Mapinduzi (CCM), and the Rwandan Patriotic Front (RPF) entrenched their positions (Booysen, 2011; O'Gorman, 2012).

The dominant parties in these countries marketed their achievements to mute domestic criticisms of their closed political systems. The parties also engaged in branding based on their liberation history. While electoral politics functioned in a limited number of countries, the same could not be said of other authoritarian civilian administrations. For example, President Robert Mugabe's Zimbabwe African National Union-Patriotic Front (Zanu PF) became increasingly unpopular and devised violent means to keep the opposition Movement for Democratic Change (MDC) from power through the rigging of elections. With limited violence, Gabon, Chad, Burundi, Equatorial Guinea, and Congo (Brazzaville) governing regimes succeeded in amending their constitutions to remove presidential term limits. Many parties that won elections during this period invested little resources in professionalizing and branding the party campaign machinery. Political marketing was confined to displaying photos of a smiling incumbent president on giant billboards in the national capitals, mostly lining the main road from the international airport into town.

The deepening of liberal democracy in Africa is likened to the Americanization of politics around the globe. Africa's brand of electoral politics mimics American presidential politics. Without a doubt, African electoral politics has embraced many American norms. More than a decade after the return of multiparty politics to the continent, American/Western liberal values had begun to impact a limited number of elections. The party system has become institutionalized in Ghana, Nigeria, Senegal, Zambia, and Malawi. Nevertheless, the question of how African voters make their choices is complex. Where previous studies had focused on clientelism, ethnicity, personalism, or valence issues (Bleck & van de Walle, 2013), Cheeseman et al. (2014) and Elischer (2013) pointed out that elections in many African countries are based on programmatic ideas. As a result, in-depth knowledge of a party's organization, structure, members, founding traditions, philosophy, ideology, performance in elections, and performance as a governing party or an opposition party is slowly beginning to influence political marketing on the continent.

At the same time, clientistic politics is still common in flawed and authoritarian regimes. But clientelism is insufficient to win political power in competitive multiparty systems. Therefore, the programmaticization of politics has necessitated the packaging of ideas and policies to enable the electorates to make informed choices. Many parties refer to political traditions and key programmatic positions to brand themselves. These brands allow the electorates with local knowledge to make choices.

Consequently, political parties have increasingly taken market research, branding, and political communication seriously, and enormous resources are now invested into making a party and its candidates and programs attractive to the electorates. This is particularly true in more competitive multiparty systems such as Ghana, Nigeria, Liberia, and Senegal. Presidential elections are keenly contested; sometimes, the margin of victory between the winning and losing parties is small. The availability of multiple platforms to market a political party also has implications for what political marketing means in the contemporary context. Political parties use traditional and new social media platforms. Therefore, governing and opposition parties have begun including brand experts in their election mobilization efforts.

The Spread of New Technologies in 2000s Revolutionizes Political Marketing in Africa

In addition to democratization, the introduction of new telecommunication technologies beginning in the early 2000s has also revolutionized political marketing in Africa. While advanced technology has made political communication much easier, it has also created new problems. As Hinson and Tweneboah-Koduah (2010) remind us, political marketing and communication agencies have been prominent in election campaigns in many African countries. South Africa has one of the continent's most advanced political marketing traditions. The telecommunication and print media have been engaged by South African political parties – the ANC and the Democratic Party (DP) to market the party's programs during elections campaigns. Similarly, Ghana's two major political parties have used the expertise of political marketers, strategists, and consultants. According to Kennedy (2009), Dr Larry Gibson, an American law professor, was hired to advise the NPP campaign team in the 2008 presidential elections. Meanwhile, the opposition party, the NDC, hired the services of the South African-based Brand Leadership Group to assist the party to package its programs for the election campaign agenda (Bob-Milliar, 2012a, 2012b).

The Nigerian political communications agency, StateCraft, has branded four presidential candidates in three West African countries successfully.[1] The PDP presidential candidate, Goodluck Jonathan, worked with the agency in 2011 and won the elections. Jonathan's opponent and the APC presidential candidate, General Muhammadu Buhari, was also branded by StateCraft. In 2016 in Ghana, Nana Akufo-Addo, a presidential candidate of the NPP, hired StateCraft services. The agency worked on the communication strategies of political parties that helped secure their victories in Nigeria, Ghana, and Senegal. Jideonwo and Williams (2018) detailed StateCraft's political marketing and communication strategies in their co-authored book, *How to Win Elections in Africa*. The strategy essentially involved polishing the presidential candidate's image and enhancing his popularity among young voters. Africa's huge population of youth is the primary target for political mobilization during election campaigns. Williams states, "We work to change narratives, shape opinion, drive a common good, and provoke action" (GhanaWeb.com, 2024). One strategy is to deploy traditional and social media platforms to promote a party's candidate and its programs. Coaching presidents to be media-savvy was another communication strategy of StateCraft. In 2014, the APC election campaign team hired StateCraft to brand its presidential candidate after his three failed attempts on different political party tickets. Buhari was a former military head of state who carried huge baggage with voters and would be challenging to sell in the democratic age. In addition, the voting demographics and generational shift are hurdles that Africa's aged politicians must contend with in their political marketing strategies.

Nevertheless, StateCraft's strategies helped to soften Buhari's military strongman's image and his campaign message of change to enable him to connect with the young voters in Nigeria. In addition, a smiling Buhari in photos through a social media campaign showing his humanity and no-nonsense legacy during his military administration was repackaged and presented positively as his stance on corruption and security. Buhari ultimately won the 2015 elections, making history as the first opposition candidate to defeat an incumbent in a general election in Nigeria.

In another example, in Ghana, Nana Akufo-Addo ran unsuccessfully twice in 2008 and 2012 (Bob-Milliar & Paller, 2018). StateCraft was hired to brand him for his third attempt at the presidency. Taking advantage of the deteriorating economic conditions and the corruption scandals drowning the Mahama administration, Nana Akufo-Addo was branded to shed his "arrogance" tag and presented as connecting with the Ghanaian youth and their pastime, celebrity, and pop culture. His anticorruption credentials were also amplified in communications. In December 2016, Nana Akufo-Addo won the elections by a landslide, defeating the incumbent (Bob-Milliar & Paller, 2023).

The internet and the widespread use of social media have also improved political marketing for the better and worse (Hassan & Hitchen, 2022; Nyabola, 2018). Parties and candidates invest in running multiple internet-based sites and social media platforms – personalized websites, Facebook accounts, X (formerly Twitter) handles, Instagram accounts, and WhatsApp groups. In Kenya, local and national politicians create WhatsApp groups for citizens in their constituencies to air their grievances and bring locally relevant issues to the attention of their representatives. Amateurs as well as party activists can now brand and package whatever information and circulate it widely on the internet and through multiple social media platforms. A positive outcome of the new media landscape is that state control of information flow has been dismantled as alternative means are used to escape censorship.

The adverse effect of the hyper-liberalization of telecommunication is that mobile phone numbers can be bought off the street without any formal document identifying the purchaser. This poses a major problem and leads to the production and unwitting consumption of fake news in Africa. Governments have capitalized on the problem of fake news to then censor news outlets and clamp down on their political opponents. Some African governments have censored websites and social media accounts. In Senegal, Uganda, and Tanzania, governments have occasionally blocked internet access, denying millions of citizens the opportunity to communicate, share information, or mobilize. These incumbent governments claim that citizens are irresponsible and abuse the freedoms associated with free speech. In Senegal, Uganda, and Tanzania, national security concerns have been invoked, and the internet completely shut down, making it impossible to communicate via FaceBook and WhatsApp.

Many African countries have practiced and perfected the minimalist version of democracy. Several decades ago, Terry Karl (1997) described this phenomenon as the "fallacy of electoralism" in her studies of Latin American politics. Periodic elections are the markers of democratization in many African states. Nevertheless, many African countries have experienced deterioration in the quality of their political liberalization and democratic practice. The recent setbacks were marked by the return of military administrations in Burkina Faso, Mali, Guinea, Niger, and Gabon. The democratic backsliding in the Sahel is a source of concern for the proponents of liberal democracy on the continent (Arriola et al., 2023). Several nominally functioning democracies have consolidated what is arguably party democracy. Current research analyzing the dysfunctional nature of electoral politics in Africa describes it as "democracy capture." According to Gyimah-Boadi (2021, p. 21), "democracy capture occurs when a few individuals or section of a supposedly democratic polity are able to systematically appropriate to themselves the institutions and processes as well as dividends of democratic governance." With specific reference to Africa, governing parties tend to entrench themselves in power and use executive powers to neutralize societal pressures that attempt to deepen democracy. The incumbent strategies that have contributed to democratic backsliding appear legitimate on the surface, but on closer inspection, one notices variants of authoritarianism creeping into democratic practices. In this regard, the judiciary is an enabler, and its rulings erode the democratic gains in many countries. Recent examples include Supreme Court rulings on the use of birth certificates to register for national identity cards in Ghana and the legibility of candidates for elected office in Senegal. Governments use legal means to stop citizens protesting in many African democracies. The law excludes the majority of citizens from exercising their democratic right of protest against state ineptitude. We contend that the spread of democratic backsliding on the continent will likely reverse the developments in political marketing, in particular, alienating young voters from increasingly out of touch and authoritarian regimes.

NEW CHALLENGES TO POLITICAL MARKETING IN AFRICA

Several new trends pose novel challenges to political marketing and the consolidation of democracy in Africa. In this section, we highlight how democratic backsliding has been associated with the decline of media freedoms. We also show how political marketing has become transnational, with a growing African diaspora participating in mobilization and support of political candidates. Finally, we highlight how rapid urbanization and an increasingly mobilized youth population shapes the efforts by political parties and states to engage voters.

Recent Decline of Media Freedoms in Africa

First, with increasing challenges to democracy in much of Africa, media freedoms have also declined. Many African states tightly control the media landscape through national communication authorities. In authoritarian regimes, civil liberties, including press freedoms, are limited (see Freedom House Media Freedom in the World, 2022). For example, Togo's regulator is the Autorité de Réglementation des Secteurs de Postes et de Télécommunications (ART&P). As the government regulator, these national communication authorities oversee the licensing, regulation, and monitoring of telecommunications operators and service providers in their respective countries. In flawed democracies such as Ghana and South Africa, the media are relatively independent and diverse. Political marketing is better even in flawed or quasi-liberal African democracies than in full-fledged authoritarian ones. Opposition parties in Ghana and Nigeria have many more avenues to market their ideologies and programs than in long-time dictator Paul Biya's Cameroon. In Togo, where the Union for the Republic (Union pour la République) dominates politics, opposition parties have struggled to market their programs during election campaigns. Togo's media landscape is rich and diverse, with 234 newspapers, 94 radio stations, and a dozen television channels. The privately owned daily, *Liberté*, has the highest daily circulation and is one of the most widely read newspapers. Yet, *Liberté* was suspended by the regulator for a month in early 2023. This is one example of how press freedoms have taken a nosedive in Africa. Journalists continue to face many hurdles, and journalism in many African countries has become more difficult in recent years. Reporters Without Borders (2023) has classified the situation in the continent as "bad" in nearly 40% of its countries.

Even Ghana, a country once lauded as having a strongly independent media, has seen a decline in press freedom over time. In 2017, Ghana recorded one of its best performances on the World Press Freedom Index, ranking 26 out of 180 countries ahead of advanced democracies such as the UK (40th) and USA (43rd). The *State of the Ghanaian Media 2023* report noted the country's media as a key pillar in its democratization journey. It was noted that Ghana had "one of the most buoyant media landscapes on the continent." Since 2017, Ghana has experienced a decline in its global standing in press freedom. In 2023, the country had fallen to 62 out of 180 countries. The factors driving Ghana's decline in press freedom are traced to the partisan environment. Still, Ghana's media ecosystem is rich and diverse. For example, in the fourth quarter of 2023, the NCA granted frequency authorizations to 747 FM broadcasting stations in Ghana. Out of the total number licensed, 550 radio stations are currently operational. The state-owned radio stations are 31 in number, while privately owned/commercial radio stations are 549 (NCA, 2024). According to the NCA data, some 175 TV stations are in operation, and more than 100 newspapers are in the traditional media space. Furthermore, several digital news, blogging, and social media platforms such as Facebook, X (formerly Twitter), Instagram, and YouTube are thriving in the Ghanaian media space.

Nevertheless, like many African countries, Ghana has experienced a decline in media freedom. Measures taken by the government to promote media pluralism have been hijacked by politicians to create a partisan media landscape. Ghanaian journalists tend to self-censor and investigative journalists now operate in fear after one prominent undercover journalist, Ahmed Hussein-Suale was murdered in January 2019 after being threatened by a governing party politician. Furthermore, between 2017 and 2019, the NCA embarked on an exercise to clean up the airwaves, which resulted in the revocation of the operational licenses of several radio stations. The opposition party protested the regulator's actions as most radio stations closed down in Accra were politically aligned with the National Democratic Congress (NDC). More importantly, the NDC and the NPP duopoly in Ghanaian politics has adversely impacted the independence of the media. There are chains of radio stations owned by politicians or their political opponents. For example, Asaase Radio (99.5FM) was established by President Akufo-Addo's cousin in 2020. The radio is headquartered in the nation's capital but has several affiliate radio stations across the country. On the opposite side is radio XYZ (93.1FM), which is aligned with the NDC. The independence of the media is compromised as these politically aligned radio and television stations become the mouthpiece of the two major political parties in Ghana.

Growing Role of African Diasporas in Home Country Politics

One positive aspect of new telecommunication technology is the opportunity it has offered Africans in the diaspora to be active citizens in their countries of origin. Transnational political networks have enriched democratization in many African countries (Taber, 2020). Many diaspora communities maintain an online presence through ethnic associations websites or through other independent digital newspaper portals. These digital platforms provide opportunities for political marketing.

Diasporans and home-based Africans are increasingly engaged in conversation about political developments on the home front. At the same time, social media platforms are used to mobilize funds for political campaigns in various African countries. For example, Nigerian, Ghanaian, and Senegalese politicians now market their programs through diasporan-based digital platforms. The engagement between Africans at home and the diaspora also allows for mobilization strategies to be shared during protests against government underperformance or state brutality.

Rapid Urbanization and Youth Mobilization Stimulate New Political Marketing Strategies

African states are also urbanizing rapidly. Urbanization and its associated problems of youth unemployment and high living costs have provided a channel for mobilizing youth energies to draw attention to governmental corruption and mismanagement, oppose police brutalities, or support opposition programs. Aalen and Oosterom (2024) draws our attention to the role youth played in popular protests which has "created high expectations about their role in countering autocratic governments and contributing to democracy." The #RhodesMustFall, #EndSARS, #FreeSenegal, #EndFinanceBill, and the #OccupyJulorbiHouse campaigns were all urban-based, youth-led protests against government policies. The 2020 #EndSARS protest saw thousands of Nigerian youths take to the streets to protest against police brutality and extrajudicial killings. The protests across major Nigerian cities were triggered by a viral video showing the notorious Special Anti-Robbery Squad (SARS) shooting and killing a robbery suspect openly. The youth demanded the disbandment of SARS and the prosecution of the police officers involved in the unlawful killing. The police unleashed more violence on the protestors to quench their demonstrations. The #EndSARS protests united Nigerians at home and abroad. Days of continuous protest yielded the desired results when the Chief of Police disbanded SARS. Young activists made their mark in the #EndSARS protest in Nigeria.

Similarly, in 2021, Senegalese youth mobilized and poured onto the streets of Dakar to protest the government arrest of Ousmane Sonko, the young leader of the opposition party and widely considered the strongest challenger to the incumbent party. The #FreeSenegal uprising broke out when Sonko was accused of rape and arrested by the regime. In response to youth protests, the courts provisionally released Sonko. He was rearrested and convicted in July 2023 "for corrupting the youth." Immediately, the court handed down its verdict, PASTEF party messaged the youth on social media to "take to the streets." The government responded by imposing restrictions on social media – Facebook, Instagram, Messenger, Telegram, TikTok, WhatsApp, and YouTube – in order, in the words of the Interior Minister to stop the "dissemination of hate and subversive messages." Young Senegalese clashed with the police in the city center. Messaging on social media allowed the youth to challenge President Macky Sall authoritarian rule in Senegal. Nevertheless, the courts were used to jail Sonko, but his supporters never relented until he was released from jail but he could not stand in the presidential elections.

In Ghana, police failed to discourage the youth from protesting against the high cost of living. Therefore, the three-day #OccupyJulorbiHouse campaign saw the youth attempting to have direct contact with high government officials at the Golden Jubilee House, but the police blocked their path.

All the youth-led protest movements across Africa have signaled the yearning of the youth for opportunities to earn decent livelihoods. As Claude Ake (2000) argued, Africans did not celebrate the return of multiparty politics for its abstractness – respect for democratic rights and enjoyment of civil liberties. Improving the social welfare of citizens was the hidden motive for the widespread demands for the institutionalization of liberal democracy. But as liberal democracy runs its course in Africa, it is apparent that party politics has become an avenue for self-aggrandizement, embezzlement of public resources, and manipulation of electoral processes to entrench a ruling clique. The democratic dividends have not been realized in many states, hence the return of the discredited military to civilian terrain in countries in the Sahel.

Politically charged youth movements shape political marketing cross the continent. Even though, the activism of the youth threatens the base of authoritarian regimes it has contributed to democratic deepening. The youth now have access to information devices and platforms more than one could ever have imagine at the start of "third wave" democratizations. The social media platforms are used effectively to mobilize and discredit government policies. On the one hand, governments monitor the online traffic on social media platforms such as Facebook, X, and WhatsApp. Personnel of the state security agencies and supporters of the governing regime infiltrate social media groups and monitor discussions in order to disrupt the strategies of protesters. On the other hand, mainstream politicians are putting investment into social media messaging to appear responsive to constituents. Indeed, constituents use messaging platforms to reach out to their representative to either advertise political goods or demand for them. These developments have implication for political marketing in the 21st century.

CONCLUSION: FUTURE RESEARCH QUESTIONS ON POLITICAL MARKETING IN AFRICA

Despite democratic backsliding and reversals, the majority of Africans maintain that they prefer liberal democracy to other political systems according to Afrobarometer public opinion surveys.[2] The political information and messaging that Africans receive from their political leaders is key for the ability of citizens to make decisions about what candidates or regimes to support or mobilize against. The rapid development of AI makes it even more difficult for citizens to adjudicate the quality and trustworthiness of information from political parties, politicians, media organizations, and a range of other political actors. The widespread suspicions of "fake news" can serve to undermine citizen trust in individual leaders but also weaken the belief in the credibility of the political institutions of the regime as a whole.

Rapid urbanization and rising inequality can further diminish the reciprocity among citizens in large cities across the continent. The growing numbers of African youth can be especially skeptical of their equitable inclusion in the political system, when they feel left behind from economic advancement and left out of political decision-making.

Moving forward, political marketing will be very important for reclaiming the vibrancy of the media environment and strengthening the quality of democracy. Scholars must continue to broaden the conceptualization and empirical study of political marketing to include a range of cases from Africa, where there is such a diversity of political regimes, demographic profiles, and levels of economic development.

Notes

1 See https://statecraftinc.com/
2 See Afrobarometer.org

REFERENCES

Aalen, L., & Oosterom, M. (2024). Young Africans could disrupt authoritarian states but they don't – Here's why. *The Conversation*. https://theconversation.com/young-africans-could-disrupt-authoritarian-states-but-they-dont-heres-why-218179. Accessed on 18 June 2024.

Abid, A., Roy, S. K., Lees-Marshment, J., Dey, B. L., Muhammad, S. S., & Kumar, S. (2023). Political social media marketing: A systematic literature review and agenda for future research. *Electronic Commerce Research*. https://doi.org/10.1007/s10660-022-09636-7

Afrobarometer. (2024). *African insights 2024 Democracy at risk – The people's perspective*. https://www.afrobarometer.org/feature/flagship-report/. Accessed on 12 September 2024.

Ake, C. (1996). *Democracy and development in Africa*. The Brookings Institution.

Ake, C. (2000). *The feasibility of democracy in Africa*. CODESRIA.

Akyeampong, E. K. (2023). *Independent Africa: The first generation of nation builders*. Indiana University Press.

Appau, S. (Ed.), (2021) *Marketing brands in Africa: Perspectives on the evolution of branding in an emerging market*. Palgrave Macmillian.

Arriola, L. R. (2013). *Multiethnic Coalitions in Africa: Business Financing of opposition election campaigns*. Cambridge University Press.

Arriola, L. R., Rakner, L., & van de walle, N. (Eds.), (2023) *Democratic backsliding in Africa? Autocratization, resilience, and contention*. Oxford University Press.

Basedau, M., & Stroh, A. (2008). *Measuring party institutionalization in developing countries: A new research instrument applied to 28 African political parties*. GIGA Working Paper.

Bleck, J., & van de Walle, N. (2013). Valence issues in African elections. *Comparative Political Studies, 46*(11), 1394–1421.

Bleck, J., & van de Walle, N. (2019). *Electoral politics in Africa since 1990: Continuity in change*. Cambridge University Press.

Bob-Milliar, G. M. (2012a). Political party activism in Ghana: Factors influencing the decision of the politically active to join a political party. *Democratization, 19*(4), 668–689.

Bob-Milliar, G. M. (2012b). *The dynamics of political party activism in Ghana: A comparative study of the activists of the NDC and NPP in Wa Central and Lawra-Nandom Constituencies, 1992–2008*. Unpublished PhD dissertation. University of Ghana.

Bob-Milliar, G. M. (2019). Activism of political parties in Africa. In *Oxford research encyclopedia of politics*. Oxford University Press. https://doi.org/10.1093/acrefore/9780190228637.013.1365

Bob-Milliar, G. M., & Paller, J. W. (2018). Democratic ruptures and electoral outcomes: Ghana 2016 general elections. *Africa Spectrum, 53*(1), 5–35.

Bob-Milliar, G. M., & Paller, J. W. (2023). The social embeddedness of elections: Ghana's 2016 and 2020 campaigns. *Commonwealth and Comparative Politics, 61*(3), 293–314.

Bogaards, M. (2004). Counting parties and identifying dominant party systems in Africa. *European Journal of Political Research, 43*(2), 173–197.

Booysen, S. (2011). *The African National Congress and the regeneration of political power*. Wits University Press.

Bratton, M., & Van de Walle, N. (1994). Neopatrimonial regimes and political transitions in Africa. *World Politics, 46*(4), 453–489. https://doi.org/10.2307/2950715

Bratton, M., & van de Walle, N. (1997). *Democratic experiments in Africa: Regime transitions in comparative perspective*. Cambridge University Press.

Bukari, Z., Hamid, A. B. A., Som, H. M., Agbemabiese, G. C., & Quansah, F. (2022). Does political issue matter in voting intention in Ghana? A political marketing perspective. *Cogent Business & Management*, *9*(1), 2034227.

Carbone, G. (2008). *No-Party democracy? Ugandan politics in comparative perspectives*. Lynne Rienner Publishers.

Chabal, P., & Daloz, J.-P. (1999). *Africa works: Disorder as political instrument*. James Currey/Indiana University Press.

Cheeseman, N. (2015). *Democracy in Africa: Successes, failures, and the struggle for political reform*. Cambridge University Press.

Cheeseman, N., et al. (2014). *Politics meets policies: The Emergence of programmatic political parties*. International Institute for Democracy and Electoral Assistance (International IDEA).

Cheeseman, N., & Fisher, J. (2021). *Authoritarian Africa: Repression, resistance, and the power of ideas*. Oxford University Press.

Department of Communication Studies. (2023). *The state of the Ghanaian media report*. University of Ghana.

Di Palma, G. (1990). *To craft demcracies: An Essay on democratic transitions*. University of California Press.

Egbunike, N. (2022). WhatsApp political campaigns in Nigerian. In I. Hassan, & J. Hitchen (Eds.), *WhatsApp and everyday life in west Africa: Beyond fake news* (pp. 3–71). Bloomsbury Academic.

Ekeh, P. (1975). Colonialism and the two publics: A theoretical statement. *Comparative Studies in Society and History*, *17*(1), 91–112.

Elischer, S. (2013). *Political parties in Africa: Ethnicity and party formation*. Cambridge University Press.

Englebert, P., & Dunn, K. C. (2013). *Inside african politics*. Lynne Rienner Publishers.

Erdmann, G. (2004). Party research: Western European bias and the 'African labyrinth. *Democratization*, *11*(3), 63–87.

GhanaWeb.com. *Meet the 31-year-old Nigerian who helped Akufo-Addo become president*. https://www.ghanaweb.com/GhanaHomePage/NewsArchive/Meet-the-31-year-old-Nigerian-who-helped-Akufo-Addo-become-President-590084. Accessed on March 4, 2024.

Gyimah-Boadi, E. (2004). *Democratic reform in Africa: The quality of progress*. Lynne Rienner Publishers.

Gyimah-Boadi, E. (2021). What is democracy capture? In *Ghana centre for democratic development, democracy capture in Africa: Benin, Ghana, Kenya, Mozambique and Nigeria* (pp. 21–32). Accra: CDD-Ghana.

Hassan, I., & Hitchen, J. (2022). Introduction: A new platform for old networks? WhatsApp and everyday life in West Africa. In I. Hassan, & J. Hitchen (Eds.), *WhatsApp and everyday life in west Africa: Beyond fake news* (pp. 1–20). Bloomsbury Academic.

Hinson, R., & Tweneboah-Koduah, E. Y. (2010). Political marketing strategies in Africa: Expert opinions of recent political elections in Ghana. *Journal of African Business*, *11*(2), 201–218.

Huntington, S. (1991). *The third wave: Democratization in the late twentieth century*. University of Oklahoma Press.

Hyden, G. (2013). *African politics in comparative perspective* (2nd ed.). Cambridge University Press.

Ishiyama, J., & Quinn, J. J. (2006). African phoenix? Explaining the electoral performance of the formerly dominant parties in Africa. *Party Politics*, *12*(3), 317–340.

Jackson, R. G., & Rosberg, C. G. (1983). *Personal rule in black Africa: Prince, autocrat, prophet, tyrant*. University of Calofornia Press.

Jideonwo, C., & Williams, A. (2018). *How to win elections in Africa: Parallel with Donald Trump*. BookBaby.

Kaid, L. L., & Holtz-Bacha, C. (Eds.). (2006). *The sage handbook of political advertising*. SAGE Publications.

Karl, T. L. (1997). *The paradox of plenty: Oil booms and petro-states*. University of California Press.

Kennedy, A. (2009). *Chasing the elephant into the bush: The politics of complacency*. Author House.

Kofi Preko, A. D., Agbanu, S. K., & Feglo, M. (2019). Political Marketing Strategy: Soundbites and Voting Behaviour in Contemporary Ghana. *Journal of African Business*, *21*(3), 375–394. https://doi.org/10.1080/15228916.2019.1641305

Kuenzi, M., & Lambright, G. (2005). Party systems and democratic consolidation in Africa's electoral regimes. *Party Politics*, *11*(4), 423–446.

LeBas, A. (2011). *From protest to parties: Party-building and democratization in Africa*. Oxford University Press.

Lees-Marshment, J. (2001a). *Political marketing and British political parties: The party's just begun*. Manchester University Press.

Lees-Marshment, J. (2024). *The human resource management of political staffers: Insights from prime ministers' Advisers and reformers*. Routledge.

Lees-Marshment, J., Conley, B., Elder, E., Pettitt, R., Raynauld, V., & Turcotte, A. (2019). *Political marketing: Principles and applications* (3rd ed.). Routledge. https://doi.org/10.4324/9781351136907

Lees-Marshment, J. (2001b). The marriage of politics and marketing. *Political Studies*, *49*(4), 692–713.

Levitsky, S., & Way, L. (2024). The resilience of democracy's third wave. *PS: Political Science & Politics*, 1–4.

Lindberg, S. I. (2006). *Democracy and elections in Africa*. Johns Hopkins University Press.

Lindberg, S. I. (2009). The power of elections in Africa revisited. In S. I. Lindberg (Ed.), *Democratization by*

elections: A new mode of transition (pp. 25–46). Johns Hopkins University Press.
Manyo, J., & Mensah, K. (2024). Political delivery marketing in Ghana. In M. Kpessa-Whyte & J. Dzisah (Eds.). *Public policy in Ghana. International series on public policy*. Palgrave Macmillan. https://doi.org/10.1007/978-3-031-33005-6_14
Mensah, K. (2017a). Political brand architecture: Towards a new conceptualization of political branding in an emerging democracy. *African Journalism Studies*, *37*(3), 61–84.
Mensah, K. (Ed.). (2017). *Political marketing and management in Ghana: A new architecture*. Palgrave Macmillan.
Michel, T., Pireaux, C., Barbé, M., & Lalou, S. (1999). *Mobutu King of Zaire: An African tragedy*. First Run/Icarus Films.
Morrison, M. K. C., & Hong, J.-W. (2006). Ghana's political parties: How ethno/regional variations sustain the national two-party system. *The Journal of Modern African Studies*, *44*(4), 623–647.
National Communication Authority (NCA). (2024). https://nca.org.gh/#. Accessed on 12 May 2024.
Ninsin, K. A. (2018). *The corrupt elites: Anatomy of power and wealth in Ghana*. Gavoss Education PLC Ltd.
Nugent, P. (1996). *Big men, small boys and politics in Ghana*. Asempa Publishers.
Nyabola, N. (2018). *Digital democracy, analogue politics: How the internet Era is transforming Politics in Kenya*. Zed Books.
O'Gorman, M. (2012). Why the CCM won't lose: The roots of single-party dominance in Tanzania. *Journal of Contemporary African Studies*, *30*(2), 313–333.
O'Cass, A. (1996). Political marketing and the marketing concept. *European Journal of Marketing*, *30*(10/11), 37–53.
Oloka-Onyango, J., & Ahikire, J. (Eds.). (2017). *Controlling consent*. Africa World Press.
Osei, A. (2013). Political parties in Ghana: Agents of democracy? *Journal of Contemporary African Studies*, *31*(4), 543–563.
Osei, A. (2016). Formal party organisation and informal relations in African parties: Evidence from Ghana. *The Journal of Modern African Studies*, *54*(1), 37–66.
Paller, J. W. (2019). *Democracy in Ghana: Everyday politics in urban Africa*. Cambridge University Press.
Riedl, R. B. (2014). *Authoritarian origins of democratic party systems in Africa*. Cambridge University Press.
Sigman, R. (2023). *Parties, Political finance, and governance in Africa: Extracting money and shaping states in Benin and Ghana*. Cambridge University Press.
Starcevic, S. (2021). The History and evolution of branding in Africa. In S. Appau (Ed.), *Marketing brands in Africa: Perspectives on the evolution of branding in an emerging market* (pp. 13–36). Palgrave Macmillian.
Taber, C. K. (2020). *Ethnicity and collective financial and democratic remittances: An analysis of transnationalism among Ghanaian Migrant associations in the American Midwest*. Indiana University. Order No. 27959775. https://proxyiub.uits.iu.edu/login?qurl=https%3A%2F%2Fwww.proquest.com%2Fdissertations-theses%2Fethnicity-collective-financial-democratic%2Fdocview%2F2405322890%2Fse-2%3Faccountid%3D11620
Van de Walle, N. (2001). *African economies and the politics of permanent crisis, 1979–1999*. Cambridge University Press.
Whitfield, L. (2009). Change for a better Ghana: Party competition, institutionalization and alternation in Ghana's 2008 elections. *African Affairs*, *108*(433), 621–641.
Zartman, W. I. (Ed.). (1995). *Collapsed states: The disintergration and restoration of legitimate authority*. Lynne Rienner Publishers, Inc
Zolberg, A. R. (1962). One-party systems and government for the people. *Africa Today*, *9*(4), 4–7.
Zolberg, A. R. (1968). The structure of political conflict in the new states of tropical Africa. *American Political Science Review*, *62*(1), 70–87.

Persuasion and Persistence: A Large-Scale Field Experiment in a Presidential Campaign

David W. Nickerson

INTRODUCTION

During the last four days of the 2012 election, the Obama campaign boasted of having completed 125 million volunteer phone calls and door knocks (Dwyer, 2012). The campaign had more than 800 staffed field offices across the country and had invested considerable staff time into assembling and organizing an army of dedicated volunteers (McKenna & Han, 2015). While volunteer engagement provides good political optics, how best to utilize the resource is not always obvious. This chapter describes a large field experiment undertaken by the 2012 Obama re-election campaign to determine whether volunteers could be used effectively to make phone calls to persuade voters in battleground state.

Volunteer door knocks have shown to be effective at boosting voter turnout (Green et al., 2003) and voter registration (Nickerson, 2015) for a wide variety of audiences (Bedolla & Michelson, 2012). Some experiments have shown volunteer phone calls are effective at increasing voter turnout (Nickerson, 2007), but the effect has been less consistent (Mann & Haenschen, 2024). If volunteers were primarily useful for mobilization at the very end of an election, finding activities to keep volunteers engaged over the entire year would be a challenge. Having volunteers recruit volunteers for months on end might start to feel like a multilevel marketing scam. Persuasion calls would offer a useful campaign activity and solve a problem maintaining volunteer engagement and morale.

However, persuading voters in a Presidential election can be difficult to the extent that there is debate whether persuasion is even possible. Sides et al. (2022) estimate that when campaigns enjoy an advantage on television ads, every 100 ads increases vote share by roughly 2 percentage points, but the evidence that volunteers can generate such large effects is weaker – even earlier in the cycle (Kalla & Broockman, 2018). Enos and Hersh (2015) provide a possible explanation for this finding by noting that campaigns are much more liberal than their intended persuasion audience. If this ideological gap prevents effective persuasion, such volunteer calling efforts would be doomed to failure.

While the 2012 Obama campaign had faith in the efficacy of its volunteers, there were questions about how best to leverage this resource. The field department partnered with the analytics in the campaign to conduct what was, at the time, the largest field experiment undertaken by a political campaign to measure the effectiveness of volunteer persuasion phone calls. Conducting experiments within a political campaign differs from doing so in academic settings and there are specific challenges to orchestrating the efforts of thousands of volunteers. This chapter describes how the experiment was conducted in detail. While the ultimate estimate – that receiving a phone call from a volunteer shifted vote choice by 5 percentage points and most of this effect persisted at least 6–12 weeks from the conversation – is interesting, understanding the details of how the campaign executed the experiment and why may also be of interest to campaign scholars.

THE PROGRAM/TREATMENT

While most Presidential campaigns struggle to recruit volunteers in each state as the primary rolls along, incumbent candidates can take advantage of volunteers from the prior election and assemble large teams of volunteers at the starting gate. Volunteer outreach was a vaunted – albeit untested – facet of the 2008 Obama campaign and one that the 2012 re-election campaign hoped to replicate. The past emphasis on grassroots mobilization provided an invaluable list of willing and experienced volunteers to make voter outreach. Even in January, the Obama team had the capacity to make nearly 1,000,000 volunteer phone calls weekly nationwide. The persuasion experiment would commandeer just over one-third of this capacity over the course of the experiment.

The script was drafted by a committee consisting of the campaign's messaging director, two training directors, leadership among field organizers, and the director of experiments. The script (see Appendix 37.1) emphasized the campaign's overarching theme of "restoring the middle-class promise." After asking specifically for the targeted voter, volunteers introduced themselves and inquired "Have you thought about who you'll support in the election for President this year? Are you 100% certain of that?" If the target indicated she was 100% for Obama, the volunteer shifted to a volunteer recruitment message. If the target indicated she was 100% for Romney, the volunteer politely signed off while requesting the target "keep an open mind." If the target provided any other response, the volunteer began the persuasion portion of the script.

The persuasion portion of the script consisted of campaign talking points and revolved around the theme of "restoring the middle-class promise." It was suggested that volunteers check off the talking points that they believe in most firmly and read only those points in order to shorten and slightly personalize the message. After reading this section of the script, the volunteers closed by thanking the target for her time and hoping the information shapes the target's thoughts on the election.

The organizational model of the Obama campaign involved highly compartmentalized levels of leadership. In each state, paid staff members were organized into distinct geographic units. Each staff member was responsible for recruiting, training, and managing a set of neighborhood team leaders (or super volunteers), who in turn were responsible for a set of team members, each of whom often had specific tasks assigned to them. The organizational structure allows for reasonably close supervision of large numbers of callers and an efficient means of disseminating information.

The national training directors prepared training materials and went from state-to-state practicing reading the script, implementing the experiment, and emphasizing the importance of accurate data entry. Large training events were held at multiple locations around each state to maximize the number of volunteers who could attend. Paid staff were provided training materials to train team members unable to attend one of the main training sessions. The net result is that callers tended to receive relatively homogeneous instruction and largely stuck to the assigned script and paid very careful attention to data entry.

The volunteers making the calls were literally anyone who showed up to a phone bank or logged into the dialing system. Nearly everyone went to a local phone bank, which would not be the case in post-pandemic campaigns, and there was no attempt to weed out volunteers. In that sense, the experiment has excellent external validity and accurately reflects the calls made by campaigns, albeit on a much larger scale than most campaigns. However, the callers at this early stage of the campaign tended to be slightly more experienced and older than the pool of volunteer who made calls for the campaign in September and October. However, that difference in experience diminishes rapidly after volunteers get a night or two of calling under their belts. Furthermore, these experienced volunteers also donate their time and skills to lower level campaigns down ballot more than the people signing up to volunteer for the Presidential campaign late in the season. Thus, it is possible that the calls used in this experiment are slightly higher quality than the average political campaign, but the difference is not sizable.

DATA AND EXPERIMENTAL DESIGN

The backbone of the persuasion experiment was the national voter file maintained by the Democratic National Committee (DNC). Since the experiment was being conducted via phone, only voters for whom the DNC had a valid landline number available were included in the experiment. Estimates of volunteer calling capacity were made across 19 states[1] and a random sample of these voters[2] were drawn to accommodate these call targets with a little cushion. A short, automated survey about media consumption was then sent to each of these targeted individuals to ensure that the phone number to be dialed was still operational. The net result was a representative sample of 750,000 registered voters with valid landlines on file with the DNC.

These targeted individuals were then matched into pairs using a cascading exact matching algorithm based on 13 traits.[3] After initial pairings were made with all 13 traits, one trait was dropped and another pairing based on exact matches were made. This process was repeated until the final set of targets were paired based only on what state they lived in.[4] Once these pairs were defined, a random number was generated for each member of the pair. The subject with the higher random number in the pair was assigned to the treatment group to be called and the subject with the lower random number in the pair was assigned to the control group. By design, the treatment and control groups were forced into perfect balance across observable traits.[5]

The subjects assigned to the treatment groups were then uploaded to the state data directors to distribute to the volunteers in the state. The numbers were placed in a random order to maintain the representativeness of the sample.[6] Most of the states printed call sheets for volunteers to use and entered the data later that night after the volunteer shifts were completed. Calls were made during the evening and began January 23rd and ended February 24th. Each night, state data directors would upload the disposition of the calls back to headquarters in Chicago for processing. Over the course of the campaign, 345,481 numbers were attempted and 54,649 calls were completed, which represents a 16% contact rate.

Once a treatment phone number was attempted, both the attempted treatment number and its paired member of the control group were sent to an independent call center to be surveyed.[7] The survey firms were not informed there was an experiment underway much less which individuals were in the treatment and control groups. The survey measurement calls were attempted two to three days after the initial volunteer call was attempted (i.e., a call Monday would be attempted by the survey firm on Wednesday or Thursday). The call center generally called a number for three days before retiring the number, so the survey would take place 48–120 hours after the initial volunteer attempt was made. Ultimately the calling houses completed 18,554 surveys with a roughly 9% response rate.

While covariate balance across treatment and control groups was assured at the time of assignment, it is possible that an imbalance could appear among survey respondents. For instance, we worried that registered voters assigned to the treatment group might be less willing to answer the survey because they were bothered on the phone a few days prior. Thankfully, there was no evidence of imbalance or differential attrition across treatment conditions among the survey respondents (see Table 37.1).

The survey was short to keep costs down and response rates high (see Appendix B for the script). The survey first asked about stated intended turnout in the November general election (yes, definitely; probably; 50/50; probably not; definitely not) to lead with a noncontroversial question and gauge voter enthusiasm. The next two questions asked the respondent "if the election were held tomorrow, would you vote for Democrat Barack Obama or the Republican nominee" and then "if the election were held tomorrow, would you vote for Democrat Barack Obama or Republican Mitt Romney."[8] Moving vote choice is obviously the Holy Grail for any political persuasion program and it was feared it may be an unrealistic goal for a single volunteer call to move Presidential vote choice. With this in mind, the survey also used five-point scales to ask whether the respondent approved of Obama's job performance and agreed that "Barack Obama had been effective as President." If the phone calls failed to move vote choice, perhaps the assessment of Barack Obama would be more malleable and able to be modeled. The final nondemographic question[9] inquired whether the respondent recalled campaign contact in the past few days. If the volunteer phone call was cutting through the background campaign and media noise, the treatment group should be more likely to report campaign contact than respondents in the control group. This question was put at the end of the survey to avoid coloring response to the earlier questions about the election.

The sample began as a representative sample of registered voters from battleground states with

Table 37.1 Balance Across Treatment Groups Among Survey Respondents

Group	*Female*	*Age*	*Black*	*White*	*Democrat*	*Unaffiliated*	*Republican*	*Support Score*	*Turnout Score*
Control	58%	60	6%	91%	30%	37%	33%	46	73
Treatment	57%	60	6%	91%	30%	37%	33%	46	74

landlines in 2012, but the pool of respondents differs from this ideal starting point. One of the most notable differences between the overall sample and the survey respondents was with regards to contact rates. While the overall contact rate by volunteers was 16%, among the survey respondents, the volunteer contact rate in the treatment group was 38%. Given that survey respondents are – by definition – the type of person who will answer the phone and talk to a stranger, this improvement in contact rate is not a surprise and improves the power of the experiment to detect treatment effects from the volunteer calls. The cost for this improvement in power is external validity; the experiment cannot speak to how nonrespondents were moved by volunteer phone call. However, the sample truncation from the survey is unavoidable and probably less important for a phone-based volunteer persuasion call that can only reach targets who answer the phone in any case. The bottom-line is that this experiment studying the actual phone calls made by a real campaign a large and representative sample of voters across states has more external validity than is typically found in a persuasion experiment.

RESULTS

The first question the Obama campaign had was whether calls from volunteers would be noticed among the media coverage and general chatter about the campaign. To gauge the extent to which targets remembered the phone calls, the campaign compared the rate the treatment and control groups recalled "receiving any contact from a political campaign" (see Table 37.2, column "Recall"). In the control group, 23.4% recalled receiving contact, which was 15.1 percentage points (se = 0.7 pp) lower than the 38.5% who recalled contact in the treatment condition. Once we adjust this intent-to-treat estimate by the 38% contact rate, we estimate that those actually contacted in the treatment group were 39.6 percentage points (s.e. = 1.7 pp) more likely to recall contact than the control group. Not only is this estimate statistically significant, it nearly perfectly matches the actual rate of contact in the treatment, which was 38%. This suggests that the volunteer contact rose above the background noise of the campaign in February of the election year despite all the coverage of and activity from the Republican primary. That is, the volunteer phone calls were memorable.

Next the campaign wanted to know whether the volunteer phone call improved approval with and assessment of effectiveness of Barack Obama's first four years in office (see Table 37.2, columns Approval and Effective). The difference in the mean assessment of Barack Obama on a five-point scale for both those traits was subtle but borderline statistically significant. For both approval and effectiveness, assignment to the volunteer call condition shifted the mean 0.04 points (s.e. = 0.02). Adjusting for the contact rate, the estimated average treatment effect is just over 0.10 (s.e. = 0.052). The standard deviation on both the approval and effective scale was 1.7 points, so a shift of 0.1 points is not a large effect. Both measures, however, demonstrate that volunteer calls could shift the opinions of a few people about Obama's presidency.

The more important question was whether the volunteer phone call could shift vote choice. While the campaign ultimately cared most about the two-way horse race[10], it was theoretically interesting whether the volunteer phone call increased support for Obama more or decreased support for Romney. On the one hand, public opinion on a sitting President should be much firmer than for a challenger – even a very prominent and experienced challenger (Gerber, 2004; Jacobson, 1990). On the other hand, the script used in the volunteer calls focused solely on Obama's accomplishment and never mentioned the Republicans. Campaign messaging would also change a great deal if the most persuasive pitch was bringing people back into the Obama tent rather than attack and define Romney before he can define himself. For this reason, the vote choice results are split into three separate columns. The first examines whether the call increases support for Obama (1 = Obama; 0 = else). The second report whether the call decreased support for

Table 37.2 Difference of Means Across Treatment and Control Groups

	Recall	*Approval*	*Effective*	*Obama*	*Romney*	*Two-Way*	*Intent to Vote*
Treatment	0.385	2.88	2.81	0.393	0.424	0.481	0.883
Control	0.234	2.84	2.77	0.380	0.445	0.460	0.873
Difference	0.151 (0.007)	0.004 (0.002)	0.004 (0.002)	0.013 (0.007)	-0.021 (0.007)	0.021 (0.008)	0.009 (0.005)
Contact Rate	38%	38%	38%	38%	38%	38%	38%
ATE	0.396 (0.017)	0.101 (0.052)	0.105 (0.052)	0.035 (0.019)	-0.055 (0.019)	0.053 (0.021)	0.025 (0.013)
p-value	<0.001	0.06	0.04	0.06	0.004	0.02	0.06
N	18,543	17,948	17,957	18,557	18,557	15,235	18,554

Numbers in parentheses represent standard errors.
Estimated p-values are two-tailed.

Romney (1 = Romney; 0 = else). The third column indicates whether the volunteer call shifted votes toward Obama and away from Romney (1 = Obama; 0 = Romney; Missing = Else). Table 37.1 reports each of the three variables in turn.[11]

The volunteer calls moved vote choice in favor of Obama (see Table 37.2, column "Obama"). Only 38% of the control group planned to vote for Obama compared to 39.3% of the treatment group. This difference of 1.3 percentage points (s.e. = 0.7pp) is statistically significant and greater than the ultimate margin of victory in Florida. Once this intent-to-treat estimate is adjusted for the 38% contact rate, we estimate that completed volunteer phone calls increased the proportion voting for Obama by 3.5 percentage points (s.e. = 1.9, $p < 0.06$). While 3.5 percentage points is less than the 5 points estimated by Gerber et al. (2011) for TV ads during a gubernatorial primary, it is sizable shift for an incumbent President about whom opinions are relatively set and larger than the estimated effect for 100 TV ads (1.8pp, Sides et al., 2022, Table 3) or the effect of ads for Presidential candidates found in on-line tests (0.85pp, Hewitt et al., 2024, Table 2).

The effect sizes for the Romney vote were larger, despite the treatment script not talking about Republicans in general or Romney in particular (see Table 37.2, column "Romney"). 44.5% of the control group planned to vote for Romney compared to only 42.4% of the treatment group. The drop of 2.1 percentage points (s.e. = 0.7pp) was 50% larger than the 1.3 percentage point gain in vote share for Obama and suggests that support for challengers is less certain than support for the incumbent and more prone to changes. The experiment estimates that completed volunteer calls decreased support for Romney by 5.5 percentage points (s.e. = 1.9pp). While we can't be certain that all 54,649 completed volunteer calls did not attack Romney, it appears likely that a large portion of the people persuaded away were supporting Romney because of dissatisfaction with Obama and the call helped to address those concerns. Again, the experiment does not have the statistical power to definitively say that opinions about challengers are more malleable than opinions about incumbents, but the evidence is consistent with that hypothesis.

Given that the volunteer calls moved voters to support Obama and away from Romney, it is not surprising that the experiment estimates that the calls positively influenced two-way horse race – the primary outcome of interest for the campaign (see Table 37.2, column "Two-way"). Among the 82% of subjects expressing an opinion on the vote choice question, 48% of subjects in the treatment group supported Obama compared to 46% in the control group. This difference of 2 percentage points was statistically significant (s.e. = 0.8, $p < 0.02$) and substantively large given that the average margin of victory/defeat in these states was less than 7 points in the final election. The magnitude of the treatment effect is even more impressive once we account for the contact rate. The people who received the volunteer phone calls were 5.3 percentage points (s.e. = 2.1, $p < 0.02$) more likely to support Obama in the two-way horse race than they would have been otherwise. By any reasonable standard, phone calls from volunteers shifted voter sentiment toward Obama.

One possible effect of the volunteer phone calls is that they could energize targets to participate in the upcoming election. The campaign measured this possible outcome by looking at the percentage of subjects responding that they will definitely vote in the November general election (see Table 37.2, column "Intent to Vote").[12] In the treatment group, 88.3% of subjects said that they would "definitely vote," which was 0.9 percentage points higher than the control group where 87.3% of respondents indicated that they would definitely vote. This jump in stated intent to vote approaches traditional thresholds for statistical significance (s.e. = 0.5, $p < 0.06$) and supports the notion that the call energized targets. Adjusting this intent-to-treat estimate for the contact rate, it appears that receiving the volunteer call boosted vote intent by 2.5 percentage points (s.e. = 1.3, $p < 0.06$). While this increase in intended participation is unlikely to have lasted through Election Day, it reassured the campaign that the call was not demobilizing.

PERSISTENCE

While changing opinion about the highest profile incumbent is impressive and the campaign required tasks for their army of volunteers to accomplish over the course of the year, the campaign was concerned that the shift in opinion was fleeting. The 48–120-hour lag between volunteer calls and the survey assured that the persuasive effect of the volunteer call lasted longer than the 2-day effect for television estimated by Gerber et al. (2011), but if the effect lasted only one week, the case for volunteer calls as a major campaign push would be much weaker.[13] With this in mind, a follow-up survey was conducted six weeks after the end of the experiment to measure the persistence of the persuasion.

Mindful of budget realities, the follow-up survey was conducted using interactive voice recording (IVR) technology (see Appendix 37.2 for the full script). After a brief introduction,[14] the respondent was asked to gauge their likelihood of voting in the general election, and then whether they would vote for Mitt Romney or Barack Obama if the election was held today. This dichotomous vote choice measure was the outcome of interest and similar to the two-way horse race measure used in the analysis of the first wave of the surveys. The campaign attempted to survey the 18,557 respondents from the first round of live surveys. Ultimately, 2,575 people responded to the survey; a response rate of 13%, which is very high for an IVR survey.

While the sample was balanced at the time of randomization and there appeared to be no differential response to the live survey, it is possible that treatment and control individuals differed in their willingness to answer the IVR survey. Looking across covariates (see Table 37.3), we see no evidence of differential attribution across treatment conditions on observable variables but cannot rule out the possibility that there was an unobservable bias in who answered the survey. That said, some subjects were clearly more likely to answer the survey than others. Compared to the original live survey conducted the week the treatment was attempted, the IVR respondents in the follow up survey are more likely to be female, partisan, voters, and older. Thus, while it does not appear the internal validity of the experiment has been compromised, the external validity of the persistence analysis may not apply to targets less likely to participate in automated surveys.

One manifestation of this more limited sample is that contact rate among people who answered the IVR poll was 46% – a full 8 percentage points higher than among the people who participated in the live survey. While it is not surprising that people who answer automated surveys are more likely to take calls from campaign volunteers, it means that we have to adjust the sample to ensure comparability of the samples. The initial average treatment effect on the treated among people who later answered the IVR survey is 6.1 percentage points (s.e. = 4.2, see Table 37.4, column 2) compared to 5.3 percentage points among the full sample (s.e. = 2.1, see Table 37.4, column 1). While the difference is not statistically significant, it increases the denominator when we estimate the persistence of the treatment effect 6–10 weeks later.

Table 37.3 Balance Across Treatment Groups Among IVR Survey Respondents

Group	*Female*	*Age*	*Black*	*White*	*Democrat*	*Unaffiliated*	*Republican*	*Support Score*	*Turnout Score*
Control	65%	66	6%	92%	37%	29%	35%	48	76
Treatment	66%	66	6%	92%	36%	28%	36%	48	76

Table 37.4 Persistence of Persuasion Effect

	Full Sample	*IVR Respondents*	*6 Weeks*	*12 Weeks*
Treatment	48.1%	49.5%	45.3%	45.5%
Control	46.0%	46.7%	43.0%	46.0%
Difference	0.021 (0.008)	0.028 (0.019)	0.023 (0.020)	-0.005 (0.017)
Contact	38%	46%	46%	42%
ATT	0.053 (0.021)	0.061 (0.042)	0.050 (0.043)	-0.012 (0.041)
Persistence			81% (0.31)	N.A.
N	15,235	2,529	2,575	3,354

Looking at the vote choice for subjects 6–10 weeks out from the attempted volunteer call, we see that 45.3% supported President Obama in the treatment group compared to 43% in the control condition (Table 37.3, column 3). That is, roughly two weeks after the campaign attempted contact, we observe an intent-to-treat effect of 2.3 percentage points (s.e. = 2.0). Adjusting for the contact rate to estimate the effect on the people actually contacted, the follow-up estimates that completed calls increased vote choice for Obama by 5 percentage points (s.e. = 4.3). This estimate is not statistically significant, but it still provides an unbiased estimate that 81% of the initial boost in support for Obama from the phone call lasts 6–10 weeks out. If we calculate this downstream persistence using treatment assignment as an instrument for opinion in the initial survey, this estimate of 81% persistence is highly significant (s.e. = 0.31, $p < 0.01$). Thus, the follow-up survey provides good evidence that the persuasive effect lasts much longer for volunteer phone calls than estimates of the effect for television ads.

To gauge whether the effect of the volunteer call persisted 12–16 weeks out, a second IVR survey was conducted June 1–9th. A random subset of 100,000 participants from the original subject pool were randomly sampled plus the 18,554 people who responded to the first wave of the survey. The response rate among the people who answered the first live survey was a robust 5% and roughly 2.5% among the 100,000 subjects who did not answer the first wave the survey for a total of 3,354 respondents. Once again, the survey pool was balanced across treatment and control conditions and observable covariates, so there is no reason to believe that either the treatment assignment or delivery was correlated with propensity to respond to the survey. However, this survey detected no treatment effect whatsoever. In every subpopulation analyzed, the control group was slightly less supportive of Obama than the treatment group. This difference never approached traditional thresholds for statistical significance, but strongly suggested that the persuasion effect detected in 12–16 weeks earlier and that persisted for 6–10 weeks had degraded to the point of being undetectable.

DISCUSSION AND CONCLUSION

Campaign fundraising in 2012 lagged behind the campaign's projections based on 2008 patterns. As a result, the Obama campaign had proposed substantial budget cuts across most facets of the campaign infrastructure. The field program was one of the areas that had been hit the hardest by the cuts and they were eager to participate in the experiment to help prove the value of the field program. The decision to participate in the experiment was extremely risky; a null finding could result in further budget cuts.[15] The results of the experiment confirmed the efficacy of the volunteer field program, so the campaign invested much more in the field program surpassing the original budget.

The campaign also used the results of the experiment to model the types of voters who appeared persuadable. Drawing on the enormous treasure trove of information the campaign and DNC maintained on voters, the analytics department found moderators that predicted people very responsive to volunteer outreach. The idea was to use the resulting persuadable model to target future outreach. Given the importance of this task, the model was validated several ways – the most obvious way was verifying that people with higher persuasion scores were more likely to answer "undecided" on the tracking polls. After validation and vetting, this persuasion score became the backbone of TV, digital, and field targeting.[16]

This experiment was conducted during the middle of the Republican primary, so it cannot really answer the critics who argue that persuasion is impossible (e.g., Kalla & Broockman, 2018). While the experiment was conducted for the highest salience and most polarized office and demonstrated a persuasive effect that lasted for at least 6–10 weeks, these persuadable voters may have broken in predictable ways and "come home" when Election Day rolled around (Holbrook, 1996). However, the volunteer experiment constitutes a strong refutation of Enos and Hersh's (2015) claim that volunteers were likely ineffective campaign surrogates for Obama. It is undoubtedly true that volunteers were more liberal than the average Democrat, much less the average undecided voter. However, this experiment shows that these volunteers could be persuasive and advance the campaign's objectives. Whether the reason is that volunteers relied on campaign approved talking points or peer-to-peer conversations can overcome differences in ideology is open to interpretation.

Notes

1 AZ, CO, FL, GA, IA, IN, ME, MI, MN, MO, NC, NH, NM, NV, OH, OR, PA, VA, and WA.

2 Prior to randomization, one randomly selected individual was selected among the set of voters sharing the phone number to "represent" the household.

3 The traits were geography, contactability score, support score, turnout score, age, gender, ethnicity, vote history, length of time on the phone with the automated survey, estimated education, missingness of data on file, party registration, and area code.

4 The pairing was computationally efficient and exhibited good balance across sample runs. Another pairing method (e.g., Mahalanobis distance) could possibly offer small gains in statistical efficiency but was not computationally feasible and would be irrelevant to causal identification.

5 We checked a few other variables that we did not match on to ensure that there was not a flaw in the randomization process. We never found a variable that appeared imbalanced.

6 Quality control checks were conducted each morning to ensure that the sample was representative.

7 The capacity of the volunteer operation outstripped the survey budget for this project, so it was not possible to survey every pairing attempted by volunteers. To maintain external validity, we randomly selected the pairs sent to the call center.

8 These two questions are so highly correlated ($r = 0.85$) that all the analysis reports the results from the Mitt Romney specific question. The results do not depend on which variable used.

9 The survey also asked the respondent for their year of birth and gender was recorded by the caller. This information was used to check the quality of the calls. Over the course of the campaign, 86% of the completed calls matched both on gender and age. The 18,554 completions reported all matched and gender.

10 The two-way horse race is defined as voting for Obama (1) or voting for the Republican (0) with undecideds being dropped from the analysis. This metric is preferred by the campaign for three reasons. First, it measures the state of the race at that moment in time without resorting to arbitrary rules for assigning undecideds. Second, the primary purpose of this experiment was to model persuadability from volunteer phone calls. Undecideds are inherently difficult to predict given standard voter file information, so their inclusion typically adds noise to a model rather than signal. Third, people who move from supporting your opponent to "undecided" are very likely to slide back to supporting your opponent by the time Election Day rolls around. Respondents will return to their circles of friends and media environments that generated the initial opposition and will naturally drift back to that opposition.

11 A comparison of means test on experimental data is unbiased. Adding on modeling assumptions through the use of ordered logistic regression, which is justified through assumptions about the distribution of the variables rather than randomization (Freedman, 2008), changes neither the magnitude nor the statistical significance of the results (see Appendix C).

12 This operationalization was agreed upon by the analytics and field staff in early planning memos. Looking at intent to vote as a five-point scale using an ordered logit does not change the substantive interpretation of the results and crosses traditional thresholds of statistical significance ($p < 0.04$, see Appendix C).

13 This persuasion experiment itself would still have value as data to help target "persuadable" voters.

14 The recorded voice was from a woman named Clare, a campaign volunteer from New York with a very soothing voice. Roughly a dozen voices were tested earlier in the campaign for automated calls, and Clare's voice very consistently led to the highest response rates and best quality of data (measured by respondent

entered age and gender matching what was listed on the voter file). She generously agreed to lend her voice to most automated calls from the campaign.

15 The importance of the outcome of the experiment caused the field team to be heavily involved in the design of the experiment. Getting complete buy-in on the research design was required so that they would accept the resulting estimates. The involvement of field team leadership greatly improved the design and execution of the experiment.

16 Large mail programs conducted their own persuasion experiments to model the persuadability for that particular flight of mail.

REFERENCES

Bedolla, L. G., & Michelson, M. R. (2012). *Mobilizing inclusion: Transforming the electorate through get-out-the-vote campaigns*. Yale University Press.

Dwyer, D. (2012, November 3). Obama camp trumpets massive ground game on election eve. *ABC News*. https://abcnews.go.com/blogs/politics/2012/11/obama-camp-trumpets-massive-ground-game-on-election-eve

Enos, R., & Hersh, E. (2015). Party activists as campaign advertisers: The ground campaign as a principal-agent problem. *American Political Science Review*, *109*(2), 252–278. https://doi.org/10.1017/S0003055415000064

Freedman, D. A. (2008). Randomization does not justify logistic regression. *Statistical Science*, *23*, 237–249.

Gerber, A. S. (2004). Does campaign spending work? Field experiments provide evidence and suggest new theory. *American Behavioral Scientist*, *47*(5), 541–574. https://doi.org/10.1177/0002764203260415

Gerber, A. S., Gimpel, J. G., Green, D. P., & Shaw, D. R. (2011). How large and long-lasting are the persuasive effects of televised campaign ads? Results from a randomized field experiment. *American Political Science Review*, *105*(1), 135–150.

Green, D. P., Gerber, A. S., & Nickerson, D. W. (2003). Getting out the vote in local elections: Results from six door-to-door canvassing experiments. *The Journal of Politics*, *65*(4), 1083–1096.

Hewitt, L., Broockman, D., Coppock, A., Tappin, B. M., Slezak, J., Coffman, V., Lubin, N., & Hamidan, M. (2024). How experiments help campaigns persuade voters: Evidence from a large archive of campaigns' own experiments. *American Political Science Review*, 1–19. https://doi.org/10.1017/S0003055423001387

Holbrook, T. M. (1996). *Do campaigns matter?* SAGE.

Jacobson, G. C. (1990). The effects of campaign spending in House elections: New evidence for old arguments. *American Journal of Political Science*, *34*(2), 334–362.

Kalla, J., & Broockman, D. (2018). The minimal persuasive effects of campaign contact in general elections: Evidence from 49 field experiments. *American Political Science Review*, *112*(1), 148–166. https://doi.org/10.1017/S0003055417000363

Mann, C. B., & Haenschen, K. (2024). A meta-analysis of voter mobilization tactics by electoral salience *Electoral Studies*, *87*. https://doi.org/10.1016/j.electstud.2023.102729

McKenna, E., & Han, H. (2015). *Groundbreakers: How Obama's 2.2 million volunteers transformed Campaigning in America*. Oxford University Press.

Nickerson, D. W. (2007). Quality is job one: Volunteer and professional phone calls. *American Journal of Political Science*, *51*(2), 269–282.

Nickerson, D. W. (2015). Do voter registration drives increase participation? For whom and when? *The Journal of Politics*, *77*(1), 88–101.

Sides, J., Vavreck, L., Warshaw, C. (2022). The effect of television advertising in United States elections. *American Political Science Review*, *116*(2) 702–718.

APPENDIX 37.1: SAMPLE VOLUNTEER CALL SCRIPT

2012 Persuasion Script

CALL RESULT KEY

NO PERSON PICKS UP	SOMEONE PICKS UP
Not Home: Phone just rings **Disconnected:** Disconnected line **Busy:** Busy, fax or other tri tone signal	**Call back:** You are told the person on your list is not available **Deceased:** You are told the person on your list has passed away **Language:** The person you reach does not speak your language **Wrong Number:** You are told that the number is incorrect **Refused:** Someone picks up but does not answer our support question

Hi. Is _________ available? [**ONCE THE PERSON ANSWERS THE PHONE]** Hi _________. My name is _____________and I'm a fellow **[STATE NAME]** volunteering with Obama for America.

Q1. **Have you thought about who you'll support in the election for President this year? [If Obama or Republicans, ask:] Are you 100% certain of that?**

[If Definitely support Obama, check the box 1 – **Support Obama]** Great! President Obama took office in the middle of the biggest economic challenge our country has faced in decades. While there's more work to do, after three years of hard work, we're moving in the right direction and we've seen twenty-two consecutive months of private sector job creation. As you know, we need to re-elect President Obama so he can continue building an economy that restores economic security to the middle class, makes sure that hard work pays, and that everyone from Wall Street to Main Street plays by the same rules.

The first step in our grass roots campaign is focused on reconnecting with every member of the Obama family. It is people like us – working together, reaching out to others to grow the movement – that will re-elect Barack Obama as President.

Q2. **Would you be willing to volunteer with the campaign?**

[If Yes, check box] Great! Thank you for your commitment to our continuing movement. Someone from the campaign will be in touch about volunteer opportunities. Thanks for your time, and have a great day.

[If No, check box] Ok. Thank you for your commitment to the President. We will keep you posted on future opportunities to get involved. Thanks for your time, and have a great day.

[If Leaning Obama, Undecided, or Leaning Republican, check the box: 2 – Lean Obama/3 – Undecided/4 – Lean Republican] Okay, we're calling people like you to talk about the important economic issues facing the country. **(Engage using the talking points below while personalizing your story.)**

- The promise of this country has always been that if you work hard and play by the rules, you can provide a decent life for your family.
- But for decades, that promise of middle-class security has been slipping away for too many Americans. Even as they worked harder, wages stagnated, health care costs soared and fewer employers offered retirement benefits. Good manufacturing jobs were shipped overseas and college tuition costs skyrocketed.
- And after a difficult decade, in late 2008, middle-class families were devastated when their 401ks were wiped out on Wall Street, the value of their houses plummeted and millions of jobs disappeared overnight.
- This is what the President has been working to turnaround.
- Our opponents are clear about their vision for the country. They have proposed a new round of tax cuts for those at the top and deep cuts to education funding. They want to take away regulations that protect our air and water and outlaw abortion in all circumstances. And they want to turn Medicare and Social Security over to insurance companies and Wall Street banks.
- Instead of new ideas, they want to double down on the same ideas that got us into this mess.
- The President wants to build on the hard work of the past three years to restore security to the middle class. He wants to extend the tax cuts that benefit middle and working-class families. He wants to make college more affordable and give people a chance to get trained for good paying jobs. He wants to continue to focus on small businesses and manufacturers so we can make things in this country to sell throughout the world. And he'll work to make sure that the Medicare and Social Security that people have worked for and earned is there for today's senior and tomorrow's.

[If Definitely supporting a Republican, check the box: 5 – Support Republican] Thank you for sharing your opinion with us. This year you'll have an opportunity to hear all the candidates debate the important economic issues facing this country. We hope you continue to listen to what the candidates have to say, watch the debates this fall, and give every candidate's views a fair chance. **(Use your best judgment about whether they are willing to engage in a polite conversation about jobs and the economy. If so, engage using the talking points while personalizing your story. If not, politely hang up.)**

[CLOSING] Thanks for taking the time to discuss these important issues facing our country. We hope you'll keep this conversation in mind next year and consider voting for President Obama. Have a great day.

Talking Points – Responses to Common Attacks

Unfortunately, when making persuasion calls, you may encounter people who have false beliefs about the President. We don't want people to think the campaign has no response to these misconceptions. If you hear someone say something false, you should respond with a short but polite comment using the talking points below.

- **Gun Rights:** The President believes, as do a majority of Americans, that the Second Amendment guarantees an individual right to bear arms and the courts have settled that as the law of land. No new gun restrictions have been passed under the President, and not one law-abiding American citizen has had a gun taken away by the federal government since Barack Obama became president.
- **Citizenship:** Barack Obama was born in Honolulu, Hawaii at Kapi'olani (kah pee oh lah nee) Maternity and Gynecological Hospital (Now called the Kapi'olani Medical Center for Women and Children) on 4 August 1961. You can view two versions of his birth certificate ("long" and "short" form) at www.FactCheck.org and the birth announcement in the Honolulu Star-Bulletin at www.snopes.com.
- **Immigration:** The President recognizes that our current immigration system is broken and he is deeply committed to building a new 21st century immigration system that meets our nation's important economic and security needs. He's pushed for a system where everyone's accountable, a system where the federal government secures the border, employers who game the system and hire undocumented workers are held accountable and those who are here illegally pay taxes, follow the law, and get on the path to earning citizenship.
- **Bailouts:** TARP was proposed by the Bush administration and signed into law in October 2008 by President Bush, months before President Obama took office. Under President Obama, banks have repaid 99% of TARP funds and any losses to taxpayers have been substantially reduced from initial estimates.
- **Taxes:** Under President Obama, income taxes for most Americans are at historically low levels. President Obama has signed dozens of tax cuts that give relief to the middle class and to small businesses.

APPENDIX 37.2: SURVEY INSTRUMENTS

Live Calls

Hello, I'm calling from [firm name]. May I speak with [name of voter specified]? [If unable to get the voter specified, terminate call.] I have just a few questions for you today that will take no more than a few minutes of your time.

1 If next year's election for President were held today, would you definitely vote, probably vote, is there a 50/50 chance you would vote, would you probably not vote or would you definitely not vote?
  1 Definitely vote
  2 Probably vote
  3 50/50
  4 Probably not vote
  5 Definitely not vote
  6 Other, don't know, no response, refused DO NOT READ
2 If next year's election for President were held today, for whom would you vote [ROTATE: Democrat Barack Obama or the Republican candidate]? [If undecided/don't know/independent] Even though you say you are undecided/don't know/independent – which way do you lean – Democrat Barack Obama, or the Republican nominee?
  1 Democrat Barack Obama
  2 Republican candidate
  3 Undecided/don't know/independent DO NOT READ
  4 Lean toward Barack Obama
  5 Lean toward Republican candidate
  6 Other candidate, refused DO NOT READ
3 If next year's election for President were held today, for whom would you vote [ROTATE: Democrat Barack Obama or Republican Mitt Romney]? [If undecided/don't know/independent] Even though you say you are undecided/don't know/independent – which way do you lean – Democrat Barack Obama or Republican Mitt Romney?
  1 Democrat Barack Obama
  2 Republican candidate
  3 Undecided/don't know/independent DO NOT READ
  4 Lean toward Barack Obama
  5 Lean toward Republican candidate
  6 Other candidate, refused DO NOT READ
4 How favorable are your views toward Barack Obama?
  1 Very Favorable
  2 Somewhat favorable
  3 Somewhat unfavorable
  4 Very Unfavorable
  5 Don't recognize, other, refused (DO NOT READ)
5 Do you APPROVE or DISAPPROVE of the way Barack Obama is handling his job as President? [PROBE: And is that STRONGLY (approve/disapprove) or SOMEWHAT (approve/disapprove)?]
  1 Strongly Approve
  2 Somewhat Approve
  3 Somewhat Disapprove
  4 Strongly Disapprove
  5 Other, don't know, refused (DO NOT READ)
6 Do you agree or disagree with the following statement: Barack Obama has been effective as President? [PROBE: And is that STRONGLY (agree/disagree) or SOMEWHAT (agree/disagree)?]
  1 Strongly Agree
  2 Somewhat Agree
  3 Somewhat Disagree
  4 Strongly Disagree
  5 Other, don't know, refused (DO NOT READ)
7 Regardless of how you are registered to vote, do you think of yourself as a Democrat, a Republican, an Independent, or something else? [IF DEMOCRAT, ASK:] Would you call yourself a strong Democrat, or a not very strong Democrat? [IF REPUBLICAN, ASK:] Would you call yourself a strong Republican, or a not very strong Republican?
  1 Democrat
  2 Not very strong Democrat
  3 Not very strong Republican
  4 Strong Republican
  5 Independent
  6 Undecided/Other/Refused (DO NOT READ)
8 For statistical purposes only, would you please tell me the year you were born? RECORD YEAR
9 Finally, in the past few days, have you received any contact from political campaigns?
  1 Yes
  2 No
  3 Other, don't know, refused (DO NOT READ)
10 RECORD RESPONDENT GENDER

Automated Calls

Hi, this is Clare calling from DNC Services Corp with just a few questions for you today.

1 In November 2012, there will be an election for US President and other offices. How likely is it that you will vote in the 2012 Presidential election – will you definitely vote, probably vote, are the chances 50–50, will you probably not vote or definitely not vote? Press 1 if you will definitely vote. Press 2 if you will probably vote. Press 3 if there is a 50/50 chance you will vote. Press 4 if you will probably not vote. Press 5 if you will definitely not vote.

Definitely Vote 1
Probably Vote 2
50–50 3
Probably Will Not Vote..4
Definitely Not Vote 5

2 If the November 2012 presidential election were held tomorrow, would you vote for [ROTATE: Democrat Barack Obama/Republican Mitt Romney] or would you vote for [ROTATE: Republican Mitt Romney/Democrat Barack Obama]? Press 1 for Democrat Barack Obama. Press 2 for Republican Mitt Romney.
   1 Democrat Barack Obama
   2 Republican Mitt Romney
3 Thinking about the November 2008 presidential election, did you vote for [ROTATE: Democrat Barack Obama or Republican John McCain] in November 2008 or did you not vote in November 2008? Press 1 for Democrat Barack Obama. Press 2 for Republican John McCain. Press 3 if you did not vote.
   1 Barack Obama
   2 John McCain
   3 Did not vote
4 Finally, and for statistical purposes only, would you please tell me your age?
5 For statistical purposes only, please enter your gender. Press 1 if you are a man and 2 if you are a woman.

Thanks for your time.

[Paid for by DNC Services Corp, 430 S Capitol ST SE, Washington, DC 20003, [telnum]. Not authorized by any candidate or candidate's committee.]

The Challenge of Responding to Populism

Wayne Steger

INTRODUCTION

Populism continues to trend upward the United States, Europe, South America, and Asia. Among the most visible populists are Boris Johnson (UK), Marine Le Pen (France), Viktor Orban (Hungary), Giorgia Meloni (Italy), Alexis Tsipras (Greece), Narendra Modi (India), Jair Bolsonaro (Brazil), and Donald Trump in the United States. Populism is a global phenomenon that poses serious challenges for established political parties and for liberal democracy. How we think about populism affects how intellectuals and the political class respond to rising populism.

The discussion in this chapter focuses on the attributes of populism in America. There are common attributes of populism that generalize to populism elsewhere, but the vein of populism that occurs in a given country evolves in a particular political, economic, and cultural history of that country. The United States is somewhat unique in that both left- and right-wing populisms are currently resurgent, whereas most countries tend to have either a left- or right-wing populism. The remainder of this chapter defines populism and explains why it is so difficult to respond to.

In one sense, the growth and spread of populism presents a serious wake-up call to political leaders and intellectuals that governments are failing to respond to rising public dissatisfactions and disaffections (Grattan, 2016). There are real grievances that fuel the spread of populism, though the underlying causes of resentments often differ from the targets or scapegoats in populist rhetoric and attacks. Supporters of populist candidates and parties are dissatisfied with existing parties and policies that are failing to relieve the economic, social, and political stresses that underpin that dissatisfaction (Norris & Inglehart, 2019; Steger, forthcoming; Tillman, 2021). Populism could be a positive force for democracy by forcing the political class to develop policies to cope with these problems. Populism serves as a wake-up call to pay attention to aggrieved populations. Populist leaders engage and mobilize people in elections to bring attention to concerns of people who perceive that their concerns are ignored by government. The problems posed by perceptions of underrepresentation are particularly challenging in the United States where both left- and right-wing populisms are challenging the political establishment. In the United States, left wing populists appeal to and mobilize people who believe that government is not doing enough to help traditionally marginalized groups, while right wing populists appeal to and mobilize people who perceive that their way of life and socio-economic status is slipping while government operates to help others at their expense (Steger, forthcoming).

Competing for the votes of these citizens pushes existing parties to address aggrieved populations and the problems that underlay populist sentiments. To do that, intellectuals and political leaders need to know the underlying causal forces driving grievances. That may not be easy when populists scapegoat groups (e.g., immigrants) or offer facile solutions (e.g., protectionist tariffs). If, however, intellectuals can discern the underlying impetuses driving populism and parties can develop responses to cope with these problems, then populism could be a positive for society and for democracy.

On the other hand, populism represents a fundamental, perhaps even existential threat to liberal democracy, understood at a basic level as governance by leaders whose claim to authority is certified by elections, and whose power is constrained by constitutional limits and the principle of the rule of law. Populists are antipluralist in that they claim that they alone represent the people (Werner-Müller, 2016). Populists are illiberal when they refuse to accept rules that constrain power or legal parameters that define as out of bounds their preferred policy actions (Riker, 1982). As president, Donald Trump repeatedly violated the Constitution, laws, and norms of democracy. For example, Donald Trump repeatedly sought to ban most people from predominantly Muslim countries, despite Court rulings that the ban amounted to an unconstitutional violation of the first amendment protection for religious freedom (Madhukar & Panduranga, 2020). In the most direct threat to the rule of law, Donald Trump refused to accept the results of the 2020 presidential election, filing numerous judicial challenges and attempting to disrupt the peaceful transfer of power on 6 January 2021 (Jacobson, 2021; Williams, 2021).

Populism also poses a serious threat to pluralist democracy since a government cannot simultaneously represent both them and those they oppose. Populists tend to see existing leaders and the procedures of government as obstacles to getting what they want. Moreover, they tend to portray opposing parties and groups as illegitimate (Norris & Inglehart, 2019, p. 19). The nationalism and Christian nationalism inherent in American right-wing populism is particularly problematic because it implies that traditionally dominant ethnic groups are legitimate while others are not (Omer & Lupo, 2023). There is a zero-sum quality to the us vs. them, good vs. evil framing of conflict in populism. The aim to use to exclude those deemed not legitimate poses a fundamental challenge to pluralist democracy and the stability of the political system.

Political elites, public intellectuals, and citizens concerned about the future of their political system need to respond to surging populism, whether the aim is to further the representation of the underrepresented, address concerns of disaffected publics, or more existentially to save democracy from the illiberalism of populist leaders and movements. That is not straightforward.

There is a counter-productive tendency to be dismissive of and condescending to populists. This tendency is reflected in how public intellectuals and political commentators discuss populist candidates. Dismissiveness and condescension are implicit in the two common uses of populism in public discourse. The first usage is what Cas Mudde calls "the politics of the pub," which refers to an emotional and simplistic discourse directed at the "gut feelings" of the people (Mudde, 2004). For example, Donald Trump's speeches, while criticized by political elites, resonate with his supporters an emotional level and how he made his supporters feel mattered as much as his policy positions (Edwards, 2021). The idea that populists are emotionally driven and ill-informed or ignorant makes it easy to dismiss and treat populists with disdain. Thinking of populism in these terms will be perceived as elitist, so responses couched in these uses of the term may reinforce rather than persuade. Indeed, intellectuals and experts are part of the elite that populists oppose (Merkley, 2020).

Public intellectuals and political commentators also use the term in a second way to refer to policy promises that might please voters in the short run, but which will make people worse off in the long-term. Donald Trump's anti-immigration and protectionist rhetoric and policies illustrate this usage (Kelly, 2017). Both of these common uses of populism are used by detractors who view populist leaders as demagogues who seek to people gain personally by taking advantage of the emotions of ill-informed people. The view that demagoguery lacks substance and that populist policies are myopic and counterproductive lends to a sense that populist ideas will be exposed as bad and thus rejected in the long run. In the meantime, much damage can be done, even to the supporters of populist leaders.

Dismissing populists also is problematic because it leads us to ignore questions about what drives the disaffection of populist voters and to underappreciate the threat to liberal democracy. Dismissing populists also leads critics to underestimate the potential appeal of populism, something that both Democrats and Republican elites have done repeatedly over the past ten years in the United States. Republican insiders and elites, for example, tended to wait on the sidelines in 2016, expecting Trump's appeal to collapse, until it was too late and Trump's supporters showed themselves to be a winning coalition within the Republican Party (Steger, 2017). Although exit polls are not a necessarily representative sample of voters, in 2016, they showed that a slight majority of Republican voters held populist views (Steger, 2018). Trump's hold on the Republican Party increased during his presidency and his supporters seem impervious to information that would bring ruin upon almost any other politician (Costa & Rucker, 2020. To respond to populism effectively, we need to think of populism in a more disciplined approach to recognize what it is and why it is surging at this time.

The essay addresses two questions. First, what is populism? Developing a response requires understanding what populism is, and why it is surging at this time in history. A great deal of the burgeoning writing on populism looks at particular aspects of populism, such as anti-elitism or nationalism. This narrow focus misses much, so responses grounded in narrow conceptions of populism are likely to fail. This essay looks at populism broadly, focusing on characteristics common to various strains of populism. It addresses differences between right-wing populists, such as Donald Trump or Viktor Orban, and left-wing populists such as Alexis Tsipras or Bernie Sanders in the United States. Responding to left- and right-wing populisms requires an understanding of populism generally and of the social and economic concerns that are prevalent in specific types of populism.

The second question addressed in this essay is why is populism so difficult to respond to? As the preceding discussion suggests, populists are not easily dissuaded. Populist parties and candidates appeal to people who have underlying grievances and concerns, and whose beliefs and values predispose them to being susceptible to populist appeals. Ambitious politicians take advantage of that for their own purposes. Ambitious populists have been aided and abetted by ideological and profit-seeking commentators and media that benefit from the populist resurgence. Populist candidates and parties are having success at this point in history, in part because they have access to technologies, fundraising, and a media environment that prior populists have lacked. We need to keep in mind that responding to populist messaging will be met with counter-vailing efforts to keep the populist momentum going.

WHAT DO WE MEAN BY POPULISM?

Populism is a multifaceted phenomenon in both form and characteristics. Richard Hofstadter (1964, pp. 2–4) viewed populism as a *paranoid style of expression* by otherwise normal people, and *as a way of seeing the world and of seeing oneself*, that motivates particular type of political behavior characterized by conspiracy theorizing and paranoia, which he defined as "a delusional perception of persecution and of own's own greatness." Margaret Canovan (1981, 1999) viewed populism as a *style* of communication or rhetorical strategy appealing to the common man in a struggle against the established structure that includes a rivalist mood. Michael Kazin (1995) and Cas Mudde (2004, 2007) defined populism as a *worldview* or as a *political frame* pitting the common man in a struggle against some elite. Jan Werner-Müller (2016) defined populism as a form of *identity politics* employing a *moralistic imagination* of politics pitting a morally pure people against corrupt elites. Paul Taggart (2000) viewed populism in terms of a *social movement.* Though different arguments, Hofstadter, Werner-Müller, and Taggert all see populism as a form of *identity politics* in which people *react to power* that they perceive as threatening to people like them framed in an "us" versus "them" conflict. Populism also is used to refer to a form of *illiberal, popular* democracy unconstrained by norms and rules that protect individuals and political minorities from the state, and which are necessary for political stability (Riker, 1982; Schumpeter, 1943).

These definitions capture aspects or dimensions of populism, but there are common threads to these various definitions that can be summarized as follows. Populists involves an *antielite* or *anti-establishment framework* or constructed reality in which populist candidates or political parties establish an ingroup *political identity* of a good or pure people who are in a struggle *against corrupt elites* in order to *disrupt the status quo and politics-as-usual* (Steger, forthcoming). Further, populists seek to mobilize people through two related mechanisms: *resistance to power* and the *politics of victimization.*

Populists see themselves as resisting some powerful elite or social, economic, or political elite or system that is short-changing them if not oppressing or persecuting them. Resistance to power often involves conspiracies (or their functional equivalent) about the actions an immoral, unjust, or illegitimate adversary. Conspiracies are a form of resistance to power (Nelson, 2015). The idea of perceived persecution was central to Hofstadter's (1964) argument about right-wing populism. Right-wing populists in America have a litany of conspiracies. For example, Hillary Clinton was the subject of numerous right-wing conspiracies, from Uranium One to Benghazi –

none of which were substantiated in multiple Republican-directed congressional investigations. Right-wing conspiracies spread through digital and social media about topics like QAnon and Deep State, in which government bureaucrats colluded to thwart Trump and subvert the will of the people (Rozsa, 2019).

Conspiracies thrive in our current media environment, in which anyone can post ideas to social media, message boards or chat rooms, YouTube or TikTok. The more extreme left- and right-wing digital media often includes conspiratorial content. Leftwing blogs in the United States like US Uncut, Addicting Info, and Natural News sensationalize and distort stories with interpretations of abuses of and outrages by oligarchs, conservatives, and Republicans. Right-wing digital media like InfoWars, Breitbart, and The Blaze are even more overtly conspiratorial, particularly with respect to deep state. Such views spread through social media and make it into more established media, lending credibility to these viewpoints and reinforcing the perspectives of followers of populist leaders and commentators.

Conspiratorial thinking appears to be more prolific among right-wing populists than left-wing populists in the United States; however, left-wing populists in the U.S. tend to use a theoretical framework that serves as the functional equivalent in calling for resistance to power. Although not conspiracy theories of the same ilk as QAnon or Deep State, the New Left and subsequent left-wing populists have long based their rhetoric and appeals in the critical theory paradigm, including its identity-based strains (Steger, forthcoming, ch. 2). These theoretical frameworks serve a similar function by providing a rationale for resistance to perceived power. Critical theorists are explicitly normative in their call to challenge perceived powerful interests and structures that leave other groups on the losing side of societal status allocations, in a way that may be plausible (e.g., Hayes et al., 2011; Morrow & Brown, 1994; Strydom, 2011; Sensoy & DiAngelo, 2011). Contemporary critical theorists have extended beyond the thinking of Adorno, Fromm, Erikson, and Marcuse to focus on economic, government, and cultural norms and institutions that confer power and social status to some groups while producing systematic oppression of other groups through institutional hierarchies or informally through norms and behaviors (Horkheimer & Adorno, 2002). The populist left engages in an economic, socio-cultural, and political struggle against the dominant forces in society. At the core of critical theories are powerful elites, social, economic, political, and economic structures that privilege some at the expense of the many, and especially racial, gendered, and sexual identity minorities. Given this premise, it is a matter of social justice to resist these structures and mobilize to upend the structures and systems that give rise to the status quo. The populist left engages in an economic, socio-cultural, and political struggle against the dominant forces in society. Opposition to these unjust and illegitimate structures and norms does not lend to compromise.

Another, related form of resistance to power involves the politics of victimization and grievance to mobilize potential supporters against the establishment. This idea also is implicit in Diana Mutz's argument that populists are motivated by threats to their social status (Mutz, 2018). While Mutz was concerned with right-wing, authoritarian populists, the threat to basic rights and sense of social justice extends this dimension to left-wing populists. Both left- and right-wing populists use the politics of victimization as a mechanism of identity formation, legitimization, and mobilization (Feher, 1996).

For example, Donald Trump consistently portrays himself as a victim of persecution by the political establishment, a "weaponized" Department of Justice, a "rigged electoral system," and more (e.g., Costa, 2023). He played the role of victim in his impeachments, the various legal actions against him, and even in response to his indictments. As Trump asserted at one political rally, "I am a victim of one of the great political smear campaigns in the history of our country. They are coming after me to try and destroy what is considered by even them the greatest movement in the history of our country" (Jones, 2016). Trump ties his victimhood to those of his supporters. Attacks on him are attacks on them. He and his followers are thus similarly victimized by liberal elites and the government. The injustice is a call to join Trump in resistance. Supporting Trump in his fight is their fight against the same forces of oppression. Importantly this messaging has been reiterated and reinforced by many other Republicans, conservative media commentators, and even some of his rivals for the 2024 Republican nomination. Reinforcing messaging across conservative media lends credibility to Trump's claims, which largely go unchallenged in the conservative media environment. While detractors accuse Trump of gas-lighting his supporters, it fits with their predispositions (see below). Not impeachment, successful lawsuits, indictments, or electoral defeat have deterred Trump's hold on the loyalties of his supporters. That speaks to the power of the populist resistance to power as a motivating influence for populist supporters.

Left-wing populism in the United States has been greatly influenced by the critical theory framework for understanding power relationships and resisting power. In particularly, critical theory evolved to form the basis of identity politics, in which oppressed groups suffer from the norms and common understandings, which are viewed as constructed realities established by the dominant groups in a society (e.g., Domhoff & Dye, 1986; Sensoy & DiAngelo, 2011). Marginalization is part of the identity in identity politics (Brown, 1995; Gitlin, 1995). Marginalization results from the victimization of oppressed groups. Leftwing populists use the politics of economic, racial, and cultural victimization at the hands of economic elites and cultural institutions like religion and social norms established by the white hetero-patriarchy. Correcting these injustices is a powerful motivator of left-wing populists, who see government as unresponsive and often view Democrats as complicit in maintaining the system.

While left- and right-wing populists have a less favorable view of their own party, they have an even more negative view of the opposition. During the 2016 presidential nominations, for example, Bernie Sanders' supporters had lower thermometer ratings of Democratic Party leaders compared to the supporters of Hillary Clinton, while Trump supporters had lower ratings of the Republican Party leaders compared to the supporters of other Republican candidates (Steger, 2017). Both Sanders and Trump supporters had more negative views of the opposing party than did other members of their own party. Sanders' supporters were the most negative toward Trump of any group in the ANES surveys, though Trump supporters' low rating of Sanders was similar to that of other Republicans. In many ways, left- and right-wing populists are most opposed to each other and seem to view the opposing party as consisting mainly of each other. This is telling, because as the country has polarized along partisan lines, there has been an increase in the intensity of partisan affect – an emotional response associated with partisanship. Within the binary part competition between Democrats and Republicans, there has been an increase in negative partisan affect in which partisan loyalties are motivated by anger, distrust, and hatred of the opposing party (Abramowitz & Webster, 2016; Lelkes et al., 2017; Sood & Iyengar, 2018; Westwood & Iyengar, 2015). Left- and right-wing populists may not like their own party, but even more they do not like the other party.

DIFFERENCES BETWEEN LEFT- AND RIGHT-WING POPULISTS

At this point, it is clear that left- and right-wing populists in the United States are distinctive, even though they have in common characteristics of an anti-establishment attitudes, the contours of an identity of an ingroup that has been victimized by, and must resist, elites and an unjust system (see Table 38.1). While both types of populism in the United States have the underlying commonalities identified above, each appeals to different groups in society that are distinct in their underlying beliefs, values, and grievances. Populist candidates and parties, like other opinion leaders, can be successful shaping public opinion when they can frame discourse in a way that resonates with people's existing values and beliefs and thus predispose them to accept the rhetoric (Nelson & Oxley, 1999; Slothuus & de Vreese, 2010). The extent to which the audience is receptive to messages depends on the existing values and beliefs of citizens, or what political scientists call latent attitudes or predispositions. Bernie Sander's attacks on billionaires and Wall Street resonated with progressive Democrats because they were already concerned with economic and social inequalities. Donald Trump's attacks on immigrants, Muslims, and liberals gain find receptive audiences among Republican voters largely because they already possessed these attitudes

Table 38.1 Anti-establishment Orientation of Left- and Right-Wing Populists

	Left-Wing Populists	*Right-Wing Populists*
Primarily oppose	Economic elites: "oligarchs," billionaires, CEOs, Wall Street.	Government elites: "deep state," "corrupt" government officials.
Secondarily oppose	"Enablers" in government: neoliberal Democrats and Republicans; religious and cultural conservative elites	Special interests above and underserving people below; urban elites, cultural liberals, liberal professors, "Hollywood"

before Trump came along (Hetherington & Weiler, 2009). Populist leaders and parties give form and direction to attitudes that otherwise might exist as noise in political commentaries and opinions expressed in social circles of a country.

Left- and right-wing populists form distinctive ingroups that oppose different elites and power structures, use different frameworks to justify their resistance to power, perceive different victimizations, and seek different ends. Left-wing populists oppose the concentration of wealth and power of economic elites, and view government as a vehicle for challenging the power of economic elites. Left-wing populists oppose the institution of capitalism, with all of its rules, structures, and norms that they view as creating inequalities. Left-wing populists also oppose traditional cultural institutions like organized religions and prevailing cultural norms that create racial, gender, and sexual orientation inequalities. The right opposes the concentration of power in government, which sits at the nexus of multiple grievances based in ethnic, cultural, religious, generational, and economic identities. The right-wing populists view government as helping undeserving others, especially immigrants, at their expense. Right-wing populists also oppose cultural and educated elites who advocate for a multicultural society, sexual liberation, and social justice for disadvantaged groups, defined in terms of race, ethnicity, gender, and sexual identity.

An important difference here is that left-wing populists, while they are distrustful of government, are primarily opposed to economic and cultural elites, institutions (religion) and structures (capitalism). Left-wing populists oppose, on a *secondary level*, the political "establishment" that serves the interests and priorities of these elites. Right-wing populists focus their anti-establishment frame on governments for "rigging the system" in ways that disadvantage or discriminates against hard-working, middle class (white) Americans in favor of "special interests" above *and* in favor of "undeserving" people – the nonworking poor, minorities, and immigrants *at their expense* (Judis, 2016). American right-wing populists oppose, on a secondary level, numerous elites in political and nonpolitical life. They see their traditions, values, beliefs – their way of life, as being under assault by multiple political, economic, and cultural institutions including government, corporations (i.e., Disney), the liberal media, educational institutions, and Hollywood (Judis, 2016; Kazin, 1995). In the right-wing populist perspective, liberals have infected these institutions with their socialism and political correctness, multiculturalism, and woke ideology.

Left- and right-wing populists have different underlying values and political beliefs on both cultural and economic dimensions (see Table 38.2). The political left generally is tolerant if not celebratory about racial, ethnic, and cultural diversity, though less tolerant of conservative religions and norms that they see as subjugating women and denying rights to sexual identity minorities. This culturally inclusive or cosmopolitan orientation is associated with multiculturalism, identity politics, diaspora, and political correctness, while being strongly opposed to nativist, white, Christian nationalism, racism, and xenophobia (Norris & Inglehart, 2019). Conversely, Republicans generally, and right-wing populists in particular, have negative views of multiculturalism, feminists, LBGTQ, and racial and ethnic minorities, particularly if those minorities are immigrants (Steger, forthcoming, ch. 9).

Perceived discrimination against whites has been a central factor in support for Trump (Tessler & Sides, 2016). White nationalism, in this sense, is white identity politics. While conservative Christians have supported Trump, his earliest and strongest support came from Evangelicals and other conservative Christians who identified as Christian but who did not frequently attend church (Scala, 2020). Among right wing populists, Christian identity blends with nationalism in a

Table 38.2 Economic and Cultural Dimensions of Left- and Right-Wing Populism in the United States

	Economic Orientation	*Cultural Orientation*
Left-wing	Socialistic (whatever reduces inequality) and protectionist	Inclusive: supportive of diversity and cultural equality; accepts modernity and cosmopolitan values
Right-wing	Conservative policies (less government, taxes and regulation); Economic nationalism with protectionism; Accept social programs services, but with exclusions for "undeserving" people	Exclusive: opposed to diversity, multi-culturalism, critical race/feminist theory, and difference with regard to sexual identity, language and culture; traditionalist and nativist

cultural and political sense more than a religious sense. Interestingly, nonchurch attendance is the one demographic trait that left- and right-wing populists have in common; more than age or self-identified ideology, Bernie Sanders' supporters are distinct from other Democrats and liberals by identification as atheist or no religion in particular (Steger, forthcoming, ch. 8). The various issue emphases of right-wing populists – tradition, capitalism, religion, and ethnic heritage pride all meld together in nationalism, which Trump's America First and Make America Great Again slogans symbolize.

In sum, Bernie Sanders' left-wing populism fused anti-establishment rhetoric with an egalitarian, socialistic economic view and cultural inclusivity. They aspire for economic and social justice for historically disadvantaged groups including people of color, immigrants, women, and LGBTQ populations. The embrace of socialism, cosmopolitan values, and secularism stands in opposition to culturally exclusive orientation of right-wing populism with its support for capitalism, cultural exclusivity, and Christian and white identities unified in a nationalistic attitude structure (Norris & Inglehart, 2019). Note that there has been relatively little said about foreign policy in this discussion. While Sanders and Trump have both been critical of global elites, foreign wars, and free trade, these issues rank low in importance to the supporters of both Sanders and Trump. At front and center are differences about socialism vs capitalism on an economic dimension, and differences between cultural inclusivity vs. cultural exclusivity on a cultural dimension.

Within their respective political camps, left- and right-wing populists are distinguished from partisans that they identify with or lean toward, mainly in terms of their anti-establishment attitudes and resistance to powerful elites, institutions, and structures that they oppose. Left wing populists are a little more liberal or progressive on economic policy, immigration, race, gender, and sexual identity but not by much. They are more likely to see these groups as victimized by dominant economic and social elites and structures. On the other side, right-wing populists are actually a little less conservative on economic policy than other Republicans. They are more accepting of Social Security, Medicare, and other programs, but exclusively for taxpayers, not for immigrants and other undeserving groups. Right wing populists are more negative than other Republicans when it comes to race, immigrants, feminists, and LBGTQ, but not much more.

In sum, left-wing populists are largely similar other progressives in economic and social attitudes and beliefs, but seek more substantial "structural" change in economic and government institutions pursuant to a more economically and culturally egalitarian society. Left wing populists want to change the system more than they want to work within the system for incremental change. Right-wing populists are a more distinctive on economic ideology compared to other conservatives, but are largely similar in their social and cultural traditionalism. Where both depart from their partisan and ideological allies is their anti-establishment frame, the want to resist oppressive powerful enemies, their sense of victimization, and the extent to which they are willing to disrupt the "system" in order to get changes that they want.

WHY DO POPULISTS ATTRACT SO MUCH SUPPORT AND WILL IT FADE?

The usual arguments for the rise of populism focus on declining economic opportunity and/or cultural backlash against socio-cultural change. There is evidence for both the economic and the cultural backlash arguments. Elsewhere, I argue more extensively that the conditions that underpin the growth of populist sentiment transcend economic and social inequality (concern of the left) or declining economic opportunity and cultural backlash (concerns of the right). There is something larger going on, and what that is may be reflected in the commonalities of the eras in which populism has peaked. The United States has experienced two eras in which populism has received widespread support. The first era in which populism peaked in the United States was the 1890s, when populists succeeded in nominating William Jennings Bryan to be the Democratic Party nominee (Kazin, 1995). The other surge has been occurring in the past two decades. Both eras have in common, three broad patterns (Steger, forthcoming).

First, the United States went through a period of substantial economic transformation in each era. The latter half of the 19th century witnessed rapid change from a largely rural and agrarian society to an urban society in which manufacturing was the main driver of employment and wealth creation. In the past fifty years, the US economy has been similarly transformed from an industrial base to a professional service, financial, and information-based economy in which technology has been used to greatly augment productivity, first through the introduction of micro-processers, then the internet and now artificial intelligence. These economic transformations have contributed to rising economic inequality, declining economic mobility for many, and have disrupted lives, social relations, and communities. These transformations have created new winners and losers with distinct social, educational, and geographic dimensions, which in turn help us understand which segments of society are attracted to left- or right-wing populism. These changes have profoundly changed patterns of employment, income, and wealth, giving rise to increasing economic inequality and declining economic mobility for people living in areas in which the new economy is not investing, and in general for people without a college degree. The onset of artificial intelligence may further exacerbate the pace and scale of economic dislocations as many jobs of college educated people will be displaced in the way that manufacturing jobs were displaced by automation and robotics. How to cope with economic dislocations and related strains on society will be a central challenge of this century.

Second, both eras in which populism has surged in popularity occurred after decades of socio-cultural transformation. In both the late 19th and the late 20th century, American society went through rapid demographic and cultural change, through immigration, migration, advances in education, changes in the religious composition of society, and the introduction of new ideas that challenged (and changed) existing social norms and social order. Some of this transformation owed to the disruptive impacts on communities and social relations by changing patterns of economic production, employment, and the distribution of wealth. Other drivers of social and cultural change include patterns of immigration, and intra- and inter-state migration that have weakened civic capital at the local level. Society has also been changed by changing levels of educational attainment and exposure to changing pop culture across generations have produced differing value systems about how people live their lives. These kinds of changes can be subsumed under the heading of modernity, which is resisted by people yearning for a more traditional social structure and cultural value system. The transition from traditional society with roots in family and community to a more modern, secular, and diverse society involves the rise of values emphasizing diversity, tolerance of the other, and other cosmopolitan values associated with liberal arts education. The liberal movements of the 1950s and 1960s under the banners of the Civil Rights movement and the New Left met with resistance from what became known as movement conservatism. The liberal political movements of the 1960s were met with resistance in a cultural backlash that began among conservative whites opposed to civil rights and desegregation, religious conservative activists like Phyllis Schlafly and Pat Buchanan, and politicians who espoused nationalism like Ronald Reagan. Older, white, less-educated, blue-collar, and rural or small-town Americans who share these values have been drawn to right-wing populist messages; while younger, college-educated, and urban (and suburban) professionals have more socially liberal attitudes and beliefs that are consistent with left-wing populism.

The combination of considerable economic and socio-cultural transformations creates considerable societal dislocations and stressed. Further, the pace of change has given societies relatively little time to adjust. The result is a great deal of economic and social dissatisfaction, social strife. These conditions form a context which makes America and other countries experiencing similar changes ripe for populist leaders and political parties. But there is more to the story, which is an inability of government to provide relief from these social stresses.

Third, both eras involved peak periods of polarized political parties, centralized party control of Congress, and intense partisan conflict. The problem of polarized political parties is that it creates dysfunctionality in a constitutional structure of government that simultaneously divides and shares political authority over policy making (Mann & Ornstein, 2016). This system of blended authority requires cooperation and compromise to enact policies and simultaneously enables political minorities to obstruct and resist the majority. In this system, polarized political parties create an impediment to the government's ability to address the economic and social stresses on society that result from transformative economic and socio-cultural change. Increasingly, American politics are a zero-sum, winner-try-to-take-all game in which losing is highly threatening to the interests and values of party constituencies, which results in greater intensity of political conflict and diminished prospects for reason and compromise. As a result, the political system is failing to provide relief to the struggles faced by people on both sides of the political spectrum. At the same time, there has been a proliferation of extremist commentary on cable, digital, and social media, encouraged and abetted by politicians seeking short-term advantage that have stoked passions and set unrealistic expectations that the political system could not meet. Populism feeds on the emotionally charged rhetoric and negative partisan affect that political polarization created. Is it any wonder that populists are frustrated with and seek to disrupt the status quo, politics as usual system?

Populism is one possible political response to societal stresses that result from diffuse, interrelated, and systemic economic, social, and cultural transformations of society, coupled with frustration with the major political parties for failing to offer relief from the stresses that result from socio-economic and cultural transformation. The disruptive forces were emergent before Sanders and Trump and the conditions that created the fertile ground for their campaigns will not fade soon. The implications of all of this will occupy our thoughts for the foreseeable future.

The populist wave of the 1890s was responded to, and dampened by, serious political change. Many of the policy ideas of populists were incorporated into the progressive era political reforms and policy innovations. Political reforms included the direct primary to nominate candidates, the secret ballot, and patronage reforms that weakened political parties, and thus arguably dampened political polarization. The operation of Congress was also transformed, with a profound weakening of the party centric powers of the Speaker of the House and a strengthening of committees, in which members of both parties had common constituency concerns. Responding to the current wave of populism will involve, in part, the generation of new ideas for political reform, perhaps including ways to restrict the influence of polarizing parties, campaign finance, and special interest groups and lobbyists. Political marketing includes not just the communication or advertising of ideas. It begins with a serious look at what consumers want and generating ideas that can help them. Generating ideas to reduce the influence of polarizing forces and of special interests that contribute to the stagnation of government are important places to start.

In terms of policy, perhaps an important place to start is thinking about what works for the political center. Conservatives with their free-market advocacy which calls for less regulation and lower taxes for corporations and the very rich, conflicts directly with the socialistic preferences of the political left. This is a stalemate, at least for now. Perhaps the way forward is to revive the mixed economy of the early progressive era, which sought to curb the excesses of capitalism while enabling it to continue (Croly, 1965). The early progressives, who were philosophically different from the more socialistic and egalitarian progressives of the modern era, blended political reforms, serious regulation of the economy, progressive taxes, and a social safety net (limited socialism) in order to curb the excesses of an unfettered free-market. Revitalizing that kind of efficiency minded government, guided by ideas of science (natural and social science), may help reduce some of the economic dislocations and societal stresses that have occurred with the economic transformations of the economy that have occurred over the past 50 years. That, however, may not be sufficient to placate either side. The mixed economy of the New Deal to the Great Society resulted in more powerful government that became excessively influenced by big monied corporations, trade associations and billionaires (e.g., Hacker & Pierson, 2017). What became of that mixed system is simultaneously big government that conservatives oppose and very rich capitalists that progressives oppose. Conservatives and progressives vehemently oppose the power that the other seeks to unleash, and both seem deeply dissatisfied by the compromises involved in the mixed economy. It may no longer be politically feasible in the polarized politics of the 21st century.

Addressing the conflicts of the culture war that divide Americans into those more tolerant of diversity and those who resist it is going to be substantially more challenging. In large part, these conflicts go well beyond what governments have traditionally attempted to do or been successful doing. Social and cultural change occur well beyond the jurisdiction of most governments, and conflicts may well continue. For many years, the idea is that increasing access to education and promoting cultural tolerance through entertainment media, would change society – essentially transforming society enough that cosmopolitan values and modernity take hold. That may still be the case, though such transformation is slow, occurring largely through generational replacement. It's becoming harder, as education itself has become a battleground of the culture war. Social conservative Republicans are seeking to curtail the emphasis on diversity, LBGTQ, and other progressive social ideas. The fragmentation of the media environment also makes it more challenging. Rather than communicating common sets of values, social media present content that is wildly divergent, enabling people who are more progressive and those who are more socially conservative to find content that conforms to their values and beliefs. The disintegration of American society, in terms of a common ethos and value system, is a distinct possibility to which the political system is not well suited.

The point is, that we do not yet have the kinds of ideas that will dampen economic, sociocultural, and political conflict in the way that the progressive era succeeded in doing a little over 100 years ago. Identifying problems to be addressed, however, may be what we can offer at this time. Thinking about solutions to competing grievances and resolving incompatible visions of social norms will be part of the response to populism.

POPULISM: RESISTANT TO POLITICAL AND INTELLECTUAL ELITE MESSAGING

We face a lot of problems and societal stresses in an economically and socially changing society, with intensely hostile political parties that can block the big ideas of the other. Even if ideas are generated to address these problems, it is going to be difficult to break through anti-establishment populisms with their resistance to perceived power.

First, the central characteristic of populism – antielite attitudes and frames of understanding limit the efficacy of elite-level messaging against candidates or parties that take advantage of populist sentiment to advance their own ambitions. People who are angry with party establishments or elites are not inclined to follow the cues of those elites. The problem may be particularly difficult with supporters of right-wing populist parties, given that the resistance is in no small part, resistance to changes associated with forces of modernity and demographic changes for which there is no way yet conceived to put the genie back in the bottle.

Another reason that it is difficult to respond to populism is that populist political leaders, like other political leaders, take advantage of the powerful cognitive effects of partisanship and cultural values. Donald Trump, in particular, attacked as unfair and deceitful news media that gave him unflattering coverage. He took advantage of it and amplified it with repeated accusations of "fake news" and characterizing journalists as "enemies of the people" (Samuels, 2019). In doing so, he took advantage of the cognitive biases of his partisan supporters who were predisposed to distrust liberal news media and trust or at least accept Trump's version. Political identities, rooted in cultural values and beliefs, shape perceptions and cognitive processes so that supporters to see what they want to see, ignore, or discount contrary information; and maintain an optimistic view of a candidate even in the face of negative information (Bolsen et al., 2014; Gastil et al., 2011; Sharot et al., 2011). Continued Republican support for Donald Trump, despite so many scandals, indictments, and criminal convictions, is a testament to the power of predispositions. It is difficult to change the opinions of people who are predisposed to resist and distrust countervailing information.

That challenge is even greater in our current, highly fragmented media environment in which anyone can find reinforcing informational content. The existence of cable, digital, and social media enables populist groups and candidates to spread messaging that countervails party or other elite messaging. Our highly divisive politics are being driven in part by "profit-driven provocateurs whose livelihoods ride on their abilities to rouse rabble, stir passions and diabolize opponents" (Blow, 2014). Political types of all sides disparage the news media when it suits them. Liberals have disparaged news media as having corporate bias (Chomsky, 2003; Herman & Chomsky, 1988). Conservatives attack the news media for liberal bias (Ladd, 2011). Research, think tanks, and centers provide evidence, selectively enough, to make something of a case for the grievances with the media. The existence of these critiques of the media and other cultural mediums provides populists of a ready rationale to dismiss countervailing information. If the news media or other elites run stories critical of a populist leader, like Donald Trump, supporters simply dismiss the information as liberal bias. Donald Trump did not create Republican antipathy toward the mainstream media. He took advantage of it and amplified it with repeated accusations of "fake news" and characterizing journalists as "enemies of the people" (Samuels, 2019).

CONCLUDING REMARKS

It may not be possible to respond to populists in the short term. We live in an economically, culturally, and politically divisive world, amped up by emotionally charged rhetoric and appeals, and in which people are motivated at a cognitive level to discount information they do not care to hear, and in which people have access to messaging that affirms their anger and discounting counter-vailing messaging. The problems that give rise to deep dissatisfactions, economic and social transformations of society, are so deep that a polarized government lacks the ideas or the capacity to address in ways that would reduce tensions. Social and cultural changes are largely beyond the scope of governments that are better at economic policy making than social engineering.

REFERENCES

Abramowitz, A. I., & Webster, S. (2016). The rise of negative partisanship and the nationalization of U.S. elections in the 21st century. *Electoral Studies*, *41*(2), 12–22.

Blow, C. M. (2014, June 15). Dangerous divisiveness. *New York Times*. https://www.nytimes.com/2014/06/16/opinion/charles-blow-politics-grow-more-partisan-than-ever.html

Bolsen, T., Druckman, J. N., & Lomax Cook, F. (2014). The influence of partisan motivated reasoning on public opinion. *Political Behavior*, *36*(2), 236–262.

Brown, W. (1995). *States of injury: Power and freedom in late modernity*. Princeton University Press.

Canovan, M. (1981). *Populism*. Harcourt.

Canovan, M. (1999). Trust the people! Populism and the two faces of democracy. *Political Studies*, *47*(1), 2–16.

Chomsky, N. (2003 [1989]). *Necessary illusions thought control in democratic societies*. House of Anansi Press.

Costa, R. (2023, June 23). Trump casting himself as victim on campaign trail in appeal to Republicans. https://www.cbsnews.com/video/trump-casting-himself-as-victim-on-campaign-trail-in-appeal-to-republicans/

Costa, R., & Rucker, P. (2020, February 8). Tempted to Despair: Trump's resilience causes democrats to sound the alarm. *Washington Post*. https://www.washingtonpost.com/politics/tempted-to-despair-trumps-resilience-causes-democrats-to-sound-the-alarm/2020/02/08/8301b71a-4906-11ea-b4d9-29cc419287eb_story.html

Croly, H. (1965). *The promise of American life*. 1911. Harvard University Press.

Domhoff, G. W., & Dye, T. R. (Eds.). (1986). *Power elites and organizations*. SAGE.

Edwards, G. C., III (2021). *Changing their Minds: Donald Trump and presidential leadership*. University of Chicago Press.

Feher, M. (1996). Empowerment hazards: Affirmative action, recovery psychology, and identity politics. *Representations*, *55*(1), 84–91.

Fenster, M. (2008). *Conspiracy theories: Secrecy and power in American culture*. University of Minnesota Press.

Gastil, J., Braham, D., Kahan, D., & Slovic, P. (2011). The cultural orientation of mass political opinion. *PS: Political Science and Politics*, *44*(3), 711–714.

Gitlin, T. (1995). *The Twilight of common dreams: Why America is wracked by culture wars*. Metropolitan.

Grattan, L. (2016). *Populism's power: Radical grassroots democracy in America*. Oxford University Press.

Hacker, J. S., & Pierson, P. (2017). *American amnesia: How the war on government led us to forget what made America prosper*. Simon & Schuster.

Hayes, K., Steinberg, S. R., & Tobin, K. (Eds.). (2011) *Key works in critical pedagogy: Joe L. Kincheloe*. Sense Publishers.

Herman, E. S., & Chomsky, N. (1988). *Manufacturing consent*. Pantheon Books.

Hetherington, M. J., & Weiler, J. D. (2009). *Authoritarianism and polarization in American politics*. Cambridge University Press.

Hofstadter, R. (1964). *The paranoid style in American politics*. Harvard University Press.

Horkheimer, M., & Adorno, T. W. (Eds.). (2002). *1947 dialectic of enlightenment: Philosophical fragments* (E. Jephcott translation). Stanford University Press.

Jacobson, G. C. (2021). Driven to extremes: Donald Trump's extraordinary impact on the 2020 elections. *Presidential Studies Quarterly*, *51*(3), 492–521.

Jones, A. (2016, November 1). *Donald Trump: The greatest victim in the history of the world*. https://billmoyers.com/story/donald-trump-greatest-victim-history-world/

Judis, J. B. (2016). *The populist explosion: How the great recession transformed American and European politics*. Columbia Global Reports.

Kazin, M. (1995). *The populist persuasion: An American history*. Cornell University Press.

Kelly, A. (2017). *Fact check: Have immigrants lowered wages for blue collar American workers?* https://www.npr.org/2017/08/04/541321716/fact-check-have-low-skilled-immigrants-taken-american-jobs

Ladd, J. (2011). *Why Americans hate the media and how it matters*. Princeton University Press.

Lelkes, Y., Sood, G., & Iyengar, S. (2017). The hostile audience: The effect of access to broadband internet on partisan affect. *American Journal of Political Science*, *61*(1), 5–20.

Madhukar, P., & Panduranga, H. (2020). *Fighting the Muslim Ban: Three years and counting*. Brennan Center for Justice. https://www.brennancenter.org/our-work/analysis-opinion/fighting-muslim-ban-three-years-and-counting

Mann, T., & Ornstein, N. (2016). *It's even worse than it looks: How the American constitutional system collided with the new politics of extremism*. Basic Books.

Merkley, E. (2020). Anti-intellectualism, populism, and motivated resistance to expert consensus. *Public Opinion Quarterly*, *84*(1), 24–48.

Morrow, R. A., & Brown, D. (1994). *Critical theory and methodology*. SAGE.

Mudde, C. (2004). The populist zeitgeist. *Government and Opposition*, *39*(4), 541–563.
Mudde, C. (2007). *Populist radical right parties in Europe*. Cambridge University Press.
Mutz, D. C. (2018). Status threat, not economic hardship, explains the 2016 presidential vote. *Proceedings of the National Academy of Sciences*, *115*(19), E4330–E4339.
Nelson, J. S. (2015). *Politics in popular movies*. Routledge.
Nelson, T. E., & Oxley, Z. M. (1999). Issue framing effects on belief importance and opinion. *The Journal of Politics*, *61*(4), 1040–1067.
Norris, P., & Inglehart, R. (2019). *Cultural backlash: Trump, Brexit, and authoritarian populism*. Cambridge University Press.
Omer, A., & Lupo, J. (Eds.). (2023). *Religion, populism, and modernity: Confronting white Christian nationalism and racism*. University of Notre Dame Pess.
Riker, W. H. (1982). *Liberalism against populism: A confrontation between the theory of democracy and the theory of social choice*. Freeman.
Rozsa, M. (2019). QAnon is the conspiracy theory that won't die. *Salon*. https://www.salon.com/2019/08/18/qanon-is-the-conspiracy-theory-that-wont-die-heres-what-they-believe-and-why-theyre-wrong/. Accessed on August 18.
Samuels, B. (2019, April 5). *Trump Ramps up Rhetoric on media, calls press 'the enemy of the people*. The Hill. https://thehill.com/homenews/administration/437610-trump-calls-press-the-enemy-of-the-people
Scala, D. J. (2020). The Skeptical faithful: How Trump gained momentum among Evangelicals. *Presidential Studies Quarterly*, *50*(4), 927–947.
Schumpeter, J. (1943). *Capitalism, socialism, and democracy*. George Allen and Unwin.
Sensoy, O., & DiAngelo, R. (2011). *Is everyone really equal?: An introduction to key concepts in social justice education*. Teachers College Press.
Sharot, T., Korn, C., & Dolan, R. J. (2011). How unrealistic optimism is maintained in the face of reality. *Nature Neuroscience*, *14*(11), 1475–1481.
Slothuus, R., & de Vreese, C. H. (2010). Political parties, motivated reasoning, and issue framing effects. *The Journal of Politics*, *72*(3), 630–645.
Sood, G., & Iyengar, S. (2018). All in the eye of the beholder: Asymmetry in ideological accountability. In H. Lavine & C. S. Tabor (Eds.), *The feeling, thinking citizen* (pp. 195–227). Routledge.
Steger, W. P. (2017). Populist challenges in the 2016 presidential nominations. In A. Cavari, R. J. Powell, & K. R. Mayer (Eds.), *The 2016 presidential elections: The causes and consequences of a political earthquake* (pp. 23–42). Lexington Books.
Steger, W. P. (2018). Populist waves in the 2016 presidential nominations: A limit to the party decides thesis. In G. C. Green (Ed.), *The state of the parties 2018* (8th ed., pp. 150–168). Roman & Littlefield.
Steger, W. P. (forthcoming). *Resurgence of American populism: Socio-economic transition and political discontent*. Routledge.
Strydom, P. (2011). *Contemporary critical theory and methodology*. Routledge.
Taggart, P. (2000). *Populism: Concepts in the social sciences*. Open University Press.
Tessler, M., & Sides, J. (2016, March 3). How political science helps explain the rise of Trump: The role of white identity and grievances. *Washington Post*. https://www.washingtonpost.com/news/monkey-cage/wp/2016/03/03/how-political-science-helps-explain-the-rise-of-trump-the-role-of-white-identity-and-grievances/
Tillman, E. R. (2021). *Authoritarianism and the evolution of West European electoral politics*. Oxford University Press.
Werner-Müller, J. (2016). *What is populism?* University of Pennsylvania Press.
Westwood, S. J., & Iyengar, S. (2015). Fear and loathing across party lines: New evidence on group polarization. *American Journal of Political Science*, *69*(3), 690–707.
Williams, B. (2021). Did President Trump's 2020 election litigation kill rule 11? *Boston University Public Interest Law Journal*, *30*, 181–214.

Index